A HISTORY
OF THE
TWENTIETH
CENTURY

BOOKS BY MARTIN GILBERT

THE CHURCHILL BIOGRAPHY

Volume III: 1914–1916
Document Volume III: (in two parts)
Volume IV: 1917–1922
Document Volume IV: (in two parts)
Volume V: 1922–1939
Document Volume V: 'The Exchequer
  Years' 1922–1929
Document Volume V: 'The Wilderness
  Years' 1929–1935
Document Volume V: 'The Coming of
  War' 1936–1939

Volume VI: 'Finest Hour' 1939–1941
Document Volume VI: 'At the Admiralty'
  1939–1940
Document Volume VI: 'Never Surrender'
  May–December 1940
Volume VII: 'Road to Victory' 1941–1945
Volume VIII: 'Never Despair' 1945–1965

Churchill: A Photographic Portrait
Churchill: A Life

OTHER BOOKS

The Appeasers (with Richard Gott)
The European Powers 1900–1945
The Roots of Appeasement
Children's Illustrated Bible Atlas
Atlas of British Charities
Atlas of American History
Atlas of the Arab-Israeli Conflict
Atlas of British History
Atlas of the First World War
Atlas of the Holocaust
The Holocaust: Maps and Photographs
Atlas of Jewish History
Atlas of Recent History (in preparation)
Atlas of Russian History
The Jews of Arab Lands: Their History
  in Maps

The Jews of Russia: Their History in Maps
Jerusalem Illustrated History Atlas
Sir Horace Rumbold: Portrait of a Diplomat
Jerusalem: Rebirth of a City
Jerusalem in the Twentieth Century
Exile and Return: The Struggle for Jewish Statehood
Auschwitz and the Allies
The Jews of Hope: The Plight of Soviet Jewry Today
Shcharansky: Hero of Our Time
The Holocaust: The Jewish Tragedy
The Boys, Triumph over Adversity
First World War
Second World War
The Day the War Ended
In Search of Churchill

EDITIONS OF DOCUMENTS

Britain and Germany Between the Wars
Plough My Own Furrow: The Life of Lord Allen of Hurtwood
Servant of India: Diaries of the Viceroy's Private Secretary 1905–1910

A HISTORY
OF THE
TWENTIETH
CENTURY

VOLUME ONE: 1900-1933

———————

MARTIN GILBERT

HarperCollins*Publishers*

HarperCollins*Publishers*
77–85 Fulham Palace Road,
Hammersmith, London w6 8jb

Published by HarperCollins*Publishers* 1997
1 3 5 7 9 8 6 4 2

ISBN 000 215867 1

Set in Garamond 3 by
Rowland Phototypesetting Ltd,
Bury St Edmunds, Suffolk

Printed and bound in Great Britain by The Bath Press, Bath

I dedicate this history to my mother, Miriam Gilbert, who was born in 1911, and who has lived through all but one decade of the century which is the subject of these three volumes.

This first volume is dedicated to my friend, Hugo Gryn, who, in his very last discussions with me before his death in 1996, was full of his usual wealth of ideas as to what ought to be included.

CONTENTS

LIST OF ILLUSTRATIONS

LIST OF MAPS

ACKNOWLEDGEMENTS

I AM GRATEFUL TO THOSE who have helped me in the collection of material for this volume: Dr Sarah Bendall, Judge Volney V. Brown Jr, Dr Richard Ward Day, Professor Peter Craig, Robert Craig, Henry K. Griesman, Rachelle Gryn, Michael Henderson, Edward Kanter, Tom Krannawitter, Leonard Mader, Michael Meredith, A. J. Peacock, Lilia Podkaminer, Inspector Robin Ford, Paul Sharma, Jay Shir, Stephen J. Solarz, Shippen Swift and Michael Williams-Jones.

In the course of my own travels, I have been fortunate to have been able to spend time in several of the more distant cities which figure in this narrative, among them Cape Town, Istanbul, New Delhi and San Francisco. I am grateful to my sons David and Joshua for accompanying me on various journeys in search of historical facts and background; among the cities which we have explored together have been Berlin, Munich, Prague, Vienna, Budapest, Trieste and Zagreb.

The text was read by my friend and former teacher, the historian Alan Palmer, who made many important suggestions as to form and content, as did Arabella Quin of HarperCollins and Bill Swainson. The Russian sections were read by Harold Shukman. The text was scrutinized by Vicky Robinson, Rachelle Gryn and Ronald S. Cohen. Tim Aspden prepared the maps from my rough drafts. Carol O'Brien encouraged me from the first days of my work on this project. Caradoc King has been supportive throughout. Kay Thomson made many important suggestions with regard to content, and also undertook the considerable task of transcribing many passages of text.

Susie Gilbert's help has been indispensable, and her guidance has been of the greatest encouragement at every stage.

I am grateful to the Robert Hunt Library and Graham Mason for the prints of the illustrations in this volume, and for permission to use them. I would also like to thank the sources from which they came: Orbis Publishing (photograph 1); Robert Hunt Library (2, 7, 8, 9, 14, 15, 16, 17, 23, 31, 37, 42, 44, 50); Bundesarchiv (3, 20, 27, 28, 38,

45); Keystone Press Agency (4); National Archives, Washington (5, 30, 35); Official US Navy Photographs (6); ABC Press, Amsterdam (10); Press Association (11); Camera Press (12, 36); Hulton Getty Picture Collection (13, 17, 32, 48); Heeresgeschichtlichen Museum, Vienna (18, 19); Foto Saporetta, Milan (21); Imperial War Museum (22, 26, 33, 34, 52); Library of Congress (24, 41); US Signal Corps (25); Black Star (39, 43, 47); Novosti, Moscow (40); Fox Photos (46); Associated Press (49); Sado, Brussels (51); United States Information Agency (53).

I am grateful to those authors, publishers, and literary executors, for permission to use extracts from published works; and to those newspapers still extant, for allowing me to quote from their past pages.

INTRODUCTION

How like a paradise the world would be, flourishing
in joy and rest, if men would cheerfully conspire in
affection, and helpfully contribute to each other's
content: and how like a savage wilderness now it is,
when, like wild beasts, they vex and persecute, worry
and devour each other.

ISAAC BARLOW, Doctor of Divinity
Sermon, *Works*, 1683

THE TWENTIETH CENTURY HAS witnessed some of humanity's
greatest achievements and some of its worst excesses. By any scale of values
it has been a century of improvement in the quality of life for millions of
people, yet also one of decline in many parts of the globe.

Every twentieth-century historian will have particular perspectives on a
period so rich in diversity of experience. Given the confines of an 846-page
book covering the century up to 1933, and a limit of three volumes for the
whole century, not much more than twenty-five pages can be devoted, on
average, to any one year. The choice of topics, the stresses, the episodes and
the focus must be personal. I have tried to give a fair balance of the different
powers, regions and conflicts.

My focus as the century starts is on the empires and ideologies which
ruled or controlled so much of the world at that time, or sought to control
it. In the coming decades these empires, dominated in Europe by Germany,
Austria-Hungary, and Russia, were to be defeated, fragmented or transformed, some by war and some by revolution, some into dictatorships and
others into parliamentary democracies. Yet even after war and revolution

had mauled them, Germany and Russia struggled to remain at the centre of the world stage.

When the century began, some of its future tyrants were already alive, and had embarked upon their destructive careers; science and medicine were making enormous strides forward; the motorcar was in its infancy, and within a decade, aircraft would take to the skies. As in previous centuries, the value placed on human life by religion and custom was almost daily confronted by the savageries of war.

This history is one in which the clash of nations and their alliances, the strivings of empires and their collapse, and the struggles of nationalities and national groups, are central to the narrative, as they are central to the century itself. No year passed without soldiers and civilians being killed in war, or struggling to recover from its ravages. By chance, while writing the chapter which includes the Armenian massacres of 1915, I walked through the Armenian Quarter of Jerusalem; there, maps pasted on the walls of houses and courtyards showed the towns and villages throughout Asia Minor in which the Armenians had been massacred. 'It is called the century of the common man,' wrote Winston Churchill, 'because in it the common man has suffered most.'

The often tragic fate of the 'common man', and woman and child, runs like a dark thread through these pages. There are also golden threads among them – the courage and perseverance of innumerable individuals, and the assertion of the equal rights of all nations, and of the rights of the individual, against the frequently crushing burdens of State oppression and military tyranny.

By 1933, air power had added another dimension of terror, presaging a time, the poet Siegfried Sassoon wrote, when 'Fear will be synonymous with Flight'. Yet that same invention of flight also brought with it great opportunities, as did most of the inventions of each decade. For example, the Bosch magneto, a small but crucial component in the working of the internal combustion engine, was essential if cars and lorries were to run at all. Without the mobility it provided, the continuing warmaking powers of the combatants would have been seriously diminished after 1914, and the domestic and commercial vehicles, which added so much to commerce and leisure once the war was over, unthinkable.

Coal, and fuel oil, which drove the destructive machinery of two world wars, likewise fuelled many of the improvements and comforts of daily life: as I write these words, more than 20 million barrels of oil are being consumed in the world every day, one third of them in the United States. Also in the twentieth century, nuclear power was to reveal its destructive and constructive sides; and, like so many of the century's scientific and industrial advances, to create massive problems of pollution and waste disposal. The planet was a much less crowded, cleaner and less scarred one when the century began than as it draws to its close. The ocean floor has suffered from the discarded detritus and rubbish of war, and even the atmosphere above the planet is crowded with man-made satellites, space stations, and the debris of space exploration. These add a new dimension even to Byron's caustic reflection of two hundred years ago:

> Man marks the earth with ruin – his control
> Stops with the shore.

I have tried in this volume to indicate the national and international efforts by which the human race sought to control its own destiny and regulate its conflicts. Treaties and agreements, promises and armistices, seemed in any year or decade to be the pointers of hope for the future. They are an integral part of this narrative. Some of them are international treaties, some were signed between a group of States, others between two States, others by would-be States and national groups and autonomous regions. The Mürzsteg Programme of 1904 which attempted to resolve Balkan conflicts, the Treaty of Portsmouth of 1905 following the Russo-Japanese war, the Balfour Declaration of 1917 which promised the Jews a National Home in Palestine, the decisions of the Paris Peace Conference of 1919, the London Ultimatum of 1921, the Geneva Protocol of 1924, the Nettuno Conventions of 1928 settling the dispute between Italy and Yugoslavia over Dalmatia, the Kellogg-Briand Pact of 1928 in which war itself was outlawed: these were only a few of the pledges and agreements that brought, every year, every month, and sometimes even at weekly intervals, a manifestation of hope in some region of the world. Often prompted by suffering and conflict, much was expected from these solemn instruments of diplomacy and negotiation.

The borders of new or established nation States are also a theme of this work: the battles to secure them, the plans to preserve them, and the designs to change them. The century began with imperialism in the ascendant, and yet already under daily threat. As empires tried to overcome that threat, national movements devised means of subverting them. Lines on the map, and regions remote from the centres of power, became the locations of national passions and international wars. Places that one is hard pressed to locate in an atlas without the use of a good gazetteer were, for a few months, or a few weeks, the centre of attention and the focal point of ambition and dissent. A small port, an obscure mountain pass, a remote monastery, an unimpressive stream, focused for a short while the patriotic hopes and nervous apprehensions of millions of people and their leaders.

The First World War, which forms the watershed of the years covered in this volume, was fought predominantly by the European empires, each of which had established, during the second half of the nineteenth century, commercial dominance and territorial control over much of the globe. In the last years of the nineteenth century and at the beginning of the twentieth these efforts to assert imperial control led to repeated wars against the local populations, mostly in Africa, but also (as the century opened) in China. The rivalries between the great industrialized and militarized nations were also to pit their peoples against each other. Starting with the Russo-Japanese war in 1904, this rivalry reached a terrible climax ten years later, with the outbreak of the First World War. At its outset a European war, it was to draw in both Japan and the United States, as well as the distant self-governing Dominions of the British Empire.

The confidence generated by industrial progress, mass industrial production, and the success of Empire-building, gave the European powers, the United States, and (increasingly) Japan, a sense that they controlled, or ought to control, the destinies of peoples not blessed with similar advantage, materially or technologically. As such advances increased – wireless telegraphy is one of the early achievements of the twentieth century – so the confidence of the Powers increased. Yet Europe's optimism in the nineteenth century, generated by tremendous effort, victories overseas, and economic expansion, was to be confronted by a very different reality.

It was Winston Churchill, who had just experienced war in three imperial conflicts – in India, the Sudan and South Africa – who warned publicly in 1901: 'The wars of peoples will be more terrible than those of kings.' Not only war – and the genocide that sometimes accompanies war – but assassination, terrorism, and later even the heavy death toll generated by the the motorcar – were to be grim counters to progress in the medical, technological and environmental sciences, and the civilizing influences of the arts.

The empires which dominated the world when the century began have all dissolved, some more recently than others. The Soviet Union, successor to the Russian Empire of the Tsars, survived into the final decade of the century. Other national groupings, such as Yugoslavia, came into being as the century moved forward, but have likewise dissolved. On 19 December 1996, *The Times* listed the diplomats who had attended a memorial service in London on the previous day. They included the Ambassadors of Macedonia, Croatia, Albania, Lithuania and Ukraine, and the Chargé d'Affaires of the Slovak Republic. None of these six countries existed as an independent State in 1900. Only one – Albania – was independent by 1914 and only one more – Lithuania – by the time this volume ends in 1933.

The ever-changing, ever-renewing drama on the world stage is the focus of this volume. Episodes in one decade reflect those of another, personalities take nations in their grip, ideologies enforce discipline and sacrifice, propaganda heightens, and knowledge questions the demands of one nation upon another. Revolutions and revolutionaries everywhere strove to change the old order, and in the process often did not respect the rights which even the worst of the old orders had established. Indeed, the secret police regimes of the old order were not necessarily any worse, and were often more benign, than those by which they were replaced in the hope of a better tomorrow.

Everywhere mankind strove, and continues to strive for that better tomorrow, while not always preserving what has been achieved for today. The 'common man', the ordinary citizen, the soldier, the prisoner and the refugee are usually anonymous, yet it remains the century in which their lives have been transformed the most, sometimes for the better, sometimes very much for the worse. Even so, as the century ends, there are still those national leaders in the world who believe that they can improve the lot of their people, and that they can do so, not at any one else's expense, but in harmony with the common good.

It was the poet Thomas Hardy who wrote, in disillusionment, after the First World War:

> After two thousand years of Mass
> We've got as far as poison gas.

This history explores the way in which the twentieth century, the culmination of many centuries of political and social evolution, was not the inevitable progress towards perfection that so many fighters for truth in previous centuries had assumed it would be.

The twentieth century began – as it is likely to end – with war being fought somewhere on the globe, with troops gathered in mortal combat, and with death and injury reported daily in the newspapers. On the day I handed in the first draft of this volume to the publishers, the morning newspapers reported the death of a hundred people, including twenty civilians, in several villages in Colombia, in battles that were being fought between government forces and 'left-wing guerrillas'. There was also a news item of a total death toll, over a three-year period, of as many as ninety thousand soldiers and civilians in the war between Russia and the would-be breakaway region of Chechnya. That day, the newspapers also reported the death on the roads, in Britain, in a single car crash, of six young people aged between seventeen and twenty-two. Two of them were the grandchildren of the First World War poet Siegfried Sassoon.

On 27 July 1996, when a minute's silence was held in the Olympic Stadium in Atlanta to commemorate the civilian killed a few days earlier by a bomb, a television commentator, Bonnie Anderson, remarked that the occasion was 'a grim reminder of what is becoming life and death in the twentieth century'. In looking at the extraordinary achievements of the century, as well as its terrible failures, the reader seeking an uplifting theme may still be forced to ask, as one reader of this book did in its early stages: 'And has it really been the century of war?'

Merton College
Oxford
1 May 1997

CHAPTER ONE

1900

A most gratifying demonstration of the common ties
which bind mankind in one great brotherhood.

OTTAWA FIRE RELIEF COMMITTEE
1900

WELCOMING THE NEW CENTURY, a writer to *The Times* expressed
the hope, 'May it be a fortunate one for our Sovereign and her people'. Even
as he wrote his letter, imperial wars were being fought on two continents:
in Africa and in Asia. In South Africa, the Boer War was entering its eleventh
week. The Boers, in their two independent republics, the Transvaal and the
Orange Free State, had taken on the might of the British Empire in
neighbouring Cape Colony and Natal. Fearing Britain's expansionist policies
towards their two republics, the Boers had launched their first attacks into
British territory at a time when there were only 12,000 British soldiers
stationed in South Africa. As the century opened, and Britain expected
a rapid reversal of its military defeats, British newspapers reported the
gifts which private companies were sending out to the troops, including
1000 barrels of stout, and 5000 tablets of Lifebuoy Royal disinfectant
soap.

In the first flush of victory, the Boers had laid siege to the British garrisons
inside the towns of Mafeking and Ladysmith. The number of British troops
seeking to lift these two sieges, to drive the Boers back, and to defeat their
two republics, was increased during the course of a year to almost a quarter
of a million. This was the largest number of British troops to have been
sent so far from home – 7000 miles by sea – since the Crimean War half a
century earlier. Each passenger liner that sailed from Britain carried further
volunteers. Reinforcements for the British war effort also came from across

the British Empire, from Canada, Australia, New Zealand, Tasmania, India and Ceylon: more than thirty thousand men in all. Britons living in South Africa – the Uitlanders – also joined in the battles against the Boers. In December, a telegram from the town of Dawson City – in the remote frozen north of Canada – to the Canadian Minister of Defence in Ottawa reported that four former policemen had begun to walk 400 miles across the snow and ice to where they could then travel a further thousand miles by rail and ship to Victoria, British Columbia, at their own expense, 'in the hope of being in time to join the forces in South Africa'.

Among those who witnessed the war in South Africa was Mohandas Karamchand Gandhi, who for several years had been leading the struggle for Indian rights in Natal. Determined to show that the despised 'coolie' labourers from India could render good service, on the outbreak of the war he helped form an Indian Ambulance Corps of more than a thousand South African Indians. Their task was to help the wounded on both sides. 'To carry the wounded seven or eight miles was part of our ordinary routine,' Gandhi later wrote. 'But sometimes we had to carry badly wounded soldiers and officers over much longer distances up to twenty-five miles.' He added: 'We were only too willing to enter the danger zone, and had never liked to remain outside it.'

Gandhi also recalled, with pride, the story of a fellow Indian who was with the besieged British troops inside Ladysmith. His name was Parbhu Singh. Before the war he had been the servant of an Englishman:

The most dangerous and most responsible work was assigned to Parbhu Singh, who was called a 'coolie'. On a hill near Ladysmith the Boers had stationed a field-gun whose operations destroyed many buildings and even occasioned some loss of life. An interval of a minute or two must pass before a shell which had been fired from the gun reached a distant objective. If the besieged got even such a short notice, they could take cover before the shell dropped in the town and thus save themselves.

Parbhu Singh was to sit perched up in a tree all the time that the gun was working, with his eyes fixed on the hill, and would ring a bell the moment he observed a flash. On hearing the bell the residents of Ladysmith instantly took cover and saved themselves from the deadly cannon-ball whose approach was thus announced.

The officer in charge of Ladysmith, in eulogizing the invaluable services rendered by Parbhu Singh, stated that he worked so zealously that not once had he failed to ring the bell. It need hardly be said that his own life was constantly in peril.

The first British defeats in South Africa were a shock to a British public brought up on the success of imperial arms. 'England, in these dark days, comported itself with a dignity that extorted admiration even from its foes,' wrote the authors of Cassell's *Illustrated History of England*, a patriotic volume published annually:

> There were no hysterics, no panic. Success might have unhinged the nation
> – later on did momentarily unhinge it – but reverse made it rigid. The
> bulldog British nature came out in its best expression – grim, silent,
> obstinate, determined. And John Bull put his hands into his pockets, deep,
> deep, deep – a sure sign that his soul was stirred. One of the best features
> of the war was the spontaneous burst of charity it gave rise to. Throughout
> the United Kingdom relief funds were opened, and subscriptions flowed
> in a strong, generous stream for widow, and orphan, and fighting man
> broke in the wars.

The first battle of 1900 in South Africa took place on January 6, when Boer forces, commanded by General Joubert, tried to drive the British from their positions inside Ladysmith. Ten thousand British troops, commanded by General Sir George White, defended the besieged town, which they had held for more than two months. Twenty thousand more British troops, under General Buller, were in camp eighteen miles to the south, unable to break out of a Boer encirclement, and powerless to affect the outcome of the battle.

The Boer attack on Ladysmith began before dawn. Quickly, the Boers overran one of the British strongpoints, Waggon Hill, and pressed in upon another, Caesar's Camp. The battle lasted for eleven hours. Cassell's history describes it thus:

> It fell to the lot of a handful of brave men – Manchesters, Gordons, a few
> sailors and Engineers, and some plucky Colonials – to sustain the brunt
> of what was actually the grand assault, and heroically defend a front which
> had been narrowed down to a quarter of a mile, against the determined
> attack of the Boers, who had advanced to within a stone's throw.
>
> The sun rose, and with it came reinforcements to our sorely pressed
> men. First the Rifles, then the 53rd and 21st Batteries of Artillery, who

served their pieces with marvellous skill and precision, notwithstanding the overwhelming metal of the Boer big guns which pounded them from Bulwana Hill, to the south-east of Ladysmith.

Presently, as the attack developed, the Border Regiment and some Natal Volunteers were sent in support. The Boers, on their side, pushed up fresh commandos, driving home an attack with a bravery and persistency they seldom showed except in defence. The hill-sides streamed with blood: for hours the strenuous fight raged: for hours the issue hung in the balance, as if the God of Battles was undecided to whom to award the palm.

General Buller's troops, 10,000 in all, were at Chieveley Camp, eighteen miles to the south of Ladysmith. From their encampment they could hear the sound of the British and Boer artillery as Joubert and White fought for mastery:

The morning was cloudy, but with occasional intervals of sunshine. During one of these – at 9 a.m. – White succeeded in heliographing to Buller that he was attacked in considerable force. At 11 o'clock came a second message 'Attack continues, and enemy has been reinforced from the south.' Whereupon Buller turned his force out and made a demonstration against Colenso.

At 3 o'clock in the afternoon White heliographed 'Very hard pressed.' After that the sun was hidden by clouds and no more messages could be flashed. Buller demonstrated until seven o'clock, when he withdrew his troops to camp.

The suspense in England when White's last ominous message reached London, and for twenty-four hours no other news arrived, was painful, almost breathless. The nation, tutored in the school of surprise and disaster, knew not what next to expect. To add to their bitterness was the reflection that whilst 10,000 men were being attacked, perhaps annihilated, at Ladysmith, an army of 20,000 a few miles away appeared to be impotent to save or even aid them. It was humiliating.

Luckily, in the sturdy men of Manchester, the gallant Gordons, the stalwart Devons, and the splendid Imperial Light Horse – recruited from the Uitlanders, whom some men had dared to call cowards – England had sons able to sustain her honour and her prestige.

If the spectacle of 10,000 British troops hemmed up in the saucer of Ladysmith was not an edifying one, the defence of Caesar's Camp and

Waggon Hill by 3000 of them deserved a page to itself in the annals of British military history. For between three of the morning clock and seven of the evening, by their own right arm they held their own and finally won victory at the point of the bayonet.

In a storm of tropical rain, that added to the dramatic intensity of the scene, to the music of crashing thunder, and with the glare of battle paling before the flashes of lightning, they scattered the Boers in rout amongst the rocks and chased them into the flooded spruits that drained the foot of the hill.

Ladysmith remained besieged. To the south, General Buller continued to try to find ways of breaking through the Boer ring, but failed to do so. To the humiliation of the British newspaper readers, he was defeated by General Louis Botha at the Battle of Spion Kop. Against Buller's imperial army, Botha used the weapon most associated with imperial conquest – the rapid-firing Maxim gun[1] – to devastating effect.

Even as a war was being fought in South Africa to defend the area of Empire, the British government announced, on the first day of 1900, that the lands hitherto controlled by the Royal Niger Company were to be added to Britain's existing Niger Coast Protectorate, forming a new imperial unit, Southern Nigeria. The first High Commissioner for the new region was Frederick Lugard, an intrepid explorer and diligent administrator who had raised and commanded since 1897, a native regiment, the West African Frontier Force. These regiments, of regular, disciplined local troops, were a feature of British – and also French – imperial control. Similar native regiments to those established by Lugard existed in India, Hong Kong, China (based on the British territorial concession at Weihaiwei), the Sudan and Somaliland.

Each of the Powers was involved not only in building up its own empire, but in seeking to influence and guide other nations. In 1900 the German armaments firm of Krupp received authorization from the Sultan of Turkey to arm eight Turkish warships.

---

[1] Hiram Maxim, an engineer, was the inventor of the automatic system of firearms that enabled extremely rapid fire to be directed from a single gun. Born in the United States (in Maine) he crossed the Atlantic to settle in England in 1881, only two years before inventing his gun. He was knighted by the British king in 1901.

In South Africa, Ladysmith and Mafeking remained under siege by the Boers. In Vienna, the Emperor of Austria, Franz Josef, had taken the unusual step, three days after the Boer attack on Ladysmith, of seeking out a British diplomat during a state ball, and telling him emphatically, 'In this war, I am completely English.' Conflict between the European Powers was a recurrent nightmare; a peaceful assurance, even with regard to a far-off colonial conflict, was always welcome.

On the day after Franz Josef voiced his support, Britain's determination to defeat the Boers was signalled by the arrival in South Africa of a new Commander-in-Chief, Field Marshal Lord Roberts, a hero of much earlier battles against the Afghans. He landed in South Africa together with his Chief-of-Staff, Lord Kitchener, who, two years earlier, had defeated a Dervish army in the Sudan. The arrival of these two imperial soldiers in South Africa was a token of national determination, stimulating patriotic zeal. Later in January, on the hundredth day of the defence of Mafeking, the mayor of the town, on behalf of troops and defenders, sent a message of loyalty to Queen Victoria: the town would not surrender. Nineteen days later, while Mafeking continued to hold out against repeated Boer bombardment, Ladysmith was relieved. Five hundred British cavalrymen broke through the Boer ring and galloped through the main street shouting 'We are here!'

One member of the Ladysmith relief column was a young cavalry officer turned war correspondent, Winston Churchill. 'Whatever victories the future may have in store,' he wrote for his newspaper that April, 'the defence and relief of Ladysmith, because they can afford, perhaps, the most remarkable examples of national tenacity and perseverance which our later history contains, will not soon be forgotten by the British people, whether at home or in the colonies.'

News of the relief of Ladysmith gave a strong boost to British patriotic morale. 'My Sheikh has just told me that Ladysmith is relieved,' the explorer Gertrude Bell wrote to her mother from the deserts of Arabia on January 11. 'I do hope it is true and that this is the beginning of good news.' Among those who congratulated Queen Victoria were four sovereigns: her grandson, Kaiser Wilhelm II, Emperor of Germany, Franz Josef of Austria-Hungary, King Umberto of Italy and Sultan Abdul Hamid, the ruler of the Ottoman Empire. Their accolades contrasted with the conclusion of an international congress, meeting that autumn in Paris, that responsibility for the war fell upon Britain for having repeatedly refused arbitration. The British ignored this conclusion, which was made public on October 2, and continued to seek British control over the whole territory of the two Boer republics. An eleven-year-old Indian boy, Jawaharlal Nehru, recalled in his autobiography thirty-six years later, 'All my sympathies were with the Boers.'

The Boer fight with Britain was Nehru's first intimation that imperialism could be challenged, even if that particular challenge was to no immediate avail. Even in Britain there were those who doubted the wisdom of the war. In mid March, local people in the North Sea coastal town of Scarborough held a private meeting to question whether Britain should seek to eliminate Boer independence. When news of the meeting became known, riots took place and shops were damaged by a mob angry at any expression of anti-war opinion. In Europe, at the annual parade of washerwomen in Paris – where students and market women competed for the style and glamour of their floats – Parisians were promised the spectacle of Joan of Arc attended by Boers on horseback. The French government, not wishing to annoy Britain, intervened to prevent so blatant an anti-British gesture.

Mafeking was relieved in May. The rejoicing in London when this news reached the capital was unprecedented, with crowds marching and singing in the streets throughout the night. They were so vociferous and enthusiastic that the verb 'to Mafeking' – to celebrate without inhibition – entered the language and remained there for several decades. Within a month of the relief of Mafeking, Johannesburg was under British control. Five days later Pretoria, the capital of the Transvaal, was occupied.

Those who defied British imperial rule elsewhere were being hunted down. In January, Osman Digna, leader of the Mahdist forces who had been defeated in the deserts of the Sudan, was captured by a military expedition sent to find him in the remote regions of southern Sudan to which he had fled.

In February, after ten days' fighting, the rebel leader in British North Borneo, Mat Salleh, was killed when one of the forts he had built to assert his authority was attacked and overrun.

In the Gold Coast, the Ashanti leader, Coomassie, having launched an attack on a local tribe loyal to Britain, sparked off a general uprising. Among those who led troops against British forces in the Gold Coast were King Prempeh, the ruler of Ashanti, and King Asibi of Kokofu. A fierce sense of tribal loyalty and independence was prepared to challenge the far superior weaponry of the colonial power. Once more British troops were sent to the coast of Africa to restore imperial control.

Within six months, the two kings, Prempeh and Asibi, were on their way, under armed guard, into exile on the British islands of the Seychelles, in the Indian Ocean. But the fighting in the Gold Coast continued until the troops commanded by Queen Ashantuah were attacked and scattered at the end of August. A week later these troops, too, surrendered.

Like the ancient British Queen Boadicea, who fought against the Romans almost two thousand years earlier, Queen Ashantuah had not been able to prevail against the superior technology of her enemies. The advantages of the imperial powers had for several decades included rapid-fire Maxim guns and artillery. But despite the imperial optimism so prevalent in Britain since the Great Exhibition of 1851 in London, resistance to imperial rule – resistance to the benefits of imperial rule, as the British saw it – did not diminish. There had not been a single year since then when some military action or other did not take place against the disaffected beneficiaries of British control. That November, for example, the Ogaden Somalis, in British East Africa, rebelled against British rule, starting yet another conflict in Africa.

While Britain fought to maintain, and to extend its imperial power, Germany, a latecomer to the imperial game, was looking for regions in which to establish German control. In March, as local chiefs quarrelled on the Pacific island of Samoa, the German flag was formally raised over the island. But during 1900 it was one of the great empires of the past, China, that came to dominate the attentions of the Powers – as the leading nations of the world were known – eclipsing even South Africa. Those Powers were generally considered to be Britain, France, Russia, Germany, Austria-Hungary, the United States and Japan. Italy sought to be one. The Ottoman Empire, despite its vast territory, was not considered a member of the club by the others, and was, indeed, soon to be imposed upon by them.

At the centre of the threat to foreign interests in China were the Boxer rebels, acting in defiance of the Chinese imperial government, whose weakness at the centre had long been a cause of concern for the Powers. In Chinese, the name of the rebels meant 'Righteous harmonious fists': hence Boxers. They had begun as a secret society whose members adopted boxing, and ritual forms of combat, and who believed that foreign weapons would not harm them. The Boxers viciously attacked foreigners, and especially foreign Christian missions, wherever they could.

The first intimations that a violent clash might be imminent between China and the Powers came on May 21, when the foreign diplomats in Peking called on the Chinese government to suppress all anti-foreigner activities of the Boxers, and to end all anti-foreign propaganda in the country.

South of Peking, on the railway line to Hankow, the Boxers raised their standard of revolt. Within a week they had driven off the Chinese government troops sent to curb them, and were marching towards Peking, under the slogan, 'Death and destruction to the foreigner and all his works.' On the last day of May, in an attempt to protect the foreign Legations in Peking, which had appealed for help, 365 marines reached Peking by train from Tientsin. The contingent was made up of troops from the United States, Britain, Russia, France and Japan.

In the Chinese province of Manchuria, the Russian Empire had been working to complete its direct railway line to Port Arthur, across several hundred miles of Chinese territory. To accelerate the work, the Russians brought in 4000 Chinese labourers every day to the building sites. In June, the Boxers attacked the Russian engineers supervising the work, and the Cossack railway guards protecting it, burning down many of the railway stations, and tearing up the new line wherever they could. They also bombarded a Russian town, Blagoveshchensk, that lay across the Amur River, which at that point was the Russo-Chinese border. The bombardment lasted for eighteen days.

Attacks on foreigners and their property intensified during June. 'Christian establishments were burnt down,' reported the senior British diplomat in Peking, Sir Claude MacDonald, 'the summer residence of the British Minister and his staff, just completed at the cost of £10,000 was similarly treated; two devoted English missionaries (Robinson and Norman) were murdered near the Peking–Tientsin line and the anti-foreign party at Court seemed to have obtained a complete ascendancy over the Empress Dowager.'

The Empress Dowager – known affectionately as the Old Buddha – had ruled China for forty years. Her support for the Boxers derived from the belief, that had gained wide currency throughout China, that the destruction of the Legations would end the European, American and Japanese influence over China and its trade. The Boxers' claim that they could not be killed by foreign bullets made this belief all the more persuasive. On June 12 they attacked the Allied naval force which, travelling by rail from Tientsin, had reached the outskirts of the Great Hunting Park a few miles south of Peking. This force consisted of just over two thousand men. More than half of them were British, but there were also German, Russian, French, American, Japanese, Italian and Austro-Hungarian soldiers and sailors. A machine gunner with the force, a British sublieutenant, Maurice Cochrane, later wrote to his parents about the Boxers: 'Their distinguishing feature is red; red caps, red socks, red sashes, and very formidable swords and spears with red on them.' He also found the Boxers hard to stop: 'They work themselves into an extreme state of hypnotism and certainly do not for the moment feel body wounds. We have all learnt that they take a tremendous lot of killing and I myself put four man-stopping revolver bullets into one man before he dropped.'

The senior American naval officer at the Great Hunting Park was Captain McCalla. He watched as another British machine gunner, Captain Jellicoe – who in the First World War would command the British naval forces in the Battle of Jutland – was himself in action. The Boxers had reached to within a few feet of the train on which the sailors were travelling. 'Recognising Captain Jellicoe's clear voice calling for the Maxim and looking out of the car window,' McCalla wrote, 'I saw the Boxers in a wedge, led by a very large Chinaman who was wielding a two-handed sword.' His account continued:

> Grasping a rifle from one of my men I sprang to the ground, opening fire myself at the flank of the enemy. I almost immediately heard the sound of Captain Jellicoe's Maxim, which cut down the head of the on-rushing column.
>
> The leader escaped the fire from the Maxim but, turning at a right-angle, he came directly towards me. At this critical moment, I was seized by one of my men, a coloured Oiler, Smith, who at first was more intent in endeavouring to haul me towards the steps of the car than on using his own rifle.
>
> It required several seconds for me to extricate myself from my would-be rescuer and direct him to open fire on the few remaining Boxers. By that time, a gallant young English signal boy armed with a rifle had also come to my assistance.
>
> The Boxer leader was within thirty yards of us, advancing gallantly and though my first shot hit him it was not entirely disabling but the second shot from my rifle proved fatal.

When the Boxers were driven off, five Italian sailors were found dead: they had been caught asleep while on guard duty several hundred yards from the train. Eighty-eight Boxers were killed, some of them only having been wounded by the Allied marines, but then having had their throats cut by fellow-Boxers who did not want them to fall alive into the hands of the 'foreign devils'.

The Boxers then moved to cut the railway link between Admiral Seymour's force and his ships. When Seymour urged his French and German commanders to move their troops and trains back to the river to secure the port of Yangtsun, they refused to do so. They were certain that sending them back was a trick so that the British could enter Peking without them: Perfidious Albion exposed. In fact, Seymour saw how vulnerable his railway link with the river was, and wanted to secure it. The Boxers took immediate advantage of this dissension in the Allied ranks, cutting the railway line and destroying Yangtsun railway station. Seymour's whole force, just over two thousand men, were trapped, unable to return to their ships, and unable to reach Peking.

On June 13 the Boxers entered Peking, destroying most of the foreign-owned buildings that were not within the protective zone of the Legations. Among the buildings burnt to the ground was the house of Sir Robert Hart, the Commissioner of the Chinese Imperial Customs, who had lived in Peking since 1864. Hart's collection of Chinese treasures, built up during his lifetime of service in China, was destroyed.

In northern China similar destruction followed immediately. In Peking, the Roman Catholic Church was burnt to the ground, and throughout the night, Chinese Christians living near it were massacred. Austrians at their Legation managed to rescue a Chinese Christian woman who was about to be burned to death near their Legation wall. After the Third Secretary of the Japanese Legation was set upon and murdered, Japan announced that she could have 'no more communication with China – except war'.

Those foreigners who could reach the security of their respective Legations were protected against attack by the 365 marines who had arrived two weeks earlier. From their position of danger inside the capital, the besieged representatives of the Powers were appealing to their respective governments for concerted action. The fate of foreigners in China was being given wide, and even lurid publicity in the newspapers. But it took time before concerted action proved possible. Britain, with its vast imperial possessions, including those in Burma, Malaya and Hong Kong, and a major stake in Shanghai, was expected to give a lead, but was instead concentrating its energies on the war in South Africa.

In Russia, the Tsar was suspicious of Japanese intentions towards Chinese Manchuria. In Germany, the Kaiser did not want to see the Tsar gain too much power in the Far East, where Germany also had growing territorial and trade interests. It was not his intention to take action in China merely to allow Russia to gain the territorial advantage. It was not until Russia made it clear that she had no territorial designs on the Chinese province of Korea that news of the perilous situation of the Legations inside Peking finally spurred the Powers into action.

Inside Peking, led by a senior Japanese officer, Colonel Goro Shiba, and a British Royal Marine, Captain Wray, an attempt was made on July 17 to rescue several thousand Chinese Christians who were under attack. An American civilian resident in Peking, Mary Hooker, described this action in her diary: 'A detachment of men from the English Legation, our Legation, and the Russian Legation started off under an English officer to rescue some of the thousands of Chinese Christians who are being burned and tortured by their enemies like rats in their holes. The tales that reached us through our servants, many of whom are Christian converts, and whose mothers, fathers and wives are undergoing this continuous St Bartholomew, made our men feel that we should try to do something for their rescue, even if we were not successful. Fortunately this party of men did not meet any large number of disciplined Chinese soldiers, finding them only in small groups. They killed a great many; and one could easily imagine how happy our men were to be able to kill these wretches in the very act of burning, looting, killing or torturing. Sergeant Walker told me he had sent eight devils to glory; many of his shots he had seen take effect, and others he hoped had done as good work.'

Dr George Morrison, the correspondent of *The Times*, accompanied the soldiers on this expedition. In his diary, he recorded his impressions. 'We made a raid,' he noted, 'on a temple thirty yards from the Austrian outpost; the Austrians coming up afterwards. Forty-five Boxers killed – butchered. Christian captives with hands tied being immolated while actually massacring, five already dead. Rescued three. One accidentally killed. All Boxers killed; only one dared to face us. I killed myself at least six. Back tired having paraded city and witnessed devastation in many places.'

Morrison's most dramatic despatch to *The Times* was published in London on June 18. Headed 'Riots in Peking, Massacre of Native Christians, Destruction of Foreign Property', it reported the burning of the Roman Catholic cathedral, the buildings of the London Mission and the American

Board of Missions, and the Maritime Customs building. 'It was an anxious night,' Morrison reported, 'for all the foreigners who were collected under the protection of foreign guards.' This was Morrison's last despatch. Shortly after it was sent, the Boxers cut the telegraph line. Peking was not only besieged, but incommunicado.

At the mouth of the Peiho River, to avoid being utterly outflanked, Admiral Seymour and his international naval force captured the Taku Forts. Russian, French, German and Japanese warships took part in the attack. Only the American paddle-steamer, the *Monocracy*, armed with two small artillery pieces and a number of Colt machine guns, remained aloof from the battle: President McKinley, in his re-election year, did not want domestic repercussions.

On board the attacking ships, as well as their own sailors, were sailors from Italy and Austria-Hungary. In the capture of the Taku Forts, two British naval officers played a leading part, Captain Christopher Cradock, who was to go down with his ship at the Battle of Coronel in 1914, and Lieutenant Roger Keyes, who was to lead a spectacular raid on German submarine pens at Zeebrugge in 1918.

The capture of the Taku Forts was hailed in Europe and the United States as a triumph of military cooperation and achievement. Thirty-one of the attacking force were killed, and as many as eight hundred Chinese. Three days later, on June 20, the German Minister-resident at Peking, Baron von Ketteler, the senior German diplomat in the city, was murdered while on his way to the Chinese foreign office. Admiral Seymour now tried to reach Peking by water, along the Peiho river, but was forced back. His adversaries on the river banks, it was noted with alarm in Europe, were not only the Boxer rebels, but detachments of Chinese Imperial troops who had abandoned their previous acceptance of foreigners. Seymour then ordered his ships' guns to bombard the Chinese fortifications at Tientsin. One of his officers, Captain von Usedom of the German Navy, supervised the bombardment. The city arsenal was destroyed, but the Allied force did not have enough men to take the town.

Japan and the United States were acting in concert with five European Empires – Russia, Germany, Austria-Hungary, France and Britain – in condemning and combating China's actions. Determined to crush the Boxers, the Powers were assembling a large military force. On July 27 France announced that she would be sending 20 warships, including 12 first-class cruisers, to Chinese waters; that the export of arms to China was forbidden; and that a special bounty would be paid to all former soldiers and marines who enlisted for service in China. That afternoon the German Kaiser was present at the North Sea port of Bremerhaven when 4000 German imperial soldiers set sail for China. In his speech wishing them good fortune, the Kaiser declared: 'When you meet the foe you will defeat him. No quarter will be given, no prisoners will be taken. Let all who fall into your hands be at your mercy. Just as the Huns, a thousand years ago, under the leadership of Attila, gained a reputation in virtue in which they will live in historical tradition, so may the name of Germany become known in such a manner in China that no Chinaman will ever again even dare to look askance at a German.'

The Kaiser's use of the word 'Huns', intended to encourage and flatter his men, was to rebound on Germany's head. Three days after his speech, a message was received from Peking that the European Legations had been under siege for three weeks, their compound subjected to continuous attack, and sixty-two Europeans killed. Such forces as could be gathered, more than twelve thousand men, moved on Tientsin. It was a combined force of British, Russian, German and Japanese troops. American troops also took part, despite McKinley's earlier refusal to allow American participation in the attack on the Taku Forts.

A German Field Marshal, Count von Waldersee, was appointed to command the German forces in China. Because of his senior military rank, he was given command of the whole Allied expedition. Among those who would be under his command, once he reached China, was the Commander-in-Chief of the American forces in China, General Chaffee.

At the end of July, the Kaiser, intent on becoming the European scourge of Asia, even if his military force was only the fourth or fifth largest, preached a sermon on board his royal yacht in which he drew the analogy, not of Attila, but of the Israelites under Moses and their heathen enemy, the Amalekites. 'The heathen spirit of the Amalekites is again astir in far-off Asia,' he said. 'With great might and with much cunning, with fire and with slaughter, is the attempt being made to bar the way of European commerce and of Christian morality and of Christian faith. And once again has the word of God gone forth, "Choose us our men, and go out and fight with Amalek." A terrible and bloody struggle has begun. Many of our brethren are already under fire – many are on their way to the hostile shore. When the word went out: "Volunteers to the front! Who is ready to defend the empire?'', you saw thousands gather together and march out with flying banners to meet the foe. But we, who are bound by sacred duties to remain behind at home, do we not hear the word of God which goes out to us and says, "Climb up to the mountain top. Raise thy hands to heaven. The prayer of the just man is mighty when it is sincere."'

Rejecting the idea that Germans could remain distant spectators of the battle which others had gone to fight, the Kaiser said, 'We will mobilize not only battalions of warriors, but also a holy force of supplicants.' He then dwelt upon the power of prayer and intercession, pointing out that 'when Moses held up his hand, Israel prevailed'.

Both Attila and Moses had been invoked in stirring words by the Kaiser. But by the time Count von Waldersee reached China, the battle was over. Before his men had crossed the Indian Ocean, a relief force of 24,000 Japanese, 6000 Russians, 3000 British (mostly Sikhs from India), 1500 Americans, and 1000 Frenchmen (mostly Zouaves from French Indo-China) was ready to advance on Peking.

On August 12, President Loubet of France was among a crowd of French dignitaries at Marseilles to witness the departure of several thousand more French troops for China. But the panoply and national pride of a military expedition was in contrast to the demand that same summer for higher wages and better conditions, a demand that was affecting all the main seaports of France, including Marseilles. In two of the strike-bound ports, Bordeaux and Dunkirk, police clashed with strikers and there were serious injuries. In Marseilles, both the mayor and the police were sympathetic to the strikers; they were later strongly condemned for their sympathy by the conservative Parties in the Chamber of Deputies.

Some of the strikers in Marseilles were ships' stokers. The government ordered them to be seized and put by force on board the ships that were about to sail for China. The needs of a distant war took precedence over civil harmony at home.

While the French troops were on their way to China, a report in the London *Daily Mail* announced that the Legations had fallen and that all the Europeans had been massacred. It was a triumph of press sensationalism, but it was untrue. Before the French troops who had set sail from Marseilles had even passed through the Suez Canal, the Allied troops who had captured Tientsin and marched rapidly towards Peking were ready to enter the city itself.

On August 14, Russian and American troops attacked the central gates.

British Indian troops, entering by the water gate, were the first to reach the besieged Legations. 'It was queer to see these great, fine-looking Indians, in khaki uniforms and huge picturesque red turbans, strutting around the compound,' Mary Hooker wrote in her diary on the following day, 'and as they entered right into our midst they all whooped a good English whoop. A little blond Englishwoman was so overcome at the relief really being here that she seized the first one she could get to and threw her arms around him and embraced him. The Sikh was dumbfounded at a mem-sahib apparently so far forgetting all caste. It seemed odd that the word "relief" should have been personified in these Eastern and heathen-looking Sikhs, but it was all the more in keeping with this extraordinary siege in Peking that they should be the first on the scene to rescue us.'

Fighting continued around the Legations for another two days. Among those killed in action was an American artillery officer, Captain Reilly. On August 16, Mary Hooker wrote in her diary: 'Captain Reilly, who was killed this morning while gallantly directing the fire of his battery, was buried this afternoon in a small open space in the American Legation. This funeral, however, was not as pitiful to me as the siege funerals we have been having all summer. Perhaps because there was some help and satisfaction to be got out of the military pomp and honours which were given him as he was laid away.'

At the end of the graveside ceremony the senior American diplomatic representative in Peking, Herbert Squiers – who had been in the city throughout the siege – stepped down into the grave and began to remove the Stars and Stripes from the casket. 'There are so few American flags in Peking,' he told the astounded onlookers, 'this one can't be spared.' A second later, General Chaffee, the Commander-in-Chief of the American forces in China, called out: 'Don't touch that flag. If it's the last American flag in China it shall be buried with Reilly.' The general, noted Mary Hooker, 'was instantly obeyed, and so his dead subordinate was tenderly cared for by him at the end, and his body was buried wrapped in the flag for which he had given his life.'

That day Japanese troops entered the Forbidden City, and on the following day all the Allied forces paraded in the former sanctuary. The siege of the Legations was over. Only the nearby Peitang Cathedral and the Roman Catholic compound around it remained under siege. In the savage and prolonged battle for its defence, four hundred Europeans were killed, more than two hundred of them children from the Catholic orphanage within the compound. Twenty-eight died when, on July 11, the Chinese managed to explode a large mine underneath one section of the compound, a further 136 (including fifty-one children) when a second mine was exploded on August 12. Four days later, Japanese troops arrived and the siege of the cathedral compound was over.

French and Italian troops had been the compound's main defenders, led by a naval sublieutenant, Paul Henry. He was killed by a sniper towards the end of the siege. 'Do not feel too much sadness,' he wrote in his last Will and letter to his family in France. 'I have died for the most beautiful of causes. I have done, I hope, all my duty. I leave to you the little that I have, and I ask you to set aside from the money that I leave the sum of two hundred francs for the Missions in China, so hard pressed at the moment . . .'

The Allied death toll in the siege of Peking was eighty. Every Power had some deaths.[1] Following the lifting of the siege, China had to submit to much fuller control by the victorious Powers. The Russians, taking advantage of the Allied attack on China, had occupied much of Manchuria during the fighting, but agreed to withdraw. Theirs had been the largest contingent to fight in China, followed by the Japanese and the British.

The Powers had gained a sense of their strength, when acting in harmony, and assumed that in future they would be able to do likewise; their own rivalries seemed small compared with the challenges facing them far beyond the borders of the industrialized world. A collective military enterprise had been effective; far more so than it was to prove against the Italians in Abyssinia in the 1930s or against the Bosnian Serbs in the 1990s.

News of the scale of the killings in China took time to reach those who had despatched the expeditionary force. It was not until late in September that one of the French missionary groups, based in Lyons, whose Chinese work had been particularly the object of Boxer hatred, learned that four of its priests and seven of its nuns had been killed at the mission in Shansi, and as many as a thousand Chinese Christians in Shansi had been beheaded. When, within a few months, a spate of books was published by individual

[1] The death toll was: French 17, Italian 13, German 12, British 11, Japanese 10, American 8, Russian 5 and Austro-Hungarian 4. On 12 September 1992 *The Times* reported the death in the United States, at the age of 106, of Nathan Cook, the oldest known United States war veteran. He had first seen action in China in 1900.

soldiers and eye-witnesses among the victorious Powers, photographs of these beheadings were included. To spare the sensitivities of readers who might find them offensive, the photographic sections containing them were often perforated by the publisher, so that they could be removed before the book was left in the drawing room for all to see.

When the Emperor of China sent the Kaiser a conciliatory message, offering to place 'drink offerings on an altar' as expiation, the Kaiser replied that this was insufficient, in view of the murder of the German diplomat and the Christian missionaries. But on October 16, Britain and Germany signed a comprehensive agreement, made public four days later, establishing a common policy in the Far East. Its basis was the upholding of an 'open door' for all trading activity, 'for the commerce of every power in China', and the repudiation of any territorial designs by the Powers. There was some critical comment at the time that this agreement, while clearly of direct interest to all the Powers, had been reached by only two of them, and would, according to its terms, be communicated to the others, who would then, but only then, be invited to accept it.

The Russian government, in the person of Tsar Nicholas II, was greatly put out by what it saw as an Anglo-German surprise, especially as the agreement would make impossible Russian hopes of annexing all or part of Chinese Manchuria. But it concurred in the end. Austria-Hungary, Italy, Japan, France and the United States had meanwhile accepted the Anglo-German initiative and policy. It was an article in the magazine *Fortnightly Review* by the most experienced of all the representatives of the interests of the Powers in China, Sir Robert Hart, which sealed the acceptance of the agreement. Even though Hart's position in control of many important public offices was a hated sign, for many Chinese, of the subservience of China to Western outsiders, he warned in his article of the dangers of the 'Yellow Peril' if the Powers did not deal leniently with the Chinese government in its moment of defeat and shame. The alternative, he wrote, was a second and even more violent anti-foreigner uprising.

Compared to China, the disturbances in Morocco were minor. But the Moors of this North African region – the Maghreb – were embarked on a persistent effort to challenge the French authorities who had declared their ultimate authority over the Sultan and his kingdom. Throughout 1900 Reuter's Agency in Tangier reported local disturbances and French counter-action. 'Great excitement reigns at Fez,' Reuter's reported on July 2, 'owing to French encroachments on the Twat oasis. The mob have killed the manager of a French business house who is an American citizen. The British Consul has demanded the assistance of the authorities to protect his house. The Jewish ghetto is besieged.'

France's struggle to assert its authority in Morocco, and to persuade the Sultan to maintain law and order wherever he could, was to be a feature of French policy and concerns for the next two decades.

The twentieth century also opened with the aspirations of working men in all countries under parliamentary governments determined to better their situation by direct participation in the political process. At a conference in London on February 27, representatives of all the British working-class organizations – the Independent Labour Party, the Fabian Society, the Social Democratic Federation, and the trade union movement – founded the Labour Representation Committee. Its aim was to work 'for the independent representation of working people in Parliament'. A quarter of a century later, the secretary of the committee, Ramsay MacDonald, was to become Britain's first Labour Prime Minister.

In monarchist Italy, which had only been unified as a single country for thirty years, a parliamentary fracas, exacerbated by both anarchist and mafia elements, had led to the fall of the government of General Luigi Pelloux and the success of the left-wing parties in the elections. Disturbances in the north of Italy, caused by the high price of bread, had to be calmed by the sale of corn from military stores. When King Umberto opened the new Parliament on June 16 he warned the deputies, some of whom boycotted his speech: 'It is my duty to defend the institutions of the country against every danger which might threaten them.' A new government was formed, headed by Giuseppe Saracco, and calm seemed to return to Italian political life. There was also an economic uplift, the signing of a Treaty of Commerce with the United States. But on July 29, at Monza near Milan, as the king was leaving a gymnastic fête at which he had distributed the prizes, he was shot three times by an anarchist, Angelo Bressi. 'One shot pierced his heart and His Majesty fell back and died in a few moments,' *The Times* reported. 'His assailant was at once arrested, and was with some difficulty saved from the fury of the people.'

The assassin was an Italian silk weaver living with his wife and seven-year-old daughter in the United States, in Paterson, New Jersey. While in America he had developed what he called 'hatred of monarchical institutions'. Travelling to Milan, he had joined a society of anarchists who had drawn lots to see who would carry out the murder.

Assassinations, and assassination attempts, were a feature of the creed of anarchism which had reached a peak in the second half of the nineteenth century. In the opening years of the twentieth century, political assassinations had come to be regarded as an abomination and an anomaly. By the final decade of the new century, however, they had become all too familiar worldwide. Among those who would succumb to the assassin's bullet in the twentieth century were the Archduke Franz Ferdinand in Sarajevo, Walther Rathenau in Berlin, King Alexander of Yugoslavia at Marseilles, Mahatma Gandhi in Delhi, Solomon Bandaranaike in Ceylon, Count Folke Bernadotte and King Abdullah of Transjordan in Jerusalem, John F. Kennedy in Dallas and his brother Robert in Los Angeles, Indira Gandhi and her son Rajiv in India, Martin Luther King in Memphis, Tennessee, Anwar Sadat in Egypt, and Yitzhak Rabin in Tel Aviv. Adolf Hitler, by contrast, survived several attempts on his life.

Any hopes that the cult of anarchism and individual assassination might have been thought to have run its course in the opening year of the new century was quickly dispelled. In 1900, at a railway station in Brussels, an anarchist, Sipido, tried to kill the British Prince of Wales, whom he held 'responsible for the Transvaal war'. In Paris an attempt was made on the life of the Shah of Persia. That October, a plot was uncovered to murder the Russian Tsar during a rail journey to his palace in the Crimea. A month later, in Johannesburg, five Italians, four Greeks and a Frenchman were arrested for planning to explode a bomb during a church service attended by Lord Roberts, the British Commander-in-Chief whose forces had crushed Boer resistance.

A past assassination was also remembered; in November, President Loubet unveiled a monument in Lyons to his predecessor, President Carnot, who had been assassinated in that city six years earlier. Two weeks after the unveiling, a woman, described in the newspapers as 'of weak intellect', threw a hatchet at the German Kaiser as he was riding in his carriage in Breslau. The missile missed its target.

The United States was steadily enhancing its position in the world, by large measures and small. German investment was highlighted in September by the placing of 80,000,000 marks' worth of treasury bonds in Washington.

The Treaty of Commerce with Italy opened up new American markets in Europe. There was also an American territorial acquisition that year. By a convention with Spain, signed on November 7, Spain's last two island possessions in the Pacific, Cagayan and Sibutu, were ceded to the United States, for $100,000. But an attempt by the United States to purchase the Danish West Indies was given up when King Christian IX of Denmark, who had been on the throne for thirty-seven years, deferred to the strong national feeling in his country against the proposed sale.

In May, the British raised the Union flag over the Pacific island of Tonga, declaring a protectorate, despite the protests by the King of Tonga, who refused to give up his claim, or that of his descendants.

It was not only in China that the imperial powers were cooperating. In German South West Africa, the British and German Governments reached agreement on the construction of a 400-mile railway into the interior, the money for which would be raised equally in Britain and Germany. It would not have seemed possible to those diplomats and engineers who negotiated this agreement – had anyone raised the prospect – that within fifteen years Britain and Germany would be at war, and that every German overseas possession would be the object of British military attack.

A German Navy Bill, passed in the Reichstag in Berlin in June, which laid down the scale and pace of German naval construction until 1920, likewise raised no alarms in London, Paris or St Petersburg. As far as the British were concerned, their fleets were the most impressive of all. The British Ambassador in Vienna, having seen the arrival of the British Mediterranean squadron at the Austrian port of Trieste, wrote back to London, about those Austrians who looked to the German Empire for inspiration: 'After their assiduous prophesying for months of our approaching decline, and their gloating over our military disasters, it has been a rough shock to the leaders of the anti-English movement to witness the arrival in Austrian waters of a fleet so clearly symbolizing our unbroken power.'

Hopes of good relations between Britain and Germany animated the governments of both countries. As a sign of his liking for Britain, in December the Kaiser issued an edict replacing French with English as a compulsory subject in the top three classes in all high schools of Prussia. In lower classes, English was to be offered as an alternative to Greek.

Anti-Semitism, which was so to scar Germany later in the century, was in evidence even as the century opened. At the beginning of March, a German schoolboy was murdered in Konitz, a small town in the province of West

Prussia. His body was afterwards discovered, dissected and bloodless, giving rise to rumours in the locality that the boy had been murdered by Jews. It was a centuries' old libel, heard most frequently in medieval Christian Europe, that Jews murdered Christian children in the period immediately before Passover, so that the blood would be preserved for ritual purposes, for the making of bread in the forthcoming Passover festival. The anti-Semitic press in Germany seized the opportunity to stir up hatred against the Jews.

Jewish homes in the town were attacked, and a large military force had to be sent to restore order. But the inflamed hostility in the town towards Jews made it difficult for the police to conduct enquiries. The reward for evidence leading to the detection of the attackers was raised to 20,000 marks, but without result. The *Germania*, the leading clerical publication in Berlin, further inflamed the anti-Semites by implying that the police authorities were not in earnest in their efforts to discover the murderers of a Christian child.

That summer a second riot took place at Konitz, when a large crowd, including many people who had come in from the surrounding countryside, attacked houses lived in by Jews, assaulted the police, and wrecked the synagogue. As the police proved unable to stop the rioters, a company of infantry was sent in, followed by a battalion. A 'state of siege' was proclaimed in the town, and all executive authority was put in the hands of the local military commander.

Following the Konitz riots, the local rabbi, Dr Fessler, asked the professors of Old Testament theology at the Protestant theological college at Halle to state whether the use of Christian blood in religious rites is prescribed in any Jewish writings or traditions. Two professors replied in the identical terms of a resolution adopted at the Congress of Orientalists held in Rome the previous year: 'In view of recent events,' the orientalists stated, they 'regard it as their duty to declare that the assertion that the use of Christian blood for ritual purposes has ever been prescribed or even hinted at in any directions which are valid for the followers of the Jewish religion is an absolutely senseless calumny, unworthy of the end of the nineteenth century.'

This academic rebuttal of what was essentially a charge against the Jews from medieval times did not end the superstitions and hatreds of centuries. Later in the year there was a further anti-Semitic cause célèbre in Berlin itself, when a Jewish banker charged with indecent offences was said, without justification, to have bribed the police to keep a crucial witness silent. The bribery charge was found to be false, but the fact that the banker was Jewish stimulated popular anti-Jewish feelings.

The internal divisions of the Habsburg Empire – with its mixture of Germans, Czechs, Slovaks, Ruthenes, Poles, Hungarians, Roumanians, Serbs, Croats and Italians – caused considerable comment among European observers that year. Any threat to the stability of the Empire was not taken too seriously, however, in Vienna, where the Emperor, his Court and his government were confident of maintaining the vast imperial structure.

The pinpricks were frequent. During a meeting of the Austrian Parliament (the Reichsrat) that summer, the Czech opposition members disrupted the proceedings by blowing toy trumpets, beating cymbals, and producing an array of catcalls and other noises. After seven hours of disruption, the Prime Minister closed the session. In a direct rebuke to the leader of the Czech parliamentarians, on another contentious matter, the Emperor said that if Czech recruits into the Austrian army continued to answer their officers in the Czech language and not in German, he would take the severest action against them. But the slowly rising tide of national self-assertion could not be halted by threats. In December 1900, after a ten-year absence, the Italian deputies resumed their seats in the regional parliament in the Tyrol, having boycotted the assembly on the grounds that they could always be outvoted by the German-speaking deputies. On their return, they insisted that their speeches and interjections, which they would only make in Italian, should be translated into German, and read out in full.

Not only in his Austrian dominions, but also in his Hungarian kingdom – the twin pillar of his Dual Monarchy – Franz Josef faced grumblings and disaffection. Speaking in the Hungarian parliament in Budapest, the Hungarian Prime Minister said that he was prepared to take the necessary measures 'to assert the rights of Hungary and its independence'. Until the time came to do so, he added, 'let us husband our strength and keep our powder dry'. Speaking at military manoeuvres in Galicia, his most eastern province, Franz Josef went so far as to praise his Polish subjects as 'the only great nationality' of his country which had always striven with loyalty to promote the welfare of Austria-Hungary. This was not very flattering, or encouraging, to the Czechs, Hungarians, Italians, Roumanians and Ruthenes within his dominions.

A domestic issue clouded Franz Josef's life that year: the marriage at the beginning of July of his nephew and heir, the Archduke Franz Ferdinand. The Archduke had fallen in love with Countess Sophie Chotek, who was not a member of any royal house, but of the Bohemian nobility which was at that very moment asserting Czech linguistic claims. The countess was not of sufficient social standing in the complex hierarchy of Habsburg aristocracy to make a suitable Empress. The marriage had therefore to be morganatic: no children of the union could succeed to the throne. For Franz Josef this was a painful setback in the fifty-second year of his reign, a reign which had seen the suicide of his son, the Crown Prince, Rudolf in 1889.

On June 28, a few days before Franz Ferdinand's marriage was to take place, a ceremony was held in the Hofburg in Vienna, at which, in the presence of the Emperor, fifteen Archdukes, the Papal Nuncio and the Cardinal-Archbishop, he renounced under oath all the claims of Countess Chotek and any children they might have to the status of royalty, or to the inheritance of the Habsburg throne. The marriage duly took place without the Emperor or any of the Archdukes being present.

That spring, on April 23, a secret meeting was held in the Georgian province of the Russian Empire to celebrate May Day, and the hopes of the workers for an end to autocracy. To prevent detection by the Tsarist police, the place chosen for the meeting was outside the capital, Tiflis. In the previous year's gathering, seventy workers had attended. In 1900 the number was two hundred. One of the speakers that day was Josef Dzhugashvili (later known as Stalin), a Georgian who had just been expelled from the Tiflis Theological Seminary, after five years studying to be a priest. He was in charge that year of Marxist propaganda among the Tiflis railway workers, and had indeed already made contact with them while at the seminary.

By July, there was an intimation of the national problems confronting the vast Russian Empire, when the Senate of Finland, which had been a Russian province since 1808, rejected an imperial manifesto making Russian the official language of Finland, a country in which only 8000 out of 2,700,000 people spoke Russian as their native tongue. Only two years had passed since the suppression of a measure of Finnish autonomy and the exile of many Finnish national leaders. Despite this rebuff by the Finnish Senate, the power of St Petersburg seemed unchallengeable.

The Ottoman Empire was likewise troubled by political agitation, murder, and civil war among its non-Turkish and non-Muslim nationalities. In the province of Macedonia, whose ethnic mix of peoples gave its name to the French fruit salad 'Macédoine de fruits', more than a hundred ethnic Bulgarians were murdered by local Greeks during 1900. Macedonia was to become a focus of concern for the Powers, none of which wanted to be dragged into a European war in order to champion one or other of the many nationalities there. The small, landlocked province was the home to Turks, Serbs, Bulgarian Christians, Bulgarian Muslims (known as Pomaks), Roumanians (known as Vlachs: some of them Greek Orthodox, others Muslim), Greeks, Albanians (Christian and Muslim), and Albanianized Serbs (known as Arnauts). A British writer, H. N. Brailsford, who championed the Bulgarian claims to the region, wrote six years later: 'The Macedonians are Bulgarian today because a free and progressive Bulgaria has known how to attract them.' The Bulgarians also resorted to the forcible conversion of the Muslim Pomaks to Christianity.

In the neighbouring Turkish province of Albania, a local Muslim chief ordered the murder of more than two hundred Christians. A Christian village was set on fire, and several Christians who had been taken hostage were murdered because no ransom was paid for them. Even in the Ottoman capital, Constantinople, violence and riots were commonplace. The European picture of the warlike Turk was expressed in 1900 by a British diplomat, Sir Charles Eliot, in his book *Turkey in Europe* (written under the pseudonym Odysseus). 'Every Turk,' he wrote, 'is born a soldier, and adopts other pursuits chiefly because the times are bad. When there is a question of fighting, if only in a riot, the stolid peasant wakes up and shows a surprising power of organization and finding expedients, and, alas, a surprising ferocity. The ordinary Turk is an honest, good-humoured soul, kind to children and animals, and very patient, but when the fighting spirit comes on him, he . . . slays, burns and ravages without mercy or discrimination.'

In the distant eastern regions of the Ottoman Empire, Kurdish villagers attacked and murdered at least sixty Armenians, and possibly as many as four hundred, in the wide swathe of mountainous countryside along the upper reach of the Tigris river. One village, Spaghank, was surrounded not only by Kurds but by a force under the direct control of the local Turkish military commander. When a group of Armenians took refuge in the village church, the troops surrounded the building and set it on fire, suffocating to death those inside, including the local priest.

Distant Constantinople, 800 miles to the west, seemed powerless to control its far-flung emissaries. In the remote town of Van, the British Vice-Consul, who had attempted to protect the local Armenians, was himself attacked by Kurds. When the British and other governments protested to Constantinople, the Sultan removed the regional military commander. But the violence against the Armenians continued.

Britain was not untroubled by dissent within its borders. At the beginning of September the Phoenix Park in Dublin – scene of the murders in 1882 of the Chief Secretary for Ireland and his Under-Secretary by a terrorist-nationalist group 'The Invincibles' – was the scene of a large Irish nationalist demonstration. The demonstrators, members of the Irish National League, demanded Home Rule for Ireland, the abolition of landlordism, and the withdrawal of Irish political representation in the Westminster Parliament, where the Irish members were a substantial group, seeking Home Rule from within the British political system.

The natural disasters of the year also have their place in the telling of the events of 1900. In January an earthquake in the Caucasus destroyed ten villages and caused severe damage in several towns, including the coastal town of Batum. As many as a thousand Georgians were killed. In September, a cyclone swept the coast of Texas, creating a tidal wave which hit the port of Galveston, killing more than four thousand people.

In the Canadian capital, Ottawa, a fire, sweeping that April through a modern city whose houses were not of wood but of stone, left more than fourteen thousand people homeless. No one was killed. But the destruction of so many houses – more than three thousand – and the plight of the homeless, led to an international response. Money was sent from Britain, France, even Chile. There was a sense of something new and special. 'This dreadful calamity,' the relief committee reported, 'awakened the sympathy of the civilized world, and evoked a spirit of generosity that completely obliterated national barriers and gave a most gratifying demonstration of the common ties which bind mankind in one great brotherhood.'

In a fire that swept through three German ships moored at the Hoboken Dock in New Jersey, two hundred people were killed, mostly German sailors. In Hong Kong, a hundred people a week died of bubonic plague during the spring and summer. But it was in India that by far the greatest death toll was recorded; during the course of a two-year famine that spanned the end of one millennium and the beginning of the new, two million people died of hunger in the Ganges region and further south.

The population of India in 1900 was 300 million. The number of famine deaths was calculated each week by the Government of India. In a gesture of Anglo-German solidarity, the German Kaiser, a grandson of the Queen-Empress, sent a substantial sum of money for the Indian famine fund. By the end of the year, 3 million Indians were being fed by the fund. The rains having failed for the second year in succession, these millions were dependent for their survival on famine relief.

In Bundi, one of the Native States in India most badly affected by famine, the senior British official was Colonel Francis Younghusband. Travelling on horseback and camelback throughout the region for which he was responsible, he later recalled the 'climax of exhaustion' as spring gave way to summer:

By May 1900 the worst began. The people ate berries and leaves and roots. I even saw men seizing burnt human remains from the funeral piles and gnawing at them.

Scorching winds blew across the parched-up plains. The sun was pitiless. The wells were nearly dry, and what water remained in them was unfit to drink, yet the people drank it, and as a result got cholera. Cholera then raged through the land. With pure water almost unobtainable, and the people in the last stage of emaciation in spirit as well as body, they were an easy prey to it. Children hideously thin and mothers like skeletons appealed piteously for help, and dead bodies lay everywhere by the roadside.

June came and passed. The heat grew intense. The monsoon ought to have arrived by now. But this year of all others it was later than usual. Not a cloud was there in the sky. The sun still burnt down like a furnace. The first week in July passed, and still no sign of rain.

In the Native State of Rajputana, another of the centres of the famine, the British Political Agent, James Dunlop-Smith, persuaded the local Indian princes and paramount chiefs that while famine might well be an act of God, its mitigation, and even its prevention, lay in the hands of men. Considerable efforts were made, throughout the famine areas, to ensure the fair distribution of what food could be found, to reduce corruption, and to embark on substantial relief and irrigation works. This was a side to British rule in India which lacked the clamour, and the conflict, of the political struggle, but was nevertheless an integral part of the imperial mission.

*   *   *

In the Russian Empire the leaders of the small, largely exiled, Russian Social Democratic Labour Party, which had been founded in 1898, were convinced that the nineteenth-century Marxist analysis, whereby the collapse of the hated capitalist system could only come about through class conflict, made revolution inevitable in the highly industrialized states. Vladimir Ulyanov, known by his underground name of Lenin, was chief contender for the Party leadership. He left Russia in 1900, at the age of thirty, after three years in exile in Siberia. From Western Europe he was determined to spread the revolutionary call through a newspaper, *Iskra* (The Spark) which was smuggled into Russia from its publishing centres in London, Geneva and Munich.

Iskra was founded in December 1900. Through it, the ideas of revolution were propagated with skill and force. Lenin, its guiding spirit, rejected the arguments of those Russian revolutionaries who wanted to take into account the diversity of territorial, ethnic and national participants in the revolutionary movement, and to cater for this diversity by separate organizations within a federal structure.

From his base of exile in Switzerland, Lenin used *Iskra* to urge, and to forge, a centralized Party structure, and to ensure that the revolutionaries who were in charge of Party policy and organization were as professional in their outlook and methods as the most professional engineer, teacher or police officer. The Party was small, and its exiles scattered; but it was determined to work for the day – and to see the day – when the Russian Empire would be no more. But in 1900 there were few, if any, outside the small circle of the revolutionaries, who could conceive that the Russian Empire, any more than the British Empire, would not survive the century that lay ahead.

No year passed in the twentieth century in which death, conflict, turmoil and destruction were not in evidence in many parts of the globe. Yet at the same time, no year passed without efforts being made, and initiatives taken, to push ahead along a path of cooperation and mutual benefit. The year 1900 was no exception. It saw, in Paris, the new century doubly welcomed, first by a World Exhibition in which the products and manufactures of many nations were exhibited with pride amid festive surroundings, and then, that July, by the first modern Olympic Games to be held outside Athens. In sport, as in trade and commerce, the spirit that was praised and lauded was not that of destructive conflict, but of healthy competition. The table of gold medal winners was headed by France with 29, the United States with 20, and Britain with 17. Austria-Hungary won 4, Germany 3, and Russia none.

A folk hero was created in the United States that year when Casey Jones, an engine driver, was killed on his footplate after having slowed down his engine as it steamed towards another engine in Mississippi. He was the only person killed in the wreck, having insisted that his fireman, Sam Webb, jump from the footplate just before the crash.

Music and inventions could each inspire enthusiasm, and at the same time foreshadow conflict. Russia's imperial problems were reflected that year when nationalism and music combined in *Finlandia* by Sibelius. In Britain, William Crookes found the means of separating uranium. In Germany, on the evening of July 2, the first airship – the creation of Count Zeppelin – made its trial flight. With five people on board – the count, two passengers and two engineers – the 'Zeppelin', as it quickly became known, left Friedrichshafen, on Lake Constance, and flew to Immenstadt, a distance of thirty-five miles. Man had found a means of powered travel through the air.

CHAPTER TWO

1901

On 22 JANUARY 1901 Queen Victoria died. She was eighty-one, and had reigned for sixty-one years. Since 1877 she had been, among her other titles, Empress of India. It was an empire that included far more than India ('the jewel in the crown') – an empire on which it was said that 'the sun never set'. It included not only the self-governing British Dominions of Canada, Newfoundland, Australia and New Zealand, but large tracts of Africa, and island groups in every ocean. The vastness of the British Empire gave the tens of thousands of Britons who served in it their sense of mission. It provided immense hinterlands for British trade, and was the focus of a substantial system of imperial defence, dominated by the warships of the Royal Navy.

The editors of Cassell's *History of England*, of which the ninth volume was published in 1901, described the Queen's death as 'the saddest of all the 145 chapters that have been devoted in this history to the reign of Queen Victoria'. The Queen's funeral was fixed for February 2. In Cassell's words:

> The sun that, in its circuit, had never ceased to shine on the Queen's dominions for half a century, now rose continuously on a world wrapped in sorrow, on flags half-mast high in distress all over the globe, on nations grave with grief. London, the capital of the Empire, was a city of dreadful black, a city mute. The Parliaments were adjourned, all public and official engagements cancelled, theatres and places of entertainment closed, functions suspended, windows shuttered, business at a standstill, except where the preparations for mourning, or the actual necessities of life, compelled trade to be carried on.
>
> Each succeeding day saw the streets draped deeper and deeper in royal purple. From every corner of the country, from the uttermost ends of the Empire, messages of condolence and grief poured in. In the churches and chapels of the Christian world, in the mosques of the Mohamedans and

the temples of the heathen, in the sanctuaries of all creeds and all castes, the prayers of priests and worshippers went up to the universal God on behalf of her, lying so still and serene, in the death chamber at Osborne.

From every foreign state in the Old World and the New, from every considerable city in both hemispheres, over steppes and prairies wrapped in snow, over savannahs and deserts glowing in sunshine, under oceans bound in ice or lashed by wintry gales, under tropic seas, calm and placid, from torrid, from temperate, from frozen zones, there flashed one single expression of universal sorrow. Never was there a touch of nature that made the whole world more kin than the death of her Majesty the Queen of England.

'The funeral,' Cassell's history added, 'was the greatest and most impressive ever known.' Five sovereigns, nine Crown Princes or Heirs Apparent, and forty other Princes and Grand Dukes rode on horseback in the funeral procession in London, leaving 'scarcely a principality in the civilized world unrepresented':

Queen Victoria, great and greatly beloved, whose reign had glorified the century just ended, and helped to make it the most brilliant epoch in the world's history, died and was buried, and her spirit passed to where 'beyond those voices there is peace'.

Peace and rest for her who had earned them by a queenly life of toil and devotion for her peoples. But for them a sorrow it must take a long time to assuage, and a memory that shall endure and be honoured so long as the sun rises on this planet, and finds it peopled with human life.

Ten days later, a letter to *The Times* commented: 'We are touched at hearing that African chiefs have ordered tom-toms to be beaten or cattle sacrificed for the repose of the soul of the Great White Queen.'

Queen Victoria's death was followed not only by the accession of her son as King Edward VII and King-Emperor, but by Edward's proclamation in the recently conquered city of Pretoria as 'Supreme Lord of, and over, the Transvaal'. The British conquest of the two Boer republics was almost complete. But with the Boer guerrilla fighters continuing to fight in outlying districts, a further 30,000 British troops, more than 10 per cent of the forces already sent out, were despatched to South Africa.

A phrase was becoming current in Britain, 'the slimness of the Boers', an indication of the begrudging admiration that was felt for the ability of the guerrillas to evade capture and defeat. Cassell's history expressed the frustration that had come to beset the imperial power:

> Week after week the British public was regaled with lists of Boers killed, Boers wounded, Boers made prisoners, Boers surrendered, not to mention reports of the taking of huge numbers of arms, ammunition, horses, and cattle – but the war went on. It seemed to be never-ending. And every now and then there came a fight fiercer than the rest, or a reverse to indicate the recuperative powers of an enemy who, harried from pillar to post, could still turn round at every advantageous opportunity and show battle. Thus, at the end of October, a very strong column under Colonel Benson was attacked near Brakenlaagte by General Botha, and a fight ensued which was described as one of the most sanguinary and determined in the campaign. Advancing under cover of a thick mist, the enemy attacked the British force with reckless and indomitable gallantry, just as it was reaching its camping ground, killing fifty-four (including Colonel Benson) and wounding 160 men, and capturing two guns.

In an attempt to force the Boer guerrillas to surrender, the British military authorities in South Africa seized thousands of Boer women and children, whose menfolk were still fighting, and detained them in seventeen special camps, known as 'concentration camps'. Conditions in the camps were bad, with almost no medical facilities, and little food. A further thirty-five camps were set up for Africans who worked on the farms of the absent fighters, so they too would be unable to plant or harvest crops, or look after livestock. But still the farmers refused to be lured or bullied out of their fighting encampments, even when they were told that the cost of maintaining those who were interned would be charged against their farms and property.

The death toll in the camps was extremely high. A British woman, Emily Hobhouse, visited them. 'I began to compare a parish I had known at home of two thousand people,' she wrote, 'where a funeral was an event – and usually of an old person. Here some twenty to twenty-five were carried away *daily*. . . The full realization of the position dawned on me – it was a death-rate such as had never been known except in the times of the Great Plagues . . . The whole talk was of death – who died yesterday, who lay dying today, who would be dead tomorrow.'

Returning to Britain, Emily Hobhouse led a campaign against the camps, which were forcefully denounced by the Liberal Party leader, Henry Camp-bell-Bannerman. 'When is a war not a war?' he asked, and gave the answer: 'When it is carried on by methods of barbarism in South Africa.' The government quickly instituted improvements, and the death rate fell. But the episode sharpened the divide between supporters and opponents of the war. The final toll was far higher than that of the battlefield: 28,000 Boer women and children died in the camps, and more than 50,000 Africans.

Among the mourners at Queen Victoria's funeral had been her grandson the German Kaiser, Wilhelm II. He had been at her side when she died; on hearing how ill she was, he had cancelled his engagements for the bicentenary celebrations of the Prussian kingdom so he could be with her. The mutually beneficial links between countries through the blood relationship of their sovereigns seemed to be underlined by this gesture. Before returning to Germany the Kaiser let it be known that he favoured an alliance between 'the two Teutonic nations', Britain and Germany. It was an alliance in which Britain would 'keep the seas' while Germany 'would be responsible for the land'. With such an alliance, he asserted, 'not a mouse will stir in Europe without our permission'.

The enthusiasm of the Kaiser was in contrast with the more cautious attitudes of the British and German foreign offices. The British Foreign Secretary, Lord Lansdowne, was to find the idea of such an alliance 'a very stiff fence to ride at', while the German Chancellor, Baron von Richthofen, thought it was a wildly irresponsible suggestion. Germany was already committed to its Triple Alliance with Austria-Hungary and Italy; and Britain could hardly, in allying itself with Germany, take on the responsibilities of Germany's commitments to defend the frontiers of its existing partners.

When Wilhelm met King Edward seven months later, the Kaiser rebuked his uncle for the sloth of those in the British Government whom he castigated as 'unmitigated noodles', who had failed to pursue his idea of 'a definite and binding treaty of alliance' between the two countries. Edward was irritated by his nephew's tone. Even if the idea of such an alliance had appealed to him, he had neither the constitutional authority nor the drive to push such a scheme forward.

The prominence of the King-Emperors centred on tradition, wealth and social hierarchy. Their travels were the scenes of magnificent and ostentatious balls, banquets and finery. But their words and actions were scrutinized for whatever they might betoken, and for the nature of the relationships between the Powers which they represented, both in the ceremonial and political life of their countries. There was relief throughout Europe when, after a meeting with the Tsar in the German Baltic city of Danzig in September, the Kaiser stated publicly that the meeting had convinced him that European peace would be preserved for many years to come. From that meeting, the Tsar went on to France, where he attended the last day of French army manoeuvres near Rheims.

Russia's alliance with France dated back to 1894. For the Germans, it represented a potential encirclement; hence the importance for them of maintaining their earlier alliances with Austria-Hungary and Italy. In this European alliance system, whereby frontiers were guaranteed and national interests linked, Britain stood aside, as did Japan and the United States. But Britain was actively seeking an alliance with Japan, not wishing, after Russia's continual strides there, to find itself outwitted by Russia in the Far East. And towards the end of the year, Britain and the United States entered into a Treaty whereby Britain acknowledged the right of the United States to build a canal across the isthmus between North and South America.

Provided no other Power was involved, the independent action of individual Powers in the opening years of the century was a regular feature of international affairs which led to no international repercussions. An example of this was the French quarrel with Turkey in 1901, about the status of French subjects and institutions on the Turkish island of Crete. A French naval expedition embarked for Crete, seized the customs house at Mytilene, and cut the telegraphic communications with Constantinople. The French force demanded the recognition by Turkey of all French charitable, scholastic and religious institutions on the island, and the repair and restoration of all Armenian property that had been destroyed or damaged during the anti-Armenian riots of 1894 and 1896. After only three days of French occupation, the Sultan yielded to France's demands, and the crisis was over. No other Power had come to Turkey's defence.

That same month, Turkey was in another clash with one of the Powers. Once again no other Power came to her aid. The issue was an attempt by the Turkish Sultan to extend his control to the small sheikhdom of Kuwait, in the Persian Gulf. Kuwait, which had never been formally incorporated into the Ottoman Empire, was adjacent to the Turkish province of Mesopotamia (now Iraq). When the Sultan tried to land a Turkish military force, the Sheikh of Kuwait, who had made a treaty with Britain two years earlier, appealed for help to his new ally. A British warship arrived in the Persian Gulf and made it clear that it would open fire should the Turkish forces try to land. This naval exercise was effective; and the Sultan abandoned his claim to sovereignty over Kuwait.

The Kaiser's peaceful assurances at Danzig, that peace in Europe would be preserved for many years, were welcome, but the Tsar's presence at French army manoeuvres was a more realistic pointer of what was to come. The Tsar was careful, though, in a speech at the end of his visit, to stress that the union between Russia and Germany was 'animated by the most peaceful intentions'.

By coincidence, the Tsar's speech was delivered eleven days before the first submarine to be built for the British navy was launched at Barrow-in-Furness; within ten years, fifty-six submarines had been built in Britain. In addition to the alliances of militarily strong Powers, and the submarine, yet another weapon was being added to the arsenal of 'peaceful intentions': the motorcar, whose internal combustion engine was likewise to transform war. It too had its peaceful and ceremonial uses. In November 1901, on the fifth anniversary of the parliamentary legislation setting out the conditions of motorcars on the roads of Britain, there was a celebratory drive by a fleet of cars on a ninety-five-mile stretch of road from London to Southsea. The journey astounded onlookers by its rapidity; it took just under seven hours.

The motorcar was also already revealing itself as a killer; in 1901 more than a thousand Americans were killed on the roads. During the thirty-three years covered by this volume, more than three hundred thousand people in the United States were to be killed in motor accidents.

Another development that was to have significance for the whole century, both in peace and war, took place on December 11. On that and the following day the electronics engineer and inventor, Guglielmo Marconi, who was in St John's, Newfoundland, managed to receive, by wireless telegraphy, what he called 'faint but conclusive' signals from his transmission station at Poldhu, Cornwall. This was just two years after he had secured a similar success across the English Channel. Now it was possible, *The Times* reported, to solve 'the problem of telegraphing across the Atlantic without wires'. The paper's New York correspondent reported that the news of Marconi's transmission 'has caused an intense sensation here'. There was also scepticism, especially on the part of Marconi's rival Edison, who said that 'until he gets further details he cannot believe the report'. The president of the Commercial

Cable Company, which stood to lose the most if Marconi's invention were successful, said that his company was 'going on with the construction of new cables as though wireless messages had never been heard of'.

During another year of attempted and successful assassinations, the President of the United States, William McKinley, who was visiting a Pan-American Exhibition at Buffalo, was shot on September 6 by an anarchist, Leon Czolgosz, with whom he was shaking hands. McKinley, who died eight days later, was a veteran of the American Civil War. Under his administration America had defeated Spain and acquired the Philippines. It was he who had agreed to the annexation of Hawaii by the United States, and the effective control by the United States of Cuba.

Czolgosz was arrested and brought to trial. McKinley was succeeded as President by Theodore Roosevelt, his relatively youthful (forty-three-year-old) Vice-President, who three years earlier had raised and commanded a volunteer cavalry regiment of cowboys and college graduates, the Rough Riders, to fight in the Spanish-American war. On his return from the war he had been elected Governor of New York State. 'Great privileges and great powers are ours,' the new President declared on taking the oath of office, 'and heavy are the responsibilities that go with these privileges and these powers. According as we do well or ill, so shall mankind in the future be raised or cast down.'

In a forecast of America's contribution to the century that lay ahead, Theodore Roosevelt continued: 'We belong to a young nation, already of giant strength, yet whose present strength is but a forecast of the power that is to come. We stand supreme in the continent, in the hemisphere. East and west we look across the two great oceans toward the larger world-life in which, whether we will or not, we must take an ever-increasing share. And as, keen-eyed, we gaze into the coming years, duties new and old rise thick and fast to confront us from within and from without.'

There was every reason, the new President added, why the United States 'should face these duties with a sober appreciation alike of their importance and of their difficulty. But there is also every reason for facing them with high-hearted resolution and eager and confident faith in our capacity to do them aright. A great work lies ready to the hand of this generation; it should count itself happy indeed that to it is given the privilege of doing such a work.'

American industrial power was becoming as great as that of all the industrial nations combined. Men like Andrew Carnegie, Pierpont Morgan and Will Schwalb had built up great steel empires. When the United States Steel Corporation was formed in 1901 it was popularly known as the Billion-Dollar Corporation. Its capital was in fact even larger: £1.3 billion. In the world of financing, John D. Rockefeller and James H. Hill were among the kings. The British philosopher Bertrand Russell later wrote: 'The ramifications of Morgan's power were endless. He controlled Armour's of Chicago, through whom he held power of life and death over the cattle of the Argentine. His shipping Combine contained most of the Atlantic liners. Edward VII, the Kaiser, and the Pope, entertained him as if he were a visiting monarch.' Russell noted a 'revised catechism' published by *Life* magazine, in which the answer to 'Who made the world?' was 'God made the world in 4004BC, but it was reorganized by James H. Hill, J. Pierpont Morgan and John D. Rockefeller.'

The imperial aspect of the new American power was never given the name 'imperial'. America's possessions were called 'dependencies'. Nearly seven million Filipinos, almost 10 per cent of the population of the continental United States, lived in the Philippines. Puerto Rico, acquired from Spain in 1898, had almost a million. Hawaii had a population of 154,000, Guam 8000, and American Samoa, in the Pacific, 6000. But the great demographic change in the United States was taking place, not through acquisition but through immigration. During the year 1901 almost half a million immigrants arrived in the United States from Europe, a figure which was to be maintained year after year. The largest single group that year were Italians, 135,996 according to the immigration statistics. Russian Jews made up more than 80,000. In Italy, the appointment of a Jew, General Giuseppe Ottolenghi, as Minister of War, a popular choice among both the government and opposition Parties, led one British observer to comment, when the appointment was announced, 'that Italy, in this respect happier than Germany and Austria, knew nothing of anti-Semitism'.

As enquiries proceeded into the assassination of McKinley, it emerged that a New York anarchist journal had published an article urging anarchists to assassinate heads of state. The editor was sentenced to a year in prison. The assassin, who to the last moment declared himself unrepentant, was executed in the electric chair. 'Anarchy is a crime against the whole human race,'

Theodore Roosevelt told Congress, 'and all mankind should band together against the Anarchist. His crime should be made an offence against the law of nations, like piracy, and that form of man-stealing known as the slave trade; for it is of far blacker infamy than either.'

In St Petersburg that year, a Russian student shot and seriously injured the Minister of Education. This attempt was followed within three weeks by riots which erupted in Moscow, St Petersburg, Kiev and Odessa. In an ominous development for the Tsarist authorities, the students were in almost every city joined during those March protests by factory and manual workers, who went on strike. Several provinces were put under martial law, and troops were sent in to restore order. Several hundreds of workers and students were imprisoned. Two months later, in both St Petersburg and Moscow, there were further demonstrations, and further arrests. In Moscow, nearly four hundred students were imprisoned. No sooner had they been locked away than a crowd of demonstrators marched to the monument of the Russian national hero, the poet Pushkin, where they sang a 'Hymn to Liberty' to the tune, but not to the sentiments, of the national anthem, 'God save the Tsar'.

During a further student protest in St Petersburg, proclamations were distributed with revolutionary slogans, among them 'Down with the Tsar', and a red flag was flown on the steps of the cathedral, in protest against a punishment being used against student rioters, their drafting into the army, not to serve as officers, as befitted their education and status, but as ordinary soldiers. There were further riots with red flags in many cities, including the southern city of Ekaterinoslav and the Caucasian capital, Tiflis, where fourteen demonstrators were injured and fifty arrested. Lenin, in exile in Switzerland, was enthusiastic when he heard of the Tiflis demonstration. 'This day marks the beginning,' he wrote, 'of an open revolutionary movement in the Caucasus.' Among those who took part in the Tiflis confrontation was Josef Stalin. Subsequent Soviet representations of the scene were to show him at the forefront of the demonstration, facing the police attacks alongside his fellow workers. But he was not among those injured or arrested; and by the end of the year he had been expelled from the Tiflis branch of the Social Democratic Party as a troublemaker.

Count Leo Tolstoy, the Russian writer and thinker, then aged seventy-three, was an active supporter of protests that took place inside as well as outside the cathedral in Moscow: the students had deliberately smoked inside the cathedral as a mark of their contempt for the religious authorities.[1] Tolstoy's sympathy with the demonstrators led to his excommunication by the Russian Orthodox church. In an appeal to the Tsar to intercede to protect civil liberties in Russia, Tolstoy wrote: 'Thousands of the best Russians, sincerely religious people, and therefore such as constitute the chief strength of every nation, have already been ruined, or are being ruined, in prison and in banishment.' Dissent, he said, should not be punished as a crime. It was quite wrong to believe that the salvation of Russia could only be found 'in a brutal and antiquated form of government'.

Tolstoy's letter of excommunication was signed by Konstantin Pobedonostsev, the Procurator of the Holy Synod, and the effective government minister controlling the Russian Orthodox church. Pobedonostsev hated Catholics, Jews and Muslims alike. His attitude to democracy was summed up in his phrase 'Parliaments are the greatest lie of our time'. It was he who made the alliance between the Orthodox Church and Tsarism so strong that, when the revolutionaries turned on the one, they inevitably turned on the other as well.

Neither the internal nor imperial policies of Russia were about to change. Throughout 1901 the Russification of Finland was continued with vigour, with Finnish citizens being forced to serve against their will in Russian regiments. Despite strong Russian opposition to this inside the Council of State in St Petersburg, where a majority were critical of the measure, the Tsar exercised his autocratic powers, and the protests were brushed aside.

The continued local resistance to Russian policy in Finland was galling in the extreme to the Tsar. Conscription, intended as a main route to compliance, Russification, and the maintenance of order elsewhere in the empire, was a failure. In Helsinki, in the following year, of 857 men summoned to the army, only fifty-six obeyed. In Senate Square, a vast crowd demonstrated against army service. The Tsar's Cossack troops, ordered to disperse the crowds, used their knotted whips, knocking to the ground those who did not disperse. A new imperial edict placed the Finnish Senate under the direct supervision of the Russian Governor General. At a further mass meeting in Helsinki, Finns from towns and countryside, including many workers and peasants, voted for a resolution that it was 'imperative, for the maintenance

[1] Thirty years later the cathedral was pulled down on the orders of Stalin. During a visit to Moscow while writing this book – four years after the fall of Soviet communism – I saw it being rebuilt by workers toiling day and night.

of our political and national existence, to continue everywhere, unswervingly, and until legal conditions are restored to the country, the passive resistance against all measures conflicting with, or calculated to abolish, our fundamental laws.'

Across the Gulf of Finland other subjects of the Tsar, the people of Estonia, were also seeking some means of national expression. In 1901 a group of young Estonians, led by a lawyer, Konstantin Päts, started a newspaper, *Teataja*, which cautiously, in order to protect itself against the censorship, urged an improvement in the economic conditions of the Estonian people as a means of raising national consciousness.

Workers' discontent was endemic in all industrialized States. In May that year, workers in Barcelona went on strike, and there were many clashes with the local Spanish police. When anarchists, separatists, anticlericals and republicans joined in the street demonstrations, chaos ensued, a state of siege was declared, and it was five days before the army could restore sufficient order to permit the city's trams to run. In Valencia, peasant farmers went on strike in protest at the taxes being levied on them when they brought their produce into town. The city was reduced to near famine, and the mayor was forced to suspend the taxes. During the voting in the subsequent Spanish national elections, a polling station director was killed in a skirmish with discontented workers, but the Socialist party candidates were widely defeated. The appeal for law and order was a powerful one among the Spanish bourgeoisie; by 1907 Spain was still the only major European country without a working-class deputy in Parliament.

In the United States, a strike of machine workers in 1901 was supported by men and women in the associated trades. That strike was followed two months later by another, in which 140,000 men working for the United States Steel Corporation took part. Throughout the industrial world, the more affluent public looked with trepidation at all manifestations of self-assertion by those who were its less fortunate fellow citizens. Socialist parties demanded a greater say in the conduct of government, but were nowhere in sufficient ascendancy to put their more egalitarian plans into effect.

Yet governments could be forced by parliamentary opposition to change their policies, even when they were affecting only the disadvantaged margin of society. In the British parliament, a defeat for the ruling Conservatives in 1901 forced them to abandon legislation whereby the hours of Saturday work for women and young people in the textile industry were to be from six in the morning until one in the afternoon. As a result of the exertions of the Liberal opposition, the end of the Saturday working day was put back by an hour, to twelve noon.

In Britain that July the House of Lords was asked to resolve an industrial dispute that had continued for almost two years. To the distress of the trade union movement, the court decided in favour of the owners, the Taff Vale Railway Company, and against the trade union which had declared a strike of railway workers. As a result of the legal decision, the trade union was judged responsible for the damage caused to the company by the strike. This decision was a major cause of division between the Conservative government, which supported it, and the Liberal opposition, which not only felt that it was unjust, but feared the rise of the Labour Party if Liberalism was unable to redress the grievance of the working class. The Liberal opposition demanded that the Taff Vale decision be reversed. The Conservatives refused. On coming to power four years later, the Liberals themselves reversed the decision, and restored the striking power of the unions.

Every empire and overseas power was facing serious problems of law and order, both from its own people and from those over whom it held dominion. In Athens, a violent demonstration against the proposed publication of the Gospels in modern Greek led to several deaths and the resignation of the Greek Prime Minister. In the German province of Alsace-Lorraine, acquired by conquest from France thirty years earlier, there was discontent when a new German Secretary of State was appointed for the province. He had hitherto ruled the Danish majority in North Schleswig, another German imperial conquest of the nineteenth century, and had been hated for his hostility to the Danes under his control; he had even placed restrictions on the use of the Danish language on all those living in the province.

The swift growth of the Polish population in those parts of East Prussia which, at the end of the eighteenth century, had been part of the Polish sovereign lands partitioned by Germany, Austria and Russia, was becoming a further cause for internal dissent. There was astonishment throughout Europe when, that December, twenty Polish schoolchildren in the town of Wreschen who refused to say their prayers in German, a language they did not understand, were flogged. On hearing the children's cries their parents broke into the school, but were expelled by the police, and several sent to prison for up to two and a half years for having used abusive language at the forces of order. The highest sentence went to a widow with six children. When asked by the president of the court what language she supposed Christ to have spoken, she replied without hesitation, 'Polish'.

The policy of trying to turn the Polish-speaking population into a German-speaking one had begun fifteen years earlier, under Bismarck.[1] It was paralleled by the German government's purchase of considerable tracts of land in the Posen region and the settlement of Germans there, but this only further exacerbated the feeling of the Poles against the Germans.

The German government was determined to suppress all Polish national sentiment. The Polish language was not allowed to be taught in schools – though it could not be forbidden in homes – and Poles were excluded from the civil service, which included the teaching professions. During a raid on several Polish-language newspaper offices, documents were found which confirmed the desire of the Poles inside the German Empire for a national future for Poland, when it would no longer be divided between three empires. Several editors and thirteen Polish students were arrested and imprisoned.

The crisis continued for many months. It was intensified when the German Chancellor, von Bülow, in an interview at the beginning of the following year with the Berlin correspondent of the Paris *Figaro*, characterized Germans as hares and Poles as rabbits, telling the journalist: 'If in this park I were to put ten hares and five rabbits, next year I should have fifteen hares and a hundred rabbits. It is against such a phenomenon that we mean to defend German national unity in the Polish provinces.' The real problem confronting the Germans was not numbers, however, but, as the chief burgomaster of Posen, a Prussian official, commented, the rise of a vigorous Polish middle class. With this group, whose activities in business and the professions were impressive, the Polish national movement was ceasing to be aristocratic, as it had been in the past, and was becoming democratic and radical. Its appeal was thus far wider than it had been half a century earlier.

Other observers noted that it was not only the Poles in East Prussia, where they constituted 10 per cent of the population, but those Poles scattered in many areas of the German Empire, including nearly 20,000 in Berlin,

[1] In Malta in 1901, after several large street demonstrations (and the pouring of a corrosive fluid on the statue of Queen Victoria at Valetta) the British authorities deferred to the demand of the local population that children in Maltese schools should be taught Maltese as the only language for their first two years of schooling; and that after that their parents could choose between English and Italian as the language to be taught in the higher grades of the school.

90,000 in Westphalia and 25,000 in the Rhineland, who were being attracted to Polish nationalism. They published their own newspapers, had their own social clubs, and generally held themselves apart from the Germans among whom they lived.

The conflict between Slav and Teuton showed itself not only among the Polish minority of Germany, but also in the Balkans, where Austria-Hungary feared the growth of Slav power and the emergence of Russia as a Balkan power. When Serb nationalists in Belgrade encouraged the Slavs under Turkish rule in Macedonia to seek their full rights as Serbs, Austria-Hungary was alarmed. There were considerable Slav minorities inside Austria-Hungary – Serbs, Croats, Slovenes, Poles, Czechs, Slovaks and Ruthenes – who might be encouraged by Slav national agitation to seek greater autonomies. In a warning to the Serbian Government, the Austro-Hungarian Foreign Minister, Count Goluchowski, was emphatic that Austria-Hungary would not allow 'any attack on the existing political order, or any changes prejudicial to her vital interests, or involving danger for her position in the future'.

As part of this Balkan imbroglio, there was considerable Russian activity within both Bulgaria and Roumania, directed at stimulating pan-Slav sentiment. Russian influence was also growing in Serbia, bringing the spectre of the Russian bear to those who guarded the southern borders of Austria-Hungary. Another Slav people, the Czechs, who lived as a fairly compact minority within the Habsburg dominions, was also being influenced by Russia. There was anger in Vienna in July 1901 when, during a Czech gymnastic festival in Prague, the Russian representative, General Rittich, a professor of tactics at the military academy in St Petersburg, published a letter in the leading Czech-language newspaper in which he promised the Czechs that they could count on Russia's power. Russia, he wrote, was always ready to help them. They should 'have faith in the God of Russia, and place their trust in Him'.

In the Philippines, the United States, having taken over a vast geographic area of the Spanish Empire after defeating Spain three years earlier, was still engaged in hunting down the leaders of the national movement who had taken up arms, and were fighting in the hills. On March 23 the rebel leader, Emilio Aguinaldo, and his whole staff, were captured. But fighting continued, forcing the Americans to maintain an army of 50,000 men in the Philippines. As in South Africa, it was the tactics of guerrilla fighting that proved impossible for even the most disciplined army to master, for the guerrilla forces could melt away into the undergrowth, forest and jungle as soon as they had made their strike, and then regroup as and when they decided to strike again. During a guerrilla attack five months after Aguinaldo's capture, three American officers and forty-eight of their men were killed.

In British Somaliland, Muhammad Abdullah, known to his adversaries as the 'Mad Mullah', led what remained of the Mahdist forces defeated at Omdurman two-and-a-half years earlier. In May, he was defeated by a British military expedition, but evaded capture. In Kabul, wedged between the expanding Russian Empire to the north and the British Empire to the south, the new Emir of Afghanistan, Habibullah, declared his adherence to his father's policy of friendship with Britain. In northern Nigeria, the Emir of Adamawa, an opponent of British rule, was attacked and defeated four months later by a British military force, and his brother crowned Emir in his place. In Belfast, Protestants and Catholics clashed during two days of riots in June, and the British army had to be called in to quell the disturbances. No one was killed, but there were several injuries. In British domestic politics there had been a ferocious upset that June when the leader of the Liberal opposition, Sir Henry Campbell-Bannerman, described the government's policy in South Africa of interning Boer women and children in special camps as 'methods of barbarism'. The Liberal opposition was not united, however, with regard to their criticism of the war. When a debate was forced in Parliament, of the 180 Liberals who might have voted against the government, almost fifty refused to do so. It was a young Liberal from Wales, David Lloyd George, who had moved the motion, and who spoke most effectively against the 'methods of barbarism'; his speech marked him out as a rising star of radical and political life. Two days later, on June 19, at a public meeting in the Queen's Hall, London, those who had become known as the 'pro-Boers' demanded the complete independence of the two defeated republics. Less than a month later, the pro-Boers were denounced during another public meeting, held in the Guildhall, for their 'unpatriotic attacks'. In the autumn, an anti-war meeting in Regent's Park was broken up by pro-war demonstrators, and at the end of the year, while speaking at Birmingham Town Hall, Lloyd George was so heckled by anti-Boer critics that he had to flee from the hall disguised as a police sergeant. In the ensuing riots, one man was killed.

The war in South Africa was also leading to a rethinking of the nature of any future war in Europe. In a lecture in London that summer, a Russian Imperial Councillor of State argued that, given the difficulties confronted by Britain in defeating two essentially weak republics, any war that might be waged between the European powers could not be fought decisively, and would provoke revolutions. This was a true forecast of what was to happen in Europe, and in particular to his own country, within two decades. Winston Churchill also spoke about the lessons of the war in South Africa when, on May 13, he made his first speech as a Member of Parliament. He was then twenty-six years old. As a war correspondent in South Africa he had been captured by the Boers, escaped from prisoner-of-war camp in Pretoria, and then fought as a soldier. To his listeners, among whom were many veterans of previous colonial wars, he warned:

We must not regard war with a modern Power as a kind of game in which we may take a hand, and with good luck and good management may play adroitly for an evening and come safe home with our winnings. It is not that, and I rejoice that it cannot be that.

A European war cannot be anything but a cruel, heartrending struggle, which, if we are ever to enjoy the bitter fruits of victory, must demand, perhaps for several years, the whole manhood of the nation, the entire suspension of peaceful industries, and the concentrating to one end of every vital energy in the community.

I have frequently been astonished since I have been in this House to hear with what composure and how glibly Members, and even Ministers, talk of a European war. I will not expatiate on the horrors of war, but there has been a great change which the House should not omit to notice.

In former days, when wars arose from individual causes, from the policy of a Minister or the passion of a King, when they were fought by small regular armies of professional soldiers, and when their course was retarded by the difficulties of communication and supply, and often suspended by the winter season, it was possible to limit the liabilities of the combatants. But now, when mighty populations are impelled on each other, each individual severally embittered and inflamed − when the resources of science and civilization sweep away everything that might mitigate their fury, a European war can only end in the ruin of the vanquished and the scarcely less fatal commercial dislocation and exhaustion of the conquerors . . .

Foreign nations know what war is. There is scarcely a capital in Europe which has not been taken in the last one hundred years, and it is the lively realization of the awful consequences of wars which maintains the peace of Europe.

We do not know what war is. We have had a glimpse of it in South Africa. Even in miniature it is hideous and appalling.

In 1901 the possibility of a European war seemed remote. The energies of the Powers were focused on their imperial and overseas ambitions, sometimes alone, sometimes in conjunction with others, as in China. That spring, the commander of the Allied expeditionary force in China, Field Marshal von Waldersee, had taken up residence in the Imperial Palace in Peking. During an accidental fire in which part of the palace was destroyed, he escaped with his life; but his Chief-of-Staff, General von Schwarzhoff, was killed.

A peace agreement between the Powers and China, which had been under negotiation for many months, was signed on September 7. In the first peace treaty of the new century, the Chinese government recognized the right of eleven foreign Powers to establish garrisons at certain points along the land and river communications between Peking and the sea. China also agreed to pay a cash indemnity for the loss of European life and property; the money was to be obtained mostly from the customs revenue and the salt tax. Prince Chun, a brother of the Emperor, agreed to go to Berlin and to express Chinese regret for the murder of Baron von Ketteler. An apology was also to be made to the Japanese for the death of their diplomat in Peking. The agreement having been signed, the American and Japanese troops who were then guarding the Forbidden City handed it over to the Chinese and returned home. But a small garrison remained in place to defend the Legations and also the approaches to Peking from the sea. At Tungchow, near Peking, a ceremony was held to bury seventy Chinese converts to Christianity who had been murdered during the rebellion.

With anti-foreigner violence at an end, a spate of foreign activity took place throughout China, centred around railway building. Russian, British, French and Belgian firms were most active in this work. That year the Russians also completed the Trans-Siberian railway, linking Moscow with the Russian Far East, and were working feverishly to build a port terminus for it on the Pacific. A German shipowner, Albert Ballin, director of the Hamburg–America shipping line, secured a major concession of land at Shanghai. He was an example, the Kaiser said, of the model he wished to uphold to all Germans 'to go forth and look for fresh points on which we can hang up our armour'.

That year the National Monument to Prince Bismarck was unveiled in Berlin. It was eighty feet high. The allegorical figures with which it abounded were criticized by German radicals, but seemed to represent the prevailing spirit not only of the Kaiser but of his people. Among the groups of sculpture were Siegfried forging the imperial sword, Germania in the chariot of victory, and an armed woman treading a panther underfoot, which Karl Baedeker's guide book queried, somewhat mischievously: 'Constitutional Power suppressing revolt?'

In South Africa, despite overwhelming British numerical strength, the Boers refused to give up their struggle, and on Christmas Day 1901, in a daring raid, attacked a British army camp, killing six officers and fifty men. A six-word telegram from the scene of the defeat gave Britons a sense of pride, however, in the behaviour of their troops. It read: 'No panic, and all did best.' The British army erected 8000 blockhouses throughout the countryside, linked by 3700 miles of barbed wire, to prevent the Boers from sending arms and reinforcements to their respective units.

Slowly the Boer detachments were being isolated and worn down. But the war had created a backlash of anti-war feeling in Britain which brought together anti-war forces from many lands: at a Universal Peace Conference held in Glasgow in 1901 the words 'pacifism' and 'pacifist' were officially adopted to describe the gathering and its participants.

Natural disasters remained a feature of Press and public concern. In a chemical factory in Germany, near Frankfurt-am-Main as many as a hundred people were killed when several cylinders of picric acid caught fire and exploded. During a heat wave in the United States, nearly a hundred New Yorkers died in twenty-four hours. But by far the worst disasters of the year were in the East. In British India more than a quarter of a million Indians died of plague. And in China drought and famine in the province of Shensi led, in one month, to an estimated two and a half million deaths – almost as great a loss of human life as that caused by the Indian famine with which the century had opened.

*   *   *

Amid the record of war, violence and death, the year 1901 had many examples of creativity and life. On January 10, oil was discovered in Texas, a historic moment for the future wealth and power of the United States. That same year, the mass production of motor cars began, also in the United States. Painting flourished: Paul Gauguin, Edvard Munch and Pablo Picasso each produced major canvases that year, Picasso's marking the start of his 'Blue Period'. The Czech composer Antonin Dvořák produced an opera, *Rusalka*. Like Sibelius in Finland, his music captured an awakening national mood. Music saw another development that year, offering the prospect of vastly increased popular availability: this was the introduction of the flat – as opposed to cylindrical – gramophone record. Made of shellac, with a spiral groove, it was compact, accessible and (relatively) hardy.

The first Nobel Prizes were awarded in 1901, in Stockholm. They were the result of a benefaction left by the Swedish inventor of dynamite, Alfred Nobel, who had died five years earlier. The prizes designated in his will were for Physics, Chemistry, Medicine, Literature and Peace. Over the coming century, these prizes were to be a universal mark of excellence, and from 1969 were to include a prize for Economics.

CHAPTER THREE

1902

At the beginning of 1902, reacting to the scathing criticisms by the German Chancellor, Count Bernhardt von Bülow, of the British conduct of the war against the Boers, the British Colonial Secretary, Joseph Chamberlain, countered with a disparaging reference to the conduct of the German army in France at the time of the Prussian invasion in 1870. Chamberlain, however, did not leave it there but went on to deepen his counterattack with the words: 'We can find precedents for anything we may do in the action of those nations who now criticize our "barbarity" and "cruelty", but whose example, in Poland, in the Caucasus, in Algeria, in Tongking, in Bosnia, in the Franco-German war – whose example we have never approached.'

By this remark, Chamberlain drew complaints from Russia (with regard to Poland and the Caucasus), France (Algeria and Tongking) and from Austria-Hungary (Bosnia), each of whom objected to his verbal attack. But it was the Germans who took official offence, and von Bülow quoted back at Chamberlain the words of Frederick the Great of Prussia, which the King had once used against one of his critics: 'Let that man alone, and don't excite yourself, he is biting on granite.'

The acrimony of the Anglo-German exchanges escalated. It did not, however, affect the cordiality with which the new Prince of Wales, Queen Victoria's grandson, was welcomed in Berlin by his cousin the Kaiser. This was not merely a family courtesy, but a deliberate attempt by both monarchs to mitigate the acerbity of the Boer War criticisms, and to assuage the bitterness of their repercussions. These efforts also took place in the political arena. When a deputy in the Reichstag, Liebermann von Sonnenberg, a leading Pan-German and anti-Semitic agitator, described the British troops in South Africa as 'gangs of robbers and packs of thieves', who were doing the bidding of Jewish businessmen who wanted to control the wealth and gold of South Africa, he was rebuked by the Foreign Minister, Baron von

Richthofen, who stressed that the Pan-Germans should not forget that, 'in spite of everything, in spite of our different judgements on many matters, we are, after all, still friends and kinsfolk'. Richthofen went on to point out the humane way in which the British were treating their high-ranking Boer prisoners. A senior German army officer, Major-General Trotha, had visited the prisoner-of-war camp set up by the British in distant Ceylon, and had spoken of it in most favourable terms. By October, when three leading Boer generals visited Berlin, in search of funds to continue the war, the Kaiser refused to receive them unless they were introduced to him by the British Ambassador, who of course was given no instructions from London to do so. A verbal battle between London and Berlin, which had threatened to escalate beyond the control of diplomacy, had been diffused.

Britain's war in South Africa had yet to end. In January, more reinforcements had been sent from Britain. That month one of the senior Boer commanders, General Viljoen, was captured. In February, yet more troops were sent out from Britain, and the last of the heavy guns in Boer hands was finally captured. The Dutch government had begun pressing the British to make a lenient peace with the Boers. But a Boer delegation crossed the Atlantic to seek help in continuing their struggle. It was received by Theodore Roosevelt, who told them, to their bitter disappointment, that the United States 'could not and would not interfere' in the struggle in South Africa. The Boers had reached the end of their powers of resistance, and agreed to lay down their arms.

When news of the end of the war reached London on the afternoon of June 1, rejoicing began in the streets and continued through the night. *The Times* reported:

Quickly following the posting of the notices came the special editions of the Sunday and evening newspapers confirming the news, and newspaper hawkers were to be seen rushing in every direction carrying huge bundles of newspapers, which were eagerly bought up by the crowds that soon after seven o'clock began to assemble in the principal thoroughfares.

Occasional light showers in the earlier part of the evening prevented any large congregation of people at first, but between nine and ten o'clock, when the weather had become more settled, large crowds thronged the streets of the West End, particularly the Strand, Pall Mall, St James's Street, and Piccadilly. It was an orderly crowd, however, and there were none of those disorderly scenes which were witnessed on 'Mafeking night'.

Here and there a gang of youths was to be seen marching four and five abreast singing snatches of popular songs, enthusiastically waving Union Jacks, and cheering at frequent intervals.

The vendors of flags, tri-coloured 'streamers', and medals were very numerous and did a good trade. Most of the omnibuses displayed Union Jacks affixed to long poles, and the outside passengers, like many of the pedestrians, carried small Union Jacks, which they waved enthusiastically. Some of the cabmen decorated their horses' heads with miniature flags, and others had flags affixed to their whips. The crowd increased in size as the time wore on, and the owners of wagonettes did a good business in conveying people to and from different points at treble the omnibus charges.

Whenever a soldier was seen he was cheered by the people.

More than six thousand British soldiers had been killed in South Africa. Sixteen thousand more had died from enteric fever. In London that December, Queen Alexandra gave a Christmas dinner to 629 women whose husbands had been killed in the Boer War, and to 836 children who had lost their fathers. Of the 16,000 Australian volunteers, 588 had been killed or had died of disease. The first war memorials of the century were being erected. Eton College announced that its memorial to those former Eton schoolboys who had been killed in action in South Africa would consist of a library, a hall, a record of names, and a memorial monument on which were inscribed the names of the 129 boys from the school who fell in action, out of 1470 who served.[1]

Nearly a century later, monuments to the century's wars are a significant feature of tens of thousands of towns and villages throughout the world. Some, like the Japanese monument to those killed at Port Arthur in 1904, the French war memorial to those killed at Verdun in 1916, the Moscow war memorial to the dead of 1941–5, and the Vietnam war memorial in Washington to American soldiers killed between 1964 and 1973, are monuments of great emotional and reflective power.

The ending of the war in South Africa did not end the military conflicts in which the British Empire was engaged that year. In East Africa, despite the victory over the Mad Mullah in Somaliland the previous year, the Mullah and his forces had regrouped, and attacked the British force that was trying

---

[1] In the First World War, 1157 Old Etonians were killed in action and, in the Second World War, 749.

to hunt them down. Two British officers and seventy British colonial troops were killed by the Mullah's forces, and although the Mullah was driven off, the black Somali soldiers who made up the bulk of the British force were reported to have been 'considerably shaken' by the battle. As the Mullah brought up reinforcements, the British force retreated. There was relief in London when it was learned that it had returned safely to its base, without being attacked. In December, in a gesture of defiance, the Mullah demanded that the British recognize his sphere of influence and cede him a port. His demands were ignored.

At the end of 1902, both Britain and Germany had begun a trading and political relationship that was beginning to flourish, now that their verbal skirmishing had been calmed. As trading partners they turned their attention to a dispute in South America. For some while, British ships trading between Trinidad and the mainland had been seized by Venezuelan warships searching for arms and supplies being smuggled to insurgents inside Venezuela; and various indignities had been carried out on the captains and their crews. At the same time, Venezuelan commercial obligations to British investors were being ignored. The German government was also supporting German banking claims against nonpayment of debts incurred during the construction of a railway from Caracas to Valencia. A year earlier Germany had warned the United States that she might be compelled to use force.

Britain and Germany entered into an alliance whereby they agreed to try jointly to seize the Venezuelan fleet and blockade the coast if their respective demands were not met. The joint Anglo-German ultimatum was issued against Venezuela on December 3, threatening naval operations. When the ultimatum was ignored, British and German cruisers, acting together, seized a number of Venezuelan warships and gunboats. In retaliation, the Venezuelan government arrested a number of British and German subjects in the capital, Caracas, but they were released following immediate representations by the United States.

After the Anglo-German seizure of the Venezuelan gunboats, the German naval commander sank three of those he had captured. There was indignation in the United States at the sinkings, which were portrayed as a gratuitous act of vandalism and vengeance. American newspapers vied in depicting German policy as aimed at securing colonies in South America, starting with Venezuela, and warned that sooner or later the United States would have to compel Germany by force of arms to respect the Monroe Doctrine, the eighty-year-old assertion of United States' interests throughout the western hemisphere.

For a while it looked as if Britain, by acting in concert with Germany, would rouse the anger of the United States at this direct involvement in an American area of influence. But a distinction was made, almost entirely spurious, between Britain's benign policy based on essential interests, and a possible sinister undertone on the part of Germany. When the Venezuelan government offered to submit the dispute to arbitration, there was relief in Britain that the crisis could be resolved without further use of force, and the risk of conflict with the United States. President Roosevelt was asked to act as arbitrator, but considerable United States opinion was against this, not wanting to be party to any decision that might favour Germany. The dispute was then transferred, at Roosevelt's suggestion, to the Hague Tribunal. France, which also had financial claims against Venezuela, had prudently accepted arbitration before the Anglo-German naval action.

One South American dispute was resolved more satisfactorily in 1902. This was the dispute between Chile and Argentina with regard to their southernmost border. They agreed to submit the dispute to British arbitration. After a survey was carried out among the inhospitable peaks and inlets of the southern Andes by a British expedition, headed by Sir Thomas Holditch, the deed of arbitration was signed in London by Edward VII on November 20. Both sides in the dispute were satisfied; Chile felt that she had obtained the larger portion of the territory involved, while Argentina was satisfied that the richer and more valuable land, though smaller in area, had fallen to her. Only towards the British in the Falkland Islands was there a sense of territorial grievance among Argentinians, but with the British Empire and its navy so powerful, any chance of Argentina acquiring the Falklands seemed remote. The hope was always there; it was the expectation of being able to hold the islands successfully against Britain that did not surface for another eighty years. But even that expectation was swiftly to be dashed in war, in 1982.

The United States took decisive action of its own in the western hemisphere during 1902, to assert its dominating interest in the stability of the region. After a revolutionary outbreak in Colombia, President Roosevelt ordered a battleship and a cruiser to the area, and a battalion of United States marines was landed. When the Colombian government restored order, the marines were withdrawn. That same year, the United States' occupation of Cuba, which had continued since the defeat of the Spaniards four years earlier, was ended, and diplomatic relations set up between the United States and the Cuban republic.

Off the coast of Haiti, it was not the United States but Germany that took action against revolutionary activity, when a German gunboat, *Panther*, sank the flagship of the Haitian revolutionary leader, Admiral Killick. The resentment in the United States was not so much that Germany had taken the action, which was certainly beneficial to the United States, but that it had been carried out in a way that was characterized by one American newspaper as 'unnecessarily brutal, wanton, and uncalled for'.

One unexpected foreign policy initiative in 1902 was the creation of the first alliance signed by Britain and a foreign power for many years. This was the Anglo-Japanese Alliance. Hitherto, Britain had stood outside the two main Power alignments, the Franco-Russian Alliance, and the Triple Alliance of Germany, Austria-Hungary and Italy. But the weakness of China, and the possibility of Russian predominance in the Far East, had led to new thinking in Britain. While still remaining aloof from the existing alliance systems, the British government now committed itself to significant support for Japan in the Far East.

The powers of the Triple Alliance were uneasy at Britain entering into any alliance system. Although the German Chancellor stated publicly that Germany had no territorial claims in the Far East, and that the Anglo-Japanese Alliance was of no concern to Germany, within a year the Triple Alliance was renewed for twelve years.

Within the German Empire, relations between the Germans and their Polish subjects remained tense. In March 1902 more than twenty Polish students who were studying at the Charlottenburg Technical College in Berlin were accused of political agitation and expelled from Prussia. A month later the Prussian government issued a decree limiting Polish immigration. Steps were also taken to prevent Germans, who had bought land cheaply from the Prussian authorities in an effort by the authorities to increase the German population in Polish areas, from selling that land to the Poles. Model German farms were established, to encourage German farmers to move to the pre-dominantly Polish regions.

To the distress of the Polish minority, the Kaiser, who had hitherto been sympathetic to their aspirations, in a speech in June 1902 at the restored fortress of Marienburg, the seat of the medieval Teutonic Knights of German imperial legend, described the fortress as 'the starting point of the civilization of the countries east of the Vistula', and as the 'symbol of Germany's mission'. Not content with setting Teuton against Slav in this way, he went on to declare that what he called 'Polish aggressiveness' was even then 'resolved to encroach upon Germanism', and that the time had come for him to summon the German people 'to preserve its national possessions'.

When, three months later, the Kaiser travelled to Posen to unveil a monument to the Emperor Frederick of Prussia, the Polish inhabitants of the city marked their distress at his Marienburg speech by boycotting the ceremonies. In what he hoped would be a conciliatory speech, even an apologetic one, he announced that restrictions on the building of Polish working-class houses in the areas around the fortress of Posen would be abolished. But there was to be no change in the law forbidding the use of the Polish language by Polish-speaking schoolchildren, or even at public meetings where Poles were gathered. Indeed, all such meetings were attended by a police officer who, if anyone began to speak Polish from the platform, would immediately close the meeting.

Even as the Polish minority in Germany continued to resent the restrictions on the use of the Polish language, especially in schools, the inhabitants of Alsace-Lorraine, which Germany had annexed from France in 1871, were being wooed by the Kaiser, who sought their enthusiastic rather than grudging incorporation into his dominions. In May 1902, on a visit to his magnificently restored imperial residence in the province, the castle of Hochkönigsburg, he issued an order abolishing the much-resented section in the 1879 constitution, known as the 'dictatorship paragraph'. This paragraph gave the governor of Alsace-Lorraine the powers to employ troops for police purposes, to expel 'undesirable persons', and to suppress newspapers judged to be subversive, that is to say, pro-French. At the same time, a theological faculty was set up at the Imperial University of Strasbourg where Roman Catholic priests could study for Holy Orders; until then, they had been forced to look to the Francophile Episcopal Seminary for their road to ordination.

In France, the repeal of the dictatorship paragraph in no way diminished the desire to regain the lost provinces. In the Place de la Concorde, at the very heart of Paris, around which eight stone figures represent the chief eighteenth-century cities of France, the statue of Strasbourg was hung with a black covering and wreaths of mourning, to symbolize the 'lost' province of Alsace. Even Frenchmen too young to remember the war were taught the words of the patriot Gambetta, with regard to the loss of Alsace-Lorraine in 1871: 'Think of it always, speak of it never.'

In German left-wing political circles, while there was no diminution of the determination to retain the territories annexed from France in 1871, there was discontent at the overseas imperial ambitions of the Kaiser and his government. A government proposal in 1902 to set up an emigration bureau to encourage and finance emigration to Germany's overseas territories was defeated in the Reichstag, where a strong argument was put forward that it would be better to promote German emigration to the independent but welcoming countries of South America, especially Brazil, where economic opportunities beckoned, rather than to the 'unhealthy' colonies in Africa which had been acquired in the previous two decades. When the government proposed an extension to the existing railway in German East Africa, this too was rejected by the Reichstag, where considerable anger was also expressed by the radical members at the recent purchase of the Caroline, Pelew and Mariana Islands in the Pacific.

It was pointed out by the critics in the Reichstag that whereas these three island groups had cost 17 million marks to buy, the annual revenue from them was a paltry 33,000 marks, and that the government were asking for 350,000 marks a year for their administration. It was also complained that the maintenance of the German administration in German South West Africa was costing an annual subsidy of nearly 5 million marks. Imperialism might look impressive on the map, but it was costly to maintain.

The one colonial German enterprise that did go ahead that year without opposition was an expedition to establish factories for German traders in the hinterland of the German Cameroons. This expedition was carried out in close cooperation with France and Britain, the two other imperial powers who were also pressing inland in that region, towards Lake Chad.

Colonial expansion did not seem to endanger in any way the peace that prevailed among the Powers. Even their alliance systems appeared more a cause for calm than for conflict. In September 1902 the Russian Tsar wrote one of his many friendly letters to the German Kaiser – they addressed each other in English as Willy and Nicky. 'As the rulers of the two leading Powers of the two great Continental Combinations,' the Tsar confided, 'we are able to exchange our views on any general questions touching their interests, and as soon as we have settled how to tackle it, we are able to bring our Allies to adopt the same views, so that the two Alliances – i.e. 5

Powers — having decided that Peace is to be kept, the World must remain at peace and will be able to enjoy blessings.'

The 'two alliances' were the Franco-Russian Alliance, and the Triple Alliance of Germany, Austria-Hungary and Italy.

Within Austria-Hungary, continual tensions arose as a result of the conflict between German-speakers and Hungarian-speakers. Hungarian nationalists wanted to sever all links with Austria other than that of a common sovereign. Under the arrangements finalized in 1867, however, political union was indissoluble. Pan-German activists were constantly seeking to advance the cause of the German-speaking population within Hungary. In April 1902 the German-based Pan-Germanic League proposed a special visit, with much publicity, to the predominantly German towns in Croatia and Transylvania. So angered were the Hungarians by this proposal that it had to be abandoned. Hungarian government activity against pan-Germanism was much in evidence that year, highlighted by the expulsion from Hungary of the editor of a German paper in Temesvar, and the imprisonment of other pan-Germans by the local courts.

The sensitivities of the Hungarians were also displayed during an outcry of indignation in the Hungarian parliament when it was announced that the heir to the Habsburg throne, Franz Ferdinand, would be accompanied to London for the coronation of Edward VII by three Austrian equerries but only one Hungarian. An accident of court procedure, for such it was, appeared to the Hungarians as a deliberate insult. That November, there was a public demonstration by Hungarians against the playing of the Austrian national anthem at a Hungarian national commemoration.

There were frequent periods of civil unrest in Europe in the opening years of the century, with troops often being used by governments to put down demonstrations, strikes and riots. An example of such labour unrest leading to troop intervention and loss of life erupted in February 1902 in the then Austrian port of Trieste, when, at the height of a series of strikes on the railways and in the port, a mass demonstration was held in support of an eight-hour working day, and twelve rioters were killed. Arbitration was agreed, the call for an eight-hour day was upheld, and the strikes were called off.

In Barcelona that month, several rioters were shot dead and a state of siege declared in the city for the second time within a year. In the Belgian city of Louvain, eight workers were killed when troops opened fire on demonstrators who were demanding an end to measures that prevented a genuinely universal suffrage. In the United States, a coal strike threatened to create a winter coal famine. The strike was only called off by the personal intervention of President Roosevelt, who first of all threatened to bring in federal troops to work the mines if the miners did not return to work, and then persuaded both the mine owners and the miners to accept the verdict of a special commission of enquiry.

Whether industrial disputes would be resolved by arbitration and compromise, or lead to violence in the streets and confrontation with the established authorities, was a question much debated in radical circles. Lenin and his Social Democratic fellow revolutionaries – most of them, like Lenin, in exile outside Russia – feared that industry in Russia was not yet far enough developed to create conditions for the revolution. But the Russian revolutionaries were encouraged during 1902 by the reluctance of soldiers to open fire on demonstrators who refused to disperse despite repeated exhortations. One regiment of Grenadiers was removed from Moscow when it was discovered that it could not be relied on to open fire on demonstrators when ordered by its officers to do so. In the city of Tula, less than a hundred miles to the south, a sergeant refused to order his men to open fire on strikers. The officer in charge then struck out at the sergeant with his sword. As a result, the soldiers mutinied.

The annual intake of soldiers into the Russian army was coming more and more from groups that were influenced by anti-Tsarist propaganda. Young university teachers, doctors and lawyers were likewise influenced by the antimonarchical, anti-aristocratic and anti-capitalist emphasis of the revolutionaries. The Jewish Social Democratic Labour League, the Bund, which had been created a year before the Social Democratic Labour Party, was growing into a party of mass protest, particularly strong in western Russia and the Polish and Lithuanian provinces of the empire. It too favoured a revolutionary solution to the social ills of Russia, to the widespread peasant poverty, and to the harsh conditions that prevailed in so many factories. A third Russian revolutionary party, founded in 1902, was the Socialist Revolutionary Party, whose 'fighting section' concentrated on the assassination of politicians, soldiers, policemen and police spies. When the head of the fighting section, Azev, was himself exposed as a police spy six years later, the assassinations came to a virtual halt. But the party continued to exert considerable influence both among the rural masses and the intellectuals.

The spread of revolutionary ideas among the peasantry was the most serious threat for the Tsarist authorities. In April 1902, in an attempt to curb unrest in the Caucasus, the Tsarist police arrested a number of Social Democratic agitators, among them Josef Stalin. After eighteen months in jail, first in Baku and then in Kutaisi, he was sentenced to three years' exile in Siberia, from which he later escaped. The conditions under which he was exiled were far more lenient than those which he himself was to impose on so many others (numbering in their millions) within three decades.

In June, the Minister of the Interior, Vyacheslav Plehve, issued a circular to the officials of his ministry, pointing out that 'clever and energetic peasants' were being trained by the revolutionary parties in sociology, and the history of political and economic movements, and then sent to rural areas to carry out antigovernment propaganda among their fellow tillers of the soil. In a memorandum for the Tsar, Plehve pointed out another conduit whereby revolutionary propaganda was being spread throughout the rural areas: educated city dwellers, temporarily employed by the provincial administrations to collect agricultural statistical data, would use the opportunity of their travels through the rural areas 'for the very injurious object of spreading aspirations for the subversion of the existing order of things'.

So struck was the Tsar by Plehve's report that he at once gave orders forbidding the collection of statistics in twelve provinces, and authorized provincial governors elsewhere to do likewise, if they felt public order was in danger. Another intervention by the Tsar was to close an ecclesiastical seminar in Odessa; the Russian clergy, too, were discovered to be taking revolutionary opinions seriously.

The revolutionary mood in Russia led, during 1902, to a brief student uprising in Moscow university, when 400 students, some armed, seized the main academic buildings, flew the red flag, and built barricades against the troops sent to evict them. They were all eventually captured and imprisoned.

The first decade of the new century was already becoming scarred by assassination, as each subsequent decade was to be. In February 1902 the Bulgarian Minister of Public Instruction was assassinated by a sacked schoolmaster, who immediately afterwards committed suicide. In April, the Russian Minister of the Interior was assassinated in St Petersburg by one of the students who had been expelled the previous year from Kiev University for his part in the antigovernment demonstrations there. But when, in November, an Italian anarchist, Rubino, shot at the King of the Belgians in Brussels, he missed, the king was unhurt.

It was not the Serb-Austrian conflict, but the Serb-Croat conflict, which erupted in the Danube region in 1902. That September, in Zagreb, the capital of the Hungarian province of Croatia-Slavonia, groups of Serbs and Croats fought each other in the streets. The clashes began after a Croat singing club, at its jubilee dinner, had addressed a telegram to Franz Josef, applauding him as 'King of Croatia'; whereupon a Belgrade journal, whose article was at once reproduced in the Zagreb Croat newspapers, denied that the Croats were a separate nationality; they were no more, it asserted, than 'a nation of lackeys'. The destiny of the Slavs of Croatia, the article insisted, was to be absorbed in Serbia; they spoke the same language as the Serbs, and differed only in their Catholicism from the Greek Orthodox Serbs; they were one people. The riots began when a large group of Croats, angered by Serb assertions, attacked a Serbian bank, newspaper offices, businesses and shops, most of which were completely wrecked. More than a hundred people were injured, some seriously. Violence only ended after martial law was declared, a curfew imposed, and imperial troops sent in to keep order.

In the Balkans that year, in the areas still under Ottoman rule, an attempt was made to assert the rights of the Bulgarian minority in Macedonia, a minority which was particularly strong in the eastern regions. In September, armed Bulgarian bands, led by a retired colonel, crossed the border into Macedonia, attacked Turkish army posts, and declared a provisional government. Those Christian villages, mostly Serb and Greek, that refused to provide the insurgents with arms and supplies were looted and burnt down. The Sultan ordered an immediate restoration of Ottoman authority. Several Christian villages were then destroyed by his troops, and some villagers massacred. A Bulgarian appeal to the Powers for support against 'Turkish atrocities' met with no response: there did not seem much to choose between the behaviour of the insurgents and the authorities.

Another area of imperial conflict that flared up in 1902 was the Dutch East Indies. A rebellion, led by a local sultan, led to heavy loss of life on both sides. Eighty-three of the sultan's followers were killed when he was driven from his main fortifications.

On the North West Frontier of India, British troops and Indian tribesmen continued to fight each other, as they had already done for almost a decade, with tribes determined not to submit to British control. In northern Nigeria, the Emir of Kano had fortified his capital and gathered together there all those forces opposed to the British Protectorate. In southern Nigeria, the Ju-Ju tribe resisted British rule. A British military force attacked the Ju-Ju villages, capturing an important chief, and pushing ahead with the opening of trade routes.

Natural disasters worldwide were no respecters of imperial boundaries. In February an earthquake in the Caucasus, where a century of Russian rule continued to be resented, killed two thousand people. Three months later, on May 7, thirty thousand people were killed when the town of St Pierre, on the French West Indian island of Martinique, was totally destroyed by the volcanic eruption of Mont Pelée. A further two thousand were killed within twenty-four hours when, on the nearby British island of St Vincent, the Souffrière volcano erupted. In Egypt, by the end of the year, 20,000 people had died of cholera; in Cairo alone, there was a time when four hundred were dying of the disease every day. When the British authorities began to put disinfectants in the water supply, in the hope of curbing the disease, they were accused by the local population of poisoning the water.

In the British Indian province of Scinde, more than a thousand people were killed during a hurricane which washed away forty miles of railway. But when the rains came to western India at the end of August, averting at the last moment the recurrence of famine, the news was greeted with understandable relief. Throughout British India that year, more than half a million people died of plague. But the efforts of the Indian Medical Services to combat the diseases that periodically ravaged the subcontinent were persistent, so much so that in 1902 the Nobel Prize for Medicine was awarded to a British medical officer, Major Ronald Ross – who had served in India for the past eighteen years – for his discovery of the malaria parasite, and for his pioneering studies on combating the disease.

In China, an imperial decree in 1902 allowed the study of western science, with the result that colleges were opened in eleven provinces. That same year, another imperial decree abolished the binding of women's feet.

*   *   *

President Theodore Roosevelt (known as Teddy), while on a hunting trip that November, was provided with a small bear to shoot. To make it easier for him, the bear was tethered to a tree. He refused to kill the cub, and it was released. Within weeks of the episode becoming known, a new toy was launched, whose popularity was to survive the century: the teddy bear. Also surviving, and enormously popular in every generation, was the story of the Wizard of Oz, the musical of which opened at the Grand Opera House in Chicago on 16 June 1902.

CHAPTER FOUR

1903

WAR BETWEEN THE POWERS was still, by most contemporary calculations, unthinkable in 1903. Yet there were ominous signs of how the
prospect of such a war could grip the public mind. In 1903 the most popular
thriller published in Britain was Erskine Childers' *The Riddle of the Sands*, a
spy story about a German invasion. Its author had fought in the Boer War,
and was later to fight in the First World War – and was to be executed by
the Irish Free State at the beginning of the Civil War in 1922.

Actual fighting took place that year in the Balkans. It followed the signing
of an agreement on February 13 at the Château d'Eau, whereby Austria-
Hungary and Russia jointly demanded that Turkey institute reforms in her
Balkan provinces. The Austro-Russian demands had been formulated on
behalf of Turkey's Bulgarian subjects, whose national aspirations extended
deep into Turkish Macedonia. After four months during which the Turks
failed to satisfy Bulgarian demands for a greater say in the administration,
an uprising broke out. But the Turkish forces were far stronger: an estimated
351,000, as against 26,000 insurrectionists. A thousand of the insurrectionists were killed in battle. Turkish retribution followed. It was itemized by
the Balkan Commission Report ten years later as 'two hundred villages
ruined by Turkish vengeance, 12,000 houses burned, 3,000 women outraged,
4,700 inhabitants slain and 71,000 without a roof'.

Among the Powers, the means whereby war could be waged more effectively were slowly being developed. In January, the headquarters of the
British First Army Corps, based at Aldershot, southwest of London, made
successful contact by wireless telegraphy with the ships of the Channel
Squadron. Later that month, President Roosevelt, who was at Cape Cod on
the Atlantic Coast of the United States, exchanged greetings by wireless
telegraphy with King Edward VII in Britain. Wireless telegraphy was to
prove the means for the most rapid transmission of messages from ship to
ship, and of orders from naval headquarters to ships at sea.

The progress of the new technologies did not always run smoothly. A motorcar race from Paris to Madrid, which began on April 23, and for which there were a record 250 entries, was stopped by the French Minister of the Interior after several fatal accidents among the competitors.

The repressive internal actions within the Russian Empire were, throughout the year, to be the subject of considerable unease among the parliamentary democracies. Even the threat of Russia overseas was cause for concern; the British Admiralty's announcement of the building of a new naval base at Rosyth, in Scotland, was in part a move designed to keep an eye on Russia's naval exit from the Baltic.

A Tsarist decree in 1903 confiscated all the property of the Armenian Church throughout the Caucasus, including property in several predominantly Armenian towns. This measure, the brainchild of the Minister of the Interior, Plehve, distressed those outside Russia for whom Armenian rights were seen as an important aspect of fair-dealing among national minorities.

The heightened political unrest inside Russia during the previous two years led the Tsar to seek means of calming the widespread tensions. On March 12 he issued a manifesto offering to improve the condition of village life. Two weeks later he abolished the system under which peasant communities were made collectively responsible for the taxes of their members. But even this measure was hedged with restrictions, a typical example of the Tsarist failure to implement reforms without at the same time qualifying or even negating them. In the same manifesto, the local self-governing bodies were made even more subservient to officials appointed by the Minister of the Interior in St Petersburg.

One repressive device put into effect by the Minister himself was to cause all reports of the debates in these self-governing bodies to be censored before they were sent on to the Tsar, in order to eliminate all expressions of local independent-minded or liberal sentiment. The right of the provincial assemblies to present petitions to the Tsar was also restricted to matters directly relating to the authority of the provincial assemblies, and strictly excluding comments about more general reforms and concerns. The gulf was widening between the Tsar 'of all the Russias' and his increasingly dissatisfied subjects.

Both urban and rural workers in Russia were turning to violence that year. In the provinces of Saratov and Tula, revolutionary literature was being distributed in the villages, and 'fraternal unions' formed for political agitation. In March there was a strike of 500 workers in the State-run ironworks at Zlatoust, in the Ufa province; only a charge by sabre-wielding mounted troops, and many broken skulls and limbs, was able to drive the strikers from the manager's house which they had occupied. In May, the governor of Ufa was assassinated. In June there were demonstrations by workers in the port cities of Batum on the Black Sea, and at Baku on the Caspian. In Baku an estimated 45,000 strikers took to the streets, halting all railway trains and trams. Troops were sent in, fighting ensued, and several hundred workers were killed. In July and August these disturbances spread to every industrial and manufacturing town in southern Russia, across a thousand-mile swathe of land from Kiev to the shores of the Caspian. Men known to be police spies were assassinated in Pinsk and Nizhni Novgorod. At Ufa, the president of the local court of assizes was assassinated.

Fifty-three of the leading figures in the Russian Social Democratic Party, most of them exiles, met that summer for two weeks in Brussels, and then for two weeks in London. From the outset there was a conflict between those led by Yuli Martov, who wanted a broadly based and large membership Party, and those, led by Lenin, who wanted a small, disciplined, professional centre. Lenin lost this vote by a narrow margin, twenty-eight to twenty-three. In his pamphlet, *What Is To Be Done?*, published the previous year, he had stressed that the Party should consist 'first and foremost of people whose profession is that of revolutionist'. At the end of the month-long meeting, Lenin's faction won by twenty-two to twenty (with two abstentions) the vote on who should control the Party newspaper *Iskra*. Being a majority on that occasion, albeit only just, Lenin's faction called themselves henceforth *Bolsheviki* – Majority-ites. But Martov's faction, the *Mensheviki*, or Minority-ites, later won control of *Iskra*. Both sections held together formally, as a single Party, for another nine years.

Inside Russia, these Bolshevik-Menshevik divisions were not allowed to distract the workers' struggle as much as they did among the exiles. That November the Social Democrat Party met secretly, with delegates coming from all parts of Russia, including delegates from the Jewish Social Democratic Labour League (the Bund), and issued a programme calling for the abolition of the autocracy and the establishment in its place of a democratic republic. The confidence of the delegates that the tide of history was turning their way (and that sooner rather than later the forces of the Tsar would find themselves on the 'rubbish heap of history') was intensified when several army recruiting depots were the scenes of antigovernment demonstrations, punctuated with cries of 'Down with the Tsar! Down with despotism and militarism!' In Baku, several thousand army recruits marched in procession through the town with a red flag inscribed 'Down with the autocracy! Long live the Republic!' University students were also rioting again. At Kiev University, students tore down the portrait of the Tsar and replaced it with one of Balamashev, the assassin of the Russian Minister of the Interior the previous year.

The Russian government decided to introduce a scapegoat against which to turn the attention of the discontented. It chose one that was traditional: the Jews. There were more than five million Jews in Russia. On April 20, in the city of Kishinev, during a whole day of deliberately unchecked violence, Jewish houses and passers-by were attacked by a sabre- and knife-wielding mob. Forty-three Jews were killed, and their bodies mutilated. Several hundred Jewish women were seized and raped. When Jewish leaders went to St Petersburg to ask Plehve for justice, he told them that he was greatly displeased with the conduct of the Jewish population of Russia, and that the existence of a Jewish revolutionary movement forced the government to take action. If the Jewish labour movement continued to grow, he warned, he would miss no opportunity 'of rendering the lives of the Jews intolerable'.

There were mass protests against the Kishinev pogrom, and against the Tsarist government's complicity, in many cities in Europe and the United States. An American clergyman, W. C. Stiles, in a book written immediately after the Kishinev massacre, appealed to Christians in the United States to condemn the killings. In an attempt to emphasize the obscenity of the attacks, he mimicked the inflammatory language of the pogromists:

Perhaps some lawless boys, bred in the fine art of tormenting the old long-beard who keeps a market in the corner of the plaza, started the delightful sport, dear to the heart of the populace. Surely this was not the first time Kishineff has had trouble about Jews. They have often been so unreasonable as to complain of the assaults, and insults, and outrages of the rough and slum populations of the town.

Does one of them incautiously creep home late in the evening where gangs assemble and villainous boys congregate? He is chased home with stones, and mud, and epithets that make his Abrahamic cheeks burn all night with anger and shame. And he knows that if he had dared retaliate, he, and not the assailants, would be a swift victim of the Czar's beautiful peace laws in Kishineff.

Being a Jew, he must not turn as other men may turn, as even a harried dog may turn, and bite back at his tormentors. A dog is far more reputable in Kishineff than a Jew. More reputable unless someone wishes to borrow! A lending Jew, in the moment when he can lend the Governor roubles to pay his debts, and make no complaint when he is defrauded, can even command a semblance of protection in Kishineff.

'Blessed saints! The Jews! Let us now have some fun with the Jews.'

Boys and men, swarming out of the cathedral where they have heard the glory chants that told how the Prince of Peace has risen from the dead, they must now have some fun with the Jews. And such excellent fun!

Under every kind of outrage they died, mostly at the door of their homes. Less men than that were killed in battle in our war with Spain. And these were not all soldiers, slain in the glory of battle. They were babes, butchered at the breasts of their mothers. They were old men beaten down in the presence of their sons. They were delicate women violated and murdered in the sight of their own children. But then they were only Jews!

A massive petition was prepared in the United States, calling on the Tsar to make any such massacre impossible in future. The Russian government, furious at this outside interference, informed the United States that it would decline to receive the petition. President Roosevelt, as a gesture of sympathy to those who had signed it, directed that it should at least be filed in the archives of the State Department.

The pogrom at Kishinev was followed by another at Gomel, which was also officially condoned. Police and soldiers formed protective lines for the rioters, who once again looted, raped and murdered with impunity. When a group of Jews took up arms in an attempt to break through to some of those who were being attacked, they were fired on by the police.

The killings in Kishinev and Gomel intensified the emigration of Russian Jews, many of whom made their way to the United States, Canada, Britain and, in small but steady numbers, Palestine. The killings also stimulated Jewish socialist and revolutionary feelings, turning many Jews into agitators for the overthrow of Tsardom.

*　　　*　　　*

The Russian Empire, in turmoil within, continued to act as an imperial power overseas, and at the extremity of its authority. At Port Arthur – on the Kwantung peninsula, at the entrance to the Gulf of Chihli – the building by Russia of thirty-five miles of coastal fortifications, docks and a new town on what had earlier been Chinese territory was continuous. Where, under Chinese rule, only small, local craft could dock, there was room by the end of 1903 for eight warships and a fleet of torpedo boats. Russia was in rapid process of becoming a Pacific naval power, a mere 600 miles from Japan.

The Germans were also building a port on former Chinese territory, at Kiaochow, on the Yellow Sea shore of the Shantung peninsula. But in the German parliament the expenditure proposed to build up the naval facilities there was strongly criticized by those Reichstag deputies who were opposed to German overseas imperial expansion. As a result of these criticisms, the expenditure was actually reduced. Even less money was being spent by the British on their port on the Gulf of Chihli, Weihaiwei, also on the Shantung peninsula, 150 miles across the water from the Russians, and 235 miles from the Germans. Indeed, the total sum budgeted by the British for Weihaiwei in 1903 was, from the point of view of the imperialist parliamentarians, a miserly £16,000.

With her previous year's alliance with Japan, Britain had no need to seek her own substantial naval bases in the region of the Yellow Sea. It was imperial Russia, not imperial Germany or Britain, that was to be Japan's naval rival in the Far East. The Korean peninsula, which had asserted its independence from Japan eight years earlier, was the main focus of Japanese popular concern. When Russia was found to have occupied a small port just inside Korea, on the southern bank of the Yalu River, opposite the Manchurian border, opinion in Japan was incensed. Japan had always regarded Korea as within its sphere of influence.

That autumn, Japanese demands that Russia respect Korean sovereignty became a part of the international battleground. Russia balked, however, at recognizing Japan's 'special interests' in Korea, even in return for a similar Japanese recognition of the Russian interests in Manchuria. A further Japanese demand, for 'equality of opportunity' for Japan in Manchuria, if the same were to be conceded to Russia in Korea, was likewise given an unfavourable response. The Japanese public, incensed by Russia's forward moves and demands, was calling for Japan to re-assert her rights over Korea by war. But although the Emperor of Japan praised the prudence of his ministers in choosing negotiations rather than war, the Japanese parliament unanimously adopted a resolution, unprecedented in Japanese parliamentary history, accusing the government of the neglect of its opportunities abroad. The Japanese government then asked the Russian government to reconsider its demands.

A serious crisis was in the making. Russia rushed troop reinforcements along its new Trans-Siberian railway to Port Arthur and Manchuria. In Japan, there were rumours that Russia intended to seize a port in southern Korea, and relief when the British government bought two Chilean warships the Russians were thought to want. The Japanese government then bought two armoured cruisers from the Argentine which were nearing completion at Genoa, and which Russia was also believed to want to buy. The British purchase, so helpful to Japan, had cost the British taxpayer more than a hundred times the cost of the British port construction at Weihaiwei.

As both Russia and Japan accelerated their preparations for war, various Powers began to take action. Britain and France were foremost in calling on both sides to negotiate rather than fight. China and the United States announced that they would remain neutral.

Japan's indignation at Russian efforts to acquire a port in Korea was real enough. But Japan was not acting to preserve the integrity of Korea, only to keep Russia out. That December, Japan herself, in conjunction with Britain and the United States, was pressing Korea to open up the port of Wiju to international trade.

International attention was focused on the Balkans in 1903, when, on the night of April 10, King Alexander and Queen Draga of Serbia were murdered in their palace in Belgrade, and their naked, mutilated bodies thrown from the palace window. Also murdered that night were the Prime Minister and the Minister of War, as well as the Queen's two brothers, an army general, and twelve men of the palace guard. 'Servia, the land of assassination, abdications, *pronunciamientos*, and *coups d'état*, has surpassed itself and caused all previous achievements to pale into insignificance beside the tragedy enacted between midnight and the small hours of this morning at Belgrade,' *The Times* commented with amazement. 'A Central Asian khanate, not a European city, would have been a fitting theatre for such ruthless and accurately planned regicide. France has seen her President, Austria her Empress, and Italy her King struck down by assassins within the last ten years; but no parallel can be found in recent European history for such wholesale extirpation of a reigning family and of its partisans. Fully and duly authenticated descriptions of the hecatomb are still waiting, but enough is known to characterize the tragedy of Belgrade as unique in contemporary history.'

'Never before,' a newspaper report from Paris pointed out, 'has the consort of a sovereign been the victim of a political assassination simultaneously with himself. Never before has a sovereign disappeared in such conditions without leaving any legitimate heir to the throne, the dynasty being thus extinguished at a single blow.'

The murdered King Alexander was twenty-six years old. Queen Draga was considerably older; indeed she had been a lady-in-waiting to the king's mother. The assassination had been masterminded by Colonel Mashin, the brother of the Queen's first husband. Mashin blamed the Queen for his brother's death from too much drinking, and resented having been retired from the army as soon as the Queen's second husband came to the throne. The immediate cause of the murders was the conflict that had arisen between the King and the Radicals a week earlier, when Alexander suspended the Liberal Constitution – which he himself had promulgated two years previously, revoked the law introducing secret ballots at the elections, and abolished freedom of the press. He had also excluded the Radical deputies from both the Senate and Council of State. Forming a majority of the educated population, the Radicals had been well represented in the Serbian parliament, and were determined not to be ousted from political life.

After the murders it was reported from Belgrade that the capital wore a 'festive aspect' and that 'intense joy' prevailed. Soldiers, horses and guns were decorated with sprigs of broom. A tyrant had been overthrown, and a new King, Peter Karageorgevic, then living in Geneva, was elected in his place by the parliament. The Karageorgevic dynasty had failed thirty-five years earlier to overthrow the Obrenovic dynasty, of which Alexander had been the last.

From Geneva, Peter Karageorgevic gave an interview to the press, in which, after denying all knowledge of the crime, he declared:

> I formally disapprove of violent measures. I especially deplore the fact that the army has had recourse to such measures – an army which has nobler tasks to accomplish than assassination. It would have sufficed to force Alexander to sign his abdication. He could have been bound, as has been done in other circumstances. It is a horrible thing to shed blood.
>
> You ask me what my attitude will be when I am in possession of the

Crown? Well, do you offer me the Crown? Take it for granted that, if I am called to the Throne, I shall not fail to take inspiration from the admirable institutions of Switzerland, which I have learned to appreciate highly.

I am in favour of absolute liberty of the Press, and I hope to see Servia prosper under the régime of the Constitution of 1889, which is very liberal. As regards foreign relations, it has been alleged that I am systematically hostile to Austria. That is false. It may be, however, that I have a special sympathy for Russia, where I have sent my boy in the hope that he would take service there.

Among those who sent their congratulations to the new monarch were Nicholas II of Russia and Franz Josef of Austria-Hungary. Franz Josef annoyed the Serbs, however, by expressing his hope that the new king would raise Serbia 'from the profound discredit in the eyes of the civilized world into which it has recently been plunged by an iniquitous and accursed crime'. In answer to Franz Josef, the Metropolitan of Belgrade, head of the national Church in Serbia, officiated at a thanksgiving Mass during which he praised the army for what it had done.

One of King Peter's first decisions was to issue a decree granting an indemnity for all acts of treason perpetrated up to that date. Despite a brief mutiny among the officers of the garrison at Nish, the murderers of King Alexander received the main civil and military appointments in his successor's government. So shocking was the murder to the leaders of the Powers that King Edward VII insisted that the British government break off diplomatic relations with Serbia. These relations were not renewed for three years.

Contrasting events in Serbia with those of her eastern neighbour, Roumania, one British commentator noted that during 1903 Roumania was 'in the happy position of a country which has no history. The only noteworthy (and a very discreditable) incident in her home politics was an extensive emigration of Jews to America, in consequence of their being denied the rights of Roumanian subjects.'

Following the revolt in Macedonia, the Turkish suppression of unrest continued on its harsh course. Macedonia was a small region, but one in which Serbs, Bulgarians and Greeks each resented Turkish rule, while at the same time wanting to be part of their own wider Serb, Bulgarian or Greek national entity. As news of the Turkish burnings and executions reached the European capitals, international protests were delivered at Constantinople against the repressive measures. The Russian Tsar, seeking to assert his position as the protector of all South Slavs, and of Eastern Orthodoxy, went so far as to order the Russian Black Sea fleet to make a demonstration off the Turkish coast. In Britain, four bishops wrote to *The Times* urging the British government to take action to prevent further Turkish 'outrages'. That same day, September 14, the newspaper's own correspondent in the Balkans, reporting from the Macedonian town of Monastir, gave a graphic account of atrocities committed by Turkish troops in the village of Smilievo eighteen days earlier, as reported by refugees from the village:

> The villagers suddenly found themselves surrounded, and all who tried to break the cordon were killed. The survivors were brought down to the village to watch it being looted and burnt. When only three houses remained standing all the women were collected together and ordered to enter them, but, thinking they were going to be burnt alive, most began to run, and in the stampede many more were killed.
>
> At this juncture a Turkish Bey from a neighbouring village appeared with his followers, and seems to have taken pity, for after some parleying about 60 of the women and 35 children were marched off by him to his own village and there fed and the next morning allowed to go to Monastir. On the following day many more fugitives appeared, in all about 200 families. Very many are, however, known to have been killed and more are missing. Every family has its own story to tell of murder, mutilation, and outrage, and tells it in such a way as to defy misbelief.

A second account published that day described an earlier Turkish attack on the village of Armensko:

> With no possible justification, the inhabitants being Greeks and not Bulgars, this village was suddenly surrounded, sacked, and burnt; not a villager escaped and many were burnt alive in the flames. This feat of arms was witnessed by a foreign officer who had left the railway station to watch the fight at Pisoder and his evidence is unimpeachable.
>
> Five days afterwards certain Sisters of Mercy were permitted to visit the village. They found about thirty of the wounded still living, mostly women and children, the dead still unburied and many of the bodies completely or partially burnt. They also found evidence of other things which cannot appear in print.

The corpses may still be seen lying in the village, but some of the wounded are now in the Greek hospital at Monastir. The description of their wounds will hardly bear repeating. One little girl, about ten years old, had eight in different parts of her body. They appear to be mostly from swords or bayonets, and it is interesting to note that only Turkish officers carry swords.

The proliferation of such newspaper reports led to mass protest meetings throughout Britain, France and the United States. Church leaders were prominent in their denunciation of Muslim savagery. The British government, pressed to take action to stop the Turkish killings, announced that it was for Austria and Russia to do what was required. At a mass meeting in London on September 29, the demand was for an end to Turkish rule in Macedonia. A telegram, sent that day from *The Times* correspondent in Bulgaria, described how, in the Turkish province that included parts of southern Macedonia, 'the march of devastation and rapine proceeds unchecked'.

Calls for action by the Powers – calls which were to be echoed ninety years later during the Bosnian conflict – were answered by the two sovereigns most closely affected, the Emperor Franz Josef and Tsar Nicholas who, meeting, with their Foreign Ministers, at Mürzsteg, in the mountains southwest of Vienna, agreed to put joint pressure on the Turkish Sultan. He must, said the two sovereigns, institute substantial and meaningful reform for the peoples of Macedonia. In support of this aim, the British government agreed to use its influence in Constantinople to put pressure on Turkey to comply. It was clear that any continuation by Turkey of its repressive policies could lead to international intervention, a full-scale war in the Balkans, and the loss of Turkish control there for ever. In Paris, a protest meeting against the Turkish atrocities in both Macedonia and Armenia was addressed by French, British, Italian and Belgian speakers, and a letter read out from German sympathizers. 'That was a splendid year of agitation for great causes, for justice, liberty and peace,' one of those present, the French senator Baron d'Estournelles de Constant, wrote ten years later.

On October 24 the Austro-Russian 'Instructions' to Turkey – known as the Mürzsteg Programme – were issued from Vienna. Not only were reforms in Macedonia essential, the instructions read, but they would be supervized by representatives of the Powers. The Turkish government hesitated to submit to the demands of two foreign powers – neither of which could claim to be a liberal democracy – and was emphatic that while the reforms were being applied 'everything calculated to humiliate Turkey should be avoided'.

The Austrians and Russians became impatient with the delay caused by the continuing exchange of diplomatic notes. On December 16 the Austro-Hungarian Foreign Minister, Count Goluchowski, issued a stern warning from Vienna, unusual in the relations between two empires, even if one of those empires was widely despised as being 'Asiatic'. Turkey, he said, 'must change if she wished to live'. If she could not carry out those changes herself, those who were interested 'in her preservation' would have to do so themselves. Turkey must beware, he said, of resistance to the Austro-Russian programme of reforms, 'lest chaos and ruin result'.

Three weeks after this warning the Turkish government agreed to the first step in carrying out the Austro-Russian Instructions, asking the Italian government to appoint an Italian officer to reorganize the Macedonian police. There was relief in Vienna and St Petersburg that the Turks had begun to comply with their demands; neither Power was all that eager to move its armies into the Balkans.

Although Austria-Hungary had been determined to make the Turks institute reforms in Macedonia, her own internal situation was far from satisfactory. The internal national tensions that had marked the year 1902 showed no signs of abating in 1903. Throughout the province of Croatia there were protests in May by Croat demonstrators against the policy of 'Magyarization' being carried out by the Hungarian governor of the Province. This included the unfair distribution of revenue raised by taxation, a distribution that had first been set down under the Magyar-Croat Compact of 1868, and the exclusive use of Hungarian names and the Hungarian language on the railways of Croatia and Slavonia.

In Austria, the Czechs were demanding their own university in Moravia, and the adoption of the Czech language in all official proceedings in Bohemia; if these demands were not granted, they said, they would obstruct all legislation. When the Minister who represented Czech interests in the Austrian Cabinet resigned, no other Czech politician was willing to take his place. It was clear that any successor would be equally frustrated in an attempt to advance any of the Czech national demands.

The Hungarians had been deeply upset that autumn by an army order issued by Franz Josef on September 16, from Chlopy in Galicia, in which the King-Emperor stressed that the army must stand above all antagonisms, 'so as to make use of all the qualities of each racial group for the benefit of all'. The Magyar version of the Chlopy Order used the word 'tribal' rather than 'racial', causing resentment in Hungary. After angry scenes in the Hungarian parliament, Franz Josef agreed to allow Hungary's national flag to be flown alongside the imperial flag on military establishments inside Hungary, and gave Hungarian officers stationed in Austria the right to transfer to regiments within Hungary.

In November the mood of discontent emerged in Bohemia, when the Czech deputies in the Reichsrat put forward a full programme of national demands. These included special lessons in primary schools in Austrian Silesia (where there was a Czech minority) 'to assist the development of the Czech national spirit', and the establishment of schools in Lower Austria – 'and especially in Vienna' – for the Czech minority there. The Czech demands were paralleled that year by demands from the Italian minority in the Tyrol, including the call for a university in Innsbruck, but the lecture in which the request for Italian schools was going to be made – on the sixteenth-century poet Petrarch, by a distinguished Italian professor – was itself banned by the Austrian authorities. There followed a German protest demonstration against the Italian demands, and an Italian counter-demonstration.

These manifestations of national discontent within the Habsburg Empire caused many outside observers to wonder how long the Dual Monarchy could survive.

Concerned about the growing closeness of Germany and Austria-Hungary, and their association with Italy, and the repercussions of such a combination in terms of naval power in the Mediterranean, Britain and France were drawing closer together. That October the two countries signed an agreement whereby disputes between them of a judicial nature, or relating to the interpretation of existing commercial treaties, would, if they proved intractable, be referred to the Permanent Court of Arbitration at The Hague. There were also areas in which one or other of the two countries felt their interest to be the dominant one, and in order that these regions should not be the source of any future conflict, negotiations were begun to reach agreements as to respective spheres of predominance. Britain wanted her rule in Egypt to be unchallenged by France, France wanted her control of Morocco to be an exclusive one. This was agreed.

On the basis of this exchange, several other smaller territorial conflicts were resolved, and an agreement was eventually signed in April 1904, known as the Entente Cordiale. While in no way a military alliance or threat to any other Power, the Entente Cordiale brought France and Britain into close harmony. In its imperial activities, Britain could rely upon not being criticized by France, since both shared a belief in the concept of the 'Mission Civilisatrice' (civilizing mission) of empire which had animated more than a century of exploration and expansion. In the Sudan, where five years earlier Britain and France had clashed over who was to control the upper regions of the Nile, a British force led by the Deputy-Governor General, Colonel Mahon, marched against a newly declared Mahdi, surrounded him and his men, tried him, and hanged him.

Another Muslim leader, Mullah Abdullah Mohammed (Britain's Mad Mullah), continued to lead a Dervish revolt against British rule in Somaliland. The Mullah claimed to act in the name of Islam, and to be asserting the right of Muslims to establish their own religious and – in the phraseology of the 1990s – fundamentalist regime. In April his forces surrounded a British military expedition, led by Lieutenant-Colonel Plunkett, that had tried to bring him to battle. They captured its two Maxim guns and killed Plunkett, eight other British officers, 48 Sikh and 128 black troops of the King's African Rifles. The Colonel was censured by the War Office in London for having gone forward without adequate support. The Mullah then attacked another British military unit nearby, killing thirteen.

Moving through the countryside with a force of 2000 armed men, and occupying several towns, the Mullah was attacked that December by 400 British, Indian and Somali troops, commanded by Colonel Kenna. The imperial forces drove the Dervishes off. Fearing, however, that the Mullah would bring even larger forces into battle, Kenna ordered a return to base. There was concern in the British camp that several of the Somali imperial troops had gone over to the Mullah's forces. The Mullah, while leaving the British alone for a while, and being left alone by them, retained control over a considerable tract of the interior.

Elsewhere in Africa, on the Nigerian-Sudanese axis, a considerable imperial acquisition was made that year, the second in the region in three years, when British forces moved against the Emir of Kano, and the Faulani tribe over whom he ruled. The Emir had refused to cooperate with a British commission which was trying to delineate the northern frontier. Kano was occupied in February, and 300 of the Emir's men killed. The Emir himself fled. 'Thus,' wrote one contemporary imperial historian, 'the great commercial city of the Western Sudan – the starting point of the caravan routes across the Continent to the north and east – fell under British control. An Emir favourable to the new Administration was installed, a Resident and a garrison stationed in the city, and authority exercised therefrom over a wide area hitherto closed against us.'

The Maxim gun played a major part not only in the British victories over the tribesmen of Nigeria, but in the subsequent maintenance of law and order. When African soldiers under British command were caught looting after the capture of Kano, the chief offender was put up against a wall and half a belt of Maxim gun ammunition – 125 rounds in all – was fired into him.

The final battle of the campaign against the Faulani took place at Sokoto on March 15. A European eye-witness recalled: 'As we approached close to the city hordes of horsemen and footmen armed with spears, swords, old guns and bows and arrows appeared, charging the square over and over again, only to be mown down by machine-gun and carbine fire.' A Faulani tribesman expressed the situation succinctly when he said: 'War now be no war.' The Emir escaped, but the tribe submitted to British rule, the other defeated Emirs being praised by their conquerors for having made a 'plucky stand'.

With the capture of Sokoto, British control in northern Nigeria stretched to the border of the French possessions in the Sahara. There was considerable relief among the British administrators in West Africa that, as one contemporary wrote, 'the fear of a Mahomedan movement which would sweep the whites back into the Delta need no longer be entertained'.

The search for the fugitive Emir of Kano continued, but without success. In June, a force that was searching for him was beaten back by the Emir's adherents, but the hunt continued and he was 'run to earth' – in the language of a British contemporary account, echoing the foxhunting idiom – and killed, before the end of the year.

One drawback for Britain in Nigeria was the paucity of soldiers and administrators with whom order could be maintained. In the Bassa Province, the British Resident and a police officer were attacked and killed at the end of the year, and a punitive military expedition sent against their attackers. The German colonial administrators in German South West Africa also faced local unrest, when, towards the end of the year, several soldiers were killed when the Hottentot tribe rose in revolt. A punitive expedition was ordered by the Kaiser, who was certain that the 4600 German residents in German

South West Africa, and the 1500 Boers who had emigrated there from South Africa, had to be protected, even if it meant the killing of hundreds, and indeed thousands, of native inhabitants.

In the western hemisphere, an anarchic situation broke out on the Caribbean island of Dominica. Two rival presidents (Morales and Jiminez) were fighting for ascendancy. In the warlike conditions that ensued, the lives of the European residents and traders were put at risk. Britain and the United States decided to act in concert, with British marines on the warship *Pallas* and American marines on the *Detroit* landing together and creating a defensive perimeter within which the Europeans could feel safe.

There was another crisis in Central America in 1903, when the government of Colombia refused to agree to United States' plans for the building of a canal across the Panama Isthmus at its narrowest point, the Colombian province of Panama. Travelling to California that summer, President Roosevelt spoke of the 'destiny' of the United States as a Pacific Power. This vision was enhanced a few weeks after his speech, when the 'All-American cable' was opened, establishing a telegraphic cable service which linked San Francisco to the Philippines. An imminent extension to Shanghai created telegraphic communication between the American and Asian continents. The new cable, linked with the existing Indo-European system, enabled President Roosevelt, on July 4, to send a message from Washington DC around the globe. By contrast, the Colombian government's refusal to sanction the Panama Isthmus canal seemed a churlish blow to the commercial interests and political influence of the United States.

The people of Panama were as keen as the United States to benefit from the enormous wealth which would be created by the building and working of the canal. On November 3, in a bloodless revolution, the Panamanians declared their independence from Colombia. As they made their move, there were several hundred armed Colombian troops in the city of Colon, on the Pacific Ocean side of the isthmus, who might have intervened, but an American gunboat, the *Nashville*, was also in harbour.

The commander of the *Nashville* had only forty troops that he could put ashore, against more than four hundred Colombian troops. Without revealing his weakness, he declared that if the Colombian troops attacked the Panamanians, he would come to the assistance of Panama. The Colombian troops withdrew, the Republic of Panama came into being, and one of the century's most significant commercial and marine developments could begin.

The new republic at once negotiated a treaty with the United States, whereby, in return for a guarantee by Washington to safeguard its independence, Panama would, for its part, cede to the United States in perpetuity a strip of land ten miles wide extending from the Atlantic to the Pacific, on which the United States could not only control a future canal, but build fortifications, maintain military garrisons, and exercise all the rights of sovereignty.

Colombia threatened war to recover its lost territory. The United States sent a large naval force to both seaboards. None of the Powers were willing to show any interest in the conflict; the Monroe Doctrine had been upheld, and was not to be challenged. 'This great enterprise of building an inter-oceanic canal,' President Roosevelt told Congress in the aftermath of Colombia's discomfiture, 'cannot be held up to gratify the whims, or out of respect to the government incompetence, or to the even more sinister and evil political peculiarities of people who, though they dwell afar off, yet, against the wish of the actual dwellers on the isthmus, assert an unreal supremacy over the territory. The possession of a territory fraught with such peculiar capacities as the isthmus in question carries with it obligations to mankind.' The course of events had shown, Roosevelt added, 'that this canal cannot be built by private enterprise, or by any other nations than our own; therefore it must be built by the United States.'

Another area of Pacific responsibility which gave cause for concern in the United States that year was the Sulu Archipelago, a 200-mile-long island area which had been the southernmost part of the Spanish Philippines conquered in 1898. In the days of Spanish rule, the authority of Spain was not strong enough to abolish the institution of slavery there, and in the first three years of American rule nothing was done to interfere. Indeed, the American government paid the local Sultan a subsidy for his loyalty, and slavery was permitted to exist on Sulu in order not to alienate him. This was so at variance with every United States' historical and ethical tenet, that in 1902 a Governor, General Wood, was appointed, with the specific instructions to bring slavery to an end.

General Wood arrived in Sulu and issued a proclamation against slavery – more than half a century after Lincoln. The Sultan would not comply and a punitive expedition was sent to fight him. The expedition was successful, but it also led to charges – laid by the most senior officer in the American army, General Miles – of military abuses. After an official investigation, several officers were charged with cruelty and maltreating the natives. Although the charges against them were not upheld in court, it was widely believed in the United States that the military expedition had shown excessive zeal.

On the northern borders of the British Empire in India, another conflict was in the making. The British authorities in India, having declared themselves dissatisfied that the government of Tibet had not sent 'properly empowered representatives' to discuss various frontier and trade questions, despatched Colonel Younghusband, an intrepid explorer, into the mountains. The government of India hoped that he would advance to the Tibetan capital, Lhasa, but the government in London refused – in this case – to sanction what would have been, in effect, the occupation of an independent state. Younghusband waited therefore on the British side of the frontier, for the Tibetan envoys, who made no appearance.

In the Sudan, from which Britain had driven the Mahdi five years earlier, peace had been restored. The successful activities of the Mullah to the southeast were almost a thousand miles away, too far away to have any repercussions. In February 1903 a young British diplomat then serving in Egypt visited Khartoum, and the battlefield at Omdurman, scene of the defeat of the Mahdi in October 1898. An unexpected sight greeted the diplomat's eyes, the local Sudanese football team setting off to play the Khartoum team in a temperature of 100 degrees Fahrenheit. The Omdurman team, he wrote, 'consisted of youths of thirteen to fifteen dressed in striped jersey, shorts, and boots of huge length – for these natives have very long feet. The sight of the football eleven brought home to me more forcibly than anything else the change brought about by our conquest of the Sudan and the extraordinary progress made in five years.' The young diplomat then played a game of polo on a ground just outside the square in Khartoum where five years earlier the Mahdi had exhorted a vast crowd to do battle against the British.

The year 1903 had its share of natural and unnatural disasters. In June more than a hundred Spaniards were killed in a train crash on the Bilbao-Zaragoza railway, and in August eighty-four Parisians were killed when a fire broke out in the Paris metro. In December, during a theatre matinee in Chicago, fire broke out on stage, the fire-proof curtain jammed half way down, and more than six hundred people, mainly women and children, were killed, some by fire, some by suffocation, and some crushed to death as they tried to escape.

That year, in India, the number of deaths from plague, calculated province by province, totalled 842,264. Of these, more than a third of a million were in Bombay province and almost a quarter of a million in the Punjab. A policy of mass inoculation was embarked upon, but with local resistance to inoculation growing, the government announced that it had become its 'settled policy' to abstain from any attempt to carry out preventative measures by force. By the end of the year, the total number of plague deaths over the previous three years reached 1,673,000.

Amid the panoply and sport of empire, news of suffering at home struck a discouraging note. Immediately after Christmas 1903, it was announced that the number of paupers in London who were receiving relief had reached 73,608, a higher total than any previously recorded. The search for a life of comfort, health and leisure was ever present among the wealthier nations of the world. In 1903 the first 'garden city' was founded, at Letchworth in England. It was the concept of Ebenezer Howard, who sought to combine urban living with pastoral and even agricultural pursuits. That same year, President Roosevelt established the first national wildlife refuge in the United States, Pelican Island, off the east coast of Florida. The glories of nature were to be protected by Federal law and maintained by Federal money.

The welfare of industrial workers was also enhanced that year. In Germany the principle of sickness benefits for workers was confirmed and extended. At Ghent, in Belgium, an infants' welfare centre was opened for working-class children. In Britain, a Labour Party candidate, Arthur Henderson, was elected to Parliament, heralding the slow eclipse of Liberalism as the party of the working class. Twenty-six years later, Henderson became Foreign Secretary in the second Labour government.

In the world of science and medicine, 1903 saw the discovery by Pierre and Marie Curie of the properties of radium, a recently discovered substance that, as *The Times* reported on March 25, 'possesses the extraordinary property of continuously emitting heat, without combustion, without chemical change of any kind, and without any change to its molecular structure'. That radium would have a dramatic influence in the treatment of cancer was not yet known, but the nature of its properties was clearly of medical significance. As the newspaper reported, 'radium emanations act powerfully upon the nerve substance, and cause the death of living things whose nerve centres do not lie deep enough to be shielded to their influence.'

Art, literature, music and architecture each saw an impressive development in 1903, the year in which Picasso painted *La Vie*, Jack London wrote *The Call of the Wild*, and Schoenberg composed *Pelléas et Mélisande*. Antonio Gaudi began work that year on the Sagrada Familia church in Barcelona, and Charles Reed and Allen Stem on Grand Central Station in New York (the impressive vastness of which the author remembers in 1944, from the perspective of a seven-year-old). Architecture and commerce combined in 1903 with the opening of the New York Chamber of Commerce and Stock Exchange. The year also saw one of the earliest feature films, *The Great Train Robbery*.

Travel, transport and sport all gained that year. The first motor taxicab was introduced to the streets of London in 1903, and the first Tour de France bicycle race was held, the winner being an Italian chimney sweep, Maurice Garin. In the United States, baseball's World Series was started, the series being won that year by the Boston Red Sox. Most dramatically for the future of the century, on December 17, at Kitty Hawk, North Carolina, two American brothers, Orville and Wilbur Wright, fitted a twelve horse-power petrol engine to one of their gliders. Thus powered, it flew in the air for forty yards. This was the first successful aeroplane flight. Its formidable consequences for the century ahead were unforeseen.

CHAPTER FIVE

1904

By THE EARLY YEARS of the century the inhabited world had been widely explored. Yet there were still many regions which remained hostile to exploration or penetration. In the Indian Ocean, off the desolate island of Masirah, the crew of a British merchant ship, the *Baron Innerdale*, landed in 1904 out of curiosity to see the remote and barren island. They were met, however, by a group of islanders who resented their presence, and in the confrontation that followed, one of the crew drew his pistol and fired a shot. In the subsequent fight, all the crew, with the exception of the ship's boy, were slaughtered.

In the Balkans the nature of the conflict between the ruling Turks and the Bulgars, Serbs, Roumanians, Greeks, Albanians and Montenegrins under their control was also a throwback – or so it seemed to educated observers – to an earlier century. Edith Durham, in her book *The Burden of the Balkans*, introduced English-language readers to some of the region's oddities with a wealth of personal experience, of which the following two episodes, first sent from the Balkans as a newspaper report, were typical:

> Politics here cover a multitude of sins. One night a man turned up mysteriously. In his village there were three traitors. Before anything further could be done they must be destroyed. They could not be shot, for this would probably bring down the authorities, and it was impossible to buy poison because the law on the sale of it was very strictly enforced. (This is interesting, as it shows that it is possible to enforce a law in Turkey when expedient.)
>
> But 'madama' (myself) was a friend of the doctor. No doubt if she asked him he would write her something that could be put in coffee. Then the three gentlemen could be asked to supper, and their political differences quietly arranged. Nor had he any doubt that I should fulfil this humble request.
>
> An episode such as this is vividly interesting. It is possible to ride hastily through the Balkan Peninsula and credit the people with Western twentieth-century feelings. A short residence among them reveals the

Middle Ages, their sentiments, morals, and point of view, all preserved alive by the overlaying stratum of Oriental rule.

There was a man in the town, a refugee from over Dibra way. When he was sober he talked Slav, but when he was drunk enough to straddle on his heels, which was not infrequently, he talked Albanian. He was a Bulgarian patriot. One day he came and begged my protection. Some soldiers had threatened last night to kill him. 'Why did the soldiers want to kill him?' I asked. 'Because they suspected him.' 'What of, and why?'

Then he related with pride that he was the man who had made the poisoned bread that had killed fifteen Turkish soldiers. I advised him to clear out, saying that if he did such things I could not possibly help him. He was astonished that I was not aware of his great achievement, and still more so that I did not admire it. This was just before I left Ochrida, so I never knew if he took my advice. Later I learnt whence the poison had been obtained, and also that few, if any, of the soldiers, had really died, though they had all been very ill.

Under the terms proposed jointly by Russia and Austria-Hungary for the better administration of Macedonia, the Turkish government agreed in 1904 that Austrian and Russian civilian officials could tour the province and question the local inhabitants about their respective grievances. An Italian general would reorganize the local police force. Race and religion were both declared to be no barrier to official employment. Administrative borders were to be redrawn to take more account of national groupings.

Macedonia seemed a region where the Powers could moderate existing grievances, and reduce chaos. Neither Russia nor any other Power was able, however, to intervene in the most eastern provinces of the Ottoman Empire, where an Armenian uprising against Turkish ill-treatment was put down by Turkish troops, helped by the local Kurds. Twelve Armenian villages were destroyed and several thousand Armenian men, women and children were killed. About four thousand Armenians, fleeing to the town of Mush, near Lake Van, were placed under the protection of the French consul.[1]

* * *

[1] Consular protection, even in the most hostile circumstances, can be a life-saving factor. In the autumn of 1944 tens of thousands of Hungarian Jews were saved by protective documents issued by the Swedish, Swiss and Spanish consuls (Wallenberg, Schutz and Perlasca) in Budapest; in 1956 the American embassy in Budapest gave sanctuary to Cardinal Mindszenty, a fugitive from Hungarian Communist persecution.

On 5 February 1904 the negotiations being conducted between Russia and Japan over Russian claims for some influence in Korea, and Japanese claims for a similar influence in Manchuria, were broken off. Japanese diplomats left St Petersburg for Tokyo, and Russian diplomats left Tokyo for St Petersburg. Three nights later, at midnight, as the diplomats began their long journeys home, Japanese torpedo boats attacked the Russian naval squadron at Port Arthur. Two Russian battleships and a cruiser were damaged. On the following evening the Tsar, who had just returned to the Winter Palace from the theatre, was handed a telegram from the Russian Viceroy and Commander-in-Chief, Admiral Alexeyev: 'About midnight, Japanese destroyers made a sudden attack on the squadron anchored in the outer harbour of Port Arthur. The battleships *Tsarevich*, *Retvizan* and the cruiser *Pallada* were torpedoed. The importance of the damage is being ascertained.' In copying the text of this telegram into his diary, Nicholas added: 'This without a declaration of war. May God come to our aid.'

Russia and Japan were at war. In the first weeks, Russian troops stationed in Manchuria crossed the Yalu River and entered Korea. Two months later, however, they were driven back across the river, and the Japanese entered Manchuria in force. At the same time, landing on the Liaotung peninsula, Japanese troops, helped by gunboats and torpedo boats, forced the Russian army back towards Port Arthur, which was effectively besieged. This left Japan free to land an army in Korea without fear of any serious Russian naval opposition, though two hundred Japanese soldiers were drowned when they refused to surrender to a Russian naval squadron that had intercepted them on their way to Korea.

Russia's position at sea was further weakened when, in April, the Russian flagship, the battleship *Petropavlovsk*, struck a Japanese mine off Port Arthur and sank; the Russian naval Commander-in-Chief, Admiral Makarov, 40 officers and 750 men were drowned. In all the wars of the twentieth century, from the loss of the *Petropavlovsk* in 1904 to the loss of the *General Belgrano* in 1982, the sinking of powerful and imposing warships, built at such cost, launched with such pomp, was to be among the most sudden, and the most final, of war's terrors.[1] The Japanese fleet suffered no losses until May, when two Japanese cruisers rammed each other in dense fog off Port Arthur, with the loss of 235 lives, and a Japanese battleship, the *Hatsuse*, struck two

[1] At the time of its sinking, the *General Belgrano* (then flying the Argentine colours) was the last survivor on active naval service of the United States Fleet which the Japanese had attacked at Pearl Harbor in 1941.

Russian mines and sank. Four hundred officers and men were drowned.

It had been difficult for Russia to increase its rather small military force – no more than 100,000 men – which was stationed in Manchuria when the war broke out. The section of the Trans-Siberian railway around Lake Baikal had not been completed, so tracks had to be laid across the ice of the lake, which ceased to be operable in the spring. As a result, it was not until eight months after the outbreak of the war that the strength of the force reached 320,000. Losses in battle were heavy, reducing even that figure. To augment the numbers, 7000 convicts doing hard labour in the remote and desolate camps of Sakhalin, nearly 3000 of whom were convicted murderers, were offered a year off their sentences for every two months that they were in action. Fifteen thousand ex-convicts, including five thousand murderers who had served their sentences, but who, according to Russia's rules for ex-convicts, had been forced after their release to live in settlements not far from their camps, were offered the right to return to Russia. They were not, however, given the right to live in any provincial capital or to own property.

Even with augmented numbers, the Russian forces were not a match for the Japanese in military skill and training. The Russian commander, General Kuropatkin, had to use all his powers of command to prevent the many Russian setbacks and defeats from becoming a rout. The army as a whole had remained on the defensive with relatively little loss of life, sections being beaten in a succession of clashes. In August, the Russian fleet bottled up in Port Arthur decided to try to seek battle with the Japanese in the open water. It was defeated. When, in October, Kuropatkin sought to curb criticisms of his inaction by launching an offensive, the boastful nature of his order of the day held him up to ridicule. The time had come, he told his troops, 'to compel the Japanese to do our will, as our forces are now strong enough to begin the forward movement'. The whole of his army then attacked, for the first time in the war, but the attack was a failure, making his order of the day appear even more ridiculous, as his troops were driven back further and further towards the tip of the Liautung peninsula.

The powerful Russian Baltic Fleet set sail for the Far East, a journey that would take it half way around the world. When, at a very early stage of its epic voyage, it reached the Dogger Bank, off the British coast of the North Sea, a case of mistaken naval identity led it to open fire, at a range of about a quarter of a mile, on a number of British fishing boats, sinking one boat and killing two fishermen. So great was British public and official indignation that the Tsar hastened to send a personal message to King Edward expressing his 'regret', though he declined to apologize. Two days later there was both indignation and ridicule in Britain when the Russian commander of the force, Admiral Rozhdestvensky, stated that his ships had opened fire on two Japanese torpedo boats that had taken up their positions in the midst of the fishing boats, and he added that he greatly regretted that British fishermen should have suffered, if indeed they were innocent.

The 'Dogger Bank Incident', as it was called, escalated. Despite the Tsar's reluctance to do so, the Russian government offered monetary compensation. An international tribunal, on which the United States and France would both have representatives, would try those sailors responsible. Anyone found guilty would be 'punished adequately'. Meanwhile the Russian Baltic Fleet continued on its way to the Far East, to redress the balance of naval power there which had so turned against the Russians. When it reached the Spanish port of Vigo, four officers were put ashore, to face the consequences of legal action. The British public was, to a certain extent, mollified.

In Manchuria, twenty countries sent military observers to watch the fighting, hoping to gain knowledge that might be helpful to them in their own military policies and preparations. This was the first time that two substantial powers had fought each other since the end of the Franco-Prussian war thirty-three years earlier. There was indignation in Russia when one of these observers, a Swiss officer, Colonel Audeoud, made disparaging remarks about the Russian army. He was at once recalled. This angered the Swiss public, who rallied to the colonel's defence and derided the Russian government's sensitivities as 'puerile'.

The foreign observers were impressed by the martial powers of Japan, and also by the tenacity of the Russian soldiers, many of them 6000 miles from home. But most of all it was the heavy loss of life which made an impact on the observers. In an attack on one Russian fortified position, 749 Japanese and 704 Russian soldiers were killed before the Russians withdrew. Another unexpected sight was the amount of valuable war equipment which the retreating Russian army was forced to leave behind. In that particular engagement the foreign observers reported sixty-eight field guns and ten Maxim guns among the Japanese spoils of war. After another battle two weeks later, the Japanese buried 1854 Russian soldiers on the battleground.

Japanese soldiers were drawing closer and closer to Port Arthur. In the port itself, which had been under sustained and heavy bombardment by Japanese naval forces, no single Russian warship remained capable of action.

On November 30 the Japanese infantry captured 203 Metre Hill, one of the main Russian defensive positions outside the port. The loss of life in these battles was heavier than in any previous conflict since the American Civil War forty years earlier. In this failed attempt to break into Port Arthur itself, an estimated six thousand Japanese soldiers were killed, and a further fifteen thousand injured. In his annual message to Congress a week later, President Roosevelt spoke of the duty of the United States to promote 'the peace of justice' throughout the world, and of the need for strong forces, especially naval forces, to back up such a firm approach. He also stressed the policeman's function that was devolving on the United States in the western hemisphere, as both Panama and Dominica had shown.

One person who was inspired by Japan's continuing victories over Russia was fourteen-year-old Jawarhalal Nehru, who saw the war as between a degenerate imperial power and a rising national one. 'Japanese victories stirred up my enthusiasm,' he later wrote, 'and I awaited eagerly for the papers for fresh news daily. Nationalistic ideas filled my mind. I mused of Indian freedom and Asiatic freedom from the thraldom of Europe. I dreamt of brave deeds, of how, sword in hand, I would fight for India and help in freeing her.'

There were other regions calling out to be freed. Since May 1903 news of a reign of terror in the Belgian Congo was reaching Europe as a result of the efforts of Edmund Morel, a shipping clerk in Liverpool. In a newspaper which he set up for that very purpose, the *West African Mail*, Morel published graphic accounts of staggering atrocities which had come to his notice during the system of forced labour which was imposed by the Belgian authorities – under the direct rule of King Leopold – on the local inhabitants. Morel wrote of women chained to posts as hostages until their menfolk returned with rubber; and of Belgian punitive expeditions which, on their return to base, brought baskets of human hands as proof of their ruthlessness. Morel estimated that by such methods King Leopold, for whom the Congo was a personal domain, drew £360,000 annually from rubber alone.

In February 1904, nine months after Morel's first foray into print, Roger Casement, the British Consul in the Belgian Congo, sent a report of Leopold's activities to the Foreign Office in London. He had seen Congolese women and children chained in sheds as hostages, and men beaten up for failure to produce sufficient rubber at collection points. He reported that the Belgian authorities kept some 10,000 soldiers under arms to police the Congo, and wrote of mass executions, and of terrible mutilations inflicted on the natives by white officials. Casement estimated that as many as three million native Congolese had died of disease, torture or shooting during the previous fifteen years. A Congolese soldier who was sent to get rubber, and had to open fire to do so, had to bring back a right hand for every bullet he expended.

Sometimes, Casement reported, when a soldier used a bullet to shoot a wild animal, 'they then cut off a hand from a living man' in order to justify the expenditure of the bullet. One hand was allowed to remain, so that the rubber could still be collected. At one rubber-collecting site, Casement reported, the soldiers had used 6000 cartridges, 'which means', he noted, 'that 6000 people are killed or mutilated; it means more than 6000, for the people have told me repeatedly that the soldiers kill children with the butt of their guns'.

As news of the Congolese atrocities spread, there was widespread outcry at King Leopold's sanction of such hideous practices and against the enormous financial profit he had made. President Theodore Roosevelt and King Edward VII among heads of State, Mark Twain and Joseph Conrad among writers, joined the chorus of Leopold's critics. But it was only after two years of international protests that the Belgian Parliament began to debate the situation in the Congo, and two years after that, that Leopold agreed to hand over his personal control of what was called the *Domaine de la Couronne* to the Belgian Parliament. In return for giving up this lucrative crown dominion he received £2 million from the Belgian exchequer. The abuse had ended, though at a price.

Leopold's rule in the Congo made a mockery of Europe's self-proclaimed 'civilizing mission' in Africa, which had always veered uneasily between exploitation of natural resources and the improvement of the conditions of the local inhabitants. Leopold had permitted cruelty on an unprecedented scale, and accumulated a vast fortune. In Belgium itself, he spent millions of pounds to provide museums, hotels, promenades, and dance halls at the North Sea post of Ostend, hoping to make it Europe's foremost resort. He spent over a million pounds beautifying his palaces. At Laeken he installed a royal bed made from malachite, and in the palace gardens he erected a Chinese restaurant and a Japanese pagoda, illuminated at night by more than 2000 light bulbs. When Prince Albert, the heir to the Belgian throne, remarked, 'But uncle, it will be a little Versailles!' Leopold growled angrily: 'Little . . . ?'

Leopold's political power was broken in 1908: the conscience of his own people and the protests of Europe demanded it. He lived three more years, nervously hiding his enormous beard in a leather bag whenever he felt that it would get damp and give him pneumonia. At the age of eighty-four he married the girl whom he had taken as his mistress several years earlier, when she was eighteen and he seventy-seven, and by whom he had a son. Leopold's death in 1909 ended a despicable episode of Europe's imperial history.

There was a postscript to the Congo scandal. The British diplomat Roger Casement, who was knighted for his skill in exposing the Congo atrocities, later became active in the struggle to liberate Ireland from British rule. During the First World War he attempted to recruit Irish prisoners of war in Berlin to fight against Britain. He was caught by the British after landing on the coast of Ireland, tried as a traitor, and shot.

The British government was engaged during 1904 in an expedition that was to draw much criticism from the Liberal opposition. A senior political officer of the Government of India, Colonel Younghusband, had waited in vain on the Tibetan frontier for Tibetan delegates to come to discuss trade and frontier questions with him. He therefore advanced across the border into Tibet, accompanied by 3000 armed British and Indian soldiers commanded by a senior British officer, General Macdonald. 'Negotiations have not progressed much,' he wrote to a friend in India on March 7, 'the Tibetans absolutely refusing to negotiate unless we return to the frontier, and as we have tried for twelve years to settle the matter before crossing the frontier, it does not look hopeful. The only thing to do is to really smack them.'

Younghusband was not pleased with General Macdonald, and complained about him to his friend: 'He sucks in every rumour, and lays out his plans as if the Tibetans were commanded by a Napoleon and were the most bloodthirsty people in the world.' Within two months General Macdonald had completed his plan of action, the British imperial force advanced, and the Tibetans, who had blocked Macdonald and Younghusband's way at the village of Guru, were defeated. Younghusband was not certain that he ought to be congratulated on the victory. 'I did my level best to prevent fighting,' he explained to his friend, 'and twice refused Macdonald's request to begin.' But the Tibetan general refused to carry out Macdonald's order to the Tibetans to lay down their weapons, began struggling with an Indian soldier, and then 'loosed off his revolver, the fat was in the fire. I was miserable at the time, for of course it was a loathsome sight, and, however much I felt even then it would probably work out well in the end, I could not but be disgusted at the sight of those poor wretched peasants mowed down by our rifles and Maxims.'

In the fighting around Guru, six hundred Tibetans were killed. There were no British or Indian deaths. But the moral tides were turning against such imperial excesses. 'Surely it is very wicked to do such things,' the twenty-nine-year-old Winston Churchill wrote to a friend when the news of the confrontation at Guru reached Britain. 'Absolute contempt for the rights of others must be wrong,' he asserted. 'Are there any people in the world so mean-spirited as not to resist under the circumstances to which these poor Tibetans have been subjected. It has been their land for centuries, and although they are only Asiatic, "liberty" and "home" mean something to them.' That the British Conservative party and the Conservative newspapers had greeted the victory at Guru 'with a howl of ferocious triumph' must, Churchill added, 'be an evil portent'.

Younghusband and Macdonald pressed on towards Lhasa. In subsequent skirmishes a further 2100 Tibetans were killed, for the loss in action of 37 British and Indian troops. Younghusband reached Lhasa, and the British flag was raised over the Himalayan kingdom. The Tibetans, Younghusband was surprised to find, were 'excellent people, quite polished and polite and genial and well-mannered, but absolutely impossible on business matters'. He had still hoped to discuss the trade and frontier question which were the purpose of his mission with the Dalai Lama, but he had 'gone into religious seclusion three days' marches away'. There was a national Assembly in the capital, but with no president and no system of voting. 'There is no executive or initiative head'.

Younghusband remained in Lhasa, waiting for someone to sit down with him and talk. The man chosen by the Dalai Lama to conduct the negotiations was Ti Rimbochi, a monk, and professor of Divinity. A month after Younghusband's arrival in Lhasa, he and Ti Rimbochi concluded an Anglo-Tibetan Convention. It was signed in the Dalai Lama's apartments in the Potala palace. The Tibetans agreed to all Britain's demands. They would accept as their southern frontier the line defined by Britain fourteen years earlier, and would erect border posts along it. They would destroy all fortifications between Lhasa and the frontier. They would open markets in two towns (Gyantse and Gartok) in which traders from British India and Tibetans would be permitted to trade. They would also pay Britain the massive sum (for them) of £500,000, in seventy-five annual instalments. 'I am in terrible hot water,' Younghusband wrote to his friend when the convention was signed, 'for getting too much.'

Under the terms which Younghusband had secured, until the Tibetan indemnity was paid, that is, until 1979, Britain would occupy the Chumbi Valley in southern Tibet. The government in London, which had given assurances both to China and Russia that Britain had no territorial aspirations against Tibet, was so alarmed at the thought of having to retain the Chumbi Valley for so long that it reduced the indemnity to £150,000 in twenty-five annual instalments. A small sliver of territory had been added, temporarily, to the British Empire.

On leaving Lhasa to return to India, General Macdonald was presented by the Tibetans with a gold image of Buddha. History does not record whether he appreciated the pacific message of the gift. But it does record that his return journey was made more difficult by the sudden drop in temperatures as he and his men made their way through steep ravines at 18,000 feet. While less than forty British and Indian soldiers had been killed in the fighting, more than two hundred died of cold and exposure.

In Somaliland, British forces had given up trying to capture the Mullah who had given them such trouble for the previous three years. Instead, the British and Italian colonial administrations in the region offered to make their peace with him. He would be assigned a settled sphere, with grazing rights for his people which would span both British and Italian territory. In return, he agreed to keep the peace, though he would receive no subsidy, as he had hoped.

Efforts were made that year to find a place elsewhere in Africa in which Jews, fleeing from persecution in Russia, and animated by the desire to have an autonomous area of their own, could be brought together. Although Jewish national sentiment was directed towards a homeland in Palestine, the Turkish imperial authorities were unwilling to make the necessary concessions there, and a homeland in Africa was suggested instead. The initiative came from the British government, whose landholdings in Africa were substantial. The commission of enquiry which went in search of suitable land was made up of a British army officer who was a well-known African explorer, and two Germans, one of them a scientific adviser to the German authorities in North West Cameroons (Kamerun) and the other a civil engineer.

The area suggested for the Jewish homeland was a high plateau, the climate of which was believed to be healthy enough for Europeans. It lay in the interior of British-administered Kenya (the area was later part of Uganda). Some Jewish leaders, confronted by the continued hostility to Jews both in Russia and Roumania, were tempted to give up Palestine, temporarily at least, for Africa. A vigorous debate ensued among them, but their conclusion was that they would prefer to wait until Palestine became a possibility. Meanwhile, largely as a result of the pioneering efforts of Russian Jewish workers inspired by Jewish national sentiment, and the wealth of the Rothschilds, as many as a thousand Russian Jews were making their way to Palestine each year, and several farming settlements were purchased there for them. Despite the prevalence of malaria, and attacks from neighbouring Arab villages, these immigrants persevered.

In Morocco, the French government, having secured by its April 1904 Entente Cordiale with Britain an essentially free hand, began strenuous efforts to assert its authority over the warring Muslim factions, whose local powers had been too great for the Sultan, Mulai Abdul Aziz, to control. But even the Sultan resented the attempt by France to assert its control, and military clashes were frequent. In French West Africa there was no such opposition to the French colonial rulers, who were envied even by the British for being able to police the port of Dakar, with its population of 18,000, with only ten men. In Lagos, on the coast of the British South Niger Protectorate, local unrest in 1904 was suppressed by force. Inland, in northern Nigeria, a punitive expedition was sent that year to avenge the murder of an earlier force, including its leader, Captain O'Riordan, sent to reconcile the Okpoto people to British rule. The new expedition succeeded in capturing the main town of the region, Ogodo, and holding it.

In Angola, where Portugal had been the colonial power for more than three hundred years, local discontent against the European settlers continued to flare. One of the native peoples, the Cuanhamas, had attacked an isolated column of Portuguese-officered troops, killing 254 of them. The Portuguese, who prided themselves on the enlightened nature of their administration, took punitive action. Five thousand soldiers set off to punish the Cuanhamas. The result was what a British report described as 'a massacre'.

In German South West Africa the Hereros had risen in revolt; their hatred of the German administration was understood in Berlin, where the Colonial Department recognized that the local German colonists, who numbered just under 5000, had been acquiring land from the Hereros by 'fraud and extortion'. The Hereros seized German-owned houses and cattle, and surrounded several German garrisons. When a small German military detachment was attacked, and twenty-six German soldiers killed, there was indignation throughout Germany. The Reichstag, a majority of the Deputies of which were normally hostile to imperial expenditure, voted money for a punitive expedition; there were no dissenters.

Before the punitive expedition could arrive, another nine German soldiers were trapped and killed. Further clashes, and the ravages of tropical disease, killed nearly three hundred of the existing German force. Just over two hundred survived to await the punitive expedition and its reinforcements. Shortly after the expedition arrived, the other large tribe in the colony, the Witbois, who had hitherto been armed by the Germans as allies in the struggle, joined the Hereros. In the months that followed there was a series of fierce engagements in which thousands of Hereros and Witbois were killed. When news of the severity of the punitive measures reached Europe, there was widespread indignation that destruction on such a scale had been inflicted by a colonial power on its subject peoples.

On the other side of the world, in German New Guinea, attempts were made by German missionaries to stamp out local tribal customs, judged savage by Christian standards, and to introduce Christianity in their place. The tribes rebelled against these efforts, and during an attack on a Christian Mission in the Baining mountains, six missionaries and five nuns were killed. The attackers were hunted down by German troops and killed.

In the Dutch East Indies, following a rebellion against Dutch rule, a military force was sent against the self-declared Sultan of Atchin. During the Dutch attack, nearly a thousand women and children were killed. In the Dutch parliament at The Hague the socialist deputies condemned the expedition and the massacre. The government tried to defend its actions by saying that those killed, members of the Gajoes and Alas tribes, had not only given protection to the hunted Sultan, but had made use of the women and children as shields during the fighting. Despite this explanation, a member of the government party declared, to the indignation of the Colonial minister, that the Dutch soldiers had behaved like 'Huns and Tatars', massacring the women and children for the commercial ends of mining and oil exploration.

So passionate did the debate become that one socialist deputy proposed the sale of all Dutch colonial possessions in order to put an end to any further military expeditions. If the Dutch colonies were governed by Britain or France, he said, they would be both better governed and more flourishing. There were large areas of both the British and French Empires where peace reigned, where benign administration flourished, where education spread, and where the participation of the local population in local government was encouraged. That was not to say that, even as such benefits of imperial rule spread, the desire of the ruled to be their own masters did not also persist, and grow – sometimes in equal proportion to the benefits granted to them.

Spain, having lost the last of her Caribbean and Pacific Ocean territories to the United States in 1898, was also seeking an imperial role, and looked for this in the area nearest to her, North Africa. But the territorial ambitions and power of France were such that, under the Franco-Spanish Agreement of 3 October 1904, Spain had to accept that France would be sovereign over most of Morocco – from Algeria to the Atlantic – with Spain confining her sovereignty to a territory no larger than Massachusetts. This area centred on the Rif mountains, where the local Moors were not willing to cede their independence lightly, and where yet another imperial struggle was about to begin, one that would last for more than two decades.

Within the Russian Empire, the government's difficulties were growing. In June the Governor General of Finland, General Bobrikov, was shot dead by the son of a Finnish senator. In July, the Minister of the Interior himself, Vyacheslav Plehve, was killed by a bomb. In November, at a conference in St Petersburg, the presidents of the provincial assemblies demanded the establishment of a constitution for Russia, and civil and religious liberties.

In Austria-Hungary, the diverse nationalities of the Empire continued to agitate for greater autonomy. Among the eleven separate peoples who chafed at Habsburg rule, the Poles dreamed of one day being part of a single Polish State, and the South Slavs dreamed of union with Serbia. But the King-Emperor of this agglomeration of peoples was confident that the Empire had a purpose. 'The monarchy is not an artificial creation,' Franz Josef told a friend in the summer of 1904, 'but an organic body. It is a place of refuge, an asylum for all those fragmented nations scattered over central Europe who, if left to their own resources, would lead a pitiful existence, becoming the playthings of more powerful neighbours.' Commenting on this reflection, the historian Alan Palmer writes: 'Ninety years later, it is the eleven peoples who are fragmented.'

The achievement of the Hungarians in 1867 in obtaining their own parliament proved an inspiration to an Irish nationalist, Arthur Griffith, who wrote in 1904: 'Hungary won her independence by refusing to send members to the Imperial Parliament at Vienna or admit any right in that Parliament to legislate for her.' A year later Griffith founded *Sinn Fein* — Ourselves Alone, an organization dedicated to an Ireland independent of the United Kingdom, even if, in his view, it would still accept the British monarch, following the Dual Monarchy concept of the Habsburgs. Fourteen years later, as a Sinn Fein member of the British Parliament, he was to be one of the leaders of the party's refusal to sit any longer in the parliament in London, seeking instead to establish its own Irish parliament in Dublin.

The death tolls from fire and disease in 1904 continued to catch the newspaper headlines alongside the political dramas as they had done in previous years. Several hundred Americans were killed when fire broke out on an excursion steamer sailing up the East River at New York. Carrying more than a thousand passengers, it had caught fire, and was well ablaze before it could be run ashore.

In British India, the incidents of plague, which each year diminished during the hot months, rose again with the beginning of the cold weather. During 1904 there were more deaths than in any previous year since the outbreak had begun at the start of the century; more than a million Indians died of plague that year. That year the disease also entered the cities, with 13,000 deaths in Bombay and nearly five thousand in Calcutta. Most of the deaths were in the rural areas of the provinces of Bombay and the Punjab. Because of peasant resistance to inoculation, the government had suspended all attempts to carry it out by compulsion. Of the precisely calculated total of 1,029,607 plague deaths in 1904, five were Europeans.

Politically, the Indian National Congress was searching for a means of challenging British rule. From South Africa, where his work on behalf of Indian rights was tireless, a young Indian lawyer, M.K. Gandhi sent advice as to the best method. It was, he believed, the method he was using in South Africa to obtain his political aims: non-cooperation, peaceful but all-embracing protest. 'It is the only weapon,' he wrote to a friend, 'that is suited to the genius of our people and our land, which is the nursery of the most ancient religions and has very little to learn from modern civilization — a civilization based on violence of the blackest type, largely a negation of the Divine in man, and which is rushing headlong to its own ruin.'

The efforts of Western civilization to exclude other influences was seen in 1904 in a United States government decision, through an amendment to the Exclusion Acts of the previous century, to prevent the immigration of Chinese into the United States, and to discriminate against Chinese immigrants already in the country. This led to an immediate reaction inside China, where American goods were boycotted by traders and merchants, and there were attacks on foreign property in several Chinese cities.

China was also on the verge of an internal transformation. A Chinese revolutionary, Sun Yat-sen, who had trained as a doctor in both Hawaii and Hong Kong, pressed, through his Society for the Revival of China, for an end to the imperial dynasty, and the 'regeneration' of China. In 1904 he and his followers published a document entitled 'Summary of the Revolution'. It was a far-ranging call, strongly influenced by European socialist doctrines:

The Revolution having been inaugurated by the people, it shall be democratic, i.e., all citizens shall possess equal rights. A President shall be elected by a Congress. Committees, composed of representatives chosen by the people, shall prepare and discuss the Constitution of the Chinese Republic. When once the Constitution has been authorized, it shall be honoured and obeyed by every citizen. Anyone attempting to restore the monarchy shall be outlawed.

All citizens shall share equally in the advantages of civilization. Land may possibly rise in value owing to social and economic changes. Experts shall therefore determine its price, which shall belong to the owner. After the inauguration of the Republic, any additional increment shall belong to the State, in order that the people may share in it. This shall be the basis of the socialistic government, which shall ensure to every citizen the wherewithal to live.

Monopolists, being a grave menace to the life of the people, shall be outlawed.

This was a revolutionary manifesto for a country where such ideals would have to be fought for in the streets and on the battlefields.

In Australia, however, a turning point in the emergence of organized labour came without violence in 1904, when John Christian Watson became Prime Minister. He was the first representative of a Labour Party to become the head of a government, only thirteen years after the foundation of the Australian Labour Party.

*   *   *

The third modern Olympic Games were held that year in St Louis, Missouri. The United States won eighty gold medals – by far the largest number – with the next largest, five each, going to Germany and Cuba, and four to Canada.

Several of the inventions of 1904 were to have a permanent place in the coming century. Among them were King C. Gillette's safety razor and Thomas Sullivan's tea bag. At the World Fair held in St Louis at the same time as the Olympics, German immigrants produced two items of food that, as a result of the Games, were popularized throughout the world: the ice cream cone and the hamburger.

CHAPTER SIX

1905

On 1 January 1905 the Russian forces, besieged by the Japanese in Port Arthur by land and sea, offered to negotiate terms of surrender. Their surrender was accepted by the Japanese on the following day. A vast quantity of military supplies was thus acquired by the Japanese, including 546 artillery pieces and 35,000 rifles, as well as 4 battleships, 2 cruisers, and 14 gunboats and torpedo boats. The Russian public was devastated that their vast empire should be so savagely mauled by such a small island and hitherto insignificant Power. The Japanese public was jubilant at having won such a decisive victory over a European Power. The European Powers were also impressed; the Kaiser, in a gesture of imperial and magnanimous impartiality, conferred on both the Russian commander of Port Arthur, General Stössel, and on the Japanese victor, General Nogi, the highest German award for bravery, the Pour le Mérite. But Russia was still at war, her troops fighting against the Japanese in Manchuria, and her leaders confident that the transfer of the Russian Baltic Fleet to the Far East would turn the balance of the war in Russia's favour.

In St Petersburg, long before news of the defeat at Port Arthur, tensions had been building up as a result of the dismissal on 20 December 1904 of four workers from the Putilov factory, the largest of all the factories in the capital. When the Putilov workers went on strike they were supported by those in dozens of other enterprises. On January 7 more than 80,000 workers were on strike in St Petersburg; as a result there was no electricity in the capital, and no newspapers. A mass demonstration was planned, to demand increased wages and the institution of liberal reforms. On January 8, the day before the demonstration was due to take place, its leader, Father Gapon, informed the Tsar that it would be peaceful, and that a petition would be presented which it was hoped the Tsar would receive in person, as the demonstrators had no faith in his ministers. But in another petition to the Tsar that day, sent to his palace at Tsarskoe Selo, outside St Petersburg

– which he had no intention of leaving – the peasant and working-class demonstrators warned that they had reached 'that terrible moment when death is to be preferred to the continuance of intolerable suffering'.

'A more perfect and lovely day never dawned,' *The Times* correspondent telegraphed from St Petersburg on January 9. 'There were five degrees of frost. The air was crisp and invigorating and the sky almost cloudless.' That Sunday, Father Gapon – whom the Tsar described in his diary as 'some kind of priest-socialist' – brought many thousands of unarmed men, women and children into the streets, following him towards the centre of the city singing hymns, and carrying crosses and religious banners. 'St Petersburg awoke this morning to find itself in a state of siege,' *The Times* correspondent wrote.

As Father Gapon led his flock to the approaches of the Winter Palace, Cossack troops tried to drive them away with their whips, but the crowd was too large, and too determined to present its grievances at the palace, to be whipped back. The Cossacks then used their rifles and their swords. It was eleven in the morning. The bridges linking the Putilov armaments factory with the city were then sealed off by police to prevent striking workers from crossing into the centre of the city. But the workmen were determined to join the crowd seeking to reach the Winter Palace. *The Times* correspondent was an eye-witness to what followed:

> The Cossacks at first used their knouts, then the flat of their sabres, and finally they fired.
>
> The strikers in the front ranks fell on their knees and implored the Cossacks to let them pass, protesting that they had no hostile intentions. They refused, however, to be intimidated by blank cartridges, and orders were given to load with ball.
>
> The passions of the mob broke loose like a bursting dam. The people, seeing the dead and dying carried away in all directions, the snow on the streets and pavements soaked with blood, cried aloud for vengeance.
>
> Meanwhile, the situation at the Palace was becoming momentarily worse. The troops were reported to be unable to control the vast masses which were constantly surging forward. Reinforcements were sent, and at 2 o'clock here also the order was given to fire.
>
> Men, women, and children fell at each volley, and were carried away in ambulances, sledges, and carts. It was no longer a workman's question. The indignation and fury of every class were aroused. At the moment of writing, firing is going on in every quarter of the city.

Several officers have been severely injured on the Nevsky Prospect. Their swords were taken from them and their epaulettes torn off. Panic and consternation reign supreme. The troops are apparently reckless, firing right and left, with or without reason. The rioters continue to appeal to them, saying 'You are Russians! Why play the part of bloodthirsty butchers?'

As the killed and wounded are borne away, men reverently raise their caps and many shout 'Hurrah! Well done!' in honour of those stricken down.

Hundreds of men, women and children lay bleeding on the cobblestones. When the fighting ended, as many as two hundred demonstrators lay dead.

Incensed by the violence against their fellow demonstrators, others tore up the cobblestones and began stoning the Cossacks. Knives and carpenters' tools were taken from shops, and barricades put up to prevent the Cossacks from riding down the streets seeking victims. An elderly general, who had ventured out to see what was happening, was trampled to death by the crowd.

On the following day, in support of those who had marched and been shot down, strikes took place all over Russia. One of Russia's most popular writers, Maxim Gorky, was arrested for expressing sympathy with the marchers. A government appeal for a return to work was in vain. During a widespread strike and mass demonstrations in Riga on January 13, troops charged the demonstrators, and seventy were killed. In Warsaw, on the following day, strikers marched through the streets looting and burning shops as they went. Russian troops fired on them, and ninety-three were killed. In Odessa, the strikers were joined by the crew of the battleship *Potemkin*. In the fighting in the port city, as many as two thousand demonstrators were killed.

To a deputation of working men whom he received at Tsarskoe Selo on February 1, the Tsar took an uncompromising attitude and said that for anyone to come to him 'as a rebel mob to declare their wants is a crime'. In Lodz, the industrial city known as the Polish Manchester, 100,000 workers went on strike. As in Warsaw, these were not Polish nationalists, who, for the moment at least, remained aloof from the conflict, but socialist revolutionaries, determined to use the opportunity of the growing strike movement to hasten the overthrow of Tsardom. In response, the whole of Russian Poland was put under a state of siege.

On February 6 the Tsar received the President of the Moscow Regional Assembly, Prince Troubetskoi, who explained to him that what was taking place in Russia was not a mere disturbance, but a revolution. As the strikes spread throughout the Empire, news came that as far east as Irkutsk, in Siberia, workers had marched in sympathy with the strikers elsewhere. On February 17 the Tsar's uncle, Grand Duke Serge, who until a few weeks earlier had been Governor of Moscow, and noted for his harshness towards any form of dissent, was assassinated; a bomb was thrown under his carriage. In Finland, as a gesture of hatred towards Russian rule, a former university student assassinated the Procurator of the Finnish Senate.

Despite the revolutionary turmoil at home, and despite the military setback of the loss of Port Arthur, Russian troops continued to fight with great tenacity against the Japanese in Manchuria. But in every confrontation their casualties were much higher than those of the Japanese. On March 9, after a three-week intensive battle, the Russian army was forced to abandon Mukden, the principal town in southern Manchuria. During those three weeks, 27,700 Russian soldiers had been killed.

Russia's one hope that the grim tide of war could be reversed lay with the Baltic Fleet, which, having left the Baltic port of Libau in mid-October 1904, and after its bizarre engagement six days later with a British fishing fleet in the North Sea, had continued its long, slow voyage towards the Far East. It was on April 3, when it reached Madagascar, in the Indian Ocean, that it learned of the fall of Port Arthur. Admiral Rozhdestvensky ordered his ships to continue eastward, maintaining the strictest secrecy. On April 11 his ships were sighted off Singapore, and two days later, despite French indignation at an 'abuse of neutral ports', they anchored in Camranh Bay in French Indo-China. There, the Admiral waited a month in order to be joined by more ships of the Third Baltic Squadron.

In the third week of May, Admiral Rozhdestvensky left the security of Camranh Bay and steamed northward along the Chinese coast towards Korea. On May 27 he reached the Tsushima Strait, the waterway between Korea and Japan. That morning, after Japanese scouting vessels signalled to Admiral Togo that the Russians were drawing near, Togo ordered his fleet to steam towards the Russians. It was shortly after midday that the two fleets came within sight of each other.

Within three-quarters of an hour of intense naval bombardment the Battle of Tsushima was decided. All eight Russian battleships were put out of action by shell and torpedo fire, as were seven of the twelve Russian cruisers and six of the nine destroyers. As the surviving Russian warships turned away, they were at once pursued. Of the thirty-six Russian vessels that had gone into action, twenty-two were sunk, six captured, and six later interned in the neutral ports to which they managed to escape. Only two reached Vladivostok.

The Battle of Tsushima sealed the fate of the Russian war effort. Admiral Togo was hailed in one Canadian newspaper as 'the Nelson of the Orient'. It was reported from Warsaw that news of the Russian defeat 'has been received with ill-concealed joy here, the Poles anticipating that it will result in their obtaining some concessions, while a Russian victory would have had precisely the opposite effect.' *The Times* correspondent in St Petersburg reported widespread hopes even among the Russians whose navy had been struck down:

> To the great majority of Russians, whether they belong to the cultured classes or to the villages, Rozhdestvensky's overthrow bodes nothing but good in its promise of peace and its assurance of reform. Such is the sad but sober truth.
>
> Russia has become a vast object lesson in the evils of government by irresponsible bureaucrats and police officials, thanks to which initiative and enterprise have been systematically eradicated from the nation. The police, who are able to promote massacres of Jews and Armenians, as in Zhitomir and Erivan, have proved quite incapable of introducing good government, but there is excellent promise for Russia's future in the outspokenness and sincerity displayed by the majority of the Press revelations daily published about the Far Eastern adventure.
>
> The fearless criticism of the evils of the present administration gives an earnest of the revival of the national energies, which, as soon as the promises of sound government are realized, will enable Russia quickly to recover from her present distress and to assume her rightful place among the great nations of the world.

The Japanese victory gave pleasure to many of those who were the enemies of great empires. Sixteen-year-old Jawaharlal Nehru, on the last lap of a journey from India to London, recalled 'reading in the train from Dover of the great Japanese sea victory at Tsushima. I was in high good humour. The next day happened to be Derby Day and we went to see the race.'

*   *   *

On land, the Japanese continued to advance, threatening the Russian positions in Korea, and even Vladivostok. In a daring move, Japanese troops landed on Russian soil for the first time in the war, occupying the island of Sakhalin.

As Russia's humiliation intensified, the United States took an initiative that was to transform America's standing and enhance her status in the rest of the world. At the invitation of President Roosevelt, both Russia and Japan were invited to lay down their arms and to open negotiations, and to do so in the United States. Both sides accepted, and Portsmouth, a coastal town in New Hampshire, was chosen for the meetings. It was the first time in the history of the United States that a peace conference to which she was not a direct party was held on American soil.

On reaching the United States, the two delegations were received separately by Roosevelt on board the government yacht *Mayflower*. He then introduced each delegation to the other, entertained them to lunch, and drank to the prosperity of both nations, and to the conclusion of a 'just and lasting peace' between them. He wanted there to be no sense of victor and vanquished, no humiliation of Russia for the terrible defeat she had suffered.

After less than three weeks of negotiations, the Treaty of Portsmouth was signed on 29 August 1905. A war in which 58,000 Japanese and 120,000 Russian soldiers had been killed in action was over. Korea was recognized as a Japanese dependency, the first successful assertion of Japanese control on the mainland of Asia. The Russian lease over Port Arthur was also ceded to Japan. The southern half of the Russian island of Sakhalin was annexed by Japan. Both warring states agreed to evacuate Manchuria, which was returned to Chinese sovereignty.

The Japanese public were discontented by several aspects of the peace treaty. There was anger that President Roosevelt had prevailed upon the Japanese negotiators to give up Japan's claim for a financial indemnity, to cover the cost of the war. There was also anger that Japan had given up the northern part of Sakhalin, which her troops had captured in the final phase of the war. Not only disappointment, but humiliation, was the emotion generated by the signing of the treaty that to the outside world represented the triumph of Japan, and her emergence as a Power.

Japanese moderation during the diplomatic negotiations, a moderation which so impressed the other Powers, distressed the Japanese people. Riots broke out in several cities, including Tokyo and Osaka. When the Minister of the Interior tried to prevent a public demonstration in Tokyo, he was forced to resign for having challenged public unease. In an extraordinary Japanese gesture of protest at the treaty, the warship that had carried Admiral Togo's flag to victory was set on fire in Tokyo harbour, and sank. When a few weeks later fire also destroyed an army storehouse in Hiroshima, it was assumed that this too was the work of opponents of the treaty.

An added benefit for Japan of the victory over Russia was the signing of a Treaty of Alliance with Britain. This transformed the Anglo-Japanese agreement reached three years earlier into a full commitment by each power to come to the aid of the other in the event of attack. This effectively insured Japan against any Russian attempt to regain what had been lost. The Anglo-Japanese Treaty also gave British recognition to Japan's new status in Korea. For her part, Britain, whose Conservative government was deeply suspicious of Russian intentions against the British Empire, felt that there could now be no Russian attempt to seek naval domination in the Pacific, or to challenge Britain's interests on the China coast.

Japan made every effort to follow up her victory over Russia by consolidating her military and naval strength. With the completion that year of a new dock at Nagasaki, the building of a new naval depot by British engineers at Yokosuka, and a programme of increased naval construction – including the construction of a battleship of 20,000 tons – it was clear that Japan would quickly become the naval power most to be reckoned with in the Pacific.

In the final months of the Russian war against Japan, strikes, riots and violence had spread throughout Russia. In many rural areas, peasants murdered landlords and looted and burned houses, factories and sugar refineries. In March a state of siege was again declared throughout the Polish provinces. In April, in St Petersburg, a meeting of lawyers and professors from all over Russia called for a democratic constitution, based on universal suffrage and secret ballot. Their call was widely supported by the many unions that had sprung up, including those of medical personnel, engineers and technicians, agronomists, journalists, writers and school teachers. But in a further use of autocratic powers, the government forbade all public discussion of the lawyers' and professors' call.

The powers of the autocracy to stifle debate were under daily challenge. On May 8 a congress of fourteen unions, meeting in Moscow, went so far as to advocate the use of a general strike throughout Russia to destroy the autocracy. That month, violence flared again in Russia's Polish provinces, when an unarmed procession, mostly of working men, was unexpectedly attacked by Russian troops. Many marchers were killed. In the Polish town of Kalish, troops burst into a church where the congregation was singing Polish patriotic songs, and ordered them to disperse. In the ensuing fracas, a woman was killed. In Lodz, Cossack troops attacked a crowd which was singing patriotic songs in front of a church.

Every part of the Russian Empire was caught up in the challenge to Tsarist authority. In Finland, resolutions were passed demanding the abolition of the dictatorship and censorship, the restoration of press freedom, and the removal of all Russian police forces. In the Baltic provinces, municipal buildings were attacked and portraits of the Tsar destroyed. On August 19, realizing that he could no longer resist the pressures of more than seven months of agitation and near-anarchy, the Tsar announced that, 'while preserving the fundamental law regarding the autocratic power' he had decided 'to summon elected representatives from the whole of Russia to take a constant and active part in the elaboration of laws.'

The new body would be called the State Council (in Russian, *Gosudarstvennaya Duma*), known simply as the Duma. It would be responsible 'for the preliminary study and discussion of legislative proposals'. These proposals, when decided upon, would be 'submitted to the supreme autocratic authority'. Members of the Duma would be elected by electoral colleges chosen from three classes: landowners, townsmen and peasants. The voting would be secret.

The promise of an elected assembly was a massive concession for the Tsar, but it was a grave disappointment for those who wanted a democratic assembly with legislative powers, independent of the Tsar's authority. Not only the Duma's authority, but the franchise of the voters, was limited: owners of property could vote, as could proprietors of industrial establishments, and also peasants. But working men and the professional classes, whose part in the demands for reform had been so strong, were both excluded. In St Petersburg, with a population of 1.5 million, there would only be 9500 voters. In addition, the Tsar could dissolve the Duma when he chose – nor were the public to be admitted to its sessions.

Within the Russian Empire, the fires of dissent that had been lit at the beginning of the year continued to smoulder and burst into flame. In Armenia, where a national uprising against Russian rule had been smouldering for most of the year, the conflict was made all the more bloody when, in September, the Tatars, a Muslim nationality, attacked Christian Armenian homes in Baku, Tiflis and Erivan. Fearing Armenian national ambitions, and noting that the Armenians had been joined in their protest in Baku by Russian revolutionaries, the Tsarist troops took the side of the Tatars. For their part, the Tatars raised the green banner of Islam and proclaimed a Holy War against the Armenians. Thousands of Armenians were massacred, and dozens of Armenian villages destroyed, and the oil wells of Baku set on fire.

After a month of mass killings, a conference of leading Armenians and Tatars, meeting in Baku, agreed to end the fighting, and accepted responsibility for the damage done by each side. Shops and homes that had been destroyed or damaged would be restored. Reparations would be paid to the families of those killed and injured. An arbitration court, consisting of five Armenians and five Tatars, would decide on the details of the agreement, the fulfilment of which was guaranteed by ten Armenian and ten Muslim millionaires. Unfortunately for the well-being of both peoples, the agreement broke down before the end of the year, and the fighting began again.

In the main cities of Russia, the Tsar's promise of a Duma had failed to curb the unrest, and in October there were strikes in both Moscow and St Petersburg, and troops again clashed with the strikers. On October 16, in the Estonian capital, Reval (now Tallinn), Russian troops opened fire on a mass meeting of Estonians, killing 150 of them. That month, while pleading the cause of freedom of speech at the Ministry of Public Instruction, Prince Trubetskoy died of a heart attack. His funeral was the scene of a massive public demonstration in favour of a legislative assembly elected by universal suffrage.

The revolutionary parties continued to believe that the autocracy could be brought to its knees and destroyed by forcing the country to a standstill. On October 26 a railway strike was declared throughout the empire, paralysing the ability of Russia to maintain trade or order. The constitutional reform parties believed that only drastic action could force the Tsar to go beyond a Duma to a truly democratic constituency assembly. Chemists closed their shops and announced that they would not prepare any more medicines until the autocracy was ended. A series of decrees forbidding open air public meetings without permission was ignored. In all large towns, gas and electricity supplies were cut off.

The Tsar appeared to bow to the storm, and on October 30 announced that the authority of the Duma would be increased, and that no law could come into force without its approval. As the Duma elections had not yet taken place, and it was not scheduled to meet for at least three months, this promise failed to calm the agitation in the streets, and a general strike persisted throughout the empire. Of fifty-two Justices of the Peace responsible for the administration of justice in St Petersburg, all but two joined the strikers. Commerce and administration were both at a halt. In Finland, the Russian police went on strike and the Russian troops pledged not to fire unless they were attacked.

In Warsaw, stirring speeches were delivered in favour of Polish independence; the scene of this demonstration was the steps of the Mickiewicz monument, the symbol of Polish patriotic endeavour. For many hours the crowd sang national hymns and anthems. Then, towards evening, Cossack troops attacked and several demonstrators were killed.

Throughout southern Russia there was again an upsurge of anti-Jewish feeling, as once more the Jews were used as a scapegoat for the failures of the regime. Jewish homes and shops were looted, and hundreds of Jews were tortured and mutilated by the mob. The initiative for these attacks had come from provincial governors who hoped to use anti-Jewish sentiment as a means of bolstering support for the regime. Several provincial governors were later removed from their positions for having instigated the atrocities.

In November it became an open question as to whether the Tsar would accede to the demands of the Liberals for constitutional reform, or be forced aside altogether by the more revolutionary parties. Political, social and economic discontent were merging into a single explosive mixture. An amnesty, declared by the Tsar on November 3, led to the release of many political prisoners and those imprisoned for their part in earlier strikes, but the most prominent liberal prisoners remained in prison, or were exiled to Siberia. On November 9 the sailors and artillerymen at the Kronstadt naval base, guarding the sea route to St Petersburg, mutinied. Troops were sent in to suppress the mutiny, but were only able to do so after severe fighting. An appeal on November 16 for workers to end the general strike was ignored. In Vladivostok, soldiers in the reserve mutinied, rampaging through the town, looting and setting ships and homes on fire. With the population desperate to be able to eat and travel, the general strike collapsed under popular pressure, but the unrest continued. On November 25 there was a revolt of soldiers, sailors and workmen in the Crimean port of Sebastopol. Twenty thousand loyal troops had to be sent to crush it. The battleship *Potemkin*, under the control of its crew, bombarded government buildings in Odessa and other Black Sea ports with its powerful naval guns.

The Tsar had decided on his course: a deputation of landlords urging him to reaffirm the principles of autocracy was graciously received. The earlier harsh restrictions on press freedom were reimposed. New Governors-General were appointed for the Baltic provinces and the Caucasus, with the widest ranging authority to repress all agitation. The unrest continued, however, with every region of the empire in turmoil. In Warsaw, a demonstration by more than four hundred Roman Catholic clergymen demanded autonomy for Poland, a separate Polish parliament, and the restoration of the Polish language in all government business.

The Tsar responded to the continuing demonstrations, and to a strike of postmen and telegraphists throughout the empire, by a new scale of penalties for those who incited people to strike. In response, the revolutionaries urged the public not to pay taxes, and to call on the soldiers to mutiny.

On December 21 revolution broke out in Moscow. The revolutionaries seized several railway stations, and set up barricades to prevent the troops who held the centre of the city from attacking them, or from bringing in reinforcements. Councils of Workers' Deputies, many of them under Bolshevik control, were set up throughout the city, to direct the revolutionary effort. But government troops, remaining loyal to the Tsar, retained control of one of the railway stations, Nikolaevsky Station, and of several fortified positions in the areas held by the revolutionaries, and were able to advance, bombarding revolutionary positions with artillery.

The reports published in Western Europe on the following day were fragmented but graphic, typified by the main news reports in *The Times*:

Normal life has ceased as though by magic. The stopping of the electric trams was the first sign that a strike had begun, so far as the general public was concerned. The *employés* of the Municipality and the *Zemstvo* left their offices almost simultaneously.

On the railways work was stopped on the stroke of noon. The principal factories followed suit, and within a few minutes 50,000 men were idle. All the printing works are closed, and no newspapers are expected to appear tomorrow.

Many of the strike leaders and workmen's delegates were arrested last night.

And a few hours later:

> The town is in darkness. The theatres and clubs are closed. The post office
> continued working until dusk, but the telegraph clerks decided to join
> the strike.
>
> A large number of shops put their shutters up at noon, and others closed
> early in the evening, owing to the want of light. The Cossacks are disper-
> sing gatherings of strikers. The organ of the proletariat is being printed
> at the Sitine works, where the *Russkoe Slovo* was published, and contains
> a violent appeal to the people to organize an armed revolution.
>
> The Union of Engineers has joined the strike. The Moscow representa-
> tives of the Union of Unions resolved to follow suit.
>
> The troops are confined to barracks and are ready for all emergencies.
> Cavalry and quick-firers are stationed in the riding school, and the town
> is patrolled by Dragoons and Cossacks.

The fighting in Moscow continued for ten days. A telegraphic report sent
to *The Times* on December 28 stated: 'A Cossack officer yesterday beheaded
a boy on the mere suspicion that he was carrying weapons. Two surgeons
were killed by the troops while tending the wounded.' That day 300 armed
revolutionaries forced their way into the house of the Chief of the Secret
Police, and killed him. But the authorities were gaining the upper hand;
that same day the Tsarist police arrested all the members of the Social
Revolutionary Committee in the city. An attack on the police barracks was
beaten off. When the fighting in Moscow ended, more than a thousand
revolutionaries had been killed.

On December 26, while fighting was still intense in Moscow, the Tsar had
issued a decree considerably widening the numbers who could vote for the
Duma. Among the new voters would be house owners, tradesmen paying
taxes, civil servants and railway employees. This concession calmed a considerable amount of liberal unease. At the same time, the Tsar ordered the
elections for the Duma to go ahead without delay.

Elsewhere in the empire, men and women were inspired by the revolution
in Moscow to believe that the whole edifice of autocracy could be overthrown.
In the Polish provinces there was fighting in Warsaw, Lodz and Lublin. In
the Baltic provinces the revolutionaries fought to seize power in Riga. East

of Moscow there were armed uprisings in Voronezh, Perm and Nizhni Novgorod. In the ironworks at Nizhni Novgorod, *The Times* reported on December 28, 'thousands of armed workmen barricaded themselves inside and offered a desperate resistance. Artillery shelled the works and set them on fire. The casualties are said to be very heavy.' In southern Russia, attempts were made to take over Ekaterinoslav. In the Caucasus, the towns of Mineraliye Vody and Piatygorsk saw revolutionary outbreaks. On the Black Sea shore, attempts were made to take over the ports of Novorossisk, Batum and Odessa. In Odessa, after the declaration of martial law, Cossack troops cleared the whole centre of the city, and an emergency military government was set up, headed by General Karangozov, described by *The Times* as 'a man of merciless habit'.

In Estonia, workers roamed through the countryside for several weeks, looting and burning manor houses until Russian troops, formed into 'punitive patrols', hunted them down. Several hundred Estonian workers were killed by the patrols. Five hundred more, arrested and courtmartialled, were then executed. Hundreds more were exiled to Siberia.

While the autocratic ruler of the Russian Empire was confronting revolution, the British Empire was confronted with a soul-searching moment in 1905, when an enquiry set up by the government of Western Australia revealed that the treatment of Aborigines in the northern part of the State had been 'of the utmost severity'. Those Aborigines who had been charged with crimes, and even female witnesses to the alleged crimes, were being chained together in gangs, and subjected to cruel and brutal treatment. The crime involved was the killing of the cattle of white settlers, who had themselves killed off the kangaroos on which the Aborigines lived, in order to rear cattle and sheep. The cattle killing had been an attempt by the Aborigines to avoid starvation. Public opinion in Britain was shocked by the severity and blatant racism of the punishments.

In the British parliament, where the Liberal opposition demanded impartial justice among colonial peoples, there was a call on May 9 for the 'gross disabilities' under which the Aborigines suffered to be removed for all time. On the following day the Archbishop of Canterbury told the House of Lords that the conditions under which the Aborigines had been put to work 'had many of the characteristics of slavery'. As to what had occurred during the criminal investigation to the women taken not as culprits but as witnesses 'was a part of the story on which he desired not to dwell'. A week later, it was the conditions under which Chinese labourers were working in the mines in South Africa that was cause for British parliamentary concern. These labourers had been brought from China under contracts which made their condition of work harsh in the extreme.

In German South West Africa the rebellion of the Herero and Witboi tribesmen continued. To the surprise of the other imperial Powers, the Germans were unable to crush the rebellion swiftly. Surprise turned to indignation when details emerged of the harsh, even brutal nature of German punitive actions against the Hereros and Witboi, who continually evaded defeat by avoiding direct confrontation. The German commander in the colony, General von Trotha, in offering a cash reward for anyone bringing in the Herero chiefs, alive or dead, threatened the whole tribe with 'extermination' if it did not surrender. By the beginning of 1905, more than ten thousand German troops were engaged in trying to put down the rebellion. There was exasperation in the German parliament when it was announced that the cost of the expedition thus far amounted to £1000 per head of the German population of the colony, but that the charge would have to be borne by the German tax-paying population at home.

The Herero leader, Morenga, having offered in vain to open negotiations with the Germans – as the Mullah had done successfully with the British and Italians a year earlier in Somaliland – attacked one of the main German army camps in South West Africa and overran it. He then challenged the Germans to a full-scale battle. When this took place, forty German soldiers were killed and much German military equipment, including a field gun, was captured.

More German troops were sent from Germany. In the fighting that winter, the Witboi chiefs surrendered. But the Hereros fought on. Against them, the Germans instituted the same policy that the British had used against the Boers, and that had been so denounced by Liberal opinion in Britain: concentration camps in which Herero women, children and old people were confined behind barbed wire, to try to force their menfolk warriors to surrender. What the colony needed, declared the newly appointed governor, Herr von Lindequist, was that German South West Africa should be reconstructed in such a way that it would become 'a stronghold of the German race, to which the Germans throughout southern Africa might look up.'

Elsewhere in Germany's African possessions, other rebellions broke out towards the end of 1905. In German East Africa the start of the revolt was the murder of a German bishop and four missionaries and nuns in Dar es Salaam. In the interior of the colony, two tribes rose in revolt, the Wangoni and the Wahebe. Although German officers, with black Askari troops, defeated the rebels in a number of engagements, they were unable to assert any control over vast areas. The tribal grievance gained some sympathy among the essentially anti-imperialist deputies in the German parliament when it was revealed that the missionaries had been employing tribal labour without payment.

When further complaints reached Berlin from the tribes in the German Cameroons, that similar exploitation of native labourers was taking place, many parliamentarians protested that the whole imperial policy was rotten, and that from both a military and financial standpoint the German colonies were the weak point in the German Empire. The statistic used to illustrate this was that while Germany's total trade with all its colonies had amounted in the previous year to £2,313,600, German expenditure on the colonies in that same period had been £6,352,600.

In the British Empire there was renewed violence on the North West Frontier of India, where the Mahsuds, a Muslim tribe, were exhorted by their religious leader, Mullah Powindah, to strike at the representatives of imperial rule wherever they could. Several British officers were killed, by gun and bayonet, in attacks by individual Mahsuds, as were several Indian soldiers serving in British Indian units.

In Morocco, where the previous year France had secured almost a free hand as a result of agreement with Britain, the Sultan's troops were fighting against a rival claimant to the throne. They were only saved from defeat by the timely arrival of a French military force. The disappointed claimant, escaping capture, turned his military powers against a fellow tribal leader who had failed to support him in his claim.

The Sultan, not perhaps as grateful as he might have been for the French intervention, declined to accept various reform measures pressed on him by the French. The German Kaiser, who on March 21 made a two-hour courtesy call to Tangier – landing from the ship in which he was cruising in the Mediterranean – annoyed the French by expressing his doubt as to the wisdom of pressing for European-style measures which might alienate Muslim feelings. He also angered the French by encouraging the Sultan to call for a conference of the Powers to decide what reforms should be introduced. German interference was so resented in the French parliament that when the French Prime Minister adopted a policy of not irritating Germany, he was forced from office.

The Kaiser's intervention in Moroccan affairs, although limited to a brief visit and verbal encouragement for the Sultan, raised in French minds the possibility of war with Germany. In the discussions at innumerable dinner tables in Paris, it was assumed that if the Germans were to make an unprovoked attack on France, Britain would come to France's aid. This was a false belief, however. The new Liberal government in Britain (from December 1905) was emphatic that the 1904 arrangement with France was a settlement of differences, not an alliance, and certainly not a military commitment. There was admiration among British Liberals for the social reform aspects of German life, with its more advanced system of national insurance; and there was still a determination not to be drawn into European conflicts.

There was another agreement, signed in 1905, that offered the prospect of settling disputes by negotiation rather than by war. For some years the people of Norway had been agitated by having to live as a national entity under the crown of Sweden. Jealous of their national territory, they had built a series of defence works along the Swedish border, covering what they conceived to be the four main possible routes of a Swedish invasion. The Swedes demanded the dismantling of these frontier posts. The Norwegians refused, and there was talk of war. Negotiations were begun, and a peaceful solution was found – the establishment of a demilitarized zone between the two countries. The Karlstad Convention, signed at Stockholm on October 26, created a demilitarized zone which extended for 200 miles, at an average depth of ten miles. It became a model to be followed, even in the final third of the century.[1]

Austria-Hungary faced a new complexity in 1905, when the three million Roumanians living in Transylvania decided to form their own political party, with strong national aspirations. Their complaint was the growing dominance of Hungarians (Magyars) and the Hungarian language throughout the Kingdom of Hungary, where they feared that their own identity was not adequately respected or protected.

In elections that were held in Hungary, the largest single group was that of the Hungarian independence party. This was a blow not only to the Roumanians, who had hoped for some greater recognition of their interests,

[1] After the October 1973 war in the Middle East, the United States Secretary of State, Henry Kissinger, negotiated a demilitarized zone between Israel and Syria which is still effective at the time of writing (1997), almost a quarter of a century later.

but to the government in Budapest, which feared any conflict with Austria. Given the election results, the Emperor had no choice but to ask the leader of the Hungarian independence party for his thoughts on how to resolve the parliamentary crisis. But no satisfactory agreement was reached as to a government that would be acceptable to the Hungarians, and in the ensuing crisis, a movement began for the complete separation of Hungary from Austria. This movement united the non-independence parties, who feared a collapse of economic prosperity if the two halves of the empire were to separate. A further demand for universal suffrage also grew, culminating in a mass Socialist demonstration in Budapest on September 15. The Emperor was indignant and prorogued the Hungarian parliament.

In the Austrian parliament, the defiance of the Hungarians provoked a counter-reaction, with demands from the Pan-German members for complete separation from Hungary, and for economic union with the German Empire.

The contrast between events in Russia and those in Austria-Hungary could not have been more marked. As part of the Hungarian demand for universal suffrage, Austrian Socialists united with their brethren in Budapest, and on November 28 a demonstration of working men, marching with red banners, assembled in front of the Austrian parliament building while parliament was in session. Inside, the Austrian Prime Minister, Baron Gautsch, said that his government would introduce a franchise reform bill based on universal suffrage. The Hungarian Prime Minister, the Emperor's nominee, General Fejervary, made a similar statement in Budapest. Austria-Hungary remained intact, and unbloodied.

The plague that had taken so many lives in India each year since the beginning of the century took even more lives in 1905, when the British government announced that 1,125,652 plague deaths had been reported in the year ending in September 1905. Even while the plague deaths were mounting, an earthquake struck northern India, killing a further 20,000 Indians and fifty Europeans.

Initially rural, the plague was spreading in the cities of British India, with more than 15,000 deaths reported in Bombay. There was satisfaction among the British officials that in the two areas over which government was able to exercise the most effective medical control – the Indian army and the prisons – plague deaths were minimal: just over a hundred in the army, and twenty-three in the prisons. But the death of more than a million people in one year was a terrifying testament to the power of disease, and the inability of even the most beneficent rulers to control it.

The growing prosperity of the industrial nations, and the desire of those who were making the wealth to live in greater comfort, was reflected in 1905 by the purchase, in the United States, south of Kansas City, of land on which to build an exclusive residential district. Such districts quickly proliferated on the outskirts of most American cities. The era of the Country Club had begun. With the growth of wealth there came, for some, a sense of communal responsibility. The year 1905 saw the founding in the United States of the Rotary Club, whose members – businessmen and professionals – met regularly both for the pleasure of each other's company, and to do beneficial work in their local communities.

Also in the United States, in 1905, President Roosevelt established a forest service within the existing Department of Agriculture, to ensure the proper management and preservation of the nation's vast woodland resources. The founding of the Audubon Society that year signalled recognition of the need to protect birds in the wild. In parallel with the protection of nature came the continued expansion of industry: that same year saw the creation in Pennsylvania of Bethlehem Steel, a giant of steel production. In Gary, Indiana, the rival steel company, the US Steel Corporation, constructed a 'company town' which could house 200,000 workers in conditions of comparative comfort. In Britain, the continuing expansion of the motorcar industry was exemplified by the founding of the Austin Motor Company, and of the Automobile Association. Cars were to be made accessible not only to the rich, but to the middle classes. And motor omnibuses – the 'bus' of today's cities worldwide – opened their first regular service in London in 1905. The internal combustion engine, which a decade earlier had been a curiosity, was becoming an integral part of the life, work and leisure of the twentieth century.

CHAPTER SEVEN

1906

On 10 JANUARY 1906 one of Britain's most popular newspapers, the *Daily Mail*, coined a new word, 'suffragette'. It referred to those women who, in search of the vote for women in national elections – one such election had just taken place, with an entirely male electorate – were adopting increasingly outspoken, even violent, tactics. It seemed an anomaly to many in Britain, and not only to women, that, as the twentieth century moved forward, British women should not have the right to vote for those who were to govern the country. In New Zealand, women, including Maori women, had received the vote more than a decade earlier, in 1893. In Australia, women were entitled to vote in the federal elections from 1902; but, unlike the Maoris of New Zealand, the Aborigines of Australia were denied the vote until 1967.

In the United States, where an all-male franchise was still in place, there had for many years been a strong tradition of campaigning for votes for women. In the State of Wyoming, women got the vote as early as 1889, in Colorado in 1893 and in Indiana and Utah in 1896. The struggle in Britain, which had begun to focus on disrupting political meetings, was led by Emmeline Pankhurst and one of her three daughters, Christabel. They were prepared to go to prison for their beliefs, and did so.

The question of the electoral franchise, which it was hoped by reformers in Britain would be looked upon sympathetically by the Liberal government that had come to power in the last days of 1905, was momentarily over-shadowed in the public mind on February 10, when King Edward VII launched a new battleship at Portsmouth. This was the *Dreadnought*, the most powerful, and the fastest, warship then in existence. Ten naval attachés were present, those of Argentina, Austria-Hungary, Chile, France, Germany, Italy, Japan, Russia, Turkey and the United States. As the launching cere-mony reached its climax, *The Times* reported:

The mallet and chisel were handed to the King by Admiral Barry, and his Majesty without difficulty performed the operation of severing the cord. There was a blast from a bugle, followed by a great thud as the heavy weights released by the cutting of the cord fell and knocked away the dog-shores holding back the ship.

It was one of those moments when thousands of people thrill with a common emotion. At first there was expectancy and anxious tension, and then the joy of the realization of hope finding expression in a common voice.

On all sides the cry went up, 'She's moving!' Every eye was fixed intently on the great vessel, as slowly at first, but every instant increasing in speed, she glided over the well-greased ways with the ease and grace of a bird.

The new class of *Dreadnought* battleship constituted a revolution in naval armaments, starting a new race between the Powers that was to divert considerable financial resources from social policies. That money was needed to curb social unrest was evident in London two days after the launching of the new battleship, when 4000 unemployed men marched through the city to Hyde Park, to demand greater financial assistance from government, the right to undertake useful public work, and a restriction on the hours of labour in factories and mines. One of the contingents had marched from as far away as Liverpool.

Among the speakers was a representative of the Tailoresses' Society, who told the assembled crowd that as a woman, she knew it was women who suffered most from unemployment: 'It was the woman who had to face the landlord, to go to the pawnshop, and to look after the starving children. If the men allowed their little ones to suffer and did not alter the present state of things they were worse than dogs.' Later in the proceedings, another speaker said that if the present government did not produce 'something tangible' the unemployed would at their next demonstration 'march to the Park in greater numbers and with a determination not to be so peaceful as they were that day'.

The Liberal government was not unsympathetic to the demands of the poor and the unemployed. Only eight days after the demonstration in Hyde Park, a Royal Commission report recommended the passing of an act of Parliament declaring Trade Union strikes to be legal, and refusing to make it a legal offence to persuade others to strike. It also proposed that Trade Union funds should not be vulnerable to legal actions taken against a union by an employer. These proposals, unpalatable to the previous Conservative administration, were much to the liking of the new Liberal government, on which the hopes of many social reformers rested.

In Russia, the turmoil of 1905 continued into the new year, despite the hopes that the Duma, which was to be elected according to the wider franchise extracted from the Tsar, would be able to institute substantial reforms. The first Duma election was to be held on April 4. Before then, in a stern attempt to curb political dissent, the government closed down seventy-eight newspapers and arrested more than fifty editors. Thousands of political agitators were sentenced to exile in Siberia or imprisoned. Thousands more fled the country for a life of exile. When the Duma elections took place, 180 out of a total of 524 elected were the Constitutional Democrats, known as 'Kadets' (from the party's Russian initials, KD), committed to wide-ranging constitutional changes. Two hundred of those elected were peasants, 30 were Octobrists, and 18 were Social Democrats. The Octobrists were right-wing deputies who wanted no concessions from the Tsar beyond his manifesto of October 1905 which granted the Duma legislative powers.

The first session of the Duma opened in the Winter Palace in St Petersburg on May 10. The Tsar's speech of welcome left the delegates puzzled that no reference was made to constitutional reform, or to the opportunities opened up by the very existence of an elected assembly. Instead, the Tsar stressed that he hoped to 'bequeath to his son as his inheritance a firmly established, well-ordered and enlightened State'.

The deputies then transferred, through cheering crowds, to the Tauride Palace, where they were to hold all future meetings of the Duma, and where, in their first session that same day, they called for an amnesty for political prisoners – 'those who have sacrificed their freedom for their country' – and the replacement of the autocracy by a constitutional monarchy. The members of the Duma then called for elections to be held by universal suffrage, free education, the distribution of some private land to the peasants, and the abolition of all privileges based on class, religion or race.

The hopes of the Duma were not to be realized. The government took the view that an amnesty, the first of the Duma's requests, would encourage another revolution. As for the distribution of land to the peasants, the Prime Minister, Ivan Goremykin, declared such a prospect to be 'absolutely inadmissible'. When the Duma asked that the death penalty be rescinded for eight workmen who had been arrested during the riots in the Baltic provinces, its plea was ignored, and the men were shot.

More than a hundred members of the Duma, representatives of workers and peasants, were not content to let the Duma struggle with the Tsar and his ministers. They formed their own Labour party (Trudoviki) and issued a manifesto, declaring that the Duma was powerless, and demanding a constituent assembly based on universal suffrage – for women as well as for men.

On June 14, in Bialystok, in Russian Poland, peasants who were in the city during Corpus Christi were told, falsely, that Jews had fired on a Catholic procession, and that two priests and several children had been killed by a bomb. Printed appeals to the local population to 'exterminate' the Jewish population were distributed by the local Tsarist police in a successful attempt to incite the Polish population to violence, hoping to divert Polish discontent away from their Russian overlords and against the Jews. When the attack on the Jewish parts of town began, Russian troops stationed in Bialystok joined in the mob, firing into Jewish homes. A hundred Jews were killed, and many Jewish-owned shops destroyed. Families were murdered in their homes.

On the following day, in the Duma, the government was criticized for not having taken steps to prevent the massacre. But government ministers were in no frame of mind to take criticism from the Duma, and rejected all its proposals. When the Duma supported the abolition of capital punishment, the Minister of Justice replied that the death penalty was needed to check anarchy and revolution. When General Pavlov, the Military Procurator-General, entered the chamber – not long after he had personally replaced a sentence for hard labour by one of execution for a young man who had been captured during the riots in Warsaw – he was met with cries of 'Hangman', 'Murderer' and 'Cain', and walked out of the chamber without answering any of the questions that the members wished to put to him.

To the fury of the Duma, the Tsar announced that he was 'cruelly disappointed' that the representatives of the nation had 'strayed into spheres beyond their competence', and he then proceeded to declare the session of the Duma closed. The elected delegates, as well as the public, were outraged at this sudden, petulant and autocratic act, which so went against the concessionary spirit which had, or so it seemed, led to the setting up of the Duma in the first place. To prevent an outbreak of street violence, the Tsar ordered troops into the centre of St Petersburg and other towns. A number of deputies, incensed that their authority had been dissolved before they had been allowed to make any legislative progress, moved to the town of Vyborg, in Russian Finland. From there, they issued a manifesto protesting against the dissolution, and urging the population to give the government neither money nor soldiers. For its part, the government sent a circular to all provincial governors, instructing them that 'disturbances must be repressed, and revolutionary movements must be put down by all legal means'.

The provincial governors, the conduit throughout Russia for the Tsarist government's instructions, themselves often lacked the authority to carry out those instructions. In Odessa, after a Jewish deputation told the city's governor it had heard that anti-Jewish riots were imminent, the governor replied that, while he could certainly prevent, and would prevent, government troops from joining in the attacks, he would be unable to control either the Cossack troops, who had their own commanders, or the 'Black Hundreds' – armed gangs of anti-Semites – or the public at large. Shortly afterwards, Cossacks and Black Hundreds joined a mob that rampaged through the Jewish districts, killing, maiming and plundering. The army stood aside. A second pogrom against Jews took place in Siedlce, east of Warsaw, in September.

Individual murders were also frequent in Russia throughout the year. One of those killed was a leading member of the Duma, Professor Hertzenstein, one of the most outspoken critics of the government's refusal to improve the lot of the peasants. Hertzenstein, a Jew, was murdered while on holiday at Terioki, in Finland, apparently by a member of the Black Hundreds. The revolutionaries, who had been temporarily crushed by the destruction of their uprising in Moscow the previous December, emerged again by August 1906 as an active force. In Warsaw they assassinated several policemen and attacked a number of infantry patrols.

On August 25 an attempt was made by means of a bomb to kill the Prime Minister, Peter Stolypin, while he was at his summer residence; he escaped, but his two children were severely injured and thirty of his visitors were killed. Three of the four would-be assassins were also killed. On the following day General Minn, who had taken a lead in the suppression of the Moscow uprising, was assassinated. Many provincial governors and police chiefs were also killed that autumn. Field courts martial were established in many provinces, at which the trial of someone accused of revolutionary activity had to be held in secret, and could take no longer than eighteen hours; and where the sentence had to be carried out within twenty-four hours. During September and October, 300 people were shot or hanged by order of these courts martial.

While Russia remained an autocracy, the Tsar made concessions to Finland, whose parliamentary representation became thereby the most democratic in Europe. The franchise included universal suffrage, a secret ballot, and votes for all women over the age of twenty-four. The Finnish revolutionaries, supporters of Lenin and the Bolsheviks, were dismayed at this development, which undermined their own attempts to win Finland for the revolutionary cause. To advance their cause, they formed a 'Red Guard', under a Finnish revolutionary, Captain Kock, which supported a mutiny of Russian soldiers in the Sveaborg garrison, and declared a general strike. The Finnish 'Red Guard' was, however, opposed by a Finnish 'White Guard' which assisted the authorities in maintaining order. Captain Kock and seventy-five of his officers and men were arrested, and the 'Red Guard' broken up.

In the Balkans, further violence took place throughout 1906, despite the attempts by Russia and Austria to persuade the Turks to adopt less harsh policies in Macedonia. It was not so much Ottoman rule, however, as deep-seated ethnic animosities between the different inhabitants of the region, that led to the worst of the violence. That May there was fighting throughout the province. Local Serbs and Albanians fought each other, as did local Greeks and Bulgarians.

Armed Greeks from the predominantly Greek villages in the region, reinforced by Greeks who had crossed the border from northern Greece, attacked the predominantly Bulgarian villages and forced them to accept Greek priests and schoolteachers. Groups of armed Muslims, drawn from the many Muslim communities in Macedonia, also attacked Bulgarian villages, killing many villagers. The main thrust of Turkish military activity was against the smaller (and more easily defeated) Bulgarian armed bands, many of whom were completely destroyed, while in an attack by Turkish soldiers on an armed Greek band, forty Greeks were killed. In two months, in that area of Turkey-in-Europe nominally being supervised by the European Powers, as many as four hundred of the rival nationalities were killed.

The Ottoman Empire was also in turmoil at its southernmost extremity, in Yemen, where Turkish control was being challenged by an Arab revolt. In March, a Turkish general, Ahmed Fevzi Pasha, managed to advance with a column of troops deep into rebel territory, but was forced back to the

Yemeni capital, Sanaa, because of lack of supplies. He was then confronted by a mutiny of Turkish troops, which he was able to suppress only after 300 of his men had been killed. His attempt that October to begin discussions with the Arab chiefs was rebuffed.

Following their victory over Russia, and despite the initial widespread humiliation felt at the moderate peace treaty sponsored by the United States, there was a growing enthusiasm in Japan at their country's new-found world respectability. During a visit to Japan, Prince Arthur of Connaught, a son of Queen Victoria, invested the Emperor with the Order of the Garter, and conferred the Order of Merit on Admiral Togo and two field marshals. That year Japan, which until then had bought its modern warships from abroad, launched the first battleship to be built in a Japanese shipyard. Trade was also making a major stride forward, with the value of Japanese exports exceeding the value of imported goods for the first time in ten years.

On the island of Formosa (Taiwan), a Japanese possession since 1895, expeditions against the Aboriginal population of the island resulted by 1906 in the mass destruction of those people, who dwelt mostly on the east coast of the island, and who were called 'savages' by both their Japanese adversaries and European observers. With the country apparently 'pacified' it was opened up to foreign investment. Gold production, the island's chief source of revenue for Japan, rose considerably. But 'pacified' proved for the Japanese in Formosa to be as relative a term as it was for some of the European Powers in Africa. Within a year of the pacification having been declared complete, new outbreaks of revolt took place, and there was heavy fighting. The Japanese used Chinese mercenaries to carry out the bulk of this fighting, but the Chinese troops mutinied, killing sixty-three Japanese soldiers and civilians. Japanese troops had to be called in to disperse the Chinese.

Japan's relations with the United States were affected adversely in 1906 by two incidents, both of which incensed Japanese public opinion, raising sensitivities with regard to American racial attitudes towards them. In July, several Japanese who were poaching in American sealing grounds off Alaska were killed, and in October, Japanese children were excluded from the public schools in San Francisco. With regard to the poachers, the United States insisted that as the men were breaking the law at the time they were killed, no legal action could be taken against those who killed them, an argument that the Japanese government had no real recourse but to accept.

The case of the schoolchildren was harder to explain away. That Japanese children had been judged unfit to sit in the same classrooms as the other children of San Franciscans was a humiliation to Japanese dignity and self-respect. President Roosevelt used all his considerable powers of diplomacy to assure the Japanese that the affront arose from local Trade Unions jealous of the success of Japanese commercial undertakings in California, and that the American view of the Japanese as a people should not be judged from such a one-sided point of view.

The Japanese government, its intellectuals and its businessmen were determined to present Japan as cultured and capable, and to acquire western knowledge. Large numbers of Japanese students were studying in Europe and the United States. Within a three-year period up to May 1906, fifteen new universities had been founded in Japan itself. In its economic growth, Japan was beginning to free itself from dependence on the industrialized nations. By 1906 she was exporting more than a million tons of coal annually. Oil production had reached well over a million barrels a year. During 1906 the government nationalized the railways; the subsequent encouragement of the local producers of rolling stock led to a sharp expansion in engineering output. Japan's water resources were being used for the generation of electricity. The worldwide spread of electric lighting was also of benefit to Japan, where the Tokyo Electric Company – reorganized by the General Electric Company of the United States – began manufacture of the Mazda lamp.

The European Powers continued to assert their imperial authority. In 1906 the French colonial government in Indo-China dethroned the King of Annam because of what were described by local officials as 'barbarities perpetrated by him on the ladies in the palace'. In South Africa, the British Government, the victor four years earlier over the Boers of the Transvaal and Orange Free State, granted both republics the full authority of responsible government, under British sovereignty. But at that moment of widespread British self-congratulation at having secured a just peace, the Zulu population in the British province of Natal rose in revolt against British colonial rule, and for four months there was considerable fighting. The cause of the uprising was blamed by the British on the teaching of what was known as 'Ethiopianism', the stated aim of which was to drive the whites out of South Africa altogether.

In an attempt to deter the rebels, the Natal government sentenced to death twelve Zulus who had been convicted of murdering two police officers at the outbreak of the rebellion. The Colonial Office in London, influenced by the new Under-Secretary of State for the Colonies, Winston Churchill, tried to stop the executions, but was told by the Natal government that this constituted unwarranted interference in the administration of the colony. The twelve men were executed, but the rebellion continued. A Zulu chief, Bambaata, with a large following, evaded capture and continued to fight for two more months, before he was killed in battle. Two other chiefs fought on but surrendered a month later.

The suppression of the Zulu revolt was conducted with severity, and more than three thousand Zulus were killed. Once again there were protests, from the local churches, and from men and women of conscience in Britain itself. The Anglican Bishop of Zululand charged that one column of British troops had robbed native women, stolen livestock, and thrown the bodies of Zulus they had murdered into ditches to rot. The conduct of the troops, he declared, was 'a deep disgrace to Englishmen'. Churchill also protested at what he called 'the disgusting butchery of natives'. The serious miscarriages of justice which had taken place in suppressing the revolt were, he believed, typical – he wrote to his Cabinet superior – of 'the kind of tyranny against which these unfortunate Zulus have been struggling'.

The government of Natal was not sympathetic to such complaints from London, whether from the newspapers or from politicians, and the surviving Zulu leaders were deported to the isolated South Atlantic island of St Helena – where Napoleon had been in exile almost a century earlier. When Churchill, as the member of the British government most directly concerned, learned of the conditions being imposed on the Zulus by the Governor of St Helena, he protested again. Their ration scale, he wrote, was 'more suited to the lowest animals than men'. As to the other conditions imposed on the Zulu exiles on the island, he wrote:

> I do not think that stone-breaking ought to be their only employment. They ought to have a moderate task upon the roads each day; but after they have done their allotted task, they should be allowed to cultivate a small patch of land on which they could grow vegetables for their own use or for sale.
>
> I do not see why they should not be taught to make baskets or carve wood, or make shoes, or some other simple form of light work, and I think that if any profit be made from the sale of these articles, the money should be given to them to buy any extra comforts they may wish.

I think that the Governor ought to be impressed by the fact that you are in earnest about the pledges which have been given to the House of Commons and that you will hold him responsible if he does not exert himself to make the lot of these unhappy Zulu exiles as little miserable as is compatible with their safe custody.

Churchill's protest received a minimal recognition by the Governor. The conscience of Liberal England did not extend as far as the imperial administrators who were the servants of king and parliament.

French efforts to assert authority over most of Morocco, an authority that had been conceded by Britain two years earlier, received further support at the beginning of 1906. A Conference at Algeciras, during which the Germans sought to restrict French authority, concluded by accepting it. French – and in the smaller area of Spanish Morocco, Spanish – authority was to be asserted without opposition from any other European Powers. The Sultan would remain sovereign, but France and Spain would be his mentors in their respective spheres, and would supervize trade through the eight Moroccan ports open to commerce. There was one concession to the wider European interest in the governance of Morocco: a Swiss army officer would serve as Inspector-General of the Police.

Asserting French authority in Morocco was not going to be easy, despite the agreement of Germany. In the south, the Sultan's right to rule was being challenged by a pretender to his throne. Around Tangier – where the Swiss Inspector-General was to reside – the insurgent national Moorish leader Raisuli was unimpeded in the havoc he was causing. He even raided Tangier itself on several occasions. At Casablanca, Maclain, another Muslim leader, described in the European press as 'a fanatical sorcerer from the Sahara', was calling on the local population to attack both Christians and Jews. At Marrakech he and his followers burst into the Jewish quarter, murdering and looting. At the port of Mogador, only the arrival of a French gunboat protected the Jews of the town from being looted by a Berber chief who had descended upon them from the hinterland. When news reached Europe that a distant relative of the Sultan, Mulai Abu, was trying to persuade all the tribal factions to combine in a Holy War against the French, it was the German government that, in accordance with its agreement at Algeciras, sent one of its diplomats, Count Friedrich Rosen – who in 1921 was to be the German Foreign Minister for five months – to see the Sultan and to urge him to assert his authority against Muslim fanaticism.

French West Africa and northern Nigeria, the French and British colonial territories to the south of the Sahara which had a common frontier, were both the subject of local disturbances in 1906, when several French and British officers, and local troops serving under them, were killed in separate skirmishes by local Muslim tribesmen reluctant to submit to colonial rule. A British expedition to find and punish the rebels in northern Nigeria was successful, the British newspapers reporting that the rebel forces at Satiru were 'almost exterminated'. One local chief, the Emir of Hadeija, was considered by the British to be 'truculent'; he was thought to be behind a raid on British territory from across the French frontier less than forty miles to the north.

A year earlier, a force of 500 men had been sent against the Emir. Giving in to superior force he had made submission to British authority, and had been allowed to remain as ruler. This time he was to face an even stronger expedition, with 20 British officers, 600 men, two field guns and six Maxims. No doubt he was unfamiliar with the jingle so popular in the British army, and which had already sustained imperial conquests for more than twenty years:

> Whatever happens we have got
> The Maxim gun, which they have not.

The emir of Hadeija decided to fight. His capital was captured and he, having been wounded in the struggle, was taken captive. There was further fighting a month later, against another rebel army. Thirty-one of the British expedition were killed, but more troops were sent, and the remaining rebels were crushed.

From an imperial perspective these were regarded as troublesome pinpricks, but no more than that. By the end of the year, a French and a British officer – Captain Tilho and Major O'Shee – were busy delineating the Franco-British frontier from the Niger to Lake Chad. Another imperial frontier line on the map of Africa was in the process of being drawn. Two European Powers, that a decade earlier would certainly have clashed, and possibly even fought, over their competing claims to an African hinterland, were working in tandem, and in amity.

The French colonial territories in and around the Sahara constituted by far the largest European presence there. When in August 1906, a French camel patrol was wiped out by Senussi tribesmen 200 miles northeast of Lake Chad, there were fears that this might be part of a general Muslim rebellion. The murder of two French officers on the southern frontier of Tripoli gave similar cause for alarm, though Turkish government complicity was also suspect.

But the main thrust of imperial penetration in Africa was confident and undeterred. A French expedition traversing the area south of Lake Chad in search of trade route links with the Congo Basin was unmolested, and in a speech in Timbuktu the Governor-General of French West Africa gave an optimistic account of what had been achieved by France in the region. The slave trade of Timbuktu had ended, he said, anarchy in the Niger region had been eliminated, and trade routes had been secured. The journey from Dakar (on the coast) to Timbuktu, that had taken three months a decade earlier, had just taken him only eleven days. Steamers had replaced barges on the River Niger. The *Pax Gallica* had been extended over all the tribes on the left bank of the Niger, and France's Algerian and West African administrations had been linked by a route across the Sahara traversible by military columns. The Governor-General looked forward 'to the pacification of the Sahara' before too long.

It was the German imperialists who were vexed that their rule in Africa was still proving less successful than that of the other European Powers. In German East Africa those other Powers continued to look critically at what they considered a harsh administration. Nor, except along the coast, were the Germans able to suppress the unrest in the regions under their sovereignty. In August a German military expedition captured the Sultan of the Wangoni tribe, his family and his cattle, forcing the surrender of the majority, but not all, of the Wangoni chiefs. In German South West Africa the war against the Hereros and the Witboi had continued with heavy casualties on both sides. The German public were shocked when they were told, in June 1906, that almost two thousand German troops had been killed in the fighting.

Slowly imperial power was able to overcome the peoples who had been so determined to resist it. German military reinforcements were sent from Hamburg. In February the last of the Witboi leaders surrendered. A month later another rebel leader, the Hottentot chief Cornelius, gave himself up. A German military force then set out against the ever-defiant Herero leader, deploying against him a formidable fifteen field guns and four machine guns. He escaped the net, but was driven across the British South African border. It was only then that he was captured by Cape police. That was not, however, the end of the rebellion; two more chiefs, refusing to surrender, inflicted heavy casualties on the Germans throughout the autumn.

In Berlin, a majority of the deputies in the Reichstag expressed their indignation at the expenditure being incurred on these military enterprises. The veteran Social Democratic leader in the Reichstag, August Bebel, said caustically of the Kaiser's imperial policy: 'Wherever in the world he can drive a nail on which he could hang his shield, he would drive it.' In a series of votes, the deputies drastically cut back the money which they would allow the government to spend against the rebels, or in favour of the German settlers. They also voted against railway expansion south of the town of Kubub. There was anger in the Reichstag against General von Deimling, Commander-in-Chief of the German forces in German South West Africa, who had mocked at the Reichstag's refusal not to continue the railway to the south by asking the deputies whether he should tell his troops, whose health was 'worse than it had ever been', that the Reichstag had left the railway 'stuck in the mud at Kubub'.

The Reichstag was also angered by what it considered the bad administration of two German colonial governors, Herr von Puttkamer in the Cameroons and Herr Horn in Togoland. They were being protected from prosecution, it was alleged, by the deliberate removal of incriminating documents from the official files. After several days of stormy debates, the Chancellor admitted that 'gross breaches of duty' had been committed by colonial officials; only the best men would be chosen in future for colonial appointments, he promised. This assurance did not prevent another debate a few days later, after some officials in the Colonial Department in Berlin had passed evidence to several deputies of 'unspeakable atrocities' that had been perpetrated by colonial officials on black women and girls.

The deputies, including those of the Centre Party on whom the government had hitherto relied for support, continued to oppose the government's colonial policy, and to demand a reduction in the number of troops in German South West Africa. The Chancellor was indignant at this attempt to curtail German imperial policy and, when a motion to increase the money allocated to South West Africa was rejected by 178 votes to 168, having obtained the prior approval of the Kaiser, he dissolved the Reichstag.

*   *   *

The Germans found themselves held up to considerable derision that year, when, in October, a cobbler by the name of Voigt, dressing himself up in the uniform of a captain in the elite 1st Regiment of Prussian Guards, used his military 'authority' to arrest the mayor of the town of Köpenick. Voigt ordered the Mayor to go immediately to Berlin, and then, with the Mayor gone, made off with the Köpenick city cash. It was not until nine days after the crime that the bogus captain was arrested and his true identity revealed. It was a perfect illustration, said many English and French observers, and many Germans, of the absurd respect accorded inside Germany to military officers and commands.

This was not the only hoax to point up with such audacity an attitude of misplaced deference. Four years later British naval traditions were also the victims of a hoax when a number of luminaries from the Bloomsbury circle of writers and artists, among them the writer Virginia Stephen (later Virginia Woolf) and the painter Duncan Grant, disguising themselves as the 'Emperor of Abyssinia and his suite', were welcomed aboard the flagship of the Home Fleet at Portland and carried out a successful inspection of the vessel. The Kaiser, delighted that the boastful mood of 'Britannia Rules the Waves' had been deflated, sent self-righteous commiserations on the incident to some of his Royal Navy friends.

The United States continued to assert its right, under the Monroe Doctrine of 1823, to be responsible for the maintenance of order in the western hemisphere. In 1906, eight years after the defeat of the Spaniards in Cuba and the withdrawal of American troops from the island, the first president of the Cuban Republic, Tomas Estrada Palma, tried to secure re-election by nullifying the franchise. His political opponents threatened revolution, and there were violent protests in the streets. President Palma appealed to President Roosevelt to send American troops to restore order and prevent a massacre. Roosevelt declined. But when the American diplomatic representative in Cuba cabled to Washington that without American intervention there was a 'grave danger' of anarchy, and of the widespread destruction of property, Roosevelt issued a public warning that the United States would have to intervene if Cuba showed that she had 'fallen into the insurrectionary habit' and lacked 'the self-restraint necessary to secure peaceful self-government'.

Roosevelt sent his Secretary for War, William Taft, to Cuba, to investigate.

It was clear to Taft that anarchy was imminent. The United States thereupon despatched a naval squadron, with 5000 troops, to occupy Havana. Taft was made Provisional Governor of Cuba. The United States had acquired a new territory, and a new responsibility. As soon as order was restored, Taft handed over the governorship to another American, the former governor of the Panama Canal Zone.

How long the United States would remain in control of Cuba was not clear. In early December, President Roosevelt said that should a new government be inaugurated in a peaceful and orderly fashion after the Cuban elections, which were to be held later that month, the provisional government would end. But if the forthcoming elections on the island became a 'farce', and the 'insurrectionary habit' was confirmed among the Cubans, the United States would remain in charge of the administration, and would 'exercise every charity and patience' with the Cubans as they trod the hard path to self-government.

In a century which was to see American presidents travel the world as war leaders and peace makers – from Versailles to Vladivostok, and from Helsinki to the Persian Gulf – it is strange to recall that from American independence in 1776 until the opening years of the twentieth century no American President had left the United States while in office. Many Americans believed that it must be part of the constitution that a President could not leave the national jurisdiction. There was puzzlement, therefore, and some anger, when President Roosevelt announced he was going to visit the Isthmus of Panama, to see for himself how the work on the Panama Canal was proceeding. Even if the President's remaining in the United States while in office was only a convention, it was argued, it was wrong of Roosevelt to break it. Undeterred, he sailed to Panama City. It was the first time that the President of the United States had set foot on foreign soil while in office.

The direct impact of literature on politics was seen twice in three years, first in the United States and then in Britain. The American writer, whose impact was made in 1906, was Upton Sinclair. His novel, *The Jungle*, was an exposé of the terrible conditions, moral as well as sanitary, in the meat stock yards and packing houses of Chicago. In a letter to Roosevelt, Sinclair urged the President to order an investigation. At first Roosevelt was reluctant to do so (just as he had been reluctant at first to send American troops to Cuba). But public pressure mounted, and when two undercover agents confirmed what Sinclair had written, namely that grave breaches of public health were involved in the slaughter and packing of meat, action was taken, and binding legislation, the Meat Inspections Act and the Pure Food and Drug Act, were passed through Congress. These acts imposed severe penalties on anyone whose tins and cans of meat were adulterated in any way, or did not clearly show the date of manufacture. With his novel, Sinclair had exposed a scandalous state of affairs, and affected a revolution in public health.

In Britain, it was John Galsworthy whose play *Justice*, an exposé of the cruelties of solitary confinement in prison, by likewise revealing an evil, led directly, four years after Sinclair's triumph, to a drastic reduction in the number of offences punishable by solitary confinement.

On the Pacific coast of Colombia, 2000 people were killed during an earthquake and tidal wave in February. In March, the world's worst colliery disaster – then or since – took place in France, in a coal mine near Lens. After 1800 miners had gone down for the morning shift, an explosion blew up the last three cages in which the men were descending, and the pit caught fire. Help was rushed to the scene, including a special German fire brigade from a mine in Westphalia. Only thirteen men were brought out alive. In Japan, later that same year, 256 miners were killed in an explosion in the Takashima mine.

In Hong Kong, in September, a typhoon more ferocious than any hitherto recorded killed 10,000 people. Ten steamers were sunk or wrecked in the harbour, several hundred fishing vessels overturned, and many wharfs, jetties and warehouses totally destroyed. Most of the dead were Chinese, but among those drowned was the Anglican Bishop, Dr Joseph Charles Hoare. Before his appointment to Hong Kong, Hoare had been the head of a Christian mission college in China for more than twenty years.

In Europe, five hundred people were killed in a number of Italian villages when Vesuvius erupted in the first week of April. Two nearby villages were completely destroyed. A black shower of volcanic ash darkened the Naples sky; the weight of the ash as it fell caused the roof of a market to collapse, killing twelve people. *The Times* reported from Naples on April 10:

It appears a grey city inhabited by grey ghosts, which is at least an improvement upon Saturday and Sunday nights, when the threatening thunder of the volcano, a thick pall of darkness torn by distant flashes of volcanic explosions, and a suffocating atmosphere made it resemble an ante-chamber of hell.

The Neapolitans, too, have taken courage again, and the pitiful little processions bearing a holy image or picture, sometimes composed of only a dozen or so half-distraught peasant women, have now deserted the streets, though even last night they were still to be seen here and there.

If the appearance of Naples is still forlorn enough, that of the threatened towns is most wretched. Torre Annunziata seems utterly abandoned save by a few carabinieri and troops, who mount guard in its empty streets. Torre del Greco is in little better ease. Resina and Portici suffered less in the general panic, but were deserted temporarily by a good many of the inhabitants, who are now returning to their homes. Bosco-Trecase is destroyed. The villages on the north-east of Vesuvius – Ottajano, San Giuseppe, and Terzigno – I have not yet been able to see, but from all reports their condition is sufficiently deplorable.

From San Giuseppe is reported the only serious loss of life. The roof of the old church, long known to be unsafe, succumbed, it is supposed, to the added weight of ashes and volcanic *débris* and fell in, burying in its ruins a great number of women and old people who were gathered in prayer to avert the destruction of their town.

According to the last accounts, thirty-seven dead bodies have been extricated.

On the evening of April 17 the New York Metropolitan Opera Company, on tour in San Francisco, performed Bizet's *Carmen*. The hero of the evening was the Italian tenor, Enrico Caruso. Despite his worries about the Vesuvius eruption, he was in fine voice. In the early hours of the following morning, while Caruso and the half million inhabitants of San Francisco slept, the city was struck by an earthquake. It was an earthquake far stronger than any that had hitherto struck any American city. Fires, breaking out from fractured gas mains, burned for four days. Four square miles in the centre of the city were devastated. There had been no warning; only an unexplained nervousness of dogs and horses on the previous evening. As buildings were evacuated, Caruso was seen sitting on his suitcase outside the Palace Hotel.

From New York, *The Times* correspondent telegraphed to London on April 19:

Frightful news is arriving from San Francisco. At present all is confusion in the reports, and only one wire to San Francisco is available intermittently. But it appears that the city was practically wrecked by an earthquake at 13 minutes past 5 this morning, San Francisco time.

It is estimated that 1,000 lives have been lost in San Francisco itself, but the area of the earthquake is quite large, and we are without news of the fate of the other cities and towns in the zone affected.

Fires have broken out all over San Francisco; the earthquake has wrecked the water connections, and the firemen are almost helpless. According to the latest report they are using dynamite as the only means of fighting the flames. It is declared that if a strong wind arises the whole city will be burned.

An hour later the correspondent telegraphed again:

I fear the San Francisco disaster will be the greatest in the history of the United States. Another earthquake has occurred, and the latest report is that, unless the wind changes and blows the flames in the direction of the Bay, nothing can save the city.

The Mayor of San Francisco has appointed a vigilance committee of 50 prominent citizens, who are guarding the banks, with orders to shoot any robber at sight.

The *employés* of the Postal Telegraph Company, the only company which has a wire working into San Francisco, have telegraphed that they must leave the building there, as it is in flames.

A thousand Federal troops were deployed throughout the burning city to stop looting. Four looters, caught in the act, were arrested and shot. When a large crowd of looters attacked the Mint, which was ablaze, fourteen of them were shot dead.

After the San Francisco earthquake, 666 corpses were found. The bodies of a further 354 people were never found. Among those who hastened to send aid were the people of Japan, who subscribed $100,000 to earthquake relief. But President Roosevelt declined all foreign help, asserting that the United States was able to help its own homeless and destitute.

The United States was not the only earthquake victim in 1906. On August 16 an earthquake struck Chile, partially destroying the two main cities,

Valparaiso and Santiago de Chile, and between forty and fifty smaller towns. Three thousand people were killed.

In British India, the ravages of plague continued, having killed nearly three million people in five years. A scientific committee appointed by the government put the responsibility for the spread of the disease on plague-carrying rats. Considerable efforts were made to hunt down and exterminate these rats, and by September 1906 the number of deaths from plague – 1,125,652 in the previous twelve months – had dropped to 296,697. This was still by far the highest death toll for 1906 from any single epidemic or natural cause. There were also several thousand deaths in India that year from cholera and smallpox.

In 1906 an eminent German zoologist, Ernst Haeckel, founded the Monist League. The main object of the league was the promotion of eugenics, with a view to achieving what Haeckel called 'racial improvement'. The eugenics movement – the first major introduction of biology into the domain of public policy – was then at its height. Five years later the first international conference of Monists was held in Hamburg. The 'race' which the Monists considered superior to all others, in physique and intellect, was the white race; and among its most impressive manifestations, the Germanic people.

In the United States, President Roosevelt's determination to protect the natural and historic wealth of his country continued to benefit from legislation. The Antiquities Act, 1906, gave the President the authority to set aside Federal lands 'for the protection of objects of scientific, prehistoric, or historic interest'. The National Forests Commission was also established in the United States that year. In Britain, the creation of rural suburbs as integral parts of a city was inaugurated with the founding of Hampstead Garden Suburb, on the northern outskirts of London. Also in Britain that year the Liberal government extended greater legal protection to inventors, under the Patents Act, and made considerable reforms in the conditions under which merchant seamen worked. Internationally, a convention was signed which forbade night-shift work for women.

In the realm of music, 1906 saw the invention of the jukebox and the debut of the singer Maurice Chevalier. The availability of major works of literature at a cheap price was pioneered that year in Britain by the establishment of the 'Everyman Library'. In the United States the W. K. Kellogg Toasted Corn Flake Company launched a new breakfast cereal, Kellogg's

Corn Flakes, and – that same year – the Coca-Cola Company replaced the cocaine in its popular drink with caffeine.

Two technological advances, both of which were to have wide repercussions in the years ahead in the life of every nation, took place in the United States in 1906: the opening in New York of the Biograph 14th Street film studio, and the first radio broadcast, on December 24, when R. A. Fessenden broadcast some music, a poem and a short talk, which were heard by ships' radio operators at sea.

CHAPTER EIGHT

1907

POLITICAL ASSASSINATIONS, which already scarred the first seven years of the new century, continued to make their mark in 1907. That January, in Russia, the Prefect of St Petersburg, General van der Launitz, and the Military Procurator-General of the Russian Empire, General Pavlov, were both assassinated. Hardly a day passed without attacks in Russian towns on government property, and much looting; or peasants setting fire to the houses, stores and woodlands of landowners. In Tiflis, on June 13, a detachment of Cossacks escorting money being taken from the State Bank was attacked by Bolshevik gunmen, and the money seized. Several passers-by were killed. This acquisition of funds by violence was condemned by Socialists throughout Europe, though it undoubtedly helped the Bolshevik cause. In Georgia that August, Prince Chavchavadze, the father of the Georgian cultural renaissance, and a leading liberal, was assassinated; he had spoken out strongly against the revolutionaries.

In the elections for a second Duma, the Constitutional Democrat seats were reduced from 185 to 108. The lost places were taken up by the main revolutionary party, the Social Democrats, and also by one of the smaller right-wing parties, the Octobrists. At the opening session in the Tauride Palace, postponed because the ceiling of the chamber collapsed, the Prime Minister, Peter Stolypin, created a sense of hope and expectation when he announced: 'Our country must be transformed into a constitutional State'.

What constituted the essential parameters of a 'constitutional State' differed in the mind of the government and that of the members of the Duma. When the Duma voted to expropriate land from landowners for distribution to needy peasants, the government refused to agree. In June, after calling for a secret session, Stolypin demanded the suspension of all the Social Democratic party members, sixteen of whom were at once arrested, and a further fifty-five of whom were charged with carrying on revolutionary propaganda in the army and navy, in the form of pamphlets, widely distributed, calling on all soldiers and sailors to disobey the orders of their officers. The Duma wanted a committee of deputies set up, before which the government could present its evidence against the Social Democratic deputies. But before the committee could meet, the Tsar dissolved the Duma, and fixed a date for new elections in three months' time.

Before the new elections could be held, the Tsar changed the basis of voting. This was itself an unconstitutional act, which violated a provision accepted when the Duma had been established in 1906, that the electoral law could not be changed without the Duma's consent. Under the new franchise, more votes were to go to landlords and fewer to peasants, and two-thirds of the seats allocated to Poland and the Caucasus were taken away. Those deputies (180 in all) who had signed the Vyborg manifesto after the dissolution of the first Duma were excluded from the right to stand.

Before the elections could take place, the nature of the autocracy was strengthened even further. Newspapers critical of the government were fined and confiscated, and more than a thousand people were exiled to Siberia. In Odessa, where the anti-Semitic Black Hundreds were protected by the Governor-General, Baron Kaulbars, the murder of Jews had escalated to a daily occurrence. In Vilna, the Polish bishop, Monsignor Roop, who had been a member of the second Duma, was removed from his bishopric for having supported the demands of the Poles in his diocese for equal treatment with the Russians.

The third Duma, its electoral basis having been so tampered with, no longer reflected the desire for constitutional change which had animated its two predecessors. Of the 422 deputies, it was the right-wing and moderate liberal parties that prevailed, the parties of the right winning 147 seats and the liberal Octobrists, 154. The Constitutional Democrats were reduced to forty-five seats and the more radical Social Democrats to nineteen.

Before the Duma could assemble on November 15 there was a spate of assassinations, and a mutiny of the garrison at Vladivostok which took several days to suppress. In his address to the Duma, Stolypin stressed that the disorder and open violence stalking Russia were demoralizing the younger generation, and that revolutionary excesses could only be met by force. The government quickly put this warning into effect. By the end of the year more than a hundred newspaper editors had been exiled to Siberia, and twenty-six left-wing members of the second Duma had been sentenced to imprisonment with hard labour. To avoid arrest, Lenin, whose uncompromising leadership of the Bolshevik faction of the Social Democratic Party had led to disputes within the party and his expulsion from its Central Committee, left Russia for exile in Europe: he was not to return for ten years.

In the Kingdom of Poland, 600 private schools that had been established, at the expense of the local Polish population, in order to give instruction in the Polish language, were closed down on orders of the Tsar. Only in the Finnish province of the Russian Empire was constitutional reform unimpeded by Tsarist interference. In April, the new Finnish Diet was elected on a basis of universal suffrage, in which women could both vote and be voted for. Of the 200 members elected, nineteen were women, the first women to sit in any twentieth-century parliament. The mood of the Diet reflected a Lutheran ethic quite alien to the Russian experience; one of its first measures was to forbid the sale of all wines, beers and spirits except for medicinal purposes, and to forbid the use of wine even in churches. When several deputies protested that it was irrational to forbid the drinking of alcohol in this way, a woman deputy, Baroness Grippenberg, answered that on such an important issue it was best 'to leave reason aside and let sentiment prevail'.

Of the parliamentary democracies, only the United States was to emulate Finland and turn to prohibition twelve years later, and to have thirteen alcohol-free years marred by illegal stills, bootlegging, clandestine drinking, vast profits, and violent crime as a result.

In Macedonia, Russia and Austria were committed, under the Mürzsteg programme to which they had subscribed in 1903, not only to enforcing a more equitable Turkish administration, but, as the programme expressed it, 'to favour the development of local autonomies'. In the Balkans, this promise offered the possibility to each of the factions to increase their areas of autonomy by killing or expelling rival groups living in the same area – a policy known ninety years later, when it took place little more than a hundred miles away in Bosnia, as 'ethnic cleansing'. This meant that the Greeks of Macedonia, encouraged to do so by Greeks from across the Greek border to the south, did their utmost to drive out the Bulgarians living in their midst. Whole villages inhabited by Bulgarians were burnt to the ground. The Bulgarians of Macedonia reciprocated by employing similar tactics. Turkish police, even under the command of their Italian inspector-general approved by Russia and Austria, were powerless to restrain these attacks, the prevention of which would have required more force than they possessed, and a greater willingness to incur their own casualties.

Serbs living in Macedonia likewise struggled to maintain control of the areas in which they lived, and to extend as much as possible the areas in which they might hope in due course to win autonomy. In Montenegro, where there was sharp division between those who wanted to retain the mountain kingdom's independence and those who wanted union with Serbia, there was unity when Turkish pressure seemed likely to result in the loss of a small strip of disputed territory. When the Turkish border commissioners who were examining the region refused to recognize the Montenegrin claim, a group of armed Montenegrins attacked a Turkish military outpost, and killed or wounded most of the garrison there.

At the other extremity of the Ottoman Empire, in Yemen, the year-long efforts of Ahmed Feizi Pasha to defeat the Arab revolt had collapsed. Not for the first time, he had done his utmost to negotiate with the Arab leaders, but they had declined even to talk to his emissaries. The Turkish troops, so far from home, and finding the Arabs more proficient at shooting, were in a mutinous mood, and could not be relied upon to face the Arabs in any engagement to which they were sent.

Social unrest was a feature of all industrial and prosperous countries in 1907. Sometimes, as in Britain, it took the form of the mounting demand by women for the vote. This could be peaceful as well as violent. In London, on February 9, a mass meeting of 2000 non-militant women marched through the city. 'The demonstration was remarkable as much for its representative character as for its size,' reported *The Times*. 'Not only were numerous political and labour organizations represented, but ladies of title and of social distinction joined in a procession through the muddy streets on a cold February afternoon, undaunted by the rain which fell at intervals, and by the jeers of amused spectators.' Conditions so impeded the march that it was known, ruefully, as the Mud March.

Nowhere in Europe had the socialist parties attained sufficient electoral strength to exert influence within the parliamentary systems – either to extend the franchise to women or to alleviate the hardship which pressed upon working men everywhere. Increasingly, therefore, it was through strikes, riots and mass demonstrations that the unease was manifested. In 1907 this unease was seen in many regions of France, where a 'crusade of beggars' served as a focal point for other discontents. During rioting in Narbonne, French troops were taunted by the crowd to use their bayonets, and did so. In Agde, the troops refused to act against the strikers. In Perpignan, the town hall was burned down. A warrant was put out for the arrest of the 'King of the Beggars', Marcellin Albert. Ignoring the warrant, he paid a personal visit on the Prime Minister, Georges Clemenceau, who urged him to go home and to surrender to the police, which he did.

In Italy, peasant farmers, and unsuccessful immigrants returning from Central and South America, demanded government help in regions where there was agrarian distress, disrupting railway services as part of their protest. At Bari, an attempt was made to institute a general strike; it was put down with some severity. In Roumania, social unrest flared in the rural areas of Moldavia and Wallachia in the spring of 1907, when thousands of peasants, who had witnessed the growing prosperity of Roumania through its grain exports, without being the beneficiaries of that prosperity, rose in revolt.

One factor that fuelled the discontent in Roumania was an increase in the tax on all smallholdings. Another was the leasing from the government, by Jewish middlemen, of state and communal lands, from which they then could obtain rents. When the peasant rising began in March, it was initially against the Jews alone; more than two thousand Jewish homes were looted. Then the peasants turned against all landowners of large properties. On a fierce rampage against those whom they accused of exploiting their labour, the peasants destroyed crops and burnt homes. In savage reprisals, the Roumanian government forces, 140,000 strong, commanded by General Averescu, killed more than eleven thousand of the peasant rebels.

A new Roumanian government tried to redress the balance of repression by reducing the land tax on smallholdings and abolishing altogether the system whereby land could be leased to middlemen. At the same time, it was made easier for the peasants to obtain credit. In a further attempt to appease peasant anger, in the counties of Dorhoi, Jassy and Bacau the government expelled thousands of Jews from the villages in which they had lived for several generations; the only Jews who were allowed to remain in those villages were military veterans of the 1877 war against the Turks.

Poverty throughout Europe belied the confidence of imperial policies overseas. To raise taxation, duties were imposed on consumer goods and even food. Yet it was these very taxes, intended to help the poor by creating welfare agencies, that fell most heavily upon them. When the German government put a tax on coffee in 1907, it was pointed out by critics of the tax that in Berlin alone there were as many as 14,000 children who existed only on bread and coffee.

The German Social Democratic Party, whose seats had been almost halved in the 1907 election, from seventy-nine to forty-three, were powerless to effect the radical changes they desired, in which the rights and conditions of life of working men and women would be dramatically improved. But at an International Socialist Congress held in Stuttgart in August, attended by the various socialist and labour party leaders, including representatives from Britain, France, India, Japan and the United States, delegates listened as the German Social Democratic Party leader, August Bebel, spoke of his conviction that wars came, not from any conflict between the working classes, but from the desire of capitalist interests to provoke international conflicts. Bebel was strongly critical, however, of a French socialist motion that was put before the Congress, advocating that in the event of war, soldiers in all armies should desert, and even revolt. Another German socialist then declared that love of humanity would never prevent his party from being 'good Germans', and he dismissed as 'foolishness' the idea of those delegates who believed that a European war could be brought to a halt by a working-class general strike.

The delegates at the Socialist Congress were agreed that colonialism should be denounced. As they described it in their manifesto, it inevitably led to 'slavery, forced labour, the extermination of the natives, and the exhaustion of the natural riches of the countries colonized', as well as increasing the danger of conflict among the colonial powers. The cost of the colonies, the Congress declared, should be born entirely by those who profited from their spoliation.

The conclusions of the Stuttgart Congress set the agenda for the next seven years. It was agreed that Socialist members of parliament should vote against all 'war budgets' and in favour of all treaties of arbitration; socialist workers should demonstrate whenever there was the 'slightest danger' of war; the working day should be shorter; conditions of work should be improved; a minimum wage should be established; and adult suffrage should be introduced for both men and women. As to the events of the day, the Congress condemned the peasant attacks on the Jews in Roumania, expressed its sympathies for the revolutionaries in Russia, and denounced the actions of the French and Spanish troops in Morocco.

An obvious divide existed, in Germany as elsewhere, between the world of the capitalist and the world of the worker, but the balance of power lay so heavily against the socialists that their programmes, like their protests, remained without any meaningful prospect of fulfilment. In Britain, where in the elections of 1906 the Labour Party had obtained thirty seats in a Parliament of 670 (in the previous election in 1900 it had won only two), it was the ruling Liberal Party that was devising a comprehensive programme of social reform. Under the reforming zeal of Winston Churchill, this included a bill to limit the hours that a coal miner could work below ground to eight hours, and a bill to provide pensions, financed by the state, for people of sixty-five and older. Churchill also introduced a system whereby industrial disputes would be settled by arbitration; by this means a serious railway strike was averted that November.

Within the Austrian lands of Austria-Hungary, an experiment took place in 1907 that ought to have boded well for the forces of liberalism and reform: the introduction of universal male suffrage. In some regions, voting was compulsory, and nonvoters were fined. In Vienna, the largest number of votes cast went to the mayor, Karl Lueger, the head of the Christian Socialist party, whose platform was a popular mixture of Roman Catholicism, anti-Semitism and socialism. As a result of the Austrian elections, the first to be held under universal male suffrage in any of the European empires, the largest single party in the Austrian parliament was the radical Social Democrats, with 90 seats. The Christian Socialists came second, with 67. The six German parties made up a total of 225 seats in a house of 516; they included eleven Pan-German members whose policy was the dissolution of the multinational empire and their own incorporation into imperial Germany.

Every nationality of the Austrian Empire was represented in the parliament in Vienna. The three Polish parties won 73 seats, the six Czech parties 81, with other seats going to the Ruthenians (28), Slovenes (25), Italians (14), Croats (9), Roumanians (5) and Jewish Zionists (3). The Serbs, hitherto unrepresented, received two seats. In addressing the newly elected members in his speech from the throne, Franz Josef spoke of his confidence that 'a comprehensive widening of the juridical foundations of political life may go hand in hand with a concentration and increase of the State's political power'. This did not bode well for the national aspirations of the minorities. He was also emphatic, much to the anger of Hungarian nationalists, about the need to maintain the political ties between Austria and Hungary. Sometimes it seemed as if these ties only existed in the head, and imperial vision, of the aged emperor.

The principal national unrest in Austria-Hungary that year came, not from the Hungarians, but from the most easterly peoples of the empire, the Ruthenians, who, never having been independent, but always under the rule of some distant capital, resented the growing German influence in their main city, Lemberg.[1] Having been refused permission by the Austrian authorities to open a university of their own, they broke into the university buildings and did considerable damage. In the parliament in Vienna, two Ruthenian deputies disrupted the proceedings by singing Ruthenian songs at the top of their voices, while another Ruthenian deputy who tried to make his speech in Russian was forced to fall silent when informed that only the eight official languages of Austria could be used in the debates.[2]

German imperialism suffered from a sense of inferiority to the British. This emerged in many ways, from the costly efforts to carve out colonial territories in Africa to the equally costly efforts to build a modern navy. Even when held in check by the anti-colonial and anti-expansionist forces in the parliament, these sentiments emerged in speech and aphorism. If Germany had been reunited, not in 1870 but a hundred years earlier, one German patriot declared, 'not Clive, but a Hamburg councillor, would command on the Ganges'.

It was the abuses of colonial rule, however, that dominated the discussions of 1907 inside Germany, highlighted by two trials. In April, the former Governor of the German Cameroons was put on trial for maladministration, and a month later the former Governor of Togoland was likewise brought to trial. He was found guilty of having caused the death of a native by ordering him to be tied to a post and exposed all day in the sun, in order to force him to confess where some money he had stolen from the official cash box had been hidden. When the German African explorer, Dr Peters, who had twice been condemned for cruelty to the natives ten years earlier, won a libel action against the editor of a socialist newspaper in Munich, the semi-official *Cologne Gazette* protested against 'the reckless and unwarrantable

---

[1] Known to its Polish minority as Lwow and to its Ukrainian minority as Lviv. An alternative, more common, spelling is the transliteration from the Russian: Lvov.
[2] The eight official languages were German, Hungarian, Czech, Slovene, Polish, Croat, Italian and Roumanian.

manner in which the reputation of the whole German colonial administration has been imperilled, both at home and abroad, to secure the rehabilitation of a single individual'.

But it was more than the reputation of individuals that was at stake. The crushing of the Witboi and Herero revolt in German South West Africa had shamed many Germans, as well as outsiders. It was as if the 'methods of barbarism' which the British had been forced to halt in South Africa seven years earlier had been taken up by Britain's colonial rival.

In Prussia, the German authorities continued to press forward with the Germanization of the Polish areas. Polish-language newspapers were confiscated and their editors arrested. Fines were imposed for holding Polish meetings, and a law was passed forbidding Polish peasants to build houses on their own land; this led to a peasant, whose case was given much publicity by the opposition in Germany, being forced to live with his family in a Gypsy caravan near his own stable and barn.

The culmination of the anti-Polish measures came on November 26, when a bill was introduced into the Prussian parliament for the compulsory expropriation of land owned by Poles. This was necessary, explained the Chancellor, Prince von Bülow, 'in the highest interests of the State'. Money would be raised through local taxation to give cash compensation to those whose land was to be taken; thus the Poles would have to pay for their own eviction. Bülow justified the comprehensiveness of the new measure by reference to Bismarck, who had started the German Colonization Commission in Prussian Poland twenty years earlier, with a view to enhancing and extending the German 'national spirit' throughout the Polish-inhabited areas.

The anti-Polish measures enacted in Berlin roused deep anger in Austria, where there was a demonstration in the parliament in which not only the Polish and Slavonic members, but also a Jewish and an Italian member, protested at what they described as 'a medieval plundering raid' by the Germans. The Austrian authorities were uneasy at such a protest against the internal policies of another State, and an ally, but were powerless to prevent it. So large were the combined Slav populations of Austria, outnumbering the German, that they felt confident in demanding an end to the Austro-German Alliance if the anti-Polish policies of Prussia were to continue.

Another Slav cloud on the Austrian horizon, small but ominous, appeared in 1907 in the province of Bosnia-Herzegovina, which since 1878 had been under Austrian military occupation. The Serbs, who formed nearly half the population – the other half being Muslims – demanded complete autonomy, the election of a popular assembly on the basis of universal suffrage, and government of the province, not by Austrian military rulers, but by parliamentary majority.

In the Hungarian portion of Austria-Hungary, it was the Croat minority that was demanding a greater voice. The issue around which the agitation centred was, as so often elsewhere, language. When Croat members of the Hungarian parliament insisted on speaking in Croat, the Hungarian deputies ostensibly refused to listen to them. In anger, the Croats walked out of the chamber. The Hungarian Ministry of Justice, in what was openly described as an attempt 'to strengthen the Magyar national idea', made the Hungarian (Magyar) language compulsory throughout Hungary, even though the non-Magyar nationalities — the Roumanians, Germans, Slovaks and Croats — made up more than half the population of the Kingdom of Hungary. When the Governor (or Ban) of Croatia, appointed by the government in Budapest, indicated his support for Croat demands, he was replaced by a governor who was known to support Magyar predominance in Croatia; one of the first ordinances that the new governor enforced, amid considerable Croat discontent, was one which made Magyar the official language on all Croatian railways. The Croat traveller from Zagreb to the Adriatic port of Fiume, or from Zagreb to Budapest, would have to discuss the surcharge of his train ticket in Hungarian; study the luncheon menu in Hungarian, and listen to all station announcements in Hungarian.

Similar language unrest affected the Slovak-speaking regions of northern Hungary. In the village of Csernova, a parish priest was sent to prison for two years for having insisted that the Slovak language be used in the schools and law courts. While the priest was in prison, the villagers built a new church for him, at their own expense, but they refused to consecrate it until he was set free. The local bishop, a Magyar, challenged this assertion of Slovak national authority by sending another priest, escorted by Hungarian troops, to consecrate the church. The villagers resisted, and the troops opened fire. Eleven villagers were killed, among them five women and two children. When the Slovak deputies in the Hungarian parliament protested against this shooting, the Minister for Home Affairs, Count Andrassy, replied in uncompromising terms that the villagers of Csernova had committed 'an act of rebellion against the State'. The subsequent debates in the parliament were repeatedly interrupted by angry Slovak deputies.

*   *   *

In Africa, the course of European colonization continued to be challenged. In Morocco, where there had been a number of attacks on Europeans in the early months of the year, eight Europeans working on the harbour at Casablanca – five Frenchmen, two Spaniards and an Italian – were massacred by Muslim tribesmen.[1] The French government despatched a military force to restore order and the town, much of which was being held by the Muslim rebels, was bombarded from the sea. Casablanca was then occupied by French forces.

The bombardment and the occupation of Casablanca aroused fury in Germany, where the annual Pan-German Congress described it as part of a French policy 'of conquest and annexation in the highest degree damaging to Germanic prestige in the Islamic world'. The German nationalists argued that if Morocco were to be seized by France, then Germany should demand an equivalent territorial compensation. Ignoring such German protests, the French began slowly to re-assert their authority. Their methods were harsh. When, in September, a French reconnaissance force drove the Muslim rebels out of the village of Teddert, the village was then burnt to the ground. In Fez, an uprising against the Sultan of Morocco proclaimed his rival, Mulai Hafid, a supporter of Muslim Holy War against 'the infidel French', as Sultan in his place. France's assertion of her colonial rights was clearly going to take a very long time indeed, and to be fought all the way by the forces of Islam.

Among the European Powers, the rise of Islamic opposition to French rule in Morocco raised fears of a Pan-Islamic uprising throughout West Africa. Comfort was taken by the British in the region from a report that among the Ashanti of the Gold Coast, the influence of Islam was waning, and that 'fetishism' and 'animism' – the original beliefs of the tribesmen – were not succumbing to what had been a considerable Islamic activity and propaganda. In the Northern Territories, however, the British officials, while successfully pacifying a number of tribes, noted that the spread of Islam was continuous, with a flourishing trade in fezzes and prayer beads. Only in the independent, black, Republic of Liberia, did the advent of Islam seem a benefit. Here the effect was a flourishing trade in alcohol which, while profitable to the traders (mostly British, with the Germans in sharp competition), was having a deleterious effect on the population. After the burning

[1] As I write these words, the newspapers report (25 May 1996) the murder of seven French monks by Muslim fundamentalists in Algeria.

alive of a Swiss citizen, M. W. Wolz, who had been captured in the interior of the republic, a British observer commented that 'a leaven of Mahomedanism is gradually but surely penetrating the hinterland' and might help to check the consumption of alcohol.

In Portugal's western Africa colonies – Guinea and Angola – native uprisings led to the despatch of troops from Lisbon and short but intense punitive expeditions. Portuguese rule in these two colonies, especially the way in which the plantations were worked, was being criticized by European Liberals as constituting a system of slavery, not unlike that which had been exposed and halted in the Belgian Congo. British Liberals were particularly agitated, but the pressure of commercial interests could sometimes be stronger than the dictates of morality. In the construction of the railway system in Angola, where fifty miles had been built but a further 1400 miles were under construction or consideration, British capital and British contractors were the principal participants.

In German South West Africa, the last of the Herero rebels were being hunted down. Reports reaching Europe suggested that, in the systematic sweeps being made against Herero villages, the whole tribe was being 'annihilated'.

In German West Africa, near Lake Chad, a rebellion in the Adamawa region was quickly crushed. In nearby French West Africa, a Muslim rebellion culminated in an attack by 5000 insurgents on the French army posts that had been established north of Lake Chad; the troops were able to beat off the attackers, and the French colonial administration announced with pride that a mission under Captain Arnaud had been able to cross the Sahara in 100 days without interference: a distance of 3125 miles, of which a fifth was by rail.

In the Far East, the Japanese were learning the problems of imperial rule. Not only had the peoples of eastern Formosa continued to resist the encroachments of civilization, but in Korea an uprising against the Japanese presence led to bloodshed, and a Korean regiment, which had refused Japanese orders to disband, opened fire on the Japanese forces that eventually overcame it. More than two hundred Japanese police and postal officials were murdered in the course of the uprising. Reprisals were severe.

*   *   *

One set of potential imperial conflicts was averted in 1907, by the signature in London and St Petersburg of the Anglo-Russian Agreement. It was three years since Britain's agreement with Russia's ally France, whereby Britain was given a free hand in Egypt in return for a French free hand in Morocco. This had been a bargain for Britain, given the enormous difficulties France was facing from Islamic national sentiment in Morocco, and Britain's existing firm hand and steady economic progress in Egypt.

The Anglo-Russian Agreement created a Russian and a British sphere of political and economic influence in Persia, with a neutral zone between them. East of Persia, Russia agreed not to push further south towards India in the region of Afghanistan, and to let Britain control the foreign policy of Afghanistan. Britain, for her part, would likewise not move closer to Russia in Central Asia. British fears of a Russian drive towards the Indian Ocean, fears that derived from Russia's Central Asian conquests of twenty years earlier, could be set aside. In a deliberate attempt to keep their frontiers apart, Britain and Russia transferred a strip of high mountain territory 150 miles long and 20 miles wide, the Wakhan, to China. 'Frontiers,' said a former Viceroy of India (and later British Foreign Secretary), Lord Curzon, that year, 'are indeed the razor's edge on which hang suspended the modern issues of war and peace, of life and death to nations.'

Natural disasters and serious accidents also took their toll in 1907. These included earthquakes and plague. In Kingston, Jamaica, more than seven hundred people were killed during an earthquake in January. Several United States ships hurried to the scene with aid, but were told by the British Governor that their help was not needed (he resigned a few months later on the grounds of old age). In February, when a North Sea steamer was driven on to the breakwater at the Hook of Holland, 128 passengers were drowned, and only sixteen saved.

In an explosion on board a French battleship in dock at Toulon, more than a hundred sailors were killed. In Canada, when a railway bridge being built over the St Lawrence River near Quebec collapsed, seventy workmen were killed. In a mining accident in Pennsylvania that year, more than two hundred men were cut off by fire from the mine entrance; none was saved. Accidents on the railways of the world were taking a steady toll as the century advanced; in Britain more than a thousand people lost their lives in railway accidents in 1907. This had been the death toll every year for the past decade.[1] Such high loss of life, which when it first becomes part of the life of a nation has the power to shock, soon becomes 'just part of life' – as a reader of these pages commented while I was writing them.

Yet the detailed accounts of natural and man-made disasters which were published in the daily newspapers throughout the world send a signal of the fragility of human life to those who had the leisure or the philosophic reflection to pause when such facts became known. One such example in 1907 was the earthquake which struck the Central Asian region of Bokhara in October. This was a predominantly Muslim region over which Tsarist Russia had been sovereign for the previous forty years. In the town of Karatagh, which was totally destroyed, an estimated fifteen thousand people were killed. The scale of death was such that it made its impact on distant Europe; as did the much smaller scale of an earthquake that took place two days later in southern Italy, when 175 people were killed in the village of Verruzano.

In India, the hopes of the previous year that the plague epidemic was on the wane, and that the number of deaths was steadily falling every year (from more than a million to less than a quarter of a million) were cruelly dashed. The death toll for the twelve months ending in September 1907 was 1,206,055, the highest recorded since statistics had been kept. It brought the death toll for the previous seven years to more than five million. Drastic measures were recommended during 1907 by the Government of India's medical experts, including the evacuation of hundreds of thousands of rat-infested houses, and the mass destruction of rats, even the possible inoculation of rats. But such was the government of India's fear of creating popular unrest, as the inoculation proposals had done three years earlier, that even these measures were made dependent on 'the full consent of the people', and this was not always possible to secure.

Famine also struck Russia in 1907, when the widespread failure of the harvest led to the deaths of more than a million people.

Inventions that bore upon the future nature of warfare attracted considerable attention in 1907. That year the Hague Convention of 1898 came up for

[1] A total of 11,440 people lost their lives in railway accidents in Britain between 1897 and 1907. In that same period, more than ten thousand people were killed on the roads in the United States in motorcar accidents.

renewal as part of President Roosevelt's suggestion to hold a peace conference of all the Powers. The 1898 Convention had outlawed the dropping of bombs from balloons 'or other kinds of aerial vessels'. Of the forty-four countries present at The Hague for the second conference, only twenty-seven supported a continuation of the ban on aerial warfare. The twenty-seven included Belgium, Britain, Portugal and the United States. Germany rejected the ban.

The one agreement reached with regard to air warfare at The Hague in 1907 concerned the targets that could be attacked. Warships in harbours could be attacked from the air, as could 'military works, military or naval establishments, depots of arms or war material' and workshops and factories 'which could be utilized for the needs of a hostile fleet or army'. By default, civilians had retained protection from the air; but war in the air as such was given international legitimacy.

Even as the delegates were in conference at The Hague, the British and German Governments were embarked on an aerial arms race with regard to airships. The Germans, thanks to the pioneering efforts of Count Zeppelin, already had the advantage. It was not until four years after the Hague Conference that the first British airship, the *Mayfly*, was ready to fly. As it was being taken out of its dock, however, it broke its back, and the designers of the project had to return to the drawing board.

Less spectacular, but quickly becoming significant for the lives of millions, 1907 saw the manufacture in the United States of the first electric washing machine, and in Germany the invention of Persil detergent. The first synthetic plastic, Bakelite, was also invented that year. In the realm of popular entertainment the film 20,000 *Leagues under the Sea* was produced, and, on July 8 in New York, *The Follies of 1907* music and dancing show had its opening night – the Ziegfeld Follies who were to entertain enthusiastic audiences for another half century.

CHAPTER NINE

1908

WHETHER THE OTTOMAN EMPIRE could transform itself from a State of sloth and corruption, as many saw it, into a dynamic modern empire, had long been a question that preoccupied the European Powers. The possibility of that transformation was suddenly pushed to the fore of European consciousness in 1908, when the Committee of Union and Progress, established in Salonika two years earlier by Turkish reformers, mostly young army officers, demanded the salvation of Turkey through constitutional reform.

One catalyst for the Young Turk revolution was the growing anarchy in Macedonia, where the continuing fighting between Greeks, Bulgarians, Serbs and Roumanians, the burning of each other's villages and the murder of civilians caught in the fighting, threatened to bring the Powers, particularly Austria and Russia, into Macedonia to restore order. Any such direct foreign intervention, as was becoming increasingly likely, would clearly end the already diminished control of the Sultan in the province.

The Young Turks were helped in their revolution by the Albanians, who, hitherto the loyal providers of troops for the Sultan, announced their support for the Committee of Union and Progress. Their grievance was great: under Turkish rule, Albania had been forbidden schools, and even a printing press. The Ottoman secret police had inklings that insurrection was afoot, and during June there were many searches and several arrests. On July 3, an insurrection broke out in the Macedonian town of Resne, led by Ahmed Niyazi Bey, who seized arms and ammunition from the local Turkish garrison (while the garrison was away from its barracks at Friday prayers) and took to the hills with 200 soldiers and 200 civilians, including the mayor, the tax-inspector and the Police Commissioner. Niyazi's idea was to set up, in the hills, an independent administration. In a manifesto issued on the day of his revolt, he declared that he would combat 'the injustices and inequalities which our fatherland has been suffering for many years'.

Niyazi Bey believed, not unreasonably, that he and his men might be hunted down and killed. 'Rather than live basely,' he wrote to his parents on the eve of his revolt, 'I have preferred to die.' But he was quickly joined by a number of young Turkish army officers stationed in nearby Monastir (now Bitola), among them the twenty-seven-year-old Major Enver, who had joined the Committee of Union and Progress in Monastir two years earlier, and whose dynamic personality was to make him one of the heroes of the Turkish revolution, and of the Turkish people.[1]

On July 6 a member of an Ottoman enquiry commission, which the Young Turks had boycotted, was assassinated in Salonika. The Sultan at once ordered one of his most trusted generals, Shemsi Pasha, to go to Macedonia and crush the rebellion. On reaching Monastir on July 7 he stopped at the main post office to send a telegram to Constantinople outlining his plan of campaign. As he was getting back into his carriage he was assassinated. The Committee for Union and Progress hastened to inform the Powers, through their Consuls in Monastir, that its sole aim was the restoration of the Turkish constitution of 1876, which had briefly instituted a parliamentary system; that it was in no way hostile to non-Muslims; and that it would only use force 'against the enemies of liberty and in self-defence'.

On July 10, the Sultan's aide-de-camp was assassinated while on his way to Constantinople by ship. A new general, Marshal Osman Pasha, reached Monastir on July 12, but his troops refused to fire on the insurrectionists, their fellow Turks and fellow soldiers. Starting on July 15, more than eighteen thousand Turkish troops were sent from Anatolia to reinforce the garrisons in Macedonia. On July 20, the Muslim population of Monastir rose up in revolt, seizing all military stores in the city. Uprisings followed in several towns. At Firzovik, in the Turkish province of Kosovo, thousands of Albanians gathered together and took an oath in favour of the Turkish constitution, demanded that it be restored, and threatened to march on Constantinople and depose the Sultan if he did not restore it.

The Young Turk revolution had begun. On July 22, Marshal Osman Pasha was kidnapped in Monastir, and on the following day the Young Turks in the city declared the constitution restored. Within a few hours, the constitution was proclaimed in several other Macedonian towns, and on July 23 the Committee of Union and Progress, meeting in Salonika, likewise

[1] When, in 1969, I was reading aloud to a group of elderly Turks in a village on the Gallipoli Peninsula an account of the early military career of Kemal Ataturk (whose statue was in the centre of their village, as in every Turkish village) they interrupted my reading to ask me, in unison: 'Tell us about Enver.'

proclaimed a constitution. Two Army Corps based in Salonika then threatened to march on Constantinople if the Sultan did not act at once to accept their demands. On learning of the force that was about to descend on the capital, Abdul Hamid ('Abdul the Damned' to his European critics) agreed to restore the constitution which had been granted to his subjects when he become Sultan in 1876 but which had been 'suspended' fourteen months later. He also agreed to abolish censorship, and to release political prisoners.

A new Grand Vizier, Kiamil Pasha, was appointed, and promised to modernize the ramshackle dominions. In Jerusalem, one of the more distant cities of the empire, the Jewish and Arab inhabitants of the city greeted the news of the new constitution with the hope that both would have their communal interests attended to. In Monastir, the Greek population, at a mass meeting, declared its support for the constitution. In the town of Seres, where the mixed population had earlier been in violent conflict, the Greek Metropolitan, the Turkish Mufti, and the leading Bulgarian Orthodox priests embraced each other after the reading of the Sultan's decree. Even the head of the Muslim religious hierarchy in the Ottoman Empire, the Sheikh-ul-Islam, took an oath to the constitution, and declared that there was nothing in the demands of the Young Turk revolutionaries that conflicted with Islamic law.

The Young Turk revolution passed with almost no bloodshed in Anatolia. An exception was the assassination of the hated Fehmi Pasha, the former military governor of Pera, whose autocratic rule of terror had led to his banishment a year earlier to Bursa, following protests by the British and German ambassadors. Further away from the centre, there was more agitation; even the Greeks and Bulgarians in Macedonia, after their initial euphoria, found it difficult to preserve their new-found amity. The Young Turks also stirred up national agitation in Macedonia when they demanded that the Turkish language be taught in Bulgarian schools, a haughty imperial demand reminiscent of the earlier, harsher days of Abdul Hamid's autocracy.

In the distant Ottoman province of Arabia, the local Turkish commander-in-chief, Ratib Pasha, and his troops, who had been sent there by the Young Turks from the Sultan's Guard at Constantinople because they were suspected of being opposed to the new constitution, revolted against the new order in Constantinople. The Bedouins of Arabia also revolted, seeing in the turmoil of the change in power at the centre an opportunity to attack Turkish military outposts. Troops loyal to the Young Turks hastened to the region. The Bedouin rebellion was suppressed, and Ratib Pasha captured.

In the remote mountainous eastern region around Lake Van, the Kurds took advantage of the transfer of power in Constantinople to join forces with another rebel Turkish general, Ibrahim Pasha, and to renew their earlier attacks on the Armenians and Nestorians in their midst – the hated 'Christian infidels' – destroying many villages. As in Arabia, troops loyal to Constantinople were sent to crush the rebellion; Ibrahim Pasha was killed, and the Kurdish troops whom he had led were dispersed.

The situation in Arabia was alleviated for the Young Turks in September, when, on the first day of the month, a historic day for the Ottoman Empire, the Hedjaz railway was opened, linking Damascus with Medina, a distance of 750 miles. The railway had been paid for as a work of religious charity by the contributions of tens of thousands of Muslims from throughout the Ottoman Empire. With the completion of the railway – a single-track, narrow-gauge construction – not only pilgrims, but also Turkish troops could at last move rapidly from Anatolia to the main centres of Arabia. The Arab tribes along the route, celebrating under the Young Turks' revolutionary banners of 'Liberty, Equality, Fraternity', took an oath to protect the railway. Even further to the south, the Turkish commander of the Yemen Field Force, Marshal Ahmed Fevzi Pasha, took an oath of loyalty to the new constitution. The vast empire, which might have been torn apart in a struggle between autocracy and reform, had held together.

The constitutional reforms instituted by the Young Turks led to an influx of European assistance. A Frenchman was appointed financial adviser to the new government, and an Englishman adviser on irrigation. Later, a senior British naval officer, Admiral Limpus, was sent out as head of the Turkish Navy, to advise particularly on the strengthening of the Turkish naval defences at the entrance to the Dardanelles. Limpus's successful efforts to protect Turkey from a hostile naval attack towards Constantinople were to help considerably, less than seven years after he had begun them, in repulsing the ships of his own navy. But a request by the Young Turks, in November 1908, for an alliance with Britain, was rejected in London. Despite its revolution, Turkey was not regarded as being the equal of the European Powers.

The Kurds, who in eastern Turkey had used the upheavals in Constantinople to attack their Christian neighbours, were also active across the Turkish border, inside Persia. In the region of Lake Urmiah, Kurdish troops, under their own national leaders, rampaged through thirty-six Armenian villages, killing an estimated two thousand villagers.

In the continuing struggle in Morocco, where France was determined to secure the ascendancy, the country's Sultan, Abdul Azziz, was challenged by his half-brother Mulai Hafid, who usurped power in Fez and declared himself Sultan. At the same time, Mulai Hafid caused considerable mirth when he exposed the absurdity of the deposed Sultan's purchases, which he put on display in an attempt to deride his half-brother's claims to continue to rule. These purchases included scores of damaged bicycles, a mound of broken cameras and rotting photographic material, a disintegrating stage coach, an uninstalled passenger lift, crates of unworn ceremonial uniforms, boxes of mechanical toys, hundreds of yards of unused wallpaper, pianos, harmoniums and street organs. The gullible Abdul Azziz had been persuaded to purchase this mass of material by European salesmen from whom he sought the symbols of 'civilization'.

Following Mulai Hafid's entrance into Fez, the citizens of Marrakech declared themselves for him. In a last attempt to regain his throne, Abdul Azziz marched on Marrakech, but was betrayed by tribal auxiliaries in his army, and overthrown. At Tangier, the principal city of Morocco, and the centre of French influence, Mulai Hafid proclaimed himself Sultan. A German attempt to act as Mulai Hafid's patron was challenged by France and Spain. The commander of the French troops in the region, General D'Amade, urged the would-be Sultan to accept French and Spanish overlordship in Morocco.

When Mulai Hafid agreed to the general's conditions, he was accepted as Sultan. France and Spain were relieved to have ensured their predominance in Morocco, and the loyalty of the new ruler. How far that loyalty could be depended upon was, however, questioned in France when what *The Times* described as Mulai Hafid's 'plausible, smooth-tongued emissaries' went to Paris and leaked a letter which he had sent to the chiefs of the Shawia tribes. These tribes had already made their submission to France, yet Mulai Hafid told them: 'I am coming towards your country like the rising sun, which lights the road with his rays. I rose up in response to the Musulman appeals in order to drive out the impure foreigners. After having thrown the French into the sea, you will proceed to Rabat, where you will wait for me.'

*   *   *

There was a further conflict between France and Germany in Morocco in 1908, when the German consulate in Casablanca tried to assist some German deserters from the French Foreign Legion to escape the country. As the consular officials were escorting them to the dockside, to embark on a German steamer, they were seized and captured by French soldiers, who threatened the consul with a revolver and struck his Moroccan guard. Germany demanded an apology. Once more, as the dispute flared, the other European powers were amused by the German protests. A situation was developing where every German action seemed a parody of the behaviour of a dignified Power.

There was also a growing sense among the Powers that the Germans would seek, wherever they could, to obtain small but significant advantage. It was Germany which was undertaking the only substantial building works in Jerusalem, including two replicas of German castles, both perched on high ground: the Augusta Victoria Hospice on the Mount of Olives and the Church of the Dormition on Mount Zion. It was Germany which persuaded the Turks to make Germany the protecting power for all Turkish subjects in China, a role hitherto exercised – under agreements signed in 1515 and 1740 – by France. There was again a certain derision when it emerged that France had 1200 troops still in China, perfectly capable of looking after the few Turkish interests in China, little more than several traders and merchants, while Germany had only 700 troops for her far larger commercial and territorial interests.[1]

The search for agreements that would limit, rather than exacerbate, conflict between the Powers was, however, still a predominant factor of European relations. In April, France and Germany signed a convention whereby they agreed to settle the line of the common frontier between the German Cameroons and the French Congo. The border was delineated in such a way, using rivers and streams as the frontier, that accidental clashes between troops could be minimized, and even averted altogether. There were also agreements in April between all those countries with Baltic and North Sea coastlines, an agreement in which Russian and Germany were prominent, in which all the countries concerned – Russia, Germany, Denmark, Norway, Sweden, Holland, Belgium and Britain – recognized the territorial status quo in the Baltic Sea and North Sea. The Germans, ever-sensitive to foreign criticism, regarded the agreements, as the *North German Gazette* expressed

---

[1] The largest military contingent still in China in 1908 was the British, 2000 men. Japan, like France, had 1200 men still garrisoned in China at that time.

it, as 'of direct importance from the German point of view, since they once and for all cut the ground from under the feet of those who have continually imputed to Germany a desire to annex the smaller neighbouring States'. This comment did not address the question of the political and national aspirations of Poles living on the Baltic Coast, or of Danes on both the Baltic and North Sea coasts of German-annexed Schleswig.

One movement that continued to gather momentum as the first decade of the twentieth century drew towards its last years was the demand by women that they should be allowed to vote for the governments that ruled them. In Europe, in the Russian province of Finland, women could already vote, and could also be elected as members of the Finnish Parliament. They also had the vote in New Zealand. In Britain, Germany and the United States, no such rights had yet been accorded them.

On 17 January 1908 there was a demonstration in Downing Street when thousands of women, and many men who were their supporters in the call, demanded women's suffrage. A few women managed to chain and padlock themselves to the railings. Two of them managed to enter 10 Downing Street itself. Among the suffragettes who were arrested and imprisoned that year, as the protests spread, was a twenty-three-year-old American woman, Alice Paul, from New Jersey. She was a student in Britain when she joined the suffragettes, and was imprisoned three times. Returning to the United States, she advocated the use of militant tactics to publicize the need for Federal women's suffrage. In 1996 she was honoured in the United States by the issue of a seventy-eight cent postage stamp.

In Britain, 'Votes for Women' became the slogan under which not only many women but many men insisted on the right of women to participate in the elections of their rulers. In June, after a meeting of the Women's Social and Political Union, one enterprising advocate of female suffrage took a small boat and, from the waters of the River Thames, harangued those Members of Parliament who were on the terrace. Two women broke windows in 10 Downing Street, one of whom declared with passion, 'It will be bombs next time'. In October a call went out from militant women to 'rush' the House of Commons. One woman managed to enter the debating chamber, and to address the Members of Parliament, but she was quickly removed.

The previous year – 1907 – women in Britain had been made eligible for election to local government. Only eleven days after the episode in the House of Commons, a woman candidate was only narrowly defeated in an election for a seat on the London County Council. At the beginning of November two women candidates were elected to local government at Oxford and Manchester, elections which marked a breakthrough in the question of women's rights. Nine days after these local elections, the first woman mayor in the United Kingdom, seventy-two-year-old Dr Garrett Anderson, was elected at Aldeburgh. Six years earlier she had been part of a women's committee sent by the British government to examine the cruelties imposed on Boers and blacks in the concentration camps in South Africa.

In December 1908, in Moscow, a Russian Women's Congress demanded universal suffrage for men and women. It also called for the prohibition of the employment of women on night work and work in the mines, and the limitation of women's work to eight hours a day.

The struggle of national aspirations inside Austria-Hungary was highlighted in 1908 when Count Potocki, the Governor of Galicia, and a Pole, was murdered by a Ruthenian student. The student's name was Siczynski; he accused the Count of oppressing the Ruthenians. The assassination caused particular anguish in Galicia as Count Potocki, one of the wealthiest men in the region and a substantial landlord, had been making a special effort to establish good relations between Poles and Ruthenians. In the Ruthenian areas, however, the assassin was hailed as a national hero.

On February 1 the King of Portugal and his heir, the Crown Prince, were both murdered in Lisbon. As a token of his grief, Edward VII attended a Requiem Mass in London; it was the first time in 220 years that an English king had attended a Roman Catholic service in Britain.

More than two years had passed since the Russian revolution of 1905 had been crushed, the Moscow insurgents put down with severity, and the Duma turned into that most mocked of Russian institutions, the 'talking shop'. Discontent, terror and repression were, however, continuous. In 1908 and 1909 more than three thousand Russians were sentenced to death, and more than four thousand to hard labour, for political crimes. The Socialist Revolutionary Party advocated assassination as a political weapon, but was penetrated at its highest ranks by a police spy, Evno Azev, whose exposure as a spy in 1908, while he was head of the Socialist Revolutionary's Battle

Organization, was a blow from which the party never fully recovered.

In March 1908 seven people were hanged in St Petersburg for planning to murder the Grand Duke Nicholas (the Tsar's uncle), and the Minister of Justice, Ivan Stcheglovitov – who survived in his post for another seven years. The Constitutional Democrats – the Kadets – denounced the hanging of political terrorists and referred to the gallows on which those found guilty were hung as 'Stolypin neckties'. In July, Leo Tolstoy published a powerful appeal, *I Cannot Keep Silent!*, in which he declared that government repression was 'a hundredfold worse' than the criminal and terrorist violence in Russia because it was carried out in cold blood. On Tolstoy's eightieth birthday that September, the Russian newspapers were forbidden by the authorities to make any mention of the anniversary.

As the German navy continued to grow, making it the largest naval force in the Baltic, Russia was drawing closer to Britain. In 1907 she had settled her disputes with Britain in Persia and Afghanistan. In June 1908, in the Russian Baltic port of Reval, King Edward VII met his cousin Tsar Nicholas II. For fear of assassination should they meet on land, the two sovereigns met at sea, in their yachts. It was the first ever visit of a British sovereign to Russian territorial waters. No reigning British sovereign was ever to set foot on Russian soil, Tsarist or Communist until in October 1994, three years after the fall of Communism, Queen Elizabeth II did so.

The importance of the Reval meeting was noted by the Russian newspaper *Novoe Vremya*:

> What seemed impossible a little while ago is now a matter of fact. Russia and Great Britain can now regard with equanimity the Tibetan, the Afghan frontier, and the Persian and Indian questions. The shadows between them have disappeared. In consequence the unsuccessful rising on the Indian frontier and events in Persia lost their international character and assumed a local character.
>
> The material for strategic railways which is lying ready on both frontiers of Afghanistan can now become a mighty factor in establishing economic unity, without which political unity loses half its value.
>
> The recent events in Asia were a test of the new Anglo-Russian relations. In time everybody will see that Russia and Great Britain, in bringing their Asiatic interests into harmony, are also animated by peaceful aims

in Europe. It is to be hoped that Macedonia will soon be pacified by common action on the part of the Powers, based on proposals agreed upon between Russia and Great Britain.

The meeting of the Monarchs at Reval is a feast of peace.

The Reval meeting was a harbinger of a feature of twentieth-century diplomacy, the meetings of Heads of State to cement, or at least to promote, changes of government policy. One result of the visit was the formation of a Russo-English Chamber of Commerce, intended to increase trade between the two countries, that had fallen steadily for many years. Russian reformers were hopeful that the warm welcome given to the sovereign of a parliamentary democracy would encourage their own autocrat to look with more favour on the Duma, and to allow it more authority; the presence of the President of the Duma at the ceremonies was thought to be a good omen in this regard. But the nervousness in Europe at the possible alignment of Britain and Russia for something other than trade and family amity was underlined by the worries expressed in Berlin and Vienna at possible deeper implications of Edward VII's journey: that Russia, France and Britain, though not bound together by any former tripartite alliance, were clearly a force capable of challenging Germany and Austria-Hungary should the need arise.

Each episode that generated friction was therefore scrutinized, not only for itself, but also for any possible wider implications. In the autumn of 1908 a retired German civil servant, Rudolf Martin, caused uproar in Britain when he advocated the construction of a fleet of Zeppelin airships that could be used for the invasion of Britain. On October 9 the London *Daily Mail* reported Martin's words, at a public meeting in Berlin, when he called his audience's attention to 'a plan for the conquest of England by airships' and 'asserted that the principal duty of aerial navigators was to induce the combined Continental Powers to construct a fleet of 10,000 "Zeppelins", each to carry twenty soldiers, which should land and capture the sleeping Britons before they could realize what was taking place'.

One result of the alert caused by Rudolf Martin's outburst was to increase interest in British Government circles in the aeroplane as a weapon of war. The French Army had just ordered fifty Wright aeroplanes that were to be built in France, and was experimenting with both petrol bombs and bombs containing inflammable liquid that might be dropped from these planes. The British Government set up a special committee on 'Aerial Navigation'. Among those who gave evidence to it was Sir Hiram Maxim, the inventor of the Maxim gun. 'If you were going to bombard a town,' Maxim told the committee, 'you might have a thousand of these machines, each one carrying a large shell, because it is the large shell that does the business. If a thousand tons of pure nitro-glycerine were dropped on to London in one night, it would make London look like a last year's buzzard's nest.'

Maxim's prophesy was thirty-two years before its time. The committee decided that there was no need for government action. Its report concluded: 'There appears to be no necessity for the Government to continue experiments in aeroplanes, provided that advantage is taken of private enterprise in this form of aviation.' Within a year, however, the Wright brothers themselves were advising the British government about the new aerial science. A new international rivalry had begun. When the First World War broke out six years later the number of effective warplanes at the disposal of the Powers was limited: Britain possessed 113, France 120 and Germany 232. When the war ended in November 1918, Britain, then with the largest air force, possessed 22,000 warplanes.

In Austria-Hungary, the racial and national animosities that had been the bane of the first eight years of the century were in no way diminished in the ninth year. When the Bohemian Diet met in Prague, the Germans, who constituted a majority, obstructed all legislation proposed by the Czech members, or in any way advantageous to the Czechs. When fighting broke out on the floor of the chamber between Czech and German deputies, the Diet was dissolved. Unable to fight in parliament, the Czech and German protagonists took their quarrel to the streets. Not only did Prague ring to the shouts of violent clashes between the rival groups, but in the southern province of Slovenia, German and Slovene citizens of the empire battled in the streets of Laibach.[1] In Vienna, it was German and Italian students who fought in the streets, the Italians demanding an Italian university in the Austrian port of Trieste, the majority of whose inhabitants were Italian (and the central square of which, today, is the Piazza Unità d'Italia).

When, in the parliament in Vienna, the Czech Radical deputies sought to prevent the passage of the annual budget measures by drowning the voices of the debaters with whistles and toy trumpets, it was only the intervention

[1] Since 1918, Ljubljana, an integral part of Yugoslavia, and, since 1993, the capital of the independent Republic of Slovenia.

of the socialist leader, Victor Adler, which enabled the debate to continue. He warned that those deputies who, by their disruptive tactics, prevented the parliament from dealing with fiscal matters and the problems of public expenditure, were inviting the return of 'the old Austrian bond of union, the common whipping block and the common gallows, and a government of strong hands and feeble brains'. The Czechs bowed to Adler's democratic reasoning, and the budget was then passed, the Polish deputies also supporting it.

There was a boost for Czech national aspirations in 1908, when the Russian Duma invited the Czech leader, Karel Kramar, to be their guest. At a banquet given in his honour in St Petersburg, the theme of all the speakers was the closer union of all Slavs; it was noted with enthusiasm that the Poles, hitherto wary, for their own patriotic reasons, of Russia's Pan-Slav aspirations, had decided to adhere to a movement whose aim was the support of Slavs in the German and Austro-Hungarian empires, and in the Balkans. The leader of the Polish party in the Duma, Roman Dmowski, acknowledged that the interests of Poland lay in working for the 'strength and greatness' of Russia. It was the Poles under German rule who were to be considered the captives. Polish aristocrats from the Austrian province of Galicia participated in the deliberations of the Parliament in Vienna, accepting that Cracow and Lemberg were two imperial cities in a multi-national empire, rather than jewels in an independent Poland's crown.

In retrospect, the national tensions within Austria-Hungary were but the prelude to that empire's territorial disintegration, even if it took a world war to accomplish this act of political evolution. At the time, however, Austria-Hungary made every effort to grow in strength and cohesiveness, even expanding its influence southward into the Balkans. In 1908 the Emperor Franz Josef celebrated sixty years on the throne. *The Times* of London reported the climax of the celebrations in Vienna:

On June 12 there passed before the Emperor, in a procession which lasted more than three hours, 12,000 of his subjects, of all races and tongues, in costumes of historic periods, shouting their loyal greetings. Nobles and warriors have assembled before the monarch before but never before has there been so complete a muster of the peoples of the empire. The Austrians, who are a nation without knowing it, found themselves that morning, and the people of Vienna cheered each race and clan, in the consciousness that not only common loyalty to a common dynasty personified in a venerable Sovereign, but also a common history, common interest, common enemies and a common destiny, all unite them.

Nor was an omen for the future wanting. Towards midday, with scarcely a cloud on the horizon, and none overhead, there appeared a rainbow, pale but distinct and lying, as it were, horizontally in the form of a crescent along the vault of the sky, the arch of the bow pointed southwards and the two extremities of the bow northwards. The rainbow, as the omen foreshadows, is pointed southward.

The historian Andrew Wheatcroft has commented: 'It turned out to be an omen of doom, pointing to 28 June 1914, to the encounter of an archduke and an assassin in the streets of Sarajevo.'

Since the beginning of 1908 the focus of the Powers' concern had been the Balkans. The decision of the Young Turks in Constantinople to call a parliament in which all national groups could be represented, created fears both in Austria-Hungary and in Bulgaria, that the provinces under their respective control, but still under nominal Turkish suzerainty, would accept representation in the Ottoman parliament, and through that body would assert their national rights. The Austrians were particularly perturbed that the people of Bosnia-Herzegovina, which Austria had occupied in 1878, would use the opportunity of the Turkish reforms to challenge the often harsh nature of Austrian rule.

To their collective alarm, the Powers realized that Austria-Hungary was planning some dramatic initiative in the Balkans, to forestall the people of Bosnia-Herzegovina, many of whom were Muslim, from any representation at Constantinople. The crisis centred, as it so often did in Europe, around railway building. In January the Austro-Hungarian Foreign Minister, Baron von Aerenthal, announced that the Sultan of Turkey had been approached to allow Austrian railway building which would enable Austrian trade, and with it the political influence that went with trade, to move through Bosnia-Herzegovina, through its principal city, Sarajevo, and down to the Adriatic and Aegean Seas.

Although Aerenthal insisted that Austria did not aim at any territorial acquisitions, the development of railway links in Bosnia-Herzegovina would clearly lay the foundations for the further development of the Austro-Hungarian monarchy in the Balkans. Russia was immediately critical of any change in the agreement between Russia and Austria-Hungary, the basis of the Balkan policy of both powers since 1903, that neither would alter the status quo in the area in any manner, least not without the consent of the other.

The measures announced by the Austrians were, said the Russian Foreign Ministry, an alteration of the status quo solely in favour of Austria-Hungary. Aerenthal replied that in Austria's view, any previous agreement about the status quo was at an end; that Austria no longer considered herself bound to act in concert with Russia. The dispute intensified; Russia went so far as to announce its support of a parallel and rival railway from the Danube to the Adriatic, to be built by Serbia, an anti-Austrian measure for which Italy also announced its support.

Since 1878 the Turkish province of Bosnia-Herzegovina, while occupied by Austria-Hungary for the purpose of maintaining order, remained under the suzrainty of the Turkish Sultan. Bulgaria, too, while autonomous, was still nominally a Turkish possession. All that was suddenly to change. On October 5 Bulgaria declared its independence from Turkey (in which bold act it was supported by Russia), with Prince Ferdinand, a German prince of the Battenberg family who had accepted the Bulgarian crown in 1887, declaring himself Tsar of Bulgaria.[1]

On the following day, October 6 – a fateful day for European stability – Austria-Hungary announced the annexation of Bosnia-Herzegovina. The annexation alarmed Serbia, which now had the full panoply of Austrian sovereign power along its longest border, from the Danube to the Adriatic Sea; and it alarmed the Powers, who feared that Austria-Hungary intended to move against Serbia, as many of the most ardent Serb nationalists lived within the borders of the annexed areas. Russian public opinion was incensed that Slav lands, even if already occupied by the Habsburgs, should be formally incorporated into the Habsburg Empire, whose Slav minorities, among them Poles, Czechs, Slovaks, Slovenes and Ruthenes, were already considerable in numbers, and considerably agitated by so many elements of inferiority of status and influence.

In a protest meeting held in the Nobles' Hall in St Petersburg, attended

---

[1] Under Austrian pressure, Ferdinand was subsequently forced to 'downgrade' his title from Tsar to King.

by almost two thousand people, speeches were made denouncing 'the final enslavement of the Bosnians under the rule of Austria'. When the Crown Prince of Serbia arrived in St Petersburg on October 28, he was met with enthusiastic crowds chanting their support for Serbian independence, and their anger against Austria's acquisition of so many Serb subjects. But Germany, taking Austria-Hungary's side, was emphatic that no action should be taken against the annexation, even though it was at variance with the 1878 Treaty of Berlin, whereby the status quo in the Balkans was established; a status quo that Austria had finally disrupted, without regard to the fragile nature of the racial and ethnic imbalance which annexation created.

Russia, Italy, France, Britain and Turkey joined together to urge Austria-Hungary to submit the annexation to the deliberation of an international conference. At this conference, they insisted, the question of 'compensation' for Turkey, Serbia and Montenegro must be on the agenda. Austria-Hungary, despite her closeness to Germany, was being isolated and, in the opinion of many of her citizens, humiliated. Five Powers had aligned against her. With the exception of Turkey, they were to be her enemies on the battlefield within seven years.

Despite the intensity of feeling expressed in St Petersburg at the Austro-Hungarian annexation of Bosnia-Herzegovina, Russia, in the aftermath of her own revolution and her defeat by Japan, was in no position to take action as the protector of the South Slavs – the position to which she had always aspired. In the aftermath of the visit of the Serbian Crown Prince to St Petersburg, the Russian government, while expressing sympathy for Serbia and offering her 'moral support' in the confrontation with Austria and the championing of the Serbs of Bosnia, urged Serbia in unambiguous language not to take any 'provocative steps' which might lead to hostilities. But a few months later, the Russian Foreign Minister, Alexander Izvolsky, speaking in the Duma, called on the three Slavonic States in the Balkans – Bulgaria, Serbia and Montenegro – to 'become imbued with the consciousness of the necessity of moral and political union'.

The Austrians had made their first territorial acquisition since 1848. In a proclamation to the people of Bosnia-Herzegovina, Franz Josef declared that in order to raise them 'to a higher level of political life' than they had hitherto known, they would be given a voice in the framing of their own legislation. But with the exception of a minority group of Serbian Roman

Catholics, the majority of the inhabitants of the province were hostile to becoming a part of Austria-Hungary, however much Austrian military occupation had been preferable to Turkish misrule. The Serbs of the Greek Orthodox church, who formed the largest single group in the province, and the Muslims, known at the time as the Muslim Serbs – or, in the contemporary language, the 'Mohammedan Serbians' – were bitterly opposed to the imposition of full Austrian rule. The Bosnian Serb dream was unity with Serbia, whose independence had been guaranteed by the settlement of 1878, a settlement which the Austrians had now challenged.

In a somewhat disingenuous attempt to assuage the anger of the Powers, and of Turkey, that the annexation of Bosnia-Herzegovina presaged a disruption of the settled order in the Balkans, the Austrians announced that they were evacuating the Sanjak of Novi Bazar, the other, far smaller portion of the Turkish Balkan territories – a tiny sliver in fact – which they had occupied in 1878. Although a small region, it was of significance, strategically, in that the Austrian presence there had kept Serbia and Montenegro territorially apart.

In an attempt to placate Serbia, Austria announced that it would support the Serbian desire to be part of the Commission that regulated trade and traffic on the Danube. There would also be an Austrian relaxation of the strict control which she had exercised, since 1878, on the Montenegrin port of Antivari, thus giving Montenegro unrestricted access to the sea. But with regard to Bosnia-Herzegovina, Austria was adamant that her sovereignty was permanent and irreversible.

Within Austria-Hungary, it was the Magyars who were the most vociferous in support of the annexation; they were glad to feel that Serbia, their neighbour to the south, was being all the more effectively hemmed in, and pressed for a greater Hungarian influence in the annexed province. The Poles and Czechs used the occasion of the annexation to press for the granting of greater legislative powers to all the provincial Diets. The Croats went so far as to demand a separate state, not unlike the Hungarian status in the Dual Monarchy, whereby Croatia, Bosnia, Herzegovina and Dalmatia would form a separate and fully independent region, transforming the Dual Monarchy of Austria-Hungary into a Triple Monarchy of Austria, Hungary and Croatia.

Serbia, fearing that Bosnia-Herzegovina would be used by Austria-Hungary as the launching pad for an attack on Serbian independence, made bellicose threats. Austria-Hungary, in response, was forced to expend a portion of its already strained budgets on reinforcing the garrisons in the province. Many more troops were in place in the sovereign territory than had been needed when it was under military occupation.

One impact of the declaration of Bulgarian independence was to stimulate Greek national aspirations. This took several forms. One was the infiltration of Greek soldiers into Turkish-ruled Macedonia, where they tried to assert Greek predominance in the region, mostly by the time-honoured tactic of attacking Bulgarian villages. Another form was the determination of the Greeks living in Albania to assert the essentially Greek nature of that Turkish province, and to demand its annexation to Greece. A third manifestation of Greek national sentiment was a vote in the Cretan Chamber, which had managed to secure the withdrawal of Turkish troops – though not an end to Turkish sovereignty – in 1898, for union with Greece. The four Powers which since 1898 had been the Protecting powers on Crete – Britain, France, Russia and Italy – while sympathetic to Cretan aspirations, offered to open negotiations with the Turks, provided order was maintained in the island, and the Muslim population protected.

More Greek national sentiment was voiced in 1908; on the Turkish island of Samos, with its predominantly Greek population, a revolt of the islanders demanded the restoration of autonomies. Although guaranteed by statute in 1832, these autonomies had been eroded by the governor's desire to turn the island into a Turkish province. To disperse the revolt, the governor threatened to use Turkish troops. He was beaten by the mob and blockaded in his house. When Turkish troops did arrive from the mainland, they were met by rifle fire. The Turkish navy was then brought into action, bombarding the port of Vathy and the hills around it. In the end, discussions began – after killing, talking – and a compromise was reached. Turkish troops would be removed, the autonomous institutions would be restored, and the islanders would affirm their loyalty to the Sultan.

The new Turkish parliament was opened on December 10 by that same Sultan whose powers had been so drastically curtailed six months earlier. In conformity with the new Turkish mood of reform and toleration, a Greek, Prince Mavrogordato, was appointed Minister of Mines, Forests and Agriculture, and an Armenian, Noura Sunghian, became Minister of Commerce and Works. The Turkish Muslim leader, the Sheikh-ul-Islam, was also given a Cabinet post. Of the 250 elected deputies, 50 were Arabs from Arabia; there were also 18 Greeks, 12 Albanians, 4 Bulgarians, 2 Serbians and 3 Jews.

These constitutional advances, which raised great hopes among the Turkish population, were paralleled by disappointment, and some anger, that the provinces of Bosnia-Herzegovina and Bulgaria had been lost.

International affairs continued to be disturbed by national extremism, and regulated by binational treaties, a dynamic that posed the crucial question of whether war would come through popular agitation, often stirred up by demagogues, or be averted through statesmanlike arrangements, resolved at the negotiating table. There were two examples of this dilemma in November. On November 23, one of Britain's most senior military figures, Field Marshal Earl Roberts, who had been Commander-in-Chief of the British forces in the Boer War, made a public, and widely published speech stating that a German invasion of Britain was possible, and calling for a much larger army in order to meet such an attack. Five days later, in an attempt to preserve peace on the other side of the globe, the United States and Japan announced that they had reached agreement on maintaining the status quo in the Pacific, in preserving the independence and integrity of China, and on the principle of equal commercial and industrial opportunities for all nations trading with China.

In the Dutch East Indies the efforts to establish Dutch rule even in remote areas were continuous, and largely successful, and a programme of road building inaugurated which it was hoped would accelerate trade between the interior and the coastal towns. Sporadic rebellions on several islands were put down, except in Achin, where, as a contemporary British commentator remarked, 'the difficulty of the complete pacification of this huge country, about the size of France, is to find the medium between kindness, which may be mistaken for fear, and firmness, giving the impression of harshness, if not of cruelty'.

British 'pacification' efforts were also much in evidence during 1908. Along the northwest frontier of India, two local Muslim tribes, the Mohmands and the Zakka Khels, whose rebellion more than a decade earlier had been crushed, rebelled again. A punitive expedition was launched against the Zakka Khels. It was successful before the Mohmands could come to their assistance, despite the call by the Mohmand mullahs for their people to participate in *Jihad*, or Holy War. When, at the end of April, some seven thousand Mohmands crossed the British border, they were driven back, and a second punitive expedition sent out against them. The expedition achieved its aim and the Mohmands, their forts and watch towers having been destroyed, gave up the struggle. As the British force returned to India, they were met by a hostile gathering of a third tribe, the Utman Khels, but these rebels were quickly dispersed by concentrated artillery fire.

The instinct of rebellion could not be entirely crushed. At the end of the year a group of armed men of the Mahsud Waziri tribe made a raid fifty miles into British territory, seizing a village only six miles from a major British military cantonment, with its garrison of 3000 men. After the initial shock caused by such a daring raid, the British drove the raiders back into the mountains.

Within India, the British rulers were confronted by increased nationalist agitation throughout 1908. A series of small incidents created considerable nervousness among the rulers. In Bombay, fighting between Sunni and Shia Muslims was only quelled when troops were called in. At Tuticorin, political agitators wanting greater Indian powers of self-government, on learning that their leader had been arrested, destroyed the Missionary College, the municipal offices and the courthouse, burning all municipal and police records. Once more, troops were sent to restore order. In Bengal, an attempt was made to blow up the train in which the Lieutenant-Governor was travelling. At Muzaffarpur, two British women were killed when a bomb was thrown at their carriage by two young Bengalis who mistook the carriage for that of a local magistrate. One of the Bengalis committed suicide; the other was captured, tried, convicted and executed.

In a garden in Calcutta, police discovered a cache of arms, bombs and bomb-making instructions. Literature was also found there, exhorting Bengali youth to be Mazzinis and Garibaldis, and to take their inspiration from Italy's struggle for unity and independence. Not only were laws passed to forbid the manufacture or possession of explosives but, following applause in the local Indian newspapers for the attacks that had been carried out, newspapers were warned that any incitement to murder on the printed page would also be severely punished. One result of this law was the trial in July of the nationalist leader, and newspaper editor, Bal Gangadhar Tilak, who was convicted for sedition and sentenced to six years' transportation.

The sentence on Tilak did not deter, and may even have stimulated nationalist agitation. In August a Bengali who had been arrested, and had agreed to tell the police what he knew of local conspiracies against the British, was murdered by two young men, Kanai Lal and Sytendra Nath Bose, who burst into his cell and shot him dead. Both were caught, tried and executed. In November an inspector of police, who had been responsible for the capture of one of the Muzaffarpur murderers, was shot dead in a Calcutta lane. His assassins were never caught. In December, the Indian Criminal Law was amended. Under the amendment the accused in any sedition, disturbance or murder case no longer had the right to be present at his trial, or to be represented by his own defence lawyer, unless the magistrate specifically allowed it. If committed for trial, the accused would be sent before a panel of three judges. He would have no right to trial by jury.

On 1 November 1908 the British in India celebrated the fiftieth anniversary of the assumption of the government of India by the British crown. The intention of the pattern of administration that had been built up over those five decades was to be beneficent and constructive. District Magistrates regarded the wellbeing of those within their local jurisdiction as their over-riding concern. Vast areas of India were the scene of peaceful and productive enterprise. But political dissent, led by the Indian National Congress, often spilled over into violence. At a ceremony held in Jodhpur on the day after the jubilee celebrations – a ceremony attended by all of the princes of India for whom Britain was the paramount power – a message was read out from Edward VII, the King-Emperor, in which he expressed his regret at the recent 'seditious agitation and disorders', and stressed his determination to suppress them. In Britain, in a debate in the House of Lords, the Secretary of State for India, Lord Morley, explained that, despite the agitation, there would be no attempt to set up parliamentary institutions in India, or any-thing that would lead to them.

A former Viceroy, Lord Curzon, told the same session of the House of Lords that one of the causes of the unrest that was 'menacing the structure of Indian society' was what he described as 'unsuitable education', which had given Indians 'the catchwords of modern civilization without its ideas or its sobriety'. Another cause of the unrest, he pointed out, was the victory of Japan over Russia. Asia's triumph over Europe had served as a clarion call to many people in Asia who wished to assert their own power and indepen-dence, as Japan had done.

The glories of empire could not disguise the widespread poverty at home. In September it was announced by the British government, with all the precision of the most modern statistical techniques, that the number of paupers at the beginning of the year in England and Wales was 928,671. If Scotland were to be included, the number was well over a million. Another million able-bodied Britons were without work. In a speech at Dundee in October, Winston Churchill declared that the tackling of unemployment required special remedies which would lead into 'new and untrodden fields in British politics'. In the sphere of social reform, new measures were being devised by the Liberal government to apply the direct and beneficent intervention of the State to the needs of the working class. Another move towards greater government regulation of the conditions under which the working class lived was the Eight Hours Bill, reducing the maximum number of hours which Britain's almost a million miners could work underground.

Another imperial anniversary took place in 1908. A month after the British India celebrations, Austrians celebrated the sixtieth anniversary of the accession of Franz Josef as Emperor of Austria. The city of Vienna celebrated with fireworks and illuminations; in Prague, however, discontented Czechs rioted, and a state of siege was proclaimed.

In the German Empire, the Poles continued to be the subject of harsh legislation and determined action. In introducing new measures to the Prussian parliament on February 26, the Prussian Minister of the Interior, Count Arnim, said that the Polish problem could not be solved by conciliation. His argument was unambiguous. History showed that no nation ever gave up its struggle for independence. The Poles – divided for more than a century between Russia, Austria and Prussia – had refused to give up their national ideals. Only a considerable increase in the number of German settlers in the region could affect the demographic balance in Germany's favour. To achieve this, land had to be expropriated.

The proposed expropriation of land from the Poles led to a stormy debate inside Germany. The mayors of Posen, Danzig and Berlin were against the measure. So, too, was a former President of the Reichstag, Count Ballestrem. But the measure was finally approved by a majority vote. One opposition newspaper, the *Frankfurter Zeitung*, denounced the expropriations 'in the name of justice and humanity'. But a majority of the members of the German Parliament supported their Prussian counterparts, refusing a Polish request to allow the use of the Polish language at public meetings.

The language battle was not over, however. After a series of tempestuous discussions in the parliament it was agreed that, in administrative districts where more than 60 per cent of the local inhabitants spoke Polish, provided three days' notice were given to the police, Polish could be the language of the meeting. When the bill passed the Reichstag for final approval in April, it was also agreed that the French language could be used at meetings in Alsace-Lorraine, subject to the same conditions. So rigidly was the law upheld, however, that where only a third – or even as many as 50 or 55 per cent – of the local population were Polish, they were not allowed to use their own language at public meetings. But, as Baron Arnim had seen, the Poles were persistent in their national cause, with the result that 'mute' public meetings were held, at which there were no speeches, but where the resolutions were written up in Polish on a large blackboard, and passed by a show of hands.

German colonial policy was also debated with vigour during 1908. There was outrage among liberal-minded Germans when mockery and laughter greeted the remark of one parliamentarian 'that negroes are human beings with immortal souls'.

In South Africa, an attempt to expel Indians who were said to have entered the country without permission was met by widespread protest, and the organization of a policy of passive resistance to the government's registration laws. The leader of the passive resistance movement was Mohandas Karam-chand Gandhi, the British-educated lawyer whose leadership of the Indians in South Africa had turned them from a despised minority into a group of political significance that could not be ignored or swept aside. When Gandhi and several other leaders of the demonstrations were sentenced to two months' imprisonment with hard labour, Jan Christian Smuts, the South African Boer leader whose courage on the battlefield had been much admired in Britain, denounced the sentences as too lenient.

In answer to criticism from Britain of the severity of the punishments, and of other fines and expulsions, Smuts replied that the Transvaal was 'a white man's country' and should be 'kept that way'. It was a question of 'life or death', declared the Transvaal Minister for Native Affairs, as Indians already formed one fifteenth of the population. 'What would England do,' he asked, 'if she were threatened with the influx of 2,500,000 Asiatics?' Smuts went further. If Indian immigration were not halted, he warned, it would overrun the whole of South Africa.

Smuts agreed to open negotiations with Gandhi, but made it clear that he hoped no more Indians would reach South Africa, and that in due course the Indian population would wither away. A new law sought to deprive the

Indians already in the country of religious teachers, doctors and educationalists. When the act came into force, Gandhi renewed his call for demonstrations and protest, always stressing that no violence should be employed. He was convinced that the morality of the case would prevail over prejudice, if another protest could be mounted. It was to be a long, and ultimately successful struggle; one which marked him out as a natural leader of Indian political activity inside India itself.

The United States continued to hold itself aloof from the conflicts in Europe and Africa. But President Roosevelt intended to pursue patiently the search for agreements that would eliminate potential causes of friction. On April 22 the United States' Senate ratified a treaty of arbitration with Britain, whereby any dispute arising between the two countries, with regard to the interpretation of treaties and agreements, which could not be settled by diplomacy, would be submitted to the Hague Court of Arbitration (which had been set up nine years earlier).

That same month, Roosevelt asked Congress to authorize the construction of four first-class battleships. Speaking as both Chief Executive of the Nation and Commander-in-Chief of the United States Navy, he told the legislators: 'This is a measure of peace and not of war. I can conceive of no circumstances under which this republic would enter into an aggressive war; most certainly, under no circumstances, would it enter into an aggressive war to extend its territory or in any other manner seek material aggrandisement. I advocate that the United States build a Navy commensurate with its powers and its needs, because I feel that such a Navy will be the surest guarantee and safeguard of peace.'

Roosevelt went on to tell Congress that Britain 'has been saved by its fleet from the necessity of facing one of the two alternatives – of submission to conquest by a foreign Power or of itself becoming a great military Power. The United States can hope for a permanent career of peace on only one condition, and that is, on condition of building and maintaining a first-class Navy; and the step to be taken toward this end at this time is to provide for the building of four additional battleships'.

Congress did not accept the pacific nature and aim of Roosevelt's proposal. Ever-reluctant to sanction increases in military or naval spending, it would give the money for only two of the four ships for which the President had asked. He did have the satisfaction, however, of seeing the impression made on many nations by the round-the-world cruise of the American battleship fleet of sixteen vessels, and the sense that the warships had, as he expressed it, 'gained far more experience in battle tactics than they would have gained had they stayed in Atlantic waters'. There was no naval service in the world, he declared, 'in which the average of character and efficiency in the enlisted men is as high as is now the case in our own.'

As well as stressing the need for an active defence policy, Roosevelt was a believer, indeed a pioneer, in the importance of preserving the natural resources of the United States. Having set up the system of National Parks, protected from urban and industrial exploitation, he called a conference at the White House of State Governors and prominent men. The conference concluded that the 'conservation of our natural resources is a subject of transcendent importance, which should engage unremittingly the attention of the nation', and called on the government to enact laws for the prevention of waste in coal, oil and gas mining and extraction, 'with a view to their wise conservation for the use of the people'. This issue, broached with such confidence in the first decade of the century, continued to be of concern, and even of alarm, in the last decade of the century.

The physical and natural disasters of 1908 were in no way less life-destroying or less widespread than in the previous year. Even the cinema, an invention that was slowly bringing more and more people into contact with the moving image of distant events, and recreated events, brought perils in its wake. At Barnsley, in Britain, sixteen children were killed on January 11 during a crush when a stairway leading from the gallery of the building being used as a cinema was blocked (the first purpose-built cinema in Britain was opened later that year, at Colne, less than thirty miles from Barnsley). Two days after the British cinema disaster, 167 people were killed at the Opera House at Boyertown, Pennsylvania, when an explosion during a film show created panic, oil lamps were overturned, and fire broke out. The tragedy was reported graphically in *The Times*:

> The Opera House was crowded with members of the St John's Lutheran Sunday School. In many cases several members of one family lost their lives. The injured number about a hundred, and many are not expected to live. The majority of those killed belonged to the most prominent families of the town.

The men endeavoured to stop the panic, but it was impossible to stem the rush of panic-stricken women and children, whose shrieks and screams rose above their voices. Burning oil was scattered in all directions, and the explosion of lamps added to the terror of the hundreds who were fighting frantically to gain the exits. In the mad rush a section of the floor collapsed, precipitating scores of persons to the basement. Scarcely five minutes after the explosion the entire heart of the building was like a roaring furnace. The stairway leading to the balcony was choked, and women and children were crushed to death. Mounting on their bodies, 40 persons leaped from the windows, and many limbs and skulls were broken.

The police and firemen worked heroically in dragging out those who were wedged in the doorway and were thus preventing many within from escaping. As the flames ate their way towards the front of the building women were seen to throw up their hands and fall back into the flames. As soon as the doorway was cleared the rescuers dragged many from the balcony and stairways. Some were so badly injured that they died on the way to the temporary hospital.

Fire was also the cause of a tragedy in a primary school at Collinwood, near Cleveland, Ohio, in March that year, when a furnace overheated, and defective exits from the school led to 180 children and nine of their teachers being burned, suffocated or crushed to death. Fire was likewise the cause of a considerable destruction in Constantinople that March, when three thousand Jews were left homeless after four hundred wooden houses burnt down in one of the poorer and more dilapidated suburbs of the Ottoman capital. In April a fire started in a Boston suburb during a gale. It left an estimated 10,000 people homeless.

The ravages of nature continued to take human life. In June, a tornado in Kansas and Nebraska killed twenty-five people. That month more than a thousand Chinese were killed when an earthquake created a fissure several miles long, swallowing up both homes and their occupants. In July, in the Canadian province of British Columbia, fire destroyed the town of Fernie, killing a hundred people. In August, a second fire at Constantinople – most of the houses of which were made of wood – destroyed four thousand homes, ten times as many as in the earlier fire that year, and led to several hundred deaths.

Mining accidents also continued to disturb the industrial nations, as the search for coal as fuel led to deeper and deeper mines. In August, seventy-six miners were killed in the north of England after an explosion and fire in a colliery at Abram, near Wigan. In November, 360 German miners were killed after an explosion in a coal mine at Hamm, in Westphalia. A message of sympathy was sent by the President of France. But when the Kaiser's son, Prince Eitel Friedrich, arrived at the mine to offer the imperial condolences, he was met by an angry demonstration of the miners against the mine owners.

Accidents at sea were frequent, sometimes through collisions, sometimes through explosions. In April, more than two hundred Japanese sailors were drowned when their training ship *Matsushima* sank after an explosion in her munitions magazine. In November, 150 Muslim pilgrims, on their way from Algiers to Mecca, were drowned in the eastern Mediterranean when their ship, the British steamer *Sardinia*, caught fire. On the railways, the worst accident on record in fifty years of rail travel in Belgium resulted in the deaths of thirty-seven people.

As in previous years, British India was the scene of natural disasters and disease on a considerable scale. In September, three thousand Indians were killed during floods in Hyderabad. Plague deaths diminished dramatically that year, however, with the twelve-month total to September being calculated at 201,575. High though this death toll was, there was a sense of relief among the British officials in India that more than a million fewer Indians had succumbed than in the previous year.

The worst natural disaster in 1908 came in Europe, when an earthquake struck the southern Italian cities of Messina and Reggio, both of which were destroyed, and an estimated 200,000 Italians were killed. Russian, American, French and British merchant ships that were in the area did their utmost to help; there was widespread appreciation in Italy for the way in which these seamen did what they could to alleviate the suffering of the survivors.

Flight, the new science, was also having its fatalities. When, at Washington, a propeller broke as Orville Wright was flying at seventy-five feet, his aeroplane crashed and he was badly injured; his passenger, Lieutenant Selfridge, was killed. But there was to be no let-up in the search for improvement. At Le Mans, four days after the American lieutenant's death, Orville Wright's brother Wilbur flew an aeroplane more than forty miles, and did so in only one minute more than an hour and a half: a speed of twenty-five miles an hour. Testing the limits of the new science was becoming an art, and a compulsion.

It was the Le Mans flight that first aroused general public interest in what the Wright brothers had achieved. Their first flight in December 1903 had been witnessed by only a few people, nor had the United States army been impressed by a flight demonstration at Dayton, Ohio, in September 1904. But following Wilbur Wright's promotional flights (for they were very much that, in commercial terms) in France in 1908, the search for better machines, for individual records, and for national participation in the new science, grew rapidly. Within a year of Wilbur Wright bringing his machine to France, the British Cabinet's Committee of Imperial Defence, at the instigation of Winston Churchill, discussed the wisdom of making contact with him, with a view to enhancing the British national interest.

The motorcar also made a significant advance in 1908, when Henry Ford announced that his Ford Motor Company would be making a Model T car which would be priced within the capacity of hundreds of thousands, even millions, of people. To the benefit of millions more, that year saw the introduction in the United States of the electric iron and the paper cup. The cinema was becoming an unexpected vehicle for the spread of culture to the masses: among the films issued that year were *Romeo and Juliet* and *Tosca*, the latter starring Sarah Bernhardt. The location of the main film studios in the United States was also about to change, from the East Coast to the West. When the filming of *The Count of Monte-Cristo* was completed that year in an open-air studio near Los Angeles, a new venue, and a new word, entered the vocabulary of entertainment – Hollywood.

A story that might have come from Hollywood had its origins in 1908. On August 4 that year, the Waterman's Fountain Pen Company of New York engraved the date of manufacture on one of its new gold-tipped fountain pens. At some point in the next few years it became the property of Alexandre Villedieu, a Frenchman. He had the pen with him in May 1915 while fighting in the Battle of Artois. During the battle he was killed. His body, like that of so many tens of thousands of others, pounded into the earth and mud by enemy shell fire, was never found and never buried; until a local farmer, ploughing the field in the spring of 1996, chanced upon it. Alongside Villedieu's body were his pipe, a pocket knife, his military belt – and the Waterman's fountain pen.

CHAPTER TEN

1909

A BRITISH WRITER, Norman Angell, wrote a book in 1909 which he called *Europe's Optical Illusion*, in which he argued that even a victorious warring Power would suffer extraordinary economic and financial loss as a result of any future war. At first, his warning of the destructive futility of war failed to reach a wide public. But when he reissued the book a year later, changing the title to *The Great Illusion*, it somehow caught the public imagination and became a bestseller. It was quickly translated into French, German, Italian and Russian.

Norman Angell stressed that the great industrial nations, Britain, the United States, Germany and France were 'losing the psychological impulse to war, just as we have lost the psychological impulse to kill our neighbours on account of religious differences'. How could it be otherwise, he asked. 'How can modern life, with its overpowering proportion of industrial activities and its infinitesimal proportion of military, keep alive the instincts associated with war as against those developed by peace?' Even the Prussian Junker 'becomes less of an energumen as he becomes more of a scientist'.

Not every Prussian was becoming less of an 'energumen' – an enthusiast or fanatic. That January, a former Chief of the German General Staff, Count von Schlieffen, who had retired from the army four years earlier, published an article in Germany in which he tried to anticipate 'the war of the future'. His forecast concerned four Powers – France, Russia, Britain and Italy – the latter then a member of Germany's alliance system. 'An endeavour is afoot,' he wrote, 'to bring all these Powers together for a concentrated attack on the Central Powers. At the given moment, the drawbridges are to be let down, the doors are to be opened, and the million-strong armies let loose, ravaging and destroying across the Vosges, the Meuse, the Niemen, the Bug, and even the Isonzo and the Tyrolean Alps. The danger seems gigantic.'

The Kaiser read von Schlieffen's article aloud to his senior generals, and commented, 'Bravo!' Von Schlieffen himself, while Chief of the German General Staff, had already devised a plan, finalized in December 1905, for the rapid swing of German troops through neutral Belgium. The aim was to reach Paris and defeat France within six weeks, before the cumbersome Russian army could have time to make any significant advance against Germany on the eastern front. With France having surrendered, Germany, master in the West, would turn, under von Schlieffen's plan, to the East, and advance with superior forces. Although subsequently modified, the von Schlieffen plan was a blueprint for conquest by Germany. Despite the graphic – and geographic – detail of von Schlieffen's published warning, no equivalent plan to his existed on the part of Britain, France, Russia and Italy.

A throwback to the Europe of the mid-nineteenth century took place early in 1909, when the French government authorized a public execution. It took place at Béthune, near Arras, when four members of a murder gang were guillotined before what was portrayed in the press as 'an exultant and disorderly crowd' which, *The Times* reported, 'notwithstanding the rain and the earliness of the hour, had come from all parts of the surrounding country, and even from Paris, in order to see the work of justice done. As the presence of vehicles of all kinds, from the humble farmer's cart to the motorcar, testified, nearly every class of society was represented, and the troops who were present in force had considerable difficulty in maintaining order. As the heads of the four criminals fell in rapid succession into the basket, the mob alternately howled and cheered. After the execution, the heads and bodies were hurried off to Lille for dissection.'

Twelve days after this public execution in France, in London two men who had seized a wage bag from a man at the door of a factory, were chased through the city by police using motorcars. The men, who were armed, tried to make their escape by commandeering first an electric tramcar, then a milk van, and finally a horse and cart. One of them, when cornered, shot himself; the other took refuge in a cottage, and was shot. During the chase, a policeman and a young boy were killed. *The Times* described the chase and the shootings as 'an amazing series of outrages, singularly rare if not entirely without parallel in a civilized country'. Both men, it emerged, were Jewish anarchists, one named Jacob Lepidus, the other, Paul Hefeldt, both from Riga. They had been engaged 'in conveying revolutionary literature' printed in Britain, to Russia. 'For this purpose,' the newspaper reported, 'they posed as seamen, and when going on voyages to Russia, would smuggle the papers about their persons.'

The inauguration of Theodore Roosevelt's successor, President William Howard Taft, took place in March. So great was the snow storm that blanketed the capital in the days before the ceremony that trains containing an estimated 30,000 participants to the inaugural celebrations were unable to reach it. In his Message to Congress, Taft stressed that while the foreign policy of the United States was 'always to promote peace', and to make every effort 'consistent with national honour' to avoid any recourse to armed conflict, nevertheless, 'with all the nations of the world armed and prepared for war, the United States must be in a similar condition.' The United States needed to secure 'respect for her just demands', such as the open-door policy for trade in 'the Orient', but she would not be able to do so 'if it is understood that she never intends to back up her assertion of right and her defence of her interest by anything but mere verbal protest and diplomatic note.'

In Alsace-Lorraine, during the unveiling in October of a memorial to French soldiers who had fallen in the war of 1870, there was a French nationalist demonstration. In November there was another such demonstration, when a local band, after playing the German national anthem, burst out with the Marseillaise. In Berlin, the new Chancellor, Theodor von Bethmann Hollweg, a distinguished Prussian official, said that measures would be taken to prevent the recurrence of such an incident in the future. Once the people of Alsace-Lorraine were 'freed from Chauvinistic exaggerations', he believed, 'the sooner will success be achieved in clearing the road for the realization of its own desire to act as a valuable member of the German family of States'. This remark was interpreted as conciliatory; but towards the national group at the other extremity of the German Empire, the Poles in the Posen district, no such conciliation was shown, and every effort continued to be made to prevent Poles from purchasing farms and smallholdings. The Prussian law forbidding Poles to build houses on land that already belonged to them was strictly enforced. When the German parliament issued a strong protest against this law, the vote and the protest were ignored by the Prussian authorities.

Overseas, German policy made a major conciliatory gesture in 1909, when a Franco-German agreement was signed, whereby Germany agreed to pursue 'only economic interests' in Morocco, while recognizing the special interests of France in the 'consolidation of order and of internal peace'. Germany also agreed not to carry out, or encourage, any measure that might lead to the creation of German 'economic privilege' in Morocco. To those in Britain and France who feared that German machinations might undermine the agreement, there was relief, and also surprise, when the German government prevented a German mining company from pursuing 600 mining claims which it had negotiated with Mulai Hafid, the Sultan, on the grounds that these claims, if upheld, would constitute a German monopoly, and thus a breach of the new agreement.

Even the Casablanca incident, when the German consul had tried to smuggle French Foreign Legion deserters out of Morocco, was settled by arbitration in 1909, at the Hague Court, when the German government accepted the censure of the court that the German consul had not been entitled to grant its protection 'even to deserters of German nationality'. For its part, France accepted the censure of the court that its soldiers ought not to have 'menaced' the consul with a revolver or struck at his Moroccan guard.

Honour was satisfied, and a new course of Franco-German relations seemed ready to be charted. But it was in the Balkans that the antagonism of the Powers flared most easily, and most frequently. Following the Serb protests against the Austro-Hungarian annexation of Bosnia-Herzegovina, the Austrians had warned Serbia against any provocative action. The Austrian threats had provoked demonstrations inside Russia in favour of Serbia. In protest against these Russian demonstrations, the German government issued a warning in St Petersburg that its sympathies were with Austria-Hungary, and that Russian demonstrations against Austria were unacceptable. The German position was spelt out with stark clarity: if, in the event of war between Austria-Hungary and Serbia, Russia were to intervene on behalf of Serbia, then Germany would be bound by treaty to take the side of her ally Austria-Hungary.

There could have been no clearer anticipation of the disastrous events of 1914. But on this occasion, faced by German pressure, the Russian government advised Serbia to halt all anti-Austrian demonstrations and to recognize without further protest the Austrian annexation of the province she had already occupied for thirty years. Serbia, too weak to act alone, deferred to Russia's advice. For many Russians, however, with their sense of solidarity with Slavs everywhere, there was a feeling of humiliation that German pressure had forced the Russian government to pressure Serbia to defuse the crisis.

So hostile had been the reaction in Serbia, Montenegro and Turkey, and initially in Russia, to Austria-Hungary's annexation of Bosnia-Herzegovina that Austria-Hungary had been forced to mobilize. Three Austro-Hungarian armies were formed, two of which were to operate against Serbia and one against Montenegro. An Austro-Hungarian naval force, the Danube River Flotilla, was also mobilized, and considerable expense incurred to maintain these military preparations. A 'war party' in Austria was demanding war with Serbia; Franz Josef opposed this. It was Britain and France that emerged as the brokers between Austria and Serbia, devising a formula for settling the dispute that would not be offensive to either side.

After prolonged negotiations, the Austrians, who had refused to grant compensation to Turkey for the annexed areas, agreed to accept a series of Turkish conditions, including the retention of Ottoman nationality by all Muslims in Bosnia, the security of religious practice for all Muslims, a cash payment, and an increase in the customs duties that Turkey could raise on goods coming from Austria.

The crisis generated by the annexation had brought Germany and Austria-Hungary closer together. The outward show of the new amity was a visit of the German Kaiser to Vienna, and a reciprocal visit of the heir to the Habsburg dominions, the Archduke Franz Ferdinand, to Berlin. These manifestations of Austro-German friendship did not help the national groups within the Habsburg Empire. There was anger in the Italian provinces when the Vienna Parliament decided to establish an Italian law faculty, not in Trieste or some other Italian city of the empire, as the Italians had hoped, but in Vienna.

Other nationalities within the Habsburg dominions were also offended during 1909. The local parliaments (Diets) of Upper and Lower Austria, Salzburg and Vorarlberg all passed laws forbidding the use of the Czech language in schools, even by Czech pupils. So indignant were the Czechs that a Czech delegation went to Warsaw to participate in a mass demonstration in support of pan-Slav solidarity. In the Vienna parliament, Czechs carried out a series of obstructive measures. In the Diet of Carniola, the Slovene deputies threw stink bombs.

The most serious challenge to the unity of the Habsburg lands came in Croatia. During 1909 an exceptionally high number of Croats, fifty-three in all, were charged with high treason and brought to trial in Agram. The charge against them was that they had been active in a movement for the separation of Croatia, Bosnia and Slavonia from the Habsburg monarchy, and their union with Serbia. The trial lasted for eight months, riveting the attention of the whole empire. Thirty-one of the accused were sentenced to imprisonment with hard labour.

The Croat deputies in the Croatian Diet were also accused, in a newspaper article by a distinguished Austrian historian, Dr Heinrich Friedjung – a personal friend of the Foreign Minister, Count Aehrenthal – of conspiring with the government of Serbia to detach Croatia from Hungary and annex it to Serbia. Forty-nine Croat deputies reacted to this charge by bringing a libel action against Dr Friedjung, and his trial likewise became a focal point of national tensions and accusations. It emerged during the trial that some of the documents on which Friedjung based his accusations were forgeries which had been provided to him by the Austrian Foreign Ministry. He was forced to admit in court that the charges in his article were without foundation. In the Reichsrat the Czech deputies denounced the Vienna government as a 'falsifier' with regard to the denigration of the Slav minorities.

In Russia, the Duma continued to debate, but the powers of the autocracy were undiminished. Official figures released in St Petersburg in 1909 revealed that 782 political offenders had been executed in the previous year, an increase of more than a hundred from the year before that. The number of those in exile for political offences, mostly in the remote regions of Siberia, was more than 180,000.

In Russia, the discovery by the Socialist Revolutionaries that their leader, Evno Azev, was a police spy who had deliberately arranged a series of assassinations by party members in order to discredit the whole revolutionary movement, had caused turmoil in the Party. It appeared that when his discovery was imminent Azev had tried to organize the assassination of the Tsar, in order to rehabilitate himself in the eyes of those whom he had earlier betrayed. When, in December 1909, the Chief of the Secret Police in St Petersburg, Colonel Karpov, was blown up by a bomb, there was concern in both liberal and revolutionary circles that his assassin might also have been a police spy working to discredit the revolutionaries.

Russians waited with nervous anticipation to see whether their internal struggle would evolve or erupt. Reflecting on the destruction of Messina the previous year, the Russian poet Alexander Blok asked what the supposed 'triumphant civilization' of modern times had really achieved. Was the earthquake Fate, he asked, wishing to show that an elemental force could at any time wreak vengeance on the pride of mankind, on man's assumption that he could control nature and rule the universe through his technology? 'We are going through a terrible crisis,' he wrote. 'We do not know exactly what is going to happen, but in our hearts the pendulum of the seismograph is already swinging.'

The struggle inside Russia between the forces of reaction and those of liberalism was carried out most publicly in the Duma. When in 1909 thirty-two workmen were sentenced to death for their part in the railway strike at Ekaterinoslav four years earlier – during the 1905 revolution – a motion was introduced in the Duma by Professor Paul Miliukov, the leader of the Constitutional Democratic Party (who had been lecturing at the University of Chicago when he learned of 'Bloody Sunday'), to overturn the death penalty. When the motion was rejected by the deputies of the Centre, the whole opposition walked out of the chamber. The Tsar then prorogued the Duma, which was his prerogative, but, bowing to the obvious strength of feeling of the deputies, cancelled the death sentences. As a result of this debate, the number of subsequent death sentences was considerably reduced. The Duma had shown itself to be more than a mere talking shop.

Efforts by the former Tsarist minister, Count Sergei Witte, and other right-wing leaders, to reduce the powers of the Duma, were unsuccessful. But those powers were not what the Duma wanted. In 1908 there had been a considerable majority in the Duma not to grant financial credit for the Tsar's proposal to build four Dreadnought-class battleships, but the Tsar's own Council of Empire having approved his request, the vote of the Duma was ignored, and the battleships' keels were laid down, in the dockyards of St Petersburg, in the summer of 1909. In order to create the most effective warships, the Tsar arranged for these new vessels to be built to British designs and under British supervision. This was a sign of the growing closeness of the Franco-Russian-British alignment which, while still not a formal alliance, and never to become one, was becoming a close liaison on working towards war preparedness.

As a gesture of solidarity with Britain and France, the Tsar visited Paris, and then, on board his yacht *Standart*, anchored off Cowes for four days, with both his Prime Minister, Peter Stolypin and his Foreign Minister,

Alexander Izvolsky (the negotiator of the Anglo-Russian entente), on board. The visit misfired somewhat, however, in view of liberal feelings in both countries for whom the autocracy was not at all admirable. The British Labour Party was particularly critical of the official welcome given to the man whom they condemned as responsible for so many political prisoners and political executions.

Hostility to the Tsar's visit to Britain was offset, to some extent, when it was followed by the visit of leading figures of the Duma, the liberal face of Russia. A sign that Anglo-Russian relations had much improved was the reaction in Britain when a Russian destroyer fired on a British steamer which had inadvertently been directed into closed water off the coast of Finland. An episode that, only four years earlier (like the Dogger Bank incident) might have led to great public indignation and talk of war, was settled by a rapid apology and no further repercussions.

A further sign of the growing closeness of Britain and Russia, despite the Liberal government's dislike of the autocracy, was the smooth and effective working of the Anglo-Russian Convention with regard to Persia. At Britain's request, the Russian officer commanding the Persian Cossack troops, Colonel Liakhov, was withdrawn in March, and in the following month, also at Britain's request, 2600 Russian troops were sent to Tabriz to protect European residents there from the depredations of Persian nationalists opposed to the Shah; in July these troops were sent to Kazvin, to try to protect Teheran from a nationalist attack.

Within Persia the situation was anarchic. At one point the Shah was forced to take refuge inside the Russian legation in Teheran. When he did so, the Persian National Council treated it as an act of abdication and he was formally deposed, to be succeeded that same day by his thirteen-year-old son, Sultan Ahmed Mirza, for whom a regency was established. The deposed Shah was escorted from the Russian Legation by Russian Cossacks and British Indian troops, and taken to the Crimea, where he was given an official residence and a yearly allowance.

Within Russia, a growing call for greater Russification, especially in the Polish provinces which had been a hotbed of revolt in 1905, alarmed the non-Russian nationalities of the empire. Even among the liberal groups in the Duma the idea of increased Russification found favour. One result was that the Polish deputies in the Duma, who represented the Kingdom of Poland which Russia had absorbed in the eighteenth century, lost half their representation. At the same time, the Polish Educational Society in Kiev, which catered for the large Polish minority living throughout the western Ukraine, was closed down. The argument used for the closure was that the aim of the society, the extension of Polish education, was 'inconsistent with the policy of the Imperial government' in its western provinces.

Anti-German feeling inside Russia was also growing. It had been exacerbated by Germany's support for Austria at the time of the annexation of Bosnia-Herzegovina. The number of German schools in Russia was considerable; they catered to the many hundreds of thousands of Germans living in the empire, who were not only determined to retain every element of their Germanism, but even to remain subjects of the German Empire. This was particularly true in the Baltic region, in cities such as Riga and Reval.

While nationalism was growing within the territories of all the European empires, another side of the imperial coin, the application of morality to imperialism, was seen in March when the leading British chocolate manufacturers, Cadbury, Fry and Rowntree, refused to use cocoa imported from the Portuguese island colonies of San Thomé and Principe. They had learned that the conditions of the workers in the cocoa plantations there amounted to slavery. 'They will watch with sympathetic interest,' *The Times* reported, 'any efforts which may be made by the Portuguese government or by the estate proprietors to remedy the evils of the existing system.'

In Turkey, an attempt was made by forces still loyal to the autocratic powers of the Sultan to overthrow the Young Turks. On April 13 they seized power in Constantinople. But the troops in Salonika, the original base of Young Turk activity, remained loyal to the constitution, and eleven days later Constantinople was recaptured. The Turkish national assembly, called together in an emergency session, voted unanimously to depose Abdul Hamid, and he was sent into exile. He had ruled Turkey, mostly with an iron hand (following the Armenian massacres of 1894–6 he was known as the 'Great Assassin') since 1876. He was succeeded by his brother, Rashid Effendi, who was proclaimed Sultan as Mohammed V.

Among those minorities inside Turkey who hoped that the Young Turk revolution would bring them the political equality they had long been denied were the Armenians. There were as many as two million Armenians in the Ottoman Empire at that time; they were by far the largest Christian group, living mostly in eastern Anatolia. Hopes of equality were dashed, however, when in 1909 several thousand Armenians were massacred in southern Turkey, the so-called Cilician Vespers.[1]

In March, the Reichstag in Berlin debated the future size of the German navy. The German Foreign Minister, Baron Wilhelm von Schön, announced that the British government had stated in general terms 'their readiness for an Anglo-German agreement concerning the strength and cost of the naval programmes', but that no British proposal for disarmament had yet been put forward. The Reichstag then voted, without debate, for three new Dreadnought-class battleships and one armoured cruiser to be built. The Chancellor, Prince von Bülow, in reiterating at a later sitting of the Reichstag that no British proposal for a mutual reduction in naval shipbuilding had been made, explained that in little more than three years' time, Germany would have ready for service 'thirteen large new ships, including three armoured cruisers'.

The British public, stirred up by several nationalist newspapers, was becoming worried about German intentions. There were rumours, so strong that in May the British government had specifically to deny them in Parliament, that 66,000 trained German soldiers were living secretly in England, and that in the centre of London ('within a quarter of a mile of Charing Cross' according to one rumour) was a secret store of 50,000 rifles and 7.5 million cartridges with which these troops would seize power in the capital.

Also in May there was an 'airship panic', with allegations that Germany intended to despatch an invading army across the North Sea by Zeppelin. Rumours of large numbers of airships crossing the East Anglian coast at night began to circulate. Innumerable Zeppelin sightings were reported, the mass circulation *Daily Mail* warning its readers: 'A hostile airship hovering over London . . . could inflict enormous damage.'

A Berlin newspaper, the *Berliner Neueste Nachtrichten*, took alarm at what the British panic seemed to portend, telling its readers:

Things which are being said and done in England these days strike us Germans as magnificent material for farce and comedy. But the ridiculousness of it all is only one side of the matter. Madness is also dangerous

---

[1] Named after the Cilician region in which the massacres took place. The Sicilian Vespers were the massacre of the French in Sicily at the outbreak of the Sicilian revolt against France in 1282. They were so called because the first killings took place during a riot inside a church at vespers (evensong) on Easter Monday 1282.

... What stands out conspicuously is the lack of any sturdy resistance to these hallucinations in the English public ... It is the mere spectacle which fills us with astonishment and regret.

Perhaps Englishmen will say this babble is only a Conservative manoeuvre against the Liberal regime. We reply that it is dangerous to permit conscienceless party politics to proceed to a point which does not hesitate to drag foreign politics and relations with a great neighbouring country into the vortex of partisan strife.

In Germany, the Zeppelin was cause for rejoicing and excitement. That summer Count Zeppelin himself flew to the capital in the most modern version of his craft, flying from Lake Constance. 'The occasion was celebrated by a huge demonstration and formal welcome by the Kaiser,' Jawaharlal Nehru, an eye-witness, recalled many years later. 'A vast multitude, estimated at between one and two million, gathered in the Tempelhof Field in Berlin, and the Zeppelin arrived to time and circled gracefully above us. The Hotel Adlon presented all its residents that day with a fine picture of Count Zeppelin, and I have still got that picture.'

The British Government, faced with the steady growth of German naval construction, took steps to ensure that Britain would not find itself at a disadvantage at sea. In October the Admiralty announced the establishment of a Navy War Council, of which the recently created Mobilization Department was to be an integral part. For his part, the Kaiser continued on his chosen path of a powerful navy; a seventh German Dreadnought-class battleship was launched that November.

In India, in the aftermath of Lord Curzon's Viceroyalty, the Liberal government sent out Lord Minto to effect reforms that would bring Indians into many levels of government. The first Indian to be appointed a member of the Viceroy's Executive Council, Satyendra Sinha, took his place on the council in March. In choosing Sinha as against Minto's own first choice, Dr A. Mukerji, the Vice-Chancellor of Calcutta University – a Bengali – Minto wrote to the Secretary of State for India in London: 'Please do not think me terribly narrow, but Sinha is comparatively white, whilst Mukerji is as black as my hat!' Even Sinha's appointment, or that of any Indian, had been strongly opposed by one member of the Viceroy's Council, Fleetwood Wilson, who warned: 'An Indian colleague would be the admission of the thin end of the wedge which is to bring about the downfall of British administration'.

In early February the Indian Public Prosecutor for Bengal, Asutosh Biswas, was shot dead by a Bengali student. That July, Indian unrest spilled over into London, when, at the end of an entertainment held at the Imperial Institute to encourage friendly relations between Indians and Europeans, a Punjabi student, Madhar Lal Dhingra – the son of a much respected civil servant in India – shot and killed the political aide-de-camp of the Secretary of State for India, Sir Curzon Wyllie. At Dhingra's trial in London, he refused to acknowledge the authority of the court. He was sentenced to death. That December, a British civilian in Bombay was shot dead by a young Mahrathi Brahmin in revenge for the transportation sentence passed on a friend of his in a sedition case.

It was among the Mahrathis and the Bengalis that the agitation seemed to reach its most intense forms. Heavy prison sentences were imposed on thirty-five Mahrathis and Bengalis who were caught in the princely State of Gwalior distributing nationalist pamphlets. An Indian nationalist who had been educated in England, Shyamji Krishnavarma, editor of the *Indian Sociologist*, wrote to *The Times* from Paris: 'During my seventeen years residence in England I made thousands of friends and acquaintances, and I solemnly warn them all, and their countrymen, against the risks they run in losing their kith and kin by allowing them to go to India in these troubled times, since every Englishman who goes there for exploiting that country directly or indirectly is regarded as a potential enemy by the Indian Nationalist party and its supporters.'

The British Liberal government was distressed when, in the discussions on the final act to constitute the Union of South Africa, which was to be signed within seven years of the ending of the Boer War, the Boers revealed their determination not to allow any form of equality for blacks, for Indians, or for those of mixed race, and were set on enforcing a colour bar as an integral part of the constitutional legislation. A delegation of blacks and Indians, the two races most affected by the colour bar, went to Britain to put their case, and to try to have race equality made a part of the Union legislation. They were supported by a former Prime Minister of the Cape Colony, W. P. Schreiner, who argued that the phrase 'of European descent' on which the new franchise was to be based was an intentional bar against blacks and Indians, and their descendants, from ever sitting in the South African parliament, or holding elected office in government.

Schreiner pointed out that in the Cape Colony there was already legislation which enabled the franchise to be exercised without regard to race, so that the new legislation was, in this regard, retrograde. If allowed, he argued, it would create a 'disastrous' separation of the population of South Africa into two hostile camps, the one with rights, the other without them. The British imperial policy of 'raising those emerging from barbarism into the light of civilization' — a policy which gave the moral justification to imperialism and imperial rule — would be 'stultified' if race or colour were made a barrier to full civic responsibilities.

These arguments were impressive when heard by many British Members of Parliament, who felt that the exclusion of blacks and Indians from the right to vote was not only wrong in itself, but an abdication of imperial responsibilities. The white population of South Africa was determined, however, that the new parliament of the Union would be a parliament of white men, elected by white men, and that there should be no prospect of this franchise being extended in the future.

The pressure on the British government to allow the reconciliation of Boer and Briton, and the need, if this was to be achieved, to encompass Boer needs and prejudices, overrode considerations of morality. Two liberal principles were in conflict, that of equality, and that of non-interference in colonial legislatures. With the passage of the Act of Union, the principle of equality with regard to whites and blacks in South Africa fell by the wayside; and was to remain at the wayside for more than eight decades, a cause of division and growing hatred.

The policy in the Transvaal of deporting Indians who had entered illegally remained in force, and since 1906, under what the Indians called the Black Act, force was used to uphold it. The Indian immigrants continued to be championed by Gandhi. He too travelled to England to seek to present Indian grievances to the Colonial Office, where he pointed out that 8000 of the 13,000 Indians living and working in the Transvaal had been deported, and that of the deportees, 2500 had been imprisoned first. He himself had been sentenced to three months' hard labour for refusing to take out a Fingerprint Certificate, one of the registration procedures against which the Indians had protested. While in London, Gandhi put the case for the Transvaal Indians with skill, but he was as unsuccessful in trying to get better conditions for the Indians in South Africa as Schreiner had been in trying to obtain the franchise for them.

Gandhi's visit to London had wider repercussions than his disillusionment with British justice. He had begun to turn away entirely from the European way of life. 'Looking at this land,' he wrote, 'I at any rate have grown disillusioned with Western civilization. The people whom you meet on the way seem half-crazy. They spend their days in luxury or in making a bare living and retire at night thoroughly exhausted. In this state of affairs, I cannot understand when they can devote themselves to prayers.'

In a powerful polemic which he first published in 1909 as an article in *Indian Opinion* and a year later as a pamphlet, Gandhi set out, not for the Indians of Natal but for the Indians of India – Hindus and Muslims alike – his total disaffection with British rule. His article was called *Hind Swaraj* (Indian Home Rule). It was immediately banned in India by the British authorities. In his article, Gandhi not only opposed the methods of British rule, but stressed the differences in civilization between the British and Indian systems. The theme of the article was one which the British rulers of India, confident of their good intentions towards the inhabitants of the subcontinent, found particularly hard to accept, but which struck deep chords among Gandhi's Indian readers:

> I must frankly confess that I am not so much concerned about the stability of the Empire as I am about that of the ancient civilization of India which, in my opinion, represents the best the world has ever seen. The British Government in India constitutes a struggle between the Modern Civilization, which is the Kingdom of Satan, and the Ancient Civilization, which is the Kingdom of God. The one is the God of War, the other is the God of Love.
>
> My countrymen impute the evils of modern civilization to the English people and, therefore, believe that the English people are bad, and not the civilization they represent. My countrymen, therefore, believe that they should adopt modern civilization and modern methods of violence to drive out the English.
>
> *Hind Swaraj* has been written in order to show that they are following a suicidal policy, and that, if they would but revert to their own glorious civilization, either the English would adopt the latter and become Indianized or find their occupation in India gone.

The fortunes of the British within the vast regions of their Empire were varied. Five years after Colonel Younghusband's successful advance to Lhasa, the Chinese had replaced British influence by their own. When a number of Tibetans, calling themselves the 'Golden Soldiers', but mostly unarmed – as Younghusband's adversaries had been – tried to challenge the Chinese troops in the capital, they were shot down in the market place. The Dalai Lama fled to India with a few of his followers. Although the Government of India received him in Calcutta with high honours, it let him know that it would not interfere between him and China. Nor would it agree to his request to visit England. With the fears of Russian expansion in Tibet laid to rest by the Anglo-Russian Convention three years earlier, Britain had abandoned its earlier policy of asserting its political influence across India's northern border.

On the Malayan peninsula, however, the British were in a mood of acquisition, prevailing over the Siamese authorities to transfer all Siamese rights in four Malay States and the islands adjacent to them, and to secure their transfer to Britain within thirty days of the signing of an agreement. It was also agreed that British subjects throughout Siam would enjoy 'the rights and privileges' of Siamese citizens, but would be exempt from military service and all forced loans and military contributions.

In Egypt the British were confronted by growing nationalist sentiment. Two years earlier the first Egyptian National Congress had been held. Believing that legislation could be an effective curb on national agitation, the British rulers passed a law on July 9, the aim of which was to place under police supervision and village confinement those who agitated for an end to British rule. The law quickly became a focal point of as much protest as it had sought to curb. Two months after the law was passed, a second Egyptian National Congress was held in Geneva. As well as 120 Egyptian delegates, several leading members of the British Labour Party, among them Keir Hardie, who had just completed two years as Party chairman, attended.

The Egyptian speakers stressed that the Egyptians were competent to govern themselves, and that conditions under the British administration were 'intolerable'. It was decided to publish a nationalist paper, *Free Egypt*, in Geneva. While the congress was in session a mass meeting of 6000 Egyptians in Cairo, gathering on the twenty-seventh anniversary of the British occupation, telegraphed to the British Prime Minister to express 'the energetic protest of the Egyptian people against the occupation' and demanding, 'from today', the evacuation of British troops and administrators.

'To gain our friendship,' the telegram ended, 'is preferable for English honour than to lose our hearts and support'.

The British had no intention of leaving Egypt. Control of the Suez Canal seemed an imperial necessity, guarding the route to India and the Far East, while the actual Egyptian administration, like that of the Anglo-Egyptian Sudan to the south, was considered a model of colonial rectitude and advanced thinking. There was also the moral imperative, as seen by the Liberal government in London, of suppressing the slave trade and the arms trade that were still being carried on in the more remote regions. In October a government agent and three policemen were murdered at the Siwa Oasis while seeking to suppress the slave traffic.

There was also the sense of an imperial mission to improve the material condition of the Egyptians; this mirrored the attitude of the British civil servants in India, who, like those in Egypt, believed implicitly that they were better suited than the local population to advance the causes of health, welfare and morality. These officials were proud of the fact that, as a result of a persistent British campaign against mosquitoes, a noted increase in infant mortality had been halted at Port Said. Railway building southward from Khartoum was a sign to the rulers that, in the Sudan, the economic benefits of imperialism would soon spread at least 120 miles into once-inaccessible regions – with three trains a week each way. All this made the Egyptian call for an end to British rule seem, in British eyes, retrogressive and subversive, harmful not only to the fabric of empire, but to the wellbeing of its native populations.

One region where the imperial moral imperative appeared to be proceeding without conflict was in Zanzibar. There, the British Consul-General, Basil Cave, was able to report in 1909 that because of the Sultan of Zanzibar's decree of 1897, of which he, Cave, was very much the originator, whereby no child born after that date could be a slave, and under which existing slaves could obtain their emancipation, as many as 11,000 slaves had been freed. There had been no violent opposition. As a result of this success, Cave felt confident enough in 1909 to persuade the Sultan to abolish slavery altogether. This was done, also by decree, that June.

In British Somaliland, the untrappable Mullah had continued his attacks on British army outposts. After reinforcements were sent, the Mullah indicated, as he had done before, that he would be content to leave the British troops alone, if his control of the hinterland was accepted. The British government, anxious to avoid the inevitably mounting expense of any attempt to take over the hinterland, and to dislodge the Mullah from the regions where he held sway, accepted this arrangement. But the Mullah was not satisfied, and after a few months resumed his activities, destroying a small army convoy, and prompting the despatch of yet more British troops. One cause of British confidence was that the army posts in neighbouring Italian Somaliland were by then equipped with the Marconi wireless telegraph system, which enabled news of the Mullah's movements, and instructions as to how to counteract them, to be transmitted without the previously frustrating, and often harmful delay of messengers.

In the Nigerian Protectorate, the British were confident that the lawlessness of earlier years was over, and that the Muslim Emirs were loyal to Britain. When, however, in May, a small British force under Lieutenant Vanrenen was travelling to the Guari town of Gussoro, a pagan area, with a new chief who was to be installed there, the force was ambushed. The lieutenant, the chief, and eleven policemen were killed. The Governor of the Protectorate, Sir Percy Girouard, hastened to assure London that he had been impressed by the 'contentment of the people' of Nigeria, that the past 'truculence' had disappeared, and that caravans were now seldom hindered 'even by pagan tribes'. The ambush of the lieutenant and his party, Girouard explained, was 'one of those unhappy incidents which must arise in dealing with raw pagans of whom the Guari population is composed'.

Every imperial power faced conflicts on the borders of empire. After disturbances in Samoa, in the hope of depriving the local Savaiins of leadership, the German authorities deported fourteen local chiefs to the distant island of New Britain. The Spaniards were also in difficulties, though the possession that caused them trouble was near to hand, in Spanish Morocco, where Moorish tribesman from the Rif mountains had attacked workers who were building a railway to the mines near Melilla. Four workmen were killed. Some six thousand Rif tribesmen then attacked the 2000-strong Spanish garrison, killing eleven Spanish soldiers before being driven off by artillery fire. Reinforcements were sent from Spain, but the Moors attacked again. In the ensuing battle, three hundred Spanish soldiers and more than a thousand Moors were killed.

As the fighting intensified, the Spaniards were effectively besieged in their camp. At the same time, inside Spain, there were anti-war demonstrations in those towns from which reservists had been called to the colours. Then, on July 18, the demonstrations spread to Barcelona. That same day, in

Morocco, Rif tribesmen launched an attack on Spanish supply lines. The news that reached Spain was inflamed by rumours that exaggerated the scale of the losses. There were anti-war demonstrations in Barcelona and Madrid which spread to railway stations in other cities from which conscripts were leaving for North Africa. In Barcelona, anarchists and socialists called a general strike for July 26.

On the following day, in the Rif, more than five hundred Spaniards were killed, including one of their senior officers, General Pintos. In Barcelona, on July 29, troops were called out to put an end to the anti-war demonstrations. Artillery fire was effective in dispersing the demonstrators, almost two thousand of whom were subsequently arrested, and five of whom were sentenced to death.

In further fighting in the Rif in October, a second Spanish general was killed. Then as the time for ploughing began, the tribesmen requested a cease-fire. Spain's military forces in Morocco then standing at 50,000, the Moors no longer had any hope of driving them out, or of stopping the railway to the mines. Negotiations were opened on November 12. Three days later the tribesmen of the Rif surrendered unconditionally. A six-month struggle was over.

Japan was also embroiled in the problems of empire; Korea, the principal Japanese territorial gain after the victory over Russia, was still a burden for the victors four years later, when the southern province, rebelling against the Japanese occupation, had to be sealed off by Japanese troops on land and its coast blockaded. When the seventy-one-year-old Prince Ito, three times Prime Minister of Japan, and a leading figure in the abolition of Japanese feudalism, was assassinated by a Korean during a visit to Manchuria, the reaction in Japan was to abandon altogether the conciliatory measures that had been attempted in Korea since 1905. Following Prince Ito's murder, as an assertion of Japanese control, the Korean army was placed under the War Department in Tokyo, the Korean law courts and prisons were put under direct Japanese jurisdiction, and the Korean railways were transferred to the Japanese railways board in Tokyo.

In another imperial area, French Indo-China, Japan was taking an initiative which the French found extremely distasteful: the military training in Japan of young Annamese, with a view to challenging French control. Inside Indo-China there were repeated assaults on French officials, and considerable bitterness at the high cost of the French administration. French officials were also reluctant to learn the language of their subjects.

In Persia, in the province of Luristan, more than five thousand people were killed in an earthquake in January. In February, during the showing of a film in Acapulco, Mexico, the wooden theatre caught fire and three hundred people were killed as panic prevented any form of orderly escape from the building. Two days later, in a coal mine in Durham, 114 miners were killed after an explosion in the pit. At Cherry, Illinois, a mine explosion and fire in November led to the deaths of 250 miners; a week after the explosion, twenty men who had sheltered in one of the underground galleries were found alive and brought to the surface; one of them died almost immediately.

In Upper Padang, Sumatra, more than two hundred people were killed during an earthquake in June. Nine days later, fifty-five people were killed in the south of France when the shocks of an earthquake struck between Marseilles and Toulon. In Mexico, floods in the north of the country in August led to 3800 deaths. They were followed by an earthquake in which all the buildings on the waterfront of the Pacific Ocean town of Acapulco collapsed, and hundreds died.

Between Port Natal and Cape Town, the steamer *Waratah*, on its way from Australia to London, foundered and sank. Despite continued searches, she was never found. All 300 passengers on board were drowned. When a German and an Argentinian steamer collided that August in the harbour at Montevideo, eighty passengers and crew were drowned.

In Uganda, figures were issued at the end of 1909 which put the number of deaths from sleeping sickness during the previous five years at almost twenty-five thousand. In British India, plague was in its tenth year, but by September 1909 the number of deaths was less than two-thirds of the previous twelve months, the total number of victims for the year being officially noted, with the extraordinary precision of the clerks of empire, as 129,756.

On July 19 a British pilot, Hubert Latham, tried to fly across the English Channel from Calais to Dover, but had been unable to take off because of an accident to his machine. Six days later, on July 25, a Frenchman, Louis Blériot successfully made the crossing; he flew from a field near Calais to a steep meadow just behind Dover Castle. Today, a concrete outline of his plane marks the spot where he landed. The flight took him just under an hour and twenty minutes. Two days later Hubert Latham made his second attempt; but when he was within a mile of Dover his engine failed and his plane fell into the sea. Latham was rescued.

In Berlin, Aviation Week was celebrated that year from September 26, with many different flying machines demonstrating their skills. In New York on September 29, while Berlin Aviation Week was still in progress, Orville Wright made two flights around the Statue of Liberty. Wright then hastened by trans-Atlantic liner to Berlin, where, on the final day of Aviation Week, he took the German Crown Prince up with him to a height of 1000 feet. In mid October, piloting a Wright aeroplane, the Comte de Lambert flew around the Eiffel Tower.

Records were being broken almost every week. In the last three months of 1909 a French aviator flew thirty-four miles in fifty-eight minutes – a speed of just over 34 miles an hour – and the British aviator, Hubert Latham, reached a height of 1320 feet.

After each war, the victors and the vanquished set up war memorials to commemorate their dead. One of the most impressive in the first decade of the century was the monument unveiled at Port Arthur in 1909 in honour of the 22,719 Japanese officers and men who had been killed in the siege and conquest of that city. The monument, 218 feet high, was surmounted by a structure made of cannon balls.[1]

Wars between States, and imperial conflicts, had scarred every year since the start of the century. But the achievements of the century's first decade were also considerable. The year 1909 was no exception. In Germany, women were admitted to the universities for the first time. In Britain the first Town Planning Act was passed, regulating the unchecked spread of urban sprawl. The first department store was also opened in Britain that year, the creation of an American, H. Gordon Selfridge. In Palestine, under Turkish rule, the first collective farm, or kibbutz, was founded, at Deganya on the southern shore of the Sea of Galilee. It was the brainchild of Arthur Ruppin, a German Jew. Most of the farmers who practised its collective ethos were Jewish immigrants from Russia.

---

[1] The monument in Berlin to the German victories over Denmark (1864), Austria (1866) and France (1870–71) is made up from the barrels of cannons captured from the defeated armies.

The year 1909 also marked a milestone in the history of the cinema. A permanent location for showing films, the nickelodeon, which had been introduced in the United States four years earlier, had raised cinema attendance by 1909 to more than twenty million a week. Civic groups found cause for criticism. 'Often the sanitary conditions of the show-rooms are bad,' one of them warned. 'Bad air, floors uncleaned, no provision of spittoons, and the people crowded closely together, all make contagion likely.' But the appeal of the cinema could not be diminished, as the quality of the films, and the range of subjects covered, steadily increased. One of the very first feature films was issued that year, Vitagraph's *The Life of Moses*. In Italy, Milano Films produced *Dante's Inferno*.

CHAPTER ELEVEN

1910

THE RUSSIAN BOLSHEVIKS, both inside Russia and in exile, were demanding the abolition of the Duma, an end to Tsarism, and its replacement by the rule of the proletariat. At the same time, the members of the Duma were demanding greater powers for themselves. Despite strenuous efforts by the Constitutional Democrat Party (the Kadets) to enhance the Duma's authority, the Duma was not making headway in its efforts to assert its authority against the autocratic power of the Tsar.

Tsarist power continued to be exercised throughout the vast territories of the Russian Empire in favour of Russification, sometimes dramatically so. During 1910 Finland was deprived of her autonomy, despite strong opposition by Paul Miliukov in the Duma. In defending the measure, the Russian Prime Minister, Peter Stolypin, pointed out that the Finns had 'persistently refused' to carry out their obligations to provide troops for the imperial army, and that either the Russian Empire must assert its 'dominant will', or accept Finland's flouting of imperial decrees. The Finnish Bill was eventually passed in the Duma, despite considerable anxiety expressed by many members with regard to those clauses which restricted press freedom, public meetings, and associations judged by the Tsarist authorities to be of a disruptive or subversive nature.

That same year, the Polish subjects of the empire, their national aspirations already hampered by language restrictions, as in the German Empire, were denied even the limited rights of local self-government that had been accorded to the Russians themselves. The legislation enshrining this, and endorsed by the Duma, was known as the 'Anti-Polish Bill'. Jewish disabilities, of residence and higher education, were similarly maintained, as was a refusal, likewise endorsed by the Duma, to allow Jews to participate in local government deliberations.

Russia's wooing of the Balkan Slavs continued throughout 1910. Both King Ferdinand of Bulgaria, and King Peter of Serbia visited St Petersburg that year, as the guests of the Tsar, and to enthusiastic public applause. As if to underline the conflicts that might be in prospect, in November, in St Petersburg, a Russian citizen, Baron Ungern-Sternberg, was sentenced to four years' hard labour for betraying military secrets to the Austrian government.

The death of Leo Tolstoy in November was a time of mourning throughout Russia. He was eighty-three years old, and had just refused to accept the Nobel Peace Prize for his attempt to make the teachings of the Sermon on the Mount the basis of national policy worldwide. He died at a small railway station while on his way to the Caucasus, where he had been determined to end his days in a monastery, or in seclusion. One of his last acts was to write an article opposing capital punishment. This led to a rally in St Petersburg by more than a thousand students demanding an end to the death penalty, followed by a student strike in protest against the ill-treatment of political prisoners.

In the last decades of his life, Tolstoy had been a beacon for many aspects of the radicalism and idealism of the new century. He was an opponent, not only of the Russo-Japanese war, but of all war. He was a strict vegetarian and nonsmoker (both Gandhi and Hitler were to follow him in this respect). He opposed church dogma and believed that the simple life of the Gospels was the true path. To this end, he lived, dressed and worked as a peasant, believing this to be the way to inner peace and spiritual salvation. He opposed all luxury and ceremony, the exploitation of others, and personal self-aggrandisement. In education, he believed in the inviolability of the liberty of the child, and opposed all physical forms of punishment, believing that moral influences alone were acceptable in child upbringing. His breach with the formal doctrines of the Russian Orthodox Church had led in 1901 to his being excommunicated by the Holy Synod. But the Russian government, despite his opposition to the war against Japan, and his pacifism, had feared to take any action against him because of his popular following.

Five months before Tolstoy's death, the Russian government had concluded an agreement with Japan, marking a stage beyond the Treaty of Portsmouth, by which, with the sponsorship of the United States, the war had been brought to an end. The Russo-Japanese agreement of 4 July 1910 was a landmark in the ability of former warring powers to reach constructive agreements, and to do so within five years of their conflict. Its aim was to enhance the trade of the two nations in Manchuria, the Chinese province which had been at the centre of their earlier dispute. The main focus of the agreement was to end competitive railway building in Manchuria, to establish cooperation in the completion of the railways there, and to abstain from injurious competition. Other Powers looked askance on what had been agreed; particularly the United States, which had hoped for an open-door policy in Manchuria, in which its own traders would be on an equal footing with all others. But when, to this end, the United States proposed the internationalization of the Manchurian railways, Russia and Japan united to reject any free-trade policy.

The confidence of the Japanese in their new-found power, stirred up by the assassination of Prince Ito in 1909 by a Korean student, and the publicity given to the assassin's trial, created the mood whereby the Japanese military occupation of Korea was transformed into annexation. This echoed Austria-Hungary's transformation of its military occupation of Bosnia-Herzegovina into annexation two years earlier.

The Japanese annexation of Korea was opposed by the Japanese Regent-General there, Viscount Sone, who was immediately replaced by a Minister at the War Office in Tokyo, General Terauchi. The day of Terauchi's arrival in Korea, July 4, was the day of the signing of the Russo-Japanese agreement over Manchuria. In practical terms, the agreement over Manchuria enabled Japan to withdraw the bulk of its forces that had remained in Manchuria since the end of the Russo-Japanese war; these forces were moved briskly to Korea.

On August 22 a Treaty of Annexation was signed between the Emperor of Japan and the Emperor of Korea. Under the terms of the treaty, the Emperor of Korea would be allowed to remain on his throne; but every important aspect of administration, including control of the police, would be delegated to Japan and directed from Tokyo. The Ministers of the Korean government would be the nominees of the Emperor of Japan.

Britain and the United States were linked by no alliance or even by a written understanding. Yet in the early years of the twentieth century a relationship – which was later given the sobriquet 'special' – had begun to flourish, strengthening Britain's sense of not being a part of the European quarrels and animosities. When, in November 1910, a United States fleet visited British ports for a three-week period, its officers and men were entertained

1. British troops in action in South Africa, 1900

2. The relief of Ladysmith, February 1900

7. Japanese sailors on the eve of battle, 1904

8. *(Left)* Japanese warships approach the Tsushima Straits, May 1905

9. *(Above right)* Admiral Togo, Commander-in-Chief of the Japanese navy during the Russo-Japanese War

10. *(Right)* The first 'fighter' plane, a pilot and a machine-gunner, 1913

11. A suffragette advertises a Votes for Women march, 1906

12. Emmeline Pankhurst

13. Winston Churchill

14. Lenin, disguised

15. Stalin, 1917

16. Rasputin

17. Gandhi

18. Sarajevo: the Archduke's car, 28 June 1914

19. Sarajevo: the immediate aftermath

warmly wherever they went ashore, and in London. At a speech at the Guildhall, the fleet's commanding officer, Admiral Sims, declared, to the deep resentment of the German press, that were Britain ever to be menaced by an external enemy, 'its people might count upon every man, every dollar, every ship, and every drop of blood of their kinsmen across the ocean'.

Many Irishmen and Germans in the United States protested about Sims's remark, so much so that he was publicly rebuked by his Commander-in-Chief, President Taft, who stated that one of the functions of officers when visiting foreign ports was to convey to all nations the goodwill of the United States, and that such officers were under special obligations not to embarrass their government.

A different form of embarrassment came to the United States from another quarter that year, when nationalist feeling in the Philippines erupted into violence. In July, the Secretary of the Interior was attacked on Palawan island. In August there was an uprising in the north of Luzon. In October, tribesmen on Mindanao rose in revolt. But the efforts of the United States to introduce a beneficial administration were continuous; road-making, water-supply and improved sanitation were much in evidence, trade in sugar and tobacco flourished, and there was pride in Washington at the end of the year when it was announced that bubonic plague had been eradicated on the islands and cholera greatly reduced. One cloud on the horizon of good deeds was an investigation insisted upon by a Congressional Committee in Washington, with regard to the purchase of a large tract of land, the property of a religious order, by the Sugar Trust. The type of land in question (known as 'Friar's Land') was meant to be protected from ownership by a single person or corporation.

In Turkey, the government under the leadership of the Young Turks, was seeking both greater armaments, and loans to improve its defences. A turning point in Turkey's search for European support came in October, when the French government declined to give a loan, which Turkey needed to modernize and expand its army, whereupon the loan was raised in Germany and Austria-Hungary.

The French refusal to grant the loan (one French condition, unacceptable to the Turks, had been the appointment of a French official as the Director of the Turkish Public Accounts) led to an outburst inside Turkey of anti-French and also anti-British feeling, so closely were France and Britain seen to be linked in international affairs. At an anti-British demonstration in Constantinople, there was much applause when it was suggested that Turkey should use her influence as a Muslim Power to win over the Muslim soldiers in British India, who would then drive the British from the subcontinent. A telegram was also sent by the Turkish government to the German Kaiser, urging him to come forward as the saviour of a Muslim State. The Turks had long admired Germany, and been wooed by her. Above all, since his visit to Jerusalem twelve years earlier, the Kaiser had been active in furthering German interests in the Holy Land, under the friendly eye of the Turkish authorities there, to whom his architects, builders and agronomists brought work and prosperity. In 1910 the Turkish government bought two German battleships for their own navy. The fact that both battleships were twenty years old, and would be no match in battle with their British or French counterparts, was overlooked.

In the Turkish province of Macedonia, almost the last possession of Turkey-in-Europe, the heavy hand of Turkish rule was much in evidence. The Young Turks were no less nationalist in their outlook than their predecessors. Bulgarian and Greek inhabitants of Macedonia who refused to give up their firearms were flogged and tortured; many fled across the borders into neighbouring Bulgaria and Greece. At the instigation of Talaat Bey, the Turkish Minister of the Interior, all Bulgarian political clubs in Macedonia were closed down, efforts were made to interfere in the lessons taught in Bulgarian schools in the province, and Muslims from Bosnia were encouraged to migrate to Turkish Macedonia, where they were settled in predominantly Bulgarian districts.

Macedonian revolutionary activity, which had been suspended when the Young Turks came to power in Constantinople in the hope of a more tolerant future, was revived during 1910, mainly in reaction to the growing Muslim influence in the province. The reaction was intensified after the hanging, following secret trials by Turkish military tribunals, of Macedonians accused of anti-Turkish activities. The main thrust of the renewed agitation was among Bulgarians in the province; they found a ready source of money and bombs for their terrorist actions across the border in Bulgaria, where the government looked with favour on their activities.

The Greeks in Turkish Macedonia, and also in Turkish Epirus, were likewise being harshly treated by both Turkish officials and troops, the Greek Patriarch declaring that the Greek regions of Turkey-in-Europe were being ruled by 'an invisible power, the aim of which is annihilation of all religion and the national existence'. One complaint was that the Turks were settling Muslims in Greek areas, as they were doing among the Bulgarians. Another cause of aggravation was that disputes among Christians could only be adjudicated by Muslim officials. For the Turks, the last vestiges of their once enormous European possessions – which had reached as far as the outskirts of Vienna – had to be held at all costs, even at the cost of alienating the local non-Turkish populations almost to the point of open and persistent revolt.

It was not only the Bulgarians and Greeks in Turkey-in-Europe who were the object of Turkish military actions in 1910. Uprisings among the Arabs in Arabia, the Druse in the Hauran, and the Albanians in the Turkish province of Albania, were each put down by force. The Albanians had taken up arms to protest against the Turkish insistence that they use the Arabic script in all Albanian schools, rather than their own Latin script.

In the Hauran it took 3000 of Turkey's most highly trained soldiers, commanded by a German-trained Turkish general, to force the Druse into submission. Even so, of the 7000 Druse warriors who had taken up arms against the Turks, more than a thousand remained at large after the submission, and found many occasions on which to harass Turkish military outposts. Explaining the Turkish failure to suppress the Druse revolt in its entirety, Talaat Bey told the parliament in Constantinople: 'A province which has been in revolt for centuries cannot be pacified in a few months.'

To add to Turkey's imperial troubles, hardly had the Druse rebellion been contained than a Bedouin rebellion broke out in Moab, east of the Dead Sea, with many Turkish soldiers and officials being killed during a Bedouin raid on the crusader fortress and town of Kerak. Nor did the Albanians give up their struggle, despite the despatch of 17,000 Turkish troops against them. In a humiliating reverse for the Turks, some three thousand Albanians ambushed a Turkish military train in the Katchanik Pass, on the railway line to Prishtina, capturing a large quantity of supplies and disarming the soldiers. They then held the pass for more than two weeks, until finally driven off, after a thirteen-hour battle, by a substantial Turkish force.

By the end of the year the Turks had 50,000 troops in Albania. But it was estimated that they would have to disarm a million men, many of whom were gathered together in remote mountain areas almost inaccessible to a military column.

On the European border of the Ottoman Empire, a small Slav principality was converted into a fully fledged kingdom in 1910, when Prince Nicholas of Montenegro (one of whose daughters was married to the King of Italy, and two to Russian Grand Dukes), who had ruled Montenegro for fifty years, declared himself king. His kingdom was recognized by all the Powers, and welcomed by the Pan-Slavist Congress held in Bulgaria a month later. But Slav unity at the Congress was tarnished during the deliberations when the Bulgarians accused the Serbs of putting undue pressure on the Bulgarians of Macedonia, in the hope of coercing them to the Serb cause. Serbia, declared the Bulgarians, was 'thrusting its knife into the body of the Bulgarian population of Macedonia'.

The death of Edward VII in Britain, after fewer than ten years on the throne, led to a show of sympathy among the monarchical powers. At his lying-in-state in London, when more than 350,000 people passed the coffin as it lay in the solemn splendour of Westminster Hall, the stream of mourners was halted only twice, once to allow a group of nurses to see it, and once for the dead King's nephew, the German Kaiser.

Eight foreign sovereigns were present at Edward's funeral; those of the Belgians, Bulgaria, Denmark, Germany, Greece, Norway, Portugal and Spain, and forty other members of royal families, including the Archduke Franz Ferdinand of Austria-Hungary and the Crown Prince of Serbia. There were complaints in British circles that the funeral was too exclusively a military and court ceremonial, and that neither the government nor the Houses of Parliament were given any part in the funeral procession.

The reign of the new King, George V, saw the Liberal Government in the fiercest of conflict with the Conservative opposition. The issues were twofold, the Liberal desire to give Home Rule to Ireland, where the Catholic majority (except in the six provinces of Ulster) was eager for a far greater measure of autonomy; and the determination of the social reformers in the government, led by the Chancellor of the Exchequer, Lloyd George, to introduce a budget that would include the central principle of State-supported national insurance.

The Conservatives were prepared to use the built-in Conservative majority in the House of Lords, a majority of whose members were hereditary peers – their peerages dating back in some cases more than two or three hundred years – to defeat the budget. The Liberals were prepared, in the event of a Lords' veto – which many of them welcomed as a catalyst – to break the power of the Upper House for all time. A year of political acrimony followed, marked by considerable ill will at public meetings and in the chamber of the House of Commons. The two general elections that year, the second held as a result of the death of Edward VII, served only to increase tensions, and revealed a nation evenly divided.

The year 1910 was also a year of considerable industrial unrest in Britain, with working men and women unconvinced that the Liberal government would really improve their pay and conditions sufficiently to make life tolerable. When violence broke out during a dock strike in South Wales, the local police, unable to control the situation themselves, arranged for troops to be sent from London to suppress the riots, which had led to looting and the destruction of property. Winston Churchill, then Home Secretary, unwilling to see troops used in industrial disputes, ordered the train with the soldiers on board to be halted before it reached the scene of the riots, and sent London policemen in their place. He was condemned by the Conservatives for having stopped the troops from proceeding.

One liberal measure which the Liberal government resisted was the enfranchisement of women. Indeed, it was much criticized for having ordered the forcible feeding of those among the 600 women who had been imprisoned for violence at demonstrations, and who had declared hunger strikes in prison. A Labour Member of Parliament introduced a women's franchise bill in the House of Commons in June. In the streets of London, 10,000 women gave the bill their support, their procession being led by one of the women who had been forcibly fed the previous year, a women's musical band, and women delegates from three countries where women already had the vote, Norway, New Zealand and Australia.

The British Prime Minister, H. H. Asquith, when asked if he would find time to give the franchise bill the government's necessary support, replied, to the distress of men and women alike who supported votes for women, that his government was determined 'not to introduce contentious legislation'. The advocates of votes for women were unlucky that Asquith's majority was so narrow, and that the two principal issues pressing in on him, Home Rule for Ireland and the curbing of the powers of the House of Lords, were themselves so divisive as to make him unwilling to tackle another contentious cause. After an acrimonious debate in which many caustic remarks were made about the capacity of women to play any constructive part in national politics, the franchise bill was shelved. The suffragettes twice marched in protest to 10 Downing Street. On the second occasion, as they were nearing the entrance to the street – which is now blocked by iron gates erected in the 1980s as a protection against IRA attack – *The Times* reported how:

A squad of about fifteen constables made their way from Scotland Yard to the entrance of Downing Street, which they reached a few seconds before the head of the suffragist column swung round the corner of Whitehall.

There was at once a seething mass of spectators and struggling police and suffragists. Reinforcements of police quickly arrived, and the process of clearing the street began. The fight was short, sharp, and decisive, and lasted only ten minutes, although there was such a wealth of incidents that the struggle seemed to be of much longer duration. The women fought much more viciously than on Friday, and their increased fierceness may be accounted for by the fact that some of them have vowed to go to prison for their cause, and are prepared to commit increasingly serious breaches of the law to achieve this object. The rioters yesterday appeared to have lost all control of themselves.

Some shrieked, some laughed hysterically, and all fought with a dogged but aimless pertinacity. Some of the rioters appeared to be quite young girls, who must have been the victims of hysterical rather than deep conviction.

A woman dressed in the uniform of a hospital nurse threw a missile through a window of the Colonial Office. Some of the suffragists carried banners, which were quickly torn down by the police, but if the bearer managed to retain the bamboo handle she used it to belabour the nearest constable.

The women behaved like demented creatures, and it was evident that their conduct completely alienated the sympathy of the crowd. The police behaved with self-control and good humour under the greatest provocation. It may be mentioned that as a result of Friday's fight, six policemen had to go on the sick list with bites and scratches.

In the United States, after a mass demonstration of supporters of votes for women in Washington, President Taft received the leaders of the demonstration with courtesy, but refused to concede to them the right of women to have the vote nationally.

In France, a rail strike that October threatened to bring the communications and commerce of the nation to a halt. It was brought to an end when the government arrested the leaders of the strike (except for one, who fled to Belgium) and ordered the mobilization into the army of all railwaymen and engine drivers, thereby making them subject to military discipline should they refuse to obey the order to start work. Railway stations were occupied by regiments known to be particularly disciplined, and bridges and tunnels were guarded by troops. A demonstration in the Bois de Vincennes in support of the strikers, which had the support of the Socialist and Radical deputies in the parliament, was banned. In parliament, deputies who supported the strike prevented the Prime Minister, Aristide Briand, from speaking by hissing, hooting and banging their desks. At one point Briand declared that if the government had not found a lawful means to stop the strike, it would have resorted to illegal means. There was such an outcry at this 'dictatorial' remark – an outcry unprecedented in living Parisian memory – that the session had to be suspended.

There was a serious outbreak of industrial unrest in Berlin in 1910, when police protected a group of non-union workers who were being employed by a coal merchant while their own men were on strike. A demonstration of workers, in sympathy with the strikers, and opposed to the strikebreaking efforts of the police, charged the police and attacked them with stones. The police then drew their swords and charged the demonstrators. The struggle continued for two days, with many policemen and workers being injured. A group of British and American journalists, who were given police permission to drive to the scene of the confrontation, were then attacked by the police with their swords, and some seriously injured. The German government, despite diplomatic pressure, refused to censure the police.

In the Reichstag, the Chancellor, von Bethmann Hollweg, caused indignation when he accused the Social Democrats of 'complicity' in the Berlin disturbances. He went on to say that the German people were 'opposed at heart' to the 'Utopian-economical ambitions of Socialism'. German social legislation, he pointed out, went further than that of any other country, but 'lawless and violent assaults' in the name of socialism would be 'beaten down by the employment of every resource the State possessed'.

A lawyer by training, and a former Prussian civil servant, Bethmann Hollweg sought to consolidate and expand the already impressive social reform measures in place in Germany while excluding the Social Democrats from power. But he could not lessen their frustration at a system which gave them all the status and prominence of a large opposition party without any authority for legislation.

*   *   *

The United States could not escape the industrial unrest that was troubling so much of Europe. In search of higher wages, shorter hours of employment, and the right for an all-union work force, there were strikes of clockmakers and expressmen in New York; of tailors in Chicago; and of streetcar men in Columbus, Ohio. An explosion which destroyed the *Los Angeles Times*, a newspaper that had attacked the trade unions, was attributed to the labour unrest.

An ominous development that year followed the swift and unexpected victory of a black boxer, Jack Johnson, over his white opponent, Jim Jeffries, at Reno, Nevada. As the news spread that Johnson had won, there were anti-black riots in dozens of cities, with whites attacking blacks for fear that the victory would give the blacks a sense of undue exaltation. Hundreds of blacks were injured, and thirteen were killed. In Portland, Oregon, the *Los Angeles Times* reported, 'Two women of colour – not white women with Ethiopian sympathies – and four Caucasians (ladies) mixed in a battle royal in the women's quarters of the City Jail today when they learned that Johnson had won the big fight.' From Clarksburg, West Virginia, the paper reported that: 'Angered at the demonstration of negroes celebrating the Reno victory, a posse of a thousand white men organized here tonight soon after the announcement of the news, and drove all the negroes off the streets. One was being led with a rope around his neck when the police intervened.'

From New York it was reported that the news of Johnson's victory 'flashed through the congested streets and squares of Manhattan, and wherever it ran, trouble followed it. Great crowds packed the open spaces in front of the bulletin boards, cheering and groaning for their favourite. The blacks were exultant and good-natured and the whites were surly and disappointed. From the moment the decisive words, "Johnson wins" went up on the bulletin boards until midnight, there were seventeen calls for police and ambulances, and in almost as many parts of the town. Four negroes were arrested, and eight whites.'

The British government, to prevent such riots occurring in London, and also in India, South Africa or New Zealand, secured a ban on cinema pictures of the fight, much of the prize money for which had been raised by selling the film rights.

Racial tensions did not prevent the mass immigration to the United States of people from lands where poverty or persecution made them desperate for a place far away, democratic and with the prospect of economic advancement. In 1900 the population of the United States had been almost 76 million. By 1910 it had increased to almost 92 million, a rise of nearly 16 million, or 17 per cent.[1] The population of New York had risen from just over three million to almost five million, a rise of 66 per cent. Peasants from southern Italy, Poles and Jews from Russia, Jews from Roumania, Irishmen from the west and midlands of Ireland, Czechs and Croats from Austria-Hungary, arrived each year in their hundreds of thousands at Ellis Island, and read, if their grasp of the English language yet allowed them to, Emma Lazarus's inspiring exhortation on the Statue of Liberty: 'Give me your tired, your hungry, your huddled masses yearning to be free'.

There was a parallel immigration movement into Canada, where, between 1901 and 1911 the population rose dramatically from more than five million to just over seven million. According to the immigration statistics, between 1910 and 1914 a total of 1,640,000 Europeans reached Canada and remained there (some of them had tried the United States first, and moved north). The figures for the year 1910 show that by far the largest single group reaching Canada, 103,798 immigrants in all, came from the United States. After them, 59,790 came from the United Kingdom.[2]

In the Hungarian half of the Dual Monarchy, there were repeated attempts by the considerable non-Magyar populations, in particular by the Roumanians, Croats, Serbs and Italians, to secure greater influence over their own lives. In the Hungarian Parliament, an attack by the opposition on the ruling coalition took the form of the throwing of inkpots and paperweights against the Prime Minister and his ministers, in which several ministers were injured. During the elections, the reduction of the non-Magyar seats was achieved by the stationing of troops in front of some of the polling booths, with orders not to let non-Magyar voters enter the booths. In his speech from the throne, Franz Josef, then in his eighty-first year, spoke of the need for a universal suffrage system that would maintain 'the unitary national character of the Hungarian State'. But for the non-Magyars in that State these fine

[1] By contrast, the population of France, which was 39,601,509 in 1906, rose by only 349,264, or less than one per cent, in the next five years.
[2] The next largest number of immigrants to Canada in 1910, 7118, were from Italy, followed by 4195 Austrians, 2746 Russian Jews, and 2156 Chinese. Among the smaller groups of immigrants were 76 Serbs, 75 Armenians and 10 Hindus.

words were without meaningful content: their national feelings were already focused on much greater rights and autonomies.

Inside the Austrian half of the Dual Monarchy, the racial strife was even more noticeable, and more acute. In Lemberg (present-day Lvov), the Ruthenian students who had already been denied a Ruthenian faculty, attacked the Polish students in the university building; a student was killed and a professor badly injured. When, later that year, the government in Vienna refused to carry out a law, passed nine years earlier, for the building of much-needed canals in Galicia, the Polish deputies then joined the opposition, voting (as they had refused to do earlier) with the Czech deputies.

The future government of Bosnia-Herzegovina was also a cause of concern in the Austrian parliament. The constitution for the newly annexed region was promulgated on 22 February 1910. Censorship, hitherto imposed by the Austrian military regime, was abolished. A Presidential Bureau was established in the capital, Sarajevo, in which the office of President of Bosnia-Herzegovina would be held by a Serb, a Muslim and a Croat in annual rotation. The seventy-two elected seats in the Bosnia-Herzegovina Diet would be allocated according to the balance of the religious denominations in the province: thirty-one to Serbs of the Orthodox faith, twenty-four to Muslims, and sixteen to the Catholic Croats. One seat would be reserved for a Jewish representative: the Jews had first reached Sarajevo after being expelled from Spain at the end of the fifteenth century.

On May 30 the Emperor Franz Josef visited Sarajevo, a special narrow-gauge imperial train having been constructed so that he could arrive by rail. After reviewing a guard of honour, he received homage from the leading religious dignitaries in the city: the Roman Catholic archbishop, the Serb Orthodox metropolitan, the Reis-ul-Ulema of the Muslim community, the Protestant pastor, and the Chief Rabbis of the Sephardi and Ashkenazi Jewish communities. During Franz Josef's drive through the city, *The Times* reported, 'troops in new blue-grey field uniform kept the route. Behind them stood several thousand spectators, who cheered lustily as the brilliant cortege passed'.

The Diet was opened in Sarajevo on 15 June 1910. The opening ceremony, intended as a celebratory one in order to welcome another autonomous region into the Habsburg patrimony, was marred when a Serb anarchist fired five shots at the governor of the Province, General Baron Varesanin. The governor was unhurt. The would-be assassin shot himself dead. Four years and thirteen days later, close to the same spot, another Serb assassin was to succeed against a royal target.

During the first session of the Bosnia-Herzegovina Diet, Serb, Muslim and Croat deputies made common cause in pointing out that, under the constitution that had been granted to them, their political and economic dependence on the Austro-Hungarian monarchy was total. This was indeed so; all bills introduced into the Diet had first to have the sanction of both the Austrian and Hungarian governments. Sarajevo was to be as subservient to Vienna and Budapest as Prague was to Vienna and as Agram was to Budapest. Their constitution, declared the Sarajevo deputies, 'does not correspond to the expectations of the country'.

A leading member of the Reichsrat in Vienna, the distinguished Austrian politician Dr Baernreither, expressed publicly his sympathy for the aspirations of the people of Bosnia-Herzegovina to be their own masters within the Habsburg frame. His point of view was that the aim of the Dual Monarchy in Bosnia-Herzegovina must not be mere administration, but the winning of the hearts and minds of the inhabitants, and to 'strive to establish within its borders the moral centre-point of the whole Serb-Croatian world'. Through its annexation of Bosnia-Herzegovina, Austria-Hungary was to challenge Serbia for the primacy of the whole region.

The concept of an important, permanent and constructive Slav place in so predominantly a German-speaking empire, and one linked in alliance with Germany, was not limited to the South Slavs alone. In the words of a leading Austrian politician, Prince Schwarzenberg, 'although my Czech fellow-countrymen fear the effects of German predominance, the truth must not be forgotten that Slavs and Slav politicians in Austria have achieved their greatest successes under the Austro-German Alliance'.

From the perspective of Vienna, not only Serbia but also Russia must not be allowed to disturb the Slav equilibrium within the Habsburg dominions. But it was the Czech leader, Karel Kramar – who in 1919 became the first Prime Minister of an independent Czechoslovakia – who exposed the fragility of the Austro-German alliance system, when he spoke of what he considered to be the folly of the annexation of Bosnia-Herzegovina. As a result of having to appeal to Germany for help against Russian hostility to the annexation, Austria-Hungary was now, Kramar said, 'entirely dependent' on Germany. She could have managed Serbia without the 'shining armour' of the annexation, because she already held the two provinces under firm occupation, and there was no way that Serbia could have taken them from her.

Kramar went on to warn that the annexation of Bosnia-Herzegovina had left Germany 'mistress of Austro-Hungarian relations with Russia', and had reduced Austria-Hungary's relations with the other Powers 'to an innocent and totally ineffectual flirtation with their amiable Ambassadors'. 'It was a singular gain,' he said, 'to have been obliged to spend more than 300 million kronen on armaments, to have thrown away the Sanjak of Novi Bazar, to have paid 54 million kronen to Turkey without having been able to check the anti-Austrian boycott, to have dislocated the finances of both halves of the Monarchy, to have lost the Serbian market for Austrian industry, to have chained Vienna to the policy of Berlin, and to have turned Austria-Hungary into a pace-maker for Germany, bound to share all the perils of German Weltpolitik.'

It was a stern indictment, but within it lay the truth of Austria-Hungary's weakness, Serbia's dissatisfaction, and Germany's ascendancy: all arising from the annexation of a Balkan province.

In French Indo-China, forces hostile to France continued to attack French military columns. In one such confrontation in April, with the Annamese leader De Tham, four hundred of his followers were left dead on the battle-field. Many of those captured were deported to French Guiana, on the other side of the globe.

In South Africa, the new Union Government, based on an exclusively white franchise, continued to refuse to allow into the Cape those Indians who were being deported from the Transvaal as illegal and undesirable. The cause of the Indian deportees, some of whom were sent back to Bombay, had been taken up by Gandhi in London in 1909. In 1910 it was advanced by an Englishman, Henry Polak, who was able, on a visit to India, to raise funds from several of the Maharajahs of the Indian Princely States. In eventually agreeing to allow those Indians who had been expelled from the Transvaal to land in the Cape, the Union Government at the same time enacted legislation excluding (on the Australian model of the time) almost all future Indian immigrants, by means of an educational test. There was anger among many officials in British India, and in Liberal circles in Britain, about this legislation, for it meant that imperial subjects were being excluded from another region of the empire. But the Union of South Africa would not be persuaded, and no means existed to coerce it.

In Egypt, British rule was under continual threat from nationalists who wanted an end to the imperial administration. Those few Egyptians who were a part of the higher reaches of that administration were as much at risk as the British. In February the Prime Minister, Boutros Ghali Pasha, was assassinated. He was the first native Prime Minister of Egypt, and a Christian Copt (eighty-two years later his grandson was to become Secretary General of the United Nations). The Prime Minister's assassin was Ibrahim Wardani, a student, and by profession a chemist, who had fired five shots from a revolver, three of which had struck their target. Wardani had been at the Egyptian nationalist Conference in Geneva the previous year, as a newspaper correspondent.

Whatever difficulties might arise in Egypt, Sir Edward Grey, the British Foreign Secretary, told the House of Commons, England would not give up her task. His words were denounced at the Congress of the Young Egyptian Party, held in Geneva, from which a message was sent to the British press pointing out that nearly thirty years earlier the British had pledged to leave Egypt no later than 1 January 1888. Grey's statement clearly meant that the British occupation of Egypt, dating from 1882, was intended to be permanent.

In British Somaliland, the arming by Britain of the local tribes, in the hope that they would keep the ever-active and ever-independent Mullah away from their territories without the need for British intervention, led the British Commissioner in the region, Sir William Manning, to withdraw all British troops and officials to the coast. This was criticized by the Conservatives in Parliament, where Lord Curzon, speaking with the imperial authority of a former Viceroy of India, warned that as a result of the withdrawal, friendly Somalis were being left to the mercy of the Mullah and that 'British prestige' had been greatly injured. Even after the British withdrawal, one observer commented at the time, the Mullah gave 'occasional evidence of his capacity to raid, and still outlives repeated reports of his death'.

In northern Nigeria there was relief when a new British governor was met, and welcomed, by all the Emirs of the vast region, and escorted by 14,000 of their cavalrymen into Kano, the capital. To bring trade to the region, a railway was being built to Kano from the Niger.[1] On the Atlantic coast of Africa, the independent black republic of Liberia was receiving the attention of the Powers. The Liberian government was taking punitive action

---

[1] It exists to this day, linking Jebba on the Niger with Kano, a journey of just over seventeen hours.

against several groups of its own people, who petitioned Britain and France for protection. It was understood in both Britain and France, however, that Liberia, although in Africa, was in the sphere of United States interests, the black population in the coastal towns – including the capital Monrovia – being made up of the descendants of liberated slaves who had returned there in 1821. United States help came, in March, in the form of a gunboat, and the offer by Washington to take over the Liberian debt, reorganize the administration, and settle the frontier disputes with Britain (Ivory Coast) and France (Guinea). In the event, given the European interest in as peaceful an Africa as possible, the financial assistance to Liberia was shared by the American, British, French and German banks.

Germany continued to have trouble in its colonial empire, though not on the scale that had earlier led to the suppression of the Witboi and Herero revolts in German South West Africa with such ferocity. In October there was a revolt of Kaffir labourers in the same region. They were protesting the low wages and meagre rations during the railway building. The revolt was quickly put down, and several of the labourers killed. In the German Cameroons, following the murder (by a tribe that practised cannibalism) of a German trader and his seventeen porters, punitive measures were swiftly put in place, and several hundred tribesmen killed in an attempt to strike at the perpetrators and their villages.

In the air, records were again broken, amid a growing sense that there was something remarkable in prospect. In January, at an airfield display in France, Hubert Latham, who had so nearly been the first man to cross the English Channel by aeroplane, broke the world aviation record for altitude, reaching 3000 feet. In May, in New York State, the American aviator Glenn Curtiss flew 150 miles with only two stops, in the space of five hours; his actual time in the air was two hours and forty-five minutes, almost 60 miles an hour, a world record for that distance. Four days later, the British aviator, and motorcar pioneer, C. S. Rolls, flew from Dover to Calais and back without landing on French soil.

Flying planes were not only an exciting but also a dangerous pursuit. There were frequent reports of pilots being killed when their planes disintegrated forty or fifty feet above the ground. Two months and ten days after his two-way cross-Channel success, C. S. Rolls was killed at an aviation meeting in Bournemouth while landing. It was announced at the end of the year that thirty-three aviators had been killed during 1910, by far the largest number in any year since the start of aviation. The death toll since the start of flying was more than fifty.

Submarines, a growing feature of the naval strength of every Power, were also vulnerable to accident. In May, all twenty-six crew members of the French submarine *Pluvoise* were drowned when it sank after being hit by a cross-Channel steamer.

Railway accidents continued to create a heavy toll. In Canada, when an express train on its way from Montreal to Minneapolis ran off the rails, forty-eight passengers were killed. Disasters at sea also led to heavy loss of life; in a Mediterranean gale a French steamer on its way from Marseille to Algiers was wrecked on the north coast of Minorca, and 154 passengers drowned; only one was saved. When a Japanese steamer sank off Korea in July, two hundred passengers were drowned. The worst natural disaster of the year was also in Japan, where more than a thousand people were drowned in August during heavy rains and floods.

The causes of death from natural and man-made disasters were widespread. In the Canadian Rockies, a gang of Japanese and Italian railway workers who were trying to clear the line of snow were caught by a snow slide; sixty-two of them were killed. In Hungary, at a dance in aid of the Protestant Church in the town of Okörito, the coach house of the inn where the dance was taking place caught fire; 320 people were killed. In Montreal twenty-nine people were killed when the *Herald* building burned down.

In India, plague, which had already taken more than six million lives since the beginning of the century, but was believed to be on the wane, suddenly increased its depredations. In the year ending September 1910, almost half a million Indians died. A committee was set up in the Punjab, the worst affected province, to investigate why none of the measures taken, such as burning the houses where plague was found, had been successful. After long and careful deliberation, the committee announced that the 'only possible conclusion', after examining all the evidence, was 'that all remedies had failed'. It appeared that once people fell ill with plague they would not go to their doctors, that the wholesale destruction of rats on which the authorities had focused was 'useless', and that inoculation, the most valuable protection, could not be used because of 'popular prejudice' against it. In the United Provinces, a similarly thorough enquiry confirmed that the attitude of the population towards inoculation varied 'from apathy to active hostility'.

Manchuria was also affected by plague in 1910; nor was any way found to prevent it from spreading southward into China. That year there was also a famine in two Chinese provinces; and in June, a fire at Hankow destroyed hundreds of boats, homes and stores along the Yangtse River; the number of deaths as a result of the fire was reported in the European press as 'enormous', but how enormous no one knew. The number of deaths from plague and famine, though also believed to run into the hundreds of thousands, if not more, was also unknown, there being no equivalent in China of the precise gathering of mortality statistics that characterized the British provincial governments in India.

The year 1910 saw a remarkable use of wireless telegraphy. On July 11, at Father Point on the St Lawrence River, the first port of call of the Canadian Pacific liner *Montrose* after its voyage from Antwerp, an American doctor resident in Britain, H. H. Crippen, and his typist Ethel le Neve (disguised as a boy), were arrested. A wireless message had alerted the ship's captain to their presence. Crippen was brought back to Britain, charged with the murder of his wife in London, by poison, tried, sentenced to death (on October 22) and hanged a month later.

Science, medicine and technology advanced rapidly in 1910. In Germany, a portion of main railway line was electrified between Magdeburg and Halle, while in Breslau a public building was erected using reinforced concrete. In the United States, radio kits went on sale that year, and a concert held in the Metropolitan Opera House in New York was broadcast over the radio: Enrico Caruso was one of the singers whose voices were thus carried into thousands of homes. The fluorescent tube was invented that year, and Marie Curie published her *Treatise on Radiography*.

Also in 1910, the causes of philanthropy and world peace were combined when Andrew Carnegie set up a trust fund of £2 million. Carnegie intended the income from his trust to be used 'to hasten the abolition of war, and to establish permanent peace in the world'.

CHAPTER TWELVE

1911

THE SPIRIT THAT ANIMATED enlightened imperial rule was one of confident superiority. It was based upon the intention of the rulers to enhance the lives of those whom they ruled. This perspective meant a great deal to those in London, Paris, Brussels, Berlin and Rome who set imperial policy. They were convinced that they were bringing the benefits of civilized life and behaviour, of trade and industry, of education and modernity, to millions who were deprived of these benefits. But this perspective was less evident in some regions than in others, where resistance to foreign control could be considerable, even by those less well armed than the conqueror, or less strong than the local forces that were cooperating with the imperial power.

The second decade of the twentieth century saw no respite in imperial activity. The year began with the Ottoman Empire being challenged once more at its furthest extremity, the Yemen. Arab rebels led by their religious leader, the Imam Yahya, attacked the Turkish garrison at the capital, Sanaa. An Englishman who happened to be in Sanaa at the time, Archibald Wavell, recalled the first moments of the attack: 'Four important chieftains and over a thousand of their followers were reported to have fallen. Great flocks of vultures could be seen circling above the battlefield for many days after. The Turkish casualties were by comparison inconsiderable. That evening a state of siege was proclaimed in Sanaa. The gates were closed; no one on pain of death was to attempt to enter or leave the town, and after sundown citizens were to remain in their houses.'

There was a prolonged siege. The Turkish Governor-General, Mohammed Ali Pasha, had 40,000 troops at his disposal in the main towns, and in blockhouses along the roads. 'Both sides,' Wavell noted, 'issued extravagant proclamations: the Imam that he would not sheathe his sword till the last Turk had been driven into the sea; the Turkish commander that he would not retreat one step, and that the Yemen question should be settled this time once and for all.'

Another religious leader, Seyyid Idrees, led a second religious revolt against the Turks along the Yemen coast. A further 40,000 men were sent from Turkey, under Izzet Pasha. In the end, the forces of the Imam and the Seyyid were defeated. But the spirit of Arab nationalism and of religious zeal were not diminished.

The first overseas military action that year by a European Power was taken by France, whose position of predominance in Morocco was threatened when Fez was attacked by Berber tribesmen who had risen in rebellion against the pro-French Sultan, Mulai Hafid. The Sultan's palace outside the city was looted, and organized government was brought to a virtual halt. A Berber attempt to break into Fez was beaten off when a French officer, Major Mangin – who in April 1918 was instrumental in checking the German advance against Compiègne – opened fire with his artillery. Fez was besieged, and a French force of 3000 men which was sent from Casablanca had to fight its way into the city.

The French forces arrived on May 22 and the Berbers were driven off. They returned, however, within a few days, led by Mulai-el-Zin, a brother of Mulai Hafid, and the claimant to his throne. A further 4000 French troops were rushed to the scene, and reinforcements ordered from France. On May 28, Fez was again relieved, and the Berbers driven off once more. Against those who agreed to accept Mulai Hafid as Sultan, no action was taken; those who refused to do so were subjected to continual attack. Thanks to a large French army in Fez, another to the east of the city, and a third at Casablanca, and a series of fortified military posts between them, Mulai Hafid retained his throne. From Fez, he then began to carry out a series of fierce attacks on his Berber enemies, attacks which the French tried to curb; but when the French troops were themselves attacked by the Berbers, they too found themselves retaliating.

A week after the second French relief of Fez, Spanish troops occupied Larache, another town under Berber attack. Spanish politics, already in a state of turmoil as a result of the growing strength of the republican movement, were further convulsed by this forward move; a crowded antiwar meeting in Barcelona was followed by a mutiny on one of the Spanish warships anchored off Tangier. The leader of the mutiny was not so concerned by the military action on the African coast as with the ending of the Spanish monarchy and the proclamation of a republic. He was arrested, condemned to death, and executed.

Within Spain, the situation was regarded as calm enough, once the mutiny had been crushed, for the King to embark on a cruise in the Atlantic. But Alfonso XIII's cruise was cut short and he hurried back when strikes broke out all over Spain: in docks, mines and factories. Troops were called in to restore order; cavalry charges broke up demonstrations, and artillery was brought up as a final intimidation. Insurrection, however, was in the air. In one small town an armed band of peasants broke into the town hall and shot dead the local magistrate.

The strikes continued to spread, and on September 19 the King signed a decree suspending the constitutional guarantees of personal liberty, and of freedom of the press. Within a few weeks the prisons were filled with republican agitators; and when there was no room left in the prisons, army barracks were converted into places of incarceration. The unrest was quelled, partly because the financial resources of the strikers ran out, but the discontent did not diminish; one result was a dramatic increase in working-class emigration, mostly to the Argentine.

In South Africa, the independence of the government, its contempt for British liberal opinion, and the racial course it intended to pursue, were highlighted in 1911 when a white man who was married to a coloured woman brought an action in the courts of Cape Colony to force the schools to accept his children. The judge decided that the white man had no such right, ruling that once it was established that a near ancestor, male or female, was black or yellow, any descendant of that ancestor must be considered as of 'non-European' descent. Coloured children, as defined by any coloured ancestor, were to be excluded from the European schools. The colour bar was to be enforced, and a society created where the colour of one's skin, or of one's ancestor's skin, was to determine every aspect of education and, in later life, of employment, and representation.[1]

In Central and West Africa, the British and French colonial forces continued to suppress what remnants of uprisings still harassed their soldiers and administrators. Small though these episodes were in terms of the

---

[1] The population of the Union of South Africa at that time was 4 million blacks, 1,278,025 whites and 600,000 Coloureds.

European lives lost, they led to substantial reprisals against the African natives. In every case, native troops were used, under European officers, to fight their fellow Africans. In southern Nigeria, the murder of a British Assistant District Commissioner, two policemen and three boat boys was followed by a punitive expedition against the tribe responsible. In the Gold Coast, tribes in the northern territories who refused to submit to British rule were 'reduced to subjection' – in the words of the official report – after one week's fighting by a native force led by a British captain.

In French West Africa, French colonial and native troops were attacked by Senussi tribesmen who crossed into French territory from the Turkish side of the border, and even went so far as to raise the Turkish flag; though it was to be only three months before the Turks were to be driven from the whole region by the Italians, leaving the Senussi to make their peace with the French, and return across the border. In German South West Africa, yet another Hottentot revolt broke out, and was suppressed.

British, French and German officials were working together throughout the year to delineate their African borders, and where necessary to make adjustments to them. In place of military confrontations came frontier commissions, ensuring that there was no place, however small or remote, on the map of that vast continent that was not the recognized territory of one or other of the European Powers. Each Power also undertook, having secured the loyalty of its new subject peoples, to introduce measures of European propriety and social behaviour. In Britain's West African colonies there was pressure from the somewhat grandly named 'United Committee for the Prevention of the Demoralizing of the Native Races by the Liquor Traffic' to stop the use of gin as currency, and to prevent the custom of pawning children in return for gin.

The number of Europeans in these vast new regions of colonial activity was small. In French West Africa, in 1911, there were just over 7000 Frenchmen, 1600 other Europeans, and more than ten million Africans.

The most distant European possessions were those in the Pacific. During 1911 there was a revolt on Espiritu Santo, one of the islands of the New Hebrides, an Anglo-French condominium. It was quickly suppressed. On one of the islands of the German Carolines – the island of Jokoz, near Ponape – a revolt of men who had been forced to work at road-making was likewise suppressed; fifteen, who were found guilty of the murder of German traders, were executed; the rest of the population was deported to the island of Gap.

Japan was seen throughout 1911 as a Power in conflict with Western values. That year a group of socialist dissidents were tried in secret and executed. The operation of a Factory Law passed that year to improve conditions in workshops and factories was postponed for at least four years, and was itself regarded as the most backward such legislation of any industrial nation. 'Generally speaking,' wrote Violet Markham, a British expert on the employment of women, 'Japanese women engaged in the cotton trade work under contracts essentially servile in character.' Feudal forms persisted; in November, while the Emperor was on a rail journey through western Japan, his railway carriage, coming slowly from a marshalling yard to a station, jumped the points and was delayed for twenty minutes. No one was hurt. The stationmaster, insisting that the fault was his, committed suicide.

The coronation of George V on June 22 was followed by a naval review at Spithead, when 167 British warships were assembled as a symbol of loyalty to the new sovereign, and as a sign of the power of Britain at sea. But it was a thousand miles to the south that a small naval episode threatened to escalate into a conflict between the Powers. The Germans had for some time been hoping to develop a port on the Atlantic coast of Morocco, and at the beginning of July sent a gunboat, the *Panther*, to the tiny port of Agadir. The reason given by the German government was that the gunboat was needed to protect German subjects in Agadir and the region whose personal safety and property were being threatened by Berber attacks, which had become more frequent after the Berbers had been driven from Fez by Mulai Hafid.

A few days later, the *Panther* was replaced by a larger warship, the *Berlin*. No attempt was made to put German troops ashore, but the warship had her guns trained on shore installations. She would leave Agadir, the Germans told the French, 'as soon as peace and order are restored to Morocco'; not, noted observers, restored to Agadir alone, but to the whole of Morocco.

The French were indignant; the appearance of a German warship, for whatever reason or pretext, was a breach of their rights in Morocco. There were rumours in Paris of impending war between France and Germany. When France called upon Britain for support, the British government demanded that the Germans withdraw their warship.

As the Agadir crisis developed, the German government tried to obtain some advantage from it, suggesting that in return for withdrawing from Agadir, Germany would be given, as 'compensation', the coast of French Congo and half of its hinterland. Not only did France refuse any such arrangement, but Britain expressed public support for the French position. In a speech in London on July 21, the Chancellor of the Exchequer, David Lloyd George, a radical Welshman, who ten years earlier had been an opponent of British participation in the Boer War, spoke words of warning to Germany. He would make great sacrifices for peace, he said, but if a situation were to be forced on Britain in which peace could only be preserved 'by the surrender of the great and beneficent position won by centuries of heroism and achievement — by allowing her to be treated where her interests were vitally affected as if it were of no account in the Cabinet of nations — peace at that price would be an intolerable humiliation'. National honour, he said, and the security of British international trade, were not Party questions.

In Britain, the opposition Conservatives rallied to the call for national unity. In France, there was deep satisfaction in government circles that Britain, to whom France was bound by no formal alliance, had been so emphatic in resisting the German action. Lloyd George's speech, declared the French *Journal des Débats*, was worth at least as much as the despatch of a cruiser. But it was not by words alone that the British government intended to show support for France. On July 26, five days after Lloyd George had spoken, the British Atlantic fleet, which was to have gone northward that week to Norwegian waters, was sent instead to the English Channel, within much shorter steaming distance of the Moroccan coast.

The British Labour Party was opposed to war, with Ramsay MacDonald, the Labour leader, expressing his regret at Lloyd George's speech, and stating that the Labour parties in Britain, France and Germany would stand together for peace.

For a short while, the Agadir crisis seemed a prelude to war. But within a month, the life of the European monarchs and leaders whose countries had become so vociferous against each other returned to its normal peacetime pattern. At an international naval regatta at Spithead in August, a yacht belonging to the Kaiser took part, and was among the victors.

Even if the family ties of the monarchs did not mean that war between the Powers was impossible, the realities of twentieth-century commercial interdependence seemed to assure peace. Many items essential for warmaking were available as a result of European cooperation. Any future conflict between the European Powers would create incredible problems, especially if the conflict were to be prolonged. Acetone, the solvent used in the manufacture of cordite – the explosive component of shells – was an example of such interdependence. It was produced almost entirely by the distillation of wood. Germany and Austria were two of the main timber-exporting countries, the other two being Canada and the United States. One ton of acetone required at least eighty tons of birch, beech or maple. It seemed as if, were Britain to go to war with Germany or Austria-Hungary, she would have to bear in mind that all her forests, cut down in their entirety, would not be able to supply the minimum of a hundred tons needed each year to sustain such a war.

Imported wood did indeed prove such an essential component of warmaking capacity that within six months of the outbreak of war in 1914, Britain began an urgent programme to develop synthetic acetone; but it was to take seventeen months before the synthetic process was in place, making use of vast quantities of potatoes. With so many able-bodied men at the front, schoolchildren had to be taken from their classes to harvest the potato crop.

The interdependence of trade and industry, although it was to create problems for European belligerents, had not made war impossible. A prewar German invention, the Bosch magneto, helped to power all motorcars and lorries. When, after heavy use in the first months of the war, replacement magnetos were needed, the British were forced to re-invent the device; a team of young engineers worked night and day to rediscover this small but crucial element in warmaking. In August 1915, in another area of total German monopoly – the manufacture of binoculars – Britain was obliged to use a Swiss intermediary in order to acquire, by ruse, 32,000 pairs of German binoculars for the Western Front.

In 1911, labour unrest was still a major problem in the industrialized States, where the contrast was growing between the conditions under which the workers toiled and lived and the way of life of the better off. A strike of dock workers, which had begun in Britain in May, spread during July and August until some 20,000 men were on strike in the London docks alone, with the docks at Liverpool and Manchester also brought to a halt.

On August 1, in the London docks, more than twenty ocean liners were unable to sail. Some workers, mostly coal porters and lightermen, agreed to accept arbitration, but the main body of the dock workers would not settle. While they were still on strike, and had set up pickets to prevent supplies reaching the docks by independent means, hundreds of carters had come out on strike in sympathy with the dockers. Like the dockers, they were demanding wages which would enable them to maintain a basic standard of living at a time when the cost of living had risen sharply. The carters agreed to continue to supply hospitals with ice and waterworks with coal; but they would not deliver paper to the newspapers, raw materials to factories, or provisions to shops.

On August 11 the government made plans to send 20,000 troops into London. That day, the Home Secretary sent a letter to Chief Constables throughout Britain, pointing out that it was illegal for workers to intimidate others from going to work, and that only 'peaceful' picketing was allowed.

The carters agreed to end their strike that day, obtaining a rise in wages and a shorter working week. But even as they went back to work, the railwaymen were coming out on strike in larger and larger numbers. Their complaint was the slowness with which their grievances about wages and hours were being dealt with by a specially established Conciliation Board. When, at the Liverpool railway stations, the porters joined the strike, large quantities of food began to rot on the platforms. At a mass meeting of transport workers in Liverpool on August 13, there was a struggle with the police, and two hundred people were injured. Troops were sent to the city, and on August 15, after stones were thrown at them, they opened fire; two men were killed. A cruiser was sent to the Mersey, and armed sailors were landed to protect the docks. There was also rioting in Glasgow, and among the black dock workers in Cardiff, who claimed that the rise in wages brought about by the strike caused shipowners to prefer white crews to black.

The railway strike, reducing Britain's rail traffic by half, and seriously affecting trade, continued. Troops were sent to guard stations and signal boxes where trains were still running. Strikers set up pickets to prevent workers who were still operating the trains from doing so. In one episode, an army officer whose train had been halted by strike pickets formed a company from soldiers travelling on the train (on their way to home leave) and, borrowing rifles from the local territorial troops who were guarding the station, drove the strike picket away by the threat of a bayonet charge.

In several towns there was rioting, and even looting. At Llanelli, in South

Wales, troops fired on a crowd of rioters, killing two men. On August 19 the strike was ended; the strikers would not be penalized, and their grievances would be settled by arbitration. Most railwaymen went back to work, though there were spasmodic outbreaks of unrest for some days to come, with further serious rioting in South Wales, where the ugly spectre of anti-Semitism was raised in a series of attacks on Jewish shops and homes. 'The ire of the demonstrators,' reported the *Jewish Chronicle*, 'was almost entirely directed against the Jewish community, who are said to monopolize, locally, certain businesses. It is alleged that a large number of the smaller houses are owned by the Jewish tradesmen, who stipulate that their tenants shall buy goods from them on the hire system. It is also alleged that exorbitant rents are charged for these tenements, and that repeated increases have been demanded in the rents when the tenants have decided to take in lodgers to swell their weekly incomes. Then, again, stories of evictions for non-payment of rents are freely circulated. Whatever be the truth, these stories are the stock in trade of the rioters.'

In fact, in the mining town of Tredegar, where the riots began, of the thirty Jewish families among a population of 20,000, seventeen were shop-keepers, one a mineral-water manufacturer, one was a rabbi, three were pedlars, and only one derived his income from rents. Under the headline 'Violent Attacks on the Jews in South Wales' the *Jewish Chronicle* reported:

> Looters could be seen in all directions laden with spoil. One man was observed carrying his bowler hat half filled with watches. Another was seen carrying away a bedstead on his back, while others played concertinas, accordions, and other musical instruments taken from the wrecked premises.
>
> The crowd were mad with excitement and most threatening in their demeanour. This wild rioting continued for several hours, the police being quite unable to cope with the disorder. Eventually police reinforcements arrived in a conveyance from Ebbw Vale. These were drawn across the main entrances to the town, to prevent the incursion of masses of people who had been attracted by the row, and after stern measures had been resorted to, the streets were cleared about four o'clock on Sunday morning.

The riots spread from Tredegar to many other towns and villages in South Wales. 'On Monday and Tuesday rioting was general in the mining valleys. Ebbw Vale, Rhymney, Tredegar, Cwm, Victoria, Brynmawr, Bargoed and

Beaufort were all more or less seriously affected, and looting was carried out on a large scale,' the *Jewish Chronicle* reported. 'In many places so serious was the aspect of the disturbances, that the Riot Act was read and the military were called out, and orders to fix bayonets and clear the streets were found to be necessary.' The newspaper added:

> Happily, up till the time of going to press, no lives have been lost, so far as is known, but hundreds of Jews have been ruined, having been robbed of their all, and many who were in good positions are now left destitute. Indeed, the happenings of the last few days in South Wales read of nothing so much as of the pogroms we have deplored in Russia.
>
> At Ebbw Vale, on Monday, rioters armed with crowbars, sticks, stones, and bottles, broke into a tobacconist's shop and entered the living apartments, so that the inhabitants – men, women and children – who were unarmed, had to secrete themselves in an attic, and were rescued only by the arrival of the military. Upon being released from their hiding-place, they found the shop totally wrecked, and the goods stolen. Gas fittings had been wrenched off and the boardings of the floor torn up.
>
> On all hands there was one cry – that the Jews must be forced out of South Wales. Many of the Jews were hastily departed from Tredegar, and the neighbouring towns, leaving their homes untended, fearing to remain because of their lives.

These British domestic upheavals had hardly abated when, on August 27, in a speech at Hamburg, the Kaiser spoke of the need for an increase in the size of the German navy. His speech rang alarm bells in Britain, where it seemed to herald a direct German challenge to British naval supremacy. Meanwhile, Britain was taking a lead in the science of flight, not only for military but for civil purposes. The first air mail experiment in India took place on February 18, when a French aviator, Henri Piquet, flew with a small bundle of letters from Allahabad to Naini, a distance of five miles, as part of the United Provinces Exhibition mounted by the local British administrators and traders. Beginning on September 9 the pioneer aviator Gustav Hamel made a series of flights between London and Windsor to deliver mail by air. Within three weeks he had carried 25,000 letters and 90,000 postcards.

Even as Hamel's experiment was coming to an end in Britain, an American aviator, Earle Ovington, flying from Nassau Boulevard to Mineola, Long

Island, likewise demonstrated, during nine days of flights, that mail could be delivered in bulk by air on a regular basis.

The human ability to exploit the invention of flight was in the end as mixed in terms of human happiness as the ability to regulate the affairs of men in a fair and harmonious fashion. With the continuing struggle inside many Russian universities between the radical and reactionary students, and with much violence between them, the Russian government announced in February 1911 that the administration of the universities would to a large extent be transferred to the police. In protest, the Rector of Moscow University resigned. Students who continued to agitate were expelled, and many conscripted into the army.

In an attempt to carry out the law of 1908, whereby peasants could have individual, as opposed to communal, ownership of land, the Russian Prime Minister, Peter Stolypin, sent members of the largely honorific Senate – the highest court of judicial appeal in Russia – throughout the empire to ensure that the ownership law was not being impeded by corrupt or incapable officials. At the same time, he persuaded the Duma to agree to spend money on compulsory education, and also on the strengthening, on liberal lines, of the operation of local self-government. He also obtained a substantial increase in shipbuilding for both the Baltic and Black Sea fleets.

Stolypin was often criticized for high-handedness, but his energies and reforming zeal were much admired. Lenin described them as 'revolutionary'. An Act for medical care which was put on the statute book in the following year was in many respects more advanced than those in Britain or Germany. Land sales to peasants were such that, within five years of Stolypin's premiership, the peasants owned – according to the 1916 agricultural census – 89.3 per cent of all arable land and more than 94 per cent of all livestock: a true revolution in a countryside traditionally dominated by landowners with large estates. But Stolypin's energies were soon to be cut short. At Kiev, on September 14, during a gala opera performance in the presence of the Tsar, he was shot by an anarchist while standing in the front row of the stalls. He died in hospital four days later.

How Stolypin's assassin had entered the hall was at first unclear. Admission was by ticket only, and the tickets were issued only by the police. But it was quickly discovered that the assassin, Bogrov, was present at the opera that night as an agent of the secret police, charged with watching over the safety of the Tsar and other members of the court during the performance. The true background to the murder was never ascertained. During his five years as Prime Minister, Stolypin had been a reformer, seeking to liberalize the administration of local government, education and taxation; but in his last years he had lost the full confidence, and hence the necessary backing, of the Tsar.

At the end of the year Russia was embroiled in a bizarre dispute with the United States. From time to time, Russian Jews who had emigrated to the United States returned for a visit to Russia to see family and friends. In cases where they had made good in America, they brought succour, usually in the form of cash donations, to the towns from which they came. The Russian government decided that its permission was required if these Jews were to leave Russia again, and refused to accept their American passports as sufficient documentation. Angered by this, the United States – more insulted by the indignity to its sovereignty than by the commercial implications of reprisal action – cancelled its commercial treaty with Russia. The nationalist deputies in the Duma then introduced a bill to the effect that no American Jew, without exception, should be admitted into Russia. A second Duma bill introduced at the same time greatly increased the tariffs charged on American goods. In the United States these measures only served to confirm the contempt felt for the autocracy of the Tsar and for the machinations of his empire.

In North Africa, there were only two areas not yet under the direct control of a European Power: Tripolitania and Cyrenaica (today combined as Libya). Both had been under Ottoman Turkish rule since the sixteenth century. The rest of the North African coastline, as well as the interior, was ruled by France, Spain and Britain. The Italian government had long coveted a place on the southern shore of the Mediterranean, the sea with which Italy, as much as any of the States around it, was intimately associated; and Italy was territorially ambitious.

A crisis came in relations between Turkey and Italy when the Turkish government, which had been reluctant to give any concessions in the two provinces to Italian applicants, granted a number of United States subjects a concession for archaeological excavations in Cyrenaica. The Italian newspapers claimed that the real aim of the Americans was to look for mineral deposits, especially sulphur, which would result in stiff competition for the Sicilian sulphur mines, even to the extent of threatening the Sicilian sulphur industry with collapse.

There was further anger in Italy when a small road-building contract, for about sixty-five miles of road, was given to the French rather than to the Italians. It was 'a vital interest of the very first order', explained the Italian government, that in a region so close to the coasts of Italy there should be no such discrimination of Italian enterprise; in addition, Tripolitania and Cyrenaica should be allowed 'to enjoy the same progress' as that attained by other parts of North Africa as a result of a European presence.

The commercial causes of Italian aggravation were followed by reports circulating in the Italian newspapers that French troops had occupied the oasis of Ghadames, on the western border of Tripolitania, across the border from the French Sahara. It emerged that the French had not occupied the oasis at all, but were paying a courtesy call on the Turkish side of the border, as part of the work of the Boundary Commission in the region. But Italian national sentiment was roused, and throughout the summer charges were made against the Turks of gross unfairness towards Italian residents in Tripolitania, of accumulating arms in the province, and of 'intriguing' with Germany, which was said to have territorial desires of its own in Cyrenaica.

On 26 September 1911 a Turkish transport ship arrived in the Tripolitanian port of Tripoli with quick-firing guns and other war munitions. On the following day the Italian government issued notices for army reservists to join their units. That same day Italy issued an ultimatum to the Turkish government, giving it forty-eight hours in which to accept the occupation of Tripolitania and Cyrenaica by Italian troops, and the establishment of an Italian administration. The Sultan's sovereignty would be assured, and an annual subsidy would be paid by the Italians to Constantinople.

On September 28, before the ultimatum expired, ten Italian battleships and cruisers took up war stations off the port of Tripoli. On the following day, when the ultimatum expired, Italy declared war on Turkey. In Italy, demonstrations by Socialists opposed to the war were hissed and booed by the populace. A general strike was called by the General Confederation of Labour, but failed. On September 30 Tripoli was blockaded, and for two days Italian naval guns bombarded the Turkish forts and fortified positions. The Turks returned fire for as long as their ammunition held out, and then withdrew. The city was occupied on October 5.

In the Adriatic, Italian warships sank a number of Turkish torpedo-destroyers and bombarded the port of Prevesa, on the coast of Epirus. To

Italy's annoyance, the Austro-Hungarian government let it be known that all warlike operations on the eastern coast of the Adriatic must cease, a strong rebuke from a fellow member of the Triple Alliance. Germany also indicated its disapproval of Italy's action. Given Italy's adherence to the German-led Triple Alliance, her attack on Turkey was not helpful to Germany's efforts to pose as Turkey's friend and benefactor.

Isolated diplomatically, the Italians were nevertheless victorious on the battlefield. Benghazi was captured on October 20. But in the interior, the local Arabs declared themselves supporters of the Turks, and called on their fellow Muslims in Tripoli to resist the Italian occupation. The call was answered; an uprising inside Tripoli led to the deaths of 374 Italian soldiers, and terrible cruelties being perpetrated on those Italians who were captured. The Italian reprisals were also cruel. Hundreds of Arabs were killed by Italian soldiers in scenes of brutality which, being fully reported by the journalists, and later supported by newspaper photographs, sent shock waves of indignation through the European capitals. 'Horrible atrocities,' a British commentator noted at the end of the year, 'were committed on both sides; that the half-savage Arab tribes should have committed them was perhaps to be expected, but one would have thought that the civilized Italian soldiers would at least have abstained from such acts as the indiscriminate slaughter of unarmed men, women, and children for three days after the attack on the Italian rear by the Arabs had been repulsed.'

On November 1 an Italian airman, flying over a Turkish military encampment at an oasis in Tripolitania, leaned out of his craft and dropped a few small bombs by hand. No serious damage was done, but a new, and in due course terrible, era had been inaugurated, that of aerial bombardment, which was to have such an impact on the twentieth century that the names of Guernica, Rotterdam, Coventry, Dresden, Hiroshima and Nagasaki were to be an integral part of the common language and fear of war.

On November 6 the Italian government announced that Tripolitania and Cyrenaica were under the 'full and entire sovereignty' of Italy. The Turkish empire in North Africa was at an end. In Turkey's European province of Macedonia, the demands of the Bulgarian inhabitants for greater autonomy, and the assassination of two Turkish officials, were answered by a Muslim riot in which several dozen Bulgarians were killed. Turkey had no intention of giving up its Balkan provinces.

The use of assassination as a weapon for political change continued. In the Austrian parliament that September, a Dalmatian workman by the name of Njegus fired several shots at the Minister of Justice. The Minister was unhurt. In British India, extreme nationalist agitators continued to use the bullet and the bomb, killing both British officials and Indians working in the police and criminal investigation department. But the confidence of empire could not easily be dented; at the end of 1911 the King-Emperor, George V, and his Queen-Empress, travelled throughout India as part of his coronation celebrations. At the coronation Durbar in Delhi, the King-Emperor inspected an impressive gathering of British and Indian troops, as well as 132 Ruling Chiefs. A hundred thousand Indians watched as he addressed the assembled dignitaries from his throne; one of the concessions announced that day was that, in future, Indian soldiers would be eligible for the highest British military award for bravery, the Victoria Cross, from which they had hitherto been excluded.

As a final gesture of imperial grandeur, George V announced that the capital of India would be moved from Calcutta to Delhi, and that a new city would be laid out, as befitted the largest of Britain's imperial possessions; on December 15 he and Queen Mary laid the foundation stones of the new city. It was to take as many years as the empire had to run for all the planned buildings of the imperial capital to be completed, but while those first foundation stones were being laid there was no doubt in the minds of the rulers that British rule in India would last until well beyond the end of the century, perhaps that it need never come to an end.

Even as British rule in India was laying its new capital's foundations, in China the 267-year rule of the Manchu dynasty was being challenged. Starting in Wuhan on October 10, revolutionaries intent on ending the rule of the emperors and establishing a republic seized towns and ports. Any Manchu garrison which resisted was massacred. Among the many students who were recruited to fight for the republican cause was the eighteen-year-old Mao Tse-tung, who fought briefly against the local Manchu troops.

One by one the provincial capitals fell to the revolutionary forces. In November, the Emperor, in an attempt to ward off disaster, agreed to accept a constitution, as demanded by the republican-dominated National Assembly. Under this constitution his powers would be limited to the formal appointment of a Prime Minister already elected by the parliament. Parliament would control all treaties and budgets.

These massive concessions were not enough. The revolutionaries were determined that the Manchu dynasty would give way altogether to a republic. Their capture of the arsenal in Shanghai was followed by the declaration of the naval commander on the River Yangtse, Admiral Sah, that he was transferring his loyalty, and that of his fleet, from the Manchus to the revolutionaries. At Canton, a republican government was proclaimed. Negotiations between the Manchus and the republicans were continuous, but inconclusive; then their respective forces took to the battlefield.

The organizer of the Chinese revolution was Dr Sun Yat-sen. A Christian by religion, and a graduate of an American university, for the previous fourteen years he had been an exile from China, where he had never held any political or administrative office. Yet he was hailed by all moderates and reformers as the man who would usher in his country's redemption. In exile he had formed a New China Party based on three principles: nationalism, democracy, and the 'people's livelihood'. Seven years earlier his 'Summary of Revolution' had pledged 'equal rights' to all Chinese. He was a supporter of a greater role for women in Chinese life, and wanted China to be freed from what he called the 'economic stranglehold' of the European Powers and the United States. Sun Yat-sen also believed that military force had a part to play in overcoming military despotism wherever it emerged, and in ensuring the unification of China under a civil administration.

Sun Yat-sen was fundraising in the United States when news of the uprising reached him. He read about it in a Denver newspaper while on his way by train to Kansas City. Even then he did not hurry back to China, but, regarding his main task as winning European support for the republicans, he sailed from the United States to Europe, to ensure that there would be no European military intervention on behalf of the Manchus, and no European financial help for the supporters of the monarchy. In this diplomatic task, which took him to London and Paris, he was successful.

The victory of the Chinese republicans was secured on the battlefield. In early December, Manchu and loyalist troops were defeated in Nanking. Sailing from France, Sun Yat-sen reached Shanghai on Christmas Day. On December 31 the republicans elected him President of the Chinese Republic. He assumed office in Nanking on the following day, marking his first day in office by abolishing the ancient Chinese calendar with its ten-day periods based on lunar calculations, and replacing it by the Western solar calendar with its weeks of seven days. The final act of the establishment of the republic in China was the abdication of the Emperor on 12 February 1912.

Natural disasters continued to take a heavy toll in life and property. In January a succession of earthquakes in Russian Turkestan killed more than two hundred people, mostly Kirghiz. In the Philippines, four weeks later, 1300 people were killed when a volcano erupted on Luzon. In June, in an earthquake in and around Mexico City, another 1300 people were killed.

More cinema fires were a feature of 1911, as they had been of several previous years. In the Russian town of Bologoe, half way between Moscow and St Petersburg, a wooden cinema-building caught fire during the showing of a film to mark the jubilee of the emancipation of slaves in Russia; ninety people, many of them children, were killed. In the United States during a cinema show at Canonsburg, near Pittsburgh, a panic arose after the cry of 'Fire' was heard and, although there was no fire, twenty-five people, mostly children, were killed in the crush to leave the building.

There was a fire of another sort in New York, which attracted considerable attention; it took place at a blouse workshop at the top of a ten-storey building, and killed 141 girls working there. Most of them were Italian, Irish and Hungarian immigrants. Two issues that had long been in the back of the public mind came to public prominence as a result of the fire: inadequate safety standards in workplaces, and the exploitation of immigrant labour.

Other disasters in 1911 included a two-day fire at Constantinople in which nearly five thousand wooden houses were destroyed, many of them in the crowded Jewish quarter, and more than 50,000 people were left homeless. In Littleton, Alabama, more than a hundred convicts were killed when there was an underground explosion in the mine in which they were working as forced labourers. In Briceville, Tennessee, a hundred coal miners were killed when an explosion entombed them in the depths of the mine. That same month, in a night shelter for the homeless in Berlin, fifty-seven paupers died of poisoning, having drunk an alcoholic drink that had been adulterated.

A social disturbance rocked the United States that year when, at Coatesville, Pennsylvania, there was a lynching that caused a gasp of dismay in many American towns, which had regarded lynchings as a thing of the past. It occurred when a black man, who had tried to commit suicide to avoid arrest for theft, was taken from hospital in his bed and burnt alive.

Three times he had tried to get out of the bed, and each time had been forced back into the flames.

The lynching was particularly shocking to the more enlightened members of the American public because those carrying it out were prominent citizens of the town, and because, when the lynch mob was brought to trial, the sympathy of the local whites was so much with them that two successive juries refused to convict.

As part of their warmaking preparations, all the Powers were developing submarines. These craft were designed to operate both on the surface, using their automatic weapons against merchant ships, and beneath the sea, using their torpedoes against warships. The cost of trials and practice could be high. In January 1911 the German submarine *U-3* sank in Kiel harbour. When she was raised on the following morning, her crew of twenty-six, including her commanding officer, were dead. It was Germany's first U-boat fatality.

Disasters at sea continued to make the headlines throughout the year. In March, when an Australian coastal steamer sank on the Barrier Reef off Queensland, all seventy crew and sixty-eight passengers were drowned. In August, when a French steamer collided with a British steamer in the Straits of Gibraltar, eighty-six crew and passengers on the French vessel were drowned. In Toulon harbour, in September, in an accidental explosion in the magazine of a French battleship, almost every other ship in the harbour was damaged by the force of the explosion, and 226 sailors were killed.

Air accidents continued to cast a pall over the excitement of the new science of flight. At the start of the Paris–Madrid aeroplane race in May, before a crowd of half a million people, a pilot who tried to avoid hitting a group of cavalrymen as he crashlanded, killed the French Minister of War, Maurice Berteaux, and badly injured the Prime Minister, Ernest Monis. In a single day, on September 2, three airmen were killed in crashes in France and one in the United States.

On the day after this group of fatal accidents, it was announced that the total number of fatalities in the air in the previous twelve months was seventy-six. The seventy-seventh aviator to die was killed at Huelva, in Spain, two days later. But the desire to conquer the skies was all-pervading; on September 4, just as these statistics were being absorbed, and the day before the Huelva crash, a French pilot, Roland Garros, flew to a record height of 13,800 feet, 2000 feet higher than the record set at Chicago by an American, Lincoln Beechey, two weeks earlier.

The need to regulate flight was becoming urgent. On November 26 the French Government announced that all aviators would be provided with flying certificates; that their machines must be numbered, and must carry lights; and that they could land only when signalled to do so. Flights over towns and crowds were forbidden. Regulations such as these coincided with the beginning of air services that were to transform many aspects of communications and commerce. That year, in the interest of aerial safety, the first aeronautical map was published, showing air routes across France.

An increasing number of accidental deaths were being caused each year on the roads. In 1911 the United States government announced that 1291 people had been killed that year in car accidents. This figure was to grow tenfold by 1922 and almost thirtyfold by 1932. Between 1911 and 1932 more than three hundred thousand Americans were killed on the roads.

In British India, the hopes that the plague deaths would diminish, and wither away, had been dashed in 1910, when the number of deaths had more than doubled. In the year ending September 1911 the figure almost doubled again, to almost three-quarters of a million. The remedy of inoculation, which could have saved so many lives, was again refused by those who still saw it as a threat to their bodies worse than the disease it could cure. The two remedial measures that the authorities were allowed to attempt, as before, the burning of houses where plague had struck and the mass extermination of rats, both proved ineffectual. The total number of plague deaths since the start of the century had risen to well over seven million.

In the United States, California gave women the vote in 1911. In Britain, the first nursery school was opened. Among the classics of literature that were turned into films that year was Tolstoy's *Anna Karenina*: it was to be remade three times in the next forty years. Also issued that year was the first, but not the last, film of *Pinocchio*. Film studios were being established in every European country. The films were all silent: but in 1911 words — in the form of separate captions on an otherwise blank screen — first appeared on the screen. Also in 1911, in the United States, the first State cinema censorship board was established, in Pennsylvania. In San Francisco a local ordinance forbade 'all films where one person was seen to strike another'.

The boundaries of exploration were reaching the furthest extremities of the globe. On 14 December 1911 the Norwegian explorer Roald Amundsen, who five years earlier had led the first expedition to sail through the North West Passage, reached the South Pole, the first man to do so. Ten days after Amundsen had left his base camp, a British explorer, Robert Falcon Scott, with ten men, left his base in a rival bid to reach the Pole. Scott and his men reached the Pole on 17 January 1912, too late to secure the triumph for Britain. He and all those with him died on the journey back to their base.

CHAPTER THIRTEEN

1912

AMID THE RIVALRIES of the Powers, the struggles of peoples were often overlooked. In January 1912 an event took place at Bloemfontein that was to have repercussions many years later on the history of South Africa: this was the foundation of the South African Native National Congress (later known as the African National Congress, and more commonly known by its initials ANC). The guiding spirit behind the congress was M. K. Gandhi, whose championship of Indian rights in South Africa now widened to include all non-whites, whose position in the society was that of political and social inferiority. Gandhi's plan was for passive resistance to rules and regulations that were judged to be discriminatory; he eschewed violent protest.

As the naval rivalry of the Powers intensified, heightened by the determination of Britain not to allow the German navy to become a serious challenge, disasters at sea continued. In February the British submarine *A-3* sank after a collision with a torpedo boat while on manoeuvres, and all fourteen men on board were drowned. As a by-product of the rivalry, espionage trials become more frequent; in February a German court, at Leipzig, convicted a London solicitor of attempting to obtain information injurious to German interests, and sentenced him to three and a half years' detention in a fortress. Six days later an English court, at Winchester, sentenced a German merchant navy captain to three years' penal servitude for espionage at Portsmouth.

Aware of the pressure in Germany for an increase in naval expenditure, the British government sent a highly regarded intermediary – the German-born Sir Ernest Cassell – to see the Kaiser early in 1912. One of his messages was a proposal from the new First Lord of the Admiralty, Winston Churchill, for an agreement to halt the building of warships for a fixed period of time on both sides of the North Sea: to institute a 'Naval Holiday'. The answer that came back was, not only that the Kaiser was not interested in a halt to the building of warships, but that a substantial increase in German naval construction was imminent. Having failed a second time to persuade the Kaiser to accept a mutual standstill in such construction, and having had the scale of the proposed German increases confirmed, Churchill, who was to speak at Glasgow, took the opportunity to refer to the British and German naval programmes, and to tell his audience that, when he reached the Admiralty a year earlier, he had set up a Naval War Staff, to ensure that in the event of war the navy had its plan ready.

Churchill assured his audience that the creation of this War Staff should end once and for all the rumours that had circulated at the time of the Agadir crisis that the British navy was unprepared for conflict. There was, he said, one difference between the German navy, then being expanded, and the Royal Navy. Britain's vast Empire depended on its navy, Germany's empire, being so much smaller did not. As Churchill expressed it in his speech: 'Naval power to them is a luxury. It is existence to us; it is expansion to them.' Churchill went on to say that he felt no anxiety, however, about the new German law. Britain had the resources and the ability, however, to build faster and cheaper, and on a larger scale, than any other power 'We shall face the future as our ancestors have faced it,' he said, 'without disquiet, without arrogance, but in solid and inflexible determination.' If there was to be a slackening of naval rivalry, Britain would be the first to respond, but if there were to be increases on the continent, Britain would have 'no difficulty in meeting them'.

There was indignation in Germany at Churchill's description of the German fleet as a luxury: henceforth the word 'Luxusflotte' – 'Luxury Fleet' – was used mockingly by those Germans who were in favour of their goverment's decision to build a larger and more powerful fleet. But Churchill was certain that naval rivalry, if it led to war, would benefit neither side. 'If two great and highly scientific nations go to war with one another,' he told the Royal Academy Banquet that year, 'they will become heartily sick of it before they come to the end of it.'

It was not only on land and at sea that the Powers were active in building up their strength, and pitting their respective programmes against each other. In both Britain and Germany aviation was extending its military usage and capability. In Britain, Churchill, whose responsibilities included naval defence and preparations against invasion, established a Naval Air Service which trained pilots and developed fighting aircraft, including the use of aeroplanes to bomb and machine-gun from the air. The British army also had its air wing. In Germany, one of the Kaiser's sons, Prince Henry of Prussia, announced on April 4 a project to raise money for the development of aviation in Germany. The money would be used, he said, to make German aircraft ready 'whether in national danger or in pacific international competition, to fulfil the demands of the time'.

Eleven days after Prince Henry's appeal, the new German army and navy bills were introduced to the Reichstag. Under the bills, the army was to be increased – in accordance with the rate of the increase of the population – from 515,321 men to 544,211. The navy was also to be increased, and significantly so, but the year set for the completion of the new naval increases was 1920, in eight years' time. By then, it was intended that there would be 41 German battleships, 20 armoured cruisers, 144 destroyers and 72 submarines.

In introducing the army and navy increases to the Reichstag, the German Chancellor, Bethmann-Hollweg, stressed that the government did not see any 'immediate menace' to Germany, or feel that the European situation gave any 'cause for uneasiness'. It was essential however, he argued, to maintain Germany's armaments on a level corresponding with Germany's resources and strength. If they failed to do that, all expenditure on armaments would ultimately prove 'useless'. This feeling, he said, 'was not founded upon a thirst for war or upon the wish to threaten other people. Germany was ready for war if war should be forced upon her, but she did not pick quarrels.' Strong armaments were needed, not only for warding off a possible attack but for guarding Germany's position in peace, and securing her welfare 'at all times'. Because of Germany's position on the continent of Europe, with 'her open frontiers on all sides', a strong defence gave the surest guarantee for peace.

He was convinced, Bethmann-Hollweg told the deputies, 'that among the other great Powers there was no government which desired or was seeking to bring about a war with Germany. Frequently, however, wars were not planned and brought about by governments, but noisy and fanatical minorities drive people into them. The danger still existed today – perhaps in even a greater degree than formerly.' In addition, Germans had not only the possibility of war to consider, whether in the near or distant future, but also 'their prestige and their welfare in time of peace'. Germany's military strength was regarded by other nations as the measure of the German people's value 'as friends and as allies, of their importance as possible enemies, of the weight of their opinion in international questions, and of the respect which others paid to their interests'.

Few speeches by a German Chancellor since the time of Bismarck were read so carefully in the capitals of Europe as this speech by Bethmann-Hollweg. Did Germany seek peace or war, prestige or protection, quarrels or reconciliation, trade or conflict? The speech could be read to give different answers, depending on which section was stressed. It was the speech of the leading statesman of a great Power, wishing to make sure that his country was indeed regarded as such, with respect, certainly, and perhaps with fear. The phrase about the 'noisy and fanatical minorities' who drove peoples into war was also instructive; it seemed a plea for governmental sanity against public hysteria.

Not every speaker who followed Bethmann-Hollweg in the Reichstag debate was able to resist a chauvinistic tinge. Count Posadowsky, a former Minister of the Interior, stressed Germany's weakness in Europe, and the dangers posed to Germany by 'French memories' and British 'suspicions of her commercial rival'. The Count was afraid that, as a result of the Agadir crisis, France and England had drawn closer together, 'in a friendship significantly expressed at every opportunity'. They were now joined by Russia, which hitherto, for half a century, had been Germany's 'open or secret friend'. The new relationship between France, Russia and Britain 'compelled Germany to look to her defences. There was no need to emphasize the obvious fact that Germany was a peaceful nation,' but he was convinced that 'as soon as she was weak she would again become the battleground of foreign nations, as she had been for centuries past'.

These words of warning were read carefully in London, Paris and St Petersburg. When the German army and navy bills were put to the vote, they passed with an overwhelming majority, almost the only opponents being the Socialists, the Polish deputies, and the deputies from Alsace. These latter were certainly among those of whom Count Posadowsky was speaking when he had warned the Reichstag of 'French memories'. The defeat of 1870, and the loss of Alsace-Lorraine, were forty-two years distant, but the memories of that defeat were being kept alive in France as well as in Alsace-Lorraine in every generation.

The agitation in Alsace-Lorraine against attempts at Germanization was intensified that year when a German official threatened to cancel the orders for locomotives at a factory in Alsace if a director of the company who had been active in promoting French sympathies was not dismissed. The agitation following this threat led the Kaiser himself to inform the Burgomaster of Strasbourg – the capital of Alsace – that if the agitation there continued he might suppress the constitution of 1871 and incorporate the two provinces into Prussia, the largest of the German States, and the one of which the Kaiser was also King. When the Kaiser's remark was debated in the Reichstag, a leading Social Democrat deputy commented with bemused irony that the Kaiser 'evidently regarded incorporation in Prussia as the worst punishment that he could inflict on a subordinate country'.

The leader of the predominantly Catholic and conservative Centre Party was equally scathing, expressing his regret that what the Kaiser had said would 'hamper the work of conciliation' in Alsace-Lorraine. But Bethmann-Hollweg stressed that if the 'anti-German machinations' in Alsace-Lorraine, with which the railway director at the centre of the dispute was the 'life and soul', were to get the upper hand, the Federal Council and the Reichstag would be 'bound in duty and in honour' to destroy those machinations.

In international relations, Germany found common ground with France during 1912, issuing a joint declaration on September 28 establishing commissions to delineate the boundaries between all French and German territories that lay contiguous to one another in Africa. The new frontiers would cover thousands of miles of remote and inhospitable territory, but they would ensure that there would be no future case for territorial clashes, and no claims made by either side on land which the other had acquired.

An attempt at German–British reconciliation was also made that year, six months after Churchill's proposal for a Naval Holiday had been rebuffed, when a senior British Liberal politician, the Lord Chancellor Lord Haldane (twelve years later he was to hold the same office in the first Labour government) visited Berlin and, in a private conversation with the Kaiser, sought to impress on him that Britain had no desire to impede Germany's legitimate colonial ambitions, or her status in the world.

Haldane's statesmanlike approach and desire for harmony between the two countries was challenged publicly by a retired German cavalry officer, General Bernhardi, who, in a book entitled *Germany and the Next War*, maintained that the duties and tasks of the German people could only be fulfilled by the sword, and that it was imperative that Germany claim 'not only a place in the sun, but a full share in the mastery of the world'. To do this, Germany must destroy the existing balance of power in Europe, set up a system of alliances with Germany at the head, and, above all, must recognize that Britain was the enemy, and would have to be beaten at sea.

The effectiveness of any alliance is determined by its weakest partner. During 1912, Germany's ally Austria-Hungary was in turmoil. Czechs and Germans in Bohemia, and Poles and Ruthenians in Galicia, continued to challenge each other's national pretensions. In Budapest, Hungarian socialists took their demands on to the streets, declaring a four-day strike in support of universal suffrage, smashing thousands of street lamps and burning dozens of trams. Many people were killed or wounded.

When the new president of the Hungarian parliament, Count Tisza, attempted to curb the opposition deputies, who were threatening to make Hungary ungovernable, one of them fired a pistol at him, and then turned it on himself; neither man was hurt. But the episode reflected the unwillingness of the non-Magyar peoples of Hungary to accept the rule of Budapest and the dominance of the Magyars. From Vienna, Franz Josef praised Tisza's 'self-sacrifice and moral courage' in trying to overcome opposition tactics. But the obstructions continued, especially in opposition both to a proposed two-year military service bill, and to the government's refusal to extend the franchise. When, on one occasion, the obstruction by the opposition brought all discussion to a halt, Tisza ordered the police to clear the opposition deputies out of the chamber. The deputies then fought the police with their fists, but were eventually removed.

Parliamentary procedures were being disrupted all over Franz Josef's dominions. In the Bohemian Diet in Prague, the German minority, feeling that its interests would be ignored as hitherto despite the German predominance in other parts of the empire, decided to show its powers of disruption on the day on which a Czech woman deputy, the distinguished novelist Madame Vyk-Kuneticka, was due to take her seat. As a result of this obstruction, the Diet was unable to hold its session. In the Galician Diet in Lemberg, Ruthenian deputies continued to obstruct the proceedings by demanding their own university, something that the Austrian and Polish deputies repeatedly combined to resist.

In Croatia, the Hungarian-appointed ruler, or Ban, continued to do everything possible to suppress Croat nationalism. His efforts only intensified Croat national feeling; there were street demonstrations in favour of greater Slav autonomy not only in the Croat capital Agram (now Zagreb), but also in Bosnia-Herzegovina, where the Serbs in Mostar (the capital of Herzegovina) burnt the Hungarian flag in protest. When, in April, Croat pupils in the secondary schools in Agram went on strike, and paraded in the streets singing Croat national songs, the Ban suspended the Croat constitution. In

June, the Ban was shot at by a Croat student; he escaped injury, but an official travelling in the motorcar with him was killed.

The governance of Austria-Hungary was triply threatened: by Italian national aspirations in the Trentino and in Trieste; by Roumanian national aspirations in Transylvania and Bukovina; and by Slav national aspirations in Croatia, Dalmatia, Bosnia-Herzegovina, Istria, Carniola and Carinthia. Each of these three national, or ethnic, groups looked for inspiration across their common borders with Italy, Roumania and Serbia, each of which was all too happy to encourage those who spoke the same language, shared the same religion, and dreamed the same dreams of greater Italy, greater Roumania and greater Serbia.

In Morocco, the problems faced by the French failed to diminish, and were in contrast to the British authority in Egypt where, despite nationalist unrest, the full apparatus of colonial rule was in place. The 1904 Anglo-French Entente had essentially been a French recognition of a situation where Britain was already in confident control, in return for British recognition of a very parlous state of affairs as far as France was concerned.

On April 1 the Sultan, Mulai Hafid, signed a treaty with France, accepting a French Protectorate over Morocco. Although the terms of the treaty gave France permission to enter into military occupation of the country 'after due notification', the establishment of French control in the interior was difficult to achieve. Even in the coastal cities, there were outbreaks of local rebellion. In Fez, less than three weeks after the protectorate had been declared, seventeen French officers and nine French civilians were murdered when some of the Sultan's soldiers mutinied. The target of the mutineers was not only French property, but the Jewish quarter, where there was heavy loss of life and much pillaging. Only after three days of street fighting was the mutiny quelled.

The French military presence in Morocco was being increased, to nearly 40,000 men, with reinforcements brought in by sea from Algeria and Senegal. Mulai Hafid's days as Sultan were numbered; he fell into a depression in which he was unable to conduct the affairs of state, and decided to abdicate. He was succeeded by his brother (and one-time contender for his throne), Mulai Yussef. In the south of Morocco a pretender to the throne, Sidi Mahomed Hiba – known as El Hiba – the son of a religious leader of high repute, took up arms against the new Sultan, seizing the port of Agadir.

French cruisers bombarded the port, where exactly a year earlier Germany had sought to achieve a naval presence. El Hiba then left the coast and retreated to Marrakech, where he was protected by the local Muslim leader, El Glawi (The Glauoi) until a French military force entered the city. El Hiba, disavowed by the local population, fled the city in disguise. El Glawi, loyal to France, remained the leading figure of the region for another two decades.

To the east of Morocco, despite the Italian success in driving the Turks from Tripoli and Benghazi, the tribes of the interior refused to accept Italian rule. As the fighting continued, the Italians used aeroplanes again, machine-gunning the tribesmen from the air. There were suggestions that Germany might intervene to act as a peacemaker between Rome and Constantinople, to bring to an end, by some form of compromise, a conflict that was beginning to hurt both sets of combatants. But neither the Italian government nor the Italian people were in a mood to give up in mid struggle.

The role of Austria-Hungary had also stirred considerable anger in Italy, driving a wedge between the two allies. The Austrians, having warned Italy not to fight the Turks either in the Adriatic or the Aegean, seemingly wanted to reserve for Austria-Hungary any benefits that might accrue from the weakening of Turkey in the Balkans. At Udine, an Italian mob attacked and injured a number of Austrian travellers, and there were anti-Austrian demonstrations in several towns inside Austria, including Trieste.

In the war against Turkey, the Italians were determined not to limit their military actions to Tripolitania and Cyrenaica, but to secure victory there by attacking the Turks elsewhere. In February 1912 the Italian navy entered the Red Sea and bombarded the Turkish port of Hodeida in the hope of preventing supplies and reinforcements from being sent across the Red Sea and overland to Tripoli. One effect of the Italian bombardment of the Yemen coast was to stimulate the anti-Turkish aspirations of the local Arabs, whose sustained rebellion had only just been crushed.

In March, as the struggle in Tripolitania and Cyrenaica continued, Italian public opinion called for a sustained attack on Turkey elsewhere, particularly in Albania, so near to Italy, and so vulnerable along its coastline to Italian naval bombardment. But Austria-Hungary was emphatic that there should be no action against Turkey in the Balkans; in an attempt to soothe Italian anger, the Kaiser intervened on behalf of Austria-Hungary, travelling to

Venice for talks with the King of Italy. In view of Germany's influence and ambitions in Turkey, the German government could hardly encourage the Italians to attack Turkey; the Kaiser made this plain, making his point, but at the same time helping to alienate Germany from Italy.

The Italian government was uneasy at appearing to bow to German and Austro-Hungarian pressure, and despite the appeals of its two allies, sent a fleet into the Aegean Sea, and made a naval demonstration at the Dardanelles, the sea entrance to Constantinople. On July 19, when Italian warships opened fire on the Turkish forts at the Dardanelles, all the Italian political parties were enthusiastic, except for the small Socialist Party, whose leader, Benito Mussolini, opposed the war on the grounds that 'We socialists are not Italians but Europeans'.

From the middle of August, the Turkish government became embroiled with the independent Kingdom of Montenegro. The dispute concerned Montenegrin claims to parts of Albania. The Italians were delighted that a new adversary had entered the anti-Turk arena. In the Montenegrin capital, Cetinje, the Italian Minister, Baron Palmeriti c Garasna, while officially advising the small kingdom to exercise moderation, in fact advised a tough Montenegrin stance.

The Italians, for all their public confidence and bluster, were wearying of the struggle with Turkey. While agitated by the pressure put on them by Austria-Hungary and Germany, they were uneasy at the weakening of the Triple Alliance, especially when France and Russia concluded a naval convention that autumn that would give France a much freer hand in the Mediterranean. At the same time, the gathering of French warships at Toulon was a reminder that France as well as Italy could lay claim to being a (if not the) naval Power in the Mediterranean. In the hope of disentangling themselves from the Turkish war, the Italians opened secret negotiations with Turkey in Switzerland. Peace was signed at Ouchy, near Lausanne, on October 15; it became known as the Peace of Lausanne. In a message to the people of the conquered regions, the Turkish Sultan explained that he wished to end a war 'ruinous to you and your families, and disastrous to the State'.

Under the terms of the peace, all Turkish forces would be withdrawn from Libya, and all Italian forces withdrawn from the Turkish islands in the Aegean on which they had landed during the conflict. The Italians would administer the conquered region, but it would remain under Turkish sovereignty. In this way, the Koranic law which forbade the cession of the lands of Islam to the 'infidel' would not be broken. Italy, having spared the

Sultan the embarrassment of losing Turkish sovereignty, then had Italian sovereignty recognized by the European Powers, including France. The French government exacted as its price for recognition the surrender of all Italian privileges in Morocco. France would lose any claims in Libya once Libya was under Italian sovereignty.

The Austro-Hungarians were relieved that Italian action against Turkey was over; the Germans were delighted that they had no longer to see their new-found friend Turkey being chastized by their historic ally, Italy; so much so that within a month of the end of the war, Germany and Austria-Hungary agreed to prolong the Triple Alliance for another three years, thus offering Italy continued protection against France.

The possibility that war would break out in the Balkans was much discussed in the early months of 1912. But in the immediate aftermath of the Italian attack on Turkey's North African possessions, the four Christian States in the Balkans – Serbia, Montenegro, Bulgaria and Greece – made no effort to exploit Turkey's difficulties, in spite of their respective claims on Turkish Macedonia and Thrace.

Only in Albania did an uprising against Turkish rule break out, with many hundreds of Albanians taking up arms against the Turks. An attempt by the Turkish Minister of the Interior, Hadji Adli Bey, to persuade his government to introduce constitutional reforms to Albania, was in vain. When the Young Turks' Committee in Constantinople gave the order for the rebellion to be crushed, many Turkish soldiers opposed to such measures joined the insurgents. In June, the Turkish troops at Monastir mutinied; they too were not willing to be the instruments of repression, or at least did not wish to risk their lives in combat.

The Albanian insurrection gained in momentum that summer, when 20,000 Albanian soldiers captured the Turkish garrison town of Prishtina, and warned, in a strident manifesto, of the inevitable destruction 'in consequence of the errors of a handful of braggarts', of an empire that 'had stood for six centuries'. In July, the Sultan tried to pacify the Albanians by announcing that from then on the use of armed force against them was categorically forbidden, and that the Albanian peasants would be indemnified for damage done to their farms and fields as a result of pillage carried out by Turkish soldiers during the recent fighting. But the Albanians were determined to acquire full autonomy, if not to see an end to Turkish rule, and in an audacious military move, occupied the principal town of Macedonia, Uskub (Skopje), and threatened to advance from it on Salonika. At this point the Turkish government sent some of its best troops, good fighters and loyal soldiers, and the Albanians were driven northward into the mountains.

Remaining in control of large tracts of territory in northern Macedonia, between Ipec (Pec) and Mitrovitza, the Albanian insurgents plundered Turkish military stores, opened the prisons, and collected taxes – for their own purposes – from the local inhabitants. Elsewhere in Macedonia, the Serb population took up arms against the efforts being made by the local Bulgarians to drive Serb peasants from the land which they and their ancestors had cultivated for centuries. Serb terrorist actions intensified, led by the Macedonian Internal Organization, which exploded bombs – known in the contemporary parlance as 'infernal machines' – in crowded streets and market places. At the town of Kotchana as many as a hundred Bulgarians were killed in one such explosion, followed by the slaughter of more Bulgarians by Serbs.

The response of the Turkish troops was not to intervene to prevent further bloodshed, but to set off to the adjoining village on a rampage of looting and burning. In response to the massacre of Bulgarians at Kotchana, the Bulgarians exploded a bomb in a Serb market at Berane, and burnt down twelve Serb-inhabited villages along the Montenegrin border. For their part, Turks attacked Serbs at Sienitza, within sight of the southern border of Serbia.

By August, the Serbs and Bulgarians in Macedonia were both clamouring for the governments of Bulgaria and Serbia to intervene militarily on their behalf, and to drive the Turks from the province. A Balkan League was established, in which, for the first time in 500 years of squabbling and fighting, Bulgaria, Serbia, Montenegro and Greece were united against the Turks. The only Balkan state not to join the new alliance was Roumania, although the Roumanians living in Macedonia – the Kutzo-Vlachs, as they were known – were also the victims of Turkish misrule. By August, Montenegro had sent troops across the Turkish frontier, attacking Turkish army posts, and bringing arms to the Serbian and Albanian inhabitants of the region.

On September 30 the armies of the Balkan League mobilized. The Turks mobilized a day later. In an attempt to deter the Balkan League from attacking Turkey, Russia and Austria-Hungary issued a joint declaration, on October 8, in their capacity as mandatories of all the European Powers, 'energetically condemning' any measures that might lead to war. It was the Powers, they said, who would 'take in hand' the interests of the Christian populations, and put forward a programme of reforms in European Turkey. But this must in no way affect the sovereignty of the Sultan or the integrity of the Ottoman Empire.

The Russian Tsar and the Austro-Hungarian Emperor had taken the side of a fellow ruler, the Ottoman Sultan. In order to underline this fact, they warned the Balkan League that, in the event of war breaking out between the Balkan States and Turkey, the Powers 'will not admit at the close of the war any modification of the territorial status quo of European Turkey'. These were stern and chilling words. But they were met by the Balkan League with contempt: for too long had the Macedonian Serbs, Bulgarians and Greeks aspired to be masters of the region once the Turks had been dislodged.

Montenegro formally declared war on Turkey on October 8. The Balkan League did not follow this lead, but decided instead to send a joint note to the Ottoman Government demanding autonomy for the Christian provinces. The Turks, determined not to accede to this demand, replied by a declaration of war against the Balkan League.

Hostilities began on October 18. For seven weeks, the armies of the Balkan League were in action, each advancing into the areas inhabited by its own people, with no coordinated plan of campaign. Only the Montenegrins failed to reach their main objective, Skutari. The Serbs were much more successful, occupying the Sanjak of Novi Bazar – which Austria-Hungary had handed back to Turkey in 1909 – and all the principal Serb towns of Macedonia. On October 26, Uskub, which had been the Serb capital in the fourteenth century in the days of the Serbian Tsar Stephen Dushan, was abandoned by the Turkish garrison, which a few months earlier had been overrun by the Albanians. The citizens of Uskub greeted the Serb troops with hymns and anthems. It was 400 years since the Serbs had lost Uskub to the Turks.

On November 18 the Turkish forces were defeated at Monastir, when 90,000 Turkish soldiers fled southward. Ten days later the Serbs and Montenegrins together drove the Turkish army from the two main Turkish ports on the Adriatic, Alessio and Durazzo. All of Macedonia, and large parts of Albania, were under Montenegrin and Serb control. Where Turkish officials had ruled over Albanians, Serbian officials were established in their place. For the Albanians, the defeat of the Turks held terrors of its own, as Serb and Montenegrin troops burned many Albanian villages and murdered hundreds, perhaps thousands of their inhabitants.

The Greek army was also successful, driving the Turks out of Thrace and towards the sea. Many Christian soldiers, whom the Turks had drafted into the army, deserted to the attackers. On November 8, Greek forces entered Salonika, the largest city in the Ottoman Empire after Constantinople. In the Aegean, every Turkish island fell to Greek assault. Greek warships were also in action in more distant waters, severely damaging a Turkish cruiser in the Black Sea, and shelling the unfortified town of Avlona (Valona) on the Albanian coast. This action prompted Italy and Austria-Hungary to inform Greece that they would not agree to the bay of Avlona being occupied by Greece after the war, or being used as a Greek naval base.

The Bulgarians advanced towards Turkey's principal European defences, the Chatalja Lines. As they did so, they twice defeated the main forces of the Turkish army, first at Kirk Kilisse and then at Lule Burgas, and the Turks were driven back to the Lines themselves. But the Turkish defences there, which had been armed by guns from the German armaments manufacturer Krupp, held firm. Nor, despite a month-long siege, were the Bulgarians able to conquer the city of Adrianople (Edirne). On November 4, Turkey appealed to the Powers for mediation, but there was no response.

On November 28, at Avlona, a meeting of Albanian delegates proclaimed 'the independence and neutrality of Albania'. The delegates were emphatic that the Roman Catholic Albanians, who had taken up arms against the Turks, and the Muslim Albanians, who had not, should be united in a single nation. A provisional government was set up, headed by Ismail Kemal Bey, a Muslim Albanian who had been a deputy for Albania in the Ottoman parliament, and had also served as Turkish Minister for Foreign Affairs.

Despite the rapid advance of four armies against them, the Turkish soldiers had held Skutari, Adrianople, Yanina, and the Chatalja Lines, and it had become clear that these places could not easily be overrun, if at all. On December 3, an armistice was signed at Chatalja. Only Greece refused to be a party to it, having decided to continue military operations against the Turks in Epirus. The Montenegrins, who signed the armistice, were forced to break it, however, when the Turkish troops in Skutari used the fort there as a base for a series of renewed attacks on Montenegrin troops.

The Turkish army having been driven back to the lines defending Constantinople, Austria-Hungary recognized that there was no way in which the declaration of October 8 could be upheld, and the Balkan States be forced to withdraw to their national borders. She did insist, however, that Serbia give up her claims to Albania and to the Turkish ports on the Adriatic. In Vienna and Budapest there was fear that once Serbia was in control of the ports at the entrance to the Adriatic her protector, Russia, would use those ports to block Austria-Hungary's maritime outlet from the Adriatic to the Mediterranean. This would effectively force Austria-Hungary into the position of a landlocked State.

An international crisis loomed as Austria-Hungary called out her army reserves in an attempt to convince Serbia that her demands were serious, and appointed as Chief-of-Staff the much-respected General Conrad von Hötzendorf, who had retired a year earlier in protest against the pacific policy of the Austrian government towards Italy. Von Hötzendorf's appointment rang alarm bells in St Petersburg. At the same time, the rulers of Austria-Hungary recognized that Russia might feel obliged, as the leading Slav state, to come to the aid of Serbia. The Austrians therefore asked Germany for military cooperation between them, should the need arise.

In November the Archduke Franz Ferdinand went to Berlin to discuss Austro-German cooperation with the Kaiser. On December 8, the Kaiser summoned a conference of three of his most trusted advisers, his Chief-of-Staff, Count von Moltke, his Chief of the Naval Staff, Admiral von Müller, and his Secretary of State for the Navy, Admiral von Tirpitz. According to the account set down by Müller in his diary, the Kaiser told them that 'Austria had to act vigorously against the foreign Slavs (Serbs), because she would otherwise lose her power over the Serbs in the Austro-Hungarian Monarchy'. The Kaiser added that if Russia were to support the Serbs, 'war would be inevitable for us'. He also told his advisers that in his view, in the event of a general European war, the German Fleet would find itself at war with Britain's Royal Navy. The Kaiser understood that the Franco-Russian alliance, if activated against Germany, could well lead to Britain being brought into the conflict through the Anglo-French Entente.

During this meeting, Count von Moltke suggested that 'the popularity of a war against Russia, as outlined by the Kaiser, should be better prepared'. The Kaiser agreed, and suggested that the newspapers must begin to 'enlighten the German people' as to Germany's 'great national interests' if a wider war were to break out following a conflict between Austria-Hungary and Serbia. According to the instructions which Admiral Müller passed on to the Chancellor, Bethmann-Hollweg: 'The people must not be in the position of asking themselves only at the outbreak of a great European war, what are the interests that Germany would be fighting for. The people ought rather to be accustomed to the idea of such a war beforehand.'

The idea of a wider European war being generated by the outbreak of war between Austria-Hungary and Serbia had arisen for the first time at the highest level of statecraft. In Vienna the prospect of a wider war was not only discussed, but welcomed. On December 14, in a letter to the Archduke Franz Ferdinand, Conrad von Hötzendorf wrote that the unification of the South Slav race 'is one of the powerful national movements which can neither be ignored nor kept down. The question can only be, whether that unification will take place within the boundaries of the Monarchy – that is, at the expense of Serbia's independence – or under Serbia's leadership at the expense of the Monarchy.'

Were Serbia to become the leader of Slav unification, von Hötzendorf warned, it would be at the cost to Austria-Hungary of all its South Slav provinces, and thus of almost its entire Adriatic coastline. Austria-Hungary would become a landlocked State. The loss of territory and prestige involved in Serbia's ascendancy would, von Hötzendorf insisted, 'relegate the Habsburg Monarchy to the status of a small Power'. Serbia would become the dominant State in the Balkans, an area over which Austria-Hungary was determined to retain its influence and power.

The Serbian government was unable to risk war with Austria-Hungary, especially as Russia, its natural – and indispensable – ally, was calling for restraint. In a speech in the Duma on December 18, the Russian Prime Minister, Vladimir Kokovtsov, while giving considerable oratorical flourish to Russia's position as Slavonic Orthodox Power, which has made innumerable sacrifices to protect her racial brothers and co-religionists', advised caution, and a settlement of the dispute between Austria-Hungary and Serbia through negotiations. What was essential, he said, was to avert 'fresh complications endangering the peace of Europe'.

Serbia recognized that she was, to all intents and purposes, on her own, and agreed to withdraw her claims to Albania, and to accept a commercial arrangement with Austria-Hungary – towards which Russia gave full diplomatic support – that would establish a secure trading outlet on the Adriatic for Serbian goods, without the need for Serb sovereign territory.

*   *   *

On 16 December 1912 a conference of delegates from the Balkan League met in London to discuss their conditions of peace with Turkey. Four days later, the Powers accepted those conditions: Albanian autonomy, Serbian commercial access to the Adriatic, and Montenegrin, Bulgarian, Greek and Serbian territorial annexations. Bulgaria's claim to Adrianople, which the Bulgarians had failed to capture, was at first rejected.

Turkey remained in Europe, but with her frontiers greatly drawn back, and her 400-year rule of Macedonia ended. Albania had obtained its autonomy, and Thrace had been divided between Bulgaria and Greece. For the first time in the twentieth century, the map of Europe had been redrawn, and the Balkans became a focal point of European interest and excitement. A wider war had been avoided; as the year ended, that was a source of relief to both Austria-Hungary and Russia, the two Powers whose interests were most in conflict in the Balkans, and whose respective Balkan friends had hoped for, or expected, their military intervention.

While the focus of international concern had been on the war and then on the peace in the Balkans, turmoil elsewhere was eclipsed in the mind of the newspaper-reading public of the imperial powers. Yet the diplomats and politicians of each of the Powers continued to assert their authority in many distant regions. In the British sphere of influence in Persia, established six years earlier by agreement with Russia, attacks on British and Indian traders had intensified. In the south of Persia, one contemporary noted, 'anarchy reigns supreme'. A British naval squadron was sent from India to maintain order in the Persian ports of the Gulf. When, at Lingah, 2400 local tribesmen gathered for an attack on the British Consulate and other European buildings, British Indian troops were landed, to drive them off. When tribesmen besieged Bushire, and cut off the port from the trade routes into the hinterland, British marines were landed to break the siege.

An attempt was made to create a local police force in southern Persia. The British wanted it to be seen to be a humanitarian rather than an imperial force, and asked the Swedish government, which agreed, if it could be commanded by Swedish officers. In the force's first action against a Persian robber gang, on August 6, the police were defeated, twenty policemen killed, and the force's field gun and most of its rifles captured. Four months later two British officers were sent with an escort of twenty-six British Indian troops to protect the trade routes around Shiraz. They were attacked by three hundred tribesmen, one of the British officers, Captain Eckford, was killed, and the troops were driven off. The tribesmen then made off with a complete caravan of merchandise that was on its way from Shiraz to Bushire.

In northern Persia, the former Shah, Mohammed Ali, in an attempt to regain his throne, had returned from his exile in the Crimea and taken up arms against the constitutionalist government that had overthrown him three years earlier. To avoid the spread of bloodshed and anarchy, Russia and Britain jointly persuaded Mohammed Ali to accept a cash sum to pay off his followers, and then to agree to an annual pension in return for leaving Persia and rejoining his family in exile in Russia. He agreed to do so. His brothers, however, carried on a spasmodic war on his behalf inside Persia for another nine months. In London, the British Foreign Secretary, Sir Edward Grey, was criticized for preventing Persia 'from working out her own salvation', and for helping Russia in her attack on Persian independence. He replied that if it had not been for the Anglo-Russian spheres of influence, and joint action, in Persia, the country would have 'fallen to pieces'. No British statesman, he added, was willing to go to war to prevent Russia's control in northern Persia.

In British India, there was again relief as, for the second time in a decade, the number of deaths from plague declined. The figure of those who succumbed to the disease in the twelve months up to September 1912 was 'only 344,053' as one contemporary report expressed it, less than half the previous year's toll.

While Europe was embroiled in the Balkan and Libyan wars, the United States was caught up in the problems of the western hemisphere, with 5000 American troops being sent by President Taft to the border with Mexico, where the revolutionary situation inside the country – Emilio Zapata was challenging the rule of President Diaz – made some form of United States intervention seem almost inevitable. During a revolt of government troops in Mexico City, Diaz was overthrown, and replaced as President by Francisco Madero. Zapata remained at large. Although United States intervention overland was avoided, British, French and United States warships maintained a naval patrol on the coast.

In Nicaragua, whose government had little effective control over the life of the country, a group of revolutionaries, led by a senior army officer, General Mena, turned in 1912 with particular anger against the British,

German, Dutch, Italian and American residents in the country, most of them traders. The United States government sent a force of marines, which captured the town of Massaya after a brief battle in which four marines were killed. It was explained from Washington that this was not technically a battle, but 'action in pursuance of American policy'. General Mena surrendered, and was removed to Panama, under American supervision.

There was also United States intervention that year in Honduras, to protect American-owned railway and wharf properties. In that instance the marines carried out their task without loss. Further south, following a revolution in Ecuador, the United States was involved in another capacity. The chaos and disruption of civic amenities created by the revolution had led to an outbreak of bubonic plague. In an attempt to prevent the mass destruction of life, the United States sent a commission of experts to advise on sanitation in towns. It was an example of two policies combined: the protection of trading and commercial interests, and the protection of life and social order.

In Peru, the revelation of atrocities committed in the rubber-yielding district of the Putomayo led to worldwide protests. The man who did the most to expose the Peruvian atrocities was Sir Roger Casement, who had earlier exposed the barbarities practised in the Belgian Congo. The Indians of the Putomayo region had, it was clear from Casement's report – which was presented to the British Parliament – been enslaved by agents of the British-based Peruvian Amazon Company. Some had been flogged, some tortured, and others murdered. There was evidence that British subjects from Barbados – blacks – had, under duress from their white overseers, committed barbarities upon Indians who had failed to satisfy the company's agents that they were producing the amount of rubber of which they were deemed capable.

One more South American country was in the news that year. In Paraguay, President Jara, who had come to power by force a year earlier, was himself deposed. He was subsequently tracked down and killed. His successor, President Roja, also fell victim to revolution. Having been taken prisoner, he was forced to resign. Stability returned to Paraguay before the end of the year, when a third President (Schaerer) came into office, not by a coup, but through elections.

In November, while Europe watched the unfolding of the Balkan imbroglio, the United States elected a new president, Woodrow Wilson, a Democrat.

Wilson was the first Democrat to have won a presidential election for twenty years, and only the second Democrat President since the Civil War half a century earlier. He was also a distinguished academic, having been a university professor, and President of Princeton University. At the time of his electoral triumph he was Governor of New Jersey.

Between Wilson's election in November and his inauguration the following March, the outgoing President Taft inspected the most powerful American fleet ever assembled under one command and in one place: 120 vessels anchored in the Hudson River, while at the same time 6000 American seamen and marines paraded through Manhattan. The United States, with no political interests or territorial ambitions in Europe, Africa or Asia, did have a determination not to allow any external influence over the American Continent, and was prepared to build up its navy to this end. There was also a growing realization that the United States had, following the acquisition of the Philippines and several Spanish islands in the Pacific Ocean, become a Pacific power, for which a navy was essential.

In 1912 two Prime Ministers of Spain were assassinated, José Canalejas on November 12 and Manuel Garcia Prieto a week later, after only three days in office. Canalejas had been Prime Minister for more than three years. During a railway strike earlier in 1912 he had called up the army reserves and put 12,000 strikers under military discipline. But he had been under constant criticism in the conservative newspapers for what they denounced as his 'soft' treatment of a short-lived republican naval mutiny, and for his reprieve of an anarchist who had murdered a judge. His liberalism was distasteful to the radical left, which denounced it as 'mere' reformism, but it was a liberalism that was bringing greater social equality in Britain.

Canalejas had altered the tax system so that it fell more heavily on the rich. He had introduced a tax on urban rents. He had abolished the system whereby the wealthy could purchase exemption from military service. None of this was impressive to the anarchist perspective, which saw assassination as a goal in itself. Canalejas was shot dead by an anarchist in Madrid. Manuel Garcia Prieto, his successor was also shot by an anarchist.

The worst cinema disaster of 1912 also took place in Spain, at Bilbao; forty-one children and three adults were killed when panic broke out as a result of a fire alarm. At a cinema in Menin, in Belgium, twelve women and children were crushed to death when a cry of 'Fire' set up a stampede to leave the building. The natural disasters of the year included the deaths of 400 Filipinos during a typhoon in October. Rail travel and aerial competitions also continued to cause loss of life; when a night express ran into a goods train in Sweden in June, twenty-six people were killed. In the United States, forty-two people were killed when an express ran into a stationary train in New York State. Two days later twenty-one people were killed in a train crash in Pennsylvania. At a colliery in Yorkshire, a series of explosions killed eighty-six people; not only miners, but a number of those who were trying to rescue them. In an explosion in a coal mine in Bochum, Westphalia, a month later, more than a hundred miners were killed.

In July, Harriet Quimby, who two-and-a-half months earlier had been the first woman to pilot a plane across the English Channel, was killed, with her passenger, when her plane fell 1000 feet into the sea off the coast of Massachusetts. In August, in separate flying accidents, two British officers, and a German officer, were killed on the same day; a British captain and lieutenant near Wallingford, on the Thames, and a German lieutenant near Munich. In December, an American airman, Horace Kearney, was killed with his passenger while trying to fly from Los Angeles to San Francisco.

In a cyclone in Regina, Saskatchewan, lasting only a few minutes, thirty-one Canadians died. In an earthquake that struck Constantinople, Adrianople and the towns around the Sea of Marmara, as many as a thousand people were killed. Accidents at sea remained another frequent occurrence, seizing both the newspaper headlines and the public imagination. When a German transatlantic liner struck a British submarine off Dover, slicing it in two, all but one of the fifteen submariners on board were drowned. When a British battleship engaged in trials in the English Channel ran into an Italian steamer, all thirty-six Italian seamen went down with their ship.

The disaster that most riveted attention that year was also at sea, when the ocean liner *Titanic*, the largest vessel afloat, struck an iceberg while on its maiden voyage from Southampton to New York. The first telegrams received in London reported that there had been no loss of life, and that the *Titanic* was making her own way, or being towed, to Halifax, Nova Scotia. These reports were false; the *Titanic* had sunk to the seabed with the loss of 1635 lives. Among the dead was one of America's wealthiest men, Colonel J. J. Astor. The value of his estate was later discovered to be more than $85 million.

Eighty-three years after the sinking of the *Titanic*, Edith Haisman, aged ninety-eight, recalled during the opening of a memorial garden to the victims, how, safe in a lifeboat, she had waved to her father, who was on deck smoking a cigar and drinking a glass of brandy. 'I will see you in New York,' he called out. But he did not survive.

From his room in the Admiralty, in London, Winston Churchill wrote to his wife: 'The Titanic disaster is the prevailing theme here. The story is a good one. The strict observance of the great traditions of the sea towards women & children reflects nothing but honour upon our civilization. Even I hope it can mollify some of the young unmarried lady teachers who are so bitter in their sex antagonism, and think men so base & vile. They are rather snuffy about Bruce Ismay – Chairman of the line – who, it is thought – on the facts available – shd have gone down with the ship & her crew. I cannot help feeling proud of our race & its traditions as proved by this event. Boat loads of women & children tossing on the sea – safe & sound – & the rest – Silence. Honour to their memory.'

Two days later Churchill wrote again: 'The whole episode fascinates me. It shows that in spite of all the inequalities and artificialities of our modern life, at the bottom – tested to its foundations, our civilization is humane, Christian & absolutely democratic. How differently Imperial Rome or Ancient Greece wd have settled the problem. The swells, the potentates would have gone off with their concubines & pet slaves & soldier guards, & then the sailors wd have had their chance headed by the captain; as for the rest – whoever cd bribe the crew the most wd have had the preference & the rest cd go to hell. But such ethics can neither build Titanics with science nor lose them with honour.'

The space accorded by the newspapers to the sinking of the *Titanic*, and the shock which the sinking caused, reflected the contrast between such a modern and remarkable ship – and the wealth and prominence of some of those on board – with its vulnerability. The more distant cruelties of nature, affecting people who were regarded as the inevitable victims of massive disasters, caused less stir. One such disaster in 1912 was the death by drowning in China, following massive floods, of an estimated thirty thousand people.

Among the industrial nations, poverty was a challenge that beset every government. Social welfare programmes brought the State increasingly into direct contact with those who were out of work, often through injuries sustained in the workplace, or who faced long periods of unemployment through illness. When poverty struck a region with particular severity, private charity and public relief were instituted side by side, in an attempt to alleviate the problems. The British writer D. H. Lawrence was involved in one such effort in Nottingham. 'I was round with a friend delivering relief tickets yesterday,' he wrote to a friend on April 3. 'It's not that the actual suffering is so great – though it's bad enough – but the men seem such big, helpless, hopeless children, and the women so impersonal – little atlases under a load that they know will crush them out at last, but it doesn't matter. They aren't conscious any more than their hearts are conscious of their endless business of beating. They have no conscious life, no windows. It makes me ill.'

One answer being advocated for the ills of capitalist society was socialist revolution. In January 1912 a small gathering took place in Prague. Organized by Lenin, it was a meeting of the Bolshevik section of the Russian Social Democratic Labour Party. Only eighteen delegates were present. These eighteen – the Bolshevik leaders who were then in exile in Western Europe – had decided to meet without the Menshevik wing of their party, to break away from their fellow Mensheviks altogether, and to form their own political party.

Two years earlier, at a meeting in Paris, the Bolsheviks had been outvoted and outmanoeuvred by a triple coalition of Mensheviks, Bundists, and Latvian and Polish Social Democrats. As a result, they had been forced to hand the Bolshevik financial treasury – which had been swelled by the Tiflis bank robbery and similar acts of which the other Social Democrats disapproved – to three German Social Democrat 'trustees'. This had curbed the Bolsheviks' activities, and greatly reduced their power within the Russian Social Democratic movement.

At the meeting in Prague, at Lenin's urging, a Bolshevik Central Committee was elected, with seven members and four 'candidate' members. This was the close-knit professional organization which Lenin believed to be essential if revolution was to be brought to Russia. During the meeting in Prague, Lenin was given the power to coopt others on to the Central Committee. He nominated two people, the metalworker, I. S. Belostotsky – of whom little more was heard – and a Georgian revolutionary then in exile in Siberia, Josef Stalin.

The zeal that drove the would-be revolutionaries, both inside Russia and in exile, was fuelled by continual excesses on the part of the Tsarist authorities and their agents. In April 1912, three months after the Prague meeting of

Bolshevik exiles, troops belonging to the Tsarist political police, the Okhrana, shot down and killed 170 desperate, half-starved workers in the Siberian gold mines on the Lena River. The men had dared to seek an improvement in their harsh and degrading conditions.

The Russian government responded not only by repression but by innovation. Two acts passed by the Third Duma on June 23 brought Russia in line with the more liberal of the industrialized States. One was a National Health Insurance system, whereby hospital funds, to which workers and employers contributed, would provide for medical assistance in the case of illness. The other was Accident Insurance, where the whole financial responsibility of compensation fell on the shoulders of the employer. This compensation included pensions for the widows and orphans of those killed in accidents in the workplace.

Would these measures help to assuage the internal Russian discontent? Social Democrats of all hues, Menshevik, Bolshevik and Bundist, were adamant that only revolution could overthrow the 'scourge' of capitalism, and that strikes and conflict, not legislation and amelioration, were the only way forward. With the right to strike persistently denied, this gave the social conflict its sharpest weapon. In a debate in the Duma, where the right to strike was put forward, it was pointed out that such a right had existed in Austria-Hungary since 1870, in England since 1875, in Italy since 1889, in Belgium since 1892 and in Germany since 1899. This did not weaken the resolve of the Tsar and his ministers not to permit such a right in Russia.

In the United States, three more States adopted women's suffrage in 1912: Arizona, Kansas and Wisconsin. In Britain, the Liberal government brought in a National Health Insurance Act, whereby the workers' right to financial support in ill-health was underpinned both by the employer and the State.

In the United States, March 1 saw the first use of a parachute for jumping from a moving aircraft, and reaching the ground safely. In France, in September, the airman Roland Garros reached 16,405 feet (5000 metres), the highest flight yet attained. 'Breathing is now very difficult, but here is 5000 metres,' he recounted to Le Matin. 'I have got it! I mean to get beyond it. An alarming shock and a great noise! I am rather astonished not to feel my wings part company from me in the air. With a movement quicker than thought, I cut my ignition and start planing down.'

That year the first regular passenger Zeppelin air service was inaugurated, using three rigid airships, between Berlin and Friedrichshaven. In the fifth Olympic Games, held in Stockholm, the races were timed electronically for the first time.

The success of radio broadcasting had created chaos on the air waves. On August 13, in the United States, the first regulation of broadcasting was brought in, the Radio Act, whereby radio operators had to obtain a licence. Films also continued to gain in popularity. In 1912 there were 400 cinemas in London, four times the number three years earlier. In the United States that year, an estimated five million people visited the cinema every day.

CHAPTER FOURTEEN

1913

On 11 JANUARY 1913 the last horse-drawn omnibus carried its passengers through the streets of Paris. Along its route, mock funeral ceremonies were held. The internal combustion engine was now master of the brightest capital of Europe. In London, some horse-drawn buses were to continue to ply their routes, but only for another three years. In the capitals of Europe, culture and commerce flourished side by side; as did the extremes of wealth and poverty. But it was the United States that had emerged as the world's most prosperous nation: in 1913 her manufacturing output exceeded that of France, Britain and Germany combined.

The spread of social policies designed to bridge the gap between rich and poor was uninterrupted. During 1913, old age and sickness insurance schemes were introduced in the United States, France and the Netherlands. In a gesture of charitable munificence, the Rockefeller Foundation was established in New York, dedicated to promote 'human wellbeing' worldwide. The profits of individual industry and investment were to be turned to the benefit of millions. To make the motorcar even more accessible to the masses, and to augment his own profits, Henry Ford introduced the conveyor-belt system of mass assembly. Architecture reflected the new mood. The Woolworth Building in New York, the highest skyscraper yet built, was to retain its pre-eminence for seventeen years. In New Delhi, Edwin Lutyens completed the construction of the Viceroy's house, a central and imposing feature of the new capital of British India.

Art, literature and music flourished. In Madrid, the guitarist Andrés Segovia made his debut. Stravinsky's ballet *The Rite of Spring* received its first performance. Thomas Mann's *Death in Venice* was published. That year, a new screen star, Charlie Chaplin, made thirty-five short films. Advertising, and the encouragement of spending, also made a leap forward that year, with the launching of a campaign throughout the United States for the sale of 'Camel' cigarettes.

Culture and commerce might affect human life for the good over many areas of the globe, but war and destruction remained an annual feature of the century, whose greatest bloodletting was yet to come. The first clash of armies in 1913 took place in European Turkey. Following the triple success of Greece, Serbia and Bulgaria on the battlefield the previous year, Bulgaria renewed her demand from the Turks for the cession of Adrianople, the most important Turkish city after Constantinople. When this demand was eventually supported by the Powers, the Turkish Grand Vizier, Kiamil Pasha, was prepared, albeit reluctantly, to accept it. Many Turks felt humiliated at the thought of surrendering the city.

A new government was formed in Constantinople, headed by Shevket Pasha, with Enver Pasha, one of the organizers of the Young Turk Revolution of 1908, serving as Minister of War. The first pronouncement of the new government was to insist on Turkish sovereignty over Adrianople, at least that part of the city which lay on the left bank of the River Maritza. The Balkan States, angered at this stiffening of the Turkish position, and seeking to exert their power, declared the armistice at an end. On February 1 the peace conference that was then in session in London broke down. Three days later the Bulgarians attacked Adrianople. The city was considered virtually unconquerable: it was one of the three fortresses of Turkey-in-Europe's so-called 'impregnable triangle', Adrianople-Skutari-Yanina.

The Balkan War was renewed, with even greater intensity than in the previous months. In a rapid advance southward towards the Sea of Marmara, the Bulgarians drove the Turks from the Isthmus of Bulair and occupied the northern shore of the Dardanelles between Bulair and Gallipoli, cutting off the Gallipoli peninsula from all land links with Turkey-in-Europe. A swift counterattack led by Enver Pasha drove the Bulgarians back. But when the Turkish troops were forced to re-embark, being needed desperately elsewhere, the Bulgarians returned to the north shore of the Dardanelles.

The Albanian port of Skutari, which the Turks had held throughout the First Balkan War, was attacked at the outset of the Second by a combined force of 36,000 Montenegrins and 14,000 Serbs. In Epirus, the Greeks renewed their attack on Yanina, which had evaded capture in 1912, and was widely considered to be impregnable. With Adrianople, Skutari and Yanina besieged, and the Gallipoli peninsula cut off, on March 2 the Turkish government made it known that it wanted to make peace. The Balkan League had not yet achieved its objectives, however, and fought on. The Greeks inflicted heavy casualties on the Turks defending Yanina, and on March 6 entered the city, making its 33,000 Turkish defenders prisoners of war, and capturing 200 guns.

The Greeks sensed that the victory which had evaded them the previous year was now theirs. On March 10 Greek forces occupied the island of Samos. But in the moment of victory, over the Turks, while Athens was still celebrating the capture of Yanina, Greek and Bulgarian forces clashed outside Salonika, with heavy loss of life. The Balkan allies were fighting for the territorial spoils of war. In the Bulgarian parliament, Greece was condemned for carrying out a policy of conquest detrimental to Bulgaria.

The Powers, responding to Turkey's appeal for mediation, approached the Balkan League, which stated, on March 16, that one condition of making peace was that the Turks should surrender Skutari. The Powers, influenced by Austria-Hungary and Germany, had decided, however, that one outcome of the defeat of Turkey in the Balkans would be the establishment of an independent State of Albania. This, the Serbs rejected. By annexing Albania they would acquire a substantial sea shore for themselves, and Skutari for Montenegro. The desire for an outlet on the Adriatic had been one of the consistent, and persistent, motives of Serbian policy.

Negotiations were interrupted on March 18 by the assassination of the King of Greece, shot down in the streets of Salonika by Alexandros Skinos. The assassin was described in one British newspaper as 'a drunken Greek degenerate'. King George (formerly Prince Wilhelm of Denmark) had ascended the Greek throne in 1863 on the nomination of England, France and Russia. His murder, at the very moment when Greece was about to make the most important territorial gains of its post-independence history, did not halt the onward march of the Greek armies. The Crown Prince, who had been fighting in the war with distinction, succeeded to the throne as King Constantine.

On March 28 the fortress of Adrianople fell to a combined Bulgarian and Serbian assault, and another 30,000 Turks were taken prisoner, including the Turkish Commander-in-Chief, Shukri Pasha, and a vast quantity of war material and stores. On the following day King Ferdinand of Bulgaria entered Adrianople in triumph. Of the three fortresses of the 'impregnable triangle', only Skutari was still held by the Turks. It was, however, closely besieged by Serbs and Montenegrins. When the Powers asked the besieging forces if the local population could leave under flag of safe conduct, the besieging forces refused. The majority of the civilian population, they said, 'are in the ranks of their enemies'. Skutari, known to its inhabitants as Skodra, was an entirely Albanian city, the centre of the Roman Catholic tribes of northern Albania. As Roman Catholics, they were under the religious protectorate of Austria-Hungary. When the Montenegrins began to bombard the city, Austria-Hungary protested, and on March 24 the Montenegrins agreed to allow the civilian population to leave. The Powers then asked the Montenegrins to end the siege, and to allow Skutari to become a part of an independent Albania.

The Turkish garrison continued to defend the 'impregnable fort', and the Montenegrins could not break into it. In an attempt to persuade the Montenegrins to withdraw, the Powers agreed to make a naval demonstration off the coast. The naval force assembled for this demonstration was an international one, made up of three Austro-Hungarian warships, two Italian, one British, one French and one German. A senior British naval officer, Admiral Burney, was given command, and on April 10 declared a close blockade of the Albanian coastline. The Montenegrin coastline on the Adriatic was also blockaded, but Montenegro, whose operations against the Turks were all by land, continued to ignore the appeals of the Powers for a withdrawal. For King Nicholas of Montenegro, this was the opportunity for him to show that he, and the Montenegrins, were an integral part of the Serbian race and its fortunes, and could win a great victory. When Serbia acceded to the appeal of the Powers for negotiations, and withdrew its troops from the siege of Skutari, King Nicholas continued with the bombardment.

The struggle for Skutari became intense, with both sides on the verge of exhaustion, and the besieged population facing starvation. On April 22 the Turkish commander of the fortress, Essad Pasha — who as well as being a general in the Ottoman army was also one of the leading Albanian chiefs — capitulated. He immediately issued a proclamation of Albanian independence.

Enormous pressure was put on Montenegro to accept Albania's right to statehood, and to withdraw. The Russian government warned King Nicholas that failure to do so would result in Montenegro 'running the risk of meeting her ruin'. The threat was taken to mean an attack by Austria-Hungary, against which Russia would take no action. At the same time as this threat, the Powers offered Montenegro a substantial financial sum in compensation for giving up Skutari. King Nicholas accepted, and in a telegram to the British Foreign Secretary, Sir Edward Grey, on May 5, placed the future of the fortress in the hands of the Powers. The town was then taken over by men from the international naval force, whose instructions (from Vienna, Rome, London, Paris and Berlin) were to maintain order until an Albanian administration could be set up.

Meanwhile, on April 20, an armistice was signed with Turkey by Greece, Bulgaria and Serbia. The terms of the armistice had been laid down by the Powers, and accepted by the three Balkan belligerents. The frontier of Turkey-in-Europe was pushed back to the Enos-Midia line running from the Aegean Sea to the Black Sea, with Greece and Bulgaria making substantial territorial gains in both Macedonia and Thrace. Turkey agreed to abandon all its claims to the island of Crete. Roumania, as compensation for having remained neutral – that is, for not having taken advantage of Bulgaria's involvement with Turkey to attack in the rear – was given a portion of Bulgarian territory on the Black Sea coast, and the fortress of Silistria. Bulgaria gained Adrianople. The Treaty of Peace was signed in London on 30 May 1913.

Turkey's defeat led to one further territorial loss: the small, fortified island of Ada-Kaleh, in the Danube. This island was within a few miles of Hungarian, Serbian and Roumanian territory. Since 1878 it had been garrisoned by Austria-Hungary, but had remained under nominal Turkish sovereignty and was administered by a Turkish official. In May 1913 Austria-Hungary annexed the island, and the Turkish administrator was replaced by a Hungarian. It was the last ever territorial acquisition by the Habsburgs.

That summer the heir to the Habsburg dominions, the Archduke Franz Ferdinand, went to the Galician region of Austria-Hungary with his wife Sophie, Duchess of Hohenberg. They were the guests of the Polish Count Potocki on his estate at Lancut. Among those present was the count's nephew Stas (Stanislas) Radziwill. The count's son, Alfred Potocki, who was also present, recorded in his memoirs:

> There had been a shooting party during the day, and the Archduke and Duchess went to bed about 11 p.m. Shortly afterwards my mother retired. The rest of us adjourned to one of the guest apartments and someone suggested a séance, an entertainment in vogue at the time. Letters of the alphabet were written on a sheet of papers and a small saucer was placed

on it and touched by two blindfolded members of the party. In answer to questions the saucer moved and stopped at various letters. These were written down until they formed sentences.

Stas Radziwill put the following question: 'What will be the most important event next year?' The startling answer came: 'Franz Ferdinand and Sophie will be assassinated at the station.' Then came the words, 'The heir,' and the sentence, 'Poland will be devastated.'

When my mother was told of the séance next day she was very angry, saying that it was bad taste to joke at the expense of guests. Sophie, Duchess of Hohenberg, was a cousin and an intimate friend of hers.

Assassination continued to bedevil, though not to affect, the evolution of the Balkan crisis. On June 11, as the Serbs and Bulgarians began seriously to dispute the division of the conquered areas of Turkey-in-Europe, and to threaten war against each other if their respective claims in Macedonia were not met, the Turkish Grand Vizier, Shevket Pasha, was shot and killed. The Young Turks took swift action, and twelve Turks said to have conspired to overthrow the government were hanged.

In the Balkans, where peace had been secured after so much fighting, the victorious nations might well have been expected to devote their energies and resources to the task of repairing the physical and human ravages of war. But they did not do so. The Bulgarians, whose losses in the war had been the highest of all the combatants, were determined not to allow Serbia to have the main territorial advantage in Macedonia. The Bulgarian army had lost 30,000 dead and 53,000 wounded. The other Balkan losses combined were 15,000 dead. But the scale of Bulgaria's losses did not deter her leaders from sending the Bulgarian army back into battle.

The Second Balkan War began on June 30, when the Bulgarian army launched an attack on both Greek and Serbian positions in Macedonia. In a twenty-hour battle with the Serbs, in which 100,000 Bulgarian troops were involved, the Serbs held their positions. The Bulgarians succeeded, however, in occupying the town of Gevgelija, driving a wedge between the Greek and Serbian armies.

The world outside the Balkans was shocked by the accounts that quickly circulated of the ill-treatment of wounded men after each battle. A Serb officer, Second Lieutenant Mihailo Stoyanovits, later gave evidence of how, during one battle, he was struck in the left leg and heel by a bullet. 'Unable to move, I had to stay where I was. Then some Bulgar soldiers came, and two of them began to rob me. They took from me a leather purse containing 115 francs, a watch worth forty-eight francs, a leather pouch, an amber cigarholder, and epaulette, a whistle, a box of matches, my cap and its cockade. Having taken all these, they made ready to go, but one of them said, "Let's kill him now!" Then he sharpened his knife against his gun and gave me three gashes, two on the left, one on the right. The other gave me a strong blow on the leg and in the right ribs. A third Bulgar came up and hit me with his musket in the chest. Then they departed.'

Accounts of ill-treatment, of mutilations, of men murdered while wounded, and, as the war continued into July, of the brutal killing of civilians, were widespread. In response to the outcries, an international commission of enquiry was sent out to the Balkans, under the auspices of the Carnegie Endowment for International Peace in Washington DC. Its instructions were to report on what had happened, and, most specifically, on 'what is or may be involved in an international war carried on under modern conditions'. The commission examined a plethora of gruesome evidence of atrocities committed by soldiers of every army, both against prisoners of war and against civilians on all sides. One of its most harrowing accounts concerned the atrocities committed in the town of Serres, the second largest town in eastern Macedonia, a town of 30,000 inhabitants, mostly Greek, but with Jewish, Turkish and Bulgarian minorities.

On July 4 the Bulgarian forces south of Serres were defeated by the Greeks. On the following day more than two hundred Bulgarians, some of them soldiers but most of them civilians, were rounded up in the town and taken to a local school building (the Greek girls high school). There, the commission reported:

The prisoners were tightly bound and beaten with the butt ends of rifles. The plan of the gaolers was apparently to slaughter their prisoners in batches, and they were led two by two to an upper room, where they were killed, usually by repeated wounds in the head and neck inflicted with a butcher's knife or a Martini bayonet. Each of the butchers aimed at accounting for fourteen men, which was apparently the number which each could bury during the night.

The massacre went on in this leisurely way until Friday, the 11th. The prisoners included a few captured Bulgarian soldiers, a few peasants taken with arms in their hands, and at least one local Bulgarian who was known to be an active associate of the Bulgarian bands. The immense majority were, however, inoffensive tradesmen or peasants whose only offence was that they were Bulgarians. Among them were four women, who were killed with the rest.

The only mitigating circumstance is that five lads were released in pity for their youth, after seeing their fathers killed before their eyes.

After seven days of Greek occupation of Serres, Bulgarian troops moved to recapture it. During the shelling, part of the town was set on fire. After the Bulgarians entered, and began burning more Greek property, the Greeks themselves opened fire with their artillery, and yet more fires were started. Of the 6000 houses in the town, 4000 were destroyed by fire within forty-eight hours. One result 'in all likelihood' – so the commission expressed it – was 'the painful death of many of the aged and infirm, who could not make good their escape'. The commission concluded: 'The episode of Serres is deeply discreditable alike to Greeks and Bulgarians.'

The Bulgarian military initiative in Macedonia failed to obtain the territory Bulgaria sought. Neighbouring Roumania, watching the renewed fighting, decided that the territorial gains she had made from Bulgaria by staying out of the First Balkan War could be enhanced if she were to enter the Second. The Roumanian government had informed the Bulgarians in June that if the Balkan allies were to engage in fighting among themselves, 'Roumania would not be able to maintain the reserve which she had hitherto observed in the interests of peace, and would be compelled to take action.' This threat opened up the possibility of Bulgaria having to face a war on two fronts, the nightmare of every strategic planner since Napoleon had faced Russia in the east and the British (in Spain) in the west.

The Bulgarian government made no reply to the Roumanian threat. Then, on July 9 the Roumanian government declared war on Bulgaria and advanced across the Bulgarian border, moving rapidly on the Bulgarian capital, Sofia. The Greeks, taking advantage of the Roumanian attack, seized the Thracian town of Drama, from which the Bulgarians had driven the Turks during the First Balkan War. The Bulgarians retreated rapidly, committing atrocities against Greek civilians which were widely reported and shocked Europe. In the town of Demir Hissar, a Bulgarian gendarmerie captain forced the bishop of the town, two priests, and a hundred leading citizens into the courtyard of a school, where they were shot down in cold blood.

Even as the Bulgarians, who had precipitated the Second Balkan War, began to flee back to their borders, appealing to the Russians to intervene to secure a cease-fire, the Turks decided to re-enter the conflict. On July 12 the order went out from Constantinople that the Turkish army was to advance. Its goal was Adrianople, still under Bulgarian occupation. Leading the Turkish forces was their most impressive military leader, Enver Pasha. Having isolated the Bulgarian garrison, which had been abandoned by the main body of the retreating Bulgarian forces, Enver entered Adrianople on July 20.

Bulgaria's call for an end to the war was answered by the Roumanians, who called a conference at Bucharest to discuss the terms for halting hostilities. As the delegates to the conference assembled, with the Serbian and Bulgarian troops accepting a cease fire, the Greek army continued its advance into territory which Bulgaria had conquered from the Turks a year earlier. Terrible atrocities were reported; the Greeks taking a savage revenge on the Bulgarians for what they had done during their retreat from Thrace.

An armistice was eventually signed, in Bucharest, on July 31, and the terms of a treaty negotiated by all those involved. The negotiations proceeded swiftly, all sides being exhausted by the fighting and fearful of further losses. On August 10 the Treaty of Bucharest was signed. All five Balkan combatants – Bulgaria, Greece, Roumania, Montenegro and Serbia – agreed to the terms. New frontiers were fixed. But the internal fighting of the Balkan States, having superseded their united quarrel against Turkey, had set a new level of internecine conflict. Edith Durham, then a British relief worker, commented: 'The savage ferocity with which Montenegrin, Greek and Bulgar are struggling for the giant's share of the lands they have devastated is enough to alienate all sympathy from the Balkan peoples.'

Under the Treaty of Bucharest, the port city of Salonika, coveted by Bulgaria, was assigned to Greece. The Greeks were the majority of the inhabitants of western Thrace, which contained more than a million Greeks, 383,000 Turks and 94,000 Bulgarians. In eastern Thrace, however, which was incorporated in Bulgaria, there was a Greek minority of 300,000.

The rest of Europe was shocked by the destruction of life in the Balkans in the fighting between nations who had so recently been allies. Not only in Europe, but in the United States, there was a sense of bewilderment and helplessness that so much misery could be inflicted by neighbours upon each other. There was also the hope that the lessons of the two Balkan Wars might be of service to mankind. In the words of the American member of the international commission of enquiry, Nicholas Murray Butler: 'If the minds of men can be turned even for a short time away from passion, from race antagonism and from national aggrandisement to a contemplation of the individual and national losses due to war and to the shocking horrors which modern warfare entails, a step and by no means a short one, will have been taken toward the substitution of justice for force in the settlement of international differences.'

The commission of enquiry consisted of an Austrian, two Frenchmen, a German, two Britons, a Russian and the American, Nicholas Murray Butler. Its presidency was entrusted to the French Senator, Baron d'Estournelles de Constant, who had been active a decade earlier in urging the Turks to grant greater autonomy to their Balkan subjects. In a letter to his colleagues on August 21, the Baron wrote to his fellow commissioners setting out Europe's responsibility for the Balkan imbroglio, and explaining their own task:

> If Europe had sincerely wished to help them in the past thirty years, she would have given them what makes the life in a country, that is, railways, tramways, roads, telegraphs and telephones, and in addition, schools. Once these fertile countries were linked to the rest of Europe, and connected like the rest of Europe, they would of themselves become peaceful by means of commerce and trade and industry, enriching themselves in spite of their inextricable divisions.
>
> Europe has chosen to make them ruined belligerents, rather than young clients of civilization, but it is not yet too late to repair this long error.
>
> You are the precursors of a new economic order, exceedingly important for each one of the governments; you will be, because you claim no such distinction and because of your disinterestedness, the auxiliaries of their salvation. After having verified the evil which is only too evident, you will assist each government in repairing it, by making known by your report the real aims and resources of the country.
>
> And thus you will reassure the public which never likes to despond, and which will not admit that even a small part of Europe must lie fallow, when it can share the general progress which is going on feverishly everywhere else.

As the commission of enquiry set about its task, the diplomats of the twice-warring powers negotiated new frontiers, and a second Treaty of Peace was signed on September 29 by Turkey, Greece and Bulgaria. Essentially, the last line of the armies became the new line of the frontiers. Bulgaria's retreat in the final stages of the war ensured that she was the loser on the map. Adrianople was returned to Turkey, whose troops had driven the Bulgarians out of the city two months earlier. Bulgaria also lost territory to Roumania. The Bulgarian-inhabited regions of Macedonia, over which so much Bulgarian (and Serbian and Greek) blood had been shed, were allocated to Serbia.

The peace that came to the Balkans after two wars was seen by some observers as an omen for world peace. Baron d'Estournelles de Constant, in his introduction to the report of the Balkan commission of enquiry, went so far as to see the Balkan Wars as having finally brought war itself 'into disrepute'. The Great Powers, he wrote, were now 'manifestly unwilling to make war'. He went on to explain that Germany, France, England and the United States 'have discovered the obvious truth that the richest country has the most to lose by war, and each country wishes for peace above all things. This is so true that these two Balkan wars have wrought us a new miracle – we must not forget it – namely, the active and sincere agreement of the Great Powers who, changing their tactics, have done everything to localize the hostilities in the Balkans and have become the defenders of the peace that they themselves threatened thirty-five years ago, at the time of the Berlin Congress.'

What had made a European war so unattractive? 'We might be tempted to attribute this evolution of public opinion and that of the governments in part to the new education which we are striving to spread,' the Baron wrote, 'but let us stick to facts: the exigencies of the universal competition, the increased means of communication, the protest of tax payers, and the dread of socialism and of the unknown, have been more efficacious in forcing the governments to think than any exhortations.'

Writing both as a French Senator and as an advocate of the drastic reduction of international armaments, Baron de Constant continued: 'France has imposed upon herself more than a hundred billion francs in unproductive expenditure during the last forty-three years, an average of more than two billion francs a year. This is the minimum price of armed peace for one country only. Several hundreds of billions in a half century for the Great Powers together!! Think what United Europe might have done with these millions, had she consecrated even half to the service of progress! Imagine Europe herself, not to speak of Africa and Asia, penetrated and regenerated by the pure air, in its more distant parts, of free intercourse, of education and security. Can we picture what might have been the position today of these unfortunate Balkan peoples, if their patrons, the Great Powers of

Europe, had competed with each other in aiding them, in giving them roads, and railways, and waterways, schools, laboratories, museums, hospitals and public works.'

Despite the Treaty of Bucharest, fighting continued in Albania, where much of the country had been occupied by Serbia. The Powers remained emphatic that an independent Albania must be one of the main achievements of the defeat of the Turks. The Serbians resisted this with great energy, excited to have acquired a considerable coastline along the Adriatic. But Austria-Hungary was determined to remove Serbia from the coastal and Albanian regions. In the courts and chancelleries of Europe, the dominant question was whether the Austro-Hungarian hostility to Serbia would lead to a war between the two countries.

Under the Treaty of Bucharest, Skutari remained in Albanian hands, and Avlona was declared the Albanian capital, but much of the rest of the country was divided between Serbia and Montenegro. There were many incidents, which angered the Powers, when Serbian soldiers shot down Albanians who came into Albanian towns on the Serb side of the border to exchange goods and find food. On September 21, in the predominantly Albanian town of Dibra, on the Serbian side of the frontier, the Serbian authorities put to death forty-eight Albanian notables and informed the Powers, in a tendentious note, that 'the Albanians were crossing the frontier to stir up and arm the Albanians in Serbia, and incite them against the Serbian authorities'.

The Albanians took the law into their own hands; on September 23 a force of 6000 Albanians crossed the Serbian frontier and occupied Dibra. Then, joining forces with a Bulgarian armed band, they marched on the Macedonian town of Ochrid. The recently appointed Albanian Minister of the Interior, Essad Pasha, the former defender of Skutari, who had his own ambitions to lead the Albanian people, refused to recognize the government at Avlona, and, establishing himself in Durazzo, declared his own Government of Albania, with himself as 'Prince of Albania'.

Serbia, watching these revolutionary changes, decided to march into the Albanian regions. Her troops advanced, but were ordered back by a severe threat from the Powers. During the course of their retreat, the Serbian forces burnt a number of Albanian villages on both sides of the frontier, put the village elders to death, and shot those whom they had taken prisoner.

The Powers decided that Albania was best governed by the prince of a

European dynasty. Their choice for the future sovereign was an officer in the Prussian army, Prince Wilhelm of Wied, a nephew of the Queen of Roumania (herself a German).

In the aftermath of the Second Balkan War, certain territorial changes assuaged the aspirations, and conflicts, of many decades; among them was the incorporation of Crete into Greece. The Greeks failed, however, to acquire the twelve Dodecanese islands, including Rhodes and Kos, which they had hoped to annex following Turkey's defeat. In a move almost unnoticed during the fighting, Italian forces had occupied the Dodecanese, and refused to be dislodged.[1]

The defeat of Turkey in Macedonia and Thrace had immediate repercussions on Turkey's Asiatic dominions. Hardly had the Turks been divested of their centuries-old European territories than the Arabs in Arabia attacked the Turkish garrisons that had so recently forced them into submission. Access to the Muslim Holy Cities of Mecca and Medina was likewise blocked by the Arabs. In the Armenian provinces of the Ottoman Empire, a movement was begun, under one of the Young Turk leaders, Nubar Pasha, for the introduction of reforms, under the supervision of the Powers. These reforms would give the Armenians a greater say in their local administration. They had been insisted upon in the Treaty of Berlin in 1878, but never implemented.

At the end of the year, Serbia, having been prevented by the Powers from achieving its territorial ambitions in Albania, came to an arrangement with Montenegro, whereby Montenegro was given two of the districts conquered from the Turks by the Serbs: the fertile district of Metoya and the Sandjak of Novi Bazar. The viability of the Montenegrin government was further assisted by two financial loans, one from the Banca Commerciale of Milan, and one from the Banque de Paris.

The disputes in the Balkans had a direct and disturbing impact on the relationship between the European Powers, even those who were allies. At the beginning of 1913 the German Chief-of-Staff, Count von Moltke, went so far as to warn the Austro-Hungarian government not to go to war with Serbia, despite the Serbian designs on Albania. Von Moltke's warning was supported by the German Chancellor, Bethmann-Hollweg. The concern in

---

[1] The Dodecanese were not acquired by Greece until after the Second World War.

Berlin was the escalation of the Balkan conflict into a wider war, in which the whole of Europe would become embroiled.

As early as February 1913, von Moltke had told Conrad von Hötzendorf, the Austro-Hungarian Chief-of-Staff, that he was convinced 'that a European war is bound to come sooner or later, in which the issue will be one of a struggle between Germandom and Slavdom'. To prepare themselves 'for that contingency' was 'the duty of all States which are the champions of Germanic ideas and culture'. But such a war, von Moltke warned, 'necessitates the readiness of the people to make sacrifices, and popular enthusiasm'. That time, in his opinion, had not yet come.

There were signs of Germany's preparations for a war in Europe, ominous signs for the British, French and Russians, even for the Italians, when, on March 28, the government bill for increasing the size of the German army was published. Under a proposal to add each year to the existing size of the army an extra 63,000 recruits, and to do so annually without respite, from a base of just over 800,000 men who would be eligible for call-up, a calculation was made, causing alarm beyond Germany, that by the year 1937 the strength of the German army would amount to 5,400,000 men.

The reason given by the Germans for this increase was that events in the Balkans had shifted the balance of power in Europe, and that 'in a war which might be forced upon her, Germany might have to protect herself against several enemy frontiers which are extended and by nature to a large extent open'. This was a reference to the new vulnerability of Austria-Hungary now that the Serbs had extended their territory, and were on a possible collision course with German-sponsored Albania. The Bulgarian frontier with Turkey was likewise an area in which Germany, with its growing links to Turkey, might have to defend. The German general, Liman von Sanders, was even then on his way to Constantinople, to act as adviser to the Turkish government about modernizing its armies. The Turkish First Army Corps, which was put under his command, was to be built up into a model corps, through which most of the junior Turkish officers would pass.

The Russians protested at this extension of German influence. The French contented themselves with several important posts to be held by Frenchmen in the Turkish Ministries of Finance and the Interior. The British were still in charge, through Admiral Limpus, of the building up of the Turkish naval defences at the Dardanelles. But it was the Turkish army that would be the main force to reckon with in any future Balkan conflict, and here the strength of the German influence could not be denied. Four years earlier, Enver Pasha had been an official guest at German army manoeuvres. What he saw then had impressed him enormously with the strength of the German army.

In introducing the new army bill on April 7, the German Chancellor, Bethmann-Hollweg, stressed that while no Great Power desired war, 'no man could know whether war might not at any moment break out'. The 'state of tension' that had existed for months within Austria-Hungary and Russia, thanks to the Balkan crisis, had only been prevented from developing into a war between them, Bethmann-Hollweg told the Reichstag, 'by the moderation and sense of responsibility of the Powers'. Europe, he added, would also 'feel grateful to the English Minister of Foreign Affairs for the extraordinary ability and spirit of conciliation with which he conducted the discussions of Ambassadors in London, and which constantly enabled him to bridge over differences'.

Would it be possible to 'bridge over' such differences the next time a Balkan crisis turned into war? That was a question being asked in every European parliament, chancellery and foreign office. The success of Serbia and Bulgaria in the Balkan Wars had made an enormous impact in Germany, where the thousand-year-old struggle between Germandom and Slavdom was a much-taught and much-recalled fact of history. In his army bill speech, Bethmann-Hollweg foreshadowed some of the dangers. 'If it should ever come to a European conflagration,' he said, 'in which the Slavs would be ranged on one side and the Germans on the other, this newly developed vitality of the Slavs in the Balkans would be a disadvantage to Germany, as they would hold the balance of forces in that quarter which had hitherto been occupied by Turkey.'

From the German perspective, Turkey's virtue in her European provinces was that she constituted a Muslim, not a Slav presence in the Balkans. That situation had changed as a result of the two Balkan Wars, whereby Germany found herself challenged by the growth of Slav nationalism, and Slav territorial gains; the Berlin-Baghdad railway now went through longer stretches of Serbian territory than it had done before 1912.

In his speech of April 7, Bethmann-Hollweg spoke of the 'most friendly relations' that Germany had with Russia. The racial differences of Teuton and Slav would not of themselves, he believed, lead to war between Germany and Russia. 'We at any rate,' he said, 'shall never stir up such a war.' Nor did he believe that those who held power in Russia 'at present' would ever do so; but, he warned, the Pan-Slavist movement had received 'a powerful stimulus from the victories of the Slav States in the Balkans' and Germany was 'compelled to take this into account' when thinking about the future, and when planning the future strength of her army and navy.

Reflecting the image of the dangers of a European war that Churchill had presented to the British House of Commons in the immediate aftermath of the Boer War, twelve years earlier, Bethmann-Hollweg warned in his speech of April 7: 'Nobody could conceive the dimensions of a world conflagration, and the misery and trouble it would bring upon the nations. All previous wars would probably be as child's play, and no responsible statesman would be disposed lightly to set the match to the powder.' On the other hand, he said, the power of 'public opinion' had increased, and 'the driving force of the noisiest elements of it tended in excited times to consist, not of majorities but of minorities'. He then pointed to a minority in France – he stressed that he was not speaking of the French people as a whole – among whom 'a Chauvinistic literature had arisen, which boasted of the superiority of the French army, and saw visions of Germany overrun by masses of Russian infantry and cavalry'. By succumbing to the forces of illusion, he said, 'France had already won in a future war with Germany'.

Both France and Russia desired to be 'as strong as possible', Bethmann-Hollweg added; and Germany would be 'challenging Providence' if she said that, although she ought to be stronger, it would cost too much, and that she should remain as she was. This is what France had done in 1870 and Turkey in 1912. He was presenting the new army bill to avoid such a situation. Although Germany desired peace, 'if war came, she wanted to win'.

Bethmann-Hollweg ended his speech by referring in favourable terms to Winston Churchill's renewed proposal for a Naval Holiday; a deliberate slowing down of new naval construction by both Britain and Germany. The fact that this proposal had been made, he said, 'constitutes a great progress'.

Two months after Bethmann-Hollweg's speech, Churchill reiterated, in a private conversation with the German Naval Attaché in London, Captain E. von Müller, his suggestion of a pause in both British and German naval expansion. Von Müller, who disliked the British – and did not want the German Foreign Office in Berlin, or the Kaiser, to follow up Churchill's conciliatory suggestion – asked Admiral Tirpitz what he should do. Tirpitz advised him to report his conversation with Churchill as briefly as possible, and to do so in such a way as to give the impression that Churchill was only seeking to delay German naval expansion because he feared that Britain would not be able to maintain her existing naval superiority.

Thus Churchill's initiative, which Bethmann-Hollweg had welcomed two months earlier, was presented in such a way as to prejudice the Kaiser against it. Almost a year later, the German Foreign Secretary, Gottlieb von Jagow, complained to the German Ambassador in London: 'Most disagreeable is the tendentious reporting of your Naval Attaché. Can you not keep him a bit more on leash?' This everlasting baiting and calumniation of English policy is extraordinarily disturbing, especially since it is always used in high places in argument against me.' The words 'high places' meant the Kaiser himself. But the Kaiser chose to listen to the anti-British views of the Naval Attaché, and wiser counsels failed to make any impression at court.

The Kaiser was supremely confident of Germany's military ascendancy. In the spring of 1913 his standing army, which a year earlier had been increased to 544,000 men, was increased further, to 661,000 men. That October, Bethmann-Hollweg introduced these new army increases to the Reichstag with words which echoed his earlier theme of Slav versus Teuton: 'One thing remains beyond doubt,' he said. 'If it should ever come to a European conflagration which set Slavdom against Germandom, it is then for us a disadvantage that the position in the balance of forces which was hitherto occupied by European Turkey is now filled in part by Slav States.'

Serbia's occupation of Albania was a short-lived triumph. On 18 October 1913 the Austro-Hungarian government, determined to show that Serbia could not extend its territory to the Adriatic, sent an ultimatum to Belgrade demanding the evacuation of Albania by all Serbian forces within eight days. The Serbs, fearing an attack from across the Danube on Belgrade, which was geographically vulnerable, and from across the long frontier of Bosnia-Herzegovina, complied with the Austrian demand. That day a British diplomat, Eyre Crowe, noted with truth, and a certain prescience: 'Austria has broken loose from the concert of Powers in order to seek a solution single-handed of a question hitherto treated as concerning all Powers.' On the following day the German Acting Foreign Minister, Dr Alfred Zimmermann, told the British ambassador in Berlin, Sir Edward Goschen, that he had been 'surprised that the Emperor of Austria endorsed a policy which, under certain circumstances, might lead to serious consequences, but he had done so, and that made it clearer still that restraining advice at Vienna on the part of Germany was out of the question'.

In those final fourteen words lay the seeds of a European war: Germany would not be willing – or able – to urge Austria-Hungary to exercise restraint. After the Austrian ultimatum was sent, the Kaiser sent telegrams of congratulations both to the Emperor Franz Josef, and to Franz Josef's Heir Apparent, the Archduke Franz Ferdinand. This German approval, commented Eyre Crowe, 'confirms the impression that Germany, pretending to us that she altogether disapproved and regretted the Austrian attitude, has throughout encouraged her ally'.

It was noted in Austria that no Russian newspaper suggested that Russia should take any action on behalf of Serbia that might lead to a Russian conflict with Austria. The day after the Austrian ultimatum, October 19, marked the hundredth anniversary of one of Germany's greatest military victories, the defeat of Napoleon at Leipzig, by the combined armies of Prussia, Austria, Russia and Sweden, in the Battle of the Nations.[1]

For three days the representatives of the dozens of youth and adult associations, with which Germany proliferated, gathered and marched on the Leipzig battle site. Among those marching with nationalistic fervour were the representatives of the Navy League. To commemorate the century-old triumph, the Kaiser unveiled a monument to the victory in a ceremony that was designed to stress Germany's traditional and historic military prowess. The outward show of German-Russian monarchical solidarity was also evident at the Leipzig celebrations, when the Grand Duke Cyril dedicated a Russian Memorial Chapel. Another of those at the ceremony was the Austrian Chief-of-Staff, Conrad von Hötzendorf, to whom the Kaiser expressed his support for any Austrian action to force Serbia out of Albania. 'I am with you there,' was the Kaiser's remark. The other Powers, he assured Conrad, were not prepared to take any retaliatory action in support of Serbia.

The Kaiser advised speed, telling von Hötzendorf: 'Within a few days you must be in Belgrade. I was always a partisan of peace; but this has its limits. I have read much more about war and know what it means. But finally a situation arises in which a great power can no longer just look on, but must draw the sword.'

---

[1] One of my Oxford tutors, Karl Leyser, pointed out to me during a tutorial in 1957 that Leipzig (like the Kaiser's favourite town of Potsdam) was originally a Slav settlement. The name Leipzig is derived from the Slav word *lipa*, a lime tree; it was founded by Slav tribes before AD 1000. Leyser, who had left Germany after 1933 because of Hitler's persecution of the Jews, was an expert on the thousand-year struggle between Germandom and Slavdom from its earliest years.

Turkey's defeats in the Balkans, and the end of her control over Macedonia, had given both Serbia and Bulgaria a renewed sense of Slav destiny. For the Poles of East Prussia, that Slav destiny was still being hampered by German policy. On October 19, at the start of the centenary celebrations of the battle of Leipzig, the Germans refused permission for the Poles under their jurisdiction to honour the memory of the Polish national hero, Prince Josef Poniatowski, who had died that day in the battle. By contrast, the Austrian authorities allowed a procession of 30,000 Poles, many of them in national costume, to march through the streets of Cracow on October 19, to place their wreaths on Poniatowski's grave. When, in German Poland, a group of Poles in Posen tried to place wreaths on the statue of the Polish national poet, Mickiewicz, they were arrested by the German police for making a patriotic demonstration, and the leaders sent to prison.

In Alsace-Lorraine, rumours of intended repressive measures by the government in Berlin led to strong protests in the Strasbourg Diet on May 22, and a unanimous resolution condemning government policy. The resolution warned that the Reichsland – as the two provinces were known – 'can resist Chauvinism with its own strength'. As in Germany's Polish-speaking regions, it was the language restrictions that were particularly resented by the local population. French was only allowed to be taught in government schools in Alsace-Lorraine for one hour a week. It could not be spoken at all in the debating chamber of the Diet. 'What might be said with impunity in German', the French-speaking members of the Diet protested, 'was to be suppressed when it was said in French, and the result would only be to strengthen nationalism, and set back the work of reconciliation.'

The German government was confident of its course, however, and focused in 1913 on the suppression of newspapers in Alsace-Lorraine which were pursuing an anti-German tone; newspapers that, in the words of Berlin, 'had a dangerous influence on the youth'. Associations were also to be restricted to those that had no national content or theme; meetings called to celebrate events connected with French rule, and the history of France, were to be banned. To a request by the Diet not to impose further restrictions on the press and public meetings, the German government replied that it would 'not recede an inch'. It also took steps to bring in to the provinces German settlers whose ultra-German sentiments could be guaranteed.

Incidents of anti-French discrimination were frequent. In Metz, a man and his wife were arrested for laughing at a passing German military patrol. But the incident that caused the greatest distress in the two provinces, and alarm among all the national minorities of Germany, took place in November in the town of Zabern (in French, Saverne). A young German lieutenant was reported to have told a group of German army recruits in the town that if they stabbed a *Wackes* – a local term for a native of Alsace – who insulted them, not only would they not be punished, but they would be given a present of ten German marks. Following these remarks, demonstrations took place outside the house where the lieutenant was billeted. Soldiers had to be called to disperse the crowd. That evening, a number of junior officers who were leaving a fencing school clashed with the local pupils coming out of a secondary school. When the secondary school pupils made what the German officers judged to be offensive remarks, troops were called, and the crowd that had gathered in support of the students was dispersed; twenty-seven citizens were taken to the police cells for the night.

When the Zabern Incident was debated in the Reichstag in Berlin, the Chancellor tried to play it down. The lieutenant would be punished, he said, but although the incident was to be regretted, 'it was not world-stirring'. It had however, in addition to making Germany look ridiculous and petty in the eyes of many outsiders, been stirring enough in Alsace-Lorraine. The indignation of the two provinces was aroused further when, during the debate, the Prussian Minister of War, General Falkenhayn, told the Reichstag that 'what they had to deal with was not the degree of a lieutenant's offence, but a determined attempt by Press agitation and abuse to exercise an unlawful influence upon the decision of the authorities'. There had been a 'great deal of talk', Falkenhayn added, 'about the preservation of the people's rights, but the Army constituted not the least important part of the people'. Unless the authorities were prepared to suppress the nationalist agitation in Alsace-Lorraine, 'they must be prepared to see life for a German at Zabern become less safe than life in the Congo'.

At the end of the Zabern debate, the Reichstag passed a vote of censure against the Imperial Chancellor, Bethmann-Hollweg. This was only the second such vote against him, the first having been the censure of the expropriation of Polish landowners in Posen. Bethmann-Hollweg admitted, at the end of the debate, that no progress would be made in Alsace-Lorraine 'unless they abandoned the fruitless attempt to turn the South Germans of the Reichsland into North German Prussians'. While his remark was intended to be conciliatory, it pointed up the fact that the inhabitants of Alsace-Lorraine did not consider themselves as 'South Germans', but as French; and their desire for a properly recognized French identity was only strengthened. There was further indignation in the two provinces when, during the lieutenant's court-martial at which he was sentenced to forty-three days in prison, it emerged that he had also told his recruits that the French Foreign Legion was 'good enough for French deserters'.

The language question also erupted that year in Schleswig – which Germany had annexed from Denmark in 1864 – when the Norwegian explorer, Captain Roald Amundsen was refused permission to give a scientific lecture in Norwegian – a language near enough to Danish to be understood by those in the province who did not speak German. The President of the Government of Schleswig, a German, stated, in defence of the language ban that 'all who had any sense of German nationality were crying out for measures which would put a check on the unbridled Danish agitation'. To those, he said, who hoped that Schleswig would be lost to Germany as a result of an unsuccessful war, her 'ready army and no less ready navy would afford the best answer'.

In June 1913, Bethmann-Hollweg told a friend: 'I am fed up with war and the clamour for war and with the perennial armaments. It is high time that the great nations calmed down again and occupied themselves with peaceful pursuits, or there will be an explosion which no one desires and which will be to the detriment of all.'

There was one diplomatic development that betokened calm, and a possible rapprochement between Britain and Germany, based on mutual self-interest. On 13 August 1913 the two countries entered into secret negotiations for the creation of potential spheres of influence in Portugal's African possessions. The agreement, for eventual Anglo-German control of Angola and Mozambique, was initialled on 20 October 1913, two days after Austria's 'Albanian' ultimatum to Serbia. To those negotiating a final partition in Africa, there seemed no reason why a Balkan crisis, even one that had been initiated by a European power close to Germany, should inhibit Anglo-German relations.

In Paris, on December 2, one of the most lavish balls of the year was given by Maurice de Rothschild, the leading French member of a family whose financial, social and charitable activities crossed all Europe's borders. The ball was given in honour of Princess Giselle of Bavaria. The aristocracies of France and Germany sat side by side as Félia Litvinne, the Russian soprano, sang their favourite arias. Also on December 2, High Mass was celebrated in Vienna to mark the sixty-fifth anniversary of the Emperor Franz Josef's succession to the throne. No previous European sovereign had held royal authority for so long. But he could neither curb the nationalist aspirations of his peoples nor prevent outsiders from encouraging them.

Inside the Russian Empire, equally divisive forces were at work, social rather than national. Strikes, reminiscent in size of those of 1905, took place in 1913 in St Petersburg, Moscow, Riga and Baku. As in 1905, the public expressed its support for the strikers and its hostility to the police by mass demonstrations in the streets. At the height of the agitation, it was calculated that more than a million Russian workers were on strike, a crippling blow to Russian industrial and factory production.

That October the trial began, in Kiev, of a Russian Jew, Mendel Beilis, who was accused of having killed a Christian boy for the purpose of using his blood for ritual purposes. This age-old 'ritual murder' accusation had been a frequent charge against the Jews in medieval times. Its revival caused fear among Russia's five million Jews, and concern among liberal Russians with regard to the independence of the courts when faced with a crude popular prejudice, and a prosecution brought with all the authority of the State to sustain it. By the time the trial began, Beilis had been held in prison in conditions of considerable hardship for more than two years.

The speech of the Crown Prosecutor caused derision far beyond the borders of Russia. The only evidence presented with regard to Beilis was that he worked near the place where the child had been murdered, and that a man with a black beard had been seen in the area at about the time of the murder. Beilis had a black beard. The prosecutor added to the indictment the charge that the Russian newspapers which had expressed indignation that the trial was taking place at all were only Russian in appearance; in reality, he said, they were 'almost entirely Jewish'. This overlooked the fact that one of the leading anti-Semitic papers in Kiev, the *Kievlianin*, had written that it was 'ashamed of the Kiev court and of Russian justice, which has ventured to come before the whole world with such wretched rubbish'.

After a trial that lasted more than a month, Beilis was acquitted. Following his release he made his way to Jerusalem, where the leading Muslim dignitaries invited him on to the Haram al-Sharif (the Holy Sanctuary) and welcomed him to the Dome of the Rock as a hero; a Jew had exposed the absurdity of Tsarist justice. But there had been a bitter moment at the end of the trial, when the jury, while acquitting Beilis, had insisted that the body of the boy had been 'drained of blood', and that this had been done near a factory owned by a Jewish family. The inference was clear: a ritual murder had been committed, though not by Beilis. This too was a lie.

Jewish fears of further such accusations, and of a renewal of pogroms against Jewish life and property, led to an upsurge in the numbers of Russian Jews emigrating to the United States and Western Europe. In 1912 the number of Russian Jews reaching the United States, landing at New York's Ellis Island, was 80,595. It rose in 1913 to 101,330. And in 1914 it rose again, to 138,051. In the course of the nine years following the 1905 revolution, more than a million Russian Jews settled in the United States. A further 200,000 made their way to Britain, and 24,000 to Palestine; Beilis himself chose to leave Palestine after a short while to settle in the United States.

The year 1913 had seen continuing disturbances far beyond the Balkans. In China, in February, thirty people had been killed when a bomb was thrown by supporters of the deposed Manchu dynasty at a newly appointed republican provincial governor. In Formosa, attempts by the Japanese to use local labour in expeditions against the Aborigines of the interior led to a labourers' revolt. In the Persian Gulf, British warships and Indian troops intervened at Muscat to protect the Sultan of Oman against the Islamic religious war declared on him by Sheikh Abdullah, who controlled much of the interior. On the North East Frontier of India, a British punitive expedition was sent against the villagers of the Naga Hills, who had earlier caused heavy casualties on a police detachment sent to punish them for a head-hunting raid. Three Naga villages were destroyed, and cattle seized. In French Indo-China, after a bomb killed two French army officers in Hanoi, a plot was uncovered to murder the Governor-General; seven Annamese were accused of conspiracy and executed.

The Somaliland Protectorate was the scene of a reversal of British fortunes in 1913, when the Mullah attacked a Camel Corps expedition which had been sent to halt what were still seen as his hostile movements in the interior. The British commander and twelve of his native Somali soldiers were killed. The Colonial Office in London called the attempt to engage the Mullah 'a rash act', and British forces were withdrawn to the coast.

In the French and Spanish spheres of Morocco the Moorish tribesmen were still challenging colonial rule on a substantial scale. Several Spanish outposts in the mountainous regions were overrun. On September 22 a

Spanish lieutenant, with a small force of Moorish mercenaries, won a victory over the tribesmen, and was awarded the Military Merit Cross. His name was Francisco Franco, the future leader and dictator of Spain – who would successfully keep Spain out of the Second World War.

There was fighting between French and Moroccan forces near Mogador in September 1913, when twenty French soldiers were killed. A punitive expedition was sent out to restore order and to receive the submission of the local tribes. In Italy's newly conquered province of Libya, Arab resistance to the transfer of sovereignty from Turkey to Italy resulted in the deaths of more than two hundred Italian soldiers. The Italian punitive expeditions that followed led to an even heavier loss of Arab lives.

In Johannesburg, there were serious riots in 1913 by white mine workers, protesting at their low wages and hard conditions of work underground. For several days the centre of the city was in turmoil, with troops called out to try to disperse the rioters. At one point cavalrymen drew their swords and charged into a crowd of demonstrators. The strikers then halted the tram service, and rushed to the power station, where they cut off the electric current to the city, and occupied the railway yards. In three days, twenty strikers were killed. At their funeral, a wreath was placed on the grave with the words: 'In memory of our martyrs who were foully murdered in cold blood by the capitalist class.'

In the Transvaal, legislation had been passed to exclude Indian immigrants, including measures forbidding Indians from trading or farming, or owning houses. Any offenders would be deported. The terms of the restrictions, explained the Transvaal Minister of the Interior, was 'a matter of self-preservation'. The Indian cause was championed, as it had been earlier, by Gandhi, who, as part of a growing passive resistance movement under his inspiration, led a non-violent protest march from the Natal coast towards the Transvaal. At the border of the province he was arrested, and sentenced to nine months in prison with hard labour. The Indians marching with him were forcibly taken back to the coast.

In Britain, considerable sympathy was expressed for the Indians of Natal. Field Marshal Lord Roberts, a former Commander-in-Chief in South Africa (and earlier in India), wrote to a friend: 'There is much to be said on behalf of the Indians. They were encouraged for many years to go to Natal. At a time when white men were scarce they were most useful – indeed, it would be difficult for the settlers in Natal to get on without them now, and the Indians, as British subjects, can scarcely be expected to realize that they should be treated differently to white men in the countries outside India which are part of the Empire. Putting the ringleaders in prison for nine months will not pacify the Indians in Natal, and will intensify the angry feelings of the people in India.'

Gandhi's sentence was reduced to two months. But the unrest continued. That November there were widespread strikes by Indian miners and sugar workers in Natal, and, in a move which encouraged the Indians but greatly upset the South African government, the Viceroy of India publicly protested about the conditions of Indians in South Africa, and spoke with sympathy of the passive resistance movement. Fifteen years later, another Viceroy, and the whole Government of India, was to be cast into turmoil by that same passive resistance movement, led by Gandhi himself.

Clashes between Indians and police continued in South Africa for several months. In a struggle on a sugar plantation in November, where police were trying to arrest a number of Indian workers, six Indians were killed. For the black South Africans, the restrictions which had been enshrined in the constitution were rigidly upheld; no black person was allowed to acquire land in an area scheduled for whites. In a speech in which he set out his philosophy of the apartheid policy that was to dominate South Africa for more than seventy years, General Botha explained that he did not believe in ruling the blacks with a truncheon; rather, they should be regarded as minors, and the whites as their guardians. He wanted a policy which would lead to peace between whites and blacks, 'but equality was not to be thought of'.

In the United States, natural and man-made disasters were a feature of the year. When a hurricane struck the city of Omaha, at least a hundred people were killed. In Finlayville, Pennsylvania, seventy coal miners were killed by an explosion in the mine. At Long Beach, California, during a celebration by local British residents of Empire Day, in May, thirty people were killed when the pier on which they were celebrating collapsed. During an indoor celebration that Christmas at Calumet, Michigan, seventy-two people were killed as a result of panic following a false alarm of fire. But the highest death toll in the United States that year – 2488 – was of Americans killed in motorcar accidents. This cause of death had risen year after year since the start of the century, making the motorcar by far the largest single cause of accidental death.

In the air, the Zeppelin was bringing the prospect of a revolution in travel: high above towns and countryside, swifter than the motorcar, and comfortable. There was also a military aspect that had begun to excite the German government: the Zeppelin could be used to bomb dockyards and munition factories from the air. Yet airships, like aeroplanes, continued to take their toll. When the German navy's first Zeppelin, *L1*, with its crew of twenty, was caught in a gale over the North Sea and brought down, fourteen men were drowned. Five weeks later a second Zeppelin, *L2*, blew up near Berlin while 650 feet above the ground. Of the crew of twenty-eight, all but one was killed. *L2* was the tenth Zeppelin to have come to grief in the air.

At sea and in the air, loss of life was a persistent feature of newspaper reports and public awareness. At Melun, in France, nearly fifty people were killed when two trains collided. In mid Atlantic, a British steamer bound for New York caught fire during a gale and 146 passengers were killed; more than five hundred other passengers were saved when ten other steamers, alerted by the distress calls, came to the rescue. During a sudden storm on the Great Lakes, thirty Canadian and American vessels sank, and 279 lives were lost. In a colliery explosion in Wales, one of the worst in the history of coal mining, 439 miners were killed. While 397 of those miners were still trapped behind a wall of fire, their supply of air cut off, *The Times* correspondent at the scene wrote:

> Thousands of people gathered today when the news travelled swiftly, as bad news does, through the adjoining valleys that there had been an explosion at the Universal Colliery. Men tramped over the hills from the parallel valleys or walked up from Caerphilly and the lowlands south of its ancient fortress to aid, to comfort, and to watch. They were massed on the colliery premises or on the surrounding hillsides from morning until night.
>
> I have never seen so silent a throng. The absence of noise was extraordinarily impressive. Few words were spoken by that vast crowd as the hours toiled slowly on. They waited for news, and the only news they got was bad news. Women and children, mothers and wives, sons and daughters of the men underground waited patiently at the pit mouths for tidings of their loved ones. There was little display of emotion – no weeping or beating of breasts – and there was a grimness in the demeanour of this anxious but strong-nerved crowd which added terribly to the poignancy

of the spectacle. The women particularly seemed to be steeling themselves against the knock-down blows which are the lot of miners' wives.

There is little more to be told tonight. We shall have to wait till tomorrow to know the full extent of the horror. The carpenters' shop on the pit bank has been turned into a mortuary, and at the top of the shaft are piled improvised stretchers hurriedly made from canvas and rough wood. The inquest was opened this afternoon and adjourned *sine die*. Hundreds watch at the pit mouths tonight with fear in their hearts but hope in the few words that are spoken. Some have not stirred from the colliery since early this morning, and have stood in the rain waiting and watching.

In Peru, 200 people were killed in an earthquake in November. But it was in British India that the highest death toll of the year was recorded, the deaths, through plague, of 181,388 people. High though this was, it was the lowest recorded annual death rate from plague for a decade.

To what extent could the United States, with its ever-growing industrial productivity, and its distance both from Europe and Asia, maintain independence from the turmoils of those two continents. The new President, Woodrow Wilson, was confident that he could do so. At his inauguration on March 4, he sought to outline a new social path for the United States, and did so in words which impressed many contemporaries by their eloquence: 'We have been proud of our industrial achievements,' he said, 'but we have not hitherto stopped thoughtfully enough to count the human cost, the cost of lives snuffed out, of energies overtaxed and broken, the fearful physical and spiritual cost to the men and women and children upon whom the dead weight and burden of it all has fallen pitilessly the years through. The groans and agony of it all had not yet reached our ears, the solemn, moving undertone of our life, coming up out of the mines and factories and out of every home where the struggle had its intimate and familiar seat.'

Wilson went on to attack what he called 'the great government' that had evolved in past years in the United States, a government, he said, with which he said 'went many deep secret things which we too long delayed to look into and scrutinize with candid, fearless eyes,' and he added: 'The great government we loved has too often been made use of for private and selfish purposes, and those who used it had forgotten the people.' Wilson continued, in ringing tones:

At last a vision has been vouchsafed us of our life as a whole. We see the bad with the good, the debased and decadent with the sound and vital. With this vision we approach new affairs. Our duty is to cleanse, to reconsider, to restore, to correct the evil without impairing the good, to purify and humanize every process of our common life without weakening or sentimentalizing it.

There has been something crude and heartless and unfeeling in our haste to succeed and be great. Our thought has been, 'Let every man look out for himself; let every generation look out for itself', while we reared giant machinery which made it impossible that any but those who stood at the levers of control should have a chance to look out for themselves.

We had not forgotten our morals. We remembered well enough that we had set up a polity which was meant to serve the humblest as well as the most powerful, with an eye single to the standards of justice and fair play, and remembered it with pride. But we were very heedless and in a hurry to be great.

We have come now to the sober second thought. The scales of heedlessness have fallen from our eyes. We have made up our minds to square every process of our national life again with the standards we so proudly set up at the beginning and have always carried at our hearts. Our work is the work of restoration.

The Cleveland *Plain-Dealer* commented: 'Not since Lincoln has there been a President so gifted in the art of expression.'

Woodrow Wilson was also determined to maintain the overseas possessions of the United States in as settled a mode as possible. Among the first efforts of his administration was the completion of the disarmament of Muslim rebels in the Philippines. Towards Latin America the President held, as had his predecessors, a careful watching brief. After President Madero of Mexico had been seized and killed by a rival to the presidency, General Huerta, Wilson refused to recognize Huerta as President. Towards Europe, Wilson remained detached, succeeding for three full years, once war had come to Europe in 1914, in keeping the United States out of the conflict. When he did commit his country to war, he did so with the conviction that, once the war was over, the United States would be able to impress upon Europe the same sense of equity and justice that he envisaged for his own people at home.

CHAPTER FIFTEEN
1914

Rapid strides were being made in adapting aerial flight to the needs of modern society. On 1 January 1914 the first daily civil air service was inaugurated. It was a flying-boat service in the United States, linking across a wide bay the Florida towns of St Petersburg and Tampa, a distance of twenty miles, saving twice that distance in the road journey around the bay. The pilot was Tony Jannus. He made two flights a day for four months, carrying a single passenger on each trip. In all, he carried 240 passengers.

On February 2, at Windsor Castle, the aviator Gustav Hamel looped the loop fourteen times in seventeen minutes – an astounding feat – before a large crowd which included King George V and Queen Mary. But death in the air continued to impinge on the new science. At the end of February two Turkish military airmen, attempting to fly the 130 miles from Damascus to Jerusalem, were killed when their aeroplane crashed near the Sea of Galilee. In May, Gustav Hamel, while flying from Paris to Hendon, disappeared over the English Channel. The crowd waiting on the cliffs near Dover realized, as dusk fell, that the aviator must have crashed into the sea.

In the general pattern of natural disasters and accidents which marked its early months, the year 1914 was no different to its predecessors. In mid January, two hundred Japanese were killed during a volcanic eruption on an island in Kagoshima Bay. Three days later, in the English Channel, eleven men were drowned when the British submarine A7 sank during naval exercises. In the Adriatic, near Venice, fifty people lost their lives when a ferry was run down by a torpedo boat. In Bolivia, several hundred people were killed when a magazine containing more than three thousand tons of dynamite exploded accidentally. In a mine at Eccles, in West Virginia, 178 coal miners died when they were entombed in the mine after an explosion. The opening of the Panama Canal that year, a momentous achievement in communications between the Atlantic and Pacific Oceans, led to several newspapers recalling that as many as six thousand workers had died during its construction.

On February 8, in a disaster that in the scale of loss recalled the fate of the *Titanic* two years earlier, the Canadian Pacific steamer *Empress of Canada*, on its way from Quebec to Liverpool, was run down in fog by a Norwegian collier, and sank in seventeen minutes; 1023 passengers were drowned. Storms also took their toll in 1914; off New Brunswick, fifty Canadian fishermen were drowned on the night of June 5–6, and in Paris, twenty-five people died during torrential rainfall on June 15. Earthquakes that June in Papua and Sumatra led to heavy loss of life.

The travails of the imperial powers continued in 1914 as before. On the North West Frontier of India, after eight British subjects had been killed during raids by the Bunerwals, a military expedition was sent against the tribe, 'inflicting', according to a contemporary account, 'exemplary punishment on the offending villages'. In the Somaliland Protectorate, despite British troop reinforcements from India and Aden, the Mullah attacked the largest of all the British garrisons, at Berbera. The British then advanced inland, using artillery against the Mullah's men for the first time, and also sending up pilots to spot from their cockpits where the Mullah's forces were gathering.

Every imperial power found the need to assert its authority by force. In that respect, 1914 mirrored the previous fourteen years of the century. On February 1 the Spanish army was again in action against the Moors at Beni Salem, on the outskirts of Tetuan. As a result of his bravery in action that day, twenty-one-year-old Lieutenant Franco was promoted Captain.

The United States also found itself in a war crisis in the spring of 1914. After their winter cruise, several warships of the American Atlantic Fleet had put in to Mexican ports to refit. On April 10 a party of American sailors landed at Vera Cruz to obtain petrol. They were arrested, and then paraded through the streets. After protests, the sailors were released and an apology was made for their ill-treatment. The United States naval commander, Admiral Mayo, was not satisfied by the apology and demanded, by way of reparation, that the Mexican authorities hoist the American flag and give it a salute of twenty-one guns. This demand was conveyed to General Huerta, the President of Mexico whom Wilson had refused to recognize a year earlier after he had killed his predecessor, President Madero. In search for a compromise, Huerta suggested that both the United States and the Mexican flags should be hoisted together, and saluted, reciprocally, gun for gun. The American government declined this suggestion on the grounds that, since Huerta's accession some months earlier, following the violent overthrow of

Madero and the Constitutionalists, the Mexican regime was a dictatorship of the worst sort. Before the flag episode could be resolved, the Mexicans arrested an American naval mail carrier.

For President Woodrow Wilson this was a testing time. In a message to Congress on April 20, he asked the legislators to approve the use of 'the armed forces of the United States in such ways and to such extent as may be necessary to obtain from General Huerta and his adherents the full recognition of the rights and the dignity of the United States.' This, the President explained, would not mean war with the Mexican people, but only with General Huerta and his supporters. The object of military action by the United States would be to restore to the Mexicans the freedom 'to set up their own laws and government'.

A resolution in support of military action was passed in the House of Representatives by 337 votes to 37. Before a vote could be taken in the Senate, American marines landed at Vera Cruz. They were met with sniper fire, and seventeen marines were killed. The naval guns of two American warships then opened fire, shelling buildings occupied by snipers, and the Naval Academy. American forces then occupied Vera Cruz.

Offers of mediation came from Argentine, Brazil and Chile, and were accepted by both the United States and Mexico. A conference (known as the ABC Conference after its convenors) was held at Niagara Falls, on the Canadian-United States border, and an armistice was arranged. Under it, the Americans were to remain in occupation of Vera Cruz. 'We have gone down to Mexico,' Woodrow Wilson told the mourners at the funeral of the American dead, 'to serve mankind if we can find a way.' The retirement of General Huerta two months later, in favour of the Constitutionalists, made the subsequent American withdrawal easier, as Mexico returned to a less dictatorial regime. General Huerta left by sea, via the British port of Avonmouth, for exile in Spain.

The ending of the Second Balkan War had left Austria-Hungary with a larger, more self-confident, Serbia on its southern frontier. Serbia had long aspired to be the leader of the South Slav peoples and regions, and to unite under a single Slav sovereignty the Slavs of three Habsburg-ruled regions, Bosnia-Herzegovina, Croatia and Dalmatia. The danger to the Habsburg Empire of the continuing, though often exaggerated, Pan-Slav agitation inside the Austro-Hungarian borders was a cause of popular as well as government concern. Many voices argued that the only way to avert a challenge from Serbia – a challenge that might even be supported militarily by Russia – was to order Serbia, if necessary by invasion, to cease all agitation in the Habsburg provinces along her border.

The Serb agitation could take a potentially bloody form. On May 29 two Serbian students tried to kill the Ban of Croatia, Baron Sterletz, whose rule in Zagreb they regarded as inimical to Pan-Slav aspirations. They were caught and sentenced to eight and five years' penal servitude respectively.

Austria-Hungary felt pressured on two sides: first by the Slavs in Serbia, who had been humiliated by having had to withdraw from Albania, but were still not giving up either their Pan-Slav hopes or their hope of an Adriatic coastline; and second by the Slavs in Galicia, who were agitating for closer links, and some even for territorial unity, with the Russian Empire along the whole length of the Galician border. The city of Lemberg, in Eastern Galicia, had a Polish and Ukrainian population that looked as much to their fellow Poles and Ukrainians across the border as to Vienna, for support and inspiration. In January, the Austrian Governor of Galicia had reported to the Ministry of the Interior in Vienna that the agitation of the Russophil party in Galicia had recently 'become more lively'. The continuing Russification of Galicia, he wrote, 'aided by Orthodoxy, requires greater attention on the part of administrative officers if they are to be able to combat it'.

On March 3, thirty-two Ruthenians who had been accused in the previous year of seeking annexation with Russia were sent to prison for terms ranging from six months to four and a half years. Six days later a second trial began, also in Lemberg, of four Ruthenians charged with spying for Russia. By a quirk of the legal system, the jury before whom the trial was held were all Poles. They gave an acquittal on the grounds, they said, that they wished to avoid interference 'with the internal affairs of the Ruthenians'.

On 3 March 1914 the British Admiralty issued a list of the naval strength of the Powers. The order of strength, calculated in number of battleships less than twenty years old which were already launched, was Britain (58), Germany (35), the United States (30), France (21), Japan (17) Austria-Hungary (14), Italy (9) and Russia (8). That year's proposed British naval expenditure was the highest on record. In addition to the thirteen battleships already under construction, four new ones would be built, and many other warships as well. A chain of seaplane bases was being established around the coast; five were already completed. Aircraft for war purposes were being developed for the navy as well as the army, with wireless telegraphy, gunnery and bomb dropping all part of the current training programme. Not only would aircraft be armed to attack ships, but ships would be armed to protect themselves from attack from the air.

In introducing the new measures, the First Lord of the Admiralty, Winston Churchill, warned that the naval battles of the future would be like 'two eggshells striking each other with hammers'. Good gunnery would be all important. In seeking to protect herself against a possible naval attack, Britain would maintain a 60 per cent superiority against the Power nearest to her in naval size, that is, Germany. What Churchill did not tell the House of Commons was that he was still making plans to push forward with his earlier proposal for a Naval Holiday, whereby both Britain and Germany would agree to a mutual reduction in the number of warships under construction. He had been invited by the Kaiser to visit Kiel during the German naval regatta at the end of June, and to meet the father of the German navy, Grand Admiral Tirpitz. Such a meeting, Churchill believed, might, as a result of 'direct personal discussions', be the prelude to an agreement.

It was Tirpitz who had in the past suggested limiting the size of the largest warships. Churchill wanted to follow up this idea, in the interests of a general reduction of tension and war expenditure. 'Even if numbers could not be touched', he told the Prime Minister, H. H. Asquith, and the Foreign Secretary, Edward Grey, 'a limitation in size would be a great saving, and is on every grounds to be desired'. Churchill wanted to go as far as to offer the German government 'the abandonment of secrecy in regard to the numbers and general characteristics (apart from special inventions) of the ships, built and building, in British and German dockyards.' Naval attachés from both navies would visit each other's dockyards and 'see what was going on'. This, Churchill argued, 'would go a long way to stopping the espionage on both sides, which is a continued cause of suspicion and ill-feeling'.

Such a scheme of confidence and naval disarmament needed time. Churchill had no reason to doubt, that May, that there was time, and so he awaited the end of June and the Kiel regatta in the hope that a new era might dawn in Anglo-German relations. But Edward Grey put a stop to the plan. He was afraid, he told Asquith in confidence, that Churchill's proposed visit to Kiel would make 'a terrible splash in the European Press'. The secret of diplomacy was that it must remain secret. Better to do nothing, than to expose national policy to public view, and then face the possibility of a humiliating rebuff.

In Germany and Austria-Hungary, it was not the British navy that was the main cause of agitation early that year, but the intentions of the Russians. Russian support for the Slavs in the Balkans was worrying to the two Germanic powers. On May 12, in the Bohemian resort town of Carlsbad, the German Chief-of-Staff, Count von Moltke, told his Austrian opposite number, Baron Conrad von Hötzendorf, that any delay in war with Russia 'meant a lessening of our chances; we could not compete with Russia in masses'. Travelling eight days later by car from Potsdam to Berlin, von Moltke told the German Secretary of State, Gottlieb von Jagow, that he was afraid that Russia, whose own military expansion had begun, would in two or three years have built up her maximum war armaments, and that no other way was left to Germany but 'to wage preventive war in order to beat the enemy while we still have some chance of winning'. Von Moltke's advice to Jagow during their drive was that the Secretary of State should 'orientate our policy at the early provocation of war'.

In contrast to the situation in the Balkans less than a year earlier, when the European Powers had used all their efforts to prevent the war spreading, the atmosphere in the early summer of 1914 was of hostility and imminent conflict. On May 29 Colonel House, President Wilson's emissary, wrote to the President from Berlin: 'The situation is extraordinary. It is militarism run stark mad. Unless someone acting for you can bring about a different understanding there is some day to be an awful cataclysm.' No one in Europe could bring about that understanding, House warned. 'There is too much hatred, too many jealousies. Whenever England consents, France and Russia will close in on Germany and Austria. England does not want Germany wholly crushed, for she would then have to reckon alone with her ancient enemy, Russia; but if Germany insists upon an ever-increasing navy, then England will have no choice.' Reaching London, House told the British Foreign Secretary how, in Berlin, 'the air seemed full of the clash of arms, of readiness to strike'.

Even as Colonel House wrote and spoke these words of foreboding, Britain and Germany were negotiating the Baghdad Railway Agreement, to share economic opportunities and avoid territorial conflicts in Asia Minor. But the economic benefits of peace were not the only benefits being argued about that summer. Early in June, the German Chancellor, Bethmann-Hollweg, told the Bavarian Minister in Berlin, Count Hugo von Lerchenfeld, that there were those in Germany who expected war to lead to an improvement in the domestic situation in Germany 'in a Conservative direction'. Bethmann-Hollweg thought, however, 'that on the contrary a World War with its incalculable consequences would strengthen the tremendous power of Social Democracy, because they preached peace, and would topple many a throne.'

In Italy, an antimilitarist demonstration culminated that June, in 'Red Week', a manifestation of socialist, anarchist and republican discontent. The agitation was stimulated by a leading left-wing journalist, Benito Mussolini, whose appeal for a popular insurrection helped to create violent rioting in several regions, most notably Romagna and Ancona.

Other Italian Socialist leaders denounced Mussolini for the absurdity of appealing to 'amorphous mass' to bring about revolution. But he saw the extent to which he was able, by his oratory and his passion, to establish a personal link with those in Italian society who were unorganized or inarticulate. 'The politics of intoxication were beginning to drive out the politics of reason,' writes the historian Adrian Lyttelton, 'and from the start Mussolini's part in this process was central.'

In his book *The Great Illusion*, Norman Angell had pointed out that the governments whose much-publicized rivalries made their public opinions so warlike were themselves tied closely together by links of free trade and industrial interdependence. This was borne out in June 1914, when a company owned jointly by British and German investors gained exclusive rights for oil exploration in Mesopotamia.

German, French, British and Russian cars and lorries, which in the event of war would have to transport troops and supplies, functioned thanks to the Bosch magneto. This small but essential part of the internal combustion engine was made exclusively in Germany and imported by the manufacturers of vehicles in every European country. If war came, and supplies of the magneto were cut off, a crucial mechanism would first have to be re-invented, and then manufactured from scratch.

The motorcar was a link between the European nations in a more prosaic way. Holiday travel by car was growing. That summer a guidebook to the 'motor routes' of Germany was published in London. On the journey into Germany there were war memorials to be seen commemorating the Franco-Prussian war of 1870–1, the guidebook commenting on the defeat of the French army at Sedan 'when the Emperor Napoleon III delivered his sword to King William I of Prussia'. But the guidebook was mostly full of touristic splendour and practical advice, as on the Bonn to Bingen road: 'Frequently a train runs along parallel with you as you are driving into one of the numerous small villages, and, owing to the noise of the train, it is advisable to slow down to a crawl, as little children (who are very plentiful) might not hear even a powerful klaxon in rivalry with the shrieking of a locomotive.'

As to the national aspect of a tour of Germany, the guidebook's author, Henry J. Hecht, wrote: 'The average Englishman is under the impression that all German officials are terrible people to deal with, but any motorist who has taken a car to Germany will agree with me when I say that the majority of German officials are particularly courteous to foreigners, and they do not raise difficulties – in accordance with popular superstition in this country – provided, of course, all papers presented to them are in order. If anything is not quite as it should be, they are apt to be difficult, but even under such circumstances they are generally polite, though obdurate; and they are not really anxious to find an excuse for flinging the unoffending foreigner into a fortress, although it is difficult to persuade many Englishmen of the truth of this fact. People frequently tell me that they avoid Germany when touring on the Continent, as they are afraid of getting into difficulties with the officials, which is absurd.'

One German city had a special recommendation. 'Hamburg', Hecht explained, 'is a city bound to appeal to every Englishman; the inhabitants are extremely English in their tastes and in their love of sport.'

The sense of the interdependence of the Powers could be felt in the social as well as in the commercial, industrial and tourist spheres. On June 11, at Kenwood House, in one of the leafier suburbs of North London, an orchestra brought specially from Vienna played to the guests at a spectacular dinner and ball. The host was the Grand Duke Michael, a great-great-grandson of Catherine the Great and a second cousin of the Russian Tsar. His guests were the aristocrats and nobility of Europe, headed by King George V and

Queen Mary. The guests, and the musicians entertaining them, were given no reason to feel anything but a sense of ease and wellbeing.

On June 12 the Kaiser went for the weekend to Konopischt, near Prague, to stay with the Archduke Franz Ferdinand. It was a time of relaxation and hunting. The main topic for serious conversation was the Kaiser's new-found liking for the Hungarian Prime Minister, Count Tisza, whose influence Franz Ferdinand disliked. The Kaiser and the Heir Apparent also discussed the visit, which was taking place that same weekend, of the Russian Tsar, to the Roumanian royal family at Constanta, on the Black Sea. The prospect of closer relations between Roumania and Russia was not to the liking of either the Hohenzollern or the Habsburg, both of whom were wary of Russia's influence in the Balkan region and along the Danube.

During their meeting at Konopischt, the Archduke also asked the Kaiser, but very much in passing, if Germany would still be willing, as the Kaiser had intimated during the Albanian crisis eight months earlier, to give Austria-Hungary her support in destroying the Serbian 'hornets' nest' from which, Austria was convinced, anti-Austrian feeling was being stirred up in Bosnia-Herzegovina. The Kaiser replied that Austria should 'do something' before the situation worsened. He doubted that Austria need fear Russian intervention on behalf of Serbia; the Russian army, he said, was not yet ready for war. Austrian action against Serbia, so it seemed to Franz Ferdinand, would have Germany's full support. The Kaiser left Konopiste and returned to his palace at Potsdam.

That weekend the Spanish government was again confronted in Morocco by the hostility of tribesmen whose independence it had repeatedly failed to subdue. 'Our intentions are peaceful,' a new High Commissioner, General Marina, declared. 'Our policy is to attract and fraternize with the Moors; but until this object is achieved, we must maintain ourselves in our positions, which we have occupied by the power and heroism of our army . . .'. On June 12, six months after General Marina had been sent, with extra troops, to 'conclude' the pacification of the Rif, his unsuccessful efforts were mocked by an opposition newspaper with the words: 'Six months of government. How many soldiers have returned home? How many more miles of territory are peacefully governed? How many Arabs have given in?'

That summer it might seem that the world's ills would be perpetually those of imperial conflicts; but a general unease was spreading in the minds of sovereigns and statesmen about the possibility of war in Europe. In May, Winston Churchill had been the guest of the King of Spain; driving together through the Spanish countryside the King suddenly asked his British guest: 'Mr Churchill, do you believe in this European war?' Churchill could only reply: 'Sir, sometimes I do, sometimes I don't.'

In Britain, the desire for naval security, if not superiority, was given a boost when Churchill, having returned to Britain, told the House of Commons on June 18 that the fuel oil needed for the most modern warships had been secured by Britain. Five years earlier, the Anglo-Persian Oil Company had obtained exclusive rights to extract oil, and prospect for oil, for the next sixty years. The British government negotiated with the oil company to become a majority shareholder, thereby securing for the next sixty years not only the oil that the warships would need, but any profit that might accrue from the sale of additional oil. In the event, the profit, like the gain in naval security, was considerable. 'The oil reserve,' Churchill told Parliament, 'obviated any fear of an oil famine in the first days of war.'

In the last week of June, the Kaiser was very much the central, and also the most bemedalled, figure at Kiel for the annual Elbe Regatta. 'Kiel Week', as it was known, was a time of races, dances and enjoyment. Although the newly opened Kiel Canal represented a German naval threat to Britain, opening as it did the North Sea to the swift transfer of German warships from the Baltic, a squadron of British warships (the one which Churchill had hoped to accompany in order to discuss naval arms reduction with Admiral Tirpitz) was present as an honoured guest. The four British battleships and three cruisers were moored alongside the German Imperial High Seas Fleet. Officers and men of both navies exchanged enthusiastic compliments as they went on board each other's ships to enjoy the pageantry. Together they stood bareheaded at the funeral of a British pilot killed in an air accident during the festivities.

On board his racing yacht *Meteor V*, the Kaiser was at the centre of the splendour of the regatta. On June 26, wearing his uniform as a British Admiral of the Fleet, the rank he had been accorded in the heyday of Anglo-German amity a decade earlier, he went on board the battleship *King George V*. Ironically, as an Admiral of the Fleet, he was the senior Royal Navy officer present.

Another royal highness who was inspecting troops that week was Archduke Franz Ferdinand, the heir to the throne of Austria-Hungary. As Inspector-General of the army, he was carrying out his task in Sarajevo, the capital of the annexed province of Bosnia. The Serbian Foreign Ministry had taken the unusual step of warning the Archduke that the visit was unwise, in view of pro-Serb agitation in Sarajevo. On June 28, as the Archduke's car was taking him and his wife, Sophie Chotek, Duchess of Hohenberg, to the town hall, a bomb was thrown at them, and exploded. They were unhurt by the blast, though one of the officers with them was wounded, and taken to the local hospital.

The unsuccessful bomb thrower had not been the only person lying in wait. The others in the plot with him, although dispirited by the failure of their colleague, bided their time. Franz Ferdinand continued with his programme. While at the town hall he decided to pay a visit to the bedside of the wounded officer. As he left the building another bomb was thrown at him, but did not explode. The Archduke continued on his way. As the car took a wrong turning, and then reversed, a third conspirator, Gavrilo Princip, was by chance at that very spot.

Princip had earlier been depressed when he had heard of the failure of the two previous attempts, and was taken by surprise when he saw the Archduke's car — which had not, of course, been scheduled to be on the way to the hospital. He at once drew his pistol and fired. Both the Archduke and his wife were hit; they died on the way to the hospital to which they had been going to give comfort to someone else.

Gavrilo Princip, the nineteen-year-old Serb student who shot Franz Ferdinand, was not a Serbian government agent, nor were his fellow would-be assassins. Nor was the Serbian government implicated in the crime. Indeed, the young men who carried out their assassination plan in Sarajevo belonged to a conspiratorial group that was in conflict with the Serbian government. Their patron was a Serbian army faction, the Black Hand; a group of officers determined to achieve the independence of the South Slav people from the Habsburg empire, who were acting independently of the army and in opposition to the government. Such factions were a common feature of Balkan political life at that time, in Greece as well as in Serbia. Even the head of the Black Hand, Colonel Dragutin Dimitrievic, known as Apis, had tried to halt the final preparations for the assassination, though he had done so in a half-hearted manner. It was through his military offices that the conspirators had first been trained, then armed — with weapons bearing the Serbian royal insignia — and smuggled across the Serbian frontier into Bosnia.

The Serbian army officers who supported the Black Hand were not themselves supported by their Commander-in-Chief, General Putnik. They had also suffered a political setback that spring, when a new government had been installed, led by Nicola Pašić, the head of the Serbian Radical Party, who was their implacable opponent. Four days before the assassination of the archduke, Pašić had called an election in Serbia, confident that he could retain his political ascendancy. The Black Hand, in as much as it had nurtured and encouraged the assassins before they crossed into Bosnia, was deeply at odds with the policies of the Serbian government, on which the full brunt of Austrian anger was about to fall.

The assassination of Franz Ferdinand, a shocking event in itself, was not dissimilar to many of the assassinations of the previous fourteen years. It proved, however, to be a turning point in the history of the twentieth century. Seven years later, the Czech novelist Jaroslav Hašek began his novel *The Good Soldier Schweik* with a satirical account of how the news of the assassination of the Archduke affected a particular denizen of Prague:

'So they've killed Ferdinand,' said the charwoman to Mr Schweik who, having left the army many years before, when a military medical board had declared him to be chronically feeble-minded, earned a livelihood by the sale of dogs – repulsive mongrel monstrosities for whom he forged pedigrees. Apart from this occupation, he was afflicted with rheumatism, and was just rubbing his knees with embrocation.

'Which Ferdinand, Mrs Müller?' asked Schweik, continuing to massage his knees. 'I know two Ferdinands. One of them does jobs for Prusa the chemist, and one day he drank a bottle of hair oil by mistake; and then there's Ferdinand Kokoska who goes round collecting manure. They wouldn't be any great loss, either of 'em.'

'No, it's the Archduke Ferdinand, the one from Konopiste, you know, Mr Schweik, the fat pious one.'

'Good Lord!' exclaimed Schweik, 'that's a fine thing. And where did this happen?'

'They shot him at Sarajevo with a revolver, you know. He was riding there with his Archduchess in a motorcar.'

'Just fancy that now, Mrs Müller, in a motorcar. Ah, a gentleman like him can afford it and he never thinks how a ride in a motor car like that can end up badly. And at Sarajevo in the bargain, that's in Bosnia, Mrs Müller. I expect the Turks did it. I reckon we never ought to have taken

Bosnia and Herzegovina away from them. And there you are, Mrs Müller. Now the Archduke's in a better land. Did he suffer long?'

'The Archduke was done for on the spot . . .'

Arthur Potocki, whose father had entertained the Archduke and his Duchess the previous year at Lancut, in Galicia, later recalled how the news of the assassination reached their estate in Austrian Poland:

After lunch my father was called to the telephone. He rejoined us looking shaken and told us that he had received the news that Archduke Franz Ferdinand and Duchess Sophie Hohenberg had been murdered. We talked and talked all through the afternoon under the shock of this horror.

Confirmation came a few hours later. We had tea, tried to play tennis but soon gave it up; there seemed nothing to do but talk. George took father for a drive. There was a muted air about everything. I think that most of us had the instant conviction that this was something more than an assassination, terrible though that was – something far more profound and convulsive.

Before and after dinner, which we had in the hall at nine o'clock, I walked in the gardens, wondering what might be the outcome. It was a beautiful evening with a high blue sky and a sunset like the mouth of a furnace. The air was sweet with the scent of flowers. These facts are noted in my diary; but I recollect no less clearly the emotional turmoil – all the more intense through being controlled – that possessed everybody in the castle.

There was nothing to do but wait for the newspapers next morning. They would give a full account of the murders and the public reaction to them; possibly also an official statement from the Government in Vienna. The newspapers, in fact, added little to our knowledge of the crime, nor were we able to measure its probable consequences. Father and I took up work early in the morning, and I remember reporting to him that out of 10,000 pheasants' eggs, nearly 7,000 had hatched out; which meant that there would be fine shoots later on.

In the British House of Commons, the Prime Minister, H. H. Asquith, described the murder of Franz Ferdinand as 'one of those incredible crimes which almost makes us despair of the progress of mankind'. There was an added sympathy in Britain for the Archduke, for on a visit to India twenty years earlier he had expressed his appreciation 'of the stupendous difficulty of governing a country as composite as the Austrian Empire'. The Austro-Hungarian Chief-of-Staff, Conrad von Hötzendorf, eager to find an excuse to attack Serbia, later said of the assassination that it 'was a godsend, or rather, a gift from Mars'. The Roman god of war was not, however, to be easily satisfied, or sated.

The Kaiser learned the news of the Archduke's assassination while he was at the Kiel regatta; a note of what had happened had been written out for him and thrown on to the royal yacht in a gold cigarette case. He returned at once to Berlin, where he was in a bellicose mood. 'The Serbs must be disposed of, *and* that right soon!' he noted in the margin of a telegram from his ambassador in Vienna on June 30. Against his ambassador's remark that 'only a mild punishment' might be imposed on Serbia, the Kaiser wrote, 'I hope not.'

The Kaiser's comments envisaged nothing more than a swift Austrian victory over Serbia, with no wider repercussions. That day, as the British naval squadron sailed from Kiel to return to Britain, the British admiral signalled to the German Fleet: 'Friends in the past, and friends for ever.' Also on June 30, Sir Arthur Nicolson, the senior civil servant at the British Foreign Office, wrote to the British Ambassador in St Petersburg, 'The tragedy which has just taken place in Sarajevo will not, I trust, lead to further complications.'

The German attitude towards Austria was crucial. On July 4 the German Ambassador to London, Prince Lichnowsky, having just returned from Berlin, told the former British Secretary of State for War, Lord Haldane, that he was 'very worried' about the state of opinion in Germany. 'The general feeling in Berlin,' Lichnowsky reported, was 'that Serbia could not be allowed to go on intriguing and agitating against Austria, and that Germany must support Austria in any action she proposed to take'. That same day the German Ambassador in Vienna, Count Tschirschky, told a senior Austrian official that Germany would support Austria-Hungary 'through thick and thin', and he added: 'The earlier Austria attacks the better. It would have been better to attack yesterday than today; and better to attack today than tomorrow.'

To this advice the Kaiser added, on July 5, an essential dimension of active German support, telling the Austrian Ambassador to Germany, Count Szogyeny, that Russia was 'in no way prepared for war' and that the Austrians would regret it if, having recognized the necessity of war against Serbia, 'we did not make use of the present moment, which is all in our favour'. The Kaiser added: 'Should war between Austria-Hungary and Russia prove unavoidable', Germany would be at Austria's side.

Later that day, while still at Potsdam, the Kaiser told the German Chancellor, Bethmann-Hollweg, and the Prussian War Minister, General Falkenhayn, that he 'did not believe that there was any prospect of great warlike developments. The Tsar would not side with the Archduke's murderers, and Russia and France were not ready for war.' For this reason, the Kaiser explained, 'there was no need to make special dispositions'. He then returned to Kiel and on the morning of July 6 departed in the imperial yacht *Hohenzollern* for his annual three-week summer cruise in Norwegian waters.

The European sovereigns, and many of their subjects, warmed by the July sunshine, were in the midst of summer activities of the most pacific, and even sybaritic sort.

CHAPTER SIXTEEN

ROADS TO WAR

The children born of thee are sword and fire
Red ruin, and the breaking up of laws

ALFRED, LORD TENNYSON

In its first weeks, the war crisis that broke out in the summer of 1914 did not seem to threaten many countries. Only in retrospect was it the start of the First World War. The two previous Balkan Wars, so fresh in the European memory, had been relatively limited in their scope both in regard to their geographic range and their human suffering. The previous conflicts involving European Powers, between Italy and Turkey, and between Russia and Japan, had in the same way been restricted in their scope. So confident were the Austro-Hungarian leaders that they could chastise Serbia without bringing down on their heads the wrath of their European rivals that, at a Cabinet meeting in Vienna on July 7, all but one of the eight members were in warlike mood, with the Austrian Foreign Minister, Count Berchtold, who presided, proposing an immediate armed attack on Serbia. The aim of such an attack, he and his colleagues were agreed, would be to reduce Serbia in size, territorially, and to make her dependent upon Austria; as Bosnia-Herzegovina had been for almost two decades. A deciding factor in the bellicose tone of the meeting was the Kaiser's assurance, two days earlier, that should war between Austria-Hungary and Russia prove unavoidable, 'Germany would be at Austria's side'. These six words were the immediate death knoll of wise counsel in Vienna, and the destruction, within a month, of peace in Europe.

The one voice of caution during the decisive July 7 Cabinet meeting in Vienna came from Count Tisza, who on the following day sent a formal written protest to Franz Josef, warning that any Austrian attack on Serbia 'would, in human possibility, provoke a world war'. Not only Russia, he warned, but also Roumania, with its territorial designs on Hungary's Transylvanian region, would be drawn into the conflict against the Habsburg lands. This would expose the fabric of the empire to a 'very unfavourable' prospect.

The German political leaders had no such hesitations. The Kaiser's mood, however provocative, infected all those who worked under him, and from whom they derived their positions and their influence. A key figure in the events that followed was the German Ambassador in Vienna, Count Tschirschky. When he called on Count Berchtold at the Austrian Foreign Ministry in the Ballhausplatz on July 7, Tschirschky stressed the German desire for Austria-Hungary to take action against Serbia. With the zeal of a diplomat at times of crisis, Tschirschky told Berchtold of a telegram that he had just received from Berlin – the cause of his visit to the Ballhausplatz – in which the Kaiser instructed him (as Berchtold reported to Count Tisza) 'to declare here, with all emphasis, that in Berlin an action against Serbia is expected, and that it would not be understood in Germany if we allowed the opportunity to pass without striking a blow'.

This was the spectre raised by Berlin: that the Germans would not 'understand' Austro-Hungarian caution, timidity, or – as a dispassionate observer might judge – sanity. The diplomats in the Wilhelmstrasse in Berlin had a different European perspective to that of the diplomats in the Ballhausplatz; and in the conflict between these two addresses, a conflict between allies, were sowed the seeds of war that would first see their alliance cemented, and then their empires shattered. For in the perspective of the German diplomats, politicians and court, it was Russia that was the great danger to their future dominance in Europe. Any chance to challenge Russia before she became even stronger was to be welcomed. Such a challenge required Austria-Hungary as an active partner. No pushing back of the Russian borders could take place without a major Austro-Hungarian commitment on the field of battle.

The German fear of a future Russian predominance was expressed privately on July 7 by Bethmann-Hollweg. 'The future lies with Russia,' he wrote, and he added: 'She grows and grows, and lies on us like a nightmare.' The nightmare of war tomorrow, it would seem, was less to be dreaded than the nightmare of a Russian hegemony in a decade's time. It was 'not only the extremists' in Berlin, Bethmann-Hollweg wrote on the following day to the German ambassador in London, Prince Lichnowsky, 'but even level-headed politicians, who are worried at the increases in Russian strength, and the imminence of Russian attack'.

Russia had no plans to attack the German or Habsburg Empires. Her army was large but cumbersome, her industries racked with discontent, her minorities, including those on her western borders, disaffected. But German fears of Russia stemmed from the age-old conflict between German and Slav, and the animosities and rivalries that were strong on both sides of the 900-mile border that stretched from the Baltic Sea to the Black Sea. A 500-year-old Russian jingle expressed the Russian side clearly enough:

> Russian, Russian, wake yourself up
> The German is coming, the uninvited guest.

As the pressure on Vienna from Berlin increased, the politicians and diplomats in London tried to calm the situation. They had no interest in pitting their naval strength against Germany, or in risking their very small professional army (Britain was the only European Power without military conscription) on the continent of Europe. On July 8, Sir Edward Grey asked Prince Lichnowsky to call on him at the Foreign Office. Answering the call, the German ambassador entered the door below the steps in Downing Street where today a plaque to Grey recalls his efforts as a peacemaker. Grey told Lichnowsky that, in the event of Austria-Hungary – inflamed as it was by the Sarajevo assassination – feeling that it must take up 'a stern attitude' towards Serbia, the British government was already trying to persuade the Russian government 'to adopt a calm view and a conciliatory attitude' towards Austria-Hungary.

Sir Edward Grey could not, however, offer the Germans a guarantee that Russia would take no action on behalf of Serbia. Indeed, he warned the German ambassador that Austria-Hungary might adopt measures against Serbia which would be so severe as to 'arouse Slav feeling' and make it impossible for Russia to remain 'passive'.

This was a perceptive warning; but it did not entirely reflect the seemingly less urgent counsels of Grey's own most senior adviser, Sir Arthur Nicolson, a diplomat of great experience and distinction. 'I have my doubts,' Nicolson wrote to the British ambassador in Vienna on July 9, 'as to whether Austria will take any action of a serious character, and I expect the storm will blow over.' But three days later the American ambassador in London, Walter H.

Page, wrote to President Wilson: 'Grey is greatly disturbed over the danger that comes of Serbian unrest against Austria. Both Russia and Germany are mobilizing on the south.'

On July 13 a secret report from Sarajevo reached the Austrian capital, stating that there was 'no evidence' to implicate the Serbian government in the assassination of the Archduke. In calmer times this report might have taken the pressure off the policy-makers in Vienna for punitive action against Serbia. The assassins could have been punished without implicating Belgrade, so there would be no call for action against a sovereign state. But calm was not the dominant feature of the Austrian mood towards Serbia. This was understood inside the British Foreign Office by a young official, Robert Vansittart, who wrote to his superiors that 'the unwisdom of a blindly anti-Serbian policy is not at all appreciated in Austria'. That, Vansittart believed, was 'the real point in a rather threatening situation'. The 'blindly anti-Serbian' policy was overriding the saner counsels that had in earlier years managed to restrain the Austrians from challenging the interests and the might of the Russian Empire, in order to punish and control the small Slav state that was so much, from their perspective, a thorn in their side.

Still there was no Austrian ultimatum to Serbia. How could there be, when those in power knew, from the secret report on July 13, that Serbia had not been directly involved in the assassination? There were also those who believed that knowledge of the dangers a European war would pose for all the inhabitants of the continent would be a restraining element as the crisis intensified. On July 16, in a talk in London on the international situation, Norman Angell, the man who had warned five years earlier that a European war would consume victors and vanquished alike, asserted that the younger generation 'are, I believe, increasingly determined not to be the victims of that supreme futility'.

The psychological desire for war was in conflict with the psychological imperative for peace. The distrust of Slav for German and German for Slav had not been assuaged by their respective leaders. The lives of millions were in the balance. The decision was to be made in Vienna, where the support of Berlin was regarded both as a spur and a security. The Austrian Council of Ministers, holding the power of peace or war, opted for neither. Instead, it decided to issue an ultimatum to Serbia, with various demands that would have to be met, or else the consequence would be war.

The decision to issue the ultimatum was made, in strictest secrecy, on July 14, but it was not to be delivered for a week. During that week, those who were not in the know continued to debate the rights and wrongs of Austria-Hungary's position as an aggrieved party. In London, the German ambassador was particularly scathing, writing in a private letter to Bethmann-Hollweg in Berlin, that the Austrian authorities had only themselves to blame for the Archduke's assassination; they had, after all, been the ones who sent him into 'an alley of bomb throwers' in Sarajevo, and had even ignored a warning from the Serbian Foreign Minister that the visit was unwise.

As soon as the leaders in Berlin were told that an Austrian ultimatum was about to be delivered against Serbia, they understood that the Serbs might reject whatever the Austrian demands might be. They saw that a war might ensue in which, once Austria had attacked Serbia, Russia would come to Serbia's defence. Germany would then be obliged, in accord with its alliance with Austria-Hungary, to attack Russia. But the obligation to make war on Russia did not worry those in Berlin who were aware of the imminent ultimatum. On July 17 the Deputy Chief of the German General Staff, who was at Bendlerstrasse in Berlin, wrote to the German Secretary of State, Gottlieb von Jagow, who was away from Berlin: 'I shall remain here ready to jump; we are all prepared at the General Staff'.

The German War Ministry building on Bendlerstrasse, just south of the Tiergarten, was humming with preparations and confidence, as was the Foreign Ministry on Wilhelmstrasse. While the citizens of the German and Austrian capitals went about the daily business of summer holidays and relaxation, the Wilhelmstrasse and the Bendlerstrasse in Berlin, and the Ballhausplatz in Vienna, were embarking on policies that would soon fill the streets with all the inflamed zeal of deeply felt patriotic fervour.

Far more than the public, the elite coterie of diplomats and politicians was aware of the dangers of a wider conflict emerging from the alliance system. Yet they also used their intellectual skills to push those dangers away, to rationalize, and to deceive themselves. Von Jagow, like his master the Kaiser, had come to the conclusion, despite Germany's desire to prevent, by war, a Russian hegemony, that Russia would not intervene in the dispute between Austria-Hungary and Serbia even if the Serbs rejected the ultimatum and Austria responded by declaring war. 'The more resolute Austria shows herself,' von Jagow informed the German Ambassador in London on July 18, 'and the more energetically we support her, the sooner will Russia stop her outcry. To be sure, they will make a great to-do in St Petersburg, but when all is said and done, Russia is at present not ready for war.'

In London, the voice of reason was also the voice of optimism. On July 23 the Chancellor of the Exchequer, David Lloyd George, who at the beginning of the year had authorized a considerable British naval expansion programme only with great reluctance, spoke with confidence of how what he called 'civilization' – a much-vaunted hallmark of the twentieth century – would have no difficulty in regulating the disputes that arose among nation states by means of what he called 'some sane and well-ordered arbitrament'. As for relations between Britain and Germany, he said, these were better than they had been for many years. His next budget would therefore need less money spent on armaments than the previous one.

The soothing words of such a passionate British Liberal, the architect only a few years earlier of wide-ranging social reforms that had not yet run their course, were deeply felt and in accordance with contemporary wisdom. Arbitration, not conflict, was the theme of Liberal Party policy in both domestic and international relations; it was the way forward by which not only British liberalism, but twentieth-century civilization, would show itself superior to the nineteenth century. On the evening of July 23, however, only a few hours after Lloyd George had spoken, the Austrian ultimatum was delivered in Belgrade.

Few documents have had such an impact on the twentieth century as the Austrian ultimatum to Serbia of 23 July 1914. The Treaty of Versailles five years later was undoubtedly another; Hitler's *Mein Kampf*, so deeply meant and at first so little read, was certainly a third. The Austrian ultimatum had been finalized four days before it was sent. It was based on the belief, expressed at the Austrian Council of Ministers meeting on July 19, that Serbia would reject the terms, and that Austrian military action against Serbia would follow. It was assumed that this action would be swift and successful: that Serbia could be defeated before any of the wider repercussions, which had been so much discussed in previous weeks, occurred.

In Vienna, one of those who was keen that the ultimatum should be rejected, and that Austrian forces should march into Serbia – the Serbian capital, Belgrade, lay just opposite the Austro-Hungarian shore of the Danube – was Conrad von Hötzendorf. He was Chief of the Austro-Hungarian General Staff, and was determined that Austria-Hungary would acquire considerable Serb territory.

*   *   *

Franz Josef had accepted the terms of the ultimatum three days after the Austrian Council of Ministers had approved it. The terms, as delivered in Belgrade on the evening of July 23, were wide-ranging. Linking the Belgrade government with the assassination – something that the secret report had specifically denied – the ultimatum consisted of a total of fifteen demands. The Serbian government must commit itself to condemnation of anti-Austrian propaganda. There must be a joint Austro-Serbian commission to investigate the Archduke's murder. There must be a Serbian army order condemning the Serbian military involvement with the murders. There must also be a firm Serbian promise of no further Serbian intrigue in Bosnia. Serbia would also have to give an undertaking to punish anyone who circulated anti-Austrian propaganda, either in schools or in the various nationalist societies. In addition, Austrian officials would participate in the judicial process, and in the process of punishment, of those connected with the plot.

Whether one sovereign State could accept such stern demands from another was much debated. Edward Grey, one of the arbiters of the Liberal conscience, went so far as to call it 'the most formidable document that was ever addressed from one State to another'. In strictest secrecy the Russian government agreed to the mobilization of thirteen army corps to be used 'eventually' against Austria-Hungary, should Austria declare war on Serbia. In a public announcement the Russian government declared that Russia 'cannot remain indifferent' to the Austro-Serbian crisis. There was a new-found scepticism among British diplomats that, if the war widened beyond the Balkans, Britain would be able to stay clear of it. 'We shall be lucky,' one British diplomat wrote to his wife two hours before the Austrian ultimatum was due to expire, 'if we get out of this without the long-dreaded European war, a general bust-up in fact'.

Anticipating a Serbian rejection of the ultimatum, Franz Josef ordered partial mobilization of the Austro-Hungarian forces, to start three days later; even partial mobilization was a process that, given the size of the Habsburg empire and the complexity of its war machinery, would take sixteen days to complete.

Serbia also mobilized, at three o'clock on the afternoon of July 25; but the Serbian government understood that even if Russia were in due course to enter the war against Austria-Hungary, Serbia's ability to resist an onslaught across her exposed eastern frontier, or even across the Danube against the capital, was limited. She therefore replied to the ultimatum in conciliatory tone. Everything demanded of her was agreed; the only qualification regarded the Austrian demand – certainly the most controversial of all – that Austrian officials would participate in the judicial process, and in the process of punishment, of those connected with the assassination. This demand, the Serbians asked, should be submitted to the International Tribunal at The Hague. If the tribunal accepted its legality, then Serbia would agree to it.

In Austria-Hungary it was assumed that it was only a matter of days before war with Serbia. 'For the first time in thirty years,' Sigmund Freud wrote in letter to a friend, 'I feel myself to be an Austrian and feel like giving this not very hopeful Empire another chance. Morale is excellent everywhere. Also the liberating effect of courageous action, and the secure prop of Germany, contribute a great deal to this.'

It was the Russian Tsar who took the initiative in trying to turn the Serbian reply into the basis of a reduction of tension and a withdrawal from the brink of conflict. The Tsar's proposal, made on July 27, was that negotiations should begin on the basis of the Serbian reply. The Austrian government rejected this proposal; they wanted full compliance to their ultimatum, without even that one condition, or they would go to war.

In every European capital the diplomatic manoeuvres were followed from day to day, and with a constantly changing focus. In Paris, on July 27, André Gide noted in his journal 'a certain easing of the strain this morning. People are relieved and at the same time disappointed to hear that Serbia is giving in'. But on the following day, while at Dieppe, he recorded that the hotel buses were 'loaded with the trunks of departing guests. Everyone expects the worst'.

The British government, like the Tsar, sought some way whereby talking rather than fighting would follow the Austrian ultimatum and the Serbian reply. What concerned Britain was the spread of the conflict beyond the Balkans, and the drawing in of Russia's ally France, exposing Britain to the need to support – or to abandon – France in its hour of need. The lack of any binding alliance with France meant that the British parliament might have the power, or the Cabinet the will, to insist upon neutrality in the case of a German attack on France. But public opinion in Britain could easily be roused by any German action against France to demand an active British response. To avert such a development, and the possible drawing in of Britain to a continental war, the British government proposed that day a four-Power conference of Britain, France, Italy and Germany, 'for the purpose of discovering an issue which would prevent complications'.

The Kaiser, fired up by the thought of a swift defeat of Russia, and oblivious to what might happen to his own country, to his rule and his dynasty if there were to be such 'complications' – and with them a two-front war – refused to accept the British call for a conference. A reply was returned from Berlin to London that such a conference was 'not practicable'. Even the British understood at last that despite their lack of treaty entanglements they too might be drawn in to the conflict. On the day of the German rejection of a conference, the British War Office instructed a senior general to take immediate measures to guard what were characterized as 'all vulnerable points' in southern Britain. Armed guards were also put on ammunitions dumps and oil storage depots throughout Britain.

In Berlin, the German government, whose pledge of support for Austria had been the crucial factor in the initial Austrian resolve to issue an ultimatum, now pressed the Austrians to strike at Serbia before any wider complications ensued. 'We are urgently advised to act at once and face the world with a *fait accompli*,' the Austrian ambassador in Berlin informed his masters in Vienna by telegram on July 28. When the Austrians pointed out to the Germans that it would be another two weeks before the Austrian mobilization was completed, and before an attack on Serbia could begin in optimum military conditions, the Germans pressed Austria not to wait so long. The mood in Berlin was clear and bellicose, but not untinged with panic; Austria must crush Serbia before the Russians could respond, and before Germany herself could be drawn in – as a result, not of her national interest, but of her alliance with Austria.

The mood in Vienna was for war with Serbia, so much so that on July 28 the British ambassador in Vienna, a diplomat of wide experience, informed London that 'postponement or prevention of war with Serbia would undoubtedly be a great disappointment in this country, which has gone wild with joy at the prospect of war'. The war envisaged by the Austrians, and causing the joy, was perceived as a swift and victorious one, more like a colonial expedition (Austria-Hungary having no colonies) than a struggle between equals; Serbia was a small, vexacious State with pretensions of grandeur that must be 'taught a lesson' once and for all, and if Serbian territory along the Austrian southern border were to be annexed as a result, so much the better.

There remained the question of how the Austrians would respond to the

Serbian reply to their ultimatum. The first Austrian instinct was to withdraw their ambassador to Serbia, Baron Giesl, from Belgrade, as a sign of their extreme displeasure. For their part, the Serbs, fearing an immediate Austrian attack across the Danube on Belgrade, withdrew their government to the southern city of Nis and their General Staff to the town of Kragujevac, seventy miles south of Belgrade. In a train approaching Budapest, Hungarian detectives arrested the Serbian Chief-of-Staff, General Putnik, who was on his way by train back to Serbia, and was being subjected to hostile demonstrations at the stations through which he passed.

Putnik had been taking the waters at a Bohemian spa, for the sake of his health, which was not good. After his arrest in the train he was held in Budapest under double guard with fixed bayonets. At Franz Josef's insistence, however, he was released, and escorted to the frontier with a considerable show of respect due to a military leader of a neighbouring State, and the victor of two Balkan Wars (an asthmatic, he was said to have gone through the Turkish campaign in his carpet slippers).

General Putnik's detention in Budapest, and his return to Serbia, caused a stir in the European press, and first consternation and then relief in Serbia; but the question that came to dominate all political and news-paper speculation was the Serbian reply to Austria. Did such an essentially conciliatory reply really provide a cause for war? Suddenly even theKaiser had his doubts, which he expressed in private, and in his own colourful prose, on the morning of July 28, when finally he read the full text of the Serbian reply (of three days earlier). Reading it side by side with the full text of the Austrian ultimatum, he could see no reason why Austria should embark on a full-scale war. 'A great moral victory for Vienna,' he wrote in the margin of his copy of the Serbian reply, 'but with it every reason for war is removed and Giesl ought to remain quietly in Belgrade. On the strength of this we should never have ordered mobilization.'

Having blown hot for so many days, the Kaiser suddenly blew cold. A full-scale Austrian invasion of Serbia was not needed; all that was necessary, he wrote, was that 'as a visible *satisfaction d'honneur* for Austria, the Austrian army should temporarily occupy Belgrade as a pledge'. Then negotiations could begin to end the brief military conflict. 'I am convinced,' the Kaiser wrote to von Jagow, 'that on the whole the wishes of the Danube monarchy have been acceded to. The few reservations that Serbia makes in regard to individual points can in my opinion be well cleared up by negotiations. But it contains the announcement *orbi et urbi* of a capitulation of the most humiliating kind, and with it every reason for war is removed.'

It was too late for such conciliatory counsel. At noon that day, scarcely an hour after the Kaiser penned these un-bellicose words, Austria declared war on Serbia, confident of German support if the war widened. The declaration of war was sent by Count Berchtold, not, as would have been usual, to the Serbian Foreign Ministry at Belgrade, but to the Serbian General Staff at Kragujevac, informing the Serbians that, as from the time of the despatch of the telegram from Vienna, 11.10 in the morning on July 28, 'the Royal Government of Serbia not having replied in a satisfactory manner to the Note which was sent to them on July 23, the Imperial and Royal Government finds itself obliged to provide for the safeguarding of its rights and interests, and for this purpose to have recourse to force of arms. Austria-Hungary therefore regards herself from this moment as in a state of war with Serbia.'

This telegram reached the Serbian General Staff one hour and forty minutes later. Although Serbian mobilization was not yet complete, strenuous efforts had been made to provide a military force that could defend Belgrade from any sudden attack. There were those who, watching the first moments of the Austro-Serbian war from afar, believed that had the Austrians launched an attack on Belgrade at once, they could have captured the city with a single battalion. But even in those opening hours, as many as 20,000 Serb soldiers and volunteers were being mustered outside the city, and on the day of the Austrian declaration of war a force of 10,000 men and 24 cannon was within marching distance of the capital. The Austrians hesitated to strike, and by their hesitation lost a chance to make a spectacular conquest, though whether they could have held Belgrade with the forces then available to them, once the Serb defence force had arrived, was an open question. It was not one which the Austrian General Staff wished to put to the test.

Serbia, weakened as she was by the bloodletting of the two Balkan wars, and short as she was of war material which was still in the process of being manufactured, mostly abroad, had the incentive of the defence of their native soil, and of the capital, as a spur to tenacious action. The Austrians, recognizing this, decided to strike instead across the River Drina, which had served for more than fifty miles as the border between Austrian-annexed Bosnia-Herzegovina and Serbia. It was the land across the Drina that Austria hoped to annex from Serbia, thus enlarging her Bosnian province.

An ambitious plan had been devised in Vienna, whereby, avoiding any attack on Belgrade, the Austrian army would cross the Drina and advance into the centre of Serbia, seizing the two principal towns of the region, Valievo and Kragujevac, and cutting Belgrade off from the south of the country. Austria, for all its talk of war, and its ultimatum, was not ready to launch this attack at the time of the declaration of war on July 28. It was to be more than a week before any forward military move could be attempted. This gave the Serbs invaluable time to prepare their defences and their strategy. Meanwhile, the Powers were no longer content to watch and warn; following the Austrian declaration of war, each Power had begun to contemplate military action of its own.

The Austrian declaration of war, leading as it did to no military advance and no battles on the ground, and to no immediate loss of Serb territory, did not necessarily call for the rushing forward of new combatants. Russia and Germany, despite their continuing preparations, were not inexorably bound to come to blows, and were far from ready to do so. In what way would the war widen? Winston Churchill, on whom the responsibility for Britain's naval war would rest, wrote to his wife on learning of the Austrian declaration of war on Serbia: 'I wondered whether those stupid Kings and Emperors could not assemble together and revivify kingship by saving the nations from hell but we all drift on in a kind of dull cataleptic trance. As if it was somebody else's operation.'

Following up this late-night thought, on the morning of July 29 Churchill proposed in the British Cabinet that a conference should be convened of all the European sovereigns, who should 'be brought together for the sake of peace'. It was a central fact of European life that the Kaiser and the Tsar, and King George V and the Tsar, and the Kaiser and King George V, were kinsmen; and that their family links were those of social and personal friendship. Surely families would not go to war with each other, however much their public opinions might be roused to nationalistic fervour?

On July 29, the day after the Austrian declaration of war on Serbia, and the day of Churchill's suggestion for a conference of European royalty, the Kaiser's brother, Prince Henry of Prussia, who was at that moment enjoying the pleasures of yachting in British waters, called on his cousin King George V at Buckingham Palace. The King told him, so the Prince reported to his brother in Berlin, 'We shall all try to keep out of this, and shall remain neutral.' When Admiral Tirpitz told the Kaiser that he doubted that Britain would in fact remain neutral, the Kaiser, basing himself on his brother's report, told the admiral: 'I have the word of a King, and that is good enough for me.' But even if George V had given his word, which seems unlikely (he certainly had no constitutional right to do so), that would only serve to liberate Germany to attack France without any British reaction. It would not prevent the entry of Germany into a European war, only limit the repercussions of German entry.

The attraction to the Kaiser of a war limited in this way made a Franco-German conflict all the more likely. No longer fearing a British intervention, Germany could contemplate defeating France first, and then turning on Russia. This had been the basis of General von Schlieffen's plan a decade earlier. The war would be widened in the expectation of then containing, and winning, it. But in widening the war by drawing in France, the conflict would in reality be on the verge of an even greater extension. British neutrality, so confidently presumed by the Kaiser, and so keenly hoped for by a majority in the Cabinet room in London, was not the outcome which British public opinion and street fervour, worked up by the mass-circulation newspapers, seemed to favour. There was also a wild card: the German military plan for the swift defeat of France depended upon a rapid movement of German forces through Belgium.

The route through Belgium had been chosen by General von Schlieffen to create the greatest surprise for France, and to by-pass the line of French fortresses defending the eastern approaches. Belgium was unlikely to put up a prolonged fight against the overwhelmingly strong forces of Germany; but her neutrality was protected by a treaty dating back more than sixty years. One of the signatories of that all-but-forgotten treaty was Britain. In striking at France across Belgian soil, the Kaiser had to convince himself that Britain would not honour a Treaty to which she had affixed her seal.

Any true, or only partial, understanding of the realities even of a limited war was eclipsed in the European public mind by the growing fervour of the mass of the population, themselves drawn from every segment of each society, from working men whose traditional ideology was antiwar, to shopkeepers and professional men and women whose sons would be among the first to be sent to the war fronts. When, during July 29, the German Crown Prince arrived at his palace in Berlin by car, a British diplomat who happened to witness the scene reported to London: 'The crowd cheered wildly. There was an indescribable feeling of excitement in the air. It was evident that some great event was about to happen'.

That 'great event' was imminent. During July 29 the Austrian naval flotilla on the Danube opened fire on Belgrade. The Tsar panicked. 'To try to avoid such a calamity as a European war,' he telegraphed (in English) to the Kaiser, 'I beg you in the name of our old friendship to do what you can to stop your allies from going too far.' But those allies, Austria-Hungary, were not to be restrained, even if the Kaiser felt able to try to restrain them. His reply – 'I am exerting my utmost influence to induce the Austrians to arrive at a satisfactory understanding with you' – showed how far he was out of touch with the warlike mood in Austria to which, less than three weeks earlier, he had himself contributed so much; and ignored, too, the warlike mood in Berlin, to which he had also been a principal contributor.

The Tsar was doing his utmost to keep Russia out of the war. That same day, July 29, he suggested to the Kaiser that the whole 'Austro-Serbian' problem, towards which both Germany and Russia had contributed their exacerbatory efforts, should be handed over to the International Court at The Hague – the very body which Serbia had sought to enlist as the arbiter of its sole disputed item in the Austrian ultimatum. The Kaiser was also casting about for means of keeping out of the war, now that Austrian guns had opened fire on the Serbian capital. His idea, which he communicated late that evening to the Tsar, was that Russia should 'remain a spectator of the Austro-Serbian conflict', thereby sparing Europe 'the most horrible war she has ever witnessed'.

A note of stark realism had entered into the correspondence between the two imperial rulers at the very moment when their respective countries were about to hurl themselves at each other's throats. The Tsar, to prove his pacific intentions, cancelled Russia's order for general mobilization. But the German General Staff refused a surprise suggestion by the Kaiser that Germany respond in similar vein. War Offices with their plans and hierarchies of command, not palaces with their volatile sovereigns, were in command of the situation in St Petersburg and Berlin. The Tsar was quickly prevailed upon to augment the mobilization measures that he had just reduced, for fear, his advisers insisted, that unless he did so, and brought yet more Russians under arms, the Polish provinces of the Russian Empire would be at risk of a German annexation.

'Monarchy and privilege and pride will have it out before they die – at what a cost!' the American ambassador in London, Walter H. Page, wrote to President Wilson on July 29. 'If they do have a general war they will set back the march of progress in Europe as to set the day forward for American leadership. Men here see that clearly. Even in this kingdom every ship is ready, every crew on duty, and every officer of the Admiralty office in London sleeps with a telephone by his bed which he expects to ring, and the telegraph men are at their instruments every minute.'

Page added: 'It's the Slav and the German. Each wants his day, and neither has got beyond the stage of tooth and claw.' Page's wife had just spoken to Prince Henry of Prussia 'who wishes to fight' – Page informed Wilson – 'who talks like a medieval man, and so loves the blood of his enemies that, if he can first kill enough of them, he is willing to be whipped. He went home last night.'

One last struggle took place in Berlin between those who felt the situation could still be restricted to an Austro-Serbian war, and those who anticipated, and did not shrink from, a much wider conflict. On the morning of July 31, Bethmann-Hollweg, once peace-loving, next bellicose, and then peace-loving (or war-fearing) again, telegraphed to Count Berchtold in Vienna, pressing the Austrians not to mobilize against Russia. That same morning, however, the Chief of the German General Staff, General von Moltke, in a message to his opposite number in Vienna, advised the Austrians to mobilize against Russia at once. 'Who rules in Berlin, Moltke or Beth-mann?' was Berchtold's wry question. The answer was that von Moltke ruled in Berlin. In vain did the German industrialist Walther Rathenau write in the *Berliner Tageblatt* that day: 'The government has left us in no doubt of the fact that Germany is intent on remaining loyal to her old ally. Without the protection of this loyalty, Austria could not have ventured on the step she has taken. Such a question as the participation of Austrian officials in investigating the Serbian plot is no reason for an international war.'

Two years later, Rathenau recalled the mood of July 31 in Berlin. 'Rejoicing in July sunshine,' he wrote, 'the prosperous and happy populace of Berlin responded to the summons of war. Brightly clad, with flashing eyes, the living and those consecrated to death felt themselves to be at the zenith of vital power and political existence . . . I could not share in the pride of the sacrifice of power. Nevertheless, this delirious exaltation seemed to me a dance of death, the overture to a doom which I had foreseen would be dark and dreadful.'

That day, confident of active German military support, Austria mobilized. The German government then made the first of its moves in direct support of Austria, sending an ultimatum to Russia to 'cease every war measure against us and Austria-Hungary' within twelve hours. Russia rejected this ultimatum.

The Kaiser and his General Staff prepared to go to war against Russia. One obstacle remained, the ten-year-old alliance between France and Russia. Germany therefore asked France to state categorically that she would remain neutral in the event of a war between Germany and Russia. But France declined to abandon her alliance with Russia, or to give Germany a free hand in marching eastward. Within hours, the orders went out to more than four million Frenchmen to make their way to their barracks.

In Paris, the socialist leader and parliamentarian Jean Jaurès had called repeatedly for the solidarity of all European socialists against war. On July 31 he was assassinated by a French nationalist fanatic. Fanaticism was becoming usual. In Munich that day, among a crowd clamouring for war, and for the chance to serve in the German army, Adolf Hitler was photographed gesticulating, hat in hand. In Paris, the crowds cheered as the cavalrymen rode by, and enthusiastic cries of 'To Berlin!' rent the air.

CHAPTER SEVENTEEN

WAR

The air is full of farewells to the dying,
And mournings for the dead;
The heart of Rachel, for her children crying,
Will not be comforted!

H. W. LONGFELLOW

THE ARMIES OF CONSCRIPTS and reservists were on the move, slowly but inexorably gathering in their barracks and being made ready to take up war stations. As well as four million French soldiers, six million Austrians had received their summons. Millions of Germans were likewise on the move. Only Britain, still uncommitted to enter the European conflict, lacked the numbers of men to contribute to the very real impression of vast forces on the move; but despite Britain's persistent neutrality, her warships were being made more and more ready for action with each passing hour.

The exhilaration in every capital, and in thousands of towns and villages, of nationalist fervour stimulated one last gasp of pacific and conciliatory activity. On August 1, the Tsar appealed for a second time to the Kaiser. 'Our long-proved friendship must succeed, with God's help, in avoiding bloodshed,' he telegraphed. The Kaiser, while determined to be the ally in arms of Austria-Hungary, still hoped to limit the conflict in the West. That day he grasped at the straw of a diplomatic message from his ambassador in London, Count Lichnowsky – a man who dreaded war between Britain and Germany. This straw was the hope that Britain would be prepared to remain neutral, and to guarantee French neutrality in the event of a German-Russian war, provided Germany would promise not to attack France in the West.

'So now we need only wage war against Russia,' the Kaiser told his Chief-of-Staff, von Moltke. 'We simply advance with the whole army in the East.' But von Moltke was not prepared to allow his sovereign to follow up this suggestion. The plan to defeat France before turning on Russia was already in operation, he pointed out. A German division was about to cross the frontier into Luxembourg and seize one of the railway lines essential for the German invasion of France. The troops whose task this was, and who had received their orders to march across the border, were already at Trier, and some had even crossed the border – by motorcar – into Luxembourg, seizing the village of Trois Vièrges.

The German army was in control of these military movements, and with them, of the imminent widening of the war. But the volatile Kaiser, in a final act aimed at finding a way out of the wider war, ordered the troops to leave Trois Vierges and return across the frontier back into Germany. All military operations were then halted. But within a few hours the Kaiser changed his mind. His Anglo-French neutrality plan was an illusion; it had no substance that day as diplomatic manoeuvring became increasingly harsh and uncompromising. It was eleven at night on August 1; the troops at Trier, the Kaiser ordered, should resume their advance westward.

With Luxembourg again the object of a German advance, it seemed only a matter of time before Belgium was attacked. Frenzied telegrams were sent from London to Berlin and St Petersburg on the evening of August 1, on the initiative of George V, pleading for 'a little respite in time' before any of the Powers declared war on a neighbour. But the telegrams were sent too late. At the very moment when the Kaiser ordered his troops at Trier to recross the border into Luxembourg, and to march as soon as possible after that across the border into France, the German ambassador in St Petersburg went to see the Russian Foreign Minister, and presented to him the German declaration of war on Russia. Germany had taken the step that her more cautious – some would say her wiser – military planners had long dreaded: a war on two fronts.

Kings and Emperors were powerless to influence events. Until a few months earlier both the Kaiser and the Tsar had seemed like autocrats whose word was law. The war crisis swept aside even the most autocratic sovereign's powers. Politicians and soldiers were the new autocrats. The delivery of ultimatums, the mobilization of armies, the declarations of war, and the crossing of frontiers, had become the primary domain of Prime Ministers, Foreign Secretaries, Ministers of War, Cabinets and Chiefs-of-Staffs. Neither sovereigns nor parliaments were part of the structures of power that, having evolved in the nineteenth century, were now imposing their conflicting ambitions, plans and prejudices on the twentieth century. 'Three hundred million people today lie under the spell of fear and fate,' a London evening newspaper editorial declared on August 1, and it went on to ask, 'Is there no one to break the spell, no gleam of light on this cold, dark scene?' The answer, to all intents and purposes, was no.

On August 2 André Gide reached Paris from the countryside. 'Crowds on the platform, both serious and vibrant,' he wrote. 'A workman shouts as he goes by: "All aboard for Berlin! And what fun we'll have there!" People smiled but did not applaud.' That morning a train carrying German soldiers entered Luxembourg. Other German soldiers seized all the railway stations on the line from Trier to Spa, and entered the principal army barracks in the Duchy. The Grand Duchess of Luxembourg protested; the German action was a violation of the Treaty of London of 1867. But the Germans remained in her capital, and no Entente army ever reached the region to drive them out. The Germans agreed to pay compensation for such crops and property as were damaged by German troops; the local civil administration was allowed to continue; but a strict German censorship was imposed on all postal, telegraphic and telephone services in the Duchy. Tiny Luxembourg was the only country fully conquered by Germany during the First World War.

At five o'clock on the afternoon of August 2, even as Luxembourg fell under German control, the senior German diplomat in Brussels, Herr von Below, presented an ultimatum from his government to the Belgian Foreign Minister. The Germans demanded that Belgium should allow German troops to pass through her territory, and that in return Germany would 'maintain the independence of Belgium and her possessions'. In the event of a Belgian refusal to allow the passage of German troops (an indispensable precondition for the success of the German defeat of France, according to the long-cherished Schlieffen Plan), Germany would 'treat Belgium as an enemy'.

The Belgian government was given twelve hours to reply: until five on the following morning. A Belgian Council of State was summoned at once; it was in session throughout the night, and decided, at four in the morning, that the Belgian reply would be a 'dignified and eloquent' refusal. Belgium had no intention of giving way to superior force. 'A nation which defends itself,' King Albert later told the Belgian parliament, 'commands the respect of all. Such a nation cannot perish.' Overnight, the British public and press, in whose affections Belgium had no particularly high place, were fulsome in their praise of Belgian courage, and in their contempt for the cynicism of German power.

German troops had made a number of sorties across the French frontier on August 2. On the morning of August 3, after the Belgian refusal to let German troops march across Belgian soil had been received in Berlin, Germany declared war on France, and prepared to move into Belgium. The sweep towards Paris – the essential lightning blow to avert the need to fight a war on two fronts, east and west, at the same time – was imminent. Belgium's neutrality was also about to be violated; this, not the German invasion of France, gave Britain the right by international treaty to declare war on Germany. These treaty rights, reinforced by an upsurge of moral indignation, underpinned the British note which was sent to Berlin. If German troops were to cross the Belgian border, the note warned, Britain would be forced to declare war on Germany. The Kaiser was unperturbed. That night the American ambassador in London, Walter H. Page, wrote to President Wilson:

In one way at least race-hatred is at the bottom of it – the Slav against the Teuton. The time to have that fight out seems favourable to Russia; the old Austrian Emperor is in his last years, the Slav States of his empire are restive, not to say rebellious, England may be drawn in now to help weaken Germany, Russia feels the need of a patriotic race cry at this stage of her growth and the need of a war to cause forgetfulness of the Russian-Japanese disaster.

I am told, too, that the Tsar – as, of course, most of his subjects – is really superstitious and that miracle-working priests – a sort of modern soothsayers – have a great influence over him; and of course the military party know how to use such machinery.

We have to stop and think of such absurd things as this to realize the deplorable mediaevalism of a large part of Europe and to understand why the criminal folly and the economic suicide of war do not have more effect on them. Russians, Germans, and even Frenchmen are, moreover, yet in that stage of evolution where the 'glory' of war makes a strong appeal to them.

On August 3 the German army moved across the Belgian border at five separate points. Another war zone had been created, and the names of yet more hitherto unknown villages – like Trois Vierges in Luxembourg –

became, for a few hours, familiar to the reading public on every continent.[1] When, at the small Belgian town of Visé, German troops were fired on by Belgian civilians, the German officer in command gave the order that the town was to be burned down. His order was obeyed. In Munich, a Habsburg subject, Adolf Hitler, petitioned the King of Bavaria to allow him to enlist in a Bavarian regiment. 'The Cabinet Office in those days certainly had its hands pretty full,' Hitler later wrote, 'and my joy was all the greater when my petition was granted the same day.'

Britain's ultimatum could no longer be delayed. The Germans must respect Belgian neutrality, the British government warned Berlin on the morning of August 4, or Britain would declare war. It would do so according to the Treaty of 1830, an eighty-four-year-old diplomatic document and solemn pledge, in which Britain and Prussia had been among the Powers acknowledging Belgian independence, and which had been endorsed in writing in 1870. A formal assurance from Germany, sent through the ambassador in London, promising that Germany would not 'under any pretext whatever' annex Belgian territory, was ignored.

The British ultimatum had not yet expired. During August 4, British minelayers in the English Channel laid mines in the expectation that, in the event of an Anglo-German war, German warships would try to enter the Channel and prevent the passage of British troops to France. Among the ships held up by the mining operations was one that had come from South Africa; among those on board was M. K. Gandhi. When war came, despite the reluctance of many Indian nationalists to become involved in what they considered an imperial conflict, Gandhi was to advise Indians living in Britain to 'take their share in the war'.

The British ultimatum was due to expire at eleven o'clock on the evening of August 4. Ignoring it, the German army continued to advance through Belgium. At eleven o'clock precisely the British government declared war on Germany. By midnight, five European empires were at war: Austria-Hungary against Serbia and Russia; Russia against Austria-Hungary and Germany; Germany against Russia, France, Belgium and Britain; France against Germany, and Britain against Germany.

[1] The German army entered Belgian territory on 3 August 1914 at Gemmenich (near Aachen), at Stavelot and Francorchamps (just south of Spa), at Dolhain (between Verviers and Herbesthal) and at Visé, on the River Meuse (between Maastricht and Liège).

Turkey and Italy bided their time, the Turks being tempted and pressured to join the Central Powers, Italy waiting to see which bloc would gain the ascendant. The soldiers of every Power at war moved to the war zones, the infantrymen and cavalrymen to fight, the artillery men to give them support, tens of thousands more to supply their transport, food and munitions needs. On August 15 a correspondent of *The Times* watched British troops who had just crossed to France, marching to their camps above Boulogne:

Watch them as they pass, every man in the prime of life, not a youth or stripling among them. Their shirts are open at the front, and as they shout you can see the working of the muscles of their throats, their wide-open mouths and rows of dazzling teeth. Every movement spells fitness for the field, for long marches by day and longer nights in the trenches.

I can see them again, with their brown, jolly faces, full of laughter, and hear them still shouting and singing, 'It's a long way to Tipperary, it's a long way to go,' while the officers, with the quiet, confident smiles ride between, raising hands in salute to their French comrades in arms on the pavements.

This morning's *France du Nord* says with justice: 'The gallant bearing of the men, their gaiety, fine looks, muscular appearance, as well as their splendid conduct, are of happy augury.' If physical strength and a happy disposition, added to fine training, can win the day, these troops will add many a battle name to their roll of victories.

A wonderful invasion. How many more thousands are to come no one knows. Transport after transport glides into the harbour or ranges along the quay where the Folkestone boats lie, and out they come each man neat and clean, as for parade, hard and fit.

Japan, her imperial ambitions stimulated at the thought of easy conquests, hesitated for less than two weeks, and on August 17 issued an ultimatum against Germany, citing her commitment to Britain under the Anglo-Japanese alliance of 1905, and demanding both the withdrawal of the German Far Eastern Fleet and the surrender of the German port city of Kiaochow. The Japanese government gave the Germans six days to reply, but the Germans declined to do so, the Kaiser telegraphing to the German governor of Kiaochow: 'It would shame me more to surrender Kiaochow to the Japanese than Berlin to the Russians'.

This patriotic assertion was to no practical avail. On August 23 Japan declared war on Germany, and that same day lay siege to Kiaochow, which had been reinforced by the German garrison in Peking. A siege ensued in which Japan's ally, Britain, sent a force of 910 Welsh and 450 Sikh soldiers commanded by a British general. The Japanese committed 22,980 men to the siege. The German force was, at its largest, 5000 men. On November 7, as a massive onslaught was being prepared, the garrison surrendered. In contrast with the fate of the prisoners of war taken by Japan in the Second World War, those taken captive at Kiaochow were well-treated.

It was not only Kiaochow that was lost by Germany to Japan in the opening months of the First World War; the German islands of the Pacific Ocean could hardly be defended by a nation that was at war on two fronts in Europe, and on October 6 Japanese troops occupied four Pacific island groups: Palau, the Marianas, the Carolines and the Marshalls (Australian and New Zealand troops had already occupied all the German island groups further to the south).

One German initiative was the sinking by the German Pacific Squadron of several hundred tons of Allied shipping, and the bombardment of a British wireless cable station at Samoa on September 10 as well as a French shore station at Papeete twelve days later. The commander of this force was Admiral von Spee. When he reached the remote shores of Easter Island, the British overseer there, who had not yet received news of the outbreak of war, willingly supplied him with fresh water and fresh meat for his onward voyage, and let him rest there for six days.[1]

On November 1, off the coast of Chile, at the Battle of Coronel, von Spee defeated a British naval force, sinking two British battle cruisers. No German sailors were killed in the action; 1440 British sailors were drowned, including the commander, Admiral Cradock, who, as a naval captain, had been in action in the capture of the Taku forts during the Boxer rebellion of 1900. Five weeks after Cradock's defeat at Coronel, von Spee himself was defeated at the Battle of the Falkland Islands on December 8, when two of his battle cruisers and two of his light cruisers – all but one of his heavy ships – were sunk, and 1800 of his sailors killed. That day the British losses were only 30 dead.

*   *   *

[1] So remote was Easter Island that when it was discovered by a Dutch sea captain in 1722 he found that the people who lived there believed they were the only people on earth. Their ancestors had lived on the island for more than a thousand years, 1600 kilometres from the nearest other island and 3218 kilometres from mainland Chile.

In Europe, four imperial sovereigns, the Emperor Franz Josef, Tsar Nicholas, Kaiser Wilhelm and King George, each of whom was the nominal head of his nation's armies and fleets, each of them holding the highest military and naval ranks, could only wait and watch as the officers and men of their respective armies and navies prepared to engage in battle. The Kaiser, who had once been so proud to hold the British forces' ranks – and even to wear the uniforms – of both Field Marshal and Admiral of the Fleet, announced that he would 'divest himself of these honours'. Those wearing them were henceforth his adversaries.

The chivalry, courtesy and panoply of power of the previous decades of European imperial magnificence were about to be swept away. Nearly six million Russian soldiers, four and a half million Germans, four million Frenchmen, more than three million Austro-Hungarians were under arms – even if, in many cases, they were poorly armed and equipped – and were awaiting their marching orders on the parade grounds, barrack squares and garrison fortress lines of Europe.

Those fortresses, hitherto believed to be impregnable, fell rapidly. Inside Belgium, their defence crucial to the protection of the French frontier, first Namur and then Liège was overrun, their defenders pulverized into submission by the weight of German artillery fire. Later, Antwerp suffered the same fate. As the German army swept through Belgium, the British Expeditionary Force was rushed across the North Sea and English Channel to the defence of its ally. The Kaiser mocked at the small size of the British contingent sent to confront his legions, calling the British force a 'contemptibly small army' – not, as was wrongly translated at the time, the even more derisory 'contemptible little army'. That army stood its ground at the Belgian border town of Mons, forcing the Germans to take note of its tenacity before it retreated into France.

In Paris, André Gide noted in his journal on August 15: 'The sky clouded over during the night, and in the early morning a big storm broke east of Paris. The first rolling of the thunder at about four o'clock seemed enough like the explosion of bombs to make one think a flight of Zeppelins had raided Paris. And in my half-sleep I imagined for some time that Paris was being bombarded and that it was even the end of the world.'

It was not the end of the world, but it was certainly the end of the civilized world that Europe had created for itself by the end of the nineteenth century. As the details of each battle reached the respective capitals, it was clear that such courtesies and niceties that war might have known in the past – the much-vaunted chivalries that were perhaps a figment of hopeful imaginations – were not to be a feature of the new warfare. The first German successes on the Western Front prompted André Gide to write in his journal on August 26: 'The French, who were playing fair, were indignant at the fact that in war the Germans did not observe the rules of the game. As for the latter, it seemed as if they were aiming to discredit war forever; and as if to prove that war was an evil thing – if it is true that in war the aim is to conquer – they won by the worst means.'

Within a month, Gide was to receive a telegram, typical of the hundreds of thousands, and indeed millions, of telegrams that were to be received by Frenchmen – as well as Britons, Germans, Russians, Austrians, Serbs, and more than a dozen other nationalities – in the years to come, announcing the death of a friend. The telegram, as almost always in such cases, was brief. It read: 'Charles Péguy fell before the enemy, Argonne.'

Péguy was a poet. The minds of millions, attuned to the civilized age in which the conflict had broken out, could grasp the enormity of the death of one human being, if it was a relative or friend, or even, perhaps, someone well-known. It was much harder to understand the meaning of the death of the hundred others – or two or three hundred others – killed that same day, and every day, somewhere on Europe's war fronts. The casualties were seen by many, however, as part of a necessary price to pay, an attitude expressed most powerfully by Rudyard Kipling, in a poem published in *The Times* on September 2:

> No easy hope or lies
>   Shall bring us to our goal.
> But iron sacrifice
>   Of body, will and soul.
> There is but one task for all –
>   For each one life to give.
> Who stands if freedom fall?
>   Who dies if England live?

Kipling's only son was later killed in action on the Western Front.

The first five months of the war saw all the expectations of the warring Powers disappointed. The German dash to Paris, successful for forty days, came to a halt on the forty-first day, when a combined British and French force halted them less than thirty miles from Paris, and drove them back across the River Marne and away from the capital. The British had only been able to put 50,000 men in the field in that first month, but their part in the Battle of the Marne was decisive.

Among the French soldiers killed on the Marne, on September 22, was Alain-Fournier, author of the recently published best-selling mystical novel *Le Grand Meaulnes*. Like so many thousands of those killed on every battlefield, his body was not found, and no individual grave could be erected. Seventy-six years later, however, some human remains found in a woodland were, after examination by doctors and battlefield archaeologists, identified as his, and his remains were reburied in a nearby cemetery, next to fifteen of his men who had been killed with him.

The Russian hope of being able to profit from Germany's efforts in the west by a swift victory in the war were also frustrated, the rapid, deep thrust of the Russian forces into East Prussia being halted on the battlefield of Tannenberg. The Austro-Hungarian forces also embarked in mid August on the intended crushing of Serbia, the State whose imminent destruction had roused Russia's concern a month earlier. But the Serbs, like the French and British on the Marne, and the Germans at Tannenberg, reversed the fortunes of war and were able to hold on to their western territories along the River Drina.

In Galicia, a rapid Russian advance threw the Austrians into consternation. News of the Russian capture of Lemberg on September 3 was kept secret from the Austro-Hungarian public for almost a week. Then panic set in much further west, in towns that were in fact far beyond the capacity of Russian arms. Cracow was one of them. 'People were leaving Cracow when I arrived,' Arthur Potocki recalled forty-five years (and two world wars) later. 'I watched whole families – men, women and children – move out of the city into the country in search of an illusory security. It was a sight to wring one's heart. The world has since become hardened to such pitiable scenes, for they are a feature of this cruel age; but in 1914 they shocked the soul of beholders. The Bishop of Cracow, with whom I discussed the matter, was moved to tears by the plight of the refugees.'

*   *   *

The scuttling of the ambitious military plans of Germany, Russia and Austria-Hungary did not lead to an end to the war. Instead, each disappointed war machine sought means of redressing the unexpectedly unfavourable balance. The Germans managed to reach the North Sea coast near the Franco-Belgian border, and, while unable to push as far west as the French Channel ports of Calais, Boulogne or Dieppe, established a defensive line that ran through a corner of Belgium and the length of eastern France. The British and French armies had to struggle on the north-western corner of Belgian soil to hold the line, and to prepare it as a base for future attempts to move eastward, while 200,000 Belgian civilians found refuge in Britain, and a further 500,000 in the Netherlands. They were the first of the war's refugees. By the war's end, the number of refugees – the dispossessed and the homeless – fleeing from all the war fronts was to be in the millions.

On the Russo-German Front, the frustrated Russian armies prepared to defend the Polish provinces of the Russian empire. The Austro-Hungarian army, driven by the Russians westward across the Carpathian Mountains, prepared to push as deep into Russia as it could, and also to renew its assault on Serbia. A sixth empire, that of Turkey, having entered the war in the hope of being at the side of a rapidly victorious Germany, found itself the target of Anglo-French naval guns, and of two military landings at the extremities of her empire: at the head of the Gulf of Akaba, and at the head of the Persian Gulf. At the port of Akaba, an Anglo-Indian force landed, destroyed the fortifications of the port, and withdrew. At Foa, at the head of the Persian Gulf, British and Indian troops (the Mesopotamia Expeditionary Force) attacked and defeated a force of 4000 Turkish soldiers, for the loss of five British officers and thirty-five Indians; the Mesopotamia Expeditionary Force then advanced to the town of Basra, which was occupied and held.

The British attacks on Turkey roused the anger of many of the sixty million Muslims in India, who saw the attack as one on Islam itself. One of the leaders of Indian Muslim protest, Maulana Mohammed Ali, editor of *The Comrade*, published a vociferous defence of Turkey. He was arrested, charged with sedition, and imprisoned for the rest of the war – and for a year afterwards.

The fighting of the last five months of 1914 failed to achieve the many much-expected decisive breakthroughs, or, as every capital had boasted, 'victory by Christmas'. Instead, trench warfare, a static but bloody form of confrontation, indicated a gruesome pattern that would continue until some means were found to break the stalemate. It was a stalemate made all the more costly in human life by the destructive power of heavy artillery, firing from well behind the lines, and adding substantially to the formidable daily casualty lists.

'No one can describe this vast wreck,' the American ambassador in London wrote to President Wilson on August 25. 'It will be ours to preserve civilization. All Europe is shooting it to pieces.' In Russia, the twenty-four-year-old Russian poet Anna Akhmatova expressed the fears, but also the hopes, of millions of Russians when she wrote (in the form of a prophesy of a one-legged beggar):

> 'Beware of terrible times . . . the earth
> opening for a crowd of corpses.
> Expect famine, earthquakes, plagues,
> and heavens darkened by eclipses.
>
> 'But our land will not be divided
> by the enemy at his pleasure:
> the Mother-of-God will spread
> a white shroud over these great sorrows.'

'What a miserable world,' D. H. Lawrence wrote on September 5, as yet more casualty lists were published. 'What colossal idiocy this war.'

Five days later a British journalist in St Petersburg wrote of how, every day, in the outer office of the Russian General Staff, long lists of those who had been killed in action on the Eastern Front were posted up for all to scrutinize:

Great crowds of women gather daily to scan these lists, and it is a heartrending sight to watch the faces of the tide going in and coming out. Peasant women with shawls over their heads jostle and crowd their sisters who have come in carriages. As they go in, one reads the great question in the haggard eyes of each, and as they come out the answer requires no interpretation. You see them with trembling hands turning over the huge sheets of the lists.

Some who fail to read the name of husband, son, or sweetheart, turn away with sighs of relief; but hardly a minute passes that some poor soul does not receive the wound that spells a life of loneliness or an old age bereft of a son.

I paused but for a moment within this dismal chamber, where even gilded aides move softly and respectfully as in the presence of death. But in this brief moment two faces stand clearly in my memory. One, a peasant woman with shawl fallen about her shoulders, her face dead white, her eyes in barren vacancy staring into space as she reeled against the wall.

No sob, no sound was there to indicate that the iron had entered into her soul; but the tragedy of a life still to be led, with none to share the responsibilities of poverty, was written in letters that none could fail to read. Like one walking in sleep, she moved slowly across the room, her eyes blind to the respectful sympathy that made a pathway towards the door; and thus she passed out and away to take up her burdens and her lonely life.

My eyes turned from her to another picture. In the antechamber is a small table where an orderly generally sits. Now he stands respectfully by while in his chair there sits a young woman. Her neatly-cut garments and smart fur collar speak of her better position in life. She, too, has made her offering on the altar of the nation's life. Too proud to show her feelings, she has almost without visible sign, read her fate within those ghastly columns, and has reached the door only to sink into the chair.

I saw her but for an instant and turned hastily away, but the picture remains ineffaceable. With head resting on the blotter, and hands clasped tightly beneath her small white forehead, she sat; deep, gasping sobs shaking her small girlish body through and through. And as she sobs her costly fur slips from her slender shoulders to the floor, and the great rough soldier, picking it up, gently places it around her neck. With an effort she stands up, speaks a courteous word to the gentle soldier, and then she too passes through the throng and is gone.

Who is it she mourns, one wonders? Sweetheart or young husband, probably, who but a few short days ago left her in the prime and beauty of manhood and who today sleeps in a far-away grave, with hundreds of others of his race and kind.

The numbers of dead rose within the first five months of the war to the highest in modern warfare, creating an ever-widening circle of war widows and war orphans, of bereaved parents and grieving relatives and friends. The

French alone were mourning 300,000 dead as the year 1914 came to an end: the equivalent of 2000 Frenchmen killed every day, and twice that number wounded. The Russian losses were as high. At sea, the loss of hundreds and even thousands of men in a few minutes soon became commonplace. On September 22, within two months of the outbreak of war, there was a particularly striking and sombre example of death at sea when in the North Sea, off the Dogger Bank, a single German submarine, *U-9*, sank three British cruisers, *Aboukir*, *Hogue* and *Cressy*, with the loss of 1459 lives.

Several European countries were able to preserve their neutrality as the main empires clashed, and as two small States, Serbia and Belgium, were drawn in. The most vulnerable was the Netherlands, where rumours of a possible German-controlled shipyard on one of the main sea approaches to Rotterdam alarmed the British and made some form of preventative occupation a possibility. On August 3, as German troops had entered Belgium, the Dutch government issued a declaration of neutrality. As a precautionary measure, its army was mobilized and its frontiers manned; plans were also made public to open the dykes and flood the low-lying areas to create a sea-bound 'Fortress Holland'. Despite considerable efforts by the Germans to win the Dutch to their cause, the occupation and fate of Belgium gave the Dutch a sense of the dangers that lay along that path.

The Swiss also sought, and maintained, neutrality, with general mobilization on August 3 serving, as it did in the Netherlands, as a caution to Germany that any attack would be resisted. Measures were then instituted to train troops, to build fortifications, to rearrange the railway timetables to give priority to military needs, and to import considerable reserves of grain, mostly from the United States.

Norway, Sweden and Spain also declared their neutrality, and discovered, as all neutrals did, that profits could be made both by individuals and the State from supplying the belligerents with goods. Denmark also maintained neutrality, and took the precaution, on August 1, to call up 19,000 men, to lay naval mines in the Fehmarn Belt – the narrow waterway between her and Germany – and to send troops to guard her land frontier with Germany, which in 1864 had annexed the southern region of the country. A pro-German movement in Denmark, paralleling one led by the Swedish explorer of Central Asia, Sven Hedin, in Sweden, had as little success in the smaller as in the larger country.

As early as June 30 the Spanish government had made it clear to its people that Spain was not bound by either an offensive or defensive alliance to any other Power. When Liberals and Republicans began, in August, to voice their sympathy for the Triple Entente of Russia, France and Britain, a vast majority of the Catholic priesthood, as well as several of the rightist parties, urged benevolent neutrality with a bias towards Germany and Austria-Hungary. Avoiding these two contrary pressures, the Spanish government managed to maintain strict impartiality. The publication of false news relating to the war was forbidden, and German-controlled clandestine wireless stations, discovered hidden in monasteries in both Barcelona and on the Atlantic coast of Spain, were suppressed. But the pro-German parties carried on an active political agitation, not only in favour of Germany, but for an 'Iberian Union' that would involve the Spanish annexation of Portugal.

Portugal was the only small European country that was prepared to enter the war while not being threatened militarily by a larger Power. On August 20, King Manuel II of Portugal let it be known that he had written to King George V, personally placing himself at the disposal of the British King.

As the war casualties rose, they began to exceed even the number of the deaths from disease that were afflicting Britain's largest imperial domain. In British India the number of plague deaths, which had fallen to 181,668 in 1913, rose sharply to 264,760 in the twelve months ending 30 September 1914. That figure, so large on the prewar scale, was overshadowed and submerged by the number of European war deaths before the end of 1914.

In South Africa, loyalty to the British crown had been a central feature of the Treaty of Vereeniging in 1902, and on 12 September 1914 General Botha announced that the Union of South Africa, being part of the British Empire, could not remain neutral in the European conflict. South Africans 'were under the British flag,' Botha was reported to have said, 'and had all the freedom they could have.' General Smuts, the Minister of Defence, who, like Botha, had led the anti-British Boer forces fifteen years earlier, ordered the capture of the coastal towns of German South West Africa. On September 15, German forces from South West Africa advanced across the Union border. At the same time, approaching by sea, Union forces seized the two South West African coastal towns of Swakopmund and Lüderitz Bay.

The reluctance of many Boers to accept the government's pro-British stance flared up on September 15 when the Commandant General of the Union Defence Forces, General Beyers, resigned his post. 'It was said that the war was being waged against the barbarity of the Germans,' he wrote in his letter of resignation to Smuts, and he added that he had 'forgiven, but not forgotten, all the barbarities' perpetrated by Britain during the South African war. This reference to British barbarity, Smuts replied, 'can only be calculated to sow hatred and division among the people of South Africa.'

A full-scale rebellion against the Union broke out on October 8, when Boer rebels, led by Lieutenant-Colonel S. G. Maritz, who had earlier fought with the German army in the crushing of the Herero revolt, took up arms and declared that his aim was to establish an independent Boer South Africa. Maritz, with German guns and a German force under his command, and with the rank of general over his German troops, sent as prisoners of war into German South West Africa those officers and men under his original command (North West Cape Province) who refused to break their oath to the Union. In a diplomatic move, Maritz signed an agreement with the Governor of German South West Africa, whereby the Kaiser undertook to take 'all possible measures' to secure the independence of any of the states of the South African Union that signed peace agreements with Germany.

In a battle with Union forces on October 27, many of Maritz's troops surrendered. At that very moment, however, a further revolt broke out among armed Boer commandos, led in the Transvaal by General Beyers and in the Orange Free State by General Christian de Wet, who had been among the signatories of the Treaty of Vereeniging, and had subsequently achieved ministerial office. De Wet denounced the 'miserable, pestilential British', and castigated the countermeasures taken by South Africa to seize the main ports of German South West Africa. 'Some of my friends,' he declared defiantly, 'have advised me to wait a little longer until England receives a bigger knock, but it is beneath me and my people to kick a dead dog.' As he moved forward towards the capital, Pretoria, De Wet told his followers that he would march on the city 'to pull down the British flag and proclaim a free South African republic'. But on November 12 the rebel force was attacked by General Botha, and its advance on Pretoria turned into flight and capitulation.

Still the anti-British rebellion continued. After De Wet's son was killed in action against the Union forces, he redoubled his efforts to attack them. By the end of November, however, he was captured, and by the end of the year such continuing rebel activity as was possible was suppressed, and 7000 men taken prisoner. The Union losses had not been heavy: 334 Union soldiers had been killed fighting the rebels and 369 fighting the Germans. The rebel dead amounted to 170. But the fact of the rebellion, and the German sympathies of the rebels, left a sour note at a time when the unity of the forces of the Entente was a part of the perception of the righteousness of their cause.

The world's potentially most powerful nation, the United States, declared its strict neutrality in the European conflict, and in its African and Pacific extensions. The main immediate cause of concern in the United States was the plight of the 80,000 Americans who were on holiday in Europe when war broke out. The rail and ferry services from Europe to Britain were badly disrupted by the movement of British troops to France and Belgium, and transatlantic liners also ran reduced services. Cash transactions were seriously impeded by the suspension of the international credit exchange system. An American Committee was set up in London, with its headquarters at the Savoy Hotel, to cash letters of credit; a group of Americans went so far as to purchase a steamer, the *Viking*, and sold tickets at a premium.

To facilitate the work of the American embassies and consulates in Europe, which were being overwhelmed by Americans trying to get home, an American cruiser, the *Tennessee*, was sent across the Atlantic with $250,000 in gold to be used by the diplomats to smooth and expedite their subjects' return. On August 26, and again three days later, special trains were chartered to transport 3000 Americans, who had gathered in Geneva, to Paris. They were put in hotels, and then allocated berths on ships leaving Le Havre for New York. Other special trains were run from various German towns to Rotterdam, and from Austro-Hungarian towns to the Italian port of Genoa.

From the first days of the war, Woodrow Wilson had offered his services, and those of the United States, as a mediator, should any of the warring powers wish to seek a peaceful solution. His offer was ignored. Both sides quickly turned to the Americans for sympathy in their cause: the Kaiser telegraphed to the President early in September to protest against the alleged use of dum-dum bullets – bullets filed down so as to expand on impact causing extensive laceration inside the body – by the French, but the use of these bullets was categorically denied by the French President, Raymond Poincaré. A Belgian mission, reaching Washington, was received by Wilson, who listened to its account of German actions against Belgian civilians, actions which created considerable indignation in the United States, as they had done in France and Britain, reinforcing the belief that the cause of the Entente was one of justice and retribution.

The cry 'German atrocities in Belgium' arose, not from Allied propaganda, but from a series of German actions, most of them carried out in the very first days of the war, which were given wide publicity not only in Britain and France, but also in the United States. An American diplomat, Brand Whitlock, was an eye-witness of the most widely publicized of these actions, the destruction in Louvain on August 26. A priest whose father's home and whose brother's home had been set on fire by the Germans after their occupation of the town, had wept in the diplomat's presence when describing the deliberate destruction of the university library, one of the most ancient in Europe. Nor was that the only destruction. In the account which he published after the war, Whitlock wrote:

On the orders of their chiefs the Germans set fire to the houses, spraying *salons* with inflammable liquid (using the apparatus they had for that purpose), lighting and flinging in their incendiary pastilles – breaking in windows with the butts of their rifles, that a draught might be provided for the flames.

The inmates of the houses thus doomed ran out, only to be shot down at their own doors, or took refuge in their cellars, to be burned to death and buried beneath the ruins of their homes. Men trying to escape over the roofs were fired at by the soldiers in the streets; women, their babies in their arms, hugging the walls, tried to reach some place of safety.

The Halles of the University, erected in 1317 by the Clothworkers as the Cloth Hall (*Halle aux Draps*), which in 1431 became the principal seat of the University, had come to be devoted almost exclusively to the libraries of the University. Therein were stored incomparable riches – more than 230,000 volumes, besides 750 manuscripts dating from the Middle Ages, and perhaps the finest collection of *incunabula* extant, more than a thousand of them.

The whole library, with all its riches, was deliberately and systematically burned; only the naked walls of the old Hall could resist the fury of the flames. No wonder the old scholar broke down and wept!

The ancient church of St Peter was set on fire. The flames of the holocaust lighted up the sky; the glare could be seen at Tervuren, fifteen kilometres away.

To the annoyance of the French and British, President Wilson was noncommittal in his replies to the complaints of German atrocities in Belgium. Instead, by presidential proclamation, he declared October 4 to be a day of prayer for the 'peace of Europe'. Two months later, on December 8, he told Congress that the United States had a reputation as a mediator – the reference was to America's mediation at the end of the Russo-Japanese War a decade earlier – which he hoped to be able to call upon to end the new war. 'It is our dearest present hope,' he told Congress, 'that this character and reputation may presently, in God's providence, bring us an opportunity, such as has seldom been vouchsafed any nation, to counsel and obtain peace in the world and reconciliation and a healing settlement of many a matter that has cooled and interrupted the friendship of nations.'

The thought of United States mediation had caused considerable anger in Britain. 'I have heard from high sources – that any talk of peace which is suspected of being inspired in Berlin would be received as an unfriendly suggestion,' Walter H. Page wrote to Wilson from the American Embassy in London on December 15, and he went on to explain: 'There is not the slightest feeling of vengeance here – only a feeling of sorrow; but the English are determined not to have this war recur. The German armed threat must disappear, and the sooner it disappears and with the least harm to the Germans, the better.' Page continued: 'There is not the slightest hatred of Germans. The moment Germany will or can give up what we call militarism forever, peace will come instantly – with no revenge, no hatred, but, of course, with the reinstatement of Belgium. But no voice will be heard except on these conditions – not to talk of merely stopping the war to let it recur ten or twenty or forty years hence, to gratify a vast military machine, which might fight somebody at some time to justify its existence.'

Thus the warring nations prepared for the New Year, confident in the rightness of their cause, and hopeful in the prospect – perhaps even the imminent prospect – of victory. Less than two weeks after the ambassador's report, the coming of Christmas saw troops in all the facing lines of trenches stop firing as darkness fell, leave their dugouts, and meet in no-man's land. Usually it was the German soldiers who started, singing carols and lighting candles on the Christmas trees which they had brought into their frontline trenches, and then suggesting that the two sides meet in no-man's land. 'We met, we swopped cigarettes, and had a good smoke,' a British soldier, Bertie Felstead, recalled eighty-two years later (at the age of 102). 'We were so pleased to be able to forget the war.'

'Hello Tommy!' 'Hello Fritz!' became the calls of the night. Cigarettes, cigars, beer, wine, cake and chocolates were exchanged. Carols were sung together. Names and addresses were exchanged, with promises to write once the war was over. Bruce Bairnsfather, one of the most popular British soldier-writers of the war, told of Christmas Eve on his sector, and of the first British soldier who went out that night to meet a German soldier halfway, exchanging cigars and cigarettes. 'After months of vindictive sniping,' he wrote, 'this little episode came as an invigorating tonic, and a welcome relief to the dull monotony of antagonism.' Then came Christmas Day:

Heads were bobbing about and showing over their parapet in a most reckless way, and, as we looked, this phenomenon became more and more pronounced.

A complete Boche figure suddenly appeared on the parapet, and looked about itself. This complaint became infectious. It didn't take 'Our Bert' long to be up on the skyline (it is one long grind to ever keep him off it). This was the signal for more Boche anatomy to be disclosed, and this was replied to by all our Alf's and Bill's, until, in less time than it takes to tell, half a dozen or so of each of the belligerents were outside their trenches and were advancing towards each other in no-man's land.

A strange sight, truly!

I clambered up and over our parapet, and moved out across the field to look. Clad in a muddy suit of khaki and wearing a sheepskin coat and Balaclava helmet, I joined the throng about half-way across to the German trenches.

It all felt most curious: here were these sausage-eating wretches, who had elected to start this infernal European fracas, and in so doing had brought us all into the same muddy pickle as themselves.

This was my first real sight of them at close quarters. Here they were – the actual, practical soldiers of the German army. There was not an atom of hate on either side that day; and yet, on our side, not for a moment was the will to war and the will to beat them relaxed. It was just like the interval between the rounds in a friendly boxing match.

The difference in type between our men and theirs was very marked. There was no contrasting the spirit of the two parties. Our men, in their scratch costumes of dirty, muddy khaki, with their various assorted headdresses of woollen helmets, mufflers and battered hats, were a light-hearted, open, humorous collection as opposed to the sombre demeanour and stolid appearance of the Huns in their grey-green faded uniforms, top boots, and pork-pie hats.

The shortest effect I can give of the impression I had was that our men, superior, broadminded, more frank, and lovable beings, were regarding these faded, unimaginative products of perverted kulture as a set of objectionable but amusing lunatics whose heads had *got* to be eventually smacked.

'Look at that one over there, Bill,' our Bert would say, as he pointed out some particularly curious member of the party.

I strolled about amongst them all, and sucked in as many impressions as I could. Two or three of the Boches seemed to be particularly interested in me, and after they had walked round me once or twice with sullen curiosity stamped on their faces, one came up and said 'Offizier?' I nodded my head, which means 'Yes' in most languages, and, besides, I can't talk German.

These devils, I could see, all wanted to be friendly; but none of them possess the open, frank geniality of our men. However, everyone was talking and laughing, and souvenir hunting.

I spotted a German officer, some sort of lieutenant I should think, and being a bit of a collector, I intimated to him that I had taken a fancy to some of his buttons.

We both then said things to each other which neither understood, and agreed to do a swap. I brought out my wire clippers and, with a few deft snips, removed a couple of his buttons and put them in my pocket. I then gave him two of mine in exchange.

Whilst this was going on a babbling of guttural ejaculations emanating from one of the laager-schifters, told me that some idea had occurred to someone.

Suddenly, one of the Boches ran back to his trench and presently reappeared with a large camera. I posed in a mixed group for several photographs, and have ever since wished I had fixed up some arrangement for getting a copy. No doubt framed editions of this photograph are reposing on some Hun mantelpieces, showing clearly and unmistakably to admiring strafers how a group of perfidious English surrendered unconditionally on Christmas Day to the brave Deutschers.

Slowly the meeting began to disperse; a sort of feeling that the authorities on both sides were not very enthusiastic about this fraternizing seemed to creep across the gathering. We parted, but there was a distinct and friendly understanding that Christmas Day would be left to finish in tranquillity.

The last I saw of this little affair was a vision of one of my machine gunners, who was a bit of an amateur hairdresser in civil life, cutting the unnaturally long hair of a docile Boche, who was patiently kneeling on the ground whilst the automatic clippers crept up the back of his neck.

Along a twenty-seven mile sector of the Western Front, twenty-one incidents were recorded of British and German soldiers meeting in this way. In some areas these meetings lasted only for a few hours, in others they continued all day, and in certain cases they persisted until the New Year and even beyond. 'Just think,' one British soldier wrote home to his family, 'that while you were eating your turkey, I was out talking and shaking hands with the very men I had been trying to kill a few hours before.'

CHAPTER EIGHTEEN

1915

After the war, the soul of the people will be so
maimed and so injured that it is horrible to think of.
And this shall be the new hope: that there shall be a
life wherein the struggle shall not be for money or for
power, but for individual freedom and common effort
towards good.

D. H. LAWRENCE
1 February 1915

THE NEUTRALITY OF THE UNITED STATES in the first months of
the war, and the expectation that it would be permanent, gave a sense of
confidence and strength to the Central Powers. Such hopes as the Entente
had that the United States would commit itself to the struggle against
Germany seemed far fetched. One American voice that called for an American
commitment of some sort was that of the former President, Theodore
Roosevelt, who wrote on 1 January 1915: 'Our country should not shirk its
duty to mankind. It can perform this duty only if it is true to itself. It can
be true to itself only by definitely resolving to take the position of the just
man armed; for a proud and self-respecting nation of freemen must scorn to
do wrong to others and must also scorn tamely to submit to wrong done
by others.'

These sentiments could not stir President Woodrow Wilson from the
neutrality he had proclaimed a month earlier, in his message to Congress,
and of which his predecessor wrote so bitterly on that first day of the new
year. 'In his over-anxiety not to offend the powerful who have done wrong,'
Theodore Roosevelt wrote, of Wilson, 'he scrupulously refrains from saying
one word on behalf of the weak who have suffered wrong. He makes no

allusion to the violation of the Hague conventions at Belgium's expense, although this nation' – the United States – 'had solemnly undertaken to be a guarantor of those conventions. He makes no protest against the cruel wrongs Belgium has suffered.'

Each of the warring European powers hoped to secure victory in 1915. Britain and France were determined to break through the newly established trench lines on the Western Front, to liberate Belgium, and to drive the Germans out of northeastern France. The Germans hoped to continue their advance on Paris, and to follow up their victory over the Russians at Tannenberg, in East Prussia, by pushing eastward deep into Russia. The Russians hoped to reverse the defeat of Tannenberg, re-enter East Prussia, and regain the already lost western provinces of Russian Poland. Austria-Hungary was determined to regain the lands lost to Russia in Eastern and Western Galicia, and to reverse the setback, amounting to humiliation, at the hands of the Serbs. Turkey had visions of reconquering the Sinai Desert, most of which had been transferred to Britain by Treaty in 1906; of capturing the Suez Canal; of restoring Turkish rule over Egypt, which had been lost to Britain thirty years earlier; and perhaps even reversing Turkey's defeat at the hands of the Italians in Libya just before the outbreak of the First World War.

In the air, the Germans launched their first Zeppelin attack over England on the night of January 19/20. Four airships flew across the North Sea to bomb British military installations on the east coast of England. One of them had to break off its mission and return to base because of a mechanical fault. The first bombs to be dropped fell on Great Yarmouth, missing by only fifty yards a drill hall filled with army reservists. One bomb, falling in a street, killed one man, a bootmaker, and destroyed his shop. Another bomb turned out to be a dud: it fell through the roof of a workman's cottage at Sheringham, broke the staircase, and, an eyewitness recalled, 'buried itself in the ground, leaving the baby alive and well in its cot upstairs and the parents eating their supper downstairs'. It was to be nearly three months before the next raid.

On the Western Front the opposing armies had dug their trenches and were facing each other across the parapets that looked out across no-man's land. 'We are still in our old positions,' a German corporal on the Messines front wrote to his landlord on January 20. 'The weather is miserable and we often spend days on end knee-deep in water and, what is more, under heavy fire. We are greatly looking forward to a brief respite. Let's hope that soon afterwards the whole front will start moving forward. Things can't go on like this forever.'

The corporal was Adolf Hitler, born in Austria, who had been among the crowd in Munich on the eve of war, supporting war and seeking to enlist. His hope that the front would move forward was dashed by events. Nine days after Hitler's letter to his landlord, a German lieutenant led his men in an assault on four French blockhouses in the Argonne; although he and his men were forced to withdraw from the blockhouses under heavy French artillery fire, his bravery in the action won him the Iron Cross, First Class. His name was Erwin Rommel. Twenty five years later, in May 1940, he was to reach the Channel Coast as part of Germany's successful thrust through France.

On the Eastern Front, two separate movements of vast forces were taking place during 1915. In the northern half of the front, where the Russians had won their resounding victory over the Germans at Tannenberg in the opening phase of the war in 1914, the Germans slowly and steadily reversed the fortunes of war, and advanced into Russian Poland. In the southern sector, it was the Russians who were advancing, pushing their Austrian adversary steadily westward. A high point of this southern advance, on Easter Day 1915, was the capture of the Austrian fortress town of Przemysl, where 120,000 Austrian soldiers were taken prisoner, and 700 artillery pieces captured by the Russians. That same day, during a Russian attack elsewhere on the southern front, Josip Broz, a Croat sergeant fighting with the Austrian forces, was pierced in the back by a lance, and was about to be cut up by Circassian cavalrymen – men from the Caucasus who formed part of the Russian army, and who habitually massacred the wounded – when some Russian troops reached the scene and ended the slaughter. The Croat sergeant was saved and sent to a prisoner-of-war camp inside Russia; in the Second World War, as Marshal Tito, he was to lead the Yugoslav communist partisan forces against the Germans.

The Russian advance through the Carpathians had disturbed the Central Powers' confidence considerably. One early Russian gain was the oil fields of Drohobycz, in Eastern Galicia. In an effort to push the Russians back to behind their frontier, the Austrians agreed to give overall command to a German general, August von Mackensen, and to put the artillery preparations in the hands of a German artillery expert. When the Austro-German attack began, it was preceded by a four-hour artillery barrage, the heaviest and longest hitherto attempted on the Eastern Front, with 700,000 shells being fired. The offensive achieved its aim; rapidly the Russians were driven from their most westerly conquests, and then back through the mountain passes to the Russian border. Przemysl, captured at heavy cost five months earlier, was recaptured, as were the oil fields of Drohobycz, the fortress of Gorlice, and Lemberg, the principal city of Eastern Galicia.

On April 28 the founding conference of the Women's International League for Permanent Peace opened at The Hague, amid the calm of a neutral capital. Three British women, each of them leading prewar campaigners for Votes for Women, were present. Forty-seven delegates came from the United States. At the end of their three-day deliberations they passed twenty resolutions, demanding 'an immediate and permanent peace', the teaching of 'peace education' in schools, and votes for women. They also appointed 'peace messengers' to be sent to all the governments at war, as well as to the United States, 'to urge the governments of the world to put an end to this bloodshed and to establish a just and lasting peace'.

Such antiwar protests were dismissed by the mass of the public in each warring country as the activities of cranks and traitors. But, in the strictest secrecy of a conversation with Robert Borden, the Canadian Prime Minister, the British Foreign Secretary, Sir Edward Grey, confided his view that if the war continued it 'must result in the overthrow of all existing forms of government'. In the equal secrecy of a message to the German Chancellor, the Austrian Foreign Minister, Count Czernin, suggested – as Austrian forces retook the towns and fortresses of Eastern Galicia from their brief Russian military occupation – that the time had come to make peace with Russia.

Austria-Hungary, argued Czernin, had regained almost all the territory which it had lost to Russia in the opening months of the war. Germany had made massive strides into Russian territory. It ought therefore, Czernin believed, to be possible to bring the conflict to an end. Both sides had shown their strength and courage, both had lost heavily in men and weaponry. Russia had shown that she was prepared to risk all for Serbia; and Serbia was still independent, the Austrians having failed to enter Belgrade or make any serious inroads into her territory.

Count Czernin's reasoning seemed to have the force of logic; in addition, Austria-Hungary did not wish to risk, by further conflict, the possibility that undue strain might be put, particularly in the event of military setbacks, on the fragile national fabric of the empire. The desertion (as it seemed from the perspective of Vienna) of Croat soldiers to the Russian side of the line, was a warning sign. But Czernin's logic held no appeal to the leaders in Berlin. For them, the victories over Russia were only just beginning. Warsaw was still in Russian hands, so too were the more easterly cities of Bialystok and Brest Litovsk, and the long-coveted Baltic provinces of Russia.

The German government therefore turned down Count Czernin's suggestion. It became even more determined to continue the war both against Russia and France when it received a petition from the six most powerful German economic and industrial groupings. The petition gave a list of territorial annexations in the East and West, including the annexation of the coal-producing region of northern France, the English Channel coastline of France as far as the River Somme, and the French border fortresses of Verdun, Longwy and Belfort, as well as, in the East, 'at least part' of Russia's Baltic provinces and the area lying to the south of them. What the industrialists called the 'great addition' to Germany's manufacturing resources to be acquired in the West would be counterbalanced, they wrote, 'by an equivalent annexation of agricultural territory in the East.' It was clear from this petition that some of the wealthiest and most powerful men in Germany were convinced that it was in Germany's imperial and economic interest for the war to continue. The Austro-Hungarian peace probe, the first of the war, was pushed aside.

One of the main forces behind the German industrialists' demands was Alfred Hugenberg, the chief director of Krupp's. Fourteen years later, when leader of the German National Party, Hugenberg provided Hitler with funds to campaign against the Versailles Treaty; and in 1933 he put the three million votes, which his party then commanded, at Hitler's disposal, gaining Hitler, for the first time, a majority in the Reichstag.

The Germans had every reason, from the military and political, as well as the economic perspective of Berlin, not to allow their Austrian ally to seek an end to the war. Considerable information had reached Berlin since the beginning of 1915 about demoralization in the Russian army, and in particular about the activities of the Bolsheviks to campaign within the Russian army against a continuation of the war. Bolshevik antiwar propaganda leaflets were being included in food parcels sent to troops at the front. A Russian army report told of the 'super-human efforts' that were required to keep the men in the trenches. The Russian Minister of War, General Poplivanov, warned his ministerial colleagues in St Petersburg: 'Demoralization, surrender and desertion are assuming huge proportions'.

The Germans took swift advantage of the Russian turmoil; in a report to Washington, the United States Ambassador in Berlin described how the Germans were 'picking out the revolutionarists and Liberals from many Russian prisoners of war, furnishing them with money and false passports and papers, and sending them back to Russia to stir up revolution'. In another exploitation of the divisions inside Russia, the Kaiser authorized the creation of a 2000-strong battalion of Finnish troops. These soldiers were recruited in Finland from among those Finns disaffected by Russian rule. They were then smuggled out of Finland through Sweden to Germany, and sent into action against the Russians on the Eastern Front. The recruiting for this battalion, recalled the Finnish national leader, General Mannerheim, 'forms one of the most thrilling chapters in recent Finnish history. Everything, of course, had to be done in the utmost secrecy, and in a country honeycombed with Russian police.'

Militarily, the Germans were making steady advances eastward into the eastern provinces of Russian Poland. A German offensive launched in July was immediately and spectacularly successful. Two German gas attacks to the west of Warsaw caused heavy casualties and panic among the Russian forces. Warsaw, the Polish capital, and one of the great cities of the Tsarist Empire, was occupied by the German army at the beginning of August. It was not to be entered by Russian troops again for thirty years.

By mid August, the German forces reached the line of the River Bug, the same line that Hitler was to use for the partition of Poland with Stalin in 1939. A month later even this line had been overrun, as German troops pushed further and further into western Russia, crossing the Pripet Marshes and reaching the fortress city of Kovno. The Russian Empire was never to regain this vast swathe of territory, and never to recover from its loss. On entering Kovno, the Germans found several million tins of preserved meat, the main Russian frontline food supply, on which the German troops were to have been fed in the months ahead.

The number of Russian soldiers captured during the advance in the summer and autumn of 1915 was greater than during any previous recorded conflict. On August 17, the day of the fall of Kovno, 726,694 Russian soldiers were being held prisoner by the Germans, and a further 699,254 by the Austrians; making a total of nearly a million and a half men in captivity. Two days after the fall of Kovno, a further 90,000 Russian officers and men were captured in the fortress of Novo-Georgievsk, which had been under German siege since the fall of Warsaw two weeks earlier. Conditions in the prisoner-of-war camps were primitive. In one of the camps in Germany, at Gardelegen, 300 Russians died during a typhus epidemic.

The Russians, while still holding Galicia and the southern part of Russian Poland in the early months of 1915, felt a military confidence that the events of the second half of the year were to belie. They had also made inroads, in the spring and early summer, into the Turkish Empire, advancing from the eastern areas of Anatolia which they had annexed in 1878.

As in all wars, there are areas on which the spotlight of public and press attention falls as the struggle is taking place, and areas which remain hidden from the public gaze until after disaster has struck. One of the hidden areas in the spring of 1915 was the remote eastern region of Turkey, where the large Armenian Christian population, long denied its national rights by the Ottomans, hoped against hope that a Russian victory over Turkey might lead to the recognition of Armenian national aspirations.

Starting on April 8, since then a day of infamy in the Armenian calendar, the Armenians were cruelly attacked by the Turks. Falsely accusing the Armenians of cooperating with the Russian invaders, Turkish soldiers shot dead tens of thousands of Armenian men, and drove hundreds of thousands of Armenian women and children from their homes, forcing them across the mountains southward to the inhospitable deserts of Syria. This was only the start of a terrible saga of suffering.

The Armenians appealed for protection to Germany, the European and Christian power whose officers and men were nearest to them, and, as the ally of Turkey, might be able to exert a restraining influence. Their appeal was rejected by the German government on the grounds that it would offend the Turkish government. By April 19 it was known in Berlin that more than fifty thousand Armenians had been murdered in the province of Van, and that the predominantly Armenian town of Van was besieged, with 1300 armed Armenians defending the 30,000 Armenian civilians in the town, many of them refugees from the surrounding countryside.

Despite the growing concern expressed by Christians in Germany at the Armenian massacres, no official German protest was forthcoming. The

Armenians then appealed to President Wilson, but the United States did not wish to become involved. Details of the Armenian massacres were now circulating far outside Turkey. The Germans, shamed by the international outcry that they were doing nothing to restrain their ally, instructed the German Vice-Consul at Erzerum, Max Erwin von Scheubner-Richter, to intervene against the massacres. But he was warned that he must not do so in any way that might give the impression that Germany wanted 'to exercise a right of protection over the Armenians, or interfere with the activities of the authorities'. The muted protest was duly made; the massacres continued.[1]

The only moment of respite for the Armenians was when Russian forces reached the besieged town of Van, and rescued those who had been trapped there under Turkish bombardment for thirty days. But in a huge area of Turkish Anatolia, from the western town of Bursa to the southern town of Aleppo, and eastward to the Russo-Turkish front line, the killings went on. In the town of Bitlis, a few miles from Van, 15,000 Armenian civilians were killed in eight days. In the Black Sea port of Trebizond, in the course of a two-week orgy of destruction, an estimated 15,000 Turkish troops murdered all but a hundred of the 17,000 Armenian inhabitants of the town.

A French naval attempt to take off as many Armenians as possible from the coast of Syria led to the rescue of four thousand, but this figure paled beside the total number of Armenian deaths: 600,000 during the massacres in Anatolia, and a further 400,000 as a result of brutalities and privation during the forced deportations from Anatolia into the deserts of Syria and Mesopotamia. A further 200,000 Armenians were forcibly converted to Islam. The Armenian nation was in despair, its only protection being in the east, within the regions conquered by Russia. 'There are no words in the dictionaries,' the Armenian poet Avetik Isahakian, wrote a few months later, 'to describe the hideousness of the terrors'. Today they are known as the Armenian Genocide.

The British, French and Russian governments, each of them at war with Turkey, issued a joint public denunciation, on May 24, of the Turkish 'mass murders' of the Armenians, describing the killings as 'a crime against humanity and civilization'. The original phrase, drafted by the Russians, had read 'a crime against Christianity and civilization'. This was changed in

---

Seven and a half years later von Scheubner-Richter was shot dead while advancing through the streets of Munich, at the side of Adolf Hitler, during the attempt in November 1923 to overthrow the Bavarian government.

order to spare the feelings of the Muslim populations in both British India and the French colonies.

Antiwar feeling was to be found among all the warring powers, but whenever it manifested itself publicly it was quickly put down by the authorities. Following an antiwar protest in Berlin on April 1, the leader of the demonstration, Polish-born Rosa Luxemburg, was arrested and imprisoned. Other German antimilitarists travelled from Germany to neutral Holland on April 18, to participate in the International Women's Peace Congress. More than a thousand women gathered to protest against the continuation of hostilities. No British women were present; the British government had prevented them from leaving Britain by the simple device of suspending the North Sea ferry service from Britain to Holland.

That month, Thomas Hardy expressed, from a very different antiwar perspective, his deep unease at the warring of two peoples whom he regarded as the same race and stock. His poem was entitled 'The Pity of It'. After the war it was to be much quoted by those in Britain who felt that there was an affinity between Britain and Germany that ought never to have been put to the test of war:

> Whosoever they be
> At root and bottom of this, who flung this flame
> Between kith folk kin-tongued as we are,
>
> Sinister, ugly, lurid be their fame;
> May their families grow to shun their name,
> And their brood perish everlastingly.

On the Western Front, as the intensity of the fighting grew, the French military authorities were confronted by antiwar feeling in a regiment of the French Foreign Legion. The regiment was disbanded, and the disaffected Russian, Belgian and Italian soldiers were sent back to the countries from which they had come to France as volunteers. Immediately conscripted into their respective national forces, these disillusioned men were then sent back to the trenches, to fight – and many to die – under their own national flags. The Italian members of the Legion arrived back in Italy just as Italy was deciding which of the two conflicting blocs to join.

After nearly eight months as a neutral, Italy was confronted by the need to enter the war or be left out when it came to the divisions of the spoils of war. Her first offer was to Austria-Hungary; she would join the Central Powers if Austria agreed to transfer to Italy the southern Austrian province of the Trentino, the Dalmatian Islands, and the towns of Gorizia and Gradisca on the Isonzo river, as well as recognizing Italian 'primacy' in Albania.

The Austrians, not wanting to give up so much territory, or to see Italy more powerful in the Adriatic, rejected the Italian terms. Italy then turned to the Allied Powers, with an even more comprehensive set of territorial demands. As diplomatic negotiations continued in Rome, the fighting in the war zones intensified.

On the Western Front, the first initiative of 1915 was taken by the British. Their aim was to drive the Germans from the village of Neuve Chapelle, and to push them back as far as possible. On the morning of March 10, the opening British artillery barrage was intended to pulverize and demoralize the German defenders. More shells were fired in that one barrage than in the whole of the Boer War. But when the British troops advanced, it emerged that one sector of the German front line had not been hit by the barrage, the guns allocated to that sector having fallen short of their target as the result of an aiming error.

Those British officers who watched the advance at Neuve Chapelle through their binoculars thought that all the attacking troops had penetrated the German lines, and that victory was assured. As not a single one of the attackers returned, 'it was thought at first,' the official British history noted, 'that the attack succeeded in reaching the German trenches'. In fact, every one of the attackers, almost a thousand men, had been killed. For three days the battle continued. Taking part were Indian troops who had been brought from India by sea. After the first disastrous attack, their commander, a British general, refused to allow them to continue. A British officer who witnessed the struggle, and who did not share his fellow officers' optimism, wrote home: 'People out here seem to think that the war is going to be quite short, why, I don't know; personally, I see nothing to prevent it going on for ever.'

A private in the London Scottish, Douglas Henderson, writing home about the risks of trench warfare, commented: 'I would not have missed doing my bit for anything, as after the war is over those that return will have a wonderful experience to look back on. I don't envy the feelings of those of my age who still hold back.' Private Henderson survived four more years of trench warfare, reaching the rank of captain and being mentioned in despatches.

The Battle of Neuve Chapelle failed to break the German lines, or to start the rolling back of the German army from the fields of Flanders. It was the Germans who attacked next, in an attempt to drive the British from the Belgian town of Ypres, and to push on to the Channel ports. On April 8, German aircraft dropped leaflets on Ypres warning the townspeople that the city was to be shelled into submission. Reporting this in his diary, a British officer, N. C. Harbutt, derided the possibility of such shelling. Nine days later, when the German bombardment began, he was nearly killed. Among the sights he saw as the artillery bombardment intensified was a woman urging her young daughter to run ahead of her to escape the shells; the girl ran right into a shell explosion. On April 20, Harbutt wrote in his diary: 'The big square a shambles. Seven stall-holders killed by one shell. The whole square littered with human remains, stones, timber, glass.'

Although the bombardment of Ypres was so heavy as to make the town virtually uninhabitable, the Germans were unable to breach its defences. To the south of Ypres, the Germans held the town of Messines, but were likewise unable to push further west. German troops were never to enter Ypres nor reach the Channel coast. The struggle had become one, not for towns or coastlines, but for small woods, individual farms, trenches and blockhouses from which the enemy could direct machine-gun fire on the opposing trenches. In the capture of such limited objectives, significant efforts were made, millions of lives lost, and bravery rewarded.

Another German initiative in April, the use of chlorine gas, was intended to break the stalemate and enable the trench lines to be pierced. It was first used on April 22, on what the official British war history described as 'a glorious spring day'. The first Allied soldiers to face it were French African troops, who immediately began running to the rear, pushing through the British reserve lines. 'It was impossible to understand what the Africans said,' the official British historian wrote, 'but from the way they coughed and pointed to their throats, it was evident that, if not suffering from the effects of gas, they were thoroughly scared.'

Extraordinary to relate, no German preparations had been made to have reserves ready to storm any gap that might be made in the Allied line. It had been an experimental, not a tactical attack. In a second German gas attack three days later, two thousand Canadian troops were killed, and French colonial troops, Africans from Senegal, were so terrified that they shot their French, white, officers. These officers already had orders to shoot the Senegalese if they turned away from the line of the advance.

The German use of gas had proved unsuccessful in creating a breakthrough against the Allied front line trenches, or beyond them. The immediate effects of the gas were, however, appalling. 'The horrible part of it is the slow lingering death of those who are gassed,' a British staff officer, Major Charteris, wrote in his diary on April 28. 'I saw some hundred poor fellows laid out in the open, in the forecourt of a church, to give them all the air they could get, slowly drowning with water in their lungs – the most horrible sight, and the doctors quite powerless.'

On May 2, four days after Charteris's comment, the Germans used gas for the first time on the Eastern Front. There too it failed to achieve the hoped-for breakthrough. The initial British response to the use of gas had been to condemn it. 'Germany has stooped to acts which vie with those of the Dervishes', declared Lord Kitchener when he heard of the first gas attack. But on the following day he sought, and obtained, the approval of the British War Council for Britain to use gas against the Germans. A new and harsh element in warfare, gas was to be used in increasing measure by both sides. But it failed to be the catalyst it was expected to be.

Despite the surprise which the use of gas created, the Germans had not devised any wider strategy to enable it to lead to the conquest of the Ypres salient. Both sides had become 'entrenched' in the belief that an advance of a few hundred yards, creating a small bulge in the line or straightening out an existing bulge, constituted a success. The line of trenches on the Western Front, along which this bloody stalemate was to be maintained for three more years, stretched from the North Sea to the Swiss border. For Britain and France, the German occupation of almost all of Belgium, and of the northeastern region of France, made an attempt to break through the trench lines, and to drive the Germans back, a political, and indeed a moral, imperative; one that was to determine the strategic plans for the next three years. But it was clear that the means to break through the German trenches did not exist in the spring of 1915.

*   *   *

The British had begun to search for a new war zone which might offer a swifter victory than in the trench lines of the Western Front. Strategic planners looked towards Turkey, the only non-Christian power among the belligerents, as an area where victory might be secured, and the Central Powers seriously weakened. The Ottoman Empire had been considered from the outset of the war to be a less effective and less powerful enemy.

The British leaders had initially been spurred into action by an appeal from the Russian Commander-in-Chief for some military action by Britain to take the pressure off the Turkish advance in eastern Anatolia. On 5 January 1915, after receiving the Russian appeal, Lord Kitchener, the Secretary of State for War – who seventeen years earlier had defeated the Mahdi and his Muslim Dervish army at Omdurman – suggested that Russia could be helped by an Anglo-French attack on the Dardanelles. If the Turks could be driven from the Dardanelles, Kitchener argued, and if Constantinople itself could be threatened, three neutral States – Greece, Bulgaria and Roumania – might come in to the war on the side of the Entente, by reason of the Turkish territory they might acquire. Italy too might join the Entente, in search of spoils. The Turkish pressure on Russia would also be lessened, as the Turks hastened to defend Constantinople.

The Secretary to the British Cabinet, Colonel M. P. A. Hankey, suggested that victory at the Dardanelles would give the Anglo-French forces access to the River Danube 'as a line of communication for an army penetrating into the heart of Austria', and thus bring British sea power to bear 'in the middle of Europe'.

The first attack at the Dardanelles was to be made by ships alone, with the enthusiastic support of the First Lord of the Admiralty, Winston Churchill, who was convinced that the naval power of Britain's warships would blast a way through the Turkish waterway known as the Narrows and penetrate the Sea of Marmara. The date of the attack was March 18, less than a week after the end of the battle of Neuve Chapelle on the Western Front, which had given the lie to the belief that there could be a rapid breakthrough across the trenches of France and Flanders.

Enormous hopes were placed by the Entente Powers in the naval attack of March 18. In the British War Council, those Cabinet Ministers who were privy to the secret of the attack spent many hours, over several weeks, listing the advantages that would result once British warships, far superior in fire power to anything available to the Turks, had penetrated the Sea of Marmara and reached the shoreline of Constantinople, putting that great city, the nerve centre of Ottoman power, at the mercy of naval guns of unprecedented power. Kitchener was of the opinion that once the British ships pushed through the Narrows, the Turkish garrison on the Gallipoli Peninsula would flee, without a single British soldier having to land. He thought that once news reached Constantinople of the arrival of the British fleet in the Sea of Marmara the Sultan, the Turkish garrison at Constantinople, and possibly even the Turkish army in Thrace, would 'decamp to the Asiatic shore', leaving Turkey-in-Europe to Anglo-French control.

Sir Edward Grey, with all his authority as Secretary of State for Foreign Affairs, was convinced that once the fleet pushed through the Dardanelles, there might be a *coup d'état* in Constantinople, whereby Turkey would abandon the Central Powers and join the Entente.

There was even talk at the British War Council of the territorial gains that Britain would make as soon as the naval attack had succeeded. Kitchener wanted Britain to annex the Ottoman Syrian towns of Aleppo and Alexandretta; the Admiralty wanted Britain to take control of the whole Euphrates valley from Urfa and Mosul in the north to Baghdad and Basra in the south. One minister wanted Britain to set up a Jewish National Home in Turkish-ruled Palestine. A counter-suggestion was to give the Holy places – Jerusalem, Nazareth and Bethlehem – as a Mandate to the United States, to show the altruism of the Entente in at least this small niche of the Ottoman Empire. Never in the history of modern warfare had so much been expected or hoped for from the efforts of so few ships and guns.

The Russian Empire also expected to be a beneficiary of the Dardanelles attack. A secret agreement was being negotiated between Russia and its allies, and was signed two days after the first naval attack. In return for Russia not making trouble with regard to the gains Britain hoped to make from the Turkish Empire in Asia and Arabia, Russia would be given substantial territorial gains: the city of Constantinople, more than half the land area of Turkey-in-Europe, the northern shore of the Sea of Marmara, the Bosphorus waterway, and the European and Asian shores of the Dardanelles, including the Gallipoli peninsula, and the town of Chanak on the Asian side of the Narrows.

Italy, which was still neutral, had begun to look at the possibility of the defeat of Turkey by the Entente with an eager eye. Her territorial demands for entering the war on the side of the Central Powers having been rejected by Austria-Hungary, she offered to commit herself to the cause of the Allies in return for the promise of specific territory. Italy's demands on the Entente were the Trentino, Gorizia, Istria and Dalmatia from Austria-Hungary; control over the 'Independent Muslim State of Albania'; the annexation of the Albanian town of Valona, and Saseno island at the entrance to the Adriatic; 'full possession' of the Dodecanese Islands, already under Italian occupation since the Italian-Turkish war of 1912; and control over the southern provinces of Turkish Asia Minor, including the ports of Marmarice and Antalya.

Italy understood that such gains depended upon the imminent defeat of Turkey, and the eventual defeat of Austria-Hungary. She was prepared to commit her manpower to the trenches in return for these tangible territorial gains. She also asked Britain for the immediate despatch of four British battleships to join the Italian fleet in the Adriatic, to protect the Italian coastal towns from Austro-Hungarian naval bombardment.

Although the British were surprised at the extent of the Italian claims, negotiations were begun. Greece, in return for entering the war, had already requested southern Albania and the Smyrna province of Asia Minor, as well as the remaining Turkish islands in the Aegean Sea. The nations that stood to gain from victory at the Dardanelles thus included three – Russian, Italy and Greece – who were not participating in the attack itself.

On March 12 the Kaiser was told that the Turks were short of ammunition at the Dardanelles. He at once telegraphed to Admiral Usedom, the German Inspector-General of Coast Defences and Mines at the Dardanelles, to assure him that 'everything conceivable is being done to arrange for the supply of ammunition'. The Kaiser added that the sending of a German or Austrian submarine to the Dardanelles was being 'seriously considered'. Turkey had no submarines.

Because of its strategic importance the Kaiser's telegram was sent by a top-secret coded radio signal. Within twenty-four hours, this signal was read by British naval intelligence (by the denizens of Room 40 at the Admiralty) and decoded. Reading it on the following day, Churchill realized that the Turkish army must be running out of ammunition. He was exhilarated. The First Sea Lord, Lord Fisher, as excited as his political master, waved the intercepted telegram above his head and cried out, 'By God, I'll go through tomorrow. We shall probably lose six ships, but I'm going through.'

On the following day, March 14, Churchill telegraphed to Admiral Carden at the Dardanelles that the Admiralty had 'information that the Turkish forts are short of ammunition, that German officers have made despondent reports and have appealed for more. Every conceivable effort is being made to supply ammunition, it is being seriously considered to send a German or an Austrian submarine, but apparently they have not started yet.' The telegram continued: 'All this makes it clear that the operation should now be pressed forward methodically and resolutely by night and day. The unavoidable losses must be accepted. The enemy is harassed and anxious now. The time is precious as the interference of submarines is a very serious complication.'

The Anglo-French naval attack on the Dardanelles took place on 18 March 1915. Despite the heavy fire power of the six British and four French battleships that moved forward towards the Narrows, accompanied by a substantial naval escort, the attack that day failed to push through the Narrows and into the Sea of Marmara. By midday most of the Turkish mines which had been laid in the waterway were destroyed, leaving only nine more such lines to be swept clear for the attack to reach the Narrows. But then the advancing fleet reached an unexpected line of twenty mines, which had not been spotted. Three of the ten battleships were sunk. On one of them, the *Bouvet*, 620 French sailors were drowned. The British losses were 47 men.

Faced with the unexpected minefield, and the loss of ships and men, the British admiral called off the attack. He was willing, however, to try a second attack in a few days' time, believing that he could sweep the remaining minefields and push past the last of the Turkish defences. Churchill also wanted one more naval push. But the balance of opinion in London, especially at the War Office, was that the next stage of the attack ought to be, not by ships, but by troops. The idea gaining greatest support in the War Council was that troops would land on the Gallipoli peninsula and advance from the shore of the Aegean Sea to the shore of the Sea of Marmara. As they advanced, they would destroy the Turkish defences facing the waterway. Once that was done, but only then, would the warships be able to push on into the Sea of Marmara, freed from the risk of unswept minefields and the harassment of Turkish artillery defences.

But the Turkish defences were being strengthened. Labour battalions, made up of Turks, Greeks, Armenians and Jews from the town of Chanak, were put to work strengthening the defences of the peninsula. Five hundred German officers and men were brought in to help with these preparations. Several German aircraft were brought to Chanak; one was destroyed in its hangar by a British aviator dropping a single bomb. Six Turkish divisions were also brought down to the peninsula. Two of them were commanded by German officers.

Repeated British air attacks by day forced many of the Turkish defences to be prepared in the hours of darkness, but the work was still done. 'Thousands of Turks work all night like beavers, constructing trenches, redoubts and barbed-wire entanglements', the British Admiral reported to the General who was to command the military landings. 'It is true that we have never seen any of them, but every dawn brings fresh evidence of their nightly activities.' At Cape Helles, the workers laid barbed wire along those beaches where it was assumed the Entente forces would land. They also dug machine-gun emplacements on the cliffs overlooking these beaches. These preparations, involving diligent planning and constant labour, were to cost the British forces dear.

The strategic thinking that made Lord Kitchener confident of overrunning the Gallipoli peninsula, opening the Dardanelles to the Allied ships, and forcing the Turks at Constantinople to surrender, was based on an underestimate of Turkish military qualities. When the question of sending trained British troops to the peninsula had been mooted at the War Council, Kitchener had set his colleagues' minds at rest concerning the diversion of such troops from the Western Front, by telling them that as only 'a cruise in the Sea of Marmara' was contemplated, Australian troops would be quite sufficient for the task. As Australian troops were even then in Egypt, on their way to the Western Front, they could be diverted to Gallipoli.

Kitchener's comment on the one hand belittled the Australians; and on the other certainly underestimated the Turkish soldiery.

The military landings on the Gallipoli peninsula took place on April 25. The troops succeeded in landing at Cape Helles, although losses on some of the beaches were heavy. The attackers were also able to scale the cliffs overlooking the beaches, and, further north at Anzac Cove, to secure a beachhead on the Aegean side of the peninsula. But the troops who fought so bravely that day were never able to reach the objective of the first day's assault, the high ground that ran along the central spine of the peninsula, with Achi Baba its highest point within view of Cape Helles, and Chunuk Bair dominating the skyline inland from Anzac Cove.

Yet the first day's battle was (as the Duke of Wellington said of Waterloo) a 'close run thing'. One group of Australian troops managed to approach the very crest of the Chunuk Bair late that first afternoon, shortly after the company of Turkish troops on guard there, having run out of ammunition, withdrew down the far slope. As the Turks pulled back, however, they met one of their divisional commanders who was reconnoitring in the area. 'Why are you running away?' he asked them. 'The enemy, sir,' they replied. The officer – his name was Mustafa Kemal – asked where the enemy troops were. The soldiers pointed out, about a thousand yards away on the slope below them, a small group of Australians approaching the crest of the hill. 'If you haven't any ammunition,' Kemal told them, 'at least you have your bayonets'. He then ordered them to lie down and prepare to repel the attack.

In later years, Kemal – when, as Kemal Ataturk, he was President of the Turkish Republic – recalled how, as soon as the Turkish soldiers lay down and took up their positions on the crest, the Australians below, having spotted them, likewise lay down. Kemal remained standing. One of the Australians, Captain Tulloch, later wrote of how he saw a Turkish officer standing under a tree, less than a thousand yards away, giving orders. Tulloch fired at him, but missed. The Turkish officer did not move.

As Kemal went down the reverse slope to find more men, the Australians rose and continued their advance up the slope. When Kemal returned to the crest, bringing with him 400 armed men from his own division, he saw an Australian column only 400 yards below, and advancing towards the summit. Kemal ordered a battery of guns to be brought up; they arrived just in time. As more and more Turks reached the crest, an Australian soldier with the group near the summit went back for reinforcements. He found a group of Australians on one of the lower slopes 'smoking and resting as if on a picnic'. When he explained to them the situation on the summit, with Turkish troops arriving in force, one of the Australians told him: 'I couldn't dream they'd come back.'

The fighting on Chunuk Bair became severe. One Turkish regiment, and two Arab regiments, were sent into action. The Australians were pushed back from the crest, and were then pinned down by rifle and artillery fire two-thirds of the way up the slope. 'There was no rest, no lull,' wrote one

Australian soldier. 'While the rotting dead lay all around us, never a pause in the whole of that long day that started at the crack of dawn. How we longed for nightfall! How we prayed for this ghastly day to end! How we yearned for the sight of the first dark shadow!'

The Turkish and Arab troops facing the Australians were equally exhausted. Despite constant urging from Kemal, the two Arab regiments did not have the strength left to dislodge the Australians from their rocky perch, or to push them down to the shore. But by his presence and persistence, Kemal had achieved one of the signal victories of the First World War. The first day's objective of the attacking forces, the summit of Chunuk Bair, was never to fall into Allied hands. The second and third days' objectives, to push down the eastern slope to the shore of the Marmara, were likewise not achieved, then or later. The defeat and dismemberment of Turkey were not to take place for another three and a half years; by which time Kemal himself was ready to emerge as the leader of a revivified and republican Turkish state, shorn of its empire, but not of its national pride and aspirations.

Twenty-four hours after the Gallipoli landings, the Allied forces were ashore, and fortifying all their beachheads. That day, April 26, Britain and France signed the Pact of London with Italy, accepting Italy's territorial demands on Austria-Hungary and Turkey, and welcoming Italy as a belligerent and an Allied Power. A French diplomat commented acerbicly: 'The Italians are hurtling to the aid of the victors.' Yet although the military leaders were still confident of an Allied victory at Gallipoli, perhaps within a few days, that victory was far from assured.

Echoing the mood of those who wanted Italy to participate as a warring and ultimately victorious nation, the poet Gabriele D'Annunzio, who had been an outspoken supporter of the war in Tripolitania three years earlier, declared: 'We will no longer be a museum of antiquities, a kind of hostelry, a pleasure resort, under a sky painted over with Prussian blue, for the benefit of international honeymooners. They think of us as powerless — we who are the inheritors of Rome!'

Having entered the war, Italy prepared to do battle with the Austro-Hungarian army the full length of the high mountain barrier between them. The British and French went on seeking the defeat of Turkey on the Gallipoli peninsula. For more than six months the struggle continued. Exhorted to do so by their German and Turkish commanders, of whom Mustafa Kemal was increasingly prominent, the Turks held the high ground despite repeated attacks against it. They did not have the strength, either on that first evening when Kemal's exhortations had been so effective, or later, to drive the invader into the sea. But from that first day on, neither the tenacity of the British, Australian, New Zealand and French troops, nor a new landing in August at Suvla Bay, were able to reach the high ground or push beyond it to the shore of the Sea of Marmara, less than four miles to the east. The Allied ships that in April had seemed so close to penetrating to the inland sea, remained outside the Dardanelles, using their massive naval guns to pound, but never to dislodge, the Turkish defenders.

The death toll among the soldiers battling on the Gallipoli peninsula, often in hand-to-hand fighting, mounted daily, with sudden rises in the casualty rate whenever the Entente forces launched another frontal attack. When the Entente forces finally withdrew, nine months after the first landings, the accumulated loss of life had been considerable. More than 28,000 British, 10,000 French, 7595 Australian and 2431 New Zealand soldiers had been killed; a total death toll on the part of the attacking forces of 48,000 men. In the course of their defence of the peninsula, more than 66,000 Turkish soldiers had been killed. The war graves and monuments to both the attackers and the defenders that mark and dominate the peninsula today are the memorial to more than 100,000 lost lives.

In the obituary lists of every nation at war were many who might have made a contribution to the wellbeing of society, and to the advancement of knowledge, for their own nation and for all mankind. Among those who were killed in the fighting at Gallipoli in August was a twenty-seven-year-old British physicist, Henry Moseley. It was he who had established, shortly before the outbreak of the war, the primacy of atomic numbers, the fundamental defining characteristic of a chemical element, on the basis of which all later developments in nuclear physics and atomic chemistry were built. Known to his fellow scientists as a born experimenter, he was killed in action at the Battle of Suvla Bay. Eighty years after his death, a physicist could write: 'He certainly was in the highest class of creative people of the time, perhaps of any time.'

Among the soldiers at Gallipoli was Geoffrey Dearmer, who wrote in his poem 'A Prayer':

> We pray in barren stress
> Where stricken men await the shrill alarm
> And nightly watch, in silent order set,
> The beckoning star enshrine the parapet
> 'Lord, keep his soul from harm
> And grant him happiness.'

Dearmer's brother was killed in the campaign that followed. Dearmer himself died only in 1996, at the age of 103.

There was one political development at Gallipoli which the Allies had not anticipated, the emergence of Arab nationalism as a potential extra force against the Turks. In October 1915 an Arab staff officer in the Turkish army, Muhammad Sharif al-Faruqi, deserted from the Turkish forces and crossed into the British lines, offering his services to help raise Arab support for the Allied cause. Al-Faruqi told his British interrogators that if an immediate declaration could be made, promising the Arabs independence in Arabia, Syria, Mesopotamia and Palestine, an Arab revolt against the Turks could begin at once.

Encouraged by the prospect of a new ally, the British began negotiations with Sherif Hussein of Mecca, the leader of the anti-Turkish forces in Arabia. An official British letter was written to Hussein whereby Britain agreed 'to recognize and support the independence of the Arabs within the territories included in the limits and boundaries proposed by the Sherif of Mecca'. These boundaries included Mesopotamia and much of Syria. The British negotiators, who in 1917 were to offer the Jews a National Home 'in Palestine', were later emphatic that Palestine, as well as the coastal region of Syria, had been excluded from the original promise.

Arab nationalism was ruthlessly crushed by the Turks. Even before al-Faruqi had crossed into the British lines at Gallipoli, the Turkish governor of Syria, Jemal Pasha, hanged eleven Arab leaders, including Abd al-Karim al-Khalil, who had hoped to organize an Arab revolt along the Lebanese coast, between Beirut and Sidon.

Throughout 1915 the war at sea resulted in heavy loss of life. When ships were sunk, their crews had to battle against fire and water. They had also to contend with the speed with which a warship could be blown apart and sink to the bottom of the sea. In January, during an Anglo-German naval battle in the North Sea, off the Dogger Bank, 782 German sailors were drowned when the *Blücher* went down. When the British cargo passenger ship *Falaba* was torpedoed, while on its way from Liverpool to West Africa, it sank in eight minutes; 104 of its 242 passengers and crew were drowned. Among the dead was a mining engineer, Leon Thrasher, the first United States citizen to be killed in the war.

In May, the main New York newspapers published an advertisement, sent to them from the German Embassy in Washington, stating that travellers intending to embark on an Atlantic voyage 'are reminded that a state of war exists between Germany and Great Britain and her allies', that the zone of war included the waters adjacent to the British Isles, and that vessels flying the British flag or a flag of her allies 'are liable to destruction in those waters'. Travellers sailing in the war zones to Great Britain or her Allies, the German notice added, 'do so at their own risk.'

This warning was published next to a British Cunard Line advertisement for the sailing, at ten that same morning, and again a month later, of the *Lusitania*. In the advertisement the liner was described as 'Fastest and Largest Steamer now in Atlantic Service.' She sailed as planned. Six days later she was attacked and sunk by a German submarine off the coast of Ireland. Of the 2000 passengers on board, 1198 were drowned; 128 of them were United States citizens.

The United States was shocked by the sinking, and by the loss of so many American lives. Referring to the German newspaper notice, President Wilson said that 'no warning that an unlawful and inhumane act will be committed' could be accepted 'as a legitimate excuse for that act'. The American ambassador in Berlin expected to be recalled, as a mark of his government's anger. But Wilson had no intention of risking or abandoning American neutrality. The ambassador remained in Berlin, and on behalf of his government sought an apology, which in due course the German government delivered. The German newspapers were in less apologetic mood. 'Every human life is, of course, valuable, and its loss deplorable,' the *Frankfurter Zeitung* wrote on the day after the sinking, 'but measured by the methods of this war, by the methods introduced by our enemies, forcing us to retaliatory measures in self-defence, the death of non-combatants is a matter of no consequence.'

One month after the sinking of the *Lusitania*, the Kaiser issued a secret instruction to all German submarine commanders. They were henceforth to spare all large passenger ships.

As the casualty lists had mounted on the Gallipoli peninsula, it was clear that the rapid defeat of Turkey, and the exposing of the Central Powers to a knockout blow from the south, along the Danube into the heart of Europe, was not in prospect, despite the hopes of February and March. On May 6 an Anglo-French assault on the high ground at Cape Helles was designed to capture the heights of Achi Baba – the first day's objective at Cape Helles – but failed to do so. Three days later, on the Western Front, French troops launched a massive attack on the German positions on the Vimy Ridge. The attack was a failure, the artillery barrage that proceeded it having fallen short of much of the German barbed-wire defences. Among the troops taking part was a regiment of the French Foreign Legion: of the 3000 men who went into the attack, the commanding officer, all three battalion commanders, and 1889 men were killed.

A British attack that same day against Aubers Ridge, the high ground they had failed to capture during the battle of Neuve Chapelle two months earlier, was also a failure. Shortage of artillery shells limited the preliminary bombardment to forty minutes, and fewer than eight per cent of the shells fired were high explosives. Once again the German wire was left virtually intact. The Germans reported from the battlefield that some of the shells were duds; they had been made in the United States and filled with sawdust, not explosives. Other shells, fired from overheated and worn-out gun barrels, fell far short of the German lines. The diary of one German regiment recounts the moment after the British artillery bombardment on the German frontline trenches when the smoke of the shellfire cleared. 'There could never before in war have been a more perfect target,' the diarist wrote, 'than this solid wall of khaki men, British and Indian side by side. There was only one possible order to give – "Fire until the barrels burst".'

The official history of the Rifle Brigade recounted a moment of the battle from the British side, when General Sir William Rawlinson, Chief of the General Staff of the British Expeditionary Force, said to one of the officers on his staff, General R. S. Oxley: 'This is most unsatisfactory. Where are the Sherwood foresters? Where are the East Lancashires on the right?' To which Oxley replied: 'They are lying in no-man's land, sir, and most of them will never stand again.'

In a single day of battle, with not one of the objectives reached, the British and Indian death toll was in excess of 11,000 men.

The failure at Aubers Ridge, attributed to the shell shortage, led to a demand in Britain for a change in the political direction of the war. Hitherto the Liberal government had excluded the Conservative opposition from all part in war direction. The Conservatives were now brought in to the highest places of war direction, with A. J. Balfour, a former Conservative Prime Minister, replacing Churchill as the minister in charge of the Royal Navy, and leaving Churchill to confront, for much of his long political career, the hostile cry: 'What about the Dardanelles!' Six months later, unable to influence British policy or strategy any further, Churchill left the government and went as a battalion commander to the Western Front.

Neither the political changes in Britain in May 1915, nor the employment of women for the first time in the growing number of munitions factories in Britain, led to any rapid improvement in Britain's military situation on the Western Front or at sea. There were no short cuts to victory. The warmaking power of every nation was being drawn into a prolonged struggle, and was, by its very success, ensuring that that struggle would be prolonged. A renewed German gas offensive on the Western Front failed to secure any breakthrough for the Germans. A British attempt to drive the Germans from the Ypres salient was likewise unsuccessful. Among the several thousand British dead in that battle was an Irish soldier, Private J. Condon, who is believed to be the youngest uniformed casualty of the First World War. He was fourteen years old.

That spring and early summer, systematic Zeppelin raids over Britain began. During a raid on the night of May 10/11 the crew of one Zeppelin, which had been driven off by gunfire from the ground, dropped a hastily scrawled card on Canvey Island, 'You English! We have come, and will come again soon – kill or cure.' One woman was killed that night and two people were killed in a raid a week later, all of them civilians. Then, on May 31, seven Londoners were killed when a single Zeppelin dropped ninety small incendiary bombs and thirty grenades on the capital. Among those killed were three-year-old Elsie Leggatt and her eleven-year-old sister May.

Also killed that night were Henry Good and his wife Caroline. Bricks had been thrown through their bedroom window to try to awake them before the fire spread. 'Mr and Mrs Good were kneeling beside the bed,' the policeman who found their bodies wrote in his report. 'They were unclothed, save that a band of cloth encircled Mr Good's arm, suggesting that a woollen jersey had been burnt from him. His right arm was about his wife's waist. A big tuft of hair was gripped firmly in Mrs Good's hand.' The policeman went on to ask: 'Were the victims asleep when the crash came, and stumbled, confused and half dazed in a room of which they had temporarily lost their bearings? Did the friendly missiles coming through the window suggest a hostile attack from the very direction in which escape was still possible? Or did the fumes, spreading swiftly from the burning staircase, overtake them too soon, and the woman in her agony and terror, faced by the resistless advance of those terrible flames, sink in prayer at the bedside, to be joined by her husband?'

Bombs also fell that night on a railway goods station, a music hall, a churchyard, a boot warehouse, a whisky distillery, a stable and a synagogue. Among those killed in the street, while on their way home from the cinema, were two Jewish Londoners, ten-year-old Samuel Reuben and thirty-year-old Leah Lehman. Immediately after the raid, local anger turned against German-born citizens and shopkeepers. An eye-witness wrote:

> In the centre of the turmoil men dragged a big, stout man, stumbling and resisting in their grasp, his clothes whitened by flour, his mouth dripping blood. They rushed him on. New throngs closed around him.
>
> From another direction arose more shouting. A woman's scream. The tail of the crowd dashed off towards the sound. Crowds raced to it from all directions. A woman was in the midst of a struggling mob; her blouse half-torn off, her fair hair fallen, her face contorted with pain and terror, blood running down her bare white arm.
>
> A big, drunken man flung her to the ground. She was lost to sight. 'Oh my God! Oh! They are kicking her!' a woman screamed.

As the stalemate in the trenches continued, it was shortage of munitions that most inhibited British military action in the summer of 1915. Despite the activities earlier in the year of the Women's International League for Permanent Peace, in which British women had participated, the employment of women for munitions work gained a rapid momentum once it became government policy. Women were urged to register, and within a few days 8000 had done so. On July 22 more than a thousand more women registered in the course of a few hours. One of the organizers of the registration, Mrs Dacre Fox, declared that 'nothing which had menaced women in other ages was comparable to the menace of Germany today'. Another of the organizers, Mrs Mansel, said that news of the registration 'would reach Germany, and would be read there as a direct challenge from the women of England'.

On the Western Front, the Germans used flame-throwers for the first time at the end of July. The men caught in the direct blast of the fire, one British eye-witness wrote, 'were never seen again'. But still the trench lines were held, the death toll mounting with every renewed attack. 'The country has now ceased to fight for the causes of war,' a British pacifist, Clifford Allen, wrote in a Labour newspaper at the end of May, 'and merely continues to fight, even more intensely and madly, because of the results of warfare.'

From Gallipoli, Churchill's brother Jack wrote to him in May: 'It has become siege warfare again, as in France.' That month the Australian and New Zealand forces had granted a ten-hour truce to the Turks on their sector, so that the Turks could come out of their trenches and bury 3000 of their men who were lying in no-man's land. Conditions on the peninsula were horrific; clouds of large blue-black flies, after feasting on the eyes and open wounds of the dead, would descend in a swarm on the bread and jam of soldiers nearby who were trying to eat their rations.

In June, in another attempt to capture the hill of Achi Baba, at Cape Helles, 4500 British and 2000 French soldiers were killed; as were 9000 of the Turkish defenders. A German officer present was convinced that with one more immediate assault, before the Turks had time to recover, the British would be able to break the Turkish morale and push through to their objective; but the British were too exhausted and decimated by the battle to make that second push, and Achi Baba remained in Turkish hands. But the failure of these assaults, and the inexorably mounting death toll, inhibited neither the commanders in their orders for renewed assaults, nor the men in their obedience to those orders. 'He fell with his face to the enemy,' Fred Tennant wrote from Gallipoli at the beginning of June, about his brother Harry, to their mother in England, 'and I am sure no man could wish for a more glorious death'. Fred Tennant was himself killed three weeks later.

At the end of June the British launched yet another attack on Achi Baba. But the Turks had reinforced their defences since the previous attack, and all that was captured were a few trench lines. In one of them the British troops found a breakfast of hard-boiled eggs and biscuits ready to be eaten, and a store of cigars. They also found the corpses of several Irish soldiers, unburied since an earlier attack on those same trenches two months earlier.

One more attempt was made to take the heights of the Gallipoli peninsula. Landing at Suvla Bay, to the north of Anzac Cove, on August 6, twenty-five British battalions were put ashore virtually unopposed. Their attack was matched by the simultaneous advance of the Australians and New Zealanders from the Anzac area. It was a moment of particular danger, not only for the Turks but for the Germans. 'Heavy fighting has been going on since yesterday at the Dardanelles,' Admiral Tirpitz wrote in his diary on the second day of the renewed assault, as British, Indian, Australian and New Zealand troops pushed inland and reached the lower slopes of the ridge. 'The situation is obviously critical,' Tirpitz added. 'Should the Dardanelles fall, the World War has been decided against us.'

At first it seemed that Admiral Tirpitz's apocalyptic vision might be a true one. On August 9, three days after the renewed battle had begun, New Zealand troops advancing from Anzac reached the summit of Chunuk Bair, the strategic height from which the Sea of Marmara was visible far below. It was Kemal who led the counterattack on the following morning, as he had done in May, driving off the crest the Lancashiremen who had replaced the New Zealanders during the night. The Lancashiremen had never been in battle before. The Turks on the ridge were experienced fighters.

Further north, on the even higher ridge of Koja Chemen Tepe, a small British and Gurkha force, which had also reached the crest on August 9, repelled a Turkish counterattack with a bayonet charge. It was about to drive the Turks down the far slope when British naval gunners, not knowing the summit was in Allied hands, and far too distant to make out the situation on the crest with binoculars, opened fire, blasting the Allied attackers with the unbearable force of naval high explosives, and forcing those who survived the bombardment to retreat down the slope whence they had come. The gains of August 9 were not to be repeated. Both crests remained in Turkish hands, and Mustafa Kemal was promoted General (becoming Mustafa Kemal Pasha).

*   *   *

The Allied forces made one further attempt at Suvla Bay to break through the Turkish trench lines and reach the high ground. Launched on August 21, the attack was aimed at two of the foothills that were held by the Turks well below the crest. The attack failed, despite the incredible bravery of many of the attackers. Two days later it was called off. There were to be no more attempts to drive the Turks from the summits from which they could look down on the Allied forces trapped below them. As the inclement winter weather approached, a particularly violent form of diarrhoea made life unbearable. The whole Allied force, wrote the official historian who served on the peninsula throughout the campaign, 'from the Commander-in-Chief downward, was affected by this complaint, and the men were so weak from it that few could walk at a quicker pace than a crawl'.

The impact of the deaths at Gallipoli, as on the Western Front, was felt in Britain, affecting more and more homes. 'Early in September,' Vera Brittain recalled, 'we heard of the first casualty to happen in our family. A cousin from Ireland, we learnt, had died of wounds after the landing at Suvla Bay; the original bullet-wound behind the ear had not been serious, but he had lain untended for a week at Mudros, and was already suffering from cerebral sepsis when operated on, too late, by an overworked surgeon on the crowded *Aquitania*. I had hardly known my cousin, but it was a shock to learn that lives were being thrown away through the inadequacy of the medical services in the Mediterranean.'

On November 27 hail and torrential rain on the Gallipoli peninsula led to at least a hundred men being drowned as water swept men, horses and supplies down the narrow gullies. The rain 'turned our trenches into moats', recalled one British officer, Captain C. R. Attlee, who was to be Britain's Deputy Prime Minister in the Second World War, and Prime Minister of the post-1945 Labour government. Two days after this rainstorm, a hundred men froze to death during a snow blizzard. For the Australians and Indians in particular, the extreme cold was a torment. The only welcome deaths at Gallipoli that November were those of the millions of flies who had lived and multiplied on the corpses of the dead; when the snow blizzard passed they had disappeared.

A spate of disasters to the Russian armies on the Eastern Front, culminating in the loss on August 15 of the town of Wlodawa, on the River Bug, and the fall of the fortress of Kovno two days later, led the Russians to appeal to Britain for some renewed offensive action on the Western Front, in the hope that such an offensive would take the pressure off Russia in the east. It was seven months since a similar Russian appeal, at a time when Russia was being hard pressed by the Turks in the Caucasus, had led Lord Kitchener to suggest a naval demonstration at the Dardanelles, the small seed from which had grown the whole Gallipoli enterprise. Kitchener responded to this second appeal by ordering a new attack to be prepared on the Western Front, despite the view of the Canadian Prime Minister, many of whose troops would be involved, and of Churchill – who was still in the government, though in relatively minor office – that the supply of munitions needed for such an offensive would not be ready for between five and nine months.

Before the new British attack could take place on the Western Front, the German government, having occupied such a large swathe of Russian territory, and hoping to be able to concentrate all its military efforts against Britain and France on the Western Front, offered to make peace with Russia on the basis of German territorial gains in the lands already captured. The Russian government replied that it would not make peace until every single German or Austrian soldier had left Russian soil. These brave words belied the seriousness of the military situation: at the end of August the Russian army was forced to abandon the fortress of Brest Litovsk, opening the provinces of White Russia (Byelorussia) and the Volhynia to immediate attack. When the Volhynian market town of Lutsk was occupied, 7000 Russian soldiers were taken prisoner.

Russia's antiwar movement was gaining in strength, as her armies fell back, and the fear of being taken prisoner was replaced by the fear of being killed in action. The Bolsheviks in Russia, and those in exile, increased their efforts to play on these fears. In Switzerland, a conference of International Socialists, meeting between September 5 and 11 at Zimmerwald, issued a manifesto demanding immediate peace and, in order to secure the movement's revolutionary aim, civil war 'between the classes' throughout Europe. Among the Russian delegates who supported the manifesto was the Bolshevik leader Vladimir Lenin and his former rival, the Menshevik revolutionary Leon Trotsky.

In White Russia – the Tsarist region of Byelorussia, today the independent State of Belarus – a British nurse, Florence Farmborough, who was serving with the Russian forces, noted in her diary in late September that 'the thousands of refugees swarming into the cities and towns were followed by pestilence and crime'. That September, in Odessa, there was an antiwar riot by 2500 wounded soldiers, due to be sent back to the front when their wounds were healed. Antiwar protests took place in other towns far behind the lines, including Rostov-on-Don and Astrakhan. The Bolsheviks encouraged soldiers to demand an end to the war, and to refuse to be sent back to the front. In St Petersburg, 500 reservists attacked the police at the railway station where they were being embarked for the war zone. 'News from Russia testifies to the growing revolutionary mood,' Lenin wrote with some satisfaction in a private letter from his exile in Switzerland.

As the calls for an end to the fighting echoed from Zimmerwald, the fighting itself continued and intensified. During a German air raid on the French town of Lunéville, on market day, forty-eight civilians were killed. During two German Zeppelin raids on London, forty people were killed. On the Eastern Front, German troops entered Vilna, the largest of the cities of Lithuania, taking 22,000 Russian soldiers captive. The occupation of Vilna, and the moving of the German High Command's Eastern Headquarters to Kovno, stimulated German hopes for the annexation of both Lithuania and Courland, or for their rule by a German prince, and their colonization by German farmers. The rapid German military advance in the east, so different to the static warfare on the Western Front, resulted in a far larger number of soldiers – Russians – being taken prisoner of war, and in large-scale territorial changes – in Germany's favour.

The Germanization of the newly conquered eastern regions was begun at once. An Intendant-General was appointed by Berlin to set up six administrative areas, in which Lithuanians, Latvians (or Letts, as they were also known) and Poles would live under martial law, and the German inhabitants be given all the benefits of a colonial administration. All school teachers had to be German. The language of instruction in schools had to be German. All courts were to be presided over by German judges. When the Poles asked the Germans to agree to the establishment of a university in Vilna, something that had been denied them by the Russians, their request was turned down.

The British and French promise – to launch an offensive on the Western Front, to take pressure off the Russians in the East – was made good on September 25. Two separate attacks were launched, one by the French in Champagne and the other by the British at Loos. Neither was able to breach the line of the trenches, but the French offensive made an unprecedented two-mile dent in the German line, along a fifteen-mile front, which resulted in 1800 German soldiers being taken prisoner. It was not a large number by the standards of the Eastern Front, but a substantial number in Western Front terms. Among those participating in the assault in Champagne were several volunteers from the still-neutral United States, who had enlisted in the French Foreign Legion. One of them, Henry Weston Farnsworth, was killed in action. He was a graduate of Harvard.

The parallel British offensive at Loos was even less successful than the French attack. Although the British used poison gas for the first time in this battle, as a direct result of which many German soldiers were killed, the German superiority in machine-gun fire brought the attack to a bloody halt a few hundred yards from its starting point. So shocked were the German machine gunners at the sight of line after line of British troops walking into their field of fire and being mown down that when the fifth British attempt to capture the first objective – the Bois Hugo – failed, and those wounded who could walk or crawl were working their way back to the British lines, no shot was fired at them. Among the British dead at Loos was Rudyard Kipling's only son, John. Among the wounded was a future British Prime Minister, Harold Macmillan, who was shot in the hand.

It was during the Battle of Loos that a British medical officer, Captain W. Johnson, noticed a phenomenon that had not been widely seen on the battlefield for two years – since the retreat from Mons, under heavy German artillery fire, in 1914. Many of the eighteen- and nineteen-year olds, all volunteers, who were sent to him after they had been in action at Loos were, he noted, suffering from 'definite hysterical manifestations (mutism and tremors)'. This was what soon became known as 'shell-shock'. It was affecting the soldiers of all armies, and was doing so in ever-increasing numbers.

A second war front had been opened against the Turks in the spring of 1915, in Mesopotamia. The initial advance from Basra towards Baghdad augured well for the British and Indian troops moving northward. But the conditions of warfare were even harsher than on the Gallipoli peninsula, with the temperature climbing by the end of June to 115 degrees Fahrenheit (45 degrees Celsius), and fierce, biting mosquitoes tormenting the advancing troops with an unexpected ferocity.

Despite these dreadful hardships, the advance continued as far as Kut, only twenty-two miles from Baghdad; at that point, the British and Indian forces had come 380 miles from the sea. When Kut was captured there was some amusement at the discovery, among the Turkish defences, of a Persian cannon dating from the time of Napoleon. But there was also a sinister aspect of the battle; those wounded men who had not been found by search parties were robbed by marauding Arabs, many of the injured men were mutilated, and some of them were murdered. The wounded in Mesopotamia were not automatically accorded the protection given to prisoners of war after the battles on the Western and Eastern Fronts.

The failure of the efforts of the Anglo-French force to break through the Turkish defences at Gallipoli led in the late autumn of 1915 to the decision to withdraw from the peninsula altogether, and to make no further effort to force the Dardanelles by ships or men. This decision to abandon the attack on the strategic and political heart of Turkey came at a time when, in the Balkans, the Austro-Hungarian army was about to renew the offensive against Serbia. Since repelling the first Austro-Hungarian assault a year earlier, Serbia had maintained its independence and been unmolested. The Austrians, determined not to be forced back as they had been in October 1914 by a vigorous Serb defence, made their preparations in such a way as to ensure German participation in the attack. To this end, a senior and hitherto successful German officer, General Mackensen, the German victor of the Austro-Hungarian recapture of Western and Eastern Galicia, was given command of the military operations.

The Austro-German attack on Serbia began on 7 October 1915. In an intensive Austrian artillery bombardment on Belgrade, the gun batteries that had been sent to the city's defence by Russia, France and Britain were quickly put out of action, and the city, defended tenaciously by Serbian infantrymen, was captured. Seven days later, as the Austro-German forces battled along Serbia's northern and western borders, the eastern border with Bulgaria erupted into war. To the last moment, Britain and France had hoped that they could persuade Bulgaria to remain neutral, even to join the Entente by an offer of Turkish territory. But the Bulgarians were aware of the failure of the Gallipoli expedition, even if they knew nothing of the imminent withdrawal of the Entente armies from the peninsula, and preferred to join in the assault of the Central Powers.

Bulgaria's participation in the attack on Serbia sealed Serbia's fate. The numerical odds of the forces arrayed against her were too great to be repelled. By November 1 the Bulgarian army had overrun the eastern half of Serbian Macedonia, and occupied its chief town, Skopje. From the west and north,

Austro-German forces captured the town of Kragujevac, the headquarters of the Serbian General Staff. In the British House of Commons, Sir Edward Grey had warned Bulgaria that if she attacked Serbia, England would come to Serbia's assistance 'without reserve and without qualification'. To implement this pledge, an Allied Expeditionary Force of 13,000 men had landed at Salonika on the day of the Austro-German attack, and moved forward to the Greek-Serbian frontier, followed nine days later by 18,000 French soldiers. The Anglo-French force failed, however, to break through the Bulgarian lines and push into central Serbia. The towns and villages along the route through which the Entente troops were expected to march put out flags and bunting to welcome them. But neither troops nor guns could reach the regions where they were so desperately needed. The first fighting between the Anglo-French force was not against the Austrians or the Germans, but against the Bulgarians, who were driven away from Strumitsa railway station, on the eastern bank of the River Vardar. Reaching a point on the River Vardar opposite the town of Negotin, the French troops made for a bridge that was marked on their maps, but found that it had been destroyed in the First Balkan War, and never repaired.

Following the fall of Kragujevac, the King of Serbia recognized that it was only a matter of time, and of a relatively short time, before the Austrian, German and Bulgarian forces would overrun his kingdom. On a visit to the frontline trenches, where peasant soldiers were holding the line, their bayonets fixed to rifles for which they had little ammunition left, he told them: 'Heroes, you have taken two oaths, one to me, your king, and one to your country. From the first I release you, from the second no man can release you. But if you decide to return to your home, and if we should be victorious, you shall not be made to suffer. As for me and my sons, we remain here.'

Not a single soldier left his post. Together with the king and his sons, the Serbian army fought on. But it was seriously outnumbered and eventually encircled; and in the crucial matter of artillery it had no chance; for every fifty shells that the Austrians had, the Serbians had only one.

When the Bulgarians entered Nish on November 5, they captured the last section of the Berlin–Baghdad railway that was not under German control or influence. By November 23, less than two months after the Austro-German attack on Serbia had begun, the Serbian army had been pushed back to a tiny corner of land in the mountains around Kosovo. To these sacred fields, the scene of Serbia's defeat at the hands of the Turks more than five centuries

before, the Serbian army came in its retreat. With it came many thousands
of civilian refugees, their plight seen from the windows of the train which
brought the foreign diplomats from Belgrade on their own flight out of
Serbia. From Kosovo, the Serbian army and the refugees fleeing with it
retreated, through the most treacherous of winter conditions, southward
across the precipitate mountain roads into Serbian Macedonia. Their hope
was to reach the sea at Salonika, where they could join the British and French
troops, regroup, and prepare for the day when Serbia could be liberated.

The nature of the route which the 200,000 retreating Serbs hoped to take
was precarious. At Ferizovich the railway line came to an end. From there,
a steep and winding road led up into the mountains to the town of Prizren.
It was when the mass of the Serbian soldiers and refugees reached Prizren
that they learned that the Bulgarians, advancing rapidly westward, had
entered Debar, cutting off the southward retreat through Bitola. The army
and the refugees could no longer get through to the south, and to Salonika.
They had, instead, to turn back, and to seek an ever more precipitous, and
in part roadless route through Djakovo, Skadar and Podgoritza to the Adriatic
Sea.

One last Serbian point of possible military resistance was the town of
Petch. Some of the Serb generals believed that a last stand could, and should
be made there, even if it meant the virtual destruction of the Serb forces.
But a majority of the generals were opposed to such a sacrifice, and decided
to follow the route that was already being taken by the diplomats and the
civilian refugees. As the troops set off along the new line of retreat, they
reached the point where the metalled road ended; there they had to destroy
their guns, which could not manage the rough tracks, and also burn many
of their stores and transport. It was imperative not to let them fall into the
hands of their pursuers. As the troops made their way out of Serbia into
Albania, Serb villagers who remained in their homes sprinkled white powder
on the roads and showed white flags and sheets, as a mark of surrender.

As the retreat continued, groups of Albanians were not above attacking
the defeated army and seizing what little they could find in the way of arms,
ammunition and food. Horses were killed for food by those in the retreat.
Typhus began to take a heavier toll than the battles had done. Dying men
were left by the roadside; there were not enough litters or makeshift stretchers
to carry them. A litter was found for the king, and was drawn by four oxen
through the mountain defiles.

The Serbian retreat to the Adriatic was one of the most painful sagas of the First World War. Making their way by precipitous paths to the port of San Giovanni di Medua, on the Adriatic, they arrived, after three weeks in the mountains, starving and racked by illness, to be confronted by Serbs an acute shortage of food in the tiny port. Of the 300,000 who set off, at least 20,000 perished on the march. As Italian and French ships reached San Giovanni from Italy with food, blankets and medicine, Austrian and German pilots bombed and sank the precious cargoes. When food did reach the quay, on board the *Ville de Brindisi*, there were those who were so far gone with hunger that they choked and died when bread was given to them.[1]

The Entente powers, hurrying their warships to the Albanian port of Durazzo, took off as many Serbian soldiers as managed to reach that port, and took them to the Greek island of Corfu. There, thousands more died of disease, and of the privations through which they had passed. A quarantine camp was set up on the island of Vido for those who were sick with contagious diseases. So great was the mortality there that it was known as the Island of Death.

Among the Serbian refugees retreating over the mountains had been 30,000 boys under military age. Several thousand died during the march. When they reached San Giovanni di Medua, and were waiting at the quayside for ships to take them to Corfu, several hundred were killed during an Austrian air bombardment. Once in Corfu, safe from enemy air attack, lack of food took its toll. A hundred boys a day died of starvation during their early days on the island. The outcry at their fate led to a massive rescue effort, with most of the survivors being taken to England and France for rehabilitation and schooling. Those who were suffering from typhus and tuberculosis were sent to a sanatorium on the French island of Corsica.

In their retreat, the Serbian soldiers took with them more than 24,000 Austrian prisoners of war, captured during the early weeks of the fighting. These Austrians were taken by Italian warships to Italy, where they were interned, mostly on the island of Sardinia. There, many of them were the victims of typhus and cholera.

Austria-Hungary occupied Serbia. The Anglo-French force remained at Salonika, with Serb reinforcements from Corfu, and with reinforcements

[1] At the end of the Second World War, many concentration-camp prisoners liberated by British and American troops died after eating the rations of chocolate and tinned meat that their liberators gave them. These rations were too rich for them, in their emaciated state, to digest.

from the Anglo-French troops who had been withdrawn from Gallipoli. Despite two years of fighting north of Salonika, however, this large Allied force succeeded in liberating only a single border town – Monastir – from the Austrian and Bulgarian occupying forces. Serbia, like Belgium, was to lie under the rule of her conqueror until the last weeks of the war.

The fate of the Serbs under Austrian rule, as that of the Belgians under German rule, was a cause of intense concern to the Entente Powers. It was imperative in the minds of the Entente governments that a sense of it being a 'just' war should be established. The German ill-treatment of the Belgian population, given massive and at times exaggerated publicity, served this purpose well, as did the publicity given to the plight of the Serbs under Austrian rule. The Austro-Hungarian newspapers were combed to find evidence of wrongdoing. The German press in occupied Belgium was similarly scrutinized, particularly after the execution of Edith Cavell, the British nurse who had been found guilty of helping British and French prisoners of war. She had also helped Belgians who wanted to serve in the Allied armies to escape from Belgium.

According to the official Bosnian newspaper, *Bosnische Post*, more than five thousand Serb families had been expelled from their homes in Bosnia. The number of Serb refugees from Serbia itself, finding refuge in Montenegro, was estimated by this same official Austrian source as 70,000. It was reported in the Entente press that in the Slav provinces of Austria-Hungary mass executions had taken place of Serbs and Croats who exhibited national aspirations. As many as seventy Serbs were said to have been executed in Sarajevo, and eighty at Trebinye and Mostar. Further executions were reported from Dalmatia, and from Croatia came reports of fifty Croats who were not only hanged, but whose bodies were left hanging for several weeks in order to terrorize the local Slav population. 'Many of these men,' one British writer reported, 'died singing their national songs, and exhorting the onlookers not to betray their race.'

Another particularly harsh fate awaited those Serbs and Croats who, being of military age, were called up to fight in the Austro-Hungarian army, the conqueror of Serbia and the enemy of their patron, Russia. Several thousand of these Slavs in Austro-Hungarian uniform changed sides as the armies clashed, joining their Russian fellow Slavs and turning against the army of which they had been an integral part. Some of those who were then left wounded on the field of battle killed each other rather than fall into the hands of the Austrians, to be tried and shot as traitors. A third of the Slavs sent into battle against the Russians were killed on the battlefield, serving in the front rank of the army they had been sent to fight against.

The realization that the continuation of the war could lead to the disintegration of each of the empires that were fighting it, led, after the Austrian conquest of Serbia, to a proposal by General von Hötzendorf, made secretly to the Emperor Franz Josef, for a negotiated peace with Russia. Austria did not have the same desire to gain vast areas of Russian territory as animated the Germans. She would be quite content to see the pre-war border restored. The defeat of Serbia completed the most ambitious of Austria's war aims. But the Emperor declined to support any such move, nor was there any way in which Austria would be able to make peace without Germany's approval. On the very day of von Hötzendorf's proposal, the Kaiser was warning the American Ambassador in Berlin that the United States 'had better look out after this war'. Although he said he would not have permitted the sinking of the *Lusitania* had he known of it – saying, 'no gentleman would kill so many women and children' – he was confident of victory in both East and West. And in the East, his troops were deep into the Russian heartland.

For the Russian government, defeats and retreats at the front were increasingly reflected in discontent and riots behind the lines. At Helsinki, fifty Russian sailors were arrested for protesting against the bad food and against the severity of their officers. To ensure that Russia could continue as an active ally, her Finance Minister, Peter Bark, went so far, during a visit to Paris, to warn the French President, Raymond Poincaré, that if Russia was not given massive economic assistance at once, she would be forced to make peace. He also warned that once peace was concluded, the German and Russian armies in the East would be free to move against the British and French in the West. France moved swiftly to give Russia the credits she needed. Within a year Russia had used them to purchase war supplies to the value of £757 million, including a million rifles and 27,000 machine guns.

To build a railway link between the northern Russian port of Murmansk and St Petersburg, along which most of these supplies had to pass, 30,000 Russian and 5000 Finnish labourers were taken to the frozen north. Their numbers were augmented, when the task proved beyond their capacity in the fearsome conditions of the Russian winter, by 15,000 German and Austrian prisoners of war and 10,000 Chinese indentured labourers. Even with this vast force, the railway line took a year and a half to complete. War supplies purchased from the United States, and from Russia's enemy of a decade earlier, Japan, were also brought in through the Far Eastern port of Vladivostok.

The war at sea had continued to exact a heavy toll throughout 1915. Six days after the sinking of the *Lusitania* off the coast of Ireland in May, a German submarine sank the British battleship *Goliath* off Gallipoli; 570 British sailors were drowned. A hundred sailors were drowned when the battleship *Triumph* was torpedoed two weeks after the *Goliath*. Between the sinkings of these two great warships, 226 people were killed when three trains crashed in Scotland; among the dead were more than two hundred solders on their way to the Gallipoli peninsula. It was the most serious accident, causing the greatest loss of life, in British railway history.

One of the worst naval disasters of the First World War took place in August, near the Dodecanese Island of Kos, when a German submarine sank an Allied troop transport on its way to the Gallipoli peninsula; 1865 soldiers were drowned. A further 300 soldiers, almost all of them Indians, were drowned a month later when their troopship, the *Ramazan*, also on the way to Gallipoli, was sunk in the Aegean Sea. In the Baltic, a British submarine sank a German warship, the *Prinz Adalbert*; 672 German sailors were drowned.

Each ship sunk represented the loss of life of men whose parents, wives and children were to live the rest of their lives with whatever nightmare vision of death at sea their imagination conjured up. There was not a week in which some naval disaster did not occur. When Austrian saboteurs blew up the Italian battleship *Benedetto Brin* in the Italian port of Brindisi, 456 Italian sailors were killed. When an Austrian submarine shelled and then torpedoed the Italian ocean liner *Ancona*, taking many Italian immigrants to New York, 208 passengers were drowned, including twenty-five United States citizens. When a British hospital ship, the *Anglia*, taking wounded men back from France to Britain, struck a mine off Dover, 139 of the crew and the wounded were drowned. In the eastern Mediterranean the passenger liner *Persia* was torpedoed without warning and 334 passengers drowned, among them the United States consul in Aden, and one other American citizen. As with the death of its citizens earlier, the United States issued a formal protest, but took no further action.

At sea, as on land, the relentlessness of war was revealed each day in the casualty lists which were a feature of the newspapers of every belligerent.

Yet the hope of victory remained a powerful inducement to continued support for the war effort in every land. In Britain, the public awaited that winter the news of the capture of Baghdad, and was excited when the troops at Kut moved forward to the ancient city of Ctesiphon, only a few hours' march from Baghdad. But of the 8500 British and Indian troops who went into battle at Ctesiphon on November 21, more than half were killed or wounded, and the advance had to be abandoned. Falling back towards Kut, the survivors of the battle were exhausted and demoralized. Their retreat was accompanied by continual shelling from a Turkish artillery battery, while Arab marauders fired from both banks of the River Tigris on those wounded men who were being taken to Kut by barge.

The defeated force reached Kut, where it was advised by telegram from the War Cabinet in London to return further down river to where British river reinforcements could reach it. But the advice came too late; Kut was already surrounded. The men inside it settled down to what was clearly going to be a long and arduous siege. They were unaware that a senior German officer, Field Marshal von der Goltz, was even then on his way from Constantinople to take command of the besieging force.

The siege of Kut began on December 5, when 25,000 British and Indian troops were surrounded by 80,000 Turks. Three days later, on December 8, the first of 83,048 British, Indian, Australian and New Zealand troops at Gallipoli were evacuated from Anzac and Suvla. The Allied attempt to defeat the Central Powers by striking at the heart of Turkey had failed.

The Western and Eastern Fronts, and the battles in Gallipoli and Mesopotamia, were not the only land campaigns being fought in 1915. The Italians having entered the war, they were embroiled in a series of battles with Austria in the Dolomites and on the Isonzo River. Among the Italian soldiers fighting in the mountains above the Isonzo was Private Benito Mussolini, still a Socialist, and a former newspaper editor who had welcomed Italy's entry into the war on the side of the Allies. 'Rain and lice,' he wrote, 'these are the two enemies of the Italian soldier. The cannon come after.'

By the end of the year, three prolonged battles had been fought for the mountain peaks of the Isonzo, but although more than 20,000 Italian soldiers were killed, the Austrians could not be dislodged beyond the initial and limited Italian advance. There was excitement, briefly, in Italy when, on the Dolomite Front, General Peppino Garibaldi, a grandson of the Italian national hero, captured the 4662-foot high mountain pass, the Col di Lana, but two nights later his men were driven off.

There was also fighting in three German imperial possessions in Africa: German East Africa, the Cameroons and German South West Africa, each of which was under attack by British and South African forces. In July 1915 the 7000 German settlers in German South West Africa, the beneficiaries only a few years earlier of the crushing of the Herero revolt, surrendered to a force of 30,000 South Africans. Sixteen days after the surrender, South Africa annexed this vast, diamond-rich region.

In Cameroon, despite the success of an Anglo-French force in landing at Duala and capturing its garrison within two months of the outbreak of war, German forces continued to fight in the interior throughout 1915; they surrendered only on 18 February 1916.

In German East Africa, the German forces commanded by General von Lettow-Vorbeck took the offensive in three directions: against the British forces in Uganda, to the north, against the Belgian forces in the Congo, to the west, and against the British forces in Northern Rhodesia, to the south. Throughout four years, this isolated but determined German army was to survive the various expeditions launched against it; indeed, it did not surrender until 23 November 1918, twelve days after the armistice in Europe.

On December 8 the magazine *Punch* published a poem, unsigned, which quickly established a new British and Allied symbol, the poppy. Millions of poppies were later to be worn every Armistice Day in memory of the dead. The author of the poem was a forty-two-year-old Canadian medical officer, John McCrae, who later died in the war, at his post. He called his poem 'In Flanders Fields':

> In Flanders fields the poppies blow
> Between the crosses, row on row,
>   That mark our place; and in the sky
>   The larks, still bravely singing, fly
> Scarce heard amid the guns below.

We are the Dead. Short days ago
We lived, felt dawn, saw sunset glow,
    Loved and were loved, and now we lie
        In Flanders fields.
Take up our quarrel with the foe:
To you from failing hands we throw
    The torch; be yours to hold it high.
        If ye break faith with us who die
We shall not sleep, though poppies grow
        In Flanders fields.

The pauses in fighting and fraternization on the Western Front that had occurred on Christmas Day in 1914 and continued in places until New Year's Day did not take place in 1915. Frontline fighting, like warmaking, had become all-consuming and unending. A British officer, Lieutenant Colin Gubbins, wrote home that second Christmas of 'being shelled right through Christmas Day when there was no attempt at peacemaking from either side'. The Germans, he added, 'left their trenches at safe points to walk across the open – and were fired on. The men had an excellent dinner of soup, pork, roast beef and plum pudding; a bottle of Bass for each man and a bottle of port between four.'

CHAPTER NINETEEN

1916

War, he sung, is toil and trouble;
Honour but an empty bubble.
Never ending, still beginning.
Fighting still, and still destroying.

JOHN DRYDEN
(1631–1701)

'A SECOND YEAR OF WAR,' the British orientalist Gertrude Bell wrote to her mother on 1 January 1916, 'and I can only wish you as I wished you last first of January that we may not see another. Never another year like the last!'

In Britain, the army's hope that the voluntary system that had existed since the outbreak of war would provide sufficient manpower for a second full year of war had faded, and a new scheme of recruitment was being put into effect. Devised by Lord Derby, it involved the registration of men who could be called up at any time. In a village in Cornwall, D. H. Lawrence had been struck by how distant the war had seemed to the villagers. 'But the war has come,' he wrote on January 5. 'Derby's scheme has wrung their withers. They are very sad.' A woman who was sewing an armlet on the sleeve of her husband's military jacket spoke for all the villagers when she said: 'It's come now. We've never had it till now, but it's come now, I'm sure. When I look at these buttons, I think, "We've got the Kaiser to thank for these." Every stitch I put in goes through my heart.'

The first military initiative of 1916 was taken by Austria-Hungary. It took place on January 8, in the Balkans, when a force of 45,000 Austrian soldiers and 5000 Bosnian Muslims invaded Montenegro, the small mountain kingdom that had won its independence from Turkey in 1878. Several thousand Serb soldiers who had found refuge in the Montenegrin town of Skadar a few months earlier were forced to flee again, southward across the border into Albania.

For nine days the Montenegrins fought to preserve their independence, but the forces arrayed against them were overwhelming. The King of Montenegro, like the King of Serbia, was forced to flee with his army, as Skadar, as well as the Black Mountain (as important emotionally to the Montenegrins as Kosovo to the Serbs) fell to the invading forces. 'It is all over with poor little Montenegro,' an American diplomat, John Coolidge, wrote in his diary on the last day of the Montenegrin resistance. 'When her emergency came, there was no one to help her, so she had to go.'

Austria-Hungary's victory over Montenegro was followed rapidly by another area of conquest: Albania, to which the remnant of the Serb army had fled. Italian troops joined the Albanians in the defence of the main city, Durazzo. But as a result of the Austro-Hungarian conquests of Serbia and Montenegro, Albania was effectively surrounded. Driving across the Albanian border from the southern Serbian city of Skopje, and attacking the coastal towns from the sea, the Austrians defeated the Italian-Albanian forces. The Albanian leader, Essad Pasha, fled to Naples, where he set up an Albanian government-in-exile. The Serbian government-in-exile remained on the Greek island of Corfu. Austria-Hungary had achieved her aim of mastery of the Balkans. But inside Hungary, poets who had been prepared during the previous year to welcome the war effort without reservation could do so no longer. One of them, Gyula Juhász, wrote at the beginning of 1916:

> We wanted something good, beautiful, brave,
> But came disaster, sorrow, anguish,
> And life lived in the pay of death,
> And happiness and love festered.
>
> The strife is still ours, the rude, the cruel,
> Sorrowful combat, but the soul is gentle
> And we feel – in every victory
> Thousands of loyal hearts must be mourned.

On January 15 the rail link between Germany and Turkey, broken when Serbia became a belligerent, was formally reopened. It had first opened more than thirty years earlier. Three days after it had been reopened, the Kaiser travelled by rail to the southern Serbian city of Nish, which the Bulgarians had captured in the final phases of the war against Serbia. In a ceremony full of military pomp, he invested King Ferdinand of Bulgaria, who had come from the Bulgarian capital, Sofia, with the rank and insignia of a Field Marshal in the German Army.

It was a time of triumph for the Central Powers. On the Western Front, repeated Anglo-French efforts during 1915 had failed to break the German trench lines, or to threaten the German occupation of Belgium. In the Aegean, the Anglo-French army completed its evacuation of the Gallipoli peninsula, with 35,268 troops being taken off Cape Helles in eleven days. At Salonika, the Anglo-French Expeditionary Force was pinned down by Bulgarian and Austrian troops south of the Serbian-Bulgarian border. Among those fighting in the ranks of the Serbian army was a British woman, Flora Sandes, who had gone out to Serbia in 1914 as a nurse, but later enlisted as a fighting soldier. She had fought alongside her fellow Serbian soldiers in the retreat of 1915. During the fighting on the Salonika Front, after being severely wounded by a Bulgarian hand grenade, she was decorated with the highest Serbian order for conspicuous bravery in the field, the Order of the Kara-George.

The Salonika Expeditionary Force was constantly being reinforced. But there was distress in the Allied camp when the troop transport *Provence II*, on its way to Salonika, was sunk by a German submarine off the island of Cerigo, and 930 soldiers drowned – one of the many grievous maritime disasters of the war.

Across Central Europe and the Balkans, the Berlin–Constantinople railway was open again to civilian, and most importantly, to military traffic. Its extension to Baghdad also enabled troops and supplies from Germany to be moved rapidly forward to confront the British-Indian forces trapped in the town of Kut, south of Baghdad. A British relief force, sent from Basra to break the siege, was defeated in battle only twenty miles away, and forced to retreat. A second attempt to relieve the siege reached to within two miles of Kut, but it too was beaten back.

Within Kut, with no means of food reaching the besieged soldiers, conditions worsened daily. 'Men on sentry-go would drop down,' noted Colonel Hehir, the Principal Medical Officer of the besieged force, 'those carrying loads would rest every few hundred yards; men availed themselves of every opportunity of lolling about or lying down. There were instances of Indians returning from trench duty in the evening seemingly with nothing the matter who lay down and were found dead in the morning.' Of the British troops, Colonel Hehir wrote: 'There was no grumbling; there was almost a complete absence of suicide and insanity.'

On the Eastern Front, as in the Balkans and Mesopotamia, the Central Powers were in the ascendant. Austro-Hungarian forces had finally driven the Russians out of the Habsburg frontier cities of Brody and Czernowitz. A two-week Russian counterattack starting in mid December, in which the opening phase was marked by 1000 Russian guns, each firing 1000 shells, not only failed to break the Austrian lines, but led to the capture of 6000 Russian soldiers.

The German army had overrun the whole of Russian Poland, Courland on the Baltic, and the Lithuanian provinces of the Russian Empire. To undermine the Russian war effort still further, on the last day of the failed Russian counterattack against Austria, the German authorities in Berlin handed a million roubles to Alexander Helphand, a Russian Jewish Bolshevik, with the aim of spreading antiwar propaganda throughout Russia. Guided by Lenin from his exile in Switzerland, Helphand and his fellow Bolsheviks strove to bring peace and revolution to Russia. Germany gave them every possible encouragement. The immediate Bolshevik aim was limited to revolution in Russia; their eventual hope was of revolution in all the warring States; but the effect of their undermining Russia's warmaking capacity was likely, in the first instance, to be of benefit primarily to Germany.

The antiwar movement in Russia grew with every setback. Even the occasional success on the battlefield could do little to counter war-weariness. An advance by General Yudenich in the Caucasus, and the capture of the Turkish city of Erzerum, was written up as a victory in the newspapers. But it was achieved at a cost of 2000 Russian soldiers incapacitated with frost-bite. It also saw the desertion on the Turkish side of the line of several thousand Arab troops who had been conscripted into the Turkish Army, and who felt no loyalty to their Ottoman masters, certainly not enough to die for.

Inside Russia, more than 10,000 workers went on strike in the Black Sea port and naval base of Nikolayev that January. Two weeks later, 45,000 dock workers in St Petersburg went on strike. On the Eastern Front, soldiers from four Russian regiments crossed into the Austrian lines during the Russian Orthodox Easter to fraternize with their fellow Christians. The

Austrians took a hundred of them prisoner. Outraged at his troops' behaviour, the Russian commander of the southern front, General Brusilov, issued an Order of the Day: 'I declare once and for all that contact with the enemy is permitted only by gun and bayonet.'

War-weariness did not just afflict the Russians. On a board which some German soldiers raised above their parapet on the Western Front were the words: 'We're all fools. Let's all go home.' A British war correspondent, Phillip Gibbs, who was in the Ypres salient, near the much-fought-over château at Hooge, commented: 'The message caused some laughter, and men repeating it said, "There's a deal of truth in those words. Why should this go on? What's it all about? Let the old men who made this war come and fight it out among themselves at Hooge. The fighting men have no real quarrel with each other. We all want to go home, to our wives and our work." But neither side was prepared to "go home" first. Each side was in a trap – a devil's trap from which there was no escape.'

The simple sentiments of the soldiers who saw the crude face of war at close quarters were sometimes echoed by the leaders. In Vienna, General von Hötzendorf again pressed his political masters to consider making peace before the whole fabric of the so far triumphant Austro-Hungarian Empire was endangered. 'England cannot be defeated,' he warned Count Tisza on 4 January 1916. 'Peace must be made in not too short a space, or we shall be fatally weakened, if not destroyed.' Von Hötzendorf's fears were dismissed as alarmist, even defeatist. The confidence of the Austro-Hungarian rulers, now that they had conquered Serbia and driven the Russian army from their soil, was considerable. That month, in an intensification of control from Vienna, the German language was declared the sole official language in Bohemia. In the streets of Prague the police used truncheons against people whom they overheard speaking Czech.

As if to counter talk of peacemaking, the British and French governments issued a declaration, on February 14, that there could be no peace with Germany until Belgian independence was restored, and financial reparations paid by Germany for the damage done inside Belgium by the German occupation forces. This declaration came at a time when plans were being made to launch a major Anglo-French offensive against the German lines on the Somme later in 1916, one which it was hoped would break through the trench lines, and enable the Allies to drive the Germans out of Belgium and back to the German border. The fact that Germany had been in occupation, not only of most of Belgium, but of northeastern France, for a year and a half, was a spur to a renewed military offensive. It was inconceivable that France could stand by impassive while so much of her soil, and many of her towns, were under enemy rule.

There was also indignation among the Allies, and in the United States, as details emerged during 1916 of the German use of Belgian forced labour. The Archbishop of Malines, Cardinal Mercier, was outspoken in his protests to the German occupation authorities, stressing in a series of letters 'the anti-judicial and anti-social character of the condemnation of the Belgian working classes to forced labour and deportation'. In one of his letters to the German Governor-General, the Archbishop wrote:

> At Rillaer, at Gelrode, at Rotselaer, young men, the supporters of a widowed mother, fathers at the head of large families – one among them who had already passed fifty years, has ten children, cultivating the ground, possessing several horned beasts, having never touched a sou of public charity – were carried away by force, despite their protestations. In the little commune of Rillaer they took as many as twenty-five young boys of seventeen years.
>
> Your excellency would have wished the communal administrations to be the accomplices of these odious seizures; by their legal situation and in all conscience they could not do it.

The Cardinal added that he hoped the authorities of the German Empire had not said their last word. 'They will think of our unmerited sufferings,' he wrote, 'of the reprobation of the civilised world, the judgement of history, and the punishment of God'.

The German military planners, whose long-cherished design for the rapid defeat of France had been left in tatters as early as September 1914, were devising a new plan to bring the fighting on the Western Front to a victorious end. Theirs was a plan for the assault on a fortified position on a scale hitherto unknown. It was based on an attack on the French fortresses defending Verdun, which the French had made clear they would hold to the last man. In that case, reasoned the German planners, chief among them General Falkenhayn, if Verdun could be under continuous attack, more and more French soldiers would be brought in to defend it, and they would be systematically destroyed. As General Falkenhayn explained to the Kaiser, in obtaining his approval for the plan, whether the Germans captured Verdun or not, 'the forces of France will bleed to death'.

The massive destruction of the soldiers of France in a deliberate trap of attrition would result, Falkenhayn believed, 'in opening the eyes of her people to the fact that in a military sense they have nothing more to hope for.' The breaking point would then be reached in French morale, 'and England's best sword knocked out of her hand'.

The German attack on Verdun began on 21 February 1916. It achieved its objective of killing as many French soldiers as possible, but the German death toll was also high. In a single day's unsuccessful fighting against one French stronghold, 2200 Germans were killed or wounded. The intensity of the fighting was such, that when a North African division, consisting mostly of Moroccans and Algerians, was thrown into the front line, and saw German troops advancing towards it, its men turned and fled. Directives to return to action on pain of the most serious penalty were ignored. Then, a French officer later wrote, a section of French machine guns 'fired at the backs of the fleeing men, who fell like flies'.

Among the French soldiers who were wounded at Verdun, and taken as prisoners of war to Germany, was Charles de Gaulle, the future leader of the Free French Forces in the Second World War. While in a prisoner-of-war camp, he taught French to a Russian prisoner of war, Mikhail Tukhachevsky, a young Tsarist officer who later managed to escape, rejoined the Russian army, and was in due course to be one of Stalin's Marshals (and to be executed in the purge of 1937).

Among the German dead at Verdun was the Expressionist painter, Franz Marc. In one of his letters home, he had exclaimed, 'The poor horses!' On one occasion, seven thousand horses were killed in a single day by French and German artillery shells, ninety-seven by a single shell from a French naval gun. On the day before Franz Marc was killed he wrote: 'For days I have seen nothing but the most terrible things that can be painted from a human mind.' The commander of the French forces, General Pétain, watching French troops returning from the battlefield, wrote: 'In their unsteady look one sensed visions of horror, while their step and bearing revealed utter despondency. They were crushed by horrifying memories.'

Forty-one years later, in the summer of 1957, a twelve-year-old American schoolboy, Richard W. Day, was taken by his father to the battlefield of Verdun. He later recalled (in a letter to the author):

> One day, we drove across an undulating landscape, still scarred by the remnants of trenches. At noon we stopped by the side of a small country lane. My father had found what he had been looking for. He took me by the hand down a steep embankment, turned and pointed to a dark entrance about four feet high just at the base of the rise.
>
> Pointing into the cave, he said, 'Forty one years ago several thousand soldiers lost their lives fighting each other in there.' It seemed unlikely to me that anything more than a fight between an owl and a field mouse could have taken place in so confined an area, but we lit newspaper torches and stood inside the entrance where we could stand erect.
>
> Even at the callow age of twelve, I immediately knew I was standing in a holy place. A shaft of light pierced the roof of the cave where a rusted piece of barbed wire stuck out. My heart was in my throat. As far as my torchlight would penetrate all I could see were hundreds and hundreds of crosses painted on the cave walls. Below the crosses were neatly stacked boots and helmets along with other rusted battle detritus.
>
> In a few seconds the torches extinguished and we had to retreat.

In the Middle East, the Arabs, for the most part unwilling participants in the Turkish army, were making plans to join the Allied armies, and to make their contribution to the defeat of Turkey, in anticipation of postwar independence. Despite the executions of Arab nationalist leaders in Damascus the previous year, the defiance of the Arabs was anathema to the Turks, threatening to destabilize their southern flank at the very moment when they had worsted the British in Mesopotamia.

At the beginning of 1916, a Maronite Christian Arab, Yusuf al-Hani, who lived in Beirut, invited the French to enter Lebanon and to liberate its population from Turkish rule. He, and those who were known to be supporting him, were arrested, and on 5 April 1916 Yusuf al-Hani was hanged in Beirut. Two other Arab nationalists, the Mufti of Gaza, Ahmed Arif al-Husseini, and his son Mustafa, were arrested by the Turks for trying to leave Gaza and make contact with the leaders of the Arab revolt in the deserts of Arabia. They too were hanged, in Jerusalem. Twenty-one other Arab national leaders were hanged in Beirut and Damascus, among them a former senator in the Ottoman Parliament in Constantinople, Abd al-Hamid al-Zahrawi. But the Arab revolt, the banner of which was formally raised by Sherif Hussein of Mecca, with British support, added another military arm – that of camel riders and desert raiders – to the anti-Turkish coalition.

In their first attack on the city of Medina, the Arab forces were driven off. Of the 50,000 who took part, only 10,000 had rifles. That day, several British officers were put ashore secretly at Jeddah, and made their way to the Arab forces. Among these officers was Captain T. E. Lawrence, later known as Lawrence of Arabia. Two British cruisers then bombarded the Turkish positions north of Jeddah, while British seaplanes bombed Turkish military positions in the port. Within a week of Sherif Hussein having declared the independence of the Hedjaz from Turkey, his troops, with British support, had driven the Turks from Mecca, Islam's holiest place, and from Jeddah.

The promises of independent principalities that had been made by the British to Sherif Hussein were refined by a secret Anglo-French plan, agreed upon in the spring of 1916, whereby the Arab sovereign state of Syria, with its capital in Damascus, would be under French protection, and whereby the Arab State south of Syria would be under British protection, with British sovereignty being retained over the port of Haifa and Haifa Bay, which would become the Mediterranean terminal of the oil pipeline that would be laid across the desert from northern Mesopotamia.

Such plans presupposed the eventual defeat of Turkey. That they might be premature with regard to Mesopotamia was evident, three days after the agreement was signed in Paris, when the British and Indian troops besieged by the Turks in Kut surrendered. The vast Ottoman province of Mesopotamia, which a few months earlier had seemed ripe for conquest, was back under Turkish control. The surrender of Kut was as important a victory for the Turks as the evacuation of Gallipoli four months earlier. More than nine thousand troops were led away into captivity, being marched northward towards Anatolia, cursed and attacked on the way, brutally ill-treated by their guards, and suffering, as the Armenians had suffered when being sent away from Anatolia, great hardship. Of the 2500 British soldiers sent on this march, 1750 died. Of the 9300 Indian soldiers, 2500 died on the march.

For several months a Russian relief force had been making its way through Persia to the Mesopotamian border, hoping to be able to reach Kut from the east. It was only when the force reached the Mesopotamian border that it learned of the surrender of Kut. The Russians continued across the border, capturing the Mesopotamian town of Khanikin, but could get no further.

*   *   *

A turning point in the morality of war – and in due course in its outcome – was reached on March 28, when the Reichstag in Berlin voted for immediate, unrestricted submarine warfare. This gave legal expression to a policy that had been in effect for some time. Five days before the Reichstag vote the Folkestone–Dieppe ferry, the *Sussex*, was torpedoed, and fifty passengers were drowned, among them two United States citizens and the Spanish composer Enrique Granados.

President Wilson ordered his ambassador in Berlin to issue several strong protests about the sinking of the *Sussex*. So strong were these protests that there was speculation in the Allied capitals that the United States might declare war on Germany. Wilson was content, however, to receive from Berlin a promise from the German government that no merchant ship, Allied or neutral, even if they were armed for defensive purposes, would be sunk by submarines without warning, or without 'due respect' for the safety of its passengers and crew.

The German government made it clear, however, that this promise was conditional on Britain and her allies giving up the close blockade of German ports, which was preventing the arrival not only of raw materials and war supplies, but also of foodstuffs. If the United States failed to secure an end to the close blockade, Germany would hold itself 'free to remove the restrictions on the activities of the submarines'.

Two days after the Reichstag vote of March 28, a Russian hospital ship, the *Portugal*, was torpedoed off the port of Rizeh, on the Black Sea. One of the survivors, a member of a Russian Red Cross ambulance detachment with the Army of the Caucasus, gave an account of the sinking – an 'outrage' as the Allied newspapers described it:

> All around me unfortunate Sisters of Mercy were screaming for help. They fell down, like myself, and some of them fainted. The deck became more down-sloping every minute, and I rolled off into the water between the two halves of the sinking steamer. I was drawn down deep into the whirlpool, and began to be whirled round and thrown about in every direction.
>
> While under the water, I heard a dull, rumbling noise, which was evidently the bursting of the boilers, for it threw me out of the vortex about a sazhen, or seven feet, away from the engulfment of the wreck. The stem and stern of the steamer had gone up until they were almost at right angles with the water, and the divided steamer was settling down.

At this moment I was again sucked under, but I exerted myself afresh, and once more rose to the surface. I then saw both portions of the *Portugal* go down rapidly, and disappear beneath the flood. A terrible commotion of the water ensued, and I was dragged under, together with the *Portugal*. I felt that I was going down deep, and for the first time I realized that I was drowning.

With the swiftness of lightning, all my past life flitted through my brain. I remembered my relatives, and it seemed as if I could see their grief and tears at the news of my death. My strength failed me, but I kept my mouth firmly shut, and tried not to take in the water. I knew that the moment of death from heart failure was near. It so happened, however, that the disturbance of the water somewhat abated, and I succeeded in swimming up again.

I glanced round. The *Portugal* was no more. Nothing but broken pieces of wreck, boxes which had contained our medicaments, materials for dressing wounds, and provisions were floating about. Everywhere I could see the heads and arms of people battling with the waves, and their shrieks for help were frightful. It is impossible to describe the horrors of that scene, and the remembrance of it will remain with me for the rest of my life.

Eight or nine sazhens (56 or 63 feet) away from where I was, I saw a life-saving raft, and I swam towards it. Although my soddened clothes greatly impeded my movements, I nevertheless reached the raft, and was taken on to it. About twenty persons were on it already, exclusively men. Amongst them was the French Mate, who assisted the Captain of the *Portugal*, and he and I at once set about making a rudder out of two of the oars which were on the raft, and we placed an oarsman on each side of it.

We had been going about eight minutes when we saw the body of a woman floating motionless, and dressed in the garb of a Sister of Mercy. I ordered the oarsmen to row towards her, but they said it was only a corpse, and we should do better to save some of the people who were still keeping themselves alive on the surface of the water. I seized hold of an oar, and as the woman floated nearer, I caught her with it, and dragged her towards us. I pulled her out of the water as far as her waist, and listened to her heart, which I found was still beating, though very slowly.

We then raised her on the raft. she was unconscious, quite blue, and with only feeble signs of life. We began to rub her, and bring her to her senses. She at last opened her eyes and enquired where she was. I told her that she was saved. Soon, however, she turned pale, said she was dying, and gave me the address of her relatives, to inform them of her death.

She began to spit blood, and was delirious, but gradually a better feeling returned, and she was soon out of danger.

Eighty-five of those on board the *Portugal* – nurses and crewmen – were drowned.

As war activities widened, antiwar activities also grew. In early April the leader of the German Social Democrats, Karl Liebknecht, angered the mass of German parliamentarians by interrupting a speech by the Chancellor to declare that the German people had not wanted war. On Easter Monday, at Kienthal, in Switzerland, members of the Second Socialist International, including delegates from Germany and France, met to denounce war as a capitalist conspiracy. An unsuccessful argument put forward at the conference was that the war was to be welcomed, as the essential and inevitable prelude to the fall of capitalism through civil war. The vast majority of the delegates thought this idea was perverse. They were against war, not for it. The man who put forward the scoffed-at theory was a Russian émigré in Switzerland, Vladimir Lenin.

In an effort to weaken the British war effort, the German government had encouraged an Irish nationalist, Sir Roger Casement (who a decade earlier, as a British diplomat, had exposed the cruelties being perpetrated in King Leopold's Belgian Congo), to return to recruit Irish soldiers in German prisoner-of-war camps to fight against the British. In this task, Casement had been unsuccessful. Of the several thousand men he had hoped to recruit into an Irish Brigade, only fifty-two had joined.

While he was in Germany, Casement was being urged by the Sinn Fein leaders in Ireland to obtain German support, including arms, for an Irish uprising. He asked for 200,000 rifles. When the Germans, who did not regard the Irish revolution as a promising one, offered only 20,000 rifles, Casement was distraught. The revolution – the seizure of power in Dublin – was fixed for April 22, Easter Sunday. Determined to warn Sinn Fein that they could not count on German support, Casement returned to Ireland, on board a German submarine, pretending that he would help foment the uprising. Casement was put ashore on the Atlantic coast of Ireland. At the same time, a small German merchant ship, the *Aud*, brought the 20,000 rifles and a million rounds of ammunition to the Irish coast. But a British ship intercepted the *Aud*, which scuttled itself, and the cargo was lost. Casement was arrested four days later, after he landed, but before he could get to Dublin. He was taken to London, brought to trial, found guilty of treason, and executed.

Despite the loss of the rifles and ammunition, the Irish national uprising went ahead. Its first objective was to seize the main buildings in Dublin, and then to take on the might of Britain with popular support. Last-minute uncertainty about the precise plan of the uprising meant that instead of five thousand men, only a thousand participated when the uprising began – two days later than planned – on April 24. A proclamation establishing 'the Provisional Government of the Irish Republic' was read out from the steps of the main Post Office. It began:

> Irishmen and Irishwomen: In the name of God and of the dead generations from which she receives her old tradition of nationhood, Ireland, through us, summons her children to her flag and strikes for her freedom.
>
> Having organized and trained her manhood through her secret revolutionary organization, the Irish Republican Brotherhood, and through her open military organizations, the Irish Volunteers and the Irish Citizen Army, having patiently perfected her discipline, having resolutely waited for the right moment to reveal itself, she now seizes that moment and, supported by her exiled children in America and by gallant allies in Europe, but relying in the first on her own strength, she strikes in full confidence of victory.
>
> We declare the right of the people of Ireland to the ownership of Ireland and to the unfettered control of Irish destinies, to be sovereign and indefeasible.

The reference to Germany as the 'gallant allies' of the new Republic was not a way to win popular support, despite the strength of Irish national sentiment.

For a week, the rebels held out against the troops sent against them, mostly men from Irish regiments that had been fighting on the Western Front for more than a year, and who were angered to find Germany described as the ally of the rebels. Armed Sinn Feiners also challenged the authorities in other places in Ireland, most strongly at Ardee in County Louth, and at Swords and Lusk near Dublin. On April 25, in a futile attempt to deter the

British government from sending reinforcements by sea to Ireland, the German navy came out of its North Sea ports and made a surprise raid on two east coast towns, Lowestoft and Yarmouth, bombarding both ports for half an hour, before returning to their bases.

On April 27 Martial Law was declared throughout Ireland, and troops moved against all the rebel outposts. By the end of a week of fighting the rebels in Dublin were crushed. Sixty-four of them had been killed, as well as more than two hundred civilians caught in the crossfire and artillery attacks on rebel-held buildings. More than a hundred troops and police had also been killed. Fifteen of the rebel leaders were tried by Field Court Martial, in secret, and sentenced to be shot. A sixteenth, Eamon de Valera, a professor of mathematics, was saved from execution because he was an American citizen. He spent the rest of the war in various English prisons.

The ongoing executions caused deep unease among many Britons. 'My own view,' the Irish writer, George Bernard Shaw, protested in the *Daily News* on May 10, 'is that the men who were shot in cold blood, after their capture, were prisoners of war, and it was therefore entirely incorrect to slaughter them'. When one of the signatories of the proclamation of independence, James Connolly, was taken to the place of execution on May 12, he was taken on a stretcher, as he was too ill to stand or walk.

The Insurgents, as they were called, gained widespread sympathy as a result of the executions. When the British authorities asked the Bishop of Limerick, Dr O'Dwyer, to remove those parish priests who had shown sympathy for the uprising, he refused to do so, writing to the General who had made the request: 'You took care that no plea for mercy should interpose on behalf of the poor young fellows who surrendered to you in Dublin. The first intimation which we got of their fate was the announcement that they had been shot in cold blood. Personally I regard your action with horror, and I believe that it has outraged the conscience of the country.'

The way in which the Irish rebellion was crushed affected Britain's relations with the United States. On May 30 the British ambassador in Washington warned London: 'The attitude towards England has changed for the worse by recent events in Ireland.'

Many Germans were disappointed by the failure of the rebellion in Ireland. Failure went against the theory that had earlier been much in vogue, that the British Empire as a whole would prove a liability to Britain once war came. A year earlier, a writer in *Der Tag* had seen how wrong this theory had been. 'We expected,' he wrote, 'that India would rise when the first shot was fired in Europe, but thousands of Indians came to fight with the British against us. We thought the British Empire would be torn to pieces, but the Colonies appear to be united closer than ever with the Mother Country. We expected a triumphant rebellion in South Africa; it was nothing but a failure. We thought there would be trouble in Ireland, but instead, she sent her best soldiers against us. We anticipated that the "peace at any price" party would be dominant in England, but it melted away in the ardour to fight Germany. We regarded England as degenerate, yet she seems to be our principal enemy.'

As the negotiations between London and Washington continued, inconclusively, with regard to a modification of the British blockade of Germany, the Germans took an initiative that might have broken the blockade altogether. Emerging again from their North Sea ports, 103 German warships steamed northwards to make an attack on Allied shipping off the Norwegian coast. The expedition, the largest German naval initiative since war broke out, was foiled when the attackers were themselves attacked by a superior force of 151 British warships.

The Battle of Jutland was potentially decisive for the Anglo-German war. The German naval commanders, and the Kaiser, had always hoped for a battle in which they might be able to break the British naval blockade on the German North Sea ports; the British had always hoped to destroy the German High Seas Fleet, leaving only the submarines as their German naval adversary. But despite the gigantic scale of the Battle of Jutland, its result was indecisive.

The number of sailors killed when their great ships went down was the highest of the whole war, eclipsing in scale the maritime disasters which were the frequent result of German submarine sinkings. The British losses at Jutland included 1017 men on the *Indefatigable*, 1266 on the *Queen Mary* and more than 2000 on the *Invincible*. In all, more than six thousand British sailors were killed. The German losses were 2551. In a jubilant mood, the Kaiser announced that 'the spell of Trafalgar is over', but although his navy suffered fewer losses than the British, it received a serious mauling, and was not to venture out again for the rest of the war.

After the Battle of Jutland, the German naval commander, Admiral Scheer, made it clear to the Kaiser that a German victory at sea could only be achieved, and with it perhaps the overall victory, by a successful submarine war against British trade.

On June 4 the Russians launched their Eastern Front offensive, under General Brusilov. It was begun with a massive artillery barrage of 1938 guns, along a 200-mile front; a barrage in which Japanese artillery officers participated alongside the Russian artillerymen. Within a few hours of the start of the bombardment it became clear that the Austrians were not going to be able to hold the line, and the Russian troops moved forward. In one day, 26,000 Austrians were taken prisoner. One Austrian soldier who was not taken prisoner was the philosopher Ludwig Wittgenstein; he was awarded a medal for valour for his work in directing an artillery battery during the Russian assault. By chance, on the day of Wittgenstein's valiant act on the Eastern Front, his friend and mentor, the British philosopher Bertrand Russell, was fined £100 in London for publishing a leaflet in support of those who refused to fight on conscientious grounds.

Among the German weapons used at Verdun that summer was a new phosgene gas, Green Cross. Its use was so effective that a whole French division, five thousand men in all, was wiped out, and one of the forts protecting Verdun captured. Only one more fort remained between the Germans and Verdun, but they did not have enough of the new gas to renew the attack, and the French defenders were able to revert to their tenacious defence. Among the German officers who took part in that Green Cross attack was Lieutenant Friedrich Paulus. Twenty-six years later, having just been promoted Field Marshal by Hitler for his part in the war against Russia, he was to surrender a whole German army to the Russians at Stalingrad, having been surrounded, outnumbered and outgunned.

Verdun remained in French hands, and its defence became a symbol for Frenchmen of their tenacity. But the French commanders knew how close the Germans had come to victory, and, in the hope of taking some German pressure off Verdun, asked the British High Command if they could bring the Somme offensive forward from June 29 to June 24. The British Commander-in-Chief, General Haig, said it was too late to advance the infantry attack, but that he could bring forward the artillery barrage.

Haig was confident that he could break through the German lines on the Somme, and did not mind bringing the artillery barrage forward. The British infantry advance, he had explained ten days earlier to the British General

Staff, would be 'pressed eastward far enough to enable our cavalry to push through into open country beyond the enemy's prepared line of defence'. The Russians, who had been making continuous inroads in eastern Turkey and along the Turkish Black Sea shore, as well as in their offensive against the Austrians, were as confident as Haig that the tide of war was about to turn in their favour.

While the British artillery bombardment began on the Somme, General Brusilov launched an attack on the Austrian town of Kolomea. The attack was successful; more than ten thousand Austrian soldiers were taken prisoner, and Kolomea fell to the Russians on June 29. In Berlin, the only antiwar deputy of the Reichstag, Karl Liebknecht, was taking part that day in a three-day protest against the war. More than 55,000 German workers joined him. This was cause for satisfaction on the part of the Allies, but the German authorities acted swiftly to prevent the protests spreading. Liebknecht, who was urging soldiers not to fight, was expelled from the Reichstag and sentenced to two years' hard labour; two months later his sentence was increased to four years.

A war unconnected with the European struggle reached a climax on June 29. This was the continuing Spanish effort to assert its authority in Spanish Morocco. Spain had remained neutral in the European conflict. But she continued to be embroiled in her own North African struggle against the local Moorish tribesmen, who, that summer, had seized and fortified the village of El Biutz, dominating the road from Ceuta to Tetuan. On the morning of June 29 the Spanish forces attacked the village.

Among the officers who led the charge was Captain Franco. That night the regimental report praised his 'incomparable bravery, gift for command, and energy deployed in combat'. The future ruler of Spain had been seriously wounded in the stomach. It was assumed by those who tended him on the battlefield that the wound would be fatal. So badly injured was he, that for two weeks he could not even be moved by stretcher from the first-aid post to a casualty clearing station. His survival gave him a conviction, if not of immortality, certainly of special protection. 'I have seen death walk by my side many times,' he later remarked, 'but fortunately she did not know me.'

*   *   *

The British barrage on the Somme, begun four days earlier than planned in order to help relieve the German pressure on Verdun, was continued an extra two days because heavy rain made an infantry attack impossible. The attack began on July 1. The weather that morning, recalled Siegfried Sassoon, 'after an early morning mist, was of the kind commonly called heavenly'.

In the hour before the infantry advanced from their trenches, almost a quarter of a million shells were fired at the German trenches, an average of sixty shells every second. Many of the German defenders were in deep and well-fortified shelters, however, and when the British soldiers moved forward, most of them weighed down by sixty-six pounds' weight of equipment, they found that as many as a hundred German machine-gun positions, hidden in armoured emplacements, had survived the ferocious bombardment. In the first day's fighting, more than a thousand officers and 20,000 men were killed, the highest death toll for any single day of the First World War.

In one sector, approaching the village of Mametz, 159 men were killed by one German machine gun, built into the base of a crucifix at the edge of the village. The officer leading the attack had predicted that the machine gun would be a fatal hazard if the preliminary artillery bombardment failed to destroy it. He was killed as he led his men into the intense and uninterrupted machine-gun fire. The thousands of wounded men returned as quickly as they could to the rear. 'Streams of wounded were coming down the road,' Lieutenant Eric Mockler-Ferryman wrote home, 'practically all with bullet wounds from machine guns. One man came along early in the morning with only one arm, as cheery as possible, saying in a laughing voice, "Souvenir!" By about nine p.m. we were back in our old front line – a terrible disaster with enormous loss.'

During the morning, Siegfried Sassoon recorded, at 7.45, a group of soldiers in reserve 'watching the show and cheering as if at a football match'. At 9.50: 'The birds seem bewildered; a lark begins to go up and then flies feebly along, thinking better of it. Others flutter above the trench with querulous cries, weak on the wing.' At 10.05: 'I am staring at a sunlit picture of Hell, and still the breeze shakes the yellow weeds, and the poppies glow under Crawley Ridge where some shells fell a few minutes ago.' At 2.30 that afternoon: 'I could see one man moving his arms up and down as he lay on his side; his face was a crimson patch.'

The football match image had an ironic echo that day. During his most recent leave in London, a company commander, Captain W. P. Nevill, had bought four footballs, one for each of his platoons, and offered a prize to the platoon which, at jump-off, first kicked its football up to the German frontline trench. An observer later wrote: 'As the gunfire died away I saw an infantryman climb onto the parapet into no-man's land, beckoning others to follow. As he did so he kicked off a football. A good kick. The ball rose and travelled well towards the German line. That seemed to be the signal to advance.'

Captain Nevill was killed instantly. Two of his five footballs are now museum pieces.

During that first day of battle on the Somme the number of those who had been seriously wounded was so great – an estimated 25,000 men – that the medical services were overwhelmed. In the dressing stations, those men who were not expected to survive were put on one side. 'It was very hard to ignore their cries for help,' wrote one medical orderly, 'but we had to concentrate on those who might live.'

The one Dominion force in action that day, a Newfoundland battalion, was almost wiped out. Of the 810 men who went into the attack, 710 were either killed or wounded. 'It was a magnificent display of trained and disciplined valour,' one of Haig's staff informed the Newfoundland Prime Minister, 'and its assault only failed of success because dead men can advance no further.'

Despite the incredibly high cost of the first day's attack, Haig did not doubt that the attack should be continued on the following day. But one of the main British objectives for that day, the village of Bapaume, less than ten miles from the starting point, was neither reached that day, nor after five months of renewed assaults. The main beneficiaries of the attack were the French, for the first day of the Battle of the Somme was the 132nd day of the German attack on Verdun, and the relief provided for the French at Verdun was immediate, with tens of thousands of German troops being transferred from Verdun to the Somme. In the French sector of the Somme battle, as in the British sector, the first day's objective was not reached, but the French were more successful than the British, and in one forward movement took 3000 German prisoners and captured 80 guns.

Among the French Foreign Legionnaires who were fighting on the Somme was the Harvard graduate and poet, Alan Seeger. A few months earlier he had written:

> I have a rendezvous with Death
> On some scarred slope of battered hill . . .
>
> And I to my pledged word am true
> I shall not fail that rendezvous.

In an attack with his detachment on a German fortified position, Seeger and his unit were caught in the fire of six German machine guns. His last words before he died were for water, and for his mother. By nightfall, the strongpoint was in the Legion's hands.

Another of those who fought on the Somme, Donald Hankey – the brother of the British Cabinet Secretary – sent an account of what he had seen to the editor of the *Spectator* magazine, for which he had written a number of articles while in France. The editor, however, in what he regarded as the interest of patriotism, refused to publish it. Hankey had written:

> Here we are where we started. Day and night we have done nothing but bring in the wounded and the dead. When one sees the dead, their limbs crushed and mangled, one can only have revulsion for war.
>
> It was easy to talk of glory and heroism when one is away from it. But here, in the presence of the mutilated and tortured dead, one can only feel the horror and wickedness of war. Indeed it is an evil harvest, sown of pride and arrogance and lust of power.

Hankey was killed later in the battle, leading his men over the top.

As the Battle of the Somme entered its second day, the Brusilov offensive on the Eastern Front entered its second month. On July 2 the German and Austrian troops launched a sustained counterattack east of Kolomea. The Russian novelist Sergeyev-Tsensky has left an account of an incident during the counterattack, and of the fate of one of his characters, Alexei Ivanovich Diveyev, newly commissioned into the Tsarist army:

> The mind beneath his high, bald crown was too feeble to subdue the roaring, stabbing horror. But his flabby muscles tensed themselves for struggle, not for terror-stricken flight. This nightmare which was more than his brain could bear, made him plant his feet more firmly in the damp soil, and throw his body forward in readiness. Then he caught sight

of the broad blade of a bayonet before him, and over the bayonet two glaring eyes and a pair of clean-shaven lips, tightly compressed. He pulled the trigger.

The broad bayonet caught at his leather belt, and ripped it in two. The belt fell to the ground, but so did the man behind the bayonet. The steel did not enter Diveyev's body. Alexei Ivanovich pulled the trigger again and again, no longer taking aim, but emptying his Browning straight into the multiple being before him which was the Enemy . . .

Soon another enemy bayonet, just like the one that lay by the side of the Hungarian he had killed, was jabbed deep into his abdomen. But his right hand still grasped his revolver, and the index finger pressed the trigger again and again, though all the bullets were long since spent.

His body writhed convulsively, his fingers relaxed, and the Browning fell to the ground. Round him, the battle raged on, fought by men with strong bodies and healthy minds.

The Austrian who had killed Diveyev was pierced immediately after by two Russian bayonets.

On the Somme, after nine days of fighting, the British and French had pushed the Germans back between one and two miles, but it had become clear that there would be no breakthrough. At Verdun, a final German assault, using gas and flamethrowers, failed to capture the last fort between the German front line and the city. In the two and a half weeks since the new gas had first been used, the French had been issued with effective gas masks. Science, which had been enlisted to shorten the war, served only to prolong it.

On the Somme, the battle continued, with South African troops in action, and with Australian troops, many of whom had fought at Gallipoli a year earlier, carrying out a diversionary attack to the north, at Fromelles. When the senior Australian officer at Fromelles, General Elliott, asked a British Staff Officer, Major Howard, how he thought the attack would go, Howard replied: 'If you put it to me like that, Sir, I must answer you in the same way, as man to man. It is going to be a bloody holocaust.' Elliott tried to have the attack cancelled, particularly as it emerged that the German troops in the area were not going to be transferred to the Somme, and that the diversionary attack would serve no diversionary purpose. But the message from headquarters was that the attack must go on, and when it ended, amid hand-to-hand fighting, bayonet against bayonet, 1708 Australians had been killed. The objective was not reached.

On July 23 the first women's mass antiwar demonstration in Britain was held in Glasgow, under the auspices of the newly created Women's Peace Crusade. As the women marched in anger against the continuation of the war, an Australian schoolteacher, Private Jack Bourne, wrote home from the Somme: 'Why go to war with one another? With these men we have no quarrel.' The men in the front line could only carry out their orders, however, and, in many cases, derive satisfaction from their successes, however limited those successes in the wider strategic context. An Australian Lance Corporal, E. Moorehead, wrote of one of the battles on the Somme – the battle at Pozières on July 25: 'When the Huns came into view over the crest, in twos or threes, or singly, some with packs, probably filled with bombs, others with fixed bayonets, we lined the parapet like an excited crowd and blazed like hell at them, knocking them over like rabbits, not a man getting away so far as I could see. The range was about four hundred, and as each man appeared he got a hundred bullets in him. One officer appeared and waved his men forward in a lordly way, and then collapsed like a bag, filled with our lead. I fired about thirty rounds and did my share.'

Could there be humour amid the slaughter? Could anything in that zone of destruction be seen as amusing? This same Lance Corporal recalled how, not long after the death of the 'lordly' officer, 'one unfortunate Boche, having run the gauntlet of our rifle fire, was getting away, apparently only slightly wounded, when one of our shells burst on him as though aimed, and he went up blown to pieces. Well, we cheered and laughed at the happening as though it was the funniest thing in the world.'

Whether the trench war would ever end was a question much in the minds of those who were its practitioners. A young British infantry officer, George Leigh-Mallory (who was to survive the war, but disappeared while climbing Mount Everest in 1924), wrote to his parents at the start of the fourth week of the battle of the Somme: 'I am not one of the optimists about the war, and shall be quite surprised if it ends before Xmas. I suppose we may at any moment hear very good news from Russia – but it's a long time coming, and the German war machine must be far from run down if he can put up the fight he has done.'

The British Commander-in-Chief, Sir Douglas Haig, was confident that the German war machine could be broken. In another six weeks, he told the Chief of the Imperial General Staff in London at the end of July, 'the enemy should be hard put to find men'. The maintenance of what Haig called 'a steady offensive pressure' on the Germans would, he wrote, 'result eventually in his complete overthrow'. The battle on the Somme continued. When a 2500-strong battalion of soldiers from Liverpool went into action on July 30, more than five hundred of them were killed.

George Leigh-Mallory's hopes of 'very good news from Russia' were answered by news of the continuing success of General Brusilov's offensive. By the end of July the Russians had re-entered the Austrian border town of Brody, inside the frontier of Eastern Galicia, and announced the capture of 40,000 Austrians. But the German High Command decided, as it had done on several earlier occasions, to intervene in the Austrian military plans and command, and a German commander, General Bothmer, was put in charge of much of the front facing Brusilov's advance. As Chief-of-Staff, Bothmer brought with him one of the most successful German officers, Hans von Seeckt, who, in the years after Germany's defeat, was to be the main force in creating the framework for a new German army.

The Bothmer–Seeckt combination was intended to dash Anglo-French hopes of a continual drain of men and munitions from the Western to the Eastern Front. One of the measures they took was to send German troops to join the battle line in mixed Austro-German battalions. Another of their measures, humiliating for the Austrians, was to bring two divisions of Turkish troops to the Eastern Front. Despite the Turkish successes at Gallipoli and in Mesopotamia, 'Johnny Turk' (as the British soldiers called him) was a despised adversary, a non-European, a Muslim who came almost as a mercenary to the Christian conflict.

Brusilov continued to advance. On August 7 he re-entered the Eastern Galician city of Stanislavov, capturing 7000 Austrian and 3500 German soldiers. The German High Command began, momentarily, to despair of its Austrian ally, even with German leadership and German and Turkish reinforcements. General Hoffman, who had been appointed by Berlin to take command of the organization of the Austrian defences, noted bitterly in his diary at the end of August that within the Austro-Hungarian army there were 'no less than twenty-three distinct languages. No one understands anyone else.' Nine of those languages – including Italian, Polish and

Roumanian – were officially permitted for military commands; the others – including Greek, Romany and two types of Albanian – were the languages of smaller groups within the Empire.

The Allies, waiting expectantly for continual Russian advances on the Eastern Front, were being hard pressed elsewhere. On the Caucasus Front, the earlier Russian successes in taking from Turkey almost the whole of the eastern Armenian provinces, were turned to nothing that August, when Mustafa Kemal pushed the Russians out of eastern Anatolia, retaking the Russian-held Armenian towns of Bitlis and Mus. On the Salonika Front, despite the arrival of Italian, Serb and Russian reinforcements, the Bulgarians, from their bases in occupied Serbia, managed to advance across the mountains, capturing the Greek town of Florina. The Greeks, desperate not to be drawn into the war, handed over to the Bulgarians a fortress on the Greek side of their border with Bulgaria, Fort Rupel, only fifty miles from Salonika. The Allies protested in vain.

On the Italian Front, Allied observers watched as Italy launched its sixth military offensive along the Isonzo River. The objective of the attack, the town of Gorizia, was reached, and three to four miles of Austrian territory gained along a fifteen-mile front. In addition, almost 50,000 Austrian soldiers had been captured. But the cost of this success was appallingly high; as many as 20,000 Italian soldiers were killed. How long would men continue to go to their deaths in this way? It was a question that was being asked on the Somme, and on the Eastern Front, in Mesopotamia and at Salonika, and on the high seas, with equal passion, and equal bewilderment.

In October 1916 a British observer with the Italian armies, Sidney Low, who four months earlier had seen at first hand the horror of the fighting, tried to give a positive, and even an inspiring gloss to the slaughter of the trenches, in a book he wrote to explain the war in Italy to British readers:

War is a monstrous evil, but from its furnace of pain and suffering Italy, with other nations, may emerge hardened and tempered. She will gain a larger unity, and that not merely by annexing the unredeemed territory. The war has gone far to obliterate that division of classes and localities which was the inheritance of the troubled past. Her children have been Sardinians, Venetians, Apulians, Tuscans, Neapolitans, Sicilians, longer than they have been Italians; they have been apt to set the old province, where their fathers were born, before the new nation to which they have themselves so lately succeeded.

The trench and the battlefield have brought them together. The Piedmontese have learnt that the Southerners too are brave and strong; the men of the South have found that they exaggerated the harshness and coldness of the Cisalpine peoples. The common effort and the common burden have crowned the edifice which the makers of Italy built up in the nineteenth century.

In Italy, as elsewhere, the war has brought divergent orders and sects together. We may hear less after it of that quarrel between the Church and the State which has caused unhappiness to so many devout and patriotic Italians. For if the Vatican, under the malign statesmanship of its chiefs, has been anti-national, the clergy as a whole have taken a noble part in the war.

Everywhere at the front I met uniformed priests comforting and consoling the soldiers in hardship and peril; at the hospitals and in the ambulances I saw the sisters of the religious orders ministering to the sick and dying. Three of them were killed by an Austrian bomb at one hospital I visited.

At sea, during a twenty-five day tour of duty in the Eastern Mediterranean, a single German submarine, *U-35*, sank fifty-four merchant ships, more than half of them Italian.

Initially most hopeful for the Allies, and rapidly to become most disappointing, was the appearance of a new ally, Roumania. For two years Roumania had remained neutral. Alerted, however, to the possibility of territorial gains as a result of the continuing Russian successes in eastern Galicia, on 27 August 1916 she declared war on Austria-Hungary. Nine days earlier the Roumanian government had signed a secret treaty with the Allies, whereby Roumania would acquire three substantial, and long sought after, regions: Transylvania, the Bukovina, and the Banat.

The initial result of Roumania's entry into the war was a shock to the Central Powers. As Roumanian troops pressed forward across the border into Austria-Hungary, the Kaiser commented, 'The war is lost'. It was a galling moment for him on personal grounds, as King Ferdinand of Roumania was not only a German by blood, but a Hohenzollern, of the same royal house as the Kaiser. Confident and relieved, however, that he was no longer beholden to his German relative, King Ferdinand told his Crown Council, as Roumanian troops crossed into Transylvania: 'Then I have conquered the Hohenzollern who was in me. I fear no one.'

The German army was already doing its utmost to strengthen Austrian military resolve on the Galician Front. In addition, the Kaiser decided to make a change at the top of his own command structure, in the hope that stronger men and more ruthless military measures would enable the Roumanian threat to be countered. The Chief of the German General Staff, General Falkenhayn, was replaced by the legendary Field Marshal, Paul von Hindenburg, who was given as his deputy the hero of Tannenberg, General Ludendorff. The Hindenburg–Ludendorff combination produced an immediate upsurge of morale in the German army, and among civilians, each searching for the hope that the war could be won, and, even more importantly, that it could be ended.

Hindenburg and Ludendorff's first initiative was to double munitions production, and treble the production of artillery and machine guns. Their second initiative was to take effective command of all the armies of the Central Powers. Not only the Austrians, but the Turks and the Bulgarians, agreed to this, recognition of the predominance of the military skills of Germany, and proof to the Allies that it was Germany that was the main enemy and driving force in the continuation of the war. Turkish troops were despatched to strengthen the Salonika Front, to prevent an Allied advance from the south into Serbia and the Austro-Hungarian heartland.

As the Roumanians drove deeper into Transylvania, the Central Powers played their trump card. This was a declaration of war against Roumania by Bulgaria, its southern neighbour. Bulgarian troops now prepared to invade Roumania in conjunction with German troops who had been gathering in Bulgaria. The spearhead of the attack was a point on the River Danube where it was only fifty miles from the Bulgarian border to the Roumanian capital, Bucharest. As the German-led attack was mounted on Roumania from the south, the Austro-Hungarian forces in the north were put under a German commander, General Falkenhayn, and, with German soldiers at their side, prepared to drive the Roumanians back to their border. As the advance began, Bulgarian aircraft bombed Roumanian military depots and munitions factories in Bucharest.

In an attempt to take pressure off the Roumanian armies, the Roumanian High Command appealed for a renewed British military offensive on the Somme. This took place, with the capture of two villages (Guillemont and Ginchy) but without any success against two other long-coveted objectives,

High Wood and the Schwaben Redoubt. Nor did the Germans withdraw any troops from the Roumanian Front to meet this renewed attack on the Somme. Indeed, on September 5, German forces overran the Danube fortress of Tutracaia, taking 25,000 Roumanian soldiers prisoner.

Still the Somme offensive continued. In a renewed attack on High Wood, almost all the members of a British machine-gun company were killed. 'With my runner I crept forward among the dead and wounded, and came to one of my guns mounted for action, its team lying dead beside it,' one of those who survived, Captain Hutchison, later recalled. 'I seized the rear leg of the tripod and dragged the gun some yards to where a little cover enabled me to load the belt through the feed-block. To the south of the wood Germans could be seen, silhouetted against the sky-line, moving forward. I fired at them and watched them fall, chuckling with joy at the technical efficiency of the machine.'

On September 10 a new weapon of war, the tank – known as a 'land battleship' – was in action with the British forces. This had been designed a year earlier, with Winston Churchill's encouragement, as an armoured, tracked vehicle which would be able to crush barbed wire and cross the lines of trenches, impervious to machine-gun bullets, while behind it infantrymen could cluster, and move forward protected by the tank itself. But the military planners had not been prepared to wait until sufficient numbers of tanks were available to offer the chance of a breakthrough.

With the tank, as with the use of Green Cross gas by the Germans at Verdun earlier in the year, a device that might have had a decisive impact was used before it was available in sufficient quantity to be effective. Among those infantrymen participating in the advance in which tanks were first used was Raymond Asquith, a son of the British Prime Minister. Shot through the chest, he did not want his men to know that he was mortally wounded, and so he lit a cigarette. He died on the stretcher, being taken to a dressing station. Badly wounded that day, his second wound in action, was a future British Prime Minister, Harold Macmillan. As a result of his wound, he had to remain on crutches until the end of the war.

In order to intensify the German war effort, Hindenburg gave orders for 700,000 Belgian and 200,000 French labourers to be deported to Germany to work in German factories. Among the many protests was one from Cardinal Farley of New York, who declared: 'You have got to go back to the times of the Medes and the Persians to find a like example of a whole people carried into bondage.'

The United States, still neutral – but with 32,000 Americans serving as volunteers in the British army and the French Foreign Legion – was becoming increasingly angered, both by the German submarine sinkings of merchant ships, and by the deportations to forced labour. Woodrow Wilson instructed the American ambassador in Berlin to protest to the German Chancellor about the use of Belgian labourers in the manufacture of shells. This, the ambassador pointed out, was 'contrary to the rules of war and the Hague Conventions'.

Hindenburg's plans to maintain Germany at war, and to lessen her vulnerability in a war that was now being fought on four Fronts (the Western, Eastern, Roumanian and Salonika Fronts), included the construction of a fortified line between five and thirty miles behind the line of trenches on the Western Front and the Belgian-German border. This meant that if the trench line should be broken, the German troops could fall back to strongly fortified positions; and could indeed, if strategy dictated it, pull back to the new line at a time of their own choosing.

The German decision to take effective charge of the battle against the Roumanians was proving effective. Only eleven days after General Mackensen's forces had crossed the Danube in the south, General Falkenhayn's forces drove the Roumanian forces out of Transylvania, taking 3000 prisoners. Among the German soldiers who distinguished themselves on this front was Lieutenant Rommel, who was instrumental in capturing a 3937-foot mountain peak. Advancing along the Black Sea shore of Roumania, General Mackensen overran the Roumanian provinces of Silistria and South Dobrudja, and on October 22 entered the port city of Constanta, capturing large quantities of oil and grain. With the defeat of the Roumanians in Wallachia, considerable economic advantages were immediately at the disposal of the Central Powers. Bulgaria, not to be outdone, took advantage of the destruction of her northern enemy to move south, driving the Greeks from the province of Thrace, which Greece had conquered from Turkey less than three years earlier, and acquiring the port of Kavalla on the Aegean Sea.

*　　*　　*

The war at sea, in which the warships and submarines of all the belligerent nations were taking part, continued to be dominated by German submarine attacks on Allied and neutral shipping. With great pride, and precision, the main German news agency reported that one British troopship, torpedoed in the Mediterranean, had gone to the bottom 'within forty-three seconds'. On October 1 the Kaiser congratulated the German submarine service on having sunk one million tons of Allied shipping. A week later the activities of the underwater raiders were extended to the Atlantic coast of the United States, where, in a few days, the U-53 sank three British, one Dutch and one Norwegian merchant ship off Nantucket Island.

The activities of German submarines off the coast, and within sight, of the United States, was a serious challenge to American neutrality, but Woodrow Wilson was emphatic, in a speech to the Cincinnati Chamber of Commerce, that his aim was, not to declare war on Germany, but 'both to keep and to make peace'. He was, however, under daily pressure to take action, and on October 26 made a statement that could not be misinterpreted in Berlin. 'I believe that the business of neutrality is over,' Wilson said. 'The nature of modern war leaves no State untouched.' As if to underline how right Wilson was, two days after his warning statement, a German submarine torpedoed the British liner *Marina* off Fastnet Rock; among the passengers who were drowned were six United States citizens. That same day, off the Atlantic coast of Portugal, a United States steamer, the *Lanao*, was attacked and sunk.

Woodrow Wilson's political appeal was to those of his fellow countrymen who wanted to keep out of the war, and in the Presidential election, held on November 7, he was very nearly defeated, achieving 276 votes to 255 in the electoral college and obtaining a popular majority of only 400,000 votes. But with his re-election he had a renewed lease of power, and no need to face the electorate again for another four years. He was by instinct a conciliator. Earlier in the year he had suggested that the United States would have a part to play in a future 'association of nations' that might be set up after the war, to secure the right of any people to choose the sovereignty under which it lived, and the right of the whole world to be freed from fear of aggression by another Power.

On December 20, within two months of his re-election, Wilson addressed a Peace Note to all the warring Powers, asking them to put forward their respective views 'as to the terms upon which the war might be concluded, and the arrangements which would be deemed satisfactory as a guarantee against its renewal, or the kindling of any similar conflict in the future'. His hope was to compare the various answers, and to see if he could find in them a basis for a negotiated peace among all the belligerents. Small nations, Wilson added, had to be made secure from any future aggression. Rival leagues and alliances had to be avoided. But a 'league of all nations' might be formed 'to preserve peace throughout the world'.

In the continuation of the war, Wilson's Peace Note warned, there was the risk that 'an injury be done to civilization itself which can never be atoned or repaired'.

Germany and Austria-Hungary had no reason to feel that the prolongation of the war spelt danger either to the fabric of their empires, or to the final outcome of the conflict. Austria-Hungary was in control of Serbia, Montenegro and Albania, and, with German help, had finally halted the Russian offensive into Galicia. Germany had four separate causes for satisfaction: she was in the process of crushing Roumania, she had achieved her objective of making the French army destroy itself at Verdun; she had also prevented the Anglo-French armies from breaking through the lines on the Somme, and she was occupying a deep swathe of Russian territory from the Baltic Sea to the Pripet Marshes. The German military leaders, from the Kaiser downward, were also satisfied that the submarine offensive would in due course force Britain to its knees.

The Allied Powers were equally confident of victory. The setback on the Somme was interpreted as a victory, in view of the few miles that had been gained, and the 72,901 German soldiers who had been taken prisoner; and there was confidence in high British military circles that the year 1917 would see opportunities to succeed still further, especially if the new weapon, the tank, was to be used in greater numbers. France, despite the heavy loss of life at Verdun, had held the town itself, thus making good the boast that 'Verdun will not fall'. Towards the end of October, the French took the first offensive action of the Verdun battle, recapturing one of the forts, and taking 6000 German soldiers prisoner.

The Italian army, although unable to drive the Austrians back across the mountains east of the Isonzo, continued trying; the ninth battle of the Isonzo was launched in November, and although it had to be called off after three days because the deep mud made any advance impossible, 9000 Austrians soldiers had been taken prisoner.

In Russia there seemed to be a storm brewing which might make the continuation of the Eastern war impossible. In October and November there were almost two hundred strikes throughout Russia, including the capital, by an estimated 200,000 men. Their demand was an end to the war. That winter the Tsar was warned by his Chief-of-Staff that there were only sufficient reserve troops for another five months' fighting. The halting of Brusilov's offensive against Austria had also been a setback; there was no chance of renewing it, or of maintaining a serious threat against the Austrians; nor was there any way in which the land lost to Germany could be recovered. The Russian army was incapable of any further offensive action. 'The plain truth,' wrote a British officer attached to Russian military headquarters, 'is that without aeroplanes, far more heavy guns and shells and some knowledge of their use, it is butchery, and useless butchery, to drive the Russian infantry against German lines.'

Yet patriotism could not easily be swept aside, even in an army under so much adverse pressure both at the front and in the rear. On the Eastern Front a young Russian cavalry officer, who had earlier won the St George's Cross for bravery, was injured by a mine while on a mounted reconnaissance patrol. Sent to hospital behind the lines, he later recalled how 'delighted' he had been when he was sent back to a combat regiment. His name was Georgi Zhukov, later Chief-of-Staff of the Soviet army, who in 1945 was to receive the surrender of Berlin.

The aspect of the war which was most horrific, the scale of the loss of life, was covered over with varying forms of deception and illusion. The statistic usually given after each battle was that of the number of 'casualties', that is, killed and wounded counted together. The number who had been killed was seldom published. Over the past decades, considerable historical research has gone into trying to find out the numbers killed, as opposed to killed and wounded, in the battles of 1916. The number of British dead on the Somme in the four months of continuous fighting has been put at 95,675 (of whom 20,000 were killed on the first day). The French death toll on the Somme was just over 50,000. The German losses have been estimated as in excess of 160,000. More than 300,000 men had been killed in one sector of the front in four months: an average of almost 3000 every day.

On December 6 General Mackensen entered the Roumanian capital, Bucharest, riding in triumph on a white horse. Germany had secured a signal victory for the Central Powers, the defeat of the largest of the Balkan States. The whole line of the Danube, from Germany to the Black Sea, was under German and Austro-Hungarian control. Bucharest was the fourth capital city to be occupied by the Central Powers; the others were Brussels, Belgrade and Cetinje. The Germans were also masters of Warsaw, the focal point of Polish national aspirations.

As 1916 ended, the Allied and Central Powers applied their minds to Woodrow Wilson's Peace Note. The British and French had been offended by a phrase in the Note about the United States 'being too proud to fight'. A senior British diplomat expressed the patriotic view when he asked, in retrospect: 'Did the President realize that to support peace at that moment was to support militarism with all the horrors it had entailed?' The new British Prime Minister, David Lloyd George, who had come to power that December pledged to fight the war with increasing vigour, declared in answer to Wilson's appeal: 'We shall put our trust rather in an unbroken army than in broken faith.'

President Wilson's Peace Note was rejected by all the belligerents. The Tsar's rejection took the form of an Order of the Day to all Russian troops, issued on Christmas Day, urging them to greater efforts on the battlefield. In a private answer to Wilson's insistence that there was no place for conquest and annexation, the Kaiser told his confidants that when the war was over 'the coast of Flanders must be ours'. In the Reichstag, the German Chancellor, Bethmann-Hollweg, asked in mocking tones if the British Prime Minister really imagined 'that Germany would ever again voluntarily surrender to the domination of reactionary Russia the peoples that had been liberated by Germany and Austria-Hungary between the Baltic Sea and the Volhynian swamps, whether they be Poles or Lithuanians, Letts or Balts. Russia would not again possess that territory.'

Bethmann-Hollweg reserved his sharpest criticism for what he described as Britain's war aims. 'Our existence as a nation is to be crushed,' he told the Reichstag. 'Militarily defenceless, economically crushed and boycotted by the world, condemned to lasting sickliness – that is the Germany which England wants to see at her feet.' Britain, he said, wanted to see France weakened by being bled to death, to have all the Allies 'doing slave work for England', and to secure the submission of all the neutral States of Europe. 'Great Britain is of all the most egotistic and fiercest, the most obstinate enemy. The German statesman who would hesitate to use against this enemy every available instrument of battle that will really shorten the war – such a statesman should be hanged.'

In the Reichstag, this pugnacious anti-British flourish was met with loud cheers. In order to increase the number of men under arms, a Patriotic Service Bill was then introduced, whereby all German men between the ages of eighteen and fifty-nine who were not already in the armed forces could be conscripted for the manufacture of munitions and other weapons of war, and all aspects of work relating to the war effort. The Bill was passed into law by 235 votes to 19, the only opponents being the small minority of antiwar Socialist deputies, followers of Karl Liebknecht.

In Austria-Hungary, the death on November 21 of the eighty-six-year-old Emperor, Franz Josef, was followed by a patriotic statement by his successor, the Emperor Charles (Karl, the twenty-nine-year-old grandson of Franz Josef's brother) that the war must be continued 'until the enemy powers realize that it is impossible to overthrow the monarchy'. In an attempt to convince their peoples that they were not responsible for prolonging the war, both the German Chancellor and the Hungarian Prime Minister announced that the defeat of the Central Powers was 'manifestly impossible', that for the Allies to continue the war was therefore 'a crime against humanity', and that as Germany and Austria-Hungary were both waging a 'war of defence', they were ready at any time for an 'equitable peace'. The Allies replied that no peace could be equitable in which the Central Powers retained their conquests.

There was a brief respite from the burdens of war when the Emperor Charles was crowned King of Hungary. Alfred Potocki, who had succeeded his father as Count, was among the leading Polish landowners invited to the ceremonies. 'The coronation scene,' he wrote in his memoirs, 'was like a page from *The Arabian Nights*. The procession was magnificent – wonderful costumes and carriages. Young Emperor Charles took the oath on a spacious square in front of the Imperial Palace. He then mounted his horse, rode up an incline to the summit of an artificial hillock, drew his sword and waved it in salute. It was a fantastic sight, very much to the taste of Hungarians who love dramatic gestures. The dinner in the palace made an unforgettable impression on me. I have never seen more animation under such brilliant costumes.'

The Hungarian poet Gyula Juhász wrote a coronation ode for the new Emperor. 'King, the glitter is fleeting,' he warned, 'the pomp short-lived, the rose wilts, and the song fades away. The legion of heroes still march towards death, and the Hungarian is still a widowed, orphaned nation, abundantly shedding its blood, the most beautiful purple, but wanting justice and peace.'

The number of men under arms gave confidence both to the sovereigns and to the military leaders of the Central and Allied Powers alike that the war could go on. Russia had 9 million men in her army, Germany 7 million, Austria nearly 5 million. Although these figures hid many elements of malaise and discontent, war-weariness and disaffection, and an unprecedented loss of life – since the beginning of the war, 800,000 German soldiers had been killed – the ability of each nation to convince its citizens that the war was just, and must go on, was considerable.

In Russia, where opposition to the war was intensified after the failure of Brusilov's offensive, the largest political grouping in the Duma, the Constitutional Democrats, issued a patriotic proclamation calling on all citizens not to hesitate in their support for the war. 'It is impossible to permit Russia to emerge from the contest curtailed, humiliated, and enslaved,' the proclamation read. 'It is impossible to permit Europe to bow to the yoke of Prussian militarism, and the great European democracies to be weakened and crushed. It is impossible that the peoples who have linked their fate with the Allies should perish, that Belgium and Serbia should be wiped from the face of Europe, that Poland and Lithuania should remain in the clutches of Germany, that tortured Armenia should be again surrendered to the enslavers.'

The Russian government also tried a historical Russian method of deflecting popular discontent. The Minister of the Interior, Alexei Khvostov, sent out circulars to the provincial governors in which he accused the Jews of being responsible for the high food prices. This was an unusual exploitation of anti-Jewish prejudice, given the large number of Russian Jews who were serving in the Tsarist army: the largest number of Jews killed in action in any of the armies, 100,000, were Russian Jews. As a result of these circulars, anger against the Jews was easily aroused. In Baku there were serious riots against the Jewish population. So effective had the Jewish scapegoat become that a Monarchist Congress, assembling in St Petersburg, petitioned the Tsar to abolish the Duma on the grounds that the majority of its members were 'in the pay of the Jews'. When it was revealed that Khvostov had offered to pay the travelling expenses of the 2000 peasant delegates to the Congress, the Duma forced him to resign.

Throughout 1916 the Duma sought to lessen the social discontent in Russia by legislation. The restrictions still imposed on the peasants, in particular their right to leave their villages without permission from the local authorities, were removed. Bills were passed aimed at reducing the bribery and corruption that teemed through Russian official life. For the first time the possibility was introduced of bringing a prosecution for bribery against an official without first needing the consent of a superior official. The restrictions on the areas in which Jews could live (the so-called Pale of Settlement) were also lifted, not least because so much of the area of the Pale had been conquered by the Germans. The only political pressure for making peace came, ironically, from the Congress of Monarchists, from the Reactionaries, who warned the Tsar that if he did not make peace, 'revolutionary elements' in Russia – by which they meant the liberals, or Progressives – would gain the ascendancy.

But peacemaking was not to be the Russian way. In November the Prime Minister, Boris Stürmer, himself a supporter of the Reactionaries, and an advocate of some kind of negotiated peace in order to prevent the slide to liberalism, was replaced, on orders of the Tsar. His successor, Alexander Trepov, had been the minister responsible for building the railway line that brought military supplies from Murmansk to Petrograd. In replacing Stürmer, the Tsar also expressed his support with the general wish of the Duma, that the war should be fought 'to a finish'.

In his first speech as Prime Minister, Trepov – who was to hold his high office for only forty-two days – stressed that when the war was over, Russia must acquire Constantinople and the Dardanelles. 'The vital interests of Russia are as well understood by our loyal Allies as by ourselves,' he said. He then revealed, for the first time, the terms of the 1915 agreement whereby Russia would be the territorial beneficiary of the defeat of Turkey, and would acquire 'sovereign possession of a free passage into the Mediterranean' (something which Stalin was to request of his Anglo-American allies in 1945, but in vain).

Trepov was insistent that Russia would continue the war until 'complete victory' had been secured, and a resolution was passed in the Duma at the end of the year stating that the Duma favoured 'a categorical refusal by the Allied Governments to enter under present conditions into any negotiations whatever'. Peace would only be possible, the resolution stated, 'after a decisive victory over the military power of the enemy, and after the definite renunciation by Germany of the aspirations which render her responsible for the world-war, and for the horrors by which it is accompanied.'

For many members of the Duma, the Empress Alexandra – Princess Alix of Hesse-Darmstadt – constituted a pro-German influence at the centre of power, allegedly seeking a separate peace that would strengthen the autocracy. The Empress, who was nicknamed 'the German woman', had for ten years been under the influence of Grigori Rasputin, a 'holy man' or 'healer', to whom she was devoted because of his efforts to help her haemophiliac son. His influence was regarded by the Duma as all the more dangerous because Tsar Nicholas was often away from Petrograd, at his military headquarters near the front. In November and December 1916 a number of Russian aristocrats, including the Grand Duke Dimitrii, a nephew of the Tsar, conspired to kill Rasputin. The chief conspirator, Prince Felix Yusupov, assured a fellow conspirator that once the Tsar had been freed of the influence of Rasputin and the Empress 'everything will change: he will turn into a good constitutional monarch'.

On the night of December 13/14, Rasputin was persuaded to visit Prince Yusupov's home. There he was given poisoned almond and chocolate pastries. They made him ill, but did not kill him. Yusupov then shot Rasputin with a revolver, but Rasputin managed to rise up and seize Yusupov by the throat. Another conspirator then shot Rasputin dead, and his body was thrown through a hole in a frozen canal on the outskirts of the city. Although the public rejoiced, the Tsar made no effort to turn towards more democratic rule; indeed, Rasputin's murder seemed to him proof of the Empress's view that there could be no compromise with those opposed to the autocracy.

Although none of the belligerent powers were willing to make peace, they were all very much involved in positioning themselves for influence in the postwar world. Following the defeat of Serbia, the heir to the Serbian throne, Prince-Regent Alexander, travelled to London, together with the Serbian Prime Minister, Nicola Pašić, in search of British support for the creation of an independent South Slav State (Yugoslavia) after the war. In both London and Paris, Czech national leaders were seeking assurances that when the war was over, an independent Czechoslovak State would emerge. In London, and Berlin, Zionist leaders were trying to persuade one or other of the warring powers to support their desire for a Jewish National Home in Palestine, either after the defeat of Turkey, or (in the case of the Berlin discussions) with Turkish approval.

Both Russia and Germany were competing to assure the Poles of their respective support for an independent Poland. The Germans, who were in occupation of Russian Poland, announced their support for Polish national aspirations, and gave the Polish language an official position – something it had hitherto refused to do in the Polish provinces of the German Empire. The Germans also agreed to the establishment of a Polish University in Warsaw – something the Russians had persistently refused. For many months the Germans did not make clear what administration the future Poland would have, only that it would not be 'returned to Russia'. One problem was that the Galician regions of Poland had not been under Russian, but under Austro-Hungarian rule, and Austria refused to part with the provinces it had ruled for more than a century.

After long negotiations between Berlin and Vienna, it was agreed that the importance to the Central Powers of Polish support made it essential to make a specific offer to the Poles in areas even more central to national self-expression than language and education. The offer came on November 5, in the form of an announcement by the German Governor of Warsaw, and his Austrian counterpart, the Austro-Hungarian Governor-General of the Lublin district, which Austria had conquered from Russia in 1915. The German and Austrian Emperors, the announcement declared, 'sustained by their firm confidence in the final victory of their arms', and wanting to see a 'happy future' for the Polish districts which had been 'snatched with heavy sacrifices from Russian power', had agreed to establish from those districts an independent Polish State with a hereditary monarchy and a constitution. Galicia would remain under Austrian rule.

For the Poles, the declaration was not as satisfactory as they had hoped. 'It settled nothing to the satisfaction of those Poles who dreamed of a new Poland which would embrace all the Polish people,' Alfred Potocki later wrote. 'At best it was a straw in the wind which was blowing through our country and raising hope.'

To the further disappointment of the Poles, the German government quickly made it clear that no part of Prussian Poland was to be ceded to the new State. 'Every inch' of Prussian Poland would be retained by Germany, the Prussian Minister of the Interior confirmed two weeks later, and this was upheld by a majority vote in the Prussian Parliament (in which the

Polish, Danish and Socialist parties voted against the retention). The precise frontier of the new Polish State, it said, 'remains reserved'.

Polish national aspirations went far beyond the borders of Russian Poland, not only with regard to Prussia and Galacia, but further east. It was known that the Germans were supporting Baltic national aspirations; but Poles had strong claims on several of the towns in the Baltic region, especially Vilna, which the Germans had placed under Lithuanian administration, having conquered it from Russia. The Germans had also separated the government of Suwalki from the German district of occupied Poland, linking this with the Lithuanian administration in Vilna, and intimating that it would be excluded from any future Polish State. But Suwalki, like Vilna, was considered by Poles to be part of their patrimony.

The extent and complexity of Polish demands, and the prospect of an entirely independent and separate Polish State, did not sit well either in Vienna or Berlin. To counter the creation of too powerful an independent entity on its northern border, the Austro-Hungarian government put forward the idea of a Polish State, including both Russian Poland and Austrian Galicia, that would be an integral part of the Habsburg dominions. The Germans were not pleased at the thought of such an increase in the size of their ally and neighbour. For their part, the German Conservatives, particularly those from Prussia, favoured the incorporation of Russian Poland, albeit with some form of Polish autonomy, into Germany, thus creating an eastward movement of German territory which, in conjunction with a future German-associated Baltic region, would greatly extend Germany's influence in the east, a long-cherished aim.

The wrangle over what Poland's status would be, and where its borders would be, was based on the premise that Germany and Austria-Hungary would win the war against Russia, and would dispose of the eastern territories as they chose. Wise Polish counsels also looked at the alternative, an Allied victory, and, like the Czechs and Slovaks, and the Serbs and South Slavs, canvassed for their future State in London, Paris and Washington, as well as in Berlin and Vienna. The Russian government, determined not to allow the Central Powers to make all the running with regard to Poland's future, or to affect her wartime allegiance, announced that it was the intention of the Tsar, once Russia had reconquered the lost Polish territories, to reunite Russian, Austrian and Prussian Poland as a self-governing province of the Russian Empire.

*   *   *

During 1916 H. G. Wells set out in his book *What is Coming?* his view of the possible territorial future of Europe, with regard both to borders and attitudes of mind. 'The first most distinctive thing about this conflict,' he wrote, 'is the exceptionally searching way in which it attacks human happiness. No war has ever destroyed happiness so widely. It has not only killed and wounded an unprecedented proportion of the male population of all the combatant nations, but it has also destroyed wealth beyond precedent. It has also destroyed freedom – of movement, of speech, of economic enterprise. Hardly anyone alive has escaped the worry of it and the threat of it. It has left scarcely a life untouched, and made scarcely a life happier. There is a limit to the principle that "everybody's business is nobody's business". The establishment of a world state, which was interesting only to a few cranks and visionaries before the war, is now the lively interest of a very great number of people. They inquire about it; they have become accessible to ideas about it.'

Wells also made a dire forecast:

I believe that this war is going to end not in the complete smashing up and subjugation of either side, but in a general exhaustion that will make the recrudescence of the war still possible but very terrifying.

Mars will sit like a giant above all human affairs for the next two decades, and the speech of Mars is blunt and plain. He will say to us all:

'Get your houses in order. If you squabble among yourselves, waste time, litigate, muddle, snatch profits and shirk obligations, I will certainly come down upon you again. I have taken all your men between eighteen and fifty, and killed and maimed such as I pleased; millions of them. I have wasted your substance – contemptuously. Now, mark you, you have multitudes of male children between the ages of nine and nineteen running about among you. Delightful and beloved boys. And behind them come millions of delightful babies. Of these I have scarcely smashed and starved a paltry hundred thousand perhaps by the way.

'But go on muddling, each for himself and his parish and his family and none for all the world, go on in the old way, stick to your "rights", stick to your "claims" each one of you, make no concessions and no sacrifices, obstruct, waste, squabble and presently I will come back again and take all that fresh harvest of life I have spared, all those millions that are now sweet children and dear little boys and youths, and I will squeeze it into red pulp between my hands, I will mix it with the mud of trenches and feast on it before your eyes, even more damnably than I have done with your grown-up sons and young men.

'And I have taken most of your superfluities already; next time I will take your barest necessities.'

Wells was convinced that 'if the exhaustion is fairly mutual, it need not be decisive for a long time. It may mean simply an ebb of vigour on both sides, unusual hardship, a general social and economic disorganization and grading down. The fact that a great killing off of men is implicit in the process, and that the survivors will be largely under discipline, militates against the idea that the end may come suddenly through a vigorous revolutionary outbreak.' Exhaustion was likely to be 'a very long and very thorough process, extending over years', and he went on to warn: 'A "war of attrition" may last into 1918 or 1919, and may bring us to conditions of strain and deprivation still only very vaguely imagined.'

With regard to the future of Poland, Wells also made a forecast. 'An entirely independent Poland,' he wrote, 'will be a feverish field of international intrigue – intrigue to which the fatal Polish temperament lends itself all too readily; it may be a battlefield again within five-and-twenty-years.' His solution was for Poland to 'determine to be Slav at any cost, and make the best of Russia', allying herself with Russia 'with all her liberal tendencies, and rise and fall with her.'

Wells also ventured a forecast of a possible political revolution in Germany, and how it would be received. 'If we take the extremest possibility, and suppose a revolution in Germany or in South Germany, and the replacement of the Hohenzollerns in all or part of Germany by a Republic, then I am convinced that for republican Germany there would be not simply forgiveness, but a warm welcome back to the comity of nations.'

Despite the fact that a democratic, non-monarchist Germany would, in Wells's view, be welcomed by the nations, he was aware of the power of Germany to regain the centre of the European stage. 'The German air fleet of 1930,' he wrote, 'may yet be something as predominant as the British navy of 1915, and capable of delivering a much more intimate blow.' In this forecast he was less than ten years out, as the German bombing of Warsaw in 1939 was to testify.

*   *   *

As the battles raged on both the Eastern and Western Fronts, the territorial discussions continued. They extended to every region conquered by the Central Powers. In Belgium, an attempt was made by the Germans to establish a Flemish University of Ghent that would be sympathetic to the future incorporation of Belgium, in some form, into Germany or the German sphere of influence. But the attempt was not successful. The repeated efforts by the German military authorities, of which the university was one, to deepen the animosities between Flemish and French-speaking Belgians was combated both inside Belgium, and by the Allies. In a declaration issued on 14 February 1916, the Allies pledged that they would not end hostilities with Germany 'until Belgium has been restored to her political and economic independence'. The Allies also promised financial aid to Belgium 'to ensure her commercial and financial recovery' from the German occupation.

The future of Luxembourg was also under discussion in 1916. The German desire to incorporate the Grand Duchy into the German Empire was bolstered by reference to the fact that Luxembourg had been a member of the German Confederation from 1815 to 1866. But there was distress in that small country, and in Britain and France, when it was made known that the Grand Duchess was not ill-disposed towards the German occupation authorities. There were even those in England who suggested that when the Germans were defeated, the Grand Duchess should be deposed, and Luxembourg handed over to Belgium.

The only European neutral to join the conflict in 1916 was Portugal, Britain's ally for five and a half centuries. When fighting had broken out the previous year between Portuguese and German troops in Africa, the German government had been at pains not to see this as a cause for war with Portugal. It did not want to face yet another belligerent. But the German submarine sinking of neutral shipping affected the Portuguese considerably, and on 23 February 1916 the Portuguese government had ordered the seizure of all German ships in Portuguese ports. In response to this, the German government declared war on Portugal. Without a common land border, the Germans could make no military move; indeed, the initiative came from the Portuguese, who first sent troops to join the Salonika Expeditionary Force, and then to the Western Front.

Among the nations of Europe, six – the Netherlands, Switzerland, Denmark, Norway, Sweden and Spain – continued to preserve their neutrality. The extent to which the fighting powers felt the burden of the war, and even resented the benefits of neutrality, was hinted at in the remark of a British commentator who wrote, in reviewing the events in Spain in 1916: 'While the six Great Powers were slaughtering their manhood and plunging into appalling debt, the Spanish nation continued on its way undisturbed by the sound of the distant storm.'

In the last days of 1916, Josef Stalin, a political exile in Siberia, appeared before a military medical commission that was conscripting prisoners into the Russian army. Because of a defect in his left arm, the result of a childhood blood infection in his left hand, he was declared unfit for military service.

Reaching the remote South Atlantic island of South Georgia at the end of 1916, the Polar explorer Ernest Shackleton – whose ship *Endurance* had been caught in the pack ice for eleven months until it was crushed and sank a year before – asked the weather-station keeper on the island when the war had ended, and who had won. He was flabbergasted to learn that the war was still being fought.

CHAPTER TWENTY

1917

Tens of millions of men, women and children slept soundly in their homes and in their beds as the year 1916 gave way to 1917. But there were millions of other men who were not so fortunate. Leon Wolff, in his book *In Flanders Fields*, wrote forty-one years later of that moment when the new year began:

> Somewhere in the limitless darkness a man coughed, a bird twittered an isolated phrase, a muffled voice spoke up. Many miles behind the front thousands of lorries, wagons, gun limbers, horses and men moving endlessly along the Belgian roads furnished a soft, pulsating background, like that of a kettledrum stirred by felt hammers while the orchestra rests and watches its score. Here in the advance zone of the dread Salient around Ypres hardly a man moved, nor did many even know or care that the old year was dying.
>
> The officer standing beside the field piece watched the glowing second hand of his wrist-watch. At the stroke of midnight he said 'Fire!' The gun roared, and a shell was lobbed somewhere into the German positions. A few seconds later there was a single, distinct, far-off explosion, following which a strained silence hung in the air. Then the enemy threw up anxious flares, ghastly green but of great beauty. These illuminated no-man's land lingeringly, froze it briefly into the aspect of a charcoal sketch and then faded away.
>
> The British battery fired nine more rounds in erratic succession, paused, and then another seven more. Thus the new year, 1917, was advertised by seventeen shells, to which the German did not respond; and the rest of the evening passed in relative peace there and elsewhere on the Western Front.
>
> A cheerless morning dawned some hours later.

In a New Year message to a group of loyal Conservatives, a senior British Cabinet Minister, Lord Curzon, stated with solemn truth: 'It is impossible to say as yet that the end is in sight. It seems likely that well into another year, perhaps longer, must we continue the dreadful tragedy that is turning the world into hell.' Yet the national aspirations that had been stimulated during 1916, and which depended for their satisfaction on the victory of one side or the other, became even stronger in 1917, as it became clear that the war was going to be fought until either the Allies or the Central Powers were totally defeated.

Large national groups such as the Poles and the Czechs could not yet know with which power bloc their future would reside. The South Slavs knew that the only hope for a Serbian renaissance was for the defeat of Austria-Hungary. An independent Armenia would depend for its existence upon the defeat of Turkey. Belgium could only be independent if Germany were defeated.

That January the German Chancellor made it clear to the American ambassador in Berlin that Germany would require the permanent occupation of Liège and Namur, and 'other forts and garrisons throughout Belgium', as well as the 'possession' of Belgium's ports and railways, and a permanent military presence. This was not a prescription for Belgian independence. The Belgians were not even to be allowed an army of their own under the German interpretation of what the Kaiser described, to the Americans, as 'withdrawal' from Belgium.

The Arabs were succeeding, as enemies of the Turks, to make their national needs known under British patronage, and to make their contribution to the Allied war effort. Several British officers, including Colonel T. E. Lawrence, took part that January in the Arab attack on the port of Yenbo, on the Red Sea; and three weeks later three British warships participated in the Arab capture of the port of Wejh, more than a hundred miles further up the Red Sea coast.

Jewish national aspirations also continued to regard a British victory over the Turks as one possible path to fulfilment; a group of Palestine Jews, led by members of the Aaronsohn family, who had emigrated to Palestine from Roumania in the 1880s, began to provide British Intelligence with the information needed to attack Turkish military positions in southern Palestine. It was information that would prove an essential prelude to one of Lloyd George's dreams, the British liberation of Jerusalem.

Alexander Aaronsohn, having made his way from Palestine to Egypt, passed on to the British detailed knowledge of the wells and springs in the southern Palestine region, to enable an attacking force to make its way across the otherwise inhospitable Negev desert. Another of the Aaronsohn group – who were known as the Nili spies – made contact from inside Palestine with an Australian military patrol on the Turkish border, passing on further military intelligence. A Royal Navy vessel, the *Managam*, sailing off the coast of Palestine, managed to send a boat ashore at the Crusader port of Athlit with money for the Nili spies. On a second visit, the *Managam* brought explosives, which the young Jews used to blow up bridges on the Haifa–Damascus railway. At the same time, Arab forces, also with British help, were blowing up sections of the Damascus–Medina line.

When one of the Jewish spies, Alexander Aaronsohn's sister Sarah, was captured by the Turks and tortured, she killed herself rather than reveal what she knew. Another of her brothers, Aaron, who managed to reach London through Germany and Denmark, helped to convince the British War Cabinet to look with favour on the idea of a Jewish National Home in Palestine once Turkey had been defeated.

On 12 January 1917 the Allied Powers, meeting in Rome, issued a declaration that sent a tremor through the higher echelons of the Austro-Hungarian government and army. The declaration promised that the Allies would strive for the national liberation of all the nationalities – or 'subject peoples' as they were described – within the Habsburg dominions. Among those who were promised the benefits of an Allied victory were the Poles, the Czechs, the Slovenes, the Croats, the Serbs, and the Roumanians.

Recognizing the impact that the Rome Declaration would have on the subject peoples of the Habsburg empire, the Austrian Foreign Minister, Count Czernin, told the Council of Ministers in Vienna that it had become urgent to seek a compromise peace. If they did not do so, he warned, the multinational empire, whose diversity was once its pride, would disintegrate. One example of the changing nature of Habsburg cohesion was that in southern Russia many Roumanian conscripts in the Austro-Hungarian army who were taken prisoner by the Russians signed an oath to fight against their former Habsburg rulers.

Nine days after the Rome Declaration, a further chill was felt in Vienna, and also in Berlin, when Woodrow Wilson, in his State of the Union Address, announced that a 'united Poland' should emerge from the war as a sovereign

State. Wilson specifically said that Poland should have access to the Baltic Sea, thus challenging the hopes of the German Conservatives that the Poles in the Prussian regions would remain inside Germany.

France also hoped to make territorial gains as a result of victory, and began secret negotiations with Russia to secure her claims. As a result of these negotiations, an agreement was signed with Russia, under which, in return for French recognition of Russia's rights in the Polish and Baltic regions, France was given three assurances by the Tsar: that Alsace-Lorraine would be 'restored to France', that France would be given a special position in the coal-rich Saar valley, and that the Rhineland districts of Germany would be 'entirely separated from Germany and freed from all political and economic dependence upon her'.

This Franco-Russian Agreement, signed in strictest secrecy on February 14, stated that the French frontier with Germany would be drawn up 'at the discretion of the French government'. In return for this, the French government began negotiations with the Russians to establish in detail what Russia's frontiers would be in western Russia and the Caucasus, and to support Russia's claims.

Each power bloc had set out its aims and territorial desires, and sought the approval of its allies, as the highest form of legitimacy. But each power needed to secure victory over its adversaries in order to attain those desires. In pursuit of victory, new strategies, and new methods of making war, were constantly under discussion. Unrestricted submarine warfare was one of those strategies. At a Crown Council held in the presence of the Kaiser on January 9, the German Naval Chief-of-Staff, Admiral von Holtzendorf, assured the Kaiser that once unrestricted submarine warfare on all ships, whatever their nationality or flag, was instituted by Germany, Britain would sue for peace within six months.

When the Kaiser asked how Germany would deal with America's inevitable entry into the war, if American ships were to be sunk on the scale which such a policy envisaged, the Admiral replied, with the fullest confidence in the abilities of his submarines to track down and sink any troop transports that might try to cross the Atlantic: 'I will give Your Majesty my word as an officer that not one American will land on the Continent.'

Field Marshal Hindenburg also spoke in favour of unrestricted submarine warfare. He supported this drastic measure on the grounds that it would lead to a substantial decrease in the amount of American manufactured munitions reaching the Allied powers across the Atlantic. When Bethmann-

Hollweg opposed unrestricted submarine warfare on the grounds that it would bring the United States into the war, the Kaiser and the Council – of which Bethmann-Hollweg was the senior civilian member – asked him to withdraw his opposition. What was required was unanimity.

The German ability to maintain a submarine offensive was formidable, as dangerous to the Allies in the First World War as it was to be in the Second. In January 1917, the last month during which attacks on ships flying the United States flag were not permitted, German submarines had sunk 59 British, 63 other Allied, and 66 neutral (though no American) ships, a total weight of shipping and cargo of 300,000 tons. Among the armoured merchant cruisers sunk that month was the *Laurentic*, a former ocean liner. It hit a German mine off the coast of Ireland, and 350 of those on board were drowned.

From February 1, when the unrestricted submarine warfare came into force, it was intended that this figure of 300,000 tons of shipping sunk would be substantially increased. Allied and neutral vessels were equally at risk. In mid February, 870 Italian soldiers on their way to join the Salonika Expeditionary Force were drowned when their troopship, the *Minas*, was torpedoed. Nine days later a French liner, the *Athos*, was torpedoed; among the dead were 543 Chinese labourers who had been recruited in China and were on their way to serve as manual labourers on the Western Front; part of a total force of 100,000 Chinese brought to the war zones to work behind the lines. On the Western Front, the graves of 1612 of them are tended to this day by the Commonwealth War Graves Commission.

As the German government prepared to embark on its campaign of unrestricted submarine warfare, and to accept that as a result the United States would almost certainly declare war, it offered an inducement to Mexico to attack the United States across its southern border. The Mexicans had cause for resentment against the United States. An American punitive expedition, commanded by General Pershing, had been on Mexican soil for many months, following the murder of seventeen American citizens in Columbus, New Mexico, by the Mexican political adventurer Pancho Villa, who had led a raid across the United States border.

Through its Foreign Minister, Dr Alfred von Zimmermann, the German government offered, in the utmost secrecy, to recognize the conquest by Mexico – if the Mexican armies were able to do so – of all the territories which Mexico had lost seventy years earlier: the States of New Mexico, Texas and Arizona. This top-secret offer, sent by a coded radio message, was deciphered in London. When it was shown to an American diplomat in London, he remarked derisively, 'Why not Illinois and New York while they are about it?'

The first United States ship to be sunk after the institution of unrestricted German submarine warfare was a cargo ship, the *Housatonic*, torpedoed off the Scilly Islands. Its crew was saved by a British ship; but its cargo of grain was lost. In Berlin, Dr von Zimmermann told the American ambassador, who had come to the Foreign Ministry to express his indignation at the sinking: 'Everything is all right. America will do nothing, for President Wilson is for peace, and nothing else. Everything will go on as before.'

This was as serious a miscalculation by Germany as the Kaiser's miscalculations on the eve of war. On the very day of Zimmermann's confident assertion that America would do nothing, Wilson told Congress that he was breaking off diplomatic relations with Germany. This was not a declaration of war. But it was a serious indication that such a declaration might not be far distant. On the following day, the Portuguese Expeditionary Force arrived in France, adding another 50,000 fighting men to the Allied cause.

Hindenburg, recognizing that a further Western Front offensive might not be held in check as the Somme offensive had been, gave the order for the German army on the Western Front to withdraw behind the Hindenburg Line – as the British and French called it; the Germans called it the Siegfried Line. As well as cheating the British and French of a chance to attack the newly dug trench lines nearest to them, the withdrawal, by straightening various kinks in the line, reduced the length of trenches to be defended by the Germans on the Western Front by twenty-five miles, releasing thirteen divisions – more than 60,000 men – for service elsewhere in the line, or as reserves. In the area from which Germany withdrew, the German army systematically destroyed every structure, including bridges and warehouses, that could be of use to the Allies.

There was also a sense of confidence in the German High Command as a result of the news from Russia. A German intelligence assessment in mid February made it clear that the Russian army 'cannot hold out longer than the autumn'. Ten days after this report reached General Hoffman in Berlin, there was another antiwar demonstration in the streets of Petrograd. From the British Military Attaché with the Russian army came a report, the details of which were also known in Berlin, that more than a million Russian soldiers had been killed in action, and that a further two million were either missing (killed in action but unidentified) or prisoners of war. More than half a million were in hospital, too badly injured to return to the front. A further million had deserted.

The number of Russian soldiers in frontline and reserve units was insufficient to meet the demands of the battlefield in 1917, if the rate of loss continued as before.

If Russia was a weak link in the military operations of the Entente, Turkey was a weak link in those of the Central Powers. Slowly but without setbacks, the British forces had moved back along the Tigris, reaching Kut, the scene of so much suffering and humiliation a year before, and entering Baghdad on March 11. Gertrude Bell, the British orientalist who was serving with the Allied Intelligence Bureau in Cairo, noted in her diary when Baghdad fell: 'That's the end of the German dream of domination in the Near East. Their place is not going to be in the sun.'

The Austrians were also confronted that spring with a setback – a rebellion of Serbs in the Nish region. The rebellion was suppressed with considerable brutality, and more than two thousand Serbs were executed.

The Allies were faced with growing antiwar feeling. Both the Russians, who had begun to send troops into action against antiwar demonstrators, and the French, were confronted by mounting public discontent against the war. In France, where the frontline soldiers were most closely affected by the mood of disillusionment, the word 'mutiny' began increasingly to be heard in the communications between officers and commanders.

The entry of the United States into the war as an active combatant would be a boost to the Allied morale. It might also – if Allied morale had not cracked before then – prove decisive on the battlefield once her troops could reach it. But the United States had still not declared war on Germany, nor had any of her troops embarked on the transatlantic voyage. She was still waiting for the outcome of Germany's unrestricted submarine warfare decision. The Allies could only watch and wait as America, its mood increasingly hostile to Germany, was unable to make the decision on which so much depended for an eventual Allied victory.

When a German submarine sank the Cunard liner *Laconia* off the Fastnet

Rock, four Americans were among the passengers who were killed. Yet Woodrow Wilson still made no greater protest than he had done before the German government's unrestricted submarine warfare decision. On March 5, nine days after the sinking, he told the United States Congress: 'We stand fast on armed neutrality', and that stance was maintained four days later, when an American steamship, the *Algonquin*, was sunk.

While America hesitated to enter the war, events in Russia provided the most severe challenge yet to the unity and confidence of the Allies. The conditions of life in the Russian cities had reached desperation point for many. The demands of the war, the loss of territory, and the loss of life, had brought hardship and hunger to every region. With the start of a strike in the Putilov munitions works in Petrograd on 3 March 1917 (February 18 in the Russian calendar) the Russian warmaking capacity, and Russia's will to continue the war, were eroded. The strike was called because, as a result of a severe shortage of fuel, the munitions works had been shut down and the men laid off.

This was not merely another antiwar protest, it was a challenge to the authority and rule of the Tsar. For three days there were riots in the streets of the Russian capital. Food was in short supply. Shortages of bread created panic among citizens who circulated rumours that bread rationing was imminent, and would be limited to one pound of bread per adult per day. Strikes spread, propelled by a collective fear of starvation. By March 9 there were between 200,000 and 300,000 factory workers on strike. Along the Nevsky Prospekt, Petrograd's main thoroughfare, crowds marched with shouts of 'Down with the autocracy!' and 'Down with the war!' Cossack troops, ordered to disperse them, refused to do so. When one unit of troops did open fire in the nearby covered market, three civilians were killed. Elsewhere, a police officer was separated from his men and beaten to death. But when Alexander Shlyapnikov, one of the few Bolshevik leaders who was in the city – most of them were in Siberian or more distant exile – was told that a revolution had begun, he replied contemptuously: 'What revolution? Give the workers a pound of bread and the movement will peter out.'

The Tsar was at his military headquarters in Mogilev, 120 miles east of the front line, and 450 miles south of Petrograd. On the orders of the Minister of the Interior, Alexander Protopopov, he was not given a full picture of the seriousness of the disturbances. Even so, on March 10, unwilling to follow the path of conciliation, he ordered the suppression of the Petrograd riots by force. 'I order you to stop tomorrow the disorders in the capital, which are unacceptable at this difficult time of war with Germany and Austria,' he telegraphed that day.

On the following morning, March 11, Petrograd was occupied by Tsarist troops. Anna Akhmatova, seeking to go by horse-drawn cab across the River Neva, was told by the driver, 'Lady, I'm not going over there. They're shooting, and I have a family.'

The Tsar himself was involved on March 11 in a major diplomatic initiative, the final phase of the Franco-Russian Agreement of 14 February 1917, whereby the French government recognized Russia's 'complete liberty in establishing her western frontiers'. Such 'liberty' proved to be of short duration. When the troops whom the Tsar had ordered to Petrograd opened fire on a crowd that was refusing to disperse, forty civilians were killed. The President of the Duma, M. V. Rodzianko, telegraphed to the Tsar: 'Position serious. Anarchy in the capital. Government paralysed. Arrangements for transport, supply and fuel in complete disorder. General discontent is increasing. Disorderly firing in the streets. Part of the troops are firing on one another. Essential to entrust some individual who possesses the confidence of the country with the formation of a new government. There must be no delay. Any procrastination fatal. I pray to God that in this hour responsibility fall not on the wearer of the crown!'

Rodzianko repeated this telegram to the military commanders on all the Army Group fronts, and to the Commander-in-Chief, General Alexeyev, at Field Headquarters, with a request for their support. That evening the long-awaited production by Meyerhold of Lermontov's *Masquerade* was having its dress rehearsal at the theatre. In the street, 'there was firing', a theatre critic who was present, Alexander Kugel, recalled. 'The trolleys stopped running, the street lamps burned dimly ... Scarce cabdrivers demanded incredible sums. Cries could be heard and crowds with flags were gathering. There were no people on the streets, and it was eerie. The theatre, however, was packed – and what prices! ... At the theatre entrance there was a solid black row of automobiles. All the wealth, all the nobility, all of Petrograd's enormous pluto-bureau-and-behind-the-front-lines-ocracy had turned out.'

Fighting continued during the night. Count Sheremetev, confronted at the gates of his eighteenth-century palace on the Fontanka Canal by a group of people searching for arms, and recognizing their determination, greeted them with the words: 'Arms? You need arms? Please, my axes and picks from the sixteenth century are at your service.'

On the morning of March 12 – February 27 in the Russian calendar –

Rodzianko telegraphed again to the Tsar: 'The situation is growing worse. Immediate steps must be taken, for tomorrow will be too late. The final hour has come when the fate of the country and the dynasty must be decided.' On receiving this telegram the Tsar left Mogilev by rail for Petrograd. His imperial train steamed slowly northward, stopping at each station and railway junction to make certain that the way ahead was passable. Nicholas hoped that he could exert his authority to bring the strikes and demonstrations to an end. But, even as he set off on his long train journey, the soldiers of the Petrograd garrison – 171,000 men in all, plus a further 152,000 in nearby towns – on whom he was hoping to rely, joined the street demonstrations whose slogans included 'Down with the Tsar!'

Those soldiers and police who were still loyal to the Tsar were outnumbered. They were unable that day to prevent the burning of the Law Courts, or a series of attacks on police stations throughout the city. In many instances the strikers prevailed on the troops who were sent against them not to open fire. In the clashes that did take place, 587 demonstrators were killed, as well as 655 soldiers and 73 policemen. The soldiers and officials loyal to the Tsar were no longer in control of the capital. The Duma decided to act, forming a Provisional Committee for the Restoration of Order in the Capital, chaired by Rodzianko, and with two Socialist members, Alexander Kerensky and N. S. Chkheidze.

On March 13 the captain of the Russian cruiser *Aurora*, which was undergoing repairs in Petrograd, was murdered by his own sailors. Forty more officers were murdered at the nearby island base of Kronstadt. That afternoon, Winston Churchill later wrote, 'the Russian Embassy in London informed us that they were no longer in contact with Petrograd. For some days the capital had been the prey to disorders which it was believed were being effectively suppressed. Now suddenly for a space there was silence.' From his exile in New York, Leon Trotsky wrote on March 13: 'The streets of Petrograd again speak the language of 1905.'

On March 14, as the Tsar's train continued on its way northwards to Petrograd, an officer went on board to tell the Tsar that the tracks ahead were in the hands of 'unfriendly troops'. The train made a detour westward to Pskov, where it was met by the commander of the Northern Front, General Ruzsky, a man whose political sympathies were entirely with the Duma opposition. Ruzsky at once urged the Tsar to make concessions to the Duma, and to acknowledge the authority of the Provisional Government.

The Tsar refused to do so, but in Petrograd, several leading monarchists, and even the Commandant of the Palace Guard at Tsarskoe Selo, the Tsar's cousin Grand Duke Cyril, recognized the Provisional Government. They did so in part out of fear: that same day a Petrograd 'Soviet' (or Council), elected by striking factory workers and disloyal soldiers, issued its Order No. 1: all saluting of officers by men who were not on duty was abolished, and all weapons would be controlled by elected committees.

The Bolsheviks, whose leaders – including Lenin – were in exile, called for an immediate end to the war, and the establishment of the 'dictatorship of the proletariat'. But the Bolshevik Party was a minority in the Petrograd Soviet, as were the Socialist Revolutionaries, who between then had less than 10 per cent of the seats. Power in the Soviet was in the hands of the Menshevik wing of the Social Democratic Party, with Alexander Kerensky and N.S. Chkheidze, both members of the Provisional Government, in prominent positions. The Mensheviks were headed by Irakli Tseretelli.

On March 15, while still at Pskov, Nicholas received a spate of telegrams, which had been orchestrated by General Alexeyev, appealing to him to abdicate. These telegrams came from every army commander. Their message was reinforced by General Ruzsky, who warned the Tsar that the turmoil inside Russia was such that only abdication could prevent anarchy. Another voice raised in favour of abdication was that of General Brusilov, the Tsar's most successful general, who doubted that the Russian army could continue the war if the Tsar remained on the throne. Brusilov was supported by General Sakharov, commanding the Russian troops on the Roumanian front, who confirmed that the troops would not fight if the Tsar remained at the helm.

Bowing to this overwhelming unanimity of senior military opinion, the Tsar abdicated. He would be succeeded as Tsar, he announced, by his brother, the Grand Duke Michael. But Michael, recognizing the strength of the anti-Tsarist upsurge, resigned from the throne on the following day. The Romanov dynasty, whose first Tsar, Michael, had come to the throne in 1613, was at an end.

The constitutional forces in the Duma, meeting in the Tauride Palace, ordered the arrest of the Tsarist ministers, and formed a Provisional Government, committed to the calling of a Constituent Assembly. It was through this Assembly that it was intended to establish democracy in Russia. But the situation in Russia was too chaotic for the Assembly to be summoned for another ten months, and by then the Provisional Government had been overthrown and any possibility of democracy in Russia had died.

The Provisional Government, established on the ruins of Tsardom and with high hopes for a democratic future for Russia, was headed by a liberal monarchist, Prince Lvov. As his Foreign Minister he appointed a liberal Professor, Paul Miliukov, a member of the Constitutional Democratic Party (the Kadets). As Minister of Justice, he appointed the left-wing former deputy – and member of the Petrograd Soviet – Alexander Kerensky. To the relief of the Allies, one of the first acts of the new government was to announce that it would continue with the war, and would do so 'to a victorious conclusion'. In this, the Provisional Government was supported by the Petrograd Soviet which, sitting elsewhere in the same palace, insisted upon being consulted on all major decisions. Most of the Menshevik majority in the Soviet supported the war as a 'defensive' war against the Germans.

A nightmare had emerged in the thinking of the Western Allies. It was that Russia would withdraw from the war, and the German troops that had been manning the Eastern Front would be transferred to the Western Front. Once transferred, they would overwhelm, by their numbers and their armaments, the Anglo-French forces; and they would do so before the United States, still neutral, had entered the war and been able to raise and transfer a significant army to Europe. But when the British Military Attaché in Petrograd, Colonel Knox, confided to the President of the Duma his fears that the Soviets would continue with their revolutionary activities until they had forced Russia out of the war, the President, M. V. Rodzianko, replied, 'My dear Knox, you must be easy. Everything is going on all right. Russia is a big country, and can wage war and manage a revolution at the same time.'

The Provisional Government was determined to assure the Allies that Russia would continue with the war. 'She will fight by their side against a common enemy until the end, without cessation and without faltering,' Miliukov declared on March 18. But although it was with the Provisional Government that the Allies dealt, and from whom they obtained repeated assurances as to Russia's determination to continue the war, throughout Russia, local Soviets were being established, based upon a working-class, peasant and soldier electorate, which reflected widespread antiwar feeling. The Bolshevik leaders were not in a position to exploit this; they had not been prepared for the revolution that had broken out so unexpectedly, or for the existence of a Provisional Government and a Petrograd Soviet side by side. Lenin, the guiding force of the Bolshevik movement and ideology, and three of his most senior colleagues, were in exile in Switzerland when the Tsar abdicated, having been outside Russia since the outbreak of war. Other leaders were in New York (including Trotsky), London and Paris. Josef Stalin and four other senior Bolshevik Party members were in Siberia, to which they had been exiled by Tsarist orders before the war.

Stalin reached Petrograd on March 25. On his arrival he found that three young Party members, among them Vyacheslav Molotov, had taken charge of Bolshevik activities in the capital. They were discontented both with the Provisional Government, and with the predominance inside the Petrograd Soviet of the Mensheviks and the Socialist Revolutionaries. The Bolsheviks, who had hoped for so long to lead the revolution, were being sidelined.

Molotov and his two companions were particularly angered by the decision of the Soviet to support the Provisional Government's call to carry on with the war, and were themselves calling, though the pages of the Bolshevik Party newspaper, *Pravda*, for the overthrow of Prince Lvov's government and the transfer of 'all power' to the Soviets. Other Bolsheviks then in Petrograd, led by V. Voytinsky, wanted to reunite the Bolshevik and Menshevik wings of the Social Democratic Party, support the Provisional Government, and support a 'defensive' war. Stalin, as the most senior Bolshevik to have reached Petrograd, took over the editorship of *Pravda* from Molotov, and tried to bridge the gap between the divergent Bolshevik factions. In doing so, Stalin supported the 'defensive' war to resist any further German and Austro-Hungarian advances. He also urged the Provisional Government 'to come out openly and in the hearing of everybody with an attempt to persuade all the belligerent powers to start immediate peace negotiations.'

Two developments fraught with uncertainty for the course of the war had come in the same month: the Russian Revolution and the German submarine attacks on American ships. On March 21 a United States tanker, the *Healdton*, was sunk by a German submarine in a specially declared 'safety zone' inside Dutch waters, and twenty American crewmen were killed. President Wilson called an emergency session of Congress for April 2. The day before that meeting an armed American steamer, the *Aztec*, was torpedoed off the French coast near Brest, and twenty-eight of her crewmen drowned.

In another region, the United States was making sure that the defence of American interests would be in its own hands. On the very day that the *Aztec* was sunk, the Danish government formally transferred to the United States the Danish West Indian Islands, which the United States had bought for $5 million. Henceforth they were known as the Virgin Islands.

'The world must be made safe for democracy,' Woodrow Wilson told Congress when both Houses assembled on April 2. The German threat to democracy – principally in American eyes the occupation of Belgium – was a high-sounding and high-meaning cause. The repeated submarine sinkings of American ships, however, created the more immediate sense of outrage. On April 4 the Senate voted in favour of war by eighty-two votes to six. The House of Representatives followed on April 6, voting in favour of war by 373 to 50. That same day the United States declared war on Germany.

The entry of the United States into the war was enthusiastically welcomed by demonstrations of support in all the Allied capitals. But in terms of the battlefield it could have no immediate effect. Indeed, it was likely to be at least a year before a meaningful number of American troops could be raised, trained and transported to the Western Front. It was to be a full month before a Commander-in-Chief of the American Expeditionary Force was appointed; the man chosen was General John J. Pershing, who had recently returned from heading the American punitive expedition in Mexico. Pershing suspected that a new command was in the offing when his father-in-law, a United States Senator, sent him a telegram asking whether he spoke French, and if so, how much.

From the German perspective, the entry of the United States into the war made the defection of Russia all the more imperative. Anxious to see the antiwar movement in Russia flourish, the German government facilitated Lenin's return across Europe. He was, even in exile, the undisputed leader and driving force of Bolshevik activity: the charismatic polemicist whose presence in Petrograd could push forward the revolutionary, disruptive path. The Germans saw clearly the power and importance of Lenin's personality. The Kaiser, told of the plan to facilitate Lenin's return, gave it his approval. The Austro-Hungarian Emperor Charles was uneasy, however, warning the Kaiser that a successful Bolshevik revolution in Russia, while it might take Russia out of the war, could also be dangerous to all monarchies, the German and Austro-Hungarian included.

On April 8, the day before leaving Switzerland, Lenin telegraphed to those Bolshevik leaders who were then in Sweden, also making their way back to Russia: 'Our tactics: absolute distrust; no support of new Government; Kerensky particularly suspect; to arm proletariat only guarantee; no rapprochement with other parties.'

Lenin had hoped to travel back to Russia through Britain, and on by sea to Murmansk, but the British government, which was desperate to see Russia remain at war, was alert to the dangers that he and the Bolsheviks posed, and refused him transit. Although he was reluctant to avail himself of the German offer, fearing that he would be portrayed by the Provisional Government as a tool or agent of the Germans, his determination to be at the centre of events in Russia as soon as possible led him to agree. On reaching Petrograd on April 16 he told the crowd that had gathered to meet him at the station: 'The hour is not far when, at the summons of Karl Liebknecht, the German people will turn their weapons against the capitalist exploiters.' Nor was it only in Germany that revolution would strike, according to Lenin's forecast. 'The robbers' imperialist war is the beginning of civil war in all Europe,' he said. 'Long live the worldwide socialist revolution.'

In this first public utterance on his return, Lenin stressed that the enemy of the proletariat was the 'imperialist war'. Stalin had just published in *Pravda* describing the Provisional Government's war aims as 'the conquest of Constantinople, the acquisition of Armenia, the dismemberment of Austria and Turkey, the acquisition of Northern Persia'. Russian soldiers, Stalin wrote, were 'shedding their blood on the battlefields not to "defend their fatherland", nor for "liberty", as the venal bourgeois press assures us, but for the conquest of foreign lands.'

Stalin had demanded that the Provisional Government give up its annexationist policies. But, in front of a vast gathering of Bolsheviks on the day after his arrival in Petrograd, Lenin declared that to demand of the 'government of the capitalists that it renounces annexations is nonsense'. To embark on talk of persuading the Provisional Government to change its mind or moderate its stance was to become involved in 'flagrant mockery' and 'a fog of deception'. Lenin wanted action. 'Have done with greetings and resolutions!' he thundered. 'It's time to get down to business.' The task ahead was to win a majority for the Bolsheviks in the Soviets, and then embark upon a new revolution. The time had come to demand that all industry, all production and all distribution be placed under the control of the workers. All banks should be merged into a single national bank. As the 'majority of the official Social Democrats' had betrayed communism, the Party should no longer be called the Bolshevik (Majority) of the Social Democrats but something else – the Communist Party. It should no longer be linked with the Mensheviks. It should pursue, within the Soviet, its own path to power.

Lenin insisted that the Communists would be the opponents of any further warmaking, whether annexationist or defensive: Europe was ripe for a socialist order; Russia, in isolation from the rest of Europe, was not yet ready for socialism, but with Europe in the throes of war, Russia could give the lead and start the European socialist revolution.

The delegates, Stalin among them, applauded the new direction. Stalin was elected to the Central Committee. He and Lenin, and the Communist Party leadership, started work to rouse the proletariat, the peasants and the soldiers to oppose the war altogether. 'Lenin's entry into Russia successful,' a German agent in Stockholm telegraphed to Berlin on April 17. 'He is working exactly as we wish.'

The leaders of the Provisional Government, Prince Lvov, Miliukov and Kerensky, continued to try to revive the warmaking spirit, and to prepare another Russian offensive on the Eastern Front. On April 18 the Provisional Government published what was known as the 'Miliukov Note', pledging Russia's commitment to the defeat of Austria-Hungary and to punitive reparations against Germany. There began at once a series of street demonstrations – known as the 'April Days' – against this pledge. The leader of the demonstrators was an army officer, Lieutenant Theodore Linde, a Social Democratic supporter who wanted the war waged only for 'democratic' ideals – he was later murdered by frontline troops whom he was urging to go into action.

On April 20, Lieutenant Linde led large numbers of armed soldiers to the seat of the Provisional Government – the Marinsky Palace – and demanded Miliukov's resignation. The Bolsheviks, caught unawares, joined the demonstration with placards declaring: 'Down with the Provisional Government' and 'All Power to the Soviets'. Lenin authorized a group of armed Bolsheviks to march into the centre of the city. They clashed with marchers demonstrating in favour of the Provisional Government, and three people were killed. Lenin took no part in the demonstration.

Miliukov was forced to resign, but the Provisional Government remained committed to the continuation of the war. That May, the former Menshevik, Leon Trotsky, reached Petrograd. In trying to get back to Russia from New York he had been interned in Canada. But the Canadians had let him continue on his journey. Once in Petrograd, he became convinced that the Menshevik course of participating in the Provisional Government and supporting the war was the wrong one, and he threw his support, and energy, behind Lenin and the Bolsheviks.

On the Western Front, the British and French repeated their offensive strategy of the previous year. During a simultaneous British and Canadian offensive at Arras and Vimy Ridge on April 9 the Hindenburg Line was pierced and 5600 German soldiers taken prisoner. The Canadians were also successful, taking 4000 German prisoners. But in the air above the battlefield the British had begun to learn the cost of aerial warfare. In the struggle for air mastery over the battlefield, in order to leave the skies free for reconnaissance work on behalf of the artillery and the infantry, seventy-five British aircraft were shot down by German pilots and anti-aircraft fire, and nineteen of the British pilots killed.

One soldier who was to come to prominence in the Second World War was learning his trade in the battle of Arras. Brigade Major Alan Brooke, a future British Chief of of the Imperial General Staff during the Second World War, had devised for the battle, and was carrying into effect, a new artillery technique known as the 'rolling' or 'creeping' barrage, whereby the artillery barrage moved steadily and systematically forward while the infantry advanced behind it, reaching each trench and strongpoint just after it had been pulverized by the artillery fire. Even this method, however, did not destroy all the wire or all the strongpoints: the Germans had created a defence in depth, with trench fortifications, concrete strongpoints, and wire entanglements, that stretched back several miles.

Despite the initial British successes at Arras, the Hindenburg Line held. One problem for the advancing artillerymen was that, not having advanced so far into a German trench system before, their horse-drawn guns had difficulty crossing the captured trench lines. The rapid advance at Arras led the British Commander-in-Chief to give an order he had hoped to be able to give during every previous offensive; to send the British cavalry forward to penetrate the gap in the German lines and ride forward into the unfortified land beyond. The order was given and the horsemen advanced; but they were halted by German barbed wire that had not been cut by the artillery, and then forced back by German machine-gunners whose fortified posts were intact despite the bombardments.

From that moment, the Battle of Arras went against the British. After three days of consecutive action, the attackers were suffering both from tiredness, and from the effects of an unexpected snow blizzard. When an infantry assault was ordered in place of the cavalry, the men, a Scottish battalion, were hit and badly mauled by a mis-timed British creeping artillery barrage and, when the barrage ended, by German machine-gunners who had been hidden from view. The attack was called off. At Vimy Ridge, 3598 Canadian soldiers had been killed. At Arras are the graves of 2395 British soldiers whose bodies were found and identified. They lie alongside Canadian, South African, New Zealand, British West Indian, Indian and Newfoundland graves, and near the monument on which are incised the names of several thousand others whose remains were never identified: most had been pulverized into the mud of the battlefield by the pounding of the artillery.

That process of identification has continued, and never quite ends. In December 1996, seventy-nine years after the battle, French workmen digging the foundations of a housing estate near Monchy-le-Preux uncovered the remains of twenty-seven British soldiers whose graves had hitherto been unknown. The site where their bodies had been laid in the ground was thought to have been next to a frontline field hospital that had itself been destroyed by German shellfire. Next to the skeletal remains were found a live round of rifle ammunition, a sixpence, a belt buckle, a tunic button, an epaulette tag and a broken pipe.

In addition to the dead on the ground at Arras, 316 British airmen had been shot down over the battlefield.

After the Battle of Arras, many of the wounded British, and also wounded German soldiers who had been captured – 9000 Germans had been taken prisoner – were taken to hospitals in Britain. Because of the indiscriminate German submarine attacks, including the sinking at night of clearly marked and illuminated hospital ships, it was considered too dangerous to mark the ships by lighting them up, and they steamed at night, with destroyer escorts, in darkness. The first hospital ship to be torpedoed after the unrestricted submarine warfare announcement from Berlin was the British *Asturias*, on the night of March 20. Thirty-one medical staff and crew were killed. Ten days later the hospital ship *Gloucester Castle* was sunk.

So strong was the anti-German feeling after this second sinking that the British government initiated reprisals. On April 14 a large squadron of

British and French bombers attacked the German university town of Freiburg, with what the British Air Ministry described as 'satisfactory results'. When the German government protested on April 16 that there was no justification for such reprisals, the British government announced another deterrent. In future, wounded German soldiers would be put on all hospital ships. 'They will naturally share with British wounded,' the announcement pointed out, 'equal risks from the attacks of German submarines'.

On the evening of April 17 two of the ships bringing wounded from Arras to Britain were torpedoed and sunk, the *Donegal* and the *Lanfranc*. On the *Donegal*, twenty-nine wounded men and twelve crewmen were drowned. On the *Lanfranc* the dead included thirteen British and fifteen German soldiers. An account of the sinking, written by a British officer, was published in the *Daily Telegraph* six days later. It was not calculated to create sympathy for the German wounded (the 'Prussians' and 'Fritzes' of wartime parlance):

The moment the torpedo struck the *Lanfranc* the Prussians made a mad rush for the lifeboats. One of their officers came up to a boat close to which I was standing. I shouted to him to go back, whereupon he stood and scowled. 'You must save us,' he begged. I told him to wait his turn. Other Prussians showed their cowardice by dropping on their knees and imploring pity. Some of them cried 'Kamerad,' as they do on the battlefield. I allowed none of them to pass me.

Meanwhile the crew and the staff had gone to their posts. The stretcher cases were brought on deck as quickly as possible, and the first boats were lowered without delay. Help had been summoned, and many vessels were hurrying to our assistance. In these moments, while wounded Tommies – many of them as helpless as little children – lay in their cots unaided, the Prussian morale dropped to zero.

Our cowardly prisoners made another crazy effort to get into a lifeboat. They managed to crowd into one, but no sooner had it been lowered than it toppled over. The Prussians were thrown into the water, and they fought with each other in order to reach another boat containing a number of gravely wounded British soldiers.

The behaviour of our own lads I shall never forget. Crippled as many of them were, they tried to stand at attention while the more serious cases were being looked after, and those who could lend a hand scurried below to help in saving friend or enemy. I have never seen so many individual illustrations of genuine chivalry and comradeship. One man I saw had had a leg severed, and his head was heavily bandaged. He was lifting himself up a staircase by the hands, and was just as keen on summoning help for Fritz as on saving himself. He whistled to a mate to come and aid a Prussian who was unable to move owing to internal injuries.

Another Tommy limped painfully along with a Prussian officer on his arm and helped the latter to a boat.

The refrain of bad behaviour by the wounded Germans, as well as of British courage, was taken up by one of those looking after the rescued men on shore:

Some of the less badly wounded Germans stampeded and jumped into a boat, partly filled with their own wounded. This they swamped, and the only person saved in it was an English boy, brought into us with a crushed hand and leg. He was caught by a chain down the ship's side, but it held him until he could be removed.

After the dockers had left, and we had got all straight and tidy, some of the wounded went to the piano and began to sing – they are wonderful! It made us feel queer to hear them sing 'Pack up your troubles in your old kit-bag,' etc.

After a little while Miss Waldegrave went to them and said that she felt they ought to give thanks for being safe – would they join in a hymn? Every man came to the piano, except one who was too bad to move (the worse cases had been taken away). They sang most wonderfully, 'O God, our help in ages past'. Then Miss Waldegrave said a short prayer, and before she could move away one of the men said, 'Might they have "for those in peril on the sea" for their mates, as they did not know where they might be?'

I have never heard anything like it. Many broke down. In the middle the cars came to take them away. They finished the hymn and then said goodbye. They gripped our hands until it was painful. Many of them ran back two or three times and said, 'Thank you, thank you; we shall never forget this morning.' We shall certainly never forget them, and the stories they told. One of those rescued had neither arms nor legs; another, who had lost both hands and both feet, managed to get on deck unaided!

Starting on April 16, the day after the Battle of Arras came to an end, a French offensive further south also failed to break the German lines or to recapture the heights above Rheims, from which the city was under continual German bombardment. The French plan, devised by General Nivelle, had been to advance six miles; but at their furthest point his men only reached 600 yards in front of their starting lines. Of the 128 French tanks in action, 32 were disabled by German artillery and machine-gun fire in the first day. Black Senegalese troops, confronted by uninterrupted German machine-gun fire and seeing their companions shot down beside them as they advanced, turned from the field of fire and ran.

After each offensive, it was hoped that lessons could be learned and failure redeemed by new efforts. After Arras, plans were made for an offensive in the Ypres Salient in three months' time. The British and French, and those fighting alongside them — or at least their commanders and rulers — were indefatigable in their efforts to push for victory. But on the side of the Central Powers, the Austrians and Bulgarians were looking for ways to detach themselves from the German war machine. The continuation of the war was destroying their economies, impoverishing their people, and threatening national, social and even revolutionary upheavals.

Secret discussions began in Switzerland between Austro-Hungarian, Bulgarian and Allied diplomats, in the hope of finding terms that would be acceptable for a cessation of hostilities. But the Allies were not willing to pursue these discussions; the entry of America into the war had created a sense of eventual, if not imminent victory. In the House of Commons, Winston Churchill, who had served for six months in Flanders as a battalion commander in the frontline trenches, and who was shortly to re-enter the government as Minister of Munitions, spoke against any renewed offensives on the Western Front in 1917. 'Is it not obvious,' he asked, 'that we ought not to squander the remaining armies of France and Britain in precipitate offensives before American power begins to be felt on the battlefield?'

Pressure to continue the offensives on the Western Front before the Americans came in was continuous. With the outbreak of several mutinies in the French lines in the last week of April, the French High Command asked the British to renew the Arras offensive, which Sir Douglas Haig had called off under pressure from his generals. The French High Command hoped that the Germans would have to move troops away from the part of the line weakened as result of the mutinies. A British soldier, Edward Brittain, one of whose friends had just been killed in the renewed British offensive, and several other friends of whom had been killed in earlier battles, wrote home, echoing the thoughts of millions of soldiers and families: 'We have lost almost all there was to lose and what have we gained? Truly as you say patriotism has worn very threadbare.'

On the Eastern Front, taking advantage of the turmoil in Russia, German troops entered Helsinki, which was never again in the twentieth century to know Russian rule. Elsewhere along the front line, whole Russian divisions were throwing down their arms and advancing into the German trenches to fraternize and to surrender. Additional soldiers were sent in drafts of a thousand men from the reserves to the front, to join in the action, but only 150 to 250 were arriving; the rest were deserting on the way. The Communist Party newspaper was persistent in its antiwar calls, stressing, as Lenin had always done, the 'imperialistic' nature of the war. 'Are you willing to fight for this,' *Pravda* asked towards the end of April, 'that the English capitalists should rob Mesopotamia and Palestine?'

The extent of the potential disintegration of Russia was seen on April 24, when the Ukraine demanded autonomy from Russia. Throughout Russia antiwar sentiment was rising. On April 27 the sailors and soldiers of the garrison at Kronstadt declared that they would no longer obey the orders issued by the Provisional Government. An all-women's battalion, raised by the Provisional Government, and expressing its willingness – indeed its keenness – to go to the front, was angrily denounced by the Bolsheviks. At Pernau, on the Baltic, the men of one regiment murdered their commanding officer when he refused to take off his badge of rank as a mark of sympathy for those sailors in Pernau who had already declared allegiance to the revolution. One Russian division, crossing into German lines, pointed out to the Germans the location of a Russian artillery battery that was still loyal to the government and the war. A Russian battalion commander, in conversation with the British Military Attaché, noted that while none of his men had deserted, and that military discipline was still holding on his sector of the front, 'everything in the rear' had gone: transport drivers, depot units, the means of bringing food and medical supplies forward. As a result, his men were 'absolutely without boots and are wasting from sickness'.

On April 29, the Russian Commander-in-Chief, General Alexeyev, informed the Ministry of War in Petrograd: 'The army is systematically falling apart.' In this process, the Germans were playing their part with all the weapons of propaganda at their disposal, urging Russian soldiers to throw down their arms and to surrender, and stressing the strength of Russian antiwar feeling in the rear. 'We are showering newspapers and leaflets on the Russians', General Hoffman noted in his diary, 'and trying to get at them in various ways'. The Russian Revolution, Hoffman added, 'is a godsend to us'.

Despite spreading demoralization, and persistent German propaganda, Lenin and the Communists continued to be unsuccessful in obtaining the majority support of the revolutionary parties. On May 4 the Petrograd Soviet, still dominated by the Mensheviks and Socialist Revolutionaries, voted to support the Provisional Government – in which there were four Menshevik ministers – and the continuation of the war. The margin was narrow, but the Bolsheviks were still in a minority.

In Berlin, the entry of the United States into the war was not seen as a fatal blow, particularly as the German navy was so confident in being able to sink the American troop transports as they crossed the Atlantic. This confidence, indeed, had been one of the factors contributing to the decision to declare unlimited submarine warfare. It looked as though the submarine offensive would be effective. The amount of Allied and neutral shipping sunk in April 1917 was the highest of the war; 373 ships totalling 873,754 tons. In fact it was to prove the highest monthly total of both world wars. In May the tonnage sunk was just over half a million, and in June it rose to 674,458 tons.

The Germans were everywhere taking the initiative. On May 15, in an attempt to detach Russia from its allies, and to relieve Germany of the need to continue fighting on the Eastern Front, Bethmann-Hollweg offered the Russians an immediate peace. This was what the Petrograd Soviet, accepting the Bolshevik position and abandoning its support for a defensive war, had finally demanded of the Provisional Government. But the Provisional Government rejected both the demand of the Petrograd Soviet and the request of the German government.

Russia's triple war against Germany, Austria-Hungary and Turkey continued. As a mark of its determination, the Provisional Government announced that all army deserters who did not return immediately to their units would be punished. This threat was in vain; a week later it was learned, from the Ukraine, that 30,000 deserters a day were reaching Kiev from the front, on their way back to their homes, and that there was no slackening in the exodus.

In May, six moderate members of the Petrograd Soviet agreed to join the

Provisional Government. After negotiations between the Kadet Party and the Petrograd Soviet, a new Cabinet was formed, in which three Mensheviks, including the Menshevik leader Irakli Tseretelli, were given posts. Tseretelli, a Georgian, had been a member of the second Duma (in 1906) at the age of twenty-four, but was subsequently arrested by the Tsarist police, imprisoned, and exiled to Siberia. Formerly opposed to continuing the war, he now agreed with Kerensky that the war must go on. The Menshevik desertion was a setback for the antiwar cause.

In France, the mutinies on the Western Front were spreading. By the end of May more than 30,000 French soldiers had left the trenches and made their way to the rear. In one town, the mutineers declared an 'Antiwar Government'. As the mutinies spread, courts martial were instituted and swift punishment imposed. Fifty of the mutineers were shot, and 350 sent to dreaded penal servitude in one of the French colonies. Later, the mutiny spread to the French troops at Salonika.

In the week in which the French mutinies were at their most intense, the first thousand American combat troops reached France. Given the need to raise, train, equip and transport so many more American soldiers across the Atlantic, it would be another twelve months, however, before they could arrive in sufficient numbers to take part in the war other than as small detachments alongside British and French units. The process whereby the Americans joined the other armies on the Western Front became fraught with controversy and acrimony. General Pershing did not want his men to be used to fill gaps in the Allied strength, but as an independent military force. He knew how dangerous the situation was in the trenches when he arrived in France. He had been told by an American friend living in Paris that 'there is a limit to what flesh and blood and endurance can stand' and that the French 'have just about reached that limit'.

One effect of the French mutinies was to put an added burden on the British offensive that was planned for the Ypres Salient at the end of July. The French troops, the British High Command were told in strict secrecy, would be willing to go into the front line on the French sector, but they would not be willing to leave their trenches and attack the enemy. The British High Command accepted that there would be little help forthcoming from the French forces when the Third Ypres battle began – unlike during the Battle of the Somme a year earlier, when the British and French armies had gone into action simultaneously. But Haig was determined to go ahead with the new offensive, and cherished hopes of a British breakthrough on the Western Front 'before the Americans arrive' – as he expressed it in his diary.

In London, General Smuts, the South African leader and former British adversary, expressed his belief, to a War Cabinet which was uneasy about a new offensive, that it was necessary from the moral point of view to attack the Germans again; and that not to do so would be to abdicate the high moral ground of the superior ideology. Smuts accepted that a breakthrough might be impossible, but, as he told the War Cabinet, 'If we could not break the enemy's front we might break his heart.'

The British Prime Minister, David Lloyd George, tried to counter these arguments. He was one of the few people in Britain fully aware of the scale of the French mutinies, and they alarmed him. He also knew of the growing awareness in Britain of the inhuman nature of trench warfare. A letter published that spring in the *Nation*, from a frontline officer, told of wounded men 'lying in the shell holes among the decaying corpses: helpless under the scorching sun and bitter nights, under repeated shelling. Men with bowels dropping out, lungs shot away, with blinded, smashed faces, or limbs blown into space. Men screaming and gibbering. Wounded men hanging in agony on the barbed wire, until a friendly spout of liquid fire shrivels them up like flies in a candle.'

Lloyd George told the War Cabinet that, before authorizing a new offensive, he would like to see if it was possible to negotiate a separate peace with Austria-Hungary. He also saw no point, he said, in British troops trying to break through the trench lines on the Western Front when 'the French were finding it difficult to go on' and their reserves were 'physically and mentally exhausted'. Smuts, unwilling to see the offensive given up, suggested that Haig should be consulted. This was done, the message being transmitted to London from the Commander-in-Chief's headquarters in France: 'Haig was hopeful'. Haig then came to London to explain in detail what he had in mind. His conviction was strong, he told the War Cabinet, that Germany was within six months of total exhaustion, and that with one more push, the war could be won in 1917. The War Cabinet deferred to the judgement of the Commander-in-Chief.

The Germans were also planning an initiative, but not on land. This was the launching of a new bombing policy, using, not Zeppelins, but aircraft. Over London, on May 25 in the first substantial bombing raid in modern warfare, five bombs dropped by a single German bomber killed 95 people.

Ten days later, in a second bombing raid, 13 more Londoners were killed. In a single raid three weeks later, more than a hundred bombs were dropped, and 162 civilians killed, among them 15 schoolchildren.

In June, in preparation for the Third Battle of Ypres, which was planned for July, the British exploded nineteen enormously powerful mines under the Messines-Wytschaete ridge. This was south of the salient in which the main attack was eventually to take place, with the aim of driving the Germans back, and making the Ypres Salient less exposed when the time for the main battle came. The explosion of the mines, which were detonated on June 7, was heard across the Channel in southern Britain. The mines fulfilled and exceeded the British expectations. Ten thousand German soldiers were killed, most of them killed by the blast or buried alive in the vast mounds of earth thrown up by each explosion. Thousands more Germans were stunned, the German frontline trenches were overrun, and more than 7000 German soldiers taken prisoner.

Among the British officers who took part in the battle for the Messines-Wytschaete ridge was Anthony Eden, a future Prime Minister, who in the Second World War was to be Secretary of State for War, and later Foreign Secretary. In the air above the battlefield, the German pilots in action during the battle included Lieutenant Hermann Goering, who from 1935 to 1945 was to be in charge of the German air force. During the German retreat from the ridge, Goering shot down his first British aircraft. At the time of the battle, Eden was twenty years old and Goering twenty-four.

Despite the shock of the French mutinies, the Allies felt an upsurge in confidence as the summer of 1917 progressed. In the Balkans, where only the Salonika army stood between the Bulgarian army and the sea, Greece, so long neutral and divided in its sympathies, finally committed itself to the Allied cause. At the same time, the Central Powers were suffering from increasing internal unrest, not least, in Germany, as a result of the widespread food shortage, intensified by the British blockade of the North Sea, which was successfully preventing foodstuffs from entering Germany.

The Habsburg dominions were plunged into nationalist upheavals. In Vienna, at the end of May and for the whole of June, the first meeting was held of the Reichsrat since March 1914. Polish deputies used the occasion to press their support for Polish independence, while Serb, Croat and Slovene deputies established a 'Yugoslav' Parliamentary Club. One of the Polish deputies, Count Alfred Potocki, later recalled:

> All through this Parliamentary sitting tension centred on the Polish question. There were many angry scenes. One deputy was struck across the face for shouting that more people should have been hanged in Galicia.
>
> Maurice Esterhazy, the Hungarian Prime Minister, threatened to dissolve Parliament if the vote went against the Government. Finally the Polish Club passed an anti-Government resolution and refused to vote for the Budget, forcing the Cabinet to resign. Dr. Seidler, speaking in the name of Czernin, made the foolish pronouncement that the Emperor alone had the right to decide peace and that the freedom of peoples was a secondary consideration, which provoked a storm of protests.
>
> I remember these tense days with particular vividness. High summer burned like a fire across Eastern Europe, grass shrivelled, the scorched earth cracked. For weeks there was absolute drought. Travel was a severe test of physical endurance. Everywhere the cry went up for water. In Vienna the people queued for it, and on one sweltering night a great munitions factory blew up, adding to their miseries. Then suddenly a new Russian offensive opened, forcing German and Austrian troops to retreat.

Near panic struck the British government in the last week of June, when it became clear that the vast sums of money being used to buy war materials in the United States were running out. Although, a year earlier, J. P. Morgan and Company had given the British government a loan of $400 million, the time had come for settlement. But the continuing arms purchases had used up the loan with no means of replenishing it. On June 28 the American ambassador in London, Walter H. Page, was summoned to an emergency meeting with the Chancellor of the Exchequer, Andrew Bonar Law, and the Foreign Secretary, A. J. Balfour.

British financial agents in the United States, the ambassador was told, 'now have enough money to keep the exchange up for only one day more.' Balfour told the ambassador to inform President Wilson: 'We are now on the brink of a precipice, and unless immediate help be given, financial collapse will follow.' Page told the President: 'I am convinced that these men are not overstating their case. Unless we come to their rescue all are in danger of disaster.'

The recent increase in German submarine activity had exacerbated the sense of danger. 'The Germans are fast winning in this crucial activity,' Page confided, 'there's no doubt about that.' There were more German submarines at sea in June 1917 – sixty-one in all – than at any other time in the war. Page's letter continued:

If the present rate of destruction of shipping goes on, the war will end before a victory is won. And time is of the essence of the problem; and the place where it will be won is in the waters of the approach to this Kingdom – not anywhere else. The full available destroyer power that can by any method be made available must be concentrated in this area within weeks (not months).

There are not in the two navies half destroyers enough: improvised destroyers must be got. There must be enough to provide convoys for every ship that is worth saving. Merely arming them affords the minimum of protection. Armed merchantmen are destroyed every day. Convoyed ships escape – almost all. That is the convincing actual experience.

If we had not come into the war when we did, and if we had not begun action and given help with almost miraculous speed, I do not say that the British would have been actually beaten (tho' this may have followed), but I do say that they would have quickly been on a paper money basis, thereby bringing down the financial situation of all the European Allies; and the submarine success of the Germans would or might have caused a premature peace. They were in worse straits than they ever confessed to themselves.

And now we are all in bad straits because of this submarine destruction of shipping. One sea-going tug now may be worth more than a dozen ships next year.

The United States came to Britain's aid. Sufficient money was advanced – $686 million – to enable Britain to continue with her war purchases, including ships, in the quantities required. In addition to the loan to Britain, France was given a loan of $310 million and Italy a loan of $100 million. But these enormous loans would have to repaid after the war, that was the condition laid down by the United States Treasury. The Allies could only watch with trepidation as the weight of their indebtedness mounted. Without the American supplies, their respective war efforts would be severely hampered, or even, as Page had warned, negated.

For Britain, the war at sea was an extreme worry throughout the spring and early summer. For the month of June, German submarine sinkings were high: 286 Allied merchant ships in all. Only two German submarines were sunk. But the Allies had found a means to protect their shipping, in particular their troop transports. This was the convoy system. The first west–east transatlantic convoy sailed from Hampton Roads, Virginia, on July 1, only three days after Ambassador Page had been summoned to the emergency conference at the Treasury.

The principle of the convoy was that a group of ships, moving together at a uniform speed, would be guarded front and rear, and on the flanks, by warships. A convoy of between ten and fifteen merchant ships, often with a large troopship in its midst, would be escorted throughout its voyage by a destroyer in the lead, with equipment that could detect the sound of a sub-marine engine, followed by a cruiser, the largest warship in the convoy, on which the Convoy Commander directed speed and course. Behind the cruiser, and also behind the whole convoy, would be torpedo boats, each with an aerial balloon attached, from which observers could look down from their baskets and detect underwater submarines, or the path of torpedoes. Flank-ing the convoy would be five or six destroyers, following a zigzag course in order to mislead submarines as to the convoy's course, and to protect the convoy in case of attack. The merchant ships in the convoy would have their hulls painted with varying camouflage designs, to make them look much smaller, or to make it seem that they were travelling in a different direction; the master-designer of this camouflage was a British artist, Solomon J. Solomon.

The convoy system was to transform the war at sea. In the first convoy which sailed from Hampton Roads, Virginia, only one merchant ship was lost; it had fallen behind the convoy. In July, sixty merchant ships crossed the Atlantic in convoy without loss. Most remarkable of all, and most distressing to the German High Command (and in due course fatal to the German ability to continue the war) more than a million American troops were brought across the Atlantic in convoy with the loss of only 637 men from torpedo attack, a tiny proportion of those brought over during twelve months of continual crossings. Of these crossings, the worst potential disaster, the torpedoing of the British troopship *Tuscania*, was averted when all but 166 of the 2397 American troops on board – and 44 British crew members – were rescued by the escorting craft and other convoy members.

Following the success of the Hampton Roads convoys, six more collecting points were set up: at Halifax, Nova Scotia, for ships coming from the American and Canadian Great Lakes; at Panama for ships from Australia and New Zealand; at Rio de Janeiro for the Argentinian foodstuffs (and army horses) on which the British war effort was much dependent; at Murmansk for supplies to Russia; at Port Said and Gibraltar for ships coming through the Suez Canal and the Mediterranean; and at Dakar, on the Atlantic coast of West Africa, for ships from South Africa and the African coast. This was a massive undertaking, one which the British Naval Staff had earlier repeatedly rejected, not wanting to divert its warships to the task of protecting merchant ships.

The convoy system ended Germany's long-cherished, and at times seemingly plausible hopes, of starving Britain to death; and it made possible the massive movement of American troops to Europe. In all, more than sixteen thousand merchant ships made their way safely in convoy, and only 154 of those convoyed ships were sunk. The total shipping tonnage sunk fell rapidly from more than 800,000 tons at its peak to 200,000 tons, and then to below 100,000 tons, while the tonnage carried rose considerably. For Britain, dependent for 100 per cent of its sugar, 80 per cent of its cheese and cereals, more than 50 per cent of its fruit, butter, margarine and eggs, and 40 per cent of its meat and vegetables on imported produce, the convoy system averted hunger, social unrest, and the possibility of defeat.

Militarily, the introduction of the convoy system, after two and a half years of war, helped turn the tide of war in favour of the Allied Powers. But it was a tide that turned only slowly. It took more than a year for the mass of the American troops to be in their place on the Western Front.

Meanwhile, the focus of the war turned to the Eastern Front. On July 1 – exactly a year since the British had launched their Somme offensive on the Western Front, and the day on which the first convoy sailed across the Atlantic – General Brusilov launched the Russian offensive to which the Provisional Government was committed, and for which the most careful preparations had been made.

The Brusilov offensive was initially successful. As the Russian armies moved forward through Eastern Galicia they captured 17,000 Austrian soldiers and approached their objective, the oil fields of Drohobycz – which Russia had overrun once before, in 1914 – and the city of Lemberg. Fighting alongside the Russian soldiers was a Czech Brigade. At one moment it found itself facing the Austrian 19th (Czech) Division, and persuaded many of the Czechs to abandon the Austrian cause.

But Brusilov's hopes were to be dashed, and with the arrival of German reinforcements, led by a German commanding officer, General Litzmann, the Austrians were able to halt the Russian advance before it reached its objective. The turn of the prisoner-of-war tide was also taking place. 'I should like a few more prisoners,' noted General Hoffman in his diary as news of the Austro-German successes reached him, and he added: 'The fellows ran away so fast that we could not catch any of them. Only six thousand to date.'

In Petrograd, the Russian failure on the Eastern Front persuaded the Provisional Government's inner Cabinet to grant wide-ranging autonomy to the Ukraine. This led to the resignation, on July 2, of the four Kadet ministers, who opposed any weakening of central 'Russian' control. On the following day, hoping to take advantage of this political crisis, the Bolsheviks, joined by anarchists, and by many soldiers and sailors in the capital, as well as by sailors from the Kronstadt naval base, tried to seize power. On July 4, at the instigation of Lenin and Trotsky, armed Bolshevik units occupied various points in the capital. Addressing the sailors from Kronstadt, Lenin told them he was happy to see that 'the theoretical slogans, launched two months earlier' – principally 'All Power to the Soviets' – were being 'translated into reality'.

The 'reality' of revolution was put down by force that July. It was also discredited at the height of the struggle in the streets by a crude but effective stratagem, adopted by the Minister of Justice – Pavel Pereverzev – of leaking documents to a Petrograd newspaper claiming to show that Lenin was a German agent. One of the Bolsheviks most active in the uprising, Pavel Lebedev, was actually arrested as a German spy – like Lenin, he had travelled that May from Switzerland to Russia through Germany, in a sealed train. He was later released, when workers at one of the Petrograd factories paid for his bail.[1]

The soldiers on whom the Provisional Government depended were outraged at the thought that Lenin was a German agent. 'Now they are going to shoot us,' Lenin told Trotsky on July 4. 'It is the most advantageous time for them.' Lenin immediately went into hiding. It was not a moment too

---

[1] Under the Communist regime, Lebedev became chairman of the Chief Directorate for Literature and Publishing (Glavlit), and made a major contribution to 'socialist realism'. Unlike most of the early Bolsheviks, he survived the Stalinist purges intact, and died in his bed in 1948, at the age of sixty-six.

soon; two days later the Provisional Government ordered his arrest, and that of ten other leading Bolsheviks, on the charge of 'high treason and organizing an armed uprising'. But he was nowhere to be found, and on the night of July 9/10 he secretly left the capital to hide in the countryside.

Although the 'July Days', as the Bolshevik attempt to seize power was known, had revealed considerable support for revolutionary and antiwar action among the workers, soldiers and sailors, they also revealed a strong turn to the 'right' by many liberals in the Provisional Government, and by the Kadets. Prince Lvov, who felt he lacked the strength of will to combat further disturbances, resigned as Prime Minister. He was succeeded, on July 7, by Kerensky, who retained the war and naval portfolios. In an attempt to enhance his authority, Kerensky moved the office of Prime Minister into Alexander III's suite of rooms in the Winter Palace (Alexander had been Tsar from 1881 to 1894). Kerensky continued to visit the front, and to urge the soldiers to carry on, gaining as a result the title 'Supreme Persuader-in-Chief'.

The German counterattack on the Eastern Front ended all hopes of a Russian military revival. The demoralization of the Russian frontline soldiers was turning the retreat into a rout. Tens of thousands of soldiers threw down their rifles and fled from the battlefield, heading for home. Hundreds of their officers, trying to halt the flight, were shot by their own men. The officers in command of two Allied armoured car units, one Belgian and one British, which were in action alongside the Russians, pleaded with the Russian soldiers to return to their units, but in vain. By the end of the month, 40,000 Russian soldiers were in flight. That day, Austrian and German forces recovered the last of the Austrian territory which Brusilov had recaptured. Having been appointed Commander-in-Chief of all the Russian armies, Brusilov was replaced on the Eastern Front by General Kornilov. But Kornilov could not reverse the defeats which had beset his comrade in arms.

The German advance on the Eastern Front gave Bethmann-Hollweg's successor as German Chancellor, Dr Georg Michaelis, the confidence to dismiss a Reichstag resolution, signed by a majority of the German parliamentarians, urging the German Government to work for 'a peace by agreement and permanent conciliation'. To the relief of the German General Staff, whose nominee he was, Dr Michaelis declared: 'I do not consider that a body like

20. Turkish troops at Gallipoli, 1915

21. Roumanian troops on their way to war, 1916

22. Jewish refugees from Russian Poland, 1915

23. Serbian troops in retreat, winter 1915-16

24. Woodrow Wilson campaigning, summer 1916

25. American tanks on their way into action, 1918

30. German prisoners of war

31. Clemenceau

32. *(Right)* Wilhelm II

33. British troops at Vladivostok, 1919

34. Canadian troops in North Russia, 1919

35. An armoured train, Russia, 1919

36. Tsar Nicholas II and his family

the German Reichstag is a fit one to decide about peace and war on its own initiative during the war.' In a talk to party representatives, the Kaiser promised them a 'Second Punic War' against England that would destroy Britain's 'world domination', just as Rome had destroyed Carthage, turning her into a dependent, tribute-paying ally. The leaders of the moderate parties were shocked by the Kaiser's belligerent attitude.

In more and more countries, the public, through its elected representatives, was calling for peace. But the political leaders and military commanders were determined to continue the war. Nor did even the elected parliamentarians always reflect the growing war-weariness of the masses. When the leader of the British Labour Party, Ramsay MacDonald, tried to persuade the House of Commons to endorse the Reichstag Peace Resolution, his proposal was defeated by 148 votes to 19. After this failure, MacDonald wrote to Woodrow Wilson that it would have been better for peace if the United States had remained neutral. MacDonald could not know that, even as he was writing his letter, Woodrow Wilson was confiding to a friend another perspective. 'England and France have not the same views with regard to peace that we have by any means,' Wilson wrote. 'When the war is over we can force them to our way of thinking, because by that time they will, among other things, be financially in our hands.'

Peacemaking proposals also came up against the national imperatives of those whose achievement of statehood depended on the defeat of Austria-Hungary. Many Bosnian Serbs were fighting alongside the Allies on the Salonika Front. Many Czech troops, who had been taken captive by the Russians on the Eastern Front, were preparing to fight against Austria-Hungary as a Czech national army.

Italy, whose ambitions with regard to Albania had been enshrined in the Pact of London when she joined the Allies, set out its intentions in greater detail in a proclamation issued on June 3, in the southern Albanian town of Argyrocastro, which was under Greek control. Under the Italian plan, Albania would, with the defeat of Austria-Hungary, be given free political institutions, law courts, schools, and an army of her own, 'under the protection of Italy', with Albania's foreign relations supervized by Rome.

The Argyrocastro Proclamation was not the only agreement that summer which looked forward to, and depended upon, the defeat and dismemberment of Austria-Hungary. On July 20 an agreement was signed on the island of Corfu, whereby, following Austria-Hungary's hoped-for defeat, the three main South Slav groups, the Slovenes, Croats and Serbs, would form a single country, ruled by the Serb royal family, with guarantees for all linguistic and religious minorities. In Sarajevo, it was proposed that the Bosnian Muslims and the Jews would be given the same protection as the Roman Catholic Croats and the Greek Orthodox Serbs. Toleration was intended to be the hallmark of the new state.

The discussions leading to the Pact of Corfu were held under the cloud of news coming from Austrian-occupied Serbia. As many as a million Serbs – a quarter of the population – had died as a result of privation and famine. Austrian-occupied Albania was similarly the scene of desperate hardship for the conquered people.

On the Western Front, two weeks before the third British offensive at Ypres was due to begin, the Germans experimented with a new gas – mustard gas. More than 50,000 gas shells were fired, eighty-seven British soldiers were killed, and more than two thousand affected. But in the attack which followed, the Germans were unable to break through the line. Retaliation came five days later, when the British fired 100,000 shells filled with chloropicrin gas, killing seventy-five Germans. The Germans then retaliated against the retaliation, killing more than six hundred British soldiers with mustard gas, and incapacitating more than nineteen thousand. Wilfred Owen, a British officer, and poet, who was later killed in action, wrote a poem about a soldier caught without his gas mask and taken to hospital in a cart. His poem was addressed to those in England far from the front line. In it he cited the Latin motto much used by patriots at home, 'It is a sweet and becoming thing to die for one's country':

> If you could hear, at every jolt, the blood
> Come gargling from the froth-corrupted lungs,
> Obscene as cancer, bitter as the cud
> Of vile, incurable sores on innocent tongues, –
> My friend, you would not tell with such high zest
> To children ardent for some desperate glory
> The old Lie: Dulce et decorum est
> Pro patria mori.

In Britain, the Women's Peace League was appealing for financial support. Its efforts were supported by the *Labour Leader*, the weekly newspaper of the

Independent Labour Party. On July 5 the paper published a message from the League. It read: 'One woman, enclosing £10, says "I have lost one son in the war, and another is in the trenches. Thank God that at last the women are waking up."' The League also reported that four soldiers' wives 'have clubbed together to send ten shillings, saying that they have not known peace of mind since the ghastly slaughter began'.

The British offensive at Ypres – Third Ypres as it became known – began on July 31 and continued for more than three months. The offensive started with the capture of more than 5000 German soldiers in the first three days. But to the great disappointment of the British High Command, it failed in its double objective: the complete breakthrough of the German trench lines; and, if German morale were then to break as well, the defeat of Germany. The Third Ypres offensive even failed, after more than three months, to take the objective of its first day, the village of Passchendaele, which lay four and a half miles from the starting point of the battle. It was the name of this Belgian village that was to become synonymous in Britain with mud and death, and failure.

A German soldier who fought at Third Ypres – his first battle – until he was wounded by British shell splinters was Erich Remarque. Twelve years later he was to draw on his frontline experiences in his novel *All Quiet on the Western Front*. Here is his account of an artillery bombardment and the resultant enemy attack, in this instance by French troops:

Our legs refuse to move, our hands tremble, our bodies are a thin skin stretched painfully over repressed madness, over an almost irresistible, bursting roar. We have neither flesh nor muscles any longer, we dare not look at one another for fear of some incalculable thing. So we shut our teeth – it will end – it will end – perhaps we will come through.

Suddenly the nearer explosions cease. The shelling continues but it has lifted and falls behind us, our trench is free. We seize the hand-grenades, pitch them out in front of the dug-out and jump after them. The bombardment has stopped and a heavy barrage now falls behind us. The attack has come.

No one would believe that in this howling waste there could still be men; but steel helmets now appear on all sides of the trench, and fifty yards from us a machine gun is already in position and barking.

The wire entanglements are torn to pieces. Yet they offer some obstacle. We see the stormtroops coming. Our artillery opens fire. Machine guns rattle, rifles crack. The charge works its way across. Haie and Kropp begin with the hand grenades. They throw as fast as they can, others pass them, the handles with the strings already pulled. Haie throws seventy-five yards. Kropp sixty, it has been measured, the distance is important. The enemy as they run cannot do much before they are within forty yards.

We recognize the distorted faces, the smooth helmets: they are French. They have already suffered heavily when they reach the remnants of the barbed-wire entanglements. A whole line has gone down before our machine guns; then we have a lot of stoppages and they come nearer.

I see one of them, his face upturned, fall into a wire cradle. His body collapses, his hands remain suspended as though he were praying. Then his body drops clean away and only his hands with the stumps of his arms, shot off, now hang in the wire.

That autumn there were several mutinous episodes behind the lines of the Western Front. A brigade of Russian troops who had been sent through Murmansk and Scotland to Europe, to strengthen the French line, not only refused to go into the trenches but also raised the Red Flag of Bolshevism. Another Russian brigade that was serving in France, and which remained loyal to Kerensky and the Provisional Government, besieged the rebel camp and shot several dozens of the antiwar protesters dead before the rest surrendered. A revolt of Chinese labourers in the British sector was also suppressed; they had wanted better conditions of work.

In neutral Spain, the conflict within a deeply divided society led that August to a strike of Socialist railway workers in Valencia. The strike quickly spread to the mining valleys of Asturias. On August 13 martial law was declared, and the army moved against the strikers. Troops of the Civil Guard, commanded by officers with experience of the fighting in North Africa, marched into the mining towns. Eighty strikers were killed and 2000 arrested, many of whom were badly beaten and even tortured by their captors. Among those who commanded a column of troops during this action was Major Franco, who the previous year had been seriously wounded in Morocco, and promoted from Captain. The official historian of the Civil Guard referred to Franco as 'the man responsible for restoring order'. The miners described the repression that had been unleashed against them by their fellow Spaniards as the 'African hatred'.

*   *   *

On the Western Front, the number of British soldiers suffering from shell-shock and nervous exhaustion was increasing: they were given the designation NYDN – Not Yet Diagnosed (Nervous) – and sent to special centres some ten to fifteen miles behind the lines, away from the noise of the front. After treatment, including games, exercises and concerts, those who were still shattered were sent back to England. Those who were judged to have recovered were returned to the trenches. On August 21 a conference at Haig's headquarters examined the means whereby every department engaged in war activities in France and Flanders was to be combed for men who could be sent to the front. All work being done on roads, railways and construction behind the lines was to cease, and the soldiers doing it sent into action. In an effort to maximize the number of men available for action in the weeks ahead, the Director-General of Medical Services considered it might be possible to send into action a certain number of men from those being treated for venereal disease, 'though this might spread infection'.

Returning to London in the first week of September for discussions with senior politicians, Haig pressed for the continuation of the Western Front offensive. In support of his appeal, he was able to cite a request from General Pétain that the pressure on the Germans be kept up, as the morale of the French troops further south was still not recovered from the mutinous discontent of four months earlier.

On the Eastern Front the Germans captured the Baltic port of Riga that month, sustained the Austrian forces on the Austro-Russian border, and advanced against the last pockets of independent Roumania. It was in this advance that Rudolf Hess, later to be Hitler's deputy, was shot through the chest, his third war wound in a year.

The Third Battle of Ypres was renewed on September 20. The village of Passchendaele was still beyond the capacity of the advancing troops, both they and the Germans suffering severely in each day's encounter. But Haig was confident. 'The enemy is tottering,' he wrote in his diary eight days later. This confidence was once again misplaced. When Haig's two most senior generals urged him to end the offensive, he declined to do so. For five days, British and Australian troops struggled to reach Passchendaele village. More than 2000 Australian soldiers were killed in the assault, and 8000 injured.

The nurses in the British military hospitals in France tended both the

British and the German wounded. One of those nurses, Vera Brittain, later wrote, of the September battle:

> In the German ward we knew only too certainly when 'the next show' began. With September the 'Fall In' resumed its embarrassing habit of repetition, and when we had no more beds available for prisoners, stretchers holding angry-eyed men in filthy brown blankets occupied an inconvenient proportion of the floor. Many of our patients arrived within twenty-four hours of being wounded; it seemed strange to be talking amicably to a German officer about the '*Putsch*' he had been in the previous morning on the opposite side of our own.
>
> Nearly all the prisoners bore their dreadful dressings with stoical fortitude, and one or two waited phlegmatically for death. A doomed twenty-year-old boy, beautiful as the young Hyacinth in spite of the flush on his concave cheeks and the restless, agonized biting of his lips, asked me one evening in a courteous whisper how long he had to wait before he died. It was not very long; the screens were round his bed by the next afternoon.
>
> Although this almost unbearable stoicism seemed to be an understood discipline which the men imposed upon themselves, the ward atmosphere was anything but peaceful. The cries of the many delirious patients combined with the ravings of the five or six that we always had coming round from an anaesthetic to turn the hut into pandemonium; cries of '*Schwester!*' and '*Kamerad!*' sounded all day. But only one prisoner – a nineteen-year-old Saxon boy with saucer-like blue eyes and a pink-and-white complexion, whose name I never knew because everybody called him 'the Fish' – demanded constant attention. He was, he took care to tell us, '*ein einziger Knabe*' (an only child). Being a case of acute empyema as the result of a penetrating chest wound, he was only allowed a milk diet, but continually besieged the orderlies for '*Fleisch, viel Brot, Kartoffeln!*'
>
> '*Nicht so viel schreien, Fisch!*' I scolded him. '*Die anderen sind auch krank, nicht Sie allein!*'
>
> But I felt quite melancholy when I came on duty one morning to learn that he had died in the night.
>
> There was no time, however, for regrets, since I had to spend half that day sitting beside a small, middle-aged Bavarian who was slowly bleeding to death from the sub-clavian artery. The haemorrhage was too deep-seated to be checked, and Hope Milroy went vehemently through the dressings

with her petrified cavalcade of orderlies while I gave the dying man water, and wiped the perspiration from his face. On the other side of the bed a German-speaking Nonconformist padre murmured the Lord's Prayer . . .

On October 2, on a day when the forward guns were being dragged up through the mud by pack mules through the Ypres Salient – and it was taking as long as fourteen hours to bring a wounded man back from the front line – Haig called another conference at his headquarters. After the conference he gave orders for preparations to be made to launch a general infantry offensive on the heels of the hoped-for retreating Germans. Behind that infantry offensive, Haig explained, the Cavalry Corps was to advance and, when the moment presented itself, the enemy was to be 'pursued and annihilated'.

By October 13, however, all hope of such a galloping through by men on horseback was ended. Heavy rain had turned the fields around Passchendaele to liquid mud. Men and horses were sucked into it and drowned. On the following day the German officers in the front line agreed to an informal truce, much as there had been at Gallipoli two years earlier, to enable the attackers to collect their dead. For several hours, unarmed British stretcher-bearers did what they could to find and bring back broken bodies. But anyone seen by the Germans coming into no-man's land with a gun was shot.

An Australian officer who went forward during the truce reported to his superiors:

The slope . . . was littered with dead, both theirs and ours. I got to one pill-box to find it just a mass of dead, and so I passed on carefully to the one ahead. Here I found about fifty men alive, of the Manchesters. Never have I seen men so broken or demoralized. They were huddled up close behind the box in the last stages of exhaustion and fear. Fritz had been sniping them off all day, and had accounted for fifty-seven that day – the dead and dying lay in piles.

The wounded were numerous – unattended and weak, they groaned and moaned all over the place . . . some had been there four days already . . .

I shifted to an abandoned pill-box. There were twenty-four wounded men inside, two dead Huns on the floor and six outside, in various stages of decomposition. The stench was dreadful . . . when the day broke I looked over the position. Over forty dead lay within twenty yards of where I stood and the whole valley was full of them.

Anyway we are out now and I don't mind much. Only I'd like to have a talk with some war correspondents – liars they are.

The war correspondents against whom the Australian officer railed were sending back what they felt the public wanted to hear. As the battle for Passchendaele became mired in mud, the *Spectator* told its readers that it had been 'a great week for the Allies in Flanders'.

On the morning of October 15, Haig and his advisers decided to halt all further attacks until the weather improved, at least to enable the artillery to make its contribution. But a new assault was in preparation, and a telegram from Lloyd George that day gave Haig great encouragement, for the Prime Minister spoke specifically of 'my confidence in your leadership'.

The new assault took place on October 26. For another four days the battle raged, and on October 30 Canadian troops entered Passchendaele, but their casualties were heavy and they were driven out. 'The horror of the shell-hole area of Verdun was surpassed,' General Ludendorff later wrote. 'It was no longer life at all. It was mere unspeakable suffering. And through this world of mud the attackers dragged themselves, slowly but steadily, and in dense masses. Caught in the advance zone of our hail of fire they often collapsed, and the lonely man in the shell-hole breathed again.'

Another grotesque aspect of trench warfare revealed itself during the battle. 'The demoralization and growing callousness of the men were reflected in their treatment of the dead,' Leon Wolff has written. 'After each attack the souvenir hunters got to work. Gradually the corpses were picked over, the whites of their pockets turned out, their tunics and shirts undone. Revolvers were the best prizes; but money, watches, rings and the crosses of Catholics were also in demand. An artillery man examining German corpses for revolvers was observed (by a writer at the front) giving one a vicious kick and snarling, 'The dirty barsted, somebody's bin 'ere before me.'' Frontline soldiers were quickest in the pursuit of loot; artillery and labour troops slower and more methodical. Letters and photos were ignored; these fluttered limply in the mud or floated away on the water.'

On November 10, after a renewed Canadian advance across 500 yards of mud in the face of a German artillery bombardment by 500 guns, and further hampered by continual German air attacks, the offensive was finally called off. Glory – and even the Son of God – were to be enlisted in the accounts of the terrible battle. The official Canadian historian of this final advance has written: 'It is not too much to compare the Canadian troops struggling forward, the pangs of hell racking their bodies, up the ridge, their dying eyes set upon the summit, with a Man who once crept up another hill, with agony in soul and body, to redeem the world and give Passchendaele its glorious name.'

On the day after the last day of the battle for Passchendaele, a senior British staff officer, Lieutenant-General Sir Launcelot Kiggell, made his first ever visit to the front line. As his staff car drew closer to the trenches, he was appalled by the conditions that he saw around him. Reaching the furthest point that his car could go, he burst into tears and said: 'Good God, did we really send men to fight in that?' The man sitting beside him, who had been in action during the campaign, replied, expressionless: 'It's worse farther on up.'

The number of British and British Empire dead in the Third Battle of Ypres has been variously estimated at between 62,000 and 66,000. German deaths have been estimated at 83,000. Commenting on the high but imprecise nature of the British figure, the official British history noted: 'The clerk-power to investigate the exact losses was not available.'

The number of wounded was enormous: about a quarter of a million Germans and 175,000 in the attacking forces. In all, 26,000 German soldiers had been taken prisoner. The new line on the map showed a clear advantage to the Allies. 'We have won great victories,' Lloyd George told the Supreme War Council of the Allies on November 12. And he added, 'When I look at the appalling casualty lists, I sometimes wish it had not been necessary to win so many.'

On the French sector of the Western Front, an American infantry battalion had been in action on November 2. It represented the first of what were to be a steadily increasing number of American support actions with the French, before the American army was ready to fight as an independent army. On this occasion a German raiding party attacked one of the American battalion's isolated outposts at Barthelémont. The Americans were outnumbered four to one, and three Americans (Corporal Gresham and Privates Enright and Hay) were killed. Twelve Americans were taken back by the Germans as prisoners of war, and one German deserted to the Americans.

On the Italian Front, German troops helping the Austrians advanced across the Isonzo river, entered the town of Caporetto, and took more than ten thousand Italian prisoners. Everywhere on the Isonzo Front the Italians fell back. Frightened that Italy might be driven to seek a separate peace, and watching as antiwar demonstrations broke out in Milan (and pro-German sentiments were expressed in Rome), Lloyd George despatched two British divisions, both of them badly needed on the Western Front, to Italy. The spectre of peacemaking had determined a military disposition potentially harmful to the successful prosecution of the war.

On the Eastern Front, the Russian collapse was intensifying. At the end of October an estimated one million Russian railway and transport workers were on strike. Supplies were unable to reach any of the Eastern war fronts. From Petrograd, the Bolsheviks were calling daily on the soldiers and sailors not to fight. In the Baltic, Admiral Altvater, the Russian defender of Moon, Dago and Osel islands, later told his German captors: 'I was defending Osel and the troops actually melted away before my eyes.'

A new Russian Minister of War, General Verkhovsky, assured the British Military Attaché that he would restore the Russian army and 'make it in a fit condition to fight by the spring'. The attaché was totally sceptical, writing in his diary that on the basis of what he knew and saw 'there is evidently not the slightest hope that the Russian Army will ever fight again'.

In issuing a declaration to the Jews of the world, on November 2, that the British government 'view with favour' the establishment of a Jewish National Home in Palestine, the British Foreign Secretary, Arthur Balfour, was hopeful that such a promise by an Allied Power would encourage the millions of Jews in Russia to take a patriotic view towards the war, and to feel the need to exert every possible influence to secure a victory over the Central Powers.

On November 3, the day after the Balfour Declaration, the British Foreign Office asked three leading Zionists then in London to go to Petrograd at once, and to rally Russian Jewry to the Allied cause. 'With skilful management of the Jews of Russia,' Balfour was told by Lord Hardinge, the head of the Foreign Office, 'the situation may still be restored by the spring.'

Neither General Verkhovsky nor Lord Hardinge were right. It was not the coming spring that was the crucial time, but that very week, the first week of November. On November 3, the day of Hardinge's note, it was learned in Petrograd that Russian troops on the Baltic Front had thrown down their arms and were fraternizing with the German soldiers facing them. On the following day, when the Provisional Government in Petrograd gave orders for the 155,000-strong Petrograd garrison to go to the front, the Bolshevik Military Revolutionary Committee persuaded them not to go. On November 5, in an attempt to get the garrison to go, Kerensky ordered troops outside Petrograd, whom he believed were still loyal to the Provisional Government, to enter the capital. A day later they refused to do so.

That same day, November 6 (October 24 in the old Russian calendar) the thousand-strong Women's Death Battalion loyal to the Provisional Government was jeered by soldiers and civilians alike as it marched through the streets to be inspected by Kerensky. During the morning Kerensky ordered troops loyal to the Provisional Government to move against various Bolshevik institutions in the capital. The Bolshevik printing presses were seized by officer cadets (known in Russian as Junkers) and closed down. The telephone lines to Bolshevik headquarters at the Smolny Institute were cut. The bridges over the River Neva were raised, to prevent Bolshevik detachments crossing them.

Confronted by these measures, the Bolsheviks took countermeasures. They had long abandoned their efforts to win a majority in the Petrograd Soviet – where they were being outvoted by four to one. The time had come to take action. That afternoon armed Bolshevik units recaptured the printing presses, lowered the bridges, and seized two crucial centres of communication in the city, the Central Telegraph Office and the Russian Telegraphic Agency. The telephone lines to the Smolny Institute were reconnected. All was ready for the seizure of power throughout the capital. Lenin, who had been in hiding since the defeat of the attempted Bolshevik uprising in July, reached the Smolny Institute that evening, his face bandaged as a disguise.

That night, without bloodshed, the Bolsheviks occupied the principal buildings and roadways in the capital. These included the railway stations, the post offices, the telephone centres, the State Bank and the bridges. At about nine o'clock in the morning Lenin drafted a proclamation, which was issued to the newspapers an hour later, deposing the Provisional Government. The declaration read:

TO THE CITIZENS OF RUSSIA!

The Provisional Government has been deposed. Government authority has passed into the hands of the organ of the Petrograd Soviet of Workers' and Soldiers' Deputies, the Military-Revolutionary Committee, which stands at the head of the Petrograd proletariat and garrison.

The task for which the people have been struggling – the immediate offer of a democratic peace, the abolition of landlord property in land, worker control over production, the creation of a Soviet Government – this task is assured.

Long Live the Revolution of Workers, Soldiers, and Peasants!

The declaration was signed: 'The Military-Revolutionary Committee of the Petrograd Soviet of Workers' and Soldiers' Deputies.' For tearing a copy of it down, Kerensky's wife was arrested and detained for forty-eight hours.

The Provisional Government met as usual the next morning, November 7, in the Winter Palace. A vast number of Bolshevik supporters – more than eighteen thousand – protected by a thousand soldiers loyal to the revolution, surrounded the Winter Palace and demanded the surrender of the deputies. During the day many more soldiers and sailors reached the capital and declared their support for the revolution, among them 9000 sailors from the Kronstadt naval base. Two Russian destroyers arrived in the Neva from Helsinki. Their crews also declared their loyalty to the revolution.

Throughout November 7 the members of the Provisional Government remained inside the Winter Palace, insisting on their sole right to govern Russia. That evening the sailors on board the cruiser *Aurora*, which had been anchored for some weeks in the Neva, announced that they would open fire on the Winter Palace if the Bolsheviks were not admitted. A few blank shells, harmless but noisy, were fired by the *Aurora* as proof of its seriousness. The Bolsheviks, who were by then supported by at least fourteen thousand soldiers and sailors, stormed the Winter Palace. By one o'clock on the morning of November 8 its defenders had fled, leaving the Bolsheviks in control.

During November 8, Lenin was elected Chairman of the Council of People's Commissars. From that moment he was the ruler of the Russian capital, and the head of the revolutionary appeal to all Russia. In Moscow, armed Bolsheviks occupied the Kremlin. Throughout Russia, hundreds of towns declared themselves for the revolution, and swore their allegiance to Lenin and his Council (or Soviet). In Petrograd, Trotsky became Commissar for Foreign Affairs, responsible for the foreign policy of the new government, and for any peacemaking negotiations with the Germans on which the Bolsheviks might embark.

To prevent the escape of leading figures of the Provisional Government from the capital, the Bolsheviks had immobilized the cars in the Winter Palace by removing their magnetos. Kerensky, hoping to rally troops loyal to the Provisional Government, was driven away in a car belonging to the American Embassy. He drove southwest, to the town of Pskov. Seven months earlier, the Tsar had attempted to make this journey in the other direction, from Pskov to Petrograd, but railway workers had refused to allow his train to pass.

Lenin did not wait to see if Kerensky could pose a threat to the capital. During November 8, in his first decree as Chairman of the Council of People's Commissars, he read out, to an enthusiastic crowd, the Decree of Peace. Russia no longer considered herself at war. The troops could come home. The Russian contribution to the 'capitalist' war was over. The Bolsheviks rejected all talk of annexation of territory. On the following day, four million copies of the Decree of Peace were sent to the soldiers at the front.

Russia was no longer a belligerent, and no longer an Ally. With the Italian army being driven back to the River Piave, a retreat of sixty miles, there was no longer anything that could be done to reactivate the Eastern Front by means of Allied pressure or enthusiasm.

On November 11 the forces loyal to the Provisional Government, having been gathered together by Kerensky, marched to within shelling distance of the capital. There they were met by a larger Bolshevik force, and after fierce fighting, were driven off. Inside Petrograd a Tsarist general being held prisoner by the Bolsheviks in the Astoria Hotel arrested the military guard that was meant to be confining him. Officer cadets loyal to the Provisional Government seized several buildings. But the Bolshevik forces were far larger than those who sought to unseat them, and were determined not to lose their three-day hold on the capital. Within a few hours the Astoria Hotel was back in Bolshevik hands and the officer cadets had been driven, by shell and machine-gun fire, from the buildings they held. Many, seeking to surrender, were brutally murdered.

At this moment of crisis for the Allies, with the possibility of the transfer of millions of German soldiers from the Eastern to the Western Front, a new leader took the helm in France – Georges Clemenceau. He was seventy-six years old, a veteran of the French political scene. Holding the posts of

Minister of War as well as of Prime Minister, 'the Tiger' demanded the greatest of exertions from all members of his government, civil servants, manufacturers, workers, and everyone involved in the war effort.

On the day after Clemenceau came to power, Trotsky informed the German government that the new government in Russia – the Council of People's Commissars – of which he was in charge of foreign policy, wished to make peace. Two days later the Bolsheviks asked Germany for an immediate armistice. In Paris, Clemenceau exhorted the French Chamber of Deputies: 'War, nothing but war.'

Like the French under Clemenceau, the British under Lloyd George were also being urged to mobilize the human and material resources of the nation. On November 20, only ten days after the Passchendaele offensive had been finally halted by mud and carnage, another British offensive was launched on the Western Front, at Cambrai. Its aim was to take advantage of the ground gained the previous year during the Battle of the Somme, and to do so making use of tanks used in substantial numbers: 376 tanks – His Majesty's Landships, they were called – took part in the opening infantry attack. 'The triple belts of wire were crossed as if they had been belts of nettles,' one British officer recalled.

Ten years later, reflecting on the Battle of Cambrai, Winston Churchill, who was Minister of Munitions at the time of the battle, wrote: 'Accusing as I do without exception all the great ally offensives of 1915, 1916, and 1917, as needless and wrongly conceived operations of infinite cost, I am bound to reply to the question, What else could be done? And I answer it, pointing to the Battle of Cambrai: "*This* could have been done". This in many variants, this in larger and better forms ought to have been done, and would have been done if only the Generals had not been content to fight machine-gun bullets with the breasts of gallant men, and think that that was waging war.'

An episode took place on the first day of the Battle of Cambrai that was unique in British (and German) military history. A German artillery officer, Lieutenant Müller, who – all alone at his gun – shot and disabled six British tanks before he was killed, was mentioned in the military despatches of the enemy. 'The great bravery of this officer aroused the admiration of all ranks,' the British citation read.

After the battle, soldiers familiar with the mud of Flanders were astounded at how different a tank battleground could be. A correspondent of *The Times* reported:

> We have forgotten that a battlefield can be anything but a hideous mass of shell holes and litter and slime. Even in the dark one could walk freely across the open with good, firm, grassy ground beneath one's feet.
>
> Soon after six o'clock, when the sky began to lighten, it was possible to see the great rolling expanse of greyish-white dead grass. In the half light of the dawn we put up two coveys of partridge, larks sprang up half visible from under our feet, and later, when the guns were thundering, a huge hare jumped up and coursed off into the distance like a stag. While the battle raged crows flew cawing across the sky, indifferent alike to guns and aeroplanes.
>
> To us the word battlefield has come to be synonymous with awful shell-hole wilderness, and to stride in the grey of the dawn across hard turf was in itself an exhilaration.

The German line on the British sector of the Western Front was broken at Cambrai, the German defenders being driven back five miles, and more than 7000 German soldiers taken prisoner. For the first time since the outbreak of war, church bells were rung throughout Britain to celebrate the victory. But German reinforcements, rushed back to the Western Front from Russia, where the enemy had collapsed, were able to prevent the long-anticipated British cavalry breakthrough, which had been denied them both on the Somme and at Passchendaele. It was now denied them a third time, and the town of Cambrai, the objective of the new attack, remained in German hands.

Among those killed in the Battle of Cambrai was one of the original American volunteers, Lieutenant A. Griggs, a pilot. He had been flying with an Australian air squadron. A company of Irish soldiers saw him in action above a German strongpoint that was pinning them down, and saw him killed. Not knowing his name or nationality, they put a notice in the 'In memoriam' column of *The Times* to thank an 'unknown airman' for his efforts. Another of those killed at Cambrai was Norman Chamberlain, whose uncle Neville, later a British Prime Minister, was deeply affected by his death. Six months earlier the young Norman had written home from the Western Front (in a letter which Neville Chamberlain later published in a memorial volume to his nephew): 'Nothing but immeasurable improvements will ever justify all the damnable waste and unfairness of this war – I only hope that those who are left will *never, never* forget at what sacrifice those improvements have been won.'

After the failure to capture Cambrai, the British withdrew in order to straighten their line. As at Gallipoli two years earlier, the withdrawal was carried out without loss. Facing the British were the first of more than half a million German soldiers (forty-two divisions) who were being transferred from the Eastern Front to the West.

The dismantling of the Russian imperial army was in its final stages. On December 1, a force of Bolshevik sailors captured the former headquarters of the Russian army at Mogilev. There they found General Dukhonin, the last of the Commanders-in-Chief of the Russian army; he was dragged from his train and killed. That day, a Bolshevik Armistice Commission left Petrograd for the Eastern Front, and on December 2, as the Commission crossed over into German lines and was taken on by train to the former Tsarist fortress of Brest Litovsk, a formal ceasefire was declared throughout the Eastern Front.

The negotiations at Brest Litovsk lasted for five days. The Bolshevik negotiators were confronted there by the delegates of four powers: Germany, Austria-Hungary, Bulgaria and Turkey, each anxious to gain the maximum advantage from Russia's collapse. Another Allied Power was also unable to continue at war: even as the negotiations continued at Brest Litovsk between Russia and her enemies, the Roumanians, who had challenged the Central Powers three months earlier, called for a cease-fire.

The negotiations at Brest Litovsk ended on December 15. The Eastern Front war was over. A week later, still at Brest Litovsk, the Bolsheviks began to negotiate peace with their former enemies. As they did so, the former Tsarist empire was breaking up under the weight of the defeat. Estonia was the first of the former imperial provinces to declare its independence, followed by Finland. They were also the first new nations to come into being as a result of the First World War. Latvia was the next to declare its independence.

In the Ukraine, fighting broke out between the Ukrainians and the Bolsheviks, while elsewhere Tsarist generals, among them Kornilov and Alexeyev, raised the banner of Russian anti-Bolshevism and proceeded to take over large areas of southern Russia. The war between the 'Reds' and the 'Whites' had begun; but the 'Reds' – the Bolsheviks – were in firm control of

Petrograd and Moscow, and were imposing their authority with considerable harshness wherever it was opposed, executing by firing squad those whom they judged to be enemies of their regime. The 'Whites', Russian officers and soldiers who had served in the Tsar's army, were divided as to their aims: some wanted to restore the Provisional Government, others wanted to restore the Tsar.

On December 9 the city of Jerusalem, which had been ruled by the adherents of Islam since the defeat of the Crusaders, surrendered to British and Australian troops commanded by General Allenby. Church bells rang out again in Britain, as they had done prematurely during the Battle of Cambrai, to celebrate a victory over Turkey. It was a victory which made up, in the public mind, for the setbacks elsewhere that winter: for Russia's defection, for Roumania's surrender, and for the high casualty lists of Passchendaele.

There were also a number of Allied disasters and setbacks that December. When, in the harbour of Halifax, Nova Scotia, a French merchant ship loaded with munitions for Europe collided with a Belgian merchant ship and blew up, more than 1600 people were killed. Six days later, in France, 543 soldiers were killed when their train came off the track; the highest death toll in a railway accident to this day. At sea, when a British destroyer, the *Attack*, was rescuing survivors of the torpedoed troopship *Aragon*, she struck a mine, and 610 soldiers and troops were drowned.

On the Italian Front, the Austrians continued to press the Italians back in the mountains around Asiago, taking 9000 Italian soldiers prisoner. More ominous for the Allies, though not made known to the public, two sets of secret talks which Lloyd George initiated with Austrian and Turkish emissaries in Switzerland in mid December, in the hope of detaching Austria and Turkey from Germany, broke down. Neither belligerent was able to see the advantage of a separate peace. With Russia out of the war and Germany in the ascendant, the Turks in particular did not want to detach themselves from Germany; they regarded the peace negotiations that were about to take place at Brest Litovsk as their chance to acquire considerable Russian territory in the Caucasus, and even further east, in the Turkic-speaking, Muslim regions of Russian Central Asia. After more than three years of war, territorial aspirations were as much a factor in making peace as they had been in making war.

CHAPTER TWENTY-ONE

1918

WHILE THE ALLIES AND the Central Powers remained at war everywhere but on the Eastern Front, the Bolshevik revolution was in difficulties. On coming to power in November 1917, Lenin had been confident that the Bolsheviks could command the support of the majority of the nation, and – carrying out what had been the intention of the March revolutionaries in their search for a democratic and parliamentary Russia – called for elections to a Constituent Assembly. To his surprise, and anger, the Bolsheviks obtained less than 10 million of the 41 million votes cast, and secured only 168 of the 703 seats. Ahead of the Bolsheviks in the poll were the Left and Right Socialist Revolutionaries, both of whom had served in the Provisional Government, and who obtained more than 15 million votes and 299 seats – 20 million votes and 380 seats if the Ukraine Social Revolutionary vote was added.

To reduce the numbers of the opposition before the Constituent Assembly met, Lenin ordered the arrest of the seventeen Constitutional Democrat (Kadet) delegates, and announced that a quorum of 400 was sufficient to enable the assembly to meet. It gathered in the Tauride Palace on 5 January 1918. The exclusion of the Kadets could not tilt the Assembly in the Bolsheviks' favour. In the election for President of the Assembly, the largest votes went to the Socialist Revolutionary candidate, Viktor Chernov, who had been Minister of Agriculture in the Provisional Government.

Inside the debating chamber a fierce struggle was going on between the elected delegates. From the galleries overlooking the delegates, drunken sailors under their anarchist-communist leader, A. G. Zhelezhnyakov, jeered and hooted. Outside the palace, Red Guards shot down Left and Right Socialist Revolutionary demonstrators who demanded that the will of the electorate and its representatives be acceded to.

As the debate inside the Constituent Assembly continued, and various laws were passed of a democratic nature (including the 'socializing' of land), the Bolshevik delegates walked out. The assembly then voted by an over-whelming majority to proclaim Russia a democratic, federal republic. This vote sealed the fate of the assembly. In the early hours of January 6, Zhelezh-nyakov and his sailor-anarchists drove the deputies out of the building. That night, two leading Kadet deputies were beaten to death by Bolshevik sailors. The Bolshevik Soviet then dissolved the assembly on the grounds that it could 'only play the role of justifying the struggle of the bourgeois counter-revolution for the overthrow of Soviet power.'

The first ever democratic rule and democratically reached decisions in Russia – derived from elections and the free votes of the elected deputies – ended twenty-four hours after they had come into existence. Democracy, born on Bolshevik sufferance, had been killed at birth by Bolshevik bayonets and decrees.

On January 8 – two days after Lenin had crushed the day-old Constituent Assembly in Russia – Woodrow Wilson, in an address to the United States Congress, issued a 'peace programme' consisting of Fourteen Points. Although the United States had been at war with Germany for more than a year, her troops were still not ready to enter the line except as small units intermingled with the British and French. The President of the most recent of the belligerents had decided, meanwhile, to set out a democratic, liberal ideology as the basis for the postwar world. All diplomacy and all treaty-making must proceed in future 'frankly and in the public view'. Freedom of navigation at sea would be assured to all. The economic barriers between States would be removed, and 'equality of trade conditions' would be estab-lished between all nations. Naval armaments – judged by Wilson to have been a cause of the world war – would be reduced by all nations.

These were the universal points, based upon a political philosophy which Woodrow Wilson hoped would transform the future relationship between States from one of suspicion and conflict to one of harmony and prosperity. There followed the points relating specifically to the Central Powers. Ger-many must evacuate all Russian territory (even as Wilson spoke, Germany was preparing to occupy even more of Russia). Belgium must be 'evacuated and restored'. All French territory occupied by Germany must be evacuated, and the 'wrong' done to France by Prussia in 1871 with the annexation of Alsace-Lorraine must be put right. No reference was made in the Fourteen Points to French hopes of detaching the Rhineland from Germany. These hopes had been revealed a few weeks earlier by the Bolsheviks, who published to the world all the secret treaties signed by the Tsar's government with the Allies.

According to the Fourteen Points, the frontiers of Italy were to be drawn 'along clearly recognizable lines of nationality'; this meant that Austria-Hungary would have to give up the South Tyrol, and perhaps parts of Istria and northern Dalmatia. The peoples of Austria-Hungary should be given what Wilson called 'the freest opportunities of autonomous development'. No mention was made of sovereignty or statehood for the peoples of the Habsburg Empire. Three States, Roumania, Serbia and Montenegro, should be restored to full sovereignty. Serbia should also be given access to the sea. The nationalities inside Turkey, like those inside Austria-Hungary, should be assured of their 'autonomous development'. Again, as with the nationalities of Austria-Hungary, nothing was said of the right to statehood. Only one new State should be created, that of Poland, 'united, independent, autonomous', with 'free, unrestricted access to the sea'. This effectively meant the acquisition by Poland of a land corridor through Prussia. In contrast to the Poles, the Czechs and Slovaks, Croats and Slovenes were each disappointed that their hopes for statehood had gone unrecognized.

Wilson's fourteenth point was the creation of a 'general association' of nations, brought together in order to guarantee political independence and territorial integrity 'to great and small States alike'. This made little appeal to those whose hope of statehood Wilson had not addressed, or to those States which hoped to acquire the territory of others as a result of victory.

There were also States whose independence would need much more than declarations in order to be sustained. In what had been the former Tsarist province of Turkestan, a Muslim government had been set up at the end of November 1917, with its capital at Kokand. Its president, Mustafa Chokaev, was a member of an aristocratic Kazakh family, and had been educated at St Petersburg University. For three months, Chokaev and his supporters maintained their independence. Then, on February 5, the Red Army attacked. For three days there was fierce fighting. Chokaev and his government were driven out, the city was burned to the ground, and hundreds – perhaps thousands – of Muslims massacred.[1]

The Red Army was also confronted that month by an uprising in the

---

[1] After the fall of Kokand, Mustafa Chokaev fled to Georgia, where he fought with the Georgians against the Bolsheviks until 1920. In exile, first in Turkey, then in France and Germany, he became the leader of the Russian Muslim emigration.

North Caucasus, led by an eighty-eight-year-old Muslim religious leader Uzun Haji, who had earlier spent fifteen years in a Siberian labour camp as a prisoner of the Tsar. An eye-witness account survives of Uzun Haji's entry into Temir Khan Shura, the town which he declared as the capital of his theocratic State:

> At 3 o'clock in the afternoon the city suddenly resounded with terrifying cries: it was the 'army' of the Imam entering Shura chanting religious hymns.
>
> It would be difficult to imagine such a vision for those who did not witness it, an endless formation stretching on the road from Kazanishch to Shura slowly marching, the advance column having already reached the city. They were dressed in rags with white bandages on their heads, horsemen, infantrymen, old and young, armed with rifles, flintlock guns or simply sticks; some fired by fanaticism, others with indifferent and tired eyes; they felt victorious.
>
> After barely an hour they seized all the government buildings. All the city, all the squares and streets were occupied by wildly picturesque turbaned groups.
>
> There was one remarkable aspect to these events: over ten thousand people had invested the city, yet there was not a single occurrence of pillage or thieving. The only casualties were a few wooden fences – it was winter, and people spending the night in the squares reluctantly had to use the fences for warmth . . . From the point of view of discipline they could be a model for any professional army units.

The Red Army diverted considerable forces to the North Caucasus to crush the new Muslim State. But it could not quench the fires of nationalism.

Total defeat of the enemy remained the aim of all the Powers still at war. Each was making its plans to win the war either in 1918 or in 1919. A massive expansion of munitions production was under way in Britain and France. The United States was about to embark on the largest shipbuilding programme in history. The German government was making increasing use of forced labourers from France and Belgium. But the peoples in every land were expressing a new type of war-weariness. Within Britain, a secret report of letters which had been intercepted by the authorities in order to gauge public opinion, revealed 'a decided increase in letters for an immediate peace'.

Six days after this secret report was compiled in Britain, more than 400,000 German workers went on strike in Berlin, demanding peace. Within two days, six other German cities were in the grip of antiwar strikes and demonstrations. Martial law was declared in Berlin and Hamburg, and striking workers were drafted into the army, becoming liable to military discipline, and court martial, should they refuse to obey orders. In Greece – like the United States, a new belligerent in the Allied ranks – troops in the town of Lamia mutinied rather than be sent to the Salonika Front. The mutiny was suppressed and two of its leaders were executed.

On the day of the Greek mutiny, 6000 Austro-Hungarian sailors, led by two Czech socialists, mutinied in the Gulf of Cattaro (Kotor). The mutineers raised the Red Flag and called for an immediate peace, and immediate demobilization. The crews of several German submarines moored alongside the Austro-Hungarian ships refused to join in the mutiny; nor would the Austro-Hungarian soldiers in the Cattaro garrison do so. Three battleships were then sent to the Gulf of Cattaro from the Austro-Hungarian naval base at Pola, at the northern end of the Adriatic. Eight hundred mutineers were arrested, forty were brought to trial, and four were executed. The Cattaro mutiny was at an end.

The almost daily manifestations of antiwar feeling did not deter the political leaders on either side. In a speech at Bad Homburg on February 10, a month after President Wilson's Fourteen Points, the Kaiser spoke of a world-wide conspiracy against Germany. Those who were working for Germany's defeat included the Bolsheviks – supported by President Wilson – 'international Jewry', and the Freemasons. The Kaiser said nothing about the fact that he had himself facilitated the return of Lenin to Russia and had approved secret German financial help for the Bolshevik newspaper, *Pravda*. Nor did he say that as many as ten thousand Jews, and many Freemasons, had already been killed on all the war fronts fighting for Germany.

The Eastern Front was erupting into turmoil. On January 28, after the Central Powers announced their support for an independent Ukraine, Russian Bolsheviks and Ukrainian forces clashed at Lutsk. That day the Third All-Russian Congress of Soviets proclaimed Russia to be a 'Federated Republic of Soviets of Workers', Soldiers' and Peasants' Deputies'. On the following day, Russian Bolshevik troops entered the Ukrainian capital, Kiev, and the Black Sea port of Odessa.

In mid February the forces of the new Soviet Republic were formed into regular fighting cadres, the Red Army and the Red Navy. Hardly was this done, than on February 17 the negotiations at Brest Litovsk between the Germans and the Bolsheviks broke down. The German terms – which included the separation of Poland from Russia, and the annexation by Germany of Lithuania and southern Latvia – were too harsh for the Bolsheviks to accept. Their control of the Ukraine gave the Bolsheviks a sense of strength that was illusory. The Ukraine was, after all, the 'bread basket' of Russia.

The Germans, determined to secure their demands, reopened hostilities. Fifty-two German divisions began to move eastward. Dvinsk, the most westerly Russian town under Soviet control, was occupied at once. 'This beast springs quickly,' was Lenin's comment to Trotsky. On February 19 Lenin and Trotsky telegraphed to General Hoffman, accepting the terms they had rejected two days earlier. But the Germans, their forces advancing as fast as their armoured cars and horses could carry them, were in no hurry to sign.

On February 20, German troops entered Minsk, the principal town of White Russia. In one twenty-four-hour period, one German unit advanced 150 miles. German infantrymen, supported by machine-gun units, travelled eastward by train, capturing the Bolshevik troops at each station they came to.

Lenin appealed to the Germans to end the fighting, and again agreed to accept the German terms. But the Germans were in no mood to go back to the earlier agreement, and set out new and harsher terms. These included the German annexation of Poland, and also of the Baltic States and parts of the Ukraine – all the territory then occupied by German forces. Many of these areas had been Russian for more than five hundred years. At a meeting of his ruling council, Lenin was bitterly attacked for urging acceptance. After threatening resignation if the German terms were rejected, he was supported by 116 to 85 votes. The terms were then discussed in the Central Committee. Again there was fierce opposition to accepting them, and Lenin was able to secure only the narrowest of majorities, seven in favour, six against. He was supported in his call for acceptance by both Trotsky and Stalin. If the Germans were to continue their advance, Stalin argued, it would strengthen the anti-Bolshevik forces in Russia and bring about conditions favourable to the 'counter-revolution'.

The Germans used delaying tactics following the Bolshevik capitulation, sending motorized German troops further and further eastward, to Dorpat, and then to Reval on the Baltic, where the Russian Tsar and British King had met amid such splendour in 1907. Further south, the deposed Tsar's military headquarters, at Mogilev, was overrun. That same day, a German aeroplane dropped its bombs on Petrograd.

In less than two weeks, 63,000 Russian soldiers had been taken prisoner, and 5000 Russian machine guns had been captured. By the time the peace treaty was signed at Brest Litovsk on March 3, the Germans were in control of almost half of Russia east of Moscow.

Under the Treaty of Brest Litovsk, Russia agreed to give up all her claims to seven of the provinces that had been an integral part of the political, economic and multi-national structure of Tsarist Russia: the Baltic provinces, Poland, White Russia, Finland, Bessarabia, Ukraine and the Caucasus. These vast areas, most of which were to be occupied by Germany under the Treaty, contained one third of Russia's prewar population, one third of her arable land, and nine-tenths of her coalfields. With the exception of Kronstadt, at the sea approaches to Petrograd, Russia was also stripped of all her naval bases in the Baltic. In the Black Sea, German troops occupied Russia's principal Black Sea port, Odessa, and the shipbuilding yards of Nikolayev.

The Armenian areas of Turkey that Russia had conquered since 1915 were to be returned to Turkey. The Turkish delegation at Brest Litovsk, headed by Talaat Pasha, a leader of the prewar Young Turk movement, was insistent on regaining the Armenian lands. As the negotiators had waited at Brest Litovsk for the final agreement, Turkish troops had driven the Armenians out of Trebizond, their main port on the Black Sea. No Russian troops had been able to protect them. Nine days after the treaty was signed, the Armenians were driven from the inland city of Erzerum. Russia's defeat marked the end of Armenia's hopes on the Anatolian plateau.

The Roumanians also signed a peace treaty with the Central Powers, at Buftea, three days after the signing of the Treaty of Brest Litovsk. The southern Dobrudja was ceded to Bulgaria, but Roumania was offered the Russian province of Bessarabia as compensation, provided she could take it from the Bolsheviks, either by negotiations or war. The Bolsheviks, meanwhile, fearing an attack by anti-Bolshevik Russians gathered not far from Petrograd, moved their capital to Moscow, where the Russian capital has remained for the rest of the century.

The Treaty of Brest Litovsk was a humiliation for Russia; but without signing it the Bolsheviks could not have retained their power for more than a few weeks. The Kaiser's armies might well have achieved the reduction of Russia to a vassal State. But those armies still had to fight on the Western Front, where the steady arrival of American troops, fresh for battle, augmented the Anglo-French armies, and where the British and French High Commands were eager to renew their earlier efforts to break the German line. Germany had transferred its troops from Russia to the Western Front before the Americans were ready to intervene in decisive numbers. A race was on for military mastery in the West.

On March 7, as the German High Command prepared to launch its first offensive on the Western Front since 1916 – supported by troops, weapons and artillery brought from the east – the German forces opened a sustained artillery bombardment along the whole length of the area of the attack. Among the first casualties were nineteen Americans of the Rainbow Division, killed in their dugout. That day, a single German aerial bomb killed twelve civilians in a residential part of London. On the following day, German bombers dropped more than ninety bombs on the French capital. Fearing more raids, 200,000 Parisians fled the city.

As the day for the launching of the German offensive drew nearer, even the peacemaking hopes of Austria-Hungary were set aside. Secret talks with the British, which had opened again in Switzerland, were broken off. On March 19 a former Austrian Foreign Minister, Baron Burian, wrote in his diary: 'No one will now listen to the word "peace". Everything is based on the forthcoming offensive, as if everyone were entrusting himself without a tremor to the decision of fate.'

As an indication of how secure the Central Powers felt in the East, on March 20 the Austro-Hungarian army opened a regular air service between Vienna and Kiev. Civilians could use it, and it also carried mail. It was, in fact, the first regular air service established anywhere since the outbreak of war. The only previous attempt was the flying boat that had plied the short distance between Tampa and St Petersburg, Florida, in the early months of 1914. The next regular air service was begun two months later, on May 15, between Washington and New York.

The German High Command, flushed with their victory and conquests in the East, were eager to put their military skills to victorious advantage in the West. Ludendorff was convinced that he could drive a wedge between the British and French armies, force the British back to the Channel coast between Calais and Dieppe, and enter Paris. The war could then end in the West, as it had just ended in the East, around the conference table. For Germany, the hope was to achieve all her territorial demands – including control of Belgium and northeastern France – with Austria-Hungary still intact as a multinational empire from the Adriatic to the Carpathians, and with the two other Central Powers, Bulgaria and Turkey, free to act as victorious powers, and to make their own territorial gains.

The German offensive was begun on March 21 with an unprecedented barrage of 6000 heavy guns and 3000 mortars. Among the shells fired were 2 million gas shells. The bombardment lasted for two and a half hours; then the German infantry advanced. Within twenty-four hours, 21,000 British soldiers had been taken prisoner. As the British were being driven rapidly back to the Somme, three German guns, made specially by Krupp, opened fire on Paris from a distance of seventy-four miles. More than twenty shells were fired, and 256 Parisians killed. That day the Kaiser announced that the battle was won, and 'the English utterly defeated'. Five French divisions, hurrying to the aid of the British, were pushed back with them.

In desperation, Lloyd George telegraphed to the British ambassador in Washington, instructing him to ask Woodrow Wilson to allow the American troops already in France to take their part with the British, even before they were numerically ready to go into action as complete brigades. This was something that Pershing had persistently refused to do. The ambassador drove straight to the White House and put the appeal to Wilson. This time, without hesitation, the President agreed. It was not a moment too soon. On the following day, German troops crossed the Somme, driving a wedge between the British and French sectors of the Front, and bringing to 45,000 the number of Allied soldiers whom they had captured in four days of fighting. But even on that fifth day of intensive German advance, the British were able to make small counterattacks, and there were several examples of German soldiers surrendering. The Germans were disheartened by the unexpected resistance that they were facing, and the ability of British units to counterattack; one British general did so, blowing a hunting horn.

On March 29, Marshal Ferdinand Foch was given overall charge of the Allied forces. When General Pétain, impressed by the continuing force of the

German advance, suggested a withdrawal twenty miles behind Amiens, Foch interrupted him, in the staccato tones for which he was already famous: 'We must fight in front of Amiens. We must stop where we are now. As we have not been able to stop the Germans on the Somme, we must not retire a single centimetre!'

As Foch wished, Amiens was defended, and the city did not fall. The nearest that the German forces reached was Moreuil Wood, only eleven miles from the city. There they were halted. Further south the French were driven out of Montdidier, only fifty miles from Paris, on March 27. Near Noyon, however, French troops halted the German advance that day, while on the Somme Front, the British, making a surprise counterattack, took 800 prisoners. When Foch was told of a dangerous ten-mile gap between the British and French lines, he ordered, 'Lose not another metre of ground!' On March 30, outside Amiens, British, Australian and Canadian troops recaptured Moreuil Wood.

After only nine days of battle, the Germans had regained all the ground which they had lost on the Somme two years earlier, and since. They had taken 90,000 prisoners and captured 1300 guns. But the line had not broken. Amiens in the north and Rheims in the south remained in Allied hands. Among the wounded men in the military hospitals in France, doctors and nurses were working with renewed energy to patch up and return 60,000 men to the battlefield each month. Every day, more American troops were reaching the battlefield, to such an extent that the 90,000 Allied troops taken prisoner in the opening phase of the battle were replaced in due course by 90,000 Americans. These fresh troops had been brought to France on board the former ocean liner *Aquitania*, which required only six transatlantic voyages to bring that vast reinforcement across.

On April 4 the Germans launched a renewed offensive against Amiens, at Villers-Bretonneux. It began with a barrage of 1200 guns and involved sending more than 60,000 men against half the number of Allied defenders. After initial panic in the Allied line, the British and Australian troops drove the attackers back. On the following day Ludendorff called off the Somme offensive altogether. 'The enemy resistance was beyond our powers,' he later wrote. That month, the Germans transferred a further 50,000 men from the Eastern to the Western Front, but they were never able to regain the full impetus of the first week's attack.

The machine gun once more played a decisive part in the April battle, serving the British defenders with the same tenacity that it had earlier served the Germans, and enabling them to go on the offensive. Captain Hutchison, who was serving with a machine-gun battalion, was exhilarated by what he later described as 'the rapidity of action, the extraordinary situation; the perfect discipline and drill; the setting of untouched farmhouses, copses and quietly grazing cattle; the flying civilians with their crazy carts piled high with household chattels and the retreating infantry behind; the magnificent targets obtained.'

During the April 4 battle, Hutchison recalled, he and his adjutant 'discovered in the Belle Croix *estaminet* behind the mill a crowd of British stragglers, fighting drunk. We routed them out, and with a machine gun trained on them, sent them towards the enemy. They perished to a man.'

Despite being deprived of the rapid victory for which they had hoped, the Germans still retained the military initiative, due largely to their numerical superiority. Having given up the Somme offensive, Ludendorff at once switched the attack to the area further north, along the River Lys, with the aim of driving the British from the Ypres Salient, and reaching the North Sea coast between Calais and Dunkirk. The attack was launched on April 9. Against the Portuguese division, the Germans sent four divisions; 6000 Portuguese were taken prisoner and a three-and-a-half mile gap was created in the Allied line. The Germans also fired 2000 tons of gas shells against the British, incapacitating 8000 men, many of whom were blinded.

On the second day of the battle of the Lys, the British were driven from the Messines-Wytschaete ridge. 'With our backs to the wall,' Haig exhorted his men, 'and believing in the justice of our cause, each one of us must fight to the end.' The Passchendaele ridge, reached at such heavy cost five months earlier, was evacuated on April 15. That day General Pershing told the 900 officers of the American 1st Division: 'You are going to meet a savage enemy, flushed with victory. Meet them like Americans. When you hit, hit hard and don't stop hitting. You don't know the meaning of the word "defeat".'

On April 20, at a crucial moment in the battle, American troops were in action in the St Mihiel Salient. They were mauled and driven back, outnumbered by the Germans, and affected, as the British were that same day south of Ypres, by the German use of gas shells.

It was French troops who prevented the Germans taking Ypres, driving them back from two villages just south of the town, Vormezeele and Locre, while to the north of Ypres, Belgian troops drove off a German attack from Langemarck. Twenty-four hours later, Ludendorff called off the attack. The Germans had failed at Ypres, as earlier at Amiens, to take the essential objective if the coast was to be reached.

The German attack in the West was not over, but its high hopes of a swift knockout blow were ended. In three weeks of intense fighting more than 30,000 German soldiers had been killed, as well as 20,000 Allied soldiers. To add to the Allied sense of success, despite the high cost, on April 23 a British naval attack on Zeebrugge succeeded in sinking blockships at the entrance to the canal used by Germany's submarines. Two hundred British sailors were killed in the raid. Its commander and hero was Vice-Admiral Roger Keyes, who had first come to the notice of the British public for his part in the attack on the Taku forts during the Boxer rebellion eighteen years earlier. The thrill of the audacious raid was mitigated somewhat three weeks later, when the German submarines managed to circumvent the obstacle, and to renew their activities in the North Sea.

During the Western Front battles of April 1918, as in the previous battles there, the Allied soldiers had a sense that they were defending – the French soldiers were literally defending – their homeland. The German troops were far from home. Equally far from home were the German troops still in the East. The signing of the Treaty of Brest Litovsk had not ended their service there. Wherever the Bolsheviks were weak, it was German troops who advanced to take control. In April the Germans occupied the eastern Ukrainian city of Kharkov, one of the main industrial and communications centres in the south, cutting the Bolsheviks off from road and rail access to the Black Sea. German troops also occupied three other former Russian cities that month: Helsinki, thereby preventing any possibility of Bolshevik rule; Simferopol, the capital of the Crimea; and Sevastopol, the Russian naval base dominating the Black Sea.

On April 29, General Groener established German military rule throughout the Ukraine. The 'bread basket' of Russia would be giving up its 1918 harvest to the German war effort. There were hopes in Berlin that 1919 might see a recovery of German strength sufficient to make a second massive push in the West. The British, French and Americans were also planning for victory in 1919. The British plan envisaged a force of nearly 5000 Allied tanks effecting the decisive breakthrough in the summer of 1919, when there would be three million American troops on the battlefield, twice as many as the 520,000 already in France.

In order to instil a sense of duty in the British public for the battles of 1919, the British Cabinet decided not to allow horse-racing during the winter season that began on 1 January 1919. The main concern, after the end of the Battle of the Lys, was a renewed German offensive in the summer of 1919. General Pershing had decided that henceforth all American troops reaching France (despite strenuous opposition to this in Washington, as well as in London and Paris) would only go into the line as an exclusively American army, not as part of the British or French armies.

An emergency Allied conference was held at Abbeville – where, in May 1940, Erwin Rommel was to reach the Channel coast, cutting off the British forces in the Calais–Dunkirk perimeter. At the conference, Lloyd George pressed Pershing to put his troops into the collective Allied strategic plan. 'The morale of the soldiers depends upon their fighting under our own flag,' was Pershing's response. The most that Pershing would agree was that the 280,000 American troops who would reach France in May and June could join the Allied line. But he refused to commit the troops who would arrive in July, and he wanted all the rest to be part of an exclusively American army, the deployment of which would be his, Pershing's, decision. 'It is maddening,' Lloyd George wrote to the British ambassador in Washington – who had helped secure the earlier, helpful agreement, of American partici-pation alongside Allied divisions – 'to think that though the men are there, the issue may be endangered because of the short-sightedness of one General and the failure of his Government to order him to carry out their under-takings.'

In India, the British were confronted with mounting discontent. Most of the Indian soldiers fighting against the Turks were from the Punjab, many of them Muslims. For them, two loyalties clashed, that to their King-Emperor and that to the Khalif, the Sultan of Turkey. When the voices of the Turkish mullahs calling the faithful to prayer were heard by the Punjabi Muslims across the trench lines, whether in Mesopotamia or Palestine, it was a disturbing moment for them.

Desertions were frequent. Those who were caught after having deserted were court-martialled and shot. Muslims in India – in Bengal and Maharash-tra as well as in the Punjab – began to protest and agitate. Several Europeans were murdered. Bitterness between the governed and the rulers increased. There was particular anger in India in that many Indians felt that the courage and the suffering of Indian soldiers at the front was not being recognized by the British people, and that the Indian soldiers were regarded as coolies and conscripts of no great loss – 'unwilling heroes' in the words of Edward Thomson, who championed their cause. The Chatri in the Downs above Brighton serves, to this day, as a memorial to the Indian losses in battle. It is little known and seldom visited. Almost 50,000 Indian soldiers lost their lives fighting for Britain.

That spring, the Central Powers were consolidating their victories in the East. Under the Treaty of Bucharest, signed on May 7, the Roumanians gave Germany and Austria-Hungary control of the mouths of the Danube. Bulgaria received all the territory it had lost to Roumania in the Balkan Wars. Five days later, on May 12, the Kaiser and the Emperor Charles, meeting at Spa, the Kaiser's Belgian headquarters, signed an agreement for the joint German-Austro-Hungarian economic exploitation of the Ukraine. They also signed a secret agreement about the postwar years, pledging to form a permanent military alliance and a customs union, and at some future date to abolish altogether the customs frontier between their two countries.

The Emperor Charles's problems within his empire were intensifying. On the very day of the Spa meeting, with its hope of a far closer union between Germany and Austria-Hungary, Slovene soldiers mutinied, demanding independence and an end to the war. The mutiny was suppressed, and six Slovenes executed. But within a week, both a Ruthenian and a Serbian unit in the Austro-Hungarian army also mutinied. They too demanded independence, and were put down. The Ruthenians had called for an independent Ruthenia, the Serbs for the greater Serbian dream of Yugoslavia, and an end to the war.

Czech troops in their barracks at Rumburg mutinied on May 21 and threatened to march on Prague. In the event, they went to Prague by train, declaring that they would 'put an end' to the war when they arrived; but they were intercepted on the journey and disarmed. Brought to trial, ten were sentenced to death, and 560 imprisoned. 'Had the rebels succeeded in advancing southward,' the local Governor warned the authorities in Vienna, 'and had they found support – and this was by no means impossible – among the civilians in these regions, we might by now have faced a regular revolution in parts of Bohemia.'

That month a final act began in the Armenian tragedy of the First World War. The Turks, masters of Eastern Anatolia and the Caucasus since the Treaty of Brest Litovsk, turned on the Armenians in the regions hitherto beyond Turkish control, and drove them from the towns and villages in which they had lived for centuries, most recently under Russian protection. More than 400,000 Armenian civilians were massacred within a few months, in a broad extent of land from the Black Sea to the Caspian Sea.

In Georgia, the largest of the Caucasian provinces of the former Tsarist Empire, an independent republic was declared on May 26. It was headed by Noi Nikolai Zhordania, who for twenty-five years had advocated Georgian national social democracy. Stalin, a fellow Georgian, had been one of Zhordania's followers at the turn of the century, before looking to Lenin for inspiration. The new nation maintained a precarious but determined independence, issued its own stamps, and promoted the Georgian language and culture.

The German failures on the Somme and the Lys did not deter Ludendorff from trying one more offensive on the Western Front, against the French and British forces along the River Aisne. If he were able to break through on this front, Paris might well be within the German grasp. A 4000-gun bombardment preceded the attack on May 27. At La-Ville-aux-Bois-les-Pontaverts, the site of a British artillery battery's resistance, a French memorial records how 'the guns continued to fire and resistance did not cease until every man was killed or captured'. The ferocity of that particular struggle can be gauged by the fact that in the Commonwealth war cemetery in the village, of the 540 graves, 413 are of 'unknown' soldiers.

The initial German attack was successful, so much so that the Allies fell back to the Marne, to the very points along the river that had seen the fiercest fighting in September 1914. An equally historic landmark was overrun by the Germans during the Aisne offensive: the 'California Position' near Craonne. This was the lookout from which, in 1814, Napoleon had witnessed one of his very last victories over the coalition ranged against him. The Kaiser, confident that his armies were on the verge of the breakthrough that had eluded them further north, himself visited the historic site, hoping that it would soon be vested with yet further historical significance.

Such significance was vested, however, that same day, in a small village elsewhere along the line, the village of Cantigny, which the Germans had captured at the end of March. Cantigny was attacked on May 28 by an American brigade. It was the first sustained American offensive of the war. Nearly four thousand men took part. Cantigny was overrun, and seven separate German counterattacks were driven off. The Germans lost an important observation point. The battle also provided – in the words of an American officer, General Hunter Liggett, who wrote a history of the American war effort in France – 'the first cold foreboding to the Germans that this was not, as they had hoped, a rabble of amateurs approaching'.

Two hundred American soldiers were killed at Cantigny, and 200 more were incapacitated by the German gas attacks. Some had become, in the words of their commander, 'half crazy, temporarily insane' after three days in action. When relief finally came, he recalled, 'they could only stagger back, hollow-eyed with sunken cheeks, and if one stopped for a moment he would fall asleep'.

The Americans secured the line at Cantigny. Further south, the Germans, advancing steadily westward, entered the town of Soissons. More than fifty thousand French soldiers were taken prisoner. German troops were now forty miles from Paris, from which tens of thousands of French civilians fled, as they had done in September 1914 and March 1918, and were to do again in May 1940. Within the ranks of the French army, demoralization re-emerged; retreating French troops called out to the Americans who passed them, moving forward, 'La guerre finie' (The war is over).

But the war continued. On June 2 the German aviator, Captain Hermann Goering, was awarded the Pour le Mérite, the highest German medal for bravery in action, for having shot down eighteen French and British aircraft on the Western Front. Twenty years later Goering would command the German Air Force as it made its plans for the blitzkrieg and conquest of his former adversaries.

On the Western Front, the Germans again used flame throwers at the end of July. The men who were caught in the direct blast of the fire, one British eye-witness wrote, 'were never seen again'. But still the trench lines held, and the death toll mounted with every renewed attack. The halting of this third German offensive within three months depended upon adequate Allied reinforcements being brought to the battlefield. Although, in the secrecy of an inter-Allied discussion at Versailles on June 2, General Pershing refused absolutely to bring forward the numbers of American troops reaching France, those American troops who were in action gave courage to those who saw them. 'We all had the impression that we were about to see a wonderful transfusion of blood,' a French Staff Officer commented. 'Life was coming in floods to re-animate the dying body of France.' More than twenty thousand French and British troops were also brought from Salonika to the Western Front, a mutiny among the Bulgarian forces having taken the pressure off the Salonika army.

Although Russia was no longer part of the Western Front equation, her problems remained the concern of both the Allies and the Central Powers. By one of those coincidences which in retrospect can be seen to mark the forward movement of history, on June 3 two landings took place at the extremities of what had been the Russian Empire. They were ordered by two of the main adversaries in the conflict on the Western Front, Britain and Germany.

The aim of the landings was the same. A small force of 150 British marines, disembarking at the northern Russian port of Pechenga, was committed not only to protecting Allied stores which had been sent there when Russia was an ally, but also helping the anti-Bolshevik Russians. These Russians were gathering at all the extremities of the former empire, under Tsarist commanders, hoping to destroy the Bolshevik regime by force of arms. Also on June 3, on instructions from Berlin, two German battalions, about 2000 men in all, landed at the Black Sea port of Poti, to support the anti-Bolshevik authorities in the Caucasus. Within two weeks, German troops had reached the Georgian capital, Tiflis, where they acted as the protectors of Noi Zhordania's newly independent Georgia against Bolshevik attack. The Germans also took 10,000 Bolshevik soldiers prisoner in southern Russia.

Britain and Germany were thus, at a great distance from each other, acting in the same cause, as the would-be destroyers of Bolshevism. At the same time, deep inside Russia, a terrible struggle was taking place between the Reds and the Whites, particularly in the Ukraine, where Bolsheviks and anti-Bolsheviks struggled for supremacy. One group of victims of the conflict was the age-old victim of chaos in Russia, the Jews. In the areas captured from the Bolsheviks, hundreds of Jews were killed each day, in a wave of pogroms, as the Jew-hatred of earlier decades was stoked up by the accusation that the Jews were secret supporters of Bolshevism. The fact that several individual Jews, among them Trotsky and the two other senior Bolshevik negotiators at Brest Litovsk – Adolf Ioffe and Lev Kamenev – were so prominent in the Bolshevik leadership, added fuel to the already blazing fire as did the prominence of Jews in the higher ranks of the CHEKA, the All-Russian Extraordinary Commission for Combating Counter-Revolution and Sabotage – the main instrument of Bolshevik repression.

On the Western Front, on June 6, British troops drove the Germans out of their fortified positions at the village of Bligny, southwest of Rheims. On the following day, a massive German assault was launched along the whole southern battle line. Three quarters of a million German gas shells were fired; 15,000 tons of gas. Although 4000 French soldiers were incapacitated, only thirty-two were killed. Nevertheless, the line broke, and the Germans, advancing five miles before nightfall, took 8000 prisoners. Even Clemenceau, the 'Tiger' of France, had a moment of panic that all might be lost. But General Pershing, who was with Clemenceau during the second day of the battle, strengthened the French leader's resolve with the words: 'Well, Mr President, it may not look encouraging just now, but we are certain to win in the end.'

On June 10 the French troops on the Noyon-Montdidier front were forced back more than five miles, from Lassigny to Antheuil-Portes. This brought the German army to within forty-five miles of Paris. But on the following day four French and two American divisions launched a counterattack, and the Germans were driven back.

Near Soissons, a German attack on June 12 by five German divisions made only minor gains. The German hope to break through to Paris was at an end. After six consecutive days of battle, Ludendorff called off the southern offensive. Each of his plans for the Somme, the Lys and the Aisne had been frustrated. Although he set about making plans for another offensive on the Western Front in a month's time, like the British and French he was beginning to believe that the decisive clash would come in 1919; that the forces were too evenly matched for a victory in 1918.

The public in all the warring nations had come to realize the enormity of trench warfare. Writers were beginning to express their feelings in print, and publishers did not shy away from publishing such books. In her very first novel, *The Return of the Soldier*, Rebecca West wrote about Christopher, a young man at the front:

> Of late I had had bad dreams about him. By night I saw Chris running across the brown rottenness of No-Man's-Land, starting back here because he trod upon a hand, not even looking there because of the awfulness of an unburied head, and not till my dreams were packed full of horror did I see him pitch forward on his knees as he reached safety – if it was that.
>
> For on the war-films I have seen men slip down as softly from the trench parapet, and none but the grimmer philosophers would say that they had reached safety by their fall. And when I escaped into wakefulness it was only to lie stiff and think of stories I had heard in the boyish voice, that rings indomitable yet has most of its gay notes flattened, of the modern subaltern. 'We were all of us in a barn one night, and a shell came along. My pal sang out, *"Help me, old man, I've got no legs!"* and I had to answer, *"I can't, old man, I've got no hands!"*'
>
> Well, such are the dreams of Englishwomen to-day; I could not complain.
>
> But I wished for the return of our soldier.

The first six months of 1918 had seen growing Allied air mastery over the battlefield. In response, Ludendorff gave orders for German aircraft production to be almost doubled, to 300 aircraft a month, between July 1918 and April 1919. The Americans also regarded 1919 as the decisive year. 'The Allies are done for,' Pershing wrote to Colonel House five days after the German offensive was called off, 'and the only thing that will hold them (especially France) in the war will be the assurance that we have enough forces to assume the initiative.'

If America could not secure a victory on the Western Front in 1919, Pershing warned, the Allies would probably make peace. To prevent this, he asked for an acceleration of the arrival of American troops in France, so that there could be two and a half million men ready for action by 1 May 1919. This alone, he argued, would tilt the balance in favour of the Allies, whose three million – French and British – soldiers on the Western Front faced three and a half million Germans. Even if the Allies could hold the line, Pershing believed, without the American reinforcements on the scale he requested they could not push the Germans back.

*   *   *

Despite the German setback on the Western Front, the Austrians still felt able to take the offensive. This was launched on June 15, when a massive force of fifty-five Austro-Hungarian divisions – almost a quarter of a million men – was sent into action against the Italians on the Asiago and Piave fronts. The objective was a line between Verona and Venice, with hopes of being able to drive the Italians back to the River Po. Supporting the Italians were British and French troops, despatched at the time of the Austrian breakthrough eight months earlier. Ludwig Wittgenstein, the Austrian philosopher and wartime artillerist, won his Gold Medal for Valour, Austria-Hungary's highest military award, when facing British troops at that time.

The Emperor Charles had gone by train to Meran, intending to travel southward as soon as his armies had broken through the Allied lines. But after a short initial advance, the Austrian offensive failed, and the Italians were able to counterattack. After five days the Austrian forces gave up their attempt to secure a victory. Downcast, the Emperor returned by train to Vienna. In Germany, the Foreign Minister (since August 1917), Richard von Kühlmann, warned the Reichstag on June 24 that Germany should not expect 'any definite end to the war from a military decision alone'. The Kaiser, outraged by what he regarded as defeatism, dismissed Kühlmann from office.

On the Western Front, on June 26, American troops drove the Germans out of Belleau Wood, in the sector of the front line nearest to Paris. Today, two war cemeteries mark the battleground. In one, at the edge of the wood, are the graves of 2288 American soldiers and the names of a further 1060 who have no known grave. A few hundred yards away is another cemetery with 8624 German graves. Like so many thousands of war cemeteries, it is a shrine for the few visitors who make the journey there today, almost eighty years after the battle. As the twentieth century draws to its close, the tranquillity of the site belies the savage fighting that once marked the rural scene and cost nearly twelve thousand lives.

North of Belleau Wood, at the village of Ambleny, the French attacked on June 30 with a new type of five-and-a-half ton tank as their surprise weapon. More than a thousand Germans were taken prisoner. For the first time in almost four years, each day witnessed some further Allied success, the capture of a wood or a village or a hillside. On July 4, American Independence Day, American troops were in action alongside Australians on the Somme, capturing the village of Hamel and taking more than a thousand German prisoners.

As the struggle for mastery was being waged on the Western Front, the war at sea continued brutally to take its toll. On June 27, when the British hospital ship, the *Llandovery Castle*, was, despite its clear Red Cross markings, torpedoed by a German submarine in the Atlantic, 283 patients and nurses died, some being fired on while in the lifeboats. Among the dead were all fourteen of the Canadian nursing sisters on board. In Japan, in an accidental explosion on the Japanese battleship *Kawachi* on July 12, more than 700 sailors were killed. Two days later – Bastille Day – 442 French sailors and troops were drowned on the French troop transport *Djemnah* when a German submarine torpedoed it off Cyrenaica.

The Italians were successful in the first days of July in pushing back the Austro-Hungarian forces in the Piave Delta. Among the casualties was an eighteen-year-old American Red Cross ambulance driver, Ernest Hemingway, hit in the foot and knee while handing out chocolate to wounded Italian soldiers in a dugout. For his bravery under fire he was awarded the Italian Silver Medal of Military Valour. Eleven years later he was to immortalize his experiences, and those of the Italians whom he saw in action, and wounded, in his novel *A Farewell to Arms*. One passage recounts:

Outside the post a great many of us lay on the ground in the dark. They carried wounded in and brought them out. I could see the light come out from the dressing station when the curtain opened and they brought some one in or out. The dead were off to one side. The doctors were working with their sleeves up to their shoulders and were red as butchers. There were not enough stretchers. Some of the wounded were noisy but most were quiet. The wind blew the leaves in the bower over the door of the dressing station and the night was getting cold. Stretcher-bearers came in all the time, put their stretchers down, unloaded them and went away. As soon as I got to the dressing station Manera brought a medical sergeant out and he put bandages on both my legs. He said there was so much dirt blown into the wound that there had not been much haemorrhage. They would take me as soon as possible. He went back inside. Gordini could not drive, Manera said. His shoulder was smashed and his head was hurt. He had not felt bad but now the shoulder had stiffened. He was sitting up beside one of the brick walls. Manera and Gavuzzi each went off with a load of wounded. They could drive all right. The British had come with three ambulances and they had two men on each ambulance. One of their drivers came over to me, brought by

Gordini who looked very white and sick. The Britisher leaned over.

'Are you hit badly?' he asked. He was a tall man and wore steel-rimmed spectacles.

'In the legs.'

'It's not serious I hope. Will you have a cigarette?'

'Thanks.'

'They tell me you've lost two drivers.'

'Yes. One killed and the fellow that brought you.'

'What rotten luck. . .'

July 14 was chosen by Ludendorff for the preliminary bombardment for one more attack on the Western Front. He had almost been forced to postpone the attack as a new scourge, influenza – known as Spanish 'Flu – had struck many of his troops. Hundreds of troops were dying of its ravages. But the offensive went ahead, and in Berlin, as the bombardment began, there were those who expected German troops to be on their way to Paris within a few days, and the Allies to sue for peace within two months.

On the eve of the attack, German artillery fired more than 17,500 gas shells against the French and American frontline trenches, 2500 more shells than before the attack of June 7. Then, on the morning itself, 500,000 rounds of gas shells were fired (9000 tons of gas in all). But at one of the main points of attack, opposite the American Rainbow Division, Pétain had set up a ruse, creating a complete line of bogus, virtually unmanned trenches, and it was against these that much of the German gas attack was expended, leaving the trenches further back fully manned, and almost untouched by the bombardment.

When the German troops reached the parapets of the real trenches, they were caught by the uncut wire, and the unimpeded machine-gun fire of the defenders; they were, one American officer in the line recalled, 'exhausted, uncoordinated, and shattered, incapable of going on without being reorganized and reinforced'. After the battle, the officer recalled, he himself was haunted by 'the vision of those writhing bodies hanging from the barbed wire'. That officer was Douglas MacArthur, the Commanding General of the United States forces in the Pacific a quarter of a century later.

Italian troops were also in action on the Western Front that July. On July 17 they were successful in preventing the Germans reaching the Marne south of Nanteuil. At German headquarters a Staff Officer noted in his diary that day: 'Fairly depressed mood. Difficult question – what is to happen from now on?' The answer came on the following day, when Foch launched the Allied counterattack along a twenty-seven-mile front. The German line was broken, and 20,000 Germans were taken prisoner. By the end of the fourth day of the French offensive, 30,000 Germans had been killed. 'Never have I seen so many dead men, never such frightful battle scenes,' a German officer later wrote. As to the wounded, an American medical officer recalled: 'Some of them cursed and raved and had to be tied to their litters. Some shook violently. Some trembled and slinked away in apparent abject fear of every incoming shell, while others simply stood speechless, oblivious to all surroundings.'

The Germans began to fall back. The German Chancellor (since November 1917), Count Georg von Hertling, recalling that on July 15 there had been those in Berlin who expected to have Paris at their mercy, wrote in his diary: 'On the 18th even the most optimistic among us knew that all was lost. The history of the world was played out in three days.'

Another element in the 'history of the world' was being played out in the third week of July, the fate of the Russian Tsar and his family. They were being held captive by the Bolsheviks in Ekaterinburg, in the Urals, a town that was suddenly on the line of advance of the Cossack and Czech anti-Bolshevik forces moving eastward. The commandant of the detachment guarding the Romanovs was a Jewish convert to Catholicism – and later to Communism – Yakov Yurovsky. He received instructions to kill the imperial family from the Commander-in-Chief of the Red Army in the Urals and Siberia, Reinhold Berzin, a Latvian Bolshevik, who realized that Ekaterinburg was about to be overrun by the Whites. As plans for the execution went ahead, Lenin was asked by telegram from Ekaterinburg, 'If your opinion is contrary, inform immediately.' He made no reply.

The killings took place at nine o'clock on the evening of July 16. One eye-witness account that has survived in the Soviet archives, kept secret for more than seventy years, is the testimony of Pavel Medvedev, the commander of the guard that was holding the Romanovs captive. This testimony was recorded by Medvedev's interviewer:

> The Tsar, the Tsaritsa, the Tsar's four daughters, the doctor, the cook and the lackey came out of their rooms. The Tsar was carrying the heir in his

arms. The sovereign Emperor and the heir were wearing field shirts and forage caps. The Empress and her daughters wore dresses but not wraps. The sovereign walked ahead with the heir.

In my presence there were no tears, no sobs and no questions. They went downstairs, out into the courtyard and from there through the second door into the downstairs quarters. They were led into the corner room adjacent to the sealed storeroom. Yurovsky ordered chairs to be brought in.

The Empress sat down by the wall where the window was – close to the rear column of the arch. Behind her stood three of her daughters. The Emperor was in the middle, next to the heir, and behind him stood Dr Botkin. The maid, a tall woman, stood by the left jamb of the storeroom door. With her stood one of the daughters. The maid had a pillow in her arms.

The Tsar's daughters had brought small pillows; they put one on the seat of the heir's chair, the other on their mother's. Simultaneously eleven men walked into the room: Yurovsky, his assistant, the two from the Cheka, and seven Latvians. According to Medvedev, Yurovsky told him: 'Go out to the street and see whether anyone's there and the shots will be heard.'

He walked out and heard the shots. By the time he returned to the house, two or three minutes had passed. Walking into the room he saw all the members of the Tsar's family lying on the floor with numerous wounds to their bodies.

The blood was gushing. The heir was still alive – and moaning. Yurovsky walked over to him and shot him two or three times at point blank range. The heir fell still. 'The scene made me want to vomit.'

The corpses were brought out to the lorry on stretchers made of a sheet stretched on shafts taken from the sleigh standing in the yard. The driver was Sergei Lyukhanov. The blood in the room and yard was washed off. By three o'clock it was all over.

The end of the killings was later described by Yurovsky himself. 'The bodies were put in a hole,' he wrote, 'and the faces and all the bodies generally doused with sulphuric acid, both so they couldn't be recognized and to prevent any stink from them rotting (it was not a deep hole). We scattered it with dirt and lime, put boards on top, and rode over it several times – no trace of the hole remained. The secret was kept.'

Edvard Radzinsky, whose researches revealed the above documents, wrote of Yurovsky's life in the 1930s: 'As before, he continued to meet in Medvedev's apartment and reminisce. About the same old thing. The execution. There was nothing else in their lives. They reminisced prosaically about the Apocalypse over a cup of tea. And they discussed who really did fire first. Yurovsky had the precedence. Precedence – for the realization of his dream. He was a Jew. Once the monarchists got the ball rolling, the Tsar's murder was declared an act of Jewish revenge.'

Medvedev's son, himself a historian, and a leading Russian dissident of post-Stalinist years, recalled: 'Once Yurovsky arrived triumphant – he had been brought a book that had come out in the West where it was written in black and white that it was he, Yurovsky, who killed Nicholas. He was happy – he had left his mark on history.'

The German Kaiser, who on July 15 had been at the front to watch his troops go into action, did not know for some days that the Tsar – the 'Nicky' of his prewar correspondence – had been murdered. His concern at the front was the most serious failure of a German offensive since the battle of the Marne almost four years earlier. It was an even more serious failure than the Marne, as the troops facing his retreating army included the Americans, fresh to battle, healthy and eager for victory.

Following the French and American successes that week, the Kaiser shared his Chancellor's sense that the end was near. 'I am a defeated War Lord to whom you must show consideration,' he told his staff on July 22. A week later, as the Germans sought to halt the accelerated Allied advance, and hold on to at least some of the gains of the summer, American soldiers defeated a regiment of the much-feared Prussian Guards at the village of Seringes. Among the Americans taking part in the advance that week was William J. Donovan, who in the Second World War was to head the Office of Strategic Services (OSS) responsible for some of the most imaginative efforts to disrupt the German war effort. Among the German soldiers who fought throughout the retreat was Corporal Hitler. On August 4 he was awarded the Iron Cross, First Class, the citation speaking of his 'personal bravery and general merit'. The officer who made this recommendation was Captain Hugo Guttman, a Jew.

After the Nazis had come to power, Captain Guttman let it be known publicly, 'I pinned the Iron Cross on Hitler.' The Nazis objected – 'No Jew could have done this' they said – and Guttman was arrested. After his release he protested again that he was indeed the man who had honoured the Führer with the decoration of which Hitler was most proud. Again Guttman was arrested. After his third arrest he left Germany for the United States, where he settled in St Louis, Missouri.

On the day that Hitler was awarded his Iron Cross, First Class, the American Assistant Secretary for the Navy, Franklin D. Roosevelt, was making his first and only visit to the battle zone. Visiting an American artillery battery, he fired one of the guns, which was aimed at a German railway junction. 'I shall never know how many, if any, Huns I killed,' he later remarked. During the day he saw 'two hundred limping, exhausted men come out of the line – the survivors of a regiment of a thousand that went forward forty-eight hours before.'

As the Allied advance continued, the Germans increasingly realized that all might indeed be lost. 'We have reached the limits of our capacity,' the Kaiser told Ludendorff on August 7. 'The war must be ended.' But it needed to be ended, in his view, at a moment when his army was gaining some sort of advantage on the battlefield, so that Germany could obtain at least a minimum of her war aims. On the following day, however, British, French and Dominion troops began a new offensive.

The Kaiser's view was reflected, a day after the renewed Allied offensive, by Ludendorff, who told a fellow officer: 'We cannot win this war any more, but we must not lose it.' But at the end of the third day of the offensive, 24,000 German soldiers had been taken prisoner. When seven fresh German divisions were sent into the line that day, a group of drunken soldiers in reserve called out to them: 'What do you war-prolongers want?'

On August 12 Ludendorff, the victor of Tannenberg almost four years earlier, told a member of his Staff, 'There is no more hope for the offensive, the generals have lost their foothold.' Two days later, at a meeting of the German Crown Council, at Spa, in the presence of the Kaiser, he recommended immediate peace negotiations. Ludendorff was supported in this by the Emperor Charles, whose senior military adviser, having journeyed to Spa, warned the Kaiser that Austria-Hungary 'could only continue the war until December'.

A major German fear was the loss of the resources available to Germany in southern Russia and the Caucasus: above all, grain and oil. When British troops, marching northward from Persia, entered the Caspian city of Baku on August 17, the principal oil resources of Russia were suddenly in the hands of the Allies. On August 25, after secret negotiations of the sort which the Bolsheviks were repeatedly denouncing, an agreement was signed between Lenin and the Kaiser, whereby the Bolsheviks, in return for a promise of no further German attacks against them in the south, agreed to fight the Allies who had landed in Northern Russia. Twenty-one years to the day before Hitler and Stalin reached agreement to partition Poland – and also, if opportunity arose, the Middle East – Germany and the Soviet Union made common cause.

Under the agreement of 25 August 1918 – which established one of the more remarkable alliances of the First World War – the Bolsheviks agreed that, if they were to capture Baku from the British, they would send one-third of Baku's oil production to Germany. For her part, Germany promised to prevent the Finns from attacking Bolshevik Russia.

Agreement with the Bolsheviks came too late to help Germany on the Western Front, where on August 17 the French had mounted an offensive, followed four days later by the British. Both offensives were successful, the British advancing two miles and taking 2000 German prisoners. Although the Germans still had a numerical superiority – forty-two divisions to thirty-one – their morale was dropping rapidly at the very moment when Allied morale was rising. From the Somme battlefield, every yard of which had been savagely contested in 1916, the Germans withdrew ten miles in a single day – August 26 – along a fifty-five mile front.

In Vienna, the Austrian Foreign Minister, Baron Burian, informed the German government on August 30 that Austria-Hungary intended to open up its own peace negotiations with the Allies, whatever Germany might say. There were, Burian pointed out, an estimated 400,000 Austro-Hungarian soldiers who had deserted from their units, a situation not unlike that which had brought the Russian war effort to a halt a year earlier.

The Germans fought on, still hoping, as Ludendorff and the Kaiser had expressed it, that if a positive change occurred in German fortunes on the battlefield, even for a short time, then Germany would be in a better position to make a negotiated peace and retain some of its goals. No such positive change seemed likely, however, as Foch gave orders on September 3 for a continuous offensive along the whole length of the Western Front. That day it was announced that in August the Allies had taken 150,000 German prisoners. 'Public feeling in Berlin is not good,' General Hoffman noted in his diary.

Ludendorff now ordered a series of evacuations, starting on September 3 with the Lys Salient, and continuing five days later with the St Mihiel Salient, which was about to be attacked by the French and Americans. When the St Mihiel attack came, before the German withdrawal had been completed, the Germans were driven out of the salient.

Among the airmen fighting in the Allied ranks at St Mihiel, under overall American command, were Americans, Frenchmen, Italians, Belgians and Portuguese. Among the American soldiers in action on the ground were two who were to rise to the highest positions in the Second World War: George S. Patton Jnr (who in 1944 commanded the United States Third Army) and George C. Marshall (Chief-of-Staff of the United States Forces throughout the Second World War).

Inside Russia, assassination had become part of the armoury of the anti-Bolsheviks. On June 20 the head of the Petrograd Cheka, V. Volodarsky (a Jew) was assassinated by a member of the self-styled Combat Organization of the Socialist Revolutionaries. On August 30 his successor, M. S. Uritsky (also Jewish), was shot dead by a young man seeking to avenge the execution of a friend. Later that same day, an attempt was made to assassinate Lenin. His assailant was Fannie Kaplan, a former anarchist who in Tsarist times had served several years' hard labour in Siberia for her part in a plot to kill the Governor-General of Kiev. Sixty years later a Soviet film opened with a blank, black screen, the sound of a shot, and the words, 'With this shot the Jewess Fannie Kaplan tried to kill the great Lenin . . .' One of the three bullets she fired hit Lenin at the juncture of his jaw and neck, permanently affecting his health. But he was able to continue to dictate Soviet policy.

Fannie Kaplan objected to Lenin's suppression of the Constituent Assembly. She also opposed the terms of the Treaty of Brest Litovsk, which she regarded as humiliating for Russia. She was executed on September 3. As a result of her unsuccessful shot, two decrees on Red Terror were issued almost at once, the first on September 4 and the second on September 5. They gave the Soviet political police full powers to arrest and imprison, and if necessary to execute, without trial.

Implementation of the two terror decrees was in the hands of Felix Dzerzhinsky (a Pole), then the head of the Cheka, and later the head of the People's Commissariat for Internal Affairs, the NKVD. Dzerzhinsky had already written, in the newspaper *Svoboda Rossii*, on June 9: 'We stand for organized terror – this should be frankly stated – terror being absolutely indispensable in current revolutionary conditions. We terrorize the enemies of the Soviet government in order to stifle crime at its inception. Terror serves as a ready deterrent.'

Massive reprisals were carried out after the attempted assassination of Lenin. Opponents of the Soviet regime, and imagined opponents, were seized and imprisoned without due process of law. Hostages were taken, to be executed as reprisals for future attacks on Bolshevik leaders. Enemies were rooted out and many old scores settled – by firing squad. In Petrograd more than five hundred opponents of the regime were executed in a single day. Even as the war continued in Western Europe, in the East a new series of horrors were replacing the horrors of war.

The forces in Germany calling openly for an immediate peace were still small. They were led by the Independent Social Democratic Party of Germany, a splinter group from the Social Democrats, from which the even more extreme Spartacus Union had been formed, led by Karl Liebknecht and Rosa Luxemburg. In an attempt to combat Spartacist propaganda among the industrial workers of the Ruhr, on September 11 the Kaiser travelled from Spa to Essen, where he addressed the Krupp workers there as 'My dear friends', and implored them to hold out to the end. But when he told them that anyone circulating antiwar leaflets ought to be hanged, the workers were silent.

Recruiting continued, with sixteen-year-olds being called to the colours. 'These mornings,' Thomas Mann wrote in his diary in Munich that week, 'mere adolescents of young soldiers are drilling in the park again. Yesterday they were doing so under the command of an extremely bourgeois middle-aged lieutenant. So far, they continue to obey . . .'

On the Salonika Front, the Bulgarian forces had continued to hold the mountain ridges which they had manned successfully for two years. But during a renewed Allied assault on September 15 they were outnumbered, with 36,000 French, Italian and Serb troops attacking 12,000 Bulgarians and Germans. The Bulgarians were ordered by their king not to retreat. On the following day, two Bulgarian regiments mutinied, and the retreat began. Elsewhere on the Salonika Front, British, French and Greek troops advanced. On September 25 British troops entered Bulgaria. That day the Bulgarians decided to ask for an armistice; they were the first of the Central Powers to do so. French forces entered the Macedonian capital, Skopje, on September

27. Austrian reinforcements, sent from the north to strengthen the Bulgarian resistance, were still fifty miles from Skopje when the city fell.

As the Bulgarian resistance collapsed in the Balkans, Turkish resistance was collapsing in Palestine. Starting on September 19, General Allenby advanced northward from Jerusalem, and within a week was in control of the Galilee. Among his tactics was the bombing and machine-gunning from the air of Turkish soldiers fleeing eastward along the precipitous slopes of the Wadi Fara, down to the River Jordan. More than 86,000 machine-gun rounds were fired at men who had no means of firing back. Some of the Allied pilots who carried out these aerial attacks were so nauseated by what they saw of the effect of their shooting that they asked to be excused any further sorties. Their request was accepted.

On September 26, the day that the Allied troops on the Salonika Front entered Skopje, Allenby's forces had already taken over the Trans-Jordanian town of Amman, among whose small population were not only desert Bedouins, but Circassian and Chechen tribes who had been settled there by the Turks as guardians of the desert frontier.[1]

That day was also the first full day of a new French and American offensive on the Western Front. The objective was to drive northward through the Argonne Forest and along the River Meuse. Among the American artillerymen in action on that first day was a battery commander, Captain Harry S. Truman, a future President. 'I slept in the edge of a wood to the right of my battery position,' he later recalled. 'If I hadn't awakened and got up at 4 a.m. I would not be here, because the Germans fired a barrage on my sleeping place!'

Within twenty-four hours of the opening of the Meuse–Argonne offensive, 23,000 German soldiers had been taken prisoner. Near Cambrai, British troops, supported by 1000 aircraft, had attacked the Hindenburg Line, taking 10,000 prisoners. Then, on the following day, September 28, Haig launched a major offensive against the Germans in the Ypres Salient – the Fourth Battle of Ypres. Swiftly, the village of Passchendaele was taken and, still advancing, the British drove the Germans from the fields beyond Passchendaele that had evaded capture a year earlier at such a heavy cost. During the day, 4000 German soldiers surrendered. The Allied forces had taken 37,000

---

[1] In the summer of 1995 the author was present (by chance) outside the Russian Embassy in Amman, when a group of local Chechens – whose grandparents and great-grandparents had been brought to Amman in Ottoman times to guard the railway – demonstrated against the Russian attacks on their fellow Chechens in the North Caucasus.

prisoners in two days, a feat that was unprecedented in the history of Allied activity on the Western Front. That evening, at Spa, Ludendorff told Hindenburg that Germany must seek an armistice, and on the following morning the two men went together to see the Kaiser.

Patiently, Ludendorff explained to his sovereign that the problem was not only the collapse of German military morale at the front, but the deep reluctance of Woodrow Wilson to negotiate either with the Kaiser or with his military chiefs. The Kaiser understood the dilemma, and in a decision unthinkable in peacetime, agreed to modify the German constitution in such a way as to introduce a parliamentary regime, something that the Social Democrats in the Reichstag had demanded in vain for more than two decades.

That September, in an attempt to support the anti-Bolshevik Russians in their efforts to win territory back from the Bolsheviks, British troops – who had originally been sent to North Russia to guard the military stores despatched from Britain for the Tsarist armies – advanced twenty-five miles inland from Murmansk, pushing back the Bolshevik forces. That same month, 4500 American troops landed at Archangel. A new war was in the making, with Petrograd and Moscow – indeed, the soul of Russia – regarded as its prize.

Germany's allies were no longer able to sustain the war efforts of the other Central Powers. On September 29 the Bulgarians were granted the armistice they had sought four days earlier, whereupon all hostilities ceased on the Salonika Front. The terms of the armistice, which Bulgaria had no military option but to accept, were severe. All Greek and Serbian territory was to be evacuated, all German and Austrian soldiers were to return home, all weapons were to be surrendered, and the Allies were to occupy strategic points inside Bulgaria.

On the Palestine Front, General Allenby reached the outskirts of Damascus, and on the following morning entered the city. An Australian officer with Allenby's army later wrote: 'The shooting by the Turks gave way, in a second, to the clapping of hands by the citizens.' The conqueror had become the liberator, and Arab national aspirations, suppressed by centuries of Turkish rule, were revived, Arab national enthusiasm being stimulated by the arrival of Arab troops among the city's liberators.

Those most at risk in Damascus on the night of liberation were Turkish soldiers who, despite having surrendered, were being killed at random by Arab zealots. One of the British officers attached to the Arab forces, Captain T. E. Lawrence, asked a fellow officer who was serving with the Arabs, Captain Alec Kirkbride, to go with him 'and help in stopping the killing of Turks in the streets'. Kirkbride's account continued:

> I expressed my willingness to go, but suggested that we should take an armed party along. He said, 'Oh no; you and I can manage, I am sure!'
>
> We must have looked an ill-assorted couple, he short and in Arab robes and with no arms but an ornamental dagger, and myself long and lanky in khaki, wearing a large Service revolver. When we found anyone butchering Turks he went up and asked them in a gentle voice to stop, while I stood by and brandished my firearm.
>
> Occasionally, someone turned nasty and I shot them at once before the trouble could spread. Lawrence got quite cross and said, 'For God's sake stop being so bloody-minded!' To which I replied, 'That is all very well, sir, but unless I act first the others could see the two of us off every time. You should have brought that armed party.'
>
> We returned to Arab headquarters leading some twenty Turkish prisoners whom we had rescued.

The First World War was not yet over, although on September 30 Ludendorff reiterated his belief that it could not go on. 'We cannot fight against the whole world,' he told a fellow general. In many of the cities of Germany, the Spartacists, inspired by what had been achieved by the Bolsheviks in Russia, were demanding the overthrow of all parliamentary power. Their aim, like Lenin's a year earlier, was Red revolution and the rule of the proletariat.

On October 2, as a thirty-mile sector of the Hindenburg Line was being overrun by the Allies, a new German Chancellor – the third in fifteen months – Prince Max of Baden, agreed to take on the task, but with one condition: that henceforth the Reichstag alone would have the power to make war and negotiate peace, and that the Kaiser's control had over the army and navy must cease. But in Berlin that day, the new Chancellor rejected Hindenburg's advice for an immediate peace; advice which Ludendorff, still in Spa, fully endorsed. 'I hoped I could fight down pessimism and revive confidence,' Prince Max later wrote, 'for I myself was still firmly convinced that in spite of the diminution of our forces we could prevent our enemy from treading the soil of the fatherland for many months.'

From Spa, Ludendorff pleaded for an immediate armistice. 'Every day lost,' he wrote to Prince Max, 'costs thousands of brave soldiers' lives.' But Prince Max hesitated. He was also worried about the loss of Alsace-Lorraine and the Polish districts of Prussia, both losses being implicit in President Wilson's Fourteen Points.

On October 3, Prince Max brought two Social Democrat deputies into his government. They too immediately urged him to seek an armistice, or to risk Red revolution in Germany. On October 4, recognizing the force of this warning, Prince Max took the step he had been so reluctant to take two days earlier, telling the Reichstag that peace was essential. Then, having obtained the agreement of the Austro-Hungarian government to contact the Allies, he telegraphed to Washington requesting an armistice. But he did so in terms that were not likely to be acceptable to Wilson. This was not a surrender, Prince Max made clear, nor even an offer of armistice terms, but an attempt to end the war without any preconditions that might be harmful to the territorial integrity of Germany or Austria-Hungary. There was not a single Allied soldier on German soil; this gave added strength to the Germany desire not to lose one inch of territory.

There were certain regions that it was unlikely Germany or Austria-Hungary would be able to retain. Even as President Wilson studied Prince Max's note, several Polish factions (one in Warsaw and one in Lublin) were declaring independence, and Polish and Ukrainian troops were fighting for control of Eastern Galicia.

On October 8, having consulted with Lloyd George and Clemenceau, President Wilson rejected the German note. The first condition of any armistice, he replied, was the evacuation of all territory occupied by Germany: the war would not end until there were no German troops on French or Belgian soil, and no Austro-Hungarian troops in Serbia. Meanwhile, the fighting on the Western Front continued. On October 9 a British cavalry unit made an unprecedented eight-mile advance, taking 500 German soldiers prisoner as it rode forward. At sea, however, the Germans were as active as ever, a German submarine sinking the Kingstown–Holyhead ferry *Leinster* on October 10, when 176 passengers and crew on their way from Ireland to Britain were drowned.

*   *   *

There were still those in Germany who felt that the war should go on. Many Social Democrats, by far the largest working-class party, continued to support the war effort. In early October their main newspaper, *Vorwärts*, proposed, as a means of preventing the collapse of the German army in the west, a call-up, or 'levée en masse', of recruits who had not yet been called to serve. But the Germans were everywhere in retreat, fleeing from Serbia as the Serbs regained their lost territory, and seeking to escape, as the Serbs had been forced to flee three years earlier, over the mountain passes into Albania. On the Western Front, despite German resistance mile by mile, the Allied armies were virtually unimpeded in their daily advance. Gas shells were now working to the Allied advantage, as earlier they had been the scourge of the Allied lines. On October 14, Adolf Hitler was temporarily blinded by a British gas shell near the Belgian village of Werwik. He was evacuated to a German military hospital at Pasewalk, north of Berlin.

On October 16, in an attempt to appease the Americans, and to comply with Woodrow Wilson's Fourteen Points, the Emperor Charles offered complete federal autonomy to the six main nationalities of his empire, the Czechs, Slovaks, Poles, Croats, Slovenes, Serbs and Roumanians. Four days later, Woodrow Wilson replied by stating – beyond anything that had been laid down in the Fourteen Points – that 'autonomy' for the subject peoples was no longer enough. The United States had incurred obligations to the Czechoslovak and South Slav peoples, the President said, that went beyond autonomy, or a federal structure within the Habsburg Empire.

The creation of a South Slav national entity was attractive to the Entente powers as well as to the United States, for it offered a counterweight that had not existed before 1914 to the influence of Germany and Austria. Early in 1918 a British expert on the future geography of Europe, Colonel Sir Thomas Holditch, wrote in favour of a future Yugoslav federation: 'Were Croats, Slovenes and Serbians united in the bonds of State federation, they would surely form a nationality strong enough to claim first rank among the powers of Middle Europe – powerful enough to face any possible Germanic federation.'

On the Western Front, despite the steady advance of the Allies, German resistance was still strong, and severe fighting was taking place. Douglas

MacArthur remembered the ferocity of the fighting on October 16 in an American battalion of 25 officers and 1450 men, led by a Major Ross. 'Officers fell and sergeants leaped to the command,' MacArthur wrote. 'Companies dwindled to platoons and corporals took over. At the end, Major Ross had only 300 men and 6 officers left.'

That same day, a German company commander wrote in his diary: 'Clouded prospects wherever one looks. Really has everything been in vain? Such a piteous finish.'

In Berlin, a final debate was taking place about whether Germany could go on fighting. Ludendorff, retreating from his earlier conviction that an armistice was essential, produced a plan on October 17 for continuing the war in 1919 by withdrawing into Belgium. But the War Minister, General Scheüch, while offering to provide 600,000 men for any such battle in Belgium, warned that if Germany's oil supply in Roumania was cut off, as it could well be within a few months – if not sooner, given that Bulgaria was out of the war – then Germany could only fight for another six weeks. There would be no way that the war could go on into 1919.

On the day after this discussion, Prince Rupprecht of Bavaria, one of the senior German commanders in the field, wrote to Prince Max that his troops, short of ammunition, artillery support, horses and officers, could not go on much longer. 'We must obtain peace,' Prince Rupprecht urged, 'before the enemy breaks into Germany.' That day, British and Belgian troops succeeded in driving the Germans away from the whole of the Belgian coast, which Germany had controlled since the end of 1914. The Belgian government immediately entered the armistice debate, demanding almost £400 million (the equivalent in 1997 of more than £10,000 million) from Germany as compensation for damage done by the German occupation forces.

On October 17, the German Social Democratic Party issued an appeal against any radical action inside Germany that might jeopardize the 'peaceful revolution' that was already taking place as a result of the constitutional changes agreed to by the Kaiser. But the revolutionary forces were beginning to feel their strength. On October 22, in the hope of lessening the social unrest, the Kaiser granted an amnesty for all political prisoners. Karl Liebknecht was among those released from prison. More than 20,000 people greeted him at the station when he returned to Berlin. 'Three months ago people used to laugh at us when we said there might be a revolution in Germany,' Lenin declared in Moscow.

In Munich, the Bavarian Social Democrat leader Kurt Eisner – a Berlin-born Jewish journalist who had just spent eight and a half months in prison for his antiwar and revolutionary appeals – told a crowd of antiwar protesters: 'If Germany were a republic and Karl Liebknecht president, peace could be concluded within twenty-four hours.'

The Habsburg Empire was disintegrating even more rapidly than the German. On October 23, Croat troops, mutinying behind the lines, seized the port of Fiume, which they wanted as a port in a South Slav state. Two days later, in Budapest, the Hungarian nationalist leader, Count Michael Karolyi, set up a Hungarian National Council, the first stage to the complete separation of Austria and Hungary.

Amid this situation of danger for the Central Powers, and with a new and massive Allied offensive opened on the Italian Front, both Ludendorff and Hindenburg panicked at the thought of the severity of the armistice terms which were likely to be acceptable. Wilson had insisted that Germany put forward terms. It was clear that these would have to be drastic curtailments of Germany's war aims and territorial situation, even from a prewar perspective. The two war leaders therefore decided to throw down the gauntlet of defiance, sending a telegram to every German army commander, warning that the armistice terms would be unworthy of Germany and unacceptable to the army, and ordering each commander to 'fight to the finish'. The front line must be held.

One army commander protested so vigorously when he received this telegram, which quite ignored the desperate military situation on the front, that the telegram was immediately cancelled. But a copy had reached the military garrison in Kovno, where it was read by a wireless operator who was opposed to the continuation of the war and who was also a member of the Independent Socialist Party. He immediately sent the text of the telegram to his Party members in the Reichstag. On October 25 it was published in the German newspapers. Outraged, Prince Max went to see the Kaiser, and told him that either Ludendorff must stand down, or the government would resign.

Ludendorff was able to win impressive support for his desire to 'fight to the finish', including from the Chief of the Naval Staff, Admiral Scheer, the Minister of War, General Scheüch, and Hindenburg. But the Kaiser had been angered that Ludendorff had telegraphed direct to the troops without imperial authority, and told him bluntly: 'Excellency, I must remind you that you are in the presence of your Emperor.'

Ludendorff resigned. Prince Max continued to negotiate with the Allies for an armistice, and the troops of both the Allies and the Central Powers continued to fight, and to die, at the front.

On October 26 the Turks began armistice talks off the island of Mudros. The talks were held on board the British battleship *Agamemnon*, which three and a half year earlier had bombarded the outer forts of the Dardanelles. In Vienna, news of further setbacks on the Italian Front were arriving daily. On October 27 the Emperor Charles telegraphed to the Kaiser: 'My people are neither capable nor willing to continue the war. I have made the unalterable decision to ask for a separate peace and an immediate armistice.'

The will of the Central Powers to fight was collapsing. Germany was the sole remaining active belligerent among them. On October 28, Admiral Scheer, determined to bring the British navy to a decisive battle in the North Sea, ordered the German High Seas Fleet to action. But when the order was given to the ships' crews for their warships to move from their berths in Kiel, they refused to take them out to sea. This, declared Scheer, was mutiny.

The Kiel mutiny was the beginning of German military disobedience on a massive scale. When the leaders of the mutiny were arrested and imprisoned, the sailors tried to free them. There were clashes, and bloodshed. Martial law was declared, but soldiers, sent to crush the naval mutineers, refused to open fire and went over to their side. As a gesture of solidarity with the sailors, the workers in Kiel declared a general strike. The war-making power of the German naval yards was over.

On October 28, Austria-Hungary asked the Allies for an armistice. In Prague, an independent Czech State was proclaimed. On the Piave, Italian troops took 3000 Austrian soldiers prisoner that day; and a further 30,000 in the following forty-eight hours. Two days later the Anglo-Turkish armistice agreement was signed on board the *Agamemnon*. It was to come into force on the following day, October 31. Under the terms of the Turkish armistice the Straits were opened and the Allies took possession of the forts that had helped keep them out in 1915. The Ottoman army was demobilized, and all Turkish railways came under control of the Allies. All German and Austro-Hungarian troops in Turkey were given a month to return home.

Many of the Young Turk leaders, who had brought Turkey into the war on the side of Germany, some of whom were tainted with their part in the Armenian massacres of 1915, fled Constantinople by German torpedo boat to the Crimea, which was then under German control. Later they made their way to different places of exile. But this did not save them from the vengeance of those whom they had so cruelly persecuted. Talaat, a former Minister of the Interior, and the Grand Vizier during the last two years of the war, was assassinated by an Armenian in Rome in 1921. Ahmed Jemal, the former commander of the Turkish forces in Syria, who in exile became the Inspector-General of the Afghan army, was assassinated by two Armenians in Tiflis in 1922, while on his way from Berlin to Kabul. Mehmet Jemal, who during the war had governed the Anatolian province of Konya, was also assassinated by Armenians in 1922, in Berlin. Enver, the best-known and most charismatic of the Young Turks, and wartime Minister of War, was killed in action in 1922 while leading a Muslim cavalry charge against Red Army troops who were then imposing Soviet rule on Uzbekistan.

Under the Turkish armistice, all Turkish relations with the Central Powers were ended. A telegram from Constantinople ordered General Liman von Sanders to hand over his military command to Mustafa Kemal. Turkey in defeat was suddenly free from the controlling hand of Germany.

In Poland there was a feeling that with the disintegration of Austria-Hungary, and the withdrawal of Habsburg authority from Galicia, the independence of Poland must come. Count Alfred Potocki recalled forty-one years later how – 'on a cold black November 1, when the Spanish influenza was taking its toll of life' – he launched a scheme on his Lancut estate whereby he would donate land to war veterans 'on a mutual basis', hoping both to preserve his own estates and to promote the fairer use of the soil:

> The day was made even more memorable because it marked also the beginning of Polish independence. Colonel Maly took over the defence of the district and a Polish authority began to function. There were scenes

of delirious joy throughout Poland. Austrian military emblems were replaced by Polish eagles, and never did our national symbols mean so much.

From this frail platform of independence, we witnessed the collapse of a world. The tides of revolution still beat against our frontiers and even lapped into our land. So near was the menace that I was forced to prepare cellars for the protection of my family and the castle staff and to post guards in the park.

Such were the first days of freedom; but the assurance that the new government would be truly national made it all the more precious. Looking back I can say with the fullest assurance that this prospect, despite the constant clashes of faction, kept our people together in circumstances of dreadful hazard.

In Berlin, Karl Liebknecht and the Spartacists were demanding an immediate end to the war, and the abdication of the Kaiser. 'I wouldn't dream of abandoning the throne because of a few hundred Jews and a thousand workers,' the Kaiser told an emissary from Prince Max on November 1. Liebknecht was not in fact Jewish, though Rosa Luxemburg and some other Spartacist leaders were. On November 2, the Americans launched a new offensive on the Western Front, themselves using mustard gas for the first time, and firing 36,000 gas shells at the German troops facing them.

A British sergeant-major, James Clarke, won the Victoria Cross that day on the Western Front, for 'conspicuous bravery'. His citation states that he 'led his men with great determination and, on being held up by heavy machine-gun fire, rushed forward through a thick, strongly held ridge, captured in succession four machine guns, and single-handed bayoneted the crews.'

The exasperation among those who had become desperate for peace is shown in an account by the poet Rainer Maria Rilke of a meeting in Munich on November 2. The sociologist and political economist Max Weber was among those on the platform, discussing the need for an immediate armistice:

The crowd was so tightly packed that the waitresses 'ate' their way through it like woodworms. One was barely aware of the alcohol and tobacco fumes or human perspiration, because it was so important that the things that mattered could be said.

Suddenly a pale young workman mounted the rostrum and said simply

'Have you, or you, made an armistice offer? Yet *we* ought to do it – not the gentlemen in office. Let us seize a radio station and let us ordinary folk address the ordinary people on the other side – right away there'll be peace.'

As he said this a problem occurred to him, and with a touching gesture in the direction of Max Weber's fellow academics on the platform the young man continued: 'Here these *Herren Professoren*, they know French! They'll know how to say it the way we mean it.'

An attempt by the German High Command to transfer troops from the Eastern to the Western Front on November 2, to meet the new American offensive, was a failure; the troops mutinied rather than go into the war zone. On the following day the Austro-Hungarian armistice was signed; all fighting on the Italian Front also ended that afternoon. From then on, only Germany was at war with the Allies. That day, the Bavarian Social Democrat leader, Kurt Eisner, told a large war-weary crowd in Munich that the peoples of both Bavaria and Austria 'proclaim peace together', and that they did so 'in the name of Germany, since in Berlin there is neither the will nor the power to reach an immediate peace settlement'.

In Berlin, the Reichstag was similarly determined that no further independent naval or military initiatives would take place. On the evening of November 3 two German politicians, the Secretary of State, Haussman, a Liberal, and, Noske, an influential Social Democrat deputy, reached Kiel as representatives of the government and were received with acclamation. Noske was appointed Governor of Kiel, and sailors, soldiers and workers felt confident that they would not be called upon to go into action.

In Berlin, Karl Liebknecht was focusing his energies on the establishment of a Soviet regime. Tens of thousands of workers were demonstrating against the three enemies of Bolshevism: the war, the monarchy and the Reichstag. Friedrich Ebert, the head of the German Social Democrat Party, desperate to avoid having to enter into an agreement of any sort with the Communist forces of Karl Liebknecht, communicated his misgivings by secret telegraphic wire to General Groener, Ludendorff's successor as First Quartermaster-General, who had just arrived in Spa from Kiev. Both Ebert and Groener agreed that the revolutionaries in Berlin must be suppressed. To do this, ten German divisions would have to be moved from the Western Front. Only with such a force could Berlin be cleared of the insurgents.

But there was no way in which ten divisions could be found, and moved.

More and more railway junctions were being seized by revolutionaries. The loyalty of the troops on the Western Front was also in doubt. On November 3, German soldiers in reserve near Metz mutinied, with a whole division of militia refusing to go forward into the war zone.

On November 4 the Allied commanders met to plan an attack into Lorraine in ten days' time. A considerable superiority of tanks and aircraft would be available, as well as troops who were excited at the prospect of being able to move forward into Germany. For the first time, a separate American army would be in action. It too had a sense of purpose that was almost entirely lacking in those against whom it would be fighting. Yet the horrors of war had never succeeded in their entirety, despite four years of agony, in diminishing the zeal for fighting on the part of men in every army for whom victory was still believed to be a prize, and not a chimera.

General Groener had supported Ebert's plan to move ten German divisions to Berlin to crush the insurgents, but the troops refused to move. Groener then spent four days on the Western Front examining the situation in the German lines. As a result of his inspection he recognized that any new Allied offensive was likely to have a catastrophic effect on Germany's ability to remain at war. On November 6 he went to see the Kaiser at Spa, not to advocate a march on Berlin by loyal troops, but to warn the Kaiser in the strongest terms that an armistice must be signed, at the latest, by Saturday November 9. Even waiting until the Monday, Groener said, would be too late.

Revolution was proving the catalyst to surrender. During November 6, as if to underline Groener's fears, the senior German officer in the submarine service, Captain Andreas Michelsen, sent a signal to all U-boats in the Baltic (the signal was read and decoded by British naval intelligence) that they must 'fire without warning on ships with the Red Flag'. The signal continued: 'The whole of Kiel is hostile. Occupy exit from Kiel harbour.' Two further signals followed: 'Use all means to break down resistance', and 'Red Flag is to be treated as enemy.'

On the morning of November 7 a German armistice delegatation, led by the Centre Party leader Matthias Erzberger, who since 1917 had advocated a peace without annexations, assembled in Spa, and then crossed over into

France. Their request that there should be 'a provisional suspension of hostilities' while talks were in progress was rejected by Marshal Foch. An erroneous news report reaching the United States that day that the war was over caused great rejoicing, with Caruso appearing on the balcony of his New York hotel and singing 'The Star-Spangled Banner' to a vast and enthusiastic crowd. In Washington, knowing that the report must be false, Woodrow Wilson refused to show himself to the crowds that were converging on the White House.

In Munich, on the afternoon of November 7, the Social Democrat leader Kurt Eisner led an estimated 50,000 Bavarian workers and soldiers from the centre of the city to the Maximilian II barracks, their banners declaring 'Peace and Freedom' and 'Down with the War'. Eisner was accompanied at the head of the marchers by Ludwig Gandorfer, the blind leader of the radical Peasants' League. The novelist Oskar Maria Graf recalled the scene:

> The silent Eisner was pale and looked deathly serious. It almost seemed as if the sudden turn of events had taken him by surprise. Every now and then he stared ahead half-fearfully and half-disturbed. Next to him the broad-shouldered and sightless Gandorfer paced with a heavy tread. He moved freely, planting his feet firmly on the ground as is the Bavarian peasant's wont.
>
> The crowd entered the barracks, freed arrested men and stripped officers of their arms. Whole units joined it as one man; they smashed windows and broke down guardhouse doors. When the crowd poured into the Maximilian II barracks an officer was drilling a squad on the barrack-square. He hardly had time to turn round before a blow from behind drove his helmet deep down over his ears. He sank down soundlessly. The soldiers, as if under orders, instantaneously threw their rifles on the ground, where they broke with a clattering sound.
>
> The crowd then reversed direction and moved back into Munich. Wherever officers got caught up in the throng they had their epaulettes torn off. None resisted; many were in a state of shock, and some even trailed along behind the demonstrators.

At seven o'clock that evening the War Minister of Bavaria, Philipp Hellingrath, left Munich, to search in vain, at the barracks in Landshut, for Prussian troops to come back with him to the city and to restore order. An hour after his departure, darkness having fallen, the Bavarian royal family left the palace unobtrusively, bringing to an abrupt end 738 years of Wittelsbach rule. Accompanied by his own military guard, Kurt Eisner then entered the Bavarian Diet, placed himself in the Speaker's chair, and proclaimed the establishment of a Bavarian Socialist Republic. Then, to the applause of his supporters, he proposed himself as provisional head of government.

The largest German State after Prussia had succumbed to revolution. As it did so, a member of the monarchist and anti-Semitic Thule Society, Rudolph von Sebottenhof, told his supporters: 'This is a revolution made by a lower race to corrupt Germans. In place of our blood-related princes we are now governed by our mortal enemy: Juda. From now on it must be an eye for an eye and a tooth for a tooth.'

On the morning of November 8 the German armistice negotiators reached the Forest of Compiègne, where the talks were to be held. Marshal Foch told them that there were no Allied proposals to be discussed. All that was required was acceptance by the German delegates of the armistice terms. Hearing the terms, the Germans were shocked at their severity. In arguing for more lenient terms they stressed the danger of Bolshevism not only in Germany but elsewhere in Europe. Foch was unmoved. 'You are suffering from a loser's malady,' he said. 'Western Europe will find the means of defending itself against the danger.'

The German delegates repeated their request for a cease-fire while the armistice terms were being settled. Foch refused. 'Hostilities cannot cease before signing the armistice,' he said. The Germans had seventy-two hours to refuse or to accept. There could be no negotiations about the terms, nor any alteration in the details. The German delegates thereupon accepted the armistice terms 'in principle' and sent a courier back across the lines to obtain approval from the German government.

The Germany that the courier reached was in disarray. In Berlin the Socialist deputies had resigned en bloc from the Reichstag when their call for the Kaiser's resignation was refused. In Cologne, sailors seized the city and ran up the Red Flag. The Bavarian Republic had entered its second day.

During November 8, Prince Max of Baden told the leader of the Social Democrat Party, Friedrich Ebert, that he was prepared to go at once to the Kaiser's headquarters at Spa and, with all the authority of the Chancellor's office, tell the Kaiser that he must abdicate. 'If I succeed in convincing him of it,' Prince Max told Ebert, 'can I count on you to support me against the social revolution?' Ebert replied: 'If the Kaiser does not abdicate there will be no preventing the social revolution any more.'

The Kaiser refused to abdicate. Instead, he told Prince Max that he would return to Germany and lead a victorious army against the forces of revolution. Eleven German cities were flying the Red Flag; he would crush the revolution in all of them. He would defeat the revolutionaries in Munich, Cologne, Kiel and Berlin. Hindenburg would command the imperial forces of law and order.

To the Kaiser's relief, Hindenburg accepted this new challenge, and did so with the same staunch sense of duty with which he had agreed to come out of retirement in 1915 to halt the Russian advance into East Prussia. But General Groener warned both the Kaiser and the Field Marshal that no military operations inside Germany could possibly succeed. Revolutionaries were in control of all the main railway junctions. Aachen, the nearest German city to Spa, only twenty miles away, was in the hands of antiwar and antimonarchist forces. Even to get as far as Aachen was impossible, as the railway junction at Verviers, a Belgian town under German occupation since 1914, was also occupied by the revolutionaries.

The Kaiser was indignant. His first instinct was to lead an immediate military expedition to drive the rebels from Verviers and Aachen. But he then proposed remaining at Spa, letting the armistice be signed at Compiègne, and only after that leading an army into Berlin. It was the pragmatic Groener who informed him bluntly that the army would not obey any such orders: the only marching they would do would be to 'march home in peace'.

In Berlin, the remaining troops loyal to the Kaiser had deserted. Prince Max, hoping to preserve the monarchy by establishing a Regency for the Kaiser's eldest son, announced that the Kaiser had abdicated, and that a Regency was in place. But the Kaiser had not abdicated, and Prince Max resigned. His last act was to hand the Chancellorship to Ebert. It was the morning of November 9. As Ebert took up his duties as Chancellor in the Imperial Chancellery, the Spartacists seized the Imperial Palace in the Unter den Linden, and Karl Liebknecht, speaking from the palace steps, declared the establishment of a German Soviet Republic.

Two embryo governments were struggling for control of Berlin, and of Germany. In his first proclamation as Chancellor, Ebert announced his intention of ruling according to parliamentary procedures, and of forming a Cabinet made up of the various political parties in the Reichstag. Another political leader, Philipp Scheidemann, the head of the Social Democratic Party, in answer to Liebknecht's proclamation of a Soviet Republic, stood on the steps of the Reichstag and proclaimed a Socialist Republic. But Germany was still a monarchy; the Kaiser had not resigned, though his mood was gloomy.

The Kaiser had reason for despondency. That November 9 he was told that even the soldiers at Spa were setting up a Revolutionary Council. One of his visitors that day, Admiral Scheer, who a few days earlier had wanted to lead the German Navy into battle, told the Kaiser that if he were to resign the navy would be without its head. 'I no longer have a navy,' was the Kaiser's comment. Nor did he any longer have the means, or the will, to remain ruler of Germany. That afternoon he decided to resign, and on the following morning, while the German delegates at Compiègne were still discussing the clauses of the armistice, he left Spa for Holland, and for exile.

The Hohenzollern dynasty was at an end, and Germany, which had been so much associated for so many centuries with monarchy and monarchism, with royal tradition, pomp and show, was a republic.

Throughout November 9 and 10 the fighting continued on the battlefield. Hundreds of soldiers were killed during those two days on both sides. On November 10 a Black American division suffered particularly heavy casualties. But Foch was confident that if the Germans refused to sign the armistice terms he could quickly crush their armies. 'The Germans are completely broken,' he said, 'even more completely than I had believed.' In three weeks he could 'beat them on the ground'.

Matthias Erzberger, as the head of the German armistice delegation, was given authority by the new government in Berlin to sign the armistice. At 2.15 in the early hours of November 11 he began one final set of talks with Foch. His aim was to try to get every clause modified in some way. To his surprise, Foch did give ground on a number of points. Fewer machine-guns, aeroplanes and lorries had to be surrendered than in the original demand. The Germans were given thirty-one days rather than twenty-five to evacuate the right bank of the Rhine. Most importantly, Erzberger persuaded Foch to allow German troops in Russia not to be evacuated immediately, as in the original armistice demand, but 'as soon as the Allies, taking into account the international situation of those territories, shall decide that the time for this had come'. Erzberger had successfully played the Bolshevik card: German troops might just protect central Europe from a Soviet onrush.

These final negotiations continued for just over two hours. Then the Germans signed the armistice. As they did so they made a formal protest: 'A nation of seventy millions suffers, but does not die.' The British admiral who was present throughout the three days of talks wrote in his diary that the German delegates were 'very quiet, very servile, and at the end cringing'.

It was half past five on the morning of November 11. The armistice was to come into effect at eleven o'clock that morning. News of the signing was broadcast from the radio transmitter at the Eiffel Tower ten minutes later. When it reached the fighting men, they were ordered to fight on until eleven o'clock. Among the artillery batteries in action that morning was the one commanded by Harry Truman. He was using a new type of shell, with a considerably longer range than the earlier shells of that type. If the war were to go on, this shell would be among several important additions to the war making power of the Allies.

Truman fired his last round at 10.45 a.m. Throughout the length of the front line running from the North Sea to the Swiss Alps, the last shots were being fired, and the last casualties incurred. At two minutes to eleven, at the village of Ville-sur-Haine, a Canadian private, George Price, was killed by a German sniper bullet. He was one of the last casualties of the First World War. At that very moment, further south, in a sector held by the South African Brigade, a German machine gunner, after firing a whole belt of ammunition without pause, was seen by the South African soldiers facing him to stand up beside his gun, bow towards the enemy line, and then walk slowly to the rear. Later that day a British officer, Captain George Eyston, who had been on the Western Front for more than four years, wrote to his mother: 'This is probably the best letter you have received for a long while! No more war! For the present at any rate.'

CHAPTER TWENTY-TWO

ARMISTICE

Those are the conditions of the Armistice. Thus at
eleven o'clock this morning came to an end the
cruellest and most terrible War that has ever scourged
mankind. I hope we may say that thus, this fateful
morning, came to an end all Wars.

DAVID LLOYD GEORGE
House of Commons
11 November 1918

'WHAT'S AN ARMISTICE, MATE?' one British soldier asked another.
'Time to bury the dead,' was the reply. Every area in which the war had
been fought was marked with its cemeteries, every town and village from
which the soldiers came has its memorial. In the summer of 1996 the author
was in the small Slovak village of Skalite. Between 1914 and 1918 it had
been an Austro-Hungarian village. Later it had been part of Czechoslovakia.
During the Second World War, and since 1994, it was in independent
Slovakia. The forty-five family names on its First World War memorial are
the names of the families who live in the village today. Though their national
allegiances have been changed four times since the end of the First World
War, their family identity remains. Skalite's memorial encapsulates suffering
and grief that knows no borders.

There are British, Australian, German and Turkish war graves in the First
World War cemetery in Gaza. There is a list of Italian village youth – often
of groups of brothers – in every Italian hill village. The names of the dead
on the war memorials in universities and schools all attest to the loss of
vital forces in every land, and in every corner of every land. In the main

cemetery in Vienna a plaque records 427 enemy soldiers buried there:

THEY DIED FOR THEIR COUNTRY
AND REST FAR AWAY FROM THEIR BELOVED HOMES IN ETERNAL PEACE,

1 Englishman
Wilson, George Alexander

426 Italians

In 1971, when Queen Elizabeth II visited the British naval war memorial at Cape Helles, there was no Turkish monument on the Gallipoli peninsula. Twenty years later a Turkish monument overlooked the Aegean Sea. On it were carved the words of a speech made in 1934 by Mustafa Kemal (Ataturk). Addressing the Allied 'heroes' who had shed their blood and lost their lives on the peninsula twenty years earlier, he declared:

> You are now lying in the soil of a friendly country. Therefore rest in peace. There is no difference between the Johnnies and the Mehmets to us where they lie side by side here in this country of ours.
>
> You, the mothers, who sent your sons from far away countries, wipe away your tears; your sons are lying now in our bosom and are in peace. After having lost their lives on this land they have become our sons as well.

On all fronts, the machine gun had been one of the most effective weapons of the war. It had mown down line after line of advancing infantrymen. Its devastating power was recognized on the post war memorial to the British Machine Gun Corps at Hyde Park Corner. Below the naked figure of 'The Boy David' – a statue which, at peak traffic times in 1997, was passed by five to six thousand motorists an hour – is the inscription:

> Saul hath slain his thousands
> But David his tens of thousands.

The First World War was over. The bloodletting that had characterized it was to affect several future generations, personally, politically and psychologically. The Allied Powers had lost more than five million men killed in action; the Central Powers lost three and a half million. The largest single death toll was that of Germany, 1,800,000 of whose soldiers were killed. Russia's losses were almost as high, 1,700,000; and Russia had still to face the continuing destruction of civil war. The French war dead were 1,400,000. Austria-Hungary lost 1,300,000 men (including the forty-five war dead of Skalite). Britain and its empire lost 947,000 men in action; Italy 615,000 (including the 426 Italian soldiers buried in the main cemetery in Vienna), Roumania 335,000 and Turkey 325,000. The Bulgarians lost 90,000, the Serbs 55,000, and the United States 48,909 men in action. The total number of men killed in action, whose graves and bones are scattered about the war zones, amounted to more than eight million.

Every nation had civilian as well as military deaths. These civilian deaths were often almost as high as the military ones. In addition to the 335,000 soldiers who had been killed, Roumania lost 275,000 civilians from privation and disease. Also to be counted in the Roumanian wartime death toll were 50,000 of the 117,000 Roumanian soldiers who had been taken prisoner of war, conditions in captivity being severe. These casualties made Roumania all the more determined to exact the highest territorial price possible at the peace table.

One other national group, the Armenians, without a country of their own when the war began, lost two million men, women and children, killed during the war in one of the century's earliest genocides. Their hopes of statehood were high, for their adversary, Turkey, had been defeated; but those hopes were not to be realized.

One other statistic gave cause for reflection: 48,909 American soldiers had been killed in action in 1917 and 1918, but in those same two years, 14,279 Americans had been killed in car accidents in the United States. They have no memorial.

The war widows and orphans in all lands mourned their lost loved ones, and bore the scars of that loss for the rest of their lives, many of them for much if not all of the century. Judge Volney V. Brown Jr wrote, seventy-eight years after the armistice, from California: 'My father, who enlisted in the United States Army on his eighteenth birthday, 22 May 1918, regretted that he missed the fighting. My two older uncles, who saw considerable action on the Western Front, generally refused to speak of it, saying it was too horrible to recall. My dear wife's father died of the effects of mustard gas before she was old enough to remember him.' Judge Brown went on to ask: 'Did the men who died suffer briefly, but the women for decades?'

*　　*　　*

The defeat of Germany not only ended the First World War, but was a major factor in the territorial and psychological changes that followed. The Armistice that was signed on November 11 encapsulated the Allied determination that Germany should be made aware of her wrongdoing, that she should make amends for it, and that she should not be able to renew the war. The terms of the Armistice were designed to ensure this. German troops were to evacuate Belgium and northern France (conquered in the opening weeks of the war), Luxembourg (occupied on the first day of the war) and Alsace-Lorraine (annexed in 1871). All inhabitants of these areas who had been deported to Germany for forced labour would be repatriated. German troops would evacuate all western Germany up to the left bank of the Rhine, which would be occupied by Allied forces. The Allies would also hold three bridgeheads across the Rhine, at Cologne, Coblenz and Mainz. All German troops in Russia would withdraw behind Germany's frontier. All Black Sea ports would be evacuated. All captured Allied merchant ships would be returned. All German submarines would be handed over to the Allies, as well several hundred warships. A vast quantity of war materials, including 25,000 machine guns and 1700 aeroplanes, would be given to the Allies. In addition, Germany would be required to make 'reparation for damage done' in Belgium and northern France.

In the last days of the war, General Pershing had advised that the fighting should go on until the Germans surrendered in the field, unconditionally. He was angered that his advice had not been taken. 'What an enormous difference a few more days would have made,' he remarked. 'What I dread is that Germany doesn't know that she is licked. Had they given us another week, we'd have *taught* them.'

Pershing's fears were not without cause. As General Groener had seen, the Armistice was the way to avoid total defeat in the field, and to avoid the German army being driven back across the border into Germany. At the moment when the Armistice was signed, and the war ended, no Allied soldiers were on German soil, except as prisoners of war. 'Firing has ceased,' one German general told his troops as the Armistice came into effect. 'Undefeated . . . you are terminating the war in enemy country.'

In his hospital bed at Pasewalk, Hitler, recovering from the effects of a British gas shell, also felt that Germany had not really been defeated, and began to cast about for villains and sinister forces inside Germany whom he could blame for having given up the fight.

*　　*　　*

With the signing of the Armistice on 11 November 1918, the war that had begun just over four years earlier was at an end. But at the very moment when, in the summer and autumn of 1918, the last battles of that war were being fought, the influenza epidemic – which had almost caused the German High Command to postpone its July offensive – began to wreak havoc among civilians and soldiers alike.

More United States soldiers died of influenza than were killed in action, adding 62,000 American military victims of disease to the soldiers' roll of honour. A million American soldiers were in Europe when the epidemic broke out. One in fifteen of them died of it. As the war came to an end, it was the spread of influenza that began to make the headlines, and to be a noticeable feature in towns and villages on both sides of the former military divide. On October 15 it was announced that 1500 Berliners had died of the disease.

That October, 2225 Londoners died of 'Spanish 'Flu'. This was more than all the deaths from four years of German Zeppelin and bomber raids over Britain. In Vienna, the Expressionist painter Egon Schiele was among the influenza victims. On the Western Front the Canadian air ace, Captain Quigley, who had shot down thirty-four German planes in combat, was another victim. Of the three thousand Eskimos living on the coast of Labrador, two thousand died of the disease. In South Africa, twenty per cent of the population of Kimberley died. 'The disease swept the country like a grass fire,' a South African reader reported to *The Times*, 'with leaps of hundreds of miles. In some places, within a few days, doctors, chemists, nurses, butchers, bakers and railway staffs were struck down and the complete paralysis of communities resulted as from a stroke.'

In Bombay, a thousand Indians were reported to have died of influenza in one month, and with each month the epidemic intensified throughout the subcontinent. Anzac soldiers, returning from Europe, carried the epidemic to Australia and New Zealand; more than 12,000 Australians died of influenza, despite two compulsory preventative measures, the wearing of face masks and the closing of theatres and cinemas.

On November 9, as negotiations for the Armistice had been taking place at Compiègne, the French poet, Guillaume Apollinaire, died of influenza. In Toronto, on the day chosen by the city fathers to mark the Allied victory, the victory parade itself had to come to a halt, during its triumphant march through the city, to allow a funeral cortege of two victims of influenza to pass.

Reaching Britain in mid December, from a prisoner-of-war camp in Germany, was one of the best known British air heroes, Lieutenant Leefe Robinson. His shooting down in 1916 of a German airship north of London had marked a high point of warmaking enthusiasm, the airship's fiery demise being witnessed by hundreds of onlookers. Later, Leefe Robinson had been shot down behind the German lines in France, and made a prisoner of war. Returning from captivity after the Armistice, he contracted influenza, and died seventeen days after reaching Britain. He was one of 150,000 British civilian and military victims of the disease.

The prisoners of war held by the Allies were not sent home as quickly as the Allied prisoners. Among the 300,000 Austrian prisoners of war being held in camps in Italy, 30,000 died of influenza while still in captivity; the philosopher Ludwig Wittgenstein was among those who were fortunate to return home unscathed. A British army officer, Captain Colin Coote, who hoped to be elected to Parliament in the election of November 1918, recalled reaching a small village in his would-be constituency, intent on encouraging the villagers to vote for him, and finding that every villager was dead.

The influenza deaths accounted, by the time the epidemic had run its course, for more deaths than the war. The worldwide death toll has been estimated at twelve million. Of these, six million died in India, the country where plague had killed a similar number at the turn of the century.

In the remote mountain terrain of Central Albania, the Austro-Hungarian commander, General Pflanzer-Balltin, was unaware that the war had ended. On November 21, ten days after the cease-fire on the Western Front, he took the salute at a march-past of imperial troops. Two days later, in East Africa, General von Lettow-Vorbeck, whose troops had never been caught or defeated in four years of war and wandering, surrendered to the British on British imperial soil, in Northern Rhodesia. During his fighting efforts, a hundred German troops and 3000 Africans had been killed. The British had lost a dozen officers, and 3000 Indian troops in trying to defeat him. Other casualties of that distant war were the African porters, labourers and bearers who had served the fighting men; of these, 20,000 had died, the victims of disease and privation.

On December 1, in Belgrade, a new State was declared, the Kingdom of the Serbs, Croats and Slovenes, later known as Yugoslavia. That same day, British and American troops crossed into Germany, the country they had defeated but on whose soil they had not fought. The occupation of Germany west of the Rhine had begun. So too had the struggle between Social Democracy and Communism in Germany; on December 5 soldiers loyal to the Social Democrat government of Friedrich Ebert opened fire on a Spartacist demonstration in Berlin. Sixteen demonstrators were killed.

In the wreckage of the empires that had so confidently embarked on the war, the political geography of Europe was being changed. In Prague, the new Czechoslovak Republic, born with the collapse of the Habsburg Empire, welcomed its first President, Thomas Masaryk, on December 21. His efforts in the United States during the last months of the war, culminating in the Pittsburgh agreement of 30 June 1918, had ensured American support for what was intended to be a model experiment in national self-determination and parliamentary democracy.

Three days before Masaryk reached Prague amid immense popular enthusiasm, Hitler returned from hospital to his regiment in Munich. What he found on his return was that Bavaria had become a Socialist Republic and that the city of Munich, his prewar home, was under the rule of Kurt Eisner, a Prussian-born Jew. On December 6 a branch of Liebknecht's Spartacists – shortly to be renamed the German Communist Party – had been established in Munich, headed by a Russian-born disciple of Lenin's, Max Levien. His enemies denounced Levien as a Jew, and derided his name as a barely disguised version of Levy or Levine. He was in fact descended from eighteenth-century Huguenot immigrants into Russia by the name of Lavigne. This fact was of no interest to Hitler. 'I thought I could no longer recognize the city,' he recalled seven years later in *Mein Kampf*. The enemy, he wrote, were the 'Hebrew corrupters of the people'. Twelve to fifteen thousand of them ought to be held 'under poison gas', together with all politicians and journalists who had taken part in the Bavarian Communist revolution; the 'jabberers', 'vermin' and 'perjuring criminals of the revolution' who deserved nothing but annihilation. 'All the implements of military power,' Hitler argued, 'should have been ruthlessly used for the extermination of that pestilence.'

CHAPTER TWENTY-THREE

1919

My name is Might-have-been;
I am also called No-more, Too-late, Farewell.

DANTE GABRIEL ROSSETTI

IN MANY LANDS the aftermath of war was a struggle for national unity and social change. It was a struggle that did not allow time for the wounds of war to be healed. In Berlin, a dramatic challenge to the parliamentary and democratic future of Germany came on January 6, when a vast crowd gathered in the capital, calling for revolution. Many of those in the crowd hoped to see the newly established republican institutions pulled down as surely as the centuries-old monarchical ones had been two months earlier, and replaced by a dictatorship of the proletariat of the sort that had established in Russia more than a year earlier. But in her address to the crowd, Rosa Luxemburg, the Polish-born, and Jewish, leader of the forces of the Left urged her Spartacist followers not to seize power. Their movement did not have sufficient popular support, she warned.

Despite her oratory and her arguments, Rosa Luxemburg was unable to dampen the revolutionary ardour of the mob, and the Spartacists seized a number of public buildings in Berlin, raised the Red Flag, and proclaimed the German Soviet Republic.

Despite the earlier fall of the monarchy, to which it had always sworn allegiance, the German army remained loyal to the young republic, even though the republic was as yet without a constitution. Paramilitary right-wing forces were also eager to crush the internal Bolshevik threat. On January 11 the revolutionaries were attacked in the streets of Berlin with artillery and machine-gun fire, and when they tried to escape, they were hunted down. On the following day the *Republik* newspaper wrote: 'Death is raging through Berlin. A socialist government made the giant engines of Prussian militarism fire on socialists who fight and die for an idea. Future historians will point to January 11 as the last result of war madness. It is worse than the insanity of the beginning of the war.'

On January 15 Karl Liebknecht, who had proclaimed the German Soviet two months earlier, was captured and killed. Rosa Luxemburg was also captured and shot. Her body was then thrown into the Landwehr Canal in the centre of the city, within sight and sound of the Zoo. Today a memorial plaque marks the spot. In all, 1200 revolutionaries were killed in Berlin in those January days.

Slowly, the German republic reasserted its authority over the whole country. But in Bavaria the Communists were biding their time for a seizure of power. The threat of provincial civil war came at a dangerous time for Germany, when the Allies were about to assemble, and to discuss the terms of peace. Nine days after the crushing of the revolution in Berlin, the delegates of the victorious powers arrived in Paris for the opening of the Peace Conference. The date chosen, January 18, was deeply offensive to many Germans; it was the anniversary of the day on which, in 1871, the German Empire had been proclaimed. Born with such high hopes of permanence and achievement, that Reich had lasted only forty-four years. Hitler, his mind fuming with its own internal and emotional discontent, was to seek a longer period of time for his Reich – a thousand years.

The opening of the Paris Peace Conference at the Quai d'Orsay highlighted the triumph of the victors and the humiliation of the vanquished. In order to ensure that the German delegates did not have second thoughts about signing the final document, the Allied naval blockade of Germany remained in force, something on which France had been insistent. As the victorious powers prepared to impose their will on those whom they had defeated, the Germans, having elected a National Assembly, were preparing to work out a new constitution. For this purpose the Assembly met on February 6 at Weimar, the town best known as Goethe's home town, and which now gave its name to the Weimar Republic. The main organizer of the move from Berlin was a leading Liberal lawyer, Hugo Pruess, who hoped that Germany would no longer be a Prussian-dominated collection of States, but a unified State with its own focus (within two years the Assembly had moved back to Berlin).

The new constitution which the Weimar Assembly devised, and by which Germany was to be ruled until 1933, guaranteed 'basic personal liberties' and introduced universal suffrage for both men and women over the age of twenty. It also introduced proportional representation, a system which was to give parties with relatively small numbers of voters a place in the Reichstag. The overlapping system of political control – which had been instituted by Bismarck – between the Reich and Prussian governments, was tackled by the creation of separate Reich and Prussian ministries, and a Prussian premiership distinct from the office of Chancellor of the Reich. The retention of Prussia, however, as one of the *Länder*, or States, of Germany, and as an administrative unit with its centre in Berlin, ensured that the conflict between Prussia and the Reich remained.

Prussia had a population the size of France. It included the Ruhr and Silesian coal mines. This made it – even without the coal mines of Upper Silesia, which were transferred to Poland – a much more powerful entity than the largest of its rivals, Bavaria. The Prussian Ministry of the Interior controlled the police in nearly two-thirds of Germany.

The Weimar Constitution confirmed the office of President of the Republic, and maintained the name 'Reich' for the Republic. As in the United States, the President was to be elected directly by the people. He would choose the Chancellor, and he would serve as Commander-in-Chief of the German armed forces. Article 48 of the constitution gave the President absolute power – with the Chancellor's assent – in an emergency, although it was specifically laid down that the Reichstag would be able to annul the President's special action when the emergency was over.

The first President was Friedrich Ebert, who was formally elected on February 11, five days after the Weimar Assembly opened. The first Chancellor, appointed on February 13, was Philipp Scheidemann. It was he who had to watch, powerless, as the victorious powers continued their deliberations in Paris. On February 15 he had also to watch, from afar, as a demonstration of 15,000 Spartacist-Communists in Munich marched under the slogans 'All Power to the Soviets', 'Remember Liebknecht and Luxemburg', 'Long Live Lenin and Trotsky', and 'No politician can forbid the sovereign people to make a revolution'.

As had happened in St Petersburg a year and a half earlier, the Munich Social Democrats and the Munich Soviet met simultaneously. They did so in the same building, the former Bavarian Diet where Kurt Eisner had proclaimed the Bavarian Socialist Republic two months earlier. An attempt by a group of armed soldiers to seize power on February 19 – they succeeded in taking over the main railway station, the post office and police headquarters, but not the Diet building – was brought to an end when Eisner persuaded them to go home. Two days later, while walking to the Diet, Eisner was shot dead by a right-wing aristocrat and army officer, Count Anton von Arco Valley. Shortly before the assassination, the count had written in his diary, about Eisner: 'He is a Jew, he is not German. He betrays the fatherland, therefore . . .' Ironically, Arco Valley was himself of part Jewish descent. This had led to the rejection of his membership application by the anti-Semitic, racist Thule Society, which had for many weeks been circulating leaflets throughout Munich demanding Eisner's death.

As a succession of weak Social Democrat governments sought to rule in Munich, and the Bavarian Communists made their own plans to seize power, revolution broke out in Hungary. Many of the Hungarian Communist leaders, like those hoping to seize power in Bavaria, were Jews. The dominant figure in the Hungarian Communist government was the Commissar for Foreign Affairs, Bela Kun, who had served in the Austro-Hungarian army from 1914. Kun, like Josip Broz (Tito) – the future Yugoslav Communist leader – had been taken prisoner by the Russians and had spent most of the war years as a prisoner of war in Russia, where he became attracted by Bolshevism.

Bela Kun seized power in Hungary on March 22. He and his government hoped to be able to link forces with Lenin and the Red Army in the east, and to serve as the harbingers of Red revolution to Munich and Vienna. They also hoped to regain the Magyar-speaking areas which were to be given to Czechoslovakia and Roumania under the treaties being negotiated in Paris.

As Bela Kun and the Communists consolidated their power in Hungary, instituting a Red Terror against their political opponents, the Bavarian Communists made their bid for power. On April 4, several thousand workers filled the Löwenbräu beer cellar in Munich and called for 'the elimination of the political parties, the arming of the proletariat and the proclamation of a Soviet Republic'. On April 5, at a meeting held in the former palace of the Wittelsbach monarchy, plans were made to proclaim a Bavarian Socialist Republic.

On April 6, as the victorious powers continued their deliberations in Paris about the future of Germany, the First (Anarchist) Bavarian Socialist Republic was proclaimed in Munich. Its head was a Jew from the Polish provinces of Prussia, Ernst Toller, a poet and playwright who had fought on the Western Front until invalided out in 1916, and who, encouraged by Albert Einstein, had sponsored a student peace appeal in 1917. Jews held several ministerial posts in Toller's government – following the Soviet Russian style, they were called Commissars.

Proclamations were sent to all the towns and villages of Bavaria: 'The die is cast, Bavaria is a Soviet Republic, the working people are masters of their fate.' But not every Bavarian town accepted the new government. In Würzburg and Regensburg, after street fighting, Munich's lead was rejected, and a rival Bavarian government was established in Bamberg, in northern Bavaria. It was headed by Johannes Hoffman, a member of Kurt Eisner's former socialist regime. On April 9 Hoffman ordered leaflets to be dropped by air over Munich stating that farmers in northern Bavaria would no longer deliver foodstuffs to Munich. From President Ebert in Berlin came the order to ensure 'the restoration of the former conditions in Bavaria as soon as possible'.

A spate of telegrams to and from Moscow now marked the progress of the Bavarian Communist regime. 'We want peace for ever', the Bavarian Commissar for Foreign Affairs informed his Soviet opposite number on April 10. A telegram from Lenin to the Bavarian Communists asked 'whether the new order is everywhere established'. The head of the newly founded Communist International, Grigory Zinoviev, telegraphed from Moscow: 'We are convinced that the time is not far off when the whole of Germany will be a Soviet republic.'

On April 13 the troops collected by Hoffman bore down on Munich and, after a morning of fighting, arrested most of the Communist leaders at the Wittelsbach Palace. But fighting continued throughout the afternoon and evening, and after twenty of the attackers had been killed in and around the railway station, the Red Flag was raised above its bullet-scarred portals. That evening, in the Hofbräuhaus Beer Cellar, the Second Bavarian Soviet Republic was declared. It was headed by Eugen Leviné, a thirty-eight-year-old Russian-born Jew who had been sent from Berlin by the German Communist Party to restore the Party's fortunes. 'The sun of world revolution has risen, long live world revolution!' Leviné declared that day, Palm Sunday.

Inspired by Russian example, Leviné informed his followers: 'As in Russia, we'll carry the class struggle into the countryside and force the farmers with punitive raids to hand over their milk and grain.' But before any such thing could be done, General Hoffman ordered the anti-Communist forces to converge on Munich. Ernst Toller, the head of the first Bavarian Communist regime, was given charge of the Red forces sent to meet the challenge. A battle was fought just outside Munich, at the town of Dachau, when the Whites (as the anti-Reds were called) were driven off. Hoffmann at once appealed to Ebert for military reinforcements.

The government in Berlin took immediate action. Ebert offered the immediate despatch of twenty thousand troops, as well as his own expert on law and order, Gustav Noske. As a result of his suppression of Communists elsewhere, including Kiel, Noske was known as Iron Gustav. Before Noske and the army could reach Munich, the Communists celebrated the ninth day of the second Bavarian Soviet Republic. Of this Victory Fête Day, the official Communist newspaper wrote:

> No elegant gentleman or well-to-do lady dared show themselves in the streets. It was as if the bourgeoisie of Munich had vanished from the surface of the globe. Only workers – wage slaves – were to be seen – but they were seen with arms.
>
> It was an unprecedented sight: a throng of armed proletarians in uniform or working clothes moving through the Ludwigstrasse in endless columns.
>
> There must have been 12,000 to 15,000 armed men – truly a number designed to inculcate respect for the armed power of the proletariat in the bourgeoisie and their helpmeets. The meeting outside the Palace presented a picture familiar from May Day demonstrations – yet how different was the spirit.
>
> Whereas the Second International had degraded the labour movement to a wage bargaining lobby Munich's Red Day bore the stamp of revolution and of struggle.

From the balcony of the Wittelsbach Palace, the headquarters of the Bavarian Soviet Republic, Eugen Leviné addressed the multitude. He was proud of his, and the revolution's, Russian origins. 'It is the West that has always called the bourgeoisie to revolution,' he said, 'but the proletarian revolution has come from the East. Our sun, our happiness has risen in the East. We thank our Russian brothers who have risen up first and have self-sacrificingly undertaken the task of storming the fortress of capital. We have followed them and others will follow us . . . Join in three cheers for Marat, Danton, Karl Marx, Friedrich Engels and Ferdinand Lassalle, for Lenin and Trotsky, the leaders of the Russian proletariat, for Bela Kun who stands in the van of the Hungarian Revolution, for our immortal leaders Karl Liebknecht and Rosa Luxemburg.'

A Hungarian revolutionary, Kovacs, reaching Vienna that month as the delegate of Bela Kun's regime, declared that Communist Hungary was prepared to feed Vienna 'even if it meant depriving the Hungarian bourgeoisie of their last morsel of bread'. Other Hungarian Communists arrived in the Austrian capital with revolutionary intent, among them two members of Bela Kun's government, Pogany and Böhm, and a man by the name of Steiner, who had in his baggage more than £83,000 in gold, jewellery and valuables. When arrested, Steiner said that the contents of the trunks were 'intended to spread Bolshevist propaganda'.

Revolution looked imminent in Vienna, as local Communists, working with emissaries from Hungary, looked for an opportunity to seize power. At a mass meeting in Vienna of Soldiers' and Danube Sailors' Soviets on April 17, the call was for the union of Austria with Hungary in a single Communist State. Then, on the afternoon of April 18, the Austrian revolution began. Its course was charted by the Vienna correspondent of *The Times*:

> The demonstration was begun by the unemployed, who, after holding a meeting in front of the Rathaus, sent a deputation to the Parliament House to lay their demands before the State Chancellor, Herr Renner.
>
> The demonstrators were joined by other demonstrations of repatriated prisoners and war invalids, and the mob seized a coal-cart and smashed the windows of the Parliament House with lumps of coal, firing also a number of shots against the building.
>
> Herr Renner soon afterwards arrived and told the deputation of unemployed that he could not alone accede to their demands, which were being considered by the Cabinet when he was summoned away.
>
> Meanwhile the crowd had tried to establish barricades against the police in the neighbouring streets, and the police replied by firing. The Parliament House was then occupied by the 2nd Company of the 41st Volkswehr Battalion, which is regarded as particularly stable, being Social-Democratic in character and commanded by Herr Frey, editor of the *Arbeiter Zeitung*.
>
> Subsequently a section of the mob threw matter impregnated with petrol through the broken windows of the Parliament House, and at least two rooms were completely burnt out or badly damaged. From time to time

bursts of firing took place, and the total casualties are estimated at five killed and forty wounded.

The Austrian revolution was at an end. Following its swift and easy suppression, Communist hopes for a territorially contiguous link between Budapest, Vienna and Munich were likewise ended. The days of the Bavarian Soviet Republic were also numbered. Volunteer Freikorps troops, wartime soldiers who had never disbanded, came from neighbouring Württemberg to join the German army troops sent from Berlin, who were commanded by General Ernst von Oven. There were also local anti-Communist militias recruited in northern Bavaria by Johannes Hoffman.

In all 35,000 armed men converged on Munich. Inside the city, the supply of food had ceased, and milk was only given to those who were seriously ill. On April 26 the divisions inside the revolutionary camp were heightened when Ernst Toller attacked both Eugen Leviné and Max Levien with the words: 'These men base their decisions not on our circumstances, but on conformity to the teachings of Russian Bolshevism. Comrades, remember 1789 and its consequences. Reflect how the Great French Revolution was ruined by the Corsican Napoleon. Whenever alien elements take over leadership of a revolution, dictatorship results.' Toller added: 'I favour the dictatorship of the proletariat – but it must be a dictatorship of love and not of hate.'

Leviné and Levien resigned. They were replaced at the helm of the revolution by Toller himself, who immediately offered to open negotiations with Johannes Hoffman's Bavarian government in exile. But the authorities in Berlin insisted that there was only one course open to the Bavarian Soviet Republic – unconditional surrender.

That day, April 26, an attack was launched against the Communist forces stationed in Dachau. The Communists drove their attackers off, helped by several hundred Russian prisoners of war who had been held in a camp at Dachau while awaiting repatriation, and who were invited to join the Bavarian revolutionary army. On the following day twenty unarmed medical orderlies working for the revolutionaries were shot down in cold blood by the White forces. This was followed within a few hours by the execution of eight Red army soldiers who had been cut off from their colleagues near Dachau and were trying to surrender.

On April 27 the revolutionaries retaliated by looking for hostages. One of those for whom they searched was a corporal then stationed at the Munich barracks of the 2nd Bavarian Infantry Regiment, who had a reputation as an anti-Communist orator. This was Adolf Hitler. He was fortunate not to be taken. Brandishing a pistol, he frightened off the three Red guards who came to arrest him. Among the hostages who were taken that day were six members of the racist Thule Society.

In all, sixteen hostages were taken by the Reds. Ten were shot, before Ernst Toller arrived and ordered a halt to the killings. The killings were denounced by the Papal Nuncio to Bavaria, Cardinal Pacelli – later Pope Pius XII – as 'bestial hostage murder'.

From Moscow, Lenin was beginning to wonder if the Bavarian Communist revolution was on the correct path. He knew Munich well, having spent several years in the city as an exile before the war. On April 29 he sent a telegram to Toller seeking enlightenment, and giving guidance: 'Have you,' Lenin asked, '(1) set up workers' councils, (2) disarmed the bourgeoisie and armed workers, (3) confiscated stores of clothing and other supplies, (4) expropriated factories and estates, (5) doubled or trebled the wages of farm labourers and unskilled workers, (6) confiscated all paper and print for the publication of popular leaflets and of mass newspapers, (7) introduced a six-hour working day with an additional two to three hours spent in administrative tasks, (8) compelled the bourgeoisie to give up accommodation to allow workers immediate access to rich apartments, (9) taken over all the banks, (10) taken bourgeois hostages, (11) introduced bigger food rations for workers than bourgeoisie, (12) mobilized all workers for the defence of the council regime and (13) mobilized the adjacent villages through propaganda.'

Only points 1, 2, 6 and 10 had been implemented. Most of the others required more time and control than the regime possessed. Lenin had put his finger on the failures and weaknesses of those who sought to emulate his example.

On May 1 the Second Soviet Republic of Bavaria was still in existence. In Moscow, Lenin told a vast crowd gathered for the May Day celebrations in Red Square: 'Today the liberated working class is celebrating its anniversary freely and openly – not only in Soviet Russia but also in Soviet Hungary and Soviet Bavaria.'

In fact, there were no celebrations in Munich that day, but deep public outrage at the shooting of the ten hostages, and fierce street fighting as the White force moved into the city and attacked Red strongpoints. When a group of Red guards took shelter behind some newspaper kiosks, the kiosks were set on fire by White troops using flame-throwers. When the Reds sought refuge in the Palace of Justice, it was pounded by White artillery fire. Some Red guards, entering the Papal Nunciature, threatened Cardinal Pacelli at pistol point. By nightfall only the railway station was in Red hands; it too fell to the Whites on the following morning.

The White revenge was swift and terrible. Among the 142 Red guard prisoners shot after being captured were fifty-five of the Russian prisoners of war who had joined the battle. Forty-four civilians were also shot. As a Freikorps major explained to his men on May 4, as the search for victims continued: 'Anyone who doesn't yet understand that there is a lot of hard work to be done here, or whose conscience bothers him, had better get out. It is a lot better to kill innocent people than to let one guilty person escape.' The major added: 'You know how to handle the problem: shoot them first and then report that they attacked you or tried to escape!'

Even these pretexts were not always followed. At Pölzing, on May 4, a Freikorps officer arrested twelve workmen whom the local Lutheran priest had described as troublemakers. They were taken into Munich on the following day and shot in the Löwenbräu beer cellar. Also in Munich, Freikorps soldiers shot and killed a young chimney sweep who, following age-old local custom, was going about his business carrying a small red flag.

Nearly a thousand soldiers and civilians were shot in Munich in the aftermath of the defeat of the revolution. Eugen Leviné was captured and brought to trial. In a moment of philosophic reflection he told his accusers, 'Communists are only dead men on leave'. He was found guilty of treason and shot. Max Levien escaped to Austria and eventually made his way to Russia: he was later a victim of one of Stalin's purges.

Johannes Hoffman, returning from Bamberg on May 13, re-established his government. He also instituted a series of trials. Ernst Toller, whose regime Hoffman had both preceded and followed, was sentenced to five years in prison. While in his cell he continued with his writing as a poet and playwright, including a dramatic representation of his own conflicts with Leviné in the final days of the Bavarian Soviet regime. In 1933, at an International writers' conference at Dubrovnik, Toller denounced Hitler's literary delegates face to face. Later, in exile in the United States, he helped those exiles who arrived from the disintegrating Spanish Republic. In May 1939, after Madrid had fallen to General Franco, he hanged himself in a New York hotel.

The poet Rilke escaped punishment for his revolutionary enthusiasm. Having been born in Prague he was able to claim the protection of Czech citizenship. Looking back a year later on the revolution he had seen in Munich at first hand, he wrote, from his home in Switzerland: 'In 1918, in the moment of collapse, Germany could have shamed and moved the world through an act of deep truthfulness and reversal. Then I hoped – for a moment.'

Kurt Eisner's assassin, Count von Arco Valley, was also brought to trial. The public prosecutor expressed his view of the assassin with the words, 'If the whole German youth were imbued with such a glowing enthusiasm we could face the future with confidence.' The count was sentenced to death. The sentence was commuted to life imprisonment, but he was released four years later.

The racist Thule Society resumed its activities, under its Grand Master, Rudolph von Sebottenhof, whose denunciation of the Jews as the 'mortal enemy' of Germany gained a small but steadily increasing following. Among those who was impressed by Sebottenhof was Adolf Hitler, who had been lucky to escape arrest by the Reds and execution as a hostage. Following the crushing of the Bavarian Communist regime, in which individual Jews had played a leading part, Munich and the Thule Society became focal points of racist rhetoric. It was in Munich that the poet Dietrich Eckhart produced a mimeographed magazine *Germany Awake – Perish Juda*.

Sebottenhof put Eckhart in charge of a daily newspaper, *Völkische Beobachter* (The People's Observer), then passed the editorship to a Baltic German architectural student, Alfred Rosenberg. It was among this group that Hitler found like-minded allies, and men whom he could harangue, inspire and lead. One of his earliest supporters, the wartime aviator Hermann Goering, had been born in nearby Rosenheim. Heinrich Himmler was from Munich. A terrible new era was in the offing.

Events in Germany and Hungary stimulated fears throughout the European democracies of extreme Socialism and Communist revolution rampant. But on March 23, the day after Bela Kun had seized power in Hungary, an event took place in Italy that was, in due course, to offer an antidote and an avenue of hope to those for whom Communism was the greatest evil: this was the foundation in Italy of the Fascist movement.

In the immediate aftermath of the war, the appeal of Fascism (*Fascismo*) was largely confined to wartime patriots who were determined that the 'generation of the trenches' – those who had fought at the Front or borne the brunt of wartime privation – should have a predominant say in government. Former soldiers were to be the elite of the movement. Paramilitary groups prepared to use violence against political opponents – against all democrats, but particularly against Socialists and Communists – were part and parcel of the organizational structure from the outset.

A main theme, and appeal, of the Fascist movement in Italy was dissatisfaction with the whole process of parliamentary government, and deep scorn for the constant changing of ministries and ministers which seemed to run in parallel with policies that failed to raise the standard of living of those who felt the State owed them something for their wartime efforts.

The State was itself exalted in Fascist arguments, as a mystical body that would ensure the goodwill of all citizens, and for which all citizens would be prepared to make sacrifices, for the common good. The leader of the State, brought to power by popular acclaim, would be the judge of what benefits the State should produce. Benito Mussolini, the former socialist newspaper editor, and frontline soldier, led the way in denouncing both socialism and 'effete' democracy; it was under his leadership that the newly formed Fascio di Combattimento met in Milan on March 23.

Among the war veterans, former socialists and other anti-democratic malcontents at this meeting were a number of 'assault troops', wearing the blackshirts which were quickly to give the vigilantes their name. One theme of the meeting was that Italy needed colonies just as Britain did, and was being cheated of her legitimate needs by the peace treaties. 'We want our place in the world because it is our right to have it,' that first meeting proclaimed. Those at the meeting pledged themselves to 'sabotaging with every means open to them the candidature of the neutralists of all parties'. The neutralists were those Italians – held up to particular scorn by the Fascists – who had opposed Italy's entry into the war in 1914 and 1915.

On June 21, while the victors of the First World War were still deliberating in Paris, and while Germany was putting the tremors of revolution behind it, Philipp Scheidemann was replaced as German Chancellor by Gustav Bauer. Like Scheidemann, Bauer could only watch helplessly as the victorious Powers, pressed to do so by Woodrow Wilson, first established a League of

Nations and then created 'mandated territories', or Mandates, nominally under the authority of the League, which would be controlled by the victors. These Mandates were carved principally from the German Empire overseas, and also from the Ottoman Empire.

From the German Empire, Britain and France divided Togoland and Cameroon between them. South Africa received its reward for participating in the European war by being given German South West Africa as a Mandate. German East Africa became a British Mandate, known henceforth as Tanganyika (and, after its independence in 1961, when it joined with Zanzibar, as Tanzania). Belgium requested part of German East Africa, but Britain refused to concede any of this vast territory. Instead, Belgium had to accept the small landlocked region of Rwanda-Urundi.

Portugal, like Belgium, had hoped to gain a portion of German East Africa, but was likewise rebuffed by Britain. Portugal's only gain was the small Kionga Triangle in northern Mozambique. Another disappointed victor was Italy. Not only did she see most of her Adriatic aspirations incorporated into the new State of Yugoslavia, but her desire for a free hand in Abyssinia was denied by the other Allies on the grounds that Abyssinia had not been a part of Germany's prewar African empire. There was no way that the Allies could transfer control to one of their number of what had been a neutral and independent State.

In Anatolian Turkey, the heartland of the Ottoman Empire, the victorious Powers asserted their respective control even before a peace treaty was negotiated. On May 15, with the prior approval of the Powers, 20,000 Greek troops landed in Asia Minor, occupied Smyrna, and proceeded into the areas that were to be transferred to Greece. The next day, the Turkish hero of Gallipoli, Mustafa Kemal Pasha, left the capital Constantinople for the eastern Anatolian cities of Sivas and Erzerum. From there, proclaiming a National Movement, he demanded the complete evacuation of Anatolia and Turkey-in-Europe by all foreign powers. These were: the British and French, who had occupied Constantinople and the Straits as part of the terms of the Armistice with Turkey; the Greeks who had marched into western Anatolia; and the Italians, who, hoping to benefit from their secret arrangement with the Allies in 1915, had occupied the southern Anatolian province of Cilicia.

The spirit of nationalism was in conflict with the spirit of victory. 'To the victors the spoils' was an ancient maxim. To back it up was the victors' undoubted military superiority. But nationalism had been a potent force in the road to victory, with Poles, Czechs, Serbs and Greeks determined to assert and to acquire their national aims. Would not the national aspirations of the defeated peoples also have a strength that, even if momentarily eclipsed, could not be fully or forever crushed? General Milne, the British officer in charge of Constantinople (his official title was Commander-in-Chief of the Army of the Black Sea), expressed this feeling when he warned the government in London of the need to evacuate Turkey-in-Europe and return it to the Turks. 'If the decisions of the Peace Conference are so drastic in the treatment of Turkey that the older men, who have the spirit of compromise, are unable to keep the wilder spirits in check,' Milne wrote, 'then it will turn out that the National Movement has prejudiced the military position of the Allies. The population is armed, and now united for the first time; and it is difficult to calculate the force which might be available in the event of a national uprising.'

In the non-Anatolian provinces of Turkey, the parcelling out of Mandates was complete. France acquired Mandates in Lebanon and Syria, including Damascus, which Hussein, Sherif of Mecca, and his sons, had hoped for as part of their reward for launching the Arab revolt. Britain acquired two Mandates, one over Mesopotamia (Iraq) and the other over Palestine. In Iraq, the British installed as ruler Hussein's son Feisal, who had hoped to be ruler in Syria. In eastern Palestine they set up Feisal's brother Abdullah as Emir of Transjordan.

West of the River Jordan, Britain's Palestine Mandate was also the place where, as a result of the Balfour Declaration of 1917, Britain proposed to establish a 'Jewish National Home'. The League of Nations confirmed this arrangement, leaving Britain to work out how to satisfy the conflicting national aspirations of Arabs and Jews. The Arabian provinces of the Ottoman Empire became the independent Arab kingdom of Saudi Arabia. A small annual tribute in gold was paid to Saudi Arabia by Britain to ensure its loyalty.

In the Pacific, the German island groups north of the Equator – the Marianas, Carolines and Marshalls – became Japanese Mandates. Japan also received the German port of Kiaochow, which had been conquered in 1914 largely by Japanese forces. German Samoa became a New Zealand Mandate, while German New Guinea and the Bismarck Archipelago became an Australian Mandate. There was a dispute between Britain, Australia and New Zealand over the phosphate-rich Nauru Island, which each of the three wished to acquire and to exploit; in a compromise which enabled the mining to continue to the benefit of all three, the island became a Mandate of the British Empire.

In Europe, the German Empire suffered less severely than overseas – where every German possession was taken away from her – but nevertheless suffered substantially. Along Germany's western border the two enclaves of Eupen and Malmédy were transferred to Belgium. The Saar was given to the League of Nations until 1935, when a plebiscite would be held for its inhabitants to determine their destiny (they voted to return to Germany). Alsace-Lorraine was returned to France after forty-seven years of German rule. A plebiscite was also ordered for northern Schleswig, which voted to be reunited with Denmark; and for southern Schleswig, which voted to remain in Germany.

The Rhineland remained sovereign German territory, though many Frenchmen had hoped it would become a separate State controlled by France. The one restriction was that no German military forces could be stationed in the area, and no military fortifications could be built. This 'demilitarization' of the Rhineland was not a territorial loss to Germany, but from the outset it was a humiliation and a thorn in the flesh for her; a reminder of defeat, and of France's historic enmity. The Rhineland was twice to become a source of conflict, first during the French occupation in 1923, and again after 1933, when Germany began to build up an army again, but was forbidden to station troops on the Rhineland border with France.

In the east, German territorial losses were much larger. As part of the creation of the new State of Poland, Germany had to give up the 'Polish Corridor' (between East Prussia and Pomerania), and the province of Posen. She had also to accept a plebiscite in Western Upper Silesia (which voted to remain German) and in Eastern Upper Silesia (which voted to become Polish). The most northeasterly region of the German Empire, Memelland, was seized by Lithuania, and annexed. Danzig, an important German prewar port, was put under League of Nations control and made a 'Free City' within the Polish tariff area.

The loss to Germany of these areas amounted to 13 per cent of her prewar territory, and 12 per cent of her prewar population. More importantly for Germany's economic future, the loss constituted 16 per cent of Germany's prewar coal production and 48 per cent of her steel production. There was also a migration of Germans away from the annexed areas. An estimated 200,000 Germans left the Polish provinces for Germany. On July 15 the

Frankfurter Zeitung reported: 'More than seventy-five per cent of the officials of the German Reich and of the Prussian State in the Eastern Marches (and almost a hundred per cent of the higher officials), when asked whether they prefer to leave the territory to be ceded to Poland or enter the Polish civil service, replied that they refuse to enter the Polish service and ask to be transferred to other Prussian provinces. Almost two thousand higher judicial officials in the area which is about to be ceded to Poland have asked for a transfer to other regions, while at this moment only a few hundred judicial positions are available in the whole of Prussia.' The newspaper added that the German position in the areas annexed by Poland could only be 'saved' if every German 'remains at his post'. Twenty years later, those Germans who had remained were to welcome Germany back as the conqueror, and to see the re-annexation of their provinces to Germany.

It was not only territorial losses that marked the defeat of the Central Powers. Twelve countries had increased their gold reserves as a result of their successful wartime trading, in particular the supply of armaments, food, shipping and raw materials. The greatest gainer was the United States, whose gold reserves increased by £278 million. The next most successful war trader was Japan, whose gold reserves increased by £183 million. Spain, which maintained its neutrality throughout the war, gained £84 million. The Argentine, which provided meat and horses to the Allies, gained £49 million. Neutral Holland was able to gain £41 million and neutral Switzerland £12 million. Other neutrals who made smaller monetary gains from the war were Sweden, Norway and Denmark. Two belligerents who also made small gains were Canada and Australia.

By contrast, the principal victors, as well as the vanquished, were saddled with a considerable depletion of their gold reserves. Germany headed the list of the vanquished by losing £123 million. Britain headed the list of the victors with a loss of £42 million. New Zealand was the only belligerent whose gold reserves neither rose nor fell as a result of the war.

As well as gold gains and losses, the victors owed massive sums of money for war supplies purchased on credit. Russia was the largest debtor, owing Britain £757 million. Lenin and Trotsky having announced that they would not honour any of the debts incurred by the Tsar, this money had to be written off. France and Italy both owed Britain almost as much. Each of the European victors owed even more to the United States, Britain's debt being in excess of £800 million and France's £600 million. It was to require considerable ingenuity, and seven years of negotiations, to have these debts settled, mostly by mutual scaling down, and by eventual cancellation.

As a result of the postwar negotiations, the United States cancelled 80 per cent of the Italian debt in 1925, and 60 per cent of the French debt a year later. Even as late as 1965 the British Treasury was allocating 1 per cent of the nation's annual income tax receipts towards the repayment of Britain's First World War debt to the United States.

Nineteen nations owed the United States money as a result of the First World War; of these nineteen, Finland alone had paid its United States debt in full by 1969. The United States' loan to Armenia for relief and reconstruction was cancelled because the Armenian State envisaged by the Allies never came into existence after the war. Belgium was the most fortunate of all the debtor nations. She was able to have its debt to Britain paid back by Germany, under the terms of the Versailles Treaty.

Germany's territorial losses under the Treaty of Versailles were considerable, but the 440 clauses of the Treaty did not just cover territorial changes. They were also physical and economic. Under article 45, exploitation of the coal mines of the Saar basin was transferred to France 'in full and absolute possession', as compensation for the destruction by Germany of the coal mines in northern France, 'and as part payment towards the reparation due from Germany for the damage resulting from the war'.

Under article 156, Germany had to give up all her 'rights, titles and privileges', including coal mining and railway concessions, in China. These were all acquired by Japan, 'free and clear of all charges and cumbrances'. Germany also gave up, mostly to Britain and France, all her pre-1914 treaty rights and commercial concessions in Morocco and Egypt (articles 141–154), in Siam (article 153) and in Liberia (article 138). Article 170 prohibited the importation into Germany of all arms, munitions and war material. Under article 177, no German clubs, even of discharged soldiers, or educational or university association, or shooting or touring clubs, were allowed to occupy themselves 'with any military matters'. In particular, under this article, they were forbidden 'to instruct or exercise their members, or allow them to be instructed or exercised, in the profession or use of arms'.

Germany could neither build nor buy submarines (article 191). Her armed forces could not include any air forces whatsoever (article 198). In the matter of fishing rights and maritime coastal trade, the victorious powers would be given 'most favoured nation' status (article 271).

The most controversial clause of all in the Treaty of Versailles was article 231. This stated that the Allied Powers affirmed, 'and Germany accepts, the responsibility of Germany and her allies for causing all the loss and damage to which the Allied and Associated Governments and their nationals have been subjected as a consequence of the war imposed upon them by the aggression of Germany and her allies.'

This clause became known as the 'war guilt' clause. It was followed by another clause (article 232), which depended upon the war guilt clause, stating that the Allies 'require, and Germany undertakes, that she will make compensation for all the damage done to the civilian population of the Allied and Associated Powers and to their property'. This was the main reparations clause of the Treaty. According to the Treaty, the amount of reparations to be levelled on Germany would be settled by a Reparation Commission, in which Germany should not take 'any part whatever'. Germany further agreed (article 236) 'to the direct application of her economic resources to reparation'.

War guilt and reparation were an integral and central part of the Treaty. To ensure compliance, the Allies would remain in military occupation of the Rhineland, and the three bridgeheads to the east of it, for fifteen years. Until the Germans signed the Treaty, the Allied naval blockade of Germany, preventing the import of any foodstuffs, would remain in force. In his opening speech in Paris, the senior German delegate, Count Brockdorff-Rantzau, spoke bitterly of the reparations clauses and their rationale. 'We are required to admit that we alone are war guilty,' he said. 'Such an admission on my lips would be a lie.' As to the continuing blockade, Brockdorff-Rantzau declared: 'The hundreds of thousands of non-combatants who have perished since November 11 by reason of the blockade were killed with cold deliberation, after our adversaries had conquered and victory been assured them. Think of that when you speak of guilt and punishment.'

This German protest was echoed by a British socialist, Norman Angell, who before the war had warned that war would cripple victor and vanquished alike. He denounced the blockade as a weapon 'against the children, the weak, the sick, the old, the women, the mothers, the decrepit'. The blockade was as wicked, he said, as the German sinking of the *Lusitania* had been. But despite such protests, the blockade continued, and Germans continued to die of hunger as a result of it.

In Paris, Lloyd George resented the strong French pressure to make the terms as harsh as possible. Even as the German delegates were studying the terms, he prepared a memorandum, which he wrote while at Fontainebleau, just south of Paris, on March 25. In it he argued that if the peace terms were too severe, Germany would turn Bolshevik. Were Bolshevism to establish itself in Germany, he warned, Lenin and his Russian Bolsheviks would have the addition to their cause 'of the organizing gift of the most successful organizers of national resources in the world'. Lloyd George had not forgotten Germany's prewar superiority in the technical and industrial spheres, or the warmaking prowess of the German factories; nor did he doubt that if Germany went Bolshevik, she would find the inner resources to reverse the verdict of defeat.

The main thought expressed in the Fontainebleau Memorandum – one of the most important documents to emerge in the immediate aftermath of war – was that the maintenance of peace would depend 'upon there being no causes of exasperation constantly stirring up either the spirit of patriotism, of justice, or of fair play, to achieve redress'. The peace being evolved in Paris, Lloyd George wrote, 'ought to be dictated in the spirit of judges sitting in a cause which does not personally engage their interests or emotions, and not in a spirit of savage vendetta, which is not satisfied without mutilation and the infliction of pain and humiliation.'

Lloyd George felt that the sooner reparations were cancelled, the better. He opposed putting Germans under the rule of others, afraid that by doing so 'we shall strew Europe with Alsace-Lorraines'. He thought it wrong that the German eastern provinces should be transferred to Polish rule, or that Danzig should be separated from Germany. The German people, he wrote, were 'proud, intelligent, with great traditions'. The people under whom they were being placed by the Treaty – which also established the independent States of Poland and Czechoslovakia – were 'races whom they regard as their inferiors, and some of whom, undoubtedly for the time being, merit that designation'. This was very much an Anglo-Saxon viewpoint of the peoples of Eastern Europe; it was not appreciated by either the Gallic French or the Slavic Poles and Czechoslovaks.

With Germany forbidden under article 80 of the Treaty of Versailles to unite with Austria, and with Czechoslovakia containing a large German-speaking minority – not former Germans, but former Austro-Hungarians – Lloyd George's most striking argument in the Fontainebleau Memorandum was this: 'I am strongly averse to transferring more Germans from German rule to the rule of some other nation than can possibly be helped'. And he added: 'I cannot conceive any greater cause of future war than that the German people, who have certainly proved themselves one of the most vigorous and powerful nations in the world, should be surrounded by a number of small States, many of them consisting of people who have never previously set up a stable government for themselves, but each of them containing large masses of Germans clamouring for reunion with their native land,' This, he warned, would bring about 'a new war in eastern Europe'.

The Fontainebleau Memorandum was discussed at Paris on March 26, the day after Lloyd George wrote it. 'If the British are so anxious to appease Germany,' Clemenceau declared, 'they should look overseas, and make colonial, naval or maritime concessions.' Three days later, the German delegates at Versailles submitted their criticisms and proposals. They wanted the victorious Powers to reduce their own armaments and military forces by the same proportion that Germany was being asked to do. They wanted a plebiscite in Alsace-Lorraine, not its transfer to France without consulting the inhabitants. While agreeing to pay reparations, they wanted the war guilt clause struck out of the Treaty, and suggested a neutral judicial or historical enquiry into the responsibility for the war.

Under French pressure, the Allies refused these requests. If it were Germany that had won the war, the Allied reply stated, the German people would have acclaimed their government's wartime policies 'with the same enthusiasm with which they welcomed the outbreak of war. They cannot now pretend, having changed their rulers after the war was lost, that it is justice that they should escape the consequence of their deeds'. This reply made clear that war guilt, and collective guilt, were to be upheld, and were to be enshrined in the Treaty. The victors were too close to their victory, and to the savagery of the fighting, to accept the leniency which Lloyd George had regarded as wise, and for which the German delegates had pleaded.

Every day brought some reminder of the fighting. On May 7, the day on which the German delegates at Versailles received the draft terms of the Treaty, Edith Cavell's body was brought back to England for burial, and for a memorial service eight days later in Westminster Abbey. Her execution by the Germans in Brussels in October 1915 had symbolized for many people in Britain a deep gulf between British and German concepts of warmaking. 'During the passing of Nurse Cavell through London,' *The Times* reported, 'a wonderful stillness rested over the streets which at the midday hour are usually clamorous with sound.' At Edith Cavell's burial in Norwich, *The Times* added, 'the difference was the vast stretch which lies between the utmost horror of war and the completed peace'.

The symbolism of postwar ceremonials was all-pervasive; on May 30, the day after the Germans presented their criticisms of the Treaty, the first of the United States' war cemeteries on the Western Front was dedicated. It contained 1551 named war graves, and a further 974 names carved on the Wall of the Missing. Three weeks later, Germans proved capable of a dramatic counter-symbolism of their own. Anticipating that the German navy would be forced to hand over its warships to the Allies, Vice-Admiral Ludwig von Reuter, the commander of the German ships that had been interned for the previous six months at Scapa Flow, off the northeast coast of Scotland, gave the order on June 21 for the ships to be scuttled.

Von Reuter's order was obeyed. Within a few hours, seventy-four German warships, among them fifteen of the most powerful warships in existence, were at the bottom of the sea. When British troops opened fire on the German sailors, hoping to force them to return to their ships and stop them sinking, eight Germans were killed. Only four ships were towed ashore by the British before they went down. 'The stain of surrender has been wiped from the escutcheon of the German Fleet,' wrote Admiral Scheer. By chance, the sinking of the warships was witnessed by a group of Scottish schoolchildren who were on an excursion on a naval tug. They were thrilled to see what they assumed was a spectacle laid on for their entertainment.

On June 22 the German delegates in Paris were asked to sign all the articles of the Versailles Treaty. They indicated that they would not sign the war guilt clause. As the discussion continued, amid considerable acrimony, news reached the delegates of the scuttling of the German Fleet on the previous day. This strengthened the Allied resolve. The Allied Powers would allow no alterations to the Treaty, they insisted, and would give the Germans only twenty-four hours to sign it. When the German delegates asked for forty-eight hours, this was refused. Lloyd George – the architect of the sympathetic Fontainebleau Memorandum – was the most emphatic of the Allied leaders in Paris that twenty-four hours were enough. The sinking of the ships, he said, was 'a breach of faith'.

*   *   *

The signing of the Versailles Treaty was clearly going to be a heavy burden for any German government to bear. Seeking to avoid this responsibility, the German republican government resigned. The President of the Republic, Friedrich Ebert, refused to accept the government's resignation. He also asked Hindenburg and Groener (who had succeeded Ludendorff as Chief of the German General Staff) if Germany had the military means to defend herself, assuming that, once Germany rejected the Treaty, the Allies were to invade. Hindenburg avoided answering the question by walking out of the room. Groener, who seven months earlier had told the Kaiser that it was hopeless to fight on, said that while the German position in the east was 'reasonable', in the west it was 'hopeless'.

With only four hours before the Allied deadline was due to expire, the German delegates signed the Treaty. They did so, they protested, 'yielding to overwhelming force, but without on that account abandoning its view in regard to the unheard of injustice of the conditions of peace.'

The Treaty of Versailles was signed on June 28. It was followed by the Treaty of St Germain, with Austria, on September 20; the Treaty of Neuilly, with Bulgaria, on November 27; and the Treaty of Trianon, with Hungary, on 4 June 1920. Under the Treaty of Neuilly, Bulgaria had to transfer the province of Thrace, her only outlet on the Aegean Sea, to the Allies, who later gave it to Greece. A strip of land on the Black Sea shore, the South Dobrudja, was transferred to Roumania. Yugoslavia got two tracts of land in Macedonia. Like Germany, Bulgaria was to have no air force, no submarines, and a limited army. Like Germany, she was to pay reparations. She was also to give Yugoslavia 50,000 tons of coal a year for five years.

Under the Treaty of St Germain, with Austria, the once widespread Empire's Austrian-ruled dominions were ceded to the nations for whom the total defeat of Austria-Hungary offered hitherto inconceivable territorial gains. The Austria that signed the Treaty was the small territorial remnant of the heartland of the Habsburg Empire; it consisted of less than eight million people in what had once been a population of twenty-eight million. Also under the Treaty of St Germain, Italy acquired the South Tyrol, Istria, part of Dalmatia, and all Austria's Adriatic islands. Roumania acquired the Austrian province of Bukovina. The Slav regions of the defunct empire – Slovenia, Croatia, much of Dalmatia, and all of Bosnia and Herzegovina – became part of the new State of Yugoslavia (Croatia's status was finalized under the Treaty of Trianon, as Croatia had been a part of Hungary in the Habsburg era).

As a result of the Treaty of St Germain, Poland acquired the former Austrian provinces of Eastern and Western Galicia, including the cities of Cracow and Lvov, and the oil fields of Drohobycz. Czechoslovakia was given the former Austrian provinces of Bohemia and Moravia, and the German-speaking Sudetenland, an area rich in coal and a hive of industry.

Austria was to have no air force, an army of no more than 30,000 men, and was forbidden to unite with Germany. This was despite a unanimous vote by the Provincial Assembly of the German-Austrian Parliament in Vienna in January 1919, declaring German Austria to be a part of the 'German realm'. In the Hungarian half of the empire, under the Treaty of Trianon, Transylvania was transferred to Roumania. The provinces of Slovakia and Ruthenia became a part of Czechoslovakia. Croatia and the Banat region were transferred to Yugoslavia. A small mountainous area in the north of Slovakia was transferred to Poland. Most of the province of Burgenland was transferred to Austria. In this way, Hungary, which lost more than two-thirds of her prewar territory, was truncated and aggrieved.

In June, the Hungarian Communist forces of Bela Kun, who had come to power three months earlier, won several victories against the Czechs, thereby recovering some Magyar-speaking territory in Slovakia. In July, Kun's forces made an attack into Roumania, again with the object of recovering the even larger Magyar-speaking regions there. But the Roumanians quickly drove the invaders back, and on August 1, Kun resigned.

The Roumanian forces continued to advance, entering Budapest three days later. The Roumanians then imposed a severe tribute, including a demand for half Hungary's railway engines and wagons, a third of all Hungary's livestock, and a third of all her agricultural machinery. When the Paris Conference protested, the Roumanians declared that this was reparation for the damage done to Roumania during its occupation by the Central Powers.

While Roumanian forces remained in Budapest, the Archduke Josef – a third cousin of the former Emperor Charles – reached the city with Roumanian support, and took charge of the administration, appointing a Prime Minister and negotiating with the Roumanians. The Czech government protested vigorously to the Paris Conference that the Habsburgs had returned, and on August 24 the Entente Powers announced that they would not recognize any Habsburg in any position of authority in Hungary. The Archduke withdrew. The Roumanians remained in Budapest until November. As soon as they left, a new Hungarian government was set up, dedicated to the elimination of what remained of Communist sympathies of the short-lived Bela Kun era.

The Minister of War (soon to be Regent of Hungary) in the new government, was Admiral Miklos Horthy. He had been the last Commander-in-Chief of the Austro-Hungarian Navy. His action against the officials of the former regime was swift: thirty Hungarian Communists were executed officially; 370 more were sought out by the mob and killed. Most of those killed by the mob, it was noted in a British Foreign Office report in May 1920, were Hungarian Jews. The reason given for their murder was that they had been killed 'for the excesses they had committed when they were in power'.

Whereas the head of the Bavarian Soviet, Kurt Eisner, had been assassinated (shot in the back on his way to the Parliament building in Munich), Bela Kun managed to escape from Budapest after the Hungarian revolution had been suppressed. Reaching Vienna, he was interned in a lunatic asylum. Later, the Allies allowed him to go to Russia, with Churchill telling the British Cabinet: 'A few additional serpents in that nest will make no appreciable difference to its poisonous character. They can bite each other if they like.'[1]

Many Hungarian Jews had participated in the Communist experiment in the hope of creating an egalitarian society, and held no brief for terror. One of these, Michael Polanyi, held a junior position in one of the cultural ministries. Fleeing to Germany after the collapse of the Bela Kun regime to avoid the White Terror, and leaving Germany for Britain in 1933 because he was a Jew, he became a distinguished chemist, philosopher and humanist. It was from him that I learned of the savagery of the conflicts in Budapest during the struggles between Red and White, and of the horrors that can ensue when a nation turns against itself.

Even as the Covenant of the League of Nations was being negotiated in Paris in 1919, with the aim of providing for the prevention of war by collective action, fighting and wars continued. The most serious point of conflict was in Russia, where Russian Bolsheviks were being surrounded by 300,000

---

[1] In Moscow, Bela Kun became a leading figure in the Communist International (the Comintern). In due course, like many western Communists who had found refuge in the Soviet Union, he was imprisoned, and in 1936 executed on Stalin's orders. Today, a plaque on the former Comintern building in Moscow records his sojourn there.

anti-Bolshevik-Russian forces, the Whites, led by former Tsarist generals.[1] Fighting alongside the Whites were more than 180,000 Allied troops: British, French, American, Serbian, Czech, Greek, Italian, Finnish, Polish, Korean and Japanese. There were times in 1919 when it looked as though the days of Bolshevik power in Russia were numbered, as the forces of the intervention pressed in upon Moscow and Petrograd, and the democratic, liberal monarchical and reactionary hopes of millions of Russians struggled against the Communist one-party state and its instruments of terror and repression, swelling the ranks of the White armies.

One object of Allied policy, strongly supported by Lloyd George, was to help maintain the newly won independence of the former Baltic and Caucasus provinces of the Tsarist Empire. The German army, in occupation of these regions since the Treaty of Brest Litovsk, had only just been withdrawn as a result of Germany's defeat in the west. But Lloyd George opposed any British initiative to make war on the Bolsheviks, whose army was at least 300,000 strong, and growing. He did not oppose, however, some help for the anti-Bolshevik forces, something for which his colleague Winston Churchill, then Secretary of State for War, was pressing hard, but he wanted the anti-Bolshevik Russians to do their own fighting. 'For Russia to emancipate herself from Bolshevism would be a redemption,' Lloyd George told the Imperial War Cabinet in London on the last day of 1918, 'but the attempt to emancipate her by foreign armies might prove a disaster to Europe as well as to Russia. The one thing to spread Bolshevism was to try to suppress it.' In addition, Lloyd George warned, 'to send our soldiers to shoot down the Bolsheviks would be to create Bolsheviks here. The best thing was to let Bolshevism fall by itself and act as a deterrent to the world.'

Each of the former Allies gave military support to the anti-Bolshevik armies, and rejoiced when the Bolsheviks were pushed deeper and deeper back into Russia. 'What sort of a Peace (!) would it be,' Churchill wrote to the British generals in North Russia in mid January 1919, 'if all Europe and Asia from Warsaw to Vladivostok were under the sway of Lenin?' Churchill's view that the Allies must give the fullest possible support to

---

[1] 'Whites' was the name by which the anti-Bolshevik Russians (Denikin, Kolchak, Wrangel, Yudenich etc) were known, as a shorthand and colour differential with the Russian Bolshevik 'Reds'. These Russian 'Whites' have no connection with White Russia (in Soviet times the Soviet Socialist Republic of Byelorussia, and now the independent State of Belarus), a region, the principal city of which is Minsk, with its own dialect and sense of nationality.

the Russian anti-Bolsheviks was expressed in mid February at Paris (where the Peace Conference was in session) as well as by Clemenceau, and by the Italian Prime Minister, Baron Sonino.

By mid February there were more than half a million anti-Bolshevik Russians under arms. In South Russia, General Denikin was advancing northwards from the North Caucasus and the Ukraine, with Cossack support, hoping to reach Moscow. In the west, General Yudenich was securing control of the Baltic region. In Siberia, Admiral Kolchak was pressing in on the Russian heartland from the east. Between the Urals and the Caspian Sea, along the Ural River, Cossack forces were pressing towards the River Volga.

Just as the anti-Bolshevik forces gathered momentum, in a dramatic reversal of policy the Allied nations decided not to support them. In Britain, Lloyd George feared a backlash, recognizing that people were weary of war, and that soldiers who had so recently returned from the Western Front were not willing to contemplate being sent to another, and to such a distant, war zone. He therefore persuaded the British Cabinet to withdraw all British troops from Archangel and Murmansk, Siberia and the Caucasus.

In France, the Under-Secretary of State for War, Léon Abrami, who had served on the Salonika Front in 1916–17, told the Chamber of Deputies, about the French contingent in North Russia, that 'not another single man would be sent to the aid of this small force'. Clemenceau, though not happy about the withdrawal, agreed that it was necessary because the French troops in Russia were 'tired, both physically and morally'. Some extra French troops were sent out, but, as was also true of the British troops who were sent out to Russia that spring, their instructions were quite specific: they were to help expedite the withdrawal of the whole force.

On April 5 the last French troops sailed from Odessa. They took with them 30,000 Russian civilians and 10,000 anti-Bolshevik Russian soldiers. Among the Russians who remained was a one-year-old girl, Lilia Podkaminer, who was later told by her mother that when the Bolsheviks first reached the city 'they came into my room and took from me my bread, my shoes and my doll'. She and her mother eventually made their way to Yugoslavia, part of the massive Russian exodus that was to see as many as 100,000 Russian refugees in camps, first in Turkey, then on the Dalmatian coast of Yugoslavia, and later dispersed throughout Western Europe. Meanwhile, secret efforts had been started to open negotiations with Lenin. At the end of February,

Woodrow Wilson had sent a young American diplomat, William C. Bullitt, to Moscow, to hold direct talks with the Bolshevik leaders.

In March, Bullitt talked for five days with Lenin and his two senior foreign policy advisers, Chicherin and Litvinov. In April he brought back several Bolshevik peace proposals for both Lloyd George and Woodrow Wilson to consider. But these two leaders, while no longer willing to commit their own forces to the anti-Bolshevik battle that was raging on all the borders of Russia, were not prepared to welcome the Bolsheviks as negotiating partners. They were fearful that Poland, and even Germany, might, by devious means, be won over to the Bolshevik cause.

The Allies, having participated in the active war against Bolshevism, were turning to the concept of a *cordon sanitaire* of countries around Russia, to prevent Bolshevism spreading outside its existing Russian confines. The idea of such a cordon made the idea of an American Mandate over Armenia an attractive one, to protect the southern flank of Allied interests. It also made Winston Churchill press, in April, for an Allied programme of feeding the Germans and ending the privations of the blockade. Churchill setting out his Russian policy in three terse phrases: 'Feed Germany; fight Bolshevism; make Germany fight Bolshevism.' He was angered a few days later when he learned that the half million Russian prisoners of war still in camps in Germany were to be repatriated to Russia, writing to his military advisers: 'Whereas we could have made out of these an army of loyal men who would have been available to sustain the defences of Archangel and Murmansk or to aid General Denikin or Kolchak, we are now I presume simply sending a reinforcement of 500,000 trained men to join the armies of Lenin and Trotsky. This appears to me to be one of the capital blunders in the history of the world.'

During 1919, Denikin's army, with Cossack support, advanced through the northern Caucasus and southern Russia. Kolchak's army reached Kazan, on the Volga, 200 miles east of Moscow. In the north, anti-Bolshevik troops won control of the whole Archangel region down to the northern shore of Lake Onega. From the west, General Yudenich came to within artillery-striking distance of Petrograd.

The anti-Bolshevik forces were not united, however, either in terms of leadership or policy. Some anti-Bolsheviks wanted to set up a constituent assembly, based on a democratic franchise, and to continue the work of agrarian reform which had been begun by the Provisional Government after the revolution of February 1917. This was very much the advice reaching them from the Allies. Others wanted to restore the monarchy. Some wanted to recognize the independence of Poland and Finland; others did not. The future independence of the former Baltic and Caucasian provinces of Russia was also a cause of disagreement among the various advancing armies, and of acrimonious disputes with the Allies. Denikin was implacably opposed to allowing the Caucasian nationalities to gain their independence. Yet the British Foreign Secretary, A. J. Balfour, had made the independence of Georgia a definite British pledge at the Paris Peace Conference. After General Yudenich had liberated all of Estonia and most of Latvia from Bolshevik control, it was by no means certain that he would agree to their independence.

These matters would only be put to the test if the anti-Bolshevik armies could defeat the Bolsheviks. This was the dominant question throughout the summer and autumn of 1919. Yet the weakness of the various Russian anti-Bolshevik armies, whether singly or collectively, was apparent at each stage of their advance. Kolchak's forces had been weakened considerably in the summer when a Ukrainian regiment under his command mutinied, and murdered all its officers. Nor would Kolchak agree to an Allied demand – on which depended the despatch to him of Allied war materials – that he convene a Constituent Assembly when he reached Moscow, or that he give assurances that Baltic and Finnish dependence would be preserved.

In July, there was a mutiny by anti-Bolshevik forces on the Onega front, where a regiment of Russian troops fighting against the Bolsheviks handed over their section of the line to the Bolshevik forces facing them. This gravely isolated the British troops who were fighting alongside them. The fate of the British in North Russia was sealed, and their withdrawal made inevitable, when the other principal Allied force on that front, an Italian force, was withdrawn on orders from Rome. The last seven hundred American troops in North Russia left a week later. On the day after the Americans left, the British withdrawal, which had been set for mid October, was brought forward. The anti-Bolshevik Russians were on their own, in part due to the anti-democratic and imperial intentions which many of them espoused. The anti-Jewish excesses perpetrated by some of the White forces had also antagonized the British and French governments. As many as 100,000 Jews were murdered during 1918 and 1919 in southern Russia and the Ukraine. Denikin's army was particularly notorious in this respect, as were the troops of the anti-Bolshevik Cossack leader, Simon Petliura. Two other anti-Bolshevik military leaders, the anarchist Nestor Makhno and the Cossack Ataman Gregoriev, were also rampaging against Jews.

Fearful though they were of the spread of Bolshevism to the west, the Allies had no desire to see the Russian Empire restored, with its social and national inequalities. Indeed, they were confident that, with the Bolshevik regimes in Hungary and Germany suppressed, they could keep Russian Bolshevism at bay.

There was also a growing admiration among the working class in Western Europe at Bolshevik tenacity. In Britain, the senior civil servant at the Ministry of Labour, Sir David Shackleton, told the War Cabinet at the end of June that the labour unrest then prevalent in Britain was being exacerbated by the British intervention in Russia. He had been surprised, he said, not just at working-class reactions, but 'at the extent to which men of all classes were now coming round to supporting the Labour view that the Soviet Government ought to be given a fair chance'.

A British naval blockade in the Gulf of Finland effectively prevented any food or supplies reaching Petrograd by sea. Two hundred British warships maintained this blockade; seventeen of them were sunk by the fledgling Red Navy. In a spectacular act of daring, a British naval officer, Lieutenant Agar, in command of a coastal motor torpedo boat, penetrated the Bolshevik naval defences outside Kronstadt and torpedoed a 6600-ton Bolshevik cruiser. For this act he was awarded the Victoria Cross, the highest British military decoration. But the balance of opinion in the British Cabinet was that such actions no longer served a purpose. 'If the Allies had decided to defeat Bolshevism,' Lloyd George told his colleagues at the end of July, 'great armies would have been required.'

The Russian anti-Bolshevik armies fought on, with dwindling material support from the Allies, and with no more Allied troops fighting actively at their side. In August a British officer, General Rawlinson, was sent to extract the British troops from North Russia. He wrote in his diary about the anti-Bolshevik Russians: 'Their troops won't fight alone and their officers are hopeless.' After meeting the Commander-in-Chief of the North Russian Army, General Evgeny Miller, Rawlinson wrote in his diary: 'The trouble with the White Russians is that they have no real leaders of character and determination.' The Bolsheviks, on the other hand, 'know what they want, and are working hard to get it.'

As the withdrawal of British troops from North Russia continued, more than a thousand Finnish troops were also evacuated, as were 262 Chinese labourers, forty-three Korean troops, and a thousand Russian civilians. On October 5 another British general, Edmund Ironside, and the last British soldiers to be evacuated from Archangel, reached Liverpool on board the steamship *Czaritza*, 'a forlorn reminder', one historian has written, 'of the crumbling empire they left behind them'. On arrival they found that all trains had halted; Britain was in the grip of a national railway strike. A special train was organized to bring the general and his staff officers to London. One of them, Colin Gubbins, recalled reaching London with 'some lovely furs'.

In all, the British brought 17,000 Russian civilians away with them in their evacuations from North and South Russia during 1919 and 1920. By 1923, as many as two million Russians were living in exile, their flight accelerated by the Red Terror, under which at least ten thousand anti-Bolshevik Russians were executed. Among the main countries of refuge were France, which took in almost a quarter of a million Russians; and Poland, China, Germany and the United States, which took in 100,000 each.

Having decided to leave the anti-Bolsheviks to their own devices, the Allies turned down a request, made in September by the Polish Prime Minister, Ignacy Paderewski, to authorize and also finance an advance of half a million Polish troops on Moscow. It was Denikin's military successes that month that made it seem that the Bolsheviks might be overthrown. On September 20 he entered Kursk, only 300 miles south of Moscow, and continued to advance rapidly, capturing 7500 Bolshevik soldiers. 'The Bolsheviks are falling,' Churchill wrote to a Cabinet colleague on October 5, 'and perhaps the end is not distant.'

On paper, the omens for the anti-Bolsheviks were good, even without direct Allied intervention. By October, a total Bolshevik force of 460,000 was facing 630,000 Whites. A British diplomat in Odessa, John Bagge, wrote of the Bolsheviks in early October: 'They may pass like a heap of snow melts under a hot sun, leaving behind only the dirt which it had gathered.' But Lenin and Trotsky controlled the interior lines, much as the Germans and Austro-Hungarians had done two years earlier; troops and supplies could be moved by rail to whatever sector of the front was in most urgent need of them.

By the first week of October, Denikin's control in southern Russia and the Ukraine contained an area inhabited by 35 million people, as well as the main food- and fuel-producing regions of Russia. On the front facing his advancing armies, the Whites outnumbered the Reds by two to one.

Other than Moscow and Petrograd, Denikin controlled all the main cities of Russia, including Kiev, Kharkov, Odessa and Rostov-on-Don. As he advanced, fifty British pilots and cavalrymen advanced with him. These were volunteers who had been allowed by the British government, as a final gesture of support to the anti-Bolshevik Russians, to help Denikin organize his aircraft and his troops. One of these Englishmen, Lieutenant Charles Roberts, later recalled how, as Denikin's troops entered Orel, only 250 miles south of Moscow, 'we were deciding which horses we should ride during the triumphal entry into Moscow'.

In northwestern Russia, General Yudenich's troops reached Luga, less than forty miles from Petrograd, on October 13. Four hundred Russian officers, who had been under training in Britain, were put on board ship for Reval, to join his army. Also on the ship, destined for Yudenich, were British tanks, aeroplanes and artillery pieces, and rifles and equipment sufficient for a force of 20,000 men. British naval units were operating on Yudenich's flank in the Gulf of Finland. On the Siberian Front, Admiral Kolchak, having been driven back several hundred miles to the east, was again advancing to the Volga.

In Moscow, the Soviet leaders discussed how to meet the accumulated, and urgent challenge. On October 15 the Politburo, the inner Cabinet of the Central Committee of the Communist Party, decided, in the words of its official minutes, 'to bring about the actual conversion of Soviet Russia into a military camp'. All able-bodied men, and even men whose physical disabilities would earlier have exempted them from the army, were called up to serve. The Moscow military district was reorganized, and allocated stocks of food, fodder and straw so that it could, in an emergency, exist as an independent military entity, cut off from the rest of the country. Trotsky was sent to Petrograd to prepare for a similar siege there.

As Denikin's troops approached the outskirts of Tula, less than a hundred miles south of Moscow, the British government agreed to send him surplus British munitions and supplies to the value of £17,500,000. But Denikin was vexed, that month, by British support for the independence of Georgia, Azerbaijan, and Trans-Caucasian Armenia, where a British diplomat, John Wardrop (who had been Consul General in Moscow at the time of the November revolution), was active in the cause of Caucasian independence from Russia. Denikin wanted these regions within his own Greater Russian patrimony.

Suddenly the seemingly unstoppable anti-Bolshevik Russians were plunged into disarray. On October 11 the Ukrainian anarchist leader, Nestor Makhno, turned his peasant army against Denikin, seeking to carve out a substantial southern Russian region for himself, and attacking Denikin's forces. That day Makhno seized the port of Berdiansk, on the Sea of Azov, then entered port after port, seizing munitions and supplies. A week later, several Cossack units at Orenburg, upon whom Denikin was dependent for his control of the Orenburg region, transferred their allegiance to the Bolsheviks. Lenin at once granted them an amnesty, and redrafted them into the Red Army. That same day, news reached Denikin that the tribesmen of Daghestan had risen against his overlordship, forcing him, at a crucial moment, to divert 15,000 troops to the south.

This accumulation of travails hit Denikin when Yudenich was only twelve miles from Petrograd. On October 19, as Yudenich was poised to assault the defences of the city, a British general was selected in London to be sent to Russia posthaste 'for the entry into Petrograd'. That night Trotsky, who had just reached Petrograd, ordered the first Bolshevik counterattack. He was unable, however, to prevent the continuing advance of Yudenich's forces, who, by the evening of October 21, were holding the heights of Pulkovo, overlooking Petrograd. Driving eastward, Yudenich then reached to within two miles of the Moscow–Petrograd railway.

It was a decisive moment in the history of the twentieth century. The future of Bolshevism hung in the balance. As Yudenich prepared to cut Moscow off from Petrograd, the anarchist leader Nestor Makhno seized two railway junctions in the south on which Denikin was dependent for all military supplies coming up from the Black Sea. As Makhno disrupted Denikin's communications in the rear, even threatening to overrun his headquarters at Taganrog, on the Sea of Azov, the Red Army launched its own counterattack against Denikin. The anti-Bolshevik hopes of reaching Moscow were dashed. The Orenburg Cossacks, the Ukrainian anarchists, and the Daghestanis had, by acting against Denikin at the same time, and in his rear, made his task impossible.

Lenin made every effort to ensure that Yudenich was likewise beaten back. On October 22 he instructed Trotsky: 'It is *damnably* important for us to finish off Yudenich (just that – finish him off: despatch him).' To ensure a successful offensive, Lenin asked Trotsky: 'Cannot 20,000 or so Petrograd workers be mobilized, plus 10,000 or so of the bourgeoisie, machine guns to be posted to the rear of them, a few hundred shot, and a real mass assault on Yudenich assured?'

As Trotsky prepared to take Lenin's advice, Lenin opened negotiations with the Estonian government. Welcoming a chance of making peace, the Estonians agreed not to give Yudenich any further support, in return for having their sovereignty accepted by the Soviets. The Soviets also agreed that all Tsarist property in Estonia would be made over to the Estonian Republic.

Trotsky launched a counterattack on Yudenich on October 23, driving the anti-Bolshevik Russians from the Pulkovo Heights. That same day, Finnish troops, advancing along the railway towards Petrograd from the north, were driven back. In the south, Makhno and his anarchists continued to disrupt Denikin's lines of communications. Bolshevik partisans were also being organized to strike at Denikin's supply lines and stores. On October 26, Lenin appealed to the Don Cossacks to abandon Denikin, and to fight against him. A Don Cossack military leader, Philip Mironov, who had been a general in the Tsarist army, and had earlier been captured by the Bolsheviks, agreed to lead his troop of 5000 men against Denikin, in return for a military command in the Red Army. Other Don Cossack leaders did the same.

In Siberia, Kolchak began to move back from Omsk to Irkutsk, a retreat of 1500 miles. On the northwest front, Yudenich was in retreat, a British naval bombardment of Bolshevik coastal positions having failed to help him. In South Russia, Denikin pulled back eighty miles. Lenin, a master of pragmatic diplomacy, then authorized secret talks with the Poles, hoping to secure their neutrality; on November 14 the Politburo authorized a full military truce with Poland. That day Yudenich and his forces reached Estonia. In accordance with the Soviet-Estonian Agreement concluded two weeks earlier, Yudenich's men were immediately interned, disarmed and disbanded.

The anti-Bolshevik Russians, in retreat on all fronts, found their international support evaporating. On November 21 the French government decided to cut off all military and financial aid. Within two weeks, the Poles, having agreed to a military truce with the Bolsheviks, advanced against Denikin in Western Russia and Eastern Galicia, acquiring substantial territory which they hoped would become part of a greater Poland. Clemenceau and Lloyd George, meeting in London on December 12, came to the conclusion 'that a strong Poland was in the interests of the Entente Powers'. They also agreed that the Poles could retain the former Austro-Hungarian province of Eastern Galicia, which Polish troops had conquered from Denikin. The Allied decision was that Eastern Galicia, with its capital, Lvov, should be an autonomous region under the protection of

Poland for twenty-five years (after which it would be at the 'disposal' of the League of Nations).

A *cordon sanitaire*, of which Poland would be an important part, would clearly be more effective than the anti-Bolshevik Russians in stemming the westward advance of Lenin's creed and power. As if to underscore that conclusion, on the day of Clemenceau's meeting with Lloyd George the Bolsheviks drove Denikin from Kharkov. Four days later, the Red Army entered Kiev. Within two weeks the Whites were in total retreat and disarray.

The year 1919 had been dominated by peacemaking in the West and Bolshevism in the East. It was also the year in which kings and emperors had given way to republican presidents. One king, however, enhanced his powers and his kingdom as a result of the war, the King of Serbia, whose sovereign control now extended to the Austrian and Italian borders in the north, and along the Adriatic coast. Even the Serbian claim to incorporate Montenegro – a nation which, with its own sovereign, King Nicholas, had been overrun by the Austrians during the war – was upheld by the Allies, the ultimate arbiters of so many boundaries and sovereignties. The French government felt particularly strongly that Montenegro should be absorbed in Yugoslavia, giving the new kingdom a further Adriatic coastline. Serbian troops accelerated the outcome by occupying Montenegro, and on April 20 King Nicholas was deposed.

The fate of Austria gave concern to those among the victorious Powers who had felt a close affinity with Austria-Hungary before the war; and also to those who still feared Red revolution in Europe. Yet the disintegration of Austria seemed to be unending. In autumn 1919 the Austrian province of the Vorarlberg announced that it had decided to detach itself from the rule of Vienna, and to seek union with Switzerland. It formed its own parliament, elected a Prime Minister (Dr Ender) and held a plebiscite on its future sovereignty. Of just over 55,000 voters, more than 45,000 voted for union with Switzerland. The Swiss government was sympathetic to this unexpected possible acquisition of new territory, but the Paris Peace Conference insisted that the integrity of Austria, which had just been established under the Treaty of St Germain, must be upheld.

Austria's territorial integrity was preserved, but hunger stalked the streets of Vienna. At one point the bread ration was reduced to a quarter of a pound per week per person. The Allies immediately organized such relief as could be sent in from new Austria's neighbours. Among the foods brought in to Vienna were eggs from Poland and meat from Yugoslavia. By the end of the year, even hungry Germany was helping to feed its former ally, with a reduction being ordered in the German bread ration so that almost 2000 tons of bread a week could be sent to Austria. When the German Field Marshal, August von Mackensen, passed through Vienna by train, he was thanked at the railway station by the Austrian Minister of War (ironically, Herr Deutsch) for Germany's assistance. During the brief ceremony, the large crowd gathered on the platform and sang the German anthem *Deutschland über Alles*.

Before the war, most of Vienna's food had been imported from Hungary. With the separation and impoverishment of Hungary, this was no longer possible. The break-up of the Habsburg dominions had left the many retired civil servants of the empire without their Habsburg state pensions. The substantial imperial civil service was likewise disbanded, leaving many wage-earners without jobs. The pleas for help on behalf of the starving Viennese, and in particular on behalf of the children of the city, also roused a considerable response in both the United States and Britain. These appeals would prove a forerunner of famine appeals that were to become more widespread and more urgent in the years to come, crossing the barriers of former enmities.

One territorial change that caused alarm, but also some ridicule, among the victors, was the seizure of the port of Fiume by a small private army led by the Italian poet and wartime aviator, Gabriele D'Annunzio. Fiume, a port on the Adriatic that had been Hungary's outlet to the sea in the Habsburg times, had been allocated by the Allies to the new State of Yugoslavia. But the port was claimed by Italy, to which it had been promised by the secret Treaty of London in 1915.

Not satisfied with seizing Fiume, in November D'Annunzio and his army appeared in the port of Zara. There was alarm in Belgrade that this was part of a scheme to deprive Yugoslavia of all its Adriatic ports. To the relief of the Yugoslavs, D'Annunzio's attempt on Zara was rejected by the Italian government, and he withdrew.

*   *   *

Unrest during 1919 took diverse forms. In March, a national uprising broke out in Egypt. Townsmen, peasants and Bedouin joined forces, attacking British property and individuals. There was rioting in Cairo. Europeans were attacked throughout the country. In one incident, eight British soldiers were killed on a train. General Allenby, the conqueror of Jerusalem a year and a half earlier, was sent to restore order. In a successful attempt to defuse Egyptian anger, he brought back from exile four Egyptian nationalist leaders whose deportation had been the spark that started the riots.

In April, passive resistance in India to British police measures against political protests led to violence in many parts of the subcontinent. This violence provoked the Government of India into passing the Anarchical and Revolutionary Crimes Act, known – by the name of its author, Sir Sidney Rowlatt – as the Rowlatt Act. Gandhi protested against the act, which effectively suspended all civil liberties in peacetime. Civil liberties had already been suspended during the war under the Defence of India Act, 1915. Basing himself on the success of his prewar activities in South Africa on behalf of the Indians there, Gandhi launched an All-India Satyagraha – literally, 'truth-force'. It was to prove the central method of the Indian struggle for political power.

Satyagraha was a peaceful protest. It involved fasting, boycotting British manufactured goods, strikes, demonstrations, and the deliberate courting of arrest. At its centre was the *hartal*, a day given up to closing all shops and stopping all work. It was non-violent. But not all Gandhi's followers were prepared to remain passive in their acts of disobedience. One group, the Ghadrites, resorted almost at once to terrorist actions, which Gandhi denounced. His protests were ignored. Railways were attacked and telephone and telegraph wires cut. To the alarm of the British administration, Hindu and Muslim protesters joined forces, in an almost unprecedented alliance. In Ahmedabad, in the Bombay Presidency, police opened fire on protesters and twenty-eight were killed.

Violence flared throughout the Punjab. It looked for a while as if British control over the province was lost. British lives were everywhere endangered. Several bank managers and officials were murdered. At Amritsar, a British missionary, Frances Sherwood, was attacked and injured; as a collective punishment, the British officer commanding the troops in the town, General Dyer, ordered all Indians passing the spot on which she had been attacked to crawl on their hands and knees. Indians protested at what the British government itself later described as 'racial humiliation'. On April 13, shortly after issuing the 'crawling order', General Dyer was confronted by a large crowd of Indian demonstrators in the confined space of the Jallianwalla Bagh. Determined, in his own words, 'to teach a moral lesson to the Punjab', he ordered his troops to open fire. The Indians in the Bagh were virtually unarmed; a few had staves. Dyer's Indian troops opened fire with machine guns and rifles.

In less than ten minutes, 379 Indians were killed, and more than a thousand injured. In the subsequent British government enquiry, Dyer was condemned, and relieved of his military command. In upholding the condemnation of the massacre, and of Dyer, Churchill – then Secretary of State for War – told the House of Commons that it was essential to make a general prohibition 'against what is called "frightfulness"', and he went on to explain: 'What I mean by frightfulness is the inflicting of great slaughter or massacre upon a particular crowd of people, with the intention of terrorizing not merely the rest of the crowd, but the whole district or the whole country.' Churchill continued: 'Our reign in India has never stood on the basis of physical force alone, and it would be fatal to the British Empire if we were to try to base ourselves only upon it.'

The bitterness inside India at what became known as the Amritsar Massacre was a strong factor in the growing Indian desire to see an end to British rule. But Gandhi had been so shocked at the way in which his non-violent Satyagraha campaign had been perverted by those of his followers who had threatened British lives that he called the campaign a 'Himalayan blunder', called it off, and fasted for three days 'as a penance'.

On the North West Frontier of India, the assassination of the Amir of Afghanistan, Habibullah, who had pursued a peaceful policy towards Britain, was followed by a concerted Afghan attack through the Khyber Pass by his son Amanullah, and much looting and pillaging. British forces launched a counterattack, using warplanes to bomb Afghan military positions in both Jellalabad and Kabul. When peace was signed on August 8, the Afghans lost their right to import arms and munitions from India, and had to accept the British line of the frontier.

The Chinese government, angered that the Paris Peace Conference had supported Japanese claims to take over all German commercial concessions on the Chinese coast, had withdrawn its delegates from Paris and refused to sign the Treaty of Versailles. Inside China, there was a nationwide boycott of Japanese goods. That August, Chinese troops entered Mongolia to drive out both Bolshevik and Cossack troops who were seeking to impose Russian authority on the country, which in Tsarist times had been a Russian sphere of influence. By the end of the year, Chinese suzerainty over Mongolia was established, yet another alteration of the boundaries drawn on the global map.

In Ireland, the efforts of the nationalists to secure independence from Britain were persistent, as were the efforts by the British government to resist the dictates of force and terror. Seventy-six Irish constituencies had returned nationalist Sinn Fein candidates to the British parliament in the British general election at the end of 1918. On 15 January 1919 they met in Dublin and decided to boycott the British parliament. They would sit, instead, in a parliament of their own creation in Dublin.

Throughout Ireland, nationalist gunmen attacked British policemen and official property. Three days after the act of defiance by the Sinn Fein Members of Parliament, the British government sent tanks, armoured cars and machine guns to prevent further violence. Sinn Fein responded by appealing for volunteers to enlarge its own military force, the Irish Republican Army (IRA). It also established an alternative government to British rule, with Cabinet ministers, including a Finance Minister, Michael Collins (the former Adjutant-General of the IRA) who took charge of raising money for the nationalist cause. Another leading nationalist, Eamon de Valera, the one leader of the Easter 1916 uprising who had not been executed (because he was an American citizen) was made President of the republican government, and went to the United States where he raised £1 million for an Irish National Loan. Britain and the Irish nationalists were on a collision course. Sympathy for the nationalist cause was strong among Irish Americans (and was to remain so for the rest of the century). The Protestants of Ulster, who had twenty-four Members of Parliament in the British House of Commons, announced their loyalty to Britain.

On September 7 a British soldier was shot dead in the predominantly Catholic town of Fermoy. On the following day a crowd of nearly two hundred soldiers, incensed by the death of their colleague, rampaged through the streets of Fermoy, smashing windows and looting shops. On September 10 the Lord Lieutenant of Ireland, Lord French (who had been Commander-in-Chief of the British Expeditionary Force in France in 1914), outlawed Sinn Fein in several of the southern Irish counties. Two days later he banned the Sinn Fein parliament, and suppressed all newspapers favourable to the Sinn Fein cause. In December several bombs were thrown at his car, but he escaped unhurt.

By the end of 1919, eighteen policemen and soldiers had been murdered by the nationalists. Britain was determined, however, not to make any political concession through force or terror. The Republicans were equally determined to end British rule altogether.

The violence of Irish nationalism, with its aim of the independence of one people, was confined to Ireland. The violence of Bolshevism, with its call for world revolution, was universal. In Buenos Aires, following the declaration of a general strike in January 1919, Communist revolutionaries, inspired and led by several Russian immigrants in the city, attempted to set up a Bolshevik regime. For three days the city was in their hands. Then, on January 11, the army, loyal to the government, was turned against the revolutionaries, and, after considerable bloodshed, the revolution was suppressed. The Russian ringleaders of the insurrection were interned in warships anchored in the harbour. As in Munich, Vienna, Budapest and Berlin, the revolution had been crushed.

In Switzerland, a general strike was declared in Basel at the beginning of August. It was followed by a confrontation between strikers and soldiers which gave hope in Moscow that a Bolshevik insurrection was imminent. When the strike spread to Zurich that hope was intensified. But public support for the strikers, which was never widespread, was weakened further because the first day of the strike action, August 1, was a Swiss national holiday. On the following day *The Times* reported:

It seems likely that what is evidently intended to be a revolutionary movement, promoted by Bolshevist elements who are attempting to create local troubles in various centres with the object of eventually linking them up and thus engineering a revolution throughout Switzerland, will prove stillborn.

The Government has taken energetic action, and a large number of troops were mobilized today, including cavalry, infantry, machine-gun corps, engineers, and the staff of the Fourth Division. Armoured cars are patrolling the streets in the affected areas.

Six people are at present reported to have been killed and several wounded at Basel. The printers have struck, the only paper continuing publication at Basel is the *Vorwärts*, but the Zurich printers have decided not to join the strike.

Three days later *The Times* was able to report the defeat of this Swiss attempt at Red revolution:

> The Bolshevist movement originating at Basel and Zurich is not receiving any support, and is now on the high road to failure, thanks to the strong action taken by the Government in promptly mobilizing troops, drawn chiefly from the peasant classes, and the occupation of the affected areas.
>
> The movement has caused the greatest indignation among the peasants, who form the backbone of the State, and this is increased since they were called up for service at a time when the crops were being harvested. All, therefore, are determined, if necessary, to deal severely with rioters.
>
> At Basel order has been maintained since the troops' occupation; the shops have re-opened and the public services are again active. Demonstrations and public meetings, in conformity with military orders, have ceased. In certain trades a strong tendency is manifested in favour of resuming work. The Basel *Vorwärts* is suspended and its office occupied by troops.
>
> The decision taken by the Workers' Union of Berne against joining the strike has produced a strong impression at Zurich, especially among the leaders of the extreme Left, who reckoned on the support of the workers here.
>
> A proclamation issued by the Commandant at Zurich forbids public meetings and warns the population, in case of insults or disturbances, that the troops are authorized to use their arms. The Zurich tramway employees have been informed that unless they immediately resume work they will be permanently dismissed and replaced temporarily by students.

The Swiss revolution was over. Switzerland had been spared the fate of Russia.

The Treaties of Versailles, Neuilly and Trianon changed almost every European boundary. They created nation States from three of the national movements that had seen their opportunities in the disintegration of the empires of the Central Powers: Poles, Czechs and South Slavs. They also created the hope that if any of the new States of Europe should be in danger, the borders established by the Treaties would be protected. It came therefore as a shock when, in August, within the United States Senate, there was considerable opposition to the Treaty of Versailles, and the possibility of a vote against it before the end of the year.

The main cause of the opposition was political. The Republicans were determined to show Wilson that he did not have the political power he craved, and that the Democrats could not determine United States policy. Wilson's Democrats were outnumbered by Republicans in the Senate by forty-seven to forty-nine. A Presidential Election was only a year away. The Republicans wanted to make clear to the nation that Wilson was not fit to be President, that he could not impose on Congress a measure that did not, so they alleged, take into account the needs of the United States, but, rather, would commit the United States to unending overseas entanglements.

Two Democrat Senators, Thomas Gore of Oklahoma and David Walsh of Massachusetts, were also opposed strongly to the Treaty. They asserted, as did many Republicans, that Wilson had not been able to prevent the ambitions of the victorious Powers from imposing unfair territorial and economic conditions on the defeated. American Liberals felt so strongly that the Treaty was unjust, particularly with regard to German reparations, that the *New Republic* republished, as a special supplement, the strongest of all the British criticisms of the Treaty, *The Economic Consequences of the Peace* by J. M. Keynes.

There were Senators on both sides of the political divide who were angry that Wilson had failed to secure self-determination for Ireland, something to which Britain had been implacably opposed. Italian-Americans resented Wilson's failure to secure the Adriatic port Fiume for Italy. German-Americans, who were numerous in several States, strongly opposed the Treaty. Both the Italian-Americans and the German-Americans were able to put considerable pressure on their Senators.

As opposition to the Treaty mounted, Wilson was presented with a possible way forward for Senatorial acceptance. A series of amendments were proposed to take into account the less extreme Senate objections, and to win over the middle ground. But Wilson refused to consider them, hoping that if there were deadlock in the Senate, sufficient waverers would come over to his side for the Treaty to pass unamended. It was a tactical error. One amendment, which might have won over half a dozen Senators with large numbers of Irish constituents, was that Ireland should 'speedily achieve a government of her own choice' and be admitted to membership of the League of Nations. Quite how the Treaty-makers in Paris would have taken this amendment is not clear; presumably they would have ignored it.

When it became clear that he could not win over a majority of the Senate, Wilson decided to appeal direct to the American people. On September 3 he left Washington by train, and in the next twenty-two days delivered forty-two speeches. Then, on September 26, while his train was at Wichita, Kansas, he collapsed with a stroke, and was forced to return to Washington. There, he faced further criticism: his attempt to appeal to the people direct had angered the Republican Senators, while his incapacity as a result of his stroke led them to question even more strongly his ability to govern. The vote on the Treaty took place only three weeks after Wilson's stroke.

The Senate vote of November 19 was a blow to those inside the United States who wished to see their country contribute to the recovery of Europe. Thirty-nine Senators voted for the resolution, fifty-five against. 'The crowded galleries sat in tense silence as the roll was called,' reported the *New York Times*. 'A murmur swept through them as the vote was announced.' The vote was particularly distressing to those Europeans who looked to America's enormous strength as a world power to serve as a counterbalance to those within Europe who might seek to disturb the peace.

During the negotiations in Paris, the Allies had been keen to establish an independent Armenia, which would be located between the Bolshevik-controlled Caucasus and the British and French Mandates in Syria and Iraq. One proposal made, with British and French support, was that Armenia should become a United States Mandate. Wilson had been attracted to the scheme, but the United States withdrew from the League of Nations before she could take up her responsibilities, and Turkey remained in control of the Armenian regions that had been allocated to the United States.

As well as Armenia, the proposed United States Mandate was to have included the Bosphorus and the Dardanelles, linking the Black Sea with the Aegean Sea, and would have included Constantinople and the Gallipoli peninsula, as well as a strip of Turkey-in-Asia along the Black Sea coast. Britain wanted this section of America's Mandate to be extended more than two hundred miles along the Black Sea shore. All this was swept away by the Senate's rejection of the Treaty.

CHAPTER TWENTY-FOUR

1920

IT WAS ON 10 JANUARY 1920, only eight weeks after the United States Senate rejected the Treaty of Versailles, that the Treaty came into force. That same day, as part of the Treaty, the League of Nations came into existence. The brainchild of Woodrow Wilson, it had lost its American patron as a result of the Senate vote. Henceforth the League was a predominantly European organization.

The importance of the League of Nations lay first in the ameliorative aspects of its Covenant. The twenty-six articles of the Covenant provided for collective consultation, arbitration and 'the acceptance of obligations not to resort to war', as well as agreements to curb the arms trade, to secure the 'just treatment' of native peoples, to combat the drug and white slave trade traffic, and to provide for the international prevention and control of disease. Of central importance was clause 16, which provided for collective action in the event of unprovoked aggression.

It was through the Covenant of the League of Nations that the Treaty of Versailles, and the other treaties, would be enforced, and that the future aggression of any of the defeated powers, or indeed of any of the victorious powers, would be prevented. Even with the unexpected withdrawal of the United States from everything connected with the Treaty, the League and the League Covenant, the early achievements of the new international body were impressive. Danzig was established as a Free City. The borders of the Saar, whose future was to be decided by plebiscite, were demarcated. A dispute between Sweden and Finland over the Aaland Islands, which at one moment seemed to threaten war between the two countries, was brought to the League Council and resolved. When actual hostilities broke out between Poland and Lithuania, over the sovereignty of the city of Vilna, the League intervened and hostilities were suspended; a referendum was then agreed upon by both sides, and neutral troops were sent to keep the peace during the referendum campaign.

It was the League Council that, following instructions in the Treaty of Versailles, carried out a detailed investigation in Eupen and Malmédy before adjudicating their transfer from Germany to Belgium. In the sphere of health, the League organized steps to reduce the spread of typhus fever in Eastern Europe. It also undertook to facilitate the considerable task of the return of Russian prisoners of war in Europe, and of German and Austro-Hungarian prisoners of war in Russia. By the time of the first meeting of the League of Nations Assembly in Geneva on November 15 there was a sense of achievement. The organization was committed to preventing wars by negotiation, to resolving disputes between nations by arbitration, and to easing the lives of all humanity. It was an ambitious task; it also seemed, that November, to be an attainable one.

At the opening of the first session, forty-two signatories of the Versailles Treaty and thirteen neutrals were present, and also China, but not the United States. In his opening address the President of Switzerland, Dr Giuseppe Motta, told the delegates: 'America should take its place in the League. The more universal the League becomes, the more its help and impartiality will be guaranteed. The victors will not for ever be able to dictate, and the collaboration of the vanquished is a vital necessity. Hate is a curse; the people are great by their generosity and repentance.'

At the first session of the League Assembly, it was agreed that all powers should undertake to limit their arms expenditure. The search for arms reduction was to become a major element of the League's activities during the next decade. One of the first fruits of the new policy was the French decision to reduce the period of national military service from two years to eighteen months.

The former Allies, however, had not disbanded their alliance. In order to secure compliance with the Treaties, they had set themselves up as a Supreme Allied Council (also known as the Supreme Council of the Allies, and, in its shorter form, as the Supreme Council). This body, on which Britain and France were the leading members, and Italy among the most active ones, met on a regular basis throughout 1920, 1921 and 1922. The United States, the Supreme Council's natural leader in many ways, had withdrawn from its deliberations, just as it had withdrawn from the League of Nations.

It was the Supreme Council that possessed the military strength which the League did not, and which threatened to use its power on a number of occasions, most dramatically when Yugoslav troops entered the Carinthian region (of which Klagenfurt is the principal town) immediately after the plebiscite there had determined, by a large majority, that the region would be part of Austria, not of Yugoslavia. The Supreme Council ordered Yugoslavia to withdraw its troops, or face an Allied expedition. The Yugoslavs complied, and Carinthia remains a part of Austria to this day.

To the League of Nations were handed every type of European problem and dispute. Thus it was the League that facilitated the transfer to Switzerland of the links (such as posts and telegraphs) hitherto maintained by the principality of Liechtenstein with the defunct Austria-Hungary. When, in December 1920, Liechtenstein applied to join the League, the League Assembly decided that she was too small a country to be given independent representation, and would be represented by Switzerland.

The republican government which had come to power in Germany following the abdication of the Kaiser had survived a year, suppressing the Spartacists, and pursuing a Socialist policy. The President since February 1919, Friedrich Ebert, was a leading Socialist. The Chancellor since the summer of 1919 was one of the leaders of the majority Socialist Party, Gustav Bauer. The Conservative Party, encouraged by its right-wing elements, contemplated the overthrow of the government, and was encouraged in its hopes by Dr Wolfgang Kapp. A former President of East Prussia, Kapp found support for his schemes from a senior army general, Baron von Lüttwitz, as well as support from another army commander, General Maercker.

On March 13 Dr Kapp made his move. Supported by a regiment of German marines, German soldiers who had earlier volunteered to fight against the national movements in the Baltic (the Freikorps) marched towards Berlin from their base at Döberitz. Realizing that the generals had betrayed the Republic, Ebert and Bauer fled from Berlin to Dresden. A few hours later Kapp entered Berlin, issued a proclamation declaring that the Ebert–Bauer administration had ceased to exist, and made himself the acting Chancellor. That day, the imperial colours – black, white and red – which had been abolished after the abdication of the Kaiser, were flown over Berlin. Emissaries were also sent to the Kaiser at his place of exile in Holland. There were fears among supporters of the Republic that the monarchy would be restored, socialism suppressed, and Prussian militarism again dominate Germany.

In Dresden, Ebert and Bauer, supported by the Minister of War, Gustav Noske – who had helped to crush the Bavarian Communist regime a year earlier – appealed to the working class throughout Germany to launch an immediate general strike. 'We refuse to bend before military compulsion,' they declared. 'We did not make this revolution in order to have again to recognize militarism. We will not cooperate with the criminals from the Baltic States. We should be ashamed of ourselves, did we act otherwise. A thousand times, No! Cease work! Stifle the opportunity of this military dictatorship! Fight with all the means at your command to retain the Republic. Put all differences of opinion aside. Only one means exists against the return of Wilhelm II. That is the cessation of all means of communication. No hand may be moved. No proletarian may assist the dictator. Strike along the whole line.'

In Berlin, the general strike brought the life of the capital to a halt. To ensure their own safety, Ebert and Bauer moved from Dresden to Stuttgart. The general strike continued for four days, making it impossible for Kapp to govern, nor did he have enough troops to take over any more cities. In Munich, Thomas Mann, who was then finishing his novel *The Magic Mountain*, welcomed what seemed to him to be the break-up of Germany into its pre-1870 component parts. 'The Berlin government seems unable to hold on much longer,' he wrote in his diary. 'Hindenburg trying to mediate, have Ebert and Kapp enter into negotiations, Lüttwitz withdraw his troops from Berlin. Both impossible. In Munich, the Landtag in permanent session. It is vacillating between Kahr and Wintersten as heads of the government. If it is the latter, the Socialists will take part. Evidently the situation is less critical here than in Prussia. But all these developments strengthen the possibility of secession. The disintegration of the Reich is unavoidable, and is a necessary step towards the realization of a Greater Germany. The French would be freed from their nightmare, understanding would be possible at last, a new peace concluded with the individual German States, and the Versailles provisions cast aside. German-speaking Austria and the Tyrol to be annexed to Southern Germany. Prussia to develop independently, in line with her own character and taste. The "Reich" will once more be an idea, a dream, a hope. Possibilities for a greater imperial Germany relegated to the background until some future date.'

That 'future date' was less than twenty years away. Meanwhile, the struggle between separatism and the centre was reaching its climax in both Berlin and Munich. On March 17, in Munich, von Kahr formed a new Bavarian government, with the Socialists excluded, and the restoration of the Bavarian monarchy on his agenda. That same day, in Berlin, Kapp resigned. The general strike had made it impossible for him to rule from Berlin. On the following day, in Stuttgart, Ebert and Bauer called a session of the National Assembly.

As members of the government returned to Berlin on March 18, Kapp's troops, including the Baltic Freikorps, left the capital. As the last units were passing the Brandenburg Gate a large crowd of onlookers followed them, mocking them with abusive catcalls. Suddenly Kapp's soldiers turned towards the crowd and opened fire. Many of the crowd were killed or wounded.

As the right-wing putsch was being frustrated by the general strike, the Spartacists sought to revive their fortunes by using the strike to their advantage. In the East End of Berlin, in the predominantly working-class area, a number of local Soviets were established, and a Communist leader, Daunig, declared himself President of a new German Communist Republic. Bauer's government at once called off the strike, and ordered the workers to return to work, but the Spartacists urged the workers to remain on strike, and continued its bid for power.

Communist governments – Soviets – were declared in several towns in western Prussia, in Bavaria and Württemberg, in Leipzig and in the Ruhr. To try to intimidate the revolutionaries in Leipzig, the government sent aircraft to fly over the city. One by one, the Soviets and the strikes were suppressed by the army, which remained loyal to the government, and obeyed the orders of Noske's successor as Minister of War, Otto Gessler. The one area to which the government's military power did not extend war was the Ruhr, Germany's industrial heartland, which lay within the area of Germany which had been demilitarized by the Treaty of Versailles, and in which Germany was not allowed to station troops.

The German government sought permission from the Allies to send troops into the Ruhr to crush the revolution there. The British, Italian and American governments were in favour of allowing German troops to take action; the French government refused. The revolutionaries, having seized control of Essen and Wesel in the Ruhr, proclaimed the 'union' of 'Red' Germany with Bolshevik Russia. In an attempt to discredit the revolutionaries in German eyes, the government in Berlin pointed out that several of the leaders of the Spartacist revolt were Russians or Russian Jews.

Fearing a repetition of January 1919, and without waiting for Allied approval, on 3 April 1920 the German government, under a new Chancellor, Hermann Müller, sent German troops into the Ruhr. After losing more than a hundred soldiers in action, they succeeded in crushing the Spartacists and in capturing the revolutionary headquarters at Mülheim on April 4. The French, incensed at this unilateral German action – which was technically a violation of the Treaty of Versailles – and without consulting the British or Italian governments, ordered French troops, as a 'penalty' for the German movement into the Ruhr, to enter the neutral zone further south. Frankfurt-am-Main, Darmstadt and Hanau were occupied by the French on April 6, and Homburg on the following day. There was intensified anger inside Germany because many of the French troops were black African soldiers from Senegal, and particular indignation that they were stationed on the campus of Frankfurt University.

After a few days of tense Anglo-French negotiations, during which the French refused a British request to invite the German government to the discussions, the French agreed to withdraw their Senegalese troops, and to act in future only with the agreement of their Allies. Meanwhile, the German troops had crushed the insurrection and withdrawn; the French troops then also withdrew.

Negotiations then began at Spa, in Belgium, the Kaiser's former military headquarters, between Germany and the Allies (meeting as the Supreme Allied Council), to proceed with the disarmament and reparations clauses of the Versailles Treaty. The percentages of reparations payments had been agreed among the Allied Powers according to the estimated scale of their losses, based upon the destruction or confiscation by Germany of their industry, shipping and natural resources. France was to receive 52 per cent of the total sum, the British Empire 22 per cent, Italy 10 per cent, Belgium 8 per cent and Serbia 5 per cent.

The Germans complied with the reparations and disarmament demands made upon them at Spa. Two million tons of coal a month were to be delivered from German coal mines to France. Four thousand heavy guns and field guns were to be destroyed. All former German soldiers were to hand in their rifles. The standing German army was to be reduced from 200,000 to 100,000. Vast quantities of livestock were also to be handed over, to France and Belgium, including 36,000 horses, 132,000 cattle and 135,000 sheep. These were part of the material price of defeat. The psychological price was to be much higher, and much less easily accounted for.

Once the disarmament clauses of the Versailles Treaty were being enforced, Germany could no longer wage war, except within its own borders, and in defence of the German Republic. Poland and Russia were under no such restraints. The year 1920 was to see a massive confrontation between these two powers, its outcome uncertain until the last, and the fate of many other nations hanging again in the balance. The issue was the survival of Bolshevism in Russia, and its ability, when triumphant, to spread its terrors and its ideals westward, towards the turmoil that was Germany.

With the collapse of the anti-Bolshevik forces in northwestern and southern Russia, the Poles hastened to fill the breach before the Bolsheviks could do so. On January 4 the Polish army captured Dvinsk. On the following day, further south, they seized Zhitomir, one of the towns evacuated by Denikin, and struck swiftly in the direction of Kiev, the capital of the Ukraine, which was then under Bolshevik control.

The Bolsheviks, unnerved, offered to negotiate peace. These offers were taken up by the Poles, but without great enthusiasm. Some Poles, including their war hero Marshal Pilsudski, hoped that even if the Polish army could not advance as far east as the more extreme Polish nationalists would have liked, some form of buffer state might be set up between the eastern border of Poland and the Bolshevik heartland. On April 27, after the negotiations with the Bolsheviks had broken down, the Polish army launched a great eastward offensive.

One of the first Polish successes was to capture a substantial portion of Russia's dwindling supply of railway rolling stock: 160 locomotives and more than 2000 railway wagons. On May 4 the Polish cavalry reached Fastov; in the previous six days 25,000 Russians had been taken prisoner, as high a Russian loss as during any similar period during the First World War. On May 8 the Polish cavalry entered Kiev, the capital of the Ukraine. There, the Polish government announced that it would transfer most of the conquered Ukrainian territory to an independent Ukraine, which would itself concede Eastern Galicia and the Volhynia to Poland.

Poland's ambition was to reestablish the frontiers that had existed before the eighteenth-century partitions, when Poland had been divided between Prussia, Austria and Russia. But within this region lived many Russians — and Ukrainians — who viewed the prospect of Polish rule with alarm, and even hatred. For this reason many anti-Bolshevik Russians were turned into Russian patriots, and when the Bolsheviks began to counterattack, the Poles found a more determined adversary than they had seen hitherto.

In June, the Russian counterattack assumed serious dimensions for the Poles, who were first driven out of Kiev, and then forced back to the Volhyn-

584 · A HISTORY OF THE TWENTIETH CENTURY

ian railway junction at Sarny. A former Tsarist officer, General Budenny, who had become a general in the Red Army, advanced westward with his cavalry as swiftly as the Poles had earlier advanced eastward, seizing the town of Rovno, the Volhynian capital. Fighting became intense. The Poles recaptured Rovno, then lost it again twenty-four hours later.

The Poles lost Minsk on July 11. The Red Army, under Trotsky's leadership as Commissar for War, was poised to enter the Polish-speaking regions of the old Tsarist Empire. The British government, alarmed at the thought that Bolshevism might reach Warsaw, even Berlin, sent a message to Moscow, requesting the Russians to conclude an armistice with the Poles. The British revealed that the Paris Peace Conference, a year earlier, had discussed a provisional eastern frontier for Poland, based on ethnographic considerations. This line was now made known: it ran from Grodno in the north, along the frontier of Lithuania, through Bialystok, along the rivers Bug and San, through Przemysl, and south to the Carpathian mountains. This was the line which Britain felt that Poland should accept; it was almost identical with the line along which Stalin and Hitler were to divide Poland in 1939, and which Britain wanted Poland to accept in 1944, rather than see Poland swallowed up by the Soviet Union. In 1920 the line was known, after the name of the British Foreign Secretary, as the Curzon Line.

Lloyd George, aware of the considerable industrial unrest in Britain, and the reluctance of the British working class to respond to an anti-Bolshevik appeal, called on Lenin and Trotsky to negotiate peace, based on the Curzon Line. Were they to accept, there would be no need to contemplate war in defence of Poland. The line would give the Bolsheviks a western border which would ensure that all rural areas with Russian and Ukrainian populations would be within the Russian border (as well as several towns with a Polish majority). Bearing in mind how recently Russia's borders had been pushed back, both by the Poles and by anti-Bolshevik Russians, this was a remarkable offer. It would also provide a territorial legitimacy that had not yet been accorded Lenin's regime. An added inducement made by Lloyd George was that General Wrangel, the one remaining anti-Bolshevik Russian who controlled a segment of Russia – in the south – would not be invited to the conference.

The Poles, fearful of losing more territory, accepted the British offer to negotiate on the basis of the Curzon Line. The Russians made no reply, and continued to advance towards it. On July 17 the Red Army entered Vilna, the largest Polish city in the east, and three days later reached the outskirts of Grodno, at the northern end of the Curzon Line. That day the Russians formally rejected Lloyd George's proposal, and as if in a gesture of contempt, entered Grodno the following day, thereby crossing the Curzon Line.

As alarming to the Supreme Council as the Russian entry into the northeast corner of the area designated to Poland was the fact that the Red Army was, at that point, within sixty miles of the German frontier. The 'spectre of Communism', which in 1848 Karl Marx had prophesied would haunt Europe, was drawing closer. In the south, the Red Army crossed the River Stryj and entered Galicia. Those whom Trotsky called the 'White Seigneurs' – the Poles who were in the forefront of the fight against Bolshevik encroachment – appealed for urgent help from the Allies. France responded by sending General Weygand, one of Marshal Foch's best known staff officers, to Warsaw, as a military adviser to the Polish army. The British also sent a distinguished general, Adrian Carton de Wiart, a holder of the Victoria Cross.

Speaking in Moscow on July 24, Trotsky declared that Poland would shortly cease to serve as a defensive barrier for Western Europe against Russia, and would become, instead, 'a bridge by means of which the social revolution could be spread from Russia to Western Europe'. That was why, he said, 'the Entente is feverishly increasing its assistance to Poland. That is why we on our side must treble our efforts in order to face the Entente – before they can send any army corps – with the absolute destruction of the White Seigneurs, a destruction which will be irreparable and hopeless.'

Unexpected help came for the Bolsheviks on July 25, when dockers in the Free City of Danzig refused to unload a Dutch merchant ship, the *Triton*, which was carrying 150,000 rifles from the Allies to the Polish army. Two days later the Red Army entered Pinsk. The Russians were so confident of victory that they set out their territorial demands – including Vilna, Minsk, Grodno and Chelm – as well as their insistence on all Polish coal and salt mines being handed over to Russian control, and the occupation of Poland for five years, for the first twelve months of which 'a Soviet regime will be instituted'.

On July 30, as the Red Army drove even further westward (reaching the line Osowiec–Suwalki–Lomza–Augustowo), Polish officers were authorized to cross the Russian lines and conclude an armistice. But the Russians, still advancing, refused to consider any armistice negotiations or terms for a cease-fire, insisting that they would only discuss the conditions for a definite peace.

Among the Soviet troops advancing into Poland was Isaac Babel, a Jew born in Odessa, who was serving as a political commissar with Budenny's cavalry. Among his published stories of the war was an account of an incident in the town of Sokal:

We took today's prisoners at dawn, at Zawada station. There were ten of them, in underclothes when we took them. Clothing lay piled beside the Poles. This was just a trick of theirs to make it impossible for us to distinguish by their uniforms between the officers and the rank and file. They had thrown off their clothes, but this time Trunov made up his mind to get at the truth.

Trunov had been wounded in the head that morning. His head was bound with a rag, and blood was dripping down from it like rain off a rick.

'Officers, own up!' he repeated, and began to push the Poles about with the butt of his revolver.

Then there stepped from the crowd a thin, aged man with big, protruding bones on his back, yellow cheek-bones, and a drooping moustache.

'Finished, this war,' said the old man with incomprehensible enthusiasm in his mutilated Russian. 'All officers run away. Finished, this war . . .'

And the Pole stretched out his blue hands to the Squadron Commander.

'Five fingers' he said, sobbing and twisting his huge, withered hand, 'with these five fingers I brought up my family . . .'.

The old man choked, swayed, burst into tears of exultation and fell on his knees before Trunov; but Trunov thrust him away with his sword.

'Your officers are damned blackguards,' said the Squadron Commander. 'Your officers have thrown their clothes down here. Well, it's all up with whoever I drop on. I'm going to make a test.'

And the Squadron Commander picked from the heap a cap with pipings and set it on the old man's head.

'Fits,' muttered Trunov, going up closer. 'Fits.' And he thrust his sword into the prisoner's throat.

The old man fell, his legs jerking. From his throat flowed a foamy coral stream. Then Andie Vosmiletov, with his shining ear-ring and round rustic neck, crept up to him. He undid the old man's buttons, shook him slightly, and began to pull the trousers off the dying man. Then he threw them over his saddle, grabbed another couple of uniforms from the heap, and rode off plying the whip.

*   *   *

On August 3 the Red Army reached the River Bug at Brest Litovsk, on the direct road and rail line to Warsaw. That day, the Russians set up a Soviet regime – the temporary Polish Revolutionary Committee – in the conquered areas of eastern Poland (just as Stalin was to set up such a regime before the Russian army reached Warsaw in 1944). Its head was Julian Marchlewski, a founder-member of the Polish Social-Democratic Party in the 1890s who later, while in Germany before and during the First World War, had been a leading Spartacist. Another of its members was the Polish-born Felix Dzerzhinsky, the future head of the Soviet secret police. These were Russia's nominees for the next rulers of Poland.

The advance of the Red Army on Warsaw, like that of the German army on Paris six years earlier, caused consternation in London and Paris, and also, this time, in Berlin. On August 8 the Red Army cut the Warsaw–Danzig railway line at Przasnysz, depriving Poland of her outlet to the sea and her main link with Allied supplies. Two days later the Russians communicated, through Britain, their peace terms: the demobilization of the Polish army, the transfer of all Polish weapons to the Red Army, the demobilization of all Polish war industries, and no further arms or assistance to Poland from abroad. In return for this, the Russians would accept a Russo-Polish frontier somewhat more favourable to the Poles than the Curzon Line on which the Supreme Council was insisting.

It was announced that peace negotiations would take place at Minsk on August 11, but the Red Army continued its advance, and no meeting took place. Instead, on August 12, the Red Army reached Pultusk, only thirty miles from Warsaw. On the following day the civilian members of the Franco-British mission were evacuated from Warsaw to Poznan. On August 14, advanced units of the Red Army reached the village of Okuniew, a mere twelve miles east of Warsaw. It seemed inevitable that the capital would fall.

As the French and British forces had done on the Marne in September 1914, so the Polish forces did on the Vistula on 15 August 1920; they launched a counteroffensive. The turn of the tide is known in Poland as the Miracle of the Vistula. The Polish unknown soldier, at whose tomb in Warsaw burns the eternal flame, is a soldier who was killed in the war of 1920.

Rapidly, the Poles pushed the Russians back from the capital. Fleeing from the advancing Polish troops, 30,000 Russian cavalrymen sought sanctuary across the German border in East Prussia, and were disarmed. By August

23 the Poles had taken 35,000 prisoners. A week later the number had increased by a further 65,000. As the Russians retreated eastward, the Lithuanians were outmanoeuvred by a Polish military force under General Zeligowski. On October 9, Zeligowski and his soldiers seized Vilna.

The Red Army continued to be pushed back. As it retreated, a Russian peasant army of up to 20,000 men, known as the Green Army, and supported by even larger numbers of peasantry, rose inside Russia against the harsh decrees of Communism. As attempts were made by Communist officials to requisition that year's harvest, the Green Army cut three main railway lines linking Moscow with the Volga and the North Caucasus. Bolshevik control was challenged throughout the Tambov province. Lenin ordered the total suppression of the revolt, setting up a Special Commission for Struggle with Banditry, and ordering the shooting, in batches, of those peasants who were suspected of supporting the rebellion. Whole villages were also burnt down, as slowly the authority of Moscow was reasserted.

Another rebellion broke out further south that August, in the North Caucasus region in which the Red Army had crushed an embryo Muslim theocratic State two and a half years earlier. The leader was Imam Najmuddin Gotsinskii. Seizing control of Daghestan and Chechnya, he led his Muslim soldiers to the Caspian Sea, where, after a nineteen-day street battle, he captured the town of Derbent. The local Soviets were quickly overrun. When Soviet reinforcements, together with the head of the Daghestan Cheka, Safar Dudarov, attacked the rebels at Arakan, they were surrounded and overwhelmed. Dudarov was taken prisoner and beheaded. Further Russian reinforcements were held at bay. At Gergebil, the Soviet forces, who had already lost more than eight hundred men in the fighting, burned down a mosque in which about a hundred rebels were besieged. All the rebels were killed.

The fighting in the North Caucasus and Daghestan continued for several months. The Muslims then formed guerrilla bands in the mountains.

On September 21 the Soviet government agreed to open peace negotiations with the Poles in Riga. But as the negotiations continued, so too did the advance of the Polish army. Its Polish and German aspirations dashed, on October 11 the Russian government accepted the Polish terms, and a day later signed the Treaty of Riga. Poland's frontier with Russia ran as far east as she could have hoped; inside it was the Baranovichi–Rovno railway, the town of Pinsk, and the whole of Eastern Galicia. In the north, a common border was established with Latvia.

Under the Treaty of Riga, whose borders were to remain in force for nineteen years (almost to the day), Poland became a country half as large again as the Poland envisaged by the Curzon Line, which, at the height of the Red Army's advance, Poland had been prepared to accept. With a substantial White Russian and Ukrainian minority (6 million out of a total population of 30 million), Poland embarked upon its independence as one of the largest countries in post-imperial Europe.

Also under the Treaty of Riga, Russia was committed to recognizing White Russia and the Ukraine as separate entities. This, given the growing strength of the Red Army in the months ahead, proved an unenforceable commitment. The forces of the Ukrainian independence movement, led by General Petliura, were unable to stand up to the advances of the Red Army, and within a month of the signing of the Treaty of Riga, Petliura sought refuge in Poland. There, as Poland had become a neutral state with regard to Russia, his troops were disarmed. Russian rule, and Soviet Communism, were imposed on the Ukraine and White Russia.

One Polish territorial hope was not realized in 1920. The League of Nations had authorized plebiscites in the Allenstein and Marienwerder districts of East Prussia, to see what their inhabitants wished; more than 90 per cent voted to remain in Germany. A plebiscite was also held, under the auspices of the League, to determine the future of the town of Teschen and the region around it (known as Teschen Silesia). Polish and Czech troops clashed there, and there was resentment in Poland when Czech troops won the upper hand. Extra bitterness was caused when a senior Polish officer, Colonel Haller, was killed in the fighting; he was the brother of one of Poland's most popular generals.

The arrival of the Allied Plebiscite Commission in Teschen did not halt the skirmishes and riots. But in July 1920, during the Spa Conference, the Supreme Council persuaded the Czech Foreign Minister, Dr Edvard Beneš, and Polish Prime Minister, Wladislaw Grabski, to reach an agreement under Allied supervision. Instead of a plebiscite, Teschen would be partitioned. Poland received the largest territorial area; Czechoslovakia received most of the coalfield.

*   *   *

That autumn, the Italians entered into negotiations with Yugoslavia to resolve their disputed claims along the Adriatic, where Italy had hoped, as a result of the 1915 Treaty of London, to make substantial territorial gains, but where the new Yugoslavia wished for the largest possible coastline. As a result of negotiations held between the two countries at Santa Margherita Ligure, agreement was reached, on November 10, whereby Italy received the whole of Istria, and the islands of Cherso, Lussin and Unie, and, further south, the islands of Lagosta and Pelagosta.

The port city of Fiume, which had been seized a year earlier by Gabriele D'Annunzio, and which he and his private army still occupied, was to be an independent city 'in territorial contiguity with Italy'. Further south, the port of Zara, which D'Annunzio had tried to seize, but without the support of the Italian people, was to have an autonomous government, under Italian suzerainty. The Yugoslavs received northern Dalmatia, which under the Treaty of London had been allocated to Italy.

These agreements were embodied in a new treaty, the Treaty of Rapallo – the town next to Santa Margherita on the Ligurian coast of Italy – to which the Allies gave their approval. D'Annunzio, styling himself the Dictator of Fiume, refused to recognize the Treaty, and, in a gesture at once romantic and absurd (the Italian government called it 'grotesque'), declared war on Italy. On December 24, Italian troops marched against the dictator; for a few hours he and his men resisted, but were outnumbered and defeated.

Immediately after the Treaty of Rapallo was signed, Italy and Yugoslavia agreed, under an arrangement not submitted for international approval, 'to act together to thwart any attempt to revive the Habsburg monarchy'. The new European States and the new European boundaries owed their existence to the collapse of the Austro-Hungarian, Russian and German Empires. They could only survive in their new and enlarged forms if those empires were to remain a part of history.

The defeat of the Ottoman Empire had created different problems; the Ottomans remained the ruling dynasty, but with virtually no powers. By October 1918 their Arab dominions had been occupied, and were subsequently to be divided, between Britain and France, acting as custodians of Arab national aspirations, and – in one small area, Palestine – of Jewish national aspirations. Various of Turkey's Anatolian provinces had been promised during the war in different ways and at different times to Italy, Greece, Russia and Armenia. The promises to Russia (including Constantinople and the Straits) had been denounced by the Bolsheviks and had lapsed, not least because the Bolsheviks were in no position to enforce them. Nor were the Bolsheviks in a position to act as the protectors – as Imperial Russia had done – of the Armenians, whose would-be new protector, and Mandatory, the United States, had withdrawn at the beginning of 1920 from all involvement in the postwar settlements. The Armenians were left to face further massacre at the hands of the Turks. That February, several thousand Armenians were murdered in the town of Marash, in Turkish Cilicia.

The withdrawal of the United States also put an end to the placing of Constantinople and the Straits under an American Mandate. The Supreme Council therefore decided to leave the Turkish capital under Turkish control. In Paris, London, Rome and Athens there were those who felt that this was an abdication of the rights of the victors. Not only did the Supreme Council insist on this (while maintaining a substantial Franco-British naval presence in the Bosphorus and Dardanelles, as well as 9500 British troops at Constantinople), but it proceeded to negotiate, in Paris, a peace treaty with the Turkish government.

The terms of the Turkish treaty were handed to the Turks by the Allies on May 11. Turkey was to cede Thrace to Greece, almost up to the Chatalja Lines – the fortifications linking the Aegean and Black seas as a protection for Constantinople – and including the city of Adrianople (Edirne), with its long historic attachment to Turkey and Islam. The Aegean islands of Tenedos and Imbros were also to go to Greece.

But it was not only the larger part of European Turkey that was to be detached from Turkey under the treaty; large parts of the Turkish heartland of Anatolia were also to be transferred to others. The Dodecanese Islands, occupied by Italy since the Italo-Turkish war of 1912, were to become Italian sovereign territory. Most drastic of all territorially, a large Anatolian region centred on Smyrna (Izmir) and running far inland was to become an autonomous region under Greek administration, with the right to attach itself, after five years, by plebiscite, to Greece.

A neutral 'Zone of the Straits' was to be created, consisting of the coastlines and waterways of the Dardanelles, the Sea of Marmara and the Bosphorus, to be controlled by a commission appointed by the League of Nations. The members of the Straits Commission would be nominated by Britain, France, Italy and Japan. There would also be Greek and Russian nominees, though with lesser powers. Turkey was not to be represented on the commission, nor would any Turkish troops be allowed in the Zone, in which Allied garrisons were to remain 'in permanent occupation'.

With regard to the southern provinces of the Ottoman Empire, the Turkish treaty enshrined what was already in place on the ground, with Syria, Mesopotamia (Iraq) and Palestine being transferred to France and Britain as Mandates, and the Hedjaz (the future Saudi Arabia) to Arab rule. In addition, an independent Armenia would be established, 'within boundaries which the President of the United States will determine as fair and just'.

Several of the conditions laid down by the Allies in the Turkish treaty were as severe as anything imposed on Germany or Austria. The Turkish navy and air force were to be abolished. The Turkish army was to be limited to 50,000 men. Tax-gathering powers throughout Turkey were to be withdrawn from the Turkish government and given to a Finance Committee made up of representatives of Britain, France and Italy.

The Turkish government tried to argue against many of the proposed terms, especially the removal of the Smyrna province from Turkish rule, but the only modification the Allies would allow was to permit a Turkish representative to join the Straits Commission. In answer to the other points of protest, the Allies informed the Turks: 'The Turkish delegation does not appear to appreciate the loss and suffering which Turkey's intervention has caused to humanity. The extent of Turkey's liability is not to be gauged merely by the cost of overcoming the Turkish armies. By gratuitously closing a great international waterway in the face of the Allies, and so cutting off the communications between Russia, Roumania and the Western Allies, Turkey certainly prolonged the war by not less than two years, and caused a loss to the Allies of several millions of lives and thousands of millions of pounds. The reparation which Turkey owes to those who, at terrible cost, have re-established liberty for the world, is far greater than she can ever pay.'

The Allied note went on to declare that the time had come 'when it is necessary to put an end once and for all to the empire of the Turks over other nations', and listed the massacre of the Armenians, the treatment of Allied prisoners of war and the deportation of Greeks and Armenians from their homes, as well as the earlier 'atrocities' against Macedonians and Bulgarians before the First World War, as justification for the total dismemberment of the Ottoman Empire. 'Not only has the Turkish Government failed to protect its subjects of other races from pillage, outrage and murder,' the Allied note continued, 'but there is abundant evidence that it has been responsible for directing and organizing savagery against people to whom it owed protection'.

Not even the Germans had been sent such a severe admonition. The Allies also made it clear that there was to be no further discussion; on July 17 the Turks were 'granted a period of ten days', at the end of which they had either to signify their acceptance of the treaty, or face the consequences of whatever action the Allied Powers 'may consider necessary in the circumstances'.

The Turkish government in Constantinople pondered what was in effect an Allied ultimatum, and came to the conclusion that it had no choice but to accept the terms of the treaty, punitive though they were. At the same time, a growing movement against the treaty was being led by Mustafa Kemal. Having gathered an army of several thousand men, he set up his headquarters at Angora (Ankara), entered Bursa, the Ottoman capital before 1453, and occupied the southern shore of the Sea of Marmara. On June 17 a specially summoned meeting of British Cabinet Ministers denounced Kemal as a 'bandit', but did not feel that it had the ability to use the British troops already in Constantinople to drive him away. The Greeks offered to do it for them.

Discovering in the Greek Prime Minister, Eleutherios Venizelos – who attended the British meeting of Ministers on June 17 – a willing partner to challenge Kemal, the British and French governments authorized Greece to take military action. Greek forces had occupied Smyrna a year earlier. They now moved rapidly northward, driving Kemal from Bursa. In Thrace, which had been occupied since the war largely by French troops, the Greek army moved to acquire the territory allocated to it under the treaty, overcoming some Turkish military opposition and occupying Adrianople.

Kemal was driven out of Bursa on July 8, and Adrianople was occupied by the Greeks on July 25. The Turkish treaty, to which the Turkish government had agreed several days before the expiry of the July 27 ultimatum, was ready to be signed. It was held up for two weeks, however, because of a dispute between two of its beneficiaries, Italy and Greece. The Greeks were incensed by the transfer of the Dodecanese Islands to Italy, as the population of the islands was predominantly Greek. After a hectic round of negotiations, while the Turks waited uneasily for their fate to be sealed, the Italians agreed to give Greece all the islands except for Rhodes, the largest, which remained Italian. At one point during the negotiations, which Britain was trying to expedite, the Italians indicated their willingness to see Rhodes transferred to Greece, but only on the condition that Britain give Cyprus to Greece, something Britain had no intention of doing.

*   *   *

The Turkish peace treaty was formally signed at Sèvres on August 10. The signatories included Armenia, which was to obtain its sovereignty as an integral part of the Treaty. In protest against the terms of the Treaty, Mustafa Kemal called a Turkish 'Parliament' in Angora, proclaiming it the Turkish Grand National Assembly. There he denounced the treaty, which he insisted had been 'imposed' on the Constantinople government, and declared war on the Allies. The Angora government would, he said, when it was ready to do so, drive the Allies, and the Greeks, from Turkish soil. Then, after negotiating a Russo-Turkish agreement with the Bolsheviks, Kemal turned his army against the area designated by the Supreme Council as the new State of Armenia. A fierce struggle began in October and continued until December.

During the fighting between the Kemalists and the Armenians, the Armenian government asked for admission to the League of Nations, but this was refused. President Wilson, whose Senate had rejected a Mandate for Armenia, proposed an extension of Armenia's borders in Anatolia (to include the Black Sea port of Trebizond and the Anatolian city of Erzerum). But these were regions where Kemal held sway, far from the weak government in Constantinople, and without Allied military intervention on a massive scale, the scheme held no prospect of fulfilment. By the end of the year Kemal's forces had overrun western Armenia; it has remained Turkish to this day.

In return for receiving Bolshevik agreement to re-establish Turkish rule in the Armenian regions of Turkey, Kemal agreed not to hamper in any way the Bolshevik incorporation of those areas of Armenia – including the new State's designated capital, Yerevan – which lay on the former Tsarist side of the border. An anti-Bolshevik republic had been set up in Russian Armenia in 1919; it had a 200-mile common border with Turkey. Kemal agreed that the Bolsheviks could act there as they chose, and Yerevan was soon occupied by Bolshevik forces. At the border, overlooked by Mount Ararat, Bolshevik and Turkish troops stood guard over the extinction of Armenian independence on both sides of the frontier.

Two other Trans-Caucasian regions had also declared their independence from Russia during 1919: Georgia – which had a common border with Turkey – and Azerbaijan, a Muslim region on the Caspian Sea. The victors in Paris had given these two new States de facto recognition, and they maintained a precarious existence. When Armenia appealed to Georgia for help against Turkey and Russia, Georgia maintained its neutrality.

Bolshevik rule was eventually established in the Georgian capital, Tbilisi, and in the Azerbaijani capital, Baku, where there was a large Russian population. Communism was then steadily, and with considerable brutality, extended throughout these two mountainous regions. These two Caucasian nations, which had briefly raised the flags of independence, held their parliamentary deliberations in their own languages, printed their own stamps, and been accepted by the rest of the world as independent entities, fell once more under the rule of Moscow. It was a rule that was to persist for seven decades, uninterrupted even by the cataclysm of the Second World War.

In Central Asia, the Bolsheviks moved against Bokhara, where, with the fall of the Tsarist regime, an independent emirate had been set up by the local Muslim leader, Sayid-Mir-Alim-Khan. In August, Lenin and Trotsky, at that very moment fighting to overrun Poland (and in the euphoria of imminent victory there), sent a a large Bolshevik army to conquer the emirate. Bokhara was defended by the Muslim forces, but swiftly overrun.

On February 7 a Red Army firing squad prepared to execute the most effective of the anti-Bolshevik leaders, Admiral Kolchak, whom the Bolsheviks had captured, and who was being held in prison in Irkutsk. With him in prison was the former Prime Minister of the independent Far Eastern region, Viktor Pepeliaev. They had been found guilty of treason by a five-man Extraordinary Investigating Commission, headed by a Bolshevik functionary, Chudnovsky. Only Kolchak's mistress, Anna Timireva, herself the daughter of a Tsarist admiral, was eventually allowed to go free. The historian Peter Fleming has described the scene:

> The prison stood, and indeed still stands, on the bank of a tributary of the Angara called the Ushakovka. Roughly a hundred yards downstream, under a slight escarpment, a hole had been cut in the ice below the bank; it was the responsibility of the prison staff to keep it from freezing over. The lip of the escarpment was illuminated by the headlamps of the lorry that had brought the firing squad; its members were drawn up on either side of the bonnet, so as not to obscure the headlamps.
>
> In the still, freezing night desultory shooting could be heard to the westward as guards under the prison commandant led Kolchak into the funnel of yellow light. Pepeliaev had to be dragged. Both men were handcuffed.

Kolchak was offered, but refused, a bandage for his eyes. There are various accounts of his last words, none reliable. Only one has, for me, the ring of truth. In this version Chudnovsky asked whether he had a last request to make. 'Would you be so good,' said Kolchak, 'as to get a message sent to my wife in Paris, to say that I bless my son?' 'I'll see what can be done,' replied Chudnovsky, 'if I don't forget about it.' Nothing was done.

A priest was there. Both prisoners said their prayers aloud. Then they were placed, side by side, on the spot where many men, and some women, had looked for the last time on the stars. Pepeliaev's eyes were shut, his face livid. Kolchak was entirely master of himself: 'like an Englishman' – the analogy oddly recurs in an official Soviet account of the execution.

The order was given, the soldiers fired raggedly, both men fell. There was a second and perhaps – visibility was poor – superfluous volley. (Timireva, alone in her cell, could hear the detonations.) The corpses were kicked or prodded over the edge of the escarpment, down the short *piste* of frozen snow discoloured by the transit of their predecessors, into the water and under the ice.

The murder of Admiral Kolchak ended all effective Russian anti-Bolshevik activity. Slowly the Bolsheviks established their authority. The chaos and anarchy with which the Bolsheviks had to contend, and which the civil war exacerbated, were later described by the Russian novelist, and Nobel Prize winner, Boris Pasternak, in his novel *Doctor Zhivago*. 'Train after train,' he wrote, 'abandoned by the Whites, stood idle, stopped by the defeat of Kolchak, by running out of fuel and by snowdrifts. Immobilized for good and buried in the snow, they stretched almost uninterruptedly for miles on end. Some of them served as fortresses for armed bands of robbers or as hideouts for escaping criminals or political fugitives – the involuntary vagrants of those days – but most of them were communal mortuaries, mass graves of the victims of the cold and typhus raging all along the railway line and mowing down whole villages in its neighbourhood.'

The American forces withdrew from Siberia in April 1920. They were followed eight months later by the Czech forces who had controlled long sections of the Trans-Siberian railway. These were former Czech soldiers in the Austro-Hungarian army who had been taken prisoner by the Russians on the Eastern Front four years earlier. After the Bolshevik revolution, and their own liberation, they had formed one of the anti-Bolshevik armies fighting alongside the Whites. Only the Japanese remained in occupation in the Russian Far East. One of the main towns they controlled was Nikolayevsk, at the mouth of the River Amur, a town with 20,000 Russian inhabitants. There were 700 Japanese soldiers and civilians in effective control of the town.

In March 1920 a ferocious assault was launched against the Japanese in Nikolayevsk by Russian troops under the command of a Bolshevik Partisan leader, Triapitsyn, and his Chief of Staff – and mistress – Nina Lebedeva. As well as killing all 700 Japanese in the town, Triapitsyn ordered the slaughter of 6000 Russian men, women and children. He specifically ordered children over the age of five to be killed, as they would otherwise remember what they had seen, and might later seek revenge.

When a Japanese punitive expedition was sent, and clearly had the strength to recapture Nikolayevsk, Triapitsyn burned the town to the ground, and then withdrew into the interior. His followers, disgusted by what he had done in Nikolayevsk, arrested him and Lebedeva. The two were given a brief trial, and then executed.

The Japanese announced that they would stay in the Russian Far East, arguing that Bolshevik activities there endangered both Manchuria and Korea. Among those captured by the Japanese after the Nikolayevsk massacre – he was found in Vladivostok – was the twenty-eight-year-old Siberian Bolshevik partisan leader Sergei Lazo (a Moldavian, of Swiss ancestry). The Japanese handed him over to the anti-Bolshevik Whites, who, in a particularly savage act of revenge, pushed him alive into the blazing furnace of a railway engine. Lazo's exploits as a partisan, and his grim fate, made him a folk hero in the Soviet Far East, and two decades later a rallying point for Russian recruitment against Japanese militarism.

After some months, the Japanese withdrew to a small Zone of Occupation around Vladivostok, and in October 1922 they withdrew from Russian soil altogether. Within weeks, Bolshevik rule was imposed throughout the region, making Lenin the master, as Tsar Nicholas had been before him, of the vast expanse of land from the Baltic Sea to the Pacific Ocean. In Petrograd, the scene of Lenin's seizure of power three years earlier, but no longer the capital, Anna Akhmatova recalled:

The old Petersburg signboards were still in place, but behind them there was nothing but dust, darkness and yawning emptiness.
Typhus, hunger, execution by firing squad, dark apartments, damp

wood, and people swollen beyond recognition. You could pick a large bouquet of wild flowers in Gostinny Dvor (the large department store). The famous Petersburg wooden pavement was rotting. The smell of chocolate still wafted from the basement windows of Kraft. All the cemeteries had been pillaged.

The city had not just changed, it had turned into its exact opposite. But people still loved poetry.

The anti-British movement in Ireland gathered momentum throughout 1920. To combat the continuing attacks by the Irish Republican Army on British soldiers and police, 40,000 British troops were sent to Ireland. In search of a political solution, the British government introduced a Home Rule Bill to Parliament on February 25, whereby there would be two Parliaments in Ireland, one, in Dublin, with 128 members, the other, in Belfast, with 52 members. Britain would retain control of foreign policy and defence, customs and excise, land and agricultural policy, and the machinery for maintaining law and order. The Dublin parliament would enable Catholic Ireland to govern itself, with the Protestant majority in Belfast in charge of its specific needs.

For Sinn Fein this was not enough; they wanted to govern the whole of Ireland, and to be free completely from British rule. Full independence, not limited autonomy, was their goal. The Home Rule Bill, they declared, was designed solely for the 'plunder and partition of Ireland'. The IRA continued to shoot at British troops. British troops continued to raid the homes of suspects. More than five hundred such raids were reported every week; often they were accompanied by considerable violence on the part of the troops. IRA violence was also shocking to the British public. In March the Resident Magistrate in Dublin, sixty-year-old Alan Bell, who was investigating the attempted assassination of the Lord Lieutenant of Ireland, was dragged from a train and shot dead. 'De Valera has practically challenged the British Empire', Lloyd George complained in a private letter.

A special Irish police force was set up, consisting of 8000 former soldiers. The force was known, from its uniform, as the Black and Tans. It served as an auxiliary arm to the existing police force, the Royal Irish Constabulary. A secret report to the British Cabinet in May stated that the Dublin police could not be relied upon to combat the IRA, nor could the civil service. Nor would Catholic judges impose the death penalty on members of the IRA who had been convicted of murder, even though Lloyd George had approved hanging as the essential punishment and deterrent. The killings by the IRA continued. On June 16 a band of Catholics besieged a Protestant club in Ennis and demanded the 'surrender' of the Protestants inside it. In the ensuing battle, seventeen people were killed. A month later a senior police officer, Colonel Smyth, who had lost an arm in the war and been twice decorated for bravery, was shot dead in Cork by thirteen or fourteen IRA men. His murder provoked riots in Belfast and Londonderry in which thirteen people were killed.

Catholics and Protestants were at war. For every IRA killing, the Black and Tans and the police carried out reprisals. In September, after a policeman was shot dead in Galway, his colleagues seized three IRA men who were asleep, had them stand against a wall, and shot them dead. It was far from an isolated incident. In one month, forty people were killed in attacks and reprisal actions. Lloyd George told his closest advisers: 'You cannot in the excited state of Ireland punish a policeman who shoots a man whom he has every reason to suspect is connected with the police murders', and in the House of Commons he declared that Britain would never allow Ireland to secede from the United Kingdom.

British reprisals had become a regular response to every IRA attack. In Dublin, after the IRA pulled six British officers out of their beds and shot them in front of their wives, the reprisal took place later that same day, when soldiers opened fire on a crowd, including several IRA men, which had gathered at a football ground in the city, killing nine people. The six murdered officers were later honoured by the British government at a memorial service in Westminster Abbey.

The strength of Irish national opinion could not be weakened, however fierce the measures introduced by the British government. In December, Lloyd George declared Martial Law in four southern Irish counties, and called for the surrender of all arms within seventeen days. Anyone found with arms after that would be tried by court martial. The penalty for carrying arms would be death.

It was felt, Lloyd George told his Cabinet on December 13, that 'the decent public in Ireland' desired a truce and an end to violence. Churchill shared this view, and suggested that once a truce could be in force for a month, and the murders stop, the situation would immediately 'light up' – and, he added, 'give a chance for the murderers to go off to America'. In the House of Commons, Churchill outlined the new policy. 'Let murder stop,' he said. 'Let constitutional dominion begin. Let the Irish people carry the debate from the squalid conditions in which it is now being pushed forward by the Irish murder gang into the field of fair discussion. Let them press their constitutional claims, as all the people of the British Isles have the right to do, in the great constitutional parliamentary assemblies of the nation, and they will find that instantly there will be a release of all those harsh and lamentable conditions which are bringing misery upon Ireland, and undoubtedly bringing discredit upon the whole of the British Empire.'

Lloyd George was impressed by Churchill's conciliatory appeal, and put him in charge of trying to reach an agreement in Ireland, even with Sinn Fein and the IRA. It was to be a long haul.

In Mesopotamia, where 14,000 British and Indian troops were stationed, more than four hundred were killed during an Arab uprising in 1920, and several towns had to be recaptured from the rebels. In India, as one British commentator expressed it, 'a very unfortunate development during the year was the capture of the Indian National Congress by the extremist politicians, headed by that notorious agitator, Mr Gandhi'.

Under Gandhi's leadership the Indian National Congress called, not for violence, but for noncooperation. British officials were to be boycotted, British rules ignored, British taxes not paid, and British orders evaded.

One contentious prewar figure who returned to challenge the power of the British Empire in 1920 was the 'Mad Mullah' of Somaliland. Despite five military campaigns against him, he took the offensive once more. Early that year the British launched their sixth campaign against him. This time, aircraft were used, and bombs were dropped on his encampments. It was not, however, to British arms or bombs that, in November 1920, the Mullah finally succumbed, but to influenza.

Fighting during 1920 had brought war casualties, and new civilian suffering to the Polish-Russian and Graeco-Turkish regions, to Armenia, to Mesopotamia and to Ireland. There was also fighting in Spanish Morocco, where the Moors continued to challenge Spanish rule, and a series of punitive raids were carried out against them by a newly established Spanish Legion. But by far the highest death toll that year was not from wars but from natural disasters, and on a scale inconceivable in Europe. In China, three provinces (Chihli, Honan and Shantung) were affected by a severe drought, the harvest failed over a vast area, and as many as fifteen million Chinese died of starvation.

The armistices and peace treaties with which the First World War had ended were not followed automatically by the spirit of reconciliation, even in what, before the war, had been a model of international participation. When, in August 1920, the VIth Olympiad was held, the city of Antwerp was chosen for the site of the Games as a gesture to 'brave little Belgium', Germany's victim of a previous decade. None of the ex-enemy countries were invited to attend the Games.

CHAPTER TWENTY-FIVE

1921

THROUGHOUT 1921 the League of Nations continued to arbitrate in international disputes. That year it mediated in a dispute that had arisen between Germany and Poland following the plebiscite in Upper Silesia. The votes cast had been divided 717,122 in favour of Germany and 483,514 in favour of Poland. The German government insisted that this vote meant that the majority favoured incorporation with Germany. The Polish government argued that the 483,514 Poles lived in a compact geographic area that could easily be annexed to Poland.

In Poland it was assumed that the Supreme Allied Council would give its decision in favour of Germany, in order to secure the Silesian coalfield for Germany, which would use it to pay the reparations demanded by the Treaty of Versailles. To challenge what he was convinced would be this cynical, self-interested outcome, a Polish insurgent, Wojciech Korfanty, began a campaign of civil disobedience, looting and violence throughout the disputed region. In response, the Germans in Upper Silesia set up their own defence force, commanded by a former German army officer who had been invalided out of the army, General Höfer, an Upper Silesian. The armies of Höfer and Korfanty fought several pitched battles. British and Italian troops who were stationed in the region also tried to suppress Korfanty's activities. On one occasion British troops, to their great annoyance, were prevented from taking military action against Korfanty by the intervention of the French Commander-in-Chief of the Allied troops in Upper Silesia, General Gratier.

A series of skirmishes threatened to turn into an all-out war. The Italian Foreign Minister, Count Sforza, alarmed at the number of Italian troops who were being killed and wounded in the Allied struggle with Korfanty, suggested to the Supreme Allied Council that the dispute be discussed by the League of Nations. This was done, the League taking its international composition seriously by appointing as the commissioners to examine the problem, and to come up with a solution, experts from Belgium, Brazil, Spain and China.

To the surprise of the Polish government, these four experts, who were supported in their decision by the League Council, did not recommend that the German majority vote be used as the legal and demographic basis for the transfer of the area to Germany. Instead, they proposed that Upper Silesia be divided between Germany and Poland (the Polish area being known as East Upper Silesia), with a third of the area going to Poland, whose votes were mostly in the rural areas. To the anger of the Germans, the partition line meant that of the sixty-one coal mines in the area, only eleven went to Germany, and one was divided between the two contenders.

In order to make this solution more palatable to the German government, the League insisted that Poland sign an economic agreement with Germany whereby there would be complete freedom of trade between the two parts of Upper Silesia, a unified railway system, and no restrictions on movement by either German or Polish Upper Silesians across their respective sides of the border. To protect the minorities on both sides of the new border, a statute for the protection of minorities was signed, with an initial duration of fifteen years. This meant that, in 1933, when the convention still had three years to run, the Jewish minority in the German area were able to appeal, successfully, to the League of Nations, against the imposition of the Nazi racial legislation.

A second territorial dispute resolved by the League in 1921 concerned the Yugoslav-Albanian border, where Yugoslav troops had occupied an area of Albania beyond the prewar border. The Yugoslav government insisted that this border had 'no relevance' to the situation of 1921, and that it wished to annex the area it had occupied. With the approval of both Yugoslavia and Albania, the League Council appointed a Commission of Inquiry, consisting of a Luxembourger, a Norwegian and a Finn, to arbitrate. But before these three experts could set off for Albania it was announced that Yugoslav troops – predominantly Serbs – were advancing deep into Albania, threatening both Durazzo and Tirana, and destroying more than a hundred Albanian villages.

The British government at once proposed activating article 16 of the League Covenant. This article, which had not been activated before, set out measures that could be taken to avert or stop wars, in this instance by imposing an economic blockade on Yugoslavia. The threat of economic sanctions, even before the League Council had agreed to them, was effective. Yugoslavia announced that its troops would withdraw. The Commission of Enquiry proceeded to the disputed border. By the end of the year, the 1913 frontier was re-established, and Yugoslav troops had withdrawn. Three small frontier rectifications were then made by the League in favour of Yugoslavia. In return, Britain, France and Italy recognized the Albanian government.

The Polish-German and Yugoslav-Albanian disputes, both of which had threatened to escalate into war, had both been resolved as a result of the intervention and authority of the the League of Nations. Another League success in 1921 was the setting up of a Permanent Court of International Justice. Its judges represented the different legal systems of the thirty participating States which initially agreed to the establishment of the court. A special League Protocol enabled those States that wished to do so to agree among themselves to submit to the Court all disputes that were capable of resolution by judicial process.

Other League activities that year included the administration of the Free City of Danzig and the Saar Valley, and efforts to secure the financial rehabilitation of Austria, to improve sanitary conditions in Mediterranean ports, and to reduce the white slave traffic (the sale of women and children for prostitution overseas) especially between Europe and South America.

In British India, the protests against British rule had begun to disrupt not only the administration which sought to improve the lot of the Indian masses, but also the smooth flow of imperial pomp and circumstance. When the Prince of Wales visited the subcontinent in 1921, there was serious rioting in the Indian quarter of Bombay, where he landed. In Poona, a town where many British troops were stationed, he received an enthusiastic welcome, but in both Allahabad and Ajmere the Indian population stayed indoors as a sign of protest. Noncooperation, as urged by Gandhi, was becoming effective even at times of ceremonial.

As the noncooperation movement gained in momentum, and also, against Gandhi's wishes, in violence, the government of India brought prosecutions wherever it could find instances of incitement. Attempts by Gandhi to persuade people not to buy foreign cloth, but to use Indian homespun materials, gained in strength; but parallel to Gandhi's noncooperation movement, which found its greatest (though not its exclusive) support among Hindus, a more aggressive Muslim independence movement, the Khilafat movement, had begun to make inroads among the Muslim population. It gained its name from opposition to Britain's policy towards the Sultan of Turkey, the Caliph, who was effectively a prisoner of the British in Constantinople. At an All-India Khilafat Committee meeting, held in Karachi in July, two of the Khilafat leaders, the brothers Mohammad and Shaukat Ali, advocated a Muslim religious ban on service in the army – Indian Muslims had distinguished themselves on all the war fronts during the First World War. Both men were arrested – as they had been in 1914 for denouncing Britain's war with Turkey – charged with incitement, convicted and imprisoned yet again.

That August, a Muslim uprising took place in the Malabar district of India, where the million-strong Moplah people, who regarded all non-Muslims as infidels, and who had been influenced by the arrival in their area of several leaders of the Khilafat movement, declared two independent Muslim kingdoms. They then attacked both Europeans and Hindus. Government offices were burnt and looted, and official records destroyed. Hindu temples were sacked, and many Hindus forced, on pain of death, to convert to Islam. Hindus who refused to convert were beheaded. Gandhi, in a moment of what many Hindus considered to be utterly misjudged even-handedness, spoke of 'the brave, God-fearing Moplahs, fighting for what they consider as religion, and in a manner which they consider as religious'. The government of India responded by putting him in prison.

As the number of Hindus murdered by the Moplahs began to rise into double and then treble figures, the government declared martial law. British and Indian troops were rushed to the district, and the Moplah insurgents attacked; 1826 Moplahs were killed, more than five thousand were captured, and 14,000 surrendered. The remnant of the rebels, about seven hundred in all, took to the hills and continued fighting. They were slowly hunted down. The government, which had gained considerable Indian sympathy in putting down the rebellion, lost some of that sympathy when, in a much-publicized incident, seventy Moplah prisoners, locked in an airless railway carriage without water, suffocated to death.

The French and Spanish governments were also embroiled during 1921 in a colonial struggle, in Morocco. In March, a French military expedition was launched against the Beni-Warian tribe in the south, which had refused to submit to French authority. Eleven engagements were fought, and the tribe forced to accept French rule. In the Rif district the Spaniards also set out to impose their rule, which had first been established there in 1909, but was under continual challenge by Abd el-Krim. The Spanish authorities were upset in their plans when, during an attempt to open the road between Melilla and Alhucemas, the Moorish troops under their command mutinied, killing five Spanish officers. The surviving Spanish troops retreated to a fortified camp at Annual, where they were besieged.

To lift the siege, a relief column was sent from Melilla, but as it approached Annual it was surrounded and destroyed by Abd el-Krim. The general in command of the column, General Fernandez Silvestre, and several of his staff, were either killed or committed suicide. Annual was then overrun by the tribesmen, as were seventy other Spanish fortified posts that had been set up since 1909, including Nador. It was only six miles from Melilla. More than nine thousand Spanish soldiers were killed during the fighting, many of them slaughtered as they sought safety inside their garrisons. Only Melilla itself was able to drive off the Moors; the part played by Major Franco in its defence made him a Spanish national hero.

In Spain, the government fell from power as a result of the disaster to Spanish arms overseas. A new Prime Minister, Antonio Maura, appointed on August 14, announced that he would re-establish the protectorate, by armed force if necessary, but would avoid all 'hazardous military enterprises'. Meanwhile, the tribesmen continued to attack the Spanish soldiers wherever they could find them. On the coast near Alcazar a colonel and fifty men were killed. In an attempt to calm tribal unrest, the government in Madrid announced that taxation would be abolished, as would the direct control over native affairs by Spanish officers. The announcement of these measures in no way diminished, however, the desire of the Moors of the Rif to get rid of Spanish rule.

Considerable Spanish military reinforcements were sent to Morocco. By the end of August more than seventy-five thousand frontline troops and a hundred thousand reservists had been assembled. Moving out of Melilla, they fought a series of battles with the Moors, uncovering evidence of Moorish mutilations on dead Spanish soldiers, recapturing Nador, and securing the promontory and high ground of the Melilla hinterland. Major Franco, who succeeded to the command of the Spanish Legion on the death of its commander in action near Nador, later wrote of 'feeling in our hearts a desire for revenge, for the most exemplary punishment ever seen down the generations'. Revenge was taken. During one engagement, each of the twelve volunteers whom Franco asked to go to the aid of a besieged blockhouse returned with a trophy – the severed head of one of the Moorish attackers.

In September, the new Spanish government announced that military operations 'on a grand scale' were over. Its policy to the rebels would be one of 'exemplary chastisement'. It would seek to occupy various points on the coast, and would pursue a policy of helping the Moors to govern themselves. A new era was dawning, and not only in Morocco. The impetus to conquer all those who resisted colonial rule was giving way, but only slowly, to an acceptance of accommodation and compromise – the essential prelude to the decolonization of later years.

In Egypt, the British government was seeking means to grant independence while at the same time securing British interests, particularly along the Suez Canal. Negotiations with the Egyptian leaders made progress in London, with agreement that the British Army of Occupation should be withdrawn from Egypt, and that British troops should be stationed only along the Canal. It was also agreed that, in order to 'safeguard foreign interests' in Egypt, the Financial Adviser of the government of Egypt, and also a senior official in the Ministry of Justice, should be British.

While these terms were being negotiated, the head of the Egyptian delegation, Zaghloul Pasha, announced his opposition to them. Returning to Egypt, he bitterly attacked the government for bowing to Britain's demands. Violence flared in the streets; for several days part of the city of Alexandria was under mob rule, and a large number of European residents, including many Greeks, were killed.

When the negotiations resumed in London, the Egyptian delegates objected to the British insistence that, for the security of British citizens and other nationals, such as the Greeks, British troops should be stationed wherever in Egypt the British military authorities thought it to be 'desirable'. The delegates, including the Egyptian Prime Minister, Adly Pasha, returned to Egypt, where Adly resigned. Zaghloul at once appealed for further demonstrations against British rule; he was arrested, and, with five of his main supporters, deported to Ceylon. Riots in Cairo, protesting against the deportations, were quickly crushed.

In the southern Sudan, which was under joint British and Egyptian rule, there was a brief Muslim uprising, led by Abdul-Laqhi-es-Soghayer. After two British officers and three British civilians were killed, the British launched a punitive expedition. Soghayer was caught, and hanged, and the uprising suppressed.

It was not in the colonial empires alone that violence marred the year 1921. In Italy, riots broke out in several cities between Socialists and the increasingly active Fascisti, who denounced not only Socialism and Communism but also parliamentary institutions. There was street fighting between the rival groups in Florence, Trieste and Pisa; it was a struggle, not merely for political ascendancy, but for the future course that Italy would take at home and abroad. Briefly that year, culture impinged on politics, when celebrations to commemorate the 600th anniversary of the death of Dante culminated in a pilgrimage to his tomb in Ravenna.

But the fighting in the streets was escalating. At Modena, five people were killed on September 26 in a street battle between the Fascisti and their opponents. A month later the Fascisti held a congress in Rome, transforming their movement into a political party (they already had 20 seats in the 535-seat parliament). Their programme was diffuse and in search of respectability. Land would belong 'to him who works it', but large 'capitalist' farms would not be dismantled. The 'practical degeneration' of Socialism would be opposed. The call for an aggressive foreign policy and an increase in the armaments needed to sustain it gave hope to the unemployed that work would be found for them in the armaments factories and war industries. The middle classes were offered the attraction of free enterprise, and even free trade. Fascism sought to appeal to the national aspirations of those who felt Italy had not received its rightful rewards from the war, calling itself 'a voluntary militia placed at the service of the nation'. A cult of discipline and leadership was also developed, with the heads of the Fascist squads gaining in authority. Even after the Fascists had constituted themselves a political party, violence underpinned reason and debate.

In Germany, the year 1921 saw another Communist uprising, just north of Weimar. On the outskirts of Halle, Merseburg and Eisleben, workers driven desperate by hunger attacked troops sent to quell their disturbances. A thirty-year-old Communist, Max Hölz, who had served in the trenches on the Western Front, put himself at the head of a military formation which, for several weeks, fought off numerous attacks by a much larger body of government troops. Reduced eventually to five hundred men, the insurgents fought their way to the town of Beesenstadt, near Halle, where they were finally defeated. Eighteen of their number were killed. Hölz escaped, and hid for a while in Berlin, but was betrayed to the police and captured. Two thousand of his fellow insurgents were captured and imprisoned.

Hölz defended the path of Communist revolution on the grounds that all other paths had failed to redress the inequalities of society. Of what use, he asked in his manifesto, were 'the noblest creations of the mind and the highest ideals of a Socrates, a Rousseau, a Kant, Fichte or Marx, so long as they remain nothing but ideas, words, dead letters; so long as they cannot be realized as the stuff of life and liberating deed?'

The trial of Hölz was turned from a political to a criminal one, and a charge, which was not substantiated, of murder, was brought against him. He was portrayed in the German press as a criminal of the lowest type. His political motives and leadership were belittled. Sentenced to life imprisonment, he was amnestied seven years later, after organizing a protest of fifty fellow political prisoners inside the prison. Among the Communists, he was a hero. When he returned to Berlin a demonstration of more than 100,000 workers came to greet him. It was assumed that he would take a prominent part in the growing Communist opposition to Hitler and National Socialism, but for internal Communist Party reasons he was sent to the Soviet Union. No more was heard of him until, in September 1933, it was given out that he had died in a boating accident somewhere in Russia. Perhaps he was among the many hundreds of foreign victims of Stalin's purges. 'It is my personal conviction,' his lawyer, Dr Alfred Apfel, later wrote, 'that if Hölz had been in Germany in 1932 and 1933, Hitler would have found his task less easy.'

It was the Right, not the Left, that was gaining the initiative in the streets of Germany that year. An estimated 40,000 former army officers were at the centre of frequent anti-government demonstrations, the abuse of the new black, gold and red flag of the Republic, and demands for a return of the monarchy, and the monarchical system.

It seemed as though, more often than not, street violence and assassination went hand in hand. In June, the leader of the Bavarian Independent Socialist Party, Gareis, was murdered in Munich. In August, two young Nationalists, a clerk and a law student, murdered Matthias Erzberger, the former German Minister of Finance who had concluded the Armistice with the Allies in

1918, and had campaigned strongly in 1919 for the acceptance of the Treaty of Versailles.

In Bavaria, Hitler was building up a small National Socialist (Nazi) Workers' Party. Denunciation of the Versailles Treaty was a main theme of all his speeches. It was not so much the terms of the Treaty that he rejected, as the implication that Germany had been defeated. At the end of 1920 he had been able to find financial backers willing to purchase the *Völkischer Beobachter*, which became the Nazi Party's newspaper. Large crowds gathered to hear him speak. In Munich, in February 1921, six and a half thousand people (five hundred more than his party membership at that time) gathered in a circus tent to hear him denounce the Allied demand for reparations. When a group within the party began talks, in his absence, to join the German Socialist Party, and proposed moving their headquarters from Munich to Berlin, Hitler resigned. He was urged to return by those who recognized his exceptional powers. He agreed to return on condition that he was made party chairman 'with dictatorial powers'. Henceforth he was not only leader of the party, but the embodiment of the leadership principle, enshrined in his title (*Führer*, leader), and in the party salute (*Heil Hitler!*)

During 1921 Hitler worked to perfect the symbols which his party would use. He took meticulous care in choosing, from various designs that he found in a Munich library, the form of an eagle which would be used on the party notepaper. He adopted the ancient Aryan swastika symbol, and he designed uniforms and party emblems which members were ordered to wear at all times. On September 17 he sent out his first circular letter to party members in his new position as party chairman. In it he gave details of the party's symbols and how they were to be used.

Hitler's oratorical skills, and his fierce denunciation of those whom he characterized as the 'enemies' of Germany – the signatories of the Versailles Treaty, the German Republic, the Jews – were combined with formidable organizational powers. As the party membership grew, he divided Germany up into districts (*Gaue*), each one under the authority of a *Gauleiter* (*Gau* leader). He also created, in 1921, a paramilitary arm, the SA; originally, in order to get round the Versailles Treaty ban on paramilitary groups, the initials stood for *Sportabteilung* (Sports Division). Later the same initials were taken to stand for a more sinister title, *Sturmabteilung* (Stormtroops).

From the uniform that the Stormtroops wore, they were also known as the Brownshirts. Their initial purpose was to beat off rival groups. They first proved their value in this regard on November 4, when Socialist Workers'

Party members attacked a Nazi Party meeting, determined to break it up. Hitler was half way through his speech when the workers attacked. There were fifty Brownshirts in the hall, and the attackers were beaten off.

The Brownshirts, Hitler explained in the first issue of their own newspaper, the SA *Gazette*, were not only an instrument for the protection of the Nazi movement, but were 'primarily the training school for the coming struggle for freedom on the domestic front'.

In Russia, the Bolsheviks, having conceded a large area of western Russia to Poland under the Treaty of Riga, and having accepted the independence of the Baltic States, consolidated their power elsewhere. Following the uprising in the Tambov province the previous year, there were further insurrections in Siberia by peasants who refused to hand over their grain and livestock. As many as 60,000 peasants took up arms, cutting several stretches of the Trans-Siberian railway in January and February 1921, and occupying two large towns, Tobolsk and Petropavlovsk. It took several months, and many executions, before the authority of the central government was restored.

To create a structure that could be controlled from Moscow, the vast area of Russia from the Gulf of Finland to the Pacific Ocean was declared a Russian Socialist Federative Soviet Republic (RSFSR). Within this area were six autonomous Soviet Republics of different nationalities, and an autonomous district. There were also two workers' communes, one of Karelians living along the Finnish border in the north, the other of Germans living on the Volga.

In what had previously been the Tsarist Empire, seven Soviet Republics were set up: Azerbaijan, Armenia, White Russia (Byelorussia), Ukraine, Georgia, Bokhara and Khiva. Most of these seven had been overrun by the Red Army in 1920, or were in the process of being conquered in 1921. Supreme authority throughout these vast regions derived from Moscow, and from the Central Committee of the Communist Party.

In her memoir *Hope Abandoned*, Nadezhda Mandelstam, wife of M – the writer Osip Mandelstam (later one of Stalin's millions of purge victims) – recalled the life of the writers and poets who were living in St Petersburg at the end of 1920 and in the first two months of 1921:

At the beginning of the twenties one could keep alive only on the rations issued by various public bodies, and there was a constant scramble to get them. The militia proved to be a powerful patron of the arts – both Georgi

Ivanov and Gumilev were fed by it. M. was also given a militia ration, either because there were no more 'academic' ones left or because he was thought unworthy of such favoured treatment. It was up to Gorky, the protector and patron in chief, to decide who got how much. He held all the keys to the modest, very relative comforts we enjoyed, and for this reason there was always a stream of people going to him to beg for things. When M. arrived after his endless wanderings and two stretches in White prisons, he found he was eligible for a little State charity. The Union of Poets applied to Gorky on his behalf for a pair of trousers and a sweater. Gorky agreed to the sweater, but the trousers he crossed out with his own hand: even then there was no nonsense about 'egalitarianism', and everybody got what the amount of his knowledge entitled him to – M.'s was not enough to earn him a pair of trousers. Gumilev let him have an extra pair of his . . .

Akhmatova also turned to Gorky for help, asking him to find her work and get her a ration, however small. She too had been refused an 'academic' ration and lived with Shileiko on the salted herring that he got from the Academy. Gorky explained to Akhmatova that she would get only the most beggarly of rations for doing office work of some kind, and then took her to see his collection of carpets. They were no doubt magnificent – you could buy things for a song at that time. When M. and I were leaving Moscow in 1921, we sold somebody a Tekin carpet of fairly good quality (we delivered it in a baby carriage). But my carpet was a quite ordinary one, not the sort you want for a collection. Akhmatova looked at Gorky's carpets, said how nice they were, and went away empty-handed. As a result of this, I believe, she took a permanent dislike to carpets. They smelled too much of dust and a kind of prosperity strange in a city that was dying so catastrophically.

M. did not stay very long – three and a half months, no more – in Petersburg. In February he fled . . . His last impression was the thunder of guns from Kronstadt . . .

Discontent with the autocratic nature of the Soviet regime had broken out in what had once been its citadel, the naval barracks at Kronstadt. It was on February 23 that the sailors raised the banner of revolt, and within a few days strikes broke out in Petrograd and Moscow. The desire everywhere was for bread, and for an end to the self-proclaimed 'dictatorship' of the Commissars through whom all authority passed.

Trotsky, as Commissar for the Army, ordered a former Tsarist officer, General Tukhachevsky, the Commander-in-Chief of the Red Forces, to crush the Kronstadt rebellion. Tukhachevsky acted with great ruthlessness. The cry of the sailors had been, 'Freely elected Soviets', but for Lenin this was a contradiction in terms. The meaning of the dictatorship of the proletariat, to which he and the Communist Party were committed, was that the Party would act in the way best suited to the needs of the proletariat. It did not mean that the voice of the proletariat, or of any other group, should have an elective value in the Western democratic sense, or that de Tocqueville's concept of the popular will should be a factor in policy-making.

In the North Caucasus the Muslim rebels led by Imam Gotsinskii continued to hold out in the mountains. Despite the Red Army's heavy casualties the previous year, it continued to track them down. The final assault came in March. On March 15 the Military Soviet at Petrovsk (Makhachkala) on the Caspian Sea issued its victory communiqué:

> At the price of innumerable victims from the Red Army, abundant blood-shed from modest unknown Red Army heroes, the backward Daghestani and Chechen masses were freed from the cabal of the White guard officer class, and the lies and deceptions of parasitic sheikhs and mullahs.
>
> The heroic units of the Red Army have endured heavy privations during the liquidation of the Terek-Daghestan uprising, fighting without interruption and bearing inhuman hardships.
>
> Hungry, cut off from the home front, overcoming all obstacles, they marched on towards their goal, breaking on the way the bitter resistance of the deceived Chechens and Daghestanis.
>
> The valiant units of the Red Army have shown to all counter-revolutionary elements of Chechnia and Daghestan the futility of their plots to overthrow Soviet power and destroy the Red Army.

Hundreds of Muslim fighters managed to withdraw into the remotest mountain regions. But the Red Army went after them with tens of thousands of men. On May 21 the last resistance was crushed. Imam Gotsinskii escaped and went into hiding. When he was caught five years later he was shot.

By the early spring of 1921, Lenin had to face up to the fact that, after more than three years, Communism had failed utterly to feed the Russian people, and that the economic methods on which he and his Party had insisted had led to bankruptcy and widespread starvation. In March, in a dramatic abandonment of Communist dogma, he introduced the New Economic Policy (NEP), designed to restore certain elements of capitalist commerce and exchange, and to enable trade to begin with the outside world. In this he was successful. A trade agreement was signed with Britain, on March 16, so trade could begin even before a peace treaty was signed. But no such peace treaty with Britain ever came into being. Under the Treaty of Riga, signed two days later, Russian trade with Poland was resumed. On May 6 a trade agreement was signed with Germany. Exports began, after a lapse of several years, to Britain, Germany, Estonia and the United States.[1]

Inside Russia, as the last of the peasant revolts in Siberia was being crushed, the compulsory requisitioning of grain was abolished, and compulsory deliveries of all agricultural produce was replaced by a tax in kind to the State amounting to just over half the produce that had been requisitioned compulsorily in 1920. Peasants were also allowed to put any surplus grain, potatoes and hay on the market.

By an Agrarian Law of March 21, small landowners were allowed to keep their land for at least nine years. Lenin recognized that he could not feed the workers in the factories if the small landowners were driven from their land, and the fields distributed in little packets to peasants who would not be able to manage them better, and would almost certainly produce less. 'We cannot prevent the progress of capitalism,' Lenin wrote in *Pravda* on May 6, 'but we can try to develop it into Russian State capitalism.' Two months later, a further decree enabled nationalized factories to be transferred to cooperatives, and even to private individuals. Shops could be opened in the towns, and trade could be conducted in the markets, without being hampered by the authorities.

The New Economic Policy gave Russia, for the first time since the 1917 revolution, a modicum of prosperity for those who could embark on trade or manufacture. But it came too late to prevent a widespread famine that summer throughout most of Central Russia. Hopes that the newly conquered Caucasus would provide the much-needed supplies of grain and food were not realized. Through inefficiency, and through the lack of economic incentives for producers, only half the quota reached the cities and towns where

[1] The main exports in 1921–2 were timber, animal hides, furs, bristles, asbestos and graphite.

food was in desperately short supply. Crop failure in Siberia added to the distress. In the Kuban, Cossacks were in revolt.

On August 5, *The Times*, under the heading 'The famine in Russia, starving hosts on the move', published an account by one of its correspondents:

> With the fields burnt dry and showing only here and there a few stalks of corn, the wretched men and women and children are making desperate attempts to support life like the beasts of the field, eating grass, dry leaves, and weeds, making cakes of acorn flour, eating the bones of animals ground to a powder, devouring at times even offal. Panic seizes them, and they flee in hundreds from their villages, nailing up their doors, and sometimes in a fit of wild despair setting their deserted dwellings on fire.
>
> Whither to flee they know not. The Cossacks from the northern districts of the Don are moving down towards the Kuban, famous for its wealth of corn, but for months past disorganized by Cossack revolts.
>
> All along the banks of the Volga great companies of starving men, women and children wait for days and days for some steamer to carry them away from the desolation. And they sicken and die whilst they wait.
>
> Then in the midst of the devastating drought cholera has appeared, has spread from the mouth of the Volga all through the famine area, and is being carried far and wide by the wandering hosts of starving peasantry.

As the famine area spread, Russian turned to the United States for immediate help, and an American Relief Administration established, which appealed to the American public. Help was forthcoming; the famine in Russia caught the imagination and sympathy of the United States, and substantial supplies were sent to alleviate it. An International Conference of all Red Cross societies agreed that two men – the League of Nations Commissioner for Refugees, Dr Fridtjof Nansen, the Norwegian scientist and explorer, and the former American President, Herbert Hoover – should exercise 'supreme control' of relief work in Russia. 'The conditions are even worse than I expected', Nansen – who was to be awarded the Nobel Peace Prize for his work in Russia – telegraphed to a British newspaper, the *Manchester Guardian*, on December 19: 'Words cannot possibly describe the misery and horrors I have seen. People are dying in their houses and in the village streets in the pitiless cold of a Russian winter without food or fuel to feed them. Millions must unavoidably die.'

Nansen was assisted, on his visit to the famine areas, by a Norwegian army officer, Captain Vidkun Quisling, who in 1940 was to welcome the German army to Norway and offer his services to them – establishing the word 'Quisling' as one of utter obloquy. Quisling's report on the famine in Russia made shocking reading. There was considerable evidence in it of cannibalism. In his report, Quisling reproduced a photograph of a young man from Zaporozhe who – according to the caption – 'has eaten his sister'. In some towns that Quisling visited thirty or forty people were dying of hunger each day; in Ekaterinoslav, eighty a day. At Kherson, of the 1197 famine dead when Quisling arrived, 836 were Jews. Throughout the Ukrainian and Black Sea regions of Russia, hundreds of thousands of Russians, Ukrainians and Jews, as well as local Germans, Poles, Roumanians, Bulgarians and Greeks had died. Hundreds of thousand more were dying.

Nansen publicized Quisling's appeals for help. A thousand tons of grain were sent from the people of Spain. The Czechoslovak government sent two trains of foodstuffs, there being a Czech minority (Ruthenians who also lived in eastern Czechoslovakia) in the famine region. The German government sent such aid as it could to the Germans of the area. From Jews in Britain and the United States came help for the Jews of the Ukraine, already ravaged by the vicious pogroms of the civil war. But Quisling warned that the situation was so bad 'that the starving population loses every hope and dies. Relief workers are also often on the point of giving up.'

Lenin had to make yet another compromise to prevent disaster, setting up an All-Russian Famine Relief Committee in which non-Communists, including Kadets and Socialist Revolutionaries, participated. On October 4 a new decree authorized private contractors to buy machinery, fuel and clothing from overseas. Cooperatives were also given the right to buy goods from abroad for the purpose of barter inside Russia. On November 23, hoping to attract foreign capital – five years after the revolution which was meant to destroy capitalism for all time – Lenin made it possible for foreign capitalists to gain concessions inside Russia, and to invest in profit-making enterprises; these included the leasing and renting of property. He also agreed that the drive to incorporate the Trade Union movement into the machinery of the State – something for which he had been pressing, as an indispensable aspect of Communist Party control, and which the Trade Unions opposed – should be slowed down. The aim of the compromise, a special commission explained, was 'to draw non-Party men into the service of the Soviet Government' and to retain the Trade Unions in a form 'in which workers of varying political and religious convictions might enter'.

A trade treaty was signed between the Soviet Union and Austria on December 7, widening yet further the areas in which Russian trade could be resumed. A week later, still searching for means whereby the peasant discontent with Communism could be assuaged, Lenin promulgated an Agrarian Law whereby peasants could retain whatever produce was needed to sustain themselves and their households. At the eighth All-Russian Congress of Soviets, which opened on December 21, he defended these measures.

Despite the famine and the New Economic Policy, Lenin had reason to be confident in the organization and development of his regime over the previous five years. The Constituent Assembly, with its rival left-wing parties, had been abolished. A secret police system was in operation, and those politicians and citizens who spoke openly against the regime were in prison; at the height of the New Economic Policy sixty-one people were executed in Petrograd, accused of conspiracy against the Soviet government, including a leading jurist, Lazarevksy, and the well-known poet Gumilev. The Kronstadt rebellion, like the conspiracy in Petrograd – if such it was – had been crushed. Wide areas of Tsarist Russia, including the Central Asian and Caucasian regions, had been retained within the territory of Bolshevik rule, and the Chechen and Daghestan revolts in the North Caucasus had been crushed. In eastern Siberia, after the execution of Admiral Kolchak, a Soviet Republic of the Far East had been set up at Vladivostok.

The last anti-Bolshevik Russians under arms, troops led by Generals Semenov, Kappel and Ungern-Sternberg, had been driven from their Siberian strongholds. The only setback, and it was no more than that, was when, on May 31, an anti-Bolshevik Russian, Merkulov, seized power in Vladivostok and declared an anti-Bolshevik government there. Lenin knew that he could reoccupy the region before too long. When, in November, Petliura emerged from his exile in Poland and tried to penetrate the Ukraine, his forces were driven out in disarray.

The forward march of Soviet Communism continued. Whenever internal danger threatened, the Bolsheviks were guided by Lenin's maxim: 'Two steps forward, one step backward' – and then two steps forward again. Nor was there any relaxation in the instruments of terror and repression. The dull, drab, poverty-stricken life of the mass of the Russian people was encumbered and controlled by the ever-present fear of the secret policeman's knock on the door.

In Ireland, the struggle by the IRA against British rule continued. The Republicans were determined to end British rule and to see an independent Ireland governed not from London but from Dublin. Thirty to forty people were being killed every week. After each IRA killing, reprisals were carried out by the British forces, principally the Black and Tans, but also by regular soldiers and the police. The British government could not decide whether to increase the military pressure on the IRA, or to approach the IRA's political umbrella, Sinn Fein, and seek a negotiated settlement. Protestant opinion in the north of Ireland was angered at the thought of London making terms with the Dublin parliament.

Some form of partition of Ireland seemed inevitable. When elections were held in southern Ireland on May 24, Sinn Fein candidates were returned unopposed in all but four of the 126 constituencies. In northern Ireland the Nationalists and Sinn Feiners won only twelve seats; the Unionists won forty. Two parliaments were set up, one in Dublin and one in Belfast. In Belfast, the Unionist leader Sir James Craig became the first Prime Minister of Northern Ireland, and the political separation of Ulster from the rest of Ireland became a reality.

In Dublin, on the day after the election, the IRA seized the Customs House and set it on fire, destroying large quantities of government records. In the ensuing battle, the police drove the IRA out, and six IRA men were killed.

The government in London had no intention of relinquishing British sovereignty over any part of Ireland. But it did seek a means of bringing the IRA to the negotiating table. With Lloyd George's approval, King George V gave the first intimation that conciliation was possible. At the opening of the Belfast Parliament on June 22 he appealed to all Irishmen 'to pause, to stretch out the hand of forbearance and conciliation, to forgive and forget, and to join in bringing for the land which they love a new era of peace, contentment, and goodwill.'

The British government called for a truce. The IRA accepted it. Under the terms of the truce, all killing would come to an end on July 11. Three days later, on July 14, De Valera met Lloyd George in the Cabinet room at 10 Downing Street. Six days after this meeting, Lloyd George presented the

British government's proposals: southern Ireland would be offered Dominion Home Rule, with complete control of her own taxation, finance, police and army. Britain would control imperial defence.

De Valera rejected the proposals and demanded complete independence. The idea of Ireland as an independent nation was, Lloyd George and his Cabinet ministers concluded, 'wholly unacceptable'. They nevertheless decided to continue with the negotiations. On October 11 the southern Irish leaders, including the leaders of the IRA, went to Downing Street to renew negotiations. Only De Valera refused to attend, claiming that as he was the 'President' of his country and Lloyd George only the Prime Minister, he was too senior to attend. The most prominent Irish delegate was Michael Collins, the Minister of Home Affairs and Finance Minister in the Sinn Fein government. He offered Britain the permanent neutrality of southern Ireland in the event of any conflict in which Britain might become involved in Europe or elsewhere. But Lloyd George wanted Britain to retain control of the Irish ports, and to retain the ability to use Ireland as part of Britain's defences in any future European conflict.

Britain was prepared to look upon southern Ireland, not as an integral part of the United Kingdom, but as part of the British Empire. The Irish delegates replied, with reference to the Irishmen who had made their lives and careers around the world, 'We too are a far-flung nation'. As the talks continued, Lloyd George told his own negotiating team: 'We do not intend to have political domination'. The Irish delegates accepted this, but rejected any British defence control.

After two months of negotiations, and many tense moments in which it looked as though the IRA would return to violence, the Sinn Fein and British delegates reached agreement. 'We had become allies in a common cause,' Churchill, one of the British negotiators of the Treaty, later wrote, 'the cause of the Irish Treaty and of peace between the two races and two islands.'

The Irish Treaty was signed on December 6. Southern Ireland became to all intents and purposes independent, but Britain remained 'solely responsible' for the security of Britain and Ireland 'and the seas around them'. The southern Irish ports would remain part of a British defence strategy in the event of war. Southern Ireland would remain under the British Crown, with Dominion Status, having the same degree of independence as Canada, Australia, New Zealand and South Africa. The oath to be taken by members of the Irish Free State Parliament would swear allegiance to the constitution of the Free State; they would also swear to be 'faithful to His Majesty King George V'. Northern Ireland would remain an integral part of the United Kingdom.

Southern Ireland was to have its own Parliament and Courts of Law. All taxes raised by the British in Southern Ireland that year were transferred to the Dublin government 'for Irish internal administration'. De Valera, angered that the Treaty had not secured full independence, resigned as President of the Dail. Seeking re-election, he was defeated. On 15 January 1922 the Dail approved the treaty and Michael Collins was appointed Prime Minister. British troops were withdrawn and the Black and Tans disbanded. The Free State government then granted an amnesty for all British forces, policemen and civil servants who had committed or assisted 'acts of hostility against the Irish people', and declared, in explanation: 'We must not suffer ourselves to be outdone by our late enemies in seeking that the wrongs of the past may be buried in oblivion.'

The Irish Treaty held. Northern Ireland remained a part of the United Kingdom, while Southern Ireland, despite its relative poverty, embarked upon all the challenges and achievements of statehood, evolving a year later into the Irish Free State, and in due course successfully negotiating her neutrality, withdrawal of the British naval bases, and transformation into a Republic. The enemies of the Treaty, led by De Valera, tried to disrupt it from its first hours, but in vain.

The United States, to which Sinn Fein had always looked for support, and where an unofficial American Commission on Ireland had regularly denounced the reprisals of the Black and Tans (though not the IRA acts which provoked them) was herself in turmoil in 1921. Although Woodrow Wilson's successor, President Warren G. Harding, maintained America's withdrawal from the European and wider responsibilities thrust upon her by her participation in the First World War, the Peace Treaties and the establishment of the League of Nations, many Americans still felt that the United States had a role to play on the international stage, most importantly in the prevention of future wars.

The catalyst to this feeling was the high military and naval budgets. General Pershing, who had commanded the American forces on the Western Front, took a lead in calling for a reduction in arms expenditure. Senator Borah, an independent Republican, proposed a conference between Britain, the United States and Japan, to negotiate some form of mutually agreed halt to naval expansion, an agreement of the sort that Churchill had twice proposed to the Germans before the First World War. In response to the growing mood, Congress cut back the size of the American army from 288,000 men to 175,000.

Whether the United States could really isolate itself from the problems of the world was uncertain. As dispute after dispute was dealt with by the Supreme Allied Council, from which America had withdrawn more than a year earlier, there was a feeling that the United States ought to exert some influence, if only as a force for moderation and common sense; and there were also American interests involved. In May, America asked to be readmitted to the Council, and was allowed to do so, sending an 'observer', the new American ambassador in London, George Harvey. This was America's first re-entry into world affairs.

Those in the United States who wanted to take a lead in world disarmament were encouraged by Harvey's position at the Supreme Council. Starting on May 17, a three-day conference was held in Chicago, at which Protestant, Catholic and Jewish leaders participated, and from which the call went out for an American disarmament initiative. In July, President Harding invited Britain, France, Italy and Japan to a conference in Washington to discuss naval disarmament with regard to the Pacific and the Far East. To ensure that this was not seen as a case of large powers ganging up on weaker ones, Belgium, Holland, Portugal and China were also invited. With the expiry of the Anglo-Japanese Alliance of 1905, there were also discussions about widening the Supreme Council to become a Four-Power agreement, with the United States and France also participating, but there was alarm in the United States that this might constitute one of the very alliances that isolationist America had spurned.

Even as the call was going out for a reduction in armaments, the United States was confronted by cause for concern in three areas under its own control. In the Philippines, agitation had begun for an end to American rule. In the Dominican Republic there were protests against the continuing American occupation. And in Haiti, there were allegations of cruelty against the American marines stationed there. Closer to home, in the American South, there had been a revival of activity by the Ku Klux Klan, with fifty-nine black Americans being lynched, five of them burnt to death, and five of them burnt after they had been killed. Mutilations, branding with acid, floggings, tarring-and-feathering, and kidnappings were frequent occurences. At Tulsa, Oklahoma, a battle between whites and blacks broke out on May 31 which resulted in the deaths of 200 people.

In reaction to these killings, a privately initiated Inter-Racial Committee was established in Tulsa. It grew in strength, with black and white members dedicated to the elimination of racial animosity. Its success by the end of the year in gaining considerable local support prompted the President to establish a Federal Inter-Racial Commission. But the evil of racism remained strong, and despite the scorn poured upon the Ku Klux Klan, especially by the northern newspapers, for its 'un-American character', it seemed to flourish on the notoriety it had obtained during the revival of its activities; in the following year, tar-and-feather parties, the murder and the torture of blacks continued, with fifty-one reported lynchings of blacks that year, thirteen of them being men who had been taken from jails, and seventeen men who had been seized from law officers outside jails. There was some encouragement for the anti-racists, when it was announced that in that same year there were fifty-eight recorded instances in which officers of the law prevented lynchings. But lynchings remained a scourge, reflecting the deep-seated racism of the South.

Another cause of concern inside the continental United States was the steady increase in the number of people out of work. In January 1921 that figure stood at 3,473,466. By August it had risen precipitately to 5,735,000. Also that year, for the first time in United States history, the size of the urban population overtook that of the rural population. While urban unemployment had risen, rural prosperity fell, with the previous year's crop, which had been gathered on the highest wages paid since the Civil War, being sold at prices lower than any since 1914. In one agricultural State alone, Ohio, 60,000 men and boys left the farms for the cities in a single year. It was the middle classes who were most strongly hurt in 1921, when a stock-market crash wiped out the savings of many millions of people.

One particular domestic event gave Americans cause for satisfaction in 1921. Few then realized how dramatically it would be extended in the years to come. On the morning of February 22 seven sacks of mail were strapped to an aeroplane in San Francisco and dropped off at Mineola, Long Island, on the following afternoon. The total flying time had been twenty-five hours and twenty-one minutes, at an average speed of 81 miles an hour. The American transcontinental domestic air-mail service was born.

Across the Pacific, in Australia, that same month saw two biplanes carrying both passengers and mail on a regular flight from western Queensland to the Northern Territory. A political aspect to flight was also in evidence in 1921. The regular air service that was operating that year between Berlin and Königsberg linked two parts of Germany that had been cut off from each other as a result of the Versailles Treaty. Within a year the Poles had also established an air link between their capital, Warsaw, and the East Galician city of Lvov, a city which, in the Austro-Hungarian days just past, had no fast rail access across what had been for so many years the Austro-Russian frontier.

On November 11 the body of America's Unknown Soldier was laid to rest in the National Cemetery at Arlington, Virginia. The oration that day, which was spoken by President Harding, was judged by one listener to have been 'among the inspired utterances' of American statesmen. In the course of his tribute, Harding declared:

I speak not as a pacifist fearing war, but as one who loves justice and hates war. I speak as one who believes the highest function of government is to give its citizens the security of peace, the opportunity to achieve, and the pursuit of happiness.

The loftiest tribute we can bestow today – the heroically earned tribute – fashioned in deliberate conviction out of unclouded thought, neither shadowed by remorse nor made vain by fancies, is the commitment of this Republic to an advancement never made before. If American achievement is a cherished pride at home, if our unselfishness among nations is all we wish it to be, and ours is a helpful example in the world, then let us give of our influence and strength, yea, of our aspiration and convictions, to put mankind on a little higher plane, exulting and exalting, with war's distressing and depressing tragedies barred from the stage of righteous civilization.

There have been a thousand defences justly and patriotically made; a thousand offences which reason and righteousness ought to have stayed. Let us beseech all men to join us in seeking the rule under which reason and righteousness shall prevail.

Standing today on hallowed ground, conscious that all America has halted to share in the tribute of heart and mind and soul to this fellow-

American, and knowing that the world is noting this expression of the Republic's mindfulness, it is fitting to say that his sacrifice, and that of the millions of dead, shall not be in vain. There must be, there shall be, the commanding voice of a conscious civilization against armed warfare.

On the day after Harding's oration, the United States put forward its proposals for a worldwide limitation of armaments. It was a proposal which Arthur Balfour called 'the basis of the greatest reform in the matter of armaments and the preparation for war that has ever been conceived or carried out by the courage and patriotism of statesmen'.

CHAPTER TWENTY-SIX

1922

THE EFFORTS BY THE UNITED STATES to secure a comprehensive naval disarmament treaty for the Pacific and the Far East reached fruition on 6 February 1922. This date was considered a landmark in the hoped-for peaceful amelioration of the postwar world. In all, seven separate treaties were concluded that day in Washington. Not only was there general agreement among the five signatories – Britain, France, Italy, Japan and the United States – for a reduction in naval armaments, but agreement was also reached denouncing the use of poison gas in warfare, and condemning as 'piratical' under international law all submarine attacks on merchant ships, whether these merchantmen were armed or not. With the stroke of a pen, two of the most hated weapons of the First World War, gas, and the submarine sinkings of merchant ships, were abolished, at least on paper.

The Washington Agreements reflected the desire of the peoples of the world, especially those who had been through the maelstrom of the First World War, to see the evils of warfare eliminated. That strong nations were capable of turning their back on the evil past in this way gave cause for optimism. That the United States' Senate, which scarcely two years earlier had turned its back on the Versailles Treaty and the League of Nations, should ratify the Washington Agreements, and in particular the Four-Power Pacific Pact, and do so by a clear vote of 67 to 27, was further cause for international optimism. So too was the agreement reached in Washington by China and Japan, whereby Japan would withdraw from all the rights and territories she had acquired in China as a result of the defeat of Germany. The port of Tsingtao was returned to China, as were all railway rights and trading concessions.

The China which was struggling, with some success, to assert its independence from foreign governments and creditors, was a divided nation. Rival governments in the north and south were fighting for power. Provincial governors, dissatisfied with their powers, ignored the centres of government, or sought to subvert them. In reaction to the corruption and conflict, the socialist ideas of Karl Marx, Louis Blanc and St Simon were beginning to take hold. Whether the Communism which was dominating Russia could likewise be imposed on China was a question as yet unanswered. But it had begun to be asked.

Another unanswered question was whether the United States would participate in the continuing regulation of the affairs of Europe after the Washington Agreements had brought her back to the centre of the world diplomatic stage. The postwar conferences which she had not attended had reached their conclusions. The principal frontiers of Europe and Asia Minor had been redrawn without her. Her League of Nations Mandates over Armenia, and over Constantinople and the Straits, had never been taken up. But still to come were two important conferences, one at Genoa to discuss Russia, and one at Lausanne to discuss Turkey.

To the surprise of those in the United States who presumed that the Washington Agreements were the beginning of greater involvement, President Harding declined, through his Secretary of State, Charles E. Hughes, to participate in the Genoa Conference. The reason given was that Russia, from the point of view of the United States, was in 'an unsatisfactory political condition'. In fact, Lenin's New Economic Policy, with its revival of various forms of private enterprise and capitalist endeavour, was exactly the opportunity which the European Powers sought to find a way to build bridges with Russia. It was agreed, however, that an American 'observer' should be present at Genoa, and henceforth no European conference took place without an American observer being present. One British commentator noted at the end of the year: 'No plant was ever of more rapid growth, for the American "observer", silent at the Genoa Conference in April and May, was freely discussing the questions raised at the Lausanne Conference for the framing of peace with Turkey.' The highly critical remarks of the American observer at the meetings of the Reparations Commission in Paris at the end of the year – remarks devoted to the 'unworkability' of the Versailles Treaty – attracted considerable public attention.

Isolationism was not in retreat. That November saw the re-election to the Senate of Robert La Follette, a leading antiwar Senator, and the outspoken champion of keeping America out of the entanglements of the globe. He had opposed both America's entry into the war and her adherence to the

League of Nations. Two years later, as a Presidential nominee, he failed in his bid, but received almost five million votes.

The shadow of what had become known as the Great War hung over all the former combatants. On May 11, King George V began a visit to the trenches and battlefields of the Western Front. The journey was officially described as a 'pilgrimage', and took the King to many of the war cemeteries whose serried rows of wooden crosses were even then being replaced by stone engraved headstones. 'In the course of my pilgrimage,' he wrote, 'I have many times asked myself whether there can be more potent advocates of peace upon earth through the years to come than this massed multitude of silent witnesses to the desolation of war.'

Thirty-six years after the King's pilgrimage, Leon Wolff recalled another aspect of the Western Front, its tourist potential, which, even as the King uttered his solemn words, was ensuring that groups of visitors made their way to the battlegrounds, guidebooks in hand, to be invited to purchase what could be retrieved of the gruesome relics of war fewer than five years after hostilities had ceased:

On Hill 60 the peasants dug up vast quantities of souvenirs – buttons, badges, pistols, boots, the bones of soldiers, holsters, wooden pipes, cartridges, shell fragments, and the like – and sold their wares out of little boxes to tourists who flowed like battalions across the ex-battlefield. Everything was priced quite methodically: twenty francs for a Smith and Wesson revolver, one penny for a brass button, and so on.

A former soldier became caretaker of one portion of the Ridge maintained as a memorial in its original state. He lived in an army hut, talked to visitors, and for one franc conducted them on his little tour of Death Trench. Each day after tea the caretaker and his dog walked down the communications trench (Princes Street) to the support line (Paradise Alley), up International Trench to the mine-crater, through formless Schenken Redoubt, and returned by way of the sap that entered the German dug-outs (Piccadilly Buildings).

He mended the duckboards, noted where the imitation concrete sandbags were split by frost, and kept the shallow trenches at the summit boarded up; and as he walked his heavy boots rasped against the remnants of rusty barbed wire and occasionally jostled a helmet, or a rifle barrel from which the wood had long since decayed. Only this, and sometimes the barking of his dog, disturbed the death-like silence where once men had screamed in fear and agony amid the clamour of the guns.

Throughout 1922, the situation in Germany was dominated by widespread discontent against reparations. This had already given Hitler one of his most popular themes for his anti-government rallies. The German government's own reluctance to pay was answered by the Allies in the London Ultimatum of 5 May 1921, in which it was made clear that Germany must begin payments at once, and according to a specific timetable. But by the beginning of 1922 Germany was suffering from an acute economic crisis. The loss of industrial territory, the loss of manpower in war casualties, and the demoralization of defeat, combined to create a downward spiral of confidence and productive economic activity. It was this economic morass that forced the German government to explain to the Allies that it did not have the financial or material resources from which to meet the reparations demands.

When the Allies rejected a German request for a postponement in the payment, there was further economic depression in Germany. The German government asked the Bank of England for a loan of £25 million. There was consternation in German financial circles when the Bank of England declined. The bank's refusal was on the grounds that no credit could be given to Germany as long as she was 'saddled with her present load of reparation debt'.

The dates set by the Allies for the first two reparations payments due in 1922 were January 15 and February 15. The German government, having already said it could only pay part of these two instalments, announced that it must seek a postponement of both amounts. The Supreme Allied Council met to discuss this impasse in an emergency session at Cannes (where Lloyd George was on holiday). As the discussions continued, German delegates were asked to attend to explain the situation. The head of the German delegation, Walther Rathenau, set out Germany's financial problems in a way that made a strong and positive impression on the Council. As a result of Rathenau's representations, the Supreme Council granted Germany a postponement on its first two monthly payments for the year, and also agreed to a small reduction in the scale of payments. The German government immediately asked for a greater reduction.

That January, an unexpected interruption in the process of reparations reduction was caused by the election, while the Cannes conference was in session, of a new French President, Raymond Poincaré. In his first speech as President he accused the German government of 'maliciously avoiding' the fulfilment of her obligations. After a month and a half of further negotiations, the Reparations Commission, recognizing Germany's dire economic situation, fixed the sums that Germany would have to pay at the amount proposed by the German government. The Commission then urged the German government to introduce stringent tax-gathering measures, in order to ensure, through the German taxpayer, that the reparations obligations could be met. The German government denounced this proposal as 'an intolerable infringement' of German sovereignty.

The German government was insisting on acting, and on responding, not as a defeated nation but as an equal one. It was the Kaiser and the monarchy that had been beaten in 1918, not the postwar Republic. In order to assert this sovereignty, and to reduce still further the reparations pressures, Rathenau asked that Germany's capacity to pay should not be laid down by the Reparations Commission, but assessed by a committee of experts. At first the Allies rejected this, but with the invitation to Germany to attend the World Economic Congress in Genoa, the German government felt that it had won a moral as well as a potential economic victory. An investigation of the world's economic problems, and their interconnection, would, the German Chancellor, Dr Wirth, told the Reichstag on January 26, 'help to put the question of reparations more and more into its true light, and so favour the reasonable and practicable solution of the problem advocated by Germany'.

At Genoa, Germany was represented by Wirth, Rathenau (who had just been appointed Foreign Minister) and Dr Hermes, the Minister of Finance. This was to be the first of a series of meetings at which the German reparations question was discussed as between equals. But the conference was overshadowed by a development which came, for all but the German delegates, as a bolt from the blue. Twenty miles along the coast from Genoa is the Italian resort town of Rapallo. There, on April 16, while the Genoa conference was still in session, the German delegates concluded, on behalf of the German government, a treaty with the Russian government, which had sent its Foreign Minister, Georgi Chicherin, to Rapallo as its chief negotiator.

The Treaty of Rapallo constituted a peace treaty between Germany and the Soviet Union. The terms of the treaty laid down that both countries, which had been so severely weakened by the war, give up all financial claims against each other arising from the war. Germany also agreed to set aside, as no longer valid, all private German claims arising out of Russian postwar 'measures of socialism' – that is, confiscation of property. Diplomatic relations were restored, and the Russian ambassador's palace in Berlin, which had been empty since 1914, was handed over to the Bolsheviks. One clause of the Treaty gave the German armaments firm of Krupp the right to manufacture war material inside Russia, for the Russian government.

The Allies at Genoa were indignant that Germany had concluded this pact with Russia under its nose, and with no prior notification. In retaliation, Germany was ejected from the commission dealing at Genoa with Russian affairs. But the Allies had to admit that they had no legal right to object to the Treaty, and Dr Hermes, proceeding to Paris, continued to negotiate the German reparations payment schedule. He reached an agreement, much to Germany's satisfaction, that the 1922 payments could be postponed, and that the German government would maintain the new schedules of payment on condition that an international loan to help her do so could be raised 'in due time'.

To help secure this loan, the United States also played its part, with the Director of the Federal Reserve Bank in New York, Benjamin Strong, joining a specially constituted Loan Committee in Paris. As discussions proceeded in Paris, leading, much to Germany's satisfaction, to a moratorium on all German reparations payments for 1922, there took place in Berlin what one contemporary British commentator called 'the most terrible event in the history of the German Republic during the year'. On the morning of June 24, just after leaving his house in an open car, Walther Rathenau was assassinated. His assassins were three nationalist extremists who considered Rathenau, as a Jew, to be a traitor to Germany. For many weeks before the assassination, the streets of Berlin had resounded with the cry of extremist marchers, "Knock off Walther Rathenau, the Goddamned, filthy Jewish sow."

An eye-witness wrote of the reaction of the working-class Berliners to Rathenau's death:

By noon on the day of the murder the news had spread, and the workers began swarming from the factories and shops to form countless processions. These soon merged into one and moved solemnly and irresistibly through the streets of the middle and upper class West. Four deep they marched in their hundred thousands, beneath their mourning banners, the red of Socialism and the black-red-gold of the Republic, in one endless disciplined procession, passing like a portent silently along the great thoroughfares lined by immense crowds, wave after wave, from the early afternoon till late into the June sunset.

The Nationalists had speculated on a rising which they hoped would have to be suppressed by force, and thus prepare public opinion for a dictatorship; the silent display of their power was the answer of the workers. It gave the German people a striking and unforgettable vision of the real forces governing its political constitution and of what had up to then been but an abstract conception, the birth of the German Republic.

That afternoon, in the Reichstag, the Chancellor, Dr Wirth, denounced the extremist organizations which touted anti-Semitism, chauvinism, nationalism and monarchism, and, pointing to the almost empty benches where normally the Nationalist deputies sat, called out angrily: 'The real enemies of our country are those who instil this poison into our people. We know where we have to seek them. The Enemy stands on the Right!'

In Munich, on the day of Rathenau's assassination, Adolf Hitler was sentenced to two weeks in prison. He had been found guilty of inciting a riot against the Bavarian authorities. That summer, his Nazi Party was banned in Prussia, Baden and Thuringia for the rest of the year.

From his exile in Holland, the former Kaiser granted an audience that month with a German visitor, Baron Clemens von Radowitz. Asked if he hoped to return to the throne, he told the Baron, in an interview published in the *New York Times*, 'I want nothing except to hide myself.' The Kaiser also praised Germany's first Chancellor, Friedrich Ebert, 'for regarding himself as the servant and not as the master of the Republic, and for not attempting to do more than his duties prescribe'.

The Kaiser was not all sweetness and light however, as the *New York Times*'s report made clear:

In his exile William has become obsessed with a deep-seated anti-Semitism. This hatred of Jews, his interviewer hints, is leading him in the direction of Roman Catholicism, the mystic side of which has always strongly appealed to the ex-Kaiser. He hears constantly from Roman Catholic Bishops on the Rhine about religious matters. His conversation invariably plays around religious questions, much to the exasperation of those in his entourage.

For the late ex-Emperor Charles of Austria he expressed profound pity to his interviewer: 'Weakened and easily led,' he observed, 'Charles suffered a hard fate. It was foolish of him to try to get back to Budapest against the wish of the Allies. Success was impossible under these conditions.'

Austria and Hungary, he believes, will never come together again, and he does not want Austria united with Germany, believing that Germany's recovery will only be retarded by association with a country in so bad a shape as Austria.

As to Czechoslovakia, the Kaiser 'does not, he says, "like republics," but admires the patriotism of Dr Masaryk, and expects that in a few years there will be a friendly understanding between the Czechs and the German Bohemians, and that the Czechs will join in an economic union with their German neighbours.'

In Austria there were repeated calls during 1922 for *Anschluss* – union with Germany – a move that was forbidden under the Austrian treaty with the Allies, and about which even the ex-Kaiser had not been enthusiastic. The League of Nations was negotiating a substantial loan to Austria, the guarantors of which were Britain, France, Italy and Czechoslovakia. The loan was meant to enable the country to restore its economic fortunes. One condition for the loan was that Austria must 'preserve her independence'. *Anschluss*, despite its emotional appeal to many Austrians, had to be set aside.

To supervize the loan, the League appointed a Dutchman as High Commissioner for Austria: Dr Zimmerman, a former mayor of Rotterdam. The League, in return for Austria putting its economic house in order, and thus averting a renewal of civil strife in the heart of Europe, abolished all reparations demands, and 'guaranteed the independence of Austria'. The one problem confronting Austria on its borders was not of its own making. An International Boundary Commission, under the auspices of the League, was tracing the border between Austria and Hungary in the Burgenland. As the commission worked, trying to find a line that would be in accord with the national composition of the Austrian and Hungarian inhabitants of the region, the Hungarian government demanded considerable rectifications in its favour, which would have deprived Austria of 23 per cent of the German-speaking parts of the region, a loss of twenty villages.

As a defeated nation, Austria still had its national pride; indeed, the writing of prewar and wartime Austrian history had begun to put substantial blame for the disintegration of the Habsburg monarchy on the policies pursued by the Hungarian half of the Empire. Fortunately for Austria's peace of mind, and for the peace of the region, the boundary commission ruled in Austria's favour.

At the very moment when the commission was ruling in Austria's favour in the Burgenland dispute, the Emperor Charles contracted pneumonia and died in exile on the Portuguese island of Madeira. He was not quite thirty-five years old. Although he had made no attempt to regain the throne of Austria since being deposed by the Austrian parliament in 1919, he had twice tried, in 1921, to regain the throne of Hungary. In Vienna, a Requiem Mass was said. It was followed by a large monarchist demonstration in favour of the restoration of Habsburg rule. The Austrian government refused, however, to lower the flags to half-mast. As in Germany, republicanism had come to stay.

Two Italian towns, Genoa and Rapallo, had been the scene of international conferences in the early months of 1922. But it was not for diplomatic activity that the focus of Europe and the United States turned to Italy in 1922. On July 13, as a culmination of the almost daily street battles which had developed between the Fascists, under the leadership of Benito Mussolini, and the Italian Socialists, Fascist forces broke into the Socialist headquarters in Cremona and looted them. They also occupied the municipal buildings, and burnt the apartment of the local parliamentary deputy representing the largest party in the Italian parliament.

In a parliamentary debate on the violence in Cremona, Mussolini said that the Fascist party might soon have to decide whether it was a constitutional or a revolutionary party. If the latter, it would no longer feel obliged to sit in parliament. The party had at its disposal, he warned, large, well-disciplined and well-organized forces.

The failure of the predominantly Liberal government of Luigi Facta to deal with the Fascist actions in Cremona led to Facta's resignation. The King, Victor Emmanuel — who had come to the throne twenty-two years earlier — then tried to put together a new administration. Mussolini might have been persuaded to join it, but the seasoned politicians, long used to jockeying for power among themselves, had nothing but scorn for the thirty-nine-year-old rabble-rouser, whose parliamentary representation was so small, and whose nationalist oratory was so bombastic.

For twelve days Italy was without a government. Then Facta was asked to form a new government. He did so, but was confronted on August 1, after being in office for only twenty-four hours, by a Socialist general strike. Mussolini gave Facta's government forty-eight hours to take action against the strikers. When Facta failed to do so, Mussolini ordered his men to take over essential public services and to keep them running. After one more day the strike collapsed.

The Fascists' success in breaking the general strike was a blow to the Socialists, to the government, and to the constitutional authority of the State. 'We must face facts,' one Socialist newspaper wrote. 'The Fascists are masters of the field. Nothing is to prevent them dealing more heavy blows, in the certainty of winning fresh victories.' Mussolini prepared his Fascist militia for a march on Rome. On August 13 the Prefect of Milan reported to the Minister of the Interior in Rome that the army could not be relied upon to challenge the Fascists in an emergency. As many as 200,000 men were in Fascist military formations; these were the Blackshirts whose uniform struck terror into those whom they assaulted, or who saw them on the rampage.

Mussolini was bolstered in his confidence by the reception he was given during a Fascist rally at Udine on September 20, when he declared that violence could be a 'moral necessity' if it was used to resolve what he called a 'cancerous' political situation. But violence was not a sport, he said; it needed to be disciplined, and to be adapted to the needs of the moment. The task of Fascism was to weld the nation into an organic whole that would work for the greatness of Italy. He had, he said, abandoned republicanism. When heckled about this, he replied that Mazzini had not thought it inconsistent with his republican beliefs to accept a united Italy under a monarchy. The Fascist aim, Mussolini declared, was not to destroy the fabric of the State, but to demolish the 'social-democratic superstructure' which had served Italy so badly in the past. Under Fascism, the Italian State would 'embrace all, protect all, and oppose all who threatened its sovereignty'. It was the State that would emerge, belatedly, from the Italian victory of 1918, and would be the guarantor of Italy's greatness in the future.

Mussolini insisted that he wanted to come to power through Parliamentary elections and the popular vote. But at the end of September, he ordered Fascist units to occupy Bolzano and Trent. Plans were made to seize Parma, and on October 6 he discussed with his closest confidants the prospects of a march on Rome itself. When he spoke at Cremona on October 11, his Fascist supporters called out in unison: 'To Rome! To Rome!'

The Blackshirt rank and file throughout Italy expected some dramatic action. Having set up their military headquarters at Perugia, the Fascist commanders established three armed columns within thirty miles of Rome, to the west, north and east of the city. Column one, near Civitavecchia, had 4000 men, column two at Monterotonda, had 2000, and column three, at Tivoli, had 8000. There was also a reserve formation of 3000 men at Foligno, seventy miles away.

On October 16, Mussolini met his senior confederates in Milan. They discussed a military move, but Mussolini refused to commit himself to a definite date, and postponed the planned seizure of Parma. On October 22 he was buoyed up when the Fascists won all seven seats at the municipal elections in Reggio Emilia. Perhaps he would still be asked to come to power by constitutional means. On October 24 he was in Naples, for a Congress of the Fascist Party. The party, he said, was at a crossroads. It would come to power either through parliamentary success or insurrection. The Fascists were not prepared 'to enter the portals of power by the tradesman's entrance and to sell their birthright for a miserable bowl of ministerial potage'.

That afternoon Mussolini told a vast gathering of 40,000 Fascists who marched past him in review in military formation: 'I assure you in all solemnity that the hour has struck. Either they give us the government or we shall take it, by marching on Rome. Now it is a matter of days or hours.' That night, in his Naples hotel room, Mussolini received the General commanding the Naples district, Frederico Baistrocchi, who assured him that the army formations in the south of Italy looked with 'great sympathy' on Fascism and its leader. For Mussolini, whose political base and main strength was in the north, this was welcome news.

On October 25 Mussolini left Naples by train for Milan. On the following day a Fascist Manifesto, issued by the Naples congress (which was still in session), announced 'the impending march on Rome, in order to cut the Gordian knot and hand over to the King and army a renewed Italy.' In secret, October 28 was the day set for the seizure of Rome by the three military columns which had been assembled at Civitavecchia, Monterotonda and Tivoli. In Rome itself, Luigi Facta spent October 26 debating whether to try to form a new government with Fascist participation, or to resign. Facta's rival for the premiership, should the leadership of Italy change yet again, was a former Prime Minister, Antonio Salandra (under whom Italy had declared war in 1915). On October 27, hoping to be able to construct a ministry of his own to replace Facta's, Salandra invited Mussolini to Rome, with the clear implication that the Fascists could have a significant place in any future Salandra government.

Mussolini declined to leave Milan. Facta's refusal to resign the premiership made it impossible for Salandra to make Mussolini a definite offer of important ministries. But during the day, news of the Fascist military preparations began to circulate in Rome. That evening Facta went to the King and resigned. He explained that he did not have the means to halt the Fascist preparations. He also proposed that the King proclaim a state of siege in the capital, but the King preferred to postpone such a drastic measure. That day, Fascist troops seized the main government buildings in Perugia.

Until Facta's successor could be found, he and his Cabinet remained in charge of the government, as provided for by the constitution. During the night of October 27/28 reports reached Facta's office of Fascist seizures of power in towns throughout Italy. On the morning of October 28 Facta asked the King to proclaim a state of siege at noon, but the King refused to do so. He had lost patience with Facta, with incompetent government, and with the chaos of the constantly changing political constellations and administrations. The King had also to face up to the reality of the military strength of Fascism, and of its rapidly spreading control of so many Italian towns.

That day, October 28, the King invited Mussolini to Rome to speak to him. The implication was that Mussolini would be asked to join the next government, possibly one headed by Salandra, in a senior position, with several other important ministerial portfolios given to other Fascists. But when the Fascist representatives in Rome urged Mussolini to accept this outcome, he replied tersely: 'It was not worth while mobilizing the Fascist army, causing a revolution, killing people, for the sake of a Salandra-Mussolini coalition. I will not accept.'

Mussolini's refusal to go to Rome led to a second appeal from the royal palace, a telephone call from the King's aide-de-camp, again inviting him to Rome to discuss the political crisis. Once again, the assumption was that several senior Ministries would be found for him and other Fascist leaders within a new government headed by someone else. Mussolini replied that the time was past for consultations of ministerial combinations. He would only leave Milan if it was he who was to be entrusted with forming a government. When Salandra also invited him to Rome that day, he returned the same reply. He would be Prime Minister or nothing.

In the early hours of October 29 several Fascist leaders in Rome telephoned

Mussolini and begged him to join a Salandra government. They were afraid that if he did not, and the march on Rome went ahead, it would fail, and they would all be arrested. Later that morning, Salandra told the King that he was unable to form a government, and he advised the King to ask Mussolini to do so. Mussolini insisted that any such request must be made in writing; he wanted a telegram sent to him in Milan, stating that the King intended to appoint him Prime Minister. The telegram arrived at noon.

As there was no train to Rome that afternoon, Mussolini had to wait in Milan until the evening. Then he took the night train, telling the stationmaster who saw him off: 'I want to leave exactly on time. From now on everything has got to function perfectly.' At 9.30 on the following morning the train stopped at Civitavecchia. Mussolini got off to inspect the Fascist militia there (no march on Rome having taken place). An hour later he reached Rome and drove to see the King, who formally entrusted him with the task of forming a government.

Italy was about to embark on two decades of Fascism. Mussolini became Prime Minister and Minister of the Interior. At the age of thirty-nine, he was the youngest of the twenty-four men who had served as Prime Minister – some more than once – in the sixty years since the unification of Italy. Of his Cabinet of fourteen, only four were Fascists; Mussolini intended to govern through parliament, but did not have enough senior followers experienced in parliamentary administration. To begin with, democratic procedures would have to be followed.

While Mussolini began to form his government, his Fascist militia were still awaiting the call to march on Rome and to seize power. They were no longer needed for this task, but had been eager for action. Mussolini invited them into the capital, where they took part in a rousing review attended by the King, and were then sent away. Mussolini did not want disorder in the streets to mar the first days of his premiership. Intervening directly with the railway administration, he ensured that the last of the enthusiastic 'victors' of the march on Rome had left the capital by the early hours on October 31.

Two weeks later, on November 16, Mussolini laid his political programme before both houses of the Italian parliament. It was said by a British observer 'that since the time of Oliver Cromwell no Prime Minister has ever spoken more haughtily to a House of Parliament', though it was noted that he treated the Upper House with respect. The new government, Mussolini told the legislators, was willing to resume full responsibility. It was therefore asking the Chamber of Deputies to grant it full powers. If the Chamber refused, the government would take the powers 'of its own accord'.

The full powers which Mussolini asked for were voted to him by the Chamber of Deputies on November 25, by 275 votes to 90. Italian Fascism, hitherto a movement of street violence, strike-breaking and the seizure of municipal power, became, by the free vote of parliament, a parliamentary dictatorship; and the future governance of Italy (initially, according to the parliamentary deputies, only until the end of 1923, in fact until the defeat of Fascism in war) was in the hands of one man and his ideological conviction that the State must rule with an iron hand.

In Turkey, a struggle was taking place to prevent the defeat of 1918 leading to the total disintegration of the national domain. Of the once widespread Ottoman lands, only Anatolia (Turkey-in-Asia) and the province of Edirne (Turkey-in-Europe) remained under Turkish sovereignty. The capital, Constantinople – the seat of the Sultan, Mehmet V – the Bosphorus and the Dardanelles, including the town of Chanak (the Neutral Zone of the Straits), were still occupied by Allied troops under the Treaty of Sèvres.

Mustafa Kemal, proclaiming himself the head of a Provisional Government, had set up the banner of national regeneration at Angora (Ankara). Denouncing the Allied partition plans, and castigating the efforts of the Sultan's government in Constantinople to work with the Allies, Kemal, from his bases in central Anatolia, built up an army. He was waiting for the moment when he would feel strong enough to drive out the foreign troops then in Anatolia, mainly the Greeks, who controlled enormous areas in the west of the country. Kemal's aim was to cross the Neutral Zone of the Straits, drive the Greeks out of Eastern Thrace, and then drive the Allies from Constantinople and the Straits. This formidable military challenge was one he was convinced he could accomplish with the impetus of his movement for Turkish national regeneration.

By August 1922, Kemal's army was driving the Greeks further and further westward in Anatolia. France, which did not wish to become embroiled in the conflict as the ally of Greece, urged the Greeks to sue for an armistice. As far as the Turks were concerned, the only acceptable terms – explained the British High Commissioner in Constantinople, Sir Horace Rumbold – were 'the immediate and orderly evacuation of Asia Minor by the Greeks'.

It was clear that once Kemal had defeated the Greeks in Anatolia, he would turn his attention to the Greeks in Eastern Thrace, and to the British, French and Italian occupation forces at Constantinople and the Zone of the Straits. The Kemalists, scornful of the Sultan's court and government, would be no respecter of the treaty which the Turkish politicians in Constantinople had signed at Sèvres, a treaty which had given the Allies their predominant position in Turkey's capital city.

In London, the Cabinet was alarmed by the thought of what would happen when Kemal's forces reached the southern shore of the Sea of Marmara, from which they had been driven by the Greeks a year earlier. There was now no Greek military force that could halt the Turks before they reached the Zone of the Straits, from which, under the Treaty of Sèvres, they were excluded. Lord Curzon, a former Viceroy of India, and the most widely travelled man in the Cabinet, told his colleagues with all his authority as Foreign Minister that he 'earnestly hoped that we would not abandon the Gallipoli peninsula or at present abandon Constantinople to the Turks'. If the Turks were to take the Gallipoli peninsula and Constantinople, Churchill (then Colonial Secretary) warned his colleagues, 'we shall have lost the whole fruits of our victory, and another Balkan war would be inevitable.' Lloyd George, who as Prime Minister had negotiated the Treaty of Sèvres, told his colleagues, as the minutes of the meeting recorded: 'In no circumstances could we allow the Gallipoli peninsula to be held by the Turks. It was the most important strategic position in the world, and the closing of the Straits in the war had prolonged the war by two years. It was inconceivable that we would allow the Turks to gain possession of the Gallipoli peninsula, and we should fight to prevent their doing so.'

In Chanak, a British force of a thousand men, protected by the fifteen-inch guns of the battleship *Ajax*, awaited the arrival of Kemal's army. The small Greek force that was stationed near the southern sections of the Zone of the Straits was driven off by the Turks on September 14. On the following day, Lloyd George suggested to Lord Curzon that Britain ought to 'organize' Balkan support, and call on Roumania, Greece and Yugoslavia – Britain's wartime Balkan allies – to send troops to prevent Kemal's forces entering Turkey-in-Europe. The existing Allied force might not be enough, Lloyd George explained. The 7600 British, French and Italian troops in the Neutral Zone faced 11,000 Turkish troops already in the region, and a further 40,000 moving northward from Smyrna. Those 40,000 Turks had just defeated the Greeks in a savage campaign. Many of the Greeks had been driven, literally, into the sea, and several hundred Armenians had been massacred. The

Armenian quarter of Smyrna had been burned down. Mainly on British warships, 180,000 Greek and Armenian refugees were embarked from the shoreline and taken to mainland Greece.

Thus, as the Graeco-Turkish war was reaching its end, a new war was in the offing between the Kemalists and the Allies. Lloyd George was determined to send military reinforcements to the Straits, and to pursue the search for Allied troops as well, telling his Cabinet colleagues on September 15 that Kemal 'ought to know that if he crossed the Straits with 60,000 rifles he would be met by 60,000 – to say nothing of the British Fleet.'

Orders were given to the British naval commander in the Mediterranean not to allow transports with Turkish troops to cross from Asia Minor to Europe. British reinforcements were sent to the Neutral Zone from Malta and Gibraltar. A press communiqué, drafted by Lloyd George and Churchill on September 16, warned of the 'deadly consequences' of the Turks taking control of the Straits, and of the possibility of a 'union' of Turkey and Bulgaria. If the Straits were closed, 'the whole trade of the Danube flowing into the Black Sea' was liable to 'strangulation'.

That same day, the British government appealed to the Dominion governments to make a military contribution to the coming struggle. Within twenty-four hours, Australia and Canada both declined to send men to the Straits. 'In a good cause, we are prepared to venture our all,' the Australian Prime Minister, William Hughes, replied, 'in a bad one, not a single man.' Only the two smallest Dominions, New Zealand and Newfoundland, agreed to send troops.

On September 18 the thousand British troops at Chanak were confronted by a considerably larger force of Turkish troops. But Lloyd George believed that war might not be necessary. 'By a show of force and firmness,' he told his Cabinet that day, 'it was possible that fighting might be prevented.' That very day, as if to underline that Britain would have to act against the Kemalists alone, both France and Italy withdrew their troops from the Asian shore of the Zone of the Straits. As the French and Italian troops left, the French High Commissioner in Constantinople, General Pellé (who had commanded an Army Corps on the Western Front during the First World War), sailed from Constantinople to Smyrna, with instructions from Paris to enter into direct negotiations with Kemal. The unity of the Allies had collapsed, even before it had been put to the test. 'French public opinion,' President Poincaré told Lord Curzon in Paris on September 20, 'would not admit of a shot being fired against a Turk.' As far as France was concerned,

Poincaré added, the Turks could 'cross to Europe when they pleased'.

France and Britain were in conflict. 'No Kemalist forces must be allowed to cross the salt water,' Lloyd George told the Cabinet Secretary on September 22. 'The moment a Kemalist gets afloat he must be dealt with.' But on September 23, without Lloyd George's knowledge, Poincaré, Count Sforza (the Italian ambassador in Paris) and Lord Curzon issued a Joint Note, in Paris, stating that they 'viewed with favour' the Turkish claim to Eastern Thrace, including the city of Adrianople, then occupied by Greece. The three statesmen also favoured, once a new peace treaty was signed with Turkey, the withdrawal of all Allied troops, High Commissioners and administrators from Constantinople.

The Paris Note (as it became known) opened up for Kemal the prospect of making a satisfactory peace with the Allies. The commander of the British forces at Constantinople and the Straits, General Harington – who remained in Constantinople throughout the crisis – and the British High Commissioner, Horace Rumbold, were both convinced that the Paris Note made a military confrontation unnecessary. On September 27, Harington made contact with Kemal, and offered to talk.

Recognizing how close he was to obtaining his aims without having to take on the military and naval power of Britain, Kemal carefully avoided any clashes with the British troops at Chanak, even though several hundred of his men had come to within a few yards of Britain's defences around the town. In London, while not wanting to give in to threats from Kemal, Churchill warned his colleagues that Chanak was not defendable, and suggested a British withdrawal to the European shore – to the Gallipoli peninsula. But Lloyd George was emphatic that, if Chanak was attacked it must be defended. The evacuation of Chanak, Lloyd George told his colleagues, 'would be the greatest loss of prestige which could possibly be inflicted on the British Empire'.

On September 28 General Harington was told that he would have the British government's 'full support' if he was 'compelled to fight'. The number of Kemalist troops in the immediate vicinity of Chanak rose from 2000 on September 28 to 4500 on September 29. At the same time, an intercepted top secret telegram from Moscow to Angora revealed to the British Cabinet, that the Bolsheviks, taking sides in a military dispute which could affect their naval access to the Mediterranean, were urging Kemal to fight. On the afternoon of September 29 a British ultimatum was sent to Harington in Constantinople, for delivery to Kemal, wherever he might be (he was thought that day to be in Angora), to tell Kemal that unless the Turks withdrew their forces from around Chanak by an hour to be determined by Harington, 'all the forces at our disposal – naval, military and aerial – will open fire.'

Britain was on the brink of making war. But Harington decided not to deliver the ultimatum. He had received a message from Kemal, on the morning of September 30, that the Turkish troops at Chanak would not 'provoke any incident' within the Neutral Zone, and that he, Kemal, was eager to negotiate the conditions of a truce. Harington informed the Cabinet in London that he had decided not to deliver the ultimatum. It would not be long, he explained, before the Allied generals in Constantinople – himself, and the French and Italian commanders – would be able to open negotiations with Kemal. Harington felt it was wrong 'that I should launch avalanche of fire . . . from which there will be no drawing back.'

While the British Cabinet debated whether or not to order Harington to deliver the ultimatum, a telegram arrived to say that Kemal had agreed to meet Harington at the town of Mudania, on the Asiatic shore of the Sea of Marmara, and to open talks on the future of the Neutral Zone, Thrace and the Straits. But the British Cabinet was uneasy, and in a telegram to Harington, which Churchill drafted, told the general that while the British government earnestly desired peace, 'we do not however desire to purchase a few days of peace at the price of actively assisting a successful Turkish invasion of Europe. Such a course would deprive us of every vestige of sympathy and respect and particularly in the United States. Nor do we believe that repeated concessions and submissions to victorious orientals is the best way to avert war.'

Believing that war could be averted, Harington steamed from Constantinople to Mudania on board the battleship *Iron Duke*. He was confident that he could persuade Kemal, without the use of an ultimatum, to withdraw from the Neutral Zone and await the outcome of peace talks in which all the Kemalist demands would be met. Harington was convinced that, if urged to do so, Kemal would agree not to cross into Turkey-in-Europe until after the peace conference had returned the territory to Turkey.

The negotiations began at Mudania on October 3. Not Kemal, but Ismet Pasha, the Commander of the Turkish troops in western Anatolia – and the victor of the battle of Inönü against the Greeks – was the principal Kemalist negotiator. Like Kemal, he had fought against the British at Gallipoli.

As the Mudania discussions began, Ismet agreed to halt all further Turkish military movements in the region of the British forces, and then to withdraw

1000 yards from the British line. But he also demanded the right to occupy Thrace immediately. The French and Italian delegates were willing to accept this. The British rejected it, and on October 6 the conference broke down. Britain once more contemplated war. But on the following day, the issue of peace and war broke the unity of British politics; a leading Conservative, Andrew Bonar Law, hitherto willing to accept Conservative participation in Lloyd George's coalition (of which he had until recently been a Minister), had a letter published in *The Times* and the *Daily Express* stating that Britain could only keep the Turks from Constantinople and Thrace if the Allied Powers, and also the United States, agreed to join in such an action. Without at least French support, Bonar Law argued, military action must be avoided: 'We cannot act alone as the policeman of the world.'

The negotiations at Mudania were resumed on October 8. After two days of discussions the Turks accepted the Paris Note of September 23. This had offered Allied recognition to the Turkish claim to Turkey-in-Europe, including Adrianople, and, once a peace treaty was signed with Turkey, committed the Allies to the withdrawal of their troops and administration from Constantinople.

The Mudania Convention was signed on October 11. The Turks agreed to withdraw their troops fifteen kilometres from Chanak. The Allies agreed that the Greeks would leave Eastern Thrace at once, and that a Franco-British-Italian administration would take over until Turkish rule was restored there. The Turks agreed that until a peace treaty was signed, no Turkish troops would enter Thrace, nor would Turkey try to raise an army from the Turkish population there. The Turks also agreed that Allied troops could remain in Constantinople and the Neutral Zone until a treaty was signed.

Britain had avoided war with Turkey, but the spectre of war had roused strong Conservative hostility against Lloyd George. On October 19 the Conservative Party Members of Parliament, meeting at the Carlton Club in London, voted to leave the coalition that had ruled Britain since 1915. In the general election which followed, the Conservatives were returned to power for the first time since 1905. Bonar Law, the man who had raised the standard of revolt against any further military action, became Prime Minister.

On November 1 the Turkish National Assembly at Angora voted to abolish the Sultanate, and to turn Turkey into a republic. Sultan Mehmet remained in Constantinople, but prepared to go into exile. On November 17 he left the city where his family had ruled for more than four hundred years; the British battleship *Malaya* took him to Malta. The Ottoman dynasty, like that of the Romanovs, the Hohenzollerns and the Habsburgs, was over, the rulers and their children condemned to a life of not always uncomfortable, but usually distant exile.[1]

At the end of November the leaders of the Allied Powers made preparations to meet in Switzerland, at Lausanne, to negotiate the last of the postwar peace treaties. The promises made to Mustafa Kemal in the Paris Note and the Mudania Convention gave the Turks the opportunity to put the hated Treaty of Sèvres behind them, and to restore Turkey's position in Anatolia and the Straits.

France was represented at Lausanne by President Poincaré, Britain by Lord Curzon, and Italy by its new Prime Minister, Benito Mussolini. The newcomer to the international scene was ill at ease with the men whose names and achievements were so well known to him, and who were a generation older than he. As neither Poincaré nor Curzon had met Mussolini before, and as they were determined to present a single Allied point of view to the Turks, they arranged to meet him in Lausanne on the evening of November 19, before the conference opened.

Mussolini had only been Prime Minister for three weeks. At each of the train stations on his journey through Italy to Switzerland he was met with great enthusiasm. Italy, bruised by her failure to secure the territory she had wanted in the Adriatic, felt that she was going to be cheated once again of the fruits of her participation in the war, and looked to Mussolini to secure from Turkey a decent share of the spoils. Hoping to make a dramatic first impression, Mussolini cancelled the meeting with Curzon and Poincaré at Lausanne. He then sent them a telegram that he would meet them instead at Teritet, a few miles away.

It was typical of the new ruler of Italy that he wanted to stage-manage the event, and upstage his two colleagues. At the meeting at Teritet he insisted that no officials were present. When the three men emerged it was with a communiqué, insisted upon by Mussolini, that Italy would be treated at the Lausanne Conference by her allies 'on a footing of equality'.

The Lausanne Conference opened on November 20. Mussolini, whose accession to power in Italy was still very much a main story in the newspapers,

[1] As a schoolboy in London in 1945, this author was taught gymnastics by Prince Fethi Sami, a nephew of the last Sultan. At the age of nine and ten, schoolboys were mesmerized both by his athletic prowess and his exotic past.

was the focus of attention. Lady Rumbold, whose husband Sir Horace was one of the British delegates, described the Italian leader in a private letter as 'most impressive and Napoleonic'. But he made little contribution to the debate, which dragged on until the following summer, with interruptions and disputes – long after the leaders had returned home. In deepest frustration, when the treaty was finally signed, Horace Rumbold wrote to a friend: 'We ought to have gone for the Turks at the time of the Chanak business, and bombed Angora with all its gasbags.'

In the new climate of peace, the aeroplane was turned to commercial purposes. Regular passenger flights began between many cities. Most of the planes could carry between six passengers (the Handley Page) and fourteen (the Farman Goliath). These two planes flew at 90 and 70 miles an hour respectively. London and Paris were among the first cities to be linked by air, with eight flights in each direction each day. Train connections were offered in Paris for Lisbon, Rome, Constantinople and Athens. The London–Paris air route was among the first on which a fatal commercial accident took place, with two planes colliding on April 7 and six passengers being killed.

Many regular air routes were linked with rail connections. The Munich–Nuremberg line was established specifically to link with rail services to Prague, Vienna and Budapest. A trans-Mediterranean passenger air service also opened in 1922 linking Alicante in Spain with Oran and Algiers. Most ambitious of the regular services that year was Paris–Warsaw, with a touchdown in Strasbourg, and an overnight stop in Prague. Each nation established its own national airline. The Hungarian Air Transport Company was formed in November 1922, the Czech national airline a year later. In the United States, the Army Air Service opened a commercial freight and passenger service, the Model Airways System, in June 1922, linking the Atlantic coast towns with the Gulf of Mexico. What had seemed before the war the extravagant hopes of the air pioneers had been realized and exceeded.

Political assassinations continued into 1922. The Polish President, Gabriel Narutowicz, was shot dead six days after his election to office, on his first public appearance as president. He had been a champion of the minorities in Poland. Also assassinated that year was a twenty-five-year-old Russian, Vladimir Nabokov, one of the leaders of the Kadet Party during the war, whose promising diplomatic career in Tsarist times had been ruined when he opposed the government-initiated pogroms against the Jews. In 1918 Nabokov had served as Minister of Justice in the anti-Bolshevik Russian government set up in the Crimea. He was murdered by an anti-Semite, a member of the Black Hundreds who resented his earlier championship of the Jews.

There were also many assassinations in Ireland in 1922. The establishment of the Irish Free State, giving southern Ireland virtual independence from Britain, had not satisfied those Irishmen who wanted complete severance from the British Crown and Empire. What they wanted was an Irish Republic, and the extension of that republic to Northern Ireland.

Many of the assassinations within Ireland in 1922 were the work of republicans against supporters of the Free State, acts of vengeance and defiance by those who wanted Ireland to cut itself off entirely from Britain. The most serious blow to the settlement, though it did not destroy it, was the murder of Michael Collins, who, following the signing of the Irish Treaty had become Commander-in-Chief of the Irish Army. Collins was ambushed while driving through the remote countryside in County Cork.

Like Matthias Erzberger, who had signed the German armistice, Collins was never forgiven by those of his fellow countrymen for having put his signature to a hated treaty. They had wanted immediate independence and a united Ireland. But ordinary citizens – those victims of so many of the century's ills – wanted peace to be preserved, and the funeral of Collins in Dublin was the scene of a demonstration in favour of a peaceful Ireland not unlike the Peace People demonstrations in Northern Ireland in the 1970s and the Marches for Peace in the 1990s. The forces of disruption, however, continued their destructive path. In December, after several officers of the new Irish army had been assassinated, the Free State government executed seven IRA men who had been found guilty of killing their fellow Irishmen.

In London, a senior British army officer and Member of Parliament, who had opposed the Free State Bill, Field Marshal Sir Henry Wilson, an Ulsterman, was shot dead on his doorstep by an IRA gunman. An hour earlier, the Field Marshal had unveiled the First World War memorial to the railwaymen of the Great Eastern Railway who had been killed in action. His murder showed that Irish hatreds would not be confined to the smaller of the two islands.

*   *   *

The use of violence to obtain political concessions, to win power, and to gain independence, was widespread. In India, twenty-one Indian policemen and rural watchmen were murdered on February 14 at Chauri-Chaura, in the United Provinces, by peasants who had earlier volunteered to pursue Gandhi's policy of noncooperation with the authorities. After the men had been murdered, their bodies were doused with petrol and set on fire.

As a token of regret at the Chauri-Chaura killings, Gandhi fasted. But he did not give up the noncooperation campaign. On the Indian railways, a strike brought the commerce of hundreds of towns to a halt. Mass civil disobedience, Gandhi declared, was the only way to bring British rule to an end. After further outbreaks of violence in Bombay and Madras, Gandhi was arrested. At his trial he made an extraordinary confession, and declaration of faith, which won him great respect from many of his most tenacious British critics. In solemn tones he told the court:

> I wish to endorse all the blame that the Advocate General has thrown on my shoulders in connection with the Bombay occurrences, the Madras occurrences and the Chauri-Chaura occurrences.
>
> Thinking over these things deeply, and sleeping over them night after night and examining my heart I have come to the conclusion that it is impossible for me to dissociate myself from the diabolical crimes of Chauri-Chaura or the mad outrages of Bombay. He is quite right when he says that as a man of responsibility, a man having received a fair share of education, having had a fair share of experience of this world, I should know the consequences of every one of my acts. I knew them. I knew that I was playing with fire. I ran the risk, and if I were set free I would still do the same. I would be failing in my duty if I did not do so. I have felt it this morning that I would have failed in my duty if I did not say all that I have said here just now.
>
> I wanted to avoid violence; I want to avoid violence. Non-violence is the first article of my faith. It is the last article of my faith. But I had to make my choice; I had either to submit to a system which I consider has done irreparable harm to my country, or incur the risk of the mad fury of my people bursting forth when they understood the truth from my lips.
>
> I know that my people have sometimes gone mad; I am deeply sorry for it; and I am therefore here to submit, not to a light penalty but to the highest penalty. I do not ask for mercy. I do not plead any extenuating act. I am here therefore to invite and submit to the highest penalty that

can be inflicted upon me for what in law is a deliberate crime and what appears to me to be the highest duty of a citizen.

Gandhi was sentenced to six years' imprisonment. A year later, when he was taken ill with appendicitis, the government of India offered him whatever medical attention he required, and then released him, so that his health might recover after the operation. His appeal had spread beyond politics. In the words of Edward Thompson, one of the those who had at first been a severe critic of Gandhi's methods, 'Some of us may have begun to see that he challenged not so much the British dominion as a thing we ourselves longed to dare to challenge, but the whole modern world, that has mechanized and arrested experience. His quarrel with us was a deeper and wider thing than we had thought. From this trial I date – and it came with startling suddenness, once it had fairly begun – the change of mood which has carried us so far from the post-Amritsar mood.' More and more Englishmen were turning with sympathy to Indian national aspirations.

The second half of the nineteenth century, and the first decade and a half of the twentieth, had seemed, to the industrialized and Christian States, to offer the prospect of continuing progress, material and moral. This was nowhere more certain than in the minds of those who governed India, who published every year a comprehensive account of British rule in the subcontinent under the heading 'the moral and material progress of the Indian people'. But the terrible killings and disintegrations of the First World War, the violence erupting even outside the war zones – most horrifically in Armenia – and the challenges to imperial systems by every national group, had by 1922 cast a pall of doubt and disillusion on the minds of the optimists of earlier years.

'What a disappointment the twentieth century has been,' Winston Churchill told his Scottish constituents at Dundee on 11 November 1922 – the fourth anniversary of the Armistice. 'How terrible and how melancholy is the long series of disastrous events which have darkened its first twenty years. We have seen in every country a dissolution, a weakening of the bonds, a challenge to those principles, a decay of faith, an abridgement of hope, on which the structure and ultimate existence of civilized society depends.' Soviet Russia, China, Mexico, India, Ireland, Egypt and India were the countries Churchill singled out. Could his listeners doubt, he asked, 'that mankind is passing through a period marked by an enormous destruction and abridgement of the human species, not only by a vast impoverishment and reduction in the means of existence, but also that the destructive tendencies have not yet run their course. And only intense, concerted and prolonged efforts among all nations can avert further and perhaps even greater calamities.'

Would those efforts be made? The omens, based on the events of the time, were not good. Yet the League of Nations existed, a structure of peace treaties had been erected, victors and vanquished were sitting down together, and economic recovery and social justice, the protection of minorities and the preservation of national independence, were the watchwords of the hour. Only in Russia, among the nations who had emerged from the First World War with hope of better things, had revolution and terror brought an era of harshness to millions of people. Enormous powers were wielded throughout the Soviet Union by the Cheka Revolutionary Tribunal (the secret police) — renamed on 6 February 1922 the State Political Administration, the GPU.

In May, Lenin explained to his Commissar of Justice, Dimitri Kursky: 'The law should not abolish terror; to promise that would be self-delusion or deception.' When Kursky remarked wrily that his department might better be named 'Commissariat for Social Extermination', Lenin replied, 'Well put, that's exactly what it should be, but we can't say that.' Terror, Lenin added, 'should be substantiated and legalized in principle, clearly, without evasion or embellishment'. Lenin's harshness shocked even those for whom the revolution and terror were synonymous. 'The more members of the reactionary bourgeoisie and clergy we manage to shoot, the better,' he said. Several thousand of these 'class enemies' were shot that year.

During 1922 the first show trial of the Soviet era was held in Moscow. It was orchestrated and prepared by the GPU, with accusations of the responsibility for the murder of millions of Russians during the civil war being based entirely on fictional evidence. Those who were put on trial were leading members of the Right Socialist Revolutionaries, whose aim, like that of the Bolsheviks, had been the liberation of the Russian people. The chief accused, Abram Gots, had himself been a Siberian exile from 1906 to 1917 and subsequently a member of the Petrograd Soviet.

At the end of the trial the death sentence was pronounced against all the accused. It was then 'postponed' until, in the judge's words, 'the Socialist Revolutionary Party continues its acts of violence against the Soviet Government.' This decision was widely condemned outside Russia. It constituted, wrote the *Frankfurter Zeitung*, 'the revival of the medieval hostage system' and a 'barbaric cruelty'. Anatole France, whose sympathy for the new Russia was well known, declared: 'I will have nothing to do with these methods. By such acts as this, an irreparable, crushing blow is dealt to every liberating movement in the world. In the name of humanity, in the name of the highest interests of the world proletariat, I protest against such actions!'

That winter, Lenin suffered his second stroke. Shortly afterwards, on December 22, he dictated a series of notes which came to be known as his Testament. In these notes he showed how acutely aware he was of the struggle for power that would follow after his death. Trotsky, he described as 'personally perhaps the most capable man in the present Central Committee', though showing 'excessive self-assurance'. The only person with similar abilities, Lenin wrote, was Stalin. But after learning of Stalin's hostile attitude towards several Georgian Communists – men whom Lenin himself had earlier characterized as intransigent – Lenin added a postscript to his Testament: 'Stalin is too rude, and this defect, though quite tolerable in our midst and in dealings among us Communists, becomes intolerable in a General Secretary. This is why I suggest that the comrades think about a way to remove Stalin from that post and appoint another man who in all respects differs from Comrade Stalin in his superiority, that is, more loyal, more courteous, and more considerate of comrades, less capricious, etc.'[1]

Lenin headed his Testament 'Letter to the Party Congress', and intended it to become widely known. In fact, it was suppressed for thirty-three years, until after Stalin's death. There was, at that very moment, another dispute with Stalin. Shortly after Lenin congratulated Trotsky on their joint victory in establishing a State monopoly on foreign trade (to which Stalin had been opposed), Stalin telephoned Lenin's wife Nadezhda Krupskaya and rebuked her violently over the telephone for having allowed Lenin to write such a letter to Trotsky, given Lenin's ill-health. As soon as he learned of Stalin's telephone call, Lenin wrote in protest direct to Stalin (sending copies to Kamenev and Zinoviev).

Lenin's letter read: 'Very respectable comrade Stalin, You allowed yourself

---

[1] One of Stalin's most recent biographers, Robert Conquest, points out that the word always translated in the Testament as 'rude' – *grub* – 'has in Russian a far broader significance than mere discourtesy: it carries a stronger implication of crudity and of a gross and bullying lack of normal social decencies'.

to be so ill-mannered as to call my wife on the telephone and to abuse her. She has agreed to forget what you said. Nevertheless she has told Zinoviev and Kamenev about the incident. I have no intention of forgetting what has been done against me, and it goes without saying what was done against my wife I also consider to have been directed against myself. Consequently, I must ask you to consider whether you would be inclined to withdraw what you said and to apologize, or whether you prefer to break off relations between us. Respectfully yours, Lenin.'

Stalin apologized. But to Krupskaya, Lenin confided that Stalin was 'devoid of the most elementary honesty, the most simple human honesty'. As General Secretary of the Communist Party since the beginning of 1922, Stalin was, however, in a commanding position, should he wish to exercise it, to outwit Trotsky. And he did choose to exercise it, and to find allies, among them Zinoviev and Kamenev. With their dislike of Trotsky, these two were prepared to support the man whom Lenin had so roundly criticized, and by whom they too, in due course, were to be condemned.

Russia, meanwhile, was undergoing yet another constitutional and territorial change. On 22 December 1922 the different Federative Socialist Republics, which were themselves made up of various autonomous regions, were joined together into a single union, the Union of Soviet Socialist Republics, or the USSR. This entity, through which the rulers in Moscow controlled with centralized power the territory of the former Tsarist Empire from the White Sea to the Caspian Sea, and from the Gulf of Finland to the Pacific Ocean, was to remain a single, imperial entity for almost seventy years.

On November 14, three days after Churchill had told his constituents what a 'terrible disappointment' the twentieth century had been, and would still be, the first regular radio news bulletin was transmitted from London, from the rooftop of the Marconi building in the Strand. Today a plaque marks the site from which this historic development took place. At first, the daily broadcasts were limited to news bulletins and dance music in the evening. But a revolution had begun, which was to bring the events of the century rapidly, with increasing frequency, and sometimes with great urgency and pain, into an ever-growing number of homes throughout the world.

Among the events of 1922 which were to gain wide notice were the public advocacy of birth control by Marie Stopes, who had established a Mothers'

Clinic for Birth Control in Holloway, London, and an advance in medical science, the first administration of insulin to diabetics. But a sign of the continuing distress caused in the aftermath of the First World War was the attempt to help hundreds of thousands of stateless refugees by the issuing of special passports. These were the Nansen passports, issued by the League of Nations' Commissioner for Refugees, Fridtjof Nansen. The Nansen passports became a byword for the hope of life free from fear.

CHAPTER TWENTY-SEVEN

1923

IN GERMANY, the burden of reparations payments was denounced throughout 1923. The British economist J. M. Keynes, one of the British negotiators at Versailles, had published a sustained attack on the reparations clauses and terms as early as December 1919, in a book entitled *The Economic Consequences of the Peace* and his criticisms – which had so influenced the American Senate's decision to reject the Treaty in 1920 – gained wide acceptance. At the beginning of 1923 the German government sought to postpone reparations payments for another year. The French Prime Minister, Raymond Poincaré, who had been angered by the previous year's postponement, announced that France would seize from Germany various productive enterprises. It would retain control of them, he said, and exploit them, until Germany fulfilled its reparations obligations. On January 10, French, and also Belgian, troops entered the Ruhr.

When, that same day, the French Communists announced that they would pursue an active opposition to the occupation policy, a number of them were arrested. The French army in Germany moved quickly to take over the factories; Essen was entered on January 11. Britain, in its most open breach with France since the end of the First World War, declined to participate in the French move.

In the factories which they occupied in the Ruhr, the French ordered German workers to continue production. But a passive resistance movement began, and spread rapidly. It was clear that France would not be able to extract reparations by actually working the German industrial system. Poincaré then announced that France would only withdraw from the Ruhr 'in proportion' as the German government paid its reparations dues.

It took almost twelve months before Britain, with the help of the United States, was able to persuade Poincaré at least to set up a committee to examine the question of Germany's capacity to pay. Meanwhile, the French occupation of the Ruhr led to the total cessation of all German reparations payments, and to considerable poverty among the striking workers. The occupation also deprived the French ironworks in Lorraine of the German coke on which they were dependent in order to maintain production. In an incident in Essen, on March 31, when French troops were trying to requisition lorries at the Krupp factory, the workers stopped work and gathered in protest outside the factory. For several hours troops and workers faced each other. Then a French soldier with a machine gun opened fire and thirteen German workers were killed. The French government blamed the factory's German managers for inciting their workers to passive resistance.

The economic distress caused by the French occupation of the Ruhr and the German passive resistance was enormous. The German government began to print money to pay subsistence wages to the two million workers who had downed tools. By August the value of the mark fell to one-fortieth of its value at the beginning of April. In many of the Ruhr towns there were repeated and widespread acts of looting and plunder. Both left-wing and right-wing extremists sought to make capital from the distress. In Frankfurt, the Communists organized a demonstration of 'fighting unions' – the Proletarian Hundreds – which led to bloodshed, and a banning order from the local government. In Munich, where the Bavarian government was less strong than its Prussian counterpart, a Fighting League of right-wing extremist forces was set up, a loose alliance of many discontented groups.

Among the members of the Fighting League, Hitler's National Socialists were prominent in denouncing five 'evils' besetting Germany: the French occupation of the Ruhr, the Berlin government, the German Republic, Socialism and Communism. In several Bavarian towns, Hitler's Brownshirts fought frequent street battles with the Proletarian Hundreds.

As Hitler's adherents gained in strength and vociferousness, dominating the Fighting League, the Bavarian government suspended civil law and placed the executive power of the State of Bavaria in the hands of a former Bavarian Prime Minister, Dr von Kahr, a supporter of the monarchy, and of enhanced provincial powers. Von Kahr at once forbade a number of Nazi meetings. When the government in Berlin, headed by a new Chancellor, Gustav Stresemann, refused to license Hitler's newspaper, the *Völkischer Beobachter*, the prohibition was not enforced in Bavaria.

Von Kahr declared that his aim was to fight against 'Marxism'. In pursuit of this aim he suppressed the local Socialist self-defence organization, as well as the Social-Democratic and Democratic newspapers. In this, he found an ally in Hitler.

Violent separatist activity immediately began to spread throughout Germany. In Munich, Hitler was building up his Brownshirt militia and denouncing his enemies in terms that won him and his Nazi Party more and more adherents. 'There are now only two alternatives before us,' he told a mass audience on September 12, 'the swastika or the Soviet star, the world despotism of the Communist International or the Holy Empire of the Germanic nation,' and he added: 'The first act of redress must be a march on Berlin and the installation of a national dictatorship.'

In Leipzig, a Communist demonstration called on the citizens to arm and establish a Soviet regime in Saxony. In Thuringia, a right-wing activist, Captain Erhardt, who had been a leader in the Kapp Putsch in Berlin three years earlier, escaped from the prison in which he had been incarcerated for his part in the Putsch, and raised a private army, intent on reactivating the forces of the right, the so-called *völkisch* (people's) forces to which Nazism was proving increasingly attractive.

The first *völkisch* uprising took place in the town of Küstrin, when 400 men who had tried in vain to enroll in the German army broke into the fortress and seized control of the town. The army, remaining loyal to the Republic, forced them to surrender. In the Rhineland, a separatist movement, encouraged by the French, also tried to seize power, organizing a mass demonstration in Düsseldorf, and attacking the German police forces sent to disperse them. Ten people were killed. In Berlin, Stresemann committed his government to bringing the disintegrating elements of Germany under the control of the Republic. Troops were despatched to Thuringia, and the *völkisch* separatist movement was put down. In Saxony, troops moved into the towns on October 22, and the Proletarian Hundreds were disbanded.

Stresemann also tried to end the anarchic situation in Bavaria. But the military commander in Bavaria, General von Lossow, sided with the Bavarian authorities, and, despite renewed pressure from Berlin, allowed the *Völkischer Beobachter*, with its vitriolic hostility to Stresemann and the Republic – which it claimed was under 'Marxist' influence – to go on being printed and circulated.

The Commander-in-Chief of the German army, General von Seeckt, ordered von Lossow to resign. Von Lossow, echoing Nazi terminology, replied that he felt no obedience to a government that was under 'Marxist' influence. Bavaria was on the verge of separating from the rest of Germany. When all the Bavarian troops who were under von Lossow's command were ordered to swear a special oath to the Bavarian government, the government in Berlin issued a manifesto accusing Bavaria of violating the German constitution. Von Kahr refused to allow the manifesto to be published in Bavaria. He also banned all fourteen mass meetings at which Hitler had planned to launch a new campaign of defiance against Bavaria as well as Berlin.

It was the success of von Kahr's independent stance in Bavaria, combined with his outright opposition to Nazi activity, that pushed Hitler to make plans for a step that he had been contemplating for many months, a Nazi seizure of power. His aim was to take power, not only in Bavaria, but throughout Germany, and to bring about what he called the 'renewal' of Germany.

By November 1923, as a result of the continuing French occupation of the Ruhr and the almost total failure of German industry, the value of the mark had collapsed. Terrible hardships affected the middle classes as the value of their savings disappeared overnight. The cost of basic foodstuffs became prohibitive. Physical hardships touched every family in the country. That month it took a million, million (1,000,000,000,000) paper marks to equal the purchasing power of a single German mark in 1914.

Hitler exploited the economic collapse by blaming it on all those whom he wished to portray as enemies. First and foremost this meant to him the government in Berlin and its alleged allies, Jewish financiers and Marxist subversives. These were the same enemies, he declared, as the 'November criminals' who had brought about Germany's defeat in 1918 – those mythical bogeymen who, from inside Germany, had deliberately brought their own country to its knees.

Hitler had an important ally in his campaign in General Ludendorff, the second most senior figure (after Hindenburg) in the German First World War military pantheon. Ludendorff, who had long been active among *völkisch* circles in Munich, stood to become the chief beneficiary of the 'stab in the back' legend, for it was he, after all, who had been at the helm when defeat came. It suited his purpose to put the blame on others. He was also the beneficiary of 100,000 gold marks, given to him by the German industrialist Fritz Thyssen, who wanted to see greater action against the Socialists, both in and out of government. Ludendorff parcelled out his money to other activists, Hitler among them.

Hitler's plan was to seize power in Munich, and, with Bavaria as his base, to launch (as he had explained in public that September) a march on Berlin, not unlike Mussolini's march on Rome of a year earlier, but without first being invited to take power, as Mussolini had been. Unlike Mussolini in 1922, Hitler in 1923 was unimportant in political terms, without a single deputy in the Reichstag, and with no accepted overall leadership of the forces of the right, such as Mussolini commanded. Still, he was determined to act, and when the conflict between Stresemann in Berlin and von Kahr and von Lossow in Munich led to what looked like a possible attempt by von Kahr and von Lossow to mount their own march on Berlin – an enterprise they did not invite Hitler to join – Hitler decided to act on his own.

Hitler knew that he could rely on the amalgamated forces of the Fighting League. Six months had passed since their first attempt to seize power. They did not want to miss out now, or to be overtaken by others, or to find that the government in Berlin was strong enough to reassert its authority over Bavaria, as it had done earlier over Saxony and Thuringia. On November 8, von Kahr and von Lossow attended a meeting of two thousand Munich citizens in the Bürgerbraü beer cellar. The heads of most Bavarian government departments were there, many industrial leaders, and the directors of various municipal and patriotic organizations. Before von Kahr and von Lossow could take the podium, however, Hitler, supported by his Brownshirts, burst in, fired a single shot into the ceiling to command attention, seized von Kahr and von Lossow at pistol point and pushed them into a side room.

'The national revolution has begun,' Hitler told the startled gathering. 'The hall is surrounded by six hundred heavily armed men. No one may leave the premises. Unless quiet is restored immediately, I shall have a machine gun placed in the gallery. The Bavarian government and the national government have been overthrown, and a provisional national government is being formed. The barracks of the Reichswehr and the state police have been occupied; the Reichswehr and the state police are already approaching under the swastika flag.'

Hitler then proclaimed a new German government. He would be its leader. Ludendorff would be the Commander-in-Chief of the German army in its march on Berlin. The 'entire might' of Bavaria was to be mustered, Hitler declared, 'for the march on that sinful Babylon, Berlin – for the German people must be saved.' And he went on to ask: 'Are you in agreement with this solution of the German question? You can see that what guides us is not self-interest, not egotism. Rather, we wish to take up the cudgels for our German fatherland, at the eleventh hour. We want to rebuild Germany as a federation in which Bavaria shall receive her rightful due. Tomorrow morning will either find Germany with a German nationalist government – or us dead!'

Hitler offered von Kahr and von Lossow positions in the new government to be established in Berlin. The two men, having been brought back on the platform, promised loyalty to Hitler. Then, as Hitler continued to declaim his policies and his programmes, they slipped away. In the heat and enthusiasm of the moment, von Kahr decided to proclaim himself 'Viceroy of the King of Bavaria'. But Hitler had no intention of restoring the Bavarian monarchy, or of making von Kahr the Viceroy. On the following day, when he learned that both von Kahr and von Lossow were mobilizing the Bavarian militia against him, he realized that he would have to act.

For many hours Hitler was in a state of panic and indecision, seeing no way in which he could possibly march on Berlin, or even hold a street rally in safety, without enlisting the support of von Kahr and von Lossow and their followers. Then, at midday on November 9, Ludendorff took charge of the forces of the Fighting League, and, standing with Hitler and the other Nazi leaders at the head of a column of several thousand Brownshirts and others, marched towards the Odeonsplatz, one of Munich's main squares.

A line of policemen stood across the road leading to the square. As the marchers approached, the police opened fire. Fourteen of the marchers were killed. Ludendorff marched on, upright and determined, right through the police cordon. Hitler, who had been pulled to the ground when the police opened fire, and had dislocated his arm, got to his feet and fled the scene, finding refuge that night at Uffing, a suburb of Munich. Two days later he was arrested by the police and taken to prison. Brought to trial accused of treason, he was sentenced to nine months' imprisonment in a Bavarian fortress.

While Berlin watched, and Stresemann's republican forces were powerless to intervene, the Bavarian separatist forces of von Kahr and von Lossow had taken on the National Socialists and beaten them. There was to be no march on Berlin, no emulation of Mussolini, no capture of the German Republic. The Nazi putsch was over, as much a part of discarded history as the Spartacist revolt, the Hölz revolution or the Kapp Putsch. In the newspaper accounts of the time, Hitler's Munich Putsch merited much space, but also much ridicule.

*   *   *

In Berlin, a new German government came to power, with Wilhelm Marx, a member of the Centre Party, as Chancellor. Stresemann remained Foreign Minister. A member of the Bavarian People's Party was made Minister of Justice, in the hope of drawing Bavaria closer to the Reich.

Since April, incidents of Nazi hooliganism had spread across the Bavarian border into Austria. Wearing swastika armbands like their German counterparts, the Austrian Nazis disrupted Social Democrat meetings. The Police President (and former Chancellor) Dr Johannes Schober advised the Social Democrats to ignore these Nazi elements. They were, he said, of 'no importance'. Another group that was emerging as a threat to Austria's parliamentary system was the *Heimwehr*, set up immediately after the war as a Citizen Defence Corps, and, as it became increasingly anti-Socialist, training the peasants in the use of arms, and strident in its Pan-German demands.

The League of Nations' international order, based on negotiations, compromise and arbitration, had received a setback with the French occupation of the Ruhr. It received a second setback later that year as a result of Italian policy. The new crisis began with the assassination, on the Greek-Albanian border, of General Tellini, Major Corti and Lieutenant Bonccini, the three Italians members of the commission delineating the Albanian-Greek frontier.

The assassinations took place on August 27. Mussolini at once sent a seven-point ultimatum to Greece, on whose territory the killings had taken place. The severity of the ultimatum reminded many observers of the Austrian ultimatum to Serbia almost a decade earlier, and raised fears of a wider war. In the ultimatum, Italy demanded an 'unreserved' public apology from Greece. A substantial cash indemnity was to be paid within five days. An enquiry was to be carried out on the spot, in the presence of the Italian Military Attaché to Greece, and was to be completed within five days. All the perpetrators of the crime were to be executed. The victims were to receive military honours. Honours were also to be conferred on the Italian fleet in the Greek port of Piraeus. A memorial service to the victims was to be held in the Roman Catholic cathedral in Athens, in the presence of the Greek government.

The Greek government had no evidence that Greeks were involved in the crime, in which there was certainly no official Greek complicity. With greater defiance than the Serbs had shown to the Austrians in 1914, the Greeks rejected several of the Italian demands. On August 31, four days after the murders, the Italian navy bombarded the island of Corfu. A number of Greek civilians were killed. The Italians then occupied the island.

There was indignation at the League of Nations in Geneva at Italy's actions. On September 1, at the League Council, the senior British delegate led the condemnation of Italy. But when, on September 4, Mussolini announced that he would take Italy out of the League if it continued to discuss the matter, the League made a rapid retreat. Only three years after its establishment as the body to avert and deter war, and punish aggression, the League had abdicated its responsibilities following a threat by one of its members.

The Corfu dispute was transferred to the Conference of Ambassadors (the successor to the Supreme Allied Council) in Paris. There, the French were sympathetic to Italy, hoping for Italian support for the continuing French occupation of the Ruhr. Within three days, the Conference drafted a milder form of seven-point demands to Greece, seeking apologies but toning them down, not (for example) the 'execution' of those responsible, but their 'punishment'. A funeral service must still be held in Athens, but without the earlier demand that members of the Greek government attend. The indemnity remained intact.

The Greeks accepted, made the apologies demanded of them, brought those responsible to trial, and paid the indemnity. Mussolini then withdrew the Italian troops from Corfu. The Italian public were impressed by Mussolini's firmness, but relieved that he had not got them into a war with Greece. They were equally impressed when, a few months later, on 27 January 1924, he signed the Pact of Rome with a Yugoslav delegation, whereby Yugoslavia recognized Italy's full sovereignty over the city and port of Fiume. In return, Yugoslavia acquired the nearby Delta and Port Barros.

The acquisition of Fiume satisfied, for the time being at least, Italy's Adriatic ambitions. It also reconciled Mussolini and Gabriele D'Annunzio. At the time of D'Annunzio's seizure of Fiume in 1919, Mussolini had not supported him, being jealous of the poet's ambitions, and fearful of being upstaged by him in the struggle for power. Mussolini had therefore (he was then a journalist and editor of the Fascist newspaper) supported the League of Nations' decision to set up Fiume as a Free City, rather than have it annexed by Italy. Now that conflict was in the past: the King of Italy gave Mussolini the highest royal decoration (the Collar of the Annunziata) for acquiring Fiume, and D'Annunzio was made a prince.

Mussolini's first year in office produced enthusiasm in conservative circles in the Western democracies. 'People have become impressed,' *The Times* wrote (on October 31) 'by the fact that Fascismo is not merely the usual successful political revolution, but also a spiritual revolution. Fascismo has abolished the game of Parliamentary chess; it has simplified the taxation system and reduced the deficit to measurable proportions; it has vastly improved the public services, particularly the railways; it has reduced a superfluously large bureaucracy without any very bad results in the way of hardship and unemployment; it has pursued a vigorous and fairly successful colonial policy. All this represents hard and useful work, but the chief bond it has conferred upon Italy are internal security and national self-respect.'

In Spain, democracy was overthrown in September 1923, less than a year after Mussolini had come to power in Rome. On September 12, Miguel Primo de Rivera, Marquis de Estella, who was both an army general and a senator, suspended the Spanish constitution and set up a Directorate of army and navy officers to take control of Spanish political life. The King of Spain, Alfonso XIII, who had come to the throne in 1886 (he was born after the death of his father, so that he had become king at birth), remained on the throne, surrounded by regal elegance, but stripped of all power.

The powers of the Spanish parliament (the Cortes) were likewise drastically curtailed. Political opponents of the new regime, including the Liberal leader Marquis Cortina, and the outstanding Spanish intellectual Don Miguel de Unamuno, were banished to an island in the Canaries. When, on November 6, King Alfonso refused to receive a petition presented by several leading Spanish politicians in defence of the constitution, there was despair among the parliamentary forces. In the provinces, the civil governorships were abolished, and Military Regions established throughout Spain, the local administrations being handed in each region to a commission of three generals.

Primo de Rivera also acted swiftly and with harshness against the separatists in Catalonia, the region which had for many years been seeking autonomy. As Captain-General of the Fourth Military Region of Catalonia before coming to power, he had already been active against these aspirations. As one of his first acts as Prime Minister, he appointed General Lossada to crush the separatist movement. Catalan extremists responded by a campaign of bomb-throwing against Spanish officials and government buildings in Barcelona. 'Determined to hispanicize Catalonia,' one British commentator noted in the following year, 'the Marquis de Estella had by the end of the first quarter of 1924 all but succeeded in reviving the movement for Catalan Separatism.' As the Directorate rejected all Catalonian requests for autonomy, Catalan extremist activities grew, culminating in a plan (which the police discovered before it could be put into operation) to blow up the train in which King Alfonso and Queen Ena would be travelling to Barcelona. The Queen – a granddaughter of Queen Victoria – commented bitterly that it looked as if she and the king 'might have to pay' for Primo de Rivera's policy towards Catalonia.

Primo de Rivera and his Directorate had also to deal with a worsening Spanish position in Morocco, where an uprising of several of the tribes of the Rif had broken out a month before the seizure of power in Madrid. During November and December more than four thousand Spanish troops were killed. Strict press censorship was imposed throughout Spain to prevent the full extent of the disaster from being known. 'The Moroccan question,' wrote the British Ambassador in Madrid, 'is like a cancer in the life of the country'. As the uprising spread on the Rif, Primo de Rivera was forced to withdraw Spanish troops from many of the forts and outposts which they had established in the interior. When the highly respected Spanish officer and politician, General Damaso Berenguer, attended a dinner for critics of the retreat in Morocco, he was arrested and sentenced to six months' confinement in a fortress.

In an attempt to bolster his prestige, Primo de Rivera proposed that Mussolini and Stanley Baldwin call an anti-Bolshevik conference, in which Spain was willing to play a prominent part. The British declined. But Primo de Rivera's imposition of dictatorial measures to secure law and order in Spain was applauded by those in Europe who feared a general disintegration of social discipline under Communist and Soviet pressure. In an article entitled 'Political Reform in Spain', the *Edinburgh Review* expressed the feelings of Conservatives generally when it wrote, two years later, in a survey of what the Spanish Directorate had achieved in its earliest days:

> The lawlessness and violence of years settled almost without a tremor into order. The police became a power again, and if a murderer was arrested, he could be sure that within a day or two, instead of being freed, he would be shot or garrotted. No one even attempted to do what had been done with impunity under the old régime. Murders and general strikes ceased. Banks were no longer held up, and courts, when they acted, began to give judgement according to the evidence.
>
> Trials of a few murderers by martial law, followed by summary

execution, had given back safety to the businessman. Disorder ceased to disturb the traffic in the three great centres where organized labour had been most provocative, Valencia, Bilbao and Barcelona. Smugglers gave up their traffic in tobacco and spirits, but there had been another contraband more lucrative, more sinister – cocaine. This now became almost impossible to find.

Not less remarkable, many of the idle men who had secured pay in government offices for doing nothing ceased to present themselves at their old places for the receipt of custom. Within a month the interior of Spain was calm.

The anarchy in China, to which Churchill had referred in 1922 in his panorama of the world's ills, increased during 1923. While north and south continued to struggle for political supremacy, violence was widespread, as the remnants of the armies of defeated warlords foraged and rampaged for food and loot, and kidnapped prosperous citizens for ransom. In the south, Dr Sun Yat-sen, the founder and leader of the Nationalist Party, the Kuomintang, made a move to seize the customs revenues of Canton, where his power was located. These revenues, which were substantial, were designated for many years to come for the repayment of loans owed to the Powers. British and French warships intervened, to prevent the seizure.

The international community was concerned throughout the year by China's refusal to pay its debts. These included the penalty imposed on China after the Boxer rebellion at the turn of the century, which was to be paid by annual instalments. During the First World War, France, Britain, Italy, Japan and Belgium had agreed (China being an ally) to postpone their share of the Boxer Indemnity until December 1922. When that date passed, the Chinese government in Peking, which was in permanent conflict with the Kuomintang government in Canton, stalled over the renewal of the payments. It wanted to retain whatever financial independence it could, and the ability to purchase warmaking supplies for its conflict with the Kuomintang. France was particularly strident in demanding that the payments be renewed, not, as the Peking government proposed, in depreciating currencies, but in gold francs. France cited the precedent of the French indemnity to Prussia after 1871, which France, under the humiliating Treaty of Frankfurt, had been forced to pay in gold francs.

With the wild inflation in Germany, and the uncertainty of many European currencies, the question of debt repayments had become a sensitive one; France was reluctant to see any diminution of the value of the money owed to her, even with a debt that went back almost a quarter of a century.

The banditry in China, which was becoming more and more brazen, reached a much-publicized climax on May 6, when a group of armed men led by a former officer in the Chinese army, Sun Mei Yao, derailed the Shanghai–Peking express at Lincheng, seized all the luggage, and captured 300 passengers. More than twenty of those captured were foreigners, mostly Americans. The captives were taken as hostages to caves some ten miles away. Government troops sent from Peking feared to attack the rebels in case of reprisals.

Yao opened negotiations with the Peking government, and with the Foreign Legations in the Chinese capital. For a month the negotiations continued, the plight of the captives being a cause of great concern in the United States. Fortunately for those whom he was holding, and for Sino-American relations, Yao's demands were not too onerous: he wanted the men under his command to be enrolled in the government forces, and himself made a brigadier-general. These demands were met, and the captives released.

The Powers now produced demands of their own. Although the victims of the 'Lincheng outrage' had been released, compensation for their month-long captivity was demanded in a stern diplomatic note. The Powers also demanded the punishment of the military governor of the region in which the kidnapping had occurred. In August, after more than two months of negotiations, the Peking government's newly elected President of China, Marshal Tsao Kun, agreed to pay compensation, and to punish the governor. The relief of the Powers at this resolution of the dispute was clouded the following day when an announcement from Peking stated that the governor had already retired – and been promoted by Peking to the rank of Marshal.

The United States was undergoing a nationwide isolationist surge. Even opera singers were vulnerable, including the German-born Johanna Gadski, who for many years had been a much-loved soprano at the Metropolitan Opera in New York, before being forced, during the First World War, to return to her native Germany. At the beginning of 1923, while Gadski was preparing for her operatic return to the United States for the first time in eight years, American Legion veterans paraded through Los Angeles under the banner, 'We Are Not Unreasonable, Only Patriotic: Gadski Shall Not Sing Tonight' and 'Real

American Money For Real American People: Gadski Shall Not Sing.'[1]

Several American state legislatures authorized the scrutiny of history text-books in order to ensure that accounts of American motives and American achievements were properly covered and expressed. A Bill introduced to the New York legislature banned from schools any textbook that 'ignores, omits, discounts or in any manner belittles, ridicules, falsifies, questions, doubts or denies the events leading up to the Declaration of American Independence or connected with the American Revolution.' The Bill failed to pass mainly because the state educational authorities did not want to transfer their exist-ing control over textbooks to the legislature. They believed they themselves could weed out inadequate accounts.

Inside the United States, one area of social change was noted in 1923 by the New York correspondent of *The Times*. It concerned the growing internal migration from South to North. In the North, the correspondent explained:

> The negro was a problem only when it came to housing and schooling. He was rarely a social problem – using 'social' in the loosest sense of the word – for generally he did not attempt to mix with white people on terms of equality. Housing was his greatest difficulty and that not an insuperable one. White people would not live in the same blocks with negroes, and when the latter began to overflow their quarters there were sometimes riots. In the schools there was seldom recognized any necessity for separating blacks and whites except where there was a preponderance or, at least, a large minority of the former. There was no distrust of the negro, as such: no suggestion, as in so much of the South, that it was only yesterday that he had come forth from the jungle.
>
> In the South, on the other hand, while his position was steadily improv-ing, there was little likelihood that it would ever be wholly satisfactory.

It was to be forty-one years before President Lyndon Johnson's Civil Rights Act prohibited racial discrimination in employment, unions, public accom-modation and schools, and even then, prejudice could not be entirely ended by legislation.

---

[1] Johanna Gadski returned to the United States to sing in 1929. She was killed in a car accident in Berlin in 1932, aged fifty-nine.

The main American grievance with the outside world in 1923 concerned the debts owed to the United States by dozens of governments. Four of the debtors – France, Italy, Belgium and Estonia – each declined even to suggest a repayment plan. Czechoslovakia, having agreed on the amount that she owed, had made no repayment. Several other countries were unwilling to embark on detailed negotiations, among them Greece, Liberia and Nicaragua. Armenia no longer existed as a country and could not pay any of the money which her leaders had been advanced at the time of the First World War, when an Armenian State seemed one of the certainties of an Allied victory. Payment by Austria of the substantial sum of $27 million had, by reason of Austria's desperate economic situation as a truncated and impoverished nation, been postponed by Act of Congress for twenty years. When that date, 6 April 1942, was reached, Austria had been annexed to Germany for four years, and the United States was at war with Germany.

Only Britain had negotiated a debt-repayment plan. So delighted was President Harding at Britain's willingness to work out a method of funding its debt – partly by borrowing more money from America to pay the interest on the debt – that he told Congress: 'This settlement means far more than the mere funding and ultimate discharge of the largest international loan ever contracted. It is the re-commitment of the English-speaking world to the validity of contract; it is, in effect, a pledge against war and war expenditure.' Harding's exuberance led him even further. The British failure to 'keep their pledge', he said, 'would have spread political and economic discouragement throughout the world, and general repudiation would have likely followed in its wake. But here is kept faith – willingly kept, be it recorded – and a covenant of peace as if joint British and American opposition to war was expressly agreed upon. It is a covenant of peace and recuperation, of respect and cooperation.'

The enthusiasm in the United States at Britain's pledge to pay was not fully reflected in Britain. The insistence by the United States on having its bond fulfilled, even under extremely favourable terms, was interpreted as mean and greedy, as were similar United States insistences half a century later, after the Second World War, which were to evoke considerable anti-American popular sentiment in Britain.

One of the worst natural disasters of the century took place in 1923, when, on September 1, an earthquake struck Japan. In Tokyo, eighty-three separate fires broke out, and almost all the government buildings were burnt down. A new Japanese Cabinet was in the process of being formed when the earthquake struck. Its first meeting took place in the open air, amid the smoking ruins of the government quarter.

In Tokyo, more than a hundred thousand people were killed. In Yokohama, where a tidal wave added to the destruction, the death toll exceeded 25,000. Another 100,000 were killed throughout the earthquake zone, which covered an area of 80 miles by 120. More than a million people were made homeless. From all over the world, money poured in for earthquake relief. Britain and the United States were particularly forthcoming in sending aid. A natural disaster, in which as many as a quarter of a million people had been killed within a few hours, succeeded, for a short while at least, in uniting the goodwill of many nations.

Not all natural disasters were awaited with inevitability. In British India, where the failure of the rains led, year after year, to famine and death, a start was made in 1923 on the construction of the Lloyd Barrage, a massive irrigation works across the River Indus. The barrage took nine years to complete. When it was in place, it served not only to regulate the flood waters of the Indus, but to distribute them over an area – twice the size of Wales – which had long suffered from the scourge of drought and famine.

CHAPTER TWENTY-EIGHT

1924

On 21 JANUARY 1924 Lenin died in the Soviet Union. He had never fully recovered from the assassination attempt four years earlier, and for the last year of his life, after a series of strokes, he had been an invalid, unable to govern. He was only fifty-three years old when he died. Under his leadership, Russia had been transformed from a monarchy into a Communist dictatorship. Following the assassination attempt on his own life in 1918, he had intensified terror as an instrument of State policy.

In the battle for Lenin's succession, Leon Trotsky, one of the main architects of the revolution in 1917 and the founder of the Red Army, was outmanoeuvred by Josef Stalin, who, as General Secretary of the Communist Party since April 1922, emerged as the strongest political figure in the State. Stalin was soon to reveal to those in the inner circle of power the disturbing characteristics of which Lenin had warned in his last will and testament. The steps which Lenin had taken towards capitalism in his New Economic Policy, in an attempt to avert famine and social disintegration, were halted, and the harsh tenets of Communist economic policy were restored.

The methods Lenin had instituted in his days of power remained the main instruments of government. The secret police organization, the State Political Administration (the GPU), which had been created in 1922, was enlarged in 1923 as the Unified State Political Administration (OGPU). As such it maintained after Lenin's death a vigilance and control over Soviet life as vigorous as before, and as harsh.

Following Lenin's death, a campaign was launched to eliminate the once-flourishing, educated and politically active Russian middle class, the source of liberalism and moderation. Children of the bourgeoisie were denied the right of attending high school or university. Apartment owners who were identified as 'bourgeois' were denied the right of voting on the house committees that determined the fate of their own apartments, in which they were invariably reduced to living in one room, with the other three or four rooms distributed to others.

Amid these extensions of Bolshevik control, the Soviet Union under Stalin sought to restore relations with the very nations which, five years earlier, had taken up arms, in Churchill's phrase, to 'strangle it at birth'. The first country to offer recognition was Britain, in February. Italy and France followed. The French recognition, in October, gave particular pleasure in Moscow, as it included a mutual agreement of noninterference in each other's internal affairs.

Despite straightforward trade agreements, and solemnly negotiated non-interference pacts, the Communist ideological imperative to spread revolution far beyond the Soviet borders was causing distress in many countries. To counter the intensification of Bolshevik propaganda in the Balkans during 1924, an Anti-Bolshevik League was formed by Yugoslavia, Bulgaria and Roumania. Yugoslavia was emphatic that it would neither recognize the Soviet Union nor trade with it. In Estonia, the Communist party was suppressed and illegal Communist groups in Dorpat and Reval arrested; on December 1 there was an attempted Bolshevik uprising in Reval, in which emissaries from Moscow played a prominent part. The main railway station and several military buildings were seized, and the Minister of Transport, in trying to prevent a coup, was shot dead at the station. The uprising was suppressed and its leaders sentenced to penal servitude for life.

So incensed was the British government by the revelation of secret Soviet financing of British Trade Union activity that year that, having recognized the Soviet Union only a year earlier, it broke off diplomatic relations with the Soviets. Mustafa Kemal's Turkey also refused to recognize Russia while Constantinople was being used as a base, not only for Bolshevik propaganda in Turkey, but also throughout the Balkans. An anti-Communist campaign in Bulgaria threatened to have such a severe backlash, encouraged from Moscow, that the former Allies allowed Bulgaria to increase the size of its army by 8000 above the limit set by the peace treaties. One of the victims of a Communist intrigue in Bulgaria that year was the Bulgarian nationalist leader, Todor Alexandroff, the head of the Macedonian Internal Revolutionary Organization, IMRO. He was assassinated. In Moscow, one of the most dynamic leaders of the Third International, Karl Radek, was removed from his post because he was considered too moderate with regard to revolutionary activity inside Germany.

Soviet control over former Russian regions far distant from Moscow was also extended in 1924, with a revolt in Turkestan crushed, and an anti-Bolshevik uprising in Georgia suppressed. So fierce were the Russian reprisals in the Georgian capital, Tbilisi, that in September a resolution was brought forward by France to the League of Nations, that the League should intervene in the Russo-Georgian conflict, and seek to mediate between the two sides. Britain supported France in this proposal, but when it was put to the Soviet Union (whose assent was essential for it to be implemented) it was ridiculed by Moscow and dismissed with contempt.

In Spanish Morocco the government of Primo de Rivera was faced during 1924 by continuous uprisings, and came to the conclusion that the Protectorate would have to be abandoned. This decision was challenged in Morocco itself by the head of the Spanish Legion, Colonel Franco, who told a dinner gathering at which Primo de Rivera was present: 'Where we tread is Spanish soil, because it has been bought at the highest price and with the most precious coin: the Spanish blood shed there. We reject the idea of pulling back, because we are convinced that Spain is in a position to dominate her zone.'

Primo de Rivera replied to Franco by defending the policy of withdrawal. His speech was interrupted by hissing from many of the officers present. When the policy of withdrawal was begun, it encouraged Abd el-Krim to attack the blockhouses that were to be evacuated, to cut the Tangier–Tetuan road, and to besiege the large but isolated garrison at Xauen. There was talk among the Spanish officers in Morocco, including Franco, of a coup against the Dictator, and of the reassertion of Spanish power in Morocco. But the withdrawal went ahead. Its most dramatic moment was the advance of Spanish forces to the besieged garrison of Xauen, where 10,000 Spanish soldiers, many of them wounded, were taken back to Tetuan in safety, together with several thousand Jewish and pro-Spanish Arab civilians who feared the harshness of Abd el-Krim's Moorish forces.

The wars and conflicts that had scarred the first five years that followed the end of the First World War brought considerable suffering to many regions already devastated and disturbed by war, and to areas such as Morocco which had been outside the European war zone, but were the scene of colonial conflict. The League of Nations was determined, however, to fulfil the hopes that had been vested in it. Its founders, and those who looked to it for succour, hoped that it would be able to reduce conflict between nations, and in due course to eliminate war altogether.

During 1924 the Fifth Assembly of the League, meeting in Geneva, completed what was known as the Geneva Protocol. This had evolved over four years, through the work of two technical commissions, and was based on the aspiration, expressed in article 8 of the League Covenant, whereby all members of the League of Nations undertook to reduce their national armaments, as a first step to the total abolition of war.

The Geneva Protocol consisted of three separate but interlinked parts: Arbitration, Security and Disarmament. The founders of the League, and those participating in its subsequent deliberations, saw disarmament as the way to avoid future wars. It was also felt that the League, not individual States, should have the right to challenge any aggressor, and to do so collectively. It was considered essential that where alliances and military guarantees existed between nations, and were in conflict with another nation or group of nations, both sides should submit to compulsory arbitration in the event of a dispute. It was only on this basis that many nations were willing to contemplate a reduction of armaments. They looked to the compulsory arbitration of the League, under the Geneva Protocol, to act as a deterrent against any threat of aggression.

At the core of the Geneva Protocol lay the willingness of both large and small nations to entrust their security to an international body rather than to their own military strength, and to have confidence in the ability of that international body to assert its collective power whenever aggression threatened. The arbitration envisioned by the Protocol would be both compulsory and pacific; those who framed it were convinced that there was an almost 'universal desire' among nations and peoples to accept compulsory arbitration, and that arbitration awards made under the Protocol would carry great weight both with the parties in dispute, and with international opinion.

The Security provisions of the Protocol were based on the abolition of the 'right' of nations to make war. All the States which were members of the League agreed that they would 'in no case' go to war unless they were called upon to do so by the Council of the League itself, in order to repress an act of aggression by a 'recalcitrant' State. War would be a collective enterprise against the aggression of a single, rogue power, not the result of conflicting alliances, pacts, ambitions and armaments. The nature of any war to be conducted by the League was spelt out clearly in the Protocol. It would start, not with actual, active hostilities, but with economic and financial pressure. If military action was required, however, the League Council would call on all its members to coordinate their land, naval and aerial forces in physical combat. Members pledged to carry out any such action, when asked to do so, 'loyally and effectively'.

Any nation that made war on another had been given notice that it would be isolated and challenged. The Geneva Protocol represented an international response to the horrors of trench warfare, and the fulfilment of the pledge of those who had sworn that the First World War would prove to be the 'war to end war'. Under the Protocol, the anarchic disturbances of the postwar period would be ended. In as much as the alliances already signed since 1918 might be seen as the creation of blocs of States capable, as the prewar alliances had been, of drifting into war, the Protocol laid down that no State could take military action in pursuance of any alliance until the Council of the League had called on it to do so. Under the Protocol, when aggression did occur, the Council of the League was instructed to summon member States to participate in such 'measures of repression' as might be needed to end the aggression.

By the end of 1924, seventeen governments had signed the Protocol. Britain hesitated to do so, fearing that it was undermining its imperial, dominion and colonial responsibilities. Meanwhile, the League worked patiently to settle the small boundary disputes that arose between nations. In 1924 it resolved a border dispute between two new States, Poland and Czechoslovakia, in the mountain district of Javorina. The dispute had aroused much anger among both Czechs and Poles, but their respective governments agreed to accept the League Council's decision to put the matter to the Permanent Court of International Justice. Attention then turned to a border dispute between Yugoslavia and Albania. It concerned the Byzantine monastery on the southern shore of Lake Ochrid, Saint Naoum, which the Court awarded to Albania.

The future of the town and territory of Memel, on the Baltic, was also approved by the League of Nations in 1924, having been the last territorial dispute to be resolved by the Allied and Associated Powers, the initiators of the postwar peace treaties. Under a convention signed on May 8, Memel was to have autonomous status, ruled by a Memel Directorate; but the autonomous region was to be under Lithuanian sovereignty, and administered by two Lithuanian officials, one appointed by Lithuania and one by the Directorate. For its part, Lithuania agreed to free transit of goods through Memel.

*   *   *

The settlement of border and territorial disputes was to be part of a wider amelioration. In all the new States, the work of establishing effective national systems of government, and working national economies, had begun. The free flow of trade, and the reduction of economic burdens, were considered by the League of Nations to be of crucial importance to protect the stability of the world. The defeated States were inevitably the main beneficiaries of this concern. To ensure that Hungary could raise enough money on the international markets to pay its reparations debt to the Allies, a League High Commissioner was appointed to go to Budapest and supervize the financial arrangements. The man chosen for the task was a distinguished American banker, Jeremiah Smith, of Boston. Within a few months, he was able to float a Hungarian government loan in London, New York, Paris and Rome, and to secure the money that was needed for Hungary's annual reparations payments.

During 1924 the League of Nations also undertook to raise the financial aid desperately needed by Greece, which had been struggling for more than a year to accommodate a million Greek-speaking refugees from Anatolia and Thrace. An International League Commission, set up by the League Council to find the money needed for the massive task of resettlement, found, as a first participant in the scheme, the Bank of England. When the scheme was launched, the Bank of England put up an initial loan of £1 million.[1] The work of resettlement was judged so effective that the bank agreed to a second instalment, also of £1 million, in May 1924. The total sum needed, a further £10 million, was then floated by the League Commission at the end of the year, and successfully raised in the money markets of London and New York.

In Poland, the largest of the new States of Europe, strenuous efforts were made during 1924 to end the inflation, culminating in the opening of the Bank of Poland, and the issue of new bank notes, which for a whole year retained their parity with gold. At the same time, Poland signed commercial treaties with Denmark, Iceland and Sweden. Efforts were also made to resolve Poland's minority problem. One long-standing demand, which had so plagued Austria-Hungary's relations with the Ukrainians of Eastern Galicia, was for a Ukrainian University in Lvov. This was granted by the Poles in 1924. At the same time, Poland's three million Jews were granted representation in the Warsaw parliament.

In Czechoslovakia, social reform was high on the domestic political agenda.

---

[1] In 1997 values, £50 million ($75 million).

A law, voted through the Czech parliament in 1924, provided for the insurance of all workers against sickness, disablement and old age – Britain and Germany had both put similar legislation on their statute books before the First World War. By the end of the year, the Czech social insurance law had been extended to include the self-employed. Czechoslovakia was fortunate economically, in that her ability to export raw materials, especially coal, enabled her to build up a favourable balance of foreign trade, and to compete with Germany. With regard to its minorities, however, Czechoslovakia had less success than Poland; both the Ruthenians in the east, and the German and Hungarian minorities elsewhere, were dissatisfied with their subordinate status, feeling that they were excluded from the inner decisions of the Czech leaders and denied the full economic benefits of citizenship.

Of all the new nations of Central Europe, Czechoslovakia was most fortunate in her leaders. Her first President, Thomas Masaryk, founder of his nation's independence, was a philosopher of broad democratic vision. The Foreign Minister, and second President, Edvard Beneš, was tenacious in maintaining his country's position as an independent State. But the problems of a small multinational State were no more easily solved than those of the much larger multinational Empire of which Czechoslovakia had once been part. Indeed, the Ruthenian, Slovak, Hungarian and Sudeten German minorities seemed at times even harder to satisfy than they had been in Habsburg times.

In Turkey, its territory reduced under the Treaty of Lausanne to Asia Minor and a small area of Thrace, Mustafa Kemal, having acquired dictatorial powers, was pursuing a revolutionary path. A year earlier, the Sultanate had been abolished, but the office of Caliphate – the spiritual head of Islam throughout the Ottoman Empire – had been retained. In March, Kemal abolished the Caliphate, closed all religious schools in Constantinople – known to the Turks as Istanbul – removed the Minister of Religion from the Cabinet, and sent the Caliph and his family into exile in Switzerland. Another religious leader in Istanbul, the Armenian Patriarch, whose jurisdiction had covered all the former Ottoman areas with Armenian inhabitants, was encouraged to transfer his patriarchate to Palestine.

Throughout 1924 Turkey was in dispute with Britain over the Mosul district on the upper Tigris. Under the Treaty of Lausanne, the question of the future of Mosul was reserved for 'friendly agreement' between the two contenders. The area had been occupied by Britain in the final phase of the war with Turkey in October 1918, and was regarded by the British, territorially, as the northernmost part of the British Mandate over Iraq. Britain insisted that Mosul, with its oilfields, should be recognized as a part of Iraq. Turkey sought the whole district for itself.

Negotiations between Britain and Turkey were opened on May 19 in Istanbul. They foundered on the question of the 450,000 Kurdish inhabitants of the region, whom the Turks claimed as Turkish, and whom the British claimed as a distinct ethnic group. Under the Treaty of Sèvres, Britain had established a Kurdish State in Eastern Anatolia, but that had been swept away with the emergence of Mustafa Kemal's national movement, and had no place in the subsequent Treaty of Lausanne. Three years earlier, when Britain was setting up the Jewish National Home in Palestine, the idea of a Kurdish National Home had been mooted for the northern province of Iraq, and was supported by Churchill. But Britain wanted control of the Mosul oilfields and felt, on reflection, that the best way to achieve this was through control of Baghdad.

The most that Britain was prepared to concede to the Turks during the negotiations that May was the transfer to Turkey of the northern third of the Mosul district. But the town of Mosul and the oilfields would be retained by Iraq, whose ruler, the Emir Feisal, was under British influence; indeed he owed his throne to Britain. The Turks rejected this, and the negotiations were broken off. In September, one of the minorities in the region, the Assyrian Christians, seized a Turkish administrator who had been passing through northern Mosul, and held him captive. Turkish troops at once attacked across the border into the Mosul region. Thousands of Assyrians and Kurds fled southward. British aircraft were sent into action against the Turks.

Repeated British demands that Turkish troops depart from the Mosul region were ignored by Turkey. Over the next few days the British insisted on the withdrawal of these troops three times: on September 26, October 6 and October 9. The third demand was a virtual ultimatum. As Turkey had no military means to challenge the might of Britain, any more than she had been able to do so at Chanak two years earlier, she agreed to accept the arbitration of the League of Nations in delineating the border between Turkey and Iraq. The League Council met in emergency session on October 15. Two weeks later it gave its judgment: Turkey would remain in possession of most of the territory which it had just occupied. Britain would retain the rest, as part of its Iraq Mandate, the oilfields of the region, and control of two-thirds of the Kurdish-inhabited areas. An independent Kurdistan would not come into being.[1]

A Republican constitution was promulgated for Turkey in April. Kemal embarked upon a rapid effort to create a secular and literate society. As part of this, the political influence of Islam was drastically curtailed. Within four years, Kemal had effected a social revolution in Turkey as remarkable as any of the postwar revolutions. The Muslim religion was separated from the State, and the State machinery secularized. The oath to be taken by newly elected deputies was changed from 'in the Name of Allah' to a secular affirmation.

The 'Western' reforms on which Kemal was so insistent were also introduced in the Muslim religion. These included the introduction of seats, instrumental music and singing in the mosques, the substitution of the Turkish language for Arabic in prayers, and the abolition of the ancient Islamic custom of removing shoes when entering a mosque. The fez was also abolished, as part of the Westernizing of all dress. Women's rights were also asserted in a way that had not taken place before in a Muslim country, culminating a decade later with votes for women.

Most revolutionary of all, a new alphabet was introduced, written in Latin characters. The Ottoman form of Arabic writing was abolished. With four-fifths of the population illiterate, and speaking a great variety of dialects, the new alphabet was to have both a unifying and educational influence, especially as it was combined with a massive campaign against illiteracy. The newspapers were ordered to publish several columns a day in the new script. Post offices and public offices were ordered to use it at once. In addition, a law was introduced, making the use of western numerals compulsory after 1 January 1929.

Kemal engaged personally in propaganda for the new alphabet, visiting hundreds of villages and explaining the new script on a blackboard. All government and semi-official employees were ordered to learn and employ it. A number of schoolmasters were arrested for 'carrying on propaganda' against it. Bank notes printed in Arabic characters continued to circulate; apart from that, Arabic characters disappeared from Turkey on 3 November

---

[1] The Turks were to pursue a consistently harsh policy towards the Kurds under their control. The Iraqis, after they became independent, could be equally harsh. In 1991 the British government of John Major established 'safe havens' in northern Iraq where the Kurdish population could be protected by Britain and the United States from attack by the Iraqi leader, Saddam Hussein.

1928, 'with the punctuality', noted one foreign observer, 'which the Ghazi Pasha has insisted on in all his reforms'.

In Italy, Mussolini's dictatorship was consolidating its power. The elections that were held in April 1924 were characterized by Fascist violence against opposition parties. Politicians and intellectuals who criticized Mussolini and Fascism were denounced as traitors to Italy. After the election, those districts where the Fascist majority had not been as high as Mussolini had hoped saw renewed Fascist violence against opponents of the regime. Parliamentary opposition continued, but suffered a severe blow when a Socialist deputy, Giacomo Matteotti, disappeared from his home. He had openly denounced the corruption and intimidation which had been practised by the Fascist Party during the elections.

Forty-eight hours after Matteotti disappeared it became clear that he had been murdered: the car into which he had been bundled was found with bloodstains.

Among those implicated in Matteotti's murder was a member of the Fascist Party Directorate. Mussolini, who many Italians assumed must have given the order, immediately denounced the murder, removed those implicated from office, and promised stringent measures to restore constitutional law in Italy. For the time being these assurances were enough to allay foreign distress; but they did not weaken for a moment Mussolini's resolve to eliminate the influence of parliament on the conduct of national policy. One of the first measures that he imposed after the murder was a strict curtailment of freedom of the press; the opposition newspapers would no longer have recourse to the courts if they were censored or shut down.

Yet the opposition to Fascism continued. On October 28 the Italian War Veterans' association refused to participate in the Fascist commemoration of the 'March on Rome'. As a reprisal, seven days later, Fascist groups attacked the veterans during the Armistice Day celebrations held on November 4 in Rome and other cities.

Abroad, Mussolini pursued the Italian imperial ambitions which had been authorized by the Allies during the war. Tripolitania and Cyrenaica were reoccupied, and the tribes who during the war had been active in attacking Allied outposts, were driven towards the Egyptian border. Mussolini also secured from Britain the annexation – which had first been envisaged in the Treaty of London in 1915 – of the Jubaland territory, between British East

Africa and Italian Somaliland. The Jubaland treaty, signed in London two months after the Italian elections, gave Mussolini's authority a boost in Rome.

The United States remained outside these conflicts. Those individual Americans who participated in the work of European amelioration, especially in the economic sphere, did so as private citizens.

In February 1924 Woodrow Wilson died. Congress adjourned in solemn memory of the man whose European (and indeed global) peace plan they had so decisively rejected, and on all American government buildings the Stars and Stripes flew at half mast. All foreign embassies also lowered their flags as a sign of respect, with one exception. The German Ambassador in Washington, Herr Wiedfeldt, decided that, as Wilson was a private citizen at the time of his death, the German flag need not be lowered. On the following day, February 6, the day of Wilson's funeral, a mob of American Army veterans besieged the German Embassy, nailed the Stars and Stripes to its door, and sang with gusto 'The Star Spangled Banner'. Herr Wiedfeldt resigned, and returned to Germany.

The French were still determined to secure reparations payments from Germany, even if it meant, as it had done in 1923, physically operating the main German industrial plants, or extracting German raw materials, lorries and railway rolling stock by force. In a defiant statement, the commander of the French occupation forces in Germany, General Dugoûte, announced that the French army would remain in the Ruhr, if necessary, for a thousand years.

On January 14 a special commission set up to resolve the Ruhr crisis met in Paris, under the auspices of the Reparations Commission. It worked without interruption until the beginning of April. Two United States experts, General Charles G. Dawes of Chicago, and Owen D. Young of Boston, although acting as private citizens, and lacking the authority they might have had if the United States had been a member of the League, managed nevertheless to impress on the other participants – from England, France, Italy and Belgium – the need to make some accommodation satisfactory to Germany. The conclusion of this committee's deliberations, under the title of the Dawes Report, gained for Germany even greater flexibility in the annual payment of reparations than she had been able to secure in earlier negotiations.

The scheme of the Dawes Report made the German repayments conditional upon a balanced German budget and a stabilized German currency. To secure these goals, the Allied nations established a Bank of Issue in Germany, which was to be the fiscal agent of the German government. Dawes wanted the bank to serve for fifty years as the only bank with the right to issue and circulate bank notes in Germany. It was to be administered by a German president and management boards, but in all matters relating to creditor nations and reparations payments was to have a General Board of Control, made up of seven Germans and seven foreigners. Thus international control would remain, and France could feel that her demand for reparations would not again be flouted.

In order to persuade the French to leave the Ruhr, and to allow the payments to be a matter of independent German economic organization, the Dawes Report set out how reparations were to be paid. First, there would be an international loan, then a mortgage on German railways, then a mortgage on German industries, and finally a transport tax and the revenues from customs, alcohol, tobacco, beer and sugar. These would be allocated as a reserve fund for reparations needs; they were known as the 'controlled revenues'. For five years, the reparations payments would rise by steady gradations from 220 million marks to 2500 million marks; after that they would be on a sliding scale to be negotiated upward or downward according to circumstances. This meant that after 1929 the subject of the amount to be paid would again be open to negotiation.

Payments were to be made through the Agent-General for Reparation Payments. The first Agent-General was Owen Young, the second was also an American, Parker Gilbert. The resolution of the reparations crisis was also helped by changes of government in both Britain and France. The British Conservative government under Stanley Baldwin, and the French government under Raymond Poincaré – known, because of his tough stance towards Germany as Poincaré la Guerre (Warrior Poincaré) – had been at loggerheads over the occupation of the Ruhr. Baldwin's Foreign Secretary, Lord Curzon, had been particularly hostile to France's action.

In January 1924, Baldwin was replaced by the Labour Party leader, Ramsay MacDonald, who became Prime Minister as well as Foreign Secretary. In May, the Poincaré government gave way to that of the Radical Party leader, Edouard Herriot. On June 22 MacDonald and Herriot met at Chequers, the British Prime Minister's country house outside London, and agreed that the Dawes Plan constituted the way forward for the amelioration of Franco-

German tension. Three weeks later, at a conference in London, the German delegates accepted the Dawes Plan, and the French government agreed to withdraw from the Ruhr. The Dawes Plan was accepted by the Reichstag that October. The French had already begun to withdraw, and on November 15 evacuated the factories which had been occupied for almost two years.

Hardly had MacDonald completed this exercise in foreign policy and the amelioration of tension between two former warring Powers than he was defeated at the polls, and Baldwin came back as Prime Minister at the head of a Conservative administration. One reason for Labour's defeat was the intense publicity created by the publication of a letter – dated 25 October 1924 – signed by the head of the Comintern, Grigori Zinoviev, and by Arthur MacManus, the one British member of the Comintern Praesidium, in which they urged the British Communist Party to 'stir up the masses of the British proletariat', to create Communist cells in the British army, navy and munitions factories, and to 'beware' of Ramsay MacDonald and the 'bourgeois' Labour Party.

The General Election was held four days after the publication of the 'Zinoviev Letter'. Labour denounced the letter as a forgery. The Conservatives won 419 seats, Labour 151, the Liberals 40 and the Communists only one. MacDonald resigned on November 4, when he was replaced as Prime Minister by Stanley Baldwin. Six weeks later, Baldwin announced that the Zinoviev Letter was genuine. Later, it was shown to have been a forgery. The Conservative Party managers, believing it to be genuine, and recognizing the impact it would have on the electorate, had paid a considerable sum of money to the men who had 'discovered' it.

Germany, not Russia, remained the principal focus of government concern in Britain. The new British Foreign Secretary, Austen Chamberlain, at once adopted a stricter attitude towards Germany. Under the Treaty of Versailles, the city of Cologne, which since 1919 had been occupied by British troops as part of the Rhineland demilitarization plan, was to be evacuated at the beginning of 1925, on January 10. It was not only the French need for reparations, however, but also France's need for security, that was at issue. The year 1924 had opened with French soldiers still in occupation of the Ruhr, and actively encouraging German separatists in the Rhineland to break away from Germany. The separatist movement, protected by the French military garrison in the Rhineland, terrorized the local inhabitants and raised the flag of independence. German police, whose presence in the Rhineland was permitted under the Treaty of Versailles, had to try to combat the separatists without antagonizing the French.

The Rhineland Palatinate was under Bavarian administration. When an independent Palatinate government was declared, headed by the separatist leader Heinz Orbis, the German police were goaded into action. On January 9 they attacked Orbis and his supporters; in the ensuing battle, Orbis was killed. The French, who favoured an autonomous Palatinate, were indignant that they should be accused of supporting the separatists. Such an accusation, Poincaré declared, was a 'slander'. France was even more indignant when the separatists seized the town of Pirmasens, occupying French Government House. It was not until February 17 that the separatists were driven out, with heavy loss of life, and the authority of the Bavarian administration was restored.

Inside Bavaria, the separatist ambitions which had surfaced with such violence during 1923 were stilled. Both von Kahr and General von Lossow, who had defied the established authorities the previous year, withdrew from public life. The Bavarian government began to rebuild its links with Berlin and to re-establish its loyalties to the German Republic.

Hitler and Ludendorff were awaiting trial for their part in the failed Munich putsch. The Nazi Party was banned by the Bavarian government. But the forces of racism and extremism found a focus in the establishment of the *völkischer* bloc, made up of Nazis and like-minded nationalists throughout Bavaria. One of the bloc's leaders, Dr Rudolph Buttman, was to devote his political life to Hitler. On January 24, Buttman declared: 'We will carry the nationalist idea into the last mountain village.' The Jews, he warned, and the other 'mortal enemies' of the *völkisch* movement, would no longer rejoice as they had done when the Putsch was crushed the previous November.

Yet another nationalist agitator, the violently anti-Semitic Julius Streicher, published a newspaper, *Der Stürmer* (The Stormer), which churned out material aimed at stimulating hatred of the Jews. On February 8, Streicher formed a new grouping in Munich, the Great German People's Community, pledging allegiance to the banned Nazi Party. The Community appealed directly to the working class to see the Jews as their enemy, and to oppose the parliamentary democracy of the Weimar Republic. Hitler, impressed by the new grouping, appointed Streicher his representative in northern Bavaria.

Throughout Bavaria, small groups of Nazis continued to gather, illegally, brandishing the swastika flag as a symbol of German regeneration, and demanding war against those whom they denounced as the 'international powers' bent on destroying Germany: the Allies, Marxism, the Jews, the Catholic church, capitalism, and parliamentary democracy.

Hitler was sentenced in April 1924 to five years in prison, on a charge of high treason. Believing that the spectre of a revolutionary, divisive and military movement had been exorcised, the Bavarian government pressed on with rebuilding its links with Berlin, and its loyalties to the German Republic. But the dangers posed by Hitler and the Nazi Party were not eliminated. Ludendorff, Hitler's co-conspirator, had been acquitted. The trial itself had been used by the Nazis to give the maximum possible exposure to their cause and to their 'heroes' – those who had fallen during the brief march into the centre of Munich. The German general election was held in the first week of May. Sixty-two Communist and thirty-six 'Racialist' members, but no Nazi Party members, were elected. Neither the Communists nor the Racialists had any political power in the wider party spectrum. Both denounced each other with equal passion.

From an outsider's view of the German public mood, there seemed to be hope for democracy in Germany. Vera Brittain, who had lost so many of those closest to her in the First World War, travelled that October to Berlin. 'Throughout Germany, we were told' – she wrote in her memoirs *Testament of Youth* – 'the Conservative Parties were declining in power except in Bavaria; the Nationalists and Communists were losing favour, and Stresemann was trying to get the pro-Dawes Plan Nationalists into his Party. The worst period of the economic and financial crisis was past; the more intelligent Germans were ceasing to wish for a war of revenge, and desired only peace and stability; one year of "sensible" politics among the Entente countries would destroy in a weary and broken people the desire for retaliation. A war-psychology had continued for so long because of the Saar provisions and the Ruhr occupation, combined with the "war-guilt" clauses of the Treaty, but now Germany was ready to accept the idea of international arbitration through a League of Nations, though her attitude towards the existing League was warped, not unnaturally, by scepticism and fear.'

From Germany, Vera Brittain travelled to Czechoslovakia, Austria and Hungary. Nine years later – and three months after Hitler had come to power in Germany – she reflected on what she had seen and felt:

. . . gradually, as the autumn weeks passed over Germany, and Austria, and Hungary, I had realized that it was not the courage and generosity of the dead which had brought about this chaos of disaster, but the failure of courage and generosity on the part of the survivors. How terrible our responsibility is! I meditated, dimly understanding that for me this journey had been the rounding off of a decade of experience which had shown, beyond all possibility of contention, the ruin and devastation wrought by international conflict in a world of mutually dependent nations. How much there was to be done for this suffering Europe, this stricken humanity; we could not, even if we would, leave it to its agony and live in the past! To find some guiding principle of action, some philosophy of life, some constructive hope upon whose wings this crippled age might swing forward into a fairer future – that at least remained and always would remain, for us who had experienced in our own souls those incalculable depths into which Germany had fallen.

It did not seem, perhaps, as though we, the War generation, would be able to do all that we had once hoped for the actual rebuilding of civilization. I understood now that the results of the War would last longer than ourselves; it was obvious, in Central Europe, that its consequences were deeper rooted, and farther reaching, than any of us, with our lack of experience, had believed just after it was over. In any case, the men who might, in cooperation with the women who were not too badly impaired by shock and anxiety, have contributed most to its recovery, the first rate, courageous men with initiative and imagination, had themselves gone down in the Flood, and their absence now meant failure and calamity in every department of human life. Perhaps, after all, the best that we who were left could do was to refuse to forget, and to teach our successors what we remembered in the hope that they, when their own day came, would have more power to change the state of the world than this bankrupt, shattered generation. If only, somehow, the nobility which in us had been turned towards destruction could be used in them for creation, if the courage which we had dedicated to war could be employed by them, on behalf of peace, then the future might indeed see the redemption of man instead of his further descent into chaos.

In the German elections held on December 7 the Communist representation fell to forty-five and the Racialists to fourteen. But the Nazi Party, even with its leader in prison, continued to spread its doctrine, spurred by the

the twin intensities of fanaticism and hatred. And on December 20, less than two weeks after the election, Hitler, who had repeatedly petitioned the Bavarian authorities, was released from prison. The prison authorities had given him a favourable report as 'a man of strict discipline and order', who had been 'at all times cooperative, modest and courteous to everyone, particularly to the officers of the institution'.

'What will you do now?' asked a friend who met Hitler at the prison gate. 'I shall start again, from the beginning,' he replied. And he did, without delay. His method was to rebuild the Nazi Party using a stratagem he had outlined while in prison: the creation, in a single town – in his case, Munich – of 'a band of absolutely reliable followers' who would be trained 'to propagate the idea of a new movement'. Hitler had also written, while in prison: 'To secure name and fame for the movement and its leader it was necessary, not only to give in this one town a striking example to shatter the belief that the Marxist doctrine was invincible, but also to show that a counter-doctrine was possible.' That counter-doctrine was Nazism, suffused with the belief in the superiority of the German race.

Under the Treaty of Versailles, the Allies had the right, if Germany was not faithfully fulfilling all its clauses of the Treaty, maintain the occupation of Cologne (and also of Mainz and Frankfurt-am-Main) for ten or even fifteen years. As 1924 came to an end, the Inter-Allied Commission of Military Control announced that the disarmament clauses of the Treaty were not being fully carried out. A Conference of Ambassadors was summoned in Paris, and concluded that the occupation must continue. At the same time, Austen Chamberlain began negotiations with the French government for a treaty of alliance between Britain and France, which would contain mutual guarantees of each other's frontiers. To the Germans, this seemed a revival of the policy encapsulated by the Anglo-French Entente of 1904, which, from the German perspective (and also from the historical one), had been one of the factors leading to the polarization of the powers before 1914, and the dragging of Britain into war.

The Germans had an unexpected ally in their opposition to an Anglo-French alliance: this was Winston Churchill, the Chancellor of the Exchequer in the new government. He argued strongly in the British Cabinet, that to link Britain and France in this way would only antagonize Germany and lead to a renewal of the confrontational aspects of the alliance system. What

Churchill advocated was a wider arrangement in which Germany would be brought in to the circle of frontier guarantees; guarantees which could serve as an instrument of both European and international peace.

Internationalization took a step forward in 1924, with a World Power Conference, held in London, to institute the standardization of electric power supplies. But the movement of peoples across borders saw a setback that year, when the Johnson–Reed Act in the United States limited the number of immigrants from Europe to 164,000 a year, and banned the Japanese altogether.

The first woman Cabinet Minister was appointed that year. She was Nina Bang, Denmark's Minister for Education. In the United States, American Indians (later called Native Americans) were allowed full citizenship for the first time. One of their number, Learned Hand, was appointed a judge in 1924 in the United States Court of Appeals. Also in the United States, the first unspoilt area of natural countryside, the Gila Wilderness in New Mexico, was given protected status.

The first Winter Olympic Games were held in 1924. The place chosen for them was Chamonix, in France. In the summer Olympics, held in Paris, the United States emerged as by far the most successful competitor, with forty-five gold medals, the next most successful being Finland with fourteen. In the cinema, the first talking film system was being developed. That same year Walt Disney produced his first film cartoon, *Alice's Wonderland*.

CHAPTER TWENTY-NINE

1925

THE LEAGUE OF NATIONS had crowned its work in 1924 with the signing of the Geneva Protocol, the aim of which was to abolish war by means of a triple fortification of arbitration, security and disarmament. The French were still unhappy at the ability of Germany to make war, the issue they regarded as central to European peace, and continued to seek a separate security in some form of alliance with Britain. As Chancellor of the Exchequer, Winston Churchill took the view that a Franco-British alliance could only deepen Franco-German animosities, and lead in due course to further conflict. Travelling to Paris at the beginning of 1925, he was told, however, by the French President, Gaston Doumerge, that it was essential for Britain and France to create a unity which the Germans would realize was 'unbreakable'.

The minutes of their meeting record that Churchill replied to the French President: 'The only real security against a renewal of war would be a complete agreement between England, France and Germany. That alone would give the security which we were all seeking, and that alone would enable the commerce of Europe to expand to such dimensions that the existing burden of debts and reparations would be supportable and not crushing.' It would be better for France to try to come to good terms with Germany, Churchill told Doumerge, and to settle their grievances, than to have, as the French wished, a defensive Anglo-French alliance 'while the fundamental antagonisms between France and Germany continued unappeased'. Churchill believed that Germany would be willing to accept the existing western frontier. It was in the east, he told Doumerge, that Germany would seek to regain the territories lost in 1918; that, he added, 'was the great cause of anxiety that brooded over Europe'.

Austen Chamberlain, the British Foreign Secretary, still favoured a direct Anglo-French alliance. Churchill feared that a return to the old alliance system of confrontation – the very system that the League Protocol was designed to avert – would pit Germany once more against France. 'This war which has occurred between France and Germany several times has broken up the world,' he told the British Committee of Imperial Defence on February 13. 'What guarantee have we got, while things are going as they are, that we shall not have another war? In fact, it seems as if we were moving towards it, although it may not be for twenty years, certainly not until Germany has been able to acquire some methods of waging war, chemically or otherwise.'

Sooner or later, Churchill wrote to his colleagues eight days later, 'Germany will be rearmed', despite the prohibitions of the Versailles Treaty. France might decide to attack Germany before this rearming process was completed. If Britain were allied to France, she would then be 'obliged to support' France. Britain would also have to support France if France were drawn in to a war against Germany elsewhere; if, for example, France were also allied to Poland, and came to the defence of a Poland that was being attacked by Germany. Britain should say to France, Churchill advised his Cabinet colleagues: 'The better friends you are with Germany, the better friends we shall be with you. The more you can settle your quarrel with Germany, the more ready we shall be to associate ourselves with your fortunes in the event of all your efforts proving unavailing.'

Churchill's argument was successful. That March, negotiations were opened in Paris between Britain and France, in which Germany was included, and also Italy and Belgium. The culmination of the negotiations was the signature, on October 16, of the Treaty of Locarno. The frontiers of Western Europe established after Germany's defeat in 1918 were accepted by the former adversaries, and protected against aggression by mutual agreement.

Contemporary cynics wondered why the first substantial postwar pact should have been negotiated outside the framework of the League of Nations, and signed elsewhere than Geneva. The treaty itself stated that its aims were 'within the framework of the Covenant' of the League, and this was so. The emphasis throughout was similar to that of the Geneva Protocol, the avoidance of war, and it was the Council of the League that was to decide whether the Locarno Treaty had been violated, and if so, by whom. Nor did the Treaty enter into force until Germany became a member of the League. The Treaty was also specifically presented only as a starting point; although limited to Western Europe, and predominantly to Germany's Rhine frontier, it envisaged a similar set of frontier acceptances and guarantees against aggression along Germany's eastern frontier. Indeed, Austen Chamberlain stressed in several speeches, the only justification for a regional pact was that ultimately the whole world would be covered with regional pacts that would then be linked up, under the Council of the League, into a general system of world security.

During 1925 the League of Nations seemed to confirm the hopes placed in it as a resolver of disputes between two potentially warring States. The States in question were Bulgaria and Greece. In October, after a Greek sentry had been killed by a Bulgarian frontier guard at the village of Demir-Hissar, Greek troops advanced across the frontier, and occupied a number of Bulgarian villages. Five Bulgarian soldiers and seven Bulgarian civilians were killed, but it was Greece that demanded an indemnity from Bulgaria for the death of the sentry. The Bulgarians offered to set up a Court of Enquiry into the Greek sentry's death. Greece rejected this, and the Bulgarians appealed to the League.

On October 26, seven days after the shooting incident, the League Council met in Paris. 'Frontier incidents,' warned Austen Chamberlain, 'might mean war.' The League Council ordered both parties to cease hostilities within twenty-four hours, and to evacuate all occupied territory within sixty hours. Both governments complied. They also agreed to accept the decision of a Commission of Enquiry, set up by the League, with regard to the resolution of the dispute and the assessment of reparations and indemnities.

Heading the Commission of Enquiry was the British diplomat, Sir Horace Rumbold. If the Graeco-Bulgarian conflict could be settled without war, he was informed by Austen Chamberlain, 'it will be a good step forward in enhancing the prestige of the League, and an effective warning to the Balkans not to embark in future on offensive operations so light-heartedly'. What Chamberlain most hoped for, Rumbold was told, was not so much 'the fixing of responsibility for what is now past' as the setting up of 'permanent measures of prevention'.

In Belgrade, the Commissioners received an assurance from the Yugoslav Foreign Minister, Momcilo Nincic, that Yugoslavia would not seek to gain any territorial advantage as a result of the Graeco-Bulgarian tensions. There would be no repetition of the Balkan War violence of 1912 and 1913. The Commissioners then went to Demir-Hissar, where the Greek sentry had been killed, and for five days took evidence from Greeks and Bulgarians on both sides of the border. They then spent four days in Athens and four in Sofia. The Bulgarians were delighted to find, only seven years after their defeat on the battlefield, that the League of Nations was treating them, not as an 'enemy' Power, their designation hitherto – whose rights had been submerged by the stigma of defeat – but as a fully independent State with rights of its own. Britain's role in chairing the Commission was particularly appreciated in Sofia. The Bulgarian government, Rumbold reported to London, 'now feel that they have one friend, and that they have emerged from their isolation'.

The Commissioners' report stressed the chaotic nature of the Graeco-Bulgarian frontier. Sentry duty on the Greek side was done by 'very young soldiers' who had received 'only a rudimentary military training'. For several hours after the shooting both sides had shown 'a desire to enter into pourparlers with a view to terminating the incident', and for several hours both the Bulgarian and Greek commanders in the field had made 'every effort to stop the affray'. Unfortunately, one of the telegrams sent from the frontier zone to Athens had been altered in transmission. One sentence had originally read: 'Bulgarian forces *amount to* one battalion.' This became, 'The Bulgarians have *attacked with* one battalion.' The Greek High Command acted accordingly, ordering an immediate advance into Bulgaria.

The Commissioners' conclusion was designed to cause a reduction of tension between the two disputants. There had been 'no question of premeditations on either side', they concluded, nor did the Greeks have any intention to follow up the operation by any further intrusion into Bulgarian territory. The population of the area, Greek and Bulgar alike, had, they wrote, been worked upon for fifty years by 'contradictory propaganda' which had led them 'to distrust one another and to seek to do each other injury'. The sufferings of more than two decades of war had 'implanted feelings of hatred which cannot be expected to disappear quickly'.

The Commissioners made several recommendations, which they hoped would avert further incidents. Frontier duty, they believed, 'should be carried out by a special body made up of picked men recruited and trained for this work'. The signalling and telegraph systems should be improved. At a political level, facilities should be put in place to enable minority groups and refugees from past wars to return to their homelands, and to give them compensation for the value of the property which they could not take with them.

A war crisis had been averted by arbitration. The Balkans, so often the scene of violence in the past, had accepted a peaceful solution. The League of Nations had enhanced its authority as a peacemaker.

*   *   *

Morocco, where the tribes of the Rif had so seriously damaged Spanish imperial rule in 1923 and 1924, became the bane of French political life in 1925. The leader of the rebels, Abd el-Krim, having taken up arms against the French in May, indicated that he was prepared to negotiate some form of autonomy for his people. The French Prime Minister, Paul Painlevé, who was also Minister of War, decided instead to crush the rebellion entirely. Troop reinforcements were sent from France, and Painlevé, in a gesture that stressed the urgency of the occasion, travelled to Morocco by plane.

The Spaniards, who had withdrawn from much of the interior of their zone in Morocco the previous year, were encouraged by the strong line being taken by France, and decided to take a new initiative of their own. The Spanish dictator, Primo de Rivera, left Madrid to take personal command of the Spanish troops. A line of fortified blockhouses was established, known as the Primo de Rivera Line, from a point on the Mediterranean near Tetuan to the border of the French Protectorate just south of Alcazar. Despite repeated attacks by the Moors, this line held.

In French Morocco, Abd el-Krim refused to give up. He had captured his main rival for power, Rasauli, who died soon afterwards in captivity. He had persuaded the tribes of the Rif to declare a Holy War (*Jihad*) against both the French and the Spanish. He had attacked and destroyed the villages of tribes still friendly to France less than fifty miles from Fez. The French continued to send reinforcements, took active steps to defend Fez, and by the end of July were pushing the Rif warriors back into the interior. A turning point came when Painlevé sent General Pétain, the 'victor' of Verdun, to prepare a plan for a major French attack.

During August, further French and Spanish troop reinforcements were sent to Morocco, bringing the total Spanish force up to 75,000 and the French to 160,000 (of whom the majority were local Moroccan troops). On September 2 a joint French and Spanish offensive was opened, and 12,000 troops landed at Alhucemas Bay, which was under Abd el-Krim's control. The first Spanish troops to go ashore were those commanded by Colonel Franco. In the face of strong Moorish opposition on the beachhead he was instrumental in obtaining a foothold, and then in securing a hill overlooking the beachhead. 'Those defenders who are too tenacious,' he wrote in his diary, 'are put to the knife.'

After a two-week delay because of inadequate ammunition and food supplies, the combined Spanish and French force moved forward. In October, recognizing that he did not have the manpower or artillery force to maintain his position, Abd el-Krim sent a British emissary, Captain Gordon Canning, to Paris, to seek terms on his behalf for the opening of negotiations. The emissary was sent back empty-handed. France, with the support of Spain, demanded unconditional surrender.

In November the joint Spanish-French offensive succeeded sufficiently for Primo de Rivera to return to Spain and take up his dictatorial duties. The Spaniards also proclaimed a new Khalifa for Spanish Morocco, to counter Abd el-Krim's religious pronouncements and popular support. The new Khalifa was Muley Mehedi, but despite Spanish military success, he failed to win Islamic support on any significant scale. Indeed, the much-publicized cruelty of the Spanish troops against their adversaries greatly aided Abd el-Krim in retaining his hold upon the spiritual and political aspirations of the Rif.

In Britain, the Spanish methods of war had also led to a reaction, and to widespread sympathy for what was seen as Abd el-Krim's struggle for independence. So supportive were many Britons of the Riffan leader that Austen Chamberlain had to issue a formal denial that Britain was giving him any assistance.

The failure of the harvest, and a typhus epidemic, provided a bitter background to Abd el-Krim's struggle. The continuing French and Spanish military offensive against him gathered in force and success. A year after raising the standard of revolt, he surrendered. Some of his followers continued to resist, but when, six months after Abd el-Krim's surrender, his former lieutenant Hamido Harari, was killed in battle, the resistance of the tribes was virtually at an end. An agreement was reached in Paris (on 13 July 1926) between Spain and France, delineating their Moroccan frontier, and giving each the right to pursue rebels across it. Abd el-Krim, who was not even mentioned in the Paris Agreement, was sent into exile on the French island of Réunion, in the Indian Ocean. Colonel Franco, the hero of the landing at Alhucemas Bay, was promoted general: aged thirty-three, he was said to be the youngest general in Europe.

In Germany, the Weimar Republic, having survived the attempted seizures of power from both Right and Left in 1923, continued to consolidate its position. The parties of the Centre, which held the balance in the Reichstag, were committed to republicanism and parliamentary democracy. In January 1925 the German Nationals, hitherto opponents of the Republic, accepted office in a government led by a non-party Chancellor, Hans Luther. As Foreign Minister, Luther retained Gustav Stresemann, the German negotiator of the Locarno Treaty. Stresemann had already been instrumental in the removal of the restrictions imposed by the Versailles Treaty against the signing of commercial agreements between Germany and other States.

Against this background of success in German foreign policy, Hitler, whose Nazi Party had thrived on denouncing the Berlin government's failure to challenge Versailles, held a meeting – two months after his release from prison – to refound his party. The meeting was held on February 27 in the Bürgerbräu beer celler in Munich. Three thousand people crammed the vaulted rooms and the street outside. 'As assailants against Marxism,' Hitler declared, 'only we National Socialists come into question. Either the enemy goes over our dead bodies, or we go over his. Just as in the war the English allegedly conducted the fight against the German Kaiser and militarism, so we will in future certainly conduct our fight against person and object, namely against the Jew as person and Marxism as the object.' What the party needed, Hitler explained, was 'fighters, not parliamentarians'.

On February 28, the day after Hitler's refounding of the Nazi Party, the first President of the German Republic, Friedrich Ebert, died. He had been in office since 1920. In contrast to the aristocratic nature of much of German politics before the war, he had begun his working life at the age of fourteen, apprenticed to a saddler. Later he had become a distinguished socialist newspaper editor. On becoming Chancellor in 1918, he had helped to ensure the triumph of the forces of moderate socialism against those of Marxist and Bolshevik extremism. His successor had to be chosen with care, to secure a continuing commitment to the republican and parliamentary process.

The candidates included Ludendorff, the candidate of the extreme national-ists and 'racialists', who had been at the forefront of Hitler's Putsch two years earlier; and Ernst Thaelmann, the German Communist leader. The main parties of the Weimar coalition chose the Prime Minister of Prussia, Wilhelm Marx, as their candidate. The Nationalists chose the seventy-seven-year-old war hero, Marshal Hindenburg, seeking someone whom they hoped would secretly harbour thoughts, as they did, of an end to the republic and a return to the monarchy.

Hindenburg was unhappy at being chosen as a candidate. He had long prided himself on being a private person, retired from all aspects of public life, and enjoying his old age as a country gentleman relaxing on his East Prussian estate. On April 6 he announced that he would not stand. Two days later, however, he was prevailed upon to change his mind. In the election, his stature as a venerable warrior was decisive. He had fought in the Franco-Prussian War of 1870–1 as a twenty-three-year-old, and had reached the rank of general a decade before the First World War. On April 26 he was elected President by 48.3 per cent of the voters (Marx received 45.4 per cent and Thaelmann only 6.3 per cent).

On May 12 Hindenburg took office, swearing on oath to support the constitution. The German Republic was in safe, if elderly hands. If, in retrospect, there was a dark cloud on the horizon, it was the publication, on July 18, of the first volume of a two-volume work, hardly noticed at the time by reviewers or readers. The book had been written in prison during the previous year and a half by Adolf Hitler. Entitled *Mein Kampf* (My Struggle), it set out the Nazi Party leader's philosophy.

It was clear from a reading of the book that Hitler had strong pretensions to ruling Germany, and that he considered Germany to be in danger. There were, he argued in the book – as he had earlier and repeatedly argued on public platforms in Munich and elsewhere in Bavaria – two perils threatening 'the existence of the German people', one was Marxism and the other was Judaism. It was while he was living in Vienna before the First World War, he wrote, that he had discovered what he called 'the truth' about the Jewish conspiracy to destroy the world of the 'Aryan' by means of political infiltration and corruption.

The word 'Aryan', hitherto a linguistic term, referring to the Indo-European group of languages, took on, in Hitler's book, a new meaning, one that within a decade was to capture the minds of millions of Germans. It was a British-born racist, Houston Stewart Chamberlain, whose work Hitler knew and admired, who at the turn of the century had given the concept of Aryan its racial connotations, using it to denote superiority over the 'Semitic' races. Yet the term 'Semitic' itself was originally not a racial but a linguistic term, and related, not to Jews and non-Jews, but to a language group which includes Hebrew and Arabic. These facts did not trouble Hitler. For him, 'Aryan' was synonymous with 'pure'. By contrast, 'Semitic' was synonymous with 'Jew', hence 'impure'.

Mein Kampf was full of appeals to German innocence and vulnerability. Considering the 'satanic skill' displayed by Jewish 'evil councillors', Hitler wrote, 'how could their unfortunate victims be blamed?' The Jewish politicians were masters of 'dialectical perfidy'. Their very mouths 'distorted the truth'. Marxism was a Jewish device, a Jewish trap. The German working class were the victims, not the advocates of Marxist doctrine. 'The more I came to know the Jew, the easier it was to excuse the workers.'

Hitler presented himself in *Mein Kampf* as a man who had seen, and who would prevent, not only the destruction of German life, but the destruction of life on earth, by 'the Jew'. The dangers, as he presented them, concerned the racial integrity of the German people, and a deliberate assault on that integrity. He told his readers:

> The black-haired Jewish youth lies in wait for hours on end, satanically glaring at and spying on the unsuspicious girl whom he plans to seduce, adulterating her blood and removing her from the bosom of her own people. The Jews use every possible means to undermine the racial foundations of a subjugated people. In his systematic efforts to ruin girls and women he strives to break down the last barriers of discrimination between him and other peoples.
>
> The Jews were responsible for bringing negroes into the Rhineland, with the ultimate idea of bastardizing the white race which they hate and thus lowering its cultural and political level so that the Jew might dominate. For as long as a people remain racially pure and are conscious of the treasure of their blood, they can never be overcome by the Jew.
>
> Never in this world can the Jew become master of any people except a bastardized people.

For this reason, Hitler told his readers, 'the Jew systematically endeavours to lower the racial quality of a people by permanently adulterating the blood of the individuals who make up that people.'

In *Mein Kampf*, Hitler outlined his mission: he would expose and then destroy the threat posed by a worldwide Jewish assault against the foundations of 'Aryan' life. 'Was there any shady undertaking,' he asked, 'any form of foulness, especially in cultural life, in which at least one Jew did not participate?' and he went on to answer his own question in these words: 'On putting the probing knife carefully to that kind of abscess, one immediately discovered, like a maggot in a putrescent body, a little Jew who was often blinded by the sudden light.'

Germany could only become a great nation again, Hitler wrote, if it first recognized, and then repelled, the Jewish danger. Germany's defeat in 1918 could have been prevented, but for 'the will of a few Jews', traitors inside the German Reich. 'There is no such thing', Hitler concluded, 'as coming to an understanding with the Jews. It must be the hard-and-fast "Either-Or".'

Hitler not only warned his readers of what he considered the life-threatening dangers to Germany; he also explained his own part in combating those dangers. His words were apocalyptic. 'Should the Jew, with the aid of his Marxist creed, triumph over the people of this world,' Hitler wrote, 'his Crown will be the funeral wreath of mankind, and this planet will once again follow its orbit through ether, without any human life on its surface, as it did millions of years ago. And so I believe today that my conduct is in accordance with the will of the Almighty creator. In standing guard against the Jew I am defending the handiwork of the Lord.'

Few heeded such hate-mongering in the summer of 1925. The Weimar Republic was halfway through its first decade, slowly establishing a democratic, parliamentary, republican regime in Germany. A venerable old soldier, with no political ambitions or disruptive ideology, had been elected President. A moderate middle-of-the-road politician was Chancellor. A master of conciliation and moderation abroad was Foreign Minister. The twin economic pressures of reconstruction and the payment of reparations to the Allies were being lessened year by year, with reparations and the means of repaying them advancing according to the conciliatory plan set out in the Dawes Report. The crisis of whirlwind inflation had passed. Employment was slowly rising. International conferences offered Germany, for the first time since her defeat, equal participation in European diplomacy.

It was on 16 October 1925, three months after the publication of Hitler's first, bitter volume, that Germany had signed the Locarno Treaty, guaranteeing, as an equal partner with Britain, France, Belgium and Italy, the frontiers of Western Europe. Under article two of the Treaty, Germany and France, as well as Germany and Belgium, mutually undertook 'that they will in no case attack or invade each other or resort to war against each other'.

Under Locarno, any disputes which could not be resolved by negotiation between the signatories would be submitted to the Council of the League of Nations for arbitration. If the Council decided that one of the signatories had breached the pledge not to go to war 'each of the other contracting parties hereby undertakes immediately to come to the help of the party against whom such a violation or breach has been directed, as soon as the said power has been able to satisfy itself that this violation constitutes an unprovoked act of aggression, and that by reason whether of the crossing of the frontier, or of the outbreak of hostilities, or the assembly of armed forces in the demilitarized zone, immediate action is necessary.'

Germany's frontiers were thus protected against aggression equally with those of France and Belgium. In seven years, Germany had transformed herself from beaten enemy to equal partner.

Also signed at Locarno were Arbitration Treaties between Germany and Poland, and Germany and Czechoslovakia. These two Treaties protected the eastern borders of Germany against what Churchill had feared would be the danger of a German eastward expansion. 'All disputes of every kind' between Germany and Poland, and Germany and Czechoslovakia, 'which it may not be possible to settle amicably by normal methods of diplomacy', the Arbitration Treaties read, 'shall be submitted for decision either to an arbitral tribunal or to the Permanent Court of International Justice'.

The undertakings signed at Locarno on 16 October 1925 offered the prospect of security for the war-weary masses of all the signatory States, including Poland and Czechoslovakia, which had emerged into statehood as a result of the war and of the defeat of Germany. Combined with the Geneva Protocol outlawing war, they represented to millions of people, for whom the scars of war were far from healed, an impressive leap forward along the path to permanent peace.

The United States was again the scene of a major natural disaster in 1925, when a tornado, passing through twenty-six towns in five States, killed more than 900 people. By contrast, 17,671 Americans were killed on the roads that year: motorcar deaths were becoming a commonplace of all prosperous societies. Elsewhere in the New World, civil and social unrest revealed a continuing and often bloody conflict between the forces of conservatism and reform. In Nicaragua, eleven people were killed when troops led by a former President, Don Diego Chamorro, marched into the city demanding the dismissal of the Liberal members of the Cabinet. Their demand was met. In Ecuador, a group of army officers, led by General Francesco Gomez, deposed the government and established a Spanish-style military regime (controlled by six military men and one civilian).

In Mexico, the reverse trend was in evidence, with the government of President Calles dismissing 500 generals from their posts – which were mostly administrative – expropriating large landed estates from their owners, and turning a blind eye to the efforts of the landless peasants (peons) to install themselves on private land. A Joint Claims Commission, set up by Mexico and the United States, to settle the claims of American citizens whose land had been expropriated illegally, made little headway; a climax to the expropriations of foreign-owned property came in April in the State of Vera Cruz, when the American-owned Light Power Traction Company at Jalapa, whose local Mexican workers were on strike, was seized by the Mexican authorities. The American government protested, but in vain.

Despite the radical expropriations, 'Red' revolution was averted. In May, President Calles strongly denied the assertion by the Soviet Foreign Minister, Georgi Chicherin, that the Soviets had a 'base' in Mexico. In the State of Vera Cruz, riots by 'Red' agitators during the municipal elections in October were put down by the army of the radical State. In November, the State Governor of the State of San Luis Potosi, Aurelio Manrique, known as the 'first Mexican disciple of Lenin', was deposed by the State Legislature.

In Chile, the predominance of the army and navy, whose nominees had driven out President Alessandri, in the autumn of 1924, led to a popular call for Alessandri's return, and for the restoration of constitutional government. Alessandri, who was in exile in Italy, returned to Chile in March, and set about creating a Constituent Assembly. He also instituted various measures of social reform, though not before troops had been sent in to put down a workers' uprising in the Nitrate Zone, and thirty-three leaders of the agitation had been banished to the Pacific island of Juan Fernandez.

A strange element of courtesy entered into the industrial life of Chile that year, when a general strike in the city of Valparaiso was postponed in order not to interfere with the city's plans to welcome a British visitor, the Prince of Wales. Less courteous was the reception by Chile of the American war commander, General Pershing, who had been appointed head of an arbitration commission, under the good offices of the American President, Calvin Coolidge, to settle a forty-year boundary dispute between Chile and Peru. The commission's decision to hand the town and province of Tarata to Chile was carried out by Chile without delay. But the plebiscite which Pershing and the commission decided upon for the other long-disputed areas, Tacna and Arica, led to friction with both the Chileans and the Peruvians. There were anti-American riots in the Peruvian capital, Lima, while in Chile, Alessandri declared that the United States had 'done nothing but foment conflict, discord and hatred between Chile and Peru'. Pershing resigned. A Peruvian request that American troops should be sent to police the plebiscite area during the voting was rejected by Coolidge; he did not want the United States to become more deeply involved.

As the plebiscite plans were being made for Tacna-Arica, under Chilean supervision, with the Americans only there as observers, the Peruvian government complained that the Chilean authorities were preventing large numbers of Peruvians from registering to vote. As a result of these complaints, the plebiscite was postponed. General Pershing's successor in charge of the American commission, General Lassiter, suggested that the holding of a plebiscite should be abandoned altogether. The Chileans, he said, were exercising 'terrorism' over the Peruvians in the region. Any plebiscite held under those conditions would not be a true indication of local feeling.

The plebiscite was abandoned, and, at the suggestion of the United States Secretary of State, Frank B. Kellogg, a remarkable solution was put forward. Chile and Peru were both asked to give up their claim to Tacna-Arica, and the territory was to be ceded to a third country, Bolivia. In return for this resolution of the conflict, the United States would use its 'good offices' to secure financial compensation for the two contending States. Arica itself would become a Free Port, and the promontory known as the Morro of Arica would be placed under international jurisdiction as 'a memorial to the valour of both Peru and Chile'.

As an exercise in diplomacy, the United States resolution of the Tacna-Arica dispute ranked with anything achieved by the League of Nations in its deployment of free ports, autonomous regions and neutral zones.

Women's participation in national life continued to find new expression in 1925. In Belgium the first woman Mayor was appointed; in the United States, the first woman State Governor. Also in the United States, an Institute for the Coordination of Women's Interests was founded.

In the world of art, the first Surrealist exhibition was held that year, in Paris. Also in Paris, the term 'Art Deco' was formulated. In Piccadilly Circus, London, the statue of Eros became a national symbol. In music, Dmitri Shostakovich published his first symphony, and Serge Prokofiev his second. But Soviet Russia's cultural life was deeply troubled. The poet Akhmatova, who refused to leave Russia for exile – 'I am not with those who abandoned their land,' she later wrote – found her poems banned. The poet Yesenin, of peasant origin, a Social Revolutionary seven years earlier, dreaming of agricultural communes of the most egalitarian sort, committed suicide in Leningrad, aged thirty, disillusioned with what the revolution had brought.

Art in the United States suffered from no such traumas. Aaron Copland published his first symphony in 1925, the year in which the first regular broadcasting of country music began – from Nashville, Tennessee – and Paul Robeson gave his first recital of negro spirituals. In an attempt to combat what he saw as the evil influence of jazz, the American industrialist Henry Ford organized a series of nationwide folk dances. But the dance that took America by storm that year was the Charleston.

Inventions continued to benefit those in more affluent lands. An American, Clarence Birdseye, made use of the existing deep-freezing process to deep-freeze food that had already been cooked. A Hungarian designer, Charles Breuer, designed the tubular steel chair. And the first motel opened that year, in California; slowly but surely the motorcar was imposing itself on the lives of the nations.

CHAPTER THIRTY

1926

A NEW DICTATOR entered the European scene in 1926. He was Marshal Jozef Pilsudski, who in 1892 had founded the Polish Socialist Party, and who had begun his service in the First World War by leading Polish troops against Russia. Contemptuous of postwar Polish parliamentary democracy, Pilsudski entered the building of the Polish Parliament (the Sejm) and told the astounded deputies: 'I shit on all of you. The time has come to treat you like children, because you behave like children.'

The arrival of Pilsudski at this dramatic point came only after he had put himself at the head of a number of army regiments, surrounded Warsaw, and marched into the city (on May 12). The Parliamentary forces, headed by the leader of the Peasants' Party, Wincenty Witos, who had been made Prime Minister two days earlier, gave battle. In the street fighting that followed, 300 Poles were killed. Witos was besieged in the President's palace. The President, Stanislaw Wojchiechowski, who was also besieged, resigned.

In the government which he formed, Pisudski made himself Minister of War. Parliament was summoned to elect a new candidate for President. Pilsudski was one; the other was a Polish landowner, Count Bninski. Pilsudski was elected by a large majority, but to the surprise of the Poles he refused to take office, saying that, under Poland's constitution, the President did not have enough powers. Five months later, Pilsudski made himself Prime Minister. For nine years – until his death in 1935 – he was to rule Poland as autocrat.

In neighbouring Lithuania there was also a coup d'état in 1926, six months after Pilsudski came to power in Poland. A Liberal-Socialist government which had been in power for most of the year was overthrown during a night attack, led by Colonel Glovatsky, on government buildings in the capital, Kovno. The insurgents claimed that a Communist coup was being planned for two months' time. About 250 leading Communists were arrested, and four were executed. A new government was then formed, in which the Clerical Party held power.

In Latvia, with its long common border with Lithuania, the Socialist government was warned by the newspapers that what had happened to the left-wing government in Kovno was the fate of all those who 'betrayed the national interest'. But although pro-Russian, the Latvian government maintained a moderate social policy, and was tenacious of Latvia's seven-year-old independence.

In Russia itself, the struggle for power that had begun with Lenin's death at the beginning of 1924 came to a climax with the Fourteenth Congress of the Communist Party of the USSR, which opened on 18 December 1925 and closed on 2 January 1926. It was Stalin, the General Secretary of the Party, who emerged victorious. Stalin put his nominees in charge of the highest offices, including that of Central Control Commission of the Party, which exercised an effective censorship over the activities of all Party members. The man whom Stalin chose to lead this commission, Valerian Kuibyshev, had been instrumental two years earlier in imposing Soviet rule on the former Tsarist provinces and Khanates of Central Asia, forcing out those local leaders who, while proclaiming themselves Communists, sought an independent, Muslim future for the region.[1] Kuibyshev's brother Nikolai was at that very moment (under the pseudonym Kisanka) serving as one of the Soviet military advisers at Kuomintang headquarters in China.

As the effect of Stalin's control spread, those Bolsheviks whom he wished to oust made an attempt to retain their influence, perhaps even to remove Stalin altogether. Near Moscow, a secret meeting of Communist Party opposition leaders – calling themselves the Joint Opposition – was held. It was organized by Mikhail Lashevich, Vice-President of the Revolutionary Military Council, who in November 1917, together with Trotsky, had persuaded the garrison in the Peter-Paul Fortress to transfer their allegiance to the Bolsheviks, and who, two days later, had helped organize the seizure of the Winter Palace and the arrest of the Provisional Government.

The opposition move was quickly countered, and at a nine-day emergency session of the Communist Party which opened in Moscow on July 14, Valerian Kuibyshev's Central Control Commission exerted its authority.

---

[1] It was not until 27 October 1991, while in the early stages of the preparation of this book, that Turkmenistan declared its independence. It had been preceded by Uzbekistan and Kirghizia (31 August 1991) and Tadzhikistan (6 September 1991) and was followed by Kazakhstan (16 December 1991).

One of Lenin's earliest supporters, Grigori Zinoviev, was charged by the commission with having tried, as head of the Moscow-based Third Communist International (the Comintern), to incite foreign Communist delegates against the Communist Party of the Soviet Union. This was a quite baseless charge of the type that was to become more and more common as Stalin sought to portray his Party critics and opponents as active enemies; it was Bismarck who, half a century earlier, had understood the effectiveness of portraying political opponents as *Reichsfeinde*: enemies of the State.

The Communist opposition did not give up hope of influencing the Party against Stalin. On October 1 a meeting was held in a small factory in Moscow, at which Trotsky was the main speaker, and where Zinoviev was among those who attacked the policies of Stalin and the Central Committee, accusing them of betraying the revolution. A similar meeting of the Party opposition took place in Leningrad.

Stalin took rapid action. At an emergency meeting of the Central Committee, held in Moscow on October 23, the leaders of the opposition were warned that they must abstain from any further 'insubordination to the rules of the Party'. Trotsky was expelled from the Politburo, and Kamenev was struck off the list of candidate members. Three days later Stalin summoned the Fifteenth Congress of the Communist Party of the USSR. Trotsky, Kamenev and Zinoviev were all allowed to speak, but the overwhelming majority of the delegates were vociferous in their support for Stalin, several of whose close colleagues were given new posts and new authority. Nikolai Bukharin was appointed both editor of the Party newspaper, *Pravda*, and Zinoviev's successor at the head of the Comintern. Anastas Mikoyan succeeded Kamenev as Commissar for Internal and Foreign Trade. Control of the secret police (OGPU) was given to another close colleague of Stalin, Vyacheslav Menzhinsky, who was soon to supervize the draconian collectivization of agriculture, and massively to extend the slave labour camp system.

By the end of 1926 the members of the Bolshevik old guard who had spoken up against Stalin had lost all their influence, as well as all their positions within the Party and administration. Zinoviev was removed from his post as President of the Leningrad Soviet, and from the Politburo, the controlling body of the Communist Party, despite the fact that in 1922 he had sided with Stalin in Stalin's first step to supreme power, the removal of Trotsky from real power. This had not helped Zinoviev in the long run to remain at the centre of policymaking.

Another of the old guard, Lev Kamenev, was also removed by Stalin in the early months of 1926 from his post as President of the Moscow Soviet, a senior position in the hierarchy of power. He too had been a close ally of Lenin. He too had helped Stalin to keep Trotsky at bay four years earlier. Now his future was uncertain.

In Italy, Mussolini continued to consolidate his power. At the beginning of 1926 there was a moment of nostalgia for the old days when the Queen Mother, Queen Margherita, died. She was seventy-five years old, the daughter of Prince Ferdinand of Savoy, Duke of Genoa. Her mother was a Saxon princess of the old German nobility. Her husband, King Umberto – whom she had married in 1868 when he was Prince of Piedmont – had been assassinated in 1900. To the people of Italy, her death in the fourth year of the Fascist era marked the passing of an epoch of aristocracy and social hierarchy whose values were as much a part of history as if they had disappeared a hundred years earlier, recalling how the death of Marie Antoinette (albeit on the guillotine) had prompted Edmund Burke to exclaim, 'The age of chivalry is dead.'

Mussolini had set as his goal the establishment of the Corporate State. Representation in the parliament would be by trades and professions, not by wealth and position. Service to the State was the overriding duty. 'The war,' Mussolini declared in March 1926, 'has imbued all Italians with the idea of Nation.' That April, a 'Law Governing Collective Labour Relations' was placed on the statute book. Strikes were made illegal. All associations, whether of workers or employers, were placed under the control of the State. All labour disputes would be resolved by compulsory arbitration. All organized corporations of workers and employers, their contracts, as well as their 'education and thrift', would come under a Ministry of Corporations, the portfolio for which was held by Mussolini himself.

The Fascist regime put great emphasis on economy. With an adverse trade balance, Italy under Mussolini looked to austerity to enhance both the economic and moral development of the nation. Spending on luxuries was officially discouraged. No further licences were to be issued for cafés, dance halls and restaurants. Expensive private housing was to be replaced by mass construction for the lower and middle classes. Italian products were to be purchased in preference to foreign imports. The currency would be strengthened by drastically reducing the amount of money in circulation. In one of those pithy (if essentially oratorical) statements of policy for which he was becoming famous, Mussolini declared in August: 'I shall never inflict upon the greatness of this nation the bankruptcy of the Lira.'

One of Mussolini's most imaginative efforts, which had begun in 1925 and was continued with effect in 1926, was the attempt to increase the harvest. The programme was known, in the military terminology favoured by Mussolini, as the Wheat Campaign, or Battle for Grain (*Battaglia del grano*). Its aim was to make Italy self-supporting in wheat, obviating the need for imports. Despite poor weather in 1926, which made it impossible to reach the previous year's target, production was still much higher than before the campaign.

In foreign policy, as in domestic policy, Mussolini sought to enhance Italy's prestige and position in the world. Both the German and Austrian governments complained that a policy of 'ruthless Italianization' was being carried out in the South Tyrol, the area – reaching as far north as the Brenner Pass – that Italy had acquired from Austria as a result of the war. Mussolini's reply was that he had no intention of 'knuckling down' to Germany or any other power, and that if necessary Fascist Italy would 'carry the Italian flag beyond the Brenner'.

For Mussolini, 1926 was the 'Napoleonic Year'. On August 7, Italy signed a treaty of friendship with Spain, in which 'mutual defence in Africa' was a feature. The Italians in Libya, like the Spaniards in Morocco, continued to be faced by tribal discontent and local uprisings. A treaty with the Yemen was signed on September 2, consolidating Italy's position as a maritime power in the Red Sea, giving her the right of economic penetration into the Yemeni hinterland, and challenging Britain's position at Aden. Two weeks later a treaty was signed with Roumania, the aim of which was to move Roumania away from her current alignment with France – her friend and patron since 1918 – and towards Italy, with whom she shared a historic and linguistic heritage. This Roumanian treaty gave Mussolini an economic interest on the lower Danube and on the shore of the Black Sea. Three more Italian treaties followed: with Greece on November 24, and with Albania five days later, creating an Italian counterweight to Yugoslav influence in the Balkans; and with Germany on December 29.

Internally, Mussolini strengthened his hold on political power during 1926 by suppressing all opposition newspapers, removing 522 opponents of the regime from their homes and placing them under preventative detention, and abolishing democratic elections (which Mussolini derided as 'paper chases') even within the Fascist Party. The system of elective mayors was also abolished; in future, a list of mayoral candidates would be submitted by the inhabitants to the government, and the government would make the choice.

In Germany, a highpoint in 1926 was the country's admission to the League of Nations. The parliamentary system established after the war was in its ninth year. But with the rise in unemployment to more than a million, the Social Democrats refused to enter the government and assume the responsibility of office for fear of driving the working class into the Communist camp. Support for the Communists was growing. There was a parliamentary crisis in May, when the government, encouraged by President Hindenburg, tried to reintroduce the prewar imperial German flag. In a Social Democrat motion of censure, the government was defeated by a single vote.

Forming a new government proved difficult; one of those who failed to do so was the President of the Prussian State Council, Konrad Adenauer, who was also mayor of Cologne – and who, in 1949, was to be the first Chancellor of the Federal Republic of Germany. The political crisis was resolved when a former Chancellor, Dr Marx, returned to office. But the economic crisis worsened, with unemployment reaching two million, and continuing to rise during the year.

It was from among the increasing number of unemployed, as well as those disillusioned with the workings of democracy, that the Nazi Party continued to recruit. At the beginning of 1926 the Party's membership stood at 17,000, but within two years it had more than doubled, to 40,000. Among the most active and most feared members of the Party were those who served in the black-uniformed Protection Squad (*Schutzstaffeln*, or SS), set up a year earlier to provide Hitler and the Nazi leadership with personal protection.

On July 6 the Hitler Youth movement was inaugurated under Hitler's personal patronage. It provided what quickly proved to be an attractive array of sporting activities, camping, rousing songs and a fiercely defended national ideology. The youngsters wore brown shirts and marched behind swastika-waving leaders. They echoed and elaborated the slogans of the many nationalist German youth movements of the day. 'We love our race, our people, our blood, and our fair upright youth,' one of these nationalist youth groups had declared two years earlier, 'but never the intellectual who is at home everywhere, who knows neither friendship nor fatherland.'

Racism was not confined to the extremist parties. On July 16 the government of Bavaria passed a Law 'For the Combating of Gypsies, Travellers and the Work-Shy', which, exploiting anti-Gypsy prejudice, gave the Bavarian police the power to send Gypsies who were not in regular employment to the workhouse – in effect to forced labour – for two years. Nazi fulminations against the Jews were to find a similar target in the Gypsies, and, in due course, to result in tens of thousands of Gypsies being sent to their deaths alongside the Jews.

On December 10, Hitler published the second volume of *Mein Kampf*. Once again anti-Jewish venom permeated its pages. 'At the beginning of the war,' Hitler wrote, 'or even during the war, if twelve or fifteen thousand of these Jews who were corrupting the nation had been forced to submit to poison gas, just as hundreds of thousands of our best German workers from every social stratum and from every trade and calling had to face it in the field, then the millions of sacrifices made at the front would not have been in vain.' On the contrary, Hitler continued, 'if twelve thousand of these malefactors had been eliminated in proper time, probably the lives of a million decent men, who would be of value to Germany in the future, would have been saved.'

These were the writings of an extremist with no prospect of political influence, let alone power. Hitler's readership was small. Every effort was being made to normalize life in Germany, to attract tourists to the many beautiful regions with which the country was endowed, and to enhance trade. A sign of the coming of more normal times had taken place at the very beginning of the year, when British troops evacuated Cologne. After seven years of occupation, a daily reminder of the defeat of 1918 was ended. Germany also negotiated a new commitment with Russia in 1926: each country agreeing – under the Russo-German Treaty signed in Berlin on April 24 – that it would remain neutral if the other was attacked, and not join in with the attacker; and each country pledging not to join any financial or economic boycott that might be imposed on the other.

There was annoyance among the Locarno Powers that Germany should have concluded a separate arrangement with Russia, and there was concern that there might be secret clauses. This was strenuously denied by both sides. In fact, a series of secret arrangements between Germany and the Soviet Union were already enabling Germany to breach the disarmament clauses of the Treaty of Versailles. Starting in 1922, and reaching a high point in 1926, nine separate facilities were set up inside the Soviet Union, at secret locations, to enable German military training and research to go ahead. At four locations – Schlüsselburg, Zlatoust, Fili and Tula – Russian armaments factories produced weapons and munitions under German supervision. At Kazan, German engineers manufactured tanks. At Trotsk, the Germans established a poison gas plant, and at Saratov a chemical warfare research centre. At Lipetsk there was a flying school for German pilots. Nearly every German air force officer who was to hold a high position in the Luftwaffe during the Second World War attended a flying course at Lipetsk between 1926 and 1931.

Aircraft production, forbidden to Germany by the Treaty of Versailles, was being undertaken in strictest secrecy both inside and outside the German borders. By 1926, with the encouragement of the German government, Hugo Junkers was operating an aircraft factory at Dessau which, while openly manufacturing civilian aircraft, was ensuring that their conversion to war purposes was an integral part of their design and construction. Also with government support, Ernst Heinkel set up an aircraft factory in Sweden, and Claude Dornier set up factories in Italy and Switzerland. Within a decade, the Junkers, Heinkel and Dornier bombers were to be an important part of the German air armament.

In Britain, 1926 was marked by a long drawn out coal strike that divided the nation. The miners were being told by the mine owners that they must accept a reduction in their already low wages, or face dismissal. With unemployment high, many miners accepted the reduced wages for fear of being unable to get other work. On May 1, when the miners' leaders insisted on no further reduction of wages throughout the industry, the whole workforce was locked out by the owners. In sympathy with the miners, the Trades Union Congress – the TUC – called a general strike, which began on May 3. Commerce and industry were brought to a standstill throughout Britain. But a massive volunteer effort was made to keep essential services running. Buses were driven by volunteers, some of them students who disapproved of the strike. In the shipbuilding yards, the construction of new vessels continued uninterrupted.

Students who supported the strike drove emergency food supplies to those families most in need. In Manchester, a demonstration of unemployed workers was dispersed by the police. At many ports, fish was unloaded by volunteers. The government refused to force the mine owners to make concessions in order to bring about a return to work in the mines. After a week of the general strike, the TUC, representing the mass of British workers, realized the urgent economic need for a return to work, and felt that it could no longer support the miners in their determination to continue on strike. On May 12 the TUC agreed to call off the general strike.

The coal strike went on throughout the summer. 'It is being a very grim world, isn't it?' Gertrude Bell wrote to her mother from Baghdad on June 30. 'What an enormous waste and loss two months' coal strike must mean. It is so amazing that the world seems to go on just the same – Ascot and parties are what I read of in *The Times*.'

In the New World, the United States was drawn into an overseas conflict in 1926. In Nicaragua, Emiliano Chamorro seized power, but was immediately faced by a counter-revolution headed by a more left-wing group. In order to 'protect American property', which was under attack by the rebel troops, President Coolidge authorized the landing of American marines. The rebels were driven out, and a nominee of Chamorro formed a government acceptable to the United States. Within a year of landing, the marines withdrew. American interests in the country, which included lumber, sugar, rice and banana plantations, had been secured, and an American collector of customs had been appointed to collect the interest on the Nicaraguan debt to the United States.

To secure control over the Panama Canal, the United States signed a treaty with Panama whereby, in the event of the United States being at war, Panama would 'turn over to the United States' control of its radio communications, aircraft, and aviation centres. Also under the treaty, Panama ceded to the United States 'in perpetuity' part of Manzanillo Island, off the Atlantic terminus of the canal.

It was in the sphere of science that the United States made the greatest progress in 1926. On January 19, more than seven hundred graduates of the Massachusetts Institute of Technology (MIT) attended a dinner at the Waldorf-Astoria Hotel in New York. The speeches and music that they heard were transmitted simultaneously to other MIT diners, twenty thousand in all, who were sitting at dinner in twenty-seven cities in the United States, Canada, Cuba and Hawaii.

As for the application of science to war, 1926, the year in which German scientists were experimenting with poison gas and chemical warfare in the Soviet Union was also the year in which American scientists at the United

States Navy Department succeeded in launching a wireless-controlled aeroplane which could unleash a self-discharging load of explosive against a target thirty-five miles away.

It was American prosperity that was the cause of the greatest comment outside the United States. As it grew, there was mounting criticism in Europe of America's continued collection of war debts. In 1926 the profits and productivity of every branch of the American economy reached record levels. In automobile production, in steel, in copper, oil and cement, in building construction, and in the manufacture of newsprint, all previous records were broken, But for the Europeans, this success story contrasted with the insistence by the United States that war debts must be paid. The Italian debt of $2000 million, though spread over sixty-two years, was confirmed by Congress. Also confirmed were debt agreements with Belgium, Czechoslovakia, Roumania, Estonia and Latvia. The French debt, of more than $4000 million, was likewise not to be reduced, but was to be paid off, like the Italian, in sixty-two annual instalments.

Hardly had the Senate confirmed the French debt than 20,000 French war veterans, many of them blind and crippled – the highly esteemed *mutilés de la guerre* – paraded through Paris in protest against the American decision. It would, they declared, 'enslave' France to the United States, and do so until 1992. The eighty-five-year-old Clemenceau (who was to die three years later) wrote an open letter to President Coolidge, denouncing America's 'hardness'. Accounts of the Paris parade, and of Clemenceau's letter, were given wide publicity in the United States, and caused considerable anger. 'If they want to cancel debts', declared Senator Borah, the Chairman of the Senate Foreign Relations Committee, 'let them cancel reparations as well, and show us that the benefits of cancellation will go to humanity and the betterment of Europe, and not to bolster up imperialistic schemes which are now crushing the life out of people who were in no sense responsible for the war.'

This was an outspoken attack on France for insisting on reparations from Germans who, in the Senator's imagery, were not those who had been the warmaking generation. It coincided with growing American pressure on the European nations to cancel their own war debts to each other. It was also pointed out in the Senate that the record of debt repayment to the United States varied among the European Powers. Under the agreements reached with the United States, Britain was repaying between 70 and 80 per cent of her debt, France 50 per cent, and Italy only 26 per cent.

Angered by the anti-Americanism of the European press, President Coolidge chose Armistice Day 1926 to reply, in his one big speech that year, to the Europeans, and to defend the record of the United States. 'I am of firm conviction,' he said, 'that there is more hope for the progress of true ideals in the modern world from a nation newly rich than there is from a nation chronically poor. Honest poverty is one thing, but lack of industry and character is quite another. While we do not need to boast of our prosperity or vaunt our ability to accumulate wealth, I see no occasion to apologize for it. They tell me that we are not liked in Europe. Such reports are undoubtedly exaggerated and can be given altogether too much importance. We are a creditor nation. We are more prosperous than some. This means that our interests have come within the European circle where distrust and suspicion, if nothing more, have been altogether too common.'

Coolidge insisted that nothing was to be gained 'from criminations and recriminations. We are attempting to restore the world to a state of better understanding and amity. We can even leave to others the discussion of who won the war. It is enough for us to know that the side on which we fought was victorious. We have maintained since the war a detached and independent position in order that we might be better prepared in our own way to serve those who need our help . . . Our assistance, when it has been sought, has been none the less valuable because we have insisted that it should not be used by one country against another, but for the fair and disinterested service of all.'

This was a deeply felt account of American altruism in the world. But Coolidge was careful, when agreeing to the participation of the United States in the World Court at The Hague, to stress that in doing so no obligation under the League of Nations was to be assumed, and no request for an opinion on any matter relating to the United States was to be entertained without American consent.

Inside the United States, organized crime continued to disturb the daily life of the major cities, as the maintenance of Prohibition since 1919 enabled considerable fortunes to be made by the illegal manufacture and distribution of alcohol. One anti-gangster solution put forward in Chicago in 1926 was the brainchild of Chief Detective William O'Connor. Asking for 500 volunteers from among policemen who had served in the American army in France in 1917 and 1918, he formed them into a special armed detachment. His address to the men as they began their duties explained why they were to use the same weapons that the gangsters were using. 'Men, the war is on,' he said. 'We have got to show society, that the Police Department, and not a bunch of dirty rats, are running this town. It is the wish of the people of Chicago that you hunt these criminals down and kill them without mercy. Your cars are equipped with machine guns and you will meet the enemies of society on equal terms. See to it that they do not have you pushing up daisies. Shoot first and shoot to kill . . . If you meet a car containing bandits pursue them and fire. When I arrive on the scene my hopes will be fulfilled if you have shot off the top of the car and killed every criminal inside it.'

Even at local election time in Chicago, the police and the criminals found themselves in conflict, as gangsters tried to influence the outcome. A British eye-witness of an episode during polling day wrote in *The Times*:

As we drove up to a booth, an excited crowd round its doors was sign enough for the squad commander. Before the car had stopped, its crew, revolver in hand, were running across the pavement.

Unceremoniously we jostled our way through the mob, to find a young and very red-faced policeman arguing with a brutal looking man who was evidently interfering with voters. The squad commander seized the offender from behind by the shoulder and, violently twisting him round, deliberately smacked him across the face with his open palm before slipping the handcuffs upon him.

Then, turning to the policemen on duty, he said equably, 'Don't argue with these birds, blow their brains out'. Our prisoner was bundled into the waiting patrol-wagon. Several other suspicious looking men were ordered to 'put 'em up', and were thoroughly 'frisked' (searched). Two men who were found to be carrying arms also went into the wagon.

Thereafter the day was occupied in frequent descents upon the polling stations. Wherever there was even the possibility of trouble, people were arrested on principle.

Three years later, on 14 February 1929, during the so-called St Valentine's Day Massacre, seven members of one Chicago gang, headed by George 'Bugsy' Moran, were shot dead by members of another gang – headed by Al 'Scarface' Capone – in a hail of machine-gun fire. The dominant weapon of the First World War had become an instrument of gangland power.

*   *   *

In China, the struggle between north and south intensified during 1926, with different warlords in command of the various provinces, and the Nationalist Party, the Kuomintang, with its headquarters in Canton, gaining considerable ground. Almost everywhere there was fighting. In April, the pro-Japanese faction holding Peking was driven out by a combination of aerial bombardment and an infantry assault by troops from Manchuria led by Marshal Chang Tso-lin. Marshal Chang also took military action against Soviet Russian interests along the Chinese Eastern railway and on the Sungari River, on the grounds that the Russian officials there were 'propagating Communism'.

In November, Marshal Chang confronted the advancing Kuomintang Nationalists, but after a series of fierce military engagements had to cede to them all the land south of the Yangtse River. On the Upper Yangtse, General Yang Sen, who was in command of an independent military force, seized a number of British merchant ships on the river off Wanhsien, and immobilized the Royal Naval vessel *Cockchafer* which had attempted to release them. A second British warship, the *Widgeon*, was sent to remonstrate and, in retaliation against heavy Chinese fire from the shore, bombarded Wanhsien. At least a hundred Chinese civilians were killed. British losses were three officers and four seamen.

General Yang Sen agreed to release the merchant ships and the *Cockchafer*. But the Wanhsien incident heightened Chinese nationalist feeling against foreigners, and there were many acts of violence against Christian missionaries in those provinces which came under Kuomintang control.

Among those who were working closely with the Kuomintang was the Chinese Communist Party. It too had a hatred of foreigners. 'Do the Chinese people only know how to hate Japan, and don't they know how to hate England?' one of their leaders, Mao Tse-tung, had asked three years earlier. 'Don't they know that the aggression of the English imperialists against China is even more atrocious than that of the Japanese imperialists?' The 'most murderous of hangmen', he added, was the United States. Deriding the government in Peking, with its foreign influences and preferences, Mao declared: 'If one of our foreign masters farts, it's a lovely perfume.'

The decision of the Chinese Communist Party to ally itself with the Kuomintang was taken in June 1923. Four months later, Stalin had sent an emissary from Moscow, Mikhail Borodin, to work closely with the Kuomintang, and to cement its alliance with the Chinese Communists. In 1924 the Soviet Union had signed a treaty with the Kuomintang leader, Sun Yat-sen, whereby the Kuomintang army was to be trained by Soviet instructors. The senior Soviet general whom Stalin sent out to Canton, Mikhail Borodin (as Mikhail Grusenberg he had been active in the Jewish Social Democratic Labour League at the turn of the century), became personal adviser to the Kuomintang generals. When the Kuomintang's Military Academy was inaugurated at Whampoa (on 16 June 1924) it was headed by one of those generals, Chiang Kai-shek – who was to lead the movement after the death of Sun Yat-sen nine months later. A Chinese Communist, Chou En-lai, was made the head of the political department of the Kuomintang army.

Mao Tse-tung's personal contribution to the advancement of Chinese nationalism, and in due course (after the break with the Kuomintang) to Communist Party strength, was his recognition of the importance of the Chinese peasantry. Stalin was sceptical of the ability of the peasants to make any practical contribution to the advancement of the Communist cause, and had little interest in Chinese nationalism as such. In March 1925 the peasants on the sea coast northeast of Canton had welcomed Chiang Kai-shek's Eastern Expedition. Two months later, after a Japanese foreman had killed a Chinese worker, the Chinese Communist Party helped organize, on May 30, a demonstration in Shanghai. The police of the International Settlement in the city, under the command of a British officer, opened fire. Ten of the demonstrators were killed. A strike was declared, and spread to Canton. There, on June 23, another mass demonstration took place. When British and French police opened fire to disperse the crowd, fifty-two people were killed. As a result, the Kuomintang organized a sixteen-month boycott of trade with Hong Kong.

Stimulated by the enthusiasm shown by the peasants in Hunan province for political activity, Mao Tse-tung consulted Mikhail Borodin as to the best way of organizing a rural Communist movement. A master of slogans, Mao pressed forward with the two which proved most effective, 'Down with the militarists!' (the hated war lords who had made peasant life a misery) and 'Down with the rich foreigners!'

By 1926 the Kuomintang-Communist alliance was at its most effective. In Canton, Mao Tse-tung ran the Propaganda Department of the Kuomintang Central Executive Committee. He also became editor of the Kuomintang political weekly newspaper. He had been among the most enthusiastic supporters of the Kuomintang military offensive against the Peking government. But he ensured that the peasant movement would not be left to the Kuomintang to lead and exploit. In July 1926 he took charge of the newly created

Peasant Department under the direct auspices of the Communist Party Central Committee, while at the same time training peasant agitators at the Kuomintang's Peasant Movement Training Institute.

The Chinese Communist Party and the Kuomintang were both elated by Chiang Kai-shek's military successes in the north. 'In the present world revolution', Chiang Kai-shek declared in August, after his troops had captured Changsha, 'there is the Third International, which is the staff of the world revolution. If we want our revolution to succeed, we must unite with Russia to overthrow imperialism.' As to the Chinese Communists, Chiang Kai-shek explained, they did not want 'to apply Communism, but rather to carry out the national revolution'.

Having used the Communists as allies and co-fighters, Chiang Kai-shek suddenly broke with them. The occasion was the dramatic seizure of Shanghai by the Communist-led workers in the city, who then handed the city over to him. He at once turned savagely against them, securing the city for the Kuomintang. With that act, a new phase began in the history of China: the isolation of the Communists and the setback to their hopes of cooperation with the Kuomintang on the road to an early revolution. At the same time, Stalin derided and denounced the Chinese Communist Party's support for and alliance with the peasants, pouring scorn on leaders like Mao Tse-tung, Communists in name and Communists by ideological conviction, who believed that it was through the peasants that Chinese Communism would triumph.

It was not only Chiang Kai-shek and Stalin who turned against the Chinese Communists in 1926. In a raid on the Soviet Embassy in Peking, Marshal Chang Tso-lin arrested a number of Chinese Communists who had taken shelter there, and executed them by strangulation. Mikhail Borodin returned to the Soviet Union. His successful efforts at strengthening the effectiveness and discipline of the Kuomintang forces – the task Stalin had given him – was to no avail. After being given a number of minor official posts, he was arrested, tried, and sent to a slave labour camp in Siberia, where, twenty years later, he died.

The ravages of nature were as fierce as ever during 1926. In Florida, 150 people were killed in a hurricane which devastated Miami and Palm Beach. Hundreds more were killed by a cyclone which struck the Pacific Ocean island of Samoa. In Australia, thirty people were killed when a bush fire swept through parts of New South Wales. But the efforts of humanity to make the globe more accessible were succeeding with every year as air routes carried passengers, mail and cargo longer and longer distances. On December 27 the main British overseas air line, Imperial Airways, opened its Desert Air Mail service from Cairo to Basra, via Gaza and Baghdad, using mainly wooden biplanes. At a desert landing strip in Iraq, H-3 – named after one of the pumping stations on the pipeline from Iraq to Haifa – this service linked with another line that took travellers to and from Europe, through Tiberias (in Palestine), Athens and Genoa.

Every month some new air route was opened. The most widespread air network, carrying the largest number of passengers worldwide, was that of Germany. Its most remarkable achievement, in conjunction with Russian aircraft, was a Berlin–Königsberg–Moscow–Kharkov–Baku–Teheran–Isfahan–Bushire route: linking the Baltic Sea with the Caspian Sea and the Persian Gulf.

During 1926, in the United States, 18,871 Americans were killed on the roads. The death toll on Britain's roads was 4,886, among them more than a thousand cyclists knocked down by motorcars. On Britain's railways, only thirteen passengers were killed in train crashes that year. But nothing could impede the annual increase in motorcar owners, or the relentless annual increase in death on the roads.

The event of 1926 with the most long-term impact on the twentieth century took place on January 26, when, from a room in London, John Logie Baird carried out the first transmission of a new invention, television.

CHAPTER THIRTY-ONE

1927

THE ANTI-FOREIGNER RIOTS in China flared up again at the beginning of 1927, when many British and other foreign traders were attacked in two of the treaty ports – in Hankow on January 4 and in Kiukiang two days later; by the end of the attacks the British Concession at Hankow had been overrun. A division of British troops was at once assembled in Britain to be sent to the Far East; the soldiers left Liverpool on an ocean liner, the *Megantic*, on January 25. Among their weaponry were gas shells.

On March 24, before the British soldiers could reach Shanghai, six British traders were murdered at Nanking. Foreign warships on the Yangtse river opened fire on the city, and six Chinese were killed. The American, French, Italian and Japanese governments hastened to send naval reinforcements to Chinese waters. But Chiang Kai-shek was determined not to risk an excuse for massive foreign intervention – 20,000 British troops were then gathered at Shanghai – and apologized for the Nanking incident.

Entering Nanking, Chiang Kai-shek established a government of his own, and opened negotiations with the foreign powers for economic assistance. He also clamped down on the Communist movement in the city, striking at his former allies with considerable ferocity. Flushed with a sense of victory, Chiang Kai-shek then continued his attempt to assert his control throughout the northern and eastern areas of China, advancing as far north as Hsuchow, an important railway junction. There, he was besieged by the Northern Army commanded by Marshal Sun Chuan-fang. In the battle that followed, and which ended with Sun Chuan-fang recapturing the town, 50,000 men were killed.

Chiang Kai-shek retreated. This was only a prelude, however, to a Kuomintang attempt to capture the capital itself, Peking. The government in Peking was still controlled by Marshal Chang Tso-lin, who declared himself, in June, Dictator, or Generalissimo. His troubles began that same month, when the Governor of Shansi province, General Yen Hsi-san, raised the nationalist flag, declared himself an adherent of the Kuomintang, and marched towards Peking. Tens of thousands of soldiers were killed in the battles which followed, but the capture of Peking was beyond the Nationalist capacity. China remained without a central government, but as the rival armies continued to battle, Chiang Kai-shek appealed for a revision of the 'unequal' treaties that had been signed by China before the war with the foreign powers. The American Secretary of State, Frank B. Kellogg, rejected the call for negotiations, arguing that only when there was a government that could speak for the whole of China could such negotiations start.

In the western hemisphere, United States intervention was decisive. Although American marines were already occupying Nicaragua at the beginning of 1927, the Liberal forces (under Sacasa) who were opposed to the Conservative government of General Díaz continued to seek the government's overthrow. On January 6, President Coolidge summoned the Congressional opposition leaders to the White House and told them that he would have to take drastic steps to restore order. It was clear that the rebels were receiving arms from Mexico. Coolidge therefore lifted the United States ban on the export of arms to the government of Nicaragua.[1]

Some $200,000 worth of United States War Department weaponry and ammunition were sold to the Díaz government. More American marines were also landed, securing several towns against rebel intrusion. A former Secretary of State, Henry L. Stimson, was then sent to Nicaragua to negotiate an agreement between the warring parties. At a meeting on May 5 with General Moncaba, the general commanding the anti-government forces, Stimson said that if the Liberals did not lay down their arms, the United States would use force against them. That same day, President Díaz offered an amnesty to all the rebel soldiers, if they would lay down their arms. Two days later they agreed to do so.

The agreement that was reached under Stimson's guidance avoided the humiliation of direct surrender, and was a masterpiece of diplomatic skill. The rebels' arms were handed over, not to the Nicaraguan government but

---

[1] A similar United States government ban sixty years later was secretly by-passed by the device of selling arms to Iran and diverting the proceeds of the arms sale to the Contra rebels in Nicaragua. This 'Iran-Contra' affair was to be one of the scandals adversely affecting the Presidency of Ronald Reagan.

to the Americans. The Conservatives had also to hand over their arms. A general peace would come into effect immediately, in order to allow the planting of a new crop in June. All those in rebellion or in exile would be amnestied. All confiscated property would be returned to its owners. The Liberals would be admitted to the administration. A Nicaraguan police force would be organized on a non-political basis, commanded by American officers. All but 2000 American marines would withdraw; those who remained would be used to guard the polling booths during new presidential elections. General Díaz would remain in office until the elections.

Stimson set off for Washington, to receive what were clearly going to be warm congratulations on what he had achieved. But no sooner had he left Nicaragua than fighting broke out again. Not only did the rebels renew their attacks on the Díaz forces, they also attacked the American marines. When rebel forces under General Sandino seized a gold mine belonging to a United States citizen, Charles Butters, at San Albino, a hundred marines were killed. The United States forces retaliated by launching an aerial attack on the rebel positions by machine-gun fire from the air – the tactic that General Allenby had used against the Turks in Palestine in 1918. 300 of the rebel force of 500 were killed, and two Americans.

The fighting in Nicaragua continued for two months. The rebels then agreed to the earlier terms which Stimson had negotiated. In November, when municipal elections were held, American marines kept watch on the polling booths. There were no untoward incidents, and calm was restored. But the continued presence of the United States forces in Nicaragua, and the part they had played in forcing the Liberal rebels to surrender, caused anger among the other countries of the region, who denounced the creation of what they considered to be an American protectorate over Nicaragua. Four Central American States – Costa Rica, Guatemala, Honduras and El Salvador – each declared that Nicaragua had ceased to be a sovereign State, and refused to recognize General Díaz as President.

Inside the United States, there was disruption of another sort during 1927, when the Ku Klux Klan staged a parade in New York. On May 30, Memorial Day (for observances in memory of the dead of all America's wars), 1000 'knights' of the Klan, in robes and white caps, together with 400 members of their women's organization, the Klavana, walked for four miles through the streets to their reviewing stand. As they marched they were jeered and attacked by hostile crowds. 'Police battle hooded Klansmen when they refuse to leave pageant,' reported the *New York Times*.

The first violence that day had nothing to do with the Klan, however. Two Italians, members of the Fascist movement in the United States, who were on their way to join a detachment of 400 black-shirted Fascists in the Memorial Day parade, were attacked by an anti-Fascist group, and killed. Both of the murdered men were war veterans, Joseph Carisi having served with the American forces in France, and Nicholas Amorrosso with the Italian army. An Italian-American anti-Fascist, Dr Charles Fama, told the *New York Times*: 'The "Black Shirts" are in direct communication with their leader in Rome, and are, in this country, opposed to Americanism. I concede that they have done a lot for Italy, but we certainly do not want them in this country, and there is absolutely no reason why their propaganda should be spread in a Memorial Day parade.'

Police clashes with the Klan continued throughout the day. At one point, the *New York Times* reported, 'a sight-seeing bus came upon the scene. It was filled with negroes bound for a picnic at Rockaway Beach'. The police, desperate to head off a group of Klan marchers who were about half a mile away, commandeered the bus and set off in successful pursuit. 'The negro picnickers, luncheons in hand, were indignant, and said so.'

No deaths took place in the New York Klan confrontation. In the South that year, following the pattern of previous years, there were sixteen recorded lynchings of blacks. But there were forty-two incidents where police prevented lynchings. The year 1927 also saw a number of defeats inside America for those Fundamentalist Christians who wanted to forbid the teaching of evolution in public schools. New Hampshire, Arkansas, Missouri and Oklahoma each passed legislation to ensure that evolution could be taught. The Tennessee Supreme Court, however, upheld the constitutionality of a law forbidding the teaching of evolution in State-supported schools, while at the same time reversing the guilty verdict on John J. Scopes, a young schoolteacher who had been sentenced for teaching evolution.

In Chicago, the campaign for mayor was livened up that autumn when William Hale Thompson, the Republican candidate, declared that he had discovered a nationwide conspiracy to turn the United States into a vassal of Great Britain. If elected, he would, he promised, 'drive King George out of Chicago'. He was elected, and immediately after his inauguration forced the resignation of the city's Superintendent of Schools for being 'pro-English'. He also instructed the Chicago Public Library to find, and burn, all pro-English books. One result of this search was the discovery – which somewhat dented his anti-English appeal – that after the library had been burned down in the Chicago fire of 1871, it had received books and money from a wide range of English sympathizers, not only the writers Thomas Carlyle and John Ruskin, but also Queen Victoria.

The year 1927 was most noteworthy in the United States, however, not for conflicts or eccentricities – or for the deaths of more than 21,000 people on the roads – but for pioneering advances in science and technology. On January 7 a telephone conversation between the President of the American Telephone and Telegraph Company, Walter S. Gifford, and the Secretary of the British Post Office, Sir Evelyn Murray, inaugurated the first commercial transatlantic telephone link. Not only was it possible to talk across the air waves, but also to hold two-way conversations with sufficient clarity as to make possible both personal and commercial communications. The only drawback was that wireless amateurs were able to 'listen in'.

On that first day, thirty-one telephone calls were made.[1] Within two months, improvements on the land-line connection between New York and San Francisco made it possible to conduct a telephone conversation between San Francisco and London, eight time zones away. Another telephone company, the Bell Telephone System, was working that year to perfect television, which had received its first successful transmission in London a year earlier. On April 7, Walter Gifford, who was then in New York, talked over the telephone to the United States Secretary of Commerce, Herbert C. Hoover, who was in Washington. Gifford's features as he talked were visible on a small disc, measuring two inches by two-and-a-half inches, which was fixed near the telephone.

Between May 10 and May 12, scarcely a month after this first American television transmission, Captain Charles Lindbergh, a twenty-four-year-old United States air mail pilot, made a record transcontinental flight across the United States, and then, eight days later, on May 20, flew nonstop from New York to Paris. This was the first ever solo flight across the Atlantic. His plane, the *Spirit of St Louis*, covered the 3610 miles in thirty-three and a half hours. Eight years had passed since the first, and faster, transatlantic flight, by two English aviators, Alcock and Brown (from Newfoundland to Ireland, in sixteen hours), but the impact of Lindbergh's solo flight was

---

[1] On the day that I wrote this sentence (15 August 1996), more than 1,800,000 transatlantic telephone calls were made between Britain and the United States.

37. Berlin 1918: revolution crushed

38. Berlin 1920: a right-wing putsch

39. The aeroplane that made the first transatlantic crossing, 1919

40. Hunger in Russia, 1920

41. A Nazi Party meeting, Munich 1923

42. Mussolini as a young fascist

43. Mao Tse-tung

44. Bela Kun

45. Edvard Beneš

. Franklin D. Roosevelt

46. Jawaharal Nehru

48. Mustapha Kemal Ataturk

49. Stalin *(left)* in Moscow with Kamenev, Rykov and Zinoviev, early 1920s

50. Hindenburg and Hitler in Berlin, 1933

51. Berlin: the night of Hitler's triumph, 1933

52. Berlin: burning books and pamphlets, 1933

53. Berlin: the burnt-out Reichstag building, February 1933

considerable, coming as it did when the commercial aspects of flight were beginning to be seriously exploited.

The worldwide excitement generated by Lindbergh's flight was comparable to that of the first moon flight in 1969. When it became known in France that his plane would be landing at Le Bourget airport after dark, the Paris police appealed for owners of cars to drive out to Le Bourget and use their headlamps to light a landing path for him. When Lindbergh returned to the United States – by sea – his reception was extraordinary, with vast crowds, many cities, and innumerable institutions, headed by Congress, seeking to do him honour. His civic reception in Washington on June 11 was followed by a ticker-tape welcome in New York two days later. He then flew to every State in the Union, visiting in all seventy-eight cities, after which he made a nonstop flight from Washington to Mexico City, and followed this by flying to sixteen countries in Latin America.

As a result of Lindbergh's achievements, writes the air historian R. E. G. Davies, 'the American people were suddenly seized with the idea that the aeroplane was a safe, speedy, and useful vehicle. This realization awoke the interest of ordinary folk who just wanted to experience the thrill of flying, and more important, perhaps, the awareness of businessmen that aircraft building and operating could be a profitable investment. There had been nothing like it since the railway boom of the previous century.' Among the most recent developments that year was a regular night-mail service from Chicago to Dallas. Within three years, three commercial air lines were operating routes from coast to coast: United from New York to San Francisco, and both TWA (Transcontinental and Western Air) and American from New York to Los Angeles. An imaginative piece of government legislation, the McNary-Watres Act – passed on 29 April 1930 – subsidized passenger air transport by federal payments based on the space which the airlines provided for mail. This both increased the use of air mail, and gave the airlines the economic boost needed to extend their services.

In Britain, 1927 saw the start, on January 17, of the first experiment in the use of broadcasting for educational purposes. It took place in Kent, where fifty schools had expressed an interest in wireless lessons. The first set of lessons focused on travel talks, elementary music, literature and history. Receiving sets were being supplied to schools, the local authority explained, 'with complete accessories, except aerial and earth, including a suitable loud speaker'.

*   *   *

On May 12 the British police raided the London premises of the Soviet Trade Delegation, and of a trading company with close links to Russia, Arcos Ltd. As a result of skilful intelligence work, the police had been made aware of efforts by members of the delegation to obtain military information. Two days later the Soviet Chargé d'Affaires was asked to leave Britain, and the British Foreign Office announced that 'the existing relations between the two governments are suspended'. They were not to be renewed for two and a half years, until after the advent of a Labour government.

Anti-Communism had become a force which made many political allies. In Italy, Mussolini found that his anti-Communist stance enabled those who might otherwise have been repelled by his Fascist regime to turn a blind eye to it. The Catholic Church was particularly distressed at the total suppression of religious worship in Stalin's Russia, and at the reiterated Marxist denunciation of religion as the 'opium of the people'.

In India, the desire of the Indian National Congress to advance towards self-government was challenged in an unusual but effective way in the summer of 1927, not by a politician but by a book. Written by an American journalist, Kathleen Mayo, the book, entitled *Mother India*, set out details of the abuse of child brides, and other cruel practices, which she had come across on a wide scale while travelling throughout the subcontinent. At the very moment when the Indian nationalists were looking forward to a renewal of their campaign for greater self-rule, *Mother India* created a backlash of anti-Hindu feeling. Writing from India, the Viceroy, Lord Irwin, told a Cabinet colleague in London: 'Miss Mayo has dropped a brick with her book *Mother India*. It will make Hindus of course see red . . . I think the general effect may be useful if it gives a shock to the unsatisfactory conditions of Hindu thought on many of these subjects.'

To what extent were the Indians yet 'ready' to rule themselves; that was a much-asked question in British political and imperial circles. Winston Churchill was 'immensely struck' by Kathleen Mayo's book. There were those who argued that it was not Britain's duty to say what customs ought to prevail among different and distant peoples; but there were others who found such aspects of Hinduism as child marriage – often as early as the age of ten – and the burning of young widows on their husband's funeral pyre, which Kathleen Mayo had documented – to be a reason for the continuation of British rule, and the elimination of these evident (from a Christian or humanitarian viewpoint) malpractices.

Inside India the year 1927 was marked, as each of its predecessors for the previous five years had been, by continual strife between Hindus and Muslims. Within the wide spectrum of Indian classes, castes, languages and ethnic groups, and political aspirations, it was this religious conflict that created the greatest tensions. The Indian National Congress, the main body of Indian national activities and agitation, was made up of Hindus and Muslims working together, and in harmony. But since 1906 an All-India Moslem League had made itself the instrument of specific Muslim hopes and the protector of Muslim interests.

As the Hindu-Muslim conflict continued, the Viceroy, Lord Irwin, announced on August 29 that in the seventeen months during which he had been in India between 250 and 300 people had been killed in Hindu-Muslim clashes, and more than 2500 injured. Violent riots had broken out in the predominantly Muslim city of Lahore after an Indian article belittled and denigrated the founder of Islam, the Prophet Mohammed. In an attempt to lessen the immediate tension, and to find a long-term solution to Hindu-Muslim violence, the head of the All-India Moslem League, Muhammad Ali Jinnah, convened a Hindu-Muslim Conference, known as the Unity Conference, at Simla. But despite the earnestness of its deliberations, it was unable to find a way forward to halt the communal riots, which continued, week by week, to take their toll in human lives.

An attempt was made by the Government of India to introduce a new section in the Indian Penal Code, to make it a criminal offence to insult the religion, or intentionally to outrage, or attempt to outrage, the religious feelings 'of any class of His Majesty's subjects'. This proposed new section of the law was submitted by the government to the Simla session of the Indian Legislative Assembly (the highest level of Indian participation in the Government of India). During the ensuing debate, it became clear that nothing could be done: the Muslim members of the assembly supported the new section, the Hindu members opposed it.

The British government in London was committed, under the Government of India Act of 1919, to set up a Statutory Commission on Indian Reforms, to review the whole future nature of British rule. The Commission was announced in November 1927, headed by a distinguished Liberal parliamentarian and jurist, Sir John Simon. Many Indian nationalists objected to the lack of any Indians on the commission, but it was made clear by the British government that the commission was to be composed entirely of members of the Westminster parliament, but that Indians would be consulted fully. One member of the commission was the Labour Member of Parliament, Clement Attlee (later Prime Minister), who had fought at Gallipoli and Mesopotamia alongside Indian soldiers.

The British Prime Minister, Stanley Baldwin, rejected pressure from the Indian National Congress that there should be equal status for the Simon Commission and the Indian Legislative Assembly. The British Parliament, he said, could not escape from its 'ultimate responsibility' for legislation. Protest meetings were held throughout India. At a meeting of Bombay citizens on November 19, eleven days after the composition of the Simon Commission was announced, it was declared to be unacceptable 'as it most flagrantly denies the right of the Indian people to participate on equal terms in framing the future constitution of the country'. Leading members of the Swarajist Party tried to persuade senior friends in the British Labour Party to withdraw from the Commission, but they declined to do so.

The Indian National Congress, meeting in Madras, decided to boycott the Simon Commission altogether. British parliamentary democracy at its most liberal, and Indian national aspirations at their least extreme, were on a collision course. One large minority group in India did welcome the Commission, and offered to cooperate fully with it. These were the 'Untouchables', those millions of Indians who were outside the rigid Hindu caste system: men, women and children forced to undertake the most menial and degrading of tasks, yet excluded from the hierarchy of social acceptability. At their own Conference of the Depressed Classes, held at Allahabad at the end of the year, the Untouchables expressed their hope that the Simon Commission would give them a better place in any future Indian constitutional arrangement, and not abandon them to their existing exclusion.

The Muslims of India were divided. Some hoped that one result of the Simon Commission would be to grant separate electorates, one of which would be for the Muslims. Other Muslims supported the decision of the Indian National Congress to boycott the Commission. Those Muslims who saw the Commission as a chance to further Muslim national and religious aspirations were led by the head of the All-India Moslem League, Muhammad Ali Jinnah. A supporter of Hindu–Muslim unity, and of cooperation between Congress and League, Jinnah had found himself for some time at variance with the Swarajist calls for civil disobedience. For this reason he had been on the verge of resigning from Congress when the Simon Commission was announced.

Jinnah did not have a clear majority within the Moslem League to participate in the work of the Simon Commission. Indeed, because the first reaction of the Moslem League after the Commission had been set up had been to join in the boycott declared by Congress, Jinnah had to challenge his fellow Muslims. Resorting to methods which his opponents denounced as unconstitutional, he moved the winter session of the League from Lahore to Calcutta, and secured support for cooperation. The result of his tactic was to split the League, and to weaken the Muslim negotiating position.

Even as the Simon Commissioners were on their way to India, the Government of India altered its policy with regard to Indian participation in the army, opening the gates to the substantial employment of Indians in the higher ranks. One important example of this was the appointment of an Indian member of the Legislative Assembly, Srinavasa Sastri, as the first Agent of the Government of India in South Africa, with responsibility to ensure the fair treatment of Indians in South Africa.

In Burma, in the remote Kachin country, which lay beyond the reach of regular British administration, the continuation of slavery had been a cause of indignation in Britain, and concern to the Government of India. At a gathering held in Myitkina at the beginning of the year – on January 10 – more than a hundred local chiefs were assembled, and told that slavery must be abolished. A military expedition to the upper reaches of the Irrawaddy River led to the release of 4000 slaves. But on March 26, when as many as six hundred more slaves remained to be liberated, a section of the expedition was ambushed, and its senior officer, Captain E. M. West, was killed. A second expedition, mounted a year later, was more successful. But these remote regions never fell fully under British rule.

In Austria, the acquittal of two Fascists on charges of murdering two Socialists in the Burgenland led to a workers' strike, and clashes with the police. On July 15 there were riots in Vienna, the Rathaus was destroyed by fire, and eighty-five people were killed.

The spread of dictatorial regimes in Europe continued. In Portugal, the government of General Carmona systematically reversed the social legislation of the Democrat Party, and the efforts of the deposed Prime Minister, Antonio Maria da Silva, to introduce a liberal regime. All town and district councils were dissolved, and replaced by Administrative Councils nominated by the dictatorship.

In Paris, a group of Portuguese exiles gathered together at the beginning of 1927 to form a focus of revolt. They were supported by the former President, Dr Bernardino Machado, who contributed to their monthly magazine, *A Revolta*. In February there were anti-government demonstrations in the Portuguese city of Oporto. General Carmona was prepared, however, to deal with such disturbances, having organized a special force of troops capable of moving swiftly to any place where trouble might occur. Taking up positions on the Serra de Pilar – a hill on the south side of the River Douro, facing the city – Carmona's troops opened fire with artillery. The rebels were quickly dispersed, and many arrested, but the leaders managed to escape, making their way to Paris, and joining the exiles there.

The suppression of the revolt in Oporto did not end the movement of protest. In the capital, Lisbon, an enormous crowd of anti-government demonstrators, including many sailors and policemen, marched through the streets to the centre of the city, seeking to take control of the main government buildings. Troops loyal to the government barred their way, and opened fire. The demonstrators then managed to make their way to the Arsenal, which they occupied. Barricades were set up, and for three days the centre of Lisbon was the scene of severe fighting. Eventually the army drove the rebels out of their positions in the streets, forcing them back into the Arsenal. Then General Carmona ordered the Portuguese air force to bomb the Arsenal, and the rebels there were forced to surrender.

One more effort at overthrowing the dictatorship in Portugal took place on August 12, when an army lieutenant, Moraes Sarmento, with the support of dissident army officers in the Oporto garrison, forced his way into General Carmona's residence during a meeting of the Cabinet and, brandishing a gun, demanded the dismissal of the Cabinet. The lieutenant's action was meant to be the signal for a new uprising, on behalf of another general, who had his own nominee for President and Dictator. General Carmona refused to be cowed, and, together with a few of his braver colleagues, tackled the lieutenant, who fired five shots at the General and his Ministers of War and Finance, but without hitting them. The lieutenant then made his escape, leaving the government shaken but intact.

In Spain, there was pressure on Primo de Rivera to broaden his government and convene a National Assembly. This was done in September, on the fourth anniversary of his coming to power. The members of the assembly were not elected, however, but nominated by the government. Senior politicians of the democratic era who were offered nomination declined to serve. The Liberals declined en bloc to serve, and the leader of the Monarchical Conservatives ostentatiously left the country on the day after the establishment of the National Assembly was announced.

The calling of the National Assembly coincided with a move among the anti-dictatorial forces to find some means of removing Primo de Rivera. On October 2 there were widespread arrests of those involved in the plot, some two hundred in all. Eight days later King Alfonso opened the National Assembly. Its deliberations were of no danger to the dictatorship; it was entirely consultative and had no power to make laws.

Two months after the opening of the National Assembly in Madrid, a daily air service was inaugurated, linking Madrid with Lisbon – the capitals of two dictatorships – and, through Barcelona, with France and the rest of Europe. Also being linked by air to the rest of Europe was the Soviet Union. The Russian-German Airship Company, Deruluft, which for three years had been operating a weekly service from Berlin to the Persian Gulf, now offered a daily passenger service London–Berlin–Königsberg–Moscow 'in comfortable Fokker III six-seaters with Rolls-Royce motors of 360 horse power'. Starting at six in the morning, the journey took just over ten hours.[1]

In its travel brochures and guidebooks the Soviet Union invited travellers and tourists from the West to explore the glories of the River Volga, the Crimea and the Caucasus: palm trees on the beaches of Sochi and Sukhumi, the snow-capped twin peaks of Mount Elbruz as seen from the North Caucasus resort towns of Piatygorsk and Kislovodsk, and the mellow riverine landscape of central Russia. The new face of the Soviet Union was also extolled. In Leningrad tourists were invited to visit the Museum of the Red Army, the Permanent Exhibition of the Supreme Economic Council, and the Museum of the Revolution. The description of the Museum of the Revolution noted that the museum offered not only material 'connected with the Russian Revolution', but that 'considerable space has also been allotted

---

[1] In 1997 the fastest commercial flying time from London to Moscow was three hours and forty minutes.

to the revolutions of Western Europe'. The Museum of Art Culture, founded in 1918, had been designed 'with the object of bringing the various currents of modern art nearer to the masses'.

The fate of those masses was nowhere even alluded to in the guidebooks, though there was a hint of an element of compulsion, or at least of propaganda, in the reference to the Young Communist League and Pioneers organizations, which, according to the official *Guide to the Soviet Union* in use in 1927, 'carry on a vigorous agitation among the rising generation of "Soviet Youth", their task being to create a considerable and constantly renewed reserve-force for the Party'.

The continuing activities of the Opposition made this 'vigorous agitation' all the more necessary to maintain Party unity, and the ascendancy of Stalin. Although driven from all positions of power or influence in the previous year, the various Opposition leaders still hoped to get a hearing. But an attack in *Pravda* by Zinoviev on Stalin's policy towards China – supporting the Kuomintang even after the Kuomintang had turned against the Chinese Communist Party – was met by a chorus of synchronized abuse. Trotsky was also active that year, publicly criticizing the Comintern policy, which had been set by Stalin, of not pushing for world revolution. He was warned that any further attacks on the Comintern would be met by his expulsion from it: it was the only Soviet body of any significance on which he was still a member of the executive.

Two other members of the opposition, V. M. Smirnov – Lenin's first Commissar of Trade and Industry – and T. B. Sapronov, published a pamphlet in which they denounced the Communist Party leaders as 'Thermidorians' – a reference to the final phase of the French Revolution – bent on turning the Party into a dictatorial monolith, following one man (Stalin), rather than expressing the will of the Russian masses, and pursuing opportunist rather than Communist policies. The Comintern, they said, had become 'merely a tool' in Stalin's hands.

At a meeting of the Central Committee that began on July 28, these voices of dissent within the Party were examined and discussed. As the discussions continued, the Opposition issued a declaration, signed by eighty-three Communist Party members, in which they set out their arguments. The Declaration of the Eighty-Three was eventually signed by more than five hundred members of the Party. When, a few days after the declaration was issued, one of the signatories, M. Smilga, left Moscow for his home in Siberia, a large gathering of his friends and supporters, led by Trotsky, not only saw him off at the station, but demonstrated there in his favour. To the cheering of the crowd, Trotsky supported the Opposition stance.

The Central Committee was outraged, and instructed the Central Control Commission to consider what to do. The commission met on August 9. That same day, thirteen leading members of the Opposition, among them Trotsky, Kamenev and Rakovsky (who had been instrumental in establishing Bolshevik rule in the Ukraine), signed a declaration denying that they wished to split the Party into two factions.

Stalin hesitated to expel his critics, whose support was widely based. Instead, he allowed *Pravda* to print a special 'debating section' of the paper, in which both the majority party view and that of the Opposition could be printed side by side. When, however, fourteen members of the Opposition set up their own printing press – an illegal act under the existing law – they were summoned to a special Party Tribunal and expelled from the Party. Among those who tried to defend them before the Tribunal were Zinoviev, Smilga and Trotsky. After Trotsky had used the occasion to make a strident attack on the Party bureaucracy, he was expelled from the Executive Committee of the Comintern.

Expulsion from the Communist Party followed rapidly. One of the first Opposition leaders to be thrown out of the Party, on October 12, was E. A. Preobrazhensky, a friend of Lenin, and a member of the Central Committee Secretariat. Two weeks later Zinoviev and Trotsky were both expelled. When the Fifteenth Congress of the Party opened in December, the Opposition had no place, and no voice. The rule of Stalin was proclaimed by every speaker. He himself demanded of the delegates 'complete acceptance' of the policies and tactics of the Party. Trotskyism was declared an 'anti-Soviet force', and Trotsky's followers were denounced in the language of ten years earlier as a 'Menshevik faction'. On December 19 a specially established Commission of Enquiry recommended to the Congress that ninety-eight leaders of the opposition should be expelled from the Party ranks. The Congress unanimously adopted this recommendation.

Those expelled included Karl Radek, one of those who had travelled to Russia with Lenin in 1917. He had been a founding member of the German Communist Party in 1918, and a member of the Bolshevik Central Committee in Moscow from 1919. As well as striking at the Opposition within the Party, Stalin's secret police were vigilant in seeking out any dissenting voices. An official manifesto, issued under the one-word signature 'Kremlin', threatened severe punishment against all those who committed offences against Soviet rule. That winter, twenty people, most of them former Tsarist officers, and including a former leader of the Kadet Party, Prince Dolgoruki, were shot without trial.

Inside Germany, the governments of both Bavaria and Saxony agreed, early in 1927, to end their ban on Hitler's public speaking. He gave both governments an assurance that he would not pursue any 'unlawful' aims or use any 'unlawful' means in his renewed political activity. His first public speech in more than three years took place on the evening of March 9, at the Krone Circus in Munich. One of the Bavarian policemen present submitted a full report:

> From the stage hangs the red swastika flag. The stage is reserved for prominent party members and the speaker. The seats in the boxes also seem to be reserved for special party members, since they are assigned by brownshirts. A band has assembled on the platform. No other decorations were to be seen.
>
> The people on the benches are excited and filled with anticipation. They talk about Hitler, about his former oratorical triumphs at the Krone Circus. The women, who are present in great numbers, still seem to be enthusiastic about him . . .
>
> There is a craving for sensation in the hot, insipid air. The band plays rousing marches while fresh crowds keep pouring in. The *Völkischer Beobachter* is hawked about. At the ticket office each visitor is given a copy of the Programme of the National Socialist Workers' Party, and at the entrance a slip is pressed into everyone's hand warning against reacting to provocations and emphasizing the need to maintain order. Small flags are sold; 'Welcoming flags, 10 pfennig apiece'. They are either black-white-red or entirely red, and show the swastika. The women are the best customers.
>
> Meanwhile the ranks are filling. 'We have to make it like the old days!' people are saying. The arena fills . . .
>
> Most of the spectators belong to the lower economic groups, workers, small artisans, small tradesmen. Many youths in windbreakers and knee socks. Few, hardly any, representatives of the radical working class are to be seen. The people are well dressed; some men are even in evening dress.

The crowd in the circus, which is nearly entirely filled, is estimated at seven thousand persons.

It is now half past eight. From the entrance come roars of *Heil*. Brownshirts march in, the band plays, the crowd cheers noisily. Hitler appears in a brown raincoat, walks swiftly, accompanied by his retinue, the whole length of the circus and up to the stage. The people gesticulate in happy excitement, wave, continually shout *Heil*, stand on the benches, stamp their feet thunderously. Then comes a trumpet blast, as in the theatre. Sudden silence.

Amid roars of welcome from the spectators, the brownshirts now march into the hall in rank and file, led by two rows of drummers and then the flag. The men salute in the manner of the Fascists, with outstretched arms. The audience cheers them.

On the stage Hitler has similarly stretched out his arm in salute. The music surges up. Flags move past, glittering standards with swastikas inside the wreath and with eagles, modelled on the ancient Roman military standards. Perhaps about two hundred men file past. They fill the arena and stand at attention while the flag-bearers and standard-bearers people the stage . . .

Hitler steps swiftly to the front of the stage. He speaks without a manuscript, at first in a slow, emphatic way; later the words come tumbling forth, and in passages spoken with exaggerated emotion his voice becomes thin and high and ceases to be intelligible. He gesticulates with arms and hands, jumps agitatedly about, and is bent on fascinating the thousands in the audience, who listen with close attention.

During the remaining ten months of 1927, Hitler spoke in public fifty-six times. But how far his Party could become a political force through parliamentary means was much in doubt. That year one of his staunchest followers, Dr Josef Goebbels, published a pamphlet in which he addressed himself to the question of what the Nazi Party should do if it could not win power through the ballot box. 'What then?' asked Goebbels, and he went on to answer his own question: 'Then we'll clench our teeth and get ready. Then we'll march against this government; then we'll dare the last great coup for Germany; then revolutionaries of the word will become revolutionaries of the deed. Then we'll make a revolution!'

*   *   *

A little-publicized event in Germany that year characterized the disturbing factors that lurked ever closer to the surface of German political life. One of the ideological fathers of modern racial theory, Houston Stewart Chamberlain, an Englishman who had made his home in Germany, was dying. His life's work had been to show that the Anglo-Saxon race was the superior one, that up till then (his principal book had been published in 1899) the cross-breeding of races had not damaged the German race, but that the German race was in danger; the threat came from the Jews. 'When the Volkish movement proclaimed the German revolution,' the historian George Mosse has commented, 'they looked to Chamberlain for the racial framework.'

Even as Houston Stewart Chamberlain was on his deathbed, he received a visitor – Hitler. Many of Hitler's own theories were based on what he had read in Chamberlain's writings. In Chamberlain's dying moments Hitler showed his homage by kissing his mentor's hand.

It was not only Hitler and the political extremists in Germany for whom racism was a central factor in their outlook. During 1927 a new scientific organization, the Kaiser Wilhelm Institute for Anthropology, Human Heredity and Eugenics, was founded in Berlin. One of its most revealing questionnaires – sent out four years later, on 5 May 1931 – asked the leaders of various professions in Germany to help solve the 'main problem' being studied in the institute, the problem of 'making reproduction discriminate'. The German Ministry of the Interior acted as distributor for the questionnaire. A science that had gained great respectability during the early years of the twentieth century – there was a Eugenics Section in the League of Nations' Health Office – was to fall, within a few years, into the hands of those for whom racial 'purity' was both a fetish and a goal.

CHAPTER THIRTY-TWO

1928

B Y THE END OF 1927, Stalin had eliminated the Left Opposition as a political force in the Soviet Union. During 1928 he turned his efforts to the destruction of the Right Opposition, those leading Communists who had supported him in the previous year against Trotsky, Kamenev and Zinoviev. When the Central Committee met in April, Stalin accused Bukharin, Rykov and Tomsky, his three main allies of the previous year's struggle, of 'dangerous deviations' and lack of Party discipline. Bukharin, he said, had been guilty of 'treacherous behaviour'.

Action was swift; Bukharin was removed from the editorship of *Pravda* and chairmanship of the Comintern, and Tomsky from the leadership of the Trade Unions. Rykov was allowed to remain as head of government, but clearly under notice. Then, in a display of the political cunning for which he became notorious, Stalin turned to the discredited Left Opposition and invited them to return to the Party. Radek, Zinoviev and Kamenev did so. Having been humiliated, they accepted the pardon and hastened to play a part once more in Party life. But their influence was small, their tasks minor, and their prospects of authority nil.

The enormous efforts that had been put into the establishment of Communism in Russia were not all cynical and opportunist; the Party had begun life before the war with many ideologists and even dreamers, men and women who were determined to create a better life for the Russian people, and to do so on the basis of perceived equalities of work and wages. Once Stalin had brought back the Left Opposition, those who had earlier feared that the true Communist ideological path had been abandoned took courage. They began to press their point of view, unaware of how little the return of the expellees meant in terms of real political change. In October, a member of the Right Opposition, Frumkin, a Party member from its first days, sent a memorandum to the Central Committee, and more bravely to the Control Committee of the Party, in which he demanded more economic freedom for the peasants, and a halt to the new policy of enforced collectivization which was being imposed on many thousands of villages. He also demanded the participation of the peasants in the State administration, and a slower pace in the process of industrialization, aspects of the spread of Communist control and economic centralization on which Stalin was insistent.

Under Stalin's instructions, the Central Committee acted against Frumkin and his memorandum in stern fashion. On October 22 a proclamation by the Central Committee warned against the 'new tendencies' which were being spread in the villages of Russia 'by people ignorant of the class antagonism in the village'. Stalin, taking up the cudgels himself, denounced Frumkin and those associated with him as hoping to 'unchain the capitalist elements of the country'.

On December 17, at the end of two weeks of deliberations in Moscow by the Executive Committee of the Central Committee, it was laid down that all rural land belonged to the community, and that the 'socialization' of agriculture was essential. The more prosperous peasants, the Kulaks – whose success was the result of the reforms of Peter Stolypin two decades earlier – were deprived of the right to be elected to the local Soviets, and declared the enemies of Socialist agriculture.

The campaign against the Kulaks, thus begun, was rapidly to evolve into one of the cruellest persecutions of the twentieth century. At the same time, a public 'show' trial, of the sort that was to set the pattern for individual persecution and mass repression in the coming decade, was being prepared. A secret police chief in the city of Shakhty had reported direct to Stalin – with whom he had been on close personal terms since the Civil War – on a network of sabotage by fifty Russian and three German engineers in the local coal mines. The charges were a deliberate fabrication. Ignoring the protests of Menzhinsky, the head of the OGPU, and Kuibyshev, the Chairman of the Council of National Economy, Stalin ordered the case to be brought to trial. The presiding judge, Andrei Vyshinsky, who was to preside over almost all the subsequent show trials, had been a prisoner with Stalin in Baku Prison twenty years earlier.

Everything at the show trial was stage-managed. The trial, which opened on May 18 and ended on July 6, was held in one of Moscow's most impressive buildings, the Hall of Columns. The slogan 'Death to the Wreckers!' was hung in banner form on many public buildings. The twelve-year-old son of one of the accused demanded the death penalty for his father. At the trial, confessions were read out that had clearly been extracted by force and fraud;

two of the accused tried to say this in court, but were derided for their courage. They had first been tortured, then promised their freedom if they signed confessions implicating not only themselves but others.

The aim of the Shakhty trial was to identify the 'class enemy', and to make any charge plausible. From that moment, the 'bourgeois specialists', men and women of pre-revolutionary upbringing and training who were loyally serving the new regime in their spheres of expertise, could be rooted out and executed (as were five of the fifty Shakhty engineers) or sentenced to long terms of imprisonment and forced labour in camps whose number, particularly in northern Russia and Siberia, was growing every year.

Although, in the Shakhty case, the charges against the three German engineers were withdrawn, it too set a pattern for linking the 'class enemy' with overseas and outside forces intent on undermining the Soviet Union. At later trials, spying for a foreign power became a standard charge.

While Russia was immersed in the travails of Stalin's evolving terror and control, Europe was seeking ways to build on the pacific intentions of the Geneva Protocol and the Locarno Treaty. The American Secretary of State, Frank B. Kellogg, in a significant change in the earlier determination of the United States to be above the European fray, promoted a Peace Pact which he invited all members of the League of Nations to sign. Its aim was no less than to outlaw war altogether: 'The unqualified renunciation of all war as an instrument of national policy'.

Even as the negotiations for the Peace Pact gathered momentum – and it was strongly supported by the French Foreign Minister, Aristide Briand – there were signs of discord between the former victors and vanquished, especially when Hungary announced its discontent at the conditions of the Treaty of Trianon, whereby Hungarian-speaking regions had been transferred to Czechoslovakia, Yugoslavia and Roumania. On the very first day of 1928, the seriousness of Hungarian revisionism was revealed in a scandal that alarmed Hungary's neighbours; five railway wagons on their way from Italy to Hungary were examined at the small town of Szent Gotthard – along the route from Budapest and Györ to the southern Austrian town of Graz, and at that point the Austrian frontier with Hungary – and were found to contain, not 'machinery', as stated on the waybill, but machine guns.

Under the Treaty of Trianon, the size of Hungary's armed forces and their weaponry were strictly limited. Three of Hungary's neighbours, Czechoslovakia, Yugoslavia and Roumania, known as the Little Entente, protested on behalf of the victorious Powers of a decade earlier. They were supported in their protest by France. Within three weeks, Hungary had been denounced at the League of Nations. The Council of the League agreed to send a Commission of Enquiry. Szent Gotthard, hitherto an unimportant border crossing, suddenly became the focus of international interest.

Before the Commission could set off, the Hungarian government stated that the railway wagons were at the Hungarian end of the Szent Gotthard station, and refused to return the machine guns to the Austrian end. It then ordered the guns to be broken up and offered for sale as metal scrap. A telegram from the League of Nations demanded that the Hungarians leave the guns where they were. But when the Commission finally arrived on the scene and made its enquiries, it came to the somewhat lame conclusion that there was no hard evidence that the guns were in fact destined for Hungary.

The incident was closed, but it raised alarm bells among the peoples of the Little Entente, which looked to its governments to protect them against Hungarian revisionism. It also weakened the authority of the League of Nations, to which the smaller States had looked for protection against just such an apparent violation of the Peace Treaties. A conference of the Little Entente States was held in Bucharest in June. The participants – Czechoslovakia, Yugoslavia and Roumania – were united in denouncing all attempts to change the borders of Eastern Europe.

The Szent Gotthard incident had shown how sensitive the postwar settlement had become. Inside Hungary, resentment at the existence of large Hungarian minorities on the other side of three of its borders was acute. In November, Czechoslovakia and Yugoslavia, which had already signed a Treaty of Alliance, renewed that Treaty for an indefinite period. A month later, a second secret shipment of arms, bound for Budapest, was discovered in Vienna. It was labelled 'oil engines', but when one of the crates accidentally broke open it was found to contain machine-gun belts.

Amid the obvious and continual smuggling of arms into its territory, Hungary was pursuing its public call for Treaty revision with tenacity. A wealthy British newspaper proprietor, Lord Rothermere, took up the revisionist cause, and did so with such enthusiasm that the Hungarians built a 'Temple of Revision' in his honour. Rothermere's son, Esmond Harmsworth, visiting Hungary in 1928, was received with adulation in more than a hundred and twenty towns. Hungarian patriots laid a wreath on the grave of one of Lord Rothermere's two other sons, both of whom had been killed in action on the Western Front. But when Rothermere himself, in a Christmas message to the people of Hungary, advocated the introduction of more liberal institutions in Hungary, and the abandonment of the idea of a restoration of the Habsburgs, his Hungarian admirers fell away.

Hungary's Prime Minister, Count Bethlen, had not assumed dictatorial powers on the scale of Pilsudski in Poland or Mussolini in Italy. He had even won an election, in 1926, although the franchise was limited to 28 per cent of the male population, with the secret ballot not widely in force. Parliamentary debates were of little consequence to him as far as legislation was concerned, though he did strike parliamentary bargains with the opposition Peasant and Social Democrat Parties. Real power resided with the Regent, Admiral Horthy, who had already ensured that liberty of assembly was curtailed, and that members of the government were forbidden to express their views publicly without previous permission from the Party executive. In a speech on January 19, Bethlen condemned both liberalism and democracy as 'antiquated political forms'.

In securing support for his policies, Bethlen formed a political alliance with the Hungarian Fascist leader, György Gömbös, who not only brought fifty more members of Parliament to the government side, but also strong ideological support. Gömbös was rewarded by being made Minister of Defence, and, under Bethlen's guidance, drew Hungary closer to Mussolini's Italy. His influence also led to a rise in anti-Jewish activities throughout Hungary. On October 20, after the admission of seventeen Jewish students to Budapest University (even this number was above the derisory quota that had been established for the admission of Hungarian Jews), there were violent attacks on Jewish students in the capital.

In Vienna, the Fascist *Heimwehr* organization had formed its own armed force, with which it attacked its opponents, principally the Social Democrats. One of the demands of the Austrian Fascists was *Anschluss*, union with Germany. Not only extremist, but much moderate opinion in Austria had continued, since 1918, to favour such a union. When, as part of the Schubert Centenary celebrations, the Tenth German Song Festival was held in Vienna, demonstrations were held in favour of *Anschluss*. Hundreds of thousands of '*Anschluss* Day' programmes were printed; the song festival became a call to the world to accept the 'racial unity' of Germans living in the two countries, with a common language, common culture and common border.

Internally, Austria's Germans had no such theme of unity. Shortly after the song festival, the Austrian Fascists announced that 40,000 of their number would assemble in the largely Socialist industrial town of Wiener Neustadt, as a gesture of defiance to the Social Democrats. The Austrian government warned that the gathering should not go ahead. The Austrian Fascist leader, Dr Steidle, who was president of the Upper House of the Austrian parliament – and who earlier had threatened to follow Mussolini's example in Italy, and march on Vienna – insisted that the march would go ahead. A Socialist counter-march was then organized by the forces of the left. Both marches took place. Only the intervention of 12,000 Austrian troops – one third of the total strength of the Austrian army as laid down by the Peace Treaties – armed with machine guns and a plentiful supply of ammunition, prevented direct confrontation. Barbed-wire barriers were erected in the town, and the two demonstrations took place without direct contact. At the moment when violence might have erupted, a heavy downpour of rain dampened the rising tempers.

Another country plagued by internal dissent in 1928 was Yugoslavia, where the Croats resented their position of inferiority, both in the general administrative scheme, and in the Belgrade Parliament, the Skupshtina. The Communist Party was also flexing its muscles; on May 1 it organized demonstrations in the Croat capital, Zagreb, and there were many arrests. Among those arrested was the city's Communist Party Secretary, Josip Broz, who was imprisoned for two weeks. The Communist Party, he declared, 'is now fighting unreservedly for the independence of Croatia'. It also supported the right of the German, Hungarian and Albanian minorities to break away from the Yugoslav State. Twenty years later, Broz, then known as Tito, was to lead a Communist Yugoslav State, of which he was Prime Minister, out of the wider orbit of the Soviet Union.

That summer, in an attempt to indicate their frustration at the Serb dominance of the legislature, Croat deputies in the Belgrade parliament disrupted the proceedings for four consecutive days, after which four of their number were dragged out of the Chamber by the police. On June 20, one of the deputies, Punisa Racic, a Montenegrin member of the Serb Radical Party, opened fire and killed a Croat deputy, Paul Radic, and at the same time seriously wounded Radic's uncle, the Croat Peasant Party leader Stephen Radic (co-founder of the Party in 1902, under the Habsburgs). Anti-Serbian riots broke out in Belgrade. The police opened fire on the rioters, five of whom were killed.

King Alexander, in an attempt to heal the wounds that were tearing his multinational kingdom apart, visited the wounded Stephen Radic in hospital in Belgrade, and, in a gesture of amity, kissed him. In a message to the funeral of the two dead Croat deputies, Radic, for his part, spoke of the importance of 'Yugoslav unity'. But many Croats felt that without autonomy for Croatia, the wider concept of Yugoslav unity was dead. On July 4 the Serbs rejected a Croat demand for the dissolution of the Belgrade parliament and for new, 'honest' elections. The King asked the wounded Radic if he would form a government, but Radic declined. Still seriously ill, he was moved back to Zagreb five days later. On August 8 he died.

Power in Belgrade passed to a coalition, in which Serbs and Slovenes came together, under a Slovene Prime Minister, Father Korosec. One of the first measures of the new government was to ratify a territorial agreement with Italy, the Nettuno Conventions, which the Croats felt was aimed at giving Italy too strong a position in the Adriatic. There was rioting in Zagreb, in which the Communist Party took a leading part, even distributing arms. Josip Broz had to go into hiding, helped by an actor friend to vary his disguises. For a while, luck was on his side. When the police came to a Trade Union building which he was at that very moment visiting, they asked him to his face, 'Is Josip Broz here?' He answered without hesitation, 'Can't you see he isn't?' and the police, saluting smartly, withdrew. But on August 4 he was caught. Throughout his trial he refused to renounce his Communist beliefs. Asked by the prosecutor, 'Are you in communication with Moscow?' he answered at once: 'Certainly we are in communication with Moscow. We are Moscow's organization.' He was sentenced to five years in prison.

On August 25, as one of the consequences of the Nettuno Conventions, Ahmed Bey Zogu was proclaimed King of Albania. The Croats at once accused the Serbs of permitting and facilitating yet another area of Italian penetration, and there were further street demonstrations in Zagreb. The new Croat leader, Dr Macek, in search of a compromise that would preserve the unity of the Yugoslav State, argued in favour of a far looser union between Croatia and Serbia, one that would be similar to that which had existed between Austria and Hungary in the Habsburg times, with separate parliaments, separate judiciaries, and separate Prime Ministers. The Crown would provide a purely personal union between the two countries. The Serbs rejected this. In Zagreb, Croat university students went on strike and the university was closed. In street riots, a man was killed and many others injured. On December 5 the Belgrade government appointed a Military Governor, Colonel Maximovic, for Zagreb. The Croats feared the imposition of a Serb dictatorship. On December 26 a Serbian secret police agent was murdered in a Zagreb café. In Belgrade there were calls for the arrest of the Croat leaders, and their trial for high treason.

The situation in Yugoslavia had become so uncertain, and the stability of the regime so in doubt, that when negotiations began for a loan with the London banking house of Rothschild, they could not be settled, and the loan was postponed indefinitely.

In Portugal, General Carmona continued to consolidate his dictatorship. Opposition groups, based in Paris, and headed by the former President, Dr Bernardino Machado, continued to demand the return of parliamentary democracy, but an outbreak of unrest inside Portugal, begun by troops in Lisbon, was crushed when their centre of revolt, St George's Castle, was bombarded by artillery until the rebels raised the white flag.

In October, on the eighteenth anniversary of the proclamation of the Portuguese republic, General Carmona issued an amnesty for the officers and civilians who had taken part in the previous revolt a year and a half earlier. The only condition was that the officers, on being reinstated in the army, should serve for two years in the Portuguese colonies overseas.

In Italy, in a measure designed to strengthen the hold of the Fascist Party, Mussolini incorporated the Fascist Grand Council, which had been in active existence since the beginning of 1923, into the Italian constitution. The Grand Council was to be 'the supreme organ coordinating all the various activities of the regime'. It would advise on any political, social or economic question 'submitted to it by the government'. No constitutional changes could be brought before parliament without prior approval of the Grand Council. Members of the Grand Council would 'enjoy freedom from arrest'. Mussolini alone would be responsible for summoning it, and he alone would set the agenda for its meetings, which would be held in secret. A new generation, Mussolini told the Italian parliament, had the right 'to make new laws suited to its needs and mentality'.

Ambitious plans were embarked upon by Mussolini to show that the power of the centralized State could be beneficial. He already boasted that under Fascism the trains 'ran on time'. In 1928 he launched an ambitious scheme to drain the malarial marshes of Italy and to put them under cultivation, providing hundreds of impoverished villages with irrigation, drainage, roads, water and electric power.

Mussolini made every effort, in carefully stage-managed appearances, to make his appeal direct to the various groups to whom he looked for support. At the end of October he gathered all the Italian newspaper editors in Rome for a 'personal conference', telling them with pride – as a former journalist himself – that in Italy the Press was free because, unlike foreign newspapers where a plutocratic owner or a political party called the tune, the Italian newspapers served a single cause and a single regime. A few days later, on November 3, he summoned 80,000 farmers to Rome, to assure them that agriculture had a 'foremost place' in the government's policies. Their loyalty had been assured beforehand by a rise in the tariff on wheat. This gave them a guaranteed minimum price when the cost of wheat – which they were producing on a much increased scale as a result of Mussolini's Battle for Grain campaign – fell as a result of the deliberate overproduction.

On the day after his speech to the farmers, Mussolini addressed an even larger gathering, a mass meeting of former soldiers. He told them that the victory in 1918 had been 'shiningly Italian', and called on them to 'do again tomorrow what you did yesterday' if it ever proved necessary for Italy to go to war.

Another dictator, Marshal Pilsudski, was briefly in trouble in 1928, when the Polish Socialist candidate, Ignacy Daszynski, received a larger vote for Speaker of the Parliament than the government candidate. So violent was the written abuse directed by Pilsudski against the Parliament in a newspaper article after the Speaker's election that it was given out that he was suffering from a 'nervous malady'. He was not too indisposed, however, to prorogue Parliament, as soon as it had voted for his budget, for six months.

In Germany, democracy continued to prevail, albeit with a proliferation of political parties that prevented any one party from securing an absolute majority in the Reichstag. Elections were called in May 1928. Thirty-one parties put forward candidates, including the Nazi Party.

One peculiarity of Hitler's election campaign was that, as an admirer of Mussolini, he did not participate in the German nationalists' call for the South Tyrol to be transferred from Italy – which had acquired it in 1918 –

to Austria. Instead, he claimed in his election speeches, as he had done three years earlier in *Mein Kampf*, that the South Tyrol issue was nothing but a 'Jewish snare' to prevent German-Italian rapprochement. It was only the 'Jews and the Marxists', he declared during the election, who made an issue of the South Tyrol. In fact, many German nationalists were concerned about the question of the South Tyrol. It was a question which, as the election campaign grew in momentum, became aggravated by the introduction of Italian as the compulsory language of religious instruction in the region. This led to a diplomatic breach between Italy and Austria. Hitler failed to exploit this; his desire for friendship with Mussolini, and his determination to make use of the spurious Jewish issue on every possible occasion, were stronger than his sense of German national unity.

More than half the parties contesting the 1928 election failed to win a single seat. After its outspoken campaign of denouncing the Republic, the Nazi Party was disappointed in securing only twelve seats. It had gained only 810,000 votes out of more than thirty million. Hitler was not downcast, however. He was confident that what he called the 'fighting spirit' of Nazism would gain him more and more adherents. 'It is there,' he declared of that fighting spirit, 'only buried under a pile of foreign theories and doctrines. A great and powerful party goes to a lot of trouble to prove the opposite, until suddenly an ordinary military band comes along and plays. Then the straggler comes to, out of his dreamy state; all at once he begins to feel himself a comrade of the marching men, and joins their columns. That's the way it is today. Our people only have to be shown this better course – and you'll see, we'll start marching.'

As a result of the 1928 election, the largest party in the new German parliament was the Social Democrats, with just under 30 per cent of the poll, and 153 seats – a gain of 22. It was they who formed the government. The next three largest parties were the German National People's Party, with 78 seats, the Centre Party with 61 and the Communist Party with 54. The new Chancellor, Hermann Müller, a member of the Council of the German Social Democratic Party since 1906, had been a well-known figure in Socialist circles abroad for many years. One of his first visitors after he took office was the British Labour Party leader, soon to be re-elected Prime Minister, Ramsay MacDonald.

Inside Germany, industrial problems were becoming acute. As foreign loans became an essential feature of industrial production, many factories were unable to continue. There was a substantial rise in liquidations and, where factories continued production, profit margins fell. Employers were unable to maintain the existing rates of wages, and men were laid off. Trade Unions battled for their workers; for several months, a strike of 50,000 dockworkers brought the German shipping industry to a virtual stop. In the Ruhr, almost a quarter of a million iron workers were locked out by their employers for a month, in protest against the government arbitrator accepting the workers' wage demands, and at the same time shortening the working week.

As a result of the Treaty of Versailles, restrictions were still imposed on German trade with the Saar, and with Upper Silesia. In the Rhineland, French troops still occupied the zone designated by the Treaty. When, at the beginning of the year, the German Foreign Minister, Gustav Stresemann, tried to negotiate an early French evacuation of the Rhineland, he was again rebuffed by his French opposite number, Aristide Briand, who linked the question of withdrawal with that of the payment of reparations. When Stresemann was in Paris in August, for the signing of the Kellogg-Briand Pact, outlawing war, he again raised the question of the Rhineland, but was put off yet again by the French.

Stresemann was also unable, while in Paris, to persuade the former victorious Powers to move forward in the direction of the disarmament clauses of the Geneva Protocol. While France, Britain and Italy remained well armed, Germany was still disarmed under the Treaty of Versailles. This rankled with all Germans, and was being exploited particularly effectively by the German National People's Party, which in 1928 replaced its relatively moderate leader, Count Westarp, with the violently anti-Versailles newspaper proprietor and advertising supremo, Alfred Hugenberg. Before the war, Hugenberg had been an active member of the Pan-German League.

Hitler, despite securing only twelve seats in the Reichstag, was certain he could win more and more adherents. He took comfort that so many votes had been won in the election by the German National People's Party and the Communists, both of them his rivals, but both, like him, opponents of the democratic system. It was his belief that if they could succeed, so could he. After the election he went to a mountain retreat that he had secured at Obersalzberg, high in the Bavarian mountains, overlooking Austria. There he began working on a new book, in which he set out both his political and philosophical convictions, and gave them a unity of focus. The book was not published until fifteen years after his death, when it was given the title *Hitler's Secret Book*.[1] Two principles combined in the account he had intended to give of what he called the 'bourgeois-national element' of German Society: the self-preservation of the German 'Aryan' race, and the need for Germany to acquire territory in the East, which Hitler termed *Lebensraum* (living space). 'The compulsion to engage in the struggle for existence,' Hitler wrote in his new book, 'lies in the limitation of the living space; but in the life-struggle for this living space lies also the basis for evolution.'

For Hitler, the consequence of this struggle for space was an 'eternal battle' between nations. It was a battle which could only be won by a people dedicated to strict racial, folk and blood values. Once standards were lowered, and pure blood was mixed with inferior blood, the end was in sight. 'Then the Jew can make his entry in any form, and this master of international poisoning and race corruption will not rest until he has thoroughly uprooted and thereby corrupted such a people.' It was not his 'task', Hitler wrote, 'to enter into a discussion of the Jewish question as such'. Jewry had 'special intrinsic characteristics which separate it from all other peoples living on the globe'. It was not a religious community with a 'territorially bounded state'; and it was parasitical rather than productive. The 'ultimate goal' of 'the Jew', which had already been achieved in the Soviet Union, was, Hitler had decided, 'the denationalization, the promiscuous bastardization of other peoples, the lowering of the racial level of the highest peoples as well as the domination of his racial mishmash through the extirpation of the folkish intelligentsia and its replacement by the members of his own people'. For Hitler, the Jews threatened mankind; their aim was conquest of the world. Hitler's battle against them, he declared, was therefore for the good, not only of Germany, but of the whole world.

Hitler intended his book to end with a survey of the 'Jewish role' in recent history. With this personal obsession he had begun to bring to the surface, and to nourish, any seed of hatred dormant in his growing public audiences. The Jewish war aim had been the destruction of Tsarism in Russia and Kaiserism in Germany, he wrote. This had been 'completely achieved'. Soviet Russia had been subjected to 'inhuman agonies and atrocities' by the Jews. In France, the Jews had entered into 'a community of interests' with 'French national chauvinism', bringing together as allies 'Jewish stock

---

[1] It would seem that Hitler's publisher had no faith in his author's selling power, and the book was not published in his lifetime. Sales of *Mein Kampf* having fallen from 10,000 in 1925 to 5,600 in 1927 and 3,015 in 1928, the publisher declined the new venture.

exchanges and French bayonets'. In Britain the struggle was undecided. 'There, the Jewish invasion still meets an old British tradition. The instincts of Anglo-Saxondom are so sharp and alive that one cannot speak of a complete victory of Jewry.' If the Jews were to triumph in Britain, 'English interests would recede into the background, just as in Germany today German interests are no longer decisive, but rather Jewish interests'. In Italy, however, Hitler wrote, the victory of Fascism had led to the 'triumph' of the Italian people over Jewry.

Hitler was not entirely wrong about the anti-Semitism to be found among other nations. By a peculiar irony, he was setting out these opinions for his new book at the very moment when the new British Ambassador in Berlin, Sir Horace Rumbold, was writing to friends in London about the situation of the Jews in Berlin (at the beginning of October 1928). 'I am appalled by the number of Jews in this place,' he wrote. 'One cannot get away from them. I am thinking of having a ham-bone amulet made "to keep off the evil nose", but I am afraid that even that would not be a deterrent.' Two months later the Ambassador wrote again: 'We have settled down here and are quite happy. The only fly in the ointment is the number of Jews in the place. One cannot get away from them.'[1]

Within five years, Rumbold was to come to hate Nazism and all its works, including the anti-Semitism whose violence he was soon to witness in Berlin, and which he utterly rejected.

Hitler's fantastic notions of the evils of Jewry might not have been dangerous if he had found no audience and no public appeal. But although the publisher seems to have decided not to publish the new book, and Hitler set his typescript aside, he made the ideas in the book known whenever he spoke in public. He had already disseminated his views to the 100,000 Nazi Party members, and they were also known to the 850,000 Germans who had voted for him. They became known additionally in 1928 to the two to three million nationalist voters, most of them Hugenberg's supporters in the election, who had begun to read Hitler's fulminations in the newspapers. Hitler was consistent and emphatic. He presented his racial ideas on every public platform he could secure.

Until the spring of 1928, Nazi Party meetings in Berlin had been banned.

[1] There were 172,672 Jews in Berlin in 1928, out of a total population of just over 4 million.

But on November 16, six months after the election, Hitler spoke in the vast Sportpalast in Berlin, asserting the need for racial and national 'regeneration'. 'The bastardization of great States has begun,' he declared. 'The negroization of culture, of customs – not only of blood – strides forward. The world becomes democratized. The value of the individual declines. The masses are apparently gaining the victory over the idea of the great leader.' Hitler was convinced that he could become the 'great leader' in Germany, just as Stalin had in Russia and Mussolini in Italy. But he set his sights on a different goal for his nation than they had for theirs; he envisaged a 'pure' Aryan nation in which the half million Jews of Germany, an integral part of German life and society, would be driven out.

Unknown to Hugenberg, or to Hitler, or to the other critics of the alleged pusillanimity of the German government with regard to German rearmament, there had been considerable strides made secretly in 1928 to begin the rebuilding of the German army. The Minister of Defence, General Groener, was assiduous in preparing the core cadres of a future substantial army. Inside the Soviet Union, the training facilities set up six years earlier for German aviators, chemical warfare specialists and other branches of army ordnance, to carry out their work in secret, continued to operate, despite Stalin's show of anti-foreigner feeling. His army, too, was the beneficiary of the work being done.

Some indication of the clandestine German military preparations was about to reach the secret services of the Western Powers. At the end of the year the British Military Attaché in Germany, Colonel James Marshall-Cornwall, informed his ambassador that the existing German army 'contained the nucleus of a very formidable fighting organization'. In reporting this to London, the ambassador, Sir Horace Rumbold, doubted that there had been any 'flagrant' breach of the Treaty of Versailles. But he went on to list several 'definite infractions' of the Treaty which Marshall-Cornwall had reported, after having been present at the autumn German army manoeuvres in Lower Silesia. In 'defiance' of article 160 of the Treaty of Versailles, Rumbold told the Foreign Office in London, 'subsidiary formations such as cavalry brigades and cyclist battalions were freely employed at manoeuvres'.

Alarmed by the report of his Military Attaché, on December 28 Rumbold discussed the development of the German army with Stresemann. The Foreign Minister protested vigorously that it could not conceivably be regarded as 'a formidable instrument of war'. But Marshall-Cornwall was persistent in his quest for hidden military facts. At manoeuvres he had seen a motor truck with canvas screens around it, designed to simulate a tank. With this machine were conducted 'tank' practice and 'tank' operations, both forbidden under the Versailles Treaty. While visiting Stockholm – he was also Military Attaché to Sweden – Marshall-Cornwall found German engineers working at the leading munitions factory. Scrutinizing the German newspapers, he found obituary notices of German pilots and tank officers accidentally killed in Russia. Although their names had earlier been removed from the German army list, it was obvious that they had not been mere tourists in the Soviet Union. In addition to his own enquiries, he obtained further information from the Swedish and American Military Attachés in Berlin, Major Berggren and Colonel Carpenter, both of whom were equally alarmed at the skilful deployment of the small, but potentially strong, German forces.

Inside Germany, efforts to maintain anger at the Treaty of Versailles were frequent among all the parties of the Centre and Right. A news item in *Die Deutsche Allgemeine* on March 3 was typical: a small, elderly and respectable looking man had entered the office of a government official who dealt with compensation. He drew a pistol, waved it at the official, and demanded to be given 112,000 marks for the farm that he had lost in the German Cameroons when the territory was taken by Britain after the war. The official refused, the elderly man fired his pistol, missed, and ran. He was soon caught. 'This pathetic episode,' a Jewish girl – now Silvia Rodgers – who was born that day in Berlin, has written, 'as well as making the headlines, was featured in a leader as yet more evidence of the desperation wrought on the German nation by the Treaty of Versailles.'

There were those in Britain who considered the Treaty of Versailles to be a blot on British policy and an unfair burden on Germany. For them, the efforts of German youth to renew the organizational efficiency and physical prowess that had marked the prewar years found echoes of support, even an ideological attraction. A young Englishman, Rolf Gardiner, expressed this feeling in book form in 1928. 'In a sense England is dying,' he wrote. 'Germany is the sole country where there is a positive challenge to the mechanism and commercialism which we associate with America, but which we in England take lying down.'

In China, the fighting between the Nationalists and their opponents during 1928 was overshadowed that April, when, in the northern province of Kansu, a revolt of the predominantly Muslim population threatened Chinese control. For eight months, the northern warlord, General Feng Yu-hsiang, battled with the insurgents. By the time he had suppressed the revolt, 200,000 Muslims had been killed. A revolt by Barga Mongols early in August, while the suppression of the Muslim revolt was still taking place, led to further slaughter.

Slowly, the Kuomintang was asserting its authority over a wider and wider area. As the head of the government established in Nanking, Chiang Kai-shek accepted the post of Generalissimo, but only, he said, for as long as Chang Tso-lin was still ruling in Peking. Chiang Kai-shek then set about securing the alliances of the two main independent warlords, General Feng Yu-hsiang, the ruler of Honan, who was in the course of suppressing the Muslim revolt, and General Li Chai-sum, the ruler of Canton.

Battle was resumed on a large scale, initiated by the Northern Army in the hope of defeating the southern coalition piecemeal. Then, as the ring of armies closed around him, Chang Tso-lin accepted that he must abandon Peking and withdraw to his military base and stronghold in Manchuria, where, with the support of the Japanese (which he had long enjoyed), he would be relatively secure.

On June 1, Chang Tso-lin gave a farewell reception to the foreign diplomats in Peking. They thanked him for having kept order in the city since the start of his dictatorship twelve months earlier. Two days later he left the capital by train, travelling northwards to Manchuria. As his train approached Mukden it was blown up by a bomb, and Chang was fatally injured.

The Kuomintang decided to transfer the capital to Nanking, their centre of power and administration. The name Peking (Northern Capital) was changed to Peiping (Northern Peace), innumerable civil servants working there were dismissed from their posts, and the government archives also transferred to Nanking.

As he had promised, Chiang Kai-shek set aside the title of Generalissimo. An economic conference of merchants and bankers was opened in Shanghai, China's largest commercial city, to advise the Nanking government on financial and economic questions. On October 3 a new constitution was promulgated in Nanking, with a State Council and five subordinate Councils for the executive, legislative, examination, judicial and supervisory functions (the Examination Council was charged with examining candidates for the civil service). Chiang Kai-shek was appointed President. By the end of the year, even Manchuria was under the control of the Nanking government, celebrating its union with the rest of China on December 31 by hoisting the Nationalist flag over the cities of Mukden, Harbin and Tsitsihar, and along its border with Japanese Korea.

China was effectively one country again, after more than a decade of fierce division and bloody struggles. As a first measure of national unity, the Nanking government announced that all 'unequal treaties' with foreign governments were abrogated, and that new ones, based on fairness and reciprocity, would be negotiated in their place. The next day, regulations were promulgated making all foreigners subject to Chinese laws and to the jurisdiction of Chinese courts.

The Danish representative in China was told that the Danish-Chinese Treaty of 1863 had expired. The Italian representative was told that the Italian-Chinese Treaty of 1866 was valid no more. France and Japan received similar communications. But just as the foreign beneficiaries of treaties signed in the previous century were becoming aggrieved to the point of wanting to take military action, the United States government announced its recognition of the Nanking government, and concluded a treaty with it, granting China complete tariff autonomy. This agreement was signed on July 25. The German government hastened to sign a similar agreement with China a few weeks later.

Suddenly the unanimity of anger of the foreign concession holders was broken. By the end of 1928 ten other nations had signed individual treaties with China, accepting that their former special status, a relic of the era of Great Power imperialism, could no longer be maintained. On December 20, the day on which the agreement with Britain was signed, the first British ambassador to the Nanking government presented his credentials. He did so in Nanking. The primacy of Peking was over. Chiang Kai-shek was the recognized ruler of China. Only Japan still fumed at having lost the special status which foreigners had come to prize, and to exploit, on the Chinese mainland. Japan refused to sign a new treaty. The loss of power of sympathetic warlords in Manchuria and Peking, as well as the demotion of Peking itself, was a blow to Japanese ambitions.

Everywhere in China the Kuomintang was in the ascendant. Having turned against the Chinese Communists a year earlier, the Kuomintang put the Communist power of organization to a severe test. From his base at Ningkang, on the River Chingkangshan, Mao Tse-tung had begun to direct a number of uprisings, calling on the peasants of the region 'to massacre the landlords'. Local Soviets were established in rural areas. In a move which paralleled the persecution of the Kulaks in Russia, Mao ordered the execution, not only of the more prosperous peasants, but of peasant landowners. It was the landless peasants, the poorest of the peasant class, who were to be the chosen ones of the new dispensation. Ironically, Mao's efforts were regarded as too moderate by the Communist Party authorities in Hunan. A Special Committee was despatched to Ningkang which, he later wrote, 'criticized us for having done too little burning and killing, and for having failed to carry out the so-called policy of "turning the petty bourgeoisie into proletarians and then forcing them into the revolution"'.

Ordered by his superiors to undertake a military expedition in southern Hunan, Mao and his forces did so, and were defeated. He was able, however, to recruit 8000 peasants into his militia, and, on returning to his base area on the Chingkangshan, to defeat a Kuomintang force which had overrun his base there in his absence. That summer he was made Secretary of a twenty-three-man Special Committee which was to supervize the military operations to which the party was now committed. Ten thousand more men, mostly poor peasants, were recruited. There were guns for only a third of them. The rest were mostly armed with long spears. It was not a cohesive force, and by the end of the year, more than two thousand of those who had been recruited by Mao in southern Hunan deserted, returning to their villages.

The Chinese Communist Party's Central Committee, located in Shanghai, had an exaggerated view of the strength and potential of the men under arms. Instructions sent to Mao at the end of June made it clear that the Party leaders believed the time had come to destroy forever the political and military power of the landlords, and to make plans for a Communist uprising throughout China. As a first step, the forces on the Chingkangshan were ordered to march south. Mao rejected this order and was removed as Secretary of the local Special Committee. Rather than believing in a seizure of power by force of arms, on the Leningrad or Moscow model of 1917, he considered revolutionary activity to be a long-term aspect of the Chinese Communist struggle. He believed it had to be conducted more on the lines of guerrilla warfare than through direct confrontations with the far superior military forces of the Kuomintang.

The main body of the forces hitherto under Mao's control were ordered south. He remained with a far smaller force, only 200 armed men, and was soon attacked by a substantial Kuomintang army. He resisted, using guerrilla tactics, for twenty-five days, after which his base was overrun. But he managed to get to southern Hunan, then to return to the Chingkangshan with a larger army, and to restore Communist control over the region. For this he was made Secretary of a five-man Front Committee, and pursued the policy he believed would alone lead to revolution. This was the slow education of the peasants, and the maintenance of a guerrilla movement that could be neither pinned down nor brought to battle by superior forces. But he was not optimistic about success, certainly not in the immediate or even medium future. 'Wherever the Red Army goes,' he wrote in November 1928, 'the masses are cold and aloof, and only after our propaganda did they slowly move into action.'

Mao had another disappointment: 'Whatever enemy units we face,' he wrote, 'there are hardly any cases of mutiny or desertion to our side, and we have to fight it out. We have an acute sense of our isolation, which we keep hoping will end.' His pessimism was almost total. 'This cannot be called an insurrection,' he explained, 'it is merely contending for the country. This method of contending for the country cannot succeed. The reason for all this is that there is absolutely no revolutionary high tide in the country as a whole.' There was worse to come. 'The vast forces of the oppressed classes have not yet been set in motion,' he wrote. 'So we are reduced to contending for the country in this cold atmosphere.' Mao's biographer Stuart Schram explains that the expression which the pessimistic revolutionary used for 'contending for the country' implied 'that one is seeking to conquer the country in an old-fashioned way, like the candidates for the imperial throne who set out in the past from a limited territorial base.'

An unusually severe winter added to the hardships facing the small and isolated Communist army, against which the Kuomintang, buoyed up by its victories elsewhere in China, launched yet another offensive. Mao had to leave his base and abandon the Chingkangshan. Hardly had he done so than the force was attacked at Tapoti on 14 January 1929, and lost half its fighting men. Mao was then forced to retreat to southern Kiangsi. With the remnants of other Communist forces joining him over the next few months, he could muster less than three thousand men. A rebuke from the Central Committee in Shanghai expressed its 'complete lack of confidence' in what he had done. He was ordered to withdraw from the army. He declined to do so. 'The more adverse the circumstances,' he replied to his distant, city-bound critics, 'the greater the need for concentrating our forces and for the leaders to be resolute in the struggle.'

In this firm, disobedient response lay the seed of the steady build-up of peasant power, the Long March, and the Chinese Communist revolution two decades later.

In India, a less violent but no less determined struggle was taking place between the British and the Indians. Although its aim was the political independence of India, it was fuelled by social hardship. In his report for the year 1927–8 the Director of Public Health in the province of Bengal, an Englishman, said that the peasants of the province were 'taking to a dietary on which even rats could not live for more than five weeks'. A British Trades Union Congress delegation that visited India in 1928 wrote in its report, with poetic power: 'In Assam tea, the sweat, hunger and despair of a million Indians enter year by year.'

The sciences of medicine and flight combined in 1928 with the foundation, in Australia, of the Aerial Medical Service (later the Flying Doctor Service). It was started by John Flynn, a Presbyterian Minister in Queensland, and the founder of his church's Australian Inland Mission. Making use of pedal-operated wireless transmitters, doctors in remote areas could summon a flying doctor, who could either administer medical help on the spot, or fly with the sick person to a hospital.

Another boost for medical science that year was the discovery of penicillin, by Alexander Fleming; but it was to take twelve years before his discovery would be turned into a medicine that could serve mankind.

CHAPTER THIRTY-THREE

1929

THE YEAR 1929 marked the tenth year of the existence of the League of Nations. It was also the year in which the Kellogg-Briand Pact, outlawing war, came into force. As if to underscore the importance of the pact, a new American President, Herbert C. Hoover, made it clear from the outset of his administration that he would look with favour upon a return of the United States to the European, and indeed global responsibilities, which it had set aside a decade earlier. Britain's new Labour government, under Ramsay MacDonald, was also pledged to a more active participation in the League, and to the main focus of the Geneva Protocol, disarmament.

Fifty-three States attended the tenth anniversary session of the League of Nations in Geneva in 1929. The United States, though not a member, participated actively in the work of the Preparatory Commission for the disarmament conference that was to seek a means of universal reduction of armaments. The United States also joined the Permanent Court that year, becoming an equal party to the settlement of all disputes between States that were capable of judicial resolution. That summer a comprehensive treaty, known as the General Act, came into force, for the peaceful settlement of all disputes between nations by conciliation. Under the General Act, the League States accepted the compulsory arbitration of the Permanent Court for all disputes where conciliation failed.

During 1929 the League also made progress on an idea put forward the previous year by the German Socialist Chancellor, Hermann Müller, and strongly supported by his British Socialist opposite number, Ramsay Mac-Donald. The idea was to create a Model Treaty, which would explicitly recognize the powers of the League Council when dealing with a dispute between two member states. Under the new treaty, it would be possible to send a commission of enquiry to the trouble spot, to request the withdrawal of troops on both sides of the frontier, and to enjoin 'peace-keeping' measures on both parties to the dispute. The final stage would be to secure a cessation of 'any movements of troops, measures of mobilization, or other acts calculated to exacerbate public opinion'.

As discussions continued on the exact wording of the Model Treaty, there was optimism in the corridors of the League that this represented yet another stage forward – the Geneva Protocol had been one stage, the Kellogg-Briand Pact another – in the central work which the League had been called into existence to secure, the prevention of future war. Disarmament, however, proved a much harder aspiration. When the detailed negotiations began in 1929, it became clear that the more heavily armed States were reluctant to reduce their arms, while those States that had been compulsorily disarmed ten years earlier were eager, in the first instance, to rearm. A series of formulae were proposed, whereby the strong would disarm in the same proportion as the weak would rearm.

The more that disarmament was discussed, the clearer it became that it was the detailed aspects of defence plans and concepts that could be obstacles to agreement. How large, for example, should reserve military forces be, and how much training could they undergo, once the regular armies were reduced? What form of international supervision would be adequate? How could the budgets and financial arrangements of member States be controlled, to prevent clandestine expenditure on arms (through apparently innocuous government departments which did not have the word 'war' or 'defence' in their title).

Trust was essential; but in the matter of national armaments, very basic concepts of national self-preservation were also involved. When, at the Preparatory Commission, various States asked for their objections not to be considered an obstacle to general agreement, and were conceded this right, Maxim Litvinov, the senior Soviet representative at the discussions (Russia, like the United States, was not a member of the League), interrupted the discussion to remark, in caustic tones, that 'one or two more' such concessions would 'make an end to the work of disarmament'.

During 1929 the League of Nations was forced to re-examine the policy of Mandates, which had been granted to various of the victorious Powers after the collapse of the German and Ottoman Empires in 1918. One of the main beneficiaries of the Mandate policy was Britain. But for more than a year the British Mandate authorities had been involved in a Jewish-Muslim dispute in Jerusalem, centering on the Western, or Wailing Wall, of the two-thousand-year-old Herodian Temple Mount. This wall, part of the original retaining wall of the Mount, was a Holy Place for the Jews. Towards the end of 1928, the Muslim authorities on the Mount – which is known to Islam as the Haram al-Sharif, or Holy Sanctuary, from which Mohammed ascended to heaven – sought to harass Jewish worshippers by opening a passageway from the Haram al-Sharif to the Wall.

Following Jewish protests, work on this passageway had been suspended by order of the British Mandatory authorities, but was later permitted by the Law Officers of the Crown in London, to whom the dispute had been submitted. On August 15 a group of young Jews and Jewesses, followers of the Zionist Revisionist leader, Zev Jabotinsky, marched to the Wall to protest at the London decision. Once there, they reiterated Jewish demands for ownership of the Wall, and swore an oath to defend it at all costs. On the following day, August 16, an Arab crowd reached the Wall, where by chance there were no Jewish worshippers at that time. The Arabs overturned a table and burned whatever religious books they could find. In the city of Jerusalem, a Jewish schoolboy was stabbed to death when he wandered by accident into a Muslim quarter.

On the following Friday, August 23, Arabs worshipping on the Mount at the al-Aksa mosque were incited to violence by a sermon warning of Jewish plots. As they left the Mount after prayers, their feelings inflamed by the political aspiration of the Mufti of Jerusalem, Haj Amin al-Husseini, they attacked, with knives and sticks, any Jews whom they could find. In the vicinity of Jerusalem, Arab villagers, many of whom had returned home after praying at the al-Aksa mosque and listening to the Mufti, attacked the Jewish villages nearest to them. The attacks quickly spread to several of the main cities in Britain's Palestine Mandate. In the southern city of Hebron, the site of the tombs of the Patriarchs – holy to both Jews and Muslims – fifty-nine Jews were murdered, and many others tortured or maimed. In the holy city of Safed, in the north, twenty Jews, mostly children and old people, were killed. It was a time of shock and fear for the Jews, and of humiliation for the British.

In all, 133 Jewish civilians were murdered in Arab attacks. The British Mandate authorities, who refused on the first night of these attacks to allow the Jews to set up armed units to protect Jewish settlements, intervened directly to prevent the Arab attacks continuing. In the process of defending Jewish homes, and driving off the Arab attackers, the British Mandate police killed 113 Arabs. Two British officials were also killed while trying to restrain the Arab attackers.

At the time of these riots there were 150,000 Jews in Palestine, of whom

100,000 had immigrated there since the establishment of the Mandate seven years earlier. The Arabs of Palestine numbered 590,000, some 100,000 of whom were also immigrants from other Arab lands, including Egypt, Syria and Saudi Arabia. Both before and after the killings, the Mufti of Jerusalem, Haj Amin al-Husseini, was strident in his call for an end to any further Jewish immigration. But the League of Nations, under its 1922 Mandate legislation, was committed to allowing Jews into Palestine, 'of right, and not on sufferance'. The Mufti also sought an end to British rule, and was supported in this by a growing body of Muslim Arab opinion. By its charter, however, the League of Nations was committed to the maintenance of British rule, and to allowing Britain, not the inhabitants (whether Jews or Arabs), to determine the nature of the administration.

In the wake of the disturbances and the deaths, the League of Nations had a constitutional part to play, asking its Permanent Mandates Commission, whose work had hitherto been somewhat bland, to hold a special session. The purpose was to hear a report on the causes of the violence in Palestine, and then to recommend measures to secure peace and order. The British government was not enamoured of this course. While administering Palestine according to the general guidelines of the League, it regarded itself as entirely competent, through two British officials, the Secretary of State for the Colonies (based in London) and the High Commissioner for Palestine (based in Jerusalem), to govern without instructions or advice from outside.

As a result of the 1929 riots, the Jews were forced to abandon seven of their settlements. The efforts that had been made among moderate Jews and Arabs in Palestine to seek common ground and to work together had suffered a severe setback. When some of the Arabs responsible for the riots were tried and imprisoned, the Arabs declared two one-day general strikes. November 2, the anniversary of the Balfour Declaration of 1917 in favour of a Jewish National Home in Palestine, was declared by the Arabs to be a day of mourning.

Amid these turmoils, the British Mandatory authorities got less credit – and gained less satisfaction – than it might otherwise have done from fighting another type of destruction on another front in Palestine. By its strenuous efforts at the beginning of the year, the Mandate authorities successfully combated a plague of locusts that had threatened to destroy the winter crops.

*   *   *

During the first four months of 1929 the British and French governments tried to find an acceptable figure for a final German reparations payment. Their efforts were made more difficult within Germany by the illness of Gustav Stresemann, and by the increasing political isolation of the Chancellor, Herman Müller. On March 11 the British Ambassador in Berlin, Sir Horace Rumbold, wrote to the Embassy's Financial Adviser that there was 'a hardening of opinion' in Berlin 'against the settlement of reparations on the basis of a large annuity'. Rumbold feared that if the British and French governments were to settle on the figure he had heard mentioned – 2 million marks – 'there may be a pretty good row over here leading perhaps to the holding of fresh elections'. In such an event, he warned, Alfred Hugenberg's German National People's Party, whose policy was to 'attack any proposal or any solution', might well win substantial support.

Despite efforts, much encouraged by Gustav Stresemann, to form a Grand Coalition of the moderate parties, there had been insufficient common ground between the Social Democrats and the German People's Party to being about a strong government of the centre. This meant that important legislation, particularly with regard to unemployment insurance, could not be put onto the statute book. Extremists on both sides of the political spectrum sought to take advantage of the government's weakness. During the May Day celebrations there were rallies in Berlin, led by the Communist fighting organization, the Red Front League. 'Huge crowds had gathered,' Silvia Rodgers was later told by her mother, a devoted Communist, 'but there were also huge numbers of police, and without warning they charged into the crowd with rubber truncheons, firearms, on horseback or in armoured cars. The workers erected barricades but the battle was uneven and many were wounded, some fatally.' Thirty-three people were killed in Berlin that day. The German government then banned the Red Front League throughout Germany. The activities of the right-wing *Stahlhelm* (Steel Helmet) ex-servicemen's organization were also declared illegal in several provinces.

Amid the continuing clashes of extremists on the right and left of the German political spectrum, the Nazi Party gained ground throughout 1929. A Party Congress, held at Nuremberg, and staged with spectacular use of swastika flags and banners, served as an emotional demonstration of loyalty to Hitler. For the first time, university graduates were admitted to Nazi Party bureaucracy, and repeated calls made to the middle classes to support the movement.

As unemployment rose in Germany, reaching three million, and affecting the middle classes as well as the working class, the Party took on a wider appeal. Small businessmen were suffering as much as the men and women on the factory floor. Hitler's repeated denunciation of Jewish 'big business' and Jewish 'wealth' found a resonance among those who were eager to find a scapegoat for their terrible misfortunes. At the same time, he made contact with wealthy German businessmen, and was able to present himself as a man who would bring order and discipline to Germany, protecting their investments.

In an attempt to win over the millions of army veterans, Hitler joined forces in 1929 with the most nationalist of all the veterans' associations, the *Stahlhelm*. With his twelve Reichstag seats, Hitler also joined forces with Hugenberg's nationalists, who had seventy-eight seats, to fight against the new United States formula for a less rigid scale of reparations. The call of the right was, 'No payments at all'. The 'shame' of Versailles had to be eliminated, not appeased. The Young Plan, they declared, like its predecessor the Dawes Plan, was a continuation of the Allied entrapment, impoverishment and humiliation of Germany. In Hitler's speeches, there was an added enemy, 'American Jewish bankers', who would profit massively, he declared, from Germany's sweat and toil.

In October, Hugenberg and Hitler presented a joint proposal to the German government, insisting on a referendum being held throughout Germany, to decide whether – as the nationalists wished – an official protest should be made by the German government against the 'war guilt' clause of the Treaty of Versailles. The referendum should also decide, as demanded by the combined Hitler–Hugenberg parliamentary forces, whether all German Ministers and civil servants who supported European 'understanding', the League of Nations, and the decisions of international conferences with regard to Germany, should be put on trial for high treason.

A few years earlier such a series of proposals would have been dismissed as beneath contempt. But Hugenberg and Hitler had, between them, 90 seats in the 491-member Reichstag, and were the masters and manipulators of a large segment of public opinion. The government, in rejecting the call for a referendum, therefore felt that it had to issue a public rebuttal of the demands. 'The whole demand for a referendum,' it announced, 'is built on a flagrant perversion of fact. It rests upon the crazy statement that German foreign policy so far has been based on an admission of Germany's war guilt, and that the German government has only to disavow the war guilt article of the Treaty of Versailles in order to free Germany from all burdens and chains.'

The government's rebuttal of the extreme nationalist demands continued: 'Germany has never admitted the sole guilt proclaimed in the Treaty of Versailles. Every German government has solemnly protested against this injustice. The belief in the fairy tale of the sole guilt of Germany is disappearing more and more.' The German people, the government declared, 'has now to choose between reason and madness'.

Hugenberg and Hitler were prepared to be denounced as mad; they both understood the appetite of many millions of people for a scapegoat, and for the reworking of a ten-year-old grievance. 'War guilt' was still a potent factor in rousing an audience to anger. The government's characterization of a war guilt referendum as 'madness' was itself a strong stimulant to further crowd and mob anger, if effectively exploited.

Despite the German government's opposition to a referendum, enough public signatures were secured – one tenth of those entitled to vote – to force a referendum. The total number of those voting was 21,000,000. Those who voted in favour of renouncing the war guilt clause totalled 5,800,000. While this was a long way from the 50 per cent needed to turn the referendum into law, it was an indication of enough hostility to the settled order to be exploited further by the Nazis for their political purposes.

During the municipal and provincial elections in Prussia, held while the 'war guilt' referendum campaign was in progress, Hitler declared that Nazism was directed, not against the Republic, but against Parliamentary democracy and Marxist socialism. In Thuringia, the first Nazi provincial government Minister was elected. By exploiting the fears of the German people, fears which he had nurtured so assiduously in his writings and speeches, Hitler gained a considerable number of local seats, and a new base of power and propaganda.

In February 1929, Trotsky, who had refused Stalin's demand to give up all political activity, was expelled from the Soviet Union. The founder of the Red Army, who twelve years earlier had returned to Russia from exile to lead the revolution, was an exile once more, the victim of the revolution he had worked so hard to establish. Trotsky went first to Turkey and then to Mexico, where he was murdered on Stalin's orders in 1940.

Throughout 1929 the instruments of Soviet terror continued to be wielded to great effect. A new atmosphere was being created in which the fear of being accused of anti-Soviet activity was as effective as the actual accusation.

The mere anticipation of a knock on the door by the members of the OGPU secret police was a powerful deterrent to criticism.

In May, amid public denunciations, three railway specialists – Meck, Velichko and Paltshinsk – were shot. The charge against them was sabotage. In October, several Red Army generals were executed on charges of having discussed a 'counter-revolutionary' plot. In the Caucasus, that same month, forty people, including several army officers, and several Kulaks, were executed for allegedly wanting to bring back the Tsar. Sabotage, anti-Communism, monarchism: every conceivable non-Communist activity, or expression of opinion – and in due course even alleged thought – was designated a crime, and punished with severity.

The forced collectivization of agriculture was not a part of the Communist creed, as envisaged by the founding fathers. Neither Marx, Engels nor Lenin had subscribed to it. The mass execution of Kulaks – the well-off and less well-off peasants who owned land, sometimes only small plots – was also not a part of that creed. During 1929 the last faint gasp of the Opposition was heard in protest against collectivization. Two professors, Slepkov and Aikhenwald, had the courage to publish a pamphlet criticizing Stalin's policy as not being in accordance with Marxist or Communist principles. The Party reacted at once, demanding, through the pages of *Pravda*, on November 15, that Bukharin and the other leaders of the Right Opposition should not only declare their support for Stalin's policy, but promise to abstain from any agitation against it, or they would face immediate expulsion from the Party.

Ten days later, Bukharin, Rykov and Tomsky recanted their criticism and swore eternal support for the leader and his policies. This undoubtedly saved their lives, or at least their membership of the Party, but within days of the recantation, Rykov was removed from the chairmanship of the Council of People's Commissars, and Bukharin was expelled from the Politburo for having 'slandered the Party with demagogic accusations'. The real demagogue, Stalin, found that accusations of demagogery levelled against others were a convenient and plausible stick with which to beat those who dared to suggest that he was the one who had exceeded his powers. Stalin may have lacked a slogan as crisp as the one favoured by Mussolini in Italy, 'Mussolini is always right', but a cult of Stalin was gaining ground. Poems in his honour, institutions bearing his name, and his portrait in public places, were joining Lenin as a regular feature of the Soviet scene.

The real thrust of Stalin's efforts at this time was to characterize the

Kulaks as an evil to be uprooted. 'Just as the Germans proclaimed that the Jews are not human,' the Soviet writer Vasily Grossman wrote in his book *Life and Fate*, 'thus did Lenin and Stalin proclaim, Kulaks are not human beings.' In fact, Lenin, for all his paranoia, cruelty and disregard for humanity, had worked to revive the agricultural independence of the peasant farmer. But Stalin was not averse to using Lenin's name in support of whatever course he chose to follow, including rural collectivization.

Grossman has left a powerful account of the demonization of the peasants (not unlike Hitler's demonization of the Jews). 'They had sold themselves on the idea that the so-called "Kulaks" were pariahs, untouchable, vermin,' Grossman recalled. 'They would not sit down at a "parasite" table; the "Kulak" child was loathsome, the young "Kulak" girl was lower than a louse. They looked on the so-called "Kulaks" as cattle, swine, loathsome, repulsive: they had no souls; they stank; they had all the venereal diseases; they were enemies of the people and exploited the labour of others. And there was no pity for them. They were not human beings, one had a hard time making out what they were – vermin evidently.'

The Russian novelist Vladimir Tendryakov described the Kulaks whom he saw in the town of Vokhrovo in northern Russia, near Vologda, where he was in exile:

> In the station square Ukrainian kulaks, expropriated and exiled from their homeland, lay down and died. One got used to seeing the dead there in the morning, and the hospital stable-boy Abram, would come along with his cart and pile the corpses in.
>
> Not everyone died. Many wandered along the dusty, sordid alleyways, dragging dropsied legs, elephantine and bloodlessly blue, and plucked at every passer-by, begging with dog-like eyes.
>
> In Vokhrovo they had no luck: the inhabitants themselves, to receive their ration, had to stand in the bread queue all night.

An official Soviet estimate of peasant deaths, in the Ukraine alone – published in Moscow in 1990, just before the disintegration of the Soviet Union – is about four million. The historian Robert Conquest put the number at about five million. The final, terrible extent of the deaths will probably never be exactly known, and could well be more.

By the end of 1929, Stalin had won his battle to root out the critics of collectivization. In the columns of *Izvestiya* he announced, on November 25, that the 'socialization of agriculture' would be continued 'at all costs' (and using, where possible, the latest tractors). A new Commissariat of Agriculture was appointed. The first Commissar, Yakov Yakovlev, was one of Stalin's most loyal supporters, endorsing with enthusiasm Stalin's statement that the object of collectivization was 'the liquidation of the Kulaks as a class', and setting a one-year target for the collectivization of those peasants who remained.

Slepkov and Aikhenwald, and several other leading economists who had criticized the collectivization of agriculture as destructive of the whole basis of agricultural life and production, were attacked in the newspapers as 'bourgeois-kulak ideologists', and removed from their teaching and advisory positions. A few years later, like so many of those in positions of authority who spoke out against Party policy, they were shot. Fifty years after their first – and as it turned out, fatal – protests, they were granted a posthumous pardon, or, in the deceptively normal-sounding language of the Soviet Union, 'rehabilitation'.

Yakovlev lost no time in fulfilling Stalin's wishes. More than fifteen million peasants were taken from their individual farms and smallholdings and forced into State farms. Rather than let their cattle fall into the hands of the State, many of these peasants, before being deported, slaughtered them. As much as half the country's herd was destroyed. The so-called 'rich' peasants, the hated and denounced Kulaks, were deported, not to State farms, but to vast labour camp zones above the Arctic Circle, in North Russia and across Siberia. An estimated 15–20 per cent of the deportees – mostly the women, children and old people – died in the cattle trucks and on the forced marches to their new 'homes'. The survivors were told that they must build their own huts and grow their own food.

Religion was also under continued attack in Stalin's Russia during 1929. On May 22, the Soviet constitution was amended, to make any 'religious' propaganda illegal, and to stress the legality of 'anti-religious' propaganda. Churches, mosques and synagogues were closed down throughout the Soviet Union, and turned into youth clubs, cinemas, or government and Party offices. Thousands of imams, priests and rabbis were imprisoned. Hundreds of monasteries and cathedrals, many of them the priceless architectural and historical treasures of medieval Russia, were pulled down.[1]

[1] In January 1996, in Moscow, even close to midnight, the main Moscow cathedral which Stalin had demolished (and which was replaced after many years by a municipal swimming pool) was being rebuilt – under floodlight – by an energetic team of construction workers.

Stalin also led a campaign against all Russian literature that might question or mock the Soviet system. Two Russian authors were particularly under attack that year, Boris Pilnyak, President of the All-Russian Union of Writers, the author of *Red Mahogany*; and Yevgeny Zamyatin, author of *We*. Both books had been published abroad in Russian, Zamyatin's in Prague, Pilnyak's in Berlin. Zamyatin's theme was that a perfectly planned State would lead to a sterile society. Pilnyak wrote of the collapse of the revolutionary ideals. Both books were banned in the Soviet Union. Pilnyak was removed from his prestigious post. Writers were warned that henceforth they must only publish, even outside Russia, books that had the Party's approval; this rule was formalized three years later.

In the Kingdom of the Serbs, Croats and Slovenes (as Yugoslavia was then officially known), the struggle between Serbs and Croats, which the unity of the country in 1918 was intended to resolve, had intensified. The Croats, the second largest group in the State, had been boycotting the Belgrade parliament (the Skupshtina) since June 1928, after their leader, Stephen Radic, had been fatally wounded on the floor of the House. They were refusing to return to the parliament building unless the country was reorganized on a federal basis, with Croatia accorded complete legislative and administrative autonomy. The least that more moderate Croats were willing to consider was for Croatia to have the same powers that were then enjoyed by the individual States of the United States.

King Alexander could see no way out of the accelerating disintegration of his kingdom but to establish military rule. When the coalition government of Serbs and Slovenes (led by the Slovene leader, Father Korosec) resigned at the very end of 1928, the King decided to take action. On the night of 5–6 January 1929 a proclamation was posted on the walls of Belgrade, signed by Alexander, stating that 'the hour has come when there can no longer be any intermediary between the King and his people. Parliamentary life has always been my ideal, but blind political passions have made it an obstacle. The confidence of the nation in the Skupshtina has been undermined. I have therefore determined that the constitution of the Kingdom of Serbs, Croats and Slovenes, of June 28, 1921, is no longer in force.'

Alexander appointed General Petar Zhivkovic, the commander of the royal bodyguard, to be Prime Minister. A Cabinet was appointed made up mostly of Serbs. The few Croats who were invited to join it were not politicians, but specialists in the field of the ministry concerned, without political experience. The King had become Dictator, and hastened to establish the apparatus of dictatorship. Freedom of the Press was abolished. The death penalty was instituted for any person working to overthrow the new regime, or taking part in, or making contact with any person or organization working to overthrow the new regime.

The very name of the State – the Kingdom of Serbs, Croats and Slovenes – was abolished. In its place came the new name by which the country was henceforth to be known (until its disintegration in the 1990s): Yugoslavia. The long-recognized borders of Serbia, Croatia and Slovenia were declared irrelevant, and new borders were established for nine specially designated regions (*Banovine*) through which the country would be governed on non-racial, non-national, grounds. The borders and the names of these new regions were determined by geographical names; most of them were named after the principal rivers (the Danube, Sava, Drina, Vardar and Morava) in order to counter local patriotism, and to promote, if that were possible, a single Yugoslav national sentiment.

The governors of each Banat were to be appointed by the King. The individual Croat, Slovene and Serb youth associations, the Sokols, which in Croatia had been a focal point of Croat national identity, were dissolved, and a single Yugoslav Sokol established. The Croat Sokol, angered at this loss of its base of influence and authority, where the Croat spirit was nurtured among the young, declared itself dissolved but refused to join the Yugoslav association.

Terrorism erupted against, but did not break, the grip of the dictatorship. Toni Schlegel, a leading Croat politician and editor, who had become a confidant of the king and a supporter of the dictatorship, was assassinated by a fellow Croat, indignant that Schlegel had accepted an official position in Belgrade. Arrests of Croat dissidents were frequent; but the newspapers were forbidden to refer to the arrests. The Croat Communist Party, which had been slowly gaining adherents since 1920, was rooted out, and its leaders, including Josip Broz, were imprisoned.

Several leading Croats fled abroad, joining a growing Croat national exile movement. One of those who fled, Dr Ante Pavelić, a leading advocate of a federal system in which Croatia would be virtually independent, went to Bulgaria, where he called for all Macedonians and Croats to make common cause against the Serbs. A Belgrade court sentenced him to death in absentia.

In the Second World War, Pavelić ruled the Independent State of Croatia, Fascist in doctrine, subservient to Mussolini politically, and brutal in the extreme towards Serbs and Jews.

On King Alexander's birthday (December 19) bombs were exploded in Zagreb. A Zagreb clergyman, Dr Rittig, who had agreed to lead a deputation of Croats to Belgrade, to demonstrate their loyalty to the King, was beaten up in the street, after which two bombs were placed on the rails on which the deputation's train was to pass – neither bomb exploded.

In India, fighting between Hindus and Muslims had continued. In February, during Hindu-Muslim riots in Bombay, 116 people were killed, and in May a further fourteen. There were also several outbreaks of Communist violence culminating in a bomb being thrown in the predominantly Indian Legislative Assembly in Delhi. Several members of the Assembly were wounded, but none fatally.

The treatment in prison of political offenders was also a contentious issue that year. Throughout India there were hunger strikes among political prisoners, culminating in the death in prison, after a hunger strike of sixty-one days, of Jatindranath Das, one of a number of Indians accused of armed conspiracy against the government. In moral support of Das, two Indian members of the Punjab Legislative Council resigned.

As a result of the uproar that had been caused by Kathleen Mayo's exposure of child marriage in her book *Mother India*, the Government of India had established an Age of Consent Committee, under the chairmanship of a distinguished Indian lawyer and civil servant, Sir Moropant Joshi. As a result of the committee's enquiries, and its report, a Child Marriage Bill was voted through that year, making fourteen the minimum age for marriage, and sixteen for the first sexual intercourse after marriage. One result of the Bill, in the short period before it became law, was a rush of marriages of girls under fourteen throughout India.

The future of British rule was about to be decided, as the work of the Commission headed by Sir John Simon on the constitutional future of India was coming to an end. But before Simon could issue his report, the Labour Prime Minister, Ramsay MacDonald, anxious to mollify Indian nationalist opinion, announced that Britain would grant India eventual self-government. Under the title Dominion Status, the inhabitants of the subcontinent would receive the same degree of independence as the inhabitants of Canada, Australia and New Zealand. They would govern their own lives, with only the broadest defence and foreign affairs considerations being retained by British officials.

The British Conservative Party accepted this Labour initiative, and, despite a hard core of dissent in Conservative ranks – led for the next five years by Churchill – worked with Labour to make the policy that of the whole British Parliament rather than of a single party. The turning point came on October 31, when the Viceroy, Lord Irwin, himself a leading figure in the Conservative Party, announced that the 'natural issue' of India's constitutional progress was 'the attainment of Dominion Status'. This had been foreshadowed, Irwin said, by a British Government pledge in the preamble to the Government of India Act of 1919, that British policy towards India was the 'progressive realization of responsible government'. It was 'important to make clear to India', Lord Irwin wrote to a friend a week after his declaration was issued, 'that the ultimate purpose for her is not one of perpetual subordination in a white Empire'.

On the morning of December 23, less than two months after Irwin's public declaration in favour of Dominion Status for India, an attempt was made by Indian nationalist extremists to kill him. As his train was entering Delhi – where he was to take up residence in the newly completed, and magnificent, Government House – a bomb placed on the tracks exploded a few seconds after the Viceregal carriage had passed over the spot. That afternoon, shaken but unharmed, Irwin received a delegation of leading members of the Indian National Congress, led by Mahatma Gandhi.

After expressing the delegation's concern at the assassination attempt, Gandhi went on to tell Irwin that the British promise of eventual Dominion Status was not enough; it must be immediate Dominion Status. As to the retention of defence policy in the hands of a British Viceroy, this too, the Congress leaders insisted, must not be allowed to stand. It was the Indians of India, not the British Parliament or its representatives, who must decide the country's defence policy. Indians were as capable of defending India from outside attack as Britain.

Before the delegation withdrew, Gandhi told Irwin that he and his colleagues were doubtful that even the Labour government, let alone the Conservative opposition, was sincere when it said that it would agree to eventual Dominion Status. Six days later, on December 29, at a full session of the All-India Congress in Lahore, anger was expressed at the idea of any delay at all in implementing the British government's pledge. 'Eventual' Dominion

Status was seen – wrongly – as having been offered by the British government as a temporary sop to nationalist sentiment, and was denounced as a promise that would not be fulfilled.

Congress then elected as its President a forty-year-old Indian lawyer, Jawaharlal Nehru, who had been educated at Harrow School in London; the schoolboy who had been on the side of the Boers. In a speech which confirmed his reputation as a brilliant and persuasive orator, Nehru declared himself to be a Socialist Republican, and pledged to work untiringly for an end to every facet of British rule. Nehru then urged all Congress members who were serving in either the Central or Provincial legislatures – the highest administrative posts open to Indians – to resign their seats. He asked them to give up cooperating with the British, and to join Congress in an all-India campaign of civil disobedience, 'including non-payment of taxes'.

There were many in the Congress Party who did not like the rejection of Dominion Status, but in a series of ballots during the three-day session they were outvoted. It was very close. A call to reject the boycott of the legislature was voted down by the relatively narrow margin of 919 votes to 769. But the Gandhi–Nehru faction held the day. They also had to deal, during their deliberations, with an angry march of 10,000 Akali Sikhs – militants led by Sirdar Kahark Singh, who had brought his followers into Lahore to protest at what they feared would be discrimination by Congress of their communal needs. Gandhi, in secret talks with the Sirdar, persuaded him that there would be no discrimination against the Sikhs when full independence was secured. As a result of this assurance, the Sirdar advised his followers to work alongside Congress in the struggle against the British for Indian independence.

At midnight on December 31, on the banks of the Ravi River, watched by a gathering of more than 1700 members of Congress, Nehru hoisted the banner of full independence atop a tall flagpole. Dominion Status had been dramatically and demonstrably rejected, whether it was to be offered then or later. Indian nationalism had moved from the phase of accommodation with British rule, to the phase of total rejection of the continuation of British India.

In the United States, an unprecedented boom had raised stock prices to their highest point ever, reducing memories of the stock market crash of 1921–2 to a bad episode that was well and truly in the past. But ominous signs were increasing during the autumn, as the prices of basic commodities began to fall, including those of timber, caused largely by the reappearance on the world market of Russia as a serious competitor, able to undercut prices. Among the countries hardest hit by the timber price collapse were Russia's neighbour Finland, Czechoslovakia and Canada. Excessive sheep farming in Australia was leading to a collapse in the price of wool. Over-production, as well as the fall in individual purchasing power, was threatening a worldwide economic crisis. At the beginning of October there was a sudden fall in the price of wheat. This affected not only the American farmers, but farmers in Canada and Australia.

Despite these ominous signs, the United States, with its vast resources of raw materials, did not seem vulnerable to economic disaster. On October 23, large-scale selling of shares took place on the New York stock market, and shares fell back to their 1927 level. President Hoover immediately took the unusual step of issuing a reassuring statement – made public on October 24 – pointing out that the 'fundamentals' of American prosperity were sound, and that the United States was 'more prosperous and more industrious than ever before'.

Hoover's reassurance came too late. On the day that it was issued, Thursday 24 October 1929 – 'Black Thursday – the New York stock market collapsed. Even those who had bought shares, not as a speculation, but as part of savings portfolios, found that the value of their funds had dropped to a third, and even to a quarter, of their value the day before. On September 3 the average price of the thirty leading American industrial shares had stood at $380. By the close of trading on October 24 it stood at $230, a loss of $150. That night, a leading American financier, dining with some of his close associates, addressed them laconically as 'Friends and *former* millionaires'.

At first, it seemed that only the rich owners of stocks would suffer – wealthy men who had been made even more wealthy by stock-market trading and speculation. But when the scale of private investment became known, it was clear, from one New York brokerage house alone, that three million families were involved in its market operations, and in the resultant loss.

A second downward lurch of the stock market on November 19, when the price of the thirty leading industrial shares fell further, to $198, accelerated the distress of millions of Americans across the country. Everyone who had set aside some savings, including the most prudent, suffered. The national income fell, to be halved within three years. Foreign trade could not be sustained. One of the first markets overseas to fall, as a result of the destruction of American purchasing power, was the diamond market in Amsterdam. Inside the United States, shopkeepers who feared that the Christmas trade would be adversely affected, cancelled their orders, thereby further weakening the manufacturing and trading base. The motorcar manufacturing centres of Michigan were badly hit.

President Hoover made every effort to calm the public and to restore some kind of confidence. At a series of conferences in the White House at the end of October, with leading bankers and industrialists, he discussed how to cushion the fall in manufacturing and halt the slide to widespread unemployment. The railway companies promised him that they would not reduce wages, and would continue, and even increase, their equipment and renewal plans. The leaders of the electricity and power industries promised to increase their construction budgets for the following year by 8 per cent. In a meeting with State Governors, Hoover secured a promise that the State expenditure on highways would be raised 'to the utmost'. Congress agreed to almost double the amount of Federal aid for the road-construction programme. Public projects, Hoover argued, should be 'pushed their hardest' during a time of threatened depression. But as the year drew to a close, the prognosis was not good. As many as eight million of the work force – some 8 per cent – were out of work.

A dangerous turning point had been reached in the leadership of the United States in the economic counsels of the world, and in its own internal ability to survive.

In the year in which the Kellogg-Briand pact outlawed war, a novel was published which was to make a great impact on antiwar feeling, *All Quiet on the Western Front*. The book's author, Erich Maria Remarque, a German Catholic, had been sent to the Western Front in 1917, ten days before his nineteenth birthday, and was wounded by a British shell during the Third Battle of Ypres, which began six weeks after he reached the front. That battle was the extent of his frontline service, but his novel, a work of powerful imagination, drew on sufficient personal experiences to make it a searing account of life and death in the trenches. 'This book', he wrote on the title page, 'is to be neither an accusation nor a confession, and least of all an adventure, for death is not an adventure to those who stand face to face with it. It will try simply to tell of a generation of men who, even though they may have escaped its shells, were destroyed by the war.'

The French-language edition of *All Quiet on the Western Front*, published in Paris in June 1929, sold 72,000 copies in ten days, and almost 450,000 copies by Christmas. It was praised by one French literary critic as 'a sort of plebiscite in favour of peace. Every volume bought is equivalent to a vote'. Remarque's impact was not forgiven by the Nazis, who were seeking to inculcate a war spirit in German youth. *All Quiet on the Western Front* was to be burned in the bonfire of 'degenerate' books in 1933 as being the 'betrayal of the German frontline soldier'. Remarque became a refugee, settling in the United States. His sister Elfriede was executed by the Nazis.

At the time of the publication of *All Quiet on the Western Front*, the German army was being steadily built up by devoted army officers, headed by General von Seekt, who were confident that one day the restrictions imposed by the Treaty of Versailles would be thrown off. Among those who saw the new German army in preparation was the veteran Spanish officer, General Franco, who in the spring of 1929 was a guest of the German Infantry Academy in Dresden. The organization and discipline of the troops he saw in training made a strong impression on him.

In 1929 the United States was again in the forefront of nature conservation. A Migratory Bird Conservation Act that year gave federal powers and funds to establish refuges for migrating birds across the United States. Also in the United States that year, the Kodak Company developed a 16-millimetre colour film, which was to revolutionize photography. On an even more domestic front, the firm of Tootal discovered a crease-resisting cotton fabric.

Amid the crash of banks and the collapse of economies, the world of the arts flourished. Not only were the first 'Oscars' presented that year, for outstanding motion pictures, but the first all-black feature film, King Vidor's *Hallelujah*, was released. Two important pieces of sculpture, Henry Moore's *Mask* and Picasso's *Woman in a Garden*, were completed. Picasso also painted *Nude in an Armchair*. In London, the playwright Sir James Barrie donated the rights of Peter Pan to the Great Ormond Street Hospital for Sick Children. Among war books, of which many hundreds were being published every year, as well as Remarque's *All Quiet on the Western Front*, Ernest Hemingway published *A Farewell to Arms* and Robert Graves *Goodbye To All That*.

Colour television was demonstrated in the United States that year at the Bell Laboratories. A new toy was also patented in 1929, the 'yoyo'. Among the songs that had their debut was 'Happy Days Are Here Again.'

CHAPTER THIRTY-FOUR

1930

As the twentieth century entered its fourth decade, violence remained a feature of the lives of millions of people in many States. The year opened with an attack by Hitler's Brownshirts on Jewish civilians in Berlin in which eight Jews were killed. They were the first Jewish victims that year of a growing campaign of spasmodic, and, within a decade, systematic killing. Throughout 1930 the Brownshirts attacked with fists and truncheons Jews who were sitting in cafés and theatres, and interrupted synagogue services with sudden incursions, beatings and derision.

In British India, a different sort of violence was becoming more and more frequent. On January 23 the Bengali nationalist leader, Subash Chandra Bose – who in 1943 was to join the Japanese in military action against the British – was sentenced to a year in prison for leading a demonstration through the streets of Calcutta under the banners 'Long Live Revolution' and 'Up with the Republic'. Three days later, on what the Indian National Congress had declared Independence Day, four Indian children were wounded by a bomb that had been placed in a school to kill a British official: the official had left the building by a door other than the one he had been expected to use.

On January 30, Gandhi offered to call off civil disobedience in return for a series of concessions by the Government of India. These included the halving of Indian military expenditure, a general amnesty for political prisoners, the reservation of coastal shipping for Indian enterprise, a free licence for firearms, and an end to the government salt monopoly. When his demands were rejected, he embarked, on March 12, on a protest march from Ahmedabad to the Indian Ocean. Reaching the sea on April 6, after a short swim, Gandhi scooped up of a handful of sand and salt water: a deliberately public and illegal act, as only the Government of India could license the gathering of salt. That same day he declared the start of a Week of Civil Disobedience.

The salt march started what one commentator called 'a tide of angry feeling' throughout India. On April 23, supporters of the Indian National Congress clashed with British and Indian troops in the city of Peshawar. A British soldier, Private Bryant, who was riding a motorcycle in front of an armoured car, was seized by the mob and hacked to death with a hatchet. Two other soldiers were burnt to death when petrol was poured over their armoured car and ignited. Several hundred European women and children living in the city were at once evacuated. Imperial rule, even when it embarked on a programme of eventual self-government for its subject peoples, was unable to relinquish its firm attitude to law and order. The loyalty of the Indian troops was uncertain. During the attempt to suppress the riots in Peshawar, one battalion of Indian troops was withdrawn, owing to the 'unsatisfactory conduct' of two of its platoons, which had refused to return to the scene of the confrontation when ordered to do so.

On May 5, Gandhi was arrested and, wearing only a loin cloth, his accustomed garb, was taken to prison in Poona. On arrival in prison, the ever-courteous leader thanked the British authorities for the arrangements they had made for his 'comfort' on the journey. For their part, the authorities issued the following statement to explain their action in making the arrest:

> The Bombay government have, ever since Mr Gandhi left his *Ashram* at Ahmedabad, pursued a policy of the utmost toleration. They have been content to risk the accusation of weakness in the firm conviction that the attack on the Salt Laws, if violence were excluded from the methods by which it was conducted, must before long come to a peaceful ending.
>
> Events have shown that Nature's laws are inexorable, and that the history of the earlier non-cooperation movements, with its accompaniments of blood and fire, would repeat itself if Mr Gandhi's campaign were allowed to continue unchecked.
>
> In these circumstances the Bombay Government concluded it was no longer possible to allow Mr Gandhi to remain at large without danger to India's tranquillity.

Riots spread rapidly throughout India. On May 8, at Sholapur, in the Bombay presidency in which Gandhi had been arrested, a large crowd attacked the police station, and several policemen were killed. Within three days, as rioting continued and several public buildings were destroyed, a police force reduced to eighty men was trying, in vain, to restrain a mob of 10,000. On May 13 martial law was proclaimed, and troops sent to the city.

That month the President of the Legislative Assembly, V. P. Patel, resigned. The British had placed high hopes on his presidency, and in the assembly; here were Indians serving at the centre of the legislative process, their highest position within the governing hierarchy. In resigning, Patel stated unequivocally that, even while he had occupied the chair of the assembly, he was in complete sympathy with 'every movement designed to create a condition which might make it difficult, if not impossible, for the British rulers to carry on in the country'.

V. P. Patel's resignation, and his words of defiance, angered the Viceroy and encouraged the nationalists, just as Gandhi's defiance had done. Patel was later sentenced to six months in prison for 'breaches of the law'. When new elections were called for the Legislative Assembly, they were boycotted by the Congress Party. On election day, Congress volunteers, including many educated women, picketed the polling booths to prevent people from voting.

Terrorist activity in India during 1930 focused on attacks against senior police officers and other officers of the law. These attacks included the attempted murder of the Calcutta Commissioner of Police, Sir Charles Tegart, on August 26, and the murder three days later in Dacca of the Inspector-General of Police, F. J. Lowman. In a raid in December on the Secretariat of the Government of Bengal, three Bengalis, armed with revolvers, shot dead the Inspector-General of Prisons, Lieutenant-Colonel N. S. Simpson. But the Government of India persevered in its attempts to return to the path of negotiations and the road to Dominion Status. In November, a Round Table Conference was opened in London. Those Congress leaders who were in prison at that time, among them Gandhi and Nehru, were allowed to meet and consult together. To this end, Nehru was taken under guard to see Gandhi in Poona jail.

The Round Table Conference continued to meet through the winter. It closed with the acceptance by Britain that Indians would be responsible for their own government both at the Legislative and Provincial level, with guarantees to protect the political liberties and rights of minorities, including the Indian Christians and the Untouchables, and with Britain in charge of foreign affairs and defence. On condition that Gandhi, Nehru, Patel, and other leaders were released from jail, Congress agreed to discuss these proposals, and set up a Working Committee to be its link with the Government of India. All was set to turn from civil disobedience to constitutional change; from revolution to reform.

*   *   *

Following the disturbances in Palestine in the previous year, a special session of the Mandates Commission of the League of Nations was held in Geneva in 1930 to review the Mandate. Without supporting the rival claims of Jews or Arabs, the Commission was critical of Britain, as the Mandatory Power. The Commission blamed the Mandatory government for not having pursued a more active policy for the development of the Mandate in the interests 'of all its inhabitants', implying that while the Jews had been motivated by Zionism to extend their landholdings and cultivation, the Arabs required the initiative of a well-disposed government in order to do so. The Mandatory authority was also criticized for not having done more to encourage cooperation between Jews and Arabs. While a British government enquiry had come to the conclusion that the attacks on Jews had been premeditated, the Mandates Commission disagreed. There was resentment in Britain at these criticisms, not least because the British taxpayer was having to pay for the growing cost of policing Palestine.

The Mandates Commission urged Britain to find a means, and a machinery, whereby the interests of the Arab population of Palestine could be safeguarded. It also stressed that, according to the interpretation of the Mandate, the obligations laid down in regard to the Jews and the Arabs 'are of equal weight'. For the Zionists, this was an ominous conclusion; as they had understood it, basing themselves on the Balfour Declaration, the prime responsibility of Britain, and hence of the Mandatory government, was to facilitate the creation of a Jewish National Home in Palestine.

That National Home was in considerable economic difficulties. The stock market crash in the United States in 1929 had lessened the amount of money being donated by American Jews – the well off and the less well off – to agricultural and social development in the Jewish towns and villages of Palestine. A plague of fieldmice in the Jezreel Valley that year destroyed much of the harvest. For the first time since the beginning of the Mandate, the number of Jews leaving the country, having tried to make a living there, exceeded the numbers coming in. For those Palestinian Jews whose hope of statehood depended upon the Jews becoming, in due course, a majority, such a 'negative' immigration rate was disastrous.

At the start of 1930, the number of unemployed in Germany reached 2.5 million. In the Reichstag, Hugenberg's German National People's Party was demanding a revision of the Polish frontier in Germany's favour; nor was this merely an extremist position. 'I have not met a single German of any authority,' the British Ambassador reported to London that February, 'who is content to accept Germany's eastern frontier as definitive.' The ambassador had other ominous news from the perspective of the Allied signatories of the Versailles Treaty. The British Air Attaché in Berlin, Group Captain Malcolm Christie, a First World War pilot, reported that the Junkers aircraft factory, which was strictly forbidden to manufacture warplanes, was offering aircraft to foreign governments 'which are readily convertible into military machines'.

In the German Reichstag, Hermann Müller's government continued to pursue a policy of conciliation with the former Allied Powers, and of fulfilment of the terms of the Versailles Treaty; terms that, in their economic aspect, had become much less onerous. On March 12 the Reichstag ratified the Hague Agreements – the last international arrangement negotiated by Stresemann before his death the previous October – whereby the 'Occupying Powers' (Britain, France and Belgium) agreed to withdraw their troops from German soil, in return for Germany's acceptance of a fixed and final reparations figure. This new reparations figure had been substantially scaled down from the original demands of a decade earlier.

This was a signal achievement for Müller, and for the predominantly Social Democrat government. Hugenberg's Nationalists and Hitler's National Socialists were vehement, however, in denouncing the fact that any reparations were still to be paid at all. They were particularly indignant, and viciously critical of the fact, that Müller had been one of the German signatories of the Treaty of Versailles (its principal German signatory, Matthias Erzberger, had been assassinated many years earlier). Even Dr Brüning, the leader of the Catholic Centre Party, which was a part of Müller's coalition, and its second largest component, denounced the Hague Agreements (also known as the Young Plan) as 'no contract between equal parties; it is a unilateral *Diktat*, and it is to this *Diktat* that we now bow'.

The Hague Agreements were passed, but the political crisis which they stirred continued for two weeks, with the Centre Party dissociating itself from the coalition. On March 27, Müller resigned. Three days later, Brüning formed a government. The days of the Social Democrat predominance were over. As before 1914, so likewise after 1918, the Social Democrat Party was unable to push its reforming policies past the barrier of German nationalism.

Brüning ruled without the help of the nationalist parties. But their activities, particularly those of the Nazi Party, were gaining in strength and disruptiveness. By the spring of 1930, Nazi Party membership had reached half a million. A senior German army officer, Colonel Erich Kühlenthal, who had served throughout the First World War, and was from 1928 to 1931 the Head of the Intelligence Department of the German General Staff, spoke of the dangers of the current political situation in a confidential talk with the British Military Attaché, Colonel Marshall-Cornwall. 'The National Socialist movement is a real danger,' Kühlenthal warned, 'and far more of a menace to the present constitution than is Communism. The trouble about the "Brown Shirts" is that their principles and theories are entirely destructive. They wish to destroy the present fabric of the State, but have no constructive programme with which to replace it, except a form of mad-dog dictatorship.'

Colonel Kühlenthal pointed out that the 'general discontent' against the previous, Müller, government, had 'turned the heads of a number of young officers towards the National Socialist movement as a means of escape from Germany's financial and political troubles.' Another 'serious feature' of the Nazi movement, the Colonel confided to his British listener, was 'the ascendancy which its leader, Adolf Hitler, has the power of exerting. He is a marvellous orator, and possesses an extraordinary gift for hypnotizing the audience and gaining adherents. Even though his policy is a negative one, his personal magnetism is such as to win over quite reasonable people to his standard, and it is this which constitutes the chief danger of the movement.'

Hitler still had only twelve seats in the Reichstag, a fact which lulled his parliamentary opponents, whose battles were those of votes and alignments inside the Chamber. But in due course a general election would have to be held, and it was clear to all observers that the Nazi Party would then much improve its parliamentary position.

That summer, the number of unemployed in Germany rose above three million. Nazi Party membership also rose, and dramatically so, from half a million to almost two million. When, at the beginning of July, the last Allied troops marched out of the Rhineland, there were bonfires, bell-ringing and torchlight processions in Berlin. But there was no praise for Britain and France; instead, the eighty-two-year-old President, Paul Hindenburg, issued a manifesto, co-signed by Brüning and all his Cabinet, pointing out that although the Rhineland was now freed from foreign troops, 'our brothers in the Saar still await the day of their return to the mother country'.

The British Ambassador was not amused. 'It is an unattractive feature of the German character to display little gratitude for favours received,' he wrote from Berlin to the Foreign Office in London, 'but when the receipt of favours is followed up by fresh demands, there are grounds for feeling impatient.' That same day, Stresemann's successor as German Foreign Minister, Dr Julius Curtius, explained to the ambassador that, for the German people, the Rhineland evacuation was 'long overdue', and that while the Saar question remained unresolved there was 'little cause' for German rejoicing. Dr Curtius added that Germany 'could not rest content with her present frontier in the East'.

In London, a diplomat of nearly thirty years' experience, Sir Robert Vansittart, set out in a confidential memorandum what he saw as the future steps of German foreign policy: these were the acquisition of colonies, union with Austria, rearmament, and a 'drastic modification' of the German-Polish frontier. Each of these demands, Vansittart believed, was inevitable; the fact that each was forbidden by the Treaty of Versailles would be irrelevant.

Brüning was unable, despite the ability of his Centre Party to build a parliamentary coalition, to pass the government's budgets. His two main objectives were to cut government expenditure as a measure of economy, and to raise taxes for the government's spending needs in the immediate present. In order to secure the budgetary measures that he believed essential, Brüning resorted to a measure that had never been used before by the Republic; emergency legislation that suspended the powers of parliament. The means whereby he did this were embedded in the Constitution of 1920: paragraph 48 of the Constitution stated, without equivocation, that 'in cases where public security and order are seriously disturbed or threatened in the German Reich, the President of the Reich is empowered to take the measures necessary for restoring public security and order'.

This Enabling Act, as it was known, was promulgated by Brüning on July 17. It was the first suspension of the rule of parliament since the creation of the German Republic more than a decade earlier. When the Reichstag met the following day, and passed a resolution, introduced by the Social Democrats, calling for the cancellation of the Enabling Act, Brüning dissolved the Reichstag.

For three months, Brüning ruled by emergency decree. Then, in the hope that a new Reichstag which he would be able to control more effectively could be elected, he called a general election. Twenty-four parties presented themselves to the electorate. The Nazi Party was one of them, with its puny base of twelve members of parliament. But it had high expectations of being able to exploit the divisions in German society, and the fragmentation of the forces of the Right. Among those who had broken away from Hugenberg's German National People's Party was Hugenberg's predecessor as the party's leader, Count Westarp. Hitler was determined to exploit this split.

The strength of nationalism was everywhere in evidence. On August 10 the leader of the People's Conservative Party, Dr Gottfried Treviranus, a member of Brüning's Cabinet, told a large crowd gathered outside the Reichstag building that the evacuation of the Rhineland was but the 'first step' on the road to Germany's true independence. 'Now,' he declared, 'the east demands the unification of all German people. In the depths of our souls we are thinking of the Vistula lands, of the unhealed wounds in the eastern flank – that withered lung of the Reich. We think of the iniquitous insistence of Wilson on the unnatural cutting off of East Prussia and of the half-breed condition to which Danzig was condemned.'

In defending his speech two days later, Treviranus spoke of Germany's 'national will to live', which could not be suppressed, nor her territorial needs ignored. The French and Polish governments protested. In reply, the German Foreign Office pointed out that in demanding a revision of Germany's eastern frontiers, Treviranus 'had only given expression to the view held by every German'.

The elections were set for September 14. During the election campaign, the efforts of the Nazi Party made a strong impression on foreign observers. 'The movement,' wrote the British Ambassador, 'is a new and vigorous one and obviously appeals to youth; and now, during the electoral campaign, its youthfulness and vigour are obviously appealing to all those in Germany who are feeling dissatisfied.' Some people were predicting that the Nazi Party would win fifty, or even sixty seats (which the ambassador thought a 'somewhat high' forecast). The Nazi Party's electoral techniques, he reported, were impressive – particularly the distribution of pamphlets, leaflets and placards – and could gain them seats 'out of proportion to their real strength'. There was, he added, much rowdyism among the Nazi supporters, 'often resulting in bloodshed'.

Nazi Brownshirts were active throughout the campaign in terrorizing Communists and Jews. In the course of a few weeks, seventy-eight Jews were injured in Brownshirt attacks. In his speeches, Hitler demanded the cancellation of reparations, the abolition of the Stock Exchange, and the abolition of interest payments. In six weeks he made twenty major speeches.

His adviser on propaganda, Dr Josef Goebbels, organized more than 6000 local Nazi party meetings. Innumerable torchlight parades were held. Among those who rallied to the Nazi Party was Prince August Wilhelm, one of the Kaiser's sons, and Prince Philipp of Hesse, a nephew of the Kaiser and a grandson of Queen Victoria. Like many others, these two princes feared the spread of Communism in Germany, and saw the Nazi Party as the best weapon against it.

When the election results were announced, there was consternation among the socialist, liberal and democratic forces. The Nazi Party had increased its number of seats in the Reichstag from 12 to 107. Its voters, just 810,000 hitherto, numbered more than six million. With 18 per cent of the electorate – 5 per cent more than the Communist Party – Hitler's was the second largest Party in the Republic. On hearing of the extent of his victory, he exclaimed, 'Heads will roll'. In Italy, Mussolini commented on the Nazi Party success with the words: 'For every country the choice of the twentieth century must lie between Fascism and Bolshevism.'

On the day that the Reichstag opened to its new political composition, Brownshirts attacked Jews in the streets of Berlin, and the windows of Jewish-owned department stores were broken. As the 107 Nazi deputies walked in a triumphant phalanx to the Reichstag, crowds of supporters lining the streets cheered them on with one of the Party's popular cries: '*Deutschland erwache, Juda verrecke!*' (Germany awake, death to Judah!)

Inside the Reichstag, the British Ambassador watched as the newly elected deputies took their seats:

> The house was crammed. When all the other deputies were in their place the Nazi deputies – over 100 strong – dressed in Khaki shirts and breeches and wearing the Swastika badge made a calculated and theatrical entry. The Communists hooted and jeered and most people laughed.
>
> The Nazis then gave their leader the Fascist salute but it was quite clear that they are really novices at the game. The whole proceeding was childish and undignified.
>
> Throughout the sitting – which only lasted one and a quarter hours and which was devoted to a roll call of the members – Nazis and Communists exchanged insults.
>
> At one moment when the Nazi leader in Parliament, Frick, was speaking

the Communists crowded up to him shouting 'Lumpenknecht' the nearest translation of which appears to be 'rag and bone merchant'. It might be freely translated, however, as 'dirty dog'. Frick remained calm.

That afternoon, the ambassador told his son, 'groups of hooligans masquerading as young Nazis milled through the main streets of Berlin breaking the windows of shops which they thought belonged to Jews'.

The balance of the parties in the Reichstag was such that a coalition would be hard to build. The largest single party was the Social Democrats, with 143 seats, a loss of 9 on the previous election. They were at loggerheads with the Communists, who won 77, an increase of 23.

In the event of a coalition being formed, Hitler's 107 seats could be amalgamated with those of two other right-wing parties: Hugenberg's German National People's Party, which had won 41 seats (a loss of 38 on the previous parliament, but still a formidable force) and Treviranus's People's Conservative Party, with 5 seats. The Centre Party, which had controlled the previous parliament until frustrated by the Social Democrats, had secured only 68 seats.

Brüning had no intention of resigning, or of letting the Hitler–Hugenberg bloc, which commanded 148 seats in all (5 more than the Social Democrats) to form a government. Instead, he continued as Chancellor, using as the basis for his authority the Emergency Decree that he had introduced before the election. The Social Democrats, alarmed at the strength of the forces of the right, no longer sought to have the Emergency Decree reversed.

Despite being the second largest party in the Reichstag, the Nazi Party was excluded from power. But it was active from the first day of the new parliament in pressing its aims and philosophy on a public that was staggered by its success. On September 30, two weeks after the election results were announced, the Nazi Party reissued a commentary on Nazi aims that had first been published eight years earlier, and virtually ignored. Its author was Alfred Rosenberg, the editor of the Nazi Party newspaper, *Völkischer Beobachter*.

According to Rosenberg's commentary, all Germans were to be consolidated into 'one great German State'. The Treaty of Versailles would be 'abolished'. Monopolies and 'living space' elsewhere would be acquired 'to feed the nation and absorb the surplus population'. No Jew would be allowed to remain a German citizen, though he could continue to live in Germany under the same rules as foreigners. No Jew could be the editor or correspondent of a German newspaper. All Jews who had entered Germany since August 1914 (this applied mostly to Jews from Poland who arrived in the 1920s) would be deported. All war profits would be confiscated. All industrial trusts and department stores, many of which were Jewish-owned, would become State property. All those found guilty of 'usury and profiteering' would be put to death. Gifted children would be educated free by the State. The physical fitness of the nation would be encouraged by compulsory gymnastics and sport. Pornographic literature would be 'abolished'.

This mixture of policies appealed to puritanism, greed, prejudice, envy and national pride. But one of Brüning's main concerns related not so much to the published programme as to the Nazi Party's private – but very visible and active – army that was growing by leaps and bounds. He realized that Hitler would gain further adherents, not only to his Party but to his Brownshirt movement, from the growing number of unemployed.

Brüning tried to counter the burdens of poverty that were the bane of unemployment, and which brought social distress and extremism in their wake. He instituted a rise of between 3.5 per cent and 6.5 per cent in the insurance contributions of employers and workers, the money from which he used to channel extra benefits to the unemployed. But by the end of the year the number of those without work in Germany had risen to four and a half million. This was too great a number to assuage by palliative economic measures that were, of financial necessity, on a small scale. The unemployed were restless and angry; the Nazi Party offered them a direction both for their emotional bitterness and for their physical energies that the government could not provide.

The question of what foreign policy Hitler might pursue if he came to power was also one that exercised, and troubled, the minds of many foreign observers. On October 18, at the German Embassy in London, Winston Churchill discussed Nazi Party foreign policy with the Councillor of Embassy, Prince Otto Bismarck (a grandson of Bismarck), who noted, in a secret memorandum which he sent to Berlin, that Churchill had been following newspaper reports of events in Germany 'in detail' and that he was 'pleased about the parliamentary victory of the Brüning government', but that he had expressed himself 'in cutting terms' on National Socialism. It was the Nazis, Churchill said, who had under their leader Adolf Hitler 'contributed towards a considerable deterioration of Germany's external position', particularly towards France.

Churchill went on to tell Bismarck that France 'was still afraid of Germany', as she had been five years before, and that it was 'no bad thing for Europe' that France had a strong army. The French 'were not an aggressive people and would never think of making an unprovoked attack on Germany'. The Maginot Line – the linked fortifications along France's eastern frontier which the French were building – was the 'tangible expression' of French fears.

Bismarck's note of Churchill's remarks continued: 'Hitler had admittedly declared that he had no intention of waging a war of aggression; he, Churchill, however, was convinced that Hitler or his followers would seize the first available opportunity to resort to armed force.'

In Austria, as in Germany, the emergence of a right-wing militia (in Germany the Brownshirts, in Austria the *Heimwehr*), and the question of reparations, was a double burden for the government. In January 1930, Dr Johann Schober, the Austrian Chancellor, travelled to The Hague, where he secured a complete liberation for Austria from the Administration Debt. These were the sums claimed by the various succession States of the Habsburg Empire (principally Czechoslovakia and Yugoslavia) on the basis of money owed at the time of the break-up of the Empire eleven years earlier. Schober caused a stir in former Allied circles, however, three months later, when on April 12, following seven weeks of negotiations in Berlin and Vienna, he announced the signature of an Austro-German treaty.

This was not the political union forbidden by the postwar treaties, or any overt move towards it; but it was a bilateral commercial treaty which, given the rise of nationalism in Germany, made foreign observers nervous. Ironically, the treaty was not well received in Austria itself, as Germany insisted on retaining the benefits of various other commercial treaties she had already signed with other countries, from which she had acquired 'most-favoured nation' status. The 'German brother' had failed to satisfy Austria's hopes of far more beneficial terms.

Austria was in conflict with the League of Nations that spring, as pressure mounted to disarm the *Heimwehr* militia. Dr Schober made a secret promise to the League that the *Heimwehr* would be disarmed. When the news of this promise leaked out in May, one of the leading Fascist activists, Prince Ernst Rüdiger von Starhemberg, stated that any attempt to put such disarmament into effect would be resisted by the *Heimwehr*. He was supported in his defiance by Major Waldemar Pabst, a Prussian who had been at the centre of the Kapp Putsch in Berlin in 1920, and who had fled from Germany to Austria to avoid arrest for high treason.

Working in the Tyrol under the name 'Peters', Pabst had helped organize the *Heimwehr* and became its Chief-of-Staff, turning it from little more than an anti-Socialist debating and beer-drinking society to a trained and vicious army. One of the features of his work was the drafting of the *Heimwehr* induction pledge (the 'Korneuburg Oath') whereby new members swore to work against the Austrian constitution and against democracy. On June 14, on the direct orders of the Chancellor, Pabst was arrested, and on the following day he was expelled from Austria as a 'dangerous alien' and flown out – to Italy, where he joined his Fascist friends in Venice.

The *Heimwehr*, alarmed at Schober's obvious determination not to give in to threats and extremism, moved its headquarters from Vienna (where Pabst had been arrested) to Graz. Its mood was one of defiance. On August 4, several thousand *Heimwehr* militiamen demonstrated in the town of St Pölten in what they brazenly called a 'civil war rehearsal'. They were surrounded by socialist counter-demonstrators, and bloodshed was only avoided by the intervention of the army, which surrounded the socialists and forced them to leave the town by train 'under the muzzles of machine guns', as a contemporary account reported. The Minister of War in Schober's coalition, Karl Vaugoin, was a sympathizer of the *Heimwehr* goal of a Fascist Austria.

Within the *Heimwehr*, a struggle for power was taking place that autumn. On September 4 the existing leaders were pushed aside by Prince Starhemberg, who had raised and illegally armed several *Heimwehr* battalions. A former officer with the German Freikorps troops who had fought against the Poles in the Baltic after the First World War, Starhemberg was also a friend of Hitler. He had visited Hitler in the early summer of 1930, and wanted to model the *Heimwehr* along the lines of Hitler's Brownshirts. Starhemberg's hope was to create a force which would enable a National Socialist style regime to seek power in Austria, as Hitler was seeking it in Germany.

A political crisis two weeks later, in which the pro-*Heimwehr* governor of Styria was particularly active, led to the fall of Dr Schober's government while he was out of the country (he was attending the League of Nations Assembly in Geneva). On September 25 – eleven days after Hitler's electoral success in Germany – the President of Austria asked the Minister of War in Schober's coalition, Karl Vaugoin, to form a government. Vaugoin's Clerical Party commanded the largest single block of seats in the Parliament: seventy-three, as against seventy-one for the Socialists.

On September 30, Vaugoin formed a government of Clericals and *Heimwehr*, an essentially Fascist coalition. Prince Starhemberg, who had just become Commander-in-Chief of the *Heimwehr*, was appointed Minister of the Interior, and the leader of the Salzburg *Heimwehr* was made Minister of Justice. Within a few days, the railways were put under *Heimwehr* and ultra-Clerical control.

Elections were fixed for November 9. Before they took place, Prince Starhemberg challenged the democratic process by declaring that whatever the election results – even if the Socialists secured a majority – the *Heimwehr* had its hands 'on the rudder of the State' and would never release it. As the election campaign continued there were repeated seizures and confiscations of any newspaper that reported adversely on *Heimwehr* plans. In Vienna, where the Socialist Governor of the city had forbidden all parades in military formation, the *Heimwehr* held a series of military demonstrations, and were protected by government troops against being dispersed by the local police.

In the four days before the election, on the orders of Vaugoin and Starhemberg, the army and the country police (who were sympathetic to the *Heimwehr*) carried out a series of raids on factories, working-men's clubs and local Socialist Party headquarters. Such intimidation did not help, however, at the polls, where Clericalism and Fascism were rejected by a majority of the voters. The Socialists were returned as the strongest party, with seventy-two seats, a gain of one. Vaugoin's Clericals won sixty-six seats, a loss of seven. Dr Schober's bloc obtained twenty seats. The *Heimwehr* and its allies, standing as the *Heimatblock* (Homeland bloc), won only eight seats.

Despite the election results, Vaugoin hung on to power for three weeks, trying, but in vain, to persuade Schober to enter a coalition in which the *Heimwehr* would be represented. Finally, on November 30, bowing to the democratic forces, Vaugoin resigned. Four days later, on December 3, a coalition was formed, headed by Dr Otto Engler, a supporter of Schober, and with Schober as Vice-Chancellor and Minister of Foreign Affairs. Vaugoin remained Minister of War, a Mephistopheles whom no one could dislodge. Democracy, however, had been preserved.

* * *

In the Soviet Union, democracy was a term of contempt. The seizure and nationalization of farms had continued without respite. On January 30 the Commissariat of Agriculture proudly announced that four million farms were already under State control; ten days later, ten million; ten days after that, more than thirteen and a half million; and by March 1, more than fourteen million.

For two and a half years there had been no Communist Party Congress. Stalin had not felt the need to have his draconian measures scrutinized, even by a carefully selected band of the Party faithful. That summer he was confident enough to summon the Sixteenth Congress. On June 26, 2000 delegates attended the opening ceremony in Moscow, and listened to a speech by Stalin which lasted an incredible ten hours.[1] The collectivization of agriculture must continue, he insisted; so also must the industrialization of the Soviet Union.

Stalin made no reference in his speech to the work of OGPU, the State Secret Police who were imposing a reign of terror that made opposition to the leader a dangerous risk. That September the OGPU declared that it had uncovered a plot of 'counter-revolutionaries' who had wanted to cut the food supplies from the working people. Three days after the announcement that the plot had been discovered, forty-eight people were shot. Half of them were officers and industrialists of the Tsarist time. A month later it was a group of eight professors – engineers and scientists – who were brought to trial, accused of having conspired with people outside the Soviet Union – including Raymond Poincaré and Aristide Briand – to bring about outside intervention and the overthrow of the Soviet State. The newspapers inside Russia whipped up a mass of indignation against the alleged plotters, who were sentenced to long periods in prison.

With deliberate slowness, but always with one aim in mind, Stalin replaced the senior and middle leadership of every branch of Soviet life, including the Party centre. On December 19, A. I. Rykov, one of the most senior members of the Party, who had earlier sided with Stalin against Trotsky, was removed from his post as President of the Council of People's Commissars, and from the presidency of the Council of Labour and Defence. His place was filled by Vyacheslav Molotov, one of those closest to Stalin, who

---

[1] Not as long as a speech by Mustafa Kemal to the Turkish parliament, which lasted three days, and for which the delegates were locked inside the parliament building for two nights.

was to remain loyal to Stalin to the end. Another of Stalin's closest confidants, Sergo Ordzonikidze, became President of the Supreme Council of the Economy, responsible for industrialization.

Britain was being pressed in 1930 by nationalist sentiment to give up its authority in Egypt. That year, a new government in Egypt, elected by a substantial popular majority, and led by Mustapha Nahas Pasha, promised 'to realize genuine independence for the country and to reach an honourable and stable agreement with Great Britain'. This call was reiterated by the Egyptian parliament at its first session. 'Real independence, internal as well as external', was the formula adopted.

Negotiations took place in England, but resulted in failure. The sticking point was the Sudan, whose government since the beginning of the century had been an Anglo-Egyptian Condominium that was an integral part of British rule and control. The British Colonial Service in the Sudan was regarded in Britain as a model for all imperial governance.

The Egyptian nationalists called for the 'unity of the Nile Valley', and the incorporation of the Sudan within the framework of their own independence. At the minimum they were prepared to share administrative and military control equally with the British. This was unacceptable to Britain, and the government of Nahas Pasha fell. He at once held a protest demonstration at Zagazig, at which 15,000 people were present. When the crowd rioted, troops opened fire, and several of the protesters were killed. Nahas then moved his protest to Mansurah, where there were further riots. As the disturbances spread to the cities, Egyptian troops opened fire on their fellow-Egyptians in Alexandria, Cairo, Suez and Port Said. British warships were sent to the Eastern Mediterranean in case British and other European residents in Egypt might be endangered.

The King of Egypt, Fuad I, turned to the European model set by Mussolini, reducing the power of parliament over public finance and legislation to a minimum, and changing the basis of membership of the Senate from primarily an elected one to one based almost entirely on royal nomination. When Fuad announced that general elections would be held with a more limited franchise (the voting age was raised from twenty-one to twenty-five) both main political parties said they would boycott them.

British rule remained the framework within which the internal Egyptian political struggle was carried out. It was to be another six years before, after many crises, Egypt – under King Fuad's sixteen-year-old successor, King Farouk – was to obtain independence.

In the United States, following the stock market crash of October 1929, there had been 22,109 business failures. President Hoover was hopeful, however, that the economy would recover, and had brought together business and industrial leaders to inject confidence, and also Federal cash, into their endeavours. For the first four months of 1930 the economy seemed to steady, and there was even some recovery; by April 1930 the steel mills that had been so hard hit six months earlier had risen from 40 to 80 per cent of their capacity.

In June, however, when it became clear that the number of those out of work was still rising, and that more and more small businesses were unable to find markets for their products in the general loss of confidence, there was another crash, and by the end of the year the number of businesses that had failed in the year – 26,355 – exceeded that of the previous year. The number of bank failures – 434 in 1929 – was multiplied threefold: in 1930 it was 1326. It was also estimated that by the end of 1930 the number of people without paid work was between two and three million (the Department of Labour's estimate) and 5,300,000 (the American Federation of Labour's estimate). The population of the United States was 122 million.

A fall in the price of grain was making it impossible for farmers to make profits. Nature also played its part in the downward spiral of confidence and the spread of distress, with severe flooding on the lower Mississippi, and a prolonged drought spreading westward from the Pacific Coast, destroying crops and driving many small farmers to bankruptcy and penury. In the cities, 'bread lines' became a familiar and distressing sight. In the rural areas, food riots took place as farmers and their families looted village food shops and demonstrated against the local authorities.

Congress passed emergency measures of food relief, and the American Red Cross, which a few years earlier had been at the forefront of sending help to the famine areas in Russia, raised $2 million for relief inside the United States, and undertook to feed three quarters of a million people. President Hoover's efforts to counter the crash were forgotten; in the midterm elections, held on November 4, the Democrats made substantial gains in both the Congress and Senate, making it difficult for Hoover to act without Democrat support.

The American economic decline was not evenly distributed or universal.

Although wages fell steadily throughout the year, savings increased, reaching a record level in October. Two products reported a considerable increase in sales in 1930: soap, and chewing gum. Manufacturers of refrigerators sold 25 per cent more than in their 'boom year' of 1929.

The year 1930 also saw the sixtieth anniversary of the founding of the Standard Oil Company. Economists and statisticians took heart, believing that the American people had the numbers and the resources to pull out of the Depression by economic resources, strength of character and national pride. The award of the Nobel Peace Prize to Frank B. Kellogg (who had become a Justice at the World Court at The Hague) for his success in having negotiated the Paris Treaty for the 'outlawry of war' was a reminder, too, of the place that the United States had in the world, despite the continuing official pursuit of a policy of isolation. Only the vehemently isolationist Chicago *Tribune* pointed out the irony that the prize for the outlawing of war was given in a year in which 'Belgium was increasing its fortifications against Germany, France is fortifying every inch of its frontier towards Italy, and Mussolini is feeding tonic to the eagles of war'.

In fact, Italy had been in the midst of negotiations for a naval agreement with France, based on mutual naval disarmament. When the negotiations broke down, the Italian Foreign Minister, Count Grandi, expressed his hope that they would be renewed, and emphasized that he was confident that Franco-Italian differences would be settled 'in the interests of a European settlement'. But a series of speeches by Mussolini served as a counter-blast to these assuring sentiments. At Livorno, on May 11, he stated that the world did not know 'to what temperature the passion of the whole Italian people would rise should the independence of Italy or the Fascist revolution be attacked', and a week later, in Florence, after praising the 'stern and warlike face of Fascist Italy', he told his audience that although 'words are beautiful things, rifles, machine-guns, ships, aeroplanes and cannon are still more beautiful'.

No wonder the Chicago *Tribune* was sceptical about the 'outlawry of war'. The 'beauty' of the implements of war, which had brought death to millions of soldiers a decade and a half earlier, and which Mussolini himself had seen on the Italian Front at their most destructive, was again a theme of many of the rulers of the modern world. Mussolini was also enhancing the power of his dictatorship. That year, many Italian Communists were arrested, tried and imprisoned. So also were two Italians who had been distributing a clandestine newspaper, calling for a coalition of all the non-Communist parties to oppose Fascism as a united front; they were both sentenced to fifteen years' imprisonment (Mussolini's Fascist regime lasted only a further thirteen years).

In 1930, nature again challenged man in its depredations when, in July, an earthquake struck a wide area of southern Italy, from Naples to Foggia, and as many as two thousand people were killed. In the United States, 319 prisoners were killed during a fire in the Ohio State Penitentiary. The prison warden, worried about escapes, had made his main task the organizing of a cordon of guards around the prison, while many of the prisoners, still in their locked cell blocks, burned to death.

In the United States, 29,080 people were killed on the roads in 1930. In Britain, the death toll that year was 6499, and in France, 2042. The motorcar had become the killer of tens of thousands every year. To protect itself against a more traditional enemy, the French government was at work on the construction of the Maginot Line, a string of fortifications from the Belgian border to the Swiss Alps, in the hope of keeping out any future German invader.

A hitherto unknown planet, Pluto, was discovered in 1930. That year a British aviator, Amy Johnson, made a solo flight from Britain to Australia. Commercial airline services were continually expanding. On April 14 a thirty-two passenger aircraft, the Fokker F-32, the roomiest hitherto, entered regular service. In Europe, the largest national carrier by far was Germany, with more than 120,000 passengers. France followed some way behind, with 55,000, Italy with 40,000, and Britain with 30,000. Even the Soviet Union was making use of airline routes, with Moscow-Tashkent and Moscow-Baku opening in 1930, giving the Communist authorities a source of rapid contact to regions that were thousands of miles from the centre of power.

More prosaically, it was in 1930 that ready-sliced bread was first marketed, under the brand name 'Wonder Bread'; yet another advance in ease of life for those in the more prosperous lands.

CHAPTER THIRTY-FIVE

1931

I N GERMANY, THROUGHOUT 1931, the Nazi Party, while holding the second largest number of seats in the Reichstag, refused in the most vulgar language to take any part in any coalition government. The only terms on which the Party would agree to enter government was if Hitler was appointed Chancellor. Brüning resolutely refused to contemplate this. But he was sufficiently worried by the scale and intensity of the Brownshirt violence that he agreed to ban the powerful antiwar film *All Quiet on the Western Front*. Based on the novel by Erich Maria Remarque, the film was a passionate portrayal of the horrors of trench warfare. Brüning was afraid that any manifestation of antiwar sentiment would provoke the Brownshirts to even greater violence, perhaps attacking cinemas showing the film, or the audiences watching it.

Within the British Foreign Office the meaning of the Nazi movement and the reasons for its success were much discussed. Robert Vansittart believed that Nazism was a resurgence of the 'Old Adam' in Germany. It was, he wrote, an amoral, primitive spirit which could not easily be satisfied, and should not be ignored. Another senior diplomat, Orme Sargent, commented on January 13 that Hitler's success pointed to 'a belief in force as opposed to cooperation in the solution of European problems'. The British ambassador in Berlin, Sir Horace Rumbold, agreed. 'In the eyes of the Nazis,' he wrote, 'Germany is like Prometheus bound, and Hitler, or the Nazi movement, is cast for the part of Hercules. This aspiration for freedom and for equality has come to stay, and is an element which every German Government must take into account. It is bound, in my opinion, to exercise an influence on the conduct of Germany's foreign policy and has begun to exercise such an influence.'

Rumbold felt that Hitler's Nazi movement had not entirely harmed Germany. It had caused both Europe and the world 'to take far more account of this efficient and industrious nation of sixty-four million inhabitants, placed in the centre of Europe, and to ask "Quo vadis Germania?"' The question of which way Germany would go was an urgent one. On January 26, unemployment passed the 4.7 million mark. In February it approached five million. Trade and industry made no recovery. The Nazi Party rank and file were pressing Hitler not to cooperate with the other political parties, but to return to the streets, and to extend their support by violence and intimidation.

On February 26, the British ambassador in Berlin sent the Foreign Secretary in London a long and pessimistic despatch. The Germans wanted an end to reparations. They were eager to rearm. They dreamed of the return of their lost territories in the east. 'A war against Poland to rectify the eastern frontiers,' the ambassador wrote, 'would be in the nature of a crusade.' The Nazis, as well as the other parties of the Right, included compulsory military service in their programme 'as a matter of course'. The ban on conscription, one of the restrictions laid down in the Versailles Treaty, was being denounced by every Nazi speaker on every public platform.

How could the Nazi Party be kept from power? That was the question in the mind and on the lips of all who wished Germany to remain a parliamentary democracy. On March 4, Sir Horace Rumbold told the British Foreign Secretary that Britain's only chance of averting a Nazi triumph was to support Brüning and to enable him to remain in power. The only way of supporting Brüning, he wrote, was to give Germany economic help, to come to an arrangement, possibly a moratorium, on reparations, or to organize some international credit operation on Germany's behalf. The least that could be done, the ambassador added two days later, was for Ramsay MacDonald to testify publicly 'to the statesmanlike and energetic manner with which Brüning is grappling with difficulties which are common to practically all the great countries of the world'. Some gesture should be made, and made soon, so that Brüning would feel that the British were willing to help him; even an invitation to London would help to lessen German fears of isolation.

Ramsay MacDonald agreed to invite Brüning to London. Before the visit could be arranged, however, the international situation worsened. On February 26, the French Minister of War, André Maginot – after whom the French fortified line along the Franco-German frontier was named – told the French deputies during a debate on the army estimates in the French Chamber that the countries 'which were the aggressors' in 1914 would have to accept a limitation of armaments 'more severe' than that of the nations who had 'committed no aggression and which refuse to commit one'.

André Maginot was insistent that there could be no question of going back on the military clauses of the Versailles Treaty. The Germans were incensed by his remarks. General Groener, in a statement to the Reichstag on March 9, insisted that 'the Versailles thesis' for Germany's sole responsibility for the war had been refuted. Dr Curtius, the German Foreign Minister, warned the British Ambassador that Maginot's remarks had 'poisoned the atmosphere' between France and Germany. The Germans would never accept that they had been responsible for the war. They rejected absolutely the war guilt charge.

Hitler had no monopoly in opposing the Treaty of Versailles. Brüning's government was as determined as any of its predecessors not to submit to the Treaty restrictions if it could find a way around them. Clandestine rearmament and military training continued without pause. Work by German engineers on the manufacture of tanks, specifically forbidden by the Versailles Treaty, continued to be carried out secretly, not only in the Soviet Union, under Stalin's benign eye, but in neutral Sweden, whose arms manufacturers were all too glad to turn any amount of profit, large or small. Over several months, the British Military Attaché, Colonel James Marshall-Cornwall, had continue to collect evidence of a number of infringements of the military restrictions. He estimated that there were about seven thousand soldiers in excess of those allowed by Treaty undergoing training in military depots. He had been shown photographs of an armoured motorcycle combination, fitted with a machine gun, which had recently been constructed in Germany.

Hitler pursued his own agenda for creating the unity of hatred. On March 15 a directive was sent to all Nazi Party officials: 'The natural hostility of the peasant against the Jews, and his hostility against the Freemason as a servant of the Jew, must be worked up to a frenzy.' That year, the SS – Hitler's personal bodyguard – which had already been enlarged by Heinrich Himmler as a 'protection squad' that could initiate violence in the streets with impunity, set up its own Intelligence Service, the *Sicherheitsdienst*, or SD, headed by Reinhard Heydrich, to keep a close watch on dissent inside the Nazi Party.

In March 1931 Brüning took a sudden initiative in foreign policy which aroused immediate antagonism in France, and deep suspicion in England. On March 19, shortly after the German Foreign Minister, Dr Curtius, returned from a visit to Vienna, it was announced that Germany and Austria intended to form a Customs Union. On the following day the French, Czechoslovak and British governments protested, the British government warning Austria that such a Union might be a direct breach of article 88 of the Treaty of Saint-Germain, whereby Austria agreed not to commit any act 'which might directly or indirectly or by any means whatsoever compromise her independence'.

On March 23, in answer to British criticisms, Dr Curtius insisted that the agreement had no political significance. It should, he said, be regarded as the first step in the creation of a free trade area, which other nations were welcome to join. 'The greater the number of States participating in such a Customs Union,' Curtius explained, 'the larger would be the free trade area between these States.' The British government was not impressed by this line of argument. If the German aim was a wider economic plan, it asked, why had it not been mentioned to some of the other nations who might be asked to participate in it?

A British commentator reflected at the end of the year: 'In Vienna, any mention of that red flag to the French bull, *Anschluss* (Austro-German union), was carefully avoided. The promoters of the Customs Union, however, were one and all the most fervent adherents of the *Anschluss* plan; it is obvious that within a few years of the Customs Union coming into operation, the two countries, whose military, educational and legal systems have, since the war, been slowly and deliberately made to work along parallel lines, could have pulled up the political frontier posts overnight without anyone being much the wiser.'

Winston Churchill, then in opposition to the Labour government of Ramsay MacDonald, was not averse to the proposed Customs Union. If it were to be a strictly economic union, he wrote in an American newspaper article eight days after the union was announced, it might help to control the new extremism in Germany. If it were to be seen, by the mass of ordinary Germans, as a success for Brüning's foreign policy, it would have an important sequel if it served to rob 'the much more dangerous Hitler movement of its mainspring'. Churchill went on to ask his readers: 'Will not the mastery of Hitlerism by the constitutional forces in Germany be a real factor in the immediate peace of Europe?'

Churchill's argument failed to influence the direction or tone of British foreign policy. On March 25 the British government warned Brüning of what it called the 'great concern' in both Britain and France that the Germans had shown an apparent disregard of their Treaty obligation in relation to Austria. It was surely not in Germany's interest, Brüning was told, that the French should be angered at the very moment when the Disarmament Conference was about to meet, and when the French Foreign Minister, Aristide Briand, was sympathetic towards the German desire for equality of armaments.

Brüning, while hastening to assure the British government that Germany 'had not had any political considerations at the back of their minds when negotiating agreement with Austria', added somewhat provocatively that Germany 'had few rights, and if she was going to be checked at every turn the position of his government would become impossible'. Brüning went on to say that he believed there would be an 'explosion' in Germany if France insisted on blocking Germany's legitimate aspirations.

The British Ambassador understood the point that Brüning was making. There would be serious repercussions in Germany, he warned the government in London, if Britain opposed the Austro-German Customs Union. 'Any outside interference which is not based on legal and convincing grounds,' he warned, 'is liable to be represented as an attempt to bully Germany, and to be exploited to the detriment of ex-allies.' In the event, it was the League of Nations, showing sharp teeth, and the Court of Arbitration at The Hague, that rejected the Customs Union and forced Germany and Austria to abandon it.

There was more to the rejection of the Austro-German Customs Union than its political aspect. In protest against the plan, the French government withdrew its considerable financial deposits from the Austrian Creditanstalt bank. This bank was already, at the request of the Austrian government, trying to bolster up another of Austria's banking institutions, the Bodencred-itanstalt. With the sudden withdrawal of French funds, the Creditanstalt was on the verge of collapse; and on May 11 notified the Austrian government that it could no longer meet its obligations. The effect in Vienna was as devastating as Black Thursday had been in New York two years earlier. First Austria, and then, in rapid succession, Germany and Hungary, were plunged into a banking crisis that left millions of small investors penniless.

Britain also suffered from the collapse of the central European banking system, so much so that the Labour government was forced to impose drastic measures, including cuts in unemployment benefits, that were unacceptable to the socialist philosophy. The result was a political crisis, and the formation, on August 24, of a National Government, still led by Ramsay MacDonald, but with four Conservative, three Labour and two Liberal Ministers forming his Cabinet. When a general election was held, the Conservatives were returned as by far the largest Party; for the sake of national economic stability they agreed that the National Government should remain in place, and that MacDonald should remain Prime Minister.

The reduction of unemployment benefit, a sign that the National Government were determined to be ruthless in putting its finances in order, led to the United States being willing to advance financial credit to the Bank of England. This staved off the possibility of national bankruptcy. Similar American economic help in 1941 was to carry Britain over a grave war emergency; and fifteen years later, during the Suez crisis of 1956, when American economic aid was deliberately withdrawn in protest against Britain's action, a major British foreign policy initiative collapsed overnight.

In Germany, Brüning had continued to rule by Emergency Decree since the elections the previous September. At the end of March 1931, after a vote of no confidence in his government narrowly missed being passed, he adjourned the Reichstag until the middle of October, and after a sitting of only a few days, when a second vote of no-confidence nearly gained approval, he adjourned the Reichstag yet again, for a further four months. The greatest fear of a majority of the deputies, that the Nazis would come to power, gave Brüning considerable strength however. This was because the Social Democrats, despite their deep disagreement on social policy with the Centre Party, gave Brüning their support in order to keep the government in office and thereby exclude the Nazis. It was clear that in any deep government crisis, the Nazi Party, with its 107 deputies, would have a strong bargaining power to join a coalition, and that Hitler might, for the sake of obtaining a share of power, give up his condition that either he would be invited to form the government as Chancellor, or else not participate in any subordinate position, even that of deputy Chancellor.

Throughout 1931 the Nazi Party continued to be the Party that promised the most to the discontented: hope for the impoverished, work for the unemployed, a revision of the Peace Treaties for the humiliated, the humiliation of the Jews for the anti-Semitic; and for those who were disillusioned by the Reichstag, parliamentary democracy and the coalition of parties governing Germany, the pledge that 'Everything will be different' under 'One nation, one people, one leader'. It was a powerful appeal to those who felt that the country, and they themselves, were not gaining from the current situation, where unemployment was rising and the international community was challenging Germany's right even to gain some small economic benefit, as in the Austro-German Customs Union.

Whereas, in the previous year's general election, the Nazi Party had secured 18 per cent of the total vote, in the local elections held during 1931 it began to secure a substantially higher share of the poll. In the election for the Diet of Oldenburg in May 1931 it secured 37.4 per cent, and in the following November, in the election to the Diet of Hesse, 37.1 per cent. An economic crisis during the summer, which resulted in considerable international support for Germany, as well as the total suspension of reparations for a year, and a suspension of all Germany's foreign debts for six months, harmed the government, despite its constructive outcome. Communists and Nazis alike hailed 'the end of capitalism', and looked forward to a new revolutionary era, though from different sides of the barricades.

That September, on the eve of the Jewish New Year, September 12, squads of young Brownshirts – the increasingly dreaded Stormtroops – attacked Jews as they were returning from synagogue. One eye-witness recorded how, in one incident, 'while three youths beat an elderly gentleman with their fists and rubber truncheons, five other young men stood round to protect them'. This scene, the strong helping the strong to attack the weak, was to become a trademark of Nazi action. So too was the deliberate choice of a holy day in the Jewish calendar for anti-Jewish violence. That year, fifty synagogues were desecrated throughout Germany, and several thousand tombstones broken or scrawled with anti-Semitic graffiti in Jewish cemeteries all over the German Republic.

In October 1931, Hitler felt strong enough to call a conference of all the parties of the Right, whose combined share in the various local elections had reached 50 per cent and even more of the poll (49.5 per cent in Oldenburg and 52.1 per cent in Hesse). The conference opened on October 11, in the small central German town of Harzburg. Not only right-wing politicians and their followers, but many leading figures from the world of commerce and industry were there, including a former President of the Reichsbank, Dr Schacht. The conference passed a resolution, throwing down the gauntlet to the moderate and democratic forces. 'We demand immediate elections,' it said, 'for replacing the present superannuated parliaments, especially in the Reich and Prussia. With the fullest sense of responsibility, we declare that the Associations which constitute the national opposition will – in the impending disturbances – protect the life and property, the homes and positions, of those who openly proclaim themselves members of one nation with us; but that we decline to defend with the sacrifice of our blood the present Government and the present ruling system. We demand a restoration of the German right to self-defence and equality of armament. We make these demands as one man, and declare outlawed anyone who seeks to break our front.'

Hitler's appeal for 'one nation' fell on fertile soil. By the end of the year, the number of unemployed in Germany had risen to 5.5 million. Unemployment relief, which itself was falling to below subsistence level, cost the government more than the money brought in, in a good year, by the taxation of wages and compulsory national insurance. Even the German social welfare system – which Bismarck had instituted half a century earlier – and which had been the model for other countries, including Britain – was proving inadequate in view of the enormous number of those without work.

Hitler reiterated throughout 1931, on many public platforms, that he had no intention of coming to power by force; he would, he said, reach his goal through the democratic system that he so despised. He would, he insisted, wait – as indeed he did wait – until summoned by the President to take on the duties of Chancellor. No such self-denying ordinance affected the Austrian Fascists. On September 13 the Styrian section of the *Heimwehr* occupied the main public buildings in Graz, declared Dr Pfrimer, a local lawyer, 'Dictator of Austria', announced the 'abolition' of the Austrian post-war constitution, and prepared to march on Vienna. But this spectacular coup was not supported by the *Heimwehr* leader, Prince Starhemberg, who had earlier ousted Dr Pfrimer from his position of leadership in the *Heimwehr*.

In scuffles between workers and *Heimwehr* forces, several workmen were killed, but the march on Vienna never took place. The revolt fizzled out, and Dr Pfrimer fled across the border into Yugoslavia. But the power of the *Heimwehr* was such that no action was taken against the many local police officers and government officials who had participated in the revolt.

Mussolini had discovered the power of overseas adventure to unite a nation in patriotic zeal. At the beginning of 1931, in Libya, Italian troops captured the Kufra Oasis, driving the Senussi tribesmen into the desert. The hoisting of the Italian flag over the Senussi stronghold, El Tag, was witnessed by two senior army officers, Marshal Badoglio and General Graziani, and caused enthusiasm throughout Italy. In September, Italian soldiers captured Omar el Mukhtar, the Senussi leader who had been their most feared opponent. He was publicly hanged.

Italian prowess in the air, something of which Mussolini was particularly proud, was demonstrated that year when a squadron of fourteen seaplanes set off from Rome to South America. Two of the planes crashed on the journey, and five lives were lost, but this was seen as the inevitable cost of pioneering aviation. The squadron was personally commanded by General Balbo, the Air Minister, who, on return to Rome, said that the loss of life was less than had been expected before the expedition set out.

While Mussolini was consolidating his imperial control in North Africa, and seeking to strengthen Italy's influence in South America, the British Empire was facing a crisis in India. Gandhi had been allowed out of prison by the Viceroy, Lord Irwin, in return for calling a halt to civil disobedience by his followers. On February 17, the two men held the first of eight meetings. Their negotiations reached a conclusion on the night of March 4, and on the following morning they announced the conclusion of the Delhi Pact. Gandhi agreed that the boycott of British goods 'as a political weapon' was to cease. Civil disobedience in all its forms would come to an end. Congress would send representatives to London to a Round Table Conference to discuss the future of India. Britain would retain 'safeguards' in the areas of defence, foreign affairs, India's overseas debts and the interest of the minorities, including the Depressed Classes (the Untouchables).

Under the Delhi Pact – also known as the Gandhi–Irwin Pact – the Government of India agreed to release all those arrested as a result of previous noncooperation and disobedience, to remit all fines, and to return all confiscated property. As a result, several thousand political prisoners were released. One phrase in the agreement – 'it has been agreed that' – gave Gandhi the status, not of a supplicant but of an equal negotiator. But throughout his discussions with the Viceroy, Gandhi had been adamant that India must have the right to ultimate withdrawal from the British Empire.

The expectations raised that the Delhi Pact would somehow prove a panacea to all ills were dissipated somewhat when the Viceroy rejected pleas for the commutation of the death sentence passed on Bhagat Singh and two companions for the murder of a police officer in Lahore three years earlier. When Hindus in Cawnpore called a strike in sympathy for the three condemned men, the Muslims in the city refused to join the strike. Riots broke out on March 24. Murder, arson and looting were their trademark. By the time the riots had been put down by the police, at least three hundred Hindus and Muslims were dead. Four months later, further Hindu–Muslim riots broke out in Kashmir. In Bengal, terrorist actions against the British grew in intensity. Three British officials were shot dead on April 7, and the District Magistrate of Midnapore on the following day. A judge was murdered (as he sat in court) on July 27. Later in the year a District Magistrate was killed by two Indian girl students as he sat in his bungalow. Two other civilians, and two Indian police inspectors, were also killed.

On the North West Frontier of India, the scene of so much fighting before the First World War, the local Pathan tribes still sought to push out the relatively slim apparatus of British rule: the British army officers, the British civilian officials headed by a Chief Commissioner, with a few dozen British civilians under him, controlling both the 'settled area' where British rule was much in evidence and the 'tribal areas' where it was less established. In August, the standard of revolt was raised in the North West Frontier Province by Abdul Ghaffar Khan, leader of the 'Red Shirt' Army.

Abdul Ghaffar Khan was one of those political prisoners who had been released from prison under the Delhi Pact. He at once demanded full independence for the North West Frontier Province. The Red Shirts issued an infantry training manual, and set up two training camps in one of the remote regions of the province. A campaign for the nonpayment of rents was launched. Lord Irwin's successor as Viceroy, Lord Willingdon, acted swiftly, increasing the Chief Commissioner's powers, and declaring the Red Shirts an illegal organization. Abdul Ghaffar and 200 of his followers were arrested. An attack by the Red Shirts on the British army barracks and civilian residential area of Kohat was driven off.

Abdul Ghaffar Khan had denounced the Round Table Conference in London, at which the British government was prepared to extend the areas of Indian self-rule even to the North West Frontier Province. Gandhi attended the conference, which opened at St James's Palace on September 8. When it ended, inconclusively, on December 1, he intimated that the Indian national movement and the British government had come to a parting of the ways, and that nonviolent civil disobedience might soon be revived. Returning by sea to India, Gandhi reached Bombay on December 28, to be met by an enormous demonstration of welcome by his supporters. But there was also a counter-demonstration, by the Depressed Classes (the Untouchables) who were angered by what they saw as Gandhi's failure, while in London, to assert their claims. Fighting broke out in the streets between the Congress supporters and the Depressed Classes – waving black flags of protest – and there were many injuries.

After discussions with the Working Committee of Congress, which had organized acts of civil disobedience in India while Gandhi was in London, Gandhi asked the Viceroy for a meeting to discuss the political situation. The Viceroy replied that the government could not have any dealings 'with persons or organizations responsible for recent subversive activities in India'. The Working Committee then announced, in the last hours of 1931, that the campaign to defy British law would be revived, that the boycott on all British manufactured goods would be reimposed, and that there would be picketing of government offices to dissuade Indians from entering them. Gandhi offered to suspend these measures if he was given an interview with the Viceroy and was allowed to tour the provinces in order to study conditions there at first hand. This was refused, and in a speech in Calcutta on December 30 the Viceroy warned both Congress and the Bengali terrorists that the government would meet their challenge to its authority 'by resolute determination'.

The 150,000 British officials in India were confident that they could rule, and rule with justice, their 353 million Indian subjects.

The Soviet Union was receding behind a barrier of secrecy and terror. Although the term Iron Curtain did not come into general use until after the Second World War, it was the phrase used by a British visitor, Ethel Snowden, in her book about a visit to Russia, *Through Bolshevik Russia*, published in 1920, and it was certainly true a decade later. On the surface, the guidebooks, and the annual *Soviet Union Year-Book*, presented a comforting picture, in which 'Inturist Limited' (later known as Intourist) offered provision of hotel accommodation, restaurants and 'guides-interpreters' for sight-seeing. 'Visits to Russian mountains and sea spas' were specially recommended, as were 'hunting tours', 'the medieval cities of Russia', 'the beautiful Crimean Riviera', and 'the Romantic Caucasus', as well as 'Siberia'.

The guidebooks and yearbooks could not hint at, let alone spell out, the other side of the coin, including the labour camps which were a blight on the Siberian landscape, or the suppression which was even then taking place in the Caucasus of all manifestations of national feeling.

Show trials were a feature of Stalin's exercise of control; the public pointing of accusatory fingers, and absurd charges, prior to the inevitable conviction and severe sentences of imprisonment and long Siberian exile. On March 1 the trial opened in Moscow of a group accused of conspiring to overthrow the Soviet government and put the 'Mensheviks' back in power. V. Groman, a leading figure of the State Planning Authority; Scher, a director of the State Bank; and Sukhanov, a member of the Commissariat of Commerce, were among those put on trial. They were accused of having joined forces with Menshevik exiles in Berlin. The 'machinations of the accused', declared the Attorney-General, N. B. Krylenko, had caused 'great damage to the Soviet economic system, but they had no support among the masses of the people'. The evidence was nonexistent, but the ten-year prison sentences were real, and the deterrent effect was considerable.

The United States was not in a strong position to give a lead in world affairs in 1931. For three years her economy had been in disarray. Bank failures were still frequent and millions of people had their savings wiped out. The number of unemployed reached as high as seven million. Destitution was widespread. Throughout the country the drill halls used by the National Guard for territorial training were turned into dormitories for homeless men and women, and even for whole families. At the baseball games to which tens of thousands came to cheer their respective sides, appeals were made and collections taken up for the unemployed. Above the skyscrapers and office blocks of New York, a loudspeaker system fitted to an airship called upon the citizens below to remember that they had jobs, and urged them to remember those less fortunate with the word: 'Give until it hurts.'

Private philanthropy was insufficient to deal with so vast a crisis. States and cities allocated taxpayers' money for relief. Wage reductions took place in every sector. On the social side, the spread of a crime wave led to lists being published of the most violent cities: Memphis, in the State of Tennessee, came first with nearly 60 murders for every 100,000 citizens. In Chicago, the equivalent figure was fourteen, in New York, only seven. Chicago launched a campaign against crime. Al 'Scarface' Capone was sent to prison for eleven years for 'evading his income tax payments'. His real crime was to have been the chief of the 'racketeers' who exploited Prohibition to make – or extort – a fortune in the illicit alcohol trade. That year, seventy 'gangsters' were killed in Chicago: twenty-nine by police, twenty-six by citizens, five by watchmen and ten in gang warfare. But the most terrible loss of life in the United States in 1931 continued to come from road accidents. The motorcar had emerged as the most persistent killer in the Western World. In 1931 alone, 30,000 Americans were killed in car accidents. This was only slightly fewer than the number of American soldiers killed on the Western Front between 1916 and 1918; and far more than the British dead on the first day of the Battle of the Somme.

The continuing economic distress led the Democrats to look for someone who could challenge the Republicans in the presidential election of the following year. The favoured candidate was the Governor of New York State, Franklin D. Roosevelt. He had already, in 1930, expressed his view that it was 'time for the country to become fairly radical for at least one generation' and he added: 'History shows that where this occurs occasionally, nations are saved from revolutions.' In New York State, where the economic distress was such that serious social unrest was a possibility, Roosevelt created a Temporary Emergency Relief Administration, to provide financial aid to the local authorities in the State, so that they could find work and relief for the unemployed. Almost one in ten families in New York State was on relief.

Starvation was avoided by a liberal distribution of funds, and of food. Not only did Roosevelt increase the State's expenditure on public works, where the unemployed could find labour building roads and other State projects, but he also encouraged a 'back-to-the-land' movement, whereby families could avert starvation, and even earn a small livelihood, as farmers and cultivators.

The economic distress in the United States, the expectations of Nazi rule in Germany, and the perpetuation of Communist tyranny in Soviet Union were matched – in their impact on the millions who hoped and prayed only for a quiet life, a job and a decent meal – by a renewal of civil upheaval in China. The authority of Chiang Kai-shek was being challenged as too dictatorial. His autocratic rule from Nanking led to an upsurge of Kuomintang discontent in Canton. On May 12, in Nanking, Chiang Kai-shek promulgated a constitution based on liberty of the person, conscience and speech, freedom of the Press and the right of association. At that very moment, the Canton nationalists declared their independence, together with that of five southern provinces.[1]

[1] Kwantung, Kweichow, Kwangsi, Fukien and Hunan.

On May 14, only two days after the promulgation of the Nanking constitution, a Kuomintang general, Chan Chai-tong, attacked two regiments loyal to Chiang Kai-shek at the Whampoa Military Academy near Canton and disarmed them. Two weeks later he was one of those nationalist rebels who, in Canton, inaugurated a new government, calling itself the National Government of China. Even as his own movement divided against him, Chiang Kai-shek was pursuing another enemy, the Chinese Communists. These, he declared, were 'bandits', and should be hunted down. For much of 1930 he had watched the activities of the Communists with alarm, when one Communist army, in which Mao Tse-tung was the political commissar, almost captured Nanchang, and two other armies had managed to hold the city of Changsha for ten days. A Communist government was established, headed by twenty-three-year-old Wang Shoudao, who had earlier been active in the countryside confiscating land from the landowners and redistributing it to the peasants. When the Kuomintang re-entered Changsha, Mao's wife and younger sister, and Wang's wife, were among those executed.[1]

One reason why the Kuomintang were nervous was that it was clear the Communist forces were operating with caution; when they were about to be outnumbered they withdrew. They were not prepared – and Mao Tse-tung was one of those most emphatic about this – to put their army at risk, or to endanger the security of their base. At the same time, Party discipline was emerging as a factor which, after initial internal perturbations, was likely to be far tighter than that which prevailed within the nationalist ranks.

In December 1930 there had been a revolt within the Communist Party and its armed forces against Mao Tse-tung's agrarian policies – which favoured the peasants and looked to the peasants as the main base of the revolution. In retaliation, Mao accused his opponents of being undercover agents of the Kuomintang (an echo of Stalin's charges against his internal Communist enemies) and hunted them down. At least 2000, and possibly as many as 3000 of the rebel Communists were killed during Mao's action. Mao's biographer Stuart Schram reflected that this was the first 'large-scale example' of Mao's ruthlessness. 'It also brought into action the very efficient secret police that he had created.'

Chiang Kai-shek set as his strategic aim the extension of his control southward to root out the Communists, whose numbers were growing, and

---

[1] Wang Shoudao served as a military commissar during the Long March. In the 1960s he was Minister of Communications of the People's Republic of China. He died in 1996, at the age of eighty-nine.

whose geographic control was widening. Within a period of twelve months, three 'Encirclement Campaigns' were launched against the Communists in the Kiangsi province by the Kuomintang. Largely as a result, however, of the guerrilla tactics devised by Mao Tse-tung – and criticized by the Communist Party's Central Executive Committee, which wanted its own troops to fight as armies, in direct confrontation with those of the enemy, in pitched battles – Chiang Kai-shek's forces were unable, despite massive efforts, to break the pattern of revolt.

Five years later, looking back on the failure of the three Kuomintang campaigns, Mao wrote in explanation, and defence of guerrilla warfare: 'Our strategy is "pit one against ten", and our tactics are "pit ten against one"; these contrary and yet complementary propositions constitute one of our principles for gaining mastery over the enemy. We use the few to defeat the many – this we say to the rulers of China as a whole. We use the many to defeat the few – this we say to the enemy on the battlefield. That is no longer a secret, and in general the enemy is by now well acquainted with our method. But, he can neither prevent our victories nor avoid his own losses, because he does not know when and where we shall act. This we keep secret. The Red Army generally operates by surprise attacks.'

The guerrilla principles that Mao adopted enabled the far smaller armies of the Communists to survive against the larger armies sent to destroy them. One principle was concealment, another was striking at the enemy at its weakest point, a third was the strategy of 'luring the enemy' deep into the base area. Even so, the Kuomintang were not defeated, and were preparing for an advance into the heartland of the Communist-controlled areas, when news came to Kuomintang and Communist alike, on September 18, of an attack by Japan on Manchuria.

The Japanese chose to invade Manchuria at the very moment when the Chiang Kai-chek nationalists were at their most stretched, in action both against the Canton separatists, and against the Communists. A quarter of a century earlier the Japanese had battled with Russia for this same region. In the face of the Japanese action, the rival Chinese nationalist factions recognized that they must give up their quarrel, and unite to defend the soil of China. Within the Kuomintang, supreme power was restored to Chiang Kai-shek, but the Cantonese rebels were given a predominant part in his administration.

*　　*　　*

The conflict between China and Japan had begun six weeks earlier when, in anti-Chinese riots in the Japanese province of Korea, 100 Chinese had been killed. Then, on July 29, a junior officer of the Japanese General Staff, Captain Nakamura, who was travelling in Inner Mongolia, had been killed by Chinese soldiers of the Mukden army. Rumours that a portion of track of the South Manchurian Railway, on which the Japanese had treaty rights, had been destroyed by Chinese soldiers from their barracks near Mukden (a rumour denied by the Chinese authorities in Mukden) led to calls inside Japan for action. Those Japanese leaders who counselled moderation were ignored.

Japanese troops guarding the railway were mobilized for fighting, and, on September 18, sent into Mukden. Within a short time they had overrun the Chinese army barracks in the city, the arsenal, and the aerodrome. The Chinese authorities in Mukden fled, and the Japanese commander of the troops guarding the railway moved his headquarters into the city. A Japanese-controlled administration was then set set up; Japan had effectively annexed a Manchurian city.

Demands by the Nanking government that Japan evacuate Mukden were ignored. The Japanese insisted that they had no territorial designs on China, but stressed that the rights of the Japanese in Manchuria had to be protected. Those rights had not in fact been violated; the death of Captain Nakamura was an isolated incident. Japanese troops remained in Mukden, while the Japanese worked to encourage a separatist movement among the local Chinese.

When the League of Nations, asked to do so by China, offered to intervene as a mediator, Japan rejected all mediation. In a military engagement in October, a Chinese force under General Ma was defeated, and the Japanese occupied Tsitsihar.

The Japanese advance into Manchuria, China's northernmost region, and an area one fourth the size of China, had taken the pressure off the Chinese Communist defence of their southern heartland. But internal Communist strife was intense. Mao Tse-tung's influence at Juilin, and over the army's guerrilla tactics, was challenged by the Communist Party Central Committee. Realizing that its instructions from Shanghai were being largely ignored by the armies in the field, the Central Committee decided to leave the dangers of Shanghai — a city in which they were always being hunted and had been forced to live a life of secrecy and fear — for the comparative security of the Kiangsi province, near the very centre of the Party's military operations.

The main figure to arrive from Shanghai, and to challenge Mao, was Chou En-lai. At the same time, the arrival in Juilin of the Shanghai leadership led, on November 7, to a strengthening of the Communist Party's inner organizational structure, and to a clarification of its aims. That day, at the opening of the First All-China Soviet Congress, the delegates proclaimed the Chinese Soviet Republic. A sixty-three-member Central Executive Committee was also elected that day, and itself elected a Council of People's Commissars. Of this latter body, Mao was chairman, but with circumscribed powers. Control over the Red Army passed to Chou En-lai, and to a more cautious policy, rejecting Mao's plans to link up the various forces fighting the Kuomintang in different areas into a solid geographic whole.

A thousand people in British Honduras were killed when a hurricane devastated the city of Belize in 1931. But no one knew how many tens of thousands of Chinese — perhaps hundreds of thousands, possibly a million — were drowned that year during the floods which turned the province of Hupeh into a lake (the size of Scotland). They were the worst floods in China in living memory. Tens of millions of people lost their homes, were destitute, and without food. From Canada and the United States, large quantities of wheat were sent out, but these were not a gift; the Chinese government had to agree to pay the market price for them, the payment to be spread over five years. The League of Nations sent a British civil servant to be in charge of the headquarters of the National Food Relief Commission. His help was received with enthusiasm; but the scale of suffering was far beyond the capacity of aid or commissions to ameliorate.

CHAPTER THIRTY-SIX

1932

IN BRITISH INDIA there was an upsurge of anti-British violence in 1932 in three provinces – Bengal, the United Provinces and the North West Frontier Province. Local government buildings were set on fire, local officials were attacked, and some officials were killed. In an attempt to bring the violence to an end, the Viceroy, Lord Willingdon, introduced emergency legislation to enable suspected agitators to be arrested and imprisoned. When the Indian National Congress asked the Viceroy to discuss this legislation with him, he refused. Following this refusal, the Working Committee of the Indian National Congress, meeting in Bombay, and chaired by Gandhi, voted unanimously to revive civil disobedience.

On January 4, as Congress called on the Indian people to refuse to obey British laws, and to resist, without violence, all British orders, the Congress Working Committee was declared an 'unlawful organization', and under a local Bombay regulation of 1827, Gandhi was arrested. Boycotts and picketing spread; the trade of Bombay was brought to a virtual halt by the declaration of *hartals* – days of mourning. An assassination attempt nearly killed the Governor of Bengal. At Midnapore, the successor to the murdered District Magistrate was himself murdered, shot dead during a meeting of his District Board. Hindu-Muslim riots also flared up again. During the first three weeks of May, more than two hundred Indians were killed.

The arrests for civil disobedience were continuous. By the end of February, 32,000 Indians had been arrested and convicted. By the end of the year the number of those arrested and convicted was in excess of 66,000. Many were sent to prison for short terms, but by the end of the year the Government of India announced that 14,815 of those arrested were still in prison, including 610 women. To have been in prison became a badge of national honour. Gandhi, from prison, spoke with great dignity of the inevitable end of British rule as a result of the will of the Indian people.

Those in Britain and India who hoped for a peaceful and constructive resolution of the conflict, and a rapid move forward to Indian self-government, urged the Viceroy to talk with Gandhi, as his predecessor had done. But the new mood in Delhi was against talks. The Government of India reiterated whenever it was asked that there could be 'no question of co-operation with anyone associated with the civil disobedience movement'. Gandhi and the others could have their liberty at any time, the government stated, by giving up noncooperation.

In Bengal, terrorism continued. On February 7 a young woman graduate of Calcutta University, Bina Das, fired five shots at the retiring Governor of Bengal, who narrowly escaped assassination. One British battalion, and six Indian battalions, were sent to Bengal to try to halt the violence. From London, three committees were established, dealing with Indian finance and with the franchise. They were sent out to India to try to find a way forward by satisfying Indian national aspirations, and the conflicting local communal aspirations within India, while at the same time not giving up the ultimate authority of British rule. Indeed, the protection of the smaller communal groups against discrimination by the larger groups was considered one of the main functions of British rule.

In Delhi, a fourth committee, known as the Consultative Committee, devised a system of elections for the Provincial Legislatures whereby six separate electorates would be created for Hindus, Muslims, Sikhs, Indian Christians, Anglo-Indians and Europeans. The Depressed Classes or Untouchables, who were held in such low esteem by their fellow Hindus, for whom they were – literally – the sweepers and scavengers of society, and who lay below the bottom of the Hindu caste hierarchy, were to have the right to vote, not only in Hindu constituencies, but also in special constituencies, for seventy-one 'reserved seats' in the Parliament.

The leader of the Depressed Classes, Dr Ambedkar, was relieved that the Consultative Committee's Award – which was published on August 17 – gave his people special representation in the Provincial Legislatures. The Indian National Congress, however, taking its lead from Gandhi – who was then in jail in Poona – saw this as a divisive move and rejected the inclusion in government of the Untouchables with their own communal rights. By contrast, many caste Hindus were relieved to have these despised people outside their own electoral process. Gandhi was outraged by what he considered this 'backward' attitude. On the day after the Award was announced he wrote to the British Prime Minister that he was totally against separate communal electorates for the Depressed Classes, who were, he argued, an integral part of Hinduism, even if so many of its adherents despised and shunned them. He would, he wrote, resist the proposal 'with his life'.

The British government, seeking to give the Untouchables what it considered their rightful place in the democratic process, rejected Gandhi's demand. On September 20 he began his fast, which would, he said, be total and 'perpetual'. Within India there was an outcry against the government: Gandhi must not die. For four days, negotiations continued in Poona jail. Then an agreement was reached, known as the Poona Pact. The 71 Untouchable constituencies of the Award would be absorbed in the general Hindu voting system. In return for this, Gandhi offered the Depressed Classes, not 71, but 147 reserved seats on the Councils. Not only had the British government given way, but the caste Hindus had also been challenged.

Angered by Gandhi's action, the caste Hindus agitated against the Poona Pact, forcing Gandhi to threaten another fast to death if the Pact were to break down 'owing to the criminal neglect of caste Hindus to implement its conditions'. When, in December, a caste Hindu who was in prison in Ratnagiri for civil disobedience was refused permission by the prison authorities to do scavenging work alongside the Untouchable prisoners in the jail, Gandhi threatened yet another hunger strike 'to death' if permission was not granted. His threat was successful. By the force of his personality, Gandhi was taking on both the British and Hindu establishments.

British soldiers were in action that year in Iraq, where a rebellion by Kurds in the north of the country, led by Sheikh Ahmed Barzani, threatened the authority of the government in Baghdad. A senior British officer, General Robinson, was sent to crush the Kurds. Freya Stark, an intrepid explorer of Arab lands, was travelling in Iraq when the rebellion broke out. On April 10 she sent a friend an account of what had occurred:

> It appears they had an awful smash up – two battalions involved in the mountains, cut off from their fodder, food, ammunition, over a thousand horses, all their baggage, all of which Sheikh Ahmed's people carried off.
>
> General RR, who is supposed to advise, but does not get his advice taken till all is in the soup, rushed up with a small force to try and extricate, and then got his wound in the foot – and very nearly got cut off with the force to be rescued, for they were all surrounded and only disentangled by some very strenuous bombing by the RAF.

So now they are where they were before except that the Kurds have lashings of stores and ammunition. This is rather sad for the first effort of Iraq to manage the Kurds on her own: I suppose it will be kept from the League of Nations, or 'arranged' at any rate – and I don't think you had better mention it around.

Two British officers were captured by the rebels. A British political officer, Captain Vyvyan Holt, was sent from Baghdad to negotiate their release with Ahmed Barzani. Freya Stark explained Holt's mission in a letter on May 8:

He went up to the Kurdish rebels in Barzan (being sent off from our bridge party on Sunday) and got off the two British officers and brought them away with him. He had nothing to offer the sheikh in exchange – but went up and talked of this and that, and said he would explain the Kurdish grievances to the government here, and then eventually added that he would take away the two prisoners. Of course they thought it a joke. But he said he could not go away without them. If they would not give them, he would stay too. They sent him out of the room and finally had him back and agreed, and he and the two (one wounded) and the doctor went back a long trek. Had a bad moment when a message came after one whole day's journey to tell them to turn back. There was nothing for it – they were marched back and spent a night in great suspense, but it was only because something else had happened meanwhile which made the sheikh (Ahmed of Barzan) anxious to see V. H. again: so they set off once more and have got here safe with great kudos.

When, in 1921, Churchill had envisaged a Kurdish National Home, he had been overruled by his officials, who insisted that Britain would always be able to exert a 'restraining hand' on Baghdad in the event of an Iraqi attack on the Kurds. In fact, the Kurds remained at the mercy of Iraqi hostility, though not without considerable tenacity of their own in maintaining some form of independence in their mountain fastnesses.

On March 31, Presidential elections were held in Germany. There were three candidates, eighty-five-year-old Field Marshal Hindenburg (the incumbent President), Hitler, and Ernst Thaelmann, the Communist candidate, a former dockworker who had been a member of the Reichstag since 1924. On the first ballot, Hindenburg secured eighteen million votes, which was insufficient for an immediate win. Hitler, who came second, with eleven million votes, would be the main challenger on the second ballot. Thaelmann, who secured five million votes, could not hope to win.

On the second ballot, held on April 10, the Field Marshal won nineteen million votes, and the former corporal more than thirteen million. Thaelmann secured less than four million. Hitler's share of the poll was 37 per cent.

At Geneva, the League of Nations Disarmament Conference was proceeding. The British Foreign Secretary, Sir John Simon, took the view that only a rapid and comprehensive disarmament treaty could avert the danger of a European war. This meant that the heavily armed nations must begin to disarm at once. Nothing could be worse, Simon warned, than for a disarmed Germany to face a well-armed France. Churchill, then at loggerheads with his own party both over India and Europe, disagreed. Nothing could be worse, he felt, than to weaken France at that particular time. 'I would very much regret,' he said during a debate in the House of Commons, 'to see any approximation in military strength between Germany and France. Those who speak of that as though it were right, or even a question of fair dealing, altogether underrate the gravity of the European situation. I would say to those who would like to see Germany and France on an equal footing in armaments: "Do you wish for war?" For my part, I earnestly hope that no such approximation will take place during my life time or that of my children.'

On May 26, in an article in the *Daily Mail*, Churchill conceded that 'millions of well-meaning English people' hoped that the Disarmament Conference at Geneva would succeed, and he went on to explain the attitude of mind which was drawn to disarmament, and determined to secure it. 'There is such a horror of war,' he wrote, 'in the great nations who passed through Armageddon, that any declaration or public speech against armaments, although it consisted only of platitudes and unrealities, has always been applauded; and any speech or assertion which set forth the blunt truths has been incontinently relegated to the category of "warmongering".'

At every disarmament conference, Churchill pointed out, each State had sought security for itself by maintaining its existing armaments, while urging all other States to disarm down to the lowest level. But was it likely, he asked, that France 'with less than forty millions, faced by Germany with sixty millions – and double the number of young men coming to military age every year – is going to deprive herself of the mechanical aids and appliances on which she relies to prevent a fourth invasion in little more than a hundred years?' Likewise, could the new States of northern and eastern Europe, like Finland, Latvia, Lithuania and Poland, be expected not to seek the most effective armaments possible, 'to protect themselves from being submerged in a ferocious deluge from Russia'.

Yet the cause of disarmament need not necessarily fail. It would be advanced 'steadily', Churchill wrote, 'by the harassing expense of fleets and armies, and by the growth of confidence in a long peace. It will be achieved only when in a favourable atmosphere half a dozen great men, with as many first class powers at their back, are able to lift world affairs out of their present increasing confusion.'

In local German elections, the Nazi Party continued to do well. In the Oldenburg assembly it won twenty-four out of the forty-six seats. Following this electoral success, Nazi bands attacked their Social Democrat and Communist opponents throughout Germany, killing not only political rivals, but also women and children. Brüning tried to take decisive action against the menace of violence. He had already ordained, in February, that members of the Nazi Party, and in particular members of the Nazi militia – the Brownshirts, or Stormtroops – would not be eligible for service in the German army. In April, as the killings in the streets intensified, Brüning decided to disband the Brownshirts altogether. But it was Hindenburg who then intervened, to say that if Hitler's Brownshirts were to be disarmed, so also should the militias of the left-wing parties. Brüning, who did not regard the left-wing militias as dangerous, refused Hindenburg's condition, and disbanded the Brownshirts. Two of his Ministers resigned, his Minister of Economy, Professor Warmold, and his Defence Minister, General Groener. In the Reichstag, Brüning struggled with difficulty to command a majority, and at the end of May he resigned.

On May 30, Brüning was replaced as German Chancellor by Count Franz von Papen. Although the Nazi leaders were not invited to join the new government, von Papen hoped that, with Hitler's tacit support, he could remain in power for several years.

Franz von Papen, the new Chancellor, appointed directly by Hindenburg, was an aristocrat, and an extreme right-wing member of the Centre Party.

He had never been a member of the Reichstag or held elected office. It was he who had been expelled from Washington in 1915 as a result of complaints that he was intriguing to win active American help for Germany. Later he had commanded a battalion on the Western Front, and served as Chief-of-Staff in Palestine to the 4th Turkish Army.

On becoming Chancellor, von Papen resigned from the Centre Party. He would rule as an individual, not as a Party adherent. His aim, he announced in a Ministerial Declaration in the first week of June, was a 'combination of all national forces'. The German people, he said, 'must be informed of the condition in which the Government finds public affairs. The finances of the Reich, of Prussia, and of most of the other Provinces and of the municipalities are in utter disorder. None of the urgently needed reforms without which there can be no recovery has passed beyond the initial stages. The social insurances are faced with bankruptcy. The continually increasing unemployment is consuming the vitals of the German people. The post-war Governments thought that by State Socialism they could relieve both employer and employed of their material anxieties. They have attempted to make the State into a kind of welfare institute. The disintegrating influence of atheistic-marxist thought has penetrated far too deeply into all cultural spheres of public life.'

At the same time as he issued this declaration, von Papen dissolved the Reichstag. He knew that he would be unable to command a majority, and so dispensed with parliamentary rule altogether. He then reversed Brüning's edict dissolving the Nazi Brownshirts, who were once more free to roam the streets. Two States, Bavaria and Baden, insisted, however, on maintaining the previous government's ban on all Brownshirt militias. But von Papen, using the Emergency Decree system which had been introduced by Brüning, forced Bavaria and Baden to allow the Nazi militias to operate legally in their States.

There was now no section of the Reich in which the Nazi uniform was not in evidence, and Nazi terror in the streets not visible. The Oldenburg government, where Nazism was strong, enrolled members of the Brownshirts into the State police force. That summer, in Prussia alone, between June 1 and July 20, seventy-two people were killed in street violence, and nearly five hundred were seriously wounded. Those murdered in street violence throughout Germany numbered several hundred.

On June 19, in the provincial elections at Hesse, the Nazi Party vote increased from 37 to 44 per cent, making it the largest single party in the province. Street violence continued. Von Papen, alarmed at the prospect of civil war, issued a Terror Emergency Decree which authorized special courts to be set up to try political offences. In order to show that even the Nazis could not break the law with impunity, five Nazis were brought to trial in Beuthen (Upper Silesia) and condemned to death for killing a Communist workman.

The international conference on reparations opened at Lausanne on June 16. The anarchic situation inside Germany was on the minds of all the participants. The aim of the conference, in the interest of what it hoped would be a return to stability in Germany, was to reduce Germany's outstanding reparations liability to an absolute minimum. Von Papen represented Germany at Lausanne, gaining a political triumph when, on July 9, the conference accepted everything the Germans had asked for. The only reparations that were retained were a final and nominal demand for 3000 marks.

Commenting on Germany's rising inflation and economic distress, Hitler mocked that those 3000 marks would be worth only 3 marks in a few months' time. In reply – for he was emerging as a leading British critic of Hitler and the Nazis – Churchill pointed out the actual benefits which Germany had gained as a result of the reparations system. These included substantial economic loans from the United States for new industrial machinery, and other aids to industrial production.

It was too late for the ending of reparations to help the moderate elements in Germany. In the streets, Nazi marchers continued to demand Germany's release from the 'shackles' of the Versailles Treaty. In a ceremony at Potsdam, more than a hundred thousand members of the Hitler Youth marched in front of Hitler, who took the salute, standing to attention for seven hours as line after line of the brownshirted youngsters passed in front of him. A General Election was set for the end of July. Hitler used new electoral techniques, including the aeroplane, flying to as many as ten different cities in a single day, speaking at each, and then flying off to his next engagement. Churchill's son Randolph, who had gone to Germany as a young journalist to report on the election campaign, travelled one afternoon in Hitler's aeroplane from meeting to meeting, amazed after every landing by the enthusiasm of the crowds for the Nazi leader.

The election was held on July 31. The Nazi Party won 230 seats, an increase of 63. The Social Democrats secured 133, a decrease of 10. The Communists made gains, but were only able to raise their number of seats from 77 to 89. While still not able to form an absolute majority in the Reichstag, the Nazi Party was by far the largest single Party, and in many ways the most cohesive and the most vociferous. On the day of Hitler's electoral success, Randolph Churchill wrote in the *Sunday Graphic*: 'The success of the Nazi Party sooner or later means war.' Hitler's lieutenants, he explained, 'burn for revenge' for the German defeat of 1918. 'They are determined once more to have an army. I am sure that once they have achieved it they will not hesitate to use it.'

Although, with more than 13.5 million votes, the Nazis were now the largest Party in the State, they had won only 37.1 per cent of the total poll. Von Papen remained Chancellor, and declined to invite them to join his government. Hitler's immediate reaction to his exclusion from power was to intensify the terror in the streets. Writing to London on August 4, the British Ambassador to Germany, Sir Horace Rumbold, described how, in the East Prussian capital, Königsberg, 'prominent Socialists and Communists were surprised at night and murdered in their beds or shot down at the doors of their houses. The windows of shops owned by Jews were smashed and their contents looted.'

On August 13, bowing to the force of terror, von Papen received Hitler in the Chancellery and offered him the post of Vice-Chancellor. Hitler refused; his aim, he said, was to be offered the Chancellorship itself, nothing less. As the 'idol' of more than thirteen million voters he insisted on 'the same degree of power' as had been granted to Mussolini after the March on Rome. Hitler added: 'I consider it my duty to mow down the Marxists.' Hitler then returned to his hotel. Later that afternoon, Hitler was invited by Hindenburg to the President's Palace. The interview lasted only fifteen minutes, during which time Hindenburg rebuked Hitler for not keeping the promises of 'toleration and cooperation' that he had made to the government. After Hitler had left the room, Hindenburg told Otto Meissner, his State Secretary: 'That man for a Chancellor? I'll make him a postmaster, and he can lick the stamps with my head on them.'

The Brownshirts continued unhindered in their work of violence and terror. In 1932 the Jewish New Year began on September 29. On that holy day in the Jewish calendar, several thousand Nazis converged on the Kurfürstendamm, the main street of Berlin's West End, attacking any Jews whom they saw, and knocking them to the ground. As they did so, they cried out with glee the Nazi slogan 'Perish Judah!' Dr Alfred Apfel, a German barrister – and war veteran – later wrote:

> I watched the proceedings from the balcony of my house. When it had been going on for almost an hour, I rang up the Polizeipräsidium and said that I could not understand why there was no police intervention now, seeing that even the smallest demonstration of unemployed was always put down and dispersed with clubs almost before it had got well under way. Finally the police did appear, and the demonstrators fled.
>
> Through the intervention of someone or other, the occurrence was passed over as a harmless incident, but this casual handling of the matter created such a fury of indignation among the dwellers in and habitual frequenters of the Kurfürstendamm that a number of the participants in the onslaught had to be brought to trial for breach of the peace.
>
> The lies of the National Socialist accused, and witnesses, at these hearings fairly raised the roof! And their conduct in the court was so outrageous in its self-assurance, insolence and contempt of the occasion, that it seemed that the very principle of authority had broken down, for neither judges nor prosecuting counsel made a gesture or said a single word to call them to order.

In an attempt to show how patriotic the Jews of Germany had been, the Reich Association of Jewish Front Line Soldiers published a memorial volume giving the names of more than 12,000 Jewish soldiers who had fallen in the First World War. To stress the significance of this Jewish contribution to the war, the first copy to be printed was presented to Hindenburg on October 2, the President's eighty-fifth birthday.

On September 12, during a session of the Reichstag, a motion of censure was brought against the government. Because of the large number of Nazi parliamentarians, the Presidency of the Reichstag had devolved on a Nazi Party member, Hermann Goering, a wartime air force pilot. Using his powers as Reichstag President, Goering refused to allow von Papen to address the Chamber. The members of the government thereupon left the Chamber, and the Reichstag was dissolved. The non-government members remained in the Chamber, and, led by the Nazis, voted massively against the government, by 512 votes to 42. Von Papen ignored the vote, refused to resign, and called new elections for November.

Germany had become a focal point of world attention. But what had seemed the inevitable advance of the Nazi Party to power received a setback in the November elections, with the Nazi share of the vote falling from 37.1 per cent to 33.1 per cent, and their number of seats in the Reichstag falling from 230 to 197. They were still a formidable popular and parliamentary force, but it seemed that their influence was on the wane. The Communists increased their seats from 89 to 100. The Social Democrat representation fell from 133 to 121. Despite the relief in liberal and democratic circles that the Nazi Party had fallen back, it remained the largest Party, and the most aggressive group, in the Reichstag.

Von Papen offered to bring Hitler into his new government. He could have several ministries for his own people, and, as he had already been offered three months earlier, the Vice-Chancellorship for himself. Hitler was not tempted. He wanted, he reiterated, the Chancellorship or nothing. He was still the leader of the largest Party in the Reichstag, and would accept nothing less. He demanded 'the same rights as Mussolini possessed in Italy'. When Von Papen put these demands to Hindenburg, and offered to make way for Hitler as Chancellor, Hindenburg refused. He could not bear the thought of Hitler at the helm. Von Papen, unable to command a majority in the Reichstag, resigned.

Hindenburg had no choice but to ask the leader of the largest Party in the Reichstag to try to form a government. This was Hitler's chance. He could take the post of Chancellor and work with some of the other right-wing and centre parties to try to build a coalition. But he refused to do so. Hitler's aim was complete power, not the sharing of power. He would form a government, Hitler told Hindenburg when they met on November 19, only if he was authorized to form a 'presidential Cabinet', one whose powers would derive, not from the will or votes of parliament, but from the Presidency. He would agree to rule Germany, Hitler informed Hindenburg, only if he could rule without the Reichstag.

Hindenburg could not accept these extraordinary terms. He therefore brought his negotiations with Hitler to an end, instructing his State Secretary to write to Hitler: 'The President of the Reich thanks you for your willingness to become head of a presidential Cabinet. He considers, however, that he would not be doing his duty to the German people if he handed over his Presidential powers to the leader of a Party which has repeatedly emphasized its exclusiveness, and which has taken up a predominantly negative attitude. In these circumstances, the President of the Reich cannot help fearing that a presidential Cabinet conducted by you would inevitably lead to a Party dictatorship, bringing in its train a bitter aggravation of the conflicts within the German people – for becoming a party to which he could not answer to his oath and his conscience.'

Hindenburg turned to a former army officer, General von Schleicher, who had been Minister of Defence under Brüning, and asked him to take over the Chancellorship, and to rule as best he could with a divided and hostile Reichstag. While von Papen had tried to dispense with the Reichstag, and to rule by Emergency Decree, von Schleicher tried to win the confidence of the political parties. 'I am a heretic enough,' he announced in a radio broadcast on December 15, 'to confess I am an adherent neither of capitalism nor of Socialism. My programme consists of a single point – to create employment.'

By the end of 1932 there were six million unemployed in Germany. Von Schleicher hoped to create work for them by means of a massive State building programme, of roads, canals and railways, not unlike Roosevelt's proposal for the reduction of unemployment in the United States. Schleicher also wanted to encourage the return of industrial workers to the land. Both these were relatively long-term projects, especially land resettlement and the creation of a rural labour market to absorb the urban unemployed.

Germany had avoided, but only just, the triumph of the Nazis in 1932, and had seen their popular vote decline. In Austria, the 'Hitlerites' (as they were called) made their first appearance that year, demanding union with Germany, and embarking on violent street demonstrations. They had no place in the parliament, but were strong in the streets. Their greatest weakness was the lack of a leader. Hitler, although Austrian-born and Austrian-educated, was across the border. Without a charismatic local Hitlerite leader, the chances of the German-orientated Austrian Nazis ousting the Austrian Fascists were slim. On April 24, however, in the elections for the provincial Diets, the Hitlerites made large gains, and, in the Vienna Diet, obtained fifteen seats where they previously had none. Their first appearance in the Diet was marked by violent pro-Nazi demonstration in the streets. But the balance of power in the Diets, as in the national Parliament, remained firmly with the *Heimwehr*, Clerical, and Socialist deputies.

On May 20, after a two-week government crisis, an Austrian administration was formed by Dr Engelbert Dollfuss, a member of the Clerical Party who had been Minister of Agriculture in the previous government. He brought two strong *Heimwehr* supporters into his Cabinet, Dr Jakconcig as Minister of Commerce, and Dr Rintelen (the Governor of Styria) as Minister of Education. He also retained another *Heimwehr* supporter, Karl Vaugoin, as Minister of War.

The Hitlerites, still without any place in the national parliament or the government, continued their activities in the streets. An anti-Semitic protest march at Vienna University on May 30 forced the university to close for a week. In search of 'wealthy Jews', a Hitlerite gang entered the International Country Club in Vienna, injuring not only Jews and other Austrians, but also the diplomats of four States. International protests followed, but the Hitlerites were not deterred. On October 16 they marched through one of the socialist quarters of Vienna, attacking the Socialist Secretariat. When the Socialists unexpectedly defended the building by force of arms, two Hitlerites were killed.

The Austrian government sought security by bringing into the Cabinet a founder of the *Heimwehr* organization and militia, Major Frey. He was made Secretary of State for Public Security, and immediately forbade all military marches, except those by the *Heimwehr*. For the moment, local Austrian Fascism was more powerful than the imported Nazi variety; but it was to be only six years before the forbidden union of Germany and Austria took place, under German Nazi rule.

In the United States, the Depression continued, and unemployment reached its highest level, as many as eleven million out of work, out of a total work-force of 58 million. As work could not be found, 'Barter Exchanges' were organized, where, in more than five hundred communities, members who enrolled would offer to work in exchange for food, clothing or shelter. Even the professional classes were drawn in. Doctors accepted chickens or eggs for their services. Some Barter Exchanges even issued their own bank-note-style 'scrip' to facilitate the work-for-goods exchange system.

As the Depression continued there were those who saw an end to the spiral of economic hardship. 'As a country descends the ladder of values,' Winston Churchill wrote to an American stockbroker friend, 'many grievances arise, bankruptcies and so forth. But one must never forget that at the same time all sorts of correctives are being applied, and adjustments being made by millions of people and thousands of firms. If the whole world except the United States sank under the ocean that community could get its living. They carved it out of the prairie and the forests. They are going to have a strong national resurgence in the near future. Therefore I wish to buy sound, low priced stocks.'

The economic distress continued. First World War veterans, forming themselves into an American Legion, demanded an immediate cash bonus. The total sum which they were calling for was $2400 million. President Hoover resisted what he feared would be a dangerous inflationary move, the equivalent to printing a vast amount of money without security. The veterans converged on Washington, 20,000 ex-soldiers in all, many of them with their wives and children. They called themselves the Bonus Expeditionary Force. Living in tents and shacks, they announced that they would not move from Washington until their demand was met. On June 14 the Bonus Expeditionary Force crowded into the Capitol building and persuaded Congress, amid rousing cheers, to vote in favour of the bill. But when the Senate rejected the bill three days later, there was disorder in the streets which continued for several days. On July 28, Hoover called out the troops. The tent camps were broken up and burned, and the marchers finally expelled by force from the capital.

The Democrats were working with great energy to take advantage of Hoover's problems, and to produce a programme of their own, determined to offer hope to America. On July 1, Franklin D. Roosevelt was nominated as the Democratic presidential candidate. Adapting a phrase made famous by Lincoln ('This nation cannot endure if it is half slave and half free') he told his supporters: 'This nation cannot endure if it is half "boom" and half "broke".' The Democrats, he said, would champion the 'forgotten man at the bottom of the economic pyramid'. And he told a cheering audience: 'I am waging a war in this campaign – a frontal attack – an onslaught – against the "Four Horsemen" of the Republican leadership: The Horsemen of Destruction, Delay, Deceit, Despair.'

Roosevelt promised to replace the high protective tariff, which made it so difficult for America to sell its goods overseas, with commercial treaties that would create a reciprocal reduction in trade barriers, and lead to the freer and faster flow of goods in both directions. He would take measures to reduce the money owed by farmers in mortgages and loans. He would do his utmost to decentralize industry, bringing industrial production, and with it greater employment and prosperity, to towns and areas at present outside the industrial belts. He wanted the Federal government to enter the power industry, and to undertake four major Federal projects to bring prosperity and employment to remote and neglected areas. 'Each one of these,' he said, 'in each of the four quarters of the United States, will be for ever a national yardstick to prevent extortion against the public, and to encourage the wider use of that servant of the people – electric power.'[1]

Roosevelt did more than offer a means to tackle unemployment and economic distress. He also pointed the way forward to a fairer society. In the language that he used in a speech at San Francisco, echoing the American Declaration of Independence, he gave hope that a fair deal could be obtained by all citizens. 'Every man has a right to life, and this means that he also has a right to make a comfortable living,' he declared. 'He may by sloth or crime decline to exercise that right; but it may not be denied him.' In addition, Roosevelt said, 'every man has a right to his own property; which means a right to be assured, to the fullest extent attainable, in the safety of his savings.' Financial and industrial leaders must combine to see that these rights were secure; government must act to restrain 'the lone wolf' who would deny them. 'Government includes the art of formulating a policy, and using the political technique to attain so much of that policy as will receive general support; persuading, leading, sacrificing, teaching always, because the greatest duty of a statesman is to educate.'

At the election, held on November 8, there was a Democratic landslide, with Roosevelt carrying forty-two States, as against only six for Hoover. The votes for the two contenders were more evenly balanced, 22 million being cast for Roosevelt and 15 million for Hoover, but this was not enough to affect the outcome in any way, given the State by State majorities for Roosevelt. Under the American system, whereby the actual succession to the Presidency does not take place until the following year, the nation and the world had to wait until 4 March 1933 before Roosevelt's inauguration, and for his presentation of a programme designed to revive America's fortunes.

While the United States looked inward and hoped for the regeneration of its economy, the world – including many Americans – looked at the Far

[1] The four hydro-electric projects proposed by Roosevelt were on the St Lawrence River in the northeast; Muscle Shoals in the southeast, on the Tennessee River; Boulder Dam in the southwest, on the Colorado River; and on the Columbia River in the northwest.

East and saw increasing danger. The Japanese, having occupied Mukden in September 1931, began a systematic advance through Manchuria. As it became clear that the Japanese aim was to occupy all Manchuria, the United States protested. Japan's action was a blow to the 'abolition of war' by the signatories of the Kellogg-Briand Pact (the Pact of Paris) of 27 August 1928; the signatories had included Japan. On 7 January 1932 the United States Secretary of State, Henry L. Stimson, announced what became known as the 'Stimson Doctrine'. Embodied in a note issued simultaneously to China and Japan, it stressed the non-recognition of all international agreements brought about by force. The note stated specifically that the United States did not intend 'to recognize any situation, treaty or agreement which may be brought about by means contrary to the covenants and obligations of the Pact of Paris'. Any agreement which threatened China's independence or territorial integrity would be in this unacceptable category.

The Japanese government replied that with the anarchy prevailing in China, Japan no longer felt bound by the Nine Power Washington Treaty of 1922, which forbade unilateral action against China, and guaranteed an 'open door' for international trade in Manchuria.

The League of Nations saw Japan's advance into Manchuria as a direct challenge to the various pacts and agreements signed since 1920 to prevent aggression, including the Covenant of the League of Nations, to which Japan was a signatory. It therefore sent a Commission of Enquiry to the Far East, headed by a British parliamentarian, Lord Lytton, with four other members, an Italian, a Frenchman, a German and an American. Unlike the international military and naval force that had been despatched in 1900 to impose the will of Europe, the United States and Japan on China, the Lytton Commission was coming as the friend of China and as a peacemaker. Those who looked to the League of Nations to avert conflicts elsewhere should they arise (perhaps as a result of a Nazi seizure of power in Germany) looked with particular concern at what Lytton and his fellow commissioners could achieve.

On February 18, while the Lytton Commission was on its way to the Far East, the Japanese government issued a proclamation in Mukden, establishing a Manchurian Republic, entirely independent of China, to be known as Manchukuo. To rule the new republic, the former Chinese boy emperor, Hsuang Tung (Pu Yi), who had been deposed in 1922, was made Chief Executive. He was twenty-six years old. Later the Japanese declared him

'Hereditary Emperor of Manchukuo', and gave him the 'honour' of a formal coronation.[1]

Anti-Japanese demonstrations took place throughout China, nowhere more actively than in Shanghai. Japanese warships were despatched to Shanghai to protect the 30,000 Japanese living there. A Japanese expeditionary force of 12,000 men, commanded by General Ueda, landed and advanced with the intention of occupying the area in which the Japanese were living. To the general's surprise, there was strong Chinese military opposition, and considerable enthusiasm inside China that the Japanese were not being allowed an easy victory.

When General Ueda issued an ultimatum to the Chinese to let his troops enter Shanghai, it was rejected. He then ordered his troops forward. He was helped in his advance by the Japanese air force, which bombed the Chinese quarter of the city. Hundreds of Chinese were killed before a cease-fire was declared, as a result of British and other European pressure. A truce was signed on March 3, and fighting ceased. Two months later the Japanese troops withdrew from Shanghai.

The British Ambassador in Washington, after a conversation with Stimson on February 9, reported the Secretary of State's view that 'no such shock as events at Shanghai had been administered to the cause of international morality since August 1914'. In elections in Japan that month, the war party gained a clear victory, 303 seats against 146. The Japanese electorate had voted for war.

Lord Lytton and his fellow commissioners had reached the Far East on the last day of February, their work overshadowed at first by the struggle in Shanghai, and the international outrage at the Japanese attacks on civilians in the city. At no time while the commission was in the region did the Japanese government suspend its activities. Instead, it continued to impose its rule on Manchuria, and to gain what advantage it could from its occupation, transferring the customs receipts of the Manchurian ports to the government of Manchukuo, and thereby depriving China of an important annual source of revenue.

[1] Pu Yi remained Emperor of Manchukuo until arrested by Soviet troops in 1945. After ten years in a Siberian prison he was handed over to the Chinese Communists in 1955. In 1959 he was given work in the botanical gardens in Peking, and was later (until his death in 1967) an assistant with the Chinese historical archives department.

Between March and September, the League of Nations commissioners visited China, Japan and Manchuria, ending their work in Peking. Their report was published early in October. It denounced the creation of the Japanese puppet State of Manchukuo, which did not represent the 'spontaneous demand' of its inhabitants. Japan's actions in conquering Manchuria, and in establishing Manchukuo, were at variance, the report insisted, with the League Covenant, and the Pact of Paris. Manchuria should be given 'a large measure' of autonomy, and Chinese sovereignty should be restored.

Japan rejected the Lytton proposals. In December, after considerable obstruction by the Japanese delegate at the League Council, the matter was put before a full meeting of the Assembly. There, twenty-three States supported the Lytton Report, two were noncommittal, and only two supported Japan. But the imposition of the Lytton proposals would require activating the League Covenant, and facing the prospect of armed conflict with Japan. Britain, seeking to avert this, proposed arbitration, another of the paths along which the League of Nations could travel. A Committee of Nineteen existed for just such a course. To put the case before the Committee of Nineteen, a special committee was set up with representatives from five of the League States: Britain, France, Czechoslovakia, Spain and Switzerland. Europe was trying to avert a conflict in which European armies would return to Asia.

Talk had replaced action. The Manchurian crisis became the symbol of the failure of the League of Nations to be able to confront a major act of aggression. The contrast with Europe's rapid and collective action against the Chinese Boxers in 1900 was palpable.

In Manchukuo, groups of Chinese soldiers – denounced by Japan as brigands – had continued throughout the year to attack the Japanese wherever they could. In November these soldiers managed to capture two towns, Anta and Hailun, but were defeated in two pitched battles north and south of Harbin. At the beginning of December the Japanese launched a major offensive against them, forcing the Chinese to retreat across the Soviet border, where they were disarmed and interned.

It was not only the Japanese military successes in Manchuria that caused aggravation to the Chinese government in Nanking. The mass of the population, the peasants and the poor, faced tribulations, hunger and death every time the contending forces marched through their villages and farmsteads. Despite Chiang Kai-shek's three military campaigns against the Chinese

Communists in 1931, the Communists had continued not only to control their base in south Kiangsi – the self-proclaimed Central Provisional Government of the Soviet Republic of China – but had managed to take a number of military initiatives. In May, a Communist army had briefly threatened the treaty port of Amoy before being driven off. In July, Communist forces were in control of hundreds of thousands of square miles in Central China, in the Kiangsi province, and along the Honan–Hupei–Anhui border.

The Chinese Communist military strength was considerable: 100,000 men and 80,000 rifles. But their greatest strength was their tactics, the fluid guerrilla movement of which Mao Tse-tung was the principal advocate. He later described it thus: 'Fluidity of battle lines leads to fluidity in the size of our Soviet areas. Our Soviet areas are constantly expanding and contracting, and often as one area falls another rises. Fluidity in the war and in our Soviet territory produces fluidity in our Soviet construction. Construction plans covering several years are out of the question. Frequent changes of plan are all in the day's work. It is to our advantage to recognize this characteristic. We must base our planning on it, and must not take illusions about a war of advance without any retreats, or take alarm at any temporary fluidity of our Soviet territory. It is only out of today's fluid way of life that tomorrow we can secure relative stability, and eventually full stability.'

Within the Communist party, Mao's guerrilla tactics were being rejected, in favour of the 'forward and offensive line': frontal attacks, army on army. This new line, which was supported by Chou En-lai, gained the ascendancy in 1932, and was formally adopted by the Twelfth Comintern Plenum in Moscow that September. It was the Comintern, sending out its directives from afar, that came to the conclusion that with 'the sharpening of the general crisis of capitalism' (as evidenced, apparently, in both Germany and the United States) the time had come for a 'revolutionary upsurge' everywhere, preparing the masses for the 'impending fight for power' in the short time that remained before capitalism collapsed. In China, according to the Moscow directives, this meant fighting directly 'for the overthrow of the Kuomintang regime'. The directive was obeyed. The result was a catastrophe for the Chinese Communists: the loss of the Kiangsi base. Through Moscow's directives, the coercive hand of Stalin had reached to the shores of the China Sea.

Inside the Soviet Union, that hand was also active in ensuring a nationwide extension of collectivization. On August 7, Stalin personally drafted a law – 'On the Safeguarding of State Property' – which defined collective farm property as all cattle, standing crops and produce, and made it a criminal offence to harm these in any way, or not to hand them over when they were demanded. The penalty for any offence was execution. Only in 'special circumstances' (which were not defined) could the sentence be reduced to a minimum of ten years in prison. The law was rigorously applied, even to those who took a few ears of corn from a field.[1]

The forcible collectivization of agriculture had led to acute peasant hardship, mass deportations, and a collapse of rural productivity. At a meeting of the Communist Party Central Committee that October, sharp criticisms of the Soviet and collective farm system of agriculture were put forward, and an agitation begun to give up collectivization. Not only did collectivization continue, however, but those who fell below the targets set by Moscow were put on trial, accused of sabotage, and shot. The law of August 7 was applied with severity. Yet the peasants could not produce the amounts demanded of them, however hard they tried. The total amount of grain deliveries demanded from them that year exceeded the total crop. As the delivery of whatever grain that had been harvested was ruthlessly enforced, starvation became widespread. That winter, famine once more stalked the fields of Russia: a famine created by State policy.

In the previous Russian famine, the first after the Bolsheviks had come to power, appeals had been launched for help, and the capitalist world had responded with massive aid, supervised by the League of Nations and the Red Cross. For this second famine, which was on an even larger scale, no such appeal was made. Any rumours of hunger were rapidly and decisively denied. When, at the beginning of 1933, the Secretary of the Kharkov Provincial Committee spoke at a closed meeting in Moscow of the scale and horror of the famine, Stalin intervened personally to belittle him. 'We have been told that you, Comrade Terekhov, are a good speaker,' Stalin said. 'It seems that you are a good storyteller, you've made up such a fable about famine, thinking to frighten us, but it won't work. Wouldn't it be better for you to leave your post of provincial committee secretary and the Ukraine Central Committee, and join the Writers' Union? Then you can write your fables and fools will read them.'

*   *   *

[1] When driving through the Ukraine in 1991 (on the road from Brody to Lvov), I stopped by the side of a large cornfield and picked an ear of corn. The Ukrainian student who was accompanying me told me, in shocked tones, that for such a 'crime' sixty years earlier I could have been shot. In the previous three years (since 1988), many articles had appeared in the Soviet press, describing the Stalinist terror of those times.

Siegfried Sassoon, who had fought in the trenches of the Western Front during the First World War, wrote a poem in the early summer of 1932 on the state of the world. It was entitled 'Thoughts in 1932':

> Alive – and forty-five – I jogged my way
> Across a dull green day,
> Listening to larks and plovers, well content
> With the pre-Roman pack-road where I went.
>
> Pastoral and pleasant was the end of May.
> But readers of the times had cause to say
> That skies were brighter for the late Victorians;
> And 'The Black Thirties' seemed a sobriquet
> Likely to head the chapters of historians.
>
> Above Stonehenge a drone of engines drew
> My gaze; there seven and twenty war-planes flew
> Manoeuvring in formation; and the drone
> Of that neat-patterned hornet-gang was thrown
> Across the golden downland like a blight.
>
> Cities, I thought, will wait them in the night
> When airmen, with high-minded motives, fight
> To save Futurity. In years to come
> Poor panic-stricken hordes will hear that hum,
> And Fear will be synonymous with Flight.

In the nineteenth century, politicians and dreamers had put great faith in the steady evolution of all things good: wealth, social harmony and international peace. The twentieth century was undermining this faith, even in years of comparative peace. 'You live in interesting times,' the French poet Paul Valéry told a graduating class in Paris on 13 July 1932. 'Interesting times are always enigmatic times that promise no rest, no prosperity or continuity or security,' and he added: 'Never has humanity joined so much power and so much disarray, so much anxiety and so many playthings, so much knowledge and so much uncertainty.'

CHAPTER THIRTY-SEVEN

1933

THE YEAR 1933 was to be a decisive turning point of the twentieth century. It opened in London with customary optimism. 'Scenes of gaiety and colour,' reported *The Times*, 'marked with joy the passing of the Old Year and with hope the coming of the New in London. There was the customary pandemonium at midnight. The whistling of trains, the ringing of bells, the cheering and yelling of the crowded streets made a discordant but cheerful noise for some minutes. That was in welcome of 1933. The wail of the sirens from ships in the river sounded like the hooting of unpopular 1932.' The newspaper continued:

> It was one of the gayest New Year's Eves that London has known. Crowds, highly good-humoured, paraded the streets. Theatres, music-halls, picture-houses were packed. Laughter, song, and dance held sway in all the West End hotels, restaurants, and cabarets.
>
> As it was also the last night of a Leap Year the hosts of many of the dinner parties were women, and at midnight the right of 'popping the question' was restored to bachelors.
>
> There were more than a thousand revellers – including many oversea visitors to London – at the Savoy, where the restaurant had been transformed into an Old English fair. Trumpeters of the Life Guards greeted 1933 with a fanfare, and after midnight showers of multi-coloured balloons descended on the guests. Royal Artillery trumpeters did likewise at Ciro's and at the Hotel Victoria the New Year was ushered in by pipers of the Scots Guards.
>
> Midnight tableaux were a feature of the festivities at some restaurants. At the Berkeley a child typifying 1933 stepped from a globe representing the World, and pretty girls in costume distributed 1933 gifts among the guests at Claridge's after midnight. The diners here included many members of the Diplomatic Corps.

Miss 1933 stepped from a huge Christmas pudding at Grosvenor House and led the singing of 'Auld Lang Syne.' At the Metropole she appeared from the face of a gigantic Big Ben as the twelve solemn strokes announced her arrival. At the Dorchester she came accompanied by two hand-maidens, Love and Charity, and was welcomed by Peace, Prosperity, and Happiness.

In Republican Spain, there were likewise hopes that the New Year would be a prosperous one. 'In general,' reported *The Times*, 'Spaniards look forward to the New Year with hope born of the moral strength and physical robustness that are outstanding characteristics of the race, mother of a score of nations. Nothing dims their fundamental optimism even if at times whole sections of the community take refuge in the enigmatic fatalism inherited during five centuries of Moorish dominion.' The left-wing press, *The Times* added, 'publishes congratulatory reviews of the principal achievements of the Republic during 1932 and outlines an ambitious programme for 1933; while the organs of the Right call upon the Conservatives to unite and organize with a view to retrieving past errors and securing during the coming year representation in the councils of the State.'

As the year began however, rioting broke out in Barcelona, led by anarchists and syndicalists, who also attacked a military barracks. Bombs were thrown, and in the resulting clash between rioters and police, three people were killed. When police tried to stop a car carrying anarchists and their bombs, there was a prolonged shoot-out and two anarchists were killed. One man was killed when police fired without warning into a shop in which several citizens had taken refuge. Another man was killed when the taxi in which he was travelling was accidentally hit in crossfire between anarchists and police. An attack on the Palace of Justice was repulsed. After three days of fighting, twenty people had been killed.

The violence, and general strikes, spread rapidly to different cities. Valencia, Cadiz and Seville were all affected, and the death toll rose. A pamphlet circulated by the National Federation of Labour and the Anarchist Federation stated that the general strike had been declared 'not merely as a revolutionary protest against the hardships and penalties imposed on the working classes by the authorities of all ranks, but with a view to promoting a social revolution by means of an answer of the people.'

On January 10 the Spanish government declared martial law in the disturbed regions. Henceforth, prisoners would be judged by military, not civilian courts. But the spirit of defiance was strong, the Syndicalist leader, Andres Nin, a Catalan and a friend of Trotsky, telling the correspondent of *The Times*:

> We began first with an educational campaign, and now we are engaged in organizing workers' soviets (councils) in anticipation of the crucial moment when the workers must be the first to arrive on the scene and seize power or lose it without hope of recovery for a considerable term of years.
>
> When the Dictatorship fell, we undertook to group the masses round the symbols of democracy, such symbols as they could understand to give the masses illusions, so that at the right moment the politico-social movement might pass to their hands from those of the *bourgeoisie*. Therefore, we organized revolutionary juntas, which in Spain have a traditional significance, and which at the right moment could be converted into soviets.
>
> We also sought to implant the idea of the expropriation of land, of separation of Church and State, of universal suffrage of both sexes, beginning at the age of eighteen. Thus power would be placed in the hands of the masses and of youth.
>
> Under the Republic we have adopted double tactics – that of conquering the workers and presenting a united front, and that of capturing the syndicates. The international situation will profoundly affect the prospects for Communism in Spain. If, for instance, German Fascism, in spite of its temporary defeat, succeeds in establishing itself before the victory is won here, it will be the death-blow to our cause.

In Germany there were expectations as 1933 began that Hitler and the Nazi Party, having suffered a setback in the polls the previous November, but still constituting the largest single party in the Reichstag and still active in the streets, would try to seize power; and that they would do so with a far greater chance of success than eight years earlier, in Munich.

Those political leaders of the German Republic who were themselves out of power sought to bring Hitler into the governing system. On January 4 the former Chancellor, Franz von Papen, met Hitler in Cologne and proposed that the two men work together against the current Chancellor, General von Schleicher, and towards the establishment of a new government in which they would both have equal powers, and some form of joint Chancellorship.

Hitler reiterated his demand that the only administration he would join was one in which he held the Chancellorship without any restrictions. Of course, he added, he would gladly bring von Papen and others of his group into the Cabinet, but the Chancellorship must be his alone.

On January 15 Hitler received a boost when, in the provincial elections in Lippe, the Nazi Party vote was increased by 20 per cent over the previous November. This was a clear sign that what his opponents had much trumpeted as a decline might not be very long lasting. President Hindenburg's State Secretary, Otto Meissner – who had served successive Presidents in that capacity since 1920 – told a foreign diplomat on January 27 that the most likely successor to von Schleicher was a majority government 'embracing all parties', in which Hitler would be Chancellor and von Papen Vice-Chancellor, and in which the Nazis would have 'one or two' Cabinet posts. With the majority of Hitler's Cabinet not being members of his party, the Nazis 'would be unable to embark on dangerous experiments'.

Otto Meissner was right about the change of government. On January 28, von Schleicher went to see Hindenburg. Von Schleicher had been Chancellor for only fifty-four days, but, unable to command a majority in the Reichstag, he asked Hindenburg if he could dissolve it. To dissolve the Reichstag, Presidential approval was needed. When Hindenburg refused, von Schleicher told the President that he wished to resign. Hindenburg accepted, and von Schleicher withdrew from political life.

Hindenburg's next act was to follow the constitutional procedure of entrusting the Chancellorship to the leader of the largest party in the Reichstag, and on January 30 he offered Hitler the post of Chancellor. Hitler accepted. In order to ensure that he could command a majority in the Reichstag, he made von Papen his Vice-Chancellor and retained von Neurath as Foreign Minister. The leader of the German National People's Party, Hugenberg, was brought in as Minister of Commerce and Food. Thus Hitler secured the loyalty of the second largest nationalist bloc in the parliament. A year later, when Hitler no longer had need of Hugenberg or his votes, he pushed him aside. Hugenberg survived the Nazi era as a private citizen, dying after the Second World War at the age of eighty-six.

The Nazi Party, while not holding an absolute majority in the Reichstag, became overnight the power in the land. Throughout Germany, as the news of Hitler's Chancellorship spread, the Brownshirts, who for so many months had been the terror of the streets, marched in triumph. They knew that their triumph was complete, and that no arrangement of Cabinet offices could reduce or restrain it. That night the watchers from the British Embassy witnessed the Nazi triumph: 'From 8 p.m. till past midnight', the ambassador's wife, Lady Rumbold, wrote to her mother two days later, 'a continuous procession went past the Embassy, of Nazis in uniform and their admirers, bands, flags, torches, over four hours of it! The old President watched from his window, and a little further down the street the new Chancellor, Hitler, and his supporters stood on a balcony, and had a stupendous ovation. On *our* steps, and perched up on the ledge with the columns, stood wild enthusiasts, singing all the old German hymns! Every now and then there were shouts of "Germany awake", "Down with the Jews", "Heil Hitler"! It seemed as tho' the whole of Berlin was processing along the Wilhelmstrasse.'

Another of those who witnessed the Nazi triumph on the night of January 30, in Berlin's West End, was Dr Alfred Apfel. 'In an uninterrupted stream', he recalled, 'huge hordes of Brownshirts marched in procession down the Kurfürstendamm where I lived, with cries of "Heil!," and singing their Party songs. Among these songs, the tunes of which were for the most part stolen from the Communists, one particularly struck my ear, because it was the one most often repeated. Later on I was to hear it not a hundred, but a thousand times more. It was made the national anthem; it resounds on every possible and impossible occasion, at official parades, at opening nights of plays, at school celebrations and at funerals. Not until some weeks later did I learn that this hymn was called the "Horst Wessel" song.'

The name Horst Wessel sounded familiar to Dr Apfel. 'I seemed to have heard it somewhere, though I could not immediately place it. I thought back. Suddenly I remembered – in one of the numerous trials I had conducted during the past years I had as client the alleged murderer of a certain Horst Wessel.' A working-class Nazi, Horst Wessel, then aged twenty-two, had been shot in January 1930 in his Berlin apartment, by a Communist, in what seems to have been an argument between two pimps. While Horst Wessel was lying badly wounded, his landlady tried to bring a doctor to attend to his wounds, but a Nazi friend who was with him refused to let the nearest doctor, a Jew, be brought to his assistance. 'Let him die,' said the friend, 'sooner than a Jewish doctor shall attend him.'

Horst Wessel died six weeks after the shooting. The Nazi leaders at once turned him into a hero. The Horst Wessel song, heard in Berlin on the night of Hitler's triumph in January 1933, reflected the Party propagandists' political skill in creating a hero of a man in the street, and in glorifying him as an innocent victim of Communist violence.

Hitler did not impress all observers. 'A stubby little Austrian with a flabby handshake, shifty brown eyes, and a Charlie Chaplin moustache' was how, in London, the Labour Party newspaper the *Daily Herald* described him on January 31. The paper was also convinced that with Hitler's appointment as Chancellor 'the way is dramatically prepared for the return of the ex-Kaiser', who, it added, had 'seven cars ready' to 'whisk him back to Germany'.

'Germany is on the brink of a great political adventure,' wrote the *Daily Mail*. 'Let us hope that it will practise moderation and prove a success.' Many observers were concerned that Hitler would act, and act quickly, to extinguish democracy in Germany. On January 31, in London, *The Times* expressed that concern in a convoluted way that betrayed its unease. 'The question is being asked by parties of the Left and upholders of the Constitution,' it wrote, 'whether, once firmly established, with the Prussian police in Captain Göring's hands, the Reichswehr no longer under General von Schleicher's control, and the Nazi "Brown Army," if not recognized by the State, at any rate conscious of being the personal guard of the Chancellor, the Government would easily be persuaded to follow the strictly constitutional path.'

The question was soon answered. On February 1 the *Manchester Guardian* reported from Berlin that 'Jews are being expelled from the University'. The first formal step to dictatorship, an Emergency Decree passed by the Reichstag on February 5, expropriated all Communist Party buildings and printing presses, and closed down all pacifist organizations. Brownshirts, buoyed up by the enthusiasm of the constitutional victory, broke into trade union buildings, and beat up political opponents in the streets.

On February 27, when fire broke out inside the Reichstag building, Hitler found the opportunity to take a second formal step towards dictatorship. Even before the blaze had been extinguished, and before any guilt could be established – the culprit was a deranged Dutchman with no political leanings – Hitler demanded new rules concerning 'protective custody'. These rules, legalizing arbitrary imprisonment without warrant or trial, came into effect on February 28. They were followed immediately by mass arrests, and a settling of accounts with political opponents. One of those arrested, a Berliner by the name of Bernstein, was given fifty lashes because he was a Communist, and then a further fifty lashes because he was 'also a Jew'.

Elections were held throughout Germany on March 5. Although the Nazi vote increased to more than seventeen million, it was still not an absolute majority of the forty million electors. The Social Democrats had secured seven million votes, and the Communists just under five million. The Centre Party, which in more settled times had been the dominant party, won less than four and a half million votes. The Nazis, with 44 per cent of the poll, obtained 288 seats in the 647-seat Reichstag. This was their largest ever number, but not enough to form a majority government. Hitler was disappointed by the results, but not deterred. In an extraordinary move, that was only possible because of the strength of the Brownshirts in the streets, the eighty-one newly elected Communist deputies were told that they would not be invited to the opening of the Reichstag on March 7.

The terror against the Jews continued. On March 9 the Brownshirts were active throughout Berlin. Many Jews were beaten. The *Manchester Guardian* reported that the beatings went on 'until the blood streamed down their heads and faces, and their backs and shoulders were bruised. Many fainted and were left lying on the streets.' The Brownshirts worked in groups of between five and thirty men, 'the whole gang often assaulting one person'.

This terror in the streets of Germany was witnessed by foreign diplomats and by journalists from the world press. But, beginning on March 9, terror found a hidden base behind barbed wire. Starting on that day, the SS sent thousands of critics of the regime, including Communists, Social Democrats, Trade Unionists, and Jews of all backgrounds, to a so-called 'concentration camp' which had been set up on the outskirts of the town of Dachau, near Munich. The camp was run by the local Dachau SS, which had already become notorious as one of the most brutal SS platoons in Bavaria. The name 'concentration camp' was taken from the camps set up by the British during the Boer War at the beginning of the century, in which more than 80,000 Boers and blacks had died. During the course of March 1933, the concentration camp at Dachau was enlarged to enable 5000 prisoners to be kept there.

Meanwhile, the terror in the streets continued. Jews were everywhere chosen for particular humiliation and brutality. On March 11, Jewish-owned department stores in Braunschweig were looted. On March 13, all Jewish lawyers and judges were expelled from court in Breslau. On March 15, in Berlin, three Jews were arrested by Brownshirts in the Café New York, taken to a local Brownshirt headquarters, robbed of all their money, beaten bloody with rubber truncheons, and then turned out into the streets semiconscious.

Hitler took rapid steps to extend his control to all the German States. The Bavarian government, which since January 30 had resisted Nazi intimidation, was forced on March 9 – the day of the opening of Dachau Concentration Camp – to replace its Minister of the Interior by a veteran Bavarian Nazi, Franz Ritter von Epp, who had commanded troops which helped to suppress the Soviet Republic of Bavaria in 1919 and the labour unrest in the Ruhr in 1920. Similar Nazi takeovers were instituted in all the States which resisted. At the same time, not only Communist but also Social Democrat newspapers were shut down. The Centre Party also felt threatened. Brüning himself found it wise to change apartments when he learned that a man resembling him had been attacked in the street. In Leipzig, the distinguished German conductor Bruno Walter was prevented from conducting a concert because he was Jewish.

Towards the end of March the British Ambassador's wife wrote home, through the safety of the diplomatic bag: 'Dreadful things happen all the time, and as the Press is muzzled are never heard by the public. All sorts of terrorizing of Jews and Socialists, and 40,000 are supposed to be in prison. Endless writers and professors etc are persecuted, while old government officials are ruthlessly turned out, often without pensions. It is hateful and uncivilized!'

The ceremonial opening of the Reichstag took place at the Garrison Church in Potsdam on March 21. For the first time since Germany's defeat in 1918, a political ceremony was given military trappings, and that harked back to the grand imperial ceremonials of the Wilhelmine era at the turn of the century. 'The entire gallery on one side of the church,' a foreign diplomat reported home, 'was filled with marshals, generals and admirals of the Imperial regime, headed by Field Marshal Mackensen, wearing the uniform of the Death's Head Hussars.' It was Mackensen who, during the First World War, had successively commanded the armies that defeated the Russians, the Austrians, the Serbians and the Roumanians; two years before the turn of the century he had accompanied the Kaiser on a triumphant visit to Palestine. Now, aged eighty-four (two years younger than President Hindenburg), and in his prewar uniform, he represented the military glories of the German past.

The members of the Reichstag walked to the Garrison Church between rows of flagpoles, on which the swastika banner and the black-and-white flag of the German Empire had been hoisted side by side. Soldiers in their German army uniforms, and Brownshirts in theirs, lined the roadway. At the opening ceremony, Hindenburg, who was dressed in the field-grey uniform of a Prussian Field Marshal (as President he was almost always seen in civilian clothes), spoke briefly, calling for 'a proud and free Germany, united in herself.' Then Hitler spoke. He promised that he would 'cherish the great traditions of the German people' and declared that Germany had neither been responsible for the First World War, nor had she lost it.

On the following day, in an article entitled 'On the New Germany', Leon Trotsky wrote from his place of exile in Turkey: 'It is clear that the twentieth century is the most disturbed century within the memory of humanity. Any contemporary of ours who wants peace and comfort above all, has chosen a bad time to be born.'

On March 23 the Reichstag opened in its new Berlin quarters, the Kroll Opera House. The corridors were patrolled by uniformed SS and SA men. Behind the dais hung a huge swastika banner. Hitler, wearing a Brownshirt uniform, promised to end unemployment and pursue peace with France and Britain – even with the Soviet Union. To do this, he said, he needed a special law to be enacted as soon as possible. He called it the Law for Alleviating the Distress of the People and Reich. It was in fact an Enabling Law, far more drastic than the one through which Brüning had ruled.

Hitler's law, should it be passed by the Reichstag, would suspend altogether the Weimar constitution under which the German Republic had been ruled since 1920, and would enable the government to pass any legislation it chose, without the need for a parliamentary majority. In order to pass into law, any Enabling Bill required, under the Weimar constitution, a two-thirds majority in the Reichstag. Hitler submitted his Bill to the Reichstag that day. The Social Democrat Party leader opposed it, but the Centre Party leader, whose party had seventy-three seats, gave it his support. As a result, the Bill passed by 441 votes to 94.

The seventy-three votes of the Centre Party gave Hitler the votes, and the power, he wanted. A week later the British ambassador to Germany telegraphed to the Foreign Minister in London, in a secret despatch: 'I understand that the reason why the Centre Party passed the Enabling Bill was because they knew their leaders would also be persecuted and sent to concentration camps on the slightest pretext.'

An era of German elections and parliamentary life had come to an end. An era of dictatorship and terror had begun.

The first changes that Hitler instituted after passing the Enabling Bill were to remove all Jews from their positions in the civil service and in the teaching professions. He was convinced that a sustained attack on the Jews would be a unifying force to win him popular support. Not only did the anti-Jewish measures seem to excite whole sections of the public, but they were something he had looked forward to in his book *Mein Kampf*, first published eight years earlier – and which, after considerable lack of success in the bookshops in the first years, had recently become a best seller.

With a fanfare of enthusiasm, in the last week of March the Nazi Party announced an imminent and open-ended Nazi boycott of Jewish shops. The proposed boycott was given considerable publicity outside Germany. There were many protests. On March 27 a vast crowd at a mass rally in New York's Madison Square Garden threatened to institute a counter-boycott of all German-made goods unless the anti-Jewish boycott was called off. The Nazi leaders bowed to the threat of economic reprisals and limited themselves to a one-day, Sabbath, boycott of all Jewish-owned shops, cafés and businesses. In every German city, posters declared: 'The Jews of the whole world are trying to destroy Germany. German people, defend yourselves! Don't buy from the Jews!'

On the eve of the boycott, the Italian Ambassador in Berlin, Vittorio Cerruti, went to see Hitler, with a request from Mussolini to soften his attitude to the Jews. Hitler told the ambassador that Mussolini did not understand the Jews, whom he, Hitler had studied 'for long years, from every angle, like no one else'. Hitler also ventured a prophesy. It was certain, he told the ambassador, that in five or six hundred years' time the name Hitler would be honoured in all lands 'as the man who once and for all exterminated the Jewish pest from the world'.

The anti-Jewish boycott began at ten in the morning on Sunday, April 1. 'I believe that today I act in unison with the Almighty Creator's intention,' Hitler declared. 'By fighting the Jews I do battle for the Lord.' Brownshirts, standing outside Jewish-owned shops, carried placards urging 'Germans' not to enter. The Star of David was painted in yellow across the doors and windows of thousands of shops, and, in crude lettering, the single word *Jude*, 'Jew', as well as the sign of the swastika and the slogans, 'Perish Judah!', 'Jews, Out!', 'Go to Palestine!' and 'Go to Jerusalem!'

On every Jewish shop, wrote the wife of the British Ambassador, 'was plastered a large notice warning people not to buy in Jewish shops. In many cases special notices were put up saying that sweated labour was employed in that particular shop, and often you saw caricatures of Jewish noses'. It was, she added, 'utterly cruel and Hunnish the whole thing, just doing down a heap of defenceless people'. To see people pilloried in this fashion, she wrote three days later, 'a very large number of them quite harmless, hard-working people, was altogether revolting, and left a very nasty taste in the mouth'.

In his diary, Hitler's Minister of Propaganda, Dr Josef Goebbels, described this organized, absurd and cruel display as 'an imposing spectacle'. During the course of the twenty-four-hour boycott, one Jew was killed. He was a lawyer named Schumm who had been arrested at Kiel after an altercation with a Brownshirt. He was then taken to the Brownshirt headquarters in the town and shot. 'As a matter of fact,' Hitler declared in his first speech after the boycott, 'the Jews in Germany have not had a hair of their heads rumpled.'

On April 7 the concept of a racial difference between German Jews and all other Germans was given legal status when the German government ordered the dismissal – called the 'retirement' – of all civil servants 'who are not of Aryan descent'. This dismissal took place immediately, irrespective of age or length of service. As teachers were civil servants in Germany, this also meant the dismissal of all Jewish schoolteachers and university lecturers and professors.

By giving German non-Jews the status of 'Aryan' – an imaginary ethnic concept based upon spurious scientific theories of racial purity – Hitler formally divided German citizens into two groups. 'The greatest achievements in intellectual life', he told the German Doctors' Union, 'can never be produced by those of an alien race, but only by those who are inspired by the Aryan and German spirit.'

German cities competed in zealous pursuit of the new 'Aryan' ideal. In Frankfurt, on the day of the 'Aryan Law', German Jewish teachers were forbidden to teach in the universities, German Jewish actors to perform on the stage, and German Jewish musicians to play in concerts. The very concept of 'German Jewish' was being denied and denounced: one could either be a German, or one could be a Jew. On April 7 *The Times* lamented 'the prostitution of a patriotic movement to the satisfaction of racial jealousies and personal spites' and added: 'There is nothing edifying in the spectacle of the incitement of a great nation, which for years defied the world in arms, against a defenceless minority of less than one per cent.'

In the British House of Commons, Austen Chamberlain – a former Foreign Secretary – spoke words of warning. 'Before we can accede to Germany's demand for Treaty revision,' he said, 'we must be quite certain that the domineering spirit has departed from Germany.' That day, it was reported in the newspapers that Marie Jankowski, a forty-six-year-old German secretary, had been taken from her home near Berlin by fourteen Nazis, stripped and beaten. She had earlier spoken out against the regime.

To terrorize all political opponents – church leaders, Communists, homosexuals and Jews – the new government set up concentration camps at Esterwegen and Sachsenhausen, in addition to the one at Dachau. In each of these camps, daily beatings and harsh treatment were the rule. By the beginning of April 1933, there were a thousand German citizens, of whom fewer than a hundred were Jews, being held at Dachau without warrant, or trial. News of conditions in the concentration camps circulated both inside and outside Germany. 'This Nazi revolution', wrote the British ambassador in Berlin to a diplomatic colleague in London, 'has brought out some of the worst characteristics in the German character, namely, a mean spirit of revenge, brutality amounting in many cases to bestiality, and complete ruthlessness.'

This letter was dated April 11. On the following day, in Dachau, four Jews died as a result of deliberate sadism. An eye-witness account of their deaths was smuggled to Britain by a non-Jewish prisoner who was later released. 'A few days ago', he wrote, 'we were going out as usual to work. All of a sudden the Jewish prisoners – Goldmann and Erwin Kahn, merchants, Benario, a lawyer from Nuremberg, and a medical student, Artur Kahn – were ordered to fall out of the ranks. Without even a word, some Stormtroop men shot at them; they had not made any attempt at escape. All were killed on the spot. All had bullet wounds in their foreheads.' The four Jews were buried openly, the SS being present. 'Then a meeting was called, and a Stormtroop leader made a speech in which he told us that it was a good thing these four Jewish sows were dead. They had been hostile elements who had no right to live in Germany; they had received their due punishment.'

On April 13, in the British House of Commons, Winston Churchill warned of the dangers of the 'odious conditions now ruling in Germany' being extended by conquest to Poland, 'and another persecution and pogrom of Jews begun in this new area'.

German Jews acted as best they could to ameliorate their situation. On April 13 a group of Jewish bankers, community leaders and Zionists established in Berlin a Central Bureau for Relief and Rehabilitation. But on that same day, at Berlin University, notices appeared on the campus: 'Against the un-German spirit'. 'Our most dangerous opponent', these notices declared, 'is the Jew. The Jew can only think Jewish. If he writes German, he is lying. The German who writes German and thinks Jewish is a traitor.'

The first Jews had reached German soil in Roman times. Jews had lived in Germany for more than a thousand years. The Jewish contribution to Germany's military sacrifices in the Great War had been a source of pride to the German Jewish community. Jews had been among the leading rebuilders of Germany after the defeat of 1918, and among those who suffered most severely from the postwar economic turmoils. All this was now to be forgotten, or denied. 'We mean to treat the Jew as a foreigner,' the Berlin University placards stated. Twelve days later, the German government passed an Act 'against the excessive number of students of foreign race in German schools and universities'. Under the Act, German Jews were to be considered 'of foreign race'.

On April 20 Hitler celebrated his forty-fourth birthday. Six days later, one of the main instruments of State control in the German Republic, the *Geheime Staatspolizei*, or Secret State Police, was taken over by the Nazi Party as its own domain. Known as the Gestapo, it was given the power to shadow, arrest, interrogate and intern, without reference to any other State authority. The apparatus of dictatorship was complete: the SS security service and its SD intelligence arm; the Gestapo secret police; and the concentration camps to which their victims could be consigned. Law courts, and due process of law, defence lawyers, and appeal courts, were, for Nazi Germany, things of the past.

*   *   *

On March 3, thirty-three days after Hitler had come to power in Germany, Franklin Roosevelt was inaugurated as President of the United States. Ironically, on that day the United States was going through yet another of its periodic banking crises, and the banks were open in only one State. But in his inaugural address Roosevelt spoke with ringing words of hope that were to mark out the mood and philosophy of his Presidency, telling the nation: 'So, first of all, let me assert my firm belief that the only thing we have to fear is fear itself – nameless, unreasoning, unjustified terror which paralyses needed efforts to convert retreat into advance.'

Roosevelt then spoke of what he called the 'dark realities of the moment', but he went on to point out – as Churchill had done the year before – that the resources of the United States were very great. 'Plenty is at our doorstep,' he said, 'but a generous use of it languishes in the very sight of supply.' He then criticized the standards and conduct of business leaders, and went on to make a number of promises. For the unemployed he promised employment on public works; for the farmer, he promised efforts to raise the prices of agricultural products. He promised measures to prevent foreclosure on farms and homes. The cost of government would be reduced.

Turning to foreign affairs, Roosevelt sought to set a new tone for the involvement of the United States. His words sounded homely and even mellifluous, not in any way ending isolation, and yet they had a moral tone to them that had been absent since the Congress's rebuff to Woodrow Wilson thirteen years earlier. 'In the field of world policy,' Roosevelt said, 'I would dedicate this nation to the policy of the good neighbour – the neighbour who resolutely respects himself and, because he does so, respects the rights of others – the neighbour who respects his obligations and respects the sanctity of his agreements in and with a world of neighbours.' Lurking in this pledge was the implication that the United States would stand aside only if each of the nations of the world 'respects the right of others'. And if not? Nothing was spelt out. But within that phrase was to lie, under Roosevelt's leadership, the greatest contribution of the United States, not only to the twentieth century, but to the survival of parliamentary democracy.

It was the immediate, urgent needs of a damaged society that opened, and ended, Roosevelt's inaugural speech. If necessary, he concluded, he would ask Congress for 'broad executive power to wage a war against the emergency, as great as the power that would be given to me if we were in fact invaded by a foreign foe.' The next day, Congress met in special session. By nightfall a proclamation was issued closing all banks for four days. When Congress met on March 9 it passed an Emergency Banking Act which gave the President the power to reopen banks only if they were proved to be sound.

Roosevelt acted both legislatively and personally to restore confidence. On March 12, only nine days after his inauguration, he broadcast to the American people the first of what were to be regular 'fireside chats', in which he explained what he was doing. He also held his first Press conference, a device that he was also to use a great deal in the months and years ahead, to good effect. The restoration of confidence was his goal, and it succeeded.

The special session of Congress that followed Roosevelt's inaugural lasted for a hundred days. That session produced more legislation than any other comparative period in American history: this was the beginning of the New Deal, whereby the United States would recover not only its economic power, its industrial productivity and its agricultural strength, but its enormous internal energy and creativity.

Dictatorship, suffused with fear, had been established in Germany; a New Deal, offering new hope, had been launched in the United States. In the Far East, an armistice was being negotiated between Japan and China. It meant that a 'demilitarized zone' would be established south of the Great Wall, to be patrolled by a special Chinese gendarmerie. The Japanese occupation of Manchuria – and of the adjacent province of Jehol – had to be accepted by China as an unwelcome but unchallengeable fact.

In the Soviet Union, as the first third of the twentieth century came to its end that April, another grim saga of the imposition of Communist rule was coming to an end. Three years earlier Stalin had given orders for the construction of a canal linking the Baltic Sea and the White Sea. This was one of the much-vaunted 'gigantic' projects of the Five Year Plan, whereby the Soviet Union was to enter the modern industrial age. The project was not placed under the authority of the Commissar for Industry, however, or under the Commissar for the Five Year Plan. Instead, it was given to the political police, the OGPU (later the KGB) to complete.

The OGPU provided the labour needed from the many hundreds of prisons and labour camps under its jurisdiction. Among the prisoners sent to dig the canal were the peasants who had been, and were still being arrested as Kulaks. There were also political prisoners, some of them opponents of the regime, but many of them Communists who had never knowingly acted against the Soviet State or its all-demanding ideology. These Communists had been selected for punishment to deter any form of dissent among those left behind. The Kulaks and political prisoners provided a continuous source of fresh labour when it was needed. They died in the labour camps along the canal in their tens of thousands. Arthur Koestler, a Hungarian-born Jew who had been attracted to Communism in his youth, reflected, in *Darkness at Noon* (1940): 'Death was no mystery in the movement; there was nothing exalted about it: it was the logical solution to political divergencies.'

As many as 300,000 slave labourers worked on the construction of the White Sea–Baltic canal at any one time. The total deaths among them are estimated at 200,000. When the canal was completed, Stalin himself visited it, and went on a short boat ride along it. Among those on the boat with him was G. G. Yagoda, the deputy head and effective chief of the OGPU, who had been associated with the Soviet terror since its earliest days.[1]

That April a public manifestation of Soviet power took place, for all the world to see. For eight days, starting on April 12, the trial took place in Moscow of several British and Russian engineers, accused of sabotage. John Cushny, Albert William Gregory, William MacDonald, Allan Monkhouse, Charles Nordwall and Leslie Thornton were British subjects, employees of the engineering firm of Metropolitan-Vickers, whose task was to maintain various power stations in the Soviet Union. Stalin wanted to show the need to combat 'wrecking and espionage' by the tightening of State control over every aspect of national life. The court was told that 'the counter-revolutionary activity of the wrecking group, which was active in a number of State power stations, consisted of: 1) Damaging equipment with the object of undermining the power of Soviet industry and weakening the Soviet State; 2) Gathering secret information of importance for the defence of the State and utilizing it to the detriment of the State; 3) Bribing and corrupting certain employees of State power stations in connection with the carrying out of counter-revolutionary wrecking activities by these employees.'

The main thrust of the trial was the need for eternal Soviet vigilance against internal and external enemies. Shortly after midnight on April 18 the verdict was delivered: guilty, with prison sentences for the Russians, and expulsion from the Soviet Union for the Britons. There was anger in

---

[1] In January 1996, driving north from St Petersburg, I crossed the White Sea–Baltic canal for the first time. It was a bright, cold winter's day, and the canal presented an idyllic scene, with frost-covered trees lining its bank. Nothing could have been further removed from the scenes of torment that must have been visible on those same canal banks sixty-three years earlier.

Britain at what was clearly a trumped-up charge. The paranoia of the Soviet leader and the isolation of the Soviet Union were complete.

By 1933, the twentieth century had failed to reverse Churchill's pessimistic description of it in 1922 as a 'terrible' century in which things could only worsen. The many hopes of the peoples of the post-war world had not been realized over much of the surface of the globe. The United States, which had looked forward to years of prosperity amid its new-found isolation, was grasping at the hope that it could emerge from the depression, but without any guarantee of success. Western Europe was faced suddenly with the prospect of a rearming and aggressive Germany.

The new States of Eastern Europe struggled, like Czechoslovakia, to maintain their democratic way of life, or, like Yugoslavia, at least to retain under dictatorship a decent standard of living. In China, the government that had with such difficulty, and through so much bloodshed, established itself at Nanking, watched as the Japanese occupation forces ruled in Manchuria, while the Chinese Communists prepared to regroup, and to fight to regain the initiative they had only just lost. People everywhere watched as their leaders embarked upon new courses, promised a better life, demanded greater sacrifices, and often paid lip service to the League of Nations as the forum through which war could be avoided – through which war had, in fact, already been outlawed.

An age of dictatorship had arisen on the ruins of the Empires destroyed in the First World War: Stalin in the Soviet Union, Mussolini in Italy, Hitler in Germany, Pilsudski in Poland, Primo de Rivera in Spain, King Alexander in Yugoslavia, Mustafa Kemal in Turkey: these were among the national leaders who trusted to their own personalities, and to the armies, police forces and secret police that supported them, and to patriots who would sacrifice individual liberty for the assertion of national power. The two largest and most tyrannical of the dictatorships, based in Moscow and Berlin, had devised, and were still devising, new and terrible varieties of control, symbolized by the Soviet labour camp and secret police system – almost a decade old – and the German concentration camp and Gestapo system – in its infancy.

The question so often asked was, would the forces of liberalism and parliamentary democracy, of equality before the law, and of reasonable debate, be able to make headway against the forces of dictatorship and terror? Would one system or the other prevail, or would the world remain divided into two vastly different systems? Would the dictatorial forces seek to impose their very different ideologies on their neighbours who did not share them, and attempt to do so by war? Would the democracies feel threatened enough to band together in defence of their way of life, or strong enough to seek an active end to tyrannies elsewhere? These questions were as yet unanswered, but they were becoming urgent.

BIBLIOGRAPHY OF WORKS CITED

Reference books

Alan Isaacs and Elizabeth Martin (eds), *Longman Dictionary of 20th Century Biography*, Longman, London, 1985.

Bruce P. Lenman and Katharine Boyd (eds), *Chambers Dictionary of World History*, Chambers Harrap, Edinburgh, 1993.

Alan Palmer, *Who's Who in Modern History*, Holt, Rinehart and Winston, New York, 1980.

Alan Palmer, *Dictionary of the British Empire and Commonwealth*, John Murray, London, 1996.

Edward Salmon and James Worsfold (eds), *The British Dominions Year Book, 1916*, The British Dominions General Insurance Company, London, 1916.

Harold Shukman (ed.), *The Blackwell Encyclopedia of the Russian Revolution*, Basil Blackwell, Oxford, 1988.

Philip Waller (ed.), *Chronology of the 20th Century*, Helicon, Oxford, 1995.

The Annual Register: A Review of Public Events at Home and Abroad for the Year 1900, Longmans, Green, London, 1901 (and subsequent annual volumes for successive years).

Cassell's *History of England*, vol. ix, Cassell, London, 1902.

Contemporary works (in chronological order)

Sir Charles Eliot (pseudonym, Odysseus), *Turkey in Europe*, London, 1900.

W. C. Stiles, *Out of Kishinev, The Duty of the American People to the Russian Jew*, G. W. Dillingham, New York, 1903.

M. Edith Durham, *The Burden of the Balkans*, Thomas Nelson, London, 1905.

Norman Angell, *The Great Illusion, A Study of the Relation of Military Power to National Advantage*, William Heinemann, London, 1909.

Mary Hooker, *Behind the Scenes in Peking, Being Experiences During the Siege of the Legations*, John Murray, London, 1910.

Karl Baedeker, *Berlin and its Environs*, T. Fisher Unwin, London, 1912.

Henry J. Hecht, *The Motor Routes of Germany*, Adam and Charles Black, London, 1914.

Report of the International Commission To Inquire into the Causes and Conduct of the Balkan Wars, Carnegie Endowment for International Peace, Washington, 1914.

Theodore Roosevelt, *America and the World War*, John Murray, London, 1915.

Stanley Washburn, *Field Notes from the Russian Front*, Andrew Melrose, London, 1915.

Bruce Bairnsfather, *Bullets and Billets*, Grant Richards, London, 1916.

Sidney Low, *Italy in the War*, Longmans, Green, London, 1916.

H. G. Wells, *What is Coming? A Forecast of Things After the War*, Cassell, London, 1916.

The War on Hospital Ships From the Narratives of Eye-witnesses, Pamphlets on the War, T. Fisher Unwin, London, 1917.

L. F. Waring, *Serbia*, Williams and Norgate, London, 1917.

Rebecca West, *The Return of the Soldier*, Nisbet, 1918.

Colonel Sir Thomas Holdich, *Boundaries in Europe and the Near East*, Macmillan, London, 1918.

President Harding's Address at the Burial of America's Unknown Soldier, Arlington Cemetery, November Eleventh 1921, Redfield-Kendrick-Odell, New York, 1921.

Frank Fox, *The King's Pilgrimage*, Hodder and Stoughton, London, 1922.

Captain Vidkun Quisling, *The Truth About the Ukrainian Horror, Official Report*, Fund for the Relief of Jewish Victims of the War in Eastern Europe, London, 1922.

George Popoff, *The Tcheka: The Red Inquisition*, A. M. Philpot, London, 1925.

Rolf Gardiner and Heinz Rocholl, *Britain and Germany*, Williams and Norgate, 1928.

Erich Maria Remarque, *All Quiet on the Western Front*, Bodley Head, London, 1929.

A. A. Santalov and Louis Segal (eds), *Soviet Union Year-Book, 1930*, George Allen and Unwin, London, 1930.

Adolf Hitler, *Mein Kampf (My Struggle)*, 1st English-language edition, Hurst and Blackett, London, 1933.

Vera Brittain, *Testament of Youth, An Autobiographical Study of the Years 1900–1925*, Victor Gollancz, London, 1933.

Wrecking Activites at Power Stations in the Soviet Union, Official Verbatim Report, 12–19 April 1933, George Allen and Unwin, London, 1933

Hitler's Secret Book, Grove Press, New York, 1961.

General histories
Feroz Ahmad, *The Young Turks, The Committee of Union and Progress in Turkish Politics, 1908–1914*, Clarendon Press, Oxford, 1969.

G. C. Allen, *A Short Economic History of Modern Japan, 1867–1937*, George Allen and Unwin, London, 1946.

Thomas A. Bailey and Paul B. Ryan, *The Lusitania Disaster, An Episode in Modern Warfare and Diplomacy*, Collier Macmillan, London, 1975.

Antonin Basch, *The Danube Basin and the German Economic Sphere*, Kegan Paul, Trench, Trubner, London, 1944.

Howard Becker, *German Youth: Bond or Free*, Kegan Paul, Trench, Trubner, London, 1946.

Patrick Beesly, *Room 40, British Naval Intelligence, 1914–18*, Hamish Hamilton, London, 1982.

Marie Bennigsen Broxup (ed.), *The North Caucasus Barrier, The Russian Advance towards the Muslim World*, Hurst, London, 1992.

Malcolm Bullock, *Austria 1918–1938, A Study in Failure*, Macmillan, London, 1939.

Raymond Carr, *Spain, 1808–1975*, Clarendon Press, Oxford, 1966.

Naomi Chazan (ed.), *Irredentism and International Politics*, Adamantine Press, London, 1991.

Winston S. Churchill, *The Unknown War, The Eastern Front*, Thornton Butterworth; London, 1931.

Basil Collier, *Arms and the Men, The Arms Trade and Governments*, Hamish Hamilton, London, 1980.

R. E. G. Davies, *A History of the World's Airlines*, Oxford University Press, London, 1964.

John Ellis, *The Social History of the Machine Gun*, Pimlico, London, 1986.

Orlando Figes, *A People's Tragedy, The Russia Revolution, 1891–1924*, Cape, London, 1996.

Paul Fussell, *The Great War and Modern Memory*, Oxford University Press, London, 1975.

Ruth Gay, *The Jews of Germany, A Historical Portrait*, Yale University Press, New Haven and London, 1992.

Alfred Gollin, *The Impact of Air Power on the British People and their Government, 1909–14*, Macmillan, London, 1989.

Roger Griffin (editor), *Fascism*, Oxford University Press, Oxford, 1995.

Richard Grunberger, *Red Rising in Bavaria*, St Martin's Press, London, 1973.

Geoffrey Hosking, *A History of the Soviet Union*, Collins, London, 1985.

Robert A. Kann, Béla K. Király and Paula S. Fichtner (eds), *The Habsburg Empire in World War I, Essays on the Intellectual, Military, Political and Economic Aspects of the Habsburg War Effort*, Columbia University Press, New York, 1977.

Donald Kenrick and Grattan Puxon, *The Destiny of Europe's Gypsies*, Chatto, Heinemann, for Sussex University Press, London, 1982.

Henry Keown-Boyd, *The Fists of Righteous Harmony, A History of the Boxer Uprising in China in the Year 1900*, Leo Cooper, London, 1991.

Peter H. Liddle, *The Soldier's War, 1914–18*, Blandford Press, London, 1988.

Wm Roger Louis, *British Strategy in the Far East, 1919–1939*, Clarendon Press, Oxford, 1971.

Bullitt Lowry, *Armistice 1918*, Kent State University Press, Kent, Ohio, 1996.

Adrian Lyttelton, *The Seizure of Power, Fascism in Italy, 1919–1929*, Weidenfeld and Nicolson, London, 1973.

Dorothy Macardle, *The Irish Republic, A Documented Chronicle of the Anglo-Irish Conflict and the Partitioning of Ireland*, Victor Gollancz, London, 1937.

Robert Machray, *The Polish-German Problem, Poland's Western Provinces and the Condition of her Independence*, George Allen and Unwin, London, 1941.

John M. Mappin, *Christmas in the Trenches, 1914*, privately printed, Montreal, 1994.

Major-General J. H. Marshall-Cornwall, *Geographic Disarmament, A Study of Regional Demilitarization*, Oxford University Press, London, 1935.

Margaret Miller, *The Economic Development of Russia, 1905–1914*, Thomas Nelson, London, 1926.

George Mosse, *The Crisis of German Ideology, The Intellectual Origins of the Third Reich*, Schocken, New York, 1981.

Jawaharlal Nehru, *The Discovery of India*, Meridian Books, London, 1956.

Geoffrey Nowell-Smith (ed.), *The Oxford History of World Cinema*, Oxford University Press, Oxford, 1996.

Neal W. O'Connor, *Aviation Awards of Imperial Germany in World War I and the Men who Earned Them*, Foundation for Aviation World War I, Princeton, New Jersey, 1990.

Thomas Pakenham, *The Boer War*, Weidenfeld and Nicolson, London, 1979.

Alan Palmer, *The Lands Between, A History of East-Central Europe since the Congress of Vienna*, Weidenfeld and Nicolson, London, 1970.

Richard Pipes, *The Russian Revolution, 1899–1919*, Harvill, London, 1990.

Richard Pipes, *Russia Under the Bolshevik Regime, 1919–1924*, Harvill, London, 1994.

A. M. Pooley, *Japan at the Cross Roads*, George Allen and Unwin, London, 1917.

Geoffrey Pridham, *Hitler's Rise to Power, The Nazi Movement in Bavaria, 1923–1933*, Hart-Davis, MacGibbon, London, 1973.

Raymond Laurence Rimell, *Zeppelin!, A Battle for Air Supremacy in World War 1*, Conway Maritime Press, London, 1984.

Bertrand Russell, *Freedom and Organisation, 1814–1914*, George Allen and Unwin, London, 1934.

G. W. Shorter, *The Ottawa-Hull Fire of 1900*, National Research Council, Ottawa, 1962.

Jonathan Spence and Annping Chin, *The Chinese Century, A Photographic History*, HarperCollins, London, 1996.

Gill Thomas, *Life on All Fronts, Women in the First World War*, Cambridge University Press, Cambridge, 1989.

Edward Thompson, *The Reconstruction of India*, Faber and Faber, London, 1930.

L. M. Thompson, *The Unification of South Africa, 1902–1910*, Clarendon Press, Oxford, 1960.

Ulrich Trumpener, *Germany and the Ottoman Empire, 1914–1918*, Princeton University Press, Princeton, New Jersey, 1968.

Evald Uustalu, *The History of the Estonian People*, Boreas, London, 1952.

Syed Razi Wasti, *Lord Minto and the Indian Nationalist Movement, 1905–1910*, Clarendon Press, Oxford, 1964.

Eugen Weber, *The Hollow Years, France in the 1930s*, Sinclair-Stevenson, London, 1995.

Andrew Wheatcroft, *The Ottomans, Dissolving Images*, Viking, London, 1993.

Andrew Wheatcroft, *The Habsburgs, Embodying Empire*, Viking, London, 1995.

H. R. Wilkinson, *Maps and Politics, A Review of the Ethnographic Cartography of Macedonia*, Liverpool University Press, Liverpool, 1951.

Elizabeth Wiskemann, *Europe of the Dictators, 1919–1945*, Fontana, London, 1966.

Leon Wolff, *In Flanders Fields, The 1917 Campaign*, Longmans, Green, London, 1958.

Biography

Neal Ascherson, *The King Incorporated, Leopold II in the Age of Trusts*, George Allen and Unwin, London, 1963.

Judith M. Brown, *Gandhi, Prisoner of Hope*, Yale University Press, New Haven and London, 1989.

Robert Conquest, *Stalin, Breaker of Nations*, Viking Penguin, New York, 1991.

Isaac Deutscher, *Stalin, A Political Biography*, Oxford University Press, London, 1949.

Joachim C. Fest, *Hitler*, Weidenfeld and Nicolson, London, 1974.

Peter Fleming, *The Fate of Admiral Kolchak*, Rupert Hart-Davis, London, 1963.

Paul Frölich, *Rosa Luxemburg: Ideas in Action*, Left Book Club, London, 1940.

E. M. Hugh-Jones, *Woodrow Wilson and American Liberalism*, Hodder and Stoughton, London, 1947.

Count Harry Kessler, *Walther Rathenau, His Life and Work*, Gerald Howe, London, 1929.

Sir Ivone Kirkpatrick, *Mussolini, Study of a Demagogue*, Odhams Books, London, 1964.

Baruch Knei-Paz, *The Social and Political Thought of Leon Trotsky*, Clarendon Press, Oxford, 1978.

Fitzroy Maclean, *Disputed Barricade, The Life and Times of Josip Broz-Tito, Marshal of Jugoslavia*, Jonathan Cape, London, 1957.

Alan Palmer, *Twilight of the Habsburgs, The Life and Times of Emperor Francis Joseph*, Weidenfeld and Nicolson, London, 1994.

Paul Preston, *Franco, A Biography*, HarperCollins, 1993.

Edvard Radzinsky, *The Last Tsar, The Life and Death of Nicholas II*, Doubleday, 1992.

Roberta Reeder, *Anna Akhmatova, Poet and Prophet*, St Martin's Press, New York, 1994.

Stuart Schram, *Mao Tse-tung*, Penguin Books, London, 1966.

George Seaver, *Francis Younghusband, Explorer and Mystic*, John Murray, London, 1952.

Robert Sencourt, *King Alfonso, a biography*, Faber and Faber, London, 1942.

John Toland, *Adolf Hitler*, Doubleday, Garden City, New York, 1976.

John W. Wheeler-Bennett, *Hindenburg, The Wooden Titan*, Macmillan, London, 1936.

Peter Wilkinson and Joan Bright Astley, *Gubbins and SOE* (the biography of Major-General Sir Colin Gubbins), Leo Cooper, London, 1993.

John A. Woods, *Roosevelt and Modern America*, English Universities Press, London, 1959.

Memoirs, diaries, journals and collected papers

C. F. Andrews (ed.), *Mahatma Gandhi: His Own Story*, George Allen and Unwin, London, 1930.

Dr Alfred Apfel, *Behind the Scenes of German Justice. Reminiscences of a German Barrister, 1882–1933*, John Lane, The Bodley Head, London, 1935.

Lady Bell (ed.), *The Letters of Gertrude Bell*, 2 vols, Ernest Benn, London, 1927.

John Gardner Coolidge, *A War Diary in Paris, 1914–1917*, Riverside Press, Cambridge, Massachusetts, 1931.

Fernand Farjenel, *Through the Chinese Revolution*, Duckworth, London, 1915.

Florence Farmborough, *Nurses at the Russian Front, A Diary, 1914–18*, Constable, London, 1974.

Mahatma Gandhi, *The Story of My Experiments with Truth*, 2 vols, Navaji-van Press, Ahmedabad, 1927, 1929.

Burton J. Hendrick, *The Life and Letters of Walter H. Page, Containing the Letters to Woodrow Wilson*, 3 vols, William Heinemann, London, 1925.

Aldous Huxley (ed.), *The Letters of D. H. Lawrence*, William Heinemann, London, 1932.

Hermann Kesten (ed.), *Thomas Mann, Diaries, 1918–1939*, Harry N. Abrams, New York, 1982.

Alec Seath Kirkbride, *A Crackle of Thorns, Experiences in the Middle East*, John Murray, London, 1956.

Nadezhda Mandelstam, *Hope Abandoned, A Memoir*, Harvill Press, London, 1974.

Jan M. Meijer (ed.), *The Trotsky Papers, 1917–1922*, 2 vols, Mouton, The Hague, 1964, 1971.

Jawaharlal Nehru, *An Autobiography*, The Bodley Head, London, 1936.

Justin O'Brien (ed.), *The Journals of André Gide, 1889–1949*, 4 vols, Alfred A. Knopf, New York, 1947–1951.

Count Alfred Potocki, *Master of Lancut*, W. H. Allen, London, 1959.

Silvia Rodgers, *Red Saint, Pink Daughter, A Communist Childhood in Berlin and London*, Andre Deutsch, London, 1996.

Siegfried Sassoon, *Memoirs of an Infantry Officer*, Faber and Faber, London, 1930.

Freya Stark, *Traveller's Prelude*, John Murray, London, 1950.

A. J. B. Wavell, *A Modern Pilgrim in Mecca and a Siege in Sanaa*, Constable, London, 1913.

Brand Whitlock, *Belgium Under The German Occupation, A Personal Memoir*, William Heinemann, 2 vols, London, 1919.

Novels, short stories, poems

I. Babel, *Red Cavalry*, 1929 (reprinted in Isaac Babel, *Collected Stories*, Methuen, London, 1957).

Vasily Grossman, *Life and Fate*, Collins Harvill, London, 1985.

Thomas Hardy, *Collected Poems*, Macmillan, London, 1932.

Jaroslav Hašek, *The Good Soldier Svejk and His Fortunes in the World War*, Thomas Y. Crowell, New York, 1974 (first published, 1930).

Ernest Hemingway, *A Farewell to Arms*, Charles Scribner's Sons, New York, 1929.

Arthur Koestler, *Darkness at Noon*, Jonathan Cape, London, 1940.

Wilfred Owen, *Poems*, Chatto & Windus, 1920.

Boris Pasternak, *Doctor Zhivago*, Collins and Harvill, London, 1957.

Siegfried Sassoon, *Rhymed Ruminations*, Faber and Faber, London, 1940.

S. Sergeyev-Tsensky, *Brusilov's Break-Through. A Novel of the First World War*, Hutchinson, London, 1944.

In addition to the books cited above, I have drawn on material from the following of my own books:

Servant of India, The correspondence and diaries of Sir James Dunlop Smith, Private Secretary to the Viceroy, 1905–1910, Longmans, London, 1966.

Winston S. Churchill, companion document volumes, Heinemann, London, 1972 (for the years 1914–1916); 1977 (1917–1922); 1979 (1922–1929); 1981 (1929–1935).

Sir Horace Rumbold, Portrait of a Diplomat, 1869–1941, Heinemann, London, 1974.

First World War, Weidenfeld and Nicolson, London, 1994.

Churchill, A Life, Heinemann, London, 1995.

MAPS

MAPS

1. Europe 1900–14

2. Germany

3. Austria-Hungary 1867–1918

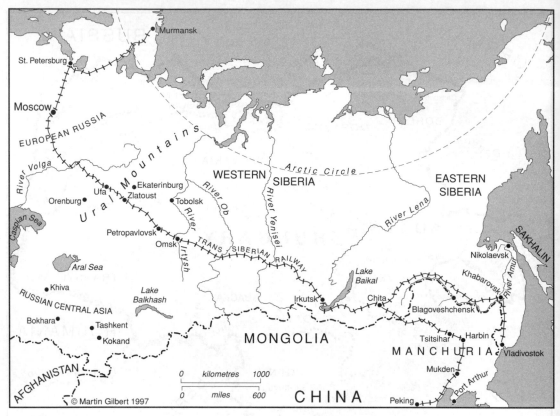

4. Siberia

5. Turkey-in-Europe 1900–14

6. The Balkans 1900–14

Map labels:

The borders of Serbia, Greece, Montenegro and Turkey in 1900
The borders of Serbia, Greece, Montenegro and Albania in 1914

BOSNIA
HERZOGOVINA
Sarajevo

River Drina

Belgrade

Valievo

Kragujevac

SERBIA

ROUMANIA

River Morava

Nish

River Danube

BULGARIA

Sofia

SANJAK
OF
NOVI BAZAR

Sienitza

MONTENEGRO

Cattaro

Berane

Mitovitza

Prishtina

Pech

METOYA

KOSOVO

Djakovo

Ferizovitch

Prizren

Kotchana

Lake Skadar
Skadar

San Giovanni
di Medua

Allesio

Skopje (Uskub)

ALBANIA

Dibra
(Debar)

Ochrid

Smilievo

MACEDONIA

River Vardar

Durazzo

Lake
Ochrid

Monastir
(Bitola)

Gevgellija

WESTERN
THRACE

Adriatic
Sea

Saint Naum
Podgor

Florina

Saseno

Avlona
(Valona)

GREECE

Salonika

Argyrocastro

VIDO

Aegean
Sea

Yanina

CORFU

EPIRUS

Ionian
Sea

Prevesa

Athens

Piraeus

0 kilometres 100

0 miles 50

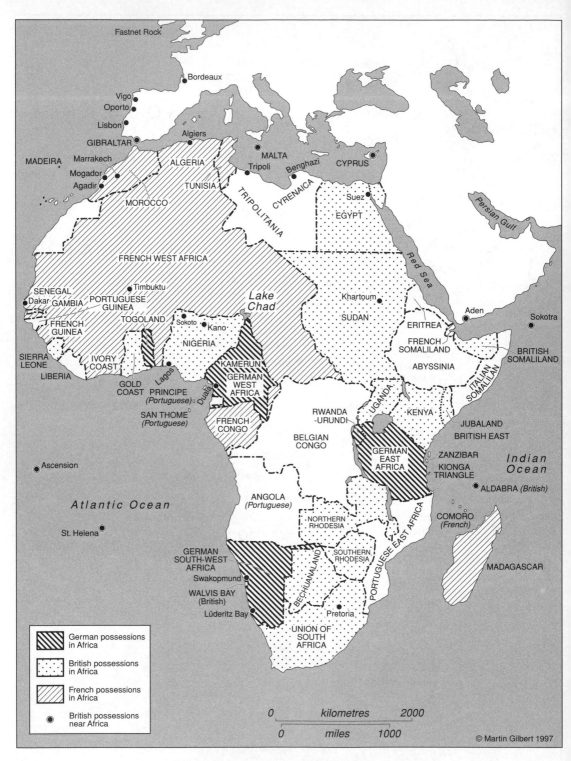

Fastnet Rock

Bordeaux

Vigo
Oporto
Lisbon
GIBRALTAR
MADEIRA
Marrakech
Mogador
Agadir
MOROCCO

Algiers
ALGERIA
TUNISIA

MALTA
Tripoli   Benghazi   CYPRUS
TRIPOLITANIA   CYRENAICA

Suez
EGYPT

Persian Gulf

FRENCH WEST AFRICA

SENEGAL
Dakar
GAMBIA
FRENCH
GUINEA
SIERRA
LEONE
LIBERIA
IVORY
COAST
GOLD
COAST

PORTUGUESE
GUINEA

TOGOLAND

Timbuktu

Lake
Chad

Sokoto   Kano
NIGERIA

Lagos

Duala

PRINCIPE
(Portuguese)

SAN THOME
(Portuguese)

KAMERUN
GERMAN
WEST
AFRICA

FRENCH
CONGO

BELGIAN
CONGO

Khartoum

SUDAN

Red Sea

Aden

Sokotra

ERITREA

FRENCH
SOMALILAND

ABYSSINIA

BRITISH
SOMALILAND

ITALIAN
SOMALILAND

RWANDA
-URUNDI

UGANDA

KENYA

JUBALAND
BRITISH EAST

Ascension

Atlantic Ocean

St. Helena

ANGOLA
(Portuguese)

NORTHERN
RHODESIA

GERMAN
EAST
AFRICA

ZANZIBAR
KIONGA
TRIANGLE

Indian
Ocean

ALDABRA (British)

COMORO
(French)

MADAGASCAR

GERMAN
SOUTH-WEST
AFRICA

Swakopmund

WALVIS BAY
(British)

Lüderitz Bay

BECHUANALAND

SOUTHERN
RHODESIA

PORTUGUESE EAST AFRICA

Pretoria

UNION OF
SOUTH
AFRICA

German possessions
in Africa

British possessions
in Africa

French possessions
in Africa

British possessions
near Africa

0   kilometres   2000

0   miles   1000

© Martin Gilbert 1997

7. Africa and the European Powers 1900–14

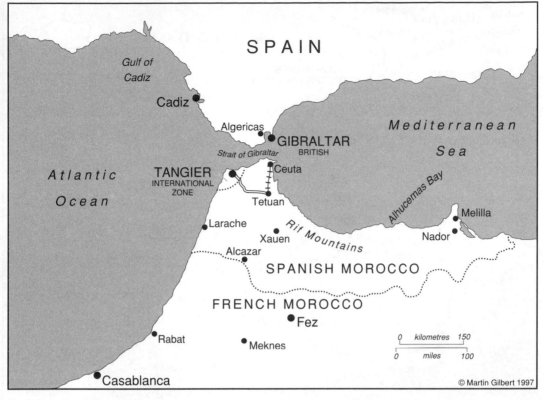

8. Morocco

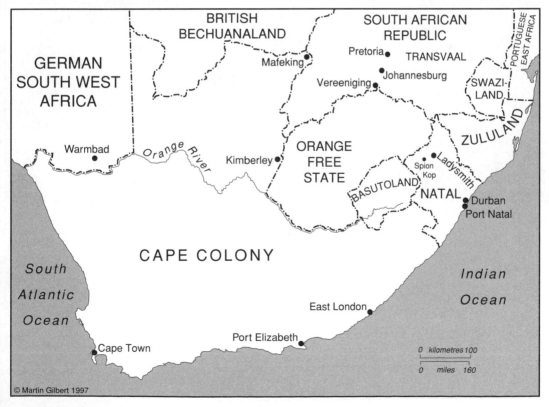

9. South Africa

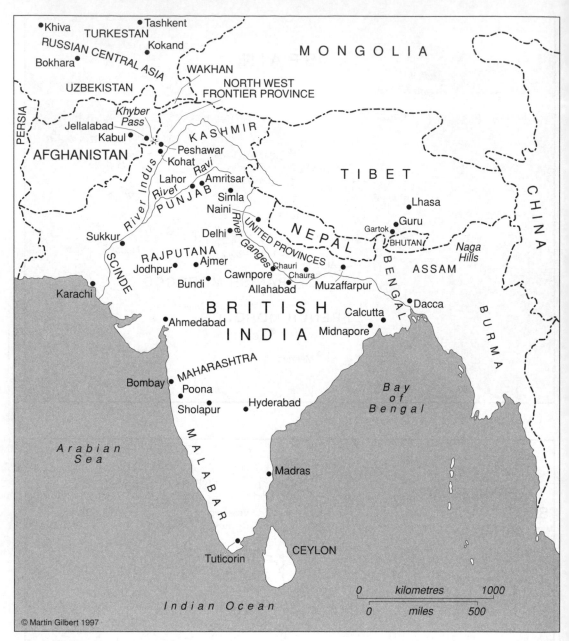

10. India

Legend:
- British
- French
- Dutch
- Japanese
- United States
- 1858 Treaty ports with opening dates

Tsitsihar · Anta · RUSSIA

Harbin

MANCHURIA

Vladivostok

Hailun

Mukden

1858
Tungchow · Wiju
Peking · Port Arthur · Weihaiwei
Tientsin

Kiaochow

JAPAN

KOREA

Tsushima Strait

Hiroshima

Nagasaki
1855

CHINA

Wuhu
1876 · Shanghai 1842

Hangkow · Ningpo
1842

Chunking · Yangtse
1895

Amoy · TAIWAN
1842 · (FORMOSA)

Canton
1842 · Hong Kong

Pacific
Ocean

INDIA · KACHIN

BURMA

Miyitkina

TONKING
Hanoi

Kiungchow
1858

HAINAN

PHILIPPINES

British
Sphere 1896

SIAM

FRENCH
INDO-
CHINA

Manila

Rangoon

French Sphere
1898

CAMBODIA

ANNAM

South China
Sea

PALAWAN

MINDANAO

Saigon

British
Sphere
1896

COCHIN
CHINA

BRITISH NORTH
BORNEO

SULU

BRUNEI

ACHIN

Malacca

MALAYA

SARAWAK

MOLUCCAS

NEW
GUINEA

SUMATRA

SINGAPORE
UPPER PADANG

BORNEO

CELEBES

Indian
Ocean

DUTCH EAST INDIES

0 kilometres 500

0 miles 300

JAVA

TIMOR

© Martin Gilbert 1997

11. The Far East

12. China

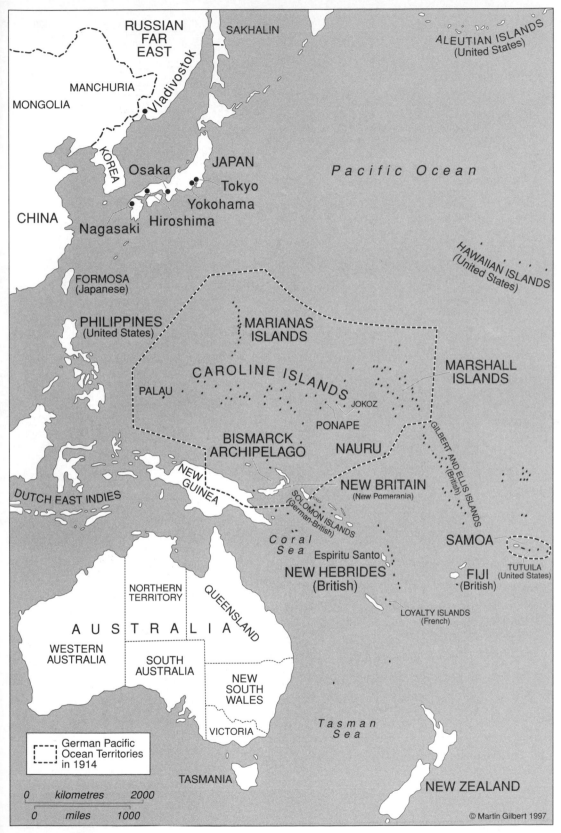

RUSSIAN FAR EAST

SAKHALIN

ALEUTIAN ISLANDS
(United States)

MANCHURIA

Vladivostok

MONGOLIA

KOREA

Pacific Ocean

JAPAN

Osaka

Tokyo

Yokohama

CHINA

Hiroshima

Nagasaki

HAWAIIAN ISLANDS
(United States)

FORMOSA
(Japanese)

PHILIPPINES
(United States)

MARIANAS
ISLANDS

CAROLINE ISLANDS

MARSHALL
ISLANDS

PALAU

JOKOZ

PONAPE

NAURU

GILBERT AND ELLIS ISLANDS
(British)

BISMARCK
ARCHIPELAGO

NEW
GUINEA

NEW BRITAIN
(New Pomerania)

DUTCH EAST INDIES

SOLOMON ISLANDS
(German-British)

*Coral
Sea*

SAMOA

Espiritu Santo

TUTUILA
(United States)

NEW HEBRIDES
(British)

FIJI
(British)

NORTHERN
TERRITORY

QUEENSLAND

LOYALTY ISLANDS
(French)

A U S T R A L I A

WESTERN
AUSTRALIA

SOUTH
AUSTRALIA

NEW
SOUTH
WALES

VICTORIA

*Tasman
Sea*

German Pacific
Ocean Territories
in 1914

TASMANIA

NEW ZEALAND

0   kilometres   2000

0   miles   1000

© Martin Gilbert 1997

13. The Pacific

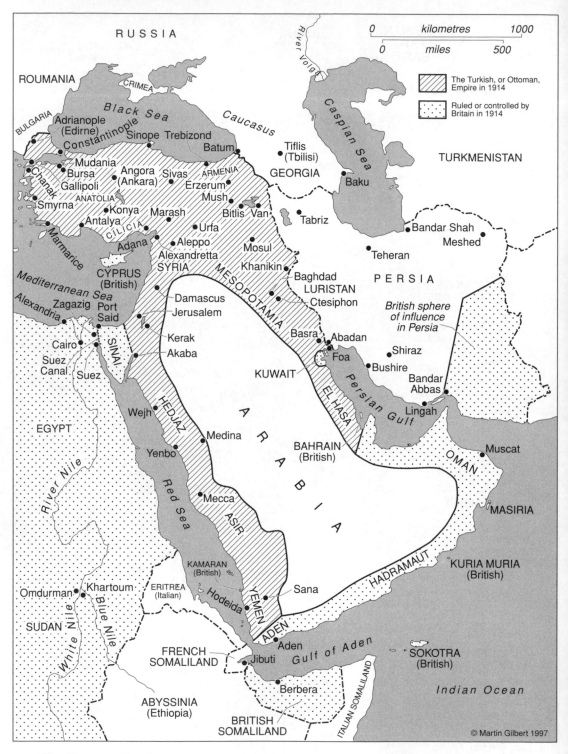

14. The Ottoman Empire 1914

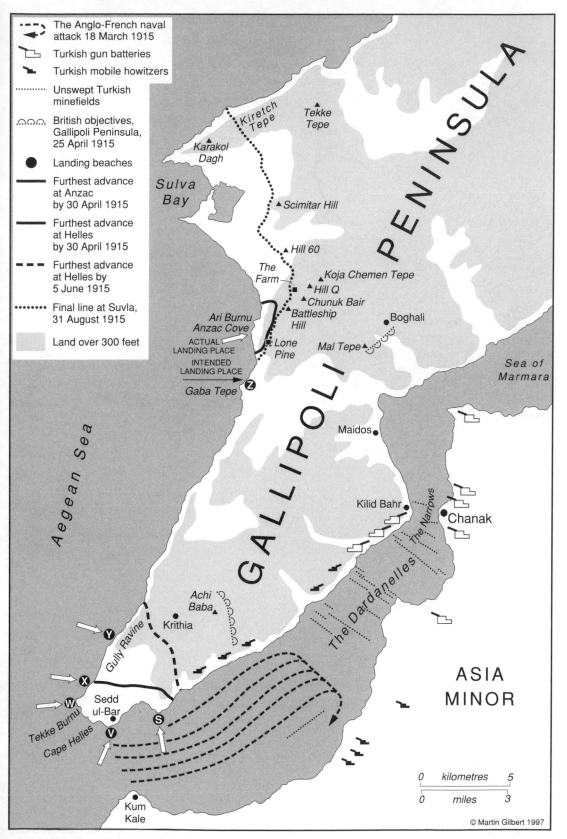

Legend

- The Anglo-French naval attack 18 March 1915
- Turkish gun batteries
- Turkish mobile howitzers
- Unswept Turkish minefields
- British objectives, Gallipoli Peninsula, 25 April 1915
- Landing beaches
- Furthest advance at Anzac by 30 April 1915
- Furthest advance at Helles by 30 April 1915
- Furthest advance at Helles by 5 June 1915
- Final line at Suvla, 31 August 1915
- Land over 300 feet

PENINSULA

GALLIPOLI

Kiretch Tepe

▲ *Tekke Tepe*

▲ *Karakol Dagh*

Sulva Bay

▲ *Scimitar Hill*

▲ *Hill 60*

The Farm

▲ *Koja Chemen Tepe*

▲ *Hill Q*

▲ *Chunuk Bair*

▲ *Battleship Hill*

● *Boghali*

Ari Burnu Anzac Cove

ACTUAL LANDING PLACE

Lone Pine

Mal Tepe ▲

INTENDED LANDING PLACE

Gaba Tepe **Z**

Sea of Marmara

Aegean Sea

Maidos ●

Kilid Bahr ●

The Narrows

Chanak ●

The Dardanelles

Achi Baba ▲

Krithia ●

Y

Gully Ravine

X

W *Sedd ul-Bar*

S

Tekke Burnu

V

Cape Helles

ASIA MINOR

Kum Kale ●

| 0 | kilometres | 5 |
| 0 | miles | 3 |

© Martin Gilbert 1997

15. Gallipoli and the Dardanelles 1915

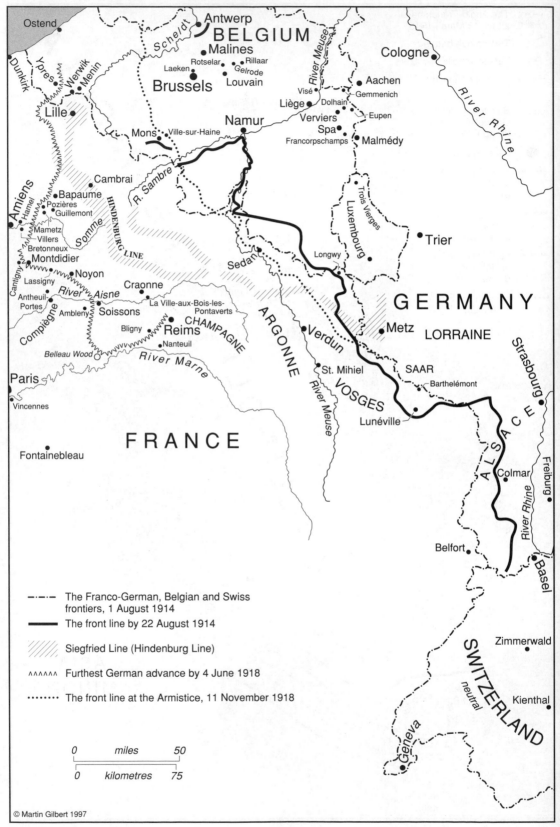

16. The Western Front 1914–18

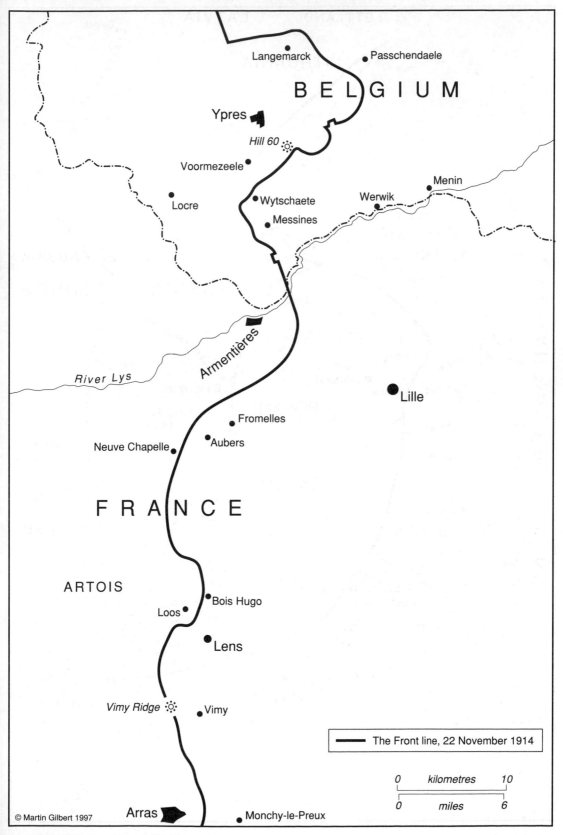

Langemarck • Passchendaele •

B E L G I U M

Ypres •

Hill 60 ☼

Voormezeele •

Menin •

Locre • Werwik •

Wytschaete • Messines •

Armentières

River Lys

Lille •

Fromelles •

Aubers •

Neuve Chapelle •

F R A N C E

A R T O I S

Bois Hugo •

Loos •

Lens •

Vimy Ridge ☼ • Vimy

━━━━ The Front line, 22 November 1914

0   kilometres   10

0   miles   6

© Martin Gilbert 1997

Arras • Monchy-le-Preux

17. The Western Front: Ypres to Arras

18. The Eastern Front 1914–16

The Salonika front,
September 1916

The Salonika front,
November 1916 to
14 September 1918

The Salonika front,
29 September 1918

SERBIA

Tsaribrod

Sofia

Vladaya

Radomir

Prizren

River Morava

Skopje

BULGARIA

ALBANIA

Veles

River Vardar

Debar

River Struma

Prilep

Negotin

Strumitsa

Strumitsa Station

Kosturino

Lake
Ochrid

Vetrenik

Doiran

Fort Rupel

WESTERN

Drama

THRACE

Monastir

Kajmackalan

Kavalla

Florina

GREECE

Salonika

0   miles   50

0   kilometres   75

Aegean

Sea

Gulf of
Salonika

© Martin Gilbert 1997

19. The Salonika Front 1916–18

Bay of
Biscay

FRANCE

La Coruna

Bilbao

Guernica

Pyrenees

ASTURIAS

Vigo

Burgos

Zaragoza

CATELONIA

Barcelona

Oporto

Salamanca

Madrid

PORTUGAL

Toledo

MAJORCA

SPAIN

Valencia

IBIZA

Lisbon

Merida

Alicante

FORMENTERA

Huelva

Seville

Granada

Mediterranean Sea

Cape
St. Vincent

Cadiz

Atlantic
Ocean

Algericas

Gibraltar (BRITISH)

Ceuta (SPANISH)

Cape Finisterre

0   kilometres   100

0   miles   160

© Martin Gilbert 1997

20. The Iberian Peninsula

Map Legend

- - - - The armistice line, December 1917
^^^^^^ Limit of German occupation, under the Treaty of Brest-Litovsk, March 1918
- · - · - Border of the Soviet Union, 1922 -1939

0 — kilometres — 500
0 — miles — 300

White Sea
Archangel
to Murmansk

Gulf of Bothnia
Vasa
FINLAND
Baltic Sea
Helsinki
Kronstadt
DAGO
Reval
OSEL
Pulkovo
Schlüsselberg
ESTONIA
Narva
Petrograd
Pernau
MOON
Tsarskoe Selo
Dorpat
Vologda
Perm
COURLAND
Pskov
Bologoe
Riga
LATVIA
BALTIC STATES
Dvinsk
Nizhni-Novgorod
Kazan
Ufa
Tver
Kovno
Moscow
Borisov
Smolensk
Fili
Vilna
Minsk
WHITE RUSSIA
Mogilev
Tula
Brest-Litovsk
Samara
Warsaw
Gomel
Orel
Lipetsk
Tambov
Orenburg
Saratov
Kursk
River Volga
Zhitomir
Kiev
Voronezh
AUSTRIA-HUNGARY
Fastov
River Don
Tsaritsyn
UKRAINE
Kharkov
Ekaterinoslav
BESSARABIA
Zaporozhe
Shakhty
Kishinev
Nikolayev
Taganrog
Astrakhan
Odessa
Berdiansk
Rostov-on-Don
Kherson
Sea of Azov
Caspian Sea
ROUMANIA
Simferopol
KUBAN
Sebastopol
Feodosiya
Novorossisk
NORTH CAUCASUS
Mineralniye Vody
Black Sea
Kislovodsk
Piatygorsk
CHECHNYA
Sochi
Mount Elbruz
Caucasus
Temir Khan Shura
Makhachkala
Sukhumi
Gergebil
DAGESTAN
Constantinople
Poti
Arakan
GEORGIA
Tiflis
Batum
AZERBAIJAN
Baku
Chanak
Bursa
Rizeh
Kars
ARMENIA
Trebizond
Erivan
TURKEY
Erzerum
Mush
Bitlis
PERSIA
ANATOLIA

© Martin Gilbert 1997

21. Russia 1917–33

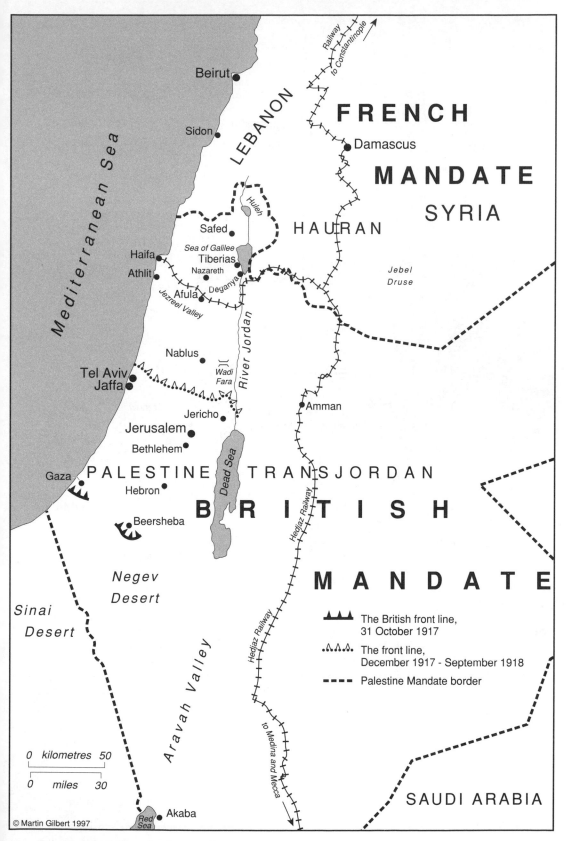

Mediterranean Sea

Beirut

LEBANON

Sidon

Railway to Constantinople

FRENCH

Damascus

MANDATE

SYRIA

HAURAN

Huleh

Safed

Jebel
Druse

Sea of Galilee
Haifa   Tiberias
Athlit   Nazareth
         Deganya
Afula
Jezreel Valley

Nablus

Wadi
Fara

River Jordan

Tel Aviv
Jaffa

Jericho

Amman

Jerusalem
Bethlehem

Dead Sea

Gaza   P A L E S T I N E   T R A N S J O R D A N
Hebron

B R I T I S H

Hedjaz Railway

Beersheba

Negev
Desert

M A N D A T E

Sinai
Desert

▲▲▲▲   The British front line,
       31 October 1917

.▲.▲.▲.   The front line,
       December 1917 - September 1918

- - - -   Palestine Mandate border

Aravah Valley

Hedjaz Railway

0   kilometres   50

0   miles   30

to Medina and Mecca

© Martin Gilbert 1997

Red
Sea   Akaba

SAUDI ARABIA

22. Palestine and Transjordan 1918–33

23. Europe 1919–33

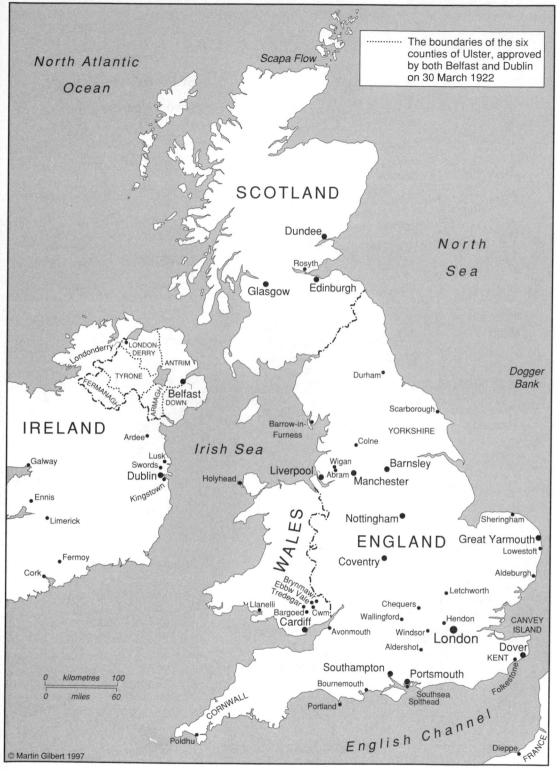

North Atlantic
Ocean

Scapa Flow

.... The boundaries of the six
counties of Ulster, approved
by both Belfast and Dublin
on 30 March 1922

SCOTLAND

Dundee

Rosyth

Glasgow   Edinburgh

North

Sea

Durham

Dogger
Bank

Scarborough

Londonderry   LONDON-
DERRY
ANTRIM
TYRONE
FERMANAGH
ARMAGH   Belfast
DOWN

YORKSHIRE

Barrow-in-
Furness

IRELAND

Ardee

Irish Sea

Colne

Lusk
Swords
Dublin

Holyhead

Wigan
Abram
Liverpool

Barnsley

Manchester

Galway

Kingstown

Ennis

Nottingham

Sheringham

Limerick

WALES

ENGLAND

Great Yarmouth
Lowestoft

Fermoy

Coventry

Aldeburgh

Cork

Letchworth

Brynmawr
Ebbw Vale
Tredegar

Chequers

Llanelli
Bargoed   Cwm
Cardiff

Wallingford

Hendon

CANVEY
ISLAND

Avonmouth

Windsor

London

Aldershot

Dover
KENT

Southampton

Portsmouth

Bournemouth

Southsea
Spithead

Folkestone

CORNWALL

Portland

Poldhu

English Channel

Dieppe
FRANCE

0   kilometres   100
0   miles   60

© Martin Gilbert 1997

24. Great Britain

25. Austria, Italy and the Adriatic 1918–33

26. The Western United States

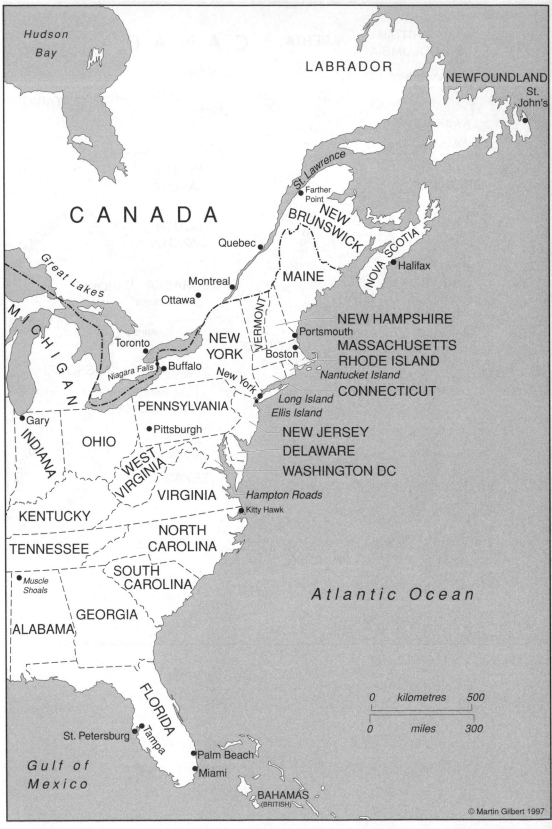

27. The Eastern United States

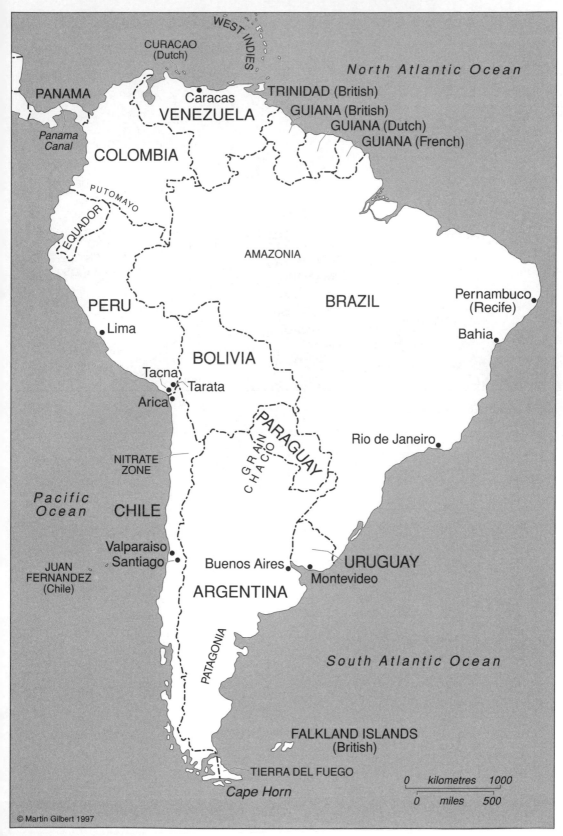

WEST INDIES

CURACAO
(Dutch)

North Atlantic Ocean

PANAMA

TRINIDAD (British)

Caracas
GUIANA (British)

VENEZUELA
GUIANA (Dutch)

GUIANA (French)

*Panama
Canal*

COLOMBIA

PUTOMAYO

EQUADOR

AMAZONIA

PERU

BRAZIL

Pernambuco
(Recife)

Lima

Bahia

BOLIVIA

Tacna

Tarata

Arica

PARAGUAY

Rio de Janeiro

NITRATE
ZONE

G
R
A
N

C
H
A
C
O

*Pacific
Ocean*

CHILE

Valparaiso

JUAN
FERNANDEZ
(Chile)

Santiago

Buenos Aires

URUGUAY

Montevideo

ARGENTINA

South Atlantic Ocean

P
A
T
A
G
O
N
I
A

FALKLAND ISLANDS
(British)

0   *kilometres*   1000

TIERRA DEL FUEGO

Cape Horn

0   *miles*   500

© Martin Gilbert 1997

28. South America

29. Central America

INDEX

compiled by the author